Bergin and Garfield's Handbook of Psychotherapy and Behavior Change

Bergin and Garfield's Handbook of Psychotherapy and Behavior Change

Fifth Edition

Michael J. Lambert
Brigham Young University

John Wiley & Sons, Inc.

• DEDICATION •

This fifth edition of the Handbook is dedicated to the distinguished editors of the previous four editions, Allen E. Bergin and Sol S. Garfield. These mentors and friends have modeled the importance of critical appraisals of the field of psychotherapy. There is no doubt that their timely and tireless efforts have been an important contribution to enhancing the effectiveness of psychotherapy and patient care.

ACQUISITIONS EDITOR	Timothy Vertovec
MARKETING MANAGER	Kevin Molloy
SENIOR PRODUCTION EDITOR	Norine M. Pigliucci
DESIGN DIRECTOR	Madelyn Lesure
PRODUCTION MANAGEMENT SERVICES	Hermitage Publishing Services
EDITORIAL ASSISTANT	Kristen Babroski

This book was set in Janson by Hermitage Publishing Services and printed and bound by Hamilton Printing. The cover was printed by Lehigh Press.

This book is printed on acid-free paper.

To Order books please call 1(800)-225-5945.

ISBN-13 978-0-471-37755-9

Printed in the United States of America

10 9 8 7 6 5

PREFACE

I am pleased to have served as editor of this new edition of Bergin and Garfield's Handbook of Psychotherapy and Behavior Change. Allen Bergin and Sol Garfield, the editors of the first four editions of this standard reference book, published their first edition in 1971, the year I received my Ph.D. I met Allen that same year as we began faculty appointments at Brigham Young University. In 1973 I met Sol Garfield at the annual meetings of the Society of Psychotherapy Research. We shared a strong interest in psychotherapy and in its scientific foundations. The Society was a meeting point for many of the great minds in the field and a stimulus for integration of research and practice. Most of the authors who have contributed chapters to the Handbook over the years discussed and debated the important issues of the day in the context of the Society and its international, multidisciplinary membership. Both Garfield and Bergin, after decades of creating the Handbook, felt it was time to step aside. Given my past contributions to the Handbook and long standing association with them, I agreed to their suggestion that I edit this fifth edition.

The influence of the Handbook on the field of psychotherapy has been enormous. The early editions of the handbook have become citation classics. Reference to psychotherapy research is not complete without considering the comprehensive work of past Handbook authors. Graduate education in psychology and the related professions would seem deficient without exposure to the empirical literature and past editions of the Handbook have set the standard for balance and completeness. Without thoughtful review of the empirical literature on psychotherapy practitioners cannot expect to deliver services of the highest quality.

I began editing this edition of the Handbook with a full understanding of the book's importance to the field over the 30 years that Garfield and Bergin devoted to it. I also realized that it needed to measure up to expectations from readers of early editions. The fifth edition is also the first to be published in the current climate of accountability that is sweeping the United States and countries across the world. I endeavored to invite outstanding authors to contribute to this edition with the hope and intention that the Handbook remains the most important overview of research findings in the field. Many of the authors that consented to write chapters have consistently contributed to the Handbook since its inception. Their work remains thorough and comprehensive. There are conflicting views about the value of certain treatment methods in relation to others, effective processes, necessary and sufficient conditions for positive change, and the interpretation of some findings. These conflicts provide an important source of discussion and wonder that will be stimulating to students and professionals. Certainly, these conflicts and their resolution will have great value for effectively treating patients.

The focus of the Handbook remains on empirical studies, but a new chapter has been added that highlights the many weaknesses of traditional science for understanding human dilemmas and emotional problems. Thus, the fifth edition includes not only chapters on traditional scientific methodology but gives attention to a philosophy of science that argues for the value of qualitative methods. The tension between therapy schools and the interpretation of empirical evidence can also be recognized as a struggle between philosophical positions.

As in past Handbooks, the current edition emphasizes practice-relevant findings, as well as, methodological issues that will help direct future research. It is therefore meant to be both a summary of accumulated knowledge and a guide for the future practice of psychotherapy. I believe the reader will find this edition of the handbook to be up to the same high standards maintained by Garfield and Bergin in the preceding four editions. The Handbook authors have done their best to keep pace with the rapid changes that are taking place in the world and attempted to be forward looking in making recommendations for future research and practice.

I would like to thank the contributing authors for their careful reviews and long hours of thoughtful work. Because of their history of accomplishments and contributions to the field over many years, their wisdom is apparent and likely to be greatly appreciated by the reader. In addition to the chapter authors, I wish to thank my research team who helped with many mundane aspects of this work. They not only contributed many hours of service but also found themselves stimulated by carefully reading the chapters. Those who helped include:

Karla Adams
Chris Allen
Joel Beckstead
Dave Bensfield, Jr.
Matthew Bishop
Derek Bowen
Lisa Brinton
Michael Cambell
Garrett Chelsey
Darin Cobia
Jonathan Cox
Mike Drebot
Joseph Farnsworth
Shelby Ferrin
Brad Forsgren
Melissa Kaye Goates
Heidi Goddard
Ann Gregerson
Cory Harmon
Quinten Harvey
Arlin Hatch
Derek Hatfield
Eric Hawkins
Jacob Hess
Lori Hughs
Robert Hunt
Brian Isakson
Elizabeth Jones
Brad Jorgeson
Meghan Kennedy
Tim Kimball
Wade Lueck
Michael Miller
Kevin Monds
Jared Morton
Rob Parker
Landon Poppleton
Bekah Richardson
Liz Richardson
Scott Seaman
Rachelle Sharp
Dave Sigmon
Kärstin Slade
Joanna Thomas
Crystal Ulibarri
Rome Walter
Kit Westbrook
Jason Whipple
Brady Wiggins
Dan Williams

I hope that readers of this new edition will be able to use the information presented to augment their work with patients and that this research compendium will stimulate and guide further examination of the scientific foundations and consequences of psychotherapeutic practice.

M.J.L.

List of Contributors

James F. Alexander
University of Utah

Shabia Alimohamed
University of California, Santa Barbara

Aaron T. Beck
University of Pennsylvania

Allen E. Bergin
Brigham Young University

Larry E. Beutler
Pacific Graduate School of Psychology

Gary M. Burlingame
Brigham Young University

John F. Clarkin
New York Hospital-Cornell Medical Center

Thomas L. Creer
Ohio University

Robert Elliott
University of Toledo

Paul M. G. Emmelkamp
University of Amsterdam

Sol L. Garfield
Washington University

Russell E. Glasgow
AMC Cancer Research Center

Leslie S. Greenberg
York University, Canada

Gordon C. Nagayama Hall
University of Oregon

T. Mark Harwood
University of California, Santa Barbara

Clara E. Hill
University of Maryland

Steven D. Hollon
Vanderbilt University

Grayson Holmbeck
Loyola University, Chicago

Kenneth A. Holroyd
Ohio University

Ripu D. Jindal
University of Pittsburgh Medical Center

Alan E. Kazdin
Yale University School of Medicine

Philip C. Kendall
Temple University

Michael J. Lambert
Brigham Young University

Kenneth N. Levy
City University of New York

Germain Lietaer
Catholic University of Leuven, Belgium

Mary Malik
University Of California,Santa Barbara

K. Roy MacKenzie
University of British Columbia

Alyson Leigh Mease
Indiana University

Sharon Noble
University of California, Santa Barbara

Joel Nunez
Pennsylvania State University

Benjamin M. Ogles
Ohio University

David E. Orlinsky
University of Chicago

Michael Helge Rønnestad
University of Oslo, Norway

Thomas L. Sexton
Indiana University

Brent D. Slife
Brigham Young University

Timothy W. Smith
University of Utah

Bernhard Strauss
Frederick Schiller University

Stanley Sue
University of California, Davis

Hani Talebi
University of California, Santa Barbara

Michael E. Thase
University of Pittsburgh Medical Center

Timothy Verduin
Temple University

Ulrike Willutzki
Ruhr-University Bochum, Germany

Eunice Wong
University of California, Santa Barbara

Kathleen Young
San Diego City College

Nolan Zane
University of California, Davis

Contents

Section 1

Historical, Methodological, Ethical, and Conceptual Foundations

CHAPTER 1

INTRODUCTION AND HISTORICAL OVERVIEW

MICHAEL J. LAMBERT
Brigham Young University
ALLEN E. BERGIN
Brigham Young University
SOL L. GARFIELD
Washington University

Psychotherapy has come a long way from its humble beginnings as a "new movement" at the beginning of the twentieth century and continues to be a field characterized by changing emphases, new developments, and considerable controversy. It receives considerable attention from the news media and has a place in the popular media including television, novels, movies, the Internet, and the "self-help" industry. It is highly regarded as an indispensable form of treatment for a variety of mental health problems and personal crises, and it remains a popular endeavor for a growing number of professionals and paraprofessionals. Its evolution has been nicely summarized in *The History of Psychotherapy: A Century of Change* by Freedheim (1992).

In contrast, research into the processes and effects of psychotherapy remains much less well known and, to some degree, represents a minor aspect of the endeavors that fall under the rubric of psychotherapy with its emphasis on theory and practical application. Nevertheless, the field of psychotherapy research is a vital and evolving enterprise, which supplements the theory-based activities of therapists and provides a foundation for practice. The forms that research has taken over the years have evolved in many of the same ways as psychotherapy itself—moving in the direction of precisely understanding the factors that lead to positive patient improvement. This evolution has been summarized in past editions of this *Handbook* (Bergin & Garfield, 1971, 1994; Garfield & Bergin, 1978, 1986).

Before discussing current trends and issues in psychotherapy research, we present a historical overview in order to put current research in the context of past research practices and changes in society at large. This overview includes comments on treatment and providers, payment systems, trends in practice, and general research directions. Finally, we provide an overview of the book's contents.

HISTORICAL BACKGROUND

From the end of the nineteenth century to around 1960, Sigmund Freud and his notable colleagues were the dominant influence in psychotherapy. Even after his death in 1939, Freud's followers persisted in defending psychoanalysis and in creating variations and significant modifications of his original scheme. Alfred Adler, Karl Jung, Karen Horney, and Harry Sullivan, while offering important modifications, retained the traditional features of Freud's thinking, such as the importance of early life experiences, repressed conflict, and unconscious motivation.

Research on these methods was published as early as 1924 (Bergin, 1971). Following the emergence of the Freudian influence, other approaches to psychotherapy began to appear. The client-centered theory, as developed by Carl Rogers (1942), was a significant departure from Freudian views, rebelling against the "therapist-as-expert" who interpreted client behavior. Rogers emphasized the client's potential for self-healing and the need for the therapist to provide an environment rich in respect, warmth, and empathic connection. Positive personality change was viewed as inevitable in such an environment.

Other more radical developments included learning-based approaches, which appeared as early as the 1920s (Jones, 1924; Mowrer & Mowrer, 1938). Learning-based procedures emphasized patient behaviors, situational contingencies, and an active/directive role for the therapist. These approaches did not begin to have a dramatic impact on psychotherapy until the publication of Wolpe's *Psychotherapy by Reciprocal Inhibition* in 1958. Since then, psychologists have been extremely influential in its development. Both the Rogerian position and that of the learning-based approaches placed greater emphasis on the importance of evaluating the effects of therapy than had been true of other orientations. Rogers's research groups applied sound recording techniques of actual sessions, allowing researchers to carefully examine the moment-by-moment encounter, thereby reducing the mystery of the therapeutic hour. Learning-based approaches put major emphasis on monitoring the treatment response and its connection to therapist-guided interventions. Both methods were relatively brief (lasting weeks or months) as compared with psychoanalysis and related techniques (often taking years), a factor that increased the feasibility of research inquiries.

The emergence of cognitive therapy was a natural outgrowth of the limitations of the learning-based approaches with their emphasis on behavior at the expense of thought, but also represented dissatisfaction with the effects of psychodynamic treatments. Cognitive therapy was most notably advocated by Ellis (1962) and Beck (1970) and came to the forefront of theory-driven treatments by the mid-1970s with the publication of Beck's (1976) *Cognitive Therapy and the Emotional Disorders.* These and related developments, such as the emergence of social learning theory (Bandura, 1969), provided rich contrasts in theory and method and carried with them a strong research emphasis.

The 1950s and 1960s marked an exciting and innovative period for the field of psychotherapy and mental health in general. The community mental health movement, along with additional forces from within psychology itself, resulted in further declines in the popularity of long-term treatments, with many of their assumptions about behavior change interventions being further challenged. These challenges were largely based on social forces that provided pressure to make affordable treatments widely available to all segments of the population. Changes toward brief interventions have even been accelerated in the last two decades due to economic pressures and the costs involved in making therapy widely available. Within psychology, theoretical issues have been the strongest driving force toward change, but research results have also been important.

The brewing theoretical controversy between systems of treatment with their underlying assumptions was crystallized in a controversial article published by British psychologist Hans Eysenck. He published an early review of 24 studies, concluding that there was no research evidence to support the effectiveness of psychotherapy compared to groups receiving no therapy and that psychoanalysis was less effective than no treatment (Eysenck, 1952). This provocative conclusion was strongly criticized by numerous psychologists (e.g., Bergin, 1971; Lambert, 1976). Nonetheless, the Eysenck article was important in sparking considerable interest in scientific investigations of psychotherapy. Since that time, there has been a dramatic increase in both the quantity and quality of research on psychotherapy, the focus of this and the previous *Handbooks.*

Since Eysenck's (1952) review, most reviews evaluating the efficacy of psychotherapy have been much more positive. By 1970, there were enough studies on the outcome of treatments that it took "the patience of Job and the mind of a bank auditor" to integrate the information (Meltzoff & Kornreich, 1970). This job was undertaken by several reviewers (Bergin, 1971; Bergin & Lambert, 1978; Meltzoff & Kornreich, 1970). With the emergence of meta-analytic statistic techniques, reviews of the growing literature were subjected to quantitative analysis, with large bodies of information summed across studies. Smith, Glass, and Miller's (1980) book was the most extensive re-analysis of the psychotherapy literature that dealt with treatment effects. Through an analysis of more than 475 studies, it reaffirmed the findings of the earlier scholarly reviews: The effects of therapy are superior to no-treatment and placebo control conditions, and therapies appear to have equivalent effects when compared with each other across a variety of disorders. Since the Smith, Glass, and Miller review, the number of studies on psychotherapy has increased so dramatically that just reviewing the reviews has become a daunting task (see Chapter 5, this volume). Some of these reviews show the superiority of some therapeutic techniques over others, the subject of numerous chapters within this text.

Several other developments in the field are worthy of note here. The number and types of psychotherapy have expanded, the practitioners of psychotherapy have increased in number and diversity along with training programs, and reimbursement systems have changed dramatically, having emerged as a powerful force in theory, practice, and research. All of these topics merit further discussion and will be highlighted both here and by the chapter authors.

The Practitioners of Psychotherapy

The practitioners of psychotherapy are becoming more numerous and diverse. This expansion and diversity can be seen across other professions as well. In medicine, for example, many services, such as writing prescriptions or administering anesthesia, were once performed solely by M.D.s but are now offered by nurses, medical assistants, and related personnel. In Freud's time, the practitioners of psychotherapy were primarily physicians, and prior to World War II, clinical psychology was a relatively small and undeveloped profession, with a major emphasis on the administration of psychological tests. After the war the shortage of psychiatrists, coupled with the unmet demand to care for veterans who had developed psychological disorders, led to government-supported graduate training in clinical and counseling psychology, with psychotherapy becoming an important part of this training. Despite subsequent conflicts with organized medicine, the independent practice of psychotherapy by psychologists became a reality (Garfield, 1983). Social workers, school psychologists, nurses, pastoral counselors, marriage and family therapists, licensed professional counselors, substance abuse counselors, as well as a host of paraprofessionals, also participated in a variety of psychotherapeutic activities—all aimed at improving the mental health of patients.

The kinds of individuals involved in psychotherapeutic services diversified to meet the demands for service, especially from underserved populations such as the poor, substance-abusing individuals, those in the criminal justice system, and the seriously and persistently mentally ill. The established professions both resisted and facilitated such developments, fearing the negative consequences to the patient who would be treated by minimally trained persons and also wary of competition from less trained providers. However, the forces at work in society and within individuals have apparently stretched boundaries of who can be considered a trustworthy provider. In addition to the needs of the underserved, as well as the fact that many treatments, once developed, can be routinely offered, economic forces have contributed to the movement toward using less trained persons (Bright, Baker, & Niemeyer, 1999; Weisz, Weisz, Ham, Granger, & Morton, 1995).

Some of the more disturbing (and promising) conclusions of psychotherapy research arose from its investigation of the effects of training on patient outcome. Within this context, research has not shown a strong link between level and type of professional training of providers and psychotherapy outcome. Durlak (1979), among others, reviewed research in this area, concluding that clients treated by paraprofessionals had essentially equivalent outcomes to those offered by professionals. This research was criticized on numerous grounds (Hattie, Sharpley, & Rogers, 1984; Nietzel & Fisher, 1981; Stein & Lambert, 1984, 1995), and detractors were quick to point out that most of this research was conducted by those who had an interest in showing the value of paraprofessionals. It was also noted that paraprofessionals were trained and supervised by professionals rather than offering independent services. Nevertheless, few studies can be found that show superiority for the highly trained professional. The study by Strupp and Hadley (1979) comparing experienced psychotherapists with college professors who had campus reputations as counselors revealed no significant differences between the two groups. An experimental program to provide therapy training for middle-aged homemakers who were college graduates also produced very positive results for the nonprofessionals (Rioch, 1971).

This research does raise questions about the value of clinical training and the uniqueness of psychotherapeutic interventions. Nevertheless, research in this area supports the value of psychotherapy regardless of the level or kind of training that typifies the separate professions and the paraprofessionals whom they train and employ as extensions of their influence. If taken seriously, such findings support the widespread application of psychotherapeutic services and will ensure that they remain widely available. On the basis of much research evidence, no one profession can claim a monopoly on superior service, and the thoughtful use of paraprofessionals should be encouraged not only for economic reasons, but also because of the proven effectiveness of paraprofessionals in a variety of roles.

Perhaps one reason for the lack of difference between professions on psychotherapy outcome is that the training given in psychotherapy is highly diverse even within professions. Psychiatrists are trained first in medicine and second in pharmacological solutions, with psychotherapy only a distant third. Psychologists have typically been trained in academic departments of psychology but now are often trained in freestanding professional schools as well. Both types of programs differ within and between themselves in the amount and intensity of didactic and supervised experience. One cannot distinguish the training a particular psychologist has received (or its quality) by simply knowing the type of degree attained. Since the various programs may emphasize different theoretical orientations and different practicum experiences, the diversity in training can be immense. In addition, knowledge of a professional's credentials will not yield information about participation in widely available postdoctoral institutes, continuing education programs, workshops, professional meetings, and the like. The personal qualities of the psychotherapist are also of great importance. Nevertheless, psychotherapy research has illuminated the widespread effectiveness of psychological interventions across a wide range of practitioners that offer services. This effectiveness is highlighted in many of the chapters that follow.

Continuing Dominance of Integrative/Eclectic Practice

A clear trend in psychotherapeutic interventions since the mid-1960s has been the proliferation not only of the types of practitioners, but also of the types and numbers of psychotherapies used alone and in combination in day-to-day practice. Garfield (1982) identified 60 forms of psychotherapy in use in the 1960s. In 1975, the Research Task Force of the National Institute of Mental Health estimated that there were 125 different forms. Herink (1980) listed over 200 separate approaches, while Kazdin (1986) noted 400 variants of psychotherapy. Research on the effectiveness of each and every emerging form of therapy was nonexistent, raising the issue of the degree to which many forms of treatment were merely experimental. Parloff (1982), for example, pointed out that "a systematic approach to dealing with a matrix of 250 psychosocial therapies and 150 classes of disorders would require approximately 47 million comparisons" (p. 723). Clearly, the invention of separate psychotherapies took place independent of research evidence, and research results have not slowed the development and advocacy of various treatment methods.

The proliferation of therapies has been accompanied by the growing trend for therapists to disavow allegiance to a single system of treatment in the form of a purely theoretically based approach. *Eclecticism*, representing the use of procedures from different theoretical systems, and *integrationism*, representing the theoretical joining of two or more positions into a consistent approach, have replaced the dominance of major theories in therapeutic practice. Surveys of practitioners repeatedly indicate that one-half to two-thirds of providers prefer using a variety of techniques that have arisen from major theoretical schools (e.g., Jensen, Bergin, & Greaves, 1990: Norcross, Karg, & Prochaska, 1997). Those therapists who identify with an eclectic orientation feel free to select techniques from any orientation that they deem to be in the best interest of the patient.

Unfortunately, eclectic therapists have come to little consensus about which techniques are most helpful, and thus there is little likelihood that two eclectic therapists would use the same techniques with the same client. Garfield and Kurtz (1977), in a study of 154 eclectic psychologists, found that 32 combinations of theoretical orientations were in use. Jensen et al. (1990) found comparable results but in addition noted a trend toward differences in preferred combinations across professional disciplines, with dynamic orientations more often used in psychiatry, systems theories in social work and marriage and family therapy, and cognitive and behavioral approaches in psychology. Since eclecticism on the whole does not represent any truly systematic approach, research on this "approach" has been minimal (Lambert, 1992); even if studies of eclectic practice were conducted, the results would probably be especially hard to replicate. Nevertheless, eclecticism reflects the existence of many diverse theoretical orientations with varying strengths. These strengths are widely recognized and supported by research evidence from the study of single-theory approaches. The movement toward the combined use and integration of these approaches is inevitable and likely to continue.

An example of this movement can be noted in attempts at theoretical integration of psychodynamic and behavioral procedures by Wachtel (1977) and Goldfried (1991). Other efforts to blend theoretical diversity include the formation of the Society for the Exploration of Psychotherapy Integration (SEPI), publication of the *Handbook of Psychotherapy Integration* (Norcross & Goldfried, 1992), and the founding of several new journals. In addition, process research aimed at examining the in-session behavior of therapists across different theoretical orientations indicates that the distinctiveness of approaches is less pronounced in practice than it is at the abstract level of theory (Ablon & Jones, 1999; Norcross & Goldfried, 1992). Thus, theories of change are somewhat independent of therapists' actual activities which show a large degree of overlap across treatments—sometimes referred to as common factors. These common factors, which account for a significant amount of patient change, include the facilitation of hope, the opportunity for emotional release, exploration and integration of one's problems, support, advice, and encouragement to try out new behaviors and thoughts. Emphasis on common factors, a phenomenon that is distinct from eclecticism (see Chapter 5 of this volume), has the potential for reducing conflicts between particular theoretic views. Polarization based on claims of unique effectiveness for specific theoretical orientations has resulted in conflict within the field that has had positive consequences (e.g., stimulation of research studies). But it has also caused considerable defensiveness and slowing of progress (e.g., through overstatement of claims of success and attempts to create lists of effective treatment). Eclectic and integrationist movements reflect attempts by many practitioners to be flexible in their approach to working with patients.

This *Handbook* has been eclectic from its inception in 1967 and its first publication by Bergin and Garfield in 1971. Empirical findings from all approaches are considered potentially important. Being open to research findings on any approach, both positive and negative, is the central mission of the *Handbook*. This focus is consistent with the ideal goals of eclecticism—fostering what works for the patient. Openness to methods of investigating psychotherapy is also valued and is represented in the chapters representing diverse and competing treatment methods and modalities that employ correlational and experimental methods, as well as in a chapter, new to the *Handbook*, advocating alternative research strategies (see Chapter 3, this volume).

Integration of Practice and Research: The Emergence of Evidence-Based Practice

Historically, the importance of research in guiding clinical practice has been limited. Theories that guide interventions have typically been developed and disseminated independent of research investigations. Despite considerable lip service to the importance of research for practice, many practitioners do not find treatment research, as reported in scientific journals, to be particularly useful to them. Research articles reporting clinical trials have not been rated highly among important sources of information on treatment (Cohen, Sargent, & Sechrest, 1986; Morrow-Bradley & Elliot, 1986). However, several dynamic forces have resulted in a renewed interest in outcome research and its integration into routine practice. These forces are both theoretical and economic. The emergence of cognitive behavioral treatments and the increasing specificity of the Diagnostic and Statistical Manual of Mental Disorders (DSM) of the American Psychiatric Association (1994) have led to increased interest in developing specific treatments for specific disorders. In recent years, we have seen more interest in what form of therapy is most effective within diagnostic classifications. Thus, research and practice have moved from an early emphasis on viewing symptoms as superficial to considering the removal of symptoms as a central goal of treatment. This trend can be noted in research designs that include only patients with a specific disorder as well as in increased use of dependent measures that operationalize outcomes for specific disorders (as noted by Hill & Lambert, Chapter 4, this volume). The result has been unambiguous evidence for the efficacy of some treatments that are transportable from the laboratory to clinical settings.

Changes in reimbursement systems in the form of managed care organizations have also had an impact on both practice and research. These organizations have emphasized the development of clinical guidelines that are intended to make treatment more uniform and, presumably, more effective. Despite a disappointing emphasis placed on cost reductions (rather than on treatment quality) by these organizations, they clearly have rekindled the need for evidence-based practice. Regardless of this misplaced financial emphasis (which will probably require legislative remedy), the resulting attention to acquiring more evidence for effective and efficient practice promises to benefit patients in the long run if the evidence is translated into policy and practice.

Based on the assumptions that society is in need of treatments with known effects and that behavioral healthcare specialists agree on the necessity of providing a firm base of empirical support for their activities, numerous efforts have been made to identify therapies that are effective with specific disorders. Beutler (2000) has provided an overview of efforts to set scientific standards both in the United States and abroad. He notes, however, that scientific standards for practice have been typically based on the subjective impressions of committee members rather than on the evidence itself (e.g., Roth & Fonagy's 1996 *What Works for Whom? A Critical Review of Psychotherapy Research;* and Nathan, Gorman, & Salkind's 1999 *Treating Mental Disorders: A Guide to What Works*). The most notorious efforts in this area were those developed by Division 12 of the American Psychological Association (the Division of Clinical Psychology), which created criteria for what constitutes empirical support for treatments. The agenda of the original Task Force on Promotion and Dissemination of Psychological Procedures (1995) was to consider methods for educating clinical psychologists, third-party funders, and the public about effective psychotherapies. This Task Force (now called the Standing Committee on Science and Practice) generated and disseminated criteria for levels of empirical support, identified relevant treatment outcome studies, and weighed evidence according to defined criteria. This resulted in highly controversial lists of treatments that met the criteria for different levels of empirical support (Chambless, 1996; Chambless & Hollon, 1998; Chambless et al., 1996) and in lists of resources for training and treatment manuals (Woody & Sanderson, 1998).

The controversies generated from the initial report came mainly from practitioners who saw the report as rigid, if not dogmatic, and as having an agenda that was biased in favor of therapies promoted by Task Force members (e.g., criteria were set up that would give an advantage to highly structured short-term behavioral and cognitive behavioral treatments advocated by many Task Force members). But strong criticism came from psychotherapy researchers as well (Garfield, 1996; Nathan, 1998; Strupp, 1997). For example, Gavin Andrews stated his view of empirically supported treatments in a recent commentary:

> This is not to deny that identifying empirically supported treatments carried out by a profession does not have important political advantages for the profession. Funders, providers, and consumers all like to pretend that efficacy is the same as effectiveness, and lists of empirically supported treatments feed this delusion. (Andrews, 2000, p.267)

The Task Force's initial response to these criticisms appeared defensive to many. For example, it insisted on retaining terms such as empirically "validated" therapies (later changed to empirically supported therapies; Chambless, 1996), and the members seemed to lack the humility of recognizing the limitations of their own work, while being especially harsh on practitioners whose practices were often seen as not being based on empirical knowledge (see Slife, this volume). This "methodolatry" did not seem to offer a hopeful way of bridging the gap between practice and research; indeed, it created greater distance rather than greater consensus. Despite the clash between "science" and "practice," the common goal of assuring positive patient outcomes and the dialogues between advocates of the two positions will hopefully prove to be in the long-term best interests of the recipients of psychotherapy. However, there is a difference between clinical trials where patient-subjects have to meet strict diagnostic criteria to be accepted for treatment and actual patients seeking therapy on their own.

The current Committee on Science and Practice now pursues a three-part agenda (Weisz, Hawley, Pilkonis, Woody, & Follette, 2000): (1) reliability of review procedures through standardization and rules of evidence; (2) improved research quality; and (3) increased relevance and dissemination to the professions and public. This work is an evolving movement, with its early productions being too limited and doctrinaire but with the important goal of rapprochement between research and practice communities. Hopefully, the damage done by the early advocates can be overcome by the apparent recognition of the positive contributions of the many forces that affect the way psychotherapy is delivered to those in need.

In our opinion, the job of the committee is a difficult one that will never be completed. Treatments evolve, as do research strategies. Therefore, the search for final conclusions that is being undertaken by this and similar committees must always recognize the tentative nature of the results forthcoming from research and practice. The current committee appears to be mindful of this reality and has been much more circumspect in its assertions than the original committee (Weisz et al., 2000). Nevertheless, the committee continues toward the goal of developing "a single list of empirically supported treatments" and setting "standards of practice" (Weisz et al., 2000, p. 249). A more practical goal, given the large number of disorders, treatment research paradigms, and means of measuring treatment effects, would be to inform both practitioners and the public of developments in the field based on current research. Lists of "empirically supported treatments" are static and seem to offer only a false guarantee of effectiveness. Although many practitioners and the public may be comforted by the notion that they are offering or receiving an empirically supported psychotherapy, the fact is that the success of treatment appears to be largely dependent on the client and the therapist, not on the use of "proven" empirically based treatments (see Chapters 6 and 7, this volume). Proof of effective treatment needs to be based on measurement of treatment response rather than provision of the "right" treatment.

Several trends in psychotherapy research appear to be more promising than the creation of treatment-for-disorder lists. These promising new research strategies are likely to make research more useful to providers and will probably have more impact on patients than offering "empirically supported treatments." Although most research has depended on statistical tests of differences between treatment and control groups, with differences reported through the use of group-based inferential statistics, there is a movement toward the use of clinically meaningful change criteria for the individual patient. Efforts to apply this alternative psychotherapy research paradigm have been recently reported in a Special Section of the *Journal of Consulting and Clinical Psychology* (Lambert, 2001).

Variously termed "patient-based research," "quality management," and "outcome management," these research strategies make use of statistical strategies for modeling expected patient treatment response in relation to actual treatment response and use definitions of clinically meaningful final outcome such as those elaborated upon by the late Neil Jacobson and his colleagues (Jacobson, Follette, & Revenstorf, 1984; Jacobson & Truax, 1991). Outcome management research strategies are aimed at helping clinicians formally monitor patient treatment response, and so these strategies make adjustments to treatments in real time. *In contrast to other research strategies, outcome management makes empiricism a viable part of routine practice rather than a distant abstraction that practitioners find difficult to incorporate in practice.*

These methods, which are being applied in numerous settings in the United States and across the world, promise to make a significant contribution to standard research paradigms. For example, if a therapist develops a treatment plan based on knowledge of empirically supported treatment outcomes, monitoring a particular patient's response to this treatment, as offered, allows one to judge the degree of this patient's response and to shift treatment strategies if the treatment is not having its usual (expected) impact. Application of statistical modeling of expected recovery (and related techniques for quality management) has already been shown to enhance treatment outcome (Lambert, Whipple, Smart, et al., 2001; Lambert, Whipple, Vermeersch et al., 2002), but as these methods are relatively new, they are in need of replication.

Based on the initial applications of these research methods, it is clear that quality management research can be integrated into routine practice, thus narrowing the gap between practice and research, while improving treatment outcomes. Already, journals are encouraging authors to report the results of traditional studies with conventions such as effect size statistics, estimates of clinical significance, and applications in clinical practice settings rather than research laboratories. Over the last decade, psychotherapy research has become more diverse and more responsive to the criticism raised by providers. Future psychotherapy research promises to be of greater use to clinicians and is more likely to trickle down to solid patient benefits. This *Handbook* is dedicated to bringing the accumulated research findings to researchers and practitioners, with the hope that the integration of research, theory, and practice will bring out the best that can be offered to those who seek and expect effective treatments.

The Continued Emphasis on Brief Therapies

A clear trend in practice has been the movement toward relatively brief treatments. For the first half of the twentieth century, effective psychotherapy was considered to be a long-term process, with brief therapy considered superficial. Although this view persists in some parts of the world, it does not represent current practice patterns in the United States and many other countries. One of the authors had the opportunity recently of going to dinner with a group of psychoanalysts from Germany where the health system continues to support long-term therapy. The discussion turned to a recent controversy within psychoanalytically oriented providers, with some advocating three sessions per week instead of the traditional four. The more traditional providers viewed this position as undermining the best interests of the patient. The author was a complete outsider in such a discussion because in the United States brief therapy has become acceptable to most practitioners and certainly is now the common experience for most patients. In fact, most research is conducted on therapy offered once a week for no more than 14 weeks, and in most practice settings treatment actually averages closer to five sessions (Hansen, Lambert, & Forman, 2002). Earlier editions of the *Handbook* included a chapter dedicated to brief therapy. No such chapter was included in the current edition because it was seen as redundant with most other chapters. Almost all therapies that are studied (particularly in the United States) are brief, lasting less than 20 sessions. For an understanding of longer-term treatments, one must consider older studies that have already been reviewed in earlier editions of the *Handbook*, or examine research from European countries (which is often not available in English) where patients continue to receive treatments that last for months and even years.

Early providers of psychoanalytically oriented therapy prescribed years of treatment that was very costly (Voth & Orth, 1973, reported an average length of 835 sessions from their study). An early impetus for change in such practices was the community mental health movement of the 1960s (Joint Commission on Mental Illness and Health, 1961) which emphasized making treatments available to underprivileged members of society, including the provision of crisis intervention and emergency services. Organized brief therapy programs tended to use interventions that lasted 6 to 10 sessions and generally reported positive results (Koss & Shiang, 1994). This trend, together with the rise of behavior therapies, stimulated greater interest in briefer therapies. Both dynamic and cognitive behavior therapies emerged over the ensuing years in various versions and forms, and, of course, all claimed to be different from the others and yet still effective.

Managed Care and Dose-Effect Research

The most profound development in recent years has been the advent of managed care organizations. Most health insurance plans place limits on the number of treatment sessions they will reimburse, and they often instigate evaluative procedures in order to make certain that therapy does not extend beyond what they deem as the basic necessary length. Because many people cannot afford private treatment that goes beyond these limits, managed care organizations determine the length of treatment received by a very large number of Americans.

Patients, for the most part, prefer to be helped as quickly as possible, and efficiency is also favored by funding services such as insurance companies and the government. Managed care itself arose, at least partially, as a response to spiraling healthcare cost in general. The amount of treatment available to those in need is often determined by the costs of providing services. Obviously, if as much can be gained from 20 sessions of treatment as 30, then curtailing the amount of therapy makes good economic sense. Brief therapy is an option that responds to the issue of efficiency, a topic important to many. At this point in time, psychotherapy researchers have not devoted much attention to cost-effectiveness studies that would simultaneously consider cost and outcome, although they have begun to investigate the relationship between "dose" of treatment and response.

Early investigations or the dose-response relationships focused on demonstrating that brief therapy was as effective as longer therapies (e.g., Luborsky, Singer, & Luborsky, 1975). Contemporary studies have been more interested in understanding this topic. This research has important implications for social policy and insurer decision making. Howard, Kopta, Krause, Merton, and Orlinsky (1986) were the first to report data in a form that was independent from comparative studies. In a meta-analysis of data from 2,431 patients drawn from previously reported studies, Howard et al. used statistical modeling techniques to estimate the number of sessions needed to meet a defined standard of improvement. Their analysis suggested that positive gains made early in treatment were followed by less dramatic changes across later sessions. They also suggested that 75% of patients had improved after 26 treatment sessions (nearly six months of once-weekly psychotherapy).

Later research following this same paradigm, but using data from patients who rated their progress on a weekly basis (obviating the need for statistical procedures that estimate weekly change), has found the same general relationships—rapid change early in therapy is followed by smaller per-session increments, but more therapy increases the likelihood of improvement and recovery in individual patients (e.g., Anderson & Lambert, 2001; Kadera, Lambert, & Andrews, 1996). It appears from this research and from related studies summarized in Chapter 5 of this volume that 50% of patients who enter treatment in clinical settings will show *clinically meaningful change* after 13 to 18 sessions of treatment. An additional 25% will meet the same standards after approximately 50 sessions of once-weekly treatment (an estimate of dosage that exceeds that provided by Howard et al., 1986).

These studies suggest that the movement toward briefer treatment is justified on empirical grounds, but that close to 50% of patients will not be well served by therapies that are arbitrarily limited to fewer than 20 sessions. They also indicate that the more disturbed a patient is when he or she begins treatment, the longer therapy will need to last in order for the patient to show adequate benefits. *Limiting treatment duration serves the interests of those patients who are least in need, but it cannot be considered a fair and equitable practice for a large minority of patients. Some recognition of this reality and its social consequences needs to find its way into the minds of the American public, employers, and government, and be integrated into managed care guidelines and future social policy decisions as well as theoretical suppositions about effective psychotherapy.*

At the same time, the limited number of sessions actually attended by patients (Garfield, 1994) predates the emergence of managed care organizations and suggests the need for healthcare providers to take steps to encourage those in need not only to seek treatment but to stay in treatment until a reliable benefit has been achieved. Hansen, Lambert, and Forman (2002) recently reported that evidence on the efficacy of psychotherapy reported in clinical trials is based on an average dosage of 12 to 16 sessions, while the actual dosage in routine practice is closer to 3 to 5 sessions. It is no wonder that they also found routine practice to be substantially less effective than clinical trials.

Ethics in Research

Interest and concern over the ethics of research activities connected to psychotherapy have a long-standing history. For example, in the 1950s Rogers and Dymond (1954) raised concerns about the use of a no-treatment control group in their study of client-centered psychotherapy. The current climate for conducting studies of psychotherapy, and psychology in general, abounds with ethical and legal issues aimed at protecting the participants of studies. The protection of "subjects" rights and welfare has been a positive development, notwithstanding the sometimes obvious inhibiting of creativity and slowing of progress in the field. These protections have obvious impact on the design and conduct of studies and have led to reductions in the use of no-treatment and placebo control groups as well as the rise in use of "standard treatment" or "usual treatment" control groups.

Other standards for conduct of research studies have remained more stable. Objectivity and honesty in recording, tabulating, analyzing, and reporting results are the mainstays of all scientific endeavors. It is important to maintain such principles if the research enterprise is to exist and flourish. So far, psychotherapy research has avoided notoriety for the kind of fraud that has been exposed in some fields (e.g., data tampering or even the creation of false data). Intentional mishandling of data and its variations must be perceived as simply intolerable. However, within the field, instances of biased interpretation of data have been noted (e.g., Bergin & Garfield, 1994); such activities can be harmful to the status of scientific information as well as the reputation and careers of those who are involved.

Some related problems though more subtle and complex, are nonetheless important to the field. For example, the presentation and interpretation of data by researchers leave considerable wiggle room for partial truths to be presented as the entire picture. In fact, journal review procedures encourage routine summaries of procedures that make it all but certain that research reports will present the strongest possible case for rigor without mention of significant limiting information. In the competitive world of publishing in the most respected journals, where editors and reviewers search for design and performance flaws, researchers are likely to emphasize the strengths of their research rather than a list of problems. Even the most rigorously executed research is imperfectly conducted, but little is to be gained by elaborating on problems when submitting manuscripts for review.

For example, a common demand in clinical trials research is to test the effects of treatment on a single disorder. In the context of writing about selection and exclusion criteria for study patients, researchers are prone to emphasize the inclusion of homogeneous patient samples. When being criticized for the lack of relevance of such research (with such carefully selected patients) for practice, however, these same researchers are likely to present a picture of these patients that is quite different. They will argue that the patients are, after all, just like the patients seen in everyday practice. Avid readers of scientific reports generally understand that the politics of publishing influence the presentation of methods and that these presentations are not an entirely accurate picture of all the findings that could be reported. Fortunately, the discussion of results (and the use of peer review) often points out many limitations of the research and softens the expression of implications for practice that might otherwise be made.

In addition, replication studies, as well as exposure of research to public scrutiny, eventually corrects many of the important errors that find their way into the field. But this corrective action often takes years. Aside from these remedies, readers of research must use caution in drawing more than tentative conclusions from any particular study. In the area of interpreting research findings, meta-analytic reviews present an opportunity to increase objectivity. Although such procedures are not entirely free of biasing choices (compare, for example, Anderson & Lambert, 1995; Crits-Christoph, 1992, Svartberg & Stiles, 1991 or results presented by Prioleau, Murdock, & Brody, 1983; Smith, Glass, & Miller, 1980), the decision rules can be explicated and made public, thereby providing a step in the direction of reducing biases in reviews of psychotherapy outcome literature (see Chapter 2 of this volume).

Psychotherapy researchers are fully aware that values are central in both the therapeutic process and the research that they conduct. An emphasis on values and their impact on research is often obscured by the focus on effective technologies and their evaluation in standard research paradigms. Yet researchers recognize that their choices about what and how to study the changes produced by psychotherapy guide the phenomena that they seek to investigate. Psychotherapy and psychotherapy research are in fact guided by a host of value choices. Change in humans is so complex that it is difficult to study the full meaning of the modifications that take place in treatment. Symptomatic changes often have a meaning component that is seldom studied in traditional research. The errors and oversimplification that inevitably arise in psychotherapy research often come from the complexity of a research task that is simply too daunting, rather than from carelessness, ignorance, or naiveté. Few studies even attempt to examine the full range of consequences of entering treatment at a propitious moment in the life of a client who is enmeshed in a family and social context. The research summaries in this book attempt to reduce the myriad of methods and results of psychotherapy to a cohesive picture that has implications for practice, but in so doing, the values of reviewers affect the conclusions that are drawn.

Out of necessity, the chapters in this text, like the research studies that informed them, sometimes emphasize relatively narrow domains of personal functioning and include research studies that vary widely in sophistication and rigor. Although there are limitations in these research summaries, they provide a foundation for broadening inquiries into the effects of psychotherapies and thereby enable future studies to move forward to more important questions. Even with these limitations, however, the research summaries included in this volume have important implications for the practice of psychotherapy and thereby for the fabric of social life in the fullest sense of the word.

Overview of the Book

This *Handbook* is divided into four sections followed by a summary chapter. As in the previous four editions, each chapter can be read by itself and makes an independent contribution to the literature. The first four chapters focus on broad issues ("Historical, Methodological, Ethical, and Conceptual Foundations"). Following the present introductory chapter is a chapter on research design that will help the reader understand terminology, procedures, statistical methods, and what types of designs are suitable for answering particular research questions. The information in Chapter 2 is essential to understanding and evaluating existing research. Chapter 3 departs from earlier editions of the *Handbook* by presenting a philosophical examination of the underlying assumptions of research methods. Written by Brent Slife, a past president of APA's Division of Philosophical Psychology, it challenges the foundation of the scientific methods most commonly employed in the research that is the focus of the *Handbook*. The fourth and final chapter in this section exposes the reader to methods of measuring the processes and outcomes of psychotherapy by reviewing measurement strategies and, like Chapter 2, is especially important for those who are planning research in this area.

The second section of this handbook, "Evaluating the Ingredients of Effective Psychotherapy", deals with evaluations of therapy in a broad context. Chapter 5 provides an overview of the efficacy and effectiveness of psychotherapy and deals with questions that are central to practice. Chapter 6 focuses on the patient's contribution to effective psychotherapy. Chapter 7 summarizes the contribution of the therapist to psychotherapy outcome. The final chapter in this section evaluates the role of processes and outcomes as studied simultaneously within a single investigation. Together, these four chapters, while overlapping to some degree, provide a broad picture of the most basic and general findings of psychotherapy research.

The third section of this handbook, "Major Approaches", reviews research findings as they have arisen within systems of psychotherapies. It includes chapters on behavior therapy with adults, cognitive behavioral therapy, and experiential/humanistic interventions.

The fourth section, "Research Applications with Special Groups and Modalities", is the longest section, with six chapters. Included are chapters on psychotherapies with child and adolescent patients, marriage and family therapies, group psychotherapies, behavioral medicine, and health psychology. The psychotherapeutic practices in these chapters represent, to a certain extent, specialty areas that are distinct from each other, both in the patient problems addressed and the interventions used. Chapter 16 reviews research on treating psychological problems with medications alone and in conjunction with psychotherapy. Finally, the last chapter in this section deals with culturally diverse populations and modifications to usual practices necessitated by the sometimes dramatic differences between members of these minority groups and the dominant culture.

In the final chapter of the *Handbook*, we summarize some highlights noted in the preceding chapters. In this context, we focus on future directions and the implications of research for the field and for society in general.

REFERENCES

Ablon, J. S., & Jones, E. E. (1999). Psychotherapy process in the National Institute of Mental Health Treatment of Depression Collaborative Research Program. *Journal of Consulting and Clinical Psychology, 67(1)*, 64–75.

American Psychiatric Association (1994). *Diagnostic and statistical manual of mental disorders: DSM* (4th ed.) New York: American Psychiatric Association Press.

Anderson, E. M., & Lambert, M. J. (1995). Short-term dynamically oriented psychotherapy: A meta-analysis. *Clinical Psychology Review, 15(5)*, 503–514.

Anderson, E. M., & Lambert, M. J. (2001). A survival analysis of clinically significant change in outpatient psychotherapy. *Journal of Clinical Psychology* 57, 875–888.

Andrews, G. (2000). A focus on empirically supported outcomes: A commentary on search for empirically supported treatments. *Clinical psychology: Science and Practice*, 7, 264–268.

Bandura, A. (1969). *Principles of behavior modification.* New York: Holt, Rinehart & Winston.

Beck, A. T. (1970). Cognitive therapy: Nature and relation to behavior therapy. *Behavior Therapy, 1*, 184–200.

Beck, A. T. (1976). *Cognitive therapy and the emotional disorders.* New York: International Universities Press.

Bergin, A. E. (1971). The evaluation of therapeutic outcomes. In A. E. Bergin & S. L. Garfield (Eds.), *Handbook of psychotherapy and behavior change: An empirical analysis* (pp. 217–270). New York: John Wiley & Sons.

Bergin, A. E., & Garfield, S. L. (Eds.). (1971). *Handbook of psychotherapy and behavior change.* New York: John Wiley & Sons.

Bergin, A. E., & Garfield, S. L. (Eds.). (1994). *Handbook of psychotherapy and behavior change* (4th ed.). New York: John Wiley & Sons.

Bergin, A. E., & Lambert, M. J. (1978). The evaluation of therapeutic outcomes. In S. L. Garfield & A. E. Bergin (Eds.), *Handbook of psychotherapy and behavior change* (2nd ed.) (pp. 139–189). New York: John Wiley & Sons.

Beutler, L. E. (2000). David and Goliath: When empirical and clinical standards of practice meet. *American Psychologist, 55*, 997–1007.

Bright, J. I., Baker, K. D., & Niemeyer, R. A. (1999). Professional and paraprofessional group treatments for depression. A comparison of cognitive behavioral and mutual support interventions. *Journal of Consulting and Clinical Psychology, 67*, 491–501.

Chambless, D. L. (1996). In defense of dissemination of empirically supported psychological interventions. *Clinical Psychology: Science and Practice, 3(3)*, 230–235.

Chambless, D. L., & Hollon, S. D. (1998). Defining empirically supported psychological interventions. *Journal of Consulting and Clinical Psychology, 66(1)*, 7–18.

Chambless, D. L., Sanderson, W. C., Shoham, V., Johnson, S. B., Pope, K. S., Crits-Christoph, P.,

Baker, M., Johnson, B., Woody, S. R., Sue, S., Beutler, L. E., Williams, D. A., & McCurry, S. (1996). An update on empirically validated therapies. *Clinical Psychology, 49(2)*, 5–14.

Cohen, L. H., Sargent, M. M., & Sechrest, L. B. (1986). Use of psychotherapy research by professional psychologists. *American Psychologist, 41(2)*, 198–206.

Crits-Christoph, P. (1992). The efficacy of brief dynamic psychotherapy: A meta-analysis. *American Journal of Psychiatry, 149(2)*, 151–158.

Durlak, J. A. (1979). Comparative effectiveness of paraprofessional and professional helpers. *Psychological Bulletin, 86*, 80–92.

Ellis, A. (1962). *Reason and emotion in psychotherapy.* New York: Lyle Stuart.

Eysenck, H. F. (1952). The effects of psychotherapy: An evaluation. *Journal of Consulting Psychology, 16*, 319–324.

Freedheim, D. K. (1992). *The History of psychotherapy: A century of change.* Washington, DC: American Psychological Association Press.

Garfield, S. L. (1983). *Clinical psychology: The study of personality and behavior* (2nd ed.). New York: Aldine.

Garfield, S. L., & Bergin, A. E. (Eds.) (1978). *Handbook of psychotherapy and behavior change* (2nd ed.). New York: John Wiley & Sons.

Garfield, S. L. (1994). Research on client variables in psychotherapy. In A. E. Bergin & S. L. Garfield (Eds.), *Handbook of psychotherapy and behavior change.* New York: John Wiley & Sons.

Garfield, S. L. (1996). Some problems associated with "validated" forms of psychotherapy. *Clinical Psychology: Science and Practice 3*, 218–229.

Garfield, S. L. (1982). Electicism and integration in psychotherapy. *Behavioral Therapy, 13*, 174–183.

Garfield, S. L., & Bergin, A. E. (Eds.) (1986). *Handbook of psychotherapy and behavior change (3rd ed.).* New York: John Wiley & Sons.

Garfield, S. L., & Kurtz, R. (1977). A study of eclectic views. *Journal of Consulting and Clinical Psychology, 45*, 78–83.

Goldfried, M. R. (1991). Research issues in psychotherapy integration. *Journal of Psychology Integration, 1*, 5–25.

Hansen, N. B., Lambert, M. J., & Forman, E. M. (2002). The psychotherapy dose-response effect and its implications for treatment delivery services. *Clinical Psychology: Science and Practice, 9*, 329–343.

Hattie, J. A., Sharpley, C. F., & Rogers, H. J. (1984). Comparative effectiveness of professional and paraprofessional helpers. *Psychological Bulletin, 95*, 534–541.

Herink, R. (Ed.). (1980). *The psychotherapy handbook: The A to Z guide to more than 250 different therapies in use today.* New York: A Meridian Book, New American Library.

Howard, K. I., Kopta, S. M., Krause, M. S., Merton, S., & Orlinsky, D. E. (1986). The dose-effect relationship in psychotherapy. *American Psychologist, 41* (2), 159–164.

Jacobson, N. S., Follette, W. C., & Revenstorf, D. (1984). Psychotherapy outcome research: Methods for reporting variability and evaluating clinical significance. *Behavior Therapy, 15(4)*, 336–352.

Jacobson, N. S., & Truax, P. (1991). Clinical significance: A statistical approach to defining meaningful change in psychotherapy research. *Journal of Consulting and Clinical Psychology, 59(1)*, 12–19.

Jensen, J. P., Bergin, A. E., & Greaves, D. W. (1990). The meaning of eclecticism: New survey and analysis of components. *Professional Psychology: Research and Practice, 21*, 124–130.

Joint Commission on Mental Illness and Health. (1961). *Action for mental health.* New York: Basic Books.

Jones, M. C. (1924). The elimination of children's fears. *Journal of Experimental Psychology*, 7, 383–390.

Kadera, S. W., Lambert, M. J., & Andrews, A. A. (1996). How much therapy is really enough? A session-by-session analysis of the psychotherapy dose-effect relationship. *Journal of Psychotherapy Practice and Research, 5*, 132–151.

Kazdin, A. E. (1986). Comparative outcome studies of psychotherapy: Methodological issues and strategies. *Journal of Consulting and Clinical Psychology, 54*, 95–105.

Koss, M. P., & Shiang, J. (1994). Research on brief psychotherapy. In A. E. Bergin & S. L. Garfield (Eds.). (1994). *Handbook of Psychology and Behavior Change* (4th ed.) (pp. 664–700). New York: John Wiley & Sons.

Lambert, M. J. (1976). Spontaneous remission in adult neurotic disorders: A revision and summary. *Psychological Bulletin, 83(1)*, 107–119.

Lambert, M. J. (1992). Psychotherapy outcome research: Implications for integrative and eclectical therapists. In J. C. Norcross & M. R. Goldfield (Eds.), *Handbook of Psychotherapy integration* (pp. 94–129). New York: Basic Books.

Lambert, M. J. (2001). Psychotherapy outcome and quality improvement: Patient-focused research. *Journal of Consulting and Clinical Psychology, 69*, 147–149.

Lambert, M. J., Whipple, J. L., Smart, D. W., Vermeersch, D. A., Nielsen, S. L., & Hawkins, E. L. (2001). The effects of providing therapists with feedback on patient progress during psychotherapy: Are outcomes enhanced? *Psychotherapy Research, 11*, 49–68.

Lambert, M. J., Whipple, J. L., Vermeersch, D. A., Smart, D. W., Hawkins, E. J., Nielsen, S. L., & Goates, M. (2002). Enhancing psychotherapy outcomes via providing feedback on client progress: A replication. *Clinical Psychology and Psychotherapy, 9*, 91–103.

Luborsky, L., Singer, B., & Luborsky, L. (1975). Comparative studies of psychotherapies: Is it true that "everyone has one and all must have prizes"? *Archive of General Psychiatry, 32*, 995–1008.

Meltzoff, J., & Kornreich, M. (1970). *Research in psychotherapy.* New York: Atherton Press.

Morrow-Bradley, C., & Elliott, R. (1986). Utilization of psychotherapy research by practicing psychotherapists. *American Psychologist, 41(2)*, 188–197.

Mowrer, O. H., & Mowrer, W. (1938). Enuresis: A method of its study and treatment. *American Journal of Orthopsychiatry, 8*, 436–459.

Nathan, P. E. (1998). Practice guidelines: Not yet ideal. *American Psychologist, 53*, 290–299.

Nathan, P. E., Gorman, J. M., & Salkind, N. J. (1999). *Treating mental disorders: A guide to what works.* New York: Oxford University Press.

Nietzel, N. T., & Fisher, S. G. (1981). Effectiveness of professional and paraprofessional helpers: A comment on Durlak. *Psychological Bulletin, 89*, 555–565.

Norcross, J. C., & Goldfried, M. R. (Eds.). (1992). *Handbook of psychotherapy integration.* New York: Basic Books.

Norcross, J. C., Karg, R. S., & Prochaska, J. O. (1997). Clinical psychologists in the 90's: Part 1. *The Clinical Psychologist, 50(2)*, 4–9.

Parloff, M. B. (1982). Psychotherapy research evidence and reimbursement decisions: Bambi meets Godzilla. *American Journal of Psychiatry, 139*, 718–727.

Prioleau, L., Murdock, M., & Brody, N. (1983). An analysis of psychotherapy versus placebo studies. *The Behavioral and Brain Sciences, 6*, 275–285.

Report of the Research Task Force of the National Institute of Mental Health. (1975). Research in the service of mental health (DHEW Publication No. ADM 75-236). Rockville, MD.

Rioch, M. J. (1971). Two pilot projects in training mental health counselors. In R. R. Holt (Ed.), *New horizon for psychotherapy* (pp. 294–311). New York: International Universities Press.

Rogers, C. R. (1942). *Counseling and psychotherapy.* Boston: Houghton Miffin.

Rogers, C. R., & Dymond, R. F. (Eds.). (1954). *Psychotherapy and personality change.* Chicago: University of Chicago Press.

Roth, A., & Fonagy, P. (1996). *What works for whom? A critical review of psychotherapy research.* New York: Guilford Press.

Smith, M. L., Glass, G. W. V., & Miller, T. L. (1980). *The benefits of psychotherapy.* Baltimore, MD: Johns Hopkins University Press.

Stein, D. M., & Lambert, M. J. (1984). On the relationship between therapist experience and psychotherapy outcome. *Clinical Psychology Review, 4(2)*, 127–142.

Stein, D. M., & Lambert, M. J. (1995). Graduate training in psychotherapy: Are therapy outcomes enhanced? *Journal of Consulting and Clinical Psychology, 63(2)*, 179–183.

Strupp, H. H. (1997). On the limitation of therapy manuals. *Clinical Psychological Science and Practice, 4(1)*, 76–82.

Strupp, H. H., & Hadley, S. W. (1979). Specific and nonspecific factors in psychotherapy. *Archives of General Psychiatry, 36*, 1125–1136.

Svartberg, M., & Stiles, T. C. (1991). Comparative effects of short-term psychodynamic psychotherapy: A meta-analysis. *Journal of Consulting and Clinical Psychology, 59(5)*, 704–714.

Task Force on Promotion and Dissemination of Psychological Procedures. (1995). Training in and dissemination of empirically validated psychologist treatments: Report and recommendations. *Clinical Psychologist, 48(1)*, 3–23.

Voth, H. M., & Orth, M. H. (1973). *Psychotherapy and the role of the environment.* New York: Behavioral Press.

Wachtel, P. L. (1977). *Psychoanalysis and behavior therapy.* New York: Basic Books.

Weisz, J. R., Hawley, K. M., Pilkonis, P. A., Woody, S. R., & Follette, W. C. (2000). Stressing the (other) three Rs in the search for empirically supported treatments: Review procedures, research quality, relevance to practice and the public interest. *Clinical Psychology: Science and Practice, 7(3)*, 243–258.

Weisz, J. R., Weisz, B., Ham, S. S., Granger, D. A., & Morton, T. (1995). Effects of psychotherapy with children and adolescents revisited: A meta-analysis of treatment outcome studies. *Psychological Bulletin, 117*, 450–468.

Wolpe, J. (1958). *Psychotherapy by reciprocal inhibition.* Stanford, CA: Stanford University Press.

Woody, S. R., & Sanderson, W. C. (1998). Manuals for empirically supported treatments: 1998 Update. *Clinical Psychology Review, 51*, 17–21.

CHAPTER 2

METHODOLOGY, DESIGN, AND EVALUATION IN PSYCHOTHERAPY RESEARCH

PHILIP C. KENDALL
Temple University
GRAYSON HOLMBECK
Loyola University, Chicago
TIMOTHY VERDUIN
Temple University

Let's face it, in many ways Kiesler (1971) was right. In the first edition of this *Handbook* (1971) in the chapter "Experimental Designs in Psychotherapy Research," he recommended that psychotherapy researchers make consistent use of designs in which patient, therapist, and type of treatment are independent variables and dependent variables are examined over time (repeated measures). Use of this approach provides the researcher with the opportunity to begin to answer the critical question, "What therapist behaviors are effective with which types of clients in producing which kinds of patient change?" In the time since this valued directive, the field of therapy outcome evaluation has progressed—our knowledge about the outcomes of clinical interventions has been advanced as we have accumulated information gathered according to this approach. Nevertheless, times have changed, new questions have been posed, and additional methodological niceties are now expected. In addition, the desire to bring empirically evaluated treatments to clinical practice has gained visibility.

In this chapter, in neo-Kiesler style, we present and discuss various topics that pertain to the evaluation of psychotherapy outcomes. We begin with a brief description of principles that guide psychotherapy researchers. We then describe and define the methodological issues that face therapy outcome researchers and discuss related questions concerning those treatments that have been evaluated. Specific methods for addressing these issues scientifically are described, and we consider both the problems that make definitive clinical outcome research difficult and the tactics developed by clinical researchers to handle these challenges. Last, we describe and comment on approaches to the cumulative examination of outcomes from multiple research studies. In general, sections of this chapter may stand alone, and the interested reader may go to any individual section for consideration of that specific content.

GUIDING PRINCIPLES: THE SCIENTIST-PRACTITIONER MODEL AND EMPIRICALLY SUPPORTED INTERVENTIONS

The Scientist-Practitioner

Therapy outcome research methods within psychology developed largely from the fundamental commitment of clinical psychologists to a scientist-practitioner model for training and professional practice (Shakow, 1976). This model has implications for research evaluations of therapy, and the empirical-clinical model of clinical practice and research developed as an operationalization of this guiding philosophy. Arguably, this model provides the framework (the adoption and refinement of the methods and guidelines of science) for continuously improving the clinical services offered to thousands of clients. Although the initial formulation of effective therapeutic strategies may result from activities other than rigorous research, such as careful observation or theoretical extrapolations, empirical evaluation of the efficacy and effectiveness of therapy is often considered necessary before widespread utilization can be sanctioned. As a result, therapy researchers developed a sophisticated array of research methods for evaluating the outcome of therapeutic intervention.

Both scientists who evaluate their work and their theories with rigor, and practitioners who utilize a research-based understanding of human behavior in social contexts to aid people in resolving psychological dysfunctions and enhancing their lives, adhere to the scientist-practitioner model. This ideal is not intended to create professional split personalities but rather to foster service providers who evaluate their interventions scientifically and researchers who study applied questions and interpret their findings with an understanding of the richness and complexity of human experience (Kendall & Norton-Ford, 1982). For the results of treatment outcome studies to be meaningful, they must reflect both a fit within the guidelines of science and an understanding of the subtleties of human experience and behavior change. Finely controlled investigations that are distant from the realities of the therapeutic experience may offer only limited conclusions. Uncontrolled studies of therapeutic results that fail to pinpoint the effects that can be accurately attributed to therapy provide, at most, speculative knowledge. The scientist-practitioner strives to develop a variety of methods for studying meaningful therapeutic interventions and outcomes in a scientific fashion. Indeed, one can find fairly widespread acceptance of the scientist-practitioner model and commitment to it when we consider the question, "What if we did not seek empirical evaluation of the effects of therapy?" (Beutler, 1998; Kendall, 1998). What process would replace it as we seek to advance our understanding of what treatments are effective for what types of client problems?

Empirically Supported Treatments

The application of research methods to treatment outcome has amassed a sizable literature. Generalized conclusions about the efficacy of treatment (based on findings from studies using clinical practitioners in mental health systems) have begun to be reached, and the field has developed a set of criteria to be used when reviewing the cumulative literature on the outcomes of therapy. These criteria help determine whether or not a treatment can be considered "empirically supported."

Empirically supported treatments may be defined as treatments shown to be efficacious in randomized clinical research trials with given populations (see American Psychological Association Task Force on Promotion and Dissemination of Psychological Procedures, 1995; Chambless & Hollon, 1998). A multitude of perspectives exist on the utility of defining and delineating validated treatments, and the topic has been much debated in recent years (e.g., see articles in *Clinical Psychology: Science and Practice*). Although the majority of researchers and clinicians would likely agree that the evaluation of treatment is necessary, not all agree on the best methods to identify these treatments (Kazdin, 1996).

The operational definition of empirically supported treatments focuses on the accumulated data on the *efficacy* of a psychological therapy. These demonstrations of treatment efficacy often involve a randomized clinical trial in which an intervention is applied to diagnosed cases and analyzed against a comparison condition (e.g., wait list, alternative treatment, treatment-as-usual) to determine the degree or relative degree of beneficial change associated with treatment. The accumulated evidence comes from studies whose purposes were to establish the presence (or absence) of a treatment effect. Note that one study does not prove the benefits of therapy, nor does a single study raise a treatment to the level of being considered empirically supported. Rather, by accumulating evaluated outcomes, one can summarize the research and suggest that the beneficial effects of a given treatment have been supported empirically. A close look at the criteria in Table 2.1 reveals the rigorous standards that have been set for labeling a treatment as empirically supported.

Even if a treatment has been supported empirically, however, the transport of the treatment from one setting (research clinic) to another (service clinic) represents a separate and important issue. One then considers the *effectiveness* of the treatment (e.g., Hoagwood, Hibbs, Brent, & Jensen, 1995). Its effectiveness has to do with the generalizability, feasibility, and cost-effectiveness of the therapeutic procedures. The investigation of treatment effectiveness necessarily grows out of studies on treatment efficacy, and it seems reasonable to assert that randomized clinical trials are useful to address questions of both efficacy and effectiveness. For the research study to be

TABLE 2.1 Summary of Criteria for Empirically Supported Psychological Therapies

- Comparison with a no-treatment control group, alternative treatment group, or placebo (a) in a randomized control trial, controlled single-case experiment, or equivalent time-samples design and (b) in which the empirically supported treatment (EST) is significantly superior to no-treatment, placebo, or alternative treatments or in which the EST is equivalent to a treatment already established in efficacy, and power is sufficient to detect moderate differences.
- These studies must have been conducted with (a) a treatment manual or its logical equivalent; (b) a population, treated for specified problems, for whom the inclusion criteria have been delineated in a reliable, valid manner; (c) reliable and valid outcome assessment measures, at minimum tapping the problems targeted for change; and (d) appropriate data analysis.
- For a designation of efficacious, the superiority of the EST must have been shown in at least two independent research settings (sample size of three or more at each site in the case of single-case experiments). If there is conflicting evidence, the preponderance of the well-controlled data must support the EST's efficacy.
- For a designation of possibly efficacious, one study (sample size of three or more in the case of single-case experiments) suffices in the absence of conflicting evidence.
- For a designation of efficacious and specific, the EST must have been shown to be statistically significantly superior to pills or psychological placebo or to an alternative bona fide treatment in at least two independent research settings. If there is conflicting evidence, the preponderance of the well-controlled data must support the EST's efficacy and specificity.

valued, however, the study must include typical patients (e.g., patients with comorbid disorders), must evaluate outcomes on more than narrow measures of improvement (i.e., focus on improvements in general functioning rather than improvements in specific symptoms), and cannot be limited to brief therapy without followup. Fortunately, contemporary evaluations of treatment outcomes include both genuine cases with comorbid conditions, and measures of general functioning, examine therapies that are not always of short duration, and evaluate the maintenance of outcomes. Moreover, the methods of a randomized clinical trial are pliable and can accommodate variations in the questions being asked. As a result, they can be used repeatedly for evaluation. When considering the efficacy and effectiveness of treatments, the evaluator of outcome needs to make informed decisions regarding both the internal and external validity of the study in question.

Managed care currently affects the mental health field. What role will treatment outcome research play in the future of mental health services vis-à-vis managed care? Although this chapter does not seek to fully address managed care, it does appear to us that the treatment outcome literature is now receiving a much more widespread readership. Parties involved in financing psychological treatment are paying increased attention to the data that inform us about the outcomes associated with types of treatments. For better or worse, in the future, treatment outcome research is likely to prosper in part as a means of distilling the preferred interventions from the larger number of practiced treatments. Recognizing the utility of treatment outcome research in the healthcare system, Lambert, Huefner, and Reisinger (2000) propose that this research should do more than simply provide evidence that some treatments are worthier of health care resources than others. Treatment outcome research can also offer valuable feedback to clinicians and healthcare providers. When integrated as part of a larger quality improvement system, outcome data can provide information about the progress of treatment gains and suggest viable treatment plans. Treatment outcome research that integrates the finely honed results of randomized clinical trials (efficacy) with the nuanced complexities found by clinicians operating in the trenches (effectiveness) is essential to the development of optimal mental health services.

DESIGN, PROCEDURE, AND MEASUREMENT ISSUES

Research evaluations of the efficacy and effectiveness of therapeutic interventions have evolved from single-subject case histories to complex multimethod experimental investigations of carefully defined treatments (or treatment components) applied to samples of genuine clients. This chapter focuses on how best to arrange these complex evaluations. Although all of the ideals outlined in the present chapter are not often achieved in a single study, our discussions provide exemplars nonetheless. Consistent attempts to incorporate these ideals into research designs must be made, although due to ethical, financial, and logistical constraints, it is recognized that not all studies achieve complete methodological rigor. This section of the chapter identifies and addresses three domains relevant to treatment outcome research: research design, research procedure, and the measurement of change over time.

Research Design

To adequately assess the causal impact of a therapeutic intervention, clinical researchers have adapted control procedures derived from experimental science. The objective is to separate the effects of the therapy per se from the changes that result from other factors (e.g., patient expectancy of change, the passage of time, therapist attention, repeated assessments, regression to the mean). These extraneous factors must be "controlled" in order to have confidence that the intervention was responsible for any observed change. To better understand this concept, we discuss the creation/selection of control conditions, random assignment, post-treatment and followup evaluations, and between-group treatment comparisons.

Creation/Selection of Control Conditions

Comparisons of persons randomly assigned to different conditions are required to ensure control of the effects of factors other than the treatment. Comparable persons are randomly placed into either the control condition or the treatment condition, and by comparing the changes evidenced by the members of both conditions, the efficacy of therapy over and above the outcome produced by the extraneous factors can be determined. However, the decision about the nature of the control conditions is not easy. Researchers have the difficult job of deciding which type of control condition (e.g., no-treatment, wait list, attention-placebo, standard treatment) to use (see Table 2.2 for recent examples).

Clients who are assigned to a no-treatment control condition are administered the assessments on repeated occasions, separated by an interval of time equal to the length of the therapy provided to those in the treatment condition. Any changes seen in the treated clients are compared to the changes seen in the nontreated clients. When treated clients evidence significantly superior improvements over nontreated clients, the treatment is credited with producing the changes. This control procedure has desirable features and eliminates several rival hypotheses (e.g., spontaneous remission, historical effects, maturation, regression to the mean). However, a no-treatment control condition does not guard against other potentially confounding factors, including client anticipation of treatment, client expectancy for change, and the act of seeing a therapist—independent of what treatment the therapist actually provided. Although a no-treatment control condition is sometimes useful in the earlier stages of the evaluation of a treatment, other control procedures are preferred.

The wait list condition, a variant of a no-treatment procedure, provides some additional control. For example, clients in a wait list control condition have taken the step of initiating treatment and may anticipate change due to therapy. The changes that occur for wait-listed clients are evaluated, as are those of the clients who received therapy. If we assume the clients in the wait list and the treatment conditions are comparable in terms of variables such as gender, age, ethnicity, severity of presenting problem, and motivation, the research may then make inferences that the changes over and above those manifested by the wait list clients are likely due to the intervention rather than to any extraneous factors that were operative for both the treated and the wait list conditions. The important demographic and other data are gathered so that statistical comparisons can be conducted to determine condition comparability. Wait list conditions, like no-treatment conditions, are of less value for treatments that have already been examined versus somewhat "inactive" comparisons.

There are potential problems with wait list controls. A wait list client might experience a life crisis that forces immediate professional attention. Each control client's status should be monitored informally but frequently. Independent of pressing distress, wait list clients are offered the therapy, or an acceptable and effective substitute, as soon as possible after the study is completed.

The withholding of treatment has been raised as a concern regarding clients assigned to

TABLE 2.2 Types of Control Conditions in Therapy Outcome Research

Control Condition	Definition	Example	Reference
No-treatment control	Clients are administered assessments on repeated occasions separated by an interval of time equal to the length of time when others receive treatment.	Male college students reporting binge drinking were randomly assigned to a brief binge drinking prevention program or a no-treatment control group.	Borsari & Carey (2000)
Wait list control	Clients are assessed before and after a designated duration of time, but receive the treatment following the waiting period. They may anticipate change due to therapy.	Clients with postpartum depression were randomly assigned to interpersonal psychotherapy or a wait list condition.	O'Hara, Stuart, Gorman, & Wenzel (2000)
Attention-placebo/ nonspecific control	Clients receive a treatment that involves nonspecific factors (e.g., attention, contact with a therapist).	Homebound caregivers of persons with dementia were assigned to a cognitive behavioral intervention or an attention-only placebo control.	Chang (1999)
Standard treatment/ Treatment-as-usual/routine care control	Clients receive an intervention that is the current practice for treatment of the problem under study.	Juvenile offenders and their families were randomly assigned to multisystemic therapy or the usual juvenile justice services.	Henggeler, Melton, Brondino, Scherer, & Hanley (1997)

wait list conditions. Consider the following: In treatment outcome studies, it is preferable that the duration of the control condition be the same as the duration of the treatment condition(s). Comparable durations help to ensure that any differential changes between the conditions would not be due to the differential passage of time. However, this design has several potential problems. For example, if a treatment is provided for 18 sessions (that take four to five months to accomplish), then clients in the control condition must wait four or five months before beginning treatment. Do ethical restraints prohibit such wait periods (see Bersoff & Bersoff, 1999)? Also, with long wait list durations, the probability of differential attrition rises, a situation that could have a compromising effect on the study results. If rates of attrition from a wait list condition are high, the sample in the control condition may be rendered sufficiently different from the treatment condition to be no longer representative of the larger sample. Control conditions are essential to demonstrate the efficacy of treatment but may not be required once a treatment has, on several occasions, been found to be more effective than wait list conditions.

Attention-placebo (or nonspecific treatment) control conditions are an alternative to the wait list control that cannot only rule out threats to internal validity but also control for the effects that might be due simply to meeting with a therapist. Participants in attention-placebo conditions have contact with and receive attention from a therapist. In addition, these participants receive a description of the treatment rationale (a statement of purpose and explanation of the treatment procedures offered at the beginning of the intervention). The rationale provided to attention-placebo clients is intended to mobilize an *expectancy* of positive gains. These nonspecific elements in the therapy (elements separate from the identified treatment strategies) may account for client change, just as medication placebos and psychological placebos have been found effective in some situations (see Hollon & DeRubeis, 1981; Jacobson & Hollon, 1996a, 1996b). Attention-placebo conditions enable clinical researchers to identify the changes produced by specific therapeutic strategies over and above the effects of nonspecific factors.

Despite their advantage, attention-placebo controls are not without limitations (Parloff, 1986). When long-term therapy is being evaluated, it is questionable from an ethical standpoint to offer some clients contact (placebo) that does not deal directly with the problems for which they have sought therapy. Attention placebos must be devoid of effective therapeutic techniques, while nevertheless providing professional contact and attention and instilling positive expectancies in clients. To offer such an intervention in the guise of effective therapy is acceptable only when clients are fully informed in advance and sign informed consent forms acknowledging their willingness to take a chance on receiving either a placebo or a therapy intervention. Even then, a true attention-placebo condition may be very difficult for the therapist to accomplish. In the absence of data to justify the provision of a treatment, clinical researchers accept the ethical mandate to conduct scientifically rigorous evaluations to examine the efficacy of practiced therapies. This may require controlling for nonspecific effects. Of course, following proper evaluations of and positive results from interventions, researchers no longer need to ask clients (some of whom may have immediate needs) to consent to the possibility of placebo treatment.

Methodologically, it is difficult to ensure that the therapists who conduct attention-placebo conditions have the same degree of positive expectancy for client gains as do therapists conducting specific interventions (O'Leary & Borkovec, 1978). Demand characteristics suggest that when therapists predict a favorable outcome, clients will tend to improve accordingly (Kazdin, 1998). Thus, therapist expectancies may not be equal for active and placebo conditions, which could produce a confounding factor. Similarly, even if clients in an attention-placebo condition have high expectations at the start, they may grow disenchanted when no specific changes are emerging. When the results suggest that the therapy condition evidenced significantly better outcomes than the attention-placebo control condition, it is essential that the researcher conduct and evaluate clients' perceptions of the credibility of the treatment rationale and their expectations for change (e.g., manipulation checks) to confirm that clients in the attention-placebo control condition perceived the treatment to be credible and expected to improve. Otherwise, differences in treatment outcome are confounded by differences in the credibility of the condition or the expectations for outcomes.

Conceptually, it is very difficult to develop procedures that researchers believe to be inert and yet are still likely to be seen as credible to clients/patients. Having been involved in attempts to create an attention-placebo control condition, we found that each credible rationale was indeed someone else's form of therapy.

The use of a standard treatment (treatment-as-usual) as a control condition involves comparing new treatments with the intervention that is currently being applied for treatment of the problems and clients involved in the therapy being evaluated. If it is demonstrated that the standard care intervention and the therapy under study are equated for nonspecific factors—for example, duration of treatment or client and therapist expectancies—this approach enables the researcher to test the relative efficacy of one type of intervention against a major contemporary competitor. It is, of course, important that researchers ensure that both the standard (routine) treatment and the new treatment are implemented in a high-quality fashion (Kendall & Hollon, 1983). Standard treatment comparisons should be used only after the standard treatment has been shown to be superior to conditions that control for alternative explanations of outcome. Without these prior tests, and an outcome where both the standard and new treatment show improvement, one would not be able to determine whether the change was due to treatment or to other factors such as the passage of time of nonspecific factors associated with seeing a therapist. One advantage arises via use of the standard treatment control condition: the ethical concerns surrounding the use of no-treatment controls are quelled, given that quality care is provided to all participants in the study; attrition is likely to be kept to a minimum as all participants receive genuine treatment procedures; and nonspecific factors are likely to be equated (Kazdin, 1998).

Random Assignment

After comparison conditions have been chosen, procedures for assigning participants to conditions must be determined. *Random assignment* of participants to the therapy or control conditions and random assignment of participants to therapists are essential steps in achieving initial comparability between conditions. For instance, random assignment of clients usually eliminates the unwanted effects of age or socioeconomic status because in most cases random assignment does not result in one condition being older, wealthier, or more educated than another condition. However, randomization does not guarantee comparability, and appropriate statistical tests should be applied to examine the comparability of the participants in the conditions.

Randomization may be accomplished by any procedure that gives every participant an equal chance of being assigned to either the control or treatment condition (e.g., assignment by a coin toss). Problems can arise when random assignment is not applied. Consider the situation when the first 30 clients seeking help at a treatment center are assigned to therapy and the next 30 clients are placed on the wait list. Such assignment is not truly random and may hide subtle selection biases. Perhaps the first 30 clients sought therapy more quickly due to stronger motivation, or more severe symptoms, than the next 30. Perhaps the first 30 clients were exposed to a temporary environmental stress that was no longer a factor when the next 30 clients applied for aid.

Although random assignment does not absolutely assure comparability of the control and therapy conditions on all measures, it does maximize the likelihood of comparability. An alternative procedure, randomized blocks assignment, or assignment by stratified blocks, involves matching prospective clients in subgroups that (a) contain clients that are highly comparable on key dimensions (e.g., initial severity) and (b) contain the same number of clients as the number of conditions. For example, if the study requires two conditions (a standard treatment and a new treatment condition), clients can be paired off so that each pair is highly comparable. The members in each pair are then randomly assigned to either condition, thus increasing the likelihood that each condition will contain relatively mirror-image participants while retaining the randomization factor. When feasible, randomized blocks assignment of clients to conditions can be a wise research strategy.

After-Treatment and During-Treatment Evaluations

Post-treatment assessments of clients are essential to examine the comparative efficacy of treatment versus control conditions. However, any evidence of treatment efficacy immediately upon therapy completion may not be indicative of more long-term success (maintenance). Treatment outcome may also be appreciable at post-treatment but fail to exhibit maintenance of the effects at followup. It is highly recommended that treatment outcome studies include in their design a followup assessment. Followup assessments (e.g., six months, one year) are a signpost of methodological rigor and are expected by funding agencies and research journals and deemed necessary in the demonstration of treatment efficacy. For evidence of maintenance, the treatment must have produced results at the followup assessment that are comparable to those evident at post-treatment (i.e., improvements from pretreatment and an absence of detrimental change since post-treatment).

Followup evaluations can identify differential effects resulting from the treatment. For example, the effects of two different treatments may be favorable and comparable at the end of treatment, but one treatment may be more effective in the prevention of relapse (see Greenhouse, Stangl, & Bromberg, 1989, for discussion of survival analysis). When two treatments are deemed comparable at the post-treatment evaluation, yet one is associated with higher relapse, the knowledge gained from the followup evaluation is a valuable rationale for selecting one treatment over another. For example, Brown, Evans, Miller, Burgess, and Mueller (1997) reported on a comparison of cognitive behavioral therapy and relaxation training as a treatment for depression in alcoholism. Using mean percent days abstinent and mean drinks per day as dependent variables, measured at pretreatment and three and six months post-treatment, the authors were able to establish that, although both treatments produced comparable initial gains, the cognitive behavioral treatment for depression was more effective than relaxation training in maintaining gains through the followup assessments.

Followup evaluations may also detect continued improvement associated with a treatment because the benefits of some therapeutic interventions may accumulate rather than lag over time. However, gains associated with followup can only be attributed to the initial treatment once one determines that the treated persons did not seek or receive additional treatments during the followup interval. Interpretation of these data requires caution, for additional treatment may be viewed either as a success (i.e., increased access to needed care) or a problem (e.g., increased costs to healthcare systems).

Followup evaluations are labor intensive and costly, but the literature suggests the need for these evaluations (e.g., Goldstein, Lopez, & Greenleaf, 1979; Nich & Carroll, 1997; Ollendick, 1986; Shapiro & Shapiro, 1982; Smith, Glass & Miller, 1980). Therefore, the current expectation is that an evaluation of treatment will include a followup (e.g., Chambless & Hollon, 1998).

As we learn more about the outcomes of treatment, we are intrigued by speculations about the process that takes place in achieving the observed outcome. Researchers are operationalizing the psychotherapy process and outcome as intertwined phenomena and are assessing change during treatment (i.e., intratreatment) as well as at post-treatment and followup. Repeated assessment of client symptoms and functional change suggests that the first several sessions of treatment constitute the period of most rapid positive change (Howard, Lueger, Maling, & Martinovich, 1993). However, change across several domains of functioning tends to be phasic and may require more extended treatment (K. Howard et al., 1993). Intratreatment assessments (see Lambert, Hansen, & Finch, 2001) not only permit a fine-grained mapping of the course of change in therapy, but also provide important clues (e.g., Jaycox, Foa, & Morral, 1998) to identify mediators of positive or adverse outcomes. We will further discuss mediators of change later in this chapter.

Comparing Alternative Treatments

The methods described thus far are typically employed to evaluate the effects of a single treatment. To determine the comparative efficacy and effectiveness of therapeutic interventions, between-groups designs with more than one treatment condition must be applied. Between-groups designs are direct comparisons of one treatment with one or more alternative treatments. Several precautions are necessary in such investigations. For example, sample size considerations are influenced by whether the comparison is between a treatment and a control condition or one treatment versus another treatment (see Kazdin & Bass, 1989).

In all between-groups comparisons, it is optimal when each client is randomly assigned to receive one and only one kind of therapy. The assignment of clients to conditions should result in the initial comparability of the clients receiving each intervention. As previously mentioned, a randomized block procedure, with participants blocked on an important variable (e.g., pretreatment severity), can be used. It is always wise to check the comparability of the clients in the different treatment conditions on other important variables (e.g., age, socioeconomic status, prior therapy experience) before continuing with the evaluation of the intervention. If not all participants are available at the outset of treatment, such as when participants come from successive clients entering a clinic, then the comparability of conditions can be checked at several intervals as the therapy outcome study progresses toward completion.

When comparing different treatments, it is important that therapists conducting each type of treatment be comparable on potentially influential factors such as (a) training background, (b) length and type of professional and clinical experience, (c) expertise in conducting the particular intervention, (d) allegiance with each of the treatments, and (e) expectation that the intervention will be effective. As one way to control for (and possibly also rigorously delineate) these therapist effects, researchers have often had each therapist conduct each type of intervention with at least one client per intervention. Stratified blocking, another viable option, assures that each intervention is conducted by several comparable therapists. The first method enables an experimental examination of the effects of differing therapists, but this evaluation is valid only if therapists are equally expert and positively oriented toward each intervention. For example, it would probably not be a valid test to ask a group of cognitive behavioral therapists to conduct both a cognitive behavioral therapy (in which their expertise is high) and an existential therapy (in which their expertise is minimal). Although therapist comparability would require documentation, the second method enables the researcher to examine the effect of a variety of therapists performing one intervention with the effect of a variety of different therapists performing an alternative intervention.

Treatment comparisons require that the intervention procedure be equated for salient variables such as (a) duration of treatment, (b) length, intensity, and frequency of therapist contacts with the client, (c) credibility of the treatment rationale given to the client, (d) setting in which treatment is provided, and (e) degree of involvement of persons significant to the client. In some cases, these factors may be the basis for two alternative therapies (e.g., conjoint vs. individual marital therapy), in which case the variable becomes part of the experimental contrast rather than a matter for control.

What is the best method of measuring change when two alternative treatments are being compared? Clearly, measures should not be differentially sensitive to one or the other treatment. The assessment measures should (a) cover the range of psychosocial functioning that is a target for therapeutic change, (b) include measures that tap the costs and possible negative side effects of the interventions, and (c) be unbiased with respect to the alternative kinds of intervention. The last precaution is necessary because the outcome of a comparison of therapies may be misleading if the assessments are not equally sensitive to the types of changes that are most likely caused by each type of intervention.

A potentially important issue in comparative therapy studies pertains to the level of efficacy of each individual therapeutic approach in relation to the "expected efficacy" of each therapy based on prior studies. This issue is worthy of closer consideration. Consider, for example, that two treatments are compared and that therapy A is found to be superior to therapy B. The question can then arise, was therapy A superior, or did therapy B fail to be efficacious in this instance? It would be desirable in demonstrating the efficacy of therapy A if the results due to therapy B reflected the level of efficacy found in earlier demonstrations of therapy B's efficacy. Interpretations of the results of comparative studies are dependent on the level of efficacy of each therapy in relation to its expected (or standard) efficacy. Effect sizes are useful in making these comparisons and in reaching sound conclusions.

Lastly, although the issues discussed nevertheless apply, comparisons of psychological therapy with medications (psychopharmacology) present special issues for consideration. For example, how and when should placebo medications be used with psychological therapy? How should expectancy effects be addressed? How should differential attrition be handled? Followups become especially important after the active treatments are discontinued. Are treatment effects maintained? This question is especially pertinent given that psychological treatment effects may persist after treatment, whereas the effects of medications may not persist when the medications are discontinued. (Readers interested in discussions of these issues are referred to Hollon, 1996; Hollon & DeRubeis, 1981; and Jacobson & Hollon, 1996a, 1996b.)

Matters of Procedure

Following decisions about the design of the research evaluation to be conducted, researchers must address procedural issues that can affect the development of treatments and the evaluations of their outcomes. In the following sections, procedural matters such as defining the independent variable (the use of manual-based treatments), checking on the independent variable (treatment fidelity or integrity checks), the issue of the transportability of treatments, and factors important in sample selection (e.g., use of select versus genuine clinical samples, ethnic diversity of clients) will be considered.

Defining the Independent Variable (Manual-Based Treatment)

To replicate an evaluation of treatment, or to be able to show and teach others how to conduct the treatment, it is essential that the treatment be adequately described. Accordingly, there is increasing interest in and need for the development and use of treatment manuals in therapy outcome research. Treatment manuals offer a number of advantages, such as enhancing internal validity and treatment integrity. They allow comparison of the treatments across contexts and formats while eliminating often potential confounds (e.g., differences in the amount of contact between therapist and client, type and amount of training required prior to implementation of the treatment, time between therapy sessions; see Dobson & Shaw, 1988). Therapist manuals facilitate training and contribute meaningfully to replication of therapy outcome studies (Dobson & Shaw, 1988). Therapy for anxiety-disordered youth is a good example: there are manuals to operationalize therapy for individual (e.g., Kendall, Kane, Howard, & Siqueland, 1990; March & Mulle, 1996), family (Howard & Kendall, 1996), and group (Flannery-Schroeder & Kendall, 1996) treatments.

Not all agree on the merits of manuals. Debate has ensued regarding the use of manual-based treatment versus the individualized approach typically found in practice. Those who discuss the limits of manual-based therapy (e.g., Garfield, 1996; Havik & VandenBos, 1996) have suggested that manuals limit therapist creativity (for other discussion, see Davidson & Lazarus, 1995; Wilson,

1996) and place restrictions on the individualization that the therapy can undergo (for other discussion, see Waltz, Addis, Koerner, & Jacobson, 1993; Wilson, 1995). The issues facing the application of manual-based treatments can be stated in testable terms (Kendall, 1998) and can be examined empirically. In a recent evaluation, use of one of the manual-based treatments noted in the earlier paragraph did not restrict therapist flexibility (Kendall & Chu, 1999). Although it is not the goal of manual-based treatments to have practitioners perform treatment in a rigid manner, this misperception has influenced some practitioners' openness to examine and use manual-based interventions.

It can be argued that manual-based treatments are preferred for the advancement of treatment outcome evaluation. However, the proper use of manual-based therapy requires flexible application and ongoing supervision. Apparently, professionals cannot become proficient in the administration of therapy simply by reading a manual. Effective use of manual-based treatments must be preceded by adequate training (Barlow, 1989). Contemporary treatment manuals allow the therapist to attend to each client's specific needs, concerns, and comorbid conditions without deviating from the manual. The goal is to include provisions for standardized implementation of therapy while utilizing a personalized case formulation (Kendall, Chu, Gifford, Hayes, & Nauta, 1998). Lastly, using manual-based treatments does not eliminate the potential for differential therapist effects. Rather, a researcher could examine those therapist variables (e.g., warmth, therapeutic relationship) that might be related to treatment outcome within a manual-based intervention.

Checking on the Independent Variable (Treatment Fidelity or Integrity Checks)

A quality research project includes checking the manipulated variable. In controlled therapy outcome evaluations, the manipulated variable is typically treatment or a characteristic of treatment. For example, a researcher may design a study in which different treatments will be provided for clients who are assigned to different conditions. By design, all clients are not treated the same. However, just because the study has been so designed does not guarantee that the independent variable (treatment) has been manipulated as intended.

Steps to help ensure that the treatments are indeed implemented as designed include requiring that a treatment plan be followed, training therapists carefully, and supervising and monitoring the treatment. Even though these steps are helpful, the research should conduct an independent check on the manipulation. For example, requiring that therapy sessions be audiotaped allows an independent rater to listen to the tapes and conduct a manipulation check. Quantifiable judgments regarding the characteristics of the treatment provide the necessary check that the described treatment was indeed provided.

Audiotapes are inexpensive, can be used for subsequent training, and can be analyzed for other research purposes. Tape recordings of the therapy sessions evaluated by outcome studies not only provide a check on the treatment within each separate study but also allow for a check on the comparability of treatments provided across studies. That is, the therapy provided as cognitive behavioral therapy in one clinician's study could be checked to determine its comparability to other clinician-researchers' cognitive behavioral therapy. Moreover, the *quality* (Kendall & Hollon, 1983) of the therapy can be examined. Treatment manuals that describe the general therapy procedures and some specific details are needed for researchers to conduct and evaluate comparable types of intervention. However, independent checks alone can document treatment comparability and examine treatment quality.

Simply because a manual was written and was said to have been the guide for therapy does not mean that the therapy provided was, in fact, the therapy described in the manual. A therapist may strictly adhere to the manual and yet fail to administer the therapy in an otherwise competent manner, or he or she may competently administer therapy while significantly deviating from the manual. In both cases, the operational definition of the independent variable (i.e., the treatment manual) has been violated, treatment integrity impaired, and replication rendered impossible (Dobson & Shaw, 1988).

Integrity checks—checking on the fidelity with which treatment was provided—are needed, but they are not a complete solution. Although manuals may foster the integrity of the independent variable, there remains the need to examine and determine that the treatment said to have been provided was indeed the treatment provided.

As part of treatment integrity, it is also of interest to study potential variations in treatment outcome that are associated with differences in the *quality* of the treatment provided (Garfield, 1998; Kendall & Hollon, 1983). Expert judges are needed to make determinations of differential quality prior to the examination of differential outcomes for high- versus low-quality therapy implementations. (For further discussion of evaluating treatment integrity, see Waltz et al., 1993.)

Selected Samples versus Genuine Clinical Samples

Debate exists over the preferred samples of participants in treatment outcome research. A highly select sample refers to a sample of participants who may need service but who may otherwise only approximate clinically disordered individuals. Clinical trials, by contrast, apply and evaluate treatments with actual clients who are seeking clinical services. Consider a study investigating the effects of treatment X on depression. It might use (a) a sample of clinically depressed clients diagnosed via structured interviews (genuine clinical sample), (b) a sample consisting of a group of adults who self-report dysphoric mood (an analogue sample), or (c) a sample of depressed persons after excluding cases with suicidal intent, economic stress, and family conflict (highly select). The last-named participants may or may not meet diagnostic criteria for depression but are nevertheless highly selected.

Those who argue for the use of analogue or select samples cite the greater ability to control various conditions and minimize sources of internal invalidity. On the other hand, those critical of select and analogue samples argue that external validity is compromised—these just are not the same people seen in actual clinical practice. With respect to depression, for instance, many question whether depression in genuine clinical populations compares meaningfully to self-reported dysphoria in adults (e.g., Coyne & Gotlib, 1983; Gotlib, 1984; Krupnick, Shea, & Elkin, 1986; Tennen, Hall, & Affleck, 1995; Vredenburg, Flett, & Krames, 1993).

Efficacy studies are preferred when they included randomized clinical trails with genuine cases. The use of analogue or select samples, though not ideal, is acceptable only when the sample size and power would otherwise be quite small and only those analogue participants who are shown to have measurable characteristics relevant to the disorder in question (e.g., depressive symptoms) are included. Researchers must consider how the results of the study will be interpreted and generalized when deciding whether to use genuine clinical cases or an analogue or select sample.

Researchers must also consider client diversity when discussing which samples to use in the study. The literature indicates ethnic and other differences in perceptions of mental health service providers and reveals that some minorities may underutilize these services (e.g., Homma-True, Greene, Lopez, & Trimble, 1993; Neal & Turner, 1991; Neighbors, 1985, 1988; Sue, Kurasaki, & Srinivasan, 1999). Investigations have also addressed the potential for bias in diagnoses and in the provision of mental health services (e.g., Flaherty & Meaer, 1980; Homma-True et al., 1993; Lopez, 1989; Simon, Fleiss, Gurland, Stiller, & Sharpe, 1973).

Despite the increased research attention given to client diversity, surprisingly few studies have investigated the role of diversity (e.g., ethnicity) as it relates to outcome. Research samples may unwittingly underrepresent certain groups and contribute to misleading conclusions (see Alvidrez, Azocar, & Miranda, 1996; Beutler, 1996; Miranda, 1996). As usual, research samples must accurately reflect the population to which the results will be generalized. To generalize to a diverse population, one must study a diverse sample. To that end, outreach efforts may be needed to inform ethnic minorities of available services. Walders and Drotar (2000) provide useful guidelines for recruiting and working with an ethnically diverse sample.

Once diversity within the sample is accomplished, statistical analyses can examine potential differential treatment outcomes (see Beutler, Brown, Crothers, Booker, & Seabrook, 1996; Treadwell, Flannery-Schroeder, & Kendall, 1994). Grouping and analyzing research participants by ethnic status is one approach. However, this approach is simplistic because it fails to address variations in an individual's degree of ethnic identity. It is often the degree to which an individual identifies with an ethnocultural group or community and not simply his or her ethnicity itself that potentially moderates treatment outcome. (See Chapter 18, this volume, for a more extensive discussion of this issue.)

Consequently, service providers should be trained in multicultural perspectives to decrease the likelihood of misunderstanding (Homma-True et al., 1993; Miranda, Azocar, Organista, Munoz, & Lieberman, 1996; Thompson, Nieghbors, Munday, & Jackson, 1996). Multicultural training could minimize the cultural gaps that may be responsible for the lack of representation of ethnic minorities in research studies. Inclusion of ethnic minorities enhances generalizability and also provides an opportunity to examine any potential between-group differences.

From Research to the Clinic: Transporting Treatments

Researchers determine the efficacy and effectiveness of treatments based on carefully evaluated outcomes. However, it is not sufficient to demonstrate treatment efficacy within a narrowly defined sample in a highly selective setting. The question of whether or not the treatment can be transported to other settings requires independent evaluation (Kendall & Southam-Gerow, 1995). In many cases, treatment outcome evaluations are conducted within research-oriented settings (compared to clinical service-oriented settings). The results of investigations conducted at research centers are valuable, but the treatments may or may not be transportable into clinical practice. One cannot assume that the treatment will be as efficacious within the clinical service setting as it was in the research setting (see Weisz, Donenberg, Han, & Weiss, 1995; Weisz, Weiss, & Donenberg, 1992).

Some initial research with panic-disordered clients treated in a service clinic using a manual-based treatment developed in a research clinic (Wade, Treat, & Stuart, 1998) suggests that the amount of beneficial change seen in the service clinic was comparable to that produced in the research clinic. These positive results were supported by similar findings at one-year followup (Stuart, Treat, & Wade, 2000). Similarly encouraging results were found in a study examining the effectiveness of an exposure and ritual prevention (EX/RP) treatment program for obsessive-compulsive disorder (Franklin, Abramowitz, Kozak, Levitt, & Foa, 2000). Franklin et al. reported that EX/RP, a treatment typically evaluated for efficacy, produced clinically significant change (effectiveness) in outpatient clients, many of whom had comorbid problems and extensive treatment histories. Although much additional applied research is needed, these studies provide initial evidence that at least some types of treatments may be transported across contexts.

Closing the gap between clinical research and clinical practice requires effort to further transport and evaluate treatments (getting "what works" into practice) and additional research into those factors (e.g., client, therapists, researcher, service delivery setting; see Kendall & Southam-Gerow, 1995) that may be involved in successful transportation. In a novel approach, Fishman (2000) suggests that an electronic journal of case studies be assembled so that patient, therapy, and environmental variables can be collected from within naturalistic therapy settings and compiled. Although the methodology has flaws (Stricker, 2000), information technology-based approaches may facilitate more seamless integration of research and practice and start a new wave of outcome research.

Assessing Treatment Outcomes: Measuring Change Over Time

It is unfortunate but true that no single measure of the outcome of therapeutic intervention is either reliable or comprehensive enough to serve as the sole indicator of clients' gains (or setbacks). Rather, a variety of methods, measures, data sources, and sampling domains (e.g., symptomatic distress, functional impairment, quality of life) is necessary to fully assess therapy outcomes (see Hill & Lambert, Chapter 4 of this volume). With reference to their contributions to the measurement of changes over time, we will now consider assessment measures, examining the intent-to-treat sample, reporting clinical significance, and testing for mediators and moderators of outcome.

Assessment Measures

A contemporary and respected study of the effects of therapy will use a variety of measures of outcome that tap a variety of sources. The list includes, but is not limited to, assessments of client self-report, client test (or task) performance, therapist judgments and ratings, archival or documentary records (e.g., healthcare visits and costs, work and school records), observations by trained, unbiased, blind observers, ratings by significant people in the client's life, and independent judgments by professionals. Outcomes have more impact when seen by independent (blind) judges than when based solely on the therapist's opinion or the client's self-reports.

A respected study will use multiple targets of assessment. For example, one can measure overall psychological adjustment, specific interpersonal skills, the presence of a diagnosis, self-reported mood, cognitive functioning, or dimensions of personality, life environment, vocational status, and the quality of interpersonal relationships. No one target captures all of the potential benefits of treatment. Using multiple targets facilitates an examination of positive therapeutic changes when changes occur, and it records the absence of change when interventions are less than successful.

Multimethod assessment permits evaluation of therapy-induced change on different levels: the specifying level and the impact level (Kendall, Pellegrini, & Urbain, 1981). The *specifying level* refers to the exact skills, cognitive or emotional processes, or behaviors that have been modified during treatment (e.g., examining the number of positive spouse statements generated during a specific marital relationship task). In contrast, the *impact level* refers to the general level of functioning of the client (e.g., absence of a diagnosis, goniometric status of the client). A compelling demonstration of beneficial treatment would include change that occurs at both the level of specific discrete skills and behaviors and the impact level of generalized functioning in which the client interacts differently within the larger environmental context. Tingey, Lambert, Burlingame, and Hansen (1996a) describe such a method for assessing clinical significance.

Missing Data

Recall that patients should be randomly assigned to treatment conditions and to the therapists providing the treatment. However, not all clients who are assigned to treatment complete their participation in the study. In clinical outcome studies, a loss of research participants may occur at any of the many points along the way (e.g., prior to post-treatment or during the followup interval) and is generally referred to as attrition. Attrition can be problematic for data analysis, such as when there is a large number of noncompleters or when attrition varies across conditions (see K. Howard, Krause, & Orlinsky, 1986). Although attrition rates vary across studies, Mason (1999) estimated that most researchers can expect nearly 20% of their sample to withdraw or be necessarily removed from the study before it is complete. Mason proposes several methods of handling the problem of attrition before it happens, including collecting extensive contact information to aid in later collection of followup data, adequately informing participants of the timetable and nature of the program, and consistently rewarding participants.

No matter how diligently researchers work to prevent attrition, data will likely still be lost. To address this matter, researchers often conduct and report two sets of analyses: analysis of outcomes for the treatment completers and analyses of outcomes for all clients who were included at the time of randomization (the intent-to-treat sample). An analysis of treatment completers involves the evaluation of only those who completed treatment: What are the effects when someone completes treatment? Treatment dropouts, treatment refusers, and clients who fail to adhere to treatment procedures would not be included in these outcome analyses. These analyses provide researchers with an estimate of treatment efficacy (Kendall & Sugarman, 1997). Intent-to-treat analyses, a more conservative approach, require evaluating the outcomes for all participants involved at the point of randomization. Intent-to-treat analyses also provide an estimate of treatment effectiveness: What are the effects of treatment for people seeking treatment for a certain problem? Both approaches can be recommended as steps toward a clearer determination of treatment outcome.

What data are used in an intent-to-treat analysis when the participant has attrited and is no longer available? Intent-to-treat analyses can be (a) end-point or "last value" analyses, (b) analyses at completion of the therapy, or (c) analyses of pretreatment scores substituted as post-treatment scores. End-point analyses involve evaluating participants at the point they drop out of the study; analyses at completion involve evaluating participants at the end of the treatment program regardless of when they dropped out. The use of pretreatment scores as post-treatment scores simply inserts the pretreatment score as the treatment outcome score.

Statistical analyses that include only treatment completers result in the most liberal estimate of the efficacy of treatment outcome. In such cases, reports of treatment outcome may be somewhat high because they represent the results for only those who adhered to and completed the treatment protocol. For those studies in which data collection is not continuous (or taking place at set intervals across time), end-point analyses can present a problem. It is likely, for example, that participants who drop out of treatment may not have completed a data collection point for a considerable amount of time (e.g., weeks or months). Thus, the last data collection point cannot be considered representative of the participant's progress or lack of progress at the time of the dropout. In addition, participants who withdrew from the study, regardless of the reason, may be unwilling to complete an assessment at that point in time. Willingness to participate in the treatment protocol and willingness to complete measurement procedures are correlated. Even if participants who dropped out are recontacted and agree to participate in an evaluation at the end of the treatment protocol, the evaluation may be confounded if the client sought an alternative treatment during the intervening period.

When conducting end-point analyses, it is important to evaluate the comparability of the completers and the dropouts not only in terms of their pretreatment scores but also the degree of change seen in the completers versus the dropouts. For example, Marks, Lowell, Noshirvani, Livanou, and Thrasher (1998) found that noncompleters in exposure-based cognitive behavioral therapy for post-traumatic stress disorder (PTSD), though not significantly different at pretreatment from completers, were significantly less improved at post-treatment than completers. Consequently, the apparent superiority at followup of the exposure-based treatments over a cognitively focused therapy may have been partially an artifact of differential attrition.

What if, when a participant drops out, the research uses the pretreatment score as the post-treatment scores? As it turns out, this solution, too, is not devoid of problems. For example, though not likely or expected, it is possible that a treatment is somewhat detrimental to participants (or to participants with certain characteristics). The use of pretreatment scores in outcome analyses when the participant actually developed more severe psychological disturbance could result in an inflated estimate of treatment effects.

Although there is currently no widely accepted solution to these problems, several strategies can be advanced. When assessing the outcomes of a treatment that is considered "probably efficacious" or "well established" (see Chambless & Hollon, 1998), using pretreatment scores as post-treatment scores is the most conservative method to assess treatment gains. Because of its very conservative nature, it is probably best when paired with reports of the outcome evaluations using treatment completers.

If it is possible for noncompleting participants to be contacted and evaluated at the time when the treatment protocol would have ended, then the best strategy is to include these data in the analyses. This method controls for the passage of time, for both dropouts and treatment completers are evaluated over time periods of the same duration. If this method is used, however, it is extremely important to determine whether or not dropouts sought and/or received alternative treatments in the time between dropout and return for assessment.

The method used to handle missing data will affect results differently depending on the type of statistical tests performed. Since the methods detailed here differ in terms of how conservative they are and how they affect power, the type of analyses should be considered when choosing a method of dealing with missing data. Each type of test performs differently with respect to statistical power and accuracy, depending on the method used to control for attrition. Delucchi and Bostrom (1999) outlined and summarized the effects of missing data on a range of statistical analyses.

Clinical Significance: Assessing the Convincingness of Outcomes

The data produced by research projects designed to evaluate the efficacy or effectiveness of therapy are submitted to statistical tests of significance. Condition means are compared, the within-group and between-group variability is considered, and the analysis produces a numerical figure, which is then checked against critical values. An outcome achieves *statistical* significance if the magnitude of the mean difference is beyond what could have resulted by chance alone. Statistical analyses and statistical significance are essential for therapy evaluation because they inform us that the degree of change was not due to chance. However, statistical tests alone do not provide evidence of *clinical significance.*

Reliance solely on statistical significance can lead to perceiving differences (i.e., treatment gains) as potent when in fact they may be clinically insignificant. For example, imagine that the results of a treatment outcome study demonstrate that mean Beck Depression Inventory (BDI) scores are significantly lower at post-treatment than pretreatment. An examination of the means, however, reveals a shift from a mean of 29 to a mean of 24. Given large sample sizes, this difference may well be statistically significant, yet perhaps be of limited practical significance. At both pre- and post-treatment, the scores are within the range considered indicative of clinical levels of depressive distress (Kendall, Hollon, Beck, Hammen, & Ingram, 1987). Furthermore, even marked changes on one or more factors may have little effect on a person's perceived quality of life (Gladis, Gosch, Dishuk, &

Crits-Christoph, 1999), and statistically meager results may disguise meaningful changes in client functioning. As Kazdin (1999) put it, sometimes a little can mean a lot, and vice versa.

Clinical significance refers to the meaningfulness or convincingness of the magnitude of change (Kendall, 1999). Clinical significance addresses the question, "Did the remediation of the presenting problem produced by treatment return the patient to the point that the initial problem was no longer troublesome?" In a depressive disorder, for example, changes in depression would have to be of the magnitude that, after therapy, the person no longer suffered from debilitating depression. Specifically, this can be made operational as changes on a measure of the presenting problem (e.g., depressive symptoms) that result in the client's being returned to within normal limits on that measure. Several approaches for measuring clinically significant change have been developed, including normative sample comparisons, social validation, and clients' own perceptions of their quality of life.

Normative Comparisons

Clinically significant improvement can be identified using normative comparisons (Kendall & Grove, 1988), a method for operationalizing clinical significance testing. Normative comparisons (Kendall, & Grove, 1988; Kendall, Marrs-Garcia, Nath, & Sheldrick, 1999) can be conducted in several steps. First, the researcher selects a normative group for post-treatment comparison. Given that several well-established measures provide normative data (e.g., the Beck Depression Inventory, the Child Behavior Checklist; see Kendall & Sheldrick, 2000), investigators may choose to rely on these preexisting normative samples. However, when normative data do not exist or when the treatment sample is qualitatively different on key factors (e.g., lower SES, presence of developmental disabilities), it may be necessary to collect one's own normative data. Other considerations in the selection of a normative group include taking care to avoid assembling a "supernormal" comparison group (e.g., through psychopathology exclusion criteria), and assuring that the error variance of the normative group is not so different from the treatment group as to introduce statistical bias.

When using statistical tests to compare groups, the investigator usually assumes that the groups are equivalent (null hypothesis) and wishes to find that they are not (alternate hypothesis). However, when the goal is to show that treated individuals are equivalent to "normal" individuals on some factor, traditional hypothesis-testing methods are inadequate. To circumvent this problem, one uses an equivalency testing method (Kendall, Marrs-Garcia, Nath, & Sheldrick, 1999) that examines whether the difference between the treatment and normative groups is within some predetermined range. When used in conjunction with traditional hypothesis testing, this approach allows for stronger conclusions about the equivalency of these groups (see e.g., Pelham et al., 2000, and Barrett, Dadds, & Rapee, 1996, for examples of normative comparisons).

The Reliable Change Index

Another approach to the examination of clinically significant change is the Reliable Change Index (RCI; Jacobson, Follette, & Revenstorf, 1984; Jacobson & Truax, 1991). This method involves calculating the number of clients moving from a dysfunctional to a normative range. The RCI is a calculation of a difference score (post-treatment minus pretreatment) divided by the standard error of measurement (calculated based on the reliability of the measure). The RCI is influenced by the magnitude of change and the reliability of the measure (for a reconsideration of the interpretation of RCI, see Hsu, 1996). The RCI has been widely used, although its originators point out that it has at times been misapplied (Jacobson, Roberts, Berns, & McGlinchey, 1999). When used in conjunction with reliable measures and appropriate cutoff scores, it can be a valuable tool for assessing clinical significance.

Clinical significance may also be examined by means of social validation (see Foster & Mash, 1999; Kazdin, 1977). Social validation may require social comparisons or subjective evaluation. Social comparison involves comparing the post-treatment behavior of the client to the behavior of a normative peer group. It is hoped that the post-treatment behavior will be indistinguishable from the behavior of the nondeviant peer group. Subjective evaluation involves an assessment by significant others as to whether or not the treatment-induced change can be detected. Individuals who interact closely with the client make qualitative judgments about behavior.

Although much progress has been made regarding clinical significance, some debate exists over how to improve the measurement of this construct. Whereas some researchers propose more advanced methods of normative comparison and analysis (e.g., using multiple normative samples), others suggest that clinical significance remain as a simple, client-focused, practical adjunct to statistical significance results (cf. Follette & Callaghan, 1996; Martinovich, Saunders, & Howard, 1996; Tingey et al., 1996a; Tingey, Lambert, Burlingame, & Hansen, 1996b).

Both clinical and statistical significance are of great importance in the assessment of treatment outcome. Given the complex nature of change, it is essential to evaluate treatment with consideration of both approaches. Statistically significant improvements are not equivalent to "cures," and clinical significance is an additional, not a substitute, evaluative strategy. Statistical significance is required to document the fact that changes were beyond those due to chance alone; yet it is also useful to consider if the changes returned dysfunctional clients to within normative limits on the measures of interest. For example, to be considered clinically significant, improvement beyond a minimum criterion could be set for dependent measures (e.g., within 1.5 standard deviations from the normative mean).

Mediators and Moderators of Therapeutic Change

In addition to examining whether psychological treatments are effective, researchers and clinicians alike are also interested in determining (1) the conditions that dictate when a treatment is more or less effective and (2) the mechanisms or processes through which a treatment produces change. Addressing such issues necessitates the specification of *moderator* and/or *mediator* variables (Baron & Kenny, 1986; Holmbeck, 1997, 2000; Shadish & Sweeney, 1991). A moderator is a variable that delineates conditions under which a given treatment is related to an outcome (see Figure 2.1), so that the nature of the treatment-to-outcome association is expected to vary as a function of the moderator. Stated in different terms, a moderator is a variable that influences either the direction or the strength of a relationship between an independent (predictor) variable and a dependent (criterion) variable. For example, if a given treatment were found to be more effective with women than with men, gender would be considered a moderator of the association between treatment and outcome (as in a significant interaction between outcome and gender). A mediator, on the other hand, is a variable that serves to explain the process by which a treatment impacts on an outcome (see Figure 2.1). If an effective treatment for child conduct problems was found to impact on the parenting behaviors of mothers and fathers, which, in turn, were found to have a significant impact on child problem behavior, then parenting behaviors would be considered to be mediators of the treatment-to-outcome relationship (provided certain statistical criteria were met; see Holmbeck, 1997). Put another way, parenting behaviors in this case would be considered one mechanism through which the treatment impacts on child conduct problems. Let's take a closer look at each of these notions.

Moderators. Moderators of treatment effectiveness have received more attention in the research literature than mediators of effectiveness. Moderator variables that have received attention include client age, client ethnicity, client gender, problem type, problem severity, therapist training, mode of delivery (e.g., individual, group), setting, and type and source of outcome measure (e.g., Durlak, Fuhrman, & Lampman, 1991; Durlak, Wells, Cotten, & Johnson, 1995; Shadish & Sweeney, 1991; Weisz, Weiss, Han, Granger, & Morton, 1995). For example, one might be interested in whether the effectiveness of therapy varies as a function of therapist training. In other words, one might ask whether professional, paraprofes-

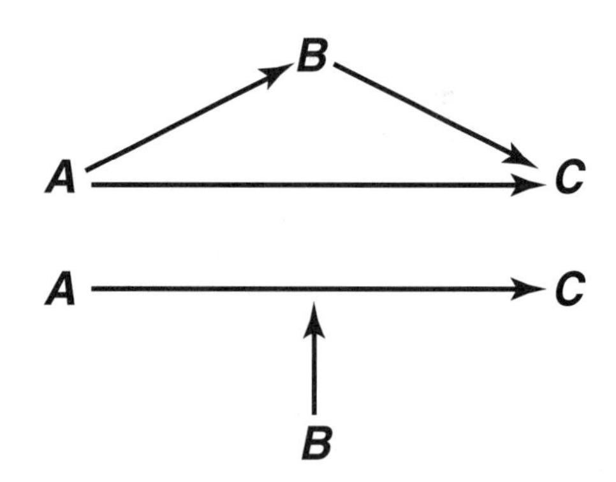

Figure 2.1 Models of mediated and moderated effects. In the top model, B mediates the relationship between A and C. In the bottom model, B moderates the relationship between A and C. From "Toward terminological, conceptual, and statistical clarity in the study of mediators and moderators: Examples for child-clinical and pediatric psychology literatures," by G. H. Holmbeck, 1997, *Journal of Consulting and Clinical Psychology, 65*, p. 600. Copyright 1997 by the American Psychological Association. Reprinted with permission.

sional, and student therapists yield different levels of treatment effectiveness. Specification of such moderator effects in psychological therapy research moves us closer to answering the critical question raised at the outset of this chapter—What therapist behaviors are effective with which types of clients in producing which kinds of patient change?

How does one test for the presence of a moderator effect? A moderator effect is an interaction effect (Holmbeck, 1997). When using multiple regression, the predictor (e.g., treatment vs. no treatment) and moderator (e.g., age of client) are main effects and are entered into the regression equation first (along with any covariates, if applicable), followed by the interaction of the predictor and the moderator. Alternatively, if one is only interested in testing the significance of the interaction effect, all of these terms can be entered simultaneously (see Aiken & West, 1991; and Holmbeck, 2000, for a discussion of the importance of "centering" the main effects when testing moderator effects within a regression context). If one is using Analysis of Variance (ANOVA), the significance of the interaction between two main effects is tested in an analogous manner. A moderator, like an interaction effect, documents that the effects of one variable are different for different levels of another variable.

Statistically significant interactions are probed by plotting and testing the significance of simple slopes of regression lines for high and low values of the moderator variable (Aiken & West, 1991; Holmbeck, 2000). Alternatively, one can test the significance of simple main effects when the predictor (e.g., treatment vs. no treatment) and moderator (e.g., gender) are both categorical variables and are tested with ANOVA. Why is "post-hoc probing" necessary? The presence of a significant interaction tells us that there is significant moderation (i.e., that the association between the treatment variable and the outcome variable is significantly different across levels of the moderator). Unfortunately, it tells us little about the specific conditions that dictate whether or not the treatment is significantly related to the outcome. For example, if a treatment X-client age interaction effect is significant in predicting change in treatment outcome, this tells us that the effect of the treatment for older clients is different from the effect of the treatment for younger clients, but it does not tell us whether the treatment effect is statistically significant for either age group.[1] In other words, one would not yet know, based on the initial significant interaction effect, whether the relationship between treatment and outcome was significant for the older group, the younger group, or both groups. Post-hoc probing of the interaction effect provides this needed information.

Mediators. When one tests the utility of a mediational model, one is attempting to answer important "why" questions, usually in relation to the mechanisms of change for a given treatment approach (Kazdin, 1995). A *mediator* is that variable that specifies the process or mechanism by which a particular outcome is produced. The mediating effect elucidates the mechanism by which the independent variable is related to the outcome variable.

Mediational models are inherently causal models; thus, significant mediational pathways are suggestive of causal pathways. As noted by Collins, Maccoby, Steinberg, Hetherington, and Bornstein (2000), studies of parenting interventions inform us not only about the effectiveness (or lack thereof) of such interventions, but also about causal relations between potential parenting mediators and child outcomes. An example will illustrate this point. Forgatch and DeGarmo (1999) administered a parent training treatment to a sample of recently divorced mothers (as well as controls) and found that treatment was associated with positive (or less negative) changes in parenting behaviors and that changes in parenting behaviors were linked with changes in child behaviors. As Collins et al. (2000) noted, past research has been inconclusive both about the causal relations between parenting and behavior problems in children and about the direction of such associations. Forgatch and DeGarmo's (1999) study not only provides preliminary evidence for the utility of their treatment approach but *also* demonstrates that there is a prospective (and perhaps causal) link in the direction of parenting impacting on child outcome. The combination of using an experimental design (i.e., random assignment) and examining a mediational model allows for such conclusions.

Similar conclusions can be drawn from the work of Huey, Henggeler, Brondino, and Pickrel (2000), although these investigators employed treatment adherence as the primary independent variable. Specifically, Huey and colleagues (2000) tested a mediational model of associations between treatment adherence to multisystemic therapy (MST) and delinquent behavior and found that *changes* in family relationships and delinquent peer affiliation mediated these associations. We see that the effectiveness of the treatment (or at least the impact of treatment adherence) can be attributed, in part, to changes made in the family and peer domains.

How does one test for such mediational effects? The researcher is usually interested in whether a variable "mediates" the association between a treatment and an outcome, such that the mediator accounts for part or all of this association. To test for mediation, one examines whether the following are significant: (1) the association between the predictor (e.g., treatment) and the outcome, (2) the association between the predictor and the mediator, and (3) the association between the mediator and the outcome, after controlling for the effect of the predictor. If all of these conditions are met, one then examines whether the predictor-to-outcome effect is less after controlling for the mediator (condition 4). A corollary of the first condition is that there initially should be a significant relationship between the treatment and the outcome for a mediator to serve its mediating role. In other words, if the treatment and outcome are not significantly associated, there is no significant effect to mediate. (Such a bivariate association between treatment and outcome is not required for moderated effects.)

The conditions necessary for mediated effects can be tested with three multiple regression analyses (Baron & Kenny, 1986). This strategy is similar to that employed when conducting a path analysis (Cohen & Cohen, 1983). The significance of the treatment-to-outcome path (condition 1 above) is examined in the first regression, after controlling for any covariates. The significance of the treatment-to-mediator path (condition 2) is examined in the second regression. Finally, treatment and mediator are employed as predictors (entered simultaneously) in the third equation where the outcome is the dependent variable. Baron and Kenny (1986) recommend using simultaneous entry (rather than hierarchical entry) in this third equation so that the effect of the mediator on the outcome is examined after controlling for the treatment and the effect of the treatment on the outcome is examined after controlling for the mediator (borrowing from path analytic methodology; Cohen & Cohen, 1983). The significance of the mediator-to-outcome path in this third equation is a test of condition 3. The relative effect of the treatment on the outcome in this equation (when the mediator is controlled) in comparison to the effect of the treatment on the outcome in the first equation (when the mediator is not controlled) is the test of the fourth condition. Specifically, the treatment should be less highly associated with the outcome in the third equation than was the case in the first equation. Consider the following example: Within a cognitive behavioral treatment for anxiety disorders in youth that has received empirical support, what changes within the clients mediate the positive outcomes? To test for mediation, Treadwell and Kendall (1996) computed three regression equations for each dependent variable. In the first, the mediating variable was based on regression equations for each dependent variable. The second equation regressed the dependent variable on the independent variable. In the third equation, the dependent variable was regressed on the mediating and independent variable. For mediation, the independent variable must predict the mediator variable, the mediator variable must predict the dependent variable, and the independent variable must predict the dependent variable. If the mediating hypothesis were correct, the effects of the independent variable (treatment) on the dependent variable (improvement) would be less in the third equation (with the mediator) than in the second equation (no mediation). The results confirmed the mediational hypothesis: Change in negative self-talk (not positive self-talk) was a mediating variable.

One question that arises with mediational analysis is this: How much reduction in the total effect is necessary to claim the presence of mediation (see Holmbeck, 2000)? Some researchers have reported whether the treatment-to-outcome effect drops from significance (e.g., $p < .05$) to nonsignificance (e.g., $p > .05$) after the mediator is introduced into the model. This strategy is flawed, however, because a drop from significance to nonsignificance may occur, for example, when a regression coefficient drops from .28 to .27 but may not occur when it drops from .75 to .35. In other words, it is possible that significant mediation *has not* occurred when the test of the treatment-to-outcome effect drops from significance to nonsignificance after taking the mediator into account. On the other hand, it is also possible that significant mediation *has* occurred even when the statistical test of the treatment-to-outcome effect continues to be significant after taking the mediator into account. It appears that a test is needed for the significance of this drop.

When one has satisfied the conditions of mediation, as described, one can test the significance of the indirect effect, which is mathematically equivalent to a test of whether the drop in the total effect (i.e., the zero-order predictor-to-outcome path) is significant upon inclusion of the mediator in the model. This mathematical relationship is demonstrated by the following (see MacKinnon & Dwyer, 1993):

If: Total Effect = Indirect Effect + Direct Effect
Then: Indirect Effect = Total Effect – Direct Effect

In this case, the direct effect is the predictor-to-outcome path with the mediator already in the model. Thus, the significance test of the indirect effect is equivalent to a significance test of the difference between the total and direct effects, with the latter representing the drop in the total effect after the mediator is in the model. The indirect effect is the product of the predictor-to-mediator and mediator-to-outcome path coefficients. (The latter path coefficient is computed with the predictor in the model; Cohen & Cohen, 1983.)

To conduct the statistical test for mediation, one needs unstandardized path coefficients from the model as well as standard errors for these coefficients (all available in computer output). One also needs the standard error of the indirect effect. Sobel (1988; also see Baron & Kenny, 1986) presents an equation for computing the standard error of the indirect effect, as follows:

Given the model: x-to-y-to-z
and
x-to-z

$$se_{\text{indirect effect}} = [(b_{yx}^2)(se_{zy.x}^2) + (b_{zy.x}^2)(se_{yx}^2)]^{1/2} \quad (1)$$

where b = unstandardized beta, se = standard error, yx = the prediction of y from x, and zy.x = the prediction of z from y, with x in the model). In other words, one needs the *b*'s and *se*'s for the x-to-y and y-to-z paths (which are available with SPSS regression output). For the y-to-z path, one computes the b and se terms with x in the model. One may also notice that the b of one path is multiplied times the se of the *other* path for each portion of the equation.

Once one has the standard error of the indirect effect, the following is computed:

$$z = \frac{b_{\text{indirect effect}}}{se_{\text{indirect effect}}} \quad (2)$$

The b for the indirect effect is simply the product of the two *b*'s used in the Sobel equation above (i.e., the b for the x-to-y path and the b for the y-to-z path). Use a z table to determine significance (significant at $p < .05$ if the absolute value of $z > 1.96$). One can also examine the following ratio to determine the percentage of the total effect that can be attributed to the mediator: $b_{\text{indirect effect}}/b_{\text{total effect}}$ (MacKinnon & Dwyer, 1993). Full mediation occurs if 100% of the total effect is accounted for by the mediator (which is very unlikely in most psychological therapy research). Thus, statistical analyses in the social sciences typically examine whether there is significant or nonsignificant *partial* mediation (Baron & Kenny, 1986). Examples of mediational analyses, with SPSS commands, are provided by Holmbeck (2000).

Cumulative Outcome Analyses

Because of the vast literature on the outcomes of diverse therapies, scholars have attempted to summarize the findings. Several major cumulative analyses have undertaken the challenging task of reviewing and reaching conclusions with regard to the effects of psychological therapy. Some of the reviews have been based on subjective conclusions, whereas others have used tabulations of the number of studies favoring one type of intervention versus that of competitors (e.g., Beutler, 1979; Luborsky, Singer, & Luborsky, 1975). This approach uses a "box score" summary of the findings, and reviewers would compare rates of treatment success to draw conclusions about outcomes. Still other reviewers have developed multidimensional multivariate analyses of the impact of potential causal factors on therapy outcome: meta-analysis (Smith & Glass, 1977). More recent attempts to summarize research findings have relied on the meta-analytic statistical techniques (for discussion of the method, see Cooper & Hedges, 1994, Durlak, 1999, and Rosenthal, 1984; for examples of meta-analyses of therapies, see Shadish, Matt, Navarro, & Phillips, 2000, and Weisz, Weiss, Han, Granger, & Morton, 1995). The meta-analytic techniques are useful because they synthesize results across multiple studies by converting the results of each investigation into a common metric (usually, the *effect size*). The outcomes of different types of treatments can then be compared with respect to the magnitude of change reflected in such statistics. The effect size is typically derived by computing the difference between the mean of the treatment group and control group at post-treatment and then dividing this difference by the pooled standard deviation of the two groups (Durlak, 1995). If group means and standard deviations are not available in a published work (and cannot be obtained from the author), an effect size can be computed from other available statistics. Interestingly, the frequent publication of meta-analytic findings has alerted authors to the importance of computing and reporting certain types of statistics that can be utilized by those seeking to conduct meta-analyses (Kazdin, 1994).

A recent approach to cumulative analysis of therapy has taken a "meet criteria" approach. That is, a set of criteria that define empirically supported treatments have been proposed (APA Task Force report, 1995; Chambless & Hollon, 1998), and authors have reviewed the published works to determine whether specific treatments for specific disorders meet the criteria (recall Table 2.1).

Several difficult choices confront the would-be reviewer of a body of research as diverse in quality, methodology, theoretical orientation, target issues and variables, and number of studies as that of the evaluation of the outcomes of psychological therapy. First, should studies of inferior methodological quality be included or omitted in a review of outcomes? The "quality selection" approach provides a reviewer with studies in which unexpected extraneous variables have the least chance of distorting results. Yet in doing so, the number of available investigations is often sufficiently reduced that it becomes difficult to assess whether or not the findings are replicated. Nevertheless, quality research is needed to answer the important questions, and additional quality research will resolve this problem.

The meta-analytic techniques have several advantages over "box score" strategies (Durlak & Lipsey, 1991). Consider the following:

1. The effectiveness of a given treatment is quantified on a continuous scale.
2. An effect size statistic can be computed for each outcome in the study (if a study includes multiple outcomes).
3. Quantitative, as opposed to qualitative, summaries of literatures are provided, such quantitative reviews are less likely to be biased (although bias is still possible, even with a meta-analysis, because numerous decisions are made during the process of conducting such an analysis; see Kazdin, 1994).
4. With meta-analysis, the influence of treatment moderator variables (see the earlier discussion above) and interactions among them can be assessed simultaneously, where the effect size is the dependent variable (Shadish & Sweeney, 1991).
5. Such analyses provide information that is of use to policymakers.

Assuming that one has decided to conduct a meta-analytic review, what are the steps involved in conducting a meta-analysis? Durlak and Lipsey (1991) suggested that six steps are necessary in conducting a thorough meta-analysis:

1. Formulating the research question.
2. Conducting a thorough literature search.
3. Coding the studies that meet inclusionary criteria.
4. Determining how one will compute effect sizes.
5. Conducting statistical analyses.
6. Interpreting the findings.

After determining that a particular research area has matured to the point where a meta-analysis is possible and the results of such an analysis would be of interest to the field, one conducts a literature search. A decision that often arises at this point is whether studies of varying quality should be included (Kendall, Flannery-Schroeder, & Ford, 1999; Kendall & Maruyama, 1985). On the one hand, one could argue that studies of poor quality should not be included in the review, since such studies would not ordinarily be used to draw conclusions about the effectiveness of a given psychological therapy. Indeed, criteria that define empirically supported treatments have been proposed (Chambless & Hollon, 1998). On the other hand, decisions concerning whether a study is of poor quality versus good quality are often not straightforward. A study may have certain exemplary features and other less desirable features. By including studies that vary in quality, one can examine whether certain "quality" variables (e.g., select versus genuine clinical cases) are associated with differential outcomes. Decisions also must be made regarding the types of unpublished work that will or will not be included in the review and the inclusionary and exclusionary criteria that will be employed. Finally, multiple methods of searching are often used (e.g., computer database searches, reviews of reference sections from relevant articles). A word of advice to the meta-analyzer: Do not rely solely on computer searches, for they routinely omit several important studies.

Coding the results of specific studies is an important part of a meta-analysis. When one codes the studies, decisions need to be made regarding what types of variables will be coded and how interrater reliability will be assessed. For example, in a study that examined the outcomes of a psychological therapy, one might code the nature of the intervention, whether the treatment was conducted in clinically representative conditions (Shadish et al., 2000), the number of sessions, the types of participants, the diagnoses of the participants, the age range, the gender distribution, the therapy administration method (e.g., group vs. individual), the qualifications of the therapists, the various features of the research design, and types of outcomes. Once variables such as these have been coded, the effect sizes are then computed. The methods employed to compute effect sizes should be specified, along with a detailing of how nonsignificant treatment effects are handled. Another consideration is whether effect sizes will be weighted, based on the sample sizes of the studies reviewed.

Meta-analysts have become interested in assessing the impact of mediator and moderator variables within a meta-analytic review. Since there is always variability in effect sizes, even within a relatively homogeneous selection of treatment outcome studies, one question that often arises is the degree to which such variability can be accounted for by various potential moderator variables. In other words, are some of the coded variables (e.g., age of client, therapist training) related to therapy effectiveness across a set of outcome studies? Examining the significance of moderator effects (see earlier discussion) would test such hypotheses. In fact, studies of moderator effects have been conducted with such frequency that meta-analytic investigations of such variables have been conducted (e.g., Durlak, Wells, Cotten, & Johnson, 1995; Shadish & Sweeney, 1991).

In their discussion of mediator and moderator effects in meta-analysis, Shadish and Sweeney (1991) examined the impact of 28 potential moderators of treatment effectiveness. Shadish and Sweeney (1991) demonstrated the utility of mediational analyses by using structural equation modeling techniques with meta-analytic data. On the one hand, a meta-analyst could simply examine the separate impact of each hypothesized predictor variable on treatment effect sizes. Unfortunately, such a strategy may not capture the underlying relations among the variables. Instead, if the meta-analyst has a theory about underlying causal mechanisms, one could propose a mediational model. Shadish and Sweeney (1991) examined a mediational model in which the impact of treatment type (i.e., behavioral vs. nonbehavioral) on treatment effect sizes was mediated by variables such as treatment standardization (i.e., whether the treatment was manualized) and treatment implementation (i.e., the degree to which the treatment was fully implemented). The model fit the data, thus supporting the mediational role that such methodological variables play in associations between the type of treatment and outcome. Alternatively, they could have examined process variables instead of methodological variables as mediators. On the other hand, process-level variables are not typically available across multiple studies, thus making it difficult to include such variables in a mediational meta-analytic model.

The merits of integration and summation of the results of related outcome studies are recognized, yet some cautions must be exercised in any meta-analysis. First, as noted earlier, one must check on the quality of the studies, eliminating those that cannot contribute meaningful findings due to basic inadequacies (Kendall & Maruyama, 1985; Kraemer, Gardner, Brooks, & Yesavage, 1998). Consider the following: Would you accept the recommendation that one treatment approach is superior to another if the recommendation was based on *inadequate* research? Probably not. Would you accept this same evidence to refute the recommendation? Again, probably not. If the research evidence is methodologically unsound, it is insufficient evidence for a recommendation; it remains inadequate as a basis for either supporting or refuting treatment recommendations, and therefore it should not be included in cumulative analyses. If a study is methodologically sound, then regardless of the outcome, it must be included.

Second, the studies that are assembled into groups for drawing conclusions about effect sizes must be comparable. Assembling groups of studies in which clients were diagnosed by different procedures, where therapists were markedly diverse, and where the length of treatment varied enormously, will not necessarily clear the picture. Initial groupings should be homogeneous. Subsequently, the generality of the conclusions can be assessed with more heterogeneous groups of studies, and the relationships between diagnostic or therapist diversity can be examined in relation to outcome.

Caution is paramount in meta-analyses in which various studies are said to provide evidence that treatment is superior to controls. The exact nature of the control condition in each specific study must be examined, especially in the case of attention-placebo control conditions. This caution arises from the indefinite definition of attention-placebo control conditions. As noted earlier, one researcher's attention-placebo control condition may be serving as another researcher's therapy condition! Meta-analyzers cannot tabulate the number of studies in which treatment was found to be efficacious in relation to controls without examining the nature of the control condition.

Currently, major efforts are being made to identify and examine those psychological treatments that can be considered empirically supported. These efforts take a set of "criteria" that have been proposed as required for a treatment to be considered empirically supported (see Table 2.1) and review the reported research literature in search of studies that can be used to meet the criteria. A series of such reviews (e.g., Baucom, Shoham, Mueser, Daiuto, & Stickle, 1998; Compas, Haaga, Keefe, Leitenberg, & Williams, 1998; DeRubeis & Crits-Christoph, 1998; Kazdin & Weisz, 1998) and reactions to the approach (e.g., Beutler, 1998; Borkovec & Castonguay, 1998; Calhoun, Moras, Pilkonis, & Rehm, 1998; Davidson, 1998; Garfield, 1998; Goldfried & Wolfe, 1998; Persons & Silberschatz, 1998) document not only that this approach is being applied, but also that there are treatments that meet the criterion of having been supported by empirical research.

Conclusions

Having reviewed several methodological considerations pertinent to treatment outcome research and having offered guidelines and recommendations for a continued accumulation of empirical findings, one recognizes that no one single study, even with optimal design and procedures, can answer the relevant questions about the efficacy and effectiveness of therapy. Rather, a series and collection of studies, with varying approaches, is necessary. The criteria for determining empirically supported treatments have been proposed, and the quest for identification of such treatments has begun. The goal is for the research to be rigorous, with the end goal that the most promising procedures serve professional practice.

Therapy outcome research plays a vital role in facilitating a dialogue between treatment providers and outcome researchers, as well as between scientist-practitioners and the public and private sector (e.g., Department of Health and Human Services, insurance payers, policymakers). Outcome research is increasingly being examined by both managed care organizations and professional associations with the intent of formulating practice guidelines for cost-effective psychological care that provides maximal service to those in need. There is the risk that psychological science and practice will be coopted and exploited in the service only of cost containment and profitability: Therapy outcome research must retain scientific rigor while enhancing the ability of practitioners to deliver effective procedures to individuals in need.

Acknowlegments

Completion of this manuscript was supported by several grants from NIMH awarded to Philip C. Kendall (NIMH MH44042; MH59087 and MH60653) and Grayson Holmbeck (NIMH MH50423; and Social and Behavioral Sciences Research Grants 12-FY93-0621, 12-FY95-0496, 12-FY97-0270, and 12-FY99-0280 from the March of Dimes Birth Defects Foundation).

Footnote

1. Change in the outcome (due to treatment effects) can be assessed in many ways. Within an ANOVA context, "time" could be used as a repeated measures variable. If there are two data collections (e.g., pre- and post-treatment) and regression is used, the Time 2 outcome variable can be used as a dependent variable and the Time 1 outcome variable can be entered first to produce a residual that represents change from Time 1 to Time 2 (or, more accurately, change over time in one's rank order on the dependent measure of interest). Finally, if there are three or more data collections (e.g., pretreatment, post-treatment, followup), slopes representing change in the dependent measure (derived from growth curve analyses) can be used (see Martinez & Forgatch, 2000, for an example of this latter strategy).

References

Aiken, L. S., & West, S. G. (1991). *Multiple regression: Testing and interpreting interactions.* Newbury Park, CA: Sage.

Alvidrez, J., Azocar, F., & Miranda, J. (1996). Demystifying the concept of ethnicity for psychotherapy researchers. *Journal of Consulting and Clinical Psychology, 64,* 903–908.

American Psychological Association Task Force on Promotion and Dissemination of Psychological Procedures. (1995). Training in and dissemination of empirically-validated psychological treatments: Report and recommendations. *Clinical Psychologist, 48*, 3–23.

Barlow, D. H. (1989). Treatment outcome evaluation methodology with anxiety disorder: Strengths and key issues. *Advances in Behavior Research and Therapy, 11*, 121–132.

Baron, R. M., & Kenny, D. A. (1986). The mediator-moderator variable distinction in social psychological research: Conceptual, strategic, and statistical consideration. *Journal of Personality and Social Psychology, 51*, 1173–1182.

Barrett, P. M., Dadds, M. R., & Rapee, R. M. (1996). Family treatment of childhood anxiety: A controlled trial. *Journal of Consulting and Clinical Psychology, 64*, 333–342.

Baucom, D., Shoham, V., Mueser, K., Daiuto, A., & Stickle, T. (1998). Empirically supported couple and family interventions for marital distress and adult mental health problems. *Journal of Consulting and Clinical Psychology, 66*, 53–88.

Bersoff, D. M., & Bersoff, D. N. (1999). Ethical perspectives in clinical research. In P C. Kendall, J. Butcher, & G. Holmbeck (Eds.), *Handbook of research methods in clinical psychology* (pp. 31–53). New York: John Wiley & Sons.

Beutler, L. E. (1979). Toward specific psychological therapies for specific conditions. *Journal of Consulting and Clinical Psychology, 47*, 882–897.

Beutler, L. E. (1996). The view from the rear: An editorial. *Journal of Consulting and Clinical Psychology, 64*, 845–847.

Beutler, L. E. (1998). Identifying empirically supported treatments: What if we didn't? *Journal of Consulting and Clinical Psychology, 66*, 37–52.

Beutler, L. E., Brown, M. T., Crothers, L., Booker, K., & Seabrook, M. K. (1996). The dilemma of fictitious demographic distinctions in psychological research. *Journal of Consulting and Clinical Psychology, 54*, 48–53.

Borkovec, T., & Castonguay, L. (1998). What is the scientific meaning of empirically supported therapy? *Journal of Consulting and Clinical Psychology, 66*, 136–142.

Borsari, B., & Carey, K. B. (2000). Effects of a brief motivational intervention with college student drinkers. *Journal of Consulting and Clinical Psychology, 68*, 728–733.

Brown, R. A., Evans, M., Miller, I., Burgess, E., & Mueller, T. (1997). Cognitive-behavioral treatment for depression in alcoholism. *Journal of Consulting and Clinical Psychology, 65*, 715–726.

Calhoun, K., Moras, K., Pilkonis, P., & Rehm, L. (1998). Empirically supported treatments: Implications for training. *Journal of Consulting and Clinical Psychology, 66*, 151–162.

Chambless, D. L., & Hollon, S. D. (1998). Defining empirically supported therapies. *Journal of Consulting and Clinical Psychology, 66*, 7–18.

Chang, B. L. (1999). Cognitive-behavioral intervention for homebound caregivers of persons with dementia. *Nursing Research, 48*, 173–182.

Cohen, J., & Cohen, P. (1983). *Applied multiple regression/correlation analysis for the behavior sciences* (2nd ed.). Hillsdale, NJ: Erlbaum.

Collins, W. A., Maccoby, E. E., Steinberg, L., Hetherington, E. M., & Bornstein, M. H. (2000). Contemporary research on parenting: The case for nature and nurture. *American Psychologist, 55*, 218–232.

Compas, B., Haaga, D., Keefe, F., Leitenberg, H., & Williams, D. (1998). Sampling of empirically supported psychological treatments from health psychology: Smoking, Chronic pain, cancer, and bulimia nervosa. *Journal of Consulting and Clinical Psychology, 66*, 89–112.

Cooper, H., & Hedges, L. V. (Eds.) (1994). *The handbook of research synthesis.* New York: Russell Sage Foundation.

Coyne, J. C., & Gotlib, I. H. (1983). The role of cognition in depression. A critical appraisal. *Psychological Bulletin, 94*, 472–505.

Davidson, G. (1998). Being bolder with the Boulder model: The challenge of education and training in empirically supported treatments. *Journal of Consulting and Clinical Psychology, 66*, 163–167.

Davidson, G. C., & Lazarus, A. A. (1995). The dialectics of science and practice. In S. C. Hayes, V. M., Follette, R. D., Dawes, & K. Grady (Eds.). *Scientific standards of psychological practice: Issues and recommendations* (pp. 95–120). Reno, NV: Context Press.

Delucchi, K., & Bostrom, A. (1999). Small sample longitudinal clinical trials with missing data: A comparison of analytic methods. *Psychological Methods, 4*, 158–172.

DeRubeis, R., & Crits-Christoph, P. (1998). Empirically supported individual and group psychological treatments for adult mental disorders. *Journal of Consulting and Clinical Psychology, 66*, 37–52.

Dobson, K., & Shaw, B. (1988). The use of treatment manuals in cognitive therapy. Experience and issues. *Journal of Consulting and Clinical Psychology, 56*, 673–682.

Durlak, J. A. (1995). Understanding meta-analysis. In L. G. Grimm, & P. R. Yarnold (Eds.), *Reading and understanding multivariate statistics* (pp. 319–352). Washington, DC: American Psychological Association.

Durlak, J. A. (1999). Meta-analytic research methods. In P. C. Kendall, J. N. Butcher, & G. N. Holmbeck (Eds.), *Research methods in clinical psychology* (pp. 419–429). New York: John Wiley & Sons.

Durlak, J. A., Fuhrman, T., & Lampman, C. (1991). Effectiveness of cognitive-behavior therapy for maladapting children: A meta-analysis. *Psychological Bulletin, 110,* 204–214.

Durlak, J. A., & Lipsey, M. W. (1991). A practitioner's guide to meta-analysis. *American Journal of Community Psychology, 19,* 291–332.

Durlak, J. A., Wells, A. M., Cotten, J. K., & Johnson, S. (1995). Analysis of selected methodological issues in child psychotherapy research. *Journal of Clinical Child Psychology, 24,* 141–148.

Fishman, D. B. (2000). Transcending the efficacy versus effectiveness debate: Proposal for a new, electronic "journal of pragmatic case studies." *Prevention & Treatment, 3,* Article 11 [Online Journal] http://journals.apa.org/prevention/volume3/pre0030012r.htm

Flaherty, J. A., & Meaer, R. (1980). Measuring racial bias in inpatient treatment. *American Journal of Psychiatry, 137,* 679–682.

Flannery-Schroeder, E., & Kendall, P. C. (1996). *Cognitive-behavioral therapy for anxious children: Therapist manual for group treatment.* Ardmore, PA: Workbook Publishing.

Follette, W. C., & Callaghan, G. M. (1996). The importance of the principle of clinical significance—defining significant to whom and for what purpose: A response to Tingey, Lambert, Burlingame, and Hansen. *Psychotherapy Research, 6,* 133–143.

Forgatch, M. S., & DeGarmo, D. S. (1999). Parenting through change: An effective prevention program for single mothers. *Journal of Consulting and Clinical Psychology, 67,* 711–724.

Foster, S. & Mash, E. (1999). Assessing social validity in clinical treatment research: Issues and procedures. *Journal of Consulting and Clinical Psychology, 67,* 308–319.

Franklin, M. E., Abramowitz, J. S., Kozak, M. J., Levitt, J. T., & Foa, E. B. (2000). Effectiveness of exposure and ritual prevention for obsessive-compulsive disorder: randomized compared with nonrandomized samples. *Journal of Consulting and Clinical Psychology, 68,* 594–602.

Garfield, S. (1996). Some problems associated with "Validated" forms of psychotherapy. *Clinical Psychology: Science and Practice, 3,* 218–229.

Garfield, S. (1998). Some comments on empirically supported psychological treatments. *Journal of Consulting and Clinical Psychology, 66,* 121–125.

Gladis, M. M., Gosch, E. A., Dishuk, N. M., & Crits-Christoph, P. (1999). Quality of Life: Expanding the scope of clinical significance. *Journal of Consulting and Clinical Psychology, 67,* 320–331.

Goldfried, M., & Wolfe, B. (1998). Toward a more clinically valid approach to therapy research. *Journal of Consulting and Clinical Psychology, 66,* 143–150.

Goldstein, A. P., Lopez, M., & Greenleaf, D. O. (1979). Introduction. In A. P. Goldstein & F. H. Kanfer (Eds.), *Maximizing treatment gains: Transfer enhancement in psychotherapy,* New York: Academic Press.

Gotlib, I. H. (1984). Depression and general psychopathology in university students. *Journal of Abnormal Psychology, 93,* 19–30.

Greenhouse, J., Stangl, D., & Bromberg, J. (1989). An introduction to survival analysis: Statistical methods for analysis of clinical trial data. *Journal of Consulting and Clinical Psychology, 57,* 536–544.

Havik, O. E., & VandenBos, G. R. (1996). Limitations of manualized psychotherapy for everyday clinical practice. *Clinical Psychology: Science and Practice, 3,* 264–267.

Henggeler, S. W., Melton, G., Brondino, M., Scherer, D., & Hanley, J. (1997). Multisystemic therapy with violent and chronic juvenile offenders and their families: The role of treatment fidelity in successful dissemination. *Journal of Consulting and Clinical Psychology, 65,* 821–833.

Hoagwood, K., Hibbs, E., Brent, D., & Jensen, P. (1995). Introduction to the special section: Efficacy and effectiveness in studies of child and adolescent psychotherapy. *Journal of Consulting and Clinical Psychology, 63,* 683–687.

Hollon, S. D. (1996). The efficacy and effectiveness of psychotherapy relative to medications. *American Psychologist, 51,* 1025–1030.

Hollon, S. D., & DeRubeis, R. J. (1981). Placebo-psychotherapy combinations: Inappropriate representation of psychotherapy in drug-psychotherapy comparative trials. *Psychological Bulletin, 90,* 467–477.

Holmbeck, G. N. (1997). Toward terminological, conceptual, and statistical clarity in the study of mediators and moderators: Examples from the child-clinical and pediatric psychology literatures. *Journal of Consulting and Clinical Psychology, 65,* 599–610.

Holmbeck, G. N. (2000). *Post-hoc probing of significant moderational and mediational effects in studies of pediatric populations.* Manuscript submitted for publication.

Homma-True, R, Greene, B., Lopez, S. R., & Trimble, J. E. (1993). Ethnocultural diversity in clinical psychology. *Clinical Psychologist, 46,* 50–63.

Howard, B., & Kendall, P. C. (1996). *Cognitive-behavioral family therapy for anxious children: Therapist manual.* Ardmore, PA: Workbook Publishing.

Howard, K. I., Krause, M. S., & Orlinsky, D. E. (1986). The attrition dilemma: Toward a new strategy for psychotherapy research. *Journal of Consulting and Clinical Psychology, 54,* 106–110.

Howard, K. I., Lueger, R., Maling, M., & Martinovich, Z. (1993). A phase model of psychotherapy. *Journal of Consulting and Clinical Psychology, 61,* 678–685.

Hsu, L. (1996). On the identification of clinically significant changes: Reinterpretation of Jacobson's cut scores. *Journal of Psychopathology and Behavioral Assessment, 18,* 371–386.

Huey, S. J., Henggeler, S. W., Brondino, M. J., & Pickrel, S. G. (2000). Mechanisms of change in multisystemic therapy: Reducing delinquent behavior through therapist adherence and improved family and peer functioning. *Journal of Consulting and Clinical Psychology, 68*, 451–467.

Jacobson, N. S., Follette, W. C., & Revenstorf, D. (1984). Psychotherapy outcome research: Methods for reporting variability and evaluating clinical significance. *Behavior Therapy, 15*, 336–352.

Jacobson, N. S., & Hollon, S. D. (1996a). Cognitive-behavior therapy versus pharmacotherapy: Now that the jury's returned its verdict, it's time to present the rest of the evidence. *Journal of Consulting and Clinical Psychology, 64*, 74–80.

Jacobson, N. S., & Hollon, S. D. (1996b). Prospects for future comparisons between drugs and psychotherapy. Lessons from the CBT-versus-pharmacotherapy exchange. *Journal of Consulting and Clinical Psychology, 64*, 104–108.

Jacobson, N. S., Roberts, L. J., Berns, S. B., & McGlinchey, J. B. (1999). Methods for defining and determining the clinical significance of treatment effects: Description, application, and alternatives. *Journal of Consulting and Clinical Psychology, 67*, 300–307.

Jacobson, N. S., & Truax, P. (1991). Clinical significance: A statistic approach to defining meaningful change in psychotherapy research. *Journal of Consulting and Clinical Psychology, 59*, 12–19.

Jaycox, L., Foa, E., & Morral, A. (1998). Influence of emotional engagement and habituation on exposure therapy for PTSD. *Journal of Consulting and Clinical Psychology, 66*, 185–192.

Kazdin, A. E. (1977). Assessing the clinical or applied importance of behavior change through social validation. *Behavior Modification, 1*, 427–451.

Kazdin, A. E. (1994). Methodology, design, and evaluation in psychotherapy research. In A. E. Bergin & S. L. Garfield (Eds.), *Handbook of psychotherapy and behavior change* (pp. 19–71). New York: John Wiley & Sons.

Kazdin, A. E. (1995). Scope of child and adolescent psychotherapy research: Limited sampling of dysfunctions, treatments, and client characteristics. *Journal of Clinical Child Psychology, 24*, 125–140.

Kazdin, A. E. (1996). Validated treatments: Multiple perspectives and issues—Introduction to the series. *Clinical Psychology: Science and Practice, 3*, 216–217.

Kazdin, A. E. (1998). *Research design in clinical psychology* (3rd ed.). Boston, MA: Allyn & Bacon.

Kazdin, A. E. (1999). The meanings and measurement of clinical significance. *Journal of Consulting and Clinical Psychology, 67*, 332–339.

Kazdin, A. E., & Bass, D. (1989). Power to detect differences between alternative treatments in comparative psychotherapy outcome research. *Journal of Consulting and Clinical Psychology, 57*, 138–147.

Kazdin, A. E., & Weisz, J. R. (1998). Identifying and developing empirically supported child and adolescent treatments. *Journal of Consulting and Clinical Psychology, 66*, 19–36.

Kendall, P. C. (1998). Empirically supported psychological therapies. *Journal of Consulting and Clinical Psychology, 66*, 1–4.

Kendall, P. C. (1999). Introduction to the special section: Clinical Significance. *Journal of Consulting and Clinical Psychology, 67*, 283–284.

Kendall, P. C., & Chu, B. (1999). Retrospective self-reports of therapist flexibility in a manual-based treatment for youths with anxiety disorders. *Journal of Clinical Child Psychology, 29*, 209–220.

Kendall, P. C., Chu, B., Gifford, A., Hayes, C., & Nauta, M. (1998). Breathing life into a manual. *Cognitive and Behavioral Practice, 5*, 177–198.

Kendall, P. C., & Flannery-Schroeder, E. C. (1998). Methodological issues in treatment research for anxiety disorders in youth. *Journal of Abnormal Child Psychology, 26*, 27–38.

Kendall, P. C., Flannery-Schroeder, E. C., & Ford, J. D. (1999). Therapy outcome research methods. In P. C. Kendall, J. N. Butcher, & G. N. Holmbeck (Eds.), *Research methods in clinical psychology* (pp. 330–363). New York: John Wiley & Sons.

Kendall, P. C., & Grove, W. (1988). Normative comparisons in therapy outcome. *Behavioral Assessment, 10*, 147 158.

Kendall, P. C., & Hollon, S. D. (1983). Calibrating therapy: Collaborative archiving of tape samples from therapy outcome trials. *Cognitive Therapy and Research, 7*, 199–204.

Kendall, P. C., Hollon, S., Beck, A. T., Hammen, C., & Ingram, R. (1987). Issues and recommendations regarding use of the Beck Depression Inventory. *Cognitive Therapy and Research, 11*, 289–299.

Kendall, P. C., Kane, M., Howard, B., & Siqueland, L. (1990). *Cognitive-behavioral therapy for anxious children: Treatment manual.* Ardmore, PA: Workbook Publishing.

Kendall, P. C., Marrs-Garcia, A., Nath, S. R., & Sheldrick, R. C. (1999). Normative comparisons for the evaluation of clinical significance. *Journal of Consulting and Clinical Psychology, 67*, 285–299.

Kendall, P. C., & Maruyama, G. (1985). Meta-analysis: On the road to synthesis of knowledge? *Clinical Psychology Review, 5*, 79–89.

Kendall, P. C., & Norton-Ford, J. D. (1982). *Clinical Psychology: Scientific and professional dimensions.* New York: John Wiley & Sons.

Kendall, P. C., Pellegrini, D. S., & Urbain, E. S. (1981). Approaches to assessment for cognitive-behavioral interventions with children. In P. C. Kendall & S. D. Hollon (Eds.), *Assessment strategies for cognitive-behavioral interventions.* New York: Academic Press.

Kendall, P. C., & Sheldrick, R. C. (2000). Normative data for normative comparisons. *Journal of Consulting and Clinical Psychology, 68*, 767–773.

Kendall, P. C., & Southam-Gerow, M. A. (1995). Issues in the transportability of treatment: The case of anxiety disorders in youth. *Journal of Consulting and Clinical Psychology, 63*, 702–708.

Kendall, P. C., & Sugarman, A. (1997). Attrition in the treatment of childhood anxiety disorders. *Journal of Consulting and Clinical Psychology, 65*, 883–888.

Kendall, P. C., & Wilcox, L. E. (1980). A cognitive-behavioral treatment for impulsivity: Concrete versus conceptual training with non-self-controlled problem children. *Journal of Consulting and Clinical Psychology, 48*, 80–91.

Kiesler, D. J. (1971). Experimental designs in psychotherapy research. In A. Bergin & S. Garfield (Eds.), *Handbook of psychotherapy and behavior change*. New York: John Wiley & Sons.

Kiesler, D. J. (1973). *The process of psychotherapy.* Chicago: Aldine.

Kraemer, H. C., Gardner, C., Brooks, J., & Yesavage, J. (1998). Advantages of excluding underpowered studies in meta-analysis: Inclusionist versus exclusionist viewpoints. *Psychological Methods, 3*, 23–31.

Krupnick, J., Shea, T., & Elkin, I. (1986). Generalizability of treatment studies utilizing solicited patients. *Journal of Consulting and Clinical Psychology, 54*, 68–78.

Lambert, M. J., Hansen, N. B., & Finch, A. E. (2001). Patient-focused research: Using patient outcome data to enhance treatment effects. *Journal of Consulting and Clinical Psychology, 69*, 159–172.

Lambert, M. J., Huefner, J. C., & Reisinger, C. W. (2000). Quality improvement: Current research in outcome management. In G. Stricker, W. G. Troy, et al., *Handbook of quality management in behavioral health: Issues in the practice of psychology* (pp. 95–110). New York: Kluwer Academic/ Plenum Publishers.

Lopez, S. R. (1989). Patient variable biases in clinical judgment: Conceptual overview and methodological considerations. *Psychological Bulletin, 106*, 184–204.

Luborsky, L., Singer, B., & Luborsky, L. (1975). Comparative studies of psychotherapy. *Archives of General Psychiatry, 32*, 995–1008.

MacKinnon, D. P., & Dwyer, J. H. (1993). Estimating mediated effects in prevention studies. *Evaluation Review, 17*, 144–158.

March, J., & Mulle, K. (1996). Cognitive-behavioral psychotherapy for obsessive-compulsive disorder. Unpublished manuscript, Duke University Medical Center, Durham, NC.

Marks, I., Lowell, L., Noshirvani, H., Livanou, M., & Thrasher, S. (1998). Treatment of posttraumatic stress disorder by exposure and/or cognitive restructuring. *Archives of General Psychiatry, 55*, 317–325.

Martinez, C. R., & Forgatch, M. S. (2000). Preventing problems with boys' noncompliance: Effects of a parent training intervention for divorcing mothers. Manuscript submitted for publication.

Martinovich, Z., Saunders, S., & Howard, K. I. (1996). Some comments on "Assessing clinical significance." *Psychotherapy Research, 6*, 124–132.

Mason, M. J. (1999). A review of procedural and statistical methods for handling attrition and missing data. *Measurement and Evaluation in Counseling and Development, 32*, 111–118.

Miranda, J. (1996). Introduction to the special section on recruiting and retaining minorities in psychotherapy research. *Journal of Consulting and Clinical Psychology, 64(5)*, 848–850.

Miranda, J., Azocar, F., Organista, K. C., Munoz, R. F., & Lieberman, A. (1996). Recruiting and retaining low-income Latinos in psychotherapy research. *Journal of Consulting and Clinical Psychology, 64*, 868–874.

Neal, A. M., & Turner, S. M. (1991). Anxiety disorders research with African Americans: Current status. *Psychological Bulletin, 109*, 400–410.

Neighbors, H. W. (1985). Seeking help for personal problems: Black Americans' use of health and mental health services. *Community Mental Health Journal, 21*, 156–166.

Neighbors, H. W. (1988). The help-seeking behavior of Black Americans. *Journal of the National Medical Association, 80*, 1009–1012.

Nich, C., & Carroll, K. (1997). Now you see it, now you don't: A comparison of traditional versus random-effects regression models in the analysis of longitudinal follow-up data from a clinical trial. *Journal of Consulting and Clinical Psychology, 65*, 252–261.

O'Hara, M. W., Stuart, S., Gorman, L. L., & Wenzel, A. (2000). Efficacy of interpersonal psychotherapy for postpartum depression. *Archives of General Psychiatry, 57*, 1039–1045.

O'Leary, K. D., & Borkovec, T. D. (1978). Conceptual, methodological, and ethical problems of placebo groups in psychotherapy research. *American Psychologist, 33*, 821–830.

Ollendick, T. H. (1986). Behavior therapy with children and adolescents. In S. L. Garfield & A. E. Bergin (Eds.), *Handbook of psychotherapy and behavior change* (3rd ed.) (pp. 525–565). New York: John Wiley & Sons.

Parloff, M. B. (1986). Placebo controls in psychotherapy research: A sine qua non or a placebo for research problems? *Journal of Consulting and Clinical Psychology, 54*, 79–87.

Pelham, W. E., Jr., Gnagy, E. M., Greiner, A. R., Hoza, B., Hinshaw, S. P., Swanson, J. M., Simpson, S., Shapiro, C., Bukstein, O., Baron-Myak, C., & McBurnett, K. (2000). Behavioral versus behavioral and pharmacological treatment in

ADHD children attending a summer treatment program. *Journal of Abnormal Child Psychology, 28,* 507–525.

Persons, J., & Silberschatz, G. (1998). Are results of randomized controlled trials useful to psychotherapists? *Journal of Consulting and Clinical Psychology, 66,* 126–135.

Rosenthal, R. (1984). *Meta-analytic procedures for social research.* Beverly Hills, CA: Sage.

Shadish, W. R., & Sweeney, R. B. (1991). Mediators and moderators in meta-analysis: There's a reason we don't let dodo birds tell us which psychotherapies should have prizes. *Journal of Consulting and Clinical Psychology, 59,* 883–893.

Shadish, W. R., Matt, G. E., Navarro, A. M., & Phillips, G. (2000). The effects of psychological therapies under clinically representative conditions: A meta-analysis *Psychological Bulletin, 126,* 512–529.

Shakow, D. (1976). What is clinical psychology? *American Psychologist, 31,* 553–560.

Shapiro, D. A., & Shapiro, D. (1982). Meta-analysis of comparative therapy outcome studies: A reply to Wilson. *Behavioural Psychotherapy, 10,* 307–310.

Simon, R., Fleiss, J., Gurland, B., Stiller, P., & Sharpe, L. (1973). Depression and schizophrenia in hospitalized Black and White mental patients. *Archives of General Psychiatry, 28,* 509–512.

Smith, M. L., & Glass, G. V. (1977). Meta-analysis of psychotherapy outcomes studies. *American Psychologist, 32,* 752–760.

Smith, M. L., Glass, G. V., & Miller, T. I. (1980). *The benefits of psychotherapy.* Baltimore, MD: Johns Hopkins University Press.

Sobel, M. E. (1988). Direct and indirect effect in linear structural equation models. In J. S. Long (Ed.), *Common problems/proper solutions: Avoiding error in quantitative research* (pp. 46–64). Beverly Hills, CA: Sage.

Stricker, G. (2000). The relationship between efficacy and effectiveness. A commentary on "Transcending the efficacy versus effectiveness research debate." *Prevention & Treatment, 3,* Article 10 [Online Journal] http://journals.apa.org/prevention/volume3/pre0030010c.htm

Stuart, G. L., Treat, T. A., & Wade, W. A. (2000). Effectiveness of an empirically based treatment for panic disorder delivered in a service clinic setting: 1-year follow-up. *Journal of Consulting and Clinical Psychology, 68,* 506–512.

Sue, S., Kurasaki, K. S., & Srinivasan, S. (1999). Ethnicity, gender, and cross-cultural issues in clinical research. In P. C. Kendall, J. N. Butcher, & G. N. Holmbeck (Eds.), *Handbook of research methods in clinical psychology* (2nd ed.) (pp. 54–71). New York. John Wiley & Sons.

Tennen, H., Hall, J. A., & Affleck, G. (1995). Depression research methodologies in the *Journal of Personality and Social Psychology:* A review and critique. *Journal of Personality and Social Psychology, 68,* 870–884.

Thompson, E. E., Neighbors, H. W., Munday, C., & Jackson, J. S. (1996). Recruitment and retention of African American patients for clinical research: An exploration of response rates in an urban psychiatric hospital. *Journal of Consulting and Clinical Psychology, 64,* 861–867.

Tingey, R. C., Lambert, M. J., Burlingame, G. M., & Hansen, N. B. (1996a). Assessing clinical significance: Proposed extensions to method. *Psychotherapy Research, 6,* 109–123.

Tingey, R. C., Lambert, M. J., Burlingame, G. M., & Hansen, N. B. (1996b). Clinically significant change: Practical indicators for evaluating psychotherapy outcome. *Psychotherapy Research, 6,* 144–153.

Treadwell, K., & Kendall, P. C. (1996). Self-talk in youth with anxiety disorders: States of mind, content specificity, and treatment outcome. *Journal of Consulting and Clinical Psychology, 64,* 941–950.

Treadwell, K., Flannery-Schroeder, E. C., & Kendall, P. C. (1994). Ethnicity and gender in a sample of clinic-referred anxious children: Adaptive functioning, diagnostic status, and treatment outcome. *Journal of Anxiety Disorders, 9,* 373–384.

VandenBos, G. R. (1996). Outcome assessment of psychotherapy. *American Psychologist, 51,* 1005–1006.

Vredenburg, K., Flett, G. L., & Krames, L. (1993). Analogue versus clinical depression: A critical reappraisal. *Psychological Bulletin, 113,* 327–344.

Wade, W., Treat, T., & Stuart, G. (1998). Transporting an empirically-supported treatment for panic disorder to a service setting: A benchmarking strategy. *Journal of Consulting and Clinical Psychology, 66,* 231–239.

Walders, N., & Drotar, D. (2000). Understanding cultural and ethnic influences in research with child clinical and pediatric psychology populations. In D. Drotar (Ed.), *Handbook of research in pediatric and clinical child psychology* (pp. 165–188). New York: Kluwer Academic/Plenum Publishers.

Waltz, J., Addis, M. E., Koerner, K., & Jacobson, N. S. (1993). Testing the integrity of a psychotherapy protocol: Assessment of adherence and competence. *Journal of Consulting and Clinical Psychology, 61,* 620–630.

Weisz, J. R., Donenberg, G. R., Han, S. S., & Weiss, B. (1995). Bridging the gap between laboratory and clinic in child and adolescent psychotherapy. *Journal of Consulting and Clinical Psychology, 63,* 688–701.

Weisz, J. R., Weiss, B., & Donenberg, G. R. (1992). The lab versus the clinic: Effects of child and adolescent psychotherapy. *American Psychologist, 47,* 1578–1585.

Weisz, J. R., Weiss, B., Han, S. S., Granger, D. A., & Morton, T. (1995). Effects of psychotherapy with children and adolescents revisited: A meta-analysis of treatment outcome studies. *Psychological Bulletin, 117*, 450–468.

Wilson, G. T. (1995). Empirically validated treatments as a basis for clinical practice: Problems and prospects. In S. C. Hayes, V. M. Follette, R. D. Dawes, & K. Grady (Eds.), *Scientific standards of psychological practice: Issues and recommendations* (pp. 163–196). Reno, NV: Context Press.

Wilson, G. T. (1996). Treatment of bulimia nervosa: When CBT fails. *Behaviour Research and Therapy, 34*, 197–212.

CHAPTER 3

THEORETICAL CHALLENGES TO THERAPY PRACTICE AND RESEARCH: THE CONSTRAINT OF NATURALISM

BRENT D. SLIFE
Brigham Young University

Contemporary therapists and therapy researchers are under intellectual siege. The conceptual life of those who practice and study psychotherapy has moved from the thoughtful and free inquiry of the personality theory tradition to what long-time observer Allen Bergin (1997) calls a "bottom line mentality" (p. 83). Bergin describes several forces—economic, medical, and scientific—that have recently coalesced to make therapists into "cookie cutters" (p. 85) and researchers into "mechanotropes" (p. 86). That is, these forces have so limited and constrained mental health professionals that they are discouraged from thinking as creatively and critically as they once did.

To be sure, many see these limits and constraints as a positive trend. The emphases on manualized techniques, standardized diagnoses, and scientific validation are considered marks of disciplinary progress, particularly in comparison to medicine (cf. APA, 1995; Calhoun, Moras, Pilkonis, & Rehm, 1998; Kendall, 1998; Luborsky & DeRubeis, 1984; Messer, 2001; Nathan & Gorman, 1998; Shoham, 1996). Also, constraining therapists in this technical manner is supposed to make them more economically accountable (Nathan, 1998). The problem is that the economic and medical tail is now wagging the therapeutic dog. Normally, we would look to our empirical researchers for critical evaluation of these constraints. Unfortunately, these researchers are themselves constrained because empirical investigation alone cannot resolve the theoretical, philosophical, and even ethical issues involved.

Therefore, this chapter—new to the fifth edition of the *Handbook*—explicates the major theoretical and philosophical challenges in the current trends of psychotherapy. Many observers have acknowledged the combination of medical, economic, and scientific factors that seem to be implicated in these professional constraints (e.g., Bergin & Garfield, 1994a; Garfield & Bergin, 1986; Goldfried & Wolfe, 1996; Messer, 2001; Richardson, Fowers, & Guignon, 1999; Russell, 1994; Strupp & Anderson, 1995). Few, however, have recognized the philosophy that underlies and fuels these factors—*naturalism.* Does this philosophy pose problems, even dangers, for the field of psychotherapy? Are the biases of naturalism leading us to ignore potentially effective factors and conceptions? Is there room for innovation in the "bottom line mentality" of today's naturalistic approach to research and treatment? Examining such questions is a primary purpose of this chapter.

BROADENING THE RELEVANCE OF THEORY

The first step in answering these questions is to broaden the conception of theory. Theory is often understood as the servant of traditional scientific method. That is, theory is typically viewed as part of the method, either as the speculation that leads to testable hypotheses or as the logical outcome of systematic observations (e.g., Heiman, 1995; cf. Slife & Williams, 1995). From this narrow perspective, theory does not have the evaluative warrant to perform the critical role needed in psychotherapy. As we shall see, for instance, traditional scientific method has itself been cast in a naturalistic light and is thus one of the scientific factors (from the combination above) that requires examination. If theory can only lead to or result from this method, how could it critically evaluate method?

Fortunately, many leading thinkers no longer understand theory in this limited manner (Bem & de Jong, 1997; Held, 1995; Messer, 2001; Polkinghorne, 1988; Richardson et al., 1999; Robinson, 1989, 1992; Slife, Williams, & Barlow, 2001; Valentine, 1992; Woolfolk, 1998). Indeed, one only needs to reflect on the rich tradition of personality theory to realize that therapy theory has meant much more than a step in the method (e.g., Hall and Lindzey, 1957; Hall, Lindzey, & Campbell, 1998). Theory also means the philosophy of the discipline, that is, its basic assumptions and values.

At first glance, this meaning might appear to put theory outside the domain of science, but the hallmark of science is investigation and examination, in *all* its forms. A scientist has no obligation to stop with empirical investigation. If the assumptions and values that are used to understand particular phenomena become problematic, creative scientists investigate those assumptions. Indeed, many of the greatest advances of science occurred through this sort of conceptual study. Einstein's theoretical investigation (and revision) of Newton's philosophical assumption of Absolute Time is a noted example (Slife, 1993).

But how does a broadened notion of theory help us to discern what is happening in psychotherapy? First, it assumes that all systems of thought have assumptions. All systems have implicit points of view that must be assumed in order to allow the system to operate. No system, whether an investigative system or a school of thought, can escape the need for assumptions. As Karl Jaspers (1954) once observed, "There is no escape from philosophy. The question is only whether [a philosophy] is good or bad, muddled or clear. Anyone who rejects philosophy is himself unconsciously practicing a philosophy" (p. 12).

Jaspers's observations mean that current models of psychotherapy, medicine, and the economy have implicit and often unexamined points of view that merit explication and examination. Even the scientific method does not escape philosophy in this sense. The scientific method has traditionally been considered free of systematic assumptions or points of view that could taint or bias its findings. Although the possibility of researcher assumptions and biases is well recognized, these possibilities are thought to be eliminatable through experimental control and/or precise measurement. As we shall see, however, some assumptions are inherent in the *logic* of these methods, in which case Jaspers's observations also apply to the core of scientific investigation (Curd & Cover, 1998; Feyerabend, 1975; Kuhn, 1970; Lakatos & Musgrave, 1970; Mahrer, 2000; Polkinghorne, 1983; Popper, 1959; Robinson, 1992; Rychlak, 2000).

The assumptions inherent in method are another reason that theory cannot be viewed as a servant of method. If method does have systematic assumptions, then the theorist must be able to metaphorically step back from method to investigate and examine those assumptions. Are they correct for the subject matter? How do they affect the ultimate findings? Method assumptions might prevent investigators from properly understanding the phenomena of interest. The science of psychotherapy, therefore, needs theoretical reflection in this broadened sense. Otherwise, its own assumptions could obstruct its investigations, a point that many leading clinical innovators have argued for years (Bergin, 1991; Kelly, 1955; Mahrer, 2000; Maslow, 1970; Polkinghorne, 1983; Rogers, 1970; Rychlak, 2000).

The Philosophy of Naturalism

What does a theoretical analysis tell us about the underlying assumptions of current trends in psychotherapy? As we shall see, it points unflinchingly to the philosophy of naturalism. This philosophy essentially postulates that natural laws and/or principles ultimately govern the events of nature, including our bodies, behaviors, and minds[1] (cf. Griffin, 2000; Honer & Hunt, 1987; Leahey, 1991; Richards & Bergin, 1997; Viney & King, 1998). Please note that this philosophy does not assume that these laws or principles have already been discovered or discerned – only that such laws exist and govern natural events. Still, to identify this *one* philosophy as the outcome of theoretical analysis is probably provocative. After all, the social sciences have traditionally been famous (or infamous) for their theoretical plurality, and thus their multiple assumptions and multiple philosophies.

More recently, however, this plurality has diminished significantly in the field of psychotherapy to allow its participation in the political and economic advantages of modern science and medicine. Central to this diminishment is the philosophy of naturalism. As Leahey (1991) notes, naturalism is "science's central dogma" (p. 379). Consequently, as psychotherapy has moved increasingly toward the natural sciences, this "central dogma" has become increasingly influential, ultimately foreclosing many conceptual and clinical options that were once open to exploration.

But where and how does this foreclosure take place? Here, the *formal* theories and methods of the psychotherapy enterprise must be distinguished from the *informal* practices and procedures of psychotherapists and researchers. This chapter claims that the philosophy of naturalism pervades the formalized theories, methods, and techniques of psychotherapy; it makes no such claim about informal practices and procedures. Informal practices are not only more difficult to pin down but also more frequently *non*-naturalistic. Formal conceptions undoubtedly inform therapy practice and actual research. However, most practitioners also sense a disconnect between formal theory and informal practice (Hoshmand & Polkinghorne, 1992; Richardson et al., 1999). That is, they frequently practice without a formal theory dictating their every therapeutic move. In fact, therapists have been known to practice *in spite of* their formally held theories. Some historians of science even hold that many scientific discoveries occur *in spite of* formally held methods (Feyerabend, 1975; Kuhn, 1970).

Consequently, this chapter makes no claims about what therapists and researchers assume in informal practice. It only makes claims about the assumptions of what therapists and researchers have been formally taught—through texts, theories, and techniques. Still, these formal teaching structures are crucial. Indeed, they can be said to comprise the formal discipline. They are, after all, the written compendium and recorded knowledge of the discipline. They also constitute our formal interface with other disciplines and institutions, such as medicine and insurance companies, as well as the first and most continuing exposure of our students in training. Yet, they are guided by a general philosophy that has enjoyed an immense and relatively unnoticed influence on the discipline—the philosophy of naturalism.

Five Assumptions of Naturalism

This philosophy can be divided into five separable assumptions that underlie and frame formal professional culture as well as current trends in psychotherapy—objectivism, materialism, atomism, hedonism, and universalism. This chapter reviews each assumption, in turn, devoting three separate sections per assumption: its *description* and relation to naturalism, its theoretical and empirical *problems*, and one of its many possible *alternatives* (see Table 3.1).

Objectivists assume that the logic inherent in the methods and techniques of science and therapy can be relatively free of systematic biases and values. *Materialists* assume that most, if not all, psychological disorders will eventually be shown to have observable and biological bases. *Hedonists* assume that the chief goal of life (and therapy) is some form of happiness, fulfillment, or well-being. *Atomists* assume that the qualities of people are contained within the self, so the basic unit of therapy is the individual. And finally, *Universalists* assume that true knowledge and valid methods are fundamentally unchangeable across time and space, whether in therapy or in science.

This last assumption—universalism—involves an important quality of all five assumptions that should be clarified at the outset: these assumptions are not situational or contextual, applying only to certain situations or particular contexts. Naturalistic assumptions, by definition, posit the nature of human nature (in all circumstances), or the nature of how human nature is investigated (in all circumstances), and thus posit the atemporal universals of humanity (cf. Slife & Reber, 2001). Consequently, these five assumptions must either be accepted or rejected; they cannot be accepted part of the time or to some degree—at least in any formal sense.

Again, no claims are made about the assumptions of informal practice. Many therapists and researchers undoubtedly hold their assumptions tentatively and even inconsistently. They may even understand formal theorizing to permit a "mixture" of incompatible assumptions. This understanding, however, is a *mis*understanding because it indicates an underestimation of the power and scope of formal theorizing and naturalistic assumptions. Naturalistic assumptions are not conceptions about how the world is *most* of the time; they are *the* way the factors of nature supposedly work *all* the time (see the section on universalism).

To help clarify the scope of naturalistic assumptions, *alternative* assumptions are developed in the following sections, along with *problems*, as part of the description of each assumption.

TABLE 3.1 The Description, Problems, and Alternatives of Five Major Assumptions of Naturalism

	Description	Problems	An Alternative
Objectivism—constrains therapy innovation and favors objectivist therapy strategies (EST, eclecticism)	The objective (natural) world of therapy occurs outside our subjectivity, and thus in a value-free world without meanings and morality. Scientific methods reveal this world through a relatively value-free logic that does not affect the outcome of the investigation and thus does not favor one type of therapy over another.	Philosophers of science have shown that scientific methods are underlain with unproven and uninvestigated assumptions and values. There is no empirical justification for empiricism. The positive empirical evaluations of some therapies may be the result of systematic bias rather than efficacy without such bias.	*Continental philosophy:* Quantitative and qualitative reseachers should critically examine the values inherent in the logic of their methods. Therapists who deny their own inescapable values risk imposing them (without awareness) on clients. Therapists should embrace their own values for therapeutic opportunities.
Materialism—accounts for many research practices and the increasing biologization of disorders and treatment	Matter is what is important and sufficient for understanding. Hence, nonobservable constructs are operationalized (translated into the material and thus observable), and psychotherapy is increasingly biologized (with treatment and diagnosis becoming increasingly medical and biological).	All findings that use operationalizations are, at best, the findings of manifestations rather than the findings of the intended phenomenon of study. Researchers often confuse the process of operationalization, which presumes no cause or basis, with the process of identification, which presumes that the cause or basis is matter.	*Holism:* Biological factors are necessary but not sufficient conditions for behavior, cognition, and even the body, accounting for materialist findings but implying the existence of nonmaterialist factors. Empirical research on agency and spirituality suggests the availability of nonmaterialistic necessary conditions.
Hedonism—dominates conceptions of therapy outcome, human nature, and human relationships	All living things seek pleasure and avoid pain, with all higher animals ultimately concerned with benefits to the self (e.g., psychoanalytic pleasure principle, behavioral reinforcement, humanistic self-actualization, cognitive rationality). Helping others and suffering are only important as means to self-benefits (e.g., well-being).	If the hedonism of therapy theory is correct, therapists and clients are capable only of a sophisticated selfishness. They can help others, but only when it ultimately benefits themselves. If therapists and clients are capable of altruism, then a core aspect of many therapy theories is wrong or severely limited in its applicability.	*Alturism:* A primary outcome of therapy is a wider sense of purpose, including ultimate concern and action for the sake of others. Even a willingness to suffer for others or cherished values, leading to deeper meaning, should be embraced. Mainstream theories of therapy will need to be significantly revised.

(continued)

TABLE 3.1 *(Continued)*

	Description	Problems	An Alternative
Atomism—accounts for emphasis on individual diagnosis and treatment as well as relativistic moral values	The natural world is comprised of self-contained "atoms" (molecules, cells), each with its own properties and qualities contained therein. In the social sciences, this means the qualities of each person originate from the self-contained individual, requiring the therapist to work within the needs and moral framework of the client.	Qualities of the self are never independent of the contexts "outside" individuals, serving as the impetus for the family therapy and social constructionist movements. Paradoxes also challenge the individualism and relativism of traditional therapy, questioning the self-containment of client needs and moral values.	*Contextualism:* At least some of the properties and qualities of things (e.g., diagnoses) come from outside the thing—in its context. None of the variables or events that science studies are self-contained. Diagnostic and outcome measures would need to be interpersonal and relational rather than personal and individual.
Universalism—explains emphasis on theoretical principles, standardized diagnoses, and manualized techniques	The most fundamental and natural things are the things that do not change—the things that are universal across both time and space. True social science knowledge approximates this universality—through standardization, generalization, and replication. The ideal is a matching of diagnostic and treatment "universals."	Emphasis on standardization and generalization discounts qualitative differences between and among clients. Some important information involves nongeneralizable, nonreplicable, and even completely unique and one-time events (e.g., trauma, "spiritual" events), but universalism leads therapists away from this vital information	*Hermeneutics:* The changeable is at least as fundamental as the unchangeable. We should search for contextual patterns of change in experiences, meanings, and relationships, rather than context-free laws, principles, or theories. This is not relativism but a changeable truth that is linked to lived experience and cultural context.

These alternatives are not intended as the "right" positions, any more than naturalistic assumptions are intended as the "wrong" positions. Indeed, naturalism is clearly important to contemporary psychotherapy. Discussing the problems and alternatives of these assumptions is only intended to help them truly *be* assumptions—*one* point of view rather than the *only* point of view—and thus raise the consciousness of therapists and researchers.

Objectivism

The first assumption to be examined in this regard is objectivism (see Table 3.1). It may seem odd to refer to objectivism as an intellectual assumption or a constraint on thinking and therapy. Being "objective" is usually associated with a lack of conceptual biases and constraints. As we shall see, however, objectivism not only constrains therapy innovation and the understanding of therapist values, but it also biases the field in favor of objectivist therapy strategies, such as technical eclecticism and empirically supported treatments. In its most basic form, objectivism is the study of "objects" that are external to the observer's mind. Naturalism requires this assumption because nature itself is presumed to exist and involve study that occurs external to the mind. In other words, the subject matter of traditional natural science is not subjectivity—the mental world of opinion, biases, values, and feelings. The subject matter of traditional science (e.g., medical research) is the objective world that presumably occurs *outside* our subjectivity—the natural world in its pristine form—and thus the world without biases and values.

But what allows objectivists to think they can get outside the biases and values of individual scientists? The scientific method is viewed as their chief tool for accomplishing this task because it ideally provides a value-free, transparent method or logic that does not affect the outcome of investigation. Although the scientists themselves may have biases and values, the ideal or logic of scientific method is to work toward eliminating these biases and values, either through experimental control or precise measurement, or some combination of the two. Objectivism, in this sense, is not the claim that all scientific research is absolutely free of values (e.g., Borkovec & Castonguay, 1998; Chambless & Hollon, 1998), but rather that all scientific research should strive to be, and thus can be, free of values.

The scientific method is thought to have this potential because it is the shotgun wedding of two, supposedly value-free systems of justification—empiricism and rationalism (Polkinghorne, 1983; Slife & Williams, 1995). That is, scientific validation implies justification not only in terms of rigorous reasoning (rationalism) but also in terms of cold, hard facts (empiricism). Neither rigorous reasoning nor hard facts are viewed as subjective because neither is thought to be controlled arbitrarily by those in power. The scientific method is itself in control, itself a neutral procedure for determining the good and the effective. In short, the scientific method is viewed as objective.

Most social sciences adopted this objectivist view of science at their inception, both in their object of study and in their method for accomplishing this study (Koch, 1959; Polkinghorne, 1983). After all, it was difficult to dispute the success of objectivism in the natural sciences. Even the science of economics (which will be touched on periodically in this chapter as one of the disciplinary forces involved in the constraints of psychotherapy) has largely adopted this objectivist view (Buchanan, 1979; Caldwell, 1994). There seemed no reason, at the time, to think that objectivism would not prove similarly successful in discerning the natural laws of the social sciences.

Many psychologists, for example, have long used the experimental and correlational methods of the natural sciences as though their scientific observations were the relatively accurate, unbiased renderings of their portion of the natural world (Slife & Williams, 1995). Values and biases are viewed as factors to be controlled, eliminated, or measured (e.g., demand characteristics) rather than inherent in the logic of the method itself. Indeed, the logic of this method is often thought to be a reasoning procedure that detects and/or eliminates any such values or biases through the rigor of control and/or measurement (e.g., Heiman, 1995).

As a result, many psychotherapy researchers have also embraced variations of objectivism. Research on therapy outcome, for example, is often conducted and reported as if the logic of the methods were transparent, that is, not itself affecting the outcome of the investigation. Indeed, *the mark of objectivists in this research is that they believe the logic of scientific method does not favor one type of therapy over another.* This belief has also been pivotal in recent moves to objectify therapy. Eclectics, for instance, have turned primarily to what has been labeled "technical eclecticism" (e.g., Lazarus & Beutler, 1993). With unsystematic eclecticism too capricious and theoretical integrationism too problematic, many eclectics now favor divorcing the techniques of therapy from their theories and then testing them for their effectiveness (cf. Beutler & Clarkin, 1990; Held, 1995; Lazarus, 1995; Lazarus, Beutler, & Norcross, 1992; Slife & Reber, 2001). Often overlooked in this eclectic enterprise, however, is the assumption of objectivism. That is, the logic of the methods used to test these eclectic techniques is assumed to be without any systematic biases of its own.

Empirically supported treatments are a similar type of professional endorsement of objectivism (APA, 1995; Chambless & Hollon, 1998; Nathan, 1998; Nathan & Gorman, 1998; Seligman, 1994). Given current trends in healthcare economics, such treatments promise greater accountability. Managed care organizations can more easily justify their use because the effectiveness of empirically supported treatments has supposedly been demonstrated through the objective methods of science. Some researchers and therapists even contend that empirically supported treatments are the most ethical form of therapy (e.g., Wilson, 1995). Treatments without empirical support are viewed as full of untested assumptions and biases that put "blinders" on therapists and subject clients to potentially less effective, if not dangerous, forms of therapy (Kendall, 1998). Empirically supported treatments, on the other hand, are supposedly objective treatments that have stood up to the rigorous, controlled science of psychotherapy research (Borkovec & Castonguay, 1998; Chambless & Hollon, 1998; Messer, 2001; Nathan, 1998).

Problems with Objectivism. Recent scholarship in the philosophy of science has challenged the value-free status of the scientific method. Philosophers of science have argued that the logic of this method is underlain with unproven and uninvestigated philosophies and assumptions (Bem and de Jong, 1997; Bernstein, 1983; Bohman, 1993; Curd & Cover, 1998; Feyerabend, 1988; Heelan 1983; Kuhn, 1970; Rorty, 1979; Taylor, 1985b; Toulmin, 1972). The gist of this argument is that the formulation of any method must assume, before investigation, a certain type of world in which that method would be effective. Indeed, every occasion that a method is applied to a new population, place, or time—and is thus, in a sense, *re*formulated—it has to make pre-investigatory assumptions about the nature of that population, place, or time.

The problem for objectivism is that when these assumptions are *already* assumed to be correct (as they must be for the method to be formulated), they are not the objects of test; they are parts of the test itself. For instance, the assumption that methods should be observable is never itself empirically tested because this assumption is part of what it *means* to test. Even if scientists take a pragmatic tack—merely hoping that such assumptions will pay off—the fact remains that method assumptions are never tested. No pay-off can be discerned because these pre-investigatory assumptions help determine what it means for something to "pay off." For example, we might agree that science should save lives. This criterion tells us how to validate the pay-off or success of science—whether it really does save lives. However, the correctness of this life-saving criterion is never itself tested. It is a value judgment that can never be decided through empirical means alone.

In this sense, the scientific method may provide empirical justification for certain therapeutic techniques, but it provides no empirical justification for itself and the philosophies that ground it. There is no empirical justification for empiricism, no scientific validation for science. Empiricism and the philosophies underlying science are just that—philosophies. Like all philosophies, they have philosophical axes to grind and pre-investigatory values to assert.

Some traditional scientists would argue that these philosophies have been successful nevertheless. There seems to be widespread agreement that the objectivist approach has worked well, at least for the natural sciences. However, it must be remembered that this claim of success is merely a claim—an opinion—however widely it is held. No scientific evidence can be gathered to substantiate this claim without already assuming the validity of the scientific method in the first place (i.e., any method must incorporate uninvestigated assumptions). Still, it is this claim that provided the original impetus for social scientists to adopt the methods of the natural sciences: they assumed these methods would be successful for understanding their own phenomena (Polkinghorne, 1983).

Unlike the natural sciences, however, the success of these methods in the social sciences appears to be more debatable (Richardson et al., 1999). After over a century of using these methods, social scientists can point to few, if any, natural laws and principles that are generally endorsed (Slife & Williams, 1995). This comparative lack of success has led some to question the appropriateness of untested method values and assumptions for the social sciences (cf. Polkinghorne, 1983). They wonder if the subject matter of the social sciences is qualitatively different from the subject matter of the natural sciences. Even here, however, these questions cannot be answered without pre-investigatory values. Recall (above) that evaluating the success of a science requires assumptions (before investigation) about what "successful" means. This is not to say that such values cannot be agreed on; it is only to say that such values are inescapable to any form of evaluation.

What types of pre-investigatory values are involved in objectivist methods? Values are usually understood to be ideas about what matters or what has relative worth or merit (Merriam-Webster, 1998). What matters, for instance, in traditional science is what is observable and replicable (see Slife & Williams, 1995, for other values in science). These aspects of reality are the ones considered "scientific" and thus the ones having relative worth or merit to scientists. It probably bears repeating, however, that there is no empirical evidence that these *should* be the values of science. The doctrines of observability and replicability are not themselves observable and replicable; they are philosophical (or moral) assertions about what should be valued, and they cannot be supported by scientific evidence because, again, such values have to be assumed to gather such evidence.

Moreover, these are not the only values available for science. Alternative formulations of science, such as qualitative research, assert different pre-investigatory values (Banister, Burman, Parker, Taylor, & Tindall, 1994; Crabtree & Miller, 1992; Denzin & Lincoln, 2000; Gilgun, Daly, & Handel, 1992; Patton, 1990). In fact, these alternative methods purport to examine and study topics that are not necessarily observable or replicable in the traditional sense (e.g., spiritual experiences; James, 1902/1994). Some traditional scientists may judge these alternative formulations to be unacceptable, but this judgment is ultimately based on opinion. That is, this judgment is not supported by empirical comparisons of the two sets of values because the validity of these values, and thus the methods, are themselves in dispute.

If science *does* contain unexamined values, it is vital to know how these values affect the subject matter being investigated. Do the original assumptions of naturalistic science, as formulated primarily about inanimate matter, work well with the animate, cultural realities of the social sciences? Can we have a complete social science based only on the observable and replicable? Existential therapists, for instance, specifically dispute that their theory or their practice follows the assumption of objectivism. Leading existential therapist Irvin Yalom (1980) questions both the observability of what is important in existential therapy—particularly through traditional scientific procedures—and its dependence on any conventional understanding of standardized (and thus replicable) techniques. If, however, certain therapies, such as existentialism, violate the assumptions of science, then these approaches are prevented from being scientifically supported *a priori*, before they are even investigated (cf. Bohart, O'Hara, & Leitner, 1998). They are scientifically *un*supported, not because of the data per se, but because of the philosophy that underlies the method and produces the data, a philosophy that is not itself scientifically supported.

Is it merely coincidental that the therapies that match the values of objectivist science are those that are the most scientifically supported? As Messer (2001) sums up the literature on empirically supported treatment (EST):

> It gives one pause to learn that the vast majority of studies that meet the criteria set forth by the [EST] task force are cognitive-behavioral in orientation, or what can be referred to as outcome-oriented therapies (Gold, 1995). To be specific, my calculation based on the task force figures is that of the 22 so-called "well established" empirically supported treatments, 19 are behavioral, and of the 7 "probably efficacious" treatments, 6 are behavioral. In the later update on the ESTs (Division 12 Task Force, 1996), I found that of the 27 treatments added to these categories, 22 are behavioral. Almost totally absent are the psychodynamic, experiential, client-centered, family, and existential therapies. (pp. 3–4)

Is it merely coincidental, in this light, that cognitive behavioral therapy has virtually the same epistemological assumptions (values) as traditional science (i.e., a wedding of empiricism and rationalism; cf. Polkinghorne, 1983; Slife & Williams 1995). The positive empirical evaluations of this therapy may be the result of systematic bias rather than efficacy without such bias. The scientific method, in this sense, is not a value-free, neutral tool of inquiry, but a set of metatheoretical criteria for deciding among theories and thus therapies. To believe that these criteria are the most correct or effective in the first place is to make a very *un*scientific assertion because this belief must be asserted before investigation even begins. The presence of pre-investigatory values also makes it difficult to hold that scientifically supported techniques are the most ethical, both because the ethical implications of these values are often unrecognized and because these values preclude a fair evaluation of therapies with nonobjectivist philosophies.

An alternative to objectivism. With these perceived problems, several alternatives to objectivism have arisen over the years. We need to understand only one alternative to help make objectivism an assumption rather than a truism of science and psychotherapy. Without some development of an alternative, it could appear that objectivism (however problematic it might be) is the only "game in town." Perhaps the most prominent alternative is a position associated with Continental philosophy—*that values are inescapable.* Philosophers such as Paul Ricoeur (1978), Hans Georg Gadamer (1960/1995), Jurgen Habermas (1973), and Charles Taylor (1985a, 1991) contend that there is no practical or intellectual position, no scientific method or therapy technique that does not have values, at least implicitly.

Objectivism, from this Continental perspective, is a good example of a careful intellectual project that has expressly attempted to escape values but ultimately failed (as described in the Problems with Objectivism section). As a result, these philosophers advocate a new attitude toward values. The objectivist attitude has us fearing and attempting to avoid values because we assume they distort our understanding through biases and obstruct our relationships through conflicts. The Continental attitude, however, is that we should *embrace* rather than fear and avoid our values, a position held by a number of contemporary theorists and therapists (Bergin, 1980; 1991; Kelly, 1955; Richardson et al., 1999; Rogers, 1951; Woolfolk, 1998).

But can we embrace values and truly advance knowledge? Would the embrace of values, and thus biases, lead to inaccurate and distorted understandings of the world? Continental thinkers first remind us that the objectivity of a method does not mean the absence of values and biases (as described above). There is no alternative to a value-laden understanding of the world. Indeed, from the Continentalist perspective, values are *required* for there to *be* understanding. Objectivist methods yield understanding, in this sense, because values and biases are already incorporated into them before investigation. Calling methods "objective" is like calling multiple-choice tests "objective"—values and biases are already built into the structure of the investigation (method or test question). The problem is, this built-in status means that values are often ignored and left unexamined.

If values are truly unavoidable—even in our methods of investigation—then is a true understanding of the world possible? Perhaps surprisingly, it is the *qualitative* researcher—within this Continental framework—who answers "yes" to this question. Qualitative researchers deliberately attempt to explicate and test any built-in values through the process of investigation (Banister et al., 1994; Crabtree & Miller, 1992; Denzin & Lincoln, 2000; Gilgun et al., 1992; Patton, 1990). Because values are inescapable, qualitative researchers do not try to eliminate, suspend, or minimize them; they attempt to remain open to the values and biases (methodological or theoretical) that make the most sense of the phenomena under investigation. Although phenomena cannot be understood (or even perceived) without values coming into play, this situation does not mean that values control the phenomena (or our perceptions). Values and phenomena *jointly* influence our perceptions, allowing us to search for the values that best fit the influence of the phenomena under investigation. As Palmer (1969) put it, "The interpreter is not so much applying a method to the text as an observed object, but rather trying to adjust his own thinking to the text" (p. 236).

Quantitative research is also a useful tool for the Continentalist, especially when its values are taken into account. As Slife and Gantt (1999) have described, the values of quantitative and qualitative research can be assembled into a complementary pluralism of methods. Interestingly, quantitative research supports the inescapability of values in psychotherapy. Even though the values inherent in quantitative methods have often been ignored, the values inherent in therapeutic methods have not. Research on the values of therapy methods dates back at least as far as Rosenthal's classic studies some 45 years ago (Rosenthal,

1955) and involves literally scores of studies (e.g., Almond, Keniston, & Boltax, 1969; Beutler, 1979; Beutler, Arizmendi, Crago, Shanfield, & Hagaman, 1983; Claiborne, Ward, & Strong, 1981; Kelly & Strupp, 1992; Landfield & Nawas, 1964; Maizlish & Hurley, 1963; Martini, 1978; Parloff, Iflund, & Goldstein, 1960).

Perhaps surprisingly, Rosenthal's findings have held up remarkably well over the years, though the methods have since been improved and refined. Rosenthal essentially found that all therapists not only held (and did not suspend or eliminate their) values but also promoted them with their clients (however unintentionally or unconsciously). Subsequent studies have made clear that no therapist is immune from this unconscious attempt to influence clients with his or her values (see Slife, Smith, & Burchfield, in press). As Kelly (1990) put it in his review of this research, "therapists [are] not value free even when they intend to be so" (p. 171).

Why are so many therapists "intending" to be "free" of values? If the conclusion of this rigorous and lengthy program of research is that psychotherapy values are inescapable, why are so many therapists (and researchers) attracted to objectivism? Being "objective," in the sense of being relatively unbiased, has long been important to many therapists. The movements of technical eclecticism and empirically supported treatments evidence this importance in evaluating therapy. There are also clear ethical injunctions against the imposition of one's values and biases on one's clients (ACA, 1995; APA, 1992). But why the desire for objectivity and the injunction against value imposition if therapist values have been shown to be inescapable, in both holding and acting on them?

Some observers explain the move toward objectivity—and thus the attempt to escape values—as a historic misunderstanding (e.g., Richardson et al., 1999; Taylor, 1985b). Modern thinkers (and therapists) are rightly sensitive about the misuse of values because of the many historic abuses that have occurred, from the Middle Ages onward. The Enlightenment solution to these abuses was to transform science into a value-free method that could arbitrate the truth without bias and thus without abuse (Polkinghorne, 1983, 1990). The problem, from a Continental perspective, is that this "solution" not only ignored the values inherent in any method but also threw the baby out with the bath water. Values in general were mistakenly identified as the problem when it was actually the abuse of values that was the problem. Therefore, the Enlightenment confounding of values and their abuse helps to explain the generalized fear of values in modern times (e.g., "bias") and in modern psychotherapy.

Still, therapists are rightfully cautious about their power in value-laden situations such as therapy. Is there a way for therapists to acknowledge their values without becoming, as Meehl (1959) once warned, "crypto-missionaries" (p. 257)—imposing their values on their clients? The objectivist approach to avoiding value imposition is to try to suspend or eliminate values in therapy, but this elimination is not only impossible, from this alternative perspective, but also dangerous. Objectivism can lead therapists to believe that their values are not involved, so they act on values of which they are unaware (e.g., the hedonism and atomism assumptions below). The Continental alternative, by contrast, recognizes that therapy cannot take place without values and actively encourages explicit value awareness and engagement. Space limitations prohibit a more complete explication (see Smith & Slife, in press). However, one key for therapists is to be more aware of their values, especially as they affect therapy, and to articulate them as they arise, so that the client has an opportunity to give an ongoing, informed consent.

Materialism

As the second assumption of naturalism (see Table 3.1), materialism helps account for the increasing emphasis on the biology of disorders and treatment (e.g., prescription privileges) as well as the problems of operationalization and inference in materialist research. Materialism is the notion that what matters (and is valued) is matter. The philosophy of naturalism does not encompass intangible constructs or entities, such as spirits and ghosts; rather, the important (and valued) things are tangible, visible, and substantial. This materialist value is based in part on the traditional natural science notion that only material things are knowable. That is, materialism is typically linked to the primary epistemology of science—empiricism. Only our sensory experiences can supposedly be known (empiricism), so only tangible and visible materials can supposedly be candidates for knowledge (materialism).

This connection between the material and the knowable is just one of the many bridges between naturalism and traditional science.

Traditional scientists have embraced empiricism because we can supposedly know only what can be observed (a sensory experience). Even if the constructs under investigation are themselves intangible and unobservable (e.g., motivation), the philosophies of empiricism and materialism require that they be *operationalized*—made into material things or processes (e.g., behavior)—so they *can* be observed. This operationalization may mean that only the material aspects of the constructs are investigated. Still, the tangible and the visible are ultimately the only things that really matter from this naturalistic perspective.

These materialist values have heavily influenced the social sciences, both in method and in application (Fisher, 1997). In research methods, the social sciences have long endorsed empiricism and the operationalization of nonobservable constructs. In therapy applications, many observers have noted that the influence of materialism has recently increased—what some have called the "biologization" of psychotherapy (e.g., Fisher, 1997, p. 46; Williams, 2001, p. 51). This biologization includes not only a greater emphasis on the biological understandings of disorder but also a greater stress on pharmacological interventions—hence the movement toward prescription privileges in psychology (e.g., DeLeon & Wiggins, 1996). These emphases are obviously different from those of the past, when distinctly psychological accounts were often advanced to explain even schizophrenic symptoms (e.g., the double-bind theory—Bateson, Jackson, Haley, & Weakland, 1956). Most therapists believe this change is due to recent research indicating the biological bases of these disorders (e.g., Silk, 1998; Valenstein, 1998; Williams, 2001; Zuckerman, 1999).

Interestingly, materialism seems to have affected other social sciences in a similar manner. For example, materialist values pervade the assumptions of many economic theorists and their models (cf. Buchanan, 1979; Caldwell, 1994). Methodologically, the science of economics has largely endorsed empiricism and the operationalization of nonmaterialist constructs. Theoretically, economists are rarely concerned with nonmaterialist matters (e.g., spirituality) in tracking the economy or predicting consumer behaviors. Economists are more interested in observable "goods," meaning things, behaviors, and products that can be turned into money and used to buy material things. Materialism, in this economic sense, is the accumulation of material things. We can only purchase a limited number of these things, so we should accumulate as much money as possible to buy as many things as possible.

This materialist view of our economic nature has had wide impact on the halls of science. Grant funds are the "coin of the realm" in many natural science and even social science disciplines—the greater the number of these "coins", the more prestigious the researcher. These materialist values are also heavily involved in the rationale for managed care. Because there is a limited supply of healthcare funds and everyone presumably wants them, the efficiency and efficacy of care are paramount. The quickest and most effective medical and psychological treatments are the "best" treatments, with long-term interventions almost a thing of the past.

Psychotherapy researchers have frequently assisted the materialism of these organizations, providing dependent measures as well as experimental designs to aid in increasing the efficiency and efficacy of therapy (cf. Bergin, 1997; Messer, 2001; Miller, 1999). This assistance comes in part because researchers have been trained in the economic materialism of grantsmanship. When the economic giants of the medical industry cry for greater "efficiency," many psychotherapy researchers heed this cry, in part because it issues from economic giants. The point is that all the variations of materialism—medical (biologization), scientific (operationalization), and economic (accumulation of goods)—coalesce and converge to facilitate current trends in psychotherapy.

Problems with Materialism. It is a testament to the pervasiveness and subtlety of these materialist values that they seem so natural. The success of the natural sciences has clearly contributed to this perception, as communicated most forcibly to psychotherapists by the financial and political power of medicine and granting agencies (e.g., Messer, 2001; Valenstein, 1998). Unfortunately, this success has sometimes prevented scientists from exploring the problems of materialism. In the social sciences especially, materialism has long been problematic, though these problems have rarely been acknowledged (cf. Slife & Williams, 1995, Ch. 6).

The social sciences, by definition, investigate social relations as well as material relations. Because these social relations cannot be observed (only the things having the relations can be observed), some of the subject matter of the social sciences is, by its very nature, *non*material. Family and marital relationships are just a few of the topics that are vital to the social sciences and psychotherapy, but they are not material, at least as traditionally understood. Such nonmaterial topics have also been a problem for the philosophy of empiricism because they are not experienced through our senses—that is, we do not observe or touch the "betweenness" of a human relationship.

These problems are the main reason the doctrine of operationalism was so readily adopted in the social sciences—it aided social scientists in studying such topics within the empiricist model (Green, 1992; Koch, 1992). The function of this doctrine, as already mentioned, is to make nonmaterial entities into material entities by translating them into their materialist manifestations. If, for example, one wanted to study love (as a feeling), operationalism would require that we observe its behavioral or neurological (materialistic) manifestations (e.g., hugs, endorphins) because the feeling of love is not itself observable (through the sense of vision). However, when we use operationalizations, we study, at best, the *manifestations* of the phenomenon of interest (e.g., hugs), not the phenomenon of interest itself (e.g., the feeling of love).

Consequently, all the findings that use operationalizations—accounting for the vast preponderance of social science investigations—are the findings of manifestations rather than the findings of the intended phenomenon of study. A program of research that is ostensibly about love is really a program of research about its material manifestations only (e.g., hugs). Sternberg and Barnes (1988), for example, attempted to establish the operationalized "structure" of love. Unfortunately, behavioral factors such as communicating well and being "supportive" did not reveal why, or even whether, people *love* certain people (Sternberg, 1998). To truly understand love, Sternberg turned away from materialist, operationalized methods and turned toward nonmaterialist, narrative methods—stories of love (Sternberg, 1998).

Another important problem with operationalizations is that we can never be sure that operationalized manifestations *are* manifestations. There can be hugs, for example (or any other specified behavior) without love, and there can be love without hugs (or any other specified behavior). *Operationalizations, in this sense, have no necessary relation to the phenomena being operationalized.* They are only postulated relations, with the experimenter free to choose literally any relation or operationalization. More importantly, the relations between the construct of study (e.g., love) and the operationalization (e.g., hugs) are never themselves empirically tested, because empiricism requires that such relations be specified *before* an investigation occurs. Even multiple-measure, multiple-source studies still function with the same pre-investigatory, operational postulates. The upshot is that we cannot know for sure with traditional scientific methods what is actually being studied in our research investigations because we cannot know with any measure of empirical certainty what a particular operationalization means (cf. Slife & Williams, 1995).

The history of attempting to objectify psychodynamic therapy illustrates this problem. In the first edition of this *Handbook*, Luborsky and Spence (1971) stated: "At this point, what can be known through clinical wisdom is far more than what can be known through quantitative, objective means" (p. 430). In the years since then, however, researchers have made a valiant effort to operationalize psychodynamic phenomena and demonstrate the efficacy of this therapeutic approach through materialist methods (e.g., Henry, Strupp, Schacht, & Gaston, 1994). Although the success of this endeavor can be debated, the nature of this struggle has vividly exposed the limitations of operationalizing (and thus materalizing) personality dynamics and human relationships. Indeed, the early descriptive studies of the therapy process (e.g., Marsden, 1971)—now relatively rare, given the emphasis on "bottom-line" efficacy studies—may have provided more understanding of important therapeutic phenomena (Bergin, Personal Communication, May 2000).

These problems with operationalism also apply to biological research on mental disorders and treatment. Any nonmaterial phenomena of the social sciences, such as love, can also be operationalized as neurological or biochemical factors (e.g., hormonal factors, serotonin levels). However, all the problems just reviewed regarding operationalism apply to these factors as well. The main problem is that we cannot know empirically the relation between the operationalization and the phenomenon of interest (e.g., love). We cannot know empirically what *type* of relationship the biochemical substrate has to the phenomenon. We also cannot know empirically whether there *is* any relationship (because the operationalization is specified before investigation).

Unfortunately, the philosophy of materialism compounds the problems of operationalism in this literature. Because the biological is often already (before investigation) assumed to be the "basis" or "cause" for whatever is "manifested" behaviorally or cognitively (the assumption of materialism), many researchers forget they are engaged in a process of operationalizing nonmaterial phenomena into material phenomena. They assume, instead, that they are engaged in a process of identifying the material basis or cause of the nonmaterial phenomenon of interest (materialism). They confuse the process of *operationalization*, which presumes no cause or basis, with the process of *identification*, which presumes (via materialism) that the cause or basis is matter.

Culbertson and Krull's (1996) use of Mirsky's (1987, 1989) materialist conceptualization of attention-deficit hyperactivity disorder (ADHD) exemplifies this type of confusion. Mirsky's phenomenon of interest is the distractibility of the ADHD client. However, Mirsky's way of understanding these attention problems is to identify their "neuroanatomic localizations" (Culbertson & Krull, 1996, p. 278). In other words, Culbertson and Krull (1996) do not view these parts of the neuroanatomy as postulated operationalizations of these attention capacities; they assume that these "neuroanatomic localizations" are the site or basis of these capacities, without any empirical test. Because ADHD involves attention, and because the reticular formation of the brain has been associated with attention, then the reticular formation must be the basis of ADHD.

Unfortunately, the logic of this inference is highly problematic—that is, an operationalization is not an identification of a basis or a cause. A counterexample reveals this problem most directly: Because a concussion involves vomiting, and because the stomach is associated with vomiting, then the stomach must be the basis of the concussion (Williams, 2001). Obviously, the stomach is not usually thought to cause a concussion, yet this materialist "logic" is vulnerable to this type of mistake. The point is that Culbertson and Krull (1996) reify an unsupported, purely theoretical postulation as though it were fact. Culbertson and Krull (1996) do consider Mirsky's speculations "preliminary" because ongoing research "will most likely provide greater specificity" (p. 279). However, this preliminary status pertains only to the "specificity" of these localizations, not to the materialism of the "localizations." The power of materialism leads researchers to *assume* the latter—an inferential leap, at best—because its correctness is not demonstrated through the empirical evidence.

As it happens, such leaps of inference occur frequently in this literature. This is not to say that all studies have these problems, but several scholars have repeatedly noted the high proportion of these inferential problems, and thus the power of this assumption (Sarbin, 1990; Slife & Williams, 1995; Sternberg, 2000; Valenstein, 1998; Williams, 2001). For instance, leading neuroscience researcher, Eliot Valenstein (1998), notes the high number of instances in which biological "correlates" are automatically assumed as causes. As he puts it, "no one would suggest that the carrying of an umbrella causes rainfall, although umbrella carrying is highly associated with rain. Yet, if some biological marker in the brain is found to correlate with a mental disorder, it is easy to fall into the trap of believing the marker is the cause of the disorder" (p. 126).

Silk (1998), for example, consistently falls into this trap while working almost exclusively with the biological correlates of personality disorders, referring to them as "bases," (p. xvii), "localizations" (p. xvi), and "underlying disturbed biological mechanisms" (p. xiv). The problem, as Valenstein (1998) notes, is that researchers routinely underestimate the power of other causes: "a person's mental state and experience can modify the brain just as surely as the other way around" (p. 126). This malleability of the brain creates obvious problems for researchers in sorting out causes and effects. Still, the main issue from Valenstein's perspective is that few researchers seem sensitive to these problems. Most researchers automatically and perhaps unconsciously make the materialist assumption, regardless of whether the experimental logic allows for this assumption.

Williams (2001) notes three breaches of experimental logic or problems of inference as a consequence of materialism in this literature—post-hoc deference, post-hoc ergo propter hoc, and argument from deficit. Each breach of logic involves an entire category of materialist research, and each illustrates the reification of materialism without empirical support. For example, the "argument from deficit" (p. 60) proceeds as follows: We know that brain damage (or some other central nervous system abnormality) results in a particular behavioral deficit. Therefore, we know that the normal brain (or other physiological) structure is responsible for normal functioning.

Often, the problems with this logic are not immediately apparent to the materialist. However, this logic would mean, via counterexample, that because damaged vocal cords prevent an orator from speaking, we should conclude that vocal cords are responsible for oratory. Obviously, there is more to "oratory" (or any speaking, for that matter) than vocal cords. The most that can be said from such evidence is that our biology is a *necessary* (but not a *sufficient*) condition for this behavior. That is, the evidence yields an important (necessary) factor that needs to be taken into account—our biology. However, the necessity of biological conditions does not mean they are sufficient alone to account for and fully understand behavior. Indeed, no set of biological conditions will, by themselves, provide us a complete account of stirring oratory. More importantly, this insufficiency implies that *this evidence does not support materialism.* Materialism implies the sufficiency of matter for understanding and explaining things, particularly understanding and explaining the body. However, evidence of the necessity of matter implies that there are *other* necessary conditions than the material for producing behavior—that is, other things matter than matter.

What would happen if these problems of inference and breaches of logic were taken into account when evaluating the empirical support for materialism—the biologization of psychotherapy? Most reviews of the materialist literature overlook these problems. However, those few reviews that *have* attempted to evaluate these problems find much of the support for materialism evaporating. This is not to say that the importance of biology evaporates—only that the support for biology as a *sufficient condition* (materialism) seems to evaporate. Valenstein (1998), for example, concludes an extensive review of the materialist literature with this statement: "I have concluded that this [materialist] theory, which is guiding much of clinical practice and our research efforts, is not supported by the evidence and may well be wrong. Yet for reasons that have little to do with science, the theory is being pursued relentlessly." (p. 241).

In summing up a similar review, Williams (2001) believes that a "much stronger statement" can be made: "There is, in fact, no evidence that a single meaningful, directed, telic behavior has ever resulted directly from any physiological state" (p. 60). Other scholars have made similar critical evaluations of materialism and reductionism with similar conclusions (Agazzi, 1991; Charles & Lennon, 1992; Davidson, 1980; Dupre, 1993; Eccles & Robinson, 1984; Lennon, 1990; Robinson, 1985, 1995; Sarbin, 1990; Slife & Williams, 1995). Such conclusions may be jarring to a mainstream materialist. So many findings and reviews have seemed so supportive of materialism. Still, the question is, are these supportive reviews and findings the result of the data? Or are they the result of an unrecognized, and perhaps even unintentional, bias toward materialism in interpreting the data, with all its accompanying problematic inferences?

It is important to note that neither Valenstein nor Williams claims that brains and chemical processes are irrelevant to therapeutic work. Nor do they claim that there are no direct relationships between the brain and psychological consequences, such as with brain injury. Their main point is that the pertinent biological data can be explained in ways that do not necessitate materialism. Our biological state is obviously a necessary condition for all behavior, but the notion of a necessary condition implies the need of other necessary conditions for complete (and sufficient) understanding. As important as biological conditions are, the data do not support our ignoring *non*materialist factors (e.g., culture) that may also be crucial to the behavior in question. Other factors than matter may matter.

This possibility also implies problems for economic materialism. Here, materialism has had a powerful synergy with hedonism, where the "bottom line" of managed care profit—materialist self-interest—has frequently overwhelmed the ethos of patient care. Obviously, a capitalist system will always endorse a profit of sorts. However, the amount of this profit, and the extent to which this profit dictates the delivery of mental health services, are other issues entirely. Part of the problem is that therapy researchers have frequently joined with these economic forces, often without questioning their philosophical or ethical origins. Part of the reason is that the materialism of economics is a philosophical bedfellow with the materialism of science. Scientific and economic materialisms coalesce to dictate the manner in which research is conducted and specify what is allowed to count as therapeutic results (e.g., observable outcome). Ultimately, this focus on "demonstrable" effects—the therapeutic results that fit the philosophies of empiricism and materialism—means that psychotherapists must "teach to the test." They must fit their care of clients within the parameters of these untested philosophies.

AN ALTERNATIVE TO MATERIALISM. These problems hint at a possible alternative to materialism. Materialism essentially asserts that all that really matters is matter. If we understand the materiality of things, then this understanding is sufficient to understand the natural world. (If it were not presumed to be sufficient, then our materialist, operationalized methods of science could not provide a complete understanding of the natural world.) In psychotherapy, this means that a biological understanding is *sufficient* to understand a disorder; biological factors are the ultimate *causes* of disorders. From this perspective, traditional theories of personality and psychotherapy are merely stopgap explanations—ultimately temporary and inadequate—until the biological bases of these disorders are understood, and biological interventions are formulated to treat them.

An interesting alternative, then, is to postulate that material factors are necessary but *not* sufficient conditions for disorders. This alternative assumes that the material and the biological are crucial, even pivotal, to understanding the issues of disorder in psychotherapy. However, this alternative does not assume that biological factors are sufficient unto themselves for causing and understanding these issues. Instead, it assumes that other, *non*material factors are *also* necessary to fully account for and explain behaviors, cognitions, and *even our bodies.* As William James (1902/1994) once put it, "The total expression of human experience . . . urges me beyond the narrow 'scientific' bounds. Assuredly the real world is . . . more intricately built than physical science allows" (p. 509).

For some, the truth of James's observation is clear and materialism is obviously untenable. It is also true that neuroscience research, as an example literature, contains few *explicit* assumptions or claims that the material is sufficient. Nevertheless, this assumption does not have to be explicit to be assumed. Merely asserting that the material explains, accounts for, or is responsible for the behavior (or cognition) in question, *especially* if no nonmaterialist factor is also included, implies sufficiency. As we will also see, the absence of clear, materialistic assertions in the neuroscience literature does not mean this assumption is not influencing many practices and findings.

A major appeal of the necessary-condition alternative, on the other hand, is its accounting of all the relevant biological data. That is, these data clearly point to the necessity of a biological element to disorders, but these data do not indicate the sufficiency of that element. The fact is, no data can indicate the sufficiency of material factors in this regard. Even the most highly controlled of experimental studies—a truly experimental design—contains factors other than the independent variables that contribute to the study's outcome. These factors may be controlled or equated across the experimental groups or conditions, but they are never eliminated. Their influence is still present and still necessary to whatever effect occurs. For instance, the influence of gravity in most earthbound experiments may be taken for granted and even measured as equal across experimental conditions. However, this control and this equation do not mean that gravity is not a necessary condition for whatever occurs or that the loss of gravity would not change whatever occurs.

Even in the biological sciences, such as medicine, the insufficiency of one set of factors is well recognized. The pathogen of disease, for example, is rarely considered a sufficient cause for the disease itself; other conditions of the body are also necessary (e.g., problems with the immune system). All the various systems of the body are necessary for health, and thus all are necessary, in some sense, for any lack of health. Indeed, many pathogens (e.g., viruses) are often already present in the body (or its environment), waiting for other conditions to change. In this sense, the pathogens themselves are never sufficient conditions for the disease; the pathogens are only a necessary condition among many other necessary conditions.

Viewing material (and nonmaterial) factors in this manner implies an alternative metaphysic—holism (e.g., Bohm, 1980). Just as a whole has many parts that are all necessary to the qualities of the whole and the qualities of each part, a biological whole (organism) has many necessary conditions that are all necessary to the qualities of the whole (and its parts). Holism also offers an alternative to materialist causation. Whereas materialism assumes that a causal factor is a *sufficient* condition for (and thus completely determines) the effect, holism assumes that a causal factor is a *necessary* condition for (and thus only partly determines) the effect. Material factors *are* causes, in this holist sense, because they are necessary. However, this type of cause does not support material*ism* because material factors are not all that ultimately matters and are not sufficient to produce the effect in question. The upshot is that nonmaterialist (and nonnaturalist) factors could be involved in materialist experiments, but traditional scientists often overlook these factors due to materialist assumptions.

Some resarchers may contend that they have never considered biological factors to be anything but necessary conditions. In other words, the philosophy of materialism does not really influence these researchers (i.e., materialism is a "straw man"). However, the necessary-condition alternative has two important implications that are often overlooked in this research literature, disputing the "straw man" assertion. First, this alternative implies that other factors matter than matter. That is, *non*material factors are also necessary for a complete understanding of mind *and* body. Rarely, however, are these nonmaterial factors investigated, or even postulated, in the literature concerning biological factors (see Libet, 1985, for an exception). The influence of materialism, however unrecognized, explains this lack of investigation.

Second, biological explanations are often considered a replacement for, and not a complement to, traditional psychological explanations (e.g., Churchland, 1994). Yet, biological explanations, in a necessary-condition sense, could never serve as a replacement for other sets of necessary conditions or for holistic explanations that attempt to specify *all* the necessary conditions—material and nonmaterial. Interestingly, psychological explanations often serve as holistic explanations in this way. The vast majority of these explanations implies, if not specifically explicates, the necessity of biological factors (cf. Rychlak, 1981). What accounts, then, for the move to replace such explanations? The tacit assumption of materialism accounts for this move. Because materialism assumes that biological factors are sufficient for explanation, no other sets of necessary conditions are needed. Materialism, in this sense, is far from being a straw man.

Consider also the compound-word conceptions, such as bio-psycho-socio-etc. models, that attempt to provide more holistic replacements for traditional psychological explanations (e.g., Paris, 1998; Silk, 1998; Zuckerman, 1999). These conceptions are rarely more than collections of materialist variables. Truly nonmaterial factors are frequently overlooked, with variables such as "socio" and "psycho" defined and operationalized in naturalistic terms (e.g., "environment"). As DeBerry (1993) shows, such compound-word conceptions typically devolve to a deterministic interaction of materialist factors.

Are truly *non*materialist factors available as necessary conditions? Considerable empirical research on spirituality and agency suggests that they may be (Howard, 1994; Howard & Conway; 1986; Richards and Bergin, 1997; Rychlak, 1988; 1994; Shafranske, 1996). Richards and Bergin (1997), for instance, review the many empirical studies that indicate the significance of spiritual factors for mental and physical health. They also explicate the nonmaterialist status of such factors, conflicting as they do with all the naturalistic assumptions of the present chapter (cf. Richards & Bergin, 1997, pp. 320–321).

This incompatibility with the assumptions of naturalism, including materialism, does not mean that spiritual "forces" cannot coexist with and even complement the necessary conditions of biology. Spiritual forces are only incongruent with the sufficiency but not the necessity of material factors. Indeed, many brain researchers view their findings as indicating the necessity of *both* spiritual and biological factors rather than the sufficiency of biological factors alone, that is, materialism (e.g., Eccles & Robinson, 1984; Popper & Eccles, 1977; Sperry, 1988, 1995). This view might seem to raise the specter of dualism, with spirit and matter unable to interact, but this philosophical issue is a product of the sufficiency notion of matter (and the philosophy of naturalism) rather than an unsolvable problem per se (e.g., Muse, 1997; Williams, 2001).

The sufficiency notion of material factors also tends to rule out agentic factors in the formal explanations of psychotherapists (Rychlak, 1988, 1994). Agentic factors typically involve a client's choices, free will, or self-generated thoughts and actions. Although these factors are often discussed in the informal practice of psychotherapy, the notion that material factors are a sufficient condition for, and thus the sole determinant of, all behaviors and cognitions has prevented most formal theories from incorporating agency (Rychlak, 1981, 1988). However, the alternative framework described here would consider material factors only necessary conditions and thus raise the possibility that agentic factors are another set of such conditions.

The problem is that many therapists and researchers affirm the predictability of thoughts and behaviors. That is, many have assumed that a free will is "free" because it is independent of biological or environmental constraints, and thus "random" or "chaotic" (e.g., Heiman, 1995, p. 5). Such independence would prevent a complementary, holistic relation among the necessary conditions of biology and agency because holism requires some *inter*dependence among the parts of the whole. However, few free will theorists advocate such independence (see special issue on free will—Howard (Ed.), 1994). Moreover, as Slife and Fisher (2000b) explain, the notion that a free will implies this independence is ultimately a misconception on the part of those who use a naturalistic (and modernistic) framework. In fact, there is considerable *empirical* evidence that a free will is itself an important, albeit overlooked, predictor of behavioral, biological, and learning variance (Howard, 1994; Howard & Conway; 1986; Libet, 1985; Rychlak, 1988, 1994). In this sense, agency could serve as a nonmaterial necessary condition that complements the necessary conditions of biology.

Hedonism

The term *hedonism* often has a negative connotation. Nevertheless, this third assumption of naturalism dominates formal disciplinary conceptions of therapy outcome, human nature, and human relationships (see Table 3.1). Hedonism is the assumption that all living things seek pleasure and avoid pain, with plants turning toward the sun and animals moving toward whatever is "pleasurable," broadly defined. In fact, hedonism is thought to be necessary to evolution and the survival of a species—with species risking evolutionary extinction when they consistently move toward pain and suffering. Higher animals, too, are viewed as hedonistic, though in more complex and sophisticated ways. Hedonism implies a certain ethic and purpose for higher animals—that well-being, happiness, or self-benefit is the sole or chief good in life (cf. Merriam-Webster, 1998).

This application of natural science conceptions to higher animals has led the social sciences to incorporate hedonism as one of its primary assumptions of formal theorizing. In a book entitled *Theory and Progress in Social Science*, Rule (1997) notes that naturalistic hedonism "offers the best—and perhaps the only—hope for meaningful progress in social science" because hedonistic explanations "tap the most fundamental levels of social reality" (p. 79). Consonant with Rule's observations, formal theorizing in psychotherapy has been consistently hedonistic. Although psychotherapy has always enjoyed considerable conceptual diversity, hedonism is amazingly pervasive, even among the "four forces" of traditional therapy theory—psychoanalysis, behaviorism, humanism, and cognitivism (cf. Slife & Williams, 1995).

Freud (1949), for example, surmised that all operations of the psyche ultimately reduce to what he termed "The Pleasure Principle." As Freud put it, "It seems as though our total mental activity is directed towards achieving pleasure and avoiding unpleasure" (Freud, 1963, p. 356). Even though the ego and superego are concerned with reality and social values, these reality-based and socially oriented strategies ultimately serve the id and its seeking of pleasure, broadly defined (Rychlak, 1981). Although psychoanalysts and behaviorists agree on little else, they agree on the importance of hedonism. Advocates of operant conditioning, for instance, have traditionally assumed that reward or "reinforcement" is a prime motivator of all animals, including humans. As Skinner (1972) explained, "We are so constituted that under certain circumstances food, water, sexual contact, and so on will make any behavior which produces them more likely to occur again." (p. 35).

Even theorists who historically reacted negatively to psychoanalysis and behaviorism—humanists and cognitivists—nevertheless affirm versions of hedonism. Rogers (1951), for example, stated rather baldly that, "Present tensions and present needs are the only ones which the organism endeavors to reduce or satisfy . . . there is no behavior except to meet a present need" (p. 492). Humanists, after all, are concerned primarily with the growth of, and thus benefits to, the "self," such as self-actualization (Maslow, 1970; Rogers, 1951; see Slife & Williams, 1995). Cognitive therapists have been equally concerned with self benefits, including the importance of engaging in pleasant activities (Beck, Rush, Shaw, & Emery, 1979). As Aaron Beck made abundantly clear, "the *goal* of cognitive therapy is to relieve emotional distress and the other symptoms of depression" (Beck et al., 1979, p. 35). Indeed, cognition itself is thought to be organized around the evolutionarily derived interests of the individual. Cognitive schemas, as they are called, cluster around "primal modes" that have "evolved to deal with the most basic needs of the organism" (Clark, Beck, & Alford, 1999, p. 89).

Some psychologists may wonder whether these hedonistic assertions are truly meant to be fundamental in nature. They might contend that these theorists are just discussing how humans are *most* of the time. The problem is, this contention would mean that all the formal theoretical assertions of these scholars should be understood similarly—for example, Freud meant that we have an id *most* of the time; Rogers believed that we have subjectivity *most* of the time. Even the hedonistic assertions quoted above would need to be understood with this qualifier. However, Freud did not say, "our total mental activity is directed '*most of the time*' towards achieving pleasure and avoiding unpleasure." Although there are conditions for many theoretical constructs (e.g., Skinner's "circumstances"), there are no temporal conditions for our ultimate motivation being self-benefit. If there *were* conditions on hedonism—conditions for those occasions on which the ultimate motivation of humans was pleasure or happiness—then these theorists would need to account for those occasions on which humans were *not* interested in benefits to the self, and they do not.

Alfred Adler (1958, 1969) is one of the few theorists of therapy to assert that clients should have a "social interest" and altruism for others. If the four theorists discussed here—Freud, Skinner, Rogers, and Beck—made similar assertions, they would have developed, along with Adler, well-articulated therapy strategies for teaching clients to benefit others. Most of these theorists are concerned, to be sure, about interpersonal relations, with some even mentioning the client's service of others. However, they mention this service because it ultimately serves the interest of the client, as a means to greater *self* (client)-benefit. The self (however it is defined) is the *ultimate* end, and others are always a means to this hedonistic end (see Richardson et al., 1999, for a review, and Slife, 2000a, for special issue on hedonism). The hedonistic assertions of these theorists are thus intended as assertions of universality—assertions of the nature of human nature (see the Universalism section below).

Recent scholars and social science commentators have also clarified the fundamental nature of hedonism in contemporary psychology. As Higgins (1997) succinctly puts it, "People are motivated to approach pleasure and avoid pain. It is the basic motivational assumption of theories across all the areas of psychology" (p. 1280). Miller (1999) seems to concur with this assessment but points to an even broader context: "With the publication of *Leviathan*, Thomas Hobbes enthroned self-interest as the cardinal human motive, a status it enjoys to this day" (p. 1053). Evolutionary psychologists also make plain the hedonistic nature of human nature (Beyers & Petersen, 2000; Buss, 1998; Reber, 2000). Indeed, many contemporary cognitive theorists argue that human rationality is itself underlain with hedonistic self-concern (cf. Gantt, 2000; Manktelow, 1999). From this perspective, there is no rational motive for acting against one's self-interest.

Many practicing psychotherapists appear to have accepted this version of human nature and rationality (Fisher Smith, 2000; Gantt, 2000). Some version of happiness or self-benefit is a standard therapeutic goal. Chronic suffering or depression is typically viewed as inherently bad. Part of the obligation of any health professional, in light of the medical (naturalistic) model, is to prevent pain and relieve suffering. A recent version of these hedonistic variations is the positive psychology movement (e.g., Diener, 1995, 2000; Myers, 2000; Seligman & Csikszentmihalyi, 2000). This movement has asserted that well-being and happiness are the fundamental purposes of life, often without any defense of this assertion. Indeed, this lack of defense is a hallmark of an implicit assumption such as hedonism—it is not explicit enough or questioned enough to be defended. Even religion and God, from this positive psychology perspective, are primarily means to hedonistic ends (Emmons, 1999; Slife & Calapp, 2000). Emmons (1999) reveals this means-ends relationship with this statement from his book on positive psychology and spirituality: "What advantage for psychological well-being is there in holding spiritual goals?" (p. 108).

These basic conceptions of human nature have, in turn, influenced other social scientists. Many economists assume a similar means-ends relationship because consumers are supposed to act in their own self-interest (cf. Buchanan, 1979; Epstein, 1991). Rational Choice Theory and Utility Maximization cast one's relationship with others and things as relative costs and benefits to the self (Gantt, 2000; Green & Shapiro, 1994). They characterize human social behavior as the result of fundamentally egoistic reasoning processes. Indeed, some view the capitalist system as fundamentally driven by hedonism (cf. Yunus, 1999), in which case the economy itself is dependent on people maximizing their own interests and benefits. However, if people are viewed as constantly maximizing their benefits, what is to prevent them from deceiving others to effect this maximization? Obviously, if hedonism is inherent in human nature and rationality, then some economic system of accountability is necessary to prevent dishonesty.

Of course, if humans are innately and wholly hedonistic, then psychotherapists are themselves hedonistic. They also act in their own self-interest, and they cannot be counted on to act in the interest of others. This unstated assumption is one of the reasons the profession of psychotherapy supposedly needs to be "managed." The economists associated with managed care assume that psychotherapists, like all hedonistic entities, must be carefully monitored and held accountable. Otherwise, these mental health professionals will maximize their own monetary standing at the expense of the insurance companies that are paying for their services. Some make the case that the managed care system is also necessary to protect the interest of clients. Left to their own devices, who knows whether psychotherapists will act in the interest of their clients, particularly when it conflicts with their own interests?

Problems with Hedonism. Some therapists may resist this hedonistic picture of themselves. They may view themselves as at least altruistic toward their clients, aiding them in many ways without the need or even the expectation of return benefits. The problem is that the *formal* theories of psychotherapy, as outlined above, do not allow this altruism; their assumptions about human nature do not explain or even permit such altruism. Consequently, the field of psychotherapy is faced with a dilemma: either the hedonistic assumptions of human nature—as manifested in these formal theories—are themselves wrong and true altruism is possible, or therapist altruism does not really exist and the therapists who think they are altruistic are merely fooling themselves. Let us examine each horn of this dilemma in turn.

If the former were true—if altruism were really possible—then major qualifications, if not whole revisions of the mainstream theories of psychotherapy would be necessary. Hedonism is not a peripheral assumption; it resides at the core of what a human is, affecting virtually all other theoretical constructs. In psychotherapy, for example, these theories extensively describe how clients can gain (and the therapist facilitate) benefits for themselves. They rarely, if ever, describe how clients can benefit *others* (and the therapist can facilitate clients in effecting these benefits). If these theoretical schools attend to "helping behaviors" at all, it is *ultimately* to benefit the person exhibiting the behaviors (i.e., hedonism). Truly altruistic motives allow self-benefits to *ensue*, as an indirect result of an altruistic action. However, truly altruistic motives cannot, by definition, allow such benefits to be *pursued* (as an ultimate motive) because this pursuit makes the helper the ultimate end (e.g., Yalom, 1980).

Altruistic motives would also throw a conceptual "wrench" into many theoretical mechanisms and principles of these schools of therapy. Operant conditioning, for example, would not operate to the degree that persons are not interested in their own benefits—their own reinforcements. This potential disruption of operant conditioning effectiveness is never discussed in the behavioral literature because this prospect is never considered possible (i.e., operant conditioning assumes the ultimate hedonism of all animals, including higher animals). Similar revisions of the theories of Freud, Beck, and Rogers would be necessary. Some of Freud's (1913/1961) criticisms of religion, for instance, depend on his theoretical assumption that religion is ultimately a means to hedonistic (id) wishes. Clearly, major revisions would be necessary if these theories were wrong about the fundamental hedonism of humans.

What if, on the other hand, these theories were basically correct, at least regarding their fundamental hedonism? Then, of course, the classical problem of hedonism would be the issue: no one can truly be altruistic. That is, if people are hedonistic by nature, then no one can truly sacrifice themselves for the sake of others. Freud would be correct: religious people would only worship God as a means to their own selfish ends (which may not be "worship" at all). If love, for instance, requires some measure of self-sacrifice, then true love would presumably be impossible. People who "love" others would really be loving themselves, ultimately (Levinas, 1987; Reber & Beyers, 2000). No one would be able to treat others as an end in themselves.

Hedonistic theorists have long disputed this classical problem by noting that many altruistic behaviors occur in order to gain self-benefit; many people serve others as a means to some hedonistic end. Although many "sacrifices" are made and even suffering is incurred, these sacrifices and sufferings are meant to actualize some benefit for the self. The ideal of this mutually beneficial hedonism is reciprocity. Reciprocity postulates that the best human relationships involve the "win-win" scenario, where mutual sacrifices yield mutual benefits. This win-win is the hedonistic ideal of many economists and therapists (Fisher Smith, 2000; Gantt, 2000). Economists assume this reciprocity of harmonious economic systems, whereas psychotherapists assume the reciprocity of harmonious therapeutic systems—the client provides monetary benefits, and the therapist provides therapeutic benefits. In addition, many therapists teach this win-win scenario as an ideal of human relationships in general. Good marriages, for instance, are supposed to work in this reciprocal fashion (Fisher Smith, 2000; Fowers, 1993; Richardson et al., 1999).

This hedonistic ideal, however, is not without its problems. For example, it means there are no benefits provided to others, whether economic or therapeutic, if there are no benefits provided to the self. Reciprocity and contractual agreement are so widely used that this might not seem to be a problem. However, reciprocal agreements do not account for the broad service orientation of the mental health profession. Although many of the relationships of the therapy enterprise consist of reciprocal agreements, therapists are also expected to act in the client's best interest, regardless of the benefits gained (APA Code of Ethics, 1992). With hedonistic reciprocity, therapists would not perform any benefits to others without a commensurate benefit in return.

Another way to put this issue is that therapists do not have to provide their services unless they can see a benefit for themselves. Indeed, if hedonism is fundamental to human nature, therapists would not *be able* to provide their services without a clear sense of comparable benefit for themselves. Consider a common set of possible interventions in a therapeutic situation. The first intervention is clearly in the best interest of the client but provides no benefit to the therapist. The second intervention, though less helpful to the client than the first intervention, provides some benefit to the therapist. The final option for intervention is actually quite harmful to the client but is the most beneficial for the therapist.

Unfortunately, the philosophy of hedonism not only predicts movement away from the first intervention—the intervention that most ethical codes would require—but movement toward the third intervention, the intervention that most ethical codes would outlaw. Some will undoubtedly respond that the third intervention will hurt therapists in the long term—that benefiting the client, even when therapists suffer, will help therapists build a clientele, and so on. However, this response assumes that the hypothetical of the third intervention (above) does not take into account long-term benefits. All this hypothetical says is that the intervention is the most beneficial for the therapist (long or short term), in which case hedonism predicts movement *toward* this intervention.

The point is that the prospect of no benefits for the therapist means there is no reason to do what is best for the client. The philosophy of hedonism only guarantees that therapists will do what is best for themselves. Reciprocity, the ideal of hedonistic human relationships, argues for some equality of benefits, but such equality is rare in practice. Moreover, hedonistic creatures will only affirm this reciprocity if it is in their interest. If there was some way to take advantage and to broker an agreement that has more benefits, presumably this way would be the path taken. In addition, therapists would not teach altruism to their clients because they would assume that such altruism was impossible. Indeed, they would assume that one should be suspicious of people acting altruistically because "altruistic" people must, of necessity, be deceptively pressing for their own advantage. This deception is also the reason economic accountability is thought to be required; therapists are considered incapable of being altruistic toward insurance companies. Consequently, they must be monitored and managed to serve the interest of the insurance company, if not the patients.

An Alternative to Hedonism. If mainstream theories of psychotherapy are any indication, naturalism is so endemic to the social sciences that the only way in which many social scientists formally explain altruistic behaviors is hedonistically (e.g., Beyers & Petersen, 2000; Reber, 2000). All behaviors are for the sake of self-interested motives, so why should behaviors that help others be any different? Obviously, such explanations are not truly an alternative to hedonism. As long as the ultimate concern or motive of the person (whether consciously or unconsciously) is some benefit to the self, then it is hedonistic. In this regard, the alternative is obvious, though seemingly improbable from the perspective of a naturalistic social scientist. The alternative is a capacity to be ultimately concerned for the other.

Altruism, in this sense, is *not* helping others with an ultimate motive to benefit one's self (however long or short the term of the benefit). Altruism is making the *other* the ultimate end—making decisions with a "neighbor's" needs as the ultimate criteria for the decisions. This capacity for altruism does not assume that *all* concerns and motives would necessarily be for the sake of the other, but it does assume that all concerns and motives *could* be for the sake of the other. That is, this alternative to hedonism does not have to mean a constant motive of altruism, though constant altruism might be the ideal from the perspective of some altruists (e.g., Adler, 1958, 1969). This alternative would merely mean the *possibility* of the ideal becoming real—clients (and therapists) can (and should) treat others as ends in themselves rather than as means to their own self-oriented ends. This assumption may, in fact, be the *informal* assumption of many therapists. However, if this is true, it is not reflected or developed in the formal theories of psychotherapy.

What would such an alternative mean if it were more formalized and developed in psychotherapy? First, as mentioned earlier, it would mean major qualifications, if not revisions, of the mainstream schools of therapy theory—psychoanalysis, behaviorism, humanism, and cognitivism. Unlike the pleasure principle of Freud, for example, a true reverence or love for others, including God, would be possible (Levinas, 1987). Also, the extent to which altruistic motives replaced self-beneficial motives is the extent to which conventional "reinforcements," at least as conceived by many behaviorists, would be less important. In addition, something besides the humanistic self would be of central interest. Instead of *self*-actualization, *other*-actualization would be the apex of the motivational hierarchy. And, contrary to many cognitivists, a client's motivation to think of others first, and to consider his or her own self-interest second, would be the epitome of rationality, regardless of the outcome for the client (e.g., suffering).

An altruistic community is also possible, where members of the community were more concerned about communal than individual benefits. Journalists, for instance, routinely assume (via hedonism) that community and political leaders act in their own self-interests (e.g., getting elected). An altruistic alternative would assume that political leaders could be ultimately concerned with what is best for the community rather than their own careers. Consequently, this possibility is as likely as hedonism when interpreting a politician's behavior. Similarly, therapists could be truly altruistic with their patients and work to instill altruistic values in their clients. Reciprocity and "win-win" relationships would not necessarily be the ideal of human connectedness. Marriages, friendships, and even therapist/client relationships could be entirely (and continually) unequal or asymmetrical in the benefits particular members of these relationships receive (e.g., Levinas, 1987).

A truly altruistic alternative would also put pain and suffering in a different light. As Jerome Frank (1978) has observed, psychotherapy currently has no room for "the redemptive power of suffering, acceptance of one's lot in life, adherence to tradition, self-restraint and moderation" (pp. 6–7). Altruism, on the other hand, would allow for the possibility of meaningful pain *for its own sake*—not just meaningful in the hedonistic sense of ultimately leading to well-being or happiness, but meaningful in its own right. Depression and other types of therapeutic suffering could have a meaning and purpose of their own, as some existentialists have argued (e.g., Yalom, 1980). Depressive symptoms and feelings would be probed for their own meaning, without automatically assuming they should be eliminated at some point. Indeed, continued suffering might be integral to continued meaning. Therapy might help clients experience greater purpose in their suffering, but this purpose would not be required to make the client "feel better" (a hedonism). This purpose would put the suffering in perspective or give it meaning, without taking away the pain or suffering in any conventional sense.

This alternative view of suffering implies perhaps the most striking contrast with a hedonistically oriented discipline—a change in orientation toward therapy outcome and efficacy. Currently, client benefit is the unquestioned ideal of nearly all therapies. An altruistic alternative, however, would imply another ideal, at least as the primary outcome—client altruism. That is, it would be better for clients to benefit others than to benefit themselves. Note that this ideal is not the same as saying that clients would be "better off" benefiting others—often meant as a hedonism again. The main outcome would, instead, be the benefit of others, even at the expense of the self. Also, this altruistic outcome would not preclude the possibility of self-benefits *ensuing*. It would, however, preclude the client *pursuing* self-benefits—at least as the primary, desired outcome. In fact, some self-benefits might not be available to the client except through true self-sacrifice (e.g., some types of meaning).

Interestingly, this alternative to hedonism would also mean that conventional outcome measures (measuring self-benefits) should be more focused on others, as the beneficiaries of clients, rather than on the clients themselves. A positive therapy outcome would mean client sacrifices for the sake of others, including helping others to be more altruistic. Presumably, measures of the clients themselves would include a client's sensitivity to others as well as a client's skills in serving others. Similarly, holistic or communitarian measures would be formulated. Has the client's sense of purpose within the community been heightened (even without the client "feeling better")? The focus would be more on how the individual serves society than on how society serves the individual, even if suffering and depression were the individual outcome.

Is such an alternative to hedonism really possible or desired? Certainly, many religious traditions contend that it is (Slife & Calapp, 2000). However, many social scientists reconstrue these traditions of altruism as ultimately self-serving (cf. Emmons, 1999; Freud, 1963; cf. Slife & Calapp, 2000). Perhaps a more pertinent question is whether the data related to altruism can be interpreted in this alternative fashion. That is, do researchers *have* to interpret apparently altruistic behaviors hedonistically? Or is hedonism an implicit assumption that is invoked automatically (and without comparison to an alternative) when interpreting these data? Some observers would contend the latter (Beyers & Petersen, 2000; Fisher Smith, 2000; Gantt, 2000; Reber, 2000). Hedonism is part of the unconsciously held naturalistic paradigm of the social sciences, and thus is typically assumed and rarely tested (at least against alternative explanations). If this dominance of data interpretation is true, then an alternative interpretation of the data is possible, perhaps even an altruistic alternative. Mental health professionals might have the capacity to follow their code of ethics, and therapists might be able to act in the best interest of their clients, regardless of their own self-interest.

What would such an alternative imply about the presumed need for economic accountability? Recall that accountability was needed, in part, because of the hedonistic nature of humans. What if humans were capable of truly altruistic motives? This capability would allow therapists to be as altruistic toward insurance companies as they are toward their clients. If therapists can act in the best interest of their clients, they could conceivably act in the best interest of the insurance company, particularly with an education about insurance company interests. However, the mere capability of altruistic motives does not mean the use of such motives. No one who champions the person's ability to act for the sake of others assumes that this ability means that persons cannot act for the sake of themselves. Although therapists are not relegated to being selfish, as with naturalistic hedonism, they are not relegated (through "natural law") to being selfless. However, this alternative approach to motives opens the possibility of alternative relationships between therapists and insurance companies.

Atomism

Atomism may be the least known of naturalism's assumptions (see Table 3.1). Still, this underlying conception accounts for some of the most popular implications of naturalism in therapy, including the emphasis on individual diagnosis and treatment (individualism), and the notion that therapists should work within the moral framework of the client (relativism). Atomism is the notion that the natural world is comprised of self-contained "atoms" (molecules, cells), each with its own properties and qualities contained therein. All the essential properties of an atom are located in the atom itself (e.g., as reflected in the periodic table of the elements). This location does not prevent atoms from interacting with other atoms, but it does imply that each atom must first exist as a self-contained entity and then cross time and space to interact with other atoms. Indeed, one of the goals of naturalism is to discover the laws or principles that govern these atomistic interactions.

Many social scientists and practitioners have adopted this assumption by viewing individual people as the "atoms" of larger communities, with each individual as a self-contained unit (cf. Richardson et al., 1999; Slife, 1993). That is, the qualities of each individual are understood as originating from the individual—from the self. Individuals are considered either in terms of their unique pasts (e.g., intrapsychic dynamics, reinforcement histories, memory storage) or in terms of their unique biochemistries (e.g., genetic makeup, neuroanatomy) or some interaction of the two. Whatever is the case, these characteristics are thought to be contained *within* the individual and carried from situation to situation *by* the individual (e.g., personality, trait, diagnosis). Atomism is so pervasive that even mainstream approaches to relationships and systems view them as collections of self-contained individuals (cf. Slife, 1993, Ch. 8).

Another important implication of atomism is the uniqueness and relativity of each "atom." If the properties of each atom or individual are self-contained, then it follows that these properties could be unique. Each individual or atom could be quite different from other individuals and atoms, each with its own individual "needs." In therapy, for instance, what some clients need is not necessarily what other clients need. Consequently, individual clients should be understood *relative* to their own personal histories and biological needs. This relativity is also thought to include values; individuals should be understood relative to their own values. As discussed previously, there are clear ethical injunctions against therapists imposing their values on clients (ACA, 1995; APA, 1992).

This relativity is also a prime reason that individual therapy has traditionally been more popular than group or family therapy. The problems that clients bring to the therapy session are considered unique and contained within the self. A group of such clients would be a collection of self-contained uniquenesses. To do their unique problems any justice is to deal with them on an individual basis, even in the group. Moreover, the common practice of having clients come to the therapist's office originates from the atomistic assumption that clients carry their problems with them. If their problems were not self-contained, then they might change from situation to situation and be qualitatively different in the therapist's office. To be sure, atomists expect some differences as situations change, but the basic qualities of individuals (e.g., personalities, traits, diagnoses) are thought to be essentially stable and self-contained.

Even the methods of science, including the methods of the social sciences, are bathed in atomism. Scientists routinely assume, for instance, that they are studying self-contained events and unique "variables." Variables are supposedly separable from and independent of other variables, each existing in their own right and having their own properties. Therefore, scientists believe they can isolate certain variables—for example, "independent variables"—by eliminating extraneous variables in the laboratory or controlling them through experimental designs. They also believe they must *sample* all the relevant variables because their findings would not contain the influence of these self-contained variables without such sampling. Natural scientists remain interested in discovering the laws that govern the interaction of these isolated variables. However, they view these multivariable interactions as first existing as self-contained individual variables.

Problems with Atomism. As popular as atomism and individualism are, these assumptions of naturalism can be very problematic. Perhaps the most obvious practical problem is the expense of individual care. If all people are unique and self-contained, then the ideal of health care is some individually tailored treatment, relative to each client's situation and needs. Atomism does not exclude group or community treatments. However, such treatments are frequently viewed as less than ideal and are often conducted as individual therapy with an audience (Slife & Lanyon, 1991; Yalom, 1983; 1985).

Unfortunately, the atomism that fuels these practices is not well supported—empirically or theoretically. In fact, there is considerable evidence that many qualities and characteristics of people are not self-contained (Richardson et al., 1999; Woolfolk, 1998). Some qualities and characteristics are inextricably intertwined with contexts and factors that are "outside" individuals. They cannot be understood without reference to the *simultaneous* context that surrounds them. The term *simultaneous* is emphasized here to distinguish self-contained qualities that interact *sequentially* with their environments (atomism) from qualities that cannot be separated and do not exist apart from their contexts, even for a moment (Slife, 1993).

For example, a moderately active child—Little Bobby—could be perceived (and perceive himself) as a "behavior problem" because everyone else in his classroom is relatively passive. Little Bobby's context—the relative passivity of his classroom—could be the sole reason he is viewed as "abnormal." If the same child, with the same behavior and "self-contained" qualities, were somehow placed in a classroom or culture of similarly active people, his activity would likely not be noticed, let alone "diagnosed" as a problem. Note also that Little Bobby's context and his behavior problem are not in sequence; the context of the classroom is not "first" and the behavior problem "second." Little Bobby's behavioral problem, in this case, is simultaneous with and inseparable from his context.

Likewise, a woman from Finland was recently enrolled in a class taught by the author. She claimed (and her family corroborated) that her emotional state and personality were the same in the United States as they were in Finland. However, in Finland she was considered a "joyous and energetic sort," whereas in the United States she was constantly asked whether she was depressed. If the culture of Finland is somewhat introverted and taciturn, as some report (Sallinen-Kuparinen, 1986, 1987; Sallinen-Kuparinen, Asikaincn, Gorlander, Kukkola, & Sihto, 1987), then someone who is less introverted and taciturn might be labeled "joyous and energetic." This same pattern of behavior could also be understood differently in the light of another culture's emotionality and behavior, in this case the United States. Diagnosis, from this perspective, does not depend entirely on one's self-contained qualities (e.g., nature/nurture). Diagnosis also depends on the simultaneous culture or context of the person being diagnosed. Even the notion that one *should* be diagnosed could be a product of culture in this sense (Fowers & Richardson, 1996).

These difficulties with atomism have served as the impetus for both the family therapy and social constructionist movements. Family therapists noticed that the "identified patients" of the family—the patients whom their families identified as being the most problematic—were better understood and treated in the context of the family itself (e.g., Becvar & Becvar, 1988). The problems were not located "inside" the identified patient, as an atomistic entity; rather, the problems were located among the relationships of the family members. Although this insight was the original impetus for the family therapy movement, many family therapy conceptions have not escaped atomism. These conceptions still assume that the family is a collection of interacting "atoms" rather than a nexus of relationships (Slife, 1993).

Social constructionists have experienced similar problems, both with individualism and with evading atomism more generally. First, the cross-cultural studies of social constructionists have revealed the ethnocentricity of individualism—the cultural factors involved in embracing atomism (e.g., Gergen & Davis, 1985). Virtually all the atomistic traits and characteristics of the self have been associated with Western culture (Gergen, 1994). Even professional notions of self-contained personalities, self-esteem, and the self in almost any capacity have been shown to be far more "Western" than previously realized. Many Asian cultures, for example, are relational and contextual. Honesty is not a trait that one carries from context to context; honesty is related to specific contexts and thus is potentially changeable, even within a particular individual (e.g., Schweder & Bourne, 1982).

Interestingly, however, social constructionists may fall prey to atomism at another level. Although they clearly eschew atomism at the level of the individual, they have been criticized for assuming atomism at the level of society (Fowers & Richardson, 1996; Slife, 1999). That is, social constructionists seem to view societies and cultures as self-contained, with their own rules, customs, and traditions. The only way to understand a society, from this widely held perspective, is to study the society itself, with all its qualities contained therein. This understanding of society is the main reason that social constructionists are thought to be relativists (e.g., Richardson et al., 1999). They believe that therapists should understand and treat people relative to their culture, and they argue that one culture has no right to impose its self-contained values on another culture, including the value of atomism.

The difficulty is that relativism at any level—whether individual or societal—is problematic, even paradoxical. The root of relativism is the notion that we should not privilege one particular individual or social value system over any other, at least in any absolute sense. If certain values are privileged, relativists believe their privileged status comes from the social power that supports them. In this sense, the relativist seems to endorse no existing value system. The problem is that there is also a sense in which this lack of endorsement is itself a value system. That is, the notion that one *should* avoid privileging a particular value system *itself* implies a host of implicit moral injunctions. First, it is wrong to claim an absolute justification for one's value system that one does not possess. (One should be honest.) Second, it is wrong to privilege one value system over another when the only basis for privileging is "might makes right." (Might should not make right.) Third, the tolerance of other value systems is a supreme virtue. (Intolerance should not be tolerated.) Fourth, it is wrong to "judge" other people from your own value framework. (One should be nonjudgmental.) And fifth, it is wrong to persuade others to abandon their own value system. (One should respect the views of others.)

The paradox of this relativistic position, then, is that it *is* a particular value position while simultaneously claiming that one should not endorse a particular value position. This paradox has very practical consequences for therapy. Although relativistic therapists are supposed to approach a client as if they have no values—to identify and work within the client's moral system—the notion that one *should* approach a client in this manner is itself a value (Fowers & Richardson, 1996; Slife & Fisher, 2000a). That is, to be tolerant or open to someone's values is to support the values of tolerance and openness. The paradox of relativism becomes clear when we consider a client who values intolerance or close-mindedness. What values do relativistic therapists use in this instance? Should relativists adopt the values of the client in the session, as relativism would demand, and abandon their own relativistic tolerance and openness, even openness to the client? Or should they uphold the values of relativism in the session and thus model how the nonrelativist can become more relativistic, possibly influencing the client to move away from their values?

The existence of these two alternatives raises an interesting empirical question: Which alternative do relativistic therapists typically pick? The research on this question is fairly unequivocal: relativists typically do *not* embrace their clients' close-mindedness and intolerance in therapy. Instead, they attempt to influence their clients (however intentionally or unintentionally) to become more open-minded and tolerant (e.g., Bergin, 1985; Kelly & Strupp, 1992; Smith, 1999; Strupp, 1980; Tjeltveit, 1986, 1999). In other words, relativistic therapists not only hold very specific values (what Bergin, 1985, calls the "freedom" values, p. 108), but they also attempt to impose these values on their clients, often without even realizing it. Indeed, they rarely view these values as stemming from their own unique philosophical positions—that is, from their own private values. They view them as the values all clients should possess. As Jensen and Bergin's (1988) survey indicates, the values related to relativism are the most endorsed values of psychotherapy. They are seen as *the* way in which all clients should be—as a kind of universal set of values.

Unfortunately, this quasi-absolutism violates the relativist ethic about *not* imposing values on clients, regardless of how widely these values are endorsed. Even values that are widely agreed upon are still values and still imposed when the therapist promotes them. Moreover, there is considerable evidence that these therapists *do* promote them (see Bergin, 1985; Beutler & Bergan, 1991; Kelly, 1990; and Slife & Fisher, 2000a, for reviews). Indeed, this promotion is the reason that many multiculturalists see therapy *in general* as a type of cultural imperialism (cf. Fowers & Richardson, 1996; Hoshmand, 2001). The paradox, again, is that such relativists (particularly social constructivists) are specifically attempting to avoid such imperialism.

AN ALTERNATIVE TO ATOMISM. One prominent alternative to atomism challenges both individualism and relativism–contextualism. Instead of the properties or qualities of a thing being contained "inside" the thing, the contextualist asserts that at least some of these properties and qualities come from "outside" the thing, in its context or situation (cf. Bohm, 1980; Slife, 1993). Just as parts get their identities from their relation to other parts (the whole), individuals get their identities from their relation to other individuals (or the community or culture). Individuals, from this perspective, are radically social creatures. They derive their identities, in large part, from the roles they play and the relationships they enjoy (e.g., Bellah, Madsen, Sullivan, Swindler, & Tipton, 1985; Eriksen, 1963). People are not first individuals and then communities—from this holistic perspective, they are parts of wholes, first and always.

This contextualist alternative has many intriguing implications. Methodologically, for example, none of the variables or events that science studies is self-contained. They do not exist, and cannot be understood, except in relation to one another, including the "variable" of the observer of the variables—the scientists themselves. Variables, in this sense, cannot be isolated or made "independent" of other variables without qualitatively altering them from their "natural" occurrence, as part of a whole. As Bergin (1997) notes, persons particularly (clients, therapists) should not be viewed as "variables" in this isolated sense (p. 84). To study an isolated subject in a laboratory setting or to counsel an isolated individual in a therapist's office is potentially to miss vital qualities of the individual that exist only in relation to his or her context.

In therapy, this context includes the therapist or observer of the individual. That is, the interpretation of the individual (e.g., diagnosis) is itself part of (a necessary condition to) the context. From this contextualist perspective, even individual therapy is always and already a "systemic" enterprise; the "client" is understood in relation to the therapist (and therapist's interpretation). Diagnostic and outcome measures, from this perspective, would need to be interpersonal and relational rather than personal and individual (cf. Kellerman, 1979; Leary, 1957; Yalom, 1985). In addition, the ideal treatment would not be individual therapy, at least in the narrow sense; the ideal treatment is a truly systemic therapy. Crucial here is distinguishing truly systemic therapy from individual therapy with an audience. Also, systemic therapy could have important economic consequences. Many people could be effectively treated at the same time both because individuals are inherently related to one another and because many of their characteristics only arise in relation to one another.

Understanding these people *relative* to one another (and their context) would seem to make relativism important. Recall, however, that relati*vism* depends ultimately on atomism. That is, relativism requires individuals or cultures to be self-contained, so that they are understandable and meaningful in isolation from one another (e.g., unique individual needs). Contextualism, on the other hand, assumes that individuals and cultures are only understandable and meaningful *in relation to one another* (the whole). For example, there would be no such thing (or word) as "culture," if there were not other cultures in which to relate and compare it. Even the qualities of cultures—for example, romantic, industrious—ultimately depend on their relations to other cultures. Without some contrast with less romantic or industrious cultures, those qualities of a culture would not stand out or get noticed. In this sense, the qualities of cultures (and individuals)—at least as understood and experienced—are not completely internal to them or relative to their self-contained properties. Indeed, to truly understand *why* a particular culture (or individual) is understood a particular way requires knowledge of comparison cultures (or individuals).

Philosophers sometimes call this type of contextualism *temporalism* to distinguish it from relativism (e.g., Faulconer & Williams, 1985; Heidegger, 1962; Slife & Reber, 2001; Widdershoven, 1992). Contextualism requires that individuals and cultures be understood in relation to their context. However, this context is not itself atomistic or self-contained. Even this context must be understood in relation to the context of contexts, and so on. From this perspective, no context is completely "local"; all contexts have at least some *trans*local characteristics that pervade many or all other contexts (Kristensen, Slife, & Yanchar, 2000; Slife, 2000b).

In therapy practice, this temporality means that individuals and their cultures are not self-contained. Individuals, regardless of their culture or unique qualities, are not "closed systems" shut off from one another. Whatever values, beliefs, and experiences individuals might have, they are relatable to and potentially understandable from the perspective of a person from another culture, race, or gender. Contextualism, in this sense, is an interesting challenge to some multicultural and feminist approaches that assume that only a therapist from the same culture, gender, or experience can truly "relate" to and understand the client (cf. Hoshmand, 2001; Maracek, 2001).

Universalism

As the final assumption of naturalism (see Table 3.1), universalism helps to account for the formal disciplinary emphasis on theoretical principles, standardized diagnoses, and manualized techniques, as well as the formal research importance of generalizability, uniform procedures, and reliability. Universalism (or atemporality, as it is sometimes called) originates from the Greek legacy to Western culture that says the most fundamental and natural things are the things that do not change—the things that are universal across both time and space (Faulconer & Williams, 1985; Slife, 1993, 1995; Slife & Williams, 1995). The common notion that truth does not change stems from this universalism (Boman, 1960). That is, if the truth is fundamental, then it cannot change. Of course, if the truth cannot change, then it cannot be a physical thing. As the Greeks knew full well, physical things do not meet this unchangeable standard because they eventually change (e.g., deteriorate, evolve). The most fundamental things, then, are *meta*physical entities or those entities that are "beyond" the physical, such as principles and laws (e.g., truth as principles).

To say that principles and laws are *beyond* the physical may seem a bit odd, particularly when we are considering *natural* laws and principles. Natural laws and principles are considered the most fundamental entities from a naturalistic perspective. After all, they are the entities that are thought to govern the events of nature (e.g., Newton, 1934). Natural laws, however, are not physical in the conventional sense. They do not fall on our retinas and they cannot be touched; only their manifestations are sensorily experienced. For example, no one has ever seen the law of gravity per se, but everyone has experienced its manifestations (e.g., scale weight, footprint in the sand).

The point is that natural laws, and thus universals, are not themselves physical; they are the unchangeable entities that supposedly control the physical (and thus control the changeable). They are thus discovered through inference rather than experienced directly.

These unchangeable laws are highly valued because they are viewed as the most fundamental and natural of all things, again courtesy of Greek philosophy. Even in the social sciences, which can boast of few natural laws, true knowledge is expected to approximate universality (i.e., change as little as possible). True knowledge must be generalizable to more than one place and time—hence the importance of replication in the social sciences. Empirical findings that are not replicated, and thus do not apply to more than one place and time, are not accepted as *real* findings (e.g., parapsychological findings; Reinsel, 1990). Indeed, a lack of replicability, in this sense, would mean a lack of scientific predictability. Part of the importance of universal laws and principles is that they allow the prediction (and determinism) of natural events across time and place.

Many social science endeavors evidence the importance of universalism (and its approximation). In fact, all the formal theories, concepts, and techniques of the social sciences are supposed to be universal. Formal theories in particular are recognized for this quality (Rychlak, 1981). Beck's theory, for example, assumes that all people (universally) have a mind (Beck, Rush, Shaw, & Emery, 1984); Skinner's (1972) theory assumes that all people can be reinforced. Although few, if any, social science theories are *proven* universals, they must be *formulated* as universals to be candidates for knowledge. All the mainstream theorists of psychotherapy postulate universals of human nature (e.g., hedonism), as if universalism is inherent in theorizing. The formal techniques of therapy are considered similarly. Although they can be tailored to some degree, they must possess universal principles that transcend the client on whom they are applied. Otherwise, they are not "techniques" in the usual sense of that term and would not be usable after being learned the first time.

Universalism, then, is a prime factor in the discipline moving to minimize professional variability (or change) through standardization and categorization (e.g., Bergin, 1997; Messer, 2001). A diagnostic system, for instance, would not be knowledge if it contained no generalities. If its categories (e.g., schizophrenia) changed qualitatively with every change in situation, it would not be viewed as knowledge in this universalist and naturalist sense. This variability would also rule out materialism because biological principles are themselves understood in universalist and thus cross-situational terms. Universalism is also the root of our professional motivation for manualized techniques and standardized tests (e.g., Strupp & Anderson, 1995). If techniques and tests changed constantly from context to context, particularly in their basic concepts and principles, they could not be viewed as knowledge. Nothing learned in one situation would seem to be transferable to the next situation.

Therefore, the ideal from this universalist perspective is a matching of "universals." Unchangeable and universal diagnostic categories should be matched to unchangeable and universal techniques, so a manualized and mechanically administered treatment can be prescribed for a known and thus predictable disorder (e.g., Koss & Shiang, 1994). This ideal, of course, is the medical (naturalist) model. Ideally (with all universal principles known), no thinking or creativity would be necessary in this model. Our knowledge of the universals, including the general principles of the matching process itself, would dictate the prescriptions given. Even the course of treatment would ideally consist of a set of principles to be followed mechanically. If tailoring to the uniqueness of the client was needed, a set of principles should also guide the tailoring, with a truly "cookie cutter" therapist as the ultimate result (Bergin, 1997, p. 85).

Problems with Universalism. The issues of tailoring and uniqueness hint at the traditional problems with universalism. The assumption of universalism is warranted only if clients and their contexts are fundamentally the same. If, however, clients and their contexts are fundamentally and qualitatively different, even at times, then generalizations and "universal" theories are not the only path to knowledge and truth. Psychologists do engage in "individual differences" research but they consider such differences to be potentially universal, and thus generalizable and replicable. In other words, the universalist assumption is still in place with such research. What if important information involved nongeneralizable, nonreplicable, and even completely unique and one-time events? What if, as many therapists report, significant client events are often one-time and possibly unique (e.g., trauma, "spiritual" events)?

A common response among universalists is that nongeneralizable information is unscientific or unsupportable and thus cannot be important to a scientifically based practice (cf. Reinsel, 1990). However, this position is questionable in light of evidence indicating that one-time events can be greatly significant to those who experience them (Jung, 1960; Stricker, 1996). Many traumatic or even "spiritual" experiences occur only once and may be irrelevant to anyone else, yet their lack of replicability and generalizability does not detract from their fundamental significance to the persons experiencing them. Artistic and creative works are often one of a kind, yet few would question their importance or potential for providing meaning and even life-altering experiences.

Another universalist response to this uniqueness is to multiply the number of universalist categories available for classifying unique experiences, people, and so on. Eclecticism is an example of a project that is intended to do just this—through the multiplication of therapeutic categories (Slife & Reber, 2001). Eclectics typically spurn single theories and single sets of interventions because they are too limiting. Their solution to these limitations is either to multiply theories (theoretical integrationism) or to multiply techniques (technical eclecticism). The diagnostic system, as another example, has been expanded and modified to make sense of the many idiosyncratic manifestations of behavior disorders and emotional difficulties. These approaches allow for some differences, to be sure, but they also deny the existence of truly one-time or wholly unique experiences and people. More and better generalities are still generalities. They still assume that clients and/or problems are *fundamentally* interchangeable parts within a particular category.

Unfortunately, this assumption is questionable in therapeutic practice (e.g., Henry, Strupp, Butler, Schacht, & Binder, 1993; Strupp & Anderson, 1995). It might be problematic to view the client who just left the consulting room as fundamentally the same as the new client—who just entered—even with the same diagnosis. Moreover, there is considerable evidence that therapists themselves are not interchangeable in this way. Although researchers have gone to great lengths, in the spirit of universalism, to "eliminate the therapist as a unique factor" (Bergin, 1997, p. 85), Lambert and his colleagues have shown that the second largest amount of variation in therapy outcome stems from therapist differences—the first largest being client differences (Lambert, 1989; Luborsky, 1995). Standardized (and universalized) techniques are *not* the strongest determinant of client change (Lambert & Okiishi, 1995).

Perhaps the best case for fundamental particularity is the relatively recent awareness of the depth of ethnic, racial, and gender differences (Fowers & Richardson, 1996). However, these differences have traditionally been understood either as categories of approximate universality (as described above) or as "add ons"—factors that are not viewed as essential to the identity or problems of the client (Hoshmand, 2001). Universals and generalities are considered more basic and essential than cultural uniquenesses and particulars. For example, a different diagnostic system is not provided for each culture: the diagnostic system is considered fundamentally universal and cross-cultural (again, following the dictates of the medical model). Generalities, after all, lead to knowledge that can be used repeatedly, whereas qualitative differences obviate knowledge advancement in this universalist sense.

However, a focus on generalities can also result in less therapist openness and creativity. If true knowledge consists of generalities and universals, then a true knowledge of clients requires a focus on the things that do not change—commonalities and samenesses—to discern universals rather than particularities and one-time occurrences. Universalism leads therapists to selectively attend to what fits the particular category of generality (e.g., diagnostic category, theoretical construct) and to selectively *in*attend to information that it does not fit. Formal theories and systems of therapy, in this sense, can obviate an authentic openness to the client. Therapists can lose vital information about what is changing in their clients in an effort to find the most fundamental aspects of their clients' conditions or to apply the generalities of the theory or system.

Fischer (2001) calls attention to similar problems in psychological assessment. The history of psychological assessment has been one of careful norming and standardization, in the universalist tradition. However, Fischer points cogently to the information being lost through such procedures. In addition, if universalized and standardized theories and manuals are to mechanically guide therapy practices, then therapists would be less able to creatively deal with client idiosyncrasies and uniquenesses. Slife and Reber (2001), for instance, cite a prototypical case in which the therapist's attention to his theory's universals (and thus techniques) obstructed his truly "seeing" his client. In fact, it was not until the client burst through the therapist's theoretical bubble that any creative interventions were available to the therapist.

AN ALTERNATIVE TO UNIVERSALISM. Hermeneutics can serve as an alternative to universalism (e.g., Messer, Sass, & Woolfolk, 1988; Packer, 1985; Packer & Addison, 1989; Richardson et al., 1999; Woolfolk, 1998). Advocates of hermeneutics, in fact, specifically challenge the universalist Greek legacy to Western culture by contending that the changeable is at least as fundamental as the unchangeable (Faulconer, 1990; Faulconer & Williams, 1990; Heidegger, 1962; Messer, Sass, & Woolfolk, 1988). Instead of searching exclusively for universal, metaphysical laws that occur without regard to context, hermeneuticists advocate the search for experiential patterns of change—for example, patterns of behavior, experiences, meanings, or relationships (e.g., Bohman, 1993).

Many of these personal or interpersonal patterns are not lawful in the conventional naturalist sense because metaphysical laws or principles are not thought to control them; there is nothing more fundamental than the patterns themselves. These patterns of behaviors or relationships pertain to and must be understood within the context in which they are found—potentially unique and nonrepeatable. Replication, in this sense, is not required, at least in the universalist sense. Indeed, some patterns may not be replicated in all or even most other contexts; some may even be limited to a very specific context or culture (e.g., family). This limitation, however, is not viewed as preventing knowledge or understanding; rather, it is considered a vital aspect of true understanding. In this sense, the hermeneutic approach is not unlike some case study methods.

Some contextual patterns, as with instructive case studies, may apply to many other conditions and contexts. Still, from this hermeneutic perspective, these patterns can never be elevated to the status of atemporal universals or natural laws because this status is always presumptuous. That is, universals and laws presume a knowledge that no human can ever have—that the pattern exists in *all* contexts. Consequently, the hermeneuticist prefers a more conservative, more humble approach that considers a pattern to be present only when it is experienced. Therapists, for instance, should never *presume* that a regularity of behavior (e.g., as connoted by a diagnostic label) is correct in another context (e.g., the next therapy session). Each new context—indeed, each new moment—means new possibilities. Even a "schizophrenic"—a diagnostic label frequently understood to cross most contexts—can have periods of symptom-free behavior. From this hermeneutic perspective, such individuals might be better labeled "intermittently schizophrenic."

Therapists, then, must be open and ready for change, at any point and under any circumstance, because change is a "natural" and fundamental way of things. Universalism, on the other hand, precludes such changeableness because it assumes that the most fundamental events of therapy can be known in advance (through universal principles). The hermeneuticist, by contrast, can never assume that the patterns observed are final or complete—particularly among humans—because they are constantly changing as our contexts shift and the interpreters of such regularities themselves change. These changes can be gradual and regular, such as a learning curve, or these changes can be discontinuous and cataclysmic, such as a sudden insight.

In either case, social science researchers would not be required to find the unchanging laws or principles that govern these changes. They could embrace experiential change for its own sake or perhaps find patterns in the change, but they would not elevate these patterns to a status that says the patterning itself (laws, principles) governs the change. In other words, the change is not necessarily determined (or governed). The regularities of change that are discerned through research would not have to be patterns of necessity; they could be patterns of possibility and meaning, permitting nondeterministic (and nonnaturalistic) constructs, such as agency and transcendence, to be part of the research enterprise.

From this perspective, treatment and research is less about discovering the universals and theoretical principles that underlie the client's behaviors and experiences and more about understanding the particular meanings of change that inhere in these behaviors and experiences. Interestingly, many qualitative researchers have explicitly advocated this approach, where the emphasis is more on *understanding* these meanings than on *explaining* underlying (naturalistic) forces (Crabtree & Miller, 1992; Denzin & Lincoln, 2000; Gilgun et al., 1992; Slife & Gantt, 1999).

Assumptions as Constraints

At this point, we have reviewed five major assumptions in the philosophy of naturalism. We have also reviewed some of the problems with, as well as one of the alternatives to, each assumption—to clarify its boundaries and counter any notions that it is an unchallengeable truism. The question now is: how do these five assumptions actually constrain therapists and therapy researchers? Recall that some prominent observers have feared that therapists and researchers are becoming technicians, without a critical and creative perspective (e.g., Messer, 2001). Some have feared they are becoming "cookie cutters" with a "bottom-line mentality" that emphasizes mechanical techniques and leads to inflexibility (e.g., Bergin, 1997). Even if this disciplinary mentality has not yet come completely to fruition, what accounts for these fears and perhaps even these trends?

First, unrecognized assumptions are the worst sort of mental constraints because they exert their influence without our awareness. We are so familiar with them (through our formal training and acculturation in the discipline) that we automatically and unconsciously assume them. Indeed, they may even appear to be *part* of our world. We are so used to organizing and interpreting the world with these assumptions that we forget they are conceptual organizations and interpretations. They become reified, stultified, and ultimately constraining to our perception, thinking, and experiencing because they are institutionalized through the discipline that informs us. They color our perceptions, direct our thinking, and imbue certain experiences with special importance. Let us briefly review each of the five assumptions of naturalism to see how they constrain psychotherapists in these ways. Again, these constraints are primarily related to institutionalized and formal conceptions of psychotherapy (as described in the introduction to the Philosophy of Naturalism). They do not necessarily pertain to the *informal* practices and conceptions of psychotherapists.

Objectivism. Although being "objective" frequently connotes a lack of mental constraints or intellectual biases, objectiv*ism* has definitely constrained the field of psychotherapy. Indeed, this connotation may be the primary constraining implication of objectivism—therapists and researchers presume they do not need to attend to implicit biases and values. The problem is that this inattention is singularly unscientific. The hallmark of science is investigation, in all its forms—including the investigation of its own assumptions and values (Slife, 2001). With objectivism, however, biases and values are viewed as either irrelevant or already settled because objectivist methods are assumed to control or eliminate them through research. Therefore, therapists can remain ignorant of the effects of assumptions in therapy as well as ignorant of the innovations available from potential alternatives.

The upshot is that unrecognized constraints and unacknowledged interpretations (e.g., naturalism) become reified. As mentioned, some assumptions and values are so familiar that they are thought to exist in the external world. As the "real" rather than the debatable, therapists typically do no thinking about them and researchers usually provide no examination of them. Doubtless, these assumptions make either positive or negative contributions (or both) to the therapeutic matter at hand. However, objectivism obstructs the active search for and test of these contributions, both in therapy and in research. In research, particularly, objectivism stymies the development of nonobjective methods and techniques—methods and techniques that do not share the values and assumptions of objectivism (e.g., qualitative methods, existentialism). This lack of development, in turn, prevents methodological pluralism, where researchers know the advantages and disadvantages of various methods (including quantitative methods) and pick and choose from among them depending on the subject matter (Bergin & Garfield, 1994b; Caldwell, 1994; Richards & Bergin, 1997; Roth, 1987; Slife & Gantt, 1999).

Materialism. Materialism constrains both research process and therapy outcome. In order to study psychotherapy outcome and process, all factors must either be material by their nature or made into material factors by proxy, that is, operationalized. This materialist requirement has several implications for therapy and research. In therapy, it means we must focus increasingly on those things that are observable and replicable—namely, the techniques and biology of therapy. Moreover, any theories of therapy that do not focus on observable techniques or biology (e.g., existentialism) are viewed either as wrong before investigation or as "unscientific"—which can amount to the same thing in a scientific discipline.

In research, materialism means the discounting of nonmaterial factors in two senses. First, it implies that material (biological) factors are more basic and thus more like causes than effects. Even before investigation, theories about material processes are presumed to involve more scientific and more fundamental processes. This presumption can account for the many inferential leaps that are permitted in materialist interpretations of data (see the Materialism section above). Second, the study of nonmaterial factors requires a translation process (operationalization) that allows only the material manifestations of these factors to be studied (and not the factors themselves). If nonmaterial factors (e.g., love, spirituality, relationship, agency) have any real import for the social sciences in general and therapy specifically, materialism hampers their development and use by therapists, and their study and understanding by researchers.

Hedonism. The assumption of hedonism, gives special importance to benefits of the self. Although there are many variations of these benefits—including happiness, well-being, and fulfillment—and many therapies urge clients to help others, the *ultimate* concern is whether the self is benefited. This concern is effectively the "bottom line" of therapy, and it is the bottom line of managed care. Client benefits lead to managed care profits. After all, the medical (naturalistic) model advocates the relieving of suffering as one of its primary tasks. Therefore, medical professionals should attempt to eliminate all types of suffering, unless the suffering itself benefits the self. Therapy, from this perspective, is the facilitation of a sophisticated selfishness because self*less*ness is either secondary or impossible.

Hedonism, in this sense, puts severe constraints on the meaning and purpose of suffering as well as the sacrifices one can make for the sake of others. Depression, for instance, can have no legitimate purpose or function in itself. It is only legitimate if it serves as a means to some greater happiness (e.g., stress inoculation). Similarly, no suffering or sacrifice for the sake of others is justified or can be recommended unless, again, it leads to benefits for the self. This constraint is also true of professionals; they can only help others if they gain a commensurate benefit for themselves. Therapists may experience altruism toward their clients, but the discipline explains this experience hedonistically. True altruism is impossible, so there is no point in therapists cultivating altruism—in themselves or in their clients. Indeed, a therapist should cultivate a suspicion of people who say that their motives are altruistic.

Atomism. Atomism restricts the disciplinary emphasis to the individual (the self). Although the interaction of individuals is clearly permitted (e.g., communities, systems), these interactions can only be conceptualized as collections of self-contained individuals. Theorizing is focused on understanding individuals (personality theory) rather than conceptualizing holistic communities or cultures. The greatest concerns of atomistic theorists are the qualities that are inherent in these individuals (e.g., reinforcement history, cognitive schema, intrapsychic conflict) and the qualities that remain relatively stable across different situations (e.g., personality traits, cognitive storage). These concerns imply, in turn, an emphasis on individual interventions and a tailoring to each individual's needs and values (e.g., relativism).

This individualism restricts the development of community-based interventions as well as conceptualizations of systems that do not consider individuals to be their most basic components. As Sandel (1996) and Fowers (1998) have noted, atomism makes communities and relationships the means to individual ends. If, for example, a married individual is no longer happy, then the marriage is no longer doing its job as a means to this individual's happiness, so divorce should be considered. Valuing individual happiness is, of course, the synergy of hedonism and atomism, where therapy is limited to the hedonistic benefits of the individual client. Clients are the "experts" on their individual needs because each client is self-contained. This expertise means that therapists are restricted to what their clients believe they need, because the community or culture (including the therapist) supposedly plays little or no part in deciding these needs.

Universalism. The assumption of universalism predisposes the therapist and researcher to attend to what is universal (generalizable) and unchangeable (permanent) because knowledge and truth are supposed to consist of, or at least approximate, what is universal and unchangeable. If therapists want to know the truth of a client's condition, they must look for and focus on the commonalties or generalities of this condition (e.g., theoretical principles). This focus places two types of constraints on the therapist. First, it means the therapist should attend primarily to what is unchangeable in the client, even when the therapist is striving to help the client to change. Second, it leads to an overreliance on therapy theory, at the expense of understanding the particulars of the client, because theory supposedly contains the more important (unchangeable) principles of therapy. Therapists are to use these theoretical principles with all clients because the universals of naturalism provide security, expertise, and authority.

A similar reliance on diagnostic labels can also occur, as is well known (e.g., Rosenhan, 1973; Woolfolk, 2001). Here a marriage of atomism and universalism can result in identifying an individual client with a diagnosis (e.g., a "schizophrenic"), as though the diagnosis were contained within the individual (atomism) and not essentially changeable across different situations (universalism). This combination of atomism and universalism also complements the materialist assumption that diagnoses are fundamentally a property of the client's matter (e.g., a self-contained and unchangeable genetic structure). This complementarity of three assumptions means that people are biologically the same within a diagnostic category. Finding this sameness is the primary task of the researcher and therapist—hence, the emphasis on standardized procedures and manualized techniques. However, as Bergin (1997) has noted this restriction to standardized procedures can lead to "cookie cutter" therapists because clients are thought to be, fundamentally, interchangeable parts.

Together, these five assumptions—the philosophy of naturalism—constrain not only what is thought to be the *desired outcome* of research and therapy but also what is viewed as the *desired process.* The most desirable outcome for research and therapy is a generalizable (universalism) and observable (materialism) benefit (hedonism) to the individual client (atomism). The fifth assumption, objectivism, enters the picture by helping therapists and researchers to assume that this desired outcome is not itself laden with questionable values and biases (i.e., it is "objective"). Significantly, managed care enters the picture by institutionalizing this outcome as the ideal and making what is considered "objective" the only process for which compensation is offered.

The coalescence of these five assumptions also restricts the desired *process* for attaining this outcome, whether that process is therapy or research. This process should isolate (atomism) and manipulate observable (materialism) and value-free variables (objectivism) to find the natural laws or theoretical principles (universalism) that govern benefits (hedonism) for our clients. This view of the desired process fits nicely the logic of traditional experimentation, particularly the medical model that is concerned primarily with dosage in relation to effect size. However, this view also fits an increasingly prevalent conception of therapy. As Bergin (1997) puts it, "the epitome of this conception is the notion that people (personalities and psychological problems) are objects (or dependent variables) to be acted upon by therapeutic interventions (independent variables) designed by experts" (p. 83).

Conclusion

Some readers may view this chapter as a diatribe against naturalism. They may assume that exposing the assumptions of naturalism and calling them "constraints" mean that they are supposed to be bad or inappropriate for psychotherapy. The problem with this assumption is that there is *no escape from assumptions.* As Jaspers (1954) was quoted as saying in the early portion of the chapter, "There is no escape from philosophy" (p. 12). If Jaspers is correct, then *no* framework associated with psychotherapy—including the alternatives described here—avoids assumptions, problems and alternatives, and theoretical and practical constraints. A similar chapter to this one could be written on each of the alternatives mentioned in this chapter.

What can we do, then, with this assumption-bound, value-laden enterprise? The first step is the purpose of this chapter—awareness. Therapy practitioners and researchers need to be aware of the assumptions they are making and the constraints they are under, so they can be examined. This awareness, however, requires more than mere exposure to the assumptions. It requires the elements incorporated into this chapter: an understanding of the problems of each assumption as well as at least one alternative with which to contrast the assumption. These elements help the assumption to be seen *as* an assumption, allowing its weaknesses to be recognized and the therapist's creativity to emerge. With an awareness of these elements, assumptions become points of view (rather than truisms) and possible ways of organizing and constraining therapy and research (rather than the *only* way).

Unfortunately, the pragmatism of many therapists and researchers thwarts this awareness of their philosophical assumptions. Such awareness is often considered more "philosophy" than "science"—as if understanding the intellectual foundations of the discipline is superfluous. Even pragmatism has its own intellectual foundations (e.g., James, 1907; Pierce, 1931); even pragmatism cannot escape its assumptions. However, many therapists and researchers have proceeded as if they could, allying themselves with "whatever works" and the "bottom line." This unreflective pragmatism—a variation on objectivism—seems to underlie many aspects of the current trends in psychotherapy. It certainly helps to explain the recent emphasis on therapy efficacy for so many factions, from researchers to managed care organizations to therapists themselves.

The thrust of this chapter, then, is not a diatribe against naturalism. It is a call for a *reflective pragmatism*, where we not only reflect on our conceptual constraints, but also move to alternatives when these constraints no longer suit us. The difficulty is, a reflective pragmatism requires more than mere awareness; it requires the active development and deliberate investigation of alternative points of view (hence, the space devoted to alternatives in this chapter). Without viable alternatives, familiar assumptions appear to be truisms. Popular points of view become reified, and *one* organization of reality becomes *the* organization of reality.

Naturalism is a case in point for formal theory, practice, and research. Many of the most familiar approaches and most common conceptions of the discipline are affiliated with this philosophy. Their affiliation with naturalism does not mean, of course, that these approaches and conceptions are bad, dumb, or ineffective. Rather, it means, that they have limitations (as do all approaches and conceptions) and that therapists and researchers should be ready to make adjustments as they encounter these limitations. It also means that these approaches and conceptions are often assumed without deliberate and rigorous examination. This lack of examination is understandable, given the seemingly divergent realms (economics, medicine, business, science) that have appeared to converge on the same vision for psychotherapy—even the same desired outcome and desired process. Such a convergence is commonly considered an indication of the truth of a shared vision. That is, if everyone sees things a certain way, then the way they are seen must be the way things really are.

Still, a convergence does not a truth make. In other words, there are alternative ways of accounting for this common vision. What is "seen" involves more than what is actually "there." What is experienced or seen, especially when considering the validity of assumptions, involves our selective attention as well as our interpretation of that selection—in short, our formal and informal theories of the world. In this sense, another way of accounting for this common vision is that these normally disparate spheres of endeavor—economics, medicine, science, business—share intellectual histories and philosophies. It was this observation, of course, that led Kuhn (1970) to postulate the existence of paradigms in the natural sciences. He believed the taken-for-granted assumptions of these paradigms were as necessary as the data for understanding the beliefs and decisions of scientists. This chapter, then, is a call to examine the usually taken-for-granted assumptions of naturalism because recent trends indicate that we no longer have the luxury of leaving them unexamined.

FOOTNOTE

1. Naturalism has been conceptualized in many ways over the centuries (cf. Griffin, 2000). Another paper would be necessary to chronicle and distinguish its various uses. However, as a brief attempt to differentiate my own use in this chapter, I would distinguish the meaning of naturalism from natural, with the former as an interpretation of the latter. In other words, the philosophy of naturalism, as I intend it here, is a particular mechanistic and reductive interpretation of the life world.

REFERENCES

Adler, A. (1958). *What life should mean to you.* New York: Capricorn Books.

Adler, A. (1969). *The theory and practice of individual psychology.* Patterson, NJ: Littlefield.

Agazzi, E. (1991) (Ed.). The problem of reductionism in science. Boston: Kluwer Academic Publishers.

Almond, R., Keniston, K., & Boltax, S. (1969). Patient value change in milieu therapy. *Archives of General Psychiatry, 20,* 339–351.

American Counseling Association (ACA). (1995). *Code of ethics and standards of practice.* Alexandria, VA: Author.

American Psychological Association. (1992). Ethical principles of psychologists and code of conduct. *American Psychologist, 47 (12),* 1597–1611.

American Psychological Association, Division of Clinical Psychology, Task Force on Promotion and Dissemination of Psychological Procedures. (1995). Training in and dissemination of empirically validated psychological treatments: Report and recommendations. *The Clinical Psychologist, 48,* 3–23.

Banister, P., Burman, E., Parker, I., Taylor, M., & Tindall, C. (1994). *Qualitative methods in psychology: A research guide.* Philadelphia: Open University Press.

Bateson, G., Jackson, D. D., Haley, J., & Weakland, J. (1956). Towards a theory of schizophrenia. *Behavior Science, 1*, 251–264.
Beck, A. T., Rush, A. J., Shaw, B. F., & Emery, G. (1979). *The cognitive therapy of depression.* New York: Guilford Press.
Beck, A., Rush, A., Shaw, F., & Emery, G. (1984). *The cognitive therapy of depression.* New York: Guilford Press.
Becvar, D. S., & Becvar, R. J. (1988). *Family therapy: A systematic integration.* Boston: Allyn & Bacon.
Bellah, R, Madsen, R., Sullivan, W., Swindler, A., & Tipton, S. (1985). *Habits of the heart: Individualism and commitment in American life.* Berkeley: University of California Press.
Bem, S., & de Jong, H. L. (1997). Theoretical issues in psychology: An introduction. London: Sage Publications.
Bergin, A. E. (1980). Psychotherapy and religious values. *Journal of Consulting and Clinical Psychology, 48*, 95–105.
Bergin, A. E. (1985). Proposed values for guiding and evaluating counseling and psychotherapy. *Counseling and Values, 29*, 99–117.
Bergin, A. E. (1991). Values and religious issues in psychotherapy and mental health. *American Psychologist, 46*, 394–403.
Bergin, A. E. (1997). Neglect of the therapist and the human dimensions of change: A Commentary. *Clinical Psychology: Science and Practice, 4(1)*, 83–89.
Bergin, A. E., & Garfield, S. L. (1994a). Overview, trends, and future issues. In A. E. Bergin & S. L. Garfield (Eds.), *Handbook of psychotherapy and behavior change* (pp. 821–830). New York: John Wiley & Sons.
Bergin, A. E., & Garfield, S. L. (Eds.) (1994b). *Handbook of psychotherapy and behavior change* (4th ed.). New York: John Wiley & Sons.
Bernstein, R. J. (1983). *Beyond objectivism and relativism: Science, hermeneutics, and praxis.* Philadelphia: University of Pennsylvania Press.
Beutler, L. E. (1979). Values, beliefs, religion and the persuasive influence of psychotherapy. *Psychotherapy: Theory, Research, and Practice, 16(4)*, 432–440.
Beutler, L. E., Arizmendi, T. G., Crago, M., Shanfield, S., & Hagaman, R. (1983). The effects of value similarity and clients' persuadability on value convergence and psychotherapy improvement. *Journal of Social and Clinical Psychology, 1(3)*, 231–246.
Beutler, L. E., & Bergan, J. (1991). Value change in counseling and psychotherapy: A search for scientific credibility. *Journal of Counseling Psychology, 38(1)*, 16–24.
Beutler, L. E., & Clarkin, J. F. (1990). *Systematic treatment selection: Toward targeted therapeutic interventions.* New York: Brunner/Mazel.
Beyers, M. S., & Petersen, M. J. (2000). A contradiction in terms: Hedonistic altruism. *General Psychologist, 35*, 78–80.
Bohart, A. C., O'Hara, M., & Leitner, L. M. (1998). Empirically violated treatments: Disenfranchisement of humanistic and other psychotherapies. *Psychotherapy Research, 8*, 141–157.
Bohm, D. (1980). *Wholeness and the implicate order.* London: Routledge.
Bohman, J. (1993). *New philosophy of social science.* Cambridge, MA: MIT Press.
Boman, T. (1960). *Hebrew thought compared with Greek.* New York: W. W. Norton.
Borkovec, T. D., & Castonguay, L. G. (1998). What is the scientific meaning of empirically supported therapy? *Journal of Consulting and Clinical Psychology, 66(1)*, 136–142.
Buchanan, J. M. (1979). *What should economists do?* Indianapolis, IN: Liberty Press.
Buss, D. M. (1998). *Evolutionary psychology: The new science of the mind.* Needham Heights, MA: Allyn & Bacon.
Caldwell, B. J. (1994). *Beyond positivism: Economic methodology in the twentieth century.* New York: Routledge.
Calhoun, K. S., Moras, K., Pilkonis, P. A., & Rehm, L. P. (1998). Empirically supported treatments: Implications for training. *Journal of Consulting and Clinical Psychology, 66*, 151–162.
Chambless, D. L., & Hollon, S. D. (1998). Defining empirically supported therapies. *Journal of Consulting and Clinical Psychology, 66(1)*, 7–18.
Charles, D., & Lennon, K. (Eds.) (1992). Reduction, explanation, and realism. Oxford, UK: Oxford University Press.
Churchland, P. (1994). Can neurobiology teach us anything about consciousness? In H. Morowitz & J. Singer (Eds.). *The mind, the brain, and complex adaptive systems: Santa Fe Institute studies in the sciences of complexity*, Vol. 22 (pp. 99–121). Reading, MA: Addison-Wesley Longman.
Claiborne, C. D., Ward, S. R., & Strong, S. R. (1981). Effects of congruence between counselor interpretations and client beliefs. *Journal of Counseling Psychology, 28*, 101–109.
Clark, D. A., Beck, A. T., & Alford, B. A. (1999). *Scientific foundations of cognitive theory and therapy of depression.* New York: John Wiley & Sons.
Crabtree, B. F., & Miller, W. L. (1992). *Doing qualitative research.* Newbury Park, CA: Sage.
Culbertson, J., & Krull, K. R. (1996). Attention deficit hyperactivity disorder. In R. L. Adams, O. A. Parsons, J. L. Culbertson, & S. J. Nixon (Eds.), *Neuropsychology for clinical practice: Etiology, assessment, and treatment of common neurological disorders* (pp. 271–330). Washington, DC: American Psychological Association.
Curd, M., & Cover, J. A. (1998). *Philosophy of science: The central issues.* New York: W. W. Norton.
Davidson, D. (1980). *Essays on actions and events.* New York: Oxford University Press.
DeBerry, S. T. (1993). *Quantum psychology: Steps to a postmodern ecology of being.* Westport, CT: Praeger.

DeLeon, P. H., & Wiggins, J. G. (1996). Prescription privileges for psychologists. *American Psychologist, 51*, 225–229.

Denzin, N. K., & Lincoln, Y. S. (Eds.). (2000). *Handbook of qualitative methods.* Thousand Oaks, CA: Sage.

Diener, E. (1995). Assessing subjective well-being: Opportunities and progress. *Social Indicators Research, 31*, 103–157.

Diener, E. (2000). Subjective well-being: The science of happiness and a proposal for a national index. *American Psychologist, 55(1)*, 34–43.

Division 12 Task Force. (1996). An update on empirically validated therapies. *The Clinical Psychologist, 49*, 5–18.

Dupre, J. (1993). *The disorder of things.* Cambridge, MA: Harvard University Press.

Eccles, J., & Robinson, D. N. (1984). *The wonder of being human: Our brain and our mind.* New York: Free Press.

Eliade, M. (1987). *The sacred and the profane: The nature of religion.* (W. R. Trask, Trans.). San Diego: Harcourt Brace & Co.

Emmons, R. (1999). *The psychology of ultimate concerns: motivation and spirituality in personality.* New York: Guilford Press.

Epstein, R. A. (1991). The varieties of self-interest. *Social Philosophy & Policy, 8*, 102–120.

Eriksen, E. H. (1963). *Childhood and society* (2nd ed.). New York: W. W. Norton.

Faulconer, J. (1990). Heidegger and psychological explanation: Taking account of Derrida. In J. Faulconer & R. Williams (Eds.), *Reconsidering psychology: Perspectives from continental philosophy* (pp. 116–135). Pittsburgh: Duquesne University Press.

Faulconer, J. E., and Williams, R. N. (1985). Temporality in human action: An alternative to positivism and historicism. *American Psychologist, 40*, 1179–1188.

Faulconer, J. E., and Williams, R. N. (Eds.). (1990). *Reconsidering psychology: Perspectives from continental philosophy.* Pittsburgh, PA: Duquesne University Press.

Feyerabend, P. (1975). *Against method.* London: Verso.

Fischer, C. (2001). Psychological assessment: From objectivism to the life world. In Slife, B., Williams, R., & Barlow, S. (Eds.), *Critical issues in psychotherapy: Translating new ideas into practice* (pp. 29–43). Thousand Oaks, CA: Sage Publications.

Fisher, A. M. (1997). Modern manifestations of materialism: A legacy of the Enlightenment discourse. *Journal of Theoretical and Philosophical Psychology, 17(1)*, 45–55.

Fisher Smith, A. M. (2000). Limitations in the psychotherapeutic relationship: Psychology's implicit commitment to hedonism. *General Psychologist, 35*, 88–91.

Fowers, B. J. (1993). Psychology as public philosophy: An illustration of the moral dimension of psychology with marital research. *Journal of Theoretical and Philosophical Psychology, 13(2)*, 124–136.

Fowers, B. J. (1998). Psychology and the good marriage: Social theory as practice. *American Behavioral Scientist, 41*, 516–541.

Fowers, B. J., & Richardson, F. C. (1996). Why is multiculturalism good? *American Psychologist, 51(6)*, 609–621.

Frank, J. D. (1978). *Psychotherapy and the human predicament: A psychosocial approach.* New York: Schocken.

Freud, S. (1913/1961). *Totem and taboo.* London: Routledge & Kegan Paul.

Freud, S. (1949). *The ego and the id.* London: Hogarth Press.

Freud, S. (1963). Introductory lectures on psychoanalysis (Part III). (J. Strachey, Trans.). London: Allen & Unwin Publishers.

Gadamer, H. G. (1995). *Truth and method.* (J. Weinsheimer & D. G. Marshall, Trans.) (Rev. ed.). New York: Continuum. (Original work published 1960.)

Gantt, E. (2000). Cognitive psychology, rationality, and the assumption of hedonism. *General Psychologist, 35*, 82–86.

Garfield, S. L., & Bergin, A. E. (1986). *Handbook of psychotherapy and behavior change* (3rd ed.). New York: John Wiley & Sons.

Gergen, K. (1994). *Realities and relationships: Soundings in social constructionism.* Cambridge, MA: Harvard University Press.

Gergen, K. J., & Davis, K. E. (Eds.) (1985). *The social construction of the person.* New York: Springer-Verlag.

Gilgun, J. F., Daly, K., & Handel, G. (Eds.) (1992). *Qualitative methods in family research.* Newbury Park: Sage.

Gold, J. R. (1995). The place of process-oriented psychotherapies in an outcome-oriented psychology and society. *Applied and Preventive Psychology, 4*, 61–74.

Goldfried, M. R., & Wolfe, B. E. (1996). Psychotherapy practice and research: Repairing a strained alliance. *American Psychologist, 51*, 1007–1016.

Green, C. D. (1992). Of immortal mythological beasts: Operationism in psychology. *Theory & Psychology, 2(3)*, 291–320.

Green, D. P., & Shapiro, I. (1994). Pathologies of rational choice theory. New Haven, CT: Yale University Press.

Griffin, D. R. (2000). *Religion and scientific naturalism: Overcoming the conflicts.* Albany: SUNY Press.

Habermas, J. (1973). *Theory and practice* (J. Viertel, Trans.). Boston: Beacon.

Hall, C. S., & Lindzey, G. (1957). *Theories of personality.* New York: John Wiley & Sons.

Hall, C. S., Lindzey, G., & Campbell, R. (1998). *Theories of personality.* New York: John Wiley & Sons.

Heelan, P. A. (1983). *Space-perception and the philosophy of science.* Berkeley: University of California Press.

Heidegger, M. (1962). *Being and time.* (J. Macquarrie & E. Robinson, Trans.). San Francisco: Harper. (Original work published 1926.)

Heiman, G. W. (1995). *Research methods in psychology.* Boston: Houghton Mifflin.

Held, B. S. (1995). *Back to reality: A critique of postmodern theory in psychotherapy.* New York: W. W. Norton.

Henry, W. P., Strupp, H. H., Butler, S. F., Schacht, T. E., & Binder, J. L. (1993). Effects of training in time-limited dynamic psychotherapy: Changes in therapist behavior. *Journal of Consulting and Clinical Psychology, 61,* 434–440.

Henry, W. P., Strupp, H. H., Schacht, T. E., & Gaston, L. (1994). Psychodynamic approaches. In A. E. Bergin & S. L. Garfield (Eds.), *Handbook of psychotherapy and behavior change* (4th ed.) (pp. 467–508). New York: John Wiley & Sons.

Higgins, E. T. (1997). Beyond the pleasure principle. *American Psychologist, 52 (12),* 1280–1300.

Honer, S. M., & Hunt, T. C. (1987). *Invitation to philosophy: Issues and options* (5th ed.). Belmont, CA: Wadsworth.

Hoshmand, L. (2001). Psychotherapy as an instrument of culture. In B. Slife, R. Williams, & S. Barlow (Eds.), *Critical issues in psychotherapy: Translating new ideas into practice* (pp. 99–113). Thousand Oaks, CA: Sage Publications.

Hoshmand, L., & Polkinghorne, D. (1992). Redefining the science-practice relationship and professional training. *American Psychologist, 47,* 55–66.

Howard, G. S. (Ed.) (special issue 1994). Free will in psychology. *Journal of Theoretical and Philosophical Psychology, 14 (1).*

Howard, G. S. (1994). Some varieties of free will worth practicing. *Journal of Theoretical and Philosophical Psychology, 14 (1),* 50–61.

Howard, G. S., & Conway, C. G. (1986). Can there be an empirical science of volitional action? *American Psychologist, 41,* 1241–1251.

James, W. (1907). *Pragmatism.* New York: Longman, Green, & Company.

James, W. (1902/1994). *The varieties of religious experience.* New York: The Modern Library.

Jaspers, K. (1954). *Way to wisdom: An introduction to philosophy.* New Haven, CT: Yale University Press.

Jensen, J. P., & Bergin, A. E. (1988). Mental health values of professional therapists: A national interdisciplinary survey. *Professional Psychology: Research and Practice, 19 (3),* 290–297.

Jung, C. G. (1960). The structure and dynamics of the psyche. In H. Read, M. Fordham, & G. Adler (Eds.), *The collected works of C. G. Jung: Vol. 8.* Bollingen Series. New York: Pantheon Books.

Kellerman, H. (1979). *Group psychotherapy and personality: Intersecting structures.* New York: Grune & Stratton.

Kelly, G. A. (1955). *The psychology of personal constructs.* New York: W. W. Norton.

Kelly, T. (1990). The role of values in psychotherapy: A critical review of process and outcome effects, *Clinical Psychology Review, 10,* 171–186.

Kelly, T. A., & Strupp, H. H. (1992). Patient and therapist values in psychotherapy: Perceived changes, assimilation, similarity, and outcome. *Journal of Consulting and Clinical Psychology, 60 (1),* 34–40.

Kendall, P. C. (1998). Empirically supported psychological therapies. *Journal of Consulting and Clinical Psychology, 66 (1),* 3–6.

Koch, S. (1959). *Psychology: A study of science* (Vols. 1–3). New York: McGraw-Hill.

Koch, S. (1992). Psychology's Bridgman vs. Bridgman's Bridgman: An essay in reconstruction. *Theory & Psychology, 2 (3),* 261–290.

Koss, M. P., & Shiang, J. (1994). Research on brief psychotherapy. In A. E. Bergin & S. L. Garfield (Eds.), *Handbook of psychotherapy and behavior change* (pp. 664–700). New York: John Wiley & Sons.

Kristensen, K., Slife, B. D., & Yanchar, S. (2000). On what basis are evaluations possible in a fragmented psychology? An alternative to objectivism and relativism. *The Journal of Mind and Behavior, 21 (3),* 273–288.

Kuhn, T. S. (1970). *The structure of scientific revolutions* (2nd ed.). Chicago: University of Chicago Press.

Lakatos, I., & Musgrave, A. (Eds.) (1970). *Criticism and the growth of knowledge.* Cambridge, England: Cambridge University Press.

Lambert, M. J. (1989). The individual therapist's contribution to psychotherapy process and outcome. *Clinical Psychology Review, 9,* 469–485.

Lambert, M. J., & Okiishi, J. (1995, June). The effects of the individual psychotherapist and implications for future research. In S. L. Garfield (Chair), *The psychotherapist as a neglected variable in psychotherapy research.* Symposium at the meeting of the Society for Psychotherapy Research, Vancouver, Canada.

Landfield, A. W., & Nawas, M. M. (1964). Psychotherapeutic improvement as a function of communication and adoption of therapists' values. *Journal of Counseling Psychology, 11,* 336–341.

Lazarus, A. A. (1995). Different types of eclecticism and integration: Let's be aware of the dangers. *Journal of Psychotherapy Integration, 5 (1),* 27–39.

Lazarus, A. A., & Beutler, L. E. (1993). On technical eclecticism. *Journal of Counseling and Development, 71 (4),* 381–385.

Lazarus, A. A., Beutler, L. E., & Norcross, J. C. (1992). The future of technical eclecticism. *Psychotherapy, 29 (1),* 11–20.

Leahey, T. H. (1991). *A history of modern psychology.* Englewood Cliffs, NJ: Prentice Hall.

Leary, T. (1957). *Interpersonal diagnosis of personality.* New York: Ronald Press.

Lennon, K. (1990). *Explaining human action.* London: Duckworth.

Levinas, E. (1987). *Time and the other.* (R. A. Cohen, Trans.). Pittsburgh, PA: Duquesne University Press.

Libet, B. (1985). Unconscious cerebral initiative and the role of conscious will in voluntary action. *The Behavioral and Brain Sciences, 8,* 529–566.

Luborsky, L. (1995, June). The psychotherapist as a less neglected variable: Studies of benefits to each therapist's caseload. In S. L. Garfield (Chair), *The psychotherapist as a neglected variable in psychotherapy research.* Symposium at the meeting of the Society for Psychotherapy Research, Vancouver, Canada.

Luborsky, L., & DeRubeis, R. J. (1984). The use of psychotherapy treatment manuals: A small revolution in psychotherapy research style. *Clinical Psychology Review, 4,* 5–14.

Luborsky, L., & Spence, D. P. (1971). Quantitative research on psychoanalytic therapy. In A. E. Bergin & S. L. Garfield (Eds.), *Handbook of psychotherapy and behavior change.* (1st ed.) (pp. 408–438). New York: John Wiley & Sons.

Mahrer, A. R. (2000). Philosophy of science and the foundations of psychotherapy. *American Psychologist, 55 (10),* 1117–1125.

Maizlish, I. L., & Hurley, J. R. (1963). Attitude changes of husbands and wives in time—limited group psychotherapy. *Psychiatric Quarterly Supplement, 37,* 230–249.

Manktelow, K. (1999). *Reasoning and thinking.* Hove, UK: Psychology Press Ltd.

Maracek, J. (2001). Bringing feminist issues to therapy. In B. Slife, R. Williams, & S. Barlow (Eds.) *Critical issues in psychotherapy: Translating new ideas into practice* (pp. 305–319). Thousand Oaks, CA: Sage Publications.

Marsden, G. (1971). Content analysis studies of psychotherapy: 1954 through 1968. In A. E. Bergin & S. L. Garfield (Eds.), *Handbook of psychotherapy and behavior change* (1st ed.) (pp. 345–407). New York: John Wiley & Sons.

Martini, J. L. (1978). Patient-therapist value congruence and ratings of client improvement. *Counseling and Values, 23,* 25–32.

Maslow, A. H. (1970). *Motivation and personality* (2nd ed.). New York: Harper & Row.

Meehl, P. (1959). Some technical and axiological problems in the therapeutic handling of religious and valuational material. *Journal of Counseling Psychology, 6,* 255–259.

Merriam-Webster collegiate dictionary. (1998). Springfield, MA: Merriam-Webster.

Messer, S. (2001). Empirically supported treatments: What's a nonbehaviorist to do? In B. Slife, R. Williams, & S. Barlow (Eds.), *Critical issues in psychotherapy: Translating new ideas into practice* (pp. 3–19). Thousand Oaks, CA: Sage Publications.

Messer, S. B., Sass, L. A., & Woolfolk, R. L. (1988). *Hermeneutics and psychological theory: Interpretive perspectives on personality, psychotherapy, and psychopathology.* New Brunswick, NJ: Rutgers University Press.

Miller, D. T. (1999). The norm of self-interest. *American Psychologist, 54,* 1053–1060.

Mirsky, A. F. (1987). Behavioral and psychophysiological markers of disordered attention. *Environmental Health Perspectives, 74,* 191–199.

Mirsky, A. F. (1989). The neuropsychology of attention: Elements of a complex behavior. Iin E. Perecman (Ed.), *Integrating theory and practice in clinical neuropsychology* (pp. 75–91). Hillsdale, NJ: Erlbaum.

Muse, M. J. (1997). The implicit dualism in eliminative materialism: What the Churchlands aren't telling you. *Journal of Theoretical and Philosophical Psychology, 17 (1),* 56–66.

Nathan, P. E. (1998). Practice guidelines: Not yet ideal. *American Psychologist, 53,* 290–299.

Nathan, P. E., & Gorman, J. M. (1998). *A guide to treatments that work.* New York: Oxford University Press.

Newton, I. (1934). *Mathematical principles of natural philosophy.* (A. Motte, Trans.). Berkeley: University of California Press.

Packer, M. J. (1985). Hermeneutic inquiry in the study of human conduct. *American Psychologist, 40,* 1081–1093.

Packer, M. J., & Addison, R. B. (Eds.). (1989). *Entering the circle: Hermeneutic investigation in psychology.* Albany, NY: SUNY Press.

Palmer, R. E. (1969). *Hermeneutic: Interpretation theory in Schleiermacher, Dilthey, Heidegger, and Gadamer.* Evanston, IL: Northwestern University Press.

Paris, J. (1998). Significance of biological research for a biopsychosocial model of personality disorders. In K. R. Silk (Ed.), *Biology of personality disorders* (pp. 129–148). Washington, DC: American Psychiatric Press.

Parloff, M. B., Iflund, B., & Goldstein, N. (1960). Communication of "therapy values" between therapist and schizophrenic patients. *Journal of Nervous and Mental Disorders, 130,* 193–199.

Patton, M. Q. (1990). *Qualitative evaluation and research methods.* (2nd ed.) Newbury Park, CA: Sage.

Pierce, C. S. (1931). *Collected papers.* New York: George Braziller.

Polkinghorne, D. E. (1983). *Methodology for the human sciences: Systems of inquiry.* Albany, NY: SUNY Press.

Polkinghorne, D. E. (1988). *Narrative knowing and the human sciences.* Albany, NY: SUNY Press.

Polkinghorne, D. (1990). Psychology after philosophy. In J. Faulconer and R. Williams (Eds.), *Reconsidering psychology: Perspectives from Continental philosophy.* Pittsburgh, PA: Duquesne University Press, pp. 92–115.

Popper, K. (1959). *The logic of discovery.* London: Unwin Hyman.
Popper, K., & Eccles, J. C. (1977). *The self and its brain.* New York: Springer.
Reber, J. (2000). Privileging hedonism: Confounds and consequences. *General Psychologist, 35*, 80–82.
Reber, J., & Beyers, M. (2000). Love is not an evolutionarily derived mechanism. In B. Slife (Ed.), *Taking sides: Clashing views on controversial psychological issues* (11th ed.) (pp. 83–89). New York: Dushkin/McGraw-Hill.
Reinsel, R. (1990). Parapsychology: An empirical science. In P. Grim (Ed.), *Philosophy of science and the occult* (pp. 187–201). New York: SUNY Press.
Richards, P. S., & Bergin, A. E. (1997). *A spiritual strategy for counseling and psychotherapy.* Washington, DC: American Psychological Association.
Richardson, F. C., Fowers, B. J., & Guignon, C. B. (1999). *Re-envisioning psychology: Moral dimensions of theory and practice.* San Francisco: Jossey-Bass.
Ricoeur, P. (1978). *The philosophy of Paul Ricoeur: An anthology of his work.* In C. E. Reagan & D. Stewart (Eds.). Boston: Beacon.
Robinson, D. N. (1985). *Philosophy of psychology.* New York: Columbia University Press.
Robinson, D. (1989). *Aristotle's psychology.* New York: Columbia University Press.
Robinson, D. (Ed.) (1992). *Social discourse and moral judgment.* San Diego: Academic Press.
Robinson, D. (1995). The logic of reductionistic models. *New Ideas in Psychology, 13*, 1–8.
Rogers, C. (1951). *Client-centered therapy: Its current practice, implications, and theory.* Boston: Houghton Mifflin.
Rogers, C. R. (1970). Toward a modern approach to values: The valuing process in the mature person. In J. T. Harr & T. M. Tomlinson (Eds.), *New directions in client-centered therapy* (pp. 430–441). Boston: Houghton Mifflin.
Rorty, R. (1979). *Philosophy and the mirror of nature.* Princeton, NJ: Princeton University Press.
Rosenthal, D. (1955). Changes in some moral values following psychotherapy. *Journal of Consulting Psychology, 19*, 431–436.
Roth, P. A. (1987). *Meaning and method in the social sciences: A case for methodological pluralism.* Ithaca, NY: Cornell University Press.
Rule, J. B. (1997). *Theory and progress in social science.* Cambridge University Press.
Russell, R. L. (Ed.) (1994). *Reassessing psychotherapy research.* New York: Guilford Press.
Rychlak, J. F. (1981). *Introduction to personality and psychotherapy: A theory-construction approach* (2nd ed.). Boston: Houghton Mifflin.
Rychlak, J. F. (1988). *The psychology of rigorous humanism* (2nd ed.). New York: New York University Press.
Rychlak, J. F. (1994). *Logical learning theory: A human teleology and its empirical support.* Lincoln: University of Nebraska Press.
Rychlak, J. F. (2000). A psychotherapist's lessons from the philosophy of science. *American Psychologist, 55 (10)*, 1126–1132.
Sallinen-Kuparinen, A. (1986). Finnish communication reticence: Perceptions and behavior. *Studia Philologica Jyvaskylaensia, 9.* Jyvaskyla: University of Jyvaskyla.
Sallinen-Kuparinen, A. (1987, February). Culture and communicator image. Paper presented at the Western Speech Communication Association Convention, Salt Lake City.
Sallinen-Kuparinen, A., Asikaincn, S., Gorlander, N., Kukkola, A., & Sihto, M. (1987). A cross-cultural comparison of instructional communication: Evaluation of an American, a Russian, a German and a Finnish Teacher's communicator style. In A. Sallinen-Kuparinen (Ed.), *Perspectives on instructional communication* (pp. 71–95). Publications of the Department of Communication S. Jyvaskyla: University of Jyvaskvla.
Sandel, M. (1996). *Democracy's discontent: America in search of a public philosophy.* Cambridge, MA: Belknap/Harvard University Press.
Sarbin, T. R. (1990). Toward the obsolescence of the schizophrenia hypothesis. *The Journal of Mind and Behavior, 11*, 259–280.
Schweder, R. A., & Bourne, E. (1982). Does the concept of the person vary cross-culturally? In A. J. Marsella & G. White (Eds.), *Cultural concepts of mental health and therapy* (pp. 97–137). Boston: Reidel.
Seligman, M. E. P. (1994). *What you can change and what you can't.* New York: Alfred A. Knopf.
Seligman, M. E., & Csikszentmihalyi, M. (2000). Positive psychology: An introduction. *American Psychologist, 55 (1)*, 5–14.
Shafranske, E. P. (1996). *Religion and the clinical practice of psychology.* Washington, DC: American Psychological Association.
Shoham, V. (1996, April). *The promise (?) of empirically validated psychotherapy integration.* Paper presented at the meeting of the Society for the Exploration of Psychotherapy Integration, Berkeley, CA.
Silk, K. R. (1998). *Biology of personality disorders.* Washington, DC: American Psychiatric Press.
Skinner, B. F. (1972). Some issues concerning the control of human behavior. In Kenneth MacCorquodale, Gardner Lindzey, and Kenneth Clark (Eds.), *Cumulative record: A selection of papers* (pp. 25–38). New York: Appleton-Century-Crofts.
Slife, B. (1993). *Time and psychological explanation.* Albany, NY: SUNY Press.
Slife, B. (1995). Information and time. *Theory and Psychology, 5(3)*, 533–550.
Slife, B. D. (1999, August). Truth in a foundationless psychology: Ontological hermeneutics. Paper presented at the meeting of the American Psychological Association, Boston, MA.

Slife, B. D. (Ed.) (2000a). Hedonism: A hidden unity and problematic of psychology. *General Psychologist, 35 (3)*, 77–80.

Slife, B. D. (2000b). Are discourse communities incommensurable in a fragmented psychology? The possibility of disciplinary coherence. *The Journal of Mind and Behavior, 21(3)*, 261–271.

Slife, B. D. (2001). Introduction. In B. Slife, R. Williams, & S. Barlow (Eds.), *Critical issues in psychotherapy: Translating new ideas into practice* (pp. xi–xvii). Thousand Oaks, CA: Sage Publications.

Slife, B. D., & Calapp, J. (2000). The ultimate concern of ultimate concern researchers. *Contemporary Psychology, 45*, 545–548.

Slife, B. D., & Fisher, A. M. (2000a, October). *Managing inescapable values in psychotherapy.* Invited address to the Department of Counseling, University of Southern California, Los Angeles, CA.

Slife, B. D., & Fisher, A. M. (2000b). Modern and postmodern approaches to the free will/determinism dilemma in psychology. *Journal of Humanistic Psychology, 40 (1)*, 80–108.

Slife, B. D., & Gantt, E. (1999). Methodological pluralism: A framework for psychotherapy research. *Journal of Clinical Psychology. 55 (12)*, 1–13.

Slife, B. D., & Lanyon, J. (1991). Accounting for the power of the here-and-now: A theoretical revolution. *International Journal of Group Psychotherapy, 41 (2)*, 145 167.

Slife, B. D., & Reber, J. (2001). Eclecticism in psychotherapy: Is it really the best substitute for traditional theories? In B. Slife, R. Williams, & S. Barlow (Eds.), *Critical issues in psychotherapy: Translating new ideas into practice* (pp. 213–234). Thousand Oaks, CA: Sage Publications.

Slife, B. D., & Richards, R. S. (2001). How separable are spirituality and theology in psychotherapy? *Counseling and Values, 45*, 190–206.

Slife, B. D., Smith, A. F., & Burchfield, C. (in press). Psychotherapists as crypto-missionaries: An exemplar on the crossroads of history, theory and philosophy. In D. B. Hill & M. J. Kral (Eds.) *About psychology: Essays at the crossroads of history, theory, and philosophy.* Albany, NY: SUNY Press.

Slife, B. D., & Williams, R. N. (1995). *What's behind the research? Discovering hidden assumptions in the behavioral sciences.* Thousand Oaks, CA: Sage Publications.

Slife, B. D., Williams, R. N., & Barlow, S. (2001). *Critical issues in psychotherapy: Translating new ideas into practice.* Thousand Oaks, CA: Sage Publications.

Smith, A. F. (1999). From value neturality to value inescapability: A qualitative inquiry into values management in psychotherapy (Doctoral dissertation, Brigham Young University, 1999). *Dissertation Abstracts International*, 60, 2337.

Smith, A. F., & Slife, B. D. (in press). *Managing inescapable values in psychotherapy.* Thousand Oaks, CA: Sage Publications.

Sperry, R. W. (1988). Psychology's mentalist paradigm and the religion/science tension. *American Psychologist, 43*, 607–613.

Sperry, R. W. (1995). The riddle of consciousness and the changing scientific worldview. *Journal of Humanistic Psychology, 35*, 7–33.

Sternberg, R. J. (1998). *Love is a story.* New York: Oxford University Press.

Sternberg, R. J. (2000). The holey grail of general intelligence. *Science, 289*, 399–401.

Sternberg, R. J., & Barnes, M. L. (Eds.) (1988). *The psychology of love.* New Haven, CT: Yale University Press.

Stricker, G. (1996, April). *Empirically validated treatment psychotherapy manuals and psychotherapy integration.* Paper presented at the meeting of the Society for the Exploration of Psychotherapy Integration, Berkeley, CA.

Strupp, H. H. (1980). Humanism and psychotherapy: A personal statement of the therapist's essential values. *Psychotherapy: Theory, research, and practice, 17 (4)*, 396–400.

Strupp, H. H., & Anderson, T. (1995, June). On the limitations of therapy manuals. In S. L. Garfield (Chair), *The psychotherapist as a neglected variable in psychotherapy research.* Symposium at the meeting of the Society for Psychotherapy Research, Vancouver, Canada.

Strupp, H. H., & Anderson, T. (1997). On the limitations of therapy manuals. *Clinical psychology: Science and Practice, 4*, 7–82.

Taylor, C. (1985a). *Human agency and language: Philosophical papers.* Cambridge, England: Cambridge University Press.

Taylor, C. (1985b). *Philosophy and the human sciences: Philosophical papers.* Cambridge, England: Cambridge University Press.

Taylor, C. (1991). *The ethics of authenticity.* Cambridge, MA: Harvard University Press.

Tjeltveit, A. C. (1986). The ethics of value conversion in psychotherapy: Appropriate and inappropriate therapist influence on client values. *Clinical Psychology Review, 6*, 515–537.

Tjeltveit, A. C. (1999). *Ethics and values in psychotherapy.* London: Routledge.

Toulmin, S. (1972). *Human understanding.* Princeton, NJ: Princeton University Press.

Valenstein, E. S. (1998). *Blaming the brain: The truth about drugs and mental health.* New York: The Free Press.

Valentine, E. R. (1992). *Conceptual issues in psychology* (2nd ed.). London: Routledge.

Viney, W., & King, D. B. (1998). *A history of psychology: Ideas and content* (2nd ed.). New York: Allyn & Bacon.

Widdershoven, G. A. M. (1992). Hermeneutics and relativism: Wittgenstein, Gadamer, Habermas. *Journal of Theoretical and Philosophical Psychology, 12*, 1–11.

Williams, R. N. (2001). The biologization of psychotherapy: Understanding the nature of influence. In B. Slife, R. Williams, and S. Barlow (Eds.), *Critical issues in psychotherapy: Translating new ideas into practice* (pp. 51–67). Thousand Oaks, CA: Sage Publications.

Wilson, G. T. (1995). Empirically supported treatments as a basis for clinical practice: Problems and prospects. In S. C. Hayes, V. M. Follette, R. M. Dawes, & K. E. Grady (Eds.), *Scientific standards of psychological practice: Issues and recommendations* (pp. 163–196). Reno, NV: Context Press.

Woolfolk, R. (1998). *The cure of souls: Science, values, and psychotherapy.* San Francisco: Jossey-Bass.

Woolfolk, R. (2001). "Objectivity" in diagnosis: A philosophical analysis. In B. Slife, R. Williams, & S. Barlow (Eds.), *Critical issues in psychotherapy: Translating new ideas into practice* (pp. 287–298). Thousand Oaks, CA: Sage Publications.

Yalom, I. D. (1980). *Existential psychotherapy.* New York: Basic Books.

Yalom, I. D. (1983). *Inpatient group psychotherapy.* New York: Basic Books.

Yalom, I. D. (1985). *Theory and practice of group psychotherapy* (3rd ed.). New York: Basic Books.

Yunus, M. (1999). Microlending: Toward a poverty-free world. *Brigham Young University Studies, 38 (2),* 149–155.

Zuckerman, M. (1999). *Vulnerability to psychopathology: A biosocial model.* Washington, DC: American Psychological Association Books.

CHAPTER 4

METHODOLOGICAL ISSUES IN STUDYING PSYCHOTHERAPY PROCESSES AND OUTCOMES

CLARA E. HILL
University of Maryland
MICHAEL J. LAMBERT
Brigham Young University

This chapter provides a resource about measures and methodological issues for researchers to use in designing and conducting process and outcome research on psychotherapy. Our readers should read the chapters by Kendall et al. (this volume) on research methodology and Slife (this volume) on conceptual issues in psychotherapy research because these chapters provide necessary background for this chapter.

First, we need to define what we mean by psychotherapy process and outcome. Process refers to what happens in psychotherapy sessions (e.g., the therapist providing interpretations), whereas outcome refers to immediate or long-term changes that occur as a result of therapy (e.g., the client decreasing in symptomatology). A typical goal is to link process to outcome (e.g., how therapist interpretations lead to changes in client functioning). The distinction between process and outcome is not always clear-cut, however, because changes in process can also be indicators of outcome (e.g., gaining insight in the session is often considered a desirable goal of therapy). Furthermore, process and outcome can be distinguished from input variables (e.g., client and therapist characteristics such as personality, demographics, expectations, and theoretical orientation/worldview, as well as setting variables such as physical arrangement of the office) and extratherapy variables (i.e., events outside of sessions such as job loss that help or hinder the therapy process).

In the first part of this chapter, we focus on methodological issues in assessing process. In the second part, we focus on the methodology of measuring outcome. We use the term *client* rather than *patient* because it has a greater psychological than medical connotation. We use the term *therapist* to refer to anyone (helper, trainee, counselor, psychotherapist, psychoanalyst) in a therapeutic or helping role. We use the term *judge* to refer to any nonparticipant (rater, observer) who evaluates therapy.

METHODOLOGICAL ISSUES IN PROCESS RESEARCH

The most frequently used methods in process research can be divided into quantitative and qualitative clusters. We define these methods, indicate some advantages and disadvantages of each, and then go into detail about the methodological issues involved in each of them.

In quantitative process research, researchers use established measures and rely on numbers to summarize and analyze findings. Using established measures is advantageous because typically there is evidence of their validity and reliability. Furthermore, results can be compared and aggregated across studies if the same measures are used. A disadvantage is that the measure might not reflect the researcher's exact interest. An advantage of using numbers is that statistical analyses can be used to answer questions; a disadvantage is that the numbers may not accurately portray reality.

A variation on the quantitative method is discovery-oriented or exploratory research (Elliott, 1984; Hill, 1990; Mahrer, 1988), in which researchers create a measure from the data for a particular study, thus allowing researchers to explore what exists in the data without preconceived theoretical biases. Once the measure is created, the researchers train a new set of judges to make the judgments reliably. The advantages of developing measures for particular studies are that researchers can "discover" the results from the data and still have some evidence of interjudge reliability; the disadvantages are that the validity of new measures is unknown and results cannot be aggregated across studies using different measures.

In qualitative research, researchers use open-ended data-gathering techniques such as interviews and then develop categories from the data. They then use words rather than numbers in summarizing data. An advantage of qualitative methods is that researchers can investigate clinically rich or infrequently occurring phenomena that are often difficult to investigate through quantitative methods, especially when minimal research exists in the area. Similar to the exploratory methods, a disadvantage is the difficulty of aggregating results across studies. Another set of limitations involves difficulties in determining the validity and reliability of the data and the judges.

Quantitative Process Research

We first focus on measures used in quantitative process research because the measures determine the results that can be obtained. Specifically, we discuss dimensions, validity, reliability, and choice of measures. We then discuss data collection issues, use of judges, data analysis within studies, and data aggregation across studies.

Dimensions of Process Measures

Many different types of measures have been created for assessing psychotherapy process. To create some order out of the different types, we can classify them on a number of dimensions (see Table 4.1). The present classification of dimensions is an extension and modification of previous classification systems (Bordin, 1974; Elliott, 1991; Greenberg, 1986; Highlen & Hill, 1984; Kiesler, 1973; Marsden, 1965, 1971; Russell, 1988; Russell & Stiles, 1979). The dimensions, which are described in some depth in this section, are the: (1) focus of evaluation, (2) aspect of process, (3) theoretical basis, (4) perspective of evaluation, (5) unit studied, (6) type of measurement, (7) level of inference required, and (8) stimulus materials required. Given that each measure can be categorized into one subtype of each dimension, there are a possible 15,360 different types of measures. Researchers can use these dimensions to describe their measures and to clarify the intent of their study, theory of change, and assumptions about process.

Focus of Evaluation. The focus or target of the investigation can be on the client (an individual, a family, a group, or a community), therapist (an individual therapist, co-therapists, or a therapist team), the client/therapist dyad/system (relationship), the supervisor, or the therapist/supervisor relationship. Most current process measures focus on the client or therapist, although there has been increased interest in a dyadic/systemic focus (e.g., Benjamin, 1974; Budman et al., 1987) and the supervision relationship (e.g., Olk & Friedlander, 1992).

Aspect of Process. Four types of processes have been measured by process measures. Most commonly, researchers have studied behaviors, which can be further subdivided into overt behaviors (e.g., therapist verbal response modes; client behaviors) and covert experiences (e.g., therapist intentions, client reactions). Second, researchers have studied the thematic content of what is said or meant (e.g., interpersonal concerns, careers concerns). Third, process can be defined in terms of the style, which is the manner or how something is said or done (e.g., empathically, judgmentally). Finally, process can be described in terms of quality or how well something is done or said (e.g., competence).

Theoretical Basis. All measures have some philosophical or theoretical underpinning. Most typically, measures are atheoretical or reflect one of the major theoretical orientations (e.g., psychoanalytic, humanistic, behavioral). For example, the Experiencing Scale (Klein, Mathieu, Gendlin, & Kiesler, 1970) was developed to measure constructs from client-centered theory related to client involvement in the therapy process. The Experiencing Scale would not be as appropriate for trying to capture the desired client behavior in cognitive behavioral therapy because cognitive behaviorists do not tend to value client experiencing. Other measures have been developed to be pantheoretical or to assess behaviors valued across therapies, for example, the Psychotherapy Process Q-Set (Jones, Cummings, & Horowitz, 1988).

Perspective of Evaluation. Process can be evaluated by clients, therapists, supervisors, or

TABLE 4.1 Dimensions of Therapy Process Measures

1. Focus of evaluation (the person being studied)
   - A. Client
   - B. Therapist
   - C. Therapist-Client Relationship
   - D. Supervisor
   - E. Therapist-Supervisor Relationship
2. Aspect of process (the part of the process that is being studied)
   - A. Type of process: the therapeutic purpose of the talk or behavior
     1. Overt behaviors (e.g., therapist techniques, client behaviors)
     2. Covert behaviors (e.g., therapist intentions, clients reactions)
   - B. Thematic content: Topic or what is said or meant (e.g., dream, adjustment to college)
   - C. Style: The manner in which the speaker talks or behaves (e.g., paralinguistic and nonverbal behaviors, vocal quality, mood, feelings about the other)
   - D. Quality: Skillfulness or competence of the speaker's talk or behavior
3. Theoretical basis (the philosophical grounding for the measure)
   - A. Atheoretical (involves no underlying theory or is meant to span several theories)
   - B. Psychodynamic (is based on psychoanalytic principles)
   - C. Humanistic (is based on person-centered, existential, or humanistic principles)
   - D. Behavioral (is based on behavioral or cognitive principles)
4. Perspective of evaluation (the person providing the evaluation)
   - A. Client (participant observer)
   - B. Therapist (participant observer)
   - C. Supervisor (responsible party but nonparticipant observer)
   - D. Judge (nonparticipant observer)
5. Unit studied (the level at which the process is studied)
   - A. Microprocess units (small units in which specific moment-by-moment behaviors can be coded)
     1. Single word or phrase
     2. Sentence: grammatical unit containing a subject and verb
     3. Speaking turn: One speaker's response bounded by the other speaker's utterances
     4. Thought unit: a unit containing a single topic
   - B. Macroprocess units (longer units that require global judgments summarizing individual behaviors)
     1. Five-minute unit: arbitrary time units
     2. Event (topic or task unit): a series of speaking turns organized by a common task
     3. Session: a unit of time usually of between 30 and 90 minutes
     4. Stage: a series of sessions marked by temporal breaks or shifts in goals or processes
     5. Treatment: the entire course of work between therapist and client
6. Type of measurement (what type of scaling or categorization is used)
   - A. Interval scale (variables are rated on Likert scales)
   - B. Nominal categories (behaviors are judged as to their presence or absence)
   - C. Q-Sorts (items are sorted into a forced distribution)
7. Level of inference required (the amount of inference required to complete the measure)
   - A. Noninferential (requires minimal inference because it is relatively straightforward)
   - B. Inferential (requires more assumptions and may result in more bias)
8. Stimulus materials required to make judgments (what the evaluator responds to in making the evaluation)
   - A. Participation (for client or therapist) or live observation (for client, therapist, judge, or supervisor)
   - B. Transcript
   - C. Audiotape or videotape
   - D. Combination of transcript and tape

judges. Hill, Nutt, and Jackson (1994) found that about half of the process measures used in the *Journal of Counseling Psychology (JCP)* and the *Journal of Consulting and Clinical Psychology (JCCP)* between 1978 and 1992 involved participants (clients and/or therapists) and about half involved nonparticipant judges.

In the past, judges were thought to be objective in evaluating process because they were not personally involved in the therapy. We are now more aware that judges are as biased as therapists and clients, although these biases differ based on the level and type of involvement in the therapy process. Hence, therapists and clients have privileged and experiential information about what happened in sessions because they participated in them, whereas nonparticipant judges have to rely on their imagination of how it felt to be involved in the sessions or on their own experience of the events (i.e., how they felt observing it). Empirical research has found low correlations among the perspectives on various measures (e.g., Caracena & Vicory, 1969; Fish, 1970; Hansen, Moore, & Carkhuff, 1968; Hill, 1974; Hill, Helms, Tichenor, et al., 1988; Kurtz & Grummon, 1972; Tichenor & Hill, 1989; Truax, 1966), supporting the view that the therapy experience varies for people in different roles in the therapy process.

The Unit Studied. Measures that focus on specific moment-by-moment experiences in units such as single words, phrases, sentences, speaking turns, and thought units can be considered *microprocess measures.* Microprocess measures have been used primarily by judges, although some researchers have asked clients and therapists to review tapes of sessions and to evaluate events within sessions (e.g., Elliott, 1986). In contrast, measures that focus globally on larger units such as sessions or treatments can be considered *macroprocess measures.* These macroprocess measures typically use questionnaires administered immediately after therapy sessions or treatments. About half of the process measures used in studies in *JCP* and *JCCP* between 1978 and 1992 involved microprocess and half involved macroprocess (Hill, Nutt, & Jackson, 1994). Units can be arranged in a hierarchy: Words, phrases, sentences, thought units, and speaking turns are embedded in therapeutic episodes, which are embedded in the therapeutic relationship, which is embedded in the client's life outside of treatment (Greenberg, 1986; Shoham-Salomon, 1990).

Researchers need to think carefully about which unit they use, so that the unit fits the construct. For example, Ekman and Friesen (1968) noted that, although nonverbal behaviors are usually measured in predetermined time units (e.g., five seconds), they do not necessarily fall into these units. Bordin et al. (1954) noted that assessing transference in a small, standard unit would destroy its essence, given that it occurs over long periods of time, but that smaller units may be needed for variables such as level of involvement that are more fleeting.

In addition, Marmar (1990) suggested that predetermined standard units have yielded little clinical information because context is ignored. In this regard, Knapp (1974) recommended demarcation of units when there is a change in some pattern. Bordin et al. (1954) warned, however, that reliability of identifying the unit is often quite low when units are defined based on meaning. Fiske (1977) noted that judgments of behavior are often less reliable with longer units because of fluctuation in behavior within units.

Widely different units have been used to study the same constructs. For example, in judging therapist intentions, Hill and O'Grady (1985) used a unit of a therapist speaking turn (all therapist speech between two client speeches), which occurs approximately once a minute. Horvath, Marx, and Kamann (1990), in contrast, allowed therapists to choose their own unit by indicating during a postsession videotape review whenever their intentions changed, which averaged about six to eight minutes. When the tape is stopped every six to eight minutes, participants combine a lot of information into their judgments, losing information about specific interventions.

A few researchers have investigated the effects on the results of different units of analysis. Kiesler, Mathieu, and Klein (1967) found that longer segments received higher ratings on the Experiencing Scale, but that reliabilities were equal across 2-, 4-, 8-, and 16-minute segments. Using the Therapist and Patient Action Checklists (Hoyt, Marmar, Horowitz, & Alvarez, 1981), Weiss, Marmar, and Horowitz (1988) found no differences between ratings of the first half of sessions compared to ratings of entire sessions. Using several process measures and data sets, Friedlander, Ellis, Siegel, Raymond, and Haase (1988) tested whether different lengths of excerpts and different starting points within sessions affected the ratings of judges. Results indicated that generalizing from any size segment to a whole session could not be done when interviews were examined individually. When interviews are aggregated across several cases, however, even small segments could be representative of whole sessions, probably because of the large variability of behavior across individuals.

In sum, it appears that the unit used can influence the results obtained. Researchers need to investigate the effects of different units for their particular measure. In general, the unit chosen needs to match the construct. Furthermore, the unit often needs to be considered in context.

TYPE OF MEASUREMENT. Interval scales, nominal category systems, and Q sorts are the types of measurement that have been used most frequently in process research. Interval rating scales can be used either by participants (after sessions) or by nonparticipant observers (judges) to rate either microprocess or macroprocess. Interval rating scales typically use five-, seven-, or nine-point Likert-type scales, although some researchers use even-numbered scales to force a decision toward one extreme of the scale or the other. Examples include the Working Alliance Inventory (Horvath & Greenberg, 1989) and the Experiencing Scale (Klein, Mathieu-Coughlan, & Kiesler, 1986). Interval rating scales are advantageous from a data analytic viewpoint because researchers can average data across judges and across data points. For example, an average score of "depth" can be calculated across all judges for a single interpretation and across all interpretations within a session (Harway, Dittman, Raush, Bordin, & Rigler, 1955). Unfortunately, many process variables do not fit the assumptions necessary for interval data in that there is not an equal difference between points on the scale, nor are some points "better than" other points. Furthermore, Coombs (1951) and Bordin et al. (1954) noted that rating scales often force data into unidimensional continua even when a single dimension does not exist. For example, the Experiencing Scale (Klein et al., 1986) involves more than a single dimension, making it difficult to determine whether a high score on the scale reflects high client, experiencing, involvement, or insight.

In nominal category systems, data are classified into categories, such that judgments are made about the presence or absence of target behaviors. Categories can be either mutually exclusive or nonmutually exclusive. In a mutually exclusive system, only one category can apply for any given behavior or observation. For example, with the Helping Skills System (Hill & O'Brien, 1999), judges assign one skill to each therapist response unit (sentence). In a nonmutually exclusive system, more than one category or item can apply for a given behavior or observation. For example, in using the Intentions List (Hill & O'Grady, 1985), therapists assign up to three intentions to each therapist speaking turn (during a videotape-assisted review of the session) because therapists often have more than one intention when delivering interventions. With nonmutually exclusive categories, definitions need to be as distinct as possible so that categories can be distinguished. Lack of separateness between categories can be determined by noting whether judges always assign the same categories together. An advantage of using nominal category systems is that they often reflect the phenomenon more accurately (i.e., we can determine presence or absence but not intensity). A disadvantage is that judgments cannot be averaged across judges (e.g., if two people say that a therapist response is an interpretation and two others say that it is a reflection of feelings, this discrepancy cannot be resolved except by discussion to determine which response mode is most "accurate").

Another type of scaling is the Q-sort method, in which participants or judges sort items about the therapy process into a number of categories in a forced distribution across a rating scale. For example, with Jones et al.'s (1988) Psychotherapy Process Q-Set, judges sort 100 items relative to each other according to their salience in describing a session. Judges use a normal distribution with 5, 8, 12, 16, 18, 16, 12, 8, and 5 items in categories 1–9 (1 = least characteristic, 5 = neutral or irrelevant, 9 = most characteristic), respectively, and then convert the data to an interval rating scale based on the category used. Jones et al. (1988) indicated that this method can capture the uniqueness of each therapy case as well as the similarities or dissimilarities of one case to another. The advantage of the Q-sort method is that it forces a distribution across a scale, compared to rating scales that generally elicit only positive ratings. The disadvantage is that Q-sorts impose a particular distribution on the items.

LEVEL OF INFERENCE REQUIRED. Measures vary in the amount of inference required to complete them. On the noninferential end, the respondent bases judgments on observable behaviors, with minimal inference about states or intentions (e.g., head nods; Hill & Stephany, 1990). On the inferential end, respondents make inferences about the speaker's intention or internal state based on observable behavior (e.g., dynamic motive states such as dependency or hostility; Dollard & Auld, 1959). A noninferential strategy tends to result in higher interjudge reliability than an inferential strategy because variables are operationally defined and rely on observation rather than inference.

Stimulus Materials Required. Respondents can make judgments about therapy sessions from different stimuli: live sessions (either as participated in or observed), transcript, audiotape, videotape, or some combination. Clients and therapists typically respond to their own memory of experiences in sessions in providing evaluations, although tapes of sessions are sometimes replayed so that clients and therapists can respond to specific parts of sessions. The majority of the theory and research about stimulus materials has been about judges, so the remainder of this section will apply only to judges.

In the process studies published that used judges, Hill, Nutt, and Jackson (1994) found that 29%, 20%, 33%, and 16% of those published in *JCP* and 45%, 12%, 32%, and 5% of those published in *JCCP*, respectively, used audiotape only, videotape only, transcript only, or some combination of tape and transcript. Bordin et al. (1954) noted that using either audiotape or videotape is necessary for variables that depend on nonlinguistic factors such as tone of voice or emphasis on different words. Lambert, DeJulio, and Stein (1978) advocated videotapes, however, because they noted that audiotapes are not sensitive to nonverbal and behavioral cues.

Several studies have examined the effects of different forms of stimulus materials. Shapiro (1968) found that audio-only and video-only ratings of facilitative conditions were correlated with the audio-video ratings but not with each other. Weiss (1979) found that judges' descriptions of personality traits were less differentiated when made from written materials than from personal contact. Waxer (1981) found that judgments of anxiety depended on nonverbal cues present in audio and video materials. McDaniel, Stiles, and McGaughey (1981) obtained higher interjudge reliability for verbal response modes using transcripts rather than audiotapes. Tracey and Guinee (1990) found that a transcript-only mode resulted in lower reliability than videotape, audiotape, videotape plus transcript, or audiotape plus transcript on the Interpersonal Communications Rating Scale. Weiss, Marmar, and Horowitz (1988) reported that more reliable ratings were made with audio/visual cues than with only audio cues on the Therapist and Patient Action Checklists (Hoyt et al., 1981). They speculated that watching videotapes holds raters' attention better and concluded that having more channels of information leads to higher reliability because raters make fewer inferences about intention, affect, and interaction.

Ideally, researchers would use videotapes accompanied by transcripts so that the judges could have nonverbal cues and accurate content from which to make judgments. We recognize that it is not always possible to use both videotapes and transcripts, but do suggest that if this is not done, researchers need to discuss the limitations of not using videotapes and transcripts on the validity of the measure and interjudge reliability.

Validity of Process Measures

Researchers need to provide evidence for the validity (e.g., face, content, construct, convergent, discriminant, predictive) of all measures used in process research to show that measures assess what we want them to assess. Face validity means that on the surface the items seem to measure the underlying construct. Content validity means that the items measure the content inherent in the construct. Face and content validity can be obtained by developing items similar to those used in past measures of the same construct, assuming that these items measure the appropriate content of interest. Face and content validity can also be obtained from experts from a range of orientations, who give feedback about the clarity and completeness of the measure after examining or using the instrument. Face and content validity are important to establish in the preliminary phases of measure development.

Construct validity (evidence that the scores reflect the desired construct) can only be established indirectly through factor analyses as well as through evidence of convergent (high correlations with related measures), discriminant (low correlations with unrelated measures), and predictive (results in the expected findings when used) validity. An example of convergent validity is Elliott et al.'s (1987) finding of high agreement among judges for six specific verbal response modes (question, information, advisement, reflection, interpretation, and self-disclosure) across six different measures of therapist response modes. Similarly, Tichenor and Hill (1989) found that three of four measures of judge-rated working alliance were highly related. An example of discriminant validity is that ratings on the Experiencing Scale were not significantly related to client activity level (Kiesler, Mathieu, & Klein, 1967). An example of predictive validity is that therapists have been found to use response modes in ways that fit their stated theoretical orientations (Elliott et al., 1987; Hill, Thames, & Rardin, 1979; Stiles, 1979; Stiles, Shapiro, & Firth-Cozens, 1988; Strupp, 1955, 1957).

Reliability of Process Measures

Reliability of the Measure Itself. For participant-rated self-report measures involving several items using interval rating scales, researchers need to provide information about reliability of the measure (e.g., internal consistency, split-half reliability). It is important to note that reliability for one-item measures is typically very low (Heppner, Kivlighan, & Wampold, 1999). Test-retest reliability is seldom reported because we would not expect stability across time in process variables (e.g., perceptions of working alliance would change over time).

For nominal category systems, cluster analyses (Borgen & Barnett, 1987) can be used to assess reliability. Alternatively, researchers can examine the overlaps between judges using a confusion matrix. For example, when two of three judges agreed on a therapist response mode category, Hill, Thames, and Rardin (1979) charted the category assigned by the third judge to determine which categories overlapped. Using either of these methods, researchers can determine categories that are difficult for judges to distinguish. Researchers might combine categories with high overlap and cluster categories that have moderate overlap (to keep conceptually similar categories together).

Reliability of Unitization. Reliability of unitization becomes an issue when the scoring unit is not automatic (such as five-minute segments) but requires some inference by raters. Rules for unitizing speech into sentences have been presented by Auld and White (1956) and modified by Hill and O'Brien (1999). Rules for segmenting narratives (stories) were presented by Angus, Levitt, and Hardtke (1999). Although words, phrases, and sentences are relatively easy to determine, longer units such as thought units and events are more difficult to determine reliably. Lower reliability should not necessarily discourage researchers from using thought units, however, because they are often clinically meaningful and relevant for some measures.

Interjudge Reliability. If judges are used, some assessment of interjudge agreement is needed. For measures involving interval rating scales, reliability among judges often is determined through some form of intraclass correlation (Shrout & Fleiss, 1979). A fixed-effects model yields an estimate of the reliability of a single or mean rating of a particular sample of raters and reflects the degree of consistency in a specific set of ratings. A random-effects model provides an estimate of the reliability of a single or mean rating that might be obtained with an independent sample of raters and represents the generalizability of the mean rating. If raters have been chosen nonrandomly because of certain characteristics, a fixed-effects model should be used. If raters have been chosen at random out of a larger population (even a population with specified characteristics) and the researcher wishes to generalize the results to the larger population of raters, a random-effects model should be chosen. Note that we generally assume that we have picked raters randomly and that another set of raters will yield similar results; so we would most often use a random effects model. Researchers should be aware, however, that random-effects models tend to yield lower estimates of reliability than fixed-effects models because higher order interactions are included in the error term and larger error terms yield less significance.

In using intraclass correlation, variance due to unrelated factors ideally needs to be partialed out, so that the result obtained is a reflection of interrater agreement rather than an inflation due to other effects (Finn, 1974). For example, when applying an intraclass correlation to determine interrater reliability for the Collaborative Study Psychotherapy Rating Scale for the NIMH Treatment of Depression Collaborative Research Program, Hill, O'Grady, and Elkin (1992) partialed out modality of treatment, therapist, client, session, site, and all possible two-way interactions between these variables, yielding an estimate of interrater reliability not confounded by these extraneous variables (although there may have been other variables that influenced the results). For intraclass correlations, 0.70 is generally considered a standard cutoff for high reliability (with higher estimates expected for judgments requiring low inference) (Heppner et al., 1999).

As an alternative to intraclass correlations, some researchers (Cronbach, Gleser, Nanda, & Rajaratnam, 1972; Gottman & Markman, 1978; Hoyt & Melby, 1999; Mitchell, 1979) have suggested that reliability and validity can be combined within the concept of generalizability. The idea of generalizability theory is to partition the total variance in a study into those facets across which one wants to generalize. As an example in assessing reliability across judges, researchers would obtain the rating of a particular item by independent judges across clients and therapists. Good reliability would mean that the total variance in this repeated measures model is mostly attributable to variation across clients and therapists rather than across judges or the interaction between judges and clients or therapists. In this method, reliability is an assessment of the work one wants the system to do (e.g., discriminate among therapists and clients) rather than a claim of no differences between judges.

For nominal category systems, the kappa statistic has become a standard in the field (Cohen, 1960; Tinsley & Weiss, 1975). Kappa is essentially the percent agreement after correcting for chance agreement. It can be computed for all the categories in a measure, or it can be computed for individual categories compared to the remainder of the categories. A weighted kappa (Cohen, 1968) can be used if some disagreements are more serious than others (e.g., disagreements outside a cluster of categories might be considered more serious than disagreements within a cluster). A caution is that kappa assumes an approximately equal distribution of data across categories. Thus, if most of the data fall into one or two out of several categories, the kappas can be artificially low. In this case, percentage agreement can be reported along with kappa. In general, kappas are lower than intraclass correlations, so the two figures are not directly comparable. Fleiss (1981) suggested that <0.40 is poor agreement; between 0.40 and 0.75 is fair-to-good agreement; and >0.75 is strong agreement. When researchers expect to obtain kappas less than 0.75, they should use more than two judges, so that the data across judges can be pooled and a better approximation of the "true" categorization can be obtained.

Consistency of Target Behavior. Researchers sometimes want to know whether the target behavior is consistent across various time periods (e.g., is therapist empathy stable or variable?). Consistency of behavior can be determined by examining random subdivisions of the data, such as odd- and even-numbered minutes or sessions, in a manner analogous to split-half reliability of a standardized test (Mitchell, 1979).

Unit for Determining Reliability. Kiesler (1973) and Mitchell (1979) noted that interjudge agreement should be presented for the "summarizing unit" used for the data analysis. Thus, if the scoring unit is the sentence but the data is reported for the whole session (e.g., 15% of therapist responses in sessions are restatements), they suggested that the reliability presented should be for the session rather than the sentence. Although agreement levels are needed only for the summarizing unit in the analyses, we recommend that researchers report agreement levels for both the scoring and summarizing units so that other researchers can be aware of problems with measures.

Limits of Relying Too Much on Reliability Estimates. Before ending this section on reliability, we must note that high reliability (>0.70) is not always necessary. Cartwright (1966) lamented that too many studies have been guided by a sheer fascination with counting at the expense of counting meaningful things; she also noted that it is an error to equate "scientific" with "reliable and quantitative." Many variables of clinical interest require inference, often resulting in low interjudge reliability. Researchers need to balance reliability, validity, and clinical relevance. Researchers might consider using qualitative strategies (such as consensus among a number of judges) instead of reliability estimates for variables that require high clinical inference (see section in this chapter on Qualitative Process Research).

Choice of Measures

After thinking through what type of measure they are interested in, researchers have to choose an existing measure or create a new measure. Kiesler (1973) and Garfield (1990) noted that many researchers develop a measure and then never use it again. Similarly, Hill, Nutt, and Jackson (1994) found that 38% and 49% of the process measures used in studies in *JCP* and *JCCP* during 1978 to 1992 were new measures developed just for those studies. Although we recognize that researchers sometimes need to develop new measures because existing measures do not reflect the dimensions of interest, it is difficult to accumulate knowledge across studies using different measures. We recommend that when possible, researchers use psychometrically sound existing measures if they fit the researcher's theoretical conceptualization. For example, we do not really need new measures of therapist verbal response modes for individual therapy, given that over 30 measures exist, and Elliott et al. (1987) found a fair amount of overlap among several of the existing systems.

In the next section, we present the measures that have been used most often in recent years, based on Hill, Nutt, and Jackson's (1994) review of studies published in *JCP* and *JCCP* during 1978–1992 (See Table 4.2). We classify these measures in terms of the focus of evaluation because this is typically the most salient dimension (along with aspect of process) for researchers in choosing a measure. For a more extended review of several common process measures, see the influential volumes by Kiesler (1973) and Greenberg and Pinsof (1986).

Measures that Focus on the Therapist. Therapist expertness, attractiveness, and trustworthiness (i.e., social influence) have been assessed by

TABLE 4.2 Most Frequently Used Process Measures

Construct Assessed	Measure	Perspective
	Measures Focusing on Therapists	
Social influence	Counselor Rating Form (Corrigan & Schmidt, 1983; LaCrosse & Barak, 1976)	C
Facilitative conditions	Barrett-Lennard Relationship Inventory (Barrett-Lennard, 1962)	C, T, J
	Empathy, genuineness, and respect scales (Carkhuff, 1969; Truax & Carkhuff, 1967)	J
Techniques	Hill Counselor Verbal Response Category System (Hill, 1986)	J
	Hill Counselor Verbal Response Category System—Revised (Friedlander, 1982)	J
	Helper Behavior Rating System (Elliott, 1979)	J
	Verbal Response Modes (Stiles, 1979, 1992)	J
Intentions	Therapist Intentions List (Hill & O'Grady, 1985)	T
Helpfulness of interventions	Helpfulness Scale (Elliott, 1985)	C, T
Nonverbal behaviors	Behavior Rating Form (Lee, Halberg, Kocsis, & Haase, 1980)	C, T
	Measures Focusing on Clients	
Experiencing	Experiencing Scale (Klein et al., 1970; Klein et al., 1986)	J
Behavior	Verbal Response Modes (Hill et al., 1981)	J
	Verbal Response Modes (Stiles, 1979, 1992)	J
	Hill Interaction Matrix (W. F. Hill, 1971)	J
Reactions	Client Reactions System (Hill et al., 1988)	C
	Measures Focusing on Therapist and Client	
Process	Vanderbilt Psychotherapy Process Scale (O'Malley et al., 1983)	J
	Vanderbilt Negative Indicators Scale (Strupp et al., 1981)	J
Control and dominance	Topic Initiation/Topic Following (Tracey, 1985)	J
	Relational Communication Control Coding System (Ericson & Rogers, 1973)	J
	Structural Analysis of Social Behavior (Benjamin, 1979)	J
	Interpersonal Communication Rating Scale (Strong & Hills, 1986)	J
Alliance	Working Alliance Inventory (Horvath & Greenberg, 1989)	C, T, J
	Couple/Family Therapeutic Alliance Scale (Pinsof & Catherall, 1986)	C
	Group Environment Scale (Moos, 1981)	C

Note. For perspective, C = client, T = therapist, J = judge. Data for this table comes from Hill, Nutt, & Williams (1994); the measures listed were the most frequently used in the *Journal of Counseling Psychology* and the *Journal of Consulting and Clinical Psychology* during 1978 to 1992.

clients and therapists after sessions using the Counselor Rating Form (Corrigan & Schmidt, 1983; LaCrosse & Barak, 1976). Therapist facilitative conditions have been assessed by clients, therapists, and judges after sessions using the Barrett-Lennard Relationship Inventory (Barrett-Lennard, 1962), and by judges rating taped segments of sessions using either the Carkhuff (1969) or Truax and Carkhuff (1967) scales of empathy, genuineness, and respect. Therapist techniques have been measured for sentences in transcripts of sessions using four different measures of verbal response modes (Elliott, 1979; Friedlander, 1982; Hill, 1986; Stiles, 1979, 1992). Covert behaviors were assessed by therapists during reviews of taped sessions using the Therapist Intentions List (Hill & O'Grady, 1985). Helpfulness of interventions has been judged by clients and therapists during reviews of taped sessions using the Helpfulness Rating Scale (Elliott, 1985). The nonverbal behaviors of therapists from the client and therapist perspectives were measured with the Behavior Rating Form (Lee, Hallberg, Kocsis, Haase, 1980).

MEASURES THAT FOCUS ON THE CLIENT. Client overt behavior has been measured most often through the Experiencing Scale (Klein et al., 1970; Klein, Mathieu-Coughlan, & Kiesler, 1986), which judges use to rate small units (e.g., speaking turns, five-minute segments) of taped sessions. Client overt behavior has also been assessed from transcripts of sessions by trained judges using the verbal response modes systems created by Hill, Siegelman, et al. (1981) or Stiles (1979, 1992). In addition, covert client behavior has been assessed by clients during reviews of taped sessions using the Client Reactions System (Hill, Helms, Spiegel, & Tichenor, 1988). Moreover, client behavior in groups has been assessed by trained judges using the Hill Interaction Matrix (W. F. Hill, 1971).

MEASURES WITH A JOINT FOCUS ON THERAPIST AND CLIENT. The Vanderbilt Psychotherapy Process Scale (O'Malley, Suh, & Strupp, 1983) and the Vanderbilt Negative Indicators Scale (Strupp, Moras, et al., 1981) have been used frequently by judges to focus on both client and therapist. In addition, judges have used the following four systems to assess control and dominance in the interaction between client and therapist: Topic initiation/Topic following (Tracey, 1985); the Relational Communication Control Coding System (Ericson & Rogers, 1973); Structural Analysis of Social Behavior (Benjamin, 1979); and the Interpersonal Communication Rating Scale (Strong & Hills, 1986). Clients, therapists, and judges have assessed the alliance after sessions for individual therapy using the Working Alliance Inventory (Horvath & Greenberg, 1989), for couples therapy using the Couple/Family Therapeutic Alliance Scale (Pinsof & Catherall, 1986), and for group therapy using the Group Environment Scale (Moos, 1981).

Data Collection Issues

When properly addressed, procedures can strengthen the results of process research, regardless of the type of process measure used in a study.

CONTROL. Researchers need to have control over data collection to ensure that their data are accurate. Rather than relying on clients and therapists to do the research tasks (which is inappropriate and often unlikely), researchers need to turn on tape recorders, monitor sessions to ensure that participants adhere to instructions, and distribute and collect measures. In addition, if participant-rated process measures that require training are used, participants need to be trained with a simulation of the therapy process prior to participation. Otherwise, there may be a "break-in" period before participants really understand how to use the measures, resulting in a loss of data or the use of inaccurate data. Finally, all data should be checked periodically during completion of tasks for missing data or inaccuracy in completion.

COOPERATION. Participants should not be burdened with having to complete too many measures and procedures. Although participants often learn from their involvement in the research, they may refuse to participate if too much time is required. Furthermore, the more time the research takes, the less generalizable the study is to naturally occurring therapy. Researchers are most likely to gain cooperation by treating therapists and clients as collaborators. If one believes and communicates to participants that they are the best informants of their experiences, a research alliance can be formed that will result in richer, more complete information. On the other hand, researchers need to guard against becoming too involved in the therapy itself, which could intrude on the therapy relationship and so bias the data as to make it less generalizable to actual therapy.

EFFECTS OF TAPING SESSIONS. Many researchers tape sessions so that participants or judges can use the tapes to evaluate the process. More accurate data can be obtained by reviewing tapes of sessions rather than by relying on client or therapist memory of what occurred in sessions (cf. Loftus, 1988, and others who have documented problems with accuracy of memory). Of concern, however, is whether taping (either audio or video) changes the nature of the session. Several early studies from the 1940s and 1950s indicated that there were no adverse effects of audiotaping on clients (see summary in Kiesler, 1973), but later evidence indicated that taping did have some effect on the process of therapy (Gelso, 1973, 1974). Roberts and Renzaglia (1965) found that when taping was introduced, Rogerian therapists behaved in less client-centered ways and clients made more favorable self-reference statements. Despite the fact that there may be some negative effects, Kielser (1973) recommended using tapes over therapist reports because tapes can be reviewed at any time and are accurate representations of the original observable events.

Carmichael (1966) noted that although most clients have no problems with being recorded, therapists are often resistant and reluctant to have others observe them, perhaps fearing damage to their self-esteem. In our research, both therapists and clients often report nervousness in anticipating the taping but generally forget the taping once they get involved in the session.

Effects of Reviewing Sessions. One method of doing process research involves having therapists and/or clients review the audio- or videotape of sessions, usually immediately after sessions (e.g., Elliott, 1984; Hill, 1989). During such reviews, researchers ask participants to remember what they were experiencing during the session. Use of such reviews raises issues about whether anticipation of the review changes sessions, whether participants can report accurately what they were feeling and thinking during the time of the session itself, and whether the review itself intrudes on or facilitates the subsequent therapy process.

Some studies have addressed issues related to concerns about reviews. Katz and Resnikoff (1977) found moderate correlations between live ratings of comfort or discomfort and ratings recalled during videotape simulation. Similarly, Hill, O'Grady et al. (1994) found high consistency for client and therapist helpfulness ratings, therapist intentions, and client reactions obtained during sessions and those obtained during videotape-assisted reviews of sessions. Hill et al. ruled out that the high consistency was due to participants remembering their in-session evaluations. These results support the validity of using videotape-assisted reviews as a means of assessing in-session experiences.

Hill, O'Grady et al. (1994) also found that, for both clients and therapist, positive mood increased from pre- to postsession but regressed back to presession levels after the tape-assisted review. This finding suggests that participating in tape-assisted reviews dampens the positive feelings gained from therapy. Hence, researchers may want to be cautious about doing too many tape-assisted reviews. Moreover, Hill, O'Grady et al. found that therapists evaluated sessions more negatively after the videotaped-assisted reviews than they had immediately after the sessions. Similarly, Walz and Johnston (1963) found that therapist assessment of their own performance tended to decrease after self-observation. Therapists seem to get anxious and self-critical when they observe themselves. Hence, evaluations of sessions should be done immediately after sessions rather than after tape-assisted reviews to make the evaluations comparable to those obtained immediately after sessions that are not reviewed.

Transcribing Sessions. Transcripts of therapy sessions are often necessary when judges need to have the verbal content to make judgments. Transcripts provide accurate depictions of the verbal process, ensuring that the judges respond to similar verbal stimuli. Furthermore, transcripts allow researchers to reliably divide the session into meaningful units, which often enhances subsequent reliability of process judgments because judges are then more likely to be evaluating the same material. Mergenthaler and Stinson (1992) developed standards for preparing transcripts, providing common symbols for spelling, pauses, paraverbal and nonverbal utterances, incomplete utterances, and punctuation.

Sampling Data from Therapy. Researchers need to think about how much and what part of the therapy needs to be rated or categorized to generalize to the entire treatment. Examining the whole course of therapy would be ideal but is often financially and practically unfeasible. Thus, the question becomes how much one needs to sample to obtain a representative portion of the treatment.

Kiesler (1973) indicated that sampling within sessions and sampling sessions across the course of therapy are separate issues. Regarding the former, Kiesler, Klein, and Mathieu (1965) found that neurotic clients showed a consistently upward trend of experiencing during a therapy hour, schizophrenics showed a sawtooth (i.e., up and down) pattern, and normals showed an inverted U-shaped trend of experiencing. Thus, the sampling decision would affect the data for different diagnostic groups in different ways. Regarding the issue of sampling sessions across the course of treatment, Rogers, Gendlin, Kiesler, and Traux (1967) and Kiesler (1971) showed that experiencing was U-shaped for schizophrenics until about session 20 and then dropped. Given this fluctuation, one could misrepresent the trend across therapy on the Experiencing Scale if only a few points were analyzed. Kiesler (1973) concluded that for the Experiencing Scale, researchers need to sample many points both within and across sessions.

In addition, Beutler, Johnson, Neville, and Workman (1973), Gurman (1973), and Karl and Abeles (1969) found that therapists differed in their behaviors across segments of sessions. Mintz and Luborsky (1971) found that judgments of empathy obtained from brief segments of sessions had low correlations with judgments of whole sessions. Hill, Carter, and O'Farrell (1983), Hill and O'Grady (1985), and O'Farrell, Hill, and Patton (1986) found that therapist and client behavior changed from the first third to the final part of sessions. Because of the fluctuation of process, researchers need to sample enough data from each case to provide a representative sample of process. Researchers also need to check the effects of their sampling strategy on the data that they obtain.

A frequently cited study that used inadequate sampling was Sloan, Staples, Cristol, Yorkston, and Whipple's (1975) comparison of psychoanalytic and behavioral therapists. They used ratings of four 4-minute segments from the fifth session to represent the entire process of therapy. Furthermore, the sampling procedure was peculiar in that behavioral therapists were not sampled randomly from within the hour but were studied when they acted like psychotherapists as opposed to times when they were using behavioral techniques. Not surprisingly, Sloan et al. found few differences between psychoanalytic and behavioral therapists.

The sampling issue needs to be considered within the context of the theoretical framework and design of the particular study (Kiesler, 1973). Thus, the amount that should be sampled depends on the question that one is asking. If one has empirical evidence that a variable occurs consistently across therapy, then only a small portion needs to be sampled. If one suspects, however, that the variable fluctuates across therapy depending on the stage of therapy and the problem being discussed, then larger portions need to be sampled.

One specific problem in terms of sampling involves infrequently occurring events, such as self-disclosure, touching, crying, or laughter, which are of interest to researchers because of their importance in therapy. When studying infrequently occurring events, researchers may need to review a large number of sessions from a variety of therapists to find enough instances of the event. For example, Gervaize, Mahrer, and Markow (1985) previewed 280 hours of therapy to extract 60 instances of strong laughter.

Controlling for Activity Level. In aggregating nominal data across sessions, Marsden, Kalter, and Ericson (1974) suggested that the proportion of each behavior to the total number of behaviors is more appropriate than the raw frequencies because proportions correct for the amount of activity. Thus, therapists who use the same amount of an intervention but differ in their overall activity would have different proportions of that intervention in relation to total utterances. Furthermore, because proportions tend to be skewed, researchers often need to transform them prior to analyses using an arc sine transformation.

Use of Judges

Many process measures rely on judges to evaluate the presence, intensity, and frequency of process events. Fiske (1977) noted that the use of human judges introduces noise and undependability in the data. Judges interpret the data on the basis of their own reactions and hence can be considered to be "two-legged meters." Similarly, Mercer and Loesch (1979) suggested that judges, rather than measures, are the actual measuring instruments. Thus, the measures cannot be considered independently of the judges who use them. Researchers must be aware of how the judgment process influences the data with observer-rated measures.

Number of Judges. The number of judges that should be used for any given measure is directly linked to issues of reliability and validity. If high reliability is expected, fewer judges can be used. But if low reliability is expected, researchers should use more judges because pooling data from several judges increases reliability and heightens the probability of approximating the "true" score.

Many researchers demonstrate minimally adequate reliability on a portion of the data and then proceed with having one judge rate the remainder of the data. This procedure is problematic from a methodological standpoint because this minimal level of reliability indicates that judges often disagree with one another. The use of just one judge could thus yield biased data. In general, it is better to err on the side of too many judges rather than too few. In the extreme, Mahrer, Paterson, Theriault, Roessler, and Quenneville (1986) advocated using 8 to 10 judges of varying orientations to provide higher validity of judgments.

Tsujimoto, Hamilton, and Berger (1990) provide a formula to estimate the gain in validity that is produced when different numbers of judges are used. In general, they noted that adding more judges is similar to adding more items on a self-report measure. They suggested that there is an inherent tradeoff in deciding how many judges to use. Using more judges increases the cost of doing the study but also enhances the expected validity of measurement. In addition, they observed that using more judges sometimes decreases the number of therapy dyads needed to attain a given level of statistical power because composite ratings decrease random error of measurement. Many researchers complain that using multiple judges is expensive or impractical. However true this may be, it is often necessary to employ multiple judges to generate credible data. Methodological shortcuts will, in the long run, be even more expensive because of the confusion that inevitably results in sorting out conflicting data across studies when such shortcuts are taken.

Selection of Judges. The capabilities and qualities of judges can have a profound effect on the validity of ratings and the ultimate expense of process research. Moras and Hill (1991), in a review of the procedures used for selecting judges for process measures, concluded that minimal research has been conducted on the qualities of judges needed for using different instruments. Most researchers simply indicate what type of judges they have used but provide no empirical evidence about the effects of their selection criteria on the data. Kiesler (1973) and Moras and Hill (1991) indicated that the level of clinical experience and/or theoretical sophistication needed by judges is directly related to the amount of inference required by the task. Trained undergraduates can rate highly operationalized variables, such as nonverbal behaviors, and are often desirable as judges for such tasks because they are more likely to attend to what they have been trained to observe rather than being biased by clinical experience (Arnhoff, 1954; Cronbach, 1960). Experienced clinicians, however, are generally required for more abstract constructs that require clinical expertise, such as transference or working alliance. Experienced clinicians are often difficult to train, however, especially when they have set beliefs about definitions of constructs and they rely on theoretical biases to judge behavior rather than on their observations of phenomena. Determining who the best judges are is somewhat circular because there is a problem of deciding who is qualified to determine whether judges are accurate (Mercer & Loesch, 1979). Nevertheless, specific selection criteria for judges for particular measures can go a long way toward increasing reliable, if not valid, judgments.

Several selection criteria have been suggested. Mercer and Loesch (1979) indicated that intelligence and unimpaired interpersonal skills are helpful in the development of valid rating skills. Furthermore, most process researchers value judges who are attentive to detail, yet not so compulsive that they cannot make decisions about gray areas. Judges who ask questions are also valued because questions help to clarify the concepts involved. Moreover, judges must be able to "buy" into the system that is being used even though it may not match their thinking style. Thus, someone who can point out the imperfections thoughtfully but can still work within the system is a desirable judge. Other desirable characteristics are dependability, trustworthiness, and a sense of ethics so that judges can do the task and do it well.

Training Judges. Training can reduce both the influence of contaminating judge characteristics and the influence of idiosyncratic interpretations of items. Training is necessary to draw valid conclusions because researchers never know how untrained judges interpret the meaning of what they are judging (Bachrach, Mintz, & Luborsky, 1971; Caracena & Vicory, 1969; Klein & Cleary, 1967; Mercer & Loesch, 1979). Thus, training can increase the similarity with which different judges approach the judgment task.

Researchers need to be careful, however, to use training to sensitize judges to the phenomena and not just to catch phrases (Bordin et al., 1954). For example, judges using the Carkhuff (1969) empathy scale were sometimes told that open questions should be rated as a 2.5 and reflections of feelings as a 3.0. Such practices increase reliability but reduce the validity of the judgment process.

Mercer and Loesch (1979) described two types of training: informal and formal. In both methods, judges are given copies of the measure, definitions of scales or categories, and tape segments to practice on. In the informal method, they practice making independent judgments on a data set other than the one used for the current study and discuss discrepancies until they reach consensus among themselves. In contrast, the goal of the formal method is to train judges to high agreement with a standard (calibrated) set of judgments of expert judges. The advantage of the formal method is that judges are trained to some standard within the field and are more likely to produce replicable judgments across trainers and sites. Unfortunately, most widely used process measures are not accompanied by such standard sets of judgments, so it is often not possible to do formal training. In both the informal and formal training methods, trainers need to be experts in the system. They should preferably have been trained by the developer of the measure or by people with demonstrated proficiency in using the measure to ensure that they train judges to use the measure as it was intended to be used.

During training, trainees should be trained until they really understand the construct that they are judging. Furthermore, they need to be given examples covering a wide range of levels of the dimension on which they are being trained (Mercer & Loesch, 1979) so that they become aware of the universe of possibilities about the target behaviors (e.g., what does very empathic or unempathic look like?). Use of "flat data" (segments representing a narrow range of levels) may lead judges to make discriminations where none should be made. Training with a wide range of examples is particularly important when there is minimal variation in the data used for the study.

Trainers also need to be aware of the social influence processes that are at work among judges. One judge sometimes dominates the process and persuades other judges to adopt his or her opinion, a problem that is exacerbated when the rating team possesses different levels of power. To handle this problem, trainees should make their initial judgments independently before interacting with the other judges. Furthermore, the order of reporting and defending judgments should be alternated in discussions among the judges to reduce the input of dominant individuals. Every judge needs to feel that his or her opinions are important. Thorough discussion helps judges sort through their thinking processes, solidify their rationales, and increase their understanding of the measure.

Kiesler (1973) noted that the amount of training required of judges varies directly with how clearly the variables are defined and how much inference is required in the judgment task. The more abstract the judgments, the longer the training will need to be to achieve desired levels of reliability.

While being trained and doing ratings, judges should not be aware of the hypotheses being studied. Judges will be aware of the variable they are judging but should not be aware of hypotheses about how that variable relates to other variables. For example, in the Hill and Stephany (1990) study, judges coded nonverbal behavior but were not informed that the researchers were relating nonverbal behavior to client reactions. After a study is completed, however, judges can be informed about the hypotheses of the study. Debriefing also provides a good opportunity for the researcher to learn from the judges about problems with measures and the judgment process.

Assigning Judges to Data. If not all judges will be rating every piece of data, members of teams should be rotated so that the error associated with each judge gets spread around. A randomized incomplete block design (Fleiss, 1981) is a useful way to rotate judges so that each person judges the same number of sessions of each type (e.g., each therapist, client, agency, etc.).

In addition, different teams of judges should be used to judge each construct in order to avoid confounding between the construct and the judges. When the same judges evaluate different dimensions, the validities of the ratings on any one dimension are contingent upon the abilities of the judges to differentiate among the dimensions (Mercer & Loesch, 1979). For example, Muehlberg, Pierce, and Drasgow (1969) found that judges were not able to distinguish between different facilitative conditions.

Judgment Task. All data should be judged independently by judges prior to discussion, with judges being given as much time as necessary to make their decisions (Rogers et al., 1967). Hence, it is often best for judges to make their judgments independently (i.e., not in a group) so that they do not feel pressured by other judges. After making the judgments independently, they come together as a team to discuss discrepancies. Reliability should be calculated on the independent judgments (which are then pooled for data analyses). Reliability for the independent judgments of actual data needs to be reported in addition to the reliability obtained during training. Mercer and Loesch (1979) noted that some studies have failed to report interjudge reliability, and others have reported reliability as established by researchers in other studies. Both procedures are clearly inadequate for determining the agreement levels for the set of judges used for a particular study.

In cases where judgments cover a long span of time (e.g., 15 minutes or an entire session), an issue arises regarding how to make the judgments. In one method, judges make global, relatively subjective judgments based on listening to or watching the entire segment. In a second method, they make tallies of each occurrence of each item and then use their judgment to decide how many tallies are needed to make a particular rating. Weiss et al. (1988) found that the tally method was superior to the global rating method for ratings on the Therapist and Patient Action Checklists (Hoyt et al., 1981). They concluded that the less inference needed, the better the judgments. Furthermore, keeping tallies or writing notes is a useful means of keeping judges alert and involved with the task.

NEED FOR CONTEXT FOR JUDGMENTS. Some controversy has arisen over whether to present segments to judges randomly or sequentially as they occur within the therapy. Bozarth and Krauft (1972) found that random presentation of segments produced greater independence between ratings than sequential presentation. When coding nonverbal behaviors (e.g., Hill, Siegelman, Gronsky, Sturniolo, & Fretz, 1981; Hill & Stephany, 1990), the sound is often also deleted so that judges are not influenced by the verbal content of the session.

We agree with the recommendation for random presentation of segments when judgments require no knowledge of context (e.g., nonverbal behavior) but not when knowledge of the context of what occurred previously in the therapy is needed to make judgments. For example, in Heatherington's (1989) measure of relational control, context is necessary for judges to be able to determine whether or not a question reflects dominant behavior. Similarly, judges need to know what has transpired between the therapist and client up until the point where they judge the depth of an interpretation (Harway et al., 1955) and empathy (Carkhuff, 1969). Messer, Tishby, and Spillman (1992) demonstrated the need for context in ratings of client progress as well as treatment plan compatibility and quality of therapist interventions.

In other cases, context does not seem to make a difference. Schoeninger, Klein, and Mathieu (1967) found no differences for client experiencing ratings when therapist speech was or was not included. Bordin et al. (1954) examined the effects of context of judgments as to whether the therapist stayed within the client's frame of reference. Judges were presented with either the entire transcript or just the therapist responses (in either the correct sequence or random sequence). They reported the "embarrassing results" (p. 81) that different contexts were a negligible source of variance in the agreement among judges. They suggested that ratings were independent of client verbalization or that judges may have relied on stylized phrases such as "You feel" to determine whether therapists stayed with the client's frame of reference. Hence, each researcher needs to establish whether context is needed for accuracy when using a particular measure.

If the scoring unit (the entity that is actually rated or coded) and the contextual unit (the portion of the interview that is considered when one judges the scoring unit) differ, it is important for researchers to specify differences in the publication (Kiesler, 1973). The contextual unit could be the same as the scoring unit (e.g., the Experiencing Scale often is used with five-minute excerpts), or it could be considerably larger than the scoring unit (e.g., when categorizing therapist response modes, judges read the entire transcript leading up to the unit.)

MAINTAINING MORALE AMONG JUDGES. Judges need to feel that what they are doing is important and that their contributions are valued. To obtain cooperation, researchers need to make the task as meaningful as possible. Having judges read about the topic (as long as they do not reveal the hypotheses of the study) and talk about therapy can be useful ways to involve the judges in the scientific endeavor. Researchers should also spend time with the judges talking about their reactions to the task, so that they know when the judges are bored or unhappy.

Drifts of Judgments. Judges are typically very conscientious initially, but judgments often become less reliable (i.e., drift) as familiarity increases and routines become established. Judges may make assumptions about the data, become less attuned to nuances, or make snap judgments after listening to small segments. Moreover, once a judgment is made, judges may listen only for evidence that confirms their viewpoint rather than assessing disconfirming evidence. In addition, judges may be more accurate when they think their behavior is being checked or monitored (Mitchell, 1979; Reid, 1970; Romanczyk, Kent, Diament, & O'Leary, 1973; Taplin & Reid, 1973). Researchers need to keep meeting with judges after training to maintain group morale, reduce drift, and prevent judges from developing idiosyncratic ways of interpreting items.

Bias. Bias occurs when judges are unable to make totally objective judgments. Fiske (1977) suggested that judgments are affected by judges' interpretation of the words used in categories or rating scales, reactions to the task of rating therapists and clients, past experiences, and mental processes as they recall past experiences and relate them to the present judgment task. In addition, variables such as mood, attitude, and personality characteristics might interfere with the ability to be objective, particularly with measures that involve inference.

Defining bias is a difficult issue, however, because, as mentioned earlier, we often have no criteria for the accuracy or validity of the judgments. After struggling with these issues in our own research, we defined bias for interval data as a deviation from the mean score of several judges, given the assumption that the mean score approximated the "true score" (Hill, O'Grady, & Price, 1988; Mahalik, Hill, O'Grady, & Thompson, 1993). For examining the bias of judges using categorical systems, Mahrer et al. (1986) examined the number of times a particular judge selected a category when the majority did not select that category.

Some studies have been conducted on bias. Hill et al. (1988) found no evidence of bias for judges on highly operationalized indices of therapist adherence to treatment manuals, but they found that judges were influenced on ratings of therapist facilitative conditions by how similar they judged themselves to be to the participants. Mahalik et al. (1993) found that perceived similarity as well as judges' personality characteristics (dominance, sociability) influenced ratings of therapist and client affiliation. Hill, O'Grady et al. (1994) found an effect of presession mood on postsession process ratings. When clients felt positive before sessions, they rated the session process more positive. In contrast, when therapists felt negatively before sessions, they rated the session process more negatively.

Reliability estimates could be improved by selecting judges who are homogeneous on whatever personality dimensions affect ratings on a given scale. Unfortunately, however, we usually do not know which personality dimensions will influence ratings on different measures. Moreover, if homogeneous groups of judges are selected, the validity of the data will be compromised because judgments would only reflect the opinions of that type of judge rather than being representative of all judges.

One solution to the bias problem is to select a large group of judges at random and thereby obtain a range on the "problematic" personality characteristics. Researchers could then statistically remove variance due to judge characteristics when conducting the analysis (cf. Mahalik et al., 1993), although removing all of the bias is probably never possible. Unfortunately, this solution is costly because it requires many judges.

Other types of judgment errors that have been identified in performance appraisal ratings in industrial psychology (Latham & Wexley, 1981; Saal, Downey, & Lahey, 1980) need to be investigated in psychotherapy process research. In addition to the perceived similarity error discussed earlier, these authors mention (1) halo, a judge's failure to discriminate among conceptually distinct and potentially independent aspects of a ratee's behavior; (2) leniency, a tendency to rate higher than the midpoint, (3) severity, a tendency to rate lower than the midpoint, (4) central tendency, a tendency to rate at the midpoint with a consequent restriction in range; (5) contrast effect, a tendency for a judge to evaluate a ratee relative to the last person rated rather than relative to the universe of possibilities, and (6) first-impression rating, the tendency to make an initial judgment and then not change based on subsequent information. Latham and Wexley (1981) and Saal et al. (1980) provide ways to analyze whether these types of errors exist and to train judges not to commit them.

Data Aggregation Across Judges. For interval data, ratings can be averaged or "pooled" across judges to yield a master rating. For nominal data, one can set an *a priori* criterion for determining a master judgment, such as using the judgment of two out of three judges; when all three judges disagree, they can discuss the judgment until they arrive at a consensus. Alternatively, Mahrer, Markow, Gervaize, and Boulet (1987) used a procedure in which 8 out of 11 judges had to agree. If this level of agreement was not reached, the piece of data was thrown back, mixed with other data, and rerated at a later time. If consensus still was not reached, the data were not used. This approach provides more accurate judgments but results in the loss of important data.

Data Aggregation Across Time. Fiske (1977) raised the issue of which aggregate of data is most representative of the process. One could use the proportion (of nominal data), the average (of interval data), the highest value (for interval data), the predominant judgment (for nominal data), or the value at critical moments. Given that a lot of noise may occur in sessions, the highest value or the value at critical moments may be the best estimate for some measures. For example, Klein et al. (1986) used peak experiencing ratings in segments to describe the highest level attained, Rice and Kerr (1986) gave preference to a focused voice quality when it occured in segments, and Hill, O'Grady, et al. (1992) used the predominant client behavior in speaking turns.

Data Analysis Within Studies

In this section, we cover several approaches that have been used for quantitative process research: descriptive approaches, correlational approaches, sequential analyses, and analyses of patterns.

Descriptive Approaches. In descriptive approaches, researchers simply describe what occurs, often in terms of frequencies or proportions of events. For example, Nagel, Hoffman, and Hill (1995) described the proportions of verbal response modes used by counselors in middle sessions of career counseling.

Correlational Approaches. Many process researchers have used a correlational strategy, in which they relate the frequency or proportion of occurrence of a process variable to some other process variable or to an outcome measure. For example, Sloan et al. (1975) correlated the occurrence of process variables in the fifth session with outcome after therapy. These correlational designs are inadequate because they do not take into account the timing, appropriateness, quality, or context of the process variable (Gottman & Markman, 1978; Hill, 1982; Hill, Helms, Tichenor et al., 1988; Russell & Trull, 1986; Stiles, 1988, 1989; Stiles & Shapiro, 1994). Thus, one moderately deep interpretation given to an introspective client who is pondering why she or he behaves in a particular way may be more helpful than 10 poorly timed interpretations (see Spiegel & Hill, 1989). Furthermore, Stiles (1988) noted that correlational designs fail to account for client needs. Disturbed clients may need more of some interventions but still may end up with poorer outcome, not because the interventions were ineffective but because clients could not use the interventions. Hence, client disturbance level may moderate process-outcome links.

The problem is not so much the correlational design per se as the fact that simplistic frequency (or proportion) data are used in the design. As a demonstration of this perspective, McCullough et al. (1991) found that when they added the client response to the therapist intervention, they were able to demonstrate a meaningful relationship between therapist interpretation and outcome. Although their findings need to be replicated, they suggest that it is not just the quantity of the specific therapist intervention that makes a difference, but how well the client is able to use the therapist intervention that may be related to outcome. A further problem with most correlational designs is that treatment outcome is used rather than more immediate outcome (see next section).

Sequential Analyses. Rather than test process variables in relation to outcome at the end of treatment, as in the traditional correlational approach, several writers have recommended using sequential analyses to study the immediate effects of process events (Bakeman, 1978; Bakeman & Gottman, 1986; Marmar, 1990; Russell & Trull, 1986). Sequential analyses allow researchers to establish the temporal contiguity of the effect in interactive data (e.g., to determine which therapist intentions lead to which client reactions). Sequential analysis is an approach to analyzing interactional data rather than a specific statistical technique (Bakeman & Gottman, 1986). Researchers can use various statistical techniques, such as analysis of variance or loglinear analyses, to test whether different process variables occur together at a level greater than chance. Russell and Trull (1986) noted advances in sequential analyses, such as testing for differences in sequences, cyclicity, and latent structures. Examples of sequential analyses include Benjamin's (1979) Markov chain analysis on interactional data, Gottman's (1979) examination of mutually criticizing cycles in married couples, and Lichtenberg and Hummel's (1976) analysis of stochastic process in counseling sessions. The effectiveness of therapist interventions was studied by examining short-term shifts in depth of experiencing, boldness, in-session anxiety (Sampson & Weiss, 1986), and shifts in alliance (Foreman & Marmar, 1985; Gaston, Marmar, & Ring, 1989). Although intuitively appealing for process research, sequential analysis is limited in that only stable, immediate effects can be determined (although researchers have some latitude in determining the window of those effects, e.g., the number of lags that they expect the effects to appear in). Furthermore, sequential analyses do not allow us to link process to longer-term outcome.

Analyses of Patterns. An extension of sequential analysis is to consider longer sequences or patterns. This type of analysis is more sophisticated because it can involve several units, can involve units that do not occur next to each other temporally, and can involve units of very different sizes. Hence, the first step is often segmenting the process into units (or stages) that can then be coded. Methods for analyzing prolonged sequences are relatively new and have been much discussed and advocated (e.g., task analysis; Greenberg, 1984, 1986, 1991). For example, Wiseman, Shefler, Caneti, and Ronen (1993) studied a central issue event, which is based on Mann's (1981) recommendation that therapists formulate the central issue for the client's present and chronically endured pain (e.g., independence vs. dependence) at the beginning of treatment and then use that central issue as the focus of the entire therapy. In studying central issue events using task analysis, Wiseman et al. found evidence for four steps (the client raises the central issue; the therapist intervenes to focus the client on the central issue and raise awareness of the conflict through interpretation, exploration, uncovering additional aspects of the conflict, and connecting it to the past; the client explores feelings raised by the conflict, deals with them, and gains awareness of other aspects of the conflict; and the client expresses awareness and acceptance of new aspects of conflicts, has new understanding, and has a more mature ability to cope with issues). Methodological issues that need to be addressed include how to identify units (stages) and transitions between stages, and how to study the relationship between resolution of events and longer-term outcome.

Challenges in Conducting Within-Session Data Analyses. Despite the advances made with sequential analyses and pattern analyses, we still do not have good methods for linking process variables at a given point in time in therapy with long-term outcome. For example, through sequential analyses we can know that accurate interpretations are particularly helpful, and we can use task analyses to study the steps of a successful interpretive sequence; but we do not have methods for determining how a particular interpretation or interpretive segment leads to change. Clients may need to be in a certain amount of pain before lasting change can occur, or change may have to be salient to become incorporated into the client's sense of self, or change may have to be supported by significant others, or the interpretive sequence may need to be repeated numerous times in therapy with slightly different problems to lead to longer-term change, or clients may have to do something different in their lives after experiencing the significant event in therapy to set the snowball of change rolling. All these and more possibilities need to be pursued if we are to understand how the therapy process leads to meaningful changes in a person's life.

Many of our process analyses have focused on understanding the relationship of a process variable with either immediate or longer-term outcome. Our energy now needs to turn to understanding more about how events combine to lead to outcome (i.e., what is the cumulative effect of all the interventions in therapy?). Furthermore, we need to examine how different individuals respond to different process events (Marmar, 1990; Shoham-Salomon, 1990; Stiles et al., 1990). For example, we need to study client pretherapy characteristics by process interactions to determine how clients react differently to different interventions. Marmar (1990) noted that high-functioning clients did best with exploratory interventions, whereas poorly functioning clients did best with supportive interventions. One caution here is that Beutler (1991) listed a myriad of client and therapist pretherapy characteristics that could influence the relationship of process and outcome.

Aggregating Data Across Studies

The accumulation of knowledge across studies can be accomplished through meta-analyses. For example, a meta-analysis of 24 studies by Horvath and Symonds (1991) found a moderate effect size ($r = .26$) between alliance and outcome. Orlinsky, Grawe, and Parks (1994 and this volume) collated results across multiple process-outcome links and reported average effect sizes. Although very appealing, it is somewhat difficult to aggregate results across existing studies because so many studies have used different definitions of variables and different measures. For example, comparing studies on the effects of therapist interpretations is very difficult given the different definitions of therapist interpretations that have been used (see also Spiegel & Hill, 1989). Hence, we have many challenges ahead of us in terms of comparing results across studies.

Qualitative Process Research

With the growing excitement about qualitative methods in the last few years, the number of methods has correspondingly proliferated. Unfortunately, each researcher seems to use a slightly different method, making it difficult even to count the number of extant methods. The approaches that have been developed outside of psychotherapy research that have had the most impact on psychotherapy process research are grounded theory (Glaser & Strauss, 1967; Rennie, Phillips, & Quartaro, 1988; Strauss & Corbin, 1990), phenomenological approaches (Giorgi, 1970, 1985), and conversation/discourse analysis (Edwards & Potter, 1992). The approaches that have been developed specifically for psychotherapy process research are comprehensive process analysis (CPA; Elliott, 1989) and consensual qualitative research (CQR; Hill, Thompson, & Williams, 1997). In CPA, researchers analyze data from psychotherapy sessions as well as data from interviews with participants. In CQR, researchers analyze data from interviews with participants about their experiences in therapy.

We do not cover methodological issues for qualitative research as thoroughly as we did for quantitative methods because methods vary so widely at this point, researchers disagree adamantly about the best methods to use, many of the same issues apply to qualitative as quantitative process research (e.g., use of judges, effects of taping sessions), and minimal research has been conducted on methodological issues. Instead, we focus on two key issues: use of interviews and criteria for evaluating qualitative process research.

Use of Interviews

Interviews are often used in qualitative process research because they allow researchers to better adapt to the individual participant, gather in-depth information, and enter into the participant's inner world and gather information about the person's phenomenological experience (McCracken, 1988). The interviewer can also monitor the participant's understanding of the questions and make sure that the information provided by the participant is relevant (McLeod, 1994).

Although interviews can be excellent for obtaining rich in-depth information from participants, researchers have to be aware of a number of issues. First, researchers need to decide whether to do face-to-face or telephone interviews. The advantage of face-to-face interviews is that interviewers can develop more rapport with interviewees and observe more of the interviewee's nonverbal behavior. The advantage of telephone interviews is that interviewers can save a substantial amount of travel time. Furthermore, it may be easier for some participants to talk about deeply personal or shameful topics in telephone interviews than in face-to-face interviews. In this regard, some research has shown that for controversial topics, such as opinions about abortions or marijuana, participants gave more socially desirable responses in face-to-face interviews, moderate amounts in telephone interviews, and the least amount in questionnaires (Wiseman, 1972).

A second issue involves the structure of the interview protocol. On the one hand, using a low-structure interview (e.g., one that contains no scripted questions, with the interviewer asking whatever questions are deemed appropriate to find out about the topic) is desirable because it allows interviewers to probe in depth into the individual participant's experiences without being constrained by preexisting notions of what is to be found. On the other hand, more structured interviews (e.g., standard questions that are asked of all participants) are desirable because interviewers can gather consistent data across interviewees. An additional advantage of structured interviews is that they are less vulnerable to interviewer expectations, which can be especially problematic when interviewers have a lot of passion for their topic. A good compromise is to use semistructured interviews, in which standard questions are asked of all participants, but interviewers also use standard probes to follow up if interviewees do not spontaneously cover certain areas and interviewers ask unstructured followup questions to delve more deeply into issues to gain more understanding of the individual.

As mentioned above, interviewer (and researcher) expectations are potentially problematic for qualitative research. Expectations are typically communicated through subtle, directive cues from the interviewer to the participant outside of the awareness of both people (Shames & Adair, 1980). Rosenthal (1966) noted that experimenter expectations are virtually always present in science. Although there is no literature on interviews in the qualitative area, there is relevant literature in social and personnel psychology. Shames and Adair (1980) found that experimenters have more influence on the performance of participants when tasks are vague and unstructured. Campion, Palmer, and Campion (1997) found that increasing the standardization of the questions in employment selection interviews decreased the possibility of interviewers influencing the interviewee. Standardized questioning may also prevent interviewers from asking questions based on personal biases instead of adapting questions to interviewees' responses (Dipboye & Gaugler, 1993). In a meta-analysis of the employment interview structure, Wiesner and Cronshaw (1988) found that structured interviews had higher validity and reliability than unstructured interviews. Many qualitative researchers suggest that researchers and interviewers should become aware of their expectations and biases and bracket them (i.e., set them aside so that they do not influence the process). Although it is laudable to be aware of biases and set them aside, it is doubtful that this completely neutralizes the effects of the biases. Using semistructured interviews helps somewhat, but researchers need to remain aware that biases do influence their work and build in mechanisms to reduce bias (e.g., having other people listen to and critique the interviews).

Finally, issues arise about whether to prompt interviewees about the questions ahead of time. On the one hand, prompting may lead interviewees to think about things in a different way. On the other hand, it may help them think through their thoughts about the topic and give more considered answers. In our experience, it is best to give the interview protocol to interviewees so that they can think through the issues ahead of time (and perhaps consult their notes in the case of therapists talking about clients).

An additional concern is that interviewees may not readily think of something during an interview but might agree if given the stimuli on a survey. For example, in asking about reasons for using silence, therapists may not spontaneously recall during an interview instances when they had used silence to relieve their own needs but might recall instances if they saw such an item on a survey. Researchers need to be aware of the constraints on recall in interpreting their data, although we would argue that this limitation of interview is not sufficiently great to preclude using it (after all, all methods have limitations).

Criteria for Evaluating Qualitative Process Research

We developed the following criteria for qualitative process research based on our review of existing criteria (Elliott, Fischer, & Rennie, 1999; Hill, Thompson, & Williams, 1997; Kirk & Miller, 1986; Lincoln & Guba, 1985; Miles & Huberman, 1994; Morrow & Smith, 2000; Stiles, 1993) and our own experience conducting qualitative research. We relied on the same overall criteria (validity, reliability, generalizability) for qualitative as we did for quantitative process research because the goals are similar, but we stress that researchers achieve the criteria in different ways.

VALIDITY. As with quantitative research, we want to know that the results of our research are valid or well grounded in logic. In quantitative research, we would estimate that we had validity if there were high correlations with measures of similar constructs and low correlations with measures of dissimilar constructs. In qualitative research, we do not use standardized measures, so we cannot assess validity in this manner. Instead, we check for validity of the findings by looking at the trustworthiness of the method and the credibility of the results. It is necessary for researchers to provide enough information about procedures and results so that readers can evaluate the credibility.

In terms of the *trustworthiness of the method*, we look for evidence that the investigators collected and analyzed the data in a manner that would give reviewers confidence that the data could be replicated and that the data were as free of investigator and judges' biases as possible. Hence, we want to be convinced that the investigators: (a) were thoroughly knowledgeable about and immersed in the previous literature, (b) did a thorough job of composing and pilot testing their interview questions, (c) trained interviewers and judges to ensure that they were performing consistently, (d) were clear about their personal biases and tried to set them aside, (e) did an adequate job of sampling from a clearly articulated, homogeneous population, (f) used consistent decision rules among judges, (g) had an equal amount of power among judges analyzing the data so that discrepant opinions could be aired and considered, and (h) recycled back to the data continually to ensure that the data were represented faithfully.

In terms of the *credibility of the results*, we look for evidence that the writeup about the results seems plausible and coherent. The results and conclusions need to be logical, account for all the data, answer the research questions, and make sense to the outside reader. In addition, the investigators need to have disclosed their perspectives and biases and how these might have influenced the data (e.g., theoretical orientation, passions about the topic, expectations about the results), so that readers can situate the results in the context of who the investigators were. Furthermore, the researchers need to present enough examples from the cases (either direct quotes or summaries of what participants said) so that readers can judge for themselves whether or not the findings make sense. Finally, it is sometimes helpful for the researchers to make connections between different parts of the data through flow charts or diagrams.

The credibility of the results can be enhanced by several things. First, the investigators can check the data with the participants to see whether they concur with the results (i.e., testimonial validity). We must mention, however, that there are not yet established criteria for what level of agreement between investigators and participants is acceptable. Second, investigators can triangulate the results with other methods (e.g., to results from a standardized measure). For example, in the Rhodes, Hill, Thompson, and Elliott (1994) study, the researchers demonstrated that their qualitatively derived resolved and unresolved groups had significantly different scores on treatment satisfaction, which provided support that these groups were indeed different. Third, researchers can divide the sample in some meaningful way and compare the results obtained for the two samples. In the above example, Rhodes et al. found different pathways of results for resolved and unresolved misunderstandings, which provided some evidence that the results were valid given that the differences between groups seemed reasonable.

Reliability. As in quantitative research, we want to know that similar results would be found with different sets of data and different judges. Although reliability is not assessed numerically, it can be assessed through evidence about the research process in terms of consensus of judgments and consensus across data sets.

First, we can look for *consensus among judges*. A number of existing qualitative studies use only one judge to analyze all the data and then have other people review the findings. Given the evidence we have from the quantitative literature, we know that judges disagree quite often on subjective judgments such as are inherent in qualitative research and that investigator biases influence the data. Hence, it is incumbent on investigators to demonstrate how they have dealt with subjectivity and bias. We contend that it is difficult for one person to fairly represent the data no matter how immersed that person is in the analysis. And having another person not completely immersed in the data analysis evaluate a subset of the data does not seem adequate to serve as a check of one judge's findings. We would be far more persuaded of reliability by using several people on a research team, all of whom were thoroughly immersed in the data. Even then, however, group processes can sway opinions and cause the team to go in the direction of one dominant person. Hence, outside auditors who are fully involved in data can lend more credibility to results. There may be other methods for demonstrating the credibility of the judgment process other than having several persons on the judgment team and using outside auditors, but the investigators must find some way to demonstrate the credibility of their judgments.

We can also look for *consensus across teams of judges or data sets*. Although no studies have yet been conducted to determine whether different teams would find similar themes on the same data set, it would be important for researchers to study this problem. Such consensus would provide credibility that our findings are not just dependent on a single team with unknown biases. We also need to establish that results would be similar across new sets of interviewees with the same interview questions. Of course, we need first to set criteria for determining a match on themes—how close does a theme have to be to consider it the same theme?

Generalizability. To whom do the results apply? We assert that qualitative researchers are typically just as interested in generalizability as quantitative researchers. They want to know that their results apply to more than just one individual. One way that generalizability can be assessed is through the *stability of results.* If participants were randomly selected from a relatively homogeneous population and stability could be demonstrated in the results, then there is some evidence that the results can be generalized from the sample to the population. Researchers are generally advised in qualitative research to continue to add cases until no new results emerge (this has also been called saturation). Although each new case provides somewhat new information, the value added after a certain mass is reached is negligible. Some researchers do this by setting aside a certain number of cases prior to doing the major analyses. Once the major analyses are done, they add each new case and see whether the structure of the results changes. If not, the results are considered stable (cf. Hill, Thompson, & Williams, 1997). Of course, there is considerable pressure to consider the results stable at this point, so researchers need to ensure that they examine the data carefully.

Other criteria. Two other criteria have been used to evaluate qualitative research, but we do not advocate them: the applicability of the results to practice ("What can therapists do differently in the practice of psychotherapy knowing these results?" "Can the results be applied?") and whether findings resonate with readers ("Do the findings make sense?"). Not all qualitative studies will be directly relevant to practice (e.g., methodological studies on the interview process). Furthermore, findings could resonate with readers because they are more easily persuaded by speaking or writing fluency than by logic and careful data analysis.

Summary

Process researchers are making strides toward developing procedures to ensure reliable, valid, and useful measurements of the therapy process, as is evident in the current research (see review in Hill & Williams, 2000). We need more studies, however, on methodology in both quantitative and qualitative process research. In the quantitative area, researchers have tended to develop a measure, use it a few times, but never think about the effects of number of judges, the stimulus materials used to collect data, the bias of judges, and so on. Hence, the results of process studies may be rife with huge amounts of error, which may be partially responsible for the lack of consistency across studies. In the qualitative area, we know almost nothing about the effects of the number of interviewers, training of interviewers, expectations and biases of interviewers, and amount of structure of interviews. We urge researchers to be more careful about the methodological decisions that they make and to study the effects of their procedures on the data they collect.

Methodological Issues in Outcome Research

We now focus on methodological issues in measuring therapeutic outcome. We discuss issues related to defining psychotherapy outcome, measuring change, conceptualizing measures and methods, assessing the psychometrics of measures, assessing clinical significance, and collecting and analyzing data.

Defining Psychotherapy Outcome

The Importance of Defining Psychotherapy Outcome

A central issue in outcome research is how to measure the changes that occur in clients as a result of their participation in therapy. A great deal of effort has been expended on understanding the effects of psychotherapy, yet the lack of agreement in what constitutes adequate outcome measurement can create many problems when interpreting study results. These problems are apparent when scholars attempt to reconcile conclusions drawn from psychotherapy research literature based on different or ambiguous criteria of success. For a classic example, the reader may recall that Eysenck (1952) and Bergin (1971) drew different conclusions regarding the effectiveness of psychoanalysis using the same data set. Eysenck came to very negative conclusions based on a selective use of change criteria, whereas Bergin found the same clients to be substantially improved and psychoanalysis to be far more effective than spontaneous remission. As another example, although it is widely believed that the success rates for clients with a circumscribed sexual dysfunction, such as premature ejaculation, range somewhere between 75 and 90% (Carson, Butcher, & Mineka, 2000), one can find substantial differences between individual studies and their reported outcomes. On careful examination of these studies, the differences between rates of successful outcome appear to be not so much a function of the techniques or therapists who offer the treatments, but result from applying different definitions of success.

The fact that our evaluation of treatment effects can be altered by the way outcome is operationalized was dramatized in a report by Levine and Argle (1978), who studied the treatment outcome of 16 male clients who were diagnosed with "chronic secondary psychological impotence." The authors noted that this dysfunction could be viewed as a performance problem only, but that it was more realistic to consider the sexual life of clients more broadly. As a result, they collected outcome data not only on changes in performance, but also on sexual desire and emotional satisfaction with sexual relations. Functioning in these three broad areas was evaluated prior to therapy, at termination, and at 3, 6, 9, and 12 months following treatment. These latter data added another dimension to those already discussed: How stable were the observed changes?

The authors noted that the outcome data collected could be summarized to show conservative and liberal views of improvement. Thus, if one were to consider the criterion of success to be "better erectile functioning at one-year follow up than at initial evaluation—regardless of any interim relapses," then 69% of the men could be considered improved. This figure is identical to the rate of 69% reported by Masters and Johnson (1970), which would suggest that their results had been replicated. This figure is misleading, however, in that a substantial portion of these clients continued to have "profound" disturbances in their sexual lives. Using a more conservative estimate of improvement (improvement in sexual functioning and satisfaction plus stability over time), we found that only one couple (6.3%) of the 16 cases was improved. This couple had achieved good sexual functioning and was able to maintain this comprehensive and substantial improvement. Since the criterion of improvement used by Masters and Johnson (1970) was never clearly defined, it is impossible to replicate their findings. The 69% improvement rate found by Levine and Argle is no more a confirmation of the Masters and Johnson figure than is the 6.3% improvement figure a refutation of it. This example illustrates the importance of conceptualizing outcome assessment and suggests: (1) that varied definitions of success can be used, (2) the possibility of drawing misleading conclusions by using only simple indices of change, (3) the need to provide operational definitions of success, and (4) the value of standardizing practices across studies so that comparisons between these studies can be made. Some uniformity in outcome measures, coupled with comparable measurement techniques, research design, and sample population, will result in more rapid advances in our knowledge about effective treatment. It could also result in greater credibility and respect for the valuable services offered by psychologists and related mental health specialists.

An Historical Perspective on Outcome Measurement

Table 4.3 suggests several dimensions on which assessments have varied during the relatively short history of studying outcome. The field has gradually moved from primary reliance on therapist ratings of gross general improvement to the use of outcome indices of specific symptoms that are quantified from a variety of viewpoints, including the client, therapist, trained observers, relatives, physiological indices, and environmental data such as employment records. None of these viewpoints is "objective" or most authoritative, but the use of multiple perspectives represents an improvement from previous measurement methods, which were based on the limited perspective of the treating therapist.

Following the use of gross post-therapy rating scales, attempts at measuring change reflected the fashionable theoretical positions of the day. Early studies relied on devices developed out of Freudian dynamic psychology, which emphasized unconscious processes. These devices (e.g., the Rorschach and TAT) are problematic because of their poor psychometric qualities and reliance on inference. Even scoring systems (e.g., Exner's 1986 scoring system for the Rorschach) that have

Table 4.3 Developmental History of Outcome Assessment

Change rated by therapist	Multiple sources
Ratings of gross change	Specific change/ multiple technology
Theory bound	Emphasis on practical
Unidirectional change	Change can be for better or worse
Unidimensional change	Multidimensional change
Stable changes	Unstable changes

overcome some of these problems are problematic for outcome studies because these measures take so much time and are costly in relation to the information they provide.

The use of these dynamic measures was followed by the use of devices consistent with client-centered theory (e.g., the Q-sort technique) and behavioral and cognitive theories (e.g., Irrational Beliefs Inventory). Theoretical interests have led to marked changes in the types of measures employed in research studies. Although theoretically specific measures hold an important place in outcome research, today they are often less important than measures of symptomatic states, which are now considered essential to measure.

Currently, the most important practices in assessing outcome involve (1) clearly specifying what is being measured, so that replication is possible; (2) measuring change from multiple perspectives, with several types of rating scales and methods; (3) employing symptom-based, atheoretical measures; and (4) examining, to some extent, patterns of change over time. These practices are an improvement over the past, and they will be further highlighted in the sections that follow.

Review of Measures Used in Assessing Outcome: Diversity or Chaos?

A seemingly endless number of measures have been used to assess outcome. Froyd, Lambert, and Froyd (1996) reviewed 348 outcome studies published in 20 selected journals from 1983 through 1988. These journals were selected to represent therapy as practiced and reported in contemporary professional literature. A total of 1,430 outcome measures were identified for a wide variety of client diagnoses, treatment modalities, and therapy types. Of this rather large number, 840 different measures were used just once, and many were unstandardized measures! In another review, which included a much more homogeneous set of studies (all clients were diagnosed with agoraphobia), published during the 1980s, 106 studies were located and found to have used 98 different outcome measures (Ogles, Lambert, Weight, & Payne, 1990). This multitude of measures occurred in studies of a well-defined, limited disorder, treated with an equally narrow range of interventions, mainly behavioral and cognitive behavioral therapies. The proliferation of outcome measures is overwhelming, if not disheartening.

It is rare to find consensus about using a specific measure within a limited disorder, even when a particular measure has been recommended at professional meetings (Ogles et al., 1990; Strupp, Horowitz, & Lambert, 1997). Wells, Hawkins, and Catalano (1988), for example, reviewed how researchers studied "drug use" in outcome studies. Ignoring the many other types of outcomes that could be and were assessed (such as employment or arrest records) and focusing only on drug usage, the authors identified five categories of use. The five categories together produced more than 25 distinct procedures and measures to assess drug use. Even when a specific scale seems to be employed across research studies, it may be modified by the researchers and therefore is the same scale in name only. Grundy, Lunnen, Lambert, Ashton, and Tovey (1994), for example, found more than a dozen versions of the Hamilton Rating Scale for Depression in usage in studies of depression outcome. This finding and the fact that we know little about the psychometrics of the various versions of this scale underscore the difficulties of comparing outcomes across studies.

The seeming disarray of instruments and procedures being used to assess outcome is partly a function of the complex and multifaceted nature of psychotherapy as reflected in the diversity of clients and their problems, treatments, and their underlying assumptions and techniques, as well as the multidimensionality of the change process itself. But it also represents the failure of researchers in this field to create a coherent applied science!

Farnsworth, Hess, and Lambert (2001) reviewed articles measuring outcome that appeared in the *Journal of Consulting and Clinical Psychology* from 1995 through June, 2000. The frequency of outcome measures categorized by source is presented in Table 4.4. As can be seen, the BDI was the most preferred self-report measure, followed by the STAI, SCL-90-R, and Inventory of Interpersonal Problems (IIP). The BDI, STAI, and SCL-90 are popular probably because symptoms of anxiety and depression occur across a wide variety of disorders. These measures were also found to be the most widely utilized measures in two previous reviews of the psychotherapy outcome literature (Froyd, Lambert, & Froyd, 1996; Lambert & McRoberts, 1993, as summarized in Table 3 of Lambert & Hill, 1994). Interestingly, the majority of self-report measures were used only one time, suggesting that researchers continue to disagree on a common set of measures.

Beyond self-report methodology, even less consensus can be found within other categories of usage. The Hamilton Rating Scale for Depres-

TABLE 4.4 Commonly Used Inventories and Methods of Assessment

Self-Report			Instrumental			Significant Others		
(*N* = 384)	No. of Times Used	Percent of total	(*N* = 50)	No.	Percent	(*N* = 15)	No.	Percent
Beck Depression Inventory	40	10.4	Heart rate	9	18	Information on specific behavior	5	33
Experimenter-created scales or questionnaires	37	9.6	Blood pressure	7	14	Problem checklist-informant	6	40
Diary-behavior and/or thoughts	27	7.0	Weight	5	10	Single use of measures of family functioning (e.g., Family Life Questionnaire, Family Environment Scale, Family Adjustment)	3	20
State-Trait Anxiety Inventory	14	3.6	Saliva composition	5	10			
Symptom Checklist 90-R	12	3.1	CO level	3	6			
Minnesota Multi-phasic Personality Inventory	6	1.6	Respiration rate	2	4			
Dysfunctional Attitude Scale	6	1.6						
Hassles Scale	5	1.3						
Schedule for Affective Disorders and Schizophrenia	5	1.3						

Trained Therapist			Observer		
(*N* = 66)	No.	Percent	(*N* = 67)	No.	Percent
Interview—Global or level of functioning ratings	35	53	Frequency of specific behavior	13	19.0
Hamilton Rating Scale for Depression[a]	14	21	Rating of client behavior or characteristics	27	40.3
			Interview of subject	12	17.9

Note: *N* = the total number of times a scale appeared within a source category.

[a] This scale was also counted as a trained observer measure when it was administered by someone other than the therapist. Based on a poster presented at the annual meetings of the Rocky Mountain Psychological Association, Farnsworth, Hess, & Lambert (2001 April) by permission of the authors.

sion (HRSD) was frequently used in the studies reviewed by Lambert (1983) and Froyd, Lambert, and Froyd (1996). In the more recent survey, the HRSD remains relatively popular, used by either therapists or expert raters. The Locke-Wallace Marital Adjustment Inventory (Locke & Wallace, 1959) was the most frequently used specific scale employed by significant others. Beyond these measures, reviews of the research literature fail to show many patterns of measurement popularity, although some consensus exists within certain specialty areas within particular research programs.

Researchers should give serious consideration to employing widely used measures to facilitate comparisons across studies and thereby allow for greater integration of results, especially within "homogeneous" client samples. Several key books provide an overview of suitable measures (Coughlin, 1997; Fischer & Corcoran, 1994; Maruish, 1999; Ogles, Lambert, & Masters, 1996; Strupp, Horowitz, & Lambert, 1997; Touliatos, Perlmutter, & Straus, 1990).

Issues in Measuring Change

Multitrait versus Monotrait Scales

A question that concerns researchers is whether to select a scale that assesses multiple symptoms such as the MMPI-2 (Butcher, Dahlstrom, Graham, Tellegen, & Kaemmer, 1989) or one that purportedly taps a single trait such as the BDI (Beck, Steer & Garbin, 1988). We discuss the advantages and disadvantages of each approach.

Multitrait scales. The advantages of using multitrait scales are that they assess a wide variety of symptoms in a single measure and thus capture elements of functioning that may not be readily apparent or identifiable prior to the study. Multitrait scales are especially useful when the clients under investigation are not presumed to be homogeneous or to have a specific limited disorder. Since scales such as the MMPI-2 are commonly and extensively used for diagnostic purposes, their selection for use as outcome measures might seem highly desirable. The major advantage of using the MMPI-2 is the massive amount of research available on it and its widespread clinical use (Piotrowski & Keller, 1989). Consequently, for many clinicians, incorporating an MMPI-2 in a pretreatment assessment is already common practice and would not require any major adjustments in their work. In addition, given that most clinicians understand how to interpret the MMPI, they do not have to learn about a new instrument and feel comfortable using the results to guide treatment.

Nevertheless, there are some disadvantages that argue against using multitrait personality scales such as the MMPI-2 as a measure of outcome. First, many clients find the task of completing the test to be aversive. Second, although the MMPI has been used relatively frequently in the past as an outcome measure, many believe that the scales are not sensitive enough to detect short-term changes (Beutler & Crago, 1983). Third, the most significant deterrent to using the MMPI-2 is its length. The test is too long to be administered repeatedly, and shortened versions have not performed adequately. Of course, some instruments have been derived from the MMPI-2 that could be used as specific measures. However, to get a general or global measure from the MMPI-2, the entire test needs to be administered, which is often difficult in actual clinical settings where samples may be large and repeated measurement may be vitally important (Kazdin, 1980).

A further disadvantage of the MMPI-2 and similar multitrait measures is their limited value with regard to statistical analysis. Unless research samples are very large, using each of the MMPI's clinical scales (not to mention special population research scales) can inflate the chances of making a Type I error because many statistical comparisons are required. In addition, the presence of so many scores increases the temptation to look for statistically significant change after the data are in, rather than formulating specific hypotheses prior to making statistical comparisons. Furthermore, not all clients are likely to show elevations on all MMPI-2 scales. The chances of finding group differences are diminished whenever individuals are already within the normal range on a particular scale. Thus, researchers handicap themselves by mixing in scale scores from low-scoring individuals with the scale scores of individuals who show psychopathology on such traits.

A solution to these problems is to consider only a limited set of scores on the MMPI-2 or to use a single composite score such as the sum of clinical scales. Nevertheless, given the time investment needed to take the MMPI-2 several times, as well as its other limitations, we do not recommend the MMPI-2 or other multitrait personality inventories such as the Millon Clinical Multiaxial Inventory (MCMI; Millon, 1983) as outcome measures.

The Symptom Checklist-90-Revised (SCL-90-R) has some advantages over the longer multitrait measures because of its brevity. The SCL-90-R (Derogatis & Meliseratos, 1983) is a 90-item self-report symptom inventory designed to reflect the psychological symptom patterns of clients. There are nine primary symptom dimensions and three global indices of distress for which the Global Severity Index (GSI) is the best single indicator of the current depth of disturbance. The GSI is often used as a single summary measure because it combines information on the number of symptoms and the intensity of distress, has high intercorrelations among the scales, and construct validity for the primary symptom dimension scales is not convincing (Parloff, Waskow, & Wolfe, 1978).

We recommend the SCL-90-R and other brief multitrait inventories when research involves a heterogeneous client sample and the researcher wants a brief assessment of a variety of psychological and physical symptoms as well as a measure that is sensitive to change. Because of their brevity, the interested researcher can concurrently use several other measures of outcome without unduly burdening clients. In addition, cutoff points to denote significant changes have been established for many of these scales, a topic we discuss later in this chapter.

Monotrait measures. The most important advantage of scales that are designed to measure a single trait or disorder is that they are brief (typically containing 20 to 30 items), usually taking only 5 to 10 minutes to complete. Because these inventories are typically easy to administer and score, they can be repeated multiple times without discomfort. They also provide fairly extensive coverage of the single dimension they are intended to measure. Many monotrait scales measure symptoms (anxiety, depression, self-esteem) that are generally important across all kinds of pathological conditions and have a substantial research base with which to compare results. Many have adequate, if not outstanding, reliability.

A disadvantage of many of these monotrait scales is the difficulty of establishing their validity. The single-trait self-report scales have precise names that provide the illusion that they precisely measure the construct of interest. Often they do not, or the constructs themselves (e.g., anxiety, depression) are not as distinct as has been assumed. Unfortunately, measures are often highly correlated with measures presumed to assess a different construct. Nevertheless, most researchers have an interest in specifying beforehand the dimensions of interest in their study. The use of multiple monotrait scales allows one to at least try to tailor outcome measures to the disorder of interest and the treatment of choice, and they are therefore desirable in studies or clinics examining outcomes within a single disorder. Nevertheless, researchers need to be aware that these scales provide less precise information than their names imply.

Use of Individualized Measures of Change

Even though current research studies focus on seemingly homogeneous samples of clients (e.g., unipolar depression, agoraphobia), it is clear that each client is unique and brings unique problems to treatment. For example, although the major complaint of a person may be summed up as "depression" and the person may meet diagnostic criteria for major depression (Axis I), this same client can have serious interpersonal problems, somatic concerns, evidence of anxiety, financial difficulties, problems at work, problems parenting children, substance abuse, Axis II disorders, and so on. All these diverse problems are often addressed in therapy, so the proper assessment of outcome requires that changes in all the areas be measured to obtain a complete picture of change for the individual.

Williams (1985) documented considerable diversity among clients in the situations that provoke panic and in the types of simple phobias (e.g., fear of flying, heights) even within the seemingly limited diagnosis of agoraphobia. The most frequent panic-provoking situation (driving on freeways) was rated as "no problem" by nearly 30% of agoraphobics. The typical agoraphobic will usually be severely handicapped in some situations, moderately handicapped in others, and not at all restricted in still others. Williams concluded that "the configuration of fears in agoraphobics is so highly idiosyncratic that it is substantially true that no two agoraphobics have exactly the same pattern of phobias, and that two people with virtually no overlapping areas of phobia disability can both be called agoraphobic" (1985, p. 112). Furthermore, agoraphobics have many fears that are common to social phobia, many somatic complaints, and associated problems (e.g., generalized anxiety disorder, depression, obsessions, compulsions, and depersonalization).

In the earliest studies of psychotherapy, a clinician (usually the therapist) viewed the progress of an individual client and noted improvement in relation to initial status. This approach was highly individualized but unreliable because the formulation of problems and symptoms was not clearly operationalized. This individualized procedure gave way to use of standardized scales applied to all clients. These different procedures for assessing change reflect the long-standing conflict in psychology between the nomothetic and the idiographic approaches.

Numerous procedures for individualizing client treatment goals have been proposed over the years. The Target Complaints measure (Battle et al., 1966) was selected for inclusion in the National Institute of Mental Health (NIMH) core battery (Waskow & Parloff, 1975) but unfortunately has not generated a great deal of research in the ensuing years. Also typical of these approaches is the "case-formulation" method by Persons (1991), which calls for individualization of outcome. A different set of measures is used to assess the set of problems presented by each client. Unfortunately, these measures have not been validated and hence have been criticized (Garfield, 1991; Herbert & Mueser, 1991; Messer, 1991; Schact, 1991; Silverman, 1991).

One method that has received widespread attention and use is Goal Attainment Scaling (GAS, Kiresuk & Sherman, 1968), which requires that a number of mental health goals be formulated prior to treatment by an individual or a combination of clinicians, client, and/or a committee assigned to the task. For each goal specified, a scale with a graded series of likely outcomes, ranging from least to most favorable, is devised. An attempt is made to formulate and specify goals with sufficient precision to allow an independent observer to determine how well a client is functioning at a given time. Each goal is weighted to give those with high priority in therapy more weight than less important goals. The procedure also allows for transformation of the overall attainment of specific goals into a standard score (Kiresuk, Smith, & Cardillo, 1994).

In using the GAS method for the treatment of obesity, for example, one goal could be the specification and measurement of weight loss. A second goal could be reduction of depressive symptoms as measured by a single symptom scale such as the Beck Depression Inventory. Or exercise goals could be set and measured through a diary. Each of these therapy goals is assigned a weight consistent with its importance for the individual client. The particular scales and behaviors examined vary from client to client, and, of course, one may include other specific types of diverse observations from additional points of view.

GAS has been recommended for use in marital and family therapy (Russell, Olson, Sprenkle, & Atilano, 1983) and continues to be applied with families as a way of expressing changes in the family as a whole, rather than limiting assessment to the identified client (Fleuridas, Rosenthal, Leigh, & Leigh, 1990). GAS has been applied in school settings (e.g., Malec, 1999; Young & Chesson 1997); with a variety of client groups and treatment methods, such as group therapy (e.g., Flowers & Booaren, 1990); and with the intellectually handicapped (e.g., Bailey & Simeonson, 1988). The most advantageous use of GAS seems to be with populations where traditional self-report instruments cannot be easily employed, as in residential care for elders or rehabilitation (e.g., Coughlan & Coughlan, 1999; Masi, Favilla, Mucci, & Millepiedi, 2000; Zaza, Stolee, & Prackin, 1999).

Many methodological issues need to be attended to when using GAS or similar methodology (Cytrynbaum, Ginath, Birdwell, & Brandt, 1979). First, research use may require that treatment goals be set by someone other than the therapist to separate therapist treatment effects from therapist goal-setting biases. The choice of goals and the attainment of goals are related to client as well as therapist characteristics that affect goal setting. Second, random assignment to condition should occur following goal setting, and, ideally, some followup raters would be independent of goal setters and therapists to increase the independence of evaluations and objectivity of ratings. Third, correlations between goals often seem to be fairly high, raising questions of independence. Fourth, goals judged either too easy or too hard to obtain are often included. Fifth, goal attainment is judged on a relative rather than an absolute basis so that behavior change is inevitably confounded with expectations. Despite a manual of instructions and ample discussion, constructing useful goals is not an easy task (Bailey & Simeonson, 1988). Sixth, examination of studies using GAS reveals widespread modification in its use by numerous researchers, so that it is misleading to consider it a single method: GAS is itself a variety of different methods for recording and evaluating client goal attainment. The units of change derived from individually tailored goals are unequal and therefore hardly comparable. It is not possible to compare accurately the goal attainment scores from one study to the next.

In summary, the status of individualized measures of change is tenuous. Effective individualization of goals for the purpose of assessing client change remains an ideal rather than a reality. The intention to individualize goals is very appealing, but the gap between intention and effective application appears to be rather large. Nevertheless, GAS and similar methodology may eventually play a central role in evaluating client change in populations that cannot be assessed through traditional methods; these methods deserve continued research.

Conceptualizing Measures and Methods

Various conceptual schemes have been proposed to bring order to outcome assessment (Schulte, 1995). For example, McLellan and Durell (1996) suggested four areas for assessment of outcome: reduction of symptoms; improvement in health, personal, and social functioning; cost of care; and reduction in public health and safety threats. Docherty and Streeter (1996), on the other hand, suggested seven dimensions that must be considered in outcome assessment: symptomatology; social/interpersonal functioning; work functioning; satisfaction; treatment utilization; health status/global well-being; and health-related quality of life. These two conceptualizations take a rather broad view of the topic. The conceptual scheme presented in Table 4.5 concerns itself more narrowly with issues that surround the collection of outcome data in research that focuses on the individual client (although the issues addressed in the other two schemes could be subsumed within the conceptualization that is offered in this table). The four major components of the scheme are content, temporality, source, and technology.

Content. Content is a dimension that reflects the need to assess changes that occur within the client (intrapersonal), in the client's intimate relationships (interpersonal), and, more broadly, in the client's participation in community and social roles (social role performance). This dimension could be considered a continuum that represents the degree to which an instrument measures intrapsychic attributes and bodily experiences versus characteristics of the client's participation in the interpersonal world. It is a matter of intel-

Table 4.5 Scheme for Organizing and Selecting Outcome Measures

Content	Temporality	Source	Technology
Intrapersonal	Single measure	Self-report	Global ratings
1		1	1
2		2	2
3		*	*
*	Repeated measure	Trained	Specific symptom index
*		Observers	1
*		1	2
Interpersonal		2	*
1		*	*
2		*	Observer ratings
*	Pattern measure	Relevant other	1
*		1	2
Social role		2	*
performance		*	*
1		*	Psychological measures
2		Therapist rating	1
*		1	2
		2	*
		*	Life records
		Institutional	1
		1	2
		2	*
		*	

Note. The numbers and asterisks below each area represent the idea that there can be subcategories such as kinds of intrapersonal events or kinds of interpersonal measures.

lectual curiosity and values, if not empirical importance, to know about the kinds of changes that are targeted in treatment efforts. Empirically, the results of outcome studies are more impressive when content is broadly measured because interventions can have extensive indirect effects as well as effects that are the target of treatment.

Temporality. Temporality reflects the fact that outcome, like process, is a dynamic state. Researchers have relied on single assessments of outcome post-therapy (Seligman, 1995), on repeated measures of outcome pre- and post-therapy, and occasionally on trying to capture the pattern of behavior during and following treatment. This latter method is most common in the study of addictions where outcome must be assessed over a long period of time and in relation to patterns of behavior such as lapses, relapses, and increased abuse of other chemicals.

When outcome assessment includes attempts to study the persistence of change and especially the persistence of behaviors over substantial periods of time in a variety of settings and in the presence of normal life stressors and opportunities, as well as the vagaries of life, a more conservative appraisal of outcome usually results. This is true whether one considers addictions, depression, marital dysfunction, or a host of other disorders (cf. Chapter 5, this volume). Studies that attempt to assess the temporal stability of change may use a variety of methods. It is often important to select measures of change that are suitable for repeated measures, such as the brief scales alluded to earlier in this chapter.

Source. In the ideal study of change, all the parties involved who have information about change can be represented, including the client, therapist, relevant (significant) others, trained judges (or observers), and societal agents that store information such as employment and educational records (Strupp & Hadley, 1977). Unlike the physical sciences, measurement in psychotherapy is highly affected by the politics, values, and biases of those providing the data. Seldom are we able to merely observe phenomena of interest to us.

In a study examining recent trends in outcome assessment, Farnsworth, Hess, and Lambert (2001) reviewed 133 outcome studies from 1996 through June 2000 published in the *Journal of Consulting and Clinical Psychology*. Specific outcome measures were classified into one of five "source" categories: self-report, trained observer, significant other, therapist, or instrumental (a category that included societal records or instruments such as physiological recording devices). Frequency data were then computed on the usage of specific instruments and instrument sources across studies (see Table 4.4). As might be expected, the most popular source for outcome data was client self-report. In fact, 41% of the studies used client self-report data as the sole source for evaluation. Of the studies that relied solely on client self-report scales, 74% used more than one self-report scale. In the next most frequent procedure, researchers employed both client self-reports and therapist ratings (23%). Significant other ratings were seldom utilized alone or in combination with all other sources. Impressively, 29% of the studies used five or more instruments to reflect changes in clients. The most ambitious effort had a combination of 11 distinct measures across three sources to assess changes following psychotherapy.

The now necessary and, to some degree, common practice of applying multiple criterion measures in research studies has made it obvious that multiple measures from different sources do not yield unitary results (e.g., Monti, Wallander, Ahern, Abrams, & Monroe, 1983). For example, a treatment used to reduce seemingly simple fears may result in a decrease in behavioral avoidance of the feared object according to observers but no change in the self-reported level of discomfort associated with the feared object (e.g., Wilson & Thomas, 1973). Similarly, a physiological indicator of fear may show no change in response to a feared object after treatment, whereas improvement in subjective self-report may be marked (e.g., Ogles et al., 1990).

The lack of agreement between sources is further supported by factor analytic studies that have analyzed a variety of outcome measures. The main factors derived from such studies tend to be associated closely with the measurement method or the source of observation used in collecting data rather than being identified by some theoretical or conceptual variable that would be expected to cut across techniques of measurement (Beutler & Hamblin, 1986; Cartwright, Kirtner, & Fiske, 1963; Forsyth & Fairweather, 1961; Gibson, Snyder, & Ray, 1955; Nichols & Beck, 1960; Pilkonis, Imber, Lewis, & Rubinsky, 1984; Shore, Massimo, & Ricks, 1965). For example, Pilkonis et al. (1984) found three factors clearly representing the source of data rather than content when they factor analyzed 15 scales representing a variety of traits and symptoms from the client, therapist, expert judges, and significant others.

The fact that differences in outcomes have been found to be a function of source rather than content has been replicated across a variety of scales and client populations and across three or four decades—suggesting that this finding is very robust. The consistency of these findings highlights the need to pay careful attention to the complexity of changes that follow psychological interventions and the way information from different perspectives is analyzed and reported. Few studies recognize or deal adequately with the complexities that result from divergence between sources, although creative efforts and some progress have been made (e.g.,, Berzins, Bednar, & Severy, 1975; Mintz, Luborsky, & Christoph, 1979; Ogles, Lambert, & Sawyer, 1995).

The lack of consensus across sources of outcome evaluation, especially when each source is presumably assessing the same phenomena, has been viewed as a threat to the validity of data. However, outcome data provide not only evidence about changes made by the individual, but also information about the differing value orientations and motivations of the individuals providing the data. This issue has been dealt with in several ways, ranging from discussion of "biasing motivations" and ways to minimize bias to discussions of the value orientation of those involved (e.g., Docherty & Streeter, 1996; Strupp & Hadley, 1977). Clearly, there are times when we want measures to converge in providing identical estimates of change, as well as times when we collect data from different sources with the hope that the sources will make a unique contribution with little or no overlap. Researchers need to collect outcome data from a variety of sources whenever possible. Finding ways to combine or compare these data in estimating overall change (when it is appropriate) remains a vital task in the continuing development of sophisticated outcome assessment.

Technology of Change Measures. The technology or format used in devising scales and collecting data can have an impact on the final index of change, although one that is not entirely independent from the source of the ratings. Table 4.5 lists several different technologies that have been employed in outcome measurement, including global ratings, specific symptom indices, observer ratings (behavioral counts), physiological measures, and life records. One broad dimension on which these technologies vary appears to be a direct-indirect dimension. Here the data are seen as possibly reflecting a bias determined by the propensity of subjects to produce effects consciously. Thus, global ratings of outcome either implicitly or explicitly call for raters to evaluate outcome directly. Their attention is drawn to the question, "Did I (the client) get better in therapy?" In contrast, specific symptom indices focus the rater's attention (before and after treatment) on the status of specific symptoms and signs at the time the rating is made without explicit references to the outcome of therapy. Whereas the client may realize at the time of post-testing that the therapy (of even the therapist) is being directly evaluated, the tendency to enter into the politics of this state of affairs is diminished if specific symptom indices are used.

Smith, Glass, and Miller (1980) suggested several reactivity factors associated with rating scales that affect estimates of psychotherapy outcome: the degree to which a measure can be influenced by either the client or therapist, the similarity between therapy goals and the measure itself, the degree of "rater awareness" in the assessment process. Relatively nonreactive measures (e.g., galvanic skin response, personality tests, and grade point average) are presumably not so easily influenced in any direction by the parties involved, whereas reactive measures (e.g., therapist ratings of improvement) are more easily influenced. Smith et al. (1980) found a correlation of .18 between reactivity ratings and effect size. Partialing out the effects of reactivity ratings substantially reduced the advantage for behavior therapies found in their review. Ogles et al. (1990), on the other hand, found no relation between reactivity and outcome within the narrow domain of agoraphobia. Other meta-analytic reviews have even found an inverse relationship between reactivity and effect size. Future research may clarify how data collection procedures consistently "over-" or "underestimate" treatment gains, thereby making estimates of change across technologies easier to compare. We now present two studies that help clarify the importance of technology in shaping our views about the effectiveness of psychotherapy.

Green, Gleser, Stone, and Siefert (1975) compared final status scores, pretreatment to post-treatment difference scores, and direct ratings of global improvement in 50 clients seen in brief crisis-oriented psychotherapy. They concluded that the percentage of clients considered improved has more to do with the type of rating scale employed than improvement per se! Global improvement ratings by therapists *and* clients showed very high rates of improvement, with no clients claiming they were worse. When clients had to rate their symptoms more specifically, however, as with the Hopkins Symptom Checklist, they were likely to indicate actual intensification of some symptoms and to provide more conservative data than gross estimates of change (see also Garfield, Prager, & Bergin, 1971).

A recent example of controversy about the importance of technology arising from assessments of the effectiveness of psychotherapy is the Consumer Reports Study (1995; Seligman, 1995), which used gross estimates of the impact of therapy based on client retrospective estimates of change and satisfaction following treatment. Among the 26 questions asked were: "How much did treatment help with the specific problem that led you to therapy?" "What was your overall state at the time you entered treatment?" and "What is your overall emotional state at the present?" (i.e., at the time of the survey 0 to 3 years following treatment). The Consumer Reports Study concluded that clients ($N = 4{,}100$) benefited very substantially from psychotherapy. Among the many criticisms of the study methodology was its retrospective nature (Mintz, Drake, & Crits-Cristoph, 1996). Reviewers doubted the ability of participants to accurately recall their pretreatment level of functioning several years after the fact, and, therefore, the accuracy of estimates of improvement based on "pre" minus "post" change scores was suspect. In addition, the validity of satisfaction ratings as useful measures of treatment response was questioned since they reflect, to a large degree, client expectations of treatment rather than outcome per se. In response to these criticisms, Seligman (1996) argued that the retrospective change scores only correlated .27 with satisfaction scores, therefore tapping a separate dimension of improvement than satisfaction. Seligman also argued that gross ratings of change based on retrospective estimates were as valid as any other measure of improvement.

In a study aimed at understanding the accuracy of retrospective gross estimates of state of functioning and satisfaction, compared to pre-post ratings, Gregersen et al. (2001) examined ratings of change gathered at followup four months to two years post-treatment), with ratings of disturbance collected at pretreatment and at followup. These researchers found a correlation of –.57 between gross estimates of the pretreatment mental state gathered at followup and actual standardized test scores filled out before clients entered treatment. This finding provides some support for Seligman's argument that post-therapy estimates of pretreatment functioning are similar to ratings of functioning gathered prior to treatment (and, therefore, represent a valid technology for collecting outcome data). However, Gregersen et al. also reported that the effect size for the retrospective procedure was 2.1, while that employing the pre-/post-procedure was 1.10—a large difference. The difference in the size of treatment effects found by Gregersen et al. suggests that the retrospective technology used in the *Consumer Reports* Study overestimated treatment effects.

The findings on satisfaction reported by Gregersen et al. were also consistent with the *Consumer Reports* finding and with more recent research. Gregerson et al. found that satisfaction at followup correlated .30 with estimates of change based on standardized test scores and .30 with change scores based on retrospective change using the *Consumer Reports* items. These findings support the *Consumer Reports*'s Study finding that improvement ratings, even when gathered retrospectively, correlate significantly, albeit weakly, with other estimates of outcome. They also suggest that measures of treatment satisfaction are largely independent of measures of treatment response as measured by the standardized scales typically used in outcome studies, a finding that has been replicated by several research groups (e.g., Lunnen & Ogles, 1998; Pekarik & Wolff, 1996).

Although measures of satisfaction and gross post-therapy estimates of change are typically not recommended in efficacy research (e.g., in clinical trials), they are often important in effectiveness research (e.g., field research) because managed care companies would like to gauge overall client satisfaction with their services (Gerarty, 1996). These types of measures seem to be favored more because of their simplicity, low cost, and propensity for making services look good than because of their high standing in the scientific community.

Observer ratings in the form of behavioral counts can supply information that is less subject to rater distortion if enough attention is devoted to the procedures that are used. These procedures can provide very convincing evidence of treatment effects, although they are costly. Ideally, these observer ratings call for counting behaviors in real-life circumstances in which the clients do not know they are being observed or have tasks to focus on that divert their attention away from their participation in an evaluation. The typical situation would be in a hospital ward or school classroom where staff count or rate client behaviors, in addition to engaging in their normal work duties. Smith et al. (1980) judged that some observer ratings were highly reactive because they were collected in circumstances that exaggerated the effectiveness of treatment. For example, the Behavioral Approach Test, often used after desensitization of phobias, calls for the client to approach a feared object. The experimenter, evaluator, and even the therapist are often in the room with the client and provide subtle cues to encourage or discourage behaviors because they know the desired outcome. The client may perform to please the evaluator (or therapist). Certain clients (e.g., those with certain personality disorders) may also behave in ways that distort ratings in the direction of denying that improvement has been achieved. Hence, we can see that observational data can be just as vulnerable to distortion as self-report measures.

The technology involved in physiological monitoring is not usually under the conscious control of the client, or at the very least it presents a real and serious challenge to conscious distortion and therefore is an important method of obtaining useful outcome data. Life records, such as grade point average and employment records, usually reflect a host of complex behaviors influenced by a wide variety of factors. Because such life records are ordinarily produced without reference to the research project, they are potentially the least reactive type of data that can be collected. Access to such data, however, can be difficult and presents many ethical and legal challenges to the researcher, so there has been a paucity of this type of data in outcome studies.

It should be obvious to the reader that the technology or procedures used to generate data on client change requires considerable thought. We hope that the conceptual scheme provided will help organize the many factors that need to be taken into consideration when selecting measures of change and that the literature presented will help illuminate some of the consequences of such important choices.

Psychometrics of Change Measurement

Researchers have to consider the psychometric qualities of assessment devices because they can have a dramatic impact on the results. Among these qualities are those that are traditionally considered relevant in psychological testing generally: reliability and validity.

Reliability

Reliability is of particular importance in measuring outcome because the most common procedure for measuring change involves administering the assessment device before and after treatment and then calculating some kind of change score. Unfortunately, the reliability of change scores is not equal to the reliability of the measure (Cronbach, 1990). Changes in test scores from one occasion to another are due not only to true differences in whatever is being measured but also to "error"—other factors that affect the score (such as item sampling, the test taker's physical and mental state, the test environment, and administrative instructions). The standard error of the difference between two scores is larger than the standard error of measurement for either score alone. Thus, the reliability of a particular measure in outcome assessment is especially critical because low reliability of a measure is compounded with computation of a change score. The problems associated with unreliability are not solved by ignoring reliability or by using experimental scales with unknown reliability. The use of unstandardized scales makes it difficult, at best, to estimate the amount of change necessary to conclude that the difference between two scores is not due to chance fluctuations in the scores.

Validity

Validity is the ability of a measure to estimate or describe the dimension, phenomenon, or construct it purports to measure. Validity is an essential component of outcome measures (and assessment procedures) and one that is at the core of most discussions of outcome measurement. Because of the limited validity of any specific measure, most researchers recommend the use of multiple measures from multiple perspectives. We refer readers to several references for more extensive coverage of the validity of several important measures (Coughlin, 1997; Fischer & Corcoran, 1994; Maruish, 1999; Ogles, Lambert, & Masters, 1996; Touliatos, Perlmutter, & Straus, 1990).

Here we deal with a neglected validity issue: sensitivity to change, or the degree to which a measure is likely to reflect changes that actually occur following participation in therapy. For example, if the Beck Depression Inventory is used as an outcome measure, will it reflect the same degree of change as the Hamilton Rating Scale for Depression or as other self-ratings of depression? Will gross ratings of overall change provided by the client show larger or smaller amounts of improvement than a scale that measures change on specific symptoms? To what extent are the conclusions drawn in comparative outcome studies determined by the specific measures selected by researchers? Do the techniques of meta-analysis actually allow us to summarize across the different outcome measures that are employed in different studies (essentially combining them) and thereby facilitate accurate conclusions about differential treatment effects?

Vermeersch, Lambert, and Burlingame (2000) provided a demonstration of test development that used statistical techniques to evaluate the sensitivity to change of items from the Outcome Questionnaire-45 (OQ-45), a self-report scale of client distress, interpersonal problems, and social role performance. The test was administered to a nonclinical sample on various schedules over nine weeks and to clients on a weekly basis over the same time period. The change slope for each of the 45 items was calculated and compared. For an item to be regarded as sensitive, it had to change significantly over the course of therapy and show a steeper recovery curve than that obtained from the untreated controls (a subset of which began the study in the clinical range). This method provided an adequate means of identifying a few items that did not show changes over the duration of the study. The 30 most sensitive items were selected for inclusion in a revised edition of the test.

Unfortunately, most outcome measures have not been developed with an eye toward choosing items that are sensitive to change, and little is known about this aspect of test validity. Yet a growing body of evidence suggests that there are reliable differences in the "sensitivity" of instruments of change. In fact, the differences between measures is not trivial but large enough to raise questions about the interpretation of research studies. Two examples of such differences will make the importance of sensitivity in instrument selection clear.

Table 4.6 presents data from a review of agoraphobia outcome studies published in the 1980s (Ogles, Lambert, Weight, & Payne, 1990). The effect sizes presented (based on pretest/post-test differences) show remarkable disparity in estimates of improvement as a function of the outcome instrument or method of measurement selected for study. Treatments appear to be more effective depending on which measure was employed rather than which treatment was truly more effective. Comparisons between the measures depicted in Table 4.6 are confounded somewhat by the fact that the data were aggregated across all studies that used either measure, but similar results can be found when only studies that give both measures to a client sample are aggregated, as was the case in this second example.

TABLE 4.6 Overall Effect Size (ES) Means and Standard Deviations by Scale

Scale	N[a]	M	SD
Phobic anxiety and avoidance	65	2.66	1.83
Global Assessment Scale	31	2.30	1.14
Self-rating severity	52	2.12	1.55
Fear Questionnaire	56	1.93	1.30
Anxiety during BAT[b]	48	1.36	.85
Behavioral Approach Test	54	1.15	1.07
Depressive measures	60	1.11	.72
Fear Survey Schedule	26	.99	.47
Heart rate	21	.44	.56

[a] *N* = the number of treatments whose effects were measured by each scale

[b] BAT = Behavioral Approach Test

Source: Based on Ogles, Lambert, Weight, and Payne (1990).

Table 4.7 presents data from a comparison of three frequently employed measures of depression: the Beck Depression Inventory (BDI) and the Zung Self-Rating Scale for Depression (ZSRS), both self-report inventories, and the Hamilton Rating Scale for Depression (HRSD), an expert judge rating (Lambert, Hatch, Kingston, & Edwards, 1986). These meta-analytic results suggest that the three measures provide reliably different pictures of change. The HRSD provides a significantly larger index of change than the BDI and ZSRS. Because the amount of actual improvement clients experience after treatment is never known, these findings can be interpreted several ways (e.g., the HRSD overestimates actual change, or the BDI and ZSRS underestimate change). It appears that there are reliable differences in the picture of outcome provided by different measures and these differences need to be explored and understood. Further research needs to clarify the various factors that inflate and deflate estimates of

TABLE 4.7 Matched Pairs of Mean Effect Size (ES Values)

Scale Pair	N[a]	Mes[b]	SD	t
HRSD/ZSRS	17	.94*/.62*	.61/.30	1.88
BDI/HRSD	49	1.16**/1.57**	.86/1.08	2.11
ZSRS/BDI	13	.70/1.03	.46/.52	1.65

HRSD = Hamilton Rating Scale for Depression, ZSRS = Zung Self-Rating Scale, BDI = Beck Depression Inventory, Mes = mean effect size, Sdes = standard deviation of effect size.

[a] N = the number of treatments whose effects were measured by each pair of depression sales.

[b] Values derived from studies in which subjects' depression was measured on two scales at a time. Effect size represents within-study comparisons.

* $p < .05$

** $p < .25$

Source: From Lambert, Hatch, Kingston, and Edwards (1986). Reprinted by permission of the American Psychological Association and authors.

change. For now, however, it is clear that dependent measures are not equivalent in their tendencies to reflect change and that meta-analysis, as it is typically used to combine different measures, cannot overcome the differences between measures that are more or less sensitive.

Several observations based on our analysis of the outcome literature are important in evaluating treatment effects: (1) Data from therapists or expert judges who are aware of the treatment status of clients produce larger effect sizes than self-report data, data produced by significant/relevant others, institutional data, or instrumental data; (2) gross ratings of change, including measures of satisfaction, produce larger estimates of change than ratings on specific dimensions or symptoms; (3) change measures based on the specific targets of therapy (e.g., individualized goals or anxiety-based measures taken in specific situations) produce larger effect sizes than more distal measures, including a wide variety of personality tests aimed at measuring trait-like factors; (4) life adjustment measures that tap social role performance in the natural setting (e.g., grade point average) produce smaller effect sizes than analogue or laboratory-based measures; (5) measures collected soon after therapy show larger effect sizes than measures collected at a later date; and (6) physiological measures such as heart rate usually show relatively small treatment effects compared to other measures across a variety of contexts even when they are specifically targeted in treatment.

Clinical versus Statistical Significance

A common criticism of outcome research is that the results of studies, as they are typically reported in terms of statistical significance, obscure both the clinical relevance of the findings and the impact of the treatment on specific individuals. Unfortunately, statistically significant improvements do not necessarily equal practically important improvements for the individual client. Statistically significant findings on a group of clients may therefore be of limited practical value. This fact raises questions about the contribution of empirical studies for the practice of psychotherapy and begs for practical solutions. The troubling fact is that in a well-designed study, small differences after treatment between large groups could produce findings that reach statistical significance, whereas the real-life difference is trivial in terms of the reduction of symptoms. For example, a treatment for obesity might create a statistically significant difference between treated and untreated groups if all treated subjects lost 10 pounds and all untreated subjects lost 5 pounds. However, the clinical utility of an extra 5-pound weight loss is debatable, especially for clinically obese clients.

Numerous attempts have been aimed at assessing the importance of the changes that are made. In the earliest studies of therapy outcome, clients were categorized post therapy with gross ratings of "improved," "cured," and the like, implying meaningful change. The lack of precision in such ratings, however, resulted in their waning use (Lambert, 1983). Those interested in operant conditioning and single-subject designs developed concepts such as social validity to describe practically important improvement (Kazdin, 1977; Wolf, 1978). Some disorders easily lend themselves to an analysis of changes because improvement can be defined as the absence of a behavior (e.g., cessation of drinking, smoking, or drug use), but most symptoms targeted in psychotherapy cannot be so easily defined and measured.

Clinical Significance and Normative Comparisons

Jacobson, Follette, and Revenstorf (1984) brought the concept of clinical significance into prominence by proposing statistical methods that would illuminate the degree to which individual clients recover at the end of therapy. Recovery was proposed to be a post-test score that was more likely to belong to the functional than the dysfunctional population of interest. Estimating clinical significance requires that norms for the functional sample are established. Furthermore, for change to be clinically significant, a client must change enough so that one can be confident that the change exceeds measurement error (calculated by a statistic titled the reliable change index). When a client moves from one distribution (dysfunctional) into another (functional) and the change reliability exceeds measurement error (calculated by dividing the absolute magnitude of change by the standard error of measurement), then change is viewed as clinically significant and the client is considered more likely to be functional than dysfunctional. A growing number of studies have employed these techniques with various treatment samples. Ogles, Lunnen, and Bonesteel (2001) reviewed the use of various forms of clinical significance in psychotherapy outcome research reports published in the *Journal of Consulting and Clinical Psychology* from 1990 through 1998. During this nine-year period, 74 studies out of more than 300 reported clinical significance, with a third (24) using both the reliable change index and a cutoff score for functional behavior.

Ankuta and Ables (1993) examined the validity of clinical significance by comparing clients who demonstrated clinically significant improvement according to Jacobson and Truax's (1991) methodology with the clients' perceived satisfaction with therapy using Strupp, Fox, and Lessler's (1969) Patient Questionnaire. They found that clients designated as having made clinically significant improvement did indeed report higher levels of satisfaction than those whose change did not meet these criteria. Lunnen and Ogles (1998) expanded on this research by performing a multiperspective, multivariable analysis of the reliable change component of Jacobson and Truax's methodology. They divided clients who were receiving outpatient therapy into one of three groups (reliably improved, no reliable change, reliably deteriorated) on the basis of their change scores on the Outcome Questionnaire (Lambert, Hansen, et al., 1996). At the time a client attained reliable change (either improvement or deterioration), she or he was matched with a client who was not reliably changed. Clients in all three groups then rated their perceived change, satisfaction, and the helping alliance as did their spouse/significant other and therapist. Perceived change and alliance were higher for individuals who reliably improved than for those who did not experience reliable change or who experienced deterioration. This finding held up across both client and therapist perspectives. Satisfaction, though higher in those who showed reliable improvement, did not differ between no-change and deteriorated clients. Clients who demonstrated reliable deterioration were not significantly different from nonchangers on any of the variables from any of the perspectives. Lunnen and Ogles concluded that the reliable change index was an effective way of evaluating symptomatic improvement but that it was less effective as an indicator of reliable worsening.

Another study that provides some evidence of validity for the concept of clinical significance was conducted by Ogles et al. (1995) using data from the Treatment of Depression Collaborative Research Program (TDCRP). They assessed the degree to which there was correspondence across measures used to assess outcome, assuming that high concordance rates would be consistent with validity for the concept of clinical significance. Over 75% of the clients in the TDCRP study were classified as making clinically significant change on all three measures used (the Beck Depression Inventory, Hamilton Depression Rating Scale, and Hopkins Symptom Checklist), but 25% of clients made changes on one of the measures but not on the other two measures. This discrepancy was of considerable clinical importance. Overall, however, the results supported the validity of clinical significance criteria.

Tingey, Lambert, Burlingame, and Hansen (1996) proposed extensions to the Jacobson method and offered a graphical method of displaying change in relation to several normative groups simultaneously. Figure 4.1 illustrates this method with normative groups who took the SCL-90. The major index of disturbance on the SCL-90 is the General Severity Index (GSI). The higher the score on this scale, the more disturbed the client. GSI scores as plotted in this figure can range from zero to two as noted on the vertical and horizontal axes. The continuous diagonal line signifies no change between pre- and post-treatment scores; a subject receiving identical pre- and post-treatment scores would fall on this line. The area above this line denotes an increase in the GSI score from pretreatment to post-treatment whereas the area below the diagonal line denotes a decrease in symptomatology following treatment. Plotted points ("A" and "B") on Figure 4.1 indicate Subject A's and Subject B's pre-and post-treatment GSI score, pretreatment along the horizontal axis, and post-treatment along the vertical. As illustrated, Subject "A" started with a GSI score

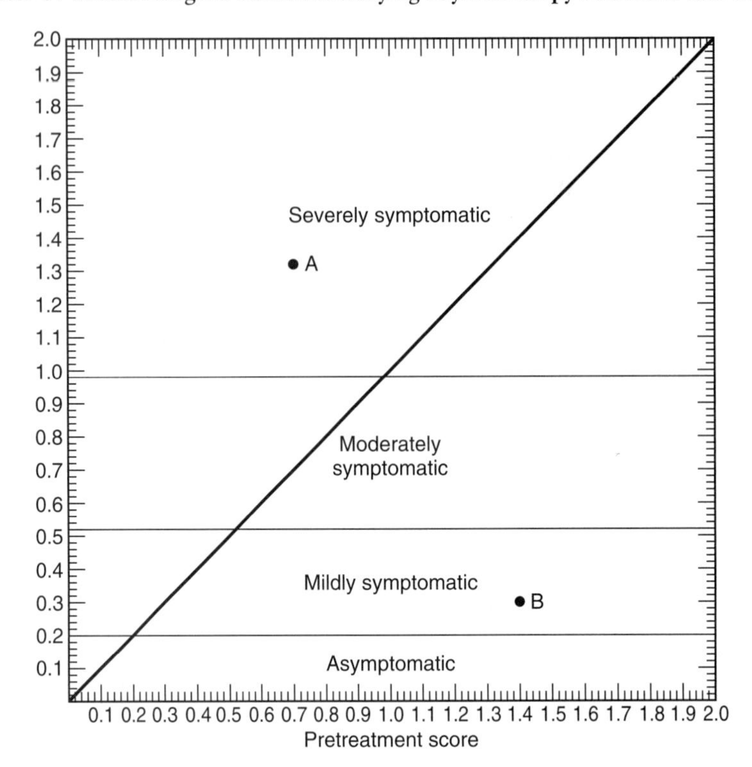

FIGURE 4.1 Sample figure illustrating cutoffs (horizontal lines) between the normative samples (continuous diagonal line indicates points of no change between pre- and post-treatment scores).
Source: From Tingey et al. (1996), used by permission of authors.

of about .7 and ended treatment with a GSI score of 1.3, indicating greater symptomatology after treatment. Subject "B" started with a GSI score of 1.4 and ended with a GSI score of .3, indicating a decrease in symptomatology.

The three horizontal lines signify the cutoff points for four normative samples at post-treatment: asymptomatic, mildly symptomatic, moderately symptomatic, and severely symptomatic. The normative data for the severely symptomatic sample in Figure 4.1 were found in existing literature on the SCL-90-R as applied to inpatients (Derogatis, 1983), outpatients (Burlingame & Barlow, 1996), and the original normative standardization sample (general population) collected by Derogatis (1983). The asymptomatic sample was collected for the purpose of identifying a group that was nominated and carefully screened to exclude persons who were not well adjusted (in contrast to the typical normative sample that is based on a random sample of persons, some of whom may evidence psychopathology). Through these procedures, the client's status in relation to clients and nonclients was carefully defined and could be observed along the dimension of mental health, with severe pathology at one end and ideal mental health (being asymptomatic) at the other end.

Efforts such as this have been carried out with other standardized measures such as the Hamilton Depression Rating Scale (Grundy, Lambert, & Grundy, 1996); the State-Trait Anxiety Inventory (Condon & Lambert, 1994); the Beck Depression Inventory (Seggar, Lambert, & Hansen, 2002); and the Outcome Questionnaire-45 (Lambert, Hansen et al., 1996). Continued efforts along these lines are needed to rate each client's change along the continuum of mental health (Kendall & Sheldrick, 2000). The use of multiple normative groups has the advantage of allowing severely disturbed clients to be considered clinically significantly improved by moving into functioning that is more typical of less disturbed clients (such as outpatients) and also allowing less disturbed (subclinical) clients' progress to be assessed with regard to their movement into high levels of functioning. This latter standard is appropriate for many students who seek help in college counseling centers or for clients who fail to meet the criteria for Axis I disorders but who might benefit from clinical services (e.g., Barkham et al., 1996).

Several methods for calculating reliable change and cutoff scores for passing into social comparison groups have been offered. However, the method outlined by Jacobson and Truax (1991) remains the most frequently used technique for examining reliable change. Speer and Greenbaum (1995) reviewed and evaluated the Jacobson method in conjunction with other methods, including Edwards-Nunnally (Edwards, Yarvis, Mueller, Zingale, & Wagman, 1978), Hsu-Linn–Lord (Hsu, 1989), and Nunnally-Kotsch (Nunnally & Kotsch, 1983). Each of these methods examines the post-treatment score in relationship to the pretreatment score while considering the reliability and distribution of test scores. In addition, Speer and Greenbaum compared a hierarchical linear modeling method that used multiple data points. They found that the Edwards-Nunnally and HLM methods identified more clients as improvers and were therefore less conservative. We recommend that researchers report the Jacobson RCI statistic and cutoff scores, either alone or in combination with other methods of evaluating meaningful change. This will allow research across sites to be evaluated with the same standard and facilitate comparisons between outcome studies of various treatment practices.

Further reading about clinical significance can be found in Kendall's (1999) special section in the *Journal of Consulting and Clinical Psychology*. Especially important is the detailed statistical procedures for calculating cutoff scores for normative comparisons summarized by Kendall, Marrs-Garcia, Nath, and Sheldrick (1999).

High End-State Functioning

High end-state functioning examines the status of clients at the end of treatment without direct reference to pretreatment status. Examples include the use of social drinking behaviors as criteria for outcome in the treatment of problem drinking or the use of adequate sexual performance (e.g., ratio of orgasms to attempts at sex; or time to orgasm following penetration; Sabalis, 1983) in the treatment of sexual dysfunction. These criteria are based on data about the normative functioning of individuals and can be easily and meaningfully applied with a number of disorders for which normal or ideal functioning is readily apparent and easily measured (e.g., obesity, bulimia).

Another method of examining the clinical meaning of change is through *a priori* derivation of high end-state functioning based on multiple measures. Jacobson, Wilson, & Tupper (1988) proposed three methods for defining high end-state functioning and compared them with their normative methods. High end-state functioning in this procedure defines clinically significant improvement as reaching normality by setting a cutoff score on each outcome measure prior to completion of therapy. These cutoffs are based on clinical judgments about normality. The advantage of this method is that it allows theoretical considerations to enter into definitions of functioning while taking into account multiple measures. High end-state functioning has the disadvantage of being based on consensus among investigators rather than being purely statistical. In their comparison of these methods with those from statistical estimates based on norm groups, Jacobson et al. (1988) found that end-state analysis depended on the reliability of the measures that were used to calculate cutoff scores. When reliability was high, the statistically based technique was more conservative. Blanchard and Schwartz (1988) applied variations of these methods in health psychology in setting standards for psychological interventions for headaches. Investigators calculate the percent improvement in headaches based on frequency and severity. A 50% reduction in headache activity in the absence of medication is defined as clinically significant improvement, but these researchers have not yet reached a standard for high end-state functioning in absolute terms. To date, researchers have just begun to formulate high end-state functioning criteria, and comparisons with other methods have seldom been published.

Cautions and Recommendations

Despite the advantages of defining clinically significant change and using standard methods for identifying clinically meaningful improvement, problems include the complexities that are created when researchers use multiple outcome measures, each one possibly providing different information regarding both the individual and the group as a whole. What shall we do with the lack of congruence between clinically significant improvement on one dependent measure but not on others? Should a client be required to change on more than one measure to be declared improved to the degree that clinical significance implies? So far no study has really addressed these issues in any substantial way.

Other problems include the use of discrete cutoff points and their derivation (how should these points be set?); the problems that result from score distributions that are not normal (how serious are violations of this assumption of normality?); and the limitations of floor and ceiling effects in many of the most frequently used tests. The problems of floor and ceiling effects are especially serious as many tests are heavily weighted toward pathology and were not developed for use with people who represent the healthy or nondisturbed end of the functioning continuum, which represents the clients' nondisturbed peers. A problem with clinical significance methodology in routine practice, as opposed to clinical trials research, is the fact that a sizable minority of clients enter treatment in the functional range and therefore cannot meet the criteria for passing a cutoff into the ranks of normal functioning. Lambert, Whipple, et al. (2001), for example, found that as many as 30% of clients were not in the clinical range on the Outcome Questionnaire (OQ-45) at pretreatment. With these nonclinical clients, only reliable change and deterioration can be estimated. In addition, considerable controversy exists about procedural and statistical analyses (Hageman & Arrindell, 1999a; Hageman & Arrindell, 1999b; Hsu, 1996; 1999; Jacobson & Truax, 1991; Kendall, 1999; Lacks & Powlista, 1989; McGlinchey & Jacobson, 1999), which have substantial impact on estimates of clinical significance. Finally, we are reminded by a special issue of *Behavioral Assessment* edited by Jacobson (1988) that, despite the precision used to assess improvement, definitions of improvement are somewhat arbitrary and culturally ascribed.

Advances in operationalizing clinical significance promise to make psychotherapy outcome assessment richer and more relevant to clinical practice, an improvement that is long overdue. Already, however, there is evidence that these methods will provide more conservative estimates of treatment effects and more modest conclusions about the efficacy of psychotherapy than we had before (Jacobson & Truax, 1991).

Issues in Data Collection and Analyses

Influence of the Assessor

The responses of clients may well be affected by the characteristics and communications of the assessor (Rosenthal, 1966). This problem is especially important in outcome research where judges, clinical experts, significant others, and therapists are involved in the assessment. Several authors have offered suggestions for enhancing the validity of therapist ratings (Newman, 1983), expert observer ratings (Auerbach, 1983), ratings by significant others (Davidson & Davidson, 1983), client self-report (Beutler & Crago, 1983; Cameron & Evers, 1990; Sobell & Sobell, 1990; Stone et al., 1999), and institutional measures (Maisto & Maisto, 1983). The general principle in all these efforts is to try to measure the actual state, beliefs, or behavior of clients. Thus, the instructions from researchers to assessors, including the client, encourage candor through some means (Rankin, 1990). Assessors are typically offered a degree of anonymity, especially with regard to telling clients that their responses will not be shared with the therapist or used to evaluate the therapist. The confidentiality offered clients encourages not only more honest responses from them, but ethical responsibility as well.

Guidelines are available in many areas of research (e.g., Babor, Brown, & Del Boca, 1990, summarized reviews of methodological studies about the accuracy of verbal reports of persons with addictive disorders). Though generally reliable, the accuracy of self-reports when compared with that coming from other assessors seems to depend on the sensitivity of the information sought (e.g., demographics vs. arrest record), specificity of validation criteria (e.g., archival data vs. urine tests), personal characteristics of the informant (e.g., sober vs. intoxicated), reference to time (e.g., immediate past vs. early life), and demand characteristics of the research situation (e.g., intake interview vs. program evaluation). Babor et al. suggested a model and an interview format that enhances the accuracy of verbal reports based on interviews, thus reducing discrepancies between assessment sources.

Psychotherapy research is usually so complex and cumbersome that the details regarding administration of instruments are vague or absent in the methodology section of most published research. One can only hope that researchers take the precautions normally assumed to be taken in the field (cf. Kazdin, 1980) or that they report deviations from accepted standards. For example, given that researchers normally inform clients that their post-therapy outcome ratings will not be shared with their therapist, deviations from this standard should be reported. The reader of these studies can then safely assume that treatment effects may be exaggerated when contrasted with anonymous ratings (e.g., Shadish & Sweeney, 1991; Smith et al., 1980).

Statistical Analyses of Change

How should the researcher analyze the possible changes in status consequent to some intervention? Probably the most commonly used procedure has been the analysis of variance of raw gain (or difference) scores (Ashcroft, 1971). Zimmerman (1997) has demonstrated that in many instances difference scores are highly reliable and can show substantial correlations with other measures. However, just as improvement ratings based on gross ratings of retrospective improvement are inordinately affected by post-therapy status, difference scores may be inordinately influenced by pretreatment status. Clients who have the highest level of pathology pre-therapy have the greatest opportunity to show positive changes (Mintz & Kiesler, 1982), so some of the change reflected in pre- minus post-difference scores may be the result of regression to the mean.

Another common procedure is analysis of covariance or multiple analysis of covariance, with pretreatment performance being the covariate (cf. Kazdin, Bass, Siegel, & Thomas, 1989). The advantage of this method is that it makes an adjustment for pretreatment differences between groups (which randomization or matching strategies has not eliminated) and reduces error variance, making it more likely that existing treatment effects will be identified.

Some researchers have proposed calculation of a true gain score or residual gain score (Cronbach & Furby, 1970). Hummel-Rossi and Weinberg (1975) recommended either the true residualized gain score (a score that is independent of pretest status) or partial correlation (multiple regression with post-test as the criterion and pretest as the covariate). The true residual gain score is used when the focus is on the change of an individual (with respect to the group), and partial correlation is used when the interest is in relating group change to other variables. Residualized gain is probably a last choice for analyzing change because its interpretation offers conclusions that are often unimportant to the clinician or administrator. Such a statement as: "After we have taken out individual differences due to initial severity of disturbance the net effect is . . ." leaves the clinician with a conclusion that holds only if the clients coming to a clinic were alike with regards to disturbance at the beginning of treatment.

Tucker, Damarin, and Messick (1966) recommended a base-free measure of change, but it has not been frequently used. Beutler and Crago (1983) recommended use of Cronbach and Gleser's (1953) D^2 transformation, which is based on the assumption that the reliability of raw change scores may, in fact, be higher than either pre- or post-measures alone. D^2 requires that the pre-post status be measured in several areas; it combines several scores, thus reducing error variance. Beutler and Crago (1983) suggested that both methods of deriving unbiased change scores should be used because they correct for different problems. Both procedures are attempts to reflect actual change accurately, and any discrepancy between the results of using either method could be explored.

Among the more promising statistical methods for studying change are those elaborated upon by Bryk and Raudenbush (1987) for the study of repeated measures on individual clients. These methods, often referred to as hierarchical linear models, allow the researcher to model the slope or speed of change for an individual over time, and then average individual slopes within larger groups of clients. These methods are based on more observations per individual and are, therefore, more reliable than the usual methods of assessing change, which are based on pre-post assessments.

In summary, no standard procedure for assessing change exists, although one is clearly needed (cf. Beutler & Hamblin, 1986). At this point in time, the raw change score remains the metric of choice for most circumstances in which client change is to be assessed.

Statistical Power

As Beutler and Hill (1992) pointed out, investigators often ignore the fact that the power of univariate comparisons to detect a difference is limited by the size of the smallest sample, the number of comparison groups, and the nature of the dependent measures. When a large number of measures are used, methods should be employed to correct for data redundancy. Rather than exploring all possibilities and thereby reducing statistical power, planned comparisons should first be employed with the theoretically important measures. Multivariate procedures should be used wherever possible, thus reducing the number of analyses and study-wise error rates.

Planned comparisons allow one to examine only the specific hypotheses under consideration and thereby limit the effects of multiple analyses on error rates, while preserving power. See Chapter 2, this volume, for additional discussions of statistical power.

Summary

The measurement of outcome is in a state of chaos, with little agreement among researchers about the specific measures to be used. We look forward to the day when researchers can agree on a minimal core outcome battery for measuring changes in clients with specific disorders. We are convinced that most of the necessary measures to be included in such batteries already exist. It remains a task for researchers in their specialty areas to agree upon a few measures while continuing to explore the possibilities of newly created measures.

Many advances have been made in outcome assessment over the years; yet, as Luborsky (1971) has suggested, outcome issues are hardy perennials in the field of psychotherapy research. At present, there is enough evidence of such divergence, and even chaos, that the time is ripe for fundamental change. No new paradigm shift is on the horizon, however, and until such a shift occurs, we will have to be content with the gradual improvements that have characterized the last five decades.

CONCLUSIONS

In our review of measures and methods that apply to process and outcome research, we were struck by the different issues confronting these related but largely independent domains of inquiry. Outcome researchers agree on many of the general targets of measurement as well as some of the procedures to be used in assessment even if they cannot agree upon the specific measures to be employed. In contrast, process researchers, perhaps because their work is more often driven by a complex theory, cannot even agree on what process should be measured, let alone what measures and methods should be employed in studying these processes. Nevertheless, one of the achievements of psychotherapy research is the increased sophistication in methods and methodology in both process and outcome research documented by this chapter. We have come a long way since the initial studies were undertaken. We hope that future research on psychotherapy and its effects will build on the foundation laid by this past research. We are optimistic that proper outcome and process assessment can build a stronger bridge between research and practice. Certainly, the field of process and outcome assessment is still in its infancy, offering abundant opportunities to curious and dedicated researchers.

REFERENCES

Angus, L., Levitt, H., & Hardtke, K. (1999). The Narrative Processes Coding System: Research applications and implications for psychotherapy practice. *Journal of Clinical Psychology, 55,* 1255–1270.

Ankuta, G. Y., & Ables, N. (1993). Client satisfaction, clinical significance, and meaningful change in psychotherapy. *Professional Psychology: Research and Practice, 24,* 70–74.

Arnhoff, F. N. (1954). Some factors influencing the unreliability of clinical judgments. *Journal of Clinical Psychology, 10,* 272–275.

Ashcroft, C. (1971). The latest school achievement of treated and untreated emotionally handicapped children. *Journal of School Psychology, 9,* 338–342.

Auerbach, A. H. (1983). Assessment of psychotherapy outcome from the viewpoint of expert observer. In M. J. Lambert, E. R. Christensen, & S. S. DeJulio (Eds.), *The assessment of psychotherapy outcome* (pp. 537–568). New York: John Wiley & Sons.

Auld, F., Jr., & White, A. (1956). Rules for dividing interviews into sentences. *Journal of Psychology, 42,* 273–281.

Babor, T. F., Brown, J., & Del Boca, F. K. (1990). Validity of self-reports in applied research on addictive behaviors: Fact or fiction? *Behavioral Assessment, 12,* 5–31.

Bachrach, H., Mintz, J., & Luborsky, L. (1971). On rating empathy and other psychotherapy variables: An experience with the effects of training. *Journal of Consulting and Clinical Psychology, 36,* 445.

Bailey, D. B., & Simeonson, R. J. (1988). Investigation of use of goal attainment scaling to evaluate individual progress of clients with severe and profound mental retardation. *Mental Retardation, 26,* 289–295.

Bakeman, R. (1978). Untangling streams of behavior: Sequential analysis of observation data. In G. P. Sackett (Ed.), *Observing behavior: Vol. 2. Data collection and analysis methods* (pp. 63–78). Baltimore, MD: University Park Press.

Bakeman, R., & Gottman, J. M. (1986). *Observing interaction: An introduction to sequential analysis.* New York: Cambridge University Press.

Barkham, M., Rees, A., Stiles, W. B., Shapiro, D. A., Hardy, G. E., & Reynolds, S. (1996). Dose effect relations in time limited psychotherapy for depression. *Journal of Consulting and Clinical Psychology, 64,* 927–935.

Barrett-Lennard, G. T. (1962). Dimensions of therapist response as casual factors in therapeutic change. *Psychological Monographs, 76* (43, Whole No. 562).

Battle, C. C., Imber, S. D., Hoehn-Saric, R., Stone, A. R., Nash, C., & Frank, J. D. (1966). Target complaints as criteria of improvement. *American Journal of Psychotherapy, 20,* 184–192.

Beck, A. T., Steer, R. A., & Garbin, M. G. (1988). Psychometric properties of the Beck Depression Inventory: Twenty-five years later. *Clinical Psychology Review, 8,* 77–100.

Benjamin, L. S. (1974). Structural analysis of social behavior. *Psychological Review, 81,* 392–425.

Benjamin, L. S. (1979). Use of structural analysis of social behavior (SASB) and Markov chains to study dyadic interactions. *Journal of Abnormal Psychology, 88,* 303–319.

Bergin, A. E. (1971). The evaluation of therapeutic outcomes. In A. E. Bergin & S. L. Garfield (Eds.), *Handbook of psychotherapy and behavior change: An empirical analysis.* (pp. 217–270). New York: John Wiley & Sons.

Berzins, J. I., Bednar, R. L., & Severy, L. J. (1975). The problem of intersource consensus in measuring therapeutic outcomes: New data and multivariate perspectives. *Journal of Abnormal Psychology, 84,* 10–19.

Beutler, L. E. (1991). Selective treatment matching: Systematic eclectic psychotherapy. *Psychotherapy, 28,* 457–462.

Beutler, L. E., & Crago, M. (1983). Self-report measures of psychotherapy outcome. In M. J. Lambert, E. R. Christensen, & S. S. DeJulio (Eds.), *The Assessment of Psychotherapy Outcome* (pp. 453–497). New York: John Wiley & Sons.

Beutler, L. E., & Hamblin, D. L. (1986). Individualized outcome measures of internal change: Methodological considerations. *Journal of Consulting and Clinical Psychology, 54,* 48–53.

Beutler, L. E., & Hill, C. E. (1992). Process and outcome research in the treatment of adult victims of childhood sexual abuse: Methodological issues. *Journal of Consulting and Clinical Psychology, 60,* 204–212.

Beutler, L. E., Johnson, D. T., Neville, C. W., & Workman, S. N. (1973). Some sources of variance in "accurate empathy" ratings. *Journal of Consulting and Clinical Psychology, 40,* 17–19.

Blanchard, E. B., & Schwartz, S. P. (1988). Clinically significant changes in behavioral medicine. *Behavioral Assessment, 10,* 171–188.

Bordin, E. S. (1974). *Research strategies in psychotherapy.* New York: John Wiley & Sons.

Bordin, E. S., Cutler, R. I., Dittmann, A. T., Harway, N. I., Rausch, H. L., & Rigler, D. (1954). Measurement problems in process research on psychotherapy. *Journal of Consulting Psychology, 18,* 79–82.

Borgen, F. H., & Barnett, D. C. (1987). Applying cluster analysis in counseling psychology research. *Journal of Counseling Psychology, 34,* 456–468.

Bozarth, J. D., & Krauft, C. J. (1972). Accurate empathy ratings: Some methodological considerations. *Journal of Clinical Psychology, 23,* 408–411.

Bryk, A. S., & Raudenbush, S. W. (1987). Application of hierarchical linear models to assessing change. *Psychological Bulletin, 101,* 147–158.

Budman, S. H., Demby, A., Feldstein, M., Redondo, J., Scherz, B., Bennett, M. J., Koppenaal, G., Daley, B. S., Hunter, M., & Ellis, J. (1987). Preliminary findings on a new instrument to measure cohesion in group psychotherapy. *International Journal of Group Psychotherapy, 37,* 75–94.

Burlingame, G. M., & Barlow, S. (1996). Outcome and process differences between professional and nonprofessional therapists in time-limited group psychotherapy. *International Journal of Group Psychotherapy, 46,* 455–478.

Butcher, J. N., Dahlstrom, W. G., Graham, J. R., Tellegen, A., & Kaemmer, B. (1989). *Minnesota Multiphasic Personality Inventory (MMPI-2). Manual for administration and scoring.* Minneapolis: University of Minnesota Press.

Cameron, R., & Evers, S. E. (1990). Self-report issues in obesity and weight management: State of the art and future directions. *Behavioral Assessment, 12,* 91–106.

Campion, M. A., Palmer, D. K., & Campion, J. E. (1997). A review of structure in the selection interview. *Personnel Psychology, 50,* 655–702.

Caracena, P. F., & Vicory, J. R. (1969). Correlates of phenomenological and judged empathy. *Journal of Counseling Psychology, 16,* 510–515.

Carkhuff, R. R. (1969). *Helping and human relations* (Vols. 1 & 2). New York: Holt, Rinehart & Winston.

Carmichael, H. T. (1966). Sound-film recording of psychoanalytic therapy: A therapist's experience and reactions. In L. A. Gottschalk & A. H. Auerbach (Eds.), *Methods of research in psychotherapy* (pp. 50–59). New York: Appleton-Century-Crofts.

Carson, R. C., Butcher, J. N., & Mineka (2000). *Abnormal psychology and modern life* (9th ed.). New York: Scott Foresman.

Cartwright, D. S., Kirtner, W. L., & Fiske, D. W. (1963). Method factors in changes associated with psychotherapy. *Journal of Abnormal and Social Psychology, 66,* 164–175.

Cartwright, R. (1966). Analysis of qualitative material. In L. Festinger & D. Katz (Eds.), *Research methods in the behavioral sciences* (pp. 421–470). New York: Holt, Rinehart & Winston.

Cohen, J. (1960). A coefficient of agreement for nominal scales. *Educational and Psychological Measurement, 20,* 37–46.

Cohen, J. (1968). Weighted kappa: Nominal scale agreement with provision for scaled disagreement or partial credit. *Psychological Bulletin, 70,* 213–220.

Condon, K. M., & Lambert, M. J. (1994, June). *Assessing clinical significance: Application to the State-Trait Anxiety Inventory.* Paper presented at the annual meeting of the Society for Psychotherapy Research, York, England.

Consumer Reports. (1995, November). Mental health: Does therapy help? pp. 734–739.

Coombs, C. H. (1951). Mathematical models in psychological scaling. *Journal of the American Statistical Association, 46,* 480–489.

Coughlan, F. J., & Coughlan, N. S. (1999). Goal Attainment Scaling: An outcomes based approach to developmental assessment for South African youth in residential settings. *Southern African Journal of Child and Adolescent Mental Health, 11,* 27–37.

Coughlin, K. M. (1997). *The 1998 behavioral outcomes handbook.* New York: Faulkner & Gray.

Corrigan, J. D., & Schmidt, L. D. (1983). Development and validation of revisions in the Counselor Rating Form. *Journal of Counseling Psychology, 30,* 64–75.

Cronbach, L. J. (1960). *Essentials of psychological testing.* New York: Harper & Row.

Cronbach, L. J. (1990). *Essentials of psychological testing* (3rd ed.) New York: Harper & Row.

Cronbach, L. J., & Furby, L. (1970). How we should measure "change"—or should we? *Psychological Bulletin, 74,* 68–80.

Cronbach, L. J., & Gleser, G. C. (1953). Assessing similarities between profiles. *Psychological Bulletin, 50,* 456–473.

Cronbach, L. J., & Gleser, G. C., Nanda, H., & Rajaratnam, N. (1972). *The dependability of behavioral measurements.* New York: John Wiley & Sons.

Cytrynbaum, S., Ginath, Y., Birdwell, T., & Brandt, L. (1979). Goal attainment scaling: A critical review. *Evaluation Quarterly, 3,* 5–40.

Davidson, C. V., & Davidson, R. H. (1983). The significant other as data source and data problem in psychotherapy outcome research. In M. J. Lambert, E. R. Christensen, & S. S. DeJulio (Eds.), *The assessment of psychotherapy outcome* (pp. 569–602). New York: John Wiley & Sons.

Derogatis, L. R. (1983). *SCL-90: Administration, scoring and procedures manual for the Revised Version.* Baltimore, MD: Clinical Psychometric Research.

Derogatis, L. R., & Melisaratos, N. (1983). The brief symptom inventory: An introductory report. *Psychological Medicine, 13,* 595–605.

Dipboye, R. L., & Gaugler, B. B. (1993). Cognitive and behavioral processes in the selection interview. In N. Schmitt & W. C. Borman, Associates, *Personnel selection in organizations* (pp. 135–170). San Francisco: Jossey-Bass.

Docherty, J. P., & Streeter, M. J. (1996). Measuring outcomes. In L. I. Sederer & B. Dickey (Eds.), *Outcome assessment in clinical practice* (pp. 8–18). Baltimore, MD: Williams & Wilkins.

Dollard, J., & Auld, F., Jr. (1959). *Scoring human motives: A manual.* New Haven, CT: Yale University Press.

Edwards, D., & Potter, J. (1992). *Discursive psychology.* London: Sage.

Edwards, D. W., Yarvis, R. M., Mueller, D. P., Zingale, H. C., & Wagman, W. J. (1978). Test-taking and the stability of adjustment scales: Can we assess patient deterioration? *Evaluation Quarterly, 2,* 275–292.

Ekman, P., & Friesen, W. V. (1968). *Nonverbal behavior in psychotherapy research.* In J. M. Sclien et al. (Eds.), *Research in psychotherapy* (Vol. 3, pp. 179–216). Washington DC: American Psychological Association.

Elliott, R. (1979). How clients perceive helper behaviors. *Journal of Counseling Psychology, 26,* 294–295.

Elliott, R. (1984). A discovery-oriented approach to significant events in psychotherapy: Interpersonal process recall and comprehensive process analysis. In L. Rice & L. Greenberg (Eds.), *Patterns of change* (pp. 249–286). New York: Guilford Press.

Elliott, R. (1985). Helpful and unhelpful events in brief counseling interviews: An empirical taxonomy. *Journal of Counseling Psychology, 32,* 302–322.

Elliott, R. (1986). Interpersonal Process Recall as a psychotherapy process recall method. In L. S. Greenberg & W. M. Pinsof (Eds.), *The psychotherapeutic process: A research handbook* (pp. 503–528). New York: Guilford Press.

Elliott, R. (1989). Comprehensive process analysis: Understanding the change process in significant therapeutic events. In M. J. Packer & R. B. Addison (Eds.), *Entering the circle: Hermaneutic investigation in psychology.* Albany, NY: SUNY Press.

Elliott, R. (1991). Five dimensions of therapy process. *Psychotherapy Research, 1,* 92–103.

Elliott, R., Fischer, C. T., & Rennie, D. L. (1999). Evolving guidelines for publication of qualitative research studies in psychology and related fields. *British Journal of Clinical Psychology, 38,* 215–229.

Elliott, R., Hill, C. E., Stiles, W. B., Friedlander, M. L., Mahrer, A. R., & Margison, F. R. (1987). Primary therapist response modes: Comparison of six rating systems. *Journal of Consulting and Clinical Psychology, 55,* 218–223.

Ericson, P. M., & Rogers, L. E. (1973). New procedures for analyzing relational communication. *Family Process, 12,* 245–267.

Exner, J. E., Jr. (1986). *The Rorschach: A comprehensive system: Vol. 1. Basic Foundation* (2nd ed.). New York: John Wiley & Sons.

Eysenck, H. J. (1952). The effects of psychotherapy: An evaluation. *Journal of Consulting Psychology, 16,* 319–324.

Farnsworth, J., Hess, J., & Lambert, M. J. (2001, April). A review of outcome measurement practices in the *Journal of Consulting and Clinical Psychology.* Paper presented at the annual meetings of the Rocky Mountain Psychological Association, Reno, NV.

Finn, J. D. (1974). *A general model for multivariate analysis.* New York: Holt, Rinehart, & Winston.

Fischer, J., & Corcoran, K. (1994). *Measures for clinical practice.* New York: The Free Press.

Fish, J. M. (1970). Empathy and the reported emotional experiences of beginning psychotherapists. *Journal of Consulting and Clinical Psychology, 35,* 64–69.

Fiske, D. W. (1977). Methodological issues in research on the psychotherapist. In A. S. Gurman & A. M. Razin (Eds.), *Effective psychotherapy* (pp. 23–43). New York: Pergamon Press.

Fleiss, J. L. (1981). Balanced incomplete block designs for interrater reliability studies. *Applied Psychological Measurement, 5,* 105–112.

Fleuridas, C., Rosenthal, D. M., Leigh, G. K., & Leigh, T. E. (1990). Family goal recording: An adaption of goal attainment scaling for enhancing family therapy and assessment. *Journal of Marital and Family Therapy, 16(4),* 389–406.

Flowers, J. V., & Booaren, C. D. (1990). Four studies toward an empirical foundation for group therapy. *Journal of Social Service Research, 13(2),* 105–121.

Foreman, S., & Marmar, C. R. (1985). Therapist actions that address initially poor therapeutic alliances in psychotherapy. *American Journal of Psychiatry, 142,* 922–926.

Forsyth, R. P., & Fairweather, G. W. (1961). Psychotherapeutic and other hospital treatment criteria: The dilemma. *Journal of Abnormal and Social Psychology, 62,* 598–604.

Friedlander, M. L. (1982). Counseling discourse as a speech event: Revision and extension of the Hill Counselor Verbal Response Category System. *Journal of Counseling Psychology, 29,* 425–429.

Friedlander, M. L., Ellis, M. V., Siegel, S. M., Raymond, L., & Haase, R. F. (1988). Generalizing from segments to sessions: Should it be done? *Journal of Counseling Psychology, 35,* 243–250.

Froyd, J. E., Lambert, M. J., & Froyd, J. D. (1996). A review of practices of psychotherapy outcome measurement. *Journal of Mental Health, 5,* 11–15.

Garfield, S. L. (1990). Issues and methods in psychotherapy process research. *Journal of Consulting and Clinical Psychology, 58,* 273–280.

Garfield, S. L. (1991). Psychotherapy models and outcome research. *American Psychologist, 46,* 1350–1351.

Garfield, S. L., Prager, R. A., & Bergin, A. E. (1971). Evaluation of outcome in psychotherapy. *Journal of Consulting and Clinical Psychology, 37,* 307–313.

Gaston, L., Marmar, C. R., & Ring, J. M. (1989, June). Engaging the difficult patient in cognitive therapy: Actions developing the therapeutic alliance. Paper presented at the annual meeting of the Society for Psychotherapy Research, Toronto, Ontario, Canada.

Gelso, C. J. (1973). The effects of audiorecording and videorecording on client satisfaction and self-exploration. *Journal of Consulting and Clinical Psychology, 40,* 455–461.

Gelso, C. J. (1974). Effects of recording on counselors and clients. *Counselor Education and Supervision, 14,* 5–12.

Gerarty, R. D. (1996). The use of outcome assessment in managed care: Past, present, and future. In L. I. Sederer & B. Dickey (Eds.), *Outcome assessment in clinical practice* (pp. 129–138). Baltimore, MD: Williams & Wilkins.

Gervaize, P. A., Mahrer, A. R., & Markow, R. (1985). Therapeutic laughter: What therapists do to promote strong laughter in patients. *Psychotherapy in Private Practice, 3,* 65–74.

Gibson, R. L., Snyder, W. U., & Ray, W. S. (1955). A factor analysis of measures of change following client-centered psychotherapy. *Journal of Counseling Psychology, 2,* 83–90.

Giorgi, A. (1970). *Psychology as human science: A phenomenologically based approach.* New York: Harper & Row.

Giorgi, A. (1985). Sketch of a psychological phenomenological method. In A. Giorgi (Ed.), *Phenomenology and psychological research* (pp. 8–22). Pittsburgh, PA: DusqueneUniversity Press.

Glaser, B., & Strauss, A. L. (1967). *The discovery of grounded theory: Strategies for qualitative research:* Hawthorne, NY: Aldine de Gruyter.

Gottman, J. M. (1979). Detecting cyclicity in social interaction. *Psychological Bulletin, 86,* 338–348.

Gottman, J. M., & Markmam, H. J. (1978). Experimental designs in psychotherapy research. In S. L. Garfield & A. E. Bergin (Eds.), *Handbook of psychotherapy and behavior change: An empirical analysis* (2nd ed., pp. 23–62.). New York: John Wiley & Sons.

Green, B. C., Gleser, G. C., Stone, W. N., & Siefert, R. F. (1975). Relationships among diverse measures of psychotherapy outcome. *Journal of Consulting and Clinical Psychology, 43,* 689–699.

Greenberg, L. S. (1984). Task analysis of interpersonal conflict. In L. N. Rice & L. S. Greenberg (Eds.), *Patterns of change: Intensive analysis of psychotherapeutic process.* New York: Guilford Press.

Greenberg, L. S. (1986). Change process research. *Journal of Consulting and Clinical Psychology, 54,* 4–9.

Greenberg, L. S. (1991). Research on the process of change. *Psychotherapy Research, 1,* 3–16.

Greenberg, L. S., & Pinsof, W. (Eds.). (1986). *The psychotherapeutic process: A research handbook.* New York: Guilford Press.

Gregerson, A. T., Nielsen, S. L., Isakson, R. L., Lambert, M. J., Smart, D. W., & Worthen, V. E. (2001, August). Recalling and estimating emotional states:

Are consumer reports accurate? Paper presented at the annual meeting of the American Psychological Association, San Francisco, CA.

Grundy, C. T., Lambert, M. J., & Grundy, E. M. (1996). Assessing clinical significance: Application to the Hamilton Rating Scale for Depression. *Journal of Mental Health, 5*, 25–33.

Grundy, C. T., Lunnen, K. M., Lambert, M. J., Ashton, J. E., & Tovey, D. R. (1994). The Hamilton Rating Scale for Depression: One scale or many? *Clinical Psychology: Science and Practice, 1*, 197–205.

Gurman, A. S. (1973). Effects of therapist and patient mood on the therapeutic functioning of high- and low-facilitative therapists. *Journal of Consulting and Clinical Psychology, 40*, 48–58.

Hageman, W.J.J.M., & Arrindell, W. A. (1999a). Clinically significant and practical! Enhancing precision does make a difference. Reply to McGlinchey and Jacobson, Hsu, and Speer. *Behavior Research and Therapy, 37*, 1219–1233.

Hageman, W.J.J.M., & Arrindell, W. A. (1999b). Establishing clinically significant change: Increment of precision and the distinction between individual and group level of analysis. *Behaviour Research and Therapy, 37*, 1169–1193.

Hansen, J. C., Moore, G. D., & Carkhuff, R. R. (1968). The differential relationships of objective and client perceptions of counseling. *Journal of Counseling Psychology, 24*, 244–246.

Harway, N., Dittman, A., Raush, H., Bordin, E., & Rigler, D. (1955). The measurement of depth of interpretation. *Journal of Counseling Psychology, 19*, 247–253.

Heatherington, L. (1989). Toward more meaningful clinical research: Taking context into account in coding psychotherapy interaction. *Psychotherapy, 26*, 436–447.

Heppner, P. P., Kivlighan, D. M., Jr., & Wampold, B. E. (1999). *Research design in counseling* (2nd ed.). New York: Brooks/Cole.

Herbert, J. D., & Mueser, K. T. (1991). Proof is in the pudding: A commentary on Persons. *American Psychologist, 46*, 1347–1348.

Highlen, P. S., & Hill, C. E. (1984). Factors affecting client change in counseling. In S. Brown & R. Lent (Eds.), *Handbook of counseling psychology* (pp. 334–396). New York: John Wiley & Sons.

Hill, C. E. (1974). A comparison of the perceptions of a therapy session by clients, therapists, and objective judges. *Catalog of Selected Documents in Psychology, 4*, 16.

Hill, C. E. (1982). Counseling process research: Philosophical and methodological dilemmas. *The Counseling Psychologist, 10(4)*, 7–19.

Hill, C. E. (1986). An overview of the Hill Counselor and Client Verbal Response Modes Category Systems. In L. S. Greenberg & W. M. Pinsof (Eds.), *The psychotherapeutic process: A research handbook* (pp. 131–160). New York: Guilford Press.

Hill, C. E. (1989). *Therapist techniques and client outcomes: Eight cases of brief psychotherapy.* Newbury Park, CA: Sage Publications.

Hill, C. E. (1990). A review of exploratory in-session process research. *Journal of Consulting and Clinical Psychology, 58*, 288–294.

Hill, C. E., Carter, J. A., & O'Farrell, M. K. (1983). A case study of the process and outcome of time-limited counseling. *Journal of Counseling Psychology, 30*, 3–18.

Hill, C. E., Helms, J., Spiegel, S. B., & Tichenor, V. (1988). Development of a system for categorizing client reactions to therapist interventions. *Journal of Counseling Psychology, 35*, 27–36.

Hill, C. E., Helms, J. E., Tichenor, V., Spiegel, S. B., O'Grady, K. E., & Perry, E. (1988). The effects of therapist response modes in brief psychotherapy. *Journal of Counseling Psychology, 35*, 222–233.

Hill, C. E., Nutt, E., & Jackson, S. (1994). Trends in psychotherapy process research: Samples, measures, researchers, and classic publications. *Journal of Counseling Psychology, 41*, 364–377.

Hill, C. E., & O'Brien, K. (1999). *Helping skills: Facilitating exploration, insight, and action.* Washington, DC: American Psychological Association. (Accompanied by a videotape)

Hill, C. E., & O'Grady, K. E. (1985). List of therapist intentions illustrated in a case study and with therapists of varying theoretical orientations. *Journal of Counseling Psychology, 32*, 3–22.

Hill, C. E., O'Grady, K. E., Balenger, V., Busse, W., Falk, D. R., Hill, M., Rios, P., & Taffe, R. (1994). Methodological examination of videotape-assisted reviews in brief therapy: Helpfulness ratings, therapist intentions, client reactions, mood, and session evaluation. *Journal of Counseling Psychology, 41*, 236–247.

Hill, C. E., O'Grady, K. E., & Elkin, I. E. (1992). Applying the Collaborative Study Psychotherapy Rating Scale to rate therapist adherence in cognitive-behavior therapy, interpersonal therapy, and clinical management. *Journal of Consulting and Clinical Psychology, 60*, 73–79.

Hill, C. E., O'Grady, K. E. & Price, P. (1988). A method for investigating sources of rater bias. *Journal of Counseling Psychology, 35*, 346–350.

Hill, C. E., Siegelman, L., Gronsky, B., Sturniolo, F., & Fretz, B. R. (1981). Nonverbal communication and counseling outcome. *Journal of Counseling Psychology, 28*, 203–212.

Hill, C. E., & Stephany, A. (1990). The relationship of nonverbal behaviors to client reactions. *Journal of Counseling Psychology, 37*, 22–26.

Hill, C. E., Thames, T. B., & Rardin, D. (1979). A comparison of Rogers, Perls, and Ellis on the Hill Counselor Verbal Response Category System. *Journal of Counseling Psychology, 26*, 198–203.

Hill, C. E., Thompson, B. J., & Williams, E. N. (1997). A guide to conducting consensual qualitative research. *The Counseling Psychologist, 25*, 517–572.

Hill, C. E., & Williams, E. N. (2000). The process of individual therapy. In R. W. Lent & S. D. Brown (Eds.), *Handbook of counseling psychology* (pp. 670–710). New York: John Wiley & Sons.

Hill, W. F. (1971). The Hill Interaction Matrix. *Personnel and Guidance Journal, 49*, 619–622.

Horvath, A. O., & Greenberg, L. S. (1989). Development and validation of the Working Alliance Inventory. *Journal of Counseling Psychology, 36*, 223–233.

Horvath, A. O., Marx, R. W., & Kamann, A. M. (1990). Thinking about thinking in therapy: An examination of clients' understanding of their therapists' intentions. *Journal of Consulting and Clinical Psychology, 58*, 614–621.

Horvath, A. O., & Symonds, B. D. (1991). Relation between working alliance and outcome in psychotherapy: A meta-analysis. *Journal of Counseling Psychology, 38*, 139–149.

Hoyt, M. F., Marmar, C. R., Horowitz, M. J., & Alvarez, W. F. (1981). The Therapist Action Scale and the Patient Action Scale: Instruments for the assessment of activities during dynamic psychotherapy. *Psychotherapy: Therapy, Research, and Practice, 18*, 109–116.

Hoyt, W. T., & Melby, J. N. (1999). Dependability of measurement in counseling psychology: An introduction to generalizability theory. *The Counseling Psychologist, 27*, 325–352.

Hsu, L. M. (1989). Reliable changes in psychotherapy: Taking into account regression towards the mean. *Behavioral Assessment, 11*, 459–467.

Hsu, L. M. (1996). On the identification of clinically significant client changes: Reinterpretation of Jacobson's cut scores. *Journal of Psychopathology and Behavioral Assessment, 18*, 371–385.

Hsu, L. M. (1999). A comparison of three methods of identifying reliable and clinically significant client changes: Commentary on Hageman and Arrindell. *Behaviour Research and Therapy, 37*, 1195–1202.

Hummel-Rossi, B. & Weinberg, S. L. (1975). Practical guidelines in applying current theories to the measurement of change. Part I: Problems in measuring change and recommended procedures. *Journal Supplement Abstract Service*, MS No. 916.

Jacobson, N. S. (1988). Defining clinically significant change: An introduction. *Behavioral Assessment. 10*, 131–132.

Jacobson, N. S., Follette, W. C., & Revenstorf, D. (1984). Psychotherapy outcome research: Methods for reporting varability and evaluating clinical significance. *Behavior Therapy, 15*, 336–352.

Jacobson, N. S., & Truax, P. (1991). Clinical significance: A statistical approach to defining meaningful change in psychotherapy research. *Journal of Consulting and Clinical Psychology, 59*, 12–19.

Jacobson, N. S., Wilson, L., & Tupper, C. (1988). The clinical significance of treatment gains resulting from exposure-based interventions for agoraphobia: A re-analysis of outcome data. *Behavior Therapy, 19*, 539–554.

Jones, E. E., Cummings, J. D., & Horowitz, M. J. (1988). Another look at the nonspecific hypothesis of therapeutic effectiveness. *Journal of Consulting and Clinical Psychology, 56*, 48–55.

Karl, N. J., & Abeles, N. (1969). Psychotherapy process as a function of the time segment sampled. *Journal of Consulting and Clinical Psychology, 33*, 207–212.

Katz, D., & Resnikoff, A. (1977). Televised self-confrontation and recalled affect: A new look at videotape recall. *Journal of Counseling Psychology, 24*, 150–152.

Kazdin, A. E. (1977). Assessing the clinical or applied importance of behavior change through social validation. *Behavior Modification, 1*, 427–452.

Kazdin, A. E. (1980). *Research design in clinical psychology*. New York: Harper & Row.

Kazdin, A. E., Bass, D., Siegel, T., & Thomas, C. (1989). Cognitive-behavioral therapy and relationship therapy in treatment of children referred for anti-social behavior. *Journal of Consulting and Clinical Psychology, 57*, 522–535.

Kendall, P. C. (1999). Clinical Significance. *Journal of Consulting and Clinical Psychology, 67(3)*, 283–284.

Kendall, P. C., Marrs-Garcia, A., Nath, S. R., & Sheldrick, R. C. (1999). Normative comparisons for the evaluation of clinical significance. *Journal of Consulting and Clinical Psychology, 67*, 285–299.

Kendall, P. C., & Sheldrick, R. C. (2000). Normative data for normative comparisons. *Journal of Consulting and Clinical Psychology, 68(5)*, 767–773.

Kiesler, D. J. (1971). Patient experiencing and successful outcome in individual psychotherapy of schizophrenics and psychoneurotics. *Journal of Consulting and Clinical Psychology, 37*, 370–385.

Kiesler, D. J. (1973). *The process of psychotherapy*. Chicago: Aldine.

Kiesler, D. J., Klein, M. H., & Mathieu, P. L. (1965). Sampling from the recorded therapy interview: The problem of segment location. *Journal of Consulting Psychology, 29*, 337–344.

Kiesler, D. J., Mathieu, P. L., & Klein, M. H. (1967). Patient experiencing level and interaction chronograph variables in therapy interview segments. *Journal of Consulting Psychology, 31*, 224.

Kiresuk, T. J., & Sherman, R. E. (1968). Goal attainment scaling: A general method for evaluating comprehensive community mental health programs. *Community Mental Health Journal, 4*, 443–453.

Kiresuk, T. J., Smith, A., & Cardillo, J. E. (1994). *Goal Attainment scaling: Applications, theory, and measurement*. Hillsdale, NJ: Erlbaum.

Kirk, J., & Miller, M. L. (1986). *Reliability and validity in qualitative research.* Newbury Park, CA: Sage.

Klein, D. F., & Cleary, T. A. (1967). Platonic true scores and error in psychiatric rating scales. *Psychological Bulletin, 68,* 77–80.

Klein, M. H., Mathieu, P. L., Gendlin, E. T., & Kiesler, D. J. (1970). *The experiencing scale: A research and training manual.* Madison: Bureau of Audio-Visual Instruction, University of Wisconsin.

Klein, M. H., Mathieu-Coughlan, P., & Kiesler, D. J. (1986). The experiencing scales. In L. Greenberg and W. Pinsof (Eds.), *The psychotherapeutic process: A research handbook* (pp. 21–72). New York: Guilford Press.

Knapp, P. H. (1974). Segmentation and structure in psychoanalysis. *Journal of the American Psychoanalytic Association, 22,* 14–36.

Kurtz, R. R., & Grummon, D. L. (1972). Different approaches to the measurement of therapist empathy and their relationship to therapy outcome. *Journal of Consulting and Clinical Psychology, 39,* 106–115.

Lacks, P., & Powlista, K. (1989). Improvement following behavioural treatment of insomnia: Clinical significance, long term maintenance and predictions of outcome. *Behavior Therapy, 20,* 117–134.

LaCrosse, M. B., & Barak, A. (1976). Differential perception of counselor behavior. *Journal of Counseling Psychology, 23,* 170–172.

Lambert, M. J. (1983). Introduction to assessment of psychotherapy outcome: Historical perspective and current issues. In M. J. Lambert, E. R. Christensen, & S. S. DeJulio (Eds.), *The assessment of psychotherapy outcome* (pp. 3–32). New York: Wiley-Interscience.

Lambert, M. J., DeJulio, S. S., & Stein, D. M. (1978). Therapist interpersonal skills: Process, outcome, methodological considerations, and recommendations for future research. *Psychological Bulletin, 85,* 467–489.

Lambert, M. J., Hansen, N. B., Umphress, V., Lunnen, K., Okiishi, J., Burlingame, G. M., Hefner, J. C., & Reisinger, C. R. (1996). *Administration and scoring manual for the Outcome Questionnaire (OQ-45.2).* Wilmington, DE: American Professional Credentialing Services LLC.

Lambert, M. J., Hatch, D. R., Kingston, M. D., & Edwards, B. C. (1986). Zung, Beck, and Hamilton rating scales as measures of treatment outcome: A meta-analytic comparison. *Journal of Consulting and Clinical Psychology, 54,* 54–59.

Lambert, M. J., & Hill, C. E. (1994). Assessing psychotherapy outcomes and processes. In A. E. Bergin & S. L. Garfield (Eds.), *Handbook of psychotherapy and behavior change* (4th ed.) (pp. 72–113). New York: John Wiley & Sons.

Lambert, M. J., & McRoberts, C. (1993, April). Survey of outcome measures used in *JCCP* 1986–1991. Poster presented at the annual meetings of the Western Psychological Association, Phoenix, AZ.

Lambert, M. J., Whipple, J. L., Smart, D. W., Vermeersch, D. A., Nielsen, S. L., & Hawkins, E. J. (2001). The effects of providing therapists with feedback on patient progress during psychotherapy: Are outcomes enhanced? *Psychotherapy Research, 11,* 49–68.

Latham, G. P., & Wexley, K. N. (1981). *Increasing productivity through performance appraisal.* Reading, MA: Addison-Wesley.

Lee, D. Y., Hallberg, E. T., Kocsis, M., & Haase, R. F. (1980). Decoding skills in nonverbal communication and perceived interviewer effectiveness. *Journal of Counseling Psychology, 27,* 89–92.

Levine, S. B., & Argle, D. (1978). The effectiveness of sex therapy for chronic secondary psychological impotence. *Journal of Sex and Marital Therapy, 4,* 235–258.

Lichtenberg, J. W., & Hummel, T. J. (1976). Counseling as a stochastic process: Fitting a Markov chain model to initial counseling interviews. *Journal of Counseling Psychology, 23,* 310–315.

Lincoln, Y. S., & Guba, E. G. (1985). *Naturalistic inquiry.* Beverly Hills, CA: Sage.

Locke, H. J., & Wallace, K. M. (1959). Short marital adjustment and prediction test: Their reliability and validity. *Marriage and Family Living, 21,* 251–255.

Loftus, E. (1988). *Memory.* New York: Ardsley House.

Luborsky, L. (1971). Perennial mystery of poor agreement among criteria for psychotherapy outcome. *Journal of Consulting and Clinical Psychology, 37,* 316–319.

Lunnen, K. M., & Ogles, B. M. (1998). A multi-perspective, multi-variable evaluation of reliable change. *Journal of Consulting and Clinical Psychology, 66,* 400–410.

Mahalik, J., Hill, C. E., O'Grady, K. E., & Thompson, B. (1993). Rater bias in the Checklist of Psychotherapy Transactions-Revised. *Psychotherapy Research, 3,* 47–56.

Mahrer, A. R. (1988). Discovery-oriented psychotherapy research. *American Psychologist, 43,* 694–702.

Mahrer, A. R., Markow, R., Gervaize, P. A., & Boulet, D. B. (1987). Strong laughter in psychotherapy: Concomitant patient verbal behavior and implications for therapeutic use. *Voices, 23,* 80–88.

Mahrer, A. R., Paterson, W. E., Theriault, A. T., Roessler, C., & Quenneville, A. (1986). How and why to use a large number of clinically sophisticated judges in psychotherapy research. *Voices: The Art and Science of Psychotherapy, 22,* 57–66.

Maisto, S. A., & Maisto, C. A. (1983). Institutional measures of treatment outcome. In M. J. Lambert, E. R. Christenson, & S. S. DeJuuo (Eds.), *The assessment of psychotherapy outcome* (pp. 603–625). New York: John Wiley & Sons.

Malec, J. F. (1999). Goal Attainment Scaling in rehabilitation. *Neuropsychology Rehabilitation, 9,* 253–275.

Mann, J. (1981). The core of time-limited psychotherapy: Time and the central issue. In S. H. Budman (Ed.), *Forms of brief therapy* (pp. 25–43). New York: Guilford Press.

Marmar, C. R. (1990). Psychotherapy process research: Progress, dilemmas, and future directions. *Journal of Consulting and Clinical Psychology, 58,* 265–272.

Marsden, G. (1965). Content analysis studies of therapeutic interviews: 1954–1964. *Psychological Bulletin, 63,* 298–321.

Marsden, G. (1971). Content analysis studies of psychotherapy: 1954 to 1968. In A. E. Bergin & S. L. Garfield (Eds.), *Handbook of psychotherapy and behavior change* (pp. 345–407). New York: John Wiley & Sons.

Marsden, G., Kalter, N., & Ericson, W. A. (1974). Response productivity: A methodological problem in content analysis studies in psychotherapy. *Journal of Consulting and Clinical Psychology, 42,* 224–230.

Maruish, M. E. (1999). *The use of psychological testing for treatment planning and outcomes assessment.* Hillsdale, NJ: Erlbaum.

Masi, G., Favilla, L., Mucci, M., & Millepiedi, S. (2000). Depressive comorbidity in children and adolescents with generalized anxiety disorder. *Child Psychiatry and Human Development, 30,* 205–215.

Masters, W. H., & Johnson, V. E. (1970). *Human sexual inadequacy.* Boston: Little, Brown.

McCracken, G. (1988). *The long interview.* Newbury Park, CA: Sage.

McCullough, L., Winston, A., Farber, B. A., Porter, F., Pollack, J., Laikin, M., Vingiano, W., & Trujillo, M. (1991). The relationship of patient-therapist interaction to outcome in brief psychotherapy. *Psychotherapy, 28,* 525–533.

McDaniel, S. H., Stiles, W. B., & McGaughey, K. J. (1981). Correlations of male college students' verbal response mode use with measures of psychological disturbance and psychotherapy outcome. *Journal of Consulting and Clinical Psychology, 49,* 571–582.

McGlinchey, J. B., & Jacobson, N. S. (1999). Clinically significant but impractical? A response to Hageman and Arrindell. *Behaviour Research and Therapy, 37,* 1211–1217.

McLellan, A. T., & Durell, J. (1996). Outcome evaluation in psychiatric and substance abuse treatment: Concepts, rationale, and methods. In L. J. Sederer & B. Dickey (Eds.), *Outcome assessment in clinical practice* (pp. 34–44). Baltimore, MD: Williams & Wilkins.

McLeod, J. (1994). *Doing counseling research.* London: Sage.

Mercer, R. C., & Loesch, L. C. (1979). Audio tape ratings: Comments and guidelines. *Psychotherapy: Theory, Research and Practice, 16,* 79–85.

Mergenthaler, E., & Stinson, C. H. (1992). Psychotherapy transcription standards. *Psychotherapy Research, 2,* 125–142.

Messer, S. B. (1991). The case formulation approach: Issues of reliability and validity. *American Psychologist, 46,* 1348–1350.

Messer, S. B., Tishby, O., & Spillman, A. (1992). Taking context seriously in psychotherapy research: Relating therapist interventions to patient progress in brief psychodynamic therapy. *Journal of Consulting and Clinical Psychology, 60,* 678–688.

Miles, M. B., & Huberman, A. M. (1994). *Qualitative data analysis: An expanded sourcebook* (2nd ed.). Thousand Oaks, CA: Sage.

Millon, T. (1983). *Millon Clinical Multiaxial Inventory Manual* (3rd ed.). Minneapolis, MN: National Computer Systems.

Mintz, J., Drake, R., & Crits-Christoph, P. (1996). The efficacy and effectiveness of psychotherapy: Two paradigms, one science. *American Psychologist, 51,* 1084–1085.

Mintz, J., & Kiesler, D. J. (1982). Individualized measures of psychotherapy outcome. In P. C. Kendall & J. N. Butcher (Eds.). *Handbook of research methods in clinical psychology* (pp. 491–534). New York: John Wiley & Sons.

Mintz, J., & Luborsky, L. (1971). Segments vs. whole sessions: Which is the better unit for psychotherapy research? *Journal of Abnormal Psychology, 78,* 180–191.

Mintz, J., Luborsky, L., & Crits-Christoph, P. (1979). Measuring the outcomes of psychotherapy: Findings of the Penn. Psychotherapy Project. *Journal of Consulting and Clinical Psychology, 47,* 319–334.

Mitchell, S. K. (1979). Inter-observer agreement, reliability, and generalizability of data collected in observational studies. *Psychological Bulletin, 86,* 376–390.

Monti, P. M., Wallander, J. L., Ahern, D. K., Abrams, D. B., & Monroe, S. M. (1983). Multi-modal measurement of anxiety and social skills in a behavioral role-play test: Generalizability and discriminant validity. *Behavioral Assessment, 6,* 15–25.

Moos, R. H. (1981). *Group Environment Scale manual.* Palo Alto, CA: Consulting Psychologists Press.

Moras, K., & Hill, C. E. (1991). Rater selection in psychotherapy process research: Observations on the state-of-the-art. *Psychotherapy Research, 1,* 113–123.

Morrow, S. L., & Smith, M. L. (2000). Qualitative research for counseling psychology. In S. D. Brown & R. W. Lent (Eds.), *Handbook of counseling psychology.* New York: John Wiley & Sons.

Muehlberg, G. N., Pierce, R., & Drasgow, J. (1969). A factor analysis of therapeutically facilitative conditions. *Journal of Clinical Psychology, 25,* 93–95.

Nagel, D. P., Hoffman, M. A., & Hill, C. E. (1995). A comparison of verbal response modes used by master's level career counselors and other helpers. *Journal of Counseling and Development, 74,* 101–104.

Newman, F. L. (1983). Therapist's evaluation of psychotherapy. In M. J. Lambert, E. R. Christensen, & S. S. DeJulio (Eds.), *The assessment of psychotherapy outcome* (pp. 498–536). New York: John Wiley & Sons.

Nichols, R. C., & Beck, K. W. (1960). Factors in psychotherapy change. *Journal of Consulting Psychology, 24,* 388–399.

Nunnally, J. C., & Kotsch, W. E. (1983). Studies of individual subjects: Logic and methods of analysis. *British Journal of Clinical Psychology, 22,* 83–93.

O'Farrell, M. K., Hill, C. E., & Patton, S. (1986). Comparison of two cases of counseling with the same counselor. *Journal of Counseling and Development, 65,* 141–145.

Ogles, B. M., Lambert, M. J., & Masters, K. S. (1996). *Assessing outcome in clinical practice.* Boston: Allyn & Bacon.

Ogles, B. M., Lambert, M. J., & Sawyer, J. D. (1995). Clinical significance of the NIMH treatment of depression collaborative research program data. *Journal of Consulting and Clinical Psychology, 63,* 321–326.

Ogles, B. M., Lambert, M. J., Weight, D. G., & Payne, I. R. (1990). Agoraphobia outcome measurement: A review and meta-analysis. *Psychological Assessment: A Journal of Consulting and Clinical Psychology, 2,* 317–325.

Ogles, B. M., Lunnen, K. M., & Bonesteel, K. (2001). Clinical significance: History, application and current practice. *Clinical Psychology Review, 21,* 421–446.

Olk, M. E., & Friedlander, M. L. (1992). Trainees' experiences in role conflict and role ambiguity in supervisory relationships. *Journal of Counseling Psychology, 39,* 389–397.

O'Malley, S. S., Suh, C. S., & Strupp, H. H. (1983). The Vanderbilt Psychotherapy Process Scale: A report on the scale development and a process-outcome study. *Journal of Consulting and Clinical Psychology, 51,* 581–586.

Orlinsky, D. E., Grawe, K., & Parks, B. K. (1994). Process and outcome in psychotherapy—Noch Einmal. In A. E. Bergin & S. L. Garfield (Eds.), *Handbook of psychotherapy and behavior change* (4th ed.). New York: John Wiley & Sons.

Parloff, M. B., Waskow, I. E., & Wolfe, B. E. (1978). Research on therapist variables in relation to process and outcome. In S. L. Garfield & A. E. Bergin (Eds.), *Handbook of psychotherapy and behavior change* (2nd ed.) (pp. 233–283). New York: John Wiley & Sons.

Pekarik, G., & Wolff, C. B. (1996). Relationship of satisfaction to symptom change, follow-up adjustment, and clinical significance. *Professional Psychology: Research and Practice, 27,* 202–208.

Persons, J. B. (1991). Psychotherapy outcome studies do not accurately represent current models of psychotherapy: A proposed remedy. *American Psychologist, 46,* 99–106.

Pilkonis, P. A., Imber, S. D., Lewis, P., & Rubinsky, P. (1984). A comparative outcome study of individual, group, and conjoint psychotherapy. *Archives of General Psychiatry, 41,* 431–437.

Pinsof, W. M., & Catherall, D. (1986). The integrative psychotherapy alliance: Family, couple, and individual therapy scales. *Journal of Marital and Family Therapy, 12,* 137–151.

Piotrowski, C., & Keller, W. (1989). Psychological testing in outpatient mental health facilities: A national study. *Professional Psychology: Research and Practice, 20,* 423–425.

Rankin, H. (1990). Validity of self-reports in clinical settings. *Behavioral Assessment, 12,* 107–116.

Reid, J. B. (1970). Reliability assessment of observation data: A possible methodological problem. *Child Development, 41,* 1143–1150.

Rennie, D. L., Phillips, J. R., & Quartaro, G. K. (1988). Grounded theory: A promising approach to conceptualization in psychology? *Canadian Psychology, 29,* 139–150.

Rhodes, R., Hill, C. E., Thompson, B. J., & Elliott, R. (1994). Client retrospective recall of resolved and unresolved misunderstanding events. *Journal of Counseling Psychology, 41,* 473–483.

Rice, L. N., & Kerr, G. P. (1986). Measures of client and therapist vocal quality. In L. S. Greenberg & W. M. Pinsof (Eds.), *The psychotherapeutic process: A research handbook* (pp. 73–105). New York: Guilford Press.

Roberts, R. R., & Renzaglia, G. A. (1965). The influence of tape recording on counseling. *Journal of Counseling Psychology, 12,* 10–16.

Rogers, C. R., Gendlin, E. T., Kiesler, D. J., & Traux, C. B. (1967). *The therapeutic relationship and its impact: A study of psychotherapy with schizophrenics.* Madison: University of Wisconsin Press.

Romanczyk, R. G., Kent, R. N., Diament, C., & O'Leary, K. D. (1973). Measuring the reliability of observational data: A reactive process. *Journal of Applied Behavior Analysis, 6,* 175–184.

Rosenthal, R. (1966). *Experimenter effects in behavioral research.* New York: Meredith.

Russell, C. S., Olson, D. H., Sprenkle, D. H., & Atilano, R. B. (1983). From family system to family system: Review of family therapy research. *The American Journal of Family Therapy, 11,* 3–14.

Russell, R. L. (1988). A new classification scheme for studies of verbal behavior in psychotherapy. *Psychotherapy, 25,* 51–58.

Russell, R. L., & Stiles, W. B. (1979). Categories for classifying language in psychotherapy. *Psychological Bulletin, 86,* 404–419.

Russell, R. L., & Trull, T. J. (1986). Sequential analysis of language variables in psychotherapy process research. *Journal of Consulting and Clinical Psychology, 54,* 16–21.

Saal, F. R., Downey, R. G., & Lahey, M. A. (1980). Rating the ratings: assessing the psychometric properties of rating data. *Psychological Bulletin, 88,* 413–428.

Sabalis, R. F. (1983). Assessing outcome in patients with sexual dysfunctions and sexual deviations. In M. J. Lambert, E. R. Christensen, & S. S. DeJulio (Eds.). *The assessment of psychotherapy outcome* (pp. 205–262). New York: John Wiley & Sons.

Sampson, H., & Weiss, J. (1986). Testing hypotheses: The approach of the Mount Zion Psychotherapy Research Group. In L. S. Greenberg & W. M. Pinsof (Eds.), *The psychotherapeutic process: A research handbook* (pp. 519–613). New York: Guilford Press.

Schact, T. E. (1991). Formulation based psychotherapy research: Some further considerations. *American Psychologist, 46,* 1346–1347.

Schoeninger, D. W., Klein, M. H., & Mathieu, P. L. (1967). Sampling from the recorded therapy interview: Patient experiencing ratings made with and without therapist speech cues. *Psychological Reports, 20,* 250.

Schulte, D. (1995). How treatment success could be assessed. *Psychotherapy Research, 5,* 281–296.

Seggar, L., Lambert, M. J., & Hansen, N. B. (2002). Assessing clinical significance: Application to the Beck Depression Inventory. *Behavior Therapy, 33,* 253–269.

Seligman, M. E. P. (1995). The effectiveness of psychotherapy: The *Consumer Reports* study. *American Psychologist, 50,* 965–974.

Seligman, M. E. P. (1996). Science as an ally of practice. *American Psychologist, 51,* 1072–1079.

Shadish, W. R., Jr., & Sweeney, R. B. (1991). Mediators and moderators in meta-analysis: There's a reason we don't let dodo birds tell us which psychotherapies should have prizes. *Journal of Consulting and Clinical Psychology, 59,* 883–893.

Shames, J. S., & Adair, B. T. (1980). Structure and experimenter expectancy effects. *Journal of Social Psychology, 34,* 119–126.

Shapiro, J. G. (1968). Relationships between visual and auditory cues of therapeutic effectiveness. *Journal of Clinical Psychology, 34,* 236–239.

Shoham-Salomon, V. (1990). Interrelating research processes of process research. *Journal of Consulting and Clinical Psychology, 58,* 295–303.

Shore, M. F., Massimo, J. L., & Ricks, D. F. (1965). A factor analytic study of psychotherapeutic change in delinquent boys. *Journal of Clinical Psychology, 21,* 208–212.

Shrout, P. E., & Fleiss, J. L. (1979). Intraclass correlations: Uses in assessing rater reliability. *Psychological Bulletin, 86,* 420–428.

Silverman, W. K. (1991). Persons' description of psychotherapy outcome studies does not accurately represent psychotherapy outcome studies. *American Psychologist, 46,* 1351–1352.

Sloan, R. B., Staples, F. R., Cristol, A. H., Yorkston, N. J., & Whipple, K. (1975). *Psychotherapy vs. behavior therapy.* Cambridge, MA: Harvard University Press.

Smith, M. L., Glass, G. V., & Miller, T. I. (1980). *The benefits of psychotherapy.* Baltimore, MD: Johns Hopkins University Press.

Sobell, L. C., & Sobell, M. B. (1990). Self-reports across addictive behaviors: Issues and future directions in clinical and research settings. *Behavioral Assessment, 12,* 1–4.

Speer, D. C., & Greenbaum, P. (1995). A comparison of five methods for computing significant individual client change and measurement rates: An individual growth curve approach. *Journal of Consulting and Clinical Psychology, 63,* 1044–1048.

Spiegel, S. B., & Hill, C. E. (1989). Guidelines for research on therapist interpretation: Toward greater methodological rigor and relevance to practice. *Journal of Counseling Psychology, 36,* 121–129.

Stiles, W. B. (1979). Verbal response modes and psychotherapeutic technique. *Psychiatry, 42,* 49–62.

Stiles, W. B. (1988). Psychotherapy process-outcome correlations may be misleading. *Psychotherapy, 25,* 27–35.

Stiles, W. B. (1989). Abuse of the drug metaphor in psychotherapy process-outcome research. *Clinical Psychology Review, 9,* 521–543.

Stiles, W. B. (1992). *Describing talk: A taxonomy of verbal response modes.* Newbury Park, CA: Sage.

Stiles, W. B. (1993). Quality control in qualitative research. *Clinical Psychology Review, 13,* 593–618.

Stiles, W. B., Elliott, R., Llewelyn, S. P., Firth-Cozens, J. A., Margison, F. R., Sharpiro, D. A., & Hardy, G. (1990). Assimilation of problematic experiences by clients in psychotherapy. *Psychotherapy, 27,* 411–420.

Stiles, W. B., & Shapiro, D. A. (1994). Drugs, recipes, babies, bathwater, and psychotherapy process-outcome relations. *Journal of Consulting and Clinical Psychology, 56,* 955–959.

Stiles, W. B., Shapiro, D. A., & Firth-Cozens, J. (1988). Verbal response mode use in contrasting psychotherapies: A within-subjects comparison. *Journal of Consulting and Clinical Psychology, 56,* 727–733.

Stone, A. A., Turkkan, J. S., Bachrach, C. A., Jobe, J. B., Kurtzman, H. S., & Cain, V. S. (1999). *The science of self report: Implications for research and practice.* Mahwah, NY: Erlbaum.

Stong, S. R., & Hills, H. (1986). *Interpersonal Communications Rating Scale.* Richmond, VA: Virginia Commonwealth University.

Strauss, A. E., & Corbin, J. (1990). *Basics of qualitative research: Grounded theory procedures and techniques.* Newbury Park, CA: Sage.

Strupp, H. H. (1955). An objective comparison of Rogerian and psychoanalytic techniques. *Journal of Consulting Psychology, 19,* 1–7.

Strupp, H. H. (1957). A multidimensional analysis of therapist activity in analytic and client-centered therapy. *Journal of Consulting Psychology, 21,* 301–308.

Strupp, H. H., Fox, R. E., & Lessler, K. (1969). *Patients view their psychotherapy.* Baltimore, MD: Johns Hopkins University Press.

Strupp, H. H., & Hadley, S. W. (1977). A tripartite model of mental health and therapeutic outcomes: With special reference to negative effects in psychotherapy. *American Psychologist, 32,* 187–196.

Strupp, H. H., Horowitz, L. M., & Lambert, M. J. (1997). *Measuring patient changes in mood, anxiety, and personality disorders: Towards a core battery.* Washington, DC: American Psychological Association Press.

Strupp, H. H., Moras, K., Sandell, J., Waterhouse, G., O'Malley, S., Keithly, L., & Gomes-Schwartz, B. (1981). Vanderbilt Negative Indicators Scale: An instrument for identification of deterrents to progress in time-limited dynamic psychotherapy. Unpublished manuscript, Vanderbilt University, Department of Psychology, Nashville, TN.

Taplin, P. S, & Reid, J. B. (1973). Effects of instructional set and experimenter influence on observer reliability. *Child Development, 44,* 547–554.

Tichenor, V., & Hill, C. E., (1989). A comparison of six measures of working alliance. *Psychotherapy, 26,* 195–199.

Tingey, R., Lambert, M. J., Burlingame, G. M., & Hansen, N. B. (1996). Assessing clinical significance: Proposed extensions to the method. *Psychotherapy Research, 6,* 109–123.

Tinsley, H.E.A., & Weiss, D. J. (1975). Interrater reliability and agreement of subjective judgments. *Journal of Counseling Psychology, 22,* 358–376.

Touliatos, J., Perlmutter, B. F., & Straus, M. A. (1990). *Family measurement techniques.* Newbury Park, CA: Sage.

Tracey, T. J. (1985). Dominance and outcome: A sequential examination. *Journal of Counseling Psychology, 32,* 119–122.

Tracey, T. J., & Guinee, J. P. (1990). Generalizability of interpersonal communications rating scale ratings across presentation modes. *Journal of Counseling Psychology, 37,* 330–336.

Traux, C. B. (1966). Therapist empathy, warmth, and genuineness and patient personality change in group psychotherapy: A comparison between interaction unit measures, time sample measures, and patient perception measures. *Journal of Clinical Psychology, 22,* 225–229.

Traux, C. B., & Carkhuff, R. R. (1967). *Toward effective counseling and psychotherapy: Training and practice.* Chicago: Aldine.

Tsujimoto, R. N., Hamilton, M., & Berger, D. E. (1990). Averaging multiple judges to improve validity: Aid to planning cost-effective clinical research. *Psychological Assessment, 2,* 432–437.

Tucker, L. R., Damarin, F., & Messick, S. (1966). A base free measure of change. *Psychometrika, 31,* 432–437, 457–473.

Vermeersch, D. A., Lambert, M. J., & Burlingame, G. M. (2000). Outcome Questionnaire: Item sensitivity to change. *Journal of Personality Assessment, 74,* 242–261.

Walz, G. R., & Johnston, J. A. (1963). Counselors look at themselves on video tape. *Journal of Counseling Psychology, 19,* 232–236.

Waskow, I. E., & Parloff, M. B. (1975). *Psychotherapy change measures.* (Dew, No. 74–120). Washington, DC: U.S. Government Printing Office.

Waxer, P. H. (1981). Channel contribution in anxiety displays. *Journal of Research in Personality, 15,* 44–56.

Weiss, D. S. (1979). The effects of systematic variations in information on judges; descriptions of personality. *Journal of Personality and Social Psychology, 37,* 2121–2136.

Weiss, D. S., Marmar, C. R., & Horowitz, M. J. (1988). Do the ways in which psychotherapy process ratings are made make a difference? The effects of mode of presentation, segment, and rating format on interrater reliability. *Psychotherapy, 25,* 44–50.

Wells, E. A., Hawkins, J. D., & Catalano, R. F. (1988). Choosing drug use measures for treatment outcome studies. 1. The influence of measurement approach on treatment results. *International Journal of Addictions, 23,* 851–873.

Wiesner, W. H., & Cronshaw, S. F. (1988). A meta-analytic investigation of the impact of interview format and degrees of structure on the validity of the employment interview. *Journal of Occupational Psychology, 61,* 275–290.

Williams, S. L. (1985). On the nature and measurement of agoraphobia. *Progress in Behavior Modification, 19,* 109–144.

Wilson, G. T., & Thomas, M. G. (1973). Self-versus drug-produced relaxation and the effects of instructional set in standardized systematic desensitization. *Behaviour Research and Therapy, 11,* 279–288.

Wiseman, F. (1972). Methodological bias in public opinion surveys. *Public Opinion Quarterly, 36,* 105–108.

Wiseman, H., Shefler, G., Caneti, L., & Ronen, Y. (1993). A systematic comparison of two cases in Mann's time-limited psychotherapy: An events approach. *Psychotherapy Research, 3,* 227–244.

Wolf, M. M. (1978). Social validity: The case for subjective measurement or how applied behavior analysis is finding its heart. *Journal of Applied Behavior Analysis, 11*, 203–214.

Young, A., & Chesson, R. (1997). Goal Attainment Scaling as a method of measuring clinical outcome for children with learning disabilities. *British Journal of Occupational Therapy. 60(3)*, 111–114.

Zaza, C., Stolee, P., & Prackin, K. (1999). The application of Goal Attainment Scaling in chronic pain settings. *Journal of Pain and Symptom Management, 17*, 55–64.

Zimmerman, D. W. (1997). A geometric interpretation of the validity and reliability of difference scores. *British Journal of Mathematical and Statistical Psychology, 50*, 73–80.

SECTION 2

EVALUATING THE INGREDIENTS OF THERAPEUTIC EFFICACY

CHAPTER 5

The Efficacy and Effectiveness of Psychotherapy

MICHAEL J. LAMBERT
Brigham Young University
BENJAMIN M. OGLES
Ohio University

In this chapter, we review the status of empirical evidence on the efficacy and effectiveness of psychotherapy, mainly with adult outpatients. We also discuss a variety of related issues, including the nature, permanence, relevance, and generalizability of therapy, curative factors, common and specific therapy factors as agents of change, and potential methods for improving the potency of therapies. With the ever growing number of interventions that are applied in a variety of contexts (e.g., medical, Internet, educational) with patients who have diverse problems, coupled with the growing number of researchers and journals showing interest in studying treatment efficacy, a complete cataloging of all studies and reviews in the area of behavior change is not possible. As a result and in keeping with previous editions of the *Handbook*, here we consider mainly the practice of individual therapy. Full accounts of the major approaches to therapy are reserved for other chapters, but in this chapter we focus on an integration and comparison of results along with issues of central importance to the effectiveness of all therapies. Occasionally, we pull from other literature (e.g., family therapy) to help emphasize the breadth and consistency of the behavior change literature.

Research on therapy outcome from the 1930s through the early 1990s was summarized in the four previous editions of this chapter (Bergin, 1971; Bergin & Lambert, 1978; Lambert & Bergin, 1994; Lambert, Shapiro, & Bergin, 1986). Our review of this literature and the related controversies is well documented. Although selected historical studies from previous chapters are included here to provide context, the interested reader is invited to review earlier editions of this chapter in order to gain an appreciation of the historical context of the current chapter, the nature and quality of prior research, and the controversies that have attended analyses of therapeutic outcomes. For the most part, however, studies conducted in the past decade are emphasized in the present chapter.

Before introducing specific studies and results, it is important to note the influence of managed care on psychotherapy research and practice. As a result of increasing healthcare costs, business management strategies were increasingly used in the 1990s to reduce the costs of medical care, including mental health services. Indeed, an industry developed specifically to manage mental health and substance abuse services—"managed behavioral healthcare." The most dramatic influence of the managed behavioral health care market was felt by practitioners who noted increased difficulty obtaining payment for services, increased paperwork, and increased scrutiny of clinical decision making.

Managed care has had a profound influence on the delivery of mental health services, mental health policy, and psychotherapy research. Several therapy research issues are front and center in the management of mental health services, including: (1) the number of sessions needed for improvement, (2) differences in treatment related to the practitioner's level of training, (3) management of the quality of care for the individual patient through outcome management or so-called patient-focused research (Howard, Moras, Brill, Martinovich, & Lutz, 1996, p. 1059), and (4) the search for empirically supported treatments (Chambless et al., 1996; Procedures, 1995). All of these issues are addressed later in the chapter through an examination of the empirical literature. The point here is that managed behavioral health care has changed the market for mental health services and influenced the direction and efforts of researchers. At times, this brings the researcher into an unfamiliar role involved in forming policy or assisting with the management of practice. As we embark on a summary of contemporary therapy research, we are more aware than ever of the need for scientifically credible statements that can also help to shape the direction of psychotherapy reimbursement, practice, and future research. Given these orienting remarks, we now turn to the business of specifically assessing the results of studies and the implications of these studies for the practice of psychotherapy.

The General Efficacy of Psychotherapy

A huge body of literature has been generated to examine the benefits of psychotherapy. It is a formidable task to broadly review the main findings produced by numerous scholars using both qualitative and quantitative techniques. In order to provide some organization to the general findings regarding the efficacy of psychotherapy, we will address a number of specific questions: (a) Is psychotherapy efficacious? (b) Do patients make changes that are clinically meaningful? (c) Do the benefits of therapy exceed placebo? (d) Do patients maintain their gains? (e) How much therapy is necessary? (f) Do some patients get worse? and (g) Does efficacy research generalize to applied settings?

Is Psychotherapy Efficacious?

The historical controversy regarding the interpretation of the psychotherapy research literature (e.g., Bergin, 1971; Bergin & Lambert, 1978; Eysenck, 1952; Rachman & Wilson, 1980) has been settled largely through the use of meta-analyses. Meta-analyses provide an efficient and maximally objective integrative summary of the primary studies and apply the methods and principles of empirical research to the process of reviewing literature. Following a systematic search of the literature to locate studies meeting predefined inclusion criteria, the findings of individual studies are quantified using a common metric (such as an effect size[1]). Salient features of each study (e.g., client population, type of treatment, and methodological strengths and weaknesses) are coded, and statistical techniques are used to arrive at summary statements of the size and statistical significance of the effects cumulated across studies. Further statistical analyses are used to identify quantitative relationships between study features and the results obtained.

Broad Meta-Analyses of Therapy Efficacy. Early applications of meta-analysis to psychotherapy outcomes (Smith & Glass, 1977; Smith, Glass, & Miller, 1980) addressed the overall question of the extent of benefit associated with psychotherapy as evidenced in the literature as a whole, compared the outcomes of different treatments, and examined the impact of methodological features of studies on the reported effectiveness of treatments. For example, Smith et al. (1980) found an average effect size of .85 standard deviation units over 475 studies comparing treated and untreated groups. This indicates that, at the end of treatment, the average treated person is better off than 80% of the untreated sample.

A second wave of meta-analytic reviews included both critical replications using the same database as Smith et al. (1980) (Andrews & Harvey, 1981; Landman & Dawes, 1982) and independent analyses of other large samples of studies (Shapiro & Shapiro, 1982). These studies substantiated the consistent effect of treatment as opposed to control. Table 5.1 lists meta-analytic studies that focus on evaluating the broad effectiveness of psychotherapy.

A large number of meta-analyses have been conducted in the intervening 20 years. Recent analyses have often focused on more narrow bodies of literature with more specific questions than the earliest meta-analyses. For example, multiple meta-analyses focus on the effects of treatments for depression and anxiety disorders (see Tables 5.2 and 5.3). Many other meta-analyses summarize the literature in other areas (see Table 5.4). One broad review and analysis of over 300 meta-analytic studies deserves specific mention. Lipsey & Wilson (1993) reviewed 302 meta-analyses of psychological, educational, and behavioral treatments and concluded that "the effect size distribution" was "so overwhelmingly positive that it hardly seems plausible that it

TABLE 5.1 Meta-Analytic Reviews of the General Effects of Therapy

Authors	Diagnosis/Treatment	No. of Studies	Effect Size
Andrews & Harvey (1981)	Neurotic	81	.72
Asay, Lambert, Christensen, & Beutler (1984)	Mixed/Mental Health Centers	9[a]	.82[b]
Belestrieri, Williams, & Wilkinson (1988)	Mixed	11	.22
Barker, Funk, & Houston (1988)	Mixed	17	1.05
Landman & Dawes (1982)	Mixed	42	.90
Lipsey & Wilson (1993)	Mixed	302[c]	.47
Nicholson & Berman (1983)	Neurotic	47[d]	.70
Shapiro & Shapiro (1982)	Mixed	143	1.03
Smith et al. (1980)	Mixed	475	.85

[a] Number of mental health centers.

[b] Pre-post effect size.

[c] Number of meta-analyses.

[d] Number of comparison groups.

presents a valid picture of the efficacy of treatment per se" (p. 1192). As a result, they selected a smaller group of meta-analyses using more stringent criteria. Even after limiting their review to this smaller sample, however, the findings were consistent. The average treatment effect for this limited sample (156 meta-analyses) was .47. Lipsey and Wilson (1993) concluded that "the evidence from meta-analysis indicates that the psychological, educational, and behavioral treatments studied by meta-analysts generally have positive effects" (p. 1198).

One obvious difference between the Smith et al. (1980) conclusions and the Lipsey and Wilson (1993) findings is the relatively large difference in overall effect size (e.g., .85 vs. .47). Some recent meta-analyses that use newer methodologies find more moderate effect sizes (e.g., in the .4 to .6 range) when compared to earlier studies, which found effect sizes in the .6 to .8 range. In fact, Shadish, Montgomery et al. (1997) suggest early meta-analyses overestimate the effects of treatment because they calculated unweighted effect sizes, giving less importance to studies with larger *N*'s. They recalculated the effect sizes for the Smith et al. (1980) data set and obtained an effect size of .60 instead of the .85 reported earlier (Shadish et al., 1997). As a result, earlier conclusions regarding the efficacy of therapy may need to be tempered given the more recent findings using refined methodologies (more specifically weighted effect sizes). Nevertheless, the broad finding of therapy benefit across a range of treatments for a variety of disorders remains.

NARROW META-ANALYSES OF THERAPY EFFICACY. With regards to more specific treatments and disorders, Table 5.2 summarizes meta-analytic reviews that quantify the outcomes of treating patients with a variety of depressive disorders, mainly unipolar depression. Results in treating depression appear to be rather consistent. In all, numerous meta-analytic reviews suggest that patients undergoing psychotherapy for depression surpassed no-treatment and wait list control patients. For example, Dobson (1989) reports that the average client treated with Beck's cognitive therapy surpassed 98% of the control patients. Similar but less dramatic results are found in the other reviews listed in Table 5.2. Robinson, Berman, and Neimeyer (1990), for example, found that behavioral, cognitive behavioral, and, to a lesser extent, general verbal therapies, all had positive effects on outcome compared to controls. Recent meta-analyses address the effectiveness of psychological interventions with a more select group of patients (e.g., geriatric patients) or a more narrow set of interventions (e.g., bibliotherapy). These studies support the finding that a range of therapeutic interventions result in improvement in mood and other symptoms for patients with depression.

Of even more interest to practicing clinicians is the consistent finding that the benefits of psychotherapy are equal to or surpass a variety of antidepressant medications. Antidepressant medication has long been considered to be the treatment of choice for depression. With the advent of the selective serotonin re-uptake inhibitors

TABLE 5.2 Meta-Analytic Reviews of Treatments for Depression

Authors	Diagnosis/Treatment	No. of Studies	Effect Size
Cuijpers (1998b)	Depression in Elderly/Outreach	8	.77[b]
Cuijpers (1998a)	Depression/Coping with Depression	10	.65[b]
Cuijpers (1997)	Depression/Bibliotherapy	6	.82
Dobson (1989)	Depression/CBT	10	2.15
Engels & Vermey (1997)	Geriatric Depression	17	
Gaffan, Tsaousis, & Kemp-Wheeler (1995)	Depression/CBT (allegiance effect)		
	Study 1 (CBT vs. wait list)	7	1.56[b]
	Study 2 (CBT vs. wait list)	11	.89[b]
Gerson, Belin, Kaufman, Mintz, & Jarvik (1999)	Geriatric Depression/Mixed		
	Drug	41	48%
	Placebo	13	31%
	Psychosocial	4	51%
Gloaguen, Cottraux, Cucherat, & Blackburn (1998)	Depression/CBT	48	
	CBT vs. wait list or placebo		.82[b,d]
	CBT vs. antidepressants		.38[b,d]
	CBT vs. behavioral treatment		.05[b,d]
	CBT vs. other treatment		.24[b,d]
Lambert, Hatch, Kingston, & Edwards (1986)	Depression	36	
	Beck Depression Inventory		1.16
	Hamilton Rating Scale		1.57
Leichsenring (2001)	Depression/Dynamic vs. CBT	6	.08
McDermut, Miller, & Brown (2001)	Depression/Group Therapy	15	1.03
Mohr (1999)	Depression in Multiple Sclerosis	5	.56[b,c]
Nietzel, Russell, Hemmings, & Gretter (1987)	Unipolar Depression	28	.71
Quality Assurance Project (1983)	Depression	10	.65
Robinson, Berman, & Neimeyer (1990)	Depression	29	.84
Scogin & McElreath (1994)	Geriatric Depression	17	.78
Steinbrueck, Maxwell, & Howard (1983)	Depression	56	1.22
Stuart & Bowers (1995)	Inpatient Depression/CBT+ meds	8	
	All studies (pre-post BDI)	8	4.34[a,d]
	Controlled studies (BDI)	4	1.13[d]
Thase et al. (1997)	Depression	6	
	Therapy (less/more severe)	6	37%/25%[e]
	Therapy plus medication	6	48%/43%[e]

[a] Pre-post effect size.

[b] Weighted effect size.

[c] Pearson *r*.

[d] Primary outcome only.

[e] Recovery rate.

(SSRIs), such as fluoxetine and other new drugs, medication for depression as the first line of treatment has been emphasized even more heavily. Indeed, the Agency for Health Care Policy and Research (AHCPR) guidelines for the treatment of depression in primary care settings suggest medication as the first line of treatment (Munoz, Hollon, McGrath, Rehm et al., 1994). As a result, a finding that psychotherapies produce comparable or superior effects would be significant.

Two early meta-analyses support the notion that psychotherapy is at a minimum equivalent to antidepressant medication (Robinson, Berman, & Neimeyer, 1990; Steinbrueck, Maxwell, & Howard, 1983). A third early meta-analysis suggested that antidepressant medications surpass psychotherapy only in the treatment of endogenous depression (Andrews, 1983). This finding was also supported by the National Institute of Mental Health (NIMH) Treatment for Depression Collaborative Research Program (TDCRP) data (Elkin, 1994), which found that medication (in this case imipramine) surpassed psychotherapy only for more severe cases of depression. A more recent meta-analysis compared therapy with combined treatment (therapy plus medication) in a sample of six studies (Thase et al., 1997). This study found that recovery rates in less severe cases were comparable between therapy alone and therapy plus medication. In more severe cases, however, the combined treatments were more effective. Finally, the most recent meta-analysis examined the comparative benefits of cognitive behavioral therapy (CBT) and medication in 17 direct comparisons (Gloaguen, Cottraux, Cucherat, & Blackburn, 1998). This study found that cognitive behavioral therapy (CBT) was more effective than antidepressant medication (comparative effect size .38). When examining eight of the studies that included a minimum of one-year followup data, CBT treatments exhibited an average relapse rate of 29.5%, while the antidepressant medication groups' average relapse rate was 60%. This suggests that, especially in the long run, CBT is superior to antidepressant medications. However, the new wave of antidepressant medications was underrepresented in the studies examined in this analysis. Further studies of the comparative efficacy of psychosocial interventions in relationship to newer medications are needed.

Table 5.3 summarizes meta-analytic reviews of a variety of treatments for anxiety-based disorders. This table summarizes data on a more diverse sample of disorders than the depression table, ranging from disorders that might be expected to show high improvement rates (e.g., public speaking anxiety) to those where improvement is more difficult to attain (e.g., obsessive compulsive disorder). But the general conclusions are the same: psychotherapies clearly show effectiveness compared to wait list and no-treatment control comparison groups. For example, in a meta-analysis of 43 treatment studies for panic disorder (Gould, Otto, & Pollack, 1995), CBT treatments were compared with pharmacological and combined CBT/pharmacological treatments. CBT treatments had fewer dropouts (5.6% versus 19.8% for pharmacological treatments and 22.0% for combined treatments). In addition, CBT produced larger effects (.68, as opposed to .47 for pharmacological treatments and .56 for combined treatments).

Meta-analyses of other bodies of literature have also been conducted. For example, Table 5.4 depicts numerous meta-analyses that investigate the efficacy of specific treatment methods (e.g., short-term dynamic psychotherapy, rational emotive therapy) or treatments for specific patient populations (e.g., insomnia, headaches, drug abuse). Several meta-analyses tackle even more specific questions such as direct comparisons of group versus individual therapy (McRoberts, Burlingame, & Hoag, 1998; Tillitski, 1990). Although widely ranging in rationale and implementation, psychological interventions for various disorders consistently produce significant outcomes when compared to various control groups.

Criticisms of Meta-Analysis. Sharpe (1997) describes three primary criticisms of meta-analysis that have been noted over the years since its inception: (1) mixing dissimilar studies, (2) publication bias, and (3) inclusion of poor quality studies. Many meta-analytic reviewers, however, have taken steps to address these potential problems. For example, more recent meta-analytic reviews tend to focus on a narrow group of studies that investigate a specific treatment or a particular disorder (addressing the dissimilarity criticism). Some writers conduct tests of effect size homogeneity to empirically investigate the similarity of the study results and to search for moderators when sufficient variability exists within the data. Recent studies have also attempted to address the publication bias by calculating a "fail safe N" or by conducting a thorough search for both published and unpublished studies. The methodological

TABLE 5.3 Meta-Analytic Reviews of Treatments for Anxiety Disorders

Authors	Diagnosis/Treatment	No. of Studies	Effect Size
Abramowitz (1996)	OCD/Exposure Response Prevention	29	1.16[b]
Abramowitz (1997)	OCD	32	
	Exposure vs. Relaxation	2	1.18
	Exposure vs. CBT	4	–.19
	Exposure vs.components	2	.59
	SRI's vs. placebo	5	.71
	Non-SRI's vs. placebo	2	.14
Allen, Hunter, & Donohue (1989)	Public Speaking Anxiety	97	.51
Bakker et al. (1998)	Panic with and without Agoraphobia	68	
	Panic		1.11[a]
	Panic + Agoraphobia		1.36[a]
Borkovec & Whisman (1996)	Generalized Anxiety Disorder	8	1.77[a]
Chambless & Gillis (1993)	Anxiety Disorders/Cognitive Therapy		
	Generalized Anxiety	5	1.69[a,b]
	Agoraphobia & Panic/Exposure	7	1.14[a,b,d]
	Agoraphobia & Panic/Cognitive	6	1.68[a,b,d]
	Social Phobia	9	1.00[a,b,d]
Christensen, Hadzi-Pavlovic, Andrews, & Mattick (1987)	OCD/Exposure	5	1.37
Christensen et al. (1987)	Behavior Therapy	10	1.16
	Control	4	.04
Clum (1989)	Panic, Agoraphobia/Behavior Therapy	283	70%
	No Therapy	46	30%
Clum, Clum, & Surls (1993)	Panic Disorder		
	Psychological Coping	4	1.41
	Antidepressants	5	.82
	Benzodiazepines	4	.29
	Other Drugs	3	.44
	Flooding	3	1.36
	Combination	8	1.09
	All Treatments Combined	28	.88
Cox, Endler, Lee, & Swinson (1992)	Panic Disorder with Agoraphobia	34	
	Alprazolam		1.21[d]
	Imipramine		.91[d]
	Exposure		3.32[d]
Cox, Swinson, Morrison, & Lee (1993)	OCD	25	
	Clomipramine	12	3.24[a]
	Fluoxetine	7	3.45[a]
	Exposure	9	2.56[a]
Feske & Chambless (1995)	CBT vs. Exposure/Social Phobia	21	
	CBT	12	.45[b]
	Exposure	9	.69[b]
Gould, Otto, & Pollack (1995)	Panic	43	
	CBT	19	.68
	Pharmacological	16	.47
	Combined	6	.56
Gould, Otto, Pollack, & Yap (1997)	Generalized Anxiety Disorder		
	CBT	22	.70
	Pharmacotherapy	39	.60

(continues)

TABLE 5.3 *(Continued)*

Authors	Diagnosis/Treatment	No. of Studies	Effect Size
Gould, Buckminster, Pollack, Otto, & Yap (1997)	Social Phobia (social anxiety outcome)	24	
	CBT	16	.74
	Pharmacological	10	.62
Hyman, Feldman, Harris, Levin, & Malloy (1989)	Relaxation Training	48	.58
Jorm (1989)	Trait Anxiety and Neuroticism	63	.53
Mattick, Andrews, Hadzi-Pavlovic, & Christensen (1990)	Agoraphobia	51	1.62
	Wait-list controls		.02
Ogles, Lambert, Weight, & Payne (1990)	Agoraphobia	42	1.93[a,d]
Quality Assurance Project (1982)	Agoraphobia	25	1.2
Quality Assurance Project (1985a)	Anxiety	81	.98
Quality Assurance Project (1985b)	OCD/Exposure	38	1.34
Sherman (1998)	PTSD	17	.52[b]
Taylor (1996)	Social Phobia/CBT	42	
	Wait list	5	–.13
	Placebo	5	.48
	Exposure	8	.82
	CBT	5	.63
	CBT + Exposure	11	1.06
	Social Skills Training	4	.65
Trull Nietzel, & Main (1988)	Agoraphobia	19	2.10[a]
van Balkom et al. (1997)	Panic with or without Agoraphobia	106	.99[a,d]
van Balkom, van Oppen Vermeulem, & van Dyck (1994)	OCD (self-rated symptoms)	86	1.15[a]

[a] Pre-post effect size.

[b] Weighted effect size.

[c] Pearson *r*.

[d] Primary outcome only.

integrity of the studies is also often examined in relationship to effect sizes. As a result, standard criticisms must be tempered by recent improvements in meta-analytic methodology.

Matt and Navarro (1997) reviewed 63 meta-analytic studies of psychotherapeutic interventions. They first replicated the finding that "the general effects of psychotherapy are overwhelmingly positive and robust despite a multitude of limitations in primary research and meta-analysis" (Matt & Navarro, 1997, p. 26). They went on to suggest that psychotherapy research reviews are limited by several weaknesses in the literature, including: (a) poor representation of diverse populations within client and therapist samples, (b) little attention to therapy effects in applied settings, (c) influence of irrelevant variables on the magnitude of effects (e.g., dependent variable reliability, meta-analytic coding reliability, insufficient data to calculate effect sizes), and (d) lack of standards for conducting and reporting meta-analytic results.

The lack of standards is worth further notation. The variability in methods among the meta-analyses listed in this chapter is significant. Decisions about which studies to include and exclude seem rather arbitrary. Studies calculate different metrics using different assumptions and formulae. Some weight the studies by sample size and examine the variability of effect sizes, whereas others do not. A few studies use more sophisticated random effects methods of analysis.

TABLE 5.4 Meta-Analytic Reviews of Miscellaneous Treatments and Disorders

Authors	Diagnosis/Treatment	No. of Studies	Effect Size
Agosti (1995)	Alcohol Consumption	12	1.17
Allison & Faith (1996)	Obesity/CBT+Hypnosis vs. CBT	6	.26
Allumbaugh & Hoyt (1999)	Grief Therapy		
Anderson & Lambert (1995)	Short-Term Dynamic Psychotherapy	11	.71/.69
Andrews, Guitar, & Howie (1980)	Stuttering	29	1.30
Beck & Fernandez (1998)	Anger/CBT	50	.70[b]
Benton & Schroeder (1990)	Schizophrenia	23	.76[a]
Berman, Miller, & Massman (1985)	Cognitive Therapy vs. Desensitization	20	.06
	Cognitive vs. No Treatment	16	.73
	Desensitization vs. No Treatment	19	.62
Blanchard, Andrasik, Ahles, Teders, & O'Keefe (1980)	Headache	35	40–80%[c]
Bowers & Clum (1988)	Behavior Therapy	69	.76
Carlson & Hoyle (1993)	Progressive Muscle Relaxation	29	.38[b,c]
Cepeda-Benito (1993)	Nicotine Chewing Gum	26	
	Gum plus Treatment	10	.28
	Gum Alone	5	.04
Crits-Christoph (1992)	Brief Dynamic Psychotherapy	11	86%/50%[f]
Devine & Pearcy (1996)	Chronic Obstructive Pulmonary Disease	65	.34[b,d]
Devine (1996)	Asthma	31	.56[b,d]
Didden, Duker, & Korzilius (1997)	Problem Behaviors (Individuals with MRDD)	482	71%[e]
Dilk & Bond (1996)	Severe Mental Illness/Skills Training	58	.40[b]
Dush, Hirt, & Schroeder (1989)	Self-Statement Modification	69	.74
Edmondson & Conger (1996)	Anger	10	
	Relaxation		.82
	Social Skills		.80
	Cognitive-relaxation		.76
	Cognitive		.64
Engels, Garnefski, & Diekstra (1993)	RET	28	1.62
Everly, Boyle, & Lating (1999)	Vicarious trauma/Debriefing	10	.54[b]
Febbaro & Clum (1998)	Self-regulation	13	.25[b]
Fettes & Peters (1992)	Bulimia/Group Therapy	40	.75
Flor, Fydrich, & Turk (1992)	Pain/Multidisciplinary Treatment	65	.62
Gould & Clum (1993)	Self-help Treatment	40	.76
Hall (1995)	Sexual Offenders	12	.12[c]
Hampton & Hulgus (1993)	Paradoxical Interventions	29	.11
Hartmann, Herzog, & Drinkmann (1992)	Bulimia	18	1.04[a,d]
Hegarty, Baldessarini, Tohen, Waternaux, et al. (1994)	Schizophrenia	320	40.2%
Hill (1987)	Paradoxical Treatment	15	.99
Holroyd & Penzien (1986)	Tension Headache	37	
	EMG biofeedback		46.0%[f]
	Relaxation		44.6%[f]
	EMG + Relaxation		57.1%[f]
	Noncontingent Control		15.3%[f]
	Headache monitoring Control		–3.9%[f]
Holroyd & Penzien (1990)	Migraine/Biofeedback	22	47.3%
	No Treatment	15	.2%

(cotninues)

TABLE 5.4 *(Continued)*

Authors	Diagnosis/Treatment	No. of Studies	Effect Size
Kazantzis, Deane, & Ronan (2000)	Homework Assignments	27	.36[c]
Kirsch (1996)	Obesity/CBT + Hypnosis vs. CBT	6	.66
Kirsch, Montgomery, & Sapirstein (1995)	CBT + Hypnosis vs. CBT	18	1.36[b]
Laessle, Zoettl, & Pirke (1987)	Bulimia	23	.95[a,b]
Lewandowski, Gebing, Anthony, & O'Brien (1997)	Bulimia/CBT	26	.64[b,c]
Lichtenstein, Glasgow, Lando, Ossip-Klein, et al. (1996)	Smoking/Telephone	10	1.34[g]
Linden & Chambers (1994)	Hypertension	166	Sys/dia
	Exercise/Weight loss		.45[a,b,c]
	Nutrition		.20[a,b,c]
	Psychological		.65[a,b,c]
	Drug Treatment		.49[a,b,c]
Lyons & Woods (1991)	RET	70	.98
Malone & Strube (1988)	Chronic Pain/Nonmedical Treatment	48	1.18[d]
Marrs (1995)	Bibliotherapy	70	.565[b]
McRoberts, Burlingame, & Hoag (1998)	Individual vs. Group Therapy	23	.01
Meyer & Mark (1995)	Cancer/Psychosocial Treatments	45	.26[b,d]
Miller & Berman (1983)	Cognitive Behavioral Therapy	38	.83
Morin, Culbert, Kowatch (1989)	Insomnia/CBT	59	.88[d]
Murtagh & Greenwood (1995)	Insomnia	66	.87[a,b]
Prendergast, Urada, & Podus (2001)	HIV Risk Reduction	18	.31[b]
Quality Assurance Project (1984)	Schizophrenia	5	.00
Scogin, Bynum, Stephens, & Calhoon (1990)	Self-Administered Treatment	40	
	Self vs. No Treatment	17	.96[b]
	Self vs. Therapist Administered	10	.07[b]
Shoham-Salomon & Rosenthal (1987)	Paradoxical Treatment	10	.42
Svartberg & Stiles (1991)	Short-term Dynamic Therapy	7	55%
	No Treatment	7	44%
Tillitski (1990)	Group vs. Individual Therapy		
	Group Therapy	9	1.35
	Individual Therapy	9	1.35
	Control	9	.18
Tonigan, Toscova, & Miller (1995)	Alcoholics Anonymous	16	.22[b,c]
Viswesvaran & Schmidt (1992)	Smoking Cessation/15 Different Categories of Treatment	633	7–42% quit rate
Walters (2000)	Problem Drinking/Self-control Training	17	.33[b]
Whittal, Agras, & Gould (1999)	Bulimia/CBT and Pharmacological		
	Pharmacological	9	.66[a,b]
	CBT	17	1.28[a,b]

[a] Either some or all of the effect sizes were pre-post effect sizes.

[b] Weighted effect size.

[c] Pearson *r*.

[d] Primary outcome variable only.

[e] Percent nonoverlapping distributions (treatment vs. control).

[f] Percent improved.

These differences are not trivial. For example, some evidence is available that different effect size estimates are not interchangeable (Ray & Shadish, 1996). Clearly, more standard meta-analytic procedures are needed.

SUMMARY. Although the methods of primary research studies and meta-analytic reviews can be improved, the pervasive theme of this large body of psychotherapy research must remain the same—psychotherapy is beneficial. This consistent finding across thousands of studies and hundreds of meta-analyses is seemingly undebatable. As a result, researchers have turned to other important questions that take us beyond the issue of whether an average positive change occurs in treated cases.

Do Patients Make Changes that are Clinically Meaningful?

The scientific study of psychotherapy focused first on testing whether the average person who received treatment had a better outcome than the average person who did not receive treatment. This type of analysis, however, masked findings regarding each individual and made no definitive statements regarding the clinical meaning of the findings (Jacobson & Truax, 1991). Consequently, some researchers suggested that tests of statistical significance should have a less immutable place in outcome research (e.g., Barlow, 1981; Bergin & Strupp, 1970). In addition, beginning in the 1970s (Bergin, 1971; Kazdin, 1977; Lick, 1973), the examination of individual changes occurring during psychotherapy became increasingly important.

CLINICAL SIGNIFICANCE. During the past two decades, many researchers have supplemented statistical comparisons between groups with followup analyses that investigate the clinical significance of the findings. Two rather independent bodies of literature evolved for designating the clinical significance of psychotherapy—social validity and clinical significance.

Social validity (Kazdin, 1977; Wolf, 1978) emerged as a method of assessing the perspective of individuals outside the therapeutic relationship regarding the importance of psychosocial interventions and outcomes. Social validity provides a cohesive rationale and two specific methodologies (subjective evaluation and social comparison) for evaluating the relevance of client change. Subjective evaluation refers to gathering data about clients by individuals who are "likely to have contact with the client or are in a position of expertise" (Kazdin, 1998, p. 387). This allows the researcher to tap whether the client has made qualitative changes that are in turn observable by others. Social comparison is evaluated based on pre- and post-evaluations of the client's behavior, with a reference group of "nondeviant" peers. The underlying premise is that socially valid changes due to the intervention in question will result in the client's post-intervention behavior being indistinguishable from a normal reference group.

In addition to the social validity data collected in behavioral studies, several parallel methods for determining the clinical significance of interventions have been developed (Gladis, Gosch, Dishuk, & Crits-Christoph, 1999; Jacobson, Roberts, Berns, & McGlinchey, 1999; Kendall, 1999). Although social validity emphasizes an examination of practical change from the perspective of both therapy participants and societal members, clinical significance takes a slightly narrower view of meaningful change by identifying methods defined by clinician-researchers (Ogles, Lunnen, & Bonesteel, 2001). The two most prominent definitions of clinically significant change are: (1) treated clients make statistically reliable improvements as a result of treatment (improvement—Jacobson et al., 1999), and (2) treated clients are empirically indistinguishable from "normal" or nondeviant peers following treatment recovery (Kendall, Marrs-Garcia, Nath, & Sheldrick, 1999). Several statistical methods are used to evaluate these propositions (see Chapter 2). For this chapter, the question is what do researchers find when they use these methods to evaluate the clinical importance of client change occurring during psychotherapy? Do clients make changes that are clinically meaningful? Several examples of typical findings may provide initial evidence of the clinical benefits of therapy.

Lipsey and Wilson (1993) addressed the issue of practical versus statistical effects of treatment in their comprehensive meta-analysis. They used the binomial effect size display (Rosenthal & Rubin, 1982) to depict the proportion of individuals who exceed a common success threshold (generally defined as the median). The effect size can be represented in table form (Wampold, 2001; see Table 5.5). Lipsey and Wilson (1993) suggest that "the practical significance of an effect, of course, is very much dependent on the nature of the outcome at issue and its importance

TABLE 5.5 Effect Sizes with Various Interpretations

Cohen's Designation and *d*	Proportion of Untreated Controls below Mean of Treated Persons	Proportion of Variability in Outcomes Due to Treatment	Success Rate of Untreated Persons	Success Rate of Treated Persons
Small				
0.0	.500	.000	.500	.500
0.1	.540	.002	.475	.525
0.2	.579	.010	.450	.550
Medium				
0.3	.618	.022	.426	.574
0.4	.655	.038	.402	.598
0.5	.691	.059	.379	.621
0.6	.726	.083	.356	.644
0.7	.758	.109	.335	.665
Large				
0.8	.788	.138	.314	.686
0.9	.816	.168	.295	.705
1.0	.841	.200	.276	.724

Source: From *The Great Psychotherapy Debate: Models, Methods, and Findings* (p. 53, Table 2.4), by B. E. Wampold, 2001, Mahwah, NJ: Erlbaum. Copyright 2001 by Lawrence Erlbaum Associates. Adapted with permission.

to patients or clients" (Lipsey & Wilson, 1993, p. 1198). They illustrate this point further by presenting the effect sizes for a variety of medical interventions, some of which have small effects but ramifications in life and death situations. Obviously, small effects in critical situations can be extremely important. While the "nature of outcomes" resulting from therapy are debatable, Lipsey and Wilson (1993) clearly demonstrate that the effect sizes for psychological interventions exceed or equal many medical interventions.

Two early meta-analytic studies addressed the issue of clinically meaningful change by examining the pre- and post-treatment scores of clients participating in treatment on specific measures of outcome (Nietzel, Russell, Hemmings, & Gretter, 1987; Trull, Nietzel, & Main, 1988). In both studies, clients moved within one standard deviation of the normative mean, suggesting that many individuals receiving treatment might be considered meaningfully improved. In a more recent meta-analysis, Abramowitz (1998) examined the clinical significance of treatment for obsessive compulsive disorder. When comparing 16 treatment groups from ten studies with nine normative samples from six additional studies, he discovered that patients with obssessive compulsive disorder (OCD) who participated in treatment made statistically and clinically meaningful improvements from pretreatment to posttreatment. The average patient with OCD started two standard deviations away from the general population mean but moved to .7 standard deviations away from the general population mean and below the cutoff (1.0 standard deviation) following treatment. At followup, the average treated client was still below the cutoff at .8 standard deviations above the general population mean. This suggests that treated patients may make clinically meaningful changes, although many have some remaining symptoms.

Ogles, Lambert, and Sawyer (1995) examined the clinical significance of the Treatment of Depression Collaborative Research Program (TDCRP) data. When combining estimates across three treatments (interpersonal psychotherapy—IPT, cognitive behavior therapy—CBT, and imipramine plus clinical management) and three measures, they found that 69 (55%) of the 125 clients who participated in a minimum of 12 sessions and 15 weeks of treatment met the criteria for clinically meaningful change on all three measures. Many other studies provide similar analyses of clinical significance following the standard statistical comparison of group averages (e.g., Freeston et al., 1997). Hansen, Lambert, and Forman (2002) summarized across 28 clinical trials and found that 58% of patients met the criteria for clinically significant change following an average of 13 treatment sessions.

Cost offset. Another related and growing body of literature regarding the medical cost offset of psychological interventions provides evidence for the clinical meaningfulness of therapy as well. Medical cost offset studies suggest that many patients who enter treatment have concurrent medical and psychological needs. Those who receive psychological interventions reduce their use of medical services more than those who do not receive interventions. As a result, the provision of psychological interventions may result in improved levels of psychological functioning and decreased need for medical services. Mumford, Schlesinger, Glass, Patrick, and Cuerdon (1984) were the first to conduct a meta-analysis regarding the cost offset effect. They concluded that those who participated in psychological interventions were less likely to use inpatient services. In a selective review of methodologically rigorous studies (Gabbard, Lazar, Hornberger, & Spiegel, 1997), a second meta-analysis found that significant cost savings, as a result of reductions in inpatient treatment, were associated with services for individuals with chronic mental illness.

Chiles, Lambert, and Hatch (1999) conducted a more recent meta-analysis to examine the cost offset effect literature. They examined 91 studies conducted in a variety of treatment settings in which different therapeutic interventions with diverse patient groups were implemented in an effort to reduce medical utilization. The primary finding suggests that on average treated clients had a 15.7% reduction in utilization of medical services as opposed to a 12.27% increase in use of medical services by individuals assigned to control conditions, for a combined 25.08% difference in medical utilization between treatment and control groups. For studies that used hospital days as the dependent variable, an average reduction of 2.52 hospital days per person was associated with participation in psychological treatment.

Summary. Not only are psychological interventions statistically superior to control conditions, but many also produce outcomes that are clinically meaningful. Both primary studies and meta-analytic reviews find that many clients improve to levels that might be considered clinically meaningful. In addition, the cost offset literature provides evidence that individuals who have emotional difficulties may also benefit medically when they participate in psychological interventions. The study of clinical significance will remain a promising field for investigation in the years to come. Especially in this age of accountability, the ability of behavioral health professionals to demonstrate that their interventions are not just statistically satisfactory is key. The establishment of clinical relevance has helped to verify that psychosocial interventions are meaningful to clients, therapists, and society.

Does Therapy Exceed Placebo?

Although psychotherapy is statistically and clinically beneficial when compared to various no-treatment control conditions and surpasses improvement based on spontaneous remission, one might conclude that the benefits of therapy are not caused by the specific treatments, but rather by a generalized placebo effect (i.e., that psychotherapists are merely "placebologists"—see Prioleau, Murdock, & Brody, 1983). As a result, a second wave of therapy research pursued the relative benefit of therapy when compared to placebo controls (cf. DeMarco, 1998; Epstein, 1995; Oei & Shuttlewood, 1996, for other contemporary discussions).

In medical research, the effects of an active pharmacological agent are contrasted with the effects of a pharmacologically inert or nontherapeutic substance—a "placebo." This contrast makes good sense with respect to drug therapies, for it allows success to be attributed to the pharmacological agent rather than to the psychological effects of being treated or taking "medicines." Placebo controls appear to make less sense, however, when extended to psychotherapy research where the benefits of treatments and placebos depend on psychological mechanisms. Many authors entirely reject the placebo concept in psychotherapy research because it is not conceptually consistent with testing the efficacy of psychological procedures (e.g., Dush, 1986; Horvath, 1988; Wilkins, 1984).

In psychology treatments, the placebo construct has taken on a variety of meanings. For example, Rosenthal and Frank (1956) defined a placebo as being theoretically inert. It is inert, however, only from the standpoint of the theory of the therapy studied. As Critelli and Neumann (1984) have pointed out, "virtually every currently established psychotherapy would be considered inert, and therefore a placebo, from the viewpoint of other established theories of cure" (p. 33). This definition of a psychological placebo is highly questionable.

Placebos have also been labeled as "nonspecific" factors (e.g., Oei & Shuttlewood, 1996). This conceptualization, however, raises serious questions about the definition of "nonspecific." For example, once a "nonspecific" factor is labeled, does it then become a specific factor and fall outside the domain of a placebo effect? Similarly, if an influence like "therapist warmth" is considered to be a placebo because it is not a specific technique, how can it also be a substantial factor in client change, as many studies show?

Others have suggested the term *common factors* in recognition that many therapies have ingredients that are not unique. Thus, research on placebo effects would be better conceptualized as research on common factors versus the specific effects of a particular technique. Common factors are those dimensions of the treatment setting (therapist, therapy, client) that are not specific to any particular technique. Research on the broader concept of common factors will be discussed later in this chapter, but here it is important to note that those factors common to most therapies (such as expectation for improvement, persuasion, warmth and attention, understanding, and encouragement) should not be viewed as theoretically inert or as trivial. Indeed, these factors are central to psychological interventions in both theory and practice. They play an active role in patient improvement (cf. Butler & Strupp, 1986; Critelli & Neumann, 1984; Parloff, 1986).

A number of historical articles address the issue of treatment superiority to placebo (e.g., Barker, Funk, & Houston, 1988; Dush, 1986; Prioleau, Murdock, & Brody, 1983; Shepherd, 1984). Two more recent and extensive meta-analyses add substantial evidence regarding the relationship between therapy and placebo. Lipsey and Wilson (1993) addressed the placebo issue as part of their extensive review of meta-analyses. A subset ($n = 30$) of the meta-analyses reviewed by Lipsey and Wilson (1993) included comparisons of treatment with no-treatment control groups and placebo control groups. Table 5.6 displays the results. As can be seen, the efficacy of treatment is clearly superior to both no-treatment and placebo treatments. They conclude that "there are quite likely some generalized placebo effects that contribute to the overall effects of psychological treatment, but their magnitude does not seem sufficient to fully account for those overall effects" (pp. 1196–1197). These findings are also supported by many of the meta-analytic reviews conducted since the Lipsey and Wilson (1993) meta-analysis.

TABLE 5.6 Comparison of Effect Sizes Based on Studies with Different Control Conditions

	Effect Size		
Control Condition	**M**	**SD**	***N***
No-treatment control	0.67	0.44	30
Placebo treatment control	0.48	0.26	30

Source: Reproduced from Lipsey & Wilson (1993). Copyright 1993 by the American Psychological Association.

In the most comprehensive examination of the placebo issue to date, Grissom (1996) examined the relationship of therapy to control, therapy to placebo, placebo to control, and therapy to therapy across 46 meta-analytic reviews. Grissom (1996) used the "probability of superior estimate" (PS) to "estimate the probability that a randomly sampled client from a population given treatment 1 will have an outcome . . . that is superior to that . . . of a randomly sampled client from a population given treatment 2" (Grissom, 1996, p. 973). A summary of the results are presented in Table 5.7. As can be seen, the overall results "are consistent with the view that the ranking for therapeutic success is generally therapy, placebo, and control (do-nothing or wait)" in that order (Grissom, 1996, p. 979).

Following the controversial and heavily debated conclusion that therapy was no more effective than placebo (Prioleau et al., 1983), a body of literature has been amassed, with results that are as might be expected: patients in so-called placebo control groups typically show greater improvement than patients who are assigned to a wait list or no-treatment control group. Indeed, a

TABLE 5.7 Summary Statistics for Grissom (1996)

	Effect Size		
Comparison	**PS**[a]	**Effect Size Equivalent**	***N***
Therapy vs. control	.70	.75	68
Therapy vs. placebo	.66	.58	21
Placebo vs. control	.62	.44	6
Therapy vs. therapy	.56	.23	32

[a] PS = probability of superiority

Source: Adapted from Grissom (1996). Copyright 1996 by the American Psychological Association.

variety of placebo treatments that emphasize the usual common factors, such as expectations for change, a prescription for activity, discussion, attention, and warmth, yield substantial effect sizes. The effects of these common-factors, placebo-comparison approaches are smaller than those of formal psychotherapy.

Do Patients Maintain Their Gains?

Although early outcome research focused primarily on the immediate post-treatment status of patients who participated in therapy, recent studies are more likely to consider the maintenance of treatment gains. Similarly, many meta-analytic reviews consider outcome following treatment and at followup. Although there is no reason to believe that a single course of psychotherapy should inoculate a person forever from psychological disturbance and the development of symptoms, many patients who undergo therapy achieve healthy adjustment for long periods of time. This is true even though they have had a long history of recurrent problems. At the same time, there is clear evidence that a portion of patients who are improved at termination do relapse and continue to seek help from a variety of mental health providers, including their former therapists. Several problems such as alcohol and drug dependence, smoking, obesity, and possibly depression are so likely to recur that they are not considered properly studied without data collection at least one year after treatment. Yet even among alcoholic patients 30% stay dry, and an additional 30% or more show a reduced level of drinking following treatment (Carroll et al., 1994).

Meta-analytic studies. Nicholson and Berman (1983) conducted the earliest and most influential meta-analysis to answer the following question: Is followup necessary in evaluating psychotherapy? In their review of research in this area, they were concerned primarily with whether followup evaluations provided different evidence and conclusions than post-treatment evaluations. They included 67 studies (21% of which evaluated a verbal therapy) of a broad range of neurotic disorders that were self-referred rather than recruited and that involved both post-testing and followup data. The results of this meta-analytic review are complicated by the divergence in the studies that were examined, but, in general, the findings suggest that treatment gains are maintained. Post-therapy status correlated with followup status; differences between treatments apparent at the end of therapy were virtually the same at followup.

The review by Nicholson and Berman (1983) was especially important because it stood in marked contrast to earlier reviews (e.g., Shapiro & Shapiro, 1982; Smith et al., 1980). The study has been criticized, however, because effect sizes were calculated only if numerical information was available (Matt & Navarro, 1997). As a result, many nonsignificant findings were not incorporated into the average effect sizes. Fortunately, many more studies have investigated the long-term benefits of therapy in the past two decades.

Many of the meta-analyses conducted in the past decade also consider the outcome of treatment at both the end of treatment and at a followup assessment period some time later. For example, Feske and Chambless (1995) conducted an analysis of 21 studies of cognitive behavioral and exposure-only treatment for social phobia. They found that both treatments produced significant pre- to post-treatment gains independent of (within-treatment) or in comparison to a (between-treatment) control group. In addition, these benefits were maintained at followup 1 to 12 months later. Similarly, Stanton and Shadish (1997) used the followup data point to calculate all effect sizes in their analysis of 15 studies comparing family and individual treatments for substance abuse because there was evidence that post-treatment outcome was not significantly different from followup outcome. Bakker et al. (1998) examined the followup status of patients engaged in treatments for panic with and without agoraphobia. Followup periods ranged from 4 weeks to 8 years (average 62 weeks). The pretreatment to followup effect size was 1.28 for panic and 1.41 for agoraphobia, indicating a remarkable endurance for treatment benefits, including a continuing gain between the end of treatment and followup for agoraphobic symptoms. Other meta-analyses also find that treatment benefits are maintained for a range of disorders over a variety of mostly short (within one year) followup periods (Carlson & Hoyle, 1993; Fettes & Peters, 1992; Gould et al., 1995; Marrs, 1995; Murtagh & Greenwood, 1995; Sherman, 1998; Taylor, 1996; van Balkom, van Oppen, Vermeulen, & van Dyck, 1994).

Despite these positive findings, several methodological problems prevent broader conclusions. First, attrition between the end of treatment and followup data collection is a significant problem. For example, in one meta-analysis, only 15% of patients (202 of 1,346) in the medication conditions were present at the followup point (Bakker et al., 1998)! Other studies also show significant amounts of attrition following treatment. Indeed, attrition during treatment presents a challenging problem in many studies, amplifying the effects of dropout that occur following treatment. Second, most studies do not continue to follow control groups after treatment ends. Thus, findings regarding followup must remain "naturalistic" in most cases (Bakker et al., 1998).

Recent studies. In addition to these meta-analyses, many recent studies present evidence for the maintenance of therapeutic gains across a broad range of clients. For example, Carroll et al., (1994) found "no significant change in the reported frequency of cocaine use from posttreatment levels" for clients participating in several treatments for cocaine dependence (p. 992). In a study comparing exposure, stress inoculation training (SIT), and a combined treatment with a wait list control group, Foa et al. (1999) examined the long-term benefit for 64 patients who completed treatment for PTSD. All three active treatments were superior to wait list at the end of the treatment period, and improvements in all three treated groups were maintained at 12-month followup. Finally, Najavits and Gunderson (1995) examined the three-year outcome of clients treated for borderline personality disorder. Although the study was uncontrolled, the evidence suggested that even clients with serious and chronic disorders maintained improvement over the course of three years (Najavits & Gunderson, 1995).

A few studies are beginning to look at the individual difference variables that may influence which patients are more likely to maintain treatment gains. Using survival analytic techniques, Ilardi, Craighead, and Evans (1997) examined the influence of Axis II psychopathology on the relapse rates of patients who were hospitalized with affective disorders. They report that "patients without a personality disorder have an expected survival (i.e., remission) period approximately 7.4 times longer than that of patients who met DSM-III-R criteria for at least one Axis II disorder" (Ilardi et al., 1997, p. 388). The greatest risk occurred in the first six months following discharge from the hospital. Patients with personality disorders had much higher rates of relapse (77%) when compared to patients with no comorbid diagnosis (14%).

Results from studies and reviews of followup are encouraging, and therefore greater selection in the application of followup designs is recommended. For example, continuing use of followup studies on depression outcome is recommended, but only if the length of the followup time is extended to at least one year. Short-term followup studies are no longer needed for establishing the durability of effects. Studies that help identify risk factors for relapse or patterns of deterioration, however, could be useful. Many high-quality studies have been conducted in the past decade that follow clients for several years after treatment. These studies generally find that treatment effects are maintained for those who continue to participate in the data collection.

Maintaining treatment gains. Some studies go beyond following clients who participate in treatment to study various strategies for maintaining treatment gains or preventing relapse. For example, one study examined the comparative effects of nortriptyline and placebo with and without once per month maintenance interpersonal psychotherapy (IPT) in the treatment of older adults with recurrent depression (Reynolds et al., 1999). From a treated sample of 187 older adults, 107 who recovered and had stable remission for 16 weeks participated in a maintenance study. The clients were randomly assigned to one of four maintenance groups: nortriptyline plus medication clinic, placebo plus medication clinic, nortriptyline plus IPT, and placebo plus IPT. The time to recurrence was slower for active treatments when compared to placebo. The combined IPT/nortriptyline treatment was superior to the IPT/placebo treatment, with recurrence rates of 20% and 64%, respectively. The combined treatment was not statistically different from the nortriptyline monotherapy, but there was a trend for its superiority (20% vs. 43% recurrence rates, respectively). They conclude that continuation of combined treatment may be "the best long-term treatment strategy for preserving recovery in elderly patients with recurrent major depression" (Reynolds et al., 1999, p. 44).

In a similar study (Jarrett et al., 2001), patients with recurrent major depression who responded to cognitive therapy were randomly assigned to continuation phase cognitive therapy or a control group. The continuation treatment phase consisted of 10 sessions of treatment over 8 months and significantly reduced relapse (10% vs. 31%) when compared to no-treatment following response to the acute phase treatment. Other findings detailed in the article further substantiated that the continuation treatment significantly reduced relapse for the patients at the highest risk of recurrence.

SUMMARY. Therapy researchers continue to make progress in the study of long-term maintenance of treatment gains. More studies are including followup data to chart the course of treatment benefits, and new studies are documenting the effects of maintenance treatments. This area of research will continue to be extremely important for the practice of psychology in the years to come. Demonstrating that treatments are beneficial for longer periods of time, identifying clients who are at risk of relapse, and developing methods of improving treatments that have acute benefits will be important future projects. For now, it appears that treatment does offer a long-term benefit for many clients. The many methodological difficulties of longitudinal research with therapy participants (e.g., dropout, uncontrolled designs, clients seeking extra-study treatment) make definitive conclusions difficult. Thus, the maintenance of treatment gains remains a rich, yet difficult, area of study.

How Much Therapy Is Necessary?

Howard, Kopta, Krause, and Orlinsky (1986) reported a meta-analysis on 2,431 patients from published research covering a 30-year period. Their analysis showed a stable pattern across studies reflecting the relationship of amount of therapy to patient improvement. They concluded that the relationship between the number of sessions and client improvement took a form similar to that evidenced by many medications—"a positive relationship characterized by a negatively accelerated curve; that is, the more psychotherapy, the greater the probability of improvement, with diminishing returns at higher doses" (Kopta, Howard, Lowry, & Beutler, 1994, p. 1009). Their analysis of the data indicated that 14% of clients improved before attending the initial session, 53% were improved following 8 weekly sessions, 75% by 26 sessions, and 83% after 52 sessions.

The Howard et al. (1986) study supports the meta-analytic findings that treatment produces a benefit that surpasses spontaneous remission rates by demonstrating that clients receiving treatments make substantial gains early in treatment. McNeilly and Howard (1991) used the same analytic methods to reconsider Eysenck's (1952) original data set from which Eysenck drew the conclusion that psychotherapy was no more effective than spontaneous remission. Using probit analysis of the untreated sample, they demonstrated that psychotherapy produced in 15 sessions the same recovery rate as spontaneous remission after two years! Ironically, Eysenck's own data confirm that therapy is beneficial. The more rapid effect of psychotherapy versus no treatment is also important because suffering is relieved faster.

A limitation of both the Howard et al. (1986) meta-analysis and the McNeilly and Howard (1991) study was their reliance on pre-post estimates of patient improvement rather than session-by-session ratings of improvement. Reliance on pre-post ratings makes it difficult to identify the exact time to recovery for individual patients. Kadera, Lambert, and Andrews (1996) analyzed change in a small group of outpatients in a training clinic by having them complete the Outcome Questionnaire-45 (OQ-45) prior to each session. This study was replicated by Anderson and Lambert (2001), who combined the Kadera data with additional data from the same clinic ($N = 140$) and included a six-month followup to see if the patients maintained their gains. This study suggests that the review by Howard et al. (1986) overestimated the speed of recovery and indicated that 50% of patients needed 13 sessions of therapy before they reached criteria for clinically significant change and 75% of patients met criteria after more than 50 sessions. Anderson and Lambert (2001) also found that patients tended to maintain or show additional improvement at followup. They noted a relationship between initial levels of distress and time to recovery, with more disturbed patients reaching criteria for recovery at a slower rate.

In an extension, Lambert, Hansen, and Finch (2001) reported recovery rates from a national sample of patients ($n = 6{,}072$) undergoing treatment in various settings (employee assistance programs, private practice, university counseling centers, and community mental health centers). Results of the analysis are illustrated in Figure 5.1. The findings suggest that 50% of patients who begin treatment in the dysfunctional range can be expected to achieve clinically significant change following 21 sessions of psychotherapy. More than double this number of treatment sessions are necessary, however, before 75% of patients reach this same criterion. Using a lesser standard of improvement (reliable change) and including patients who began treatment in the functional range, they found that 50% are esti-

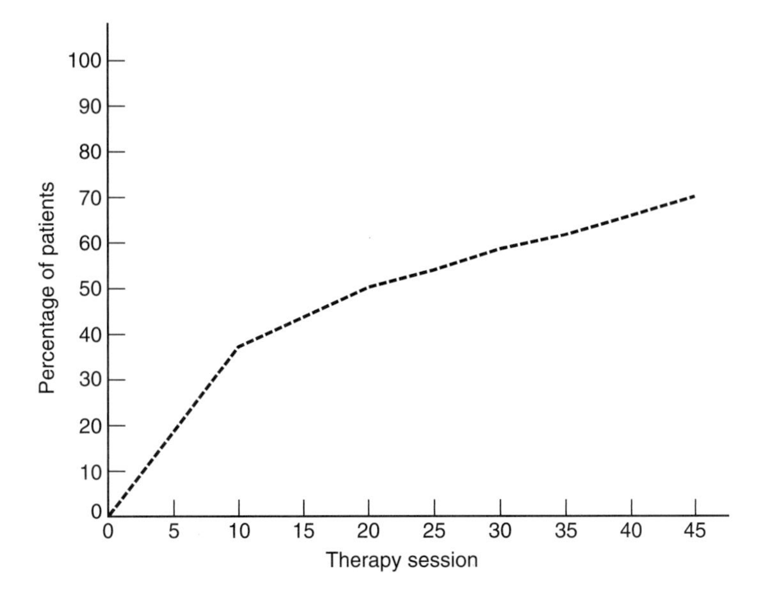

FIGURE 5.1 Time to recovery using clinically significantly improved criteria. (Reprinted by permission of the *American Psychological Association* and the authors.)

mated to improve following 7 sessions and 75% following 14 sessions.

As can be seen, the dosage of therapy needed to meet the criterion of success depends on the criterion selected. Results are also a function of the setting in which therapy occurs as well as the degree of initial patient disturbance. Thus, rather than a general recovery curve such as that provided in Figure 5.1, it might be best to rely on more specific curves based on variables of particular interest such as diagnosis. Some research beyond that provided by Lambert, Hansen, and Finch (2001) is available for this purpose. Kopta et al. (1994) followed the progress of 854 outpatient clients using one of three versions of the Symptom Checklist-90-R (Derogatis, 1983). The symptoms were clustered into three groups (acute distress, chronic distress, and characterological) based on probit analyses of the results. The researchers then examined differences in rates of change across the three categories. For acute distress items, clients reached a 50% recovery level within 10 sessions, for chronic distress items the number of sessions was extended to 14, and for characterological items fewer than 59% of the clients recovered on any of the items at 52 sessions (mean >104 sessions). Again, the recovery rates are more conservative than those found in earlier studies—50% of the clients would recover by 11 sessions, and 58 sessions would be necessary for 75% of clients to recover (Kopta et al., 1994).

In a similar study, rates of improvement in different sets of interpersonal problems (control, detached, and self-effacing) were examined over the course of therapy (Maling, Gurtman, & Howard, 1995). In this study, patients were first compared to nonpatients in order to identify interpersonal problems that were most relevant to therapy. Patients endorsed higher rates of social detachment and self-effacing traits, while few differences were evident in problems of over control. Ironically, interpersonal problems responded differentially to therapy, "and in a manner inverse to their apparent salience in patients" (p. 71). Control problems responded rapidly to treatment, with nearly 50% of the clients improving in the first 10 sessions and a steady monotonic rate of change following a clear inflection point at session 10. Problems of social detachment improved at a slower rate (30% improved in the first 17 sessions), with a clear inflection point at session 17 and a steady rate of change thereafter increasing to approximately 55% after 38 sessions. Items tapping the self-effacing problems were unresponsive to therapy. By session 4, about 25% of the patients had improved, but beyond that little improvement was observable.

Barkham et al. (1996) examined the responses of depressed clients involved in psychodynamic-interpersonal or CBT treatment administered in 8 or 16 sessions. They found that some classes of symptoms responded more quickly than others, as evidenced by (a) higher rates of change across clients on the Beck Depression Inventory (BDI) as opposed to the Inventory of Interpersonal Problems (IIP), (b) faster rates of change on acute symptoms as opposed to chronic symptoms within the BDI, and (c) faster changes on symptoms when compared to self-esteem using an individualized outcome measure. They also demonstrated that therapy outcome does proceed at a decelerating pace. Clients involved in the 8-session treatment had recovery rates that were slightly higher than half that of the clients involved in the 16-session treatment. This also suggests that "change occurred more rapidly when tighter time limits were imposed" (Barkham et al., 1996, p. 933).

Thompson, Thompson, and Gallagher-Thompson (1995) examined the session-by-session changes in mood of 91 older patients receiving therapy for depression. They noted that, while the average rate of change across patients was linear and steady, many clients had unsteady rates of change, with significant between-session decreases or increases in depressed mood. In fact, "those who showed the greatest rate of improvement were the most likely to experience a 'bumpy ride' or unsteady rates of depression reduction" (p. 334). Surprisingly, those who experienced more significant episodes of worsening or improvement (that is, relatively large changes in mood scores between sessions) were more vulnerable to an early relapse. Thompson et al. conclude that the findings of their study combined with others suggest "it may be worthwhile for psychotherapy research to attend to individual trajectories of change. Such descriptive and experimental research can increase our understanding of what constitutes 'the road to recovery' for depressed patients" (Thompson, Thompson, & Gallagher-Thompson, 1995, p. 334).

Haas, Hill, Lambert, and Morrell (2002) evaluated the relationship between rapid early response to treatment and maintenance of treatment gains at followup. In contrast to the findings of Thompson et al. (1995) and studies of antidepressants (Quitkin, McGrath, Stewart, Taylor, & Klein, 1996) that show early rapid response is related to relapse at followup, these researchers found that early (within the first three sessions) extreme positive response to psychotherapy predicted final treatment status as well as followup status. The most rapidly responding patients made up the bulk (80% at termination) of patients who made clinically significant gains. They suggested that this finding argued against the idea that early treatment response was merely a placebo effect. Many patients who respond to therapy make gains early on, and these gains precede rather than follow the specific techniques deemed to be essential by most theories of psychotherapeutic intervention. These findings also underscore the general findings on the dose-response relationship and phase model of psychotherapy—more improvement comes from earlier rather than later treatment sessions.

Several meta-analyses also provide data regarding the amount of therapy needed to bring about meaningful change. Carlson and Hoyle (1993) found that the clinical effectiveness of progressive muscle relaxation improved with an increase in the number of sessions. They speculated that the asymptote of efficacy and length of treatment was not far beyond the 12-session mark. Thase et al. (1997) examined the recovery rates of clients receiving treatment for depression across six large randomized clinical trials for the treatment of depression. After dividing clients into more and less severe groups (based on initial depression severity measures), the recovery rates of clients receiving psychotherapy with and without medication were compared. They found that "the 75th percentile of the time to recovery was reached by 9 weeks in the more severe-combined therapy group, compared with 13 weeks for patients in the more severe-psychotherapy alone group" (Thase et al., 1997, p. 1012). They concluded that "the current study provides the strongest empirical evidence ever marshaled to indicate that combined therapy is superior to psychotherapy alone for treatment of severely depressed outpatients, in terms of both overall recovery rates and shorter time to recovery" (Thase et al., 1997, pp. 1012–1013). Fettes and Peters's (1992) meta-analysis of treatments for bulimia suggested that more intense treatment (i.e., more hours of therapy per week) produced larger effects.

The question, how much therapy is enough, is important for both practical and theoretical reasons. Research on this topic can help therapists and patients make reasonable decisions for treatment planning. It can inform policy decisions about the amount of services that are necessary for sufficient medical coverage. It also allows for theory-driven exploration of variables that modify dosage models. Significant progress has been made in this area over the last decade and a half. Research suggests that a sizable portion of patients reliably improve after 10 sessions and that 75% of patients will meet more rigorous criteria for success after about 50 sessions of treatment. Limiting treatment sessions to less than 20 will mean that about 50% of patients will not achieve a substantial benefit from therapy (as measured by standard self-report scales). Aspects of patient functioning show differential response to treatment, with more characterological and interpersonal aspects of functioning responding more slowly than psychological symptoms. Future research may illuminate which, if any, specific interventions are more efficient in producing patient change. At this point in time, the results of research into the dose-effect relationship should serve as a guide to employers, government agencies, and insurance companies. Most patients are being underserved by current session limits. Managed care, if it is interested in quality care, should do more to encourage greater, not less, utilization of psychotherapy service.

Do Some Patients Get Worse?

Although negative effects are difficult, if not impossible, to study in an experimentally controlled way, research clearly indicates that some patients are worse as a result of psychotherapy. This does not mean that all instances of worsening are the product of therapy. Some cases may be on a progressive decline that no therapist effort could stop. The extent or rate of such negative change or of "spontaneous" deterioration in untreated groups has never been determined, so there is no baseline from which to judge deterioration rates observed in treated groups. The alternative is to observe negative change in experiments using treated versus control conditions and in studies of specific connections between therapy processes and patient responses. It appears that negative outcomes can be observed across a variety of treatment modalities, including group and family therapies as well as theoretical orientations.

Prior work (Bergin & Lambert, 1978; Lambert, Bergin, & Collins, 1977) described evidence (based on over 50 studies) about the incidence, prevalence, and magnitude of negative change. That process involved piecing together obscure bits of evidence since there are few, if any, definitive studies. There has been considerable hesitation to address this issue directly, and most early outcome studies did not include a category of "worse." However, the evidence is slowly changing as studies improve. There is a paradoxical fact, however, that as precision of inquiry into this question is improving, quality of therapy is also improving. The research itself stimulates better quality control and inclusion of competent therapy in outcome studies, so the study of negative effects may decrease its extent and its visibility.

Many early studies documented rates of deterioration in patients, even in those who participated in carefully controlled research protocols (cf. Beutler, Frank, Schieber, Calvert & Gaines, 1984; Doherty, Lester, & Leigh, 1986; Emmelkamp, de Haan, & Hoogduin, 1990; Henry, Schacht, & Strupp, 1986; Jacobson et al., 1984; Mohr et al., 1990; Orlinsky & Howard, 1980). Those studies that use controls usually show that deterioration is lower in controls than in treated samples. For example, Ogles, Lambert, and Sawyer (1995) in a re-analysis of the NIMH TDCRP data found that 8% of the clients in the completer sample (the 162 clients who completed at least 12 sessions and 15 weeks of treatment) deteriorated as measured with the Hamilton Rating Scale for Depression (HRSD). None of the clients who deteriorated participated in the placebo plus clinical management control group.

Recent studies also document the occurrence of negative outcomes during treatment. For example, Scogin et al. (1996) used a very liberal definition of negative outcome: any client making even a 1-point increase in scores on the self-report or clinician measures. They found that 1% of clients were identified as having a negative outcome using the clinician rated outcome, and 9% were identified as having a negative outcome using the self-report measure of outcome. Mohr (1995) examined a large number of studies to investigate factors related to negative outcome in psychotherapy. He found evidence for increased rates of negative outcome among patients treated for borderline personality disorder and obsessive compulsive disorder. Two client variables were related to negative outcome: interpersonal difficulties and more severe problems at intake. Therapist variables that were identified as potential contributors to negative outcome included lack of empathy, underestimation of patient's problem severity, and negative countertransference. Finally, there was evidence that experiential therapies may have a higher propensity to produce negative outcome and that minimal intervention for severely distressed patients may result in deterioration (Mohr, 1995). These findings were strikingly similar to earlier reviews (e.g., Lambert, Bergin, & Collins, 1977).

It is our view that, although the data contain many methodological shortcomings and ambiguities, the evidence suggests that psychotherapy can and does harm a portion of those it is intended to help. A relatively consistent portion of individuals (5 to 10%) deteriorate while participating in treatment. At this time, the research literature does not suggest the degree to which client deterioration reduces the overall estimate of positive treatment effects. At the same time, the study of negative change has important implications for the selection of clients for treatment, the suitability of specific procedures for some clients, and the selection, training, and monitoring of therapists. Several of these issues will be discussed later in the chapter.

Does Efficacy Research Generalize to Practice?

Readers who are familiar with the earlier versions of this chapter may have noticed the change in title for this chapter. Use of the term *efficacy* in addition to *effectiveness* was deliberate, based on an increasing interest in the empirical substantiation of treatments in applied versus laboratory settings (Hollon, 1996; Howard et al., 1996; Jacobson & Christensen, 1996; Seligman, 1995; Shadish et al., 1997; Shadish, Navarro, Matt, & Phillips, 2000; Shadish, Ragsdale, Glaser, & Montgomery, 1995). In the past decade, therapy researchers have applied more distinct definitions for these terms (Seligman, 1995). The efficacy of treatment is determined by a clinical trial or trials in which many variables are carefully controlled in order to demonstrate that the relationship between the treatment and outcome are relatively unambiguous. Efficacy studies emphasize the internal validity of the experimental or quasi-experimental design through a variety of means, including (a) controlling the types of patients included in the study (e.g., limiting the number of clients with comorbid disorders), (b) using manuals to standardize treatment delivery, (c) training therapists prior to the study, monitoring therapist adherence to the treatment during the study, and supervising therapists who deviate from the treatment protocol, (d) managing the "dose" of treatment through analyses that include only patients who have received a specified amount of treatment, and (e) random assignment to treatments and the use of blinding procedures for raters (Seligman, 1995). These and other strategies are used to enhance the investigator's ability to make causal inferences based on the findings.

In contrast, the effectiveness of a treatment is considered in clinical situations when the intervention is implemented without the same level of internal validity. Effectiveness studies emphasize the external validity of the experimental design and attempt to demonstrate that the treatment can be beneficial in a clinical setting. Typically, clients are not preselected, treatment dose is not controlled, and therapist adherence is neither monitored nor modified to be a pure-form, manually determined treatment. Therapists tend to be those working in the settings and may or may not receive the same level of prestudy training as that of the efficacy study. At the same time, many clinically representative studies have high internal validity because they have random assignment and minimize attrition (Shadish, Navarro, Matt, & Phillips, 2000). Nevertheless, effectiveness studies differ from efficacy studies based on "the joint effects of a constellation of variables that might pertain to clinical relevance" (Shadish, Matt et al., 1997, p. 356).

Much of the research concerning the benefits of treatment is not easily categorized. For example, the numerous studies included in the Smith, Glass, and Miller (1980) meta-analysis have extremely varied experimental designs, some of which may be viewed as efficacy studies and others of which may be viewed as effectiveness studies. With the increasing use of meta-analysis, however, many reviewers narrowed the focus of their meta-analyses to include only methodologically superior studies with specified experimental controls. As a result, the strongest findings for the benefits of psychotherapy involve the efficacy of treatments in controlled conditions. Fewer studies have examined the effectiveness of treatments. Several of the original meta-analyses examined the relationship of therapy setting, therapist experience, or other variables that are related to this issue, but few studies directly examined the differences related to efficacy versus effectiveness studies.

Weisz, Weiss, and Donenberg (1992) examined four meta-analyses of the child and adolescent treatment literature. A consistent positive benefit for treatment was noted across more than 200 studies. When comparing the effect sizes for treatments conducted in research settings with treatments conducted in clinic settings, however, they found significant differences. They suggested that "most clinic studies have not shown significant effects" (Weisz et al., 1992, p. 1578). Spurred by the findings of Weisz et al. (1992), several important studies consider whether treatment works in clinically representative conditions. Shadish et al. (1997, 2000) conducted two secondary analyses to consider the benefits of therapy conducted in clinically representative conditions. The first meta-analysis identified 54 studies from 15 previous meta-analyses that varied in the degree to which they were conducted in clinically representative conditions. For example, studies conducted in community settings with patients entering treatment using typical routes were considered to be more representative of clinical settings than studies conducted in university settings with patients recruited through ads and carefully screened to select a homogeneous sample. When comparing outcome studies along the continuum of representativeness, Shadish et al. (1997) found that the effects of clinically representative studies were the same as effects reported in the original meta-analyses.

The second meta-analysis (Shadish et al., 2000) improved upon the first study with several methodological changes and the inclusion of a larger sample of studies. Three samples were analyzed to investigate the influence of clinical representativeness of studies on their effects. Criteria for determining clinical representativeness included the following study characteristics: (a) client problems, (b) setting, (c) referral source, (d) therapists, (e) treatment structure, (f) treatment monitoring, (g) problem heterogeneity, (h) pre-therapy training, (i) therapy freedom, and (j) flexible number of sessions. Both random and fixed-effect analyses found that studies that were representative of clinical conditions produced similar effects to those that were not representative of clinical conditions.

Another, yet completely different, method of investigating the effectiveness of treatment is illustrated by one of the more controversial studies conducted in the past decade. This study used a survey methodology and was conducted by the popular magazine *Consumer Reports* (*Consumer Reports*, 1994 November). The *Consumer Reports* staff included a supplementary survey with questions regarding psychotherapy and drugs in one version of their annual survey of readers. Approximately 180,000 readers received the questionnaire: 22,000 responded, and 7,000 answered the mental health questions (Seligman, 1995). More than half (4,100) of the respondents reported receiving assistance from some combination of mental health professionals, family doctors, or support groups. Of those, 2,900 received services from a mental health professional. Based on the readers' responses to the mental health questions, several findings were reported (Seligman, 1995). First, participants in mental health treatment reported benefiting from treatment. Second, longer duration of therapy was reported to be more beneficial than shorter duration of therapy. Third, there were no differences between psychotherapy alone or psychotherapy plus medication. Fourth, psychologists, psychiatrists, and social workers performed equally well, and all of them performed better than marriage counselors. Fifth, family doctors performed as well as mental health professionals in the short term but performed worse in the long term. Sixth, people attending Alcoholics Anonymous reported the highest rates of improvement. Seventh, clients who carefully selected therapists and actively participated in therapy did better in treatment. Eighth, no specific modality of therapy was more effective than any other mode of treatment. And ninth, clients whose therapy was limited in some manner by their insurance (e.g., choice of therapist or duration of therapy) reported less improvement.

Taken together, this array of findings provides important evidence that individuals who receive uncontrolled treatments from a variety of professionals and in various settings report benefits from treatment. Although the findings may be criticized because the methodological shortcomings of this survey were numerous (Seligman, 1995, who served as a consultant to the *Consumer Reports* staff, identified no less than eight headings of methodological flaws within the study), the survey makes a unique and important contribution regarding an externally valid sample of therapy consumers. At the same time, Gregerson et al. (2001) suggest that the measure of improvement used (post-therapy retrospective ratings) tends to overstate improvement and produces double the effect size reported in studies that employ the usual pre-post self-report scales.

One important note concerning the direction of psychotherapy research is in order. Shadish et al. (2000) suggest that studies are becoming less representative of clinical conditions. As investigators get more proficient at conducting randomized trials that isolate causal factors in treatment, they risk losing the potential benefits of the therapy under more representative conditions. Clearly, both efficacy and effectiveness research (including surveys such as the *Consumer Reports* study) will contribute different and important perspectives on the benefit of psychotherapy (Seligman, 1996). However, "it is the high quality randomized experiments about clinic therapy that are currently lacking" (Shadish et al., 1997, p. 361). Hansen, Lambert, and Forman (2002) have shown that clinical trials provide doses of treatment that far exceed the doses offered in routine practice (M = 3 to 5 sessions). They also note that patients in routine practice experience much less benefit than patients in clinical trials when the criterion of success is clinically significant change. Rates of clinically significant change tended to be about 10% in routine practice, based on an analysis of over 6,000 patients treated in various settings across the United States. This contrasts with rates of clinically significant change in clinical trials (around 40% to 60% of patients), where the typical patient receives about 12 to 14 sessions of treatment.

One exception to the move toward less representative studies is referred to as "patient profiling" or "patient-oriented research" (Howard et al., 1996). These studies investigate client improvement within clinical settings under more naturalistic conditions. Indeed, some of the studies discussed earlier relating to the dose-response effect were conducted in these naturalistic settings. Another area of research that may contribute to the effectiveness literature has not typically been part of the psychologist's domain—mental health services research (Howard et al., 1996). Service evaluation, however, remains an important potential source of data for the external validity of therapeutic methods as they are disseminated in various settings (Donenberg, Lyons, & Howard, 1999). Speer and Newman (1996) examined mental health service evaluation studies conducted over a five-year period. This group of studies was largely uninformative with respect to outpatient psychotherapy, inasmuch as the majority of studies focused on innovative services for individuals from unique groups (e.g., severe mental illness, sex offenders, juvenile offenders, etc.).

During the past decade, the issue of treatment effectiveness in applied settings has become an important area of study. The dissemination or transportability of efficacious treatments may be one of the most fertile areas of study for the next decade. With diminishing resources and increasing accountability, those who fund the delivery of mental health services are clamoring for "best practices" and empirically supported interventions. The ability of researchers and evaluators to demonstrate that laboratory treatments also work in the real world will eventually lead to a better understanding of the effects of therapy as it is typically offered.

Summary

When treatment groups are compared to no-treatment groups under controlled conditions in which the quality, amount, and type of treatment are carefully monitored and patients are carefully selected, therapy works. Not only is psychotherapy superior to no treatment, but the benefits of therapy exceed the benefits accrued through administration of a placebo treatment. Although placebo treatments incorporate and use many factors that are important in bona fide treatments, treatments produce superior results to placebo treatments alone. Many patients who participate in treatment also maintain their gains. The degree to which they maintain meaningful gains over extended periods of time, however, must continue to be a focus of study. Indeed, the difficulties with attrition that attend long-term outcome studies are a significant challenge that must be addressed. Of the patients who improve, many improve enough that they can be categorized as meaningfully improved using any of several possible definitions. Unfortunately, some participants (approximately 5 to 10%) deteriorate while enrolled in therapy. Although therapy is clearly effective under tightly controlled conditions, less evidence is available to support its utility in practice. The few studies available, however, suggest that therapy can be beneficial in clinical settings. Taken together, these findings provide an impressive array of evidence for the efficacy, effectiveness, and utility of psychotherapy if it is given in substantial doses. This latter observation suggests that concerted efforts should be made to keep patients in treatment long enough for benefits to be observed. Terminations of treatment should be based on patient treatment response rather than arbitrary session limits.

Comparison and Causative Factors

In this section, we review research that further clarifies the factors associated with improvement during psychotherapy. This research, to a large extent, employs research designs that are aimed at discovering the effects of specific therapeutic factors by contrasting an established treatment with a new treatment, an effective treatment with one or more of its component factors, or an effective treatment with a different effective treatment on a group of patients with special characteristics. First, we explore evidence that deals with the differential effectiveness of different schools of therapy. Then we examine studies comparing components that have been added to or separated from an efficacious intervention. Finally, we consider studies that examine the effects of therapists within various treatments. We then return to the possibility that factors common across therapies may account for many of the therapeutic gains that are apparent in treatment groups.

Is One Treatment Preferable to Another?

Historically, there has been a clear difference of approach between "schools" of therapy associated with psychodynamic and humanistic theories on the one hand ("verbal" or "insight" therapies), and behavioral and cognitive theories ("action" therapies), on the other. Of course, it cannot be assumed that such global and philosophical divisions between treatment approaches are faithfully or functionally represented in the actual procedures implemented in the delivery of their respective therapies. The use of "manuals" to specify treatment techniques characteristic of the different schools results in objectively discriminable therapist behaviors (Luborsky & DeRubeis, 1984; Rousaville, O'Malley, Foley, & Weissman, 1988). The use of therapy manuals and more experienced therapists also has been found to reduce the variability in outcome due to the therapist, allowing for more appropriate comparisons in comparative outcome studies (Crits-Christoph et al., 1991). Whether these differences hold up in everyday routine clinical practice, however, is an open question.

Many older reviews have analyzed studies comparing the psychotherapies (e.g., Bergin & Lambert, 1978; Bergin & Suinn, 1975; Beutler, 1979; Goldstein & Stein, 1976; Kellner, 1975; Lambert & Bergin, 1973; Meltzoff & Kornreich, 1970; Rachman & Wilson, 1980). The conclusion of most, but not all, of these reviews is similar to that drawn by Luborsky, Singer, and Luborsky (1975), who suggested a verdict similar to that of the Dodo bird in Alice in Wonderland: "Everyone has won and all must have prizes." These reviews used traditional scholarly methods of reaching conclusions without reference to meta-analytic procedures. However, meta-analytic methods have now been extensively applied to large groups of comparative studies, and these reviews generally offer similar conclusions, that is, little or no difference between therapies (Wampold, 2001).

Early meta-analytic reviews often showed a small, but consistent, advantage for cognitive and behavioral methods over traditional verbal and relationship-oriented therapies (e.g., Dobson, 1989; Dush, Hirt, & Schroeder, 1989; Nicholson & Berman, 1983; Robinson et al., 1990; Shapiro & Shapiro, 1982; Smith et al., 1980; Svartberg & Stiles, 1991). This was not always the case (e.g., Shoham-Salomon & Rosenthal, 1987), but certainly when differences are found they often favor cognitive or behavioral approaches across a variety of patient diagnostic categories.

Such differences are, however, often explainable in terms of methodological artifacts. Let us try to explain and clarify these issues, providing illustrations of the way they may impact evaluations of comparative outcomes. Smith et al. (1980) reported some substantial differences between behavior therapy and other approaches. However, the relatively large effect sizes reported for behavior therapy were reduced when the analysis took into account the fact that behavior therapy studies used outcome measures that were judged to be more reactive to experimental demand. This resulted in Smith et al. (1980) concluding that the differences between therapies were minimal. However, the Smith et al. review relied on cross-study comparisons in which behavior therapy in one study was compared with verbal therapy in another study. In this situation, many variables besides treatment modality also differ across studies. Comparisons like this, of which there are many in the Smith et al. report, cannot be as conclusive as comparisons in which the compared treatments are offered within a given study. These studies are much more likely to hold numerous variables constant while comparing one type of therapy with another.

Shapiro and Shapiro's (1982) extensive meta-analysis focused exclusively on studies comparing two or more active treatments with control conditions. Their data contained more replicated comparisons between treatment methods and permitted more definitive statements concerning the comparative efficacy of treatments. Based on 143 studies, Shapiro and Shapiro (1982) found that cognitive and various behavioral treatments yielded more favorable outcomes (1.00 and 1.06 effect size, respectively) than dynamic and humanistic therapies, which yielded inferior outcomes (effect size = .40). These authors also attributed the larger behavioral effect sizes to strong biases in the behavioral and cognitive literature toward analogue studies, mild cases, and highly reactive criteria. They stated that the treatments and cases studied were not representative of clinical practice because they were frequently conducted in university settings. Although such criticisms must be taken into account, they are based on post-hoc analyses that may not do justice to cognitive and behavioral interventions.

Some meta-analytic reviews present evidence for the superiority of one treatment over another without considering potential reasons for the differences (e.g., analogue studies, measurement biases). For example, (Svartberg & Stiles, 1991) examined the effects of short-term dynamic psychotherapy (STDP) in 19 studies published in the period between 1978 and 1988. Their analysis showed that while STDP was superior to no-treatment, it was less effective than alternative therapies even at a one-year followup. However, two subsequent meta-analyses updated this review (Anderson & Lambert, 1995; Crits-Christoph, 1992). Both newer meta-analyses found short-term dynamic therapy to be equivalent to other treatments using a larger database of studies.

Many of the meta-analyses in Tables 5.1–5.4 examine the comparative benefit of different treatments. Pharmacological treatments are frequently compared to psychological treatments. Different forms of pharmacological or psychological treatments are also compared to one another. Many of these comparisons are cross-study comparisons with numerous potential confounds. A smaller number of meta-analyses conduct within-study comparisons of treatment effectiveness. Most of these studies do not consider the potential impact of the allegiance effect or other potential methodological artifacts (e.g., measurement or sample bias) on treatment comparisons. Nevertheless, differences between various therapeutic approaches are typically small (Wampold, 2001).

One issue of particular interest to practitioners and researchers is the relative effectiveness of cognitive versus behavioral methods. The Shapiro and Shapiro (1982) report showed a significantly larger effect size for cognitive therapy over systematic desensitization. This conclusion, however, was challenged by Miller and Berman (1983) and later by Berman, Miller, and Massman (1985), who compared cognitive behavior therapy with various therapies, mainly behavioral. These meta-analyses showed no difference between cognitive and desensitization therapies. The second study also revealed that the larger effect sizes for cognitive therapy occurred in studies conducted by investigators having an allegiance to that method. Finally, the combination of desensitization with a cognitive method did not increase effects beyond that obtainable by either treatment alone.

In a similar review, Dobson (1989) examined the effects of Beck's cognitive therapy for depression with a variety of other treatments, including mostly behavioral therapy and pharmacotherapy as measured by changes in Beck Depression Inventory scores. Of the nine studies that compared cognitive and behavioral therapies, the average cognitive therapy client had an outcome that was superior to 67% of the behavior therapy clients. Gaffan, Tsauousis, and Kemp-Wheeler (1995) reexamined and then extended the findings of Dobson's (1989) study of comparative outcomes with depressive disorders using meta-analytic strategies. They also considered the potential relationship of investigator allegiance to the effects of treatment. Using weighted effect sizes, cognitive therapy remained superior to behavior therapy, other psychotherapy, or pharmacotherapy (average effect size = .27). When adjusted for investigator allegiance, the effect size was reduced to .17. Thus, the superiority of cognitive therapy for this set of studies persisted but was significantly attenuated by calculating effect sizes differently and considering investigator allegiance.

Robinson, Berman, and Neimeyer (1990) conducted a comprehensive review of comparative outcome studies of treatments with depressive disorders. In their analysis of direct comparisons (i.e., within-study comparisons) of cognitive, behavioral, cognitive behavioral, or general verbal therapies, they found equivalence between cognitive and cognitive behavioral approaches, with the latter treatment showing some superiority to a strictly behavioral approach. Verbal therapies were less effective than all three alternative therapies with which they were compared. However, when two independent raters judged investigator allegiance toward a treatment on a five-point scale, the differences between treatments vanished. Ratings were based on reading and rating the introduction of the study. Some investigators had strong theoretical preferences for a particular treatment. In some cases, preferences had to be inferred. Preferred therapies produced more improvement than their less favored counterparts, but when this bias was eliminated through statistical adjustments, therapies were equivalent. Similar results were reported for analysis of drug versus psychotherapy comparisons. The evidence that favored psychotherapies over medication disappeared when comparisons took into account experimenter allegiance.

In addition to re-analyzing Dobson's meta-analysis, Gaffan et al. (1995) conducted a second analysis using 35 new published studies of cognitive therapy for depression that used the Beck Depression Inventory as the measure of outcome. Within this second set of studies, cognitive therapy was again superior to psychotherapy and pharmacotherapy. However, behavior therapy produced larger effect sizes than cognitive therapy (with just four comparisons). Importantly, ratings of investigator allegiance were not correlated with effect sizes in this more recent sample of studies. As a result, Gaffan et al. (1995) suggest that the allegiance effect may be "a historical phenomenon" (p. 978).

Since allegiance effects were alleged to account for differences between treatments, no fewer than six studies have specifically investigated the relationship of the outcome of treatment to the allegiance of the researcher (Luborsky et al., 1999). Luborsky et al. (1999) reviewed the findings of all earlier studies of the allegiance effect and then conducted an analysis of 29 studies, with two additions to the measurement of allegiance: (1) colleague ratings, and (2) self-ratings of their allegiance by the researchers themselves. When examining the relationship of researcher allegiance to the comparative outcome of the treatment, all three measures of allegiance (reprint ratings, colleague ratings, and self-ratings) were highly correlated (r = .59, .73, and .68 respectively) with the comparative outcome effect sizes. The linear combination of the three measures correlated with effect sizes at r = .85. A variety of explanations for this relationship are possible; however, the main point here is that even when well-designed studies provide evidence that one treatment is preferrable to another, extra-treatment factors (such as the allegiance of the investigator) may be responsible for the finding.

We have noted three prominent artifacts: the demand characteristics associated with more specific measures, the more frequent use of analogue designs and mild cases within certain treatments, and investigator allegiance. When these factors are controlled, comparative studies yield remarkably similar findings: "all have won and all must have prizes." In essence, the dodo bird verdict has been "fortified by the allegiance effect bias" (Shoham & Rohrbaugh, 1999, p. 122). One of the subtle points of the Luborsky et al. (1999) study is evident when we examine the effect sizes between the treatments. The effect sizes describing treatment differences ranged from –.20 to .10 even before taking into account the allegiance of the researcher (a success rate difference between groups of less than 10%). Thus, little variation in comparative treatment outcomes among the studies reviewed existed in the first place.

Wampold et al. (1997) conducted the most recent meta-analysis comparing treatments. This meta-analysis differed from earlier comparisons between treatments in several ways. First, only studies that directly compared two or more treatments were included in the meta-analysis. This eliminates the potential confounds associated with comparing treatments administered in different studies (Shadish & Sweeney, 1991). Second, the treatments were not divided into general types or categories. Third, only "bona fide" treatments were included in the meta-analysis. That is, studies in which the treatment was delivered "by trained therapists and were based on psychological principles, were offered to the psychotherapy community as viable treatments . . ., or contained specified components" were included in the meta-analysis. Thus, studies in which a viable treatment was compared to an alternative therapy that was "credible to participants in the study but not intended to be therapeutic" were excluded (Wampold et al., 1997, p. 205).

To test whether one treatment was superior to another, effect sizes calculated comparing two treatments were randomly given a positive or negative sign. The distribution of effects was then tested to see if variability in effects was homogeneously centered around zero. Using several databases with different numbers of effect sizes, "none of the databases yielded effects that vaguely approached the heterogeneity expected if there were true differences among bona fide psychotherapies" (Wampold et al., 1997, p. 205). Further analyses also indicated that more sophisticated methods associated with more recent studies were not related to increased differences between treatments and theoretically dissimilar treatments did not produce larger effect sizes. Both of these findings provide additional evidence for the substantial equivalence of bona fide treatments.

In addition to studies comparing various orientations or methods of treatment, some studies examine the comparative benefit of differing modes of therapy (e.g., family versus individual treatment). Some of the earliest meta-analyses compared the various modalities of therapy using between-group comparisons (Robinson et al., 1990; Smith et al., 1980). The potential confounding variables of between-study comparisons, however, led to several recent meta-analyses that eliminated this confound. Although the number of studies is typically small and the detailed results vary somewhat, these studies generally find no difference between group and individual therapy (McRoberts et al., 1998; Tillitski, 1990), marital/family therapies and individual therapy (Shadish, Montgomery, Wilson, Wilson, et al., 1993), and bibliotherapy and therapist-administered treatments (Marrs, 1995). One study did find a difference between modes of treatment. When examining treatments for adolescent and adult drug abuse, there were differences between couples-family treatments and individual therapy (Stanton & Shadish, 1997). In a sample of 15 studies, family-couples therapy produced larger effects (d = .55) relative to individual therapy. This rather large and interesting difference suggests the need for further research on this topic, with the hope of finding consistent evidence of unique superiority with this disorder when family members are involved in treatment.

The foregoing meta-analyses that examine the comparative effectiveness of differing theories of psychotherapy or modes of psychotherapy reveal a mixed picture. There is a strong trend toward no differences between techniques or modes in amount of change produced, which is counterbalanced by indications that, under some circumstances, certain methods (generally cognitive behavioral) or modes (family therapy) are superior. The potential confounds of cross-study comparisons, differences in measurement and samples, and investigator allegiance complicate the process of making general conclusions. An examination of selected exemplary studies allows us to explore this matter further. But even this research, carried out with the intent of contrasting two or more bona fide treatments, shows surprisingly small differences between the outcomes for patients who undergo a treatment that is fully intended to be therapeutic. Several studies illustrate this point.

Illustrative Comparative Studies

The work of Sloane, Staples, Cristol, Yorkston, and Whipple (1975) established a historical standard of methodological sophistication that provided evidence for the notion that experts using their favorite method, whether behavioral or psychodynamic, could produce substantial therapeutic change. Since the Sloane et al. (1975) study, additional well-designed comparative studies have been published. One of the more important studies is the NIMH Collaborative Depression study. This study was the collaborative effort of investigators who were equally interested in each of the two psychotherapies that were investigated as well as the treatment of patients with medication. This study clearly exemplified change in research strategies, from examining therapy as usually practiced to studying "ideal" therapy as guided by manuals and competency ratings.

Elkin et al. (1989) and Imber et al. (1990) reported on the comparative outcomes of this study, which compared a standard reference treatment (imipramine plus clinical management) with two psychotherapies (cognitive behavior therapy and interpersonal psychotherapy). These three treatments were contrasted with a drug placebo plus clinical management control group. This study was the first head-to-head comparison of these two psychotherapies that had been shown in previous research to be specifically effective with depression. Since the initial publications, a large number of papers have been published regarding various aspects of the study (e.g., Elkin, 1994; Krupnick et al., 1996; Ogles, Lambert, & Sawyer, 1995).

The 250 patients seen in this study were randomly assigned to the four treatments that were offered at three research sites. Clients met Research Diagnostic Criteria for a major depressive episode and had a score of 14 or more on the 17-item Hamilton Rating Scale for Depression along with meeting other inclusion criteria. The therapists were 28 psychiatrists and psychologists who were carefully selected, trained, and monitored in the specific treatment offered. Each therapist saw between one and eleven patients. The treatments were carefully administered based on treatment manuals. Treatments were intended to last 16 to 20 weeks. In fact, the total sample averaged 13 sessions. Those who completed therapy averaged 16.2 sessions. The battery of outcome measures included symptomatic and adjustment ratings from multiple perspectives.

Numerous comparisons were made, and the results of this study are complex. Among the more interesting findings were comparisons of the two psychotherapies with the medication and placebo plus clinical management (PLA-CM). There was limited evidence of the specific effectiveness of the interpersonal psychotherapy (IPT) and no evidence for the specific effectiveness of cognitive behavioral therapy (CBT). Surprisingly, there was little evidence for superiority of the therapies in contrast to the placebo plus clinical management. The therapies were effective, but patients who received the placebo plus clinical management also improved.

In head-to-head comparisons of IPT and CBT, no significant differences were found in any of the major analyses or in comparisons with more and less severely disturbed patients. This similarity held up even on measures that were thought to be differentially sensitive to the therapies. A random regression analysis also verified the finding of no differences between CBT and IPT (Elkin, 1994). In some post-hoc comparisons, modest evidence of specific effects could be found. Although all patient groups improved by the end of treatment, superior recovery rates were found for both interpersonal psychotherapy and imipramine plus clinical management, when compared to the placebo plus clinical management.

Several other large multisite collaborative clinical trials have been conducted since the NIMH TDCRP study. For example, Project MATCH (Project Match Research Group, 1998) examined the effects of client-treatment matching in a study of treatments for clients with alcohol abuse or dependence. Clients in an outpatient setting ($N = 952$) or participating in aftercare treatment following an inpatient or intensive day treatment placement ($N = 774$) were randomly assigned to one of three manualized treatment conditions: Twelve-Step Facilitation (TSF), Cognitive Behavioral Coping Skills Training (CBT), or Motivational Enhancement Therapy (MET). Treatment was provided at ten sites associated with nine clinical research units. Clients on average showed sustained reductions in drinking frequency and severity at both post-treatment and at one year followup. Despite clear and perhaps dramatic differences in philosophies, there were few differences across treatments for all three groups of clients. Clients with more severe psychiatric symptoms, however, had poorer outcomes overall.

In another NIMH-sponsored collaborative study, Crits-Christoph et al. (1999) examined the efficacy of four treatments for cocaine dependence. Clients ($N = 487$) with a primary diagnosis of cocaine dependence were randomly assigned to individual drug counseling (IDC) plus group drug counseling (GDC), cognitive therapy (CT) plus GDC, supportive-expressive therapy (SE) plus GDC, or GDC alone. As in the NIMH TDCRP study, therapists were carefully trained, monitored, and supervised in order to ensure the consistency of treatments across sites. Although a large battery of research instruments were completed, the primary outcome measure was the Drug Use Composite score from the Addiction Severity Index. Clients in the SE plus GDC and CT plus GDC were more likely to be retained in treatment, but the individual drug counseling plus GCD produced superior reductions in overall drug use and cocaine use and higher rates of abstinence. This was a surprising outcome given that nonprofessionals provided both treatments.

Shapiro et al. (1994) examined the effects of treatment duration within cognitive behavioral (CBT) and psychodynamic interpersonal (PI) psychotherapy for the treatment of depression. Clients were carefully screened and interviewed. Clients with major depression were included, but divided into severity categories and randomized into the treatment cells. While 150 clients were randomly assigned to treatments, 117 completed both treatments and provided sufficient data to be included in the final analysis of outcomes. Unlike many studies in which therapists are nested within treatment groups, the therapists were five (three male, two female) investigator-clinicians who conducted treatment within all four conditions. The five therapists also completed at least two training cases in each condition prior to the start of the study. The four treatments were 8- and 16-session CBT and PI. This study is typical of the larger clinical trials being conducted in the last 15 years with controlled and manualized treatments, carefully selected clients, and multiple-outcome measures.

When considering the efficacy of the four treatments together, clients made substantial improvements both at the end of treatment and at three-month followup. Unfortunately, there were some differences (severity of depression) in the groups prior to treatment, suggesting that random assignment failed to produce equivalence across groups. As a result, the investigators used each client's first assessment scores as covariates in subsequent analyses. Although one or two specific comparisons with individual outcome measures suggested otherwise, the predominant finding was that there were no differences in outcome or rate of change between PI and CBT. Similarly, there were no differences between the 8- and 16-session treatment durations. This suggests that therapist-client dyads adjust the pace of therapy based on the amount of time allotted to them (Shapiro et al., 1994). When examining the impact of pretreatment severity of depressive symptoms on treatment outcome, a consistent interaction effect was identified. For clients with the most severe depression, the 16-session treatment was consistently superior. For clients with mild or moderate depression, the 8- and 16-session treatments were equally beneficial. Overall, this study supports the general finding that PI and CBT are equivalent. This finding was further substantiated by a replication study (Barkham, 1996) in which PI and CBT were again equivalent. In the second study, however, the 16-session treatment produced statistically better outcomes than the 8-session treatment.

When examining these well-designed studies that compare different therapeutic orientations, the findings are consistently small or negligible. Indeed, studies comparing two bona fide verbal therapeutic approaches that find significantly different outcomes may be more unusual than not. The finding of relative equivalence of differing approaches has significant implications for theories regarding the processes of change and the relative importance of theory-specific techniques versus common factors as agents of change. Before addressing these issues, however, we first examine a study that compared the various components of treatment. This study approached the question of treatment effects through the isolation of various components and is exemplary of research using this design strategy. By separating components from or adding components to existing treatments, the relative benefit of certain aspects of treatment can be determined.

Illustrative Dismantling Study

As therapy research has evolved, some researchers have taken a closer look at the components of the various approaches rather than comparing different orientations or theories of psychotherapy. The dismantling and constructive research designs are especially useful for considering the comparative effectiveness of adding to or eliminating certain techniques from a typical treatment package. Some researchers vigorously advocate for this type of design rather than the comparative treatment approach (e.g., Borkovec, 1993).

A recent component analysis of cognitive behavioral treatment for depression provides an interesting example of this type of study (Jacobson et al., 1996). The sample in this study consisted of 152 clients who met the criteria for major depression and scored at least 20 on the BDI and 14 on the 17-item HRSD. Eighty percent of the clients were referred by a large HMO, while the remainder were recruited through public service announcements. Individuals who had concurrent psychiatric disorders or who were receiving treatment were excluded from the study.

Clients were randomly assigned to one of three treatments using a constructive design: behavioral activation (BA), activation and modification of dysfunctional thoughts (AT), or cognitive therapy (CT). The BA treatment included behavioral interventions designed to activate people in their natural environment and included interventions such as monitoring activities, pleasant event scheduling and rating, and specific behavioral techniques for specific problems (e.g., trouble sleeping). The AT treatment added the identification and modification of automatic thoughts to the behavioral activation treatment and incorporated interventions such as daily recording and examination of thoughts associated with events. The CT treatment included both the BA and AT treatment components, with the addition of the identification and modification of patterns of thought (schema).

All four therapists provided treatment in the three conditions. The therapists were experienced cognitive therapists who had formal training in CT and an average of 9.5 years of experience providing CT. In addition, all four therapists had participated in an earlier clinical trial of CT. The therapists were also supervised, and adherence was routinely evaluated.

Although all the therapists thought that the CT condition would be the most effective, no differences in the treatments emerged through analysis of the entire sample (including dropouts) or other samples (including only clients who participated in the complete treatment). Similarly, no differences in treatment were evident in an analysis of recovery or improvement rates. Finally no treatment differences emerged at the 6-month or 24-month followup (Gortner, Gollan, Dobson, & Jacobson, 1998). Remarkably, there were no differences in outcomes thought to be specifically targeted by the treatments (e.g., pleasant events, automatic thoughts, and attributional styles). The behavioral activation treatment produced changes in automatic thoughts and attributional styles that were equivalent to the more complete cognitive treatments. Jacobson et al. (1996) concluded that the findings raise questions about the theory of change associated with cognitive therapy for depression and the administration of cognitive therapy for the treatment of depression.

Although the Jacobson et al. (1996) component analysis found that the cognitive components of treatment did not add to the activation treatment, the finding might be interpreted in two ways. From one perspective, the finding suggests that the behavioral component of treatment is the only necessary component for a beneficial outcome and that cognitive interventions make no significant contributions to the effectiveness of treatment. From another point of view, one might argue that this study is similar to other studies comparing behavioral with cognitive behavioral treatments in which the treatments are equivalent. In this way, the study confirms the dodo bird verdict. Indeed, had the study included a CT-only group, the experimenters may have found that the CT-only group also improved. In short, the results of this component study might confirm or disconfirm the common-factors hypothesis depending on one's perspective.

In general, the results from comparative, dismantling, and components analysis studies suggest the general equivalence of treatments based on different theories and techniques. Ahn and Wampold (2001) examined component analyses conducted over an 18-year period and found that adding or removing components of treatment did not change the effects of the core treatment. Wampold (2001) believes that the lack of findings within these dismantling and constructive designs suggests that "there is little evidence that specific ingredients are necessary to produce psychotherapeutic change" (p. 126). These findings also argue against the current trend of identifying empirically supported therapies that purport to be uniquely effective. Decades of research have not produced support for one superior treatment or set of techniques for specific disorders.

Is One Therapist More Effective Than Another Therapist?

In addition to the comparison of treatment orientations, modalities, and components, differences among therapists within treatments (so-called therapist effects) is another avenue of investigation into causal factors in therapy research. The specific therapist contributions to client outcome have long been a concern of the therapy researcher and are widely accepted in clinical practice. Few clinicians refer patients to just any practitioner. It is assumed that some therapists obtain large positive effects, many obtain modest effects, and a few may cause a number of patients to worsen in adjustment. What research evidence can be brought to bear on this issue?

Several historical studies have examined this issue. Orlinsky and Howard (1980) conducted a retrospective study based on case files to examine differences among therapists. The outcome ratings of 143 female cases seen by 23 traditional verbal psychotherapists were listed therapist by therapist. Six of the 23 therapists were rated ✓+, which means that at least 70% of their cases were improved and none was rated worse. Overall, 84% of patients treated by these six therapists were improved at termination. Five of the 23 therapists, on the other hand, were x-rated, which means that 50% or fewer of their cases improved, while more than 10% were worse. Overall, 44% of their 25 cases improved. The study provided some of the first evidence showing significant differences in effectiveness among therapists.

Some outcome studies have actually studied therapist competence and used competence ratings to select therapists. For example, Rousaville et al. (1988) reported results related to training therapists in interpersonal therapy for the Collaborative Depression project. The decisions concerning therapist inclusion in the treatment phase of the project were made by expert independent evaluators who had not participated in the training or supervision of the original group of 11 carefully selected experienced therapists. On the basis of ratings made from viewing two randomly selected, videotaped sessions, 2 of the 11 therapists were judged as not performing interpersonal therapy at an acceptable level. Later ratings resulted in dropping one therapist from the study. Unsatisfactory ratings resulted from a failure either to apply techniques consistently or to refrain from using techniques incompatible with interpersonal therapy. This finding suggests that a small number of therapists who received relatively intense training, although highly motivated to learn, may not be able to achieve competent performance. It should be noted, however, that patient outcome was not used for exclusion purposes.

Perhaps more surprising were the relatively large differences among the therapists in the study even after this rigorous selection process (Blatt, Sanislow, Zuroff, & Pilkonis, 1996). Therapists were divided into three groups (more effective, moderately effective, and less effective) based on an examination of the average composite outcome score for their clients. There were significant differences among therapists, but these differences were independent of the type of treatment, the research site, and the general experience level of the clinician. More effective therapists had a more psychological approach (rather than biological) to treatment of depression, and more psychologists (and fewer psychiatrists) were included in the more effective group.

Most outcome studies have not provided such data on therapists, so it is impossible to estimate the breadth and depth of this phenomenon. Therapist variability can be found across a variety of treatment modalities and within very narrow treatments, as well as treatments that focus on more general patient problems. In perhaps the most influential early study of therapist effects, Luborsky, McClellan, Woody, O'Brien, and Auerbach (1985) reported the results of their analysis of the differential outcome of clients seen by nine different therapists. The patients were opiate-dependent males who underwent drug counseling alone or in combination with either supportive-expressive psychotherapy or cognitive behavioral psychotherapy. The therapists were trained to offer the prescribed treatment using detailed treatment manuals. Thus, we have a situation (common in contemporary research) in which the individual differences between therapists within a treatment are intentionally minimized. Despite this, Luborsky et al. report that "profound differences were discovered in the therapists' success with the patients in their case load" (p. 602). Despite careful selection, training, monitoring, and supervision, patients of therapists offering the same treatments had highly divergent results. Most notable were the differences between therapist A and C who saw 10 and 8 patients, respectively. While A's patients showed substantial improvement on a wide variety of outcomes, C's patients averaged little improvement and on some criterion actually showed an average negative change.

In their analysis of the therapy process, Luborsky et al. (1985) found that the differences in outcome between therapists could be attributed to a number of interactional variables. No general patterns of favorable or unfavorable patient qualities were associated with a particular therapist. Three therapist qualities, however, were identified as distinguishing the more helpful from the less helpful therapists: (1) the therapist's adjustment, skill, and interest in helping patients; (2) the purity of the treatment they offered; and (3) the quality of the therapist/patient relationship.

Crits-Christoph and Mintz (1991) presented further evidence that the contribution of individual therapists should not be ignored in research designs and statistical analysis of data. Their meta-analysis of 15 studies and 27 treatment groups revealed an average therapist effect accounting for 9% of outcome variance. One study showed therapist effects accounting for 49% of the outcome variance, while other studies showed no independent therapist effect. The highest partial correlation between independent variables and size of therapist effect was produced by use of a treatment manual and therapist experience level, where manuals and higher experience were associated with smaller therapist differences and smaller effect sizes. The authors argue further that "by ignoring the therapist factor, some investigators may have reported differences between treatments that were actually a function of therapist differences" (p. 89).

The area of substance abuse treatment has also been studied in relationship to therapist effects (Najavits & Weiss, 1994). In Project MATCH, therapists conducted treatment within three treatment groups: 12-step facilitation, motivational enhancement therapy, and cognitive behavior therapy. As a result, therapist effects were examined within treatment groups. Nevertheless, significant differences among therapists were identified in terms of both client satisfaction and outcome (Project Match Research Group, 1998). Importantly, six of seven observed therapist effects were attributable to one of five outlier therapists. One therapist's clients showed better outcomes, and four therapists (accounting for five effect sizes) had poorer outcomes. In short, four out of eighty therapists produced substantial therapist effects as a result of poorer outcomes. This suggests that outlier therapists were responsible for most of therapist effects rather than a wide distribution of therapist ineffectiveness.

Of course, the studies cited here constitute a mere beginning to examining the contribution of the individual therapist. We simply do not know enough yet about the therapist factor to specify when and how it makes a difference, nor when it matters more than technique. What we do know is that there are intriguing possibilities for new discoveries here and that this issue has been ignored to a surprising degree. Researchers, influenced by mechanistic models, have placed their bets more on technique factors as the powerful ones in therapeutic change. Of course, technique is still likely to be important even if reliable therapist differences are found. The differences in effectiveness between therapists not only result from personal qualities but are likely to reflect variations in technical skill as well. Thus, therapist differences may well be partly reflections of technique differences. To the extent that this is true, studies of techniques have been contaminated by heterogeneity in the purity or quality of techniques being applied. Findings like those just cited suggest that even treatment manuals have not consistently remedied this problem. Consequently, monitoring of individual therapist variation in skill (and personal qualities like warmth) is essential in outcome studies in which specific causal mechanisms are explored.

It is possible that too much energy is being devoted to technique studies at the expense of examining therapists as persons and in interaction with techniques, as well as patient characteristics. Study of interaction effects (therapist × technique × patient) will need to be more carefully conducted. Such studies may well show not only potent therapist outcome but also that technique differences are inseparably bound with therapist and patient differences. A logical extension of research on therapist outcome is to encourage research focused on the "empirically validated psychotherapist" rather than on empirically supported treatment. This type of research might have an immediate impact on practice and might also lend to a greater probability of ensuring positive patient outcomes.

Comparative Effectiveness of Professional versus Paraprofessional

One subset of the therapist effects literature involves the comparative effectiveness of professionals and paraprofessionals. The effects of psychotherapy offered by experienced clinicians have been contrasted with the effects of helping efforts made by lay therapists, paraprofessionals, and inexperienced clinicians. Many of the studies in this area have been aimed at sorting out the value of therapy beyond the contribution of warm and caring human encounters and wise advice. Other studies have investigated and helped to establish the boundaries of therapeutic procedures, for example, the level of training and skill required to be effective with specific problems. Most typically, researchers have merely examined the relationship of amount of therapist experience to outcome in studies that were designed to study other variables.

The available literature on such efforts has been reviewed and debated for several decades. Bergin and Lambert (1978), for example, suggested that more experienced clinicians obtain superior outcomes to those of less experienced therapists. Auerbach and Johnson (1977) found less support for this conclusion and suggested that the empirical base for differential outcomes as a function of level of experience was meager.

Some meta-analytic reviews (e.g., Lyons & Woods, 1990; Quality Assurance Project, 1982; Robinson et al., 1990; Shapiro & Shapiro, 1983; Smith, et al., 1980) have analyzed the relationship of experience and outcome by correlating effect size data with experience level. Occasionally, these analyses turn up relationships that favor experience or formal training. For example, in their meta-analysis of the effectiveness of psychotherapy with children and adolescents, Weisz, Weiss, Alicke, and Klotz (1987) reported a significant interaction between client age and therapist training. Trained professionals (either masters or doctoral degree) were found to be equally effective with all age groups, while graduate students and paraprofessionals were more effective with younger than with older clients. In addition, it was reported that professionals differed from graduate students and paraprofessionals in their effectiveness with overcontrol problems (i.e., phobias and shyness); as amount of formal training increased, so did effectiveness.

Despite these findings, overall, the meta-analytic reviews of psychotherapy that have provided correlational data find little evidence for a relationship between experience and outcome. However, experience levels were usually compared across studies rather than within studies, and comparisons within studies often were between inexperienced and slightly experienced clinicians. Differences in outcome between highly experienced and inexperienced therapists have generally not been tested. Some reviews have considered the body of studies that directly study professional status or experience level, and these reviews and studies are considered next.

Hattie, Sharpley, and Rogers (1984) re-analyzed the studies reviewed by Durlak (1979) using meta-analytic methods. One hundred fifty-four comparisons from 39 studies indicated that clients who seek help from paraprofessionals are more likely to achieve resolution of their problems than those who consult professionals (effect size = .34). Several problems in methodology (cf. Lambert, 1979; Nietzel & Fisher, 1981; Stein, 1980), however, raise questions about this study's findings.

Berman and Norton (1985), Stein (1980), and Stein and Lambert (1984) used a more selective group of methodologically superior studies and more careful definitions of paraprofessionals (e.g., they excluded studies that counted social workers as paraprofessionals). In general, however, all of these studies found that there were no differences between the outcome of patients treated by trained and untrained persons. At the same time, Stein and Lambert (1984) found that differences in outcome were most likely to occur when there was a large discrepancy in experience between the therapists offering treatment within a study and when the treatment modality involved more than simple counseling or specific behavioral techniques (e.g., psychodynamic therapy, marital therapy). Based on this body of literature, several reviewers concluded that professional training does not make a difference (e.g., Bickman, 1999; Dawes, 1996; Mahrer, 1999).

The most recent meta-analysis of this literature (Stein & Lambert, 1995), however, finds some evidence that training is beneficial. Like their earlier meta-analysis, Stein and Lambert (1995) reviewed studies and calculated effect sizes where more and less trained therapists were directly compared within the same study. They found that training was related to lower dropout rates (more training = lower dropout) in settings other than university counseling centers. Similarly, they found a modest yet consistent effect size associated with level of training across several measures of client improvement. The effect is strongest for client reports of satisfaction ($d = .27$) and pre-post testing on psychological measures ($d = .30$). Judges' ratings of improvement in relationship to training level was only available in three studies but also supported these conclusions ($d = .33$). In all cases, therapists with more training had better outcomes. This meta-analysis stands in contrast to earlier reviews in that training appears to result in both better outcomes and lower dropout rates.

Surprisingly, the study of training effects remains a peripheral issue in the therapy literature. Very few studies are designed to specifically investigate the issue of training effects. Most studies of training effects are conducted as a secondary analysis within a study designed to investigate other hypotheses. As a result, some of the best studies are decades old. To further support this point, it should be noted that most of the studies included in the Stein and Lambert (1995) meta-analysis were conducted several decades earlier.

The historical precedent for this research (Strupp, 1980a, 1980b, 1980c, 1980d) contrasted the effectiveness of professionally trained expert therapists with the effectiveness of a select group of college professors who had no formal training. Surprisingly, both therapists and professors had outcomes that exceeded controls, and there were no significant differences between the groups on any of the measures (patient, therapist, or clinical judges).

A second study using a time-limited therapy framework examined the relationship between treatment outcome and level of clinical experience, as well as the relationship between training methods and treatment outcome (Burlingame, Fuhriman, Paul, & Ogles, 1989). In this study, clients of experienced therapists had consistently superior outcomes when compared with the clients of less experienced therapists. The study also reported that rates of client improvement paralleled the intensity of the therapists' training, regardless of therapist experience. Greater improvement on several measures of outcome was demonstrated by clients who had been assigned to therapists receiving more training, suggesting that both experienced and less experienced therapists benefited from skill training in time-limited therapy.

A more recent study has yet to be published, but preliminary results have been presented at psychotherapy research conferences (Anderson et al., 1999). In the Anderson study, graduate students enrolled in a doctoral program in clinical psychology (with at least two years of training), and graduate students from other disciplines (e.g., history, chemistry) were asked to conduct therapy with distressed undergraduate students. The therapists were asked to respond in a tape recorder to difficult therapy situations presented to them via videotaped scenarios. Therapists were then selected if they were in the high or low interpersonal skills groups based on a combination of their responses on the Social Skills Inventory and ratings of the performance analysis. The therapists provided seven 50-minute therapy sessions to students who had been selected because their scores on the Symptom Checklist-90-R were elevated (at least two standard deviations above the normative sample mean). Therapists were instructed to verbally assist the clients in a way that they believed would ultimately help the clients to resolve their problems. Sessions were recorded and monitored to assure ethical practice and the safety of participants. Therapy outcome was assessed using the Outcome Questionnaire (OQ–45), Inventory of Interpersonal Problems (IIP), and the SCL-90-R. Data were collected at sessions 1, 3, 5, and 7, and at 3-month followup as well. In addition, the Working Alliance Inventory (WAI) was administered at the same intervals.

As predicted, therapist training was not related to therapy outcome or the therapeutic alliance. Graduate students in training and from other disciplines had equivalent outcomes on average. The level of interpersonal skills, however, was related to both outcome and the therapeutic alliance. Therapists with high interpersonal skills (regardless of training) had better outcomes on the OQ–45 and IIP, but not the SCL-90-R. Similarly, therapists with high interpersonal skills had better alliances with the clients as assessed via the WAI. This suggests that individual therapist variables, such as interpersonal skills, may be more important than training. At the same time, these early findings must be replicated using samples of clinicians with more experience.

Over the past decade there have been surprisingly few research studies in the area of experience, training, and client outcome. This is especially true when one considers the small number of studies that have directly examined this question through the use of appropriate and relevant designs. As was the case with much early research, even when this topic commanded considerable interest and controversy, most recent studies have failed to achieve acceptable levels of internal validity, external validity, and construct validity—thus limiting the interpretations and generalizations that can be made on the basis of reported findings. Designs have generally failed to adequately address the differential effects of professionals versus paraprofessional, experienced versus less experienced therapists, trained versus untrained individuals, and so forth. Problems such as inadequate controls, the unclear influence of supervision, confounding of treatment technique with level of experience, and unclear definition of categories (professional, paraprofessional, trained, untrained, etc.) continue to jeopardize the quality of research findings. With the exception of results provided by a few higher quality studies, it would seem that little empirically solid data has been added to the debate over whether experience and professional training make a difference in client outcome. At the same time, the promising findings of the Stein and Lambert (1995) meta-analysis suggest that training may make a difference.

Common Factors and Outcome

Although there are a large number of therapies, each containing its own rationale and specific techniques, there is little evidence to suggest the superiority of one school over another. The general finding of no difference in the outcome of therapy for clients who have participated in highly diverse therapies has a number of alternative explanations: (a) different therapies can achieve similar goals through different processes; (b) different outcomes do occur but are not detected by past research strategies; and (c) different therapies embody common factors that are curative, though not emphasized by the theory of change central to a particular school. At this time, any of the above interpretations can be advocated and defended because there is not enough evidence available to rule out alternative explanations.

Clearly, different therapies require the client to undergo different experiences and to engage in different behaviors. Diverse therapies could be effective for different reasons, but we do not yet know enough about the boundaries of effectiveness for each therapy to discuss alternative (a) and its merits. Alternative (b), the inadequacy of past research, will not be fully discussed here. Suffice it to say that there are many methodological reasons for failing to reject the null hypothesis. Kazdin and Bass (1989), for example, have questioned the value of the majority of past comparative studies on the basis of a "lack of statistical power." There are also serious problems in accurately measuring behavioral change (see Hill & Lambert, this volume). In fact, any of a host of methodological problems could result in a failure to detect differences between therapies. The third alternative (c), emphasizing common factors in different therapies, is the possibility that has received the most research attention and that has the clearest implications for practice. It was first hypothesized by Rosenzweig (1936). It is not only an interpretation of the results of comparative outcome literature, but is based on other research aimed at discovering the active ingredients of psychotherapy. Alternative (c) is also consistent with the results of the placebo literature discussed earlier.

The literature presents a number of views on the possible role of common factors in the psychotherapeutic change process. Some consider common factors to be both "necessary and sufficient" (e.g., Patterson, 1984), whereas others view them as being an important component of change but do not rule out the possible role of more unique variables (e.g. Garfield, 1973). Weinberger (1995) suggests that different schools or theories of psychotherapy emphasize different common factors. For example, whereas psychodynamic theory places heavier emphasis on the therapeutic relationship, cognitive and behavioral therapies give greater attention to confronting or facing "the problem." At the same time, both factors may be empirically important processes within both therapies.

Regardless of the theory, however, it seems impossible to declare any of these contrasting positions as "truth"—for their accuracy can only be determined through further empirical investigation. As an example of contemporary research, we present a study that examined the relationship of three process variables (two common and one unique) to the outcome of cognitive therapy for depression (Castonguay, Goldfried, Wiser, & Raue, 1996). These investigators found that the two common factors, the therapeutic alliance and client emotional experiencing, were related to client improvement. The finding that client emotional involvement is important within a cognitive treatment approach is important evidence of common change processes. Surprisingly, the unique factor in this study, focus on intrapersonal consequences (e.g., linking distorted thoughts to negative emotions), which is a key aspect of cognitive treatment, was inversely related to improvement. Through further descriptive analysis of the data, the researchers suggest two potential explanations for this unexpected finding. First, it appeared that therapists were more likely to focus on intrapersonal consequences when there were problems in the therapeutic alliance. Second, there was some evidence that the therapists who focused more on intrapersonal consequences may have been applying the manualized treatment in an inflexible manner. Regardless of the reasons for the inverse relationship between the unique factor and outcome, however, the study provides evidence that common factors are important mediators of outcome.

In another recent study, Ilardi and Craighead (1994) examined several studies of cognitive behavioral treatment for depression. They argue that temporal changes in cognitive therapy (early rapid response) observed during the first four weeks of therapy support the notion that common factors are the predominant causal force in cognitive therapy. Indeed, they suggest that most changes in cognitive therapy occur before specific CBT techniques have been administered in any relevant dose. They further argue that giving a rationale for treatment to the client and administering homework early in treatment provide the client with hope (corresponding with Frank's notion of remoralization and Howard's phase model of psychotherapy) and that these interventions (rationale and homework) are the common factors. Tang and DeRubeis (1999) disagree with this hypothesis and suggest that since CBT therapies typically include two sessions per week in the first four weeks of treatment a relatively large dose of specific techniques is administered early in treatment. Wilson (1998), while agreeing with Ilardi and Craighead, has noted that the bulimia and alcohol abuse treatment literature also supports the notion that early (and relatively large) improvements occur before specific cognitive techniques are thoroughly implemented in treatment. Such client changes may not be attributable to the hypothesized cognitive pathways to improvement. We would argue that early rapid response is another piece of evidence for the common-factors hypothesis (Haas et al., 2002).

Beyond these individual studies and based on a review of the evidence, it appears that what can be firmly stated is that factors common across treatments are accounting for a substantial amount of improvement found in psychotherapy patients. These so-called common factors may even account for most of the gains that result from psychological interventions. So, while we do not rule out the possibility that variables specific to one school or technique might be found to make an additional contribution, at this point it is important to recognize that the common factors are contributing a great deal to positive outcome. Therefore, it is crucial for therapists to intentionally incorporate them. Thus, the question becomes, what are these common factors?

Common factors can be conceptualized in a variety of ways (see Grencavage & Norcross, 1990; Oei & Shuttlewood, 1996; Weinberger, 1995), and unfortunately, this term has been used to mean a variety of things. To organize and clarify this broad term, we have grouped common factors into Support, Learning, and Action categories in Table 5.8. These categories were chosen to represent a sequence that we presume operates in many psychotherapies. The developmental sequence is at least partially mediated through factors common across therapies. The developmental nature of this sequence presumes that the supportive functions precede changes in beliefs and attitudes, which precede the therapist's attempts to encourage patient action.

This table lists a variety of common factors attributable to the therapist, therapy procedures, and the client. As already mentioned, these factors would seem to operate most powerfully during the process of therapy. Together they provide for a cooperative working endeavor in which the patient's increased sense of trust, security, and safety, along with decreases in tension, threat, and anxiety, lead to changes in conceptualizing his or her problems and ultimately in acting differently by reframing fears, taking risks, and working through problems in interpersonal relationships. The variables and constructs organized in Table 5.8 were derived from our reading of empirical research, and have been operationally defined and correlated with outcome in research studies of therapy.

Several alternative conceptualizations are available (e.g., Karasu, 1986; Stiles, Shapiro, & Elliot, 1986). Regardless of the conceptual scheme used to organize common factors, however, emphasizing the study of common factors in addition to specific techniques will encourage greater cooperation and harmony between competing approaches, ultimately increasing the effectiveness of psychotherapy. The conceptual schemes offer a plausible explanation for the failure to find differences in outcome between different therapies. However, empirical evidence is still needed to examine the importance of common factors.

Weinberger (1995) summarizes the theoretical and empirical conclusions regarding five common factors: the therapeutic relationship, expectations, confronting problems, mastery, and attributions of outcome. He finds evidence for these factors in both the clinical and experimental psychology literatures. In a comprehensive examination of substantial portions of the psychotherapy research literature, Wampold (2001) provides strong evidence for a "contextual model" of therapy. This model relies heavily on common factors as agents of change. Through a book-length review of many of the same bodies of literature examined in this chapter, Wampold (2001) suggests that there is little evidence for the medical model of therapy (i.e., that specific treatment ingredients lead to change) and strong evidence for a contextual model.

Perhaps the common factors most frequently studied are those identified by the client-centered school as "necessary and sufficient conditions" for patient personality change: accurate empathy, positive regard, nonpossessive warmth, and congruence or genuineness. Virtually all schools of therapy accept the notion that these or related therapist relationship variables are important for significant progress in psychotherapy and, in fact, fundamental in the formation of a working cooperative effort between patient and therapist

TABLE 5.8 Sequential Listing of Factors

Support Factors	Learning Factors	Action Factors
Catharsis	Advice	Behavioral regulation
Identification with therapist	Affective experiencing	Cognitive mastery
Mitigation of isolation	Assimilating problematic experiences	Encouragement of facing fears
Positive relationship	Cognitive learning	Taking risks
Reassurance	Corrective emotional experience	Mastery efforts
Release of tension	Feedback	Modeling
Structure	Insight	Practice
Therapeutic alliance	Rationale	Reality testing
Therapist/client active participation	Exploration of internal frame of reference	Success experience
Therapist expertness	Changing expectations of personal effectiveness	Working through
Therapist warmth, respect, empathy, acceptance, genuineness		
Trust		

(Lambert, 1983). Studies showing both positive and equivocal support for the hypothesized relationship between therapist attitudes and outcome have been reviewed elsewhere (cf. Lambert, DeJulio, & Stein, 1978; Orlinsky, Grawe, & Parks, 1994). Reviewers are virtually unanimous in their opinion that the therapist-patient relationship is critical to positive outcome.

Therapeutic Alliance

The importance of the therapeutic relationship has been bolstered in recent years by investigations of the therapeutic alliance. Although most of the early work was generated by psychodynamically oriented researchers, more recent studies include all orientations. The therapeutic alliance has been conceptualized and defined differently by a host of interested investigators. Like the "necessary and sufficient" client-centered dimensions, it is measured by client ratings, therapist ratings, and judges' ratings.

There is more disagreement about the therapeutic alliance construct than there was with the client-centered conditions. This lack of consensus may prove to be a hindrance in drawing conclusions in this area because there are now several popular methods for measuring this construct, rather than the limited number of scales evidenced in the client-centered literature (cf. Martin, Garske, & Davis, 2000). In addition, the alliance is seen as a necessary, but not sufficient, condition for personality change, and so it assumes a less important theoretical position. Ratings of the therapeutic alliance also contain a heavy emphasis on patient variables and focus mainly on the client's ability to participate productively in therapy. Since alliance ratings go well beyond measuring therapist behaviors, they can be expected to correlate more highly with outcome than the client-centered measures, but have fewer implications for training since alliance ratings may not lead directly to modification of specific therapist attitudes and behavior.

In an important conceptual article, Gaston (1990) integrated the various constructs that have been offered to describe the therapeutic alliance and suggested that four core components of the alliance are measured by some but not all current rating scales: (1) the patient's affective relationship to the therapist; (2) the patient's capacity to purposefully work in therapy; (3) the therapist's empathic understanding and involvement; and (4) the patient-therapist agreement on the goals and tasks of therapy. These core components are considered in many of the conceptual and research articles published since that time.

Research literature on the alliance has been reviewed elsewhere (Chapter 6, this volume; Horvath & Symonds, 1991; Martin, Garske, & Davis, 2000). For example, Martin, Garske, and Davis (2000) updated an earlier meta-analysis conducted by Horvath and Symonds (1991) and found that the therapeutic alliance was consistently related ($d = .22$) to outcome across a broad range of published and unpublished studies ($N = 79$). In our view, the evidence on the alliance strengthens arguments for common factors as mediators of change since outcome can be predicted from early alliance ratings. These ratings produce data very similar to the client-centered data (Frank & Gunderson, 1991; Gaston, Marmar, Gallagher, & Thompson, 1991; Salvio, Beutler, Wood, & Engle, 1992; Tichener & Hill, 1989) and indicate that the alliance not only reflects positive change but may produce it as well. The alliance is consistently related to outcome (Martin et al., 2000), although it sometimes fails to predict or it produces associations that are quite small (see Lambert, 1992).

There is some evidence that common factors (such as the alliance) are more important in control conditions than in specified treatments. For example, Carroll, Nich, and Rounsaville (1997) examined the relationship of the therapeutic alliance to outcome in an active treatment (cognitive behavioral treatment) for cocaine dependence in relationship to a control condition (clinical management). Although the overall alliance scores were higher for the active treatment, the relationship between alliance and outcome was stronger within the control condition. Surprisingly, the alliance was also found to be important in pharmacotherapy (Krupnick et al., 1996). In the NIMH depression study, both the placebo and imipramine plus clinical management groups had equivalent levels of the therapeutic alliance to the two psychotherapies (CBT and IPT). Perhaps even more surprisingly, the relationship between the alliance and outcome was consistent across both pharmacological and psychological treatments (accounting for 21% of the variance in combined self-report and expert-rated outcome).

Summary. Common factors loom large as mediators of treatment outcome. The research base for this conclusion is substantial and multidimensional (Wampold, 2001), and so we must attend to its import. Although there is some resistance to acknowledging the importance of common factors, possibly as Frank (1976) states because "little glory derives from showing that the particular method one has mastered with so much effort may be indistinguishable from other methods in its effects" (p. 74), it seems imperative that we continue moving toward an understanding of how change occurs in psychotherapy—whether through common or unique mechanisms.

Common and Specific Factors, Therapy Manuals, Preferred Practices, and Treatment Protocols

One of the more recent and controversial shifts within the practice of psychotherapy involves the use of treatment manuals or practice guidelines and protocols (Ogles, Anderson, & Lunnen, 1999). This new emphasis on specifying treatments for certain populations has evolved in part from the continuing effort to manage healthcare costs. Perhaps the strictest version of this emphasis is found in the creation of empirically validated (or supported) treatments. In the early 1990s, the Task Force on the Promotion and Dissemination of Psychological Procedures was formed within Division 12 of the American Psychological Association. This group set out to identify efficacious psychological interventions and to select strategies for educating various constituencies about these "empirically-validated (or supported)" treatments (Chambless & Ollendick, 2001). Treatment guidelines for eating disorders, major depression, substance use, and bipolar affective disorder were either in the process of being developed or had already been proposed by a special committee within the American Psychiatric Association (1993). The American Psychological Association's response was in part related to the need to emphasize the potential use of psychological interventions in many disorders.

In ironic contrast to the evidence regarding common factors and their role in treatment, however, the focus on developing or identifying specific treatments that have empirical support clearly emphasizes a theory of therapeutic effectiveness based on specified techniques. Similarly, with the rise of managed healthcare over the last decade, increased emphasis has been placed on developing specific protocols or practice guidelines for behavioral healthcare. Both movements, empirically supported treatments and practice guidelines, are based on the assumption that specific therapist technical operations are largely responsible for client improvement. Both movements also evolved out of the possibility of creating greater standardization through the use of treatment manuals to guide the delivery of mental health services. The earliest uses of therapy manuals can be traced back to the 1960s (e.g., Lang & Lazovik, 1963). Therapy manuals became common with some treatment approaches in the 1970s (Beck, Rush, Shaw, & Emery, 1979). During that phase of therapy research development, manuals were an important development (even a "minor revolution"—Luborsky & DeRubeis, 1984). Their initial use was in group workshops that emphasized training and teaching more than therapy (e.g., assertiveness training with shy college students, behavior therapy with overweight clients). Through the 1980s, there was an increased interest in using such manuals in individual psychosocial therapies. Manuals have now become so common in some forms of therapy that outcome studies that do not employ them are rare.

The development and use of treatment manuals in the TDCRP (Elkin, Parloff, Hadley, & Autry, 1985) illustrates the possibilities of manuals and associated rating scales in psychotherapy research. Cognitive Therapy, Interpersonal Therapy, and Clinical Management manuals were used to (a) guide the selection of therapists; (b) train therapists; (c) develop various rating scales to assess the effects of training; (d) test the degree to which the therapy offered conformed to the manual; and (e) measure the degree to which therapies can be discriminated. Many studies since this time employ therapy manuals in order to limit variability among therapists.

Treatment manuals have several advantages that have implications for therapy, research, training, and practice, including enhancing the internal validity of comparative outcome studies, providing a precise and organized way of training and supervising therapists, facilitating the development of rating scales for treatment integrity (adherence or conformance) and therapist competence, speeding up the process of training, enhancing the possibility of replication, and helping to sort out the active ingredients of psychotherapy by facilitating the comparison of the common components of treatments. The use of therapy manuals might also be viewed critically. Some suggest that manuals may promote therapeutic rigidity or eliminate the need for more detailed understanding.

Within the past decade, several studies have been conducted to begin evaluating the potential benefits of using treatment manuals for training purposes. For example, Wade, Treat, and Stuart (1998) examined the "transportability" of a manualized cognitive behavioral treatment for panic disorder. Using a 15-session CBT treatment protocol (Barlow & Craske, 1994), 110 clients diagnosed with panic with or without agoraphobia were treated in group sessions at a community mental health center. Treatment outcomes were then compared to two clinical trials of CBT for panic disorder (Barlow, 1989; Telch et al., 1993) using a "benchmarking" strategy. When comparing the results, clients who received the treatment within the community mental health center improved on every measure, and the magnitudes of improvement were comparable to the clinical trials. The investigators suggest that these findings support the idea that manualized treatments used in efficacy studies can be transported into clinical settings (Wade et al., 1998). A similar study was conducted using a treatment manual for bulimia, again revealing outcomes that were comparable to controlled research (Tuschen-Caffier, Pook, & Frank, 2001). Unfortunately, neither study contained a control group, and no measures of treatment integrity were gathered. Although the clients improved, it is not clear that the treatments delivered were indeed the transported treatment. At the same time, this early research on the dissemination of treatments is promising.

On the other hand, there is some evidence that therapists may learn a manualized treatment without competently delivering the treatment (Bein et al., 2000; Castonguay et al., 1996). The Vanderbilt II project examined the effects of training in Time Limited Dynamic Psychotherapy (TLDP) for 16 therapists. These therapists provided services to two clients prior to the training, one client during training (a training case), and two clients in the year following training. The treatment was brief (25-session) therapy conducted in the therapist's typical fashion prior to training and in accordance with the TLDP model following training. During the year of training, therapists participated in weekly group supervision along with workshops regarding the manualized treatment. Evaluation of the training phase data found that the therapists learned the manualized protocol (Henry, Strupp et al. 1993; Henry, Schacht et al. 1993). However, the extensive training and supervision did not result in improved treatment outcomes. Rather, clients seen by therapists prior to their manualized training were as likely to improve as those seen after training (Bein et al., 2000).

The failure to find differences in such a carefully controlled study raises serious questions about using treatment manuals in clinical settings. For example, in spite of having successfully completed the manualized training and having at least two years of postdoctoral experience, many of the therapists in the study displayed measurable deficits in basic clinical skills (Ogles et al., 1999). In addition, only 9 of the 32 post-training cases were judged to have been conducted in a minimally competent fashion (Bein et al., 2000). One can only speculate about the effectiveness of such training under less optimal conditions.

Clearly, more research is needed regarding the utility of training therapists using therapy manuals. Although the field appears to be moving in the direction of more specific treatments for certain diagnoses or populations, little evidence exists that efficacious treatments are readily transportable. Similarly, little evidence supports the notion that specific techniques make a substantial contribution to treatment effects. Indeed, a line of research that centers on further specifying common factors may ultimately result in a larger harvest.

The Search for Larger Effects

Several areas of research are directed at improving and increasing the potency of treatments. Research directed at decreasing the variability of responses to treatment (particularly eliminating deterioration) may push the average treatment gain in the direction of improvement. As a result, several lines of research have evolved in an attempt to better understand within-group variation in therapy studies and to make treatments more powerful. In this section, we will consider four research areas: treatment integration, therapist effects, dropout, and deterioration.

Treatment Modifications and Integration. One constant effort being made to increase the effects of treatment includes the modification or integration of current treatments in the hope of increasing potency. For example, after conducting many years of behavioral marital therapy research, Jacobson and Christensen (1996) identified a set of couples that consistently did not respond to treatment. These couples tended to be older, less emotionally engaged, less committed to one another, more traditional in their roles, and had more divergent goals. As a result, the behavioral treatment was substantially modified to include acceptance as a major component of a combined acceptance and change-focused couples therapy. The acceptance component of change has many features of existential therapies and was specifically included to target those couples who did not respond to the traditional behavioral marital change-focused therapy. The combined treatment is hypothesized to be more broadly powerful as a result of benefiting a larger portion of couples receiving treatment (Jacobson & Christensen, 1996).

Other treatments are evolving in a similar fashion. For example, as a result of findings that therapist adherence to cognitive interventions in the midst of problems with the alliance may be damaging in treatment, interpersonal interventions are being examined in the context of CBT as a potential method of healing ruptures in the alliance (Safran & Muran, 2000). The examples given here represent only a passing brush of the huge literature regarding psychotherapy integration. Some integrative approaches are more conceptually based, whereas others are more empirically based. In either case, however, integrative therapies may increase therapy effect sizes through more broad effects, fewer dropouts, and the like. At the same time, much more research is needed in regards to the potential benefits of integrative approaches. One might predict that results would match those of past comparative and component analyses studies in which added features produce relatively little benefit beyond the original treatment. Only time will tell.

Therapist Effects. When examining the differences among therapists in an earlier section of this chapter, we discovered clear evidence that some therapists perform significantly better or worse than other therapists. In some cases differences among therapists were larger than differences among various treatments. These findings reveal how much improvement rates may vary as a function of therapist factors and suggest that outcomes in some samples may improve when poorer therapists are dropped out of the studies. It is possible that outcome statistics, especially from poorly controlled studies, are deflated by the use of practitioners who are conducting only a mere semblance of psychotherapy.

Information like the foregoing suggests that when effective therapists are used, outcomes may be more homogeneous around a high average improvement rate or effect size. It may be that the outcome studies that have been meta-analyzed embrace a number of small effect sizes engendered by incompetent or even deleterious therapy. As standards of therapist selection and training continue to improve, and as well-trained therapists whose effectiveness has been demonstrated in the past are included more frequently in research studies, we can expect average effect sizes to improve. It is also possible that the effective use of treatment manuals may eventually help with these problems by more carefully training therapists in skills and by allowing supervisors to monitor the application of therapy more carefully.

Effect sizes are also likely to be increased by eliminating or moderating the influence of therapist maladjustment and personality problems. Beutler, Crago, and Arizmendi (1986), for example, have suggested the negative correlation between the therapist's personal difficulties and client progress. Of course, treatment outcome also varies with severity of client disturbance; however, it is not yet clear how much this variation can be reduced by careful therapist selection. Evidence from the Landman and Dawes (1982) meta-analysis provides evidence that patients with severe problems (schizophrenia, depression, alcoholism, and delinquency) in 20 studies showed an average effect size of .68, while those with circumscribed problems (snake phobias, test anxiety, etc.) in 22 studies showed an effect size of 1.11. It is conceivable that therapists with appropriate styles or skills could improve the outcome for severe cases considerably. Crits-Christoph et al. (1991) point out, for instance, that greater experience (or skill) may be crucial in treating borderline patients via dynamic therapy, whereas successful treatment of simple phobias via behavior therapy may be achieved with less experience since the technique is more uniform and easily learned. This is a difficult and complicated problem. Suffice it to say here that client levels or kinds of disturbances are not absolute predictors of outcome and that variability among therapists continues to diminish the power of therapeutic effects in both research and practice.

Methods for more carefully scrutinizing therapist effects and modifying or improving therapists with poorer outcomes may serve to improve the potency of therapy. Interestingly, the methods for helping therapists with poorer outcomes may coincide with the research on common factors. Although most research has focused on using manuals to standardize therapist techniques, less focus or effort addresses the core, common interpersonal factors that may be relevant.

Dropout. One of the persistent problems in therapy outcome research that reduces the effects of treatments is the fact that many individuals do not complete treatment. Indeed, the rates of dropout in clinical trials can be quite significant. For example, 249 clients participated in the intake process of the NIMH TDCRP study, but only 169 completed 12 sessions and 15 weeks of treatment. Rates of dropout in clinical settings are even higher (Hansen, Lambert, & Forman, 2002). In a meta-analysis of 125 outpatient psychotherapy studies examining factors related to dropout, the mean rate of dropout was 47% (Wierzbicki & Pekarik, 1993).

Attrition is a significant problem for the generalizability of therapy outcome studies. To handle some of the data analytic problems raised by attrition, some recent studies have conducted two sets of analyses. Because of the discrepant findings that are produced when comparing study results including all clients who start treatment versus only clients who complete treatment, two sets of analyses allow a comparison of treatment effects between the data sets. One analysis examines the outcome of treatment for an "intent to treat" sample (i.e., all clients starting treatment). A second analysis examines the outcome for clients who complete treatment (completer sample). Although data analytic methods may produce a better understanding of treatment effects, they do not address the need to improve treatment and reduce dropout. One way of increasing the effects of therapy is to focus on clients who do not complete treatment. By addressing the issues that result in dropout, the effects of treatment may be enhanced. Of course, some clients may drop out of treatment because of increased hope, symptomatic improvement, or no further need of treatment. It is equally likely, however, that some clients may drop out because of treatment failure.

One interesting line of research provides some evidence that treatment dropout can be effectively addressed. The multisystemic therapy (MST) approach (Henggeler, Schoewald, Borduin, Rowland, & Cunningham, 1998) actively seeks to engage families in treatment. Specified interventions target the initial engagement of families in the treatment process, and weekly supervision and consultation (i.e., quality assurance) include active problem solving of issues that may prevent families from participating in treatment (Cunningham & Henggeler, 1999). Therapy teams seek creative ways to engage the families, and the therapy sessions are scheduled in places (typically home-based) and at times that are convenient for the family. As a result of this emphasis on engagement, studies of the MST approach have produced remarkable rates of treatment completion. For example, recent trials of MST resulted in 98% (57 of 58) and 97% (77 of 79) completion of a full course of treatment in a study of MST for adolescent substance abuse and for adolescents referred for psychiatric hospitalization (Henggeler, Pickrel, Brondino, & Crouch, 1996; Henggeler, Rowland, et al., 1999).

Although not every approach can incorporate the rather extraordinary efforts that are used in the intensive, home-based MST model, a greater emphasis on dropout may lead to improved methods for identifying clients who are at risk for treatment noncompletion along with interventions to help ensure that clients receive a complete "dose" of treatment. For example, recent studies that consider ruptures in the alliance have identified typical patterns and signs of alliance ruptures along with potentially useful interventions for resolving alliance difficulties (Safran & Muran, 2000). These approaches may also be useful when clients are deteriorating.

Deterioration and Negative Effects. Negative treatment effects are (or should be) the central focus of a variety of procedures subsumed under the topic of quality assurance/quality improvement. Efforts to identify patients who are at risk for having a poor treatment response have been recently summarized in a special section of the *Journal of Consulting and Clinical Psychology* (Lambert, 2001). Each of these methods shares the goal of preventing treatment failures; the methods identify the failing patient early enough that some action can be taken to reverse the negative trend. One rationale for developing statistical methods for identifying cases prone to a negative outcome is based on evidence that suggests therapists are poor at identifying and predicting who has or will have a poor treatment response (Breslen, Sobell, Sobell, Buchan, & Cunningham, 1997; Lunnen & Ogles, 1998; Meyer & Schulte, 2002).

In general, these quality management procedures have involved the use of patient monitoring systems, information on expected recovery trajectories, and decision rules that give an "alarm signal" when a patient is identified as making insufficient progress or heading toward potential treatment failure. Richard and Kordy (2001) have developed recovery models for use in the treatment of bulimia. Four trajectories of change describe patients who respond early to treatment and have a positive final outcome, respond early but have a poor outcome, respond slowly but have a positive outcome, or respond slowly and have a poor outcome. Like systems developed by Lueger et al. (2001) and Finch, Lambert, and Schaalje (2001), expected recovery is modeled and tolerance bands are placed around the expected trajectory of change. Outliers are then identified with the purpose of providing feedback to therapists. Feedback takes many forms but has been shown to enhance outcomes for cases that are predicted to fail. For example, Lambert, Whipple, Smart et al. (2001) found that they could identify potential treatment failures based on the patient's initial level of disturbance and early negative response to treatment. Therapists were given feedback in the form of a colored marker and written message. Green and white markers indicated the patient was responding as expected or had entered the ranks of normally functioning individuals (based on normative samples on the symptom measure). Red and yellow markers were given for patients whose progress was negative, along with a message that instructed therapists to review the case, have more frequent contact, consider alterations in the treatment plan, or initiate discussions with the patients about their worsening condition.

In this study, 12% of patients were identified as alarm signal cases (red or yellow markers). Providing feedback to therapists about the patients' condition enhanced outcomes and reduced deterioration (compared to a randomly assigned control group) for these cases. Those patients identified as potential treatment failures whose therapists received feedback remained in therapy longer than no-feedback controls identified as potential treatment failures.

A replication of this study (Lambert, Whipple, Vermeersch et al., 2001) resulted in essentially the same findings and reinforces the notion that patient deterioration can be reduced if therapists are alerted to the possibility early in treatment. The effect size for the intervention was larger than those reported for comparative outcome studies (.40 and .43 in the two studies). This finding suggests that a greater investment in such methods promises greater dividends than investment in comparative outcome studies. This and related quality improvement methods aimed at reducing deterioration are not yet widely employed by managed care or by practitioners. Their use should, however, increase over the next decade and is likely to be linked to greater understanding of treatment failures and methods of reversing negative outcome.

Studying dropout and deterioration may be difficult methodologically because the base rates are relatively low. For example, because approximately 10% of clients deteriorate, studies must include a large number of total clients in order to find sufficient numbers who deteriorate in any given study. This methodological problem may hinder rapid progress in this area of research. On the other hand, this research may be ideal for mental health services researchers who study all cases receiving any treatment.

Summary. Several areas of current research focus on increasing the effects of current psychological interventions. Integrating treatment methods and identifying the key ingredients of effective treatment are the main objectives of most programmatic research on psychological interventions. Indeed, the success of psychological interventions can largely be attributed to the gradual shift in treatment methods that has occurred through research. At the same time, there is a need to further specify the common factors of treatment. It is clear that much of what makes one treatment effective is common to other forms of treatment. Further specification of these common factors may facilitate strengthening the core, central features of all effective treatments. It is also clear that some therapists are more effective than other therapists. Continued research is needed to identify, and perhaps modify, therapist characteristics that contribute to treatment efficacy. Therapy dropout has plagued therapy researchers and is commonplace in clinical settings. Finding methods for identifying and intervening with clients who are at risk of dropping out before they improve may enhance the reputation of therapy and improve its effects. Similarly, warning systems need to be consistently applied to identify clients who are getting worse during treatment. As therapy researchers work to strengthen treatment effects, methods for addressing treatment dropout and deterioration must be developed and tested.

Conclusions

Research on psychotherapy outcomes has resulted in a number of conclusions that have implications for theory, research, and clinical practice.

1. Many psychotherapies that have been subjected to empirical study have been shown to have demonstrable effects on a variety of clients, which surpass gains made in those who get a placebo or go untreated. These effects are not only statistically significant but also clinically meaningful. From 40% to 70% of clients show a substantial benefit in clinical trials, although far fewer attain this degree of benefit in routine practice. Psychotherapy facilitates the remission of symptoms and improves functioning. It not only speeds up the natural healing process but also often provides additional coping strategies and methods for dealing with future problems. Providers as well as patients can be assured that a broad range of therapies, when offered by skillful, wise, and stable therapists, are likely to result in appreciable gains for the client.

2. We now have better general estimates of the amount of therapy needed in order to bring about clinically meaningful change. For patients who begin therapy in the dysfunctional range, 50% can be expected to achieve clinically significant change following 21 sessions of psychotherapy. Over 50 sessions are needed for 75% of patients to meet criteria. Therapists and policymakers should use this estimate in order to develop treatment plans and make policy decisions. Patients should be encouraged to anticipate a course of therapy that is sufficient to provide meaningful change. Data support the use of brief therapies for some problems and cast doubt on their value for other problems. The issue of efficiency promises to be an important area of future study because of its practical, economic, and ethical consequences. Therapy is highly efficient for a large minority of clients.

3. The effects of therapy tend to be lasting. Although some problems, such as addictive disorders, tend to recur, the gains many patients make in therapy endure. This is probably because most therapists are interested in enduring changes rather than temporary improvements. Research suggests that therapists should expend greater systematic efforts on helping patients solidify the gains made in therapy and focus attention near the end of treatment on the meaning of improvement to the patient and methods of coping with future problems. As difficult as it is to study the long-term effects of therapy, continued effort should be expended on long-term followup studies and on strategies that are intended to increase the permanence of change in patients who have recurrent disorders.

4. Although research continues to support the efficacy of those therapies that have been rigorously tested, differences in outcome between various forms of therapy are not as pronounced as might have been expected. Behavioral therapy, cognitive therapy, and eclectic mixtures of these methods have shown superior outcomes to traditional verbal therapies in several studies on specific disorders, but this is by no means the general case. When this superiority is evidenced, the results have been attributed to the bias of the researchers and the selectivity in criteria of change; however, the critics can be biased and selective as well. The current interest in generating lists of "empirically supported" therapies for specific disorders is controversial and misguided. To advocate empirically supported therapies as preferable or superior to other treatments would be premature. Not only is this endeavor impractical, but research support is lacking. Advocation at this level is not supported by past or current research evidence. Although there is little evidence of one form of psychotherapy having clinically significant superiority to another form with respect to moderate outpatient disorders, behavioral and cognitive methods appear to add a significant increment of efficacy with respect to a number of problems (e.g., panic, phobias, and compulsion) and to provide useful methods with a number of nonneurotic problems with which traditional therapies have shown little effectiveness (e.g., childhood aggression, psychotic behavior, and health-related behaviors).

5. Given the growing evidence that there are probably some specific technique effects as well as large common effects across treatments, the vast majority of therapists have become eclectic in orientation. This appears to reflect a healthy response to empirical evidence and a rejection of previous trends toward rigid allegiances to schools of treatment. It also opens up the possibility of more carefully matching techniques to client dispositions, personality traits, and other diagnostic differences. Most outcome research has focused on the main effects of techniques, but there is still the potential for delineating differential interaction effects between therapy method and client type.

6. Interpersonal, social, and affective factors common across therapies still loom large as stimulators of patient improvement. It should come as no surprise that helping others deal with depression, inadequacy, anxiety, and inner conflicts, as well as helping them form viable relationships and meaningful directions for their lives, can be greatly facilitated in a therapeutic relationship that is characterized by trust, warmth, understanding, acceptance, kindness, and human wisdom. These relationship factors are probably crucial even in the more technical therapies that generally ignore relationship factors and emphasize the importance of technique in their theory of change. This is not to say that techniques are irrelevant but that their power for change is limited when compared with personal influence. Common factors that are currently popular for explaining improvement in therapy also include exposure to anxiety-provoking stimuli, encouragement to participate in other risk-taking behavior, and efforts at mastery. Research suggests that clients would be wise to pick a therapist as-a-person in parity with the selection of a therapeutic technique.

7. Although the individual therapist can play a surprisingly large role in treatment outcome even when treatment is being offered within the stipulations of manual-guided therapy, recognition of the important place held by a therapist should in no way be construed as suggesting that technical proficiency has no unique contribution to make. Future research should focus not only on the important factors common across therapies but also on the specific effects of particular interventions. The current trend to provide therapy in a systematic way, as characterized by the use of treatment manuals, and further studies of the process of therapy may yet allow for more definitive conclusions regarding the contribution of technique factors.

8. Research on the effects of less experienced clinicians and paraprofessionals complements the conclusion drawn about schools of therapy and common factors. Paraprofessionals, who in many cases are selected, trained, and supervised by professional therapists, are often able to be as helpful as practicing clinicians. Thus, paraprofessionals should continue to play an important role in providing some mental health services. They are especially useful in providing social support and in offering structured treatment programs under supervision.

9. The development and use of meta-analytic procedures for integrating outcome research is a methodological advancement that has enabled scholars and clinicians to better understand research findings. As more meta-analytic reviews are published, it is becoming obvious that this group of techniques has not reduced the controversies surrounding the interpretation of research findings. Meta-analysis is not a panacea and cannot be used to create worthwhile information if it is based on poorly designed studies. An important task of future meta-analytic reviews will be to translate the abstract review into clinically meaningful terms.

10. Although the foregoing broad, positive statements about psychotherapy can be made with more confidence than ever before, it is still important to point out that average positive effects mask considerable variability in outcomes. Wide variations exist among therapists. The therapist factor, as a contributor to outcome, looms large in the assessment of outcomes. Some therapists appear to be unusually effective, while others may not even help the majority of patients who seek their services. It is apparent that a portion of those whom therapy is intended to help are actually harmed through inept application of treatments, negative attitudes, or poor combinations of treatment technique and patient problem. Current research, based on monitoring patient treatment response following each treatment session, can provide a powerful method of reducing negative change and enhancing outcome through timely feedback to providers. Such quality management efforts may be well worth the cost of employing them in routine practice.

Much more research needs to be conducted before the exact relationship between the process of therapy and its outcome will be known. The public deserves treatments that are based not only on our best clinical judgment but also on systematic research conducted under controlled and naturalistic conditions. It is our duty to be sensitive to both the positive and negative effects of therapy and to base our treatment efforts on a broad empirical foundation as well as study of the effects of our ongoing efforts.

Footnotes

1. See Chapter 2, this volume, for an explanation of the effect size statistic.

References

Abramowitz, J. S. (1996). Variants of exposure and response prevention in the treatment of obsessive-compulsive disorder: A meta-analysis. *Behavior Therapy*, *27*, 583–600.

Abramowitz, J. S. (1997). Effectiveness of psychological and pharmacological treatments for obsessive-compulsive disorder: A quantitative review.

Journal of Consulting and Clinical Psychology, 65, 44–52.

Agosti, V. (1995). The efficacy of treatments in reducing alcohol consumption: A meta-analysis. *International Journal of the Addictions, 30*, 1067–1077.

Ahn, H., & Wampold, B. E. (2001). Where oh where are the specific ingredients? A meta-analysis of component studies in counseling and psychotherapy. *Journal of Counseling Psychology, 48*, 251–257.

Alexander, C. N., Robinson, P., & Rainforth, M. (1994). Treating and preventing alcohol, nicotine, and drug abuse through Transcendental Meditation: A review and statistical meta-analysis. *Alcoholism Treatment Quarterly, 11*, 13–87.

Allen, M., Hunter, J. E., & Donohue, W. A. (1989). Meta-analysis of self-report data on the effectiveness of public speaking anxiety treatment techniques. *Communication Education, 38*, 54–76.

Allison, D. B., & Faith, M. S. (1996). Hypnosis as an adjunct to cognitive-behavioral psychotherapy for obesity: A meta-analytic reappraisal. *Journal of Consulting and Clinical Psychology, 64*, 513–516.

Allumbaugh, D. L., & Hoyt, W. T. (1999). Effectiveness of grief therapy: A meta-analysis. *Journal of Counseling Psychology, 46*, 370–380.

American Psychiatric Association. (1993). *Diagnostic and statistical manual of mental disorders* (4th ed.). Washington, DC: Author.

Anderson, E. M., & Lambert, M. J. (1995). Short-term dynamically oriented psychotherapy: A review and meta-analysis. *Clinical Psychology Review, 15*, 503–514.

Anderson, E. M., & Lambert, M. J. (2001). A survival analysis of clinically significant change in outpatient psychotherapy. *Journal of Clinical Psychology, 57*, 875–888.

Anderson, T. (1999). Specifying non-"specifics" in therapists: The effect of facilitative interpersonal skills in outcome and alliance formation. Paper presented at the 30th annual meeting of the International Society for Psychotherapy Research, Braga, Portugal.

Andrews, G. (1983). A treatment outline for depressive disorders: The Quality Assurance Project. *Australian and New Zealand Journal of Psychiatry, 17*, 129–146.

Andrews, G., & Harvey, R. (1981). Does psychotherapy benefit neurotic patients: A re-analysis of the Smith, Glass, & Miller data. *Archives of General Psychiatry, 38*, 1203–1208.

Andrews, G., Guitar, B., & Howie, P. (1980). Meta-analysis of the effects of stuttering treatment. *Journal of Speech and Hearing Disorders, 45*, 287–307.

Asay, T. P., Lambert, M. J., Christensen, E. R., & Beutler, L. E. (1984). A meta-analysis of mental health treatment outcome. Unpublished Manuscript: Brigham Young University.

Auerbach, A. H., & Johnson, M. (1977). Research on the therapist's level of experience. In A. S. Gurman & A. M. Razin (Eds.), *Effective psychotherapy: A handbook of research* (pp. 84–102). New York: Pergamon Press.

Bakker, A., van Balkom, A.J.L.M., Spinhoven, P., Blaauw, B.M.J.W., & van Dyck, R. (1998). Follow-up on the treatment of panic disorder with or without agoraphobia. *The Journal of Nervous and Mental Disease, 186*, 414–419.

Balestrieri, M., Williams, P., & Wilkinson, G. (1988). Special mental health treatment in general practice: A meta-analysis. *Psychological Medicine, 18*, 717.

Barker, S. L., Funk, S. C., & Houston, B. K. (1988). Psychological treatment versus nonspecific factors: A meta-analysis of conditions that engender comparable expectations for improvement. *Clinical Psychology Review, 8*, 579–594.

Barkham, M. (1996). Quantitative research on psychotherapeutic interventions: Methodological issues and substantive findings across three research generations. *Handbook of counseling psychology* (pp. 23–64). Thousand Oaks, CA: Sage Publications.

Barkham, M., Rees, A., Shapiro, D. A., Stiles, W. B., Agnew, R. M., Halstead, J., Culverwell, A., and Harrington, V.M.G. (1996). Outcomes of time-limited psychotherapy in applied settings: Replicating the second Sheffield psychotherapy project. *Journal of Consulting and Clinical Psychology, 64*, 1079–1085.

Barkham, M., Rees, A., Stiles, W. B., Shapiro, D. A., Hardy, G. E., & Reynolds, S. (1996). Dose effect relations in time limited psychotherapy for depression. *Journal of Consulting and Clinical Psychology, 64*, 927–935.

Barlow, D. H. (1981). On the relation of clinical research to clinical practice: Current issues, new directions. *Journal of Consulting and Clinical Psychology, 49*, 147–155.

Barlow, D. H. (1989). Treatment outcome evaluation methodology with anxiety disorders: Strengths and key issues. *Advances in Behavior Research and Therapy, 11*, 121–132.

Barlow, D. H., & Craske, M. G. (1994). *Mastery of your anxiety and panic II.* Albany, NY: Graywind.

Barlow, D. H., Craske, M. G., Cerny, J. A., and Klosko, J. S. (1989). Behavioral treatment of panic disorder. *Behavior Therapy, 20*, 261–282.

Beck, A. T., Rush, A. J., Shaw, F. B., & Emery, G. (1979). *The cognitive therapy of depression.* New York: Guilford Press.

Beck, R., & Fernandez, E. (1998). Cognitive-behavioral therapy in the treatment of anger: A meta-analysis. *Cognitive Therapy and Research, 22*, 63–74.

Bein, E., Anderson, T., Strupp, H. H., Henry, W. P., Schacht, T. E., Binder, J. L., & Butler, S. F. (2000). The effects of training in time-limited dynamic psychotherapy: Changes in therapeutic outcome. *Psychotherapy Research, 10*, 119–132.

Benton, M. K., & Schroeder, H. E. (1990). Social skills training with schizophrenics: A meta-analytic evaluation. *Journal of Consulting and Clinical Psychology, 58,* 741–747.

Bergin, A. E. (1971). The evaluation of therapeutic outcomes. In A. E. Bergin & S. L. Garfield (Eds.), *Handbook of psychotherapy and behavior change* (pp. 217–270). New York: John Wiley & Sons.

Bergin, A. E., & Lambert, M. J. (1978). The effectiveness of psychotherapy. In S. L. Garfield & A. E. Bergin (Eds.), *Handbook of psychotherapy and behavior change* (2nd ed., pp. 139–190). New York: John Wiley & Sons.

Bergin, A. E., & Strupp, H. H. (1970). *Future directions in psychotherapy research. Journal of Abnormal Psychology, 76,* 13–26.

Bergin, A. E., & Suinn, R. M. (1975). Individual psychotherapy and behavior therapy. *Annual Review of Psychology, 26,* 509–556.

Berman, J. S., & Norton, N. C. (1985). Does professional training make a therapist more effective? *Psychological Bulletin, 98,* 401–407.

Berman, J. S., Miller, C., & Massman, P. J. (1985). Cognitive therapy versus systematic desensitization: Is one treatment superior? *Psychological Bulletin, 97,* 451–461.

Beutler, L. E. (1979). Toward specific psychological therapies for specific conditions. *Journal of Consulting and Clinical Psychology, 47,* 882–897.

Beutler, L. E., Crago, M., & Arizmendi, T. G. (1986). Research on therapist variables in psychotherapy. In S. L. Garfield & A. E. Bergin (Eds.), *Handbook of psychotherapy and behavior change* (pp. 257–310). New York: John Wiley & Sons.

Beutler, L. E., Frank, M., Schieber, S. C., Calvert, S., & Gaines, J. (1984). Comparative effects of group psychotherapies in a short-term inpatient setting: An experience with deterioration effects. *Psychiatry, 47,* 66–76.

Bickman, L. E. (1999). Practice makes perfect and other myths about mental health services. *American Psychologist, 54,* 965–978.

Blanchard, E. B., Andrasik, F., Ahles, T. A., Teders, S. J., & O'Keefe, D. (1980). Migraine and tensions headache: A meta-analytic review. *Behavior Therapy, 11,* 613–631.

Blatt, S. J., Sanislow, C. A., Zuroff, D. C., & Pilkonis, P. A. (1996). Characteristics of effective therapists: Further analysis of data from the National Institute of Mental Health treatment of depression collaborative research program. *Journal of Consulting and Clinical Psychology, 64,* 1276–1284.

Borkovec, T. D. (1993). Between-group therapy outcome research: Design and methodology. In L. S. Onken, J. D. Blaine, & J. J. Boren (Eds.), *Behavioral treatments for drug abuse and dependence* (pp. 249–290). Rockville, MD: National Institute on Drug Abuse.

Borkovec, T. D., & Whisman, M. A. (1996). Psychosocial treatments for generalized anxiety disorder. In M. Mavissakalian & R. Prien (Eds.), *Long-term treatment of anxiety disorders.* Washington, DC: American Psychiatric Association.

Bowers, T., & Clum, G. (1988). Relative contribution of specific and nonspecific treatment effects: Meta-analysis of placebo-controlled behavior therapy research. *Psychological Bulletin, 103,* 315–323.

Breslan, F., Sobell, M. B., Sobell, L. C., Buchan, G., & Cunningham, J. (1997). Toward a stepped-up care approach to treating problem drinkers: The predictive validity of written treatment variables and therapist prognostic ratings. *Addiction, 92,* 1479–1489.

Burlingame, G. M., Fuhriman, A., Paul, S., & Ogles, B. (1989). Implementing a time-limited therapy program: Differential effects of training and experience. *Psychotherapy: Theory, Research, Practice, Training, 23,* 303–313.

Butler, S. F., & Strupp, H. H. (1986). Specific and nonspecific factors in psychotherapy: A problematic paradigm for psychotherapy research. *Psychotherapy: Theory, Research, Practice, Training, 23,* 30–40.

Carlson, C. R., & Hoyle, R. H. (1993). Efficacy of abbreviated progressive muscle relaxation training: A quantitative review of behavioral medicine research. *Journal of Consulting and Clinical Psychology, 61,* 1059–1067.

Carroll, K. M., Nich, C., & Rounsaville, B. J. (1997). Contribution of the therapeutic alliance to outcome in active versus control psychotherapies. *Journal of Consulting and Clinical Psychology, 65,* 510–514.

Carroll, K. M., Rounsaville, B. J., Nich, C., Gordon, L. T., Wirtz, P. W., & Gawin, F. (1994). One-year follow-up of psychotherapy and pharmacotherapy for cocaine dependence. *Archives of General Psychiatry, 51,* 989–997.

Castonguay, L. G., Goldfried, M. R., Wiser, S., & Raue, P. J. (1996). Predicting the effect of cognitive therapy for depression: A study of unique and common factors. *Journal of Consulting and Clinical Psychology, 64,* 497–504.

Cepeda-Benito, A. (1993). Meta-analytical review of the efficacy of nicotine chewing gum in smoking treatment programs. *Journal of Consulting and Clinical Psychology, 61,* 822–830.

Chambless, D. L., & Gillis, M. M. (1993). Cognitive therapy of anxiety disorders. *Journal of Consulting and Clinical Psychology, 61,* 248–260.

Chambless, D. L., & Ollendick, T. H. (2001). Empirically supported psychological interventions: Controversies and evidence. *Annual Review of Psychology, 52,* 685–716.

Chambless, D. L., Sanderson, W. C., Shoham, V., Bennett Johnson, S., Pope, K. S., Crits-Cristoph, P., Baker, M., Johnson, B., Woody, S. R., Sue, S., Beutler, L., Williams, D. A., & McCurry, S.

(1996). An update on empirically validated therapies. *The Clinical Psychologist, 49,* 5–18.

Chiles, J. A., Lambert, M. J., & Hatch, A. L. (1999). The impact of psychological interventions on medical cost offset: A meta-analytic review. *Clinical Psychology: Science and Practice, 6,* 204–220.

Christensen, H., Hadzi-Pavlovic, D., Andrews, G., & Mattick, R. (1987). Behavior therapy and tricyclic medication in the treatment of obsessive-compulsive disorder: A qualitative review. *Journal of Consulting and Clinical Psychology, 55,* 701–711.

Clum, G. A. (1989). Psychological interventions vs. drugs in the treatment of panic. *Behavior Therapy, 20,* 429–457.

Clum, G. A., Clum, G. A., & Surls, R. (1993). A meta-analysis of treatments for panic disorder. *Journal of Consulting and Clinical Psychology, 61,* 317–326.

Consumer Reports. (1995, November). Mental health: Does therapy help? pp. 734–739.

Cox, B. J., Endler, N. S., Lee, P. S., & Swinson, R. P. (1992). A meta-analysis of treatments for panic disorder with agoraphobia: Imipramine, alprazolam, and in vivo exposure. *Journal of Behavior Therapy and Experimental Psychiatry, 23,* 175–182.

Cox, B. J., Swinson, R. P., Morrison, B., & Lee, P. S. (1993). Clomipramine, fluoxetine, and behavior therapy in the treatment of obsessive-compulsive disorder: A meta-analysis. *Journal of Behavior Therapy and Experimental Psychiatry, 24,* 149–153.

Critelli, J. W., & Neumann, K. F. (1984). The placebo: Conceptual analysis of a construct in transition. *American Psychologist, 39,* 32–39.

Crits-Christoph, P. (1992). The efficacy of brief dynamic psychotherapy: A meta-analysis. *American Journal of Psychiatry, 149,* 151–158.

Crits-Christoph, P., Baranackie, K., Kurcias, J. S., Beck, A. T., et al. (1991). Meta-analysis of therapist effects in psychotherapy outcome studies. *Psychotherapy Research, 1,* 81–91.

Crits-Christoph, P., & Mintz, J. (1991). Implications of therapist effects for the design and analysis of comparative studies of psychotherapies. *Journal of Consulting and Clinical Psychology, 59,* 20–26.

Crits-Christoph, P., Siqueland, L., Blaine, J., Frank, A., Luborsky, L., Onken, L. S., Muenz, L. R., Thase, M. E., Weiss, R. D., Gastfriend, D. R., Woody, G. E., Barber, J. P., Butler, S. F., Daley, D., Salloum, I., Bishop, S., Najavits, L. M., Lis, J., Mercer, D., Griffin, M. L., Moras, K., & Beck, A. T. (1999). Psychosocial treatments for cocaine dependence: National Institute on Drug Abuse Collaborative Cocaine Treatment Study. *Archives of General Psychiatry, 56,* 493–502.

Cuijpers, P. (1997). Bibliotherapy in unipolar depression: A meta-analysis. *Journal of Behavior Therapy and Experimental Psychiatry, 28,* 139–147.

Cuijpers, P. (1998a). A psychoeducational approach to the treatment of depression: A meta-analysis of Lewinsohn's "Coping with Depression" course. *Behavior Therapy, 29,* 521–533.

Cuijpers, P. (1998b). Psychological outreach programmes for the depressed elderly: A meta-analysis of effects and dropout. *International Journal of Geriatric Psychiatry, 13,* 41–48.

Cunningham, P. B., & Henggeler, S. W. (1999). Engaging multiproblem families in treatment: Lessons learned throughout the development of multisystemic therapy. *Family Process, 38,* 265–286.

Dawes, R. M. (1996). *House of cards: Psychology and psychotherapy built on myth.* New York: The Free Press.

DeMarco, C. W. (1998). On the impossibility of placebo effects in psychotherapy. *Philosophical Psychology, 11,* 207–227.

Derogatis, L. R. (1983). *SCL-90-R: Administration, scoring, and procedural manual—II.* Baltimore, MD: Clinical Psychometric Research.

Devine, E. C. (1996). Meta-analysis of the effects of psychoeducational care in adults with asthma. *Research in Nursing and Health, 19,* 367–376.

Devine, E. C., & Pearcy, J. (1996). Meta-analysis of the effects of psychoeducational care in adults with chronic obstructive pulmonary disease. *Patient Education & Counseling, 29,* 167–178.

Didden, R., Duker, P. C., & Korzilius, H. (1997). Meta-analytic study on treatment effectiveness for problem behaviors with individuals who have mental retardation. *American Journal on Mental Retardation, 101,* 387–399.

Dilk, M. N., & Bond, G. (1996). Meta-analytic evaluation of skills training research for individuals with severe mental illness. *Journal of Consulting and Clinical Psychology, 64,* 1337–1346.

Dobson, K. S. (1989). A meta-analysis of the efficacy of cognitive therapy for depression. *Journal of Consulting and Clinical Psychology, 57,* 414–419.

Doherty, W. J., Lester, M. E., & Leigh, G. K. (1986). Marriage encounter weekends: Couples who win and couples who lose. *Journal of Marital and Family Therapy, 12,* 49–61.

Donenberg, G. R. (1999). Reconsidering "Between-group psychotherapy outcome research and basic science": Applications to child and adolescent psychotherapy outcome research. *Journal of Clinical Psychology, 55,* 181–190.

Donenberg, G. R., Lyons, J. S., & Howard, K. I. (1999). Clinical trials versus mental health services research: Contributions and connections. *Journal of Clinical Psychology, 55,* 1135–1146.

Durlak, J. A. (1979). Comparative effectiveness of paraprofessional and professional helpers. *Psychological Bulletin, 86,* 80–92.

Dush, D. M. (1986). The placebo in psychosocial outcome evaluations. *Evaluation & the Health Professions, 9,* 421–438.

Dush, D. M., Hirt, D. M., & Schroeder, H. E. (1983). Self-statement modification with adults: A meta-analysis. *Psychological Bulletin, 94,* 408–422.

Dush, D. M., Hirt, M. L., & Schroeder, H. E. (1989). Self-statement modification with adults: A meta-analysis. *Journal of Consulting and Clinical Psychology, 94,* 408–442.

Edmondson, C. B., & Conger, J. C. (1996). A review of treatment efficacy for individuals with anger problems: Conceptual, assessment, and methodological issues. *Clinical Psychology Review, 16,* 251–275.

Elkin, I. (1994). The NIMH treatment of depression collaborative research program: Where we began and where we are. In A. E. Bergin & S. L. Garfield (Eds.), *Handbook of psychotherapy and behavior change* (4th ed.) (pp. 114–142). New York: John Wiley & Sons.

Elkin, I., Parloff, M. B., Hadley, S. W., & Autry, J. H. (1985). NIMH treatment of Depression Collaborative Research Program: Background and research plan. *Archives of General Psychiatry, 42,* 305–316.

Elkin, I., Shea, M. T., Watkins, J. T., Imber, S. D., Stosky, S. M., Collins, J. F., Glass, D. R., Pilkonis, P. A., Weber, W. R., Docherty, J. P., Fiester, S. J., & Parloff, M. B. (1989). National Institute of Mental Health treatment of Depression Collaborative Research Program: General effectiveness of treatments. *Archives of General Psychiatry, 46,* 971–982.

Emmelkamp, P. M., de Haan, E., & Hoogduin, C. A. (1990). Marital adjustment and obsessive-compulsive disorder. *British Journal of Psychiatry, 156,* 55–60.

Engels, G. I., Garnefski, N., & Diekstra, R.F.W. (1993). Efficacy of rational-emotive therapy: A quantitative analysis. *Journal of Consulting and Clinical Psychology, 61,* 1083–1090.

Engels, G. I., & Vermey, M. (1997). Efficacy of nonmedical treatments of depression in elders: A quantitative analysis. *Journal of Clinical Geropsychology, 3,* 17–35.

Epstein, W. M. (1995). *The illusion of psychotherapy.* New Brunswick, NJ: Transaction.

Everly, G. S., Boyle, S. H., & Lating, J. M. (1999). The effectiveness of psychological debriefing with vicarious trauma: A meta-analysis. *Stress Medicine, 15,* 229–233.

Eysenck, H. J. (1952). The effects of psychotherapy: An evaluation. *Journal of Consulting Psychology, 16,* 319–324.

Febbaro, G.A.R., & Clum, G. A. (1998). Meta-analytic investigation of the effectiveness of self-regulatory components in the treatment of adult problem behaviors. *Clinical Psychology Review, 18,* 143–161.

Feske, U., & Chambless, D. L. (1995). Cognitive behavioral versus exposure only treatment for social phobia: A meta-analysis. *Behavior Therapy, 26,* 695–720.

Fettes, P. A., & Peters, J. M. (1992). A meta-analysis of group treatments for bulimia nervosa. *International Journal of Eating Disorders, 11,* 97–110.

Finch, A. E., Lambert, M. J., & Schaalje, B. G. (2001). Psychotherapy quality control: The statistical generation of expected recovery curves for integration into an early warning system. *Clinical Psychology and Psychotherapy, 8,* 231–242.

Flor, H., Fydrich, T., & Turk, D. C. (1992). Efficacy of multidisciplinary pain treatment centers: A meta-analytic review. *Pain, 49,* 221–230.

Foa, E. B., Dancu, C. V., Hembree, E. A., Jaycox, L. H., Meadows, E. A., & Street, G. P. (1999). A comparison of exposure therapy, stress inoculation training, and their combination for reducing posttraumatic stress disorder in female assault victims. *Journal of Consulting and Clinical Psychology, 67,* 194–200.

Frank, A. F., & Gunderson, J. G. (1991). The role of the therapeutic alliance in the treatment of schizophrenia: Relationship to course and outcome. *Archives of General Psychiatry, 47,* 228–236.

Frank, J. D. (1976). Psychotherapy and the sense of mastery. In R. L. Spitzer & D. F. Klein (Eds.), *Evaluation of psychotherapies: Behavioral therapies, drug therapies, and their interactions* (pp. 47–56). Baltimore, MD: Johns Hopkins University Press.

Freeston, M. H., Ladouceur, R., Gagnon, F., Thibodeau, N., Rheaume, J., Letarte, H., & Bujold, A. (1997). Cognitive-behavioral treatment of obsessive thoughts: A controlled study. *Journal of Consulting and Clinical Psychology, 65,* 405–413.

Gabbard, G. O., Lazar, S. G., Hornberger, J., & Spiegel, D. (1997). The economic impact of psychotherapy: A review. *American Journal of Psychiatry, 154,* 147–155.

Gaffan, E. A., Tsaousis, I., & Kemp-Wheeler, S. M. (1995). Researcher allegiance and meta-analysis: The case of cognitive therapy for depression. *Journal of Consulting and Clinical Psychology, 63,* 966–980.

Garfield, S. L. (1973). Basic ingredients or common factors in psychotherapy? *Journal of Consulting and Clinical Psychology, 41,* 9–12.

Gaston, L. (1990). The concept of the alliance and its role in psychotherapy: Theoretical and empirical considerations. *Psychotherapy, 27,* 143–153.

Gaston, L., Marmar, C. R., Gallagher, D., & Thompson, L. W. (1991). Alliance prediction of outcome beyond in-treatment symptomatic change as psychotherapy progresses. *Psychotherapy Research, 1,* 104–112.

Gerson, S., Belin, T. R., Kaufman, A., Mintz, J., & Jarvik, L. (1999). Pharmacological and psychological treatments for depressed older patients: A meta-analysis and overview of recent findings. *Harvard Review of Psychiatry, 7,* 1–28.

Gladis, M. M., Gosch, E. A., Dishuk, N. M., & Crits-Christoph, P. (1999). Quality of life: Expanding the scope of clinical significance. *Journal of Consulting and Clinical Psychology, 67*, 320–331.

Gloaguen, V., Cottraux, J., Cucherat, M., & Blackburn, I.-M. (1998). A meta-analysis of the effects of cognitive therapy in depressed patients. *Journal of Affective Disorders, 49*, 59–72.

Goldstein, A. P., & Stein, N. (1976). *Prescriptive psychotherapies.* New York: Pergamon.

Gortner, E. T., Gollan, J. K., Dobson, K. S., & Jacobson, N. S. (1998). Cognitive-behavioral treatment for depression: Relapse prevention. *Journal of Consulting and Clinical Psychology, 66*, 377–384.

Gould, R. A., Buckminster, S., Pollack, M. H., Otto, M. W., & Yap, L. (1997). Cognitive-behavioral and pharmacological treatment for social phobia: A meta-analysis. *Clinical Psychology: Science & Practice, 4*, 291–306.

Gould, R. A., & Clum, G. A. (1993). A meta-analysis of self-help treatment approaches. *Clinical Psychology Review, 13*, 169–186.

Gould, R. A., Otto, M. W., & Pollack, M. H. (1995). A meta-analysis of treatment outcome for panic disorder. *Clinical Psychology Review, 15(8)*, 819–844.

Gould, R. A., Otto, M. W., Pollack, M. H., & Yap, L. (1997). Cognitive behavioral and pharmacological treatment of generalized anxiety disorder: A preliminary meta-analysis. *Behavior Therapy, 28*, 285–305.

Gregerson. A., Nielsen, S. L., Lambert, M. J., Isakson, R., Smart, D., & Worthen, V. (2001, April). Testing the *Consumer Reports* effectiveness scale: What can consumers report? Paper presented at the annual meeting of the Western Psychological Association, Honolulu, Hawaii.

Grencavage, L. M., & Norcross, J. C. (1990). Where are the commonalties among the therapeutic common factors? *Professional Psychology: Research and Practice, 21*, 372–378.

Grissom, R. J. (1996). The magical number .7 +– .2: Meta-meta-analysis of the probability of superior outcome in comparisons involving therapy, placebo, and control. *Journal of Consulting and Clinical Psychology, 64*, 973–982.

Haas, E., Hill, R., Lambert, M. J., & Morrell, B. (2002). Do early responders to psychotherapy maintain treatment gains? *Journal of Clinical Psychology, 58*, 1157–1172.

Hall, G.C.N. (1995). Sexual offender recidivism revisited: A meta-analysis of recent treatment studies. *Journal of Consulting and Clinical Psychology, 63*, 802–809.

Hampton, B. R., & Hulgus, Y. F. (1993). The efficacy of paradoxical strategies: A quantitative review of the research. *Psychotherapy in private practice, 12*, 53–71.

Hansen, N., Lambert, M. J., & Forman, E. M. (2002). The psychotherapy dose-response effect and its implication for treatment delivery services. *Clinical Psychology: Science and Practice, 9*, 329–343.

Hartmann, A., Herzog, T., & Drinkmann, A. (1992). Psychotherapy of bulimia nervosa: What is effective? A meta-analysis. *Journal of Psychosomatic Research, 36*, 159–167.

Hattie, J. A., Sharpley, C. F., & Rogers, H. F. (1984). Comparative effectiveness of professional and paraprofessional helpers. *Psychological Bulletin, 95*, 534–541.

Hegarty, J. D., Baldessarini, R. J., Tohen, M., Waternaux, C., et al. (1994). One hundred years of schizophrenia: A meta-analysis of the outcome literature. *American Journal of Psychiatry, 151*, 1409–1416.

Henggeler, S. W., Pickrel, S. G., Brondino, M. J., & Crouch, J. L. (1996). Eliminating (almost) treatment dropout of substance abusing or dependent delinquents through home-based multisystemic therapy. *American Journal of Psychiatry, 153*, 427–428.

Henggeler, S. W., Rowland, M. D., Randall, J., Ward, D. M., Pickrel, S. G., Cunningham, P. B., Miller, S. L., Edwards, J., Zealberg, J., Hand, L. D., & Santos, A. B. (1999). Home-based multisystemic therapy as an alternative to the hospitalization of youths in psychiatric crisis: Clinical outcomes. *Journal of the American Academy of Child and Adolescent Psychiatry, 38*, 1331–1339.

Henggeler, S. W., Schoewald, S. K., Borduin, C. M., Rowland, M. D., & Cunningham, P. B. (1998). *Multisystemic treatment of antisocial behaviors in children and adolescents.* New York: Guilford Press.

Henry, W. P., Schacht, T. E., & Strupp, H. H. (1986). Structural analysis of social behavior: Application to a study of interpersonal process in differential psychotherapeutic outcome. *Journal of Consulting and Clinical Psychology, 54*, 27–31.

Henry, W. P., Schacht, T. E., Strupp, H. H., Butler, S. F., & Binder, J. L. (1993). Effects of training in time-limited psychotherapy: Mediators of therapist's responses to training. *Journal of Consulting and Clinical Psychology, 61*, 441–447.

Henry, W. P., Strupp, H. H., Schacht, T. E., Binder, J. L., & Butler, S. F. (1993). The effects of training in time-limited dynamic psychotherapy: Changes in therapist behavior. *Journal of Consulting and Clinical Psychology, 61*, 434–440.

Hill, K. A. (1987). Meta-analysis of paradoxical interventions. *Psychotherapy, 24*, 266–270.

Hollon, S. D. (1996). The efficacy and effectiveness of psychotherapy relative to medications. *American Psychologist, 51*, 1025–1030.

Holroyd, K. A., & Penzien, D. B. (1986). Client variables and the behavioral treatment of recurrent tension headache: A meta-analytic review. *Journal of Behavioral Medicine, 9*, 515–536.

Holroyd, K. A., & Penzien, D. B. (1990). Pharmacological versus non-pharmacological prophylaxis of recurrent migraine headache: A meta-analytic review of clinical trials. *Pain, 42*, 1–13.

Horvath, A. O., & Symonds, B. D. (1991). Relationship between working alliance and outcome in psychotherapy: A meta-analysis. *Journal of Counseling Psychology, 38*, 139–149.

Horvath, P. (1988). Placebos and common factors in two decades of psychotherapy research. *Psychological Bulletin, 104*, 214–225.

Howard, K. I., Kopta, S. M., Krause, M. S., & Orlinsky, D. E. (1986). The dose-effect relationship in psychotherapy. *American Psychologist, 41*, 159–164.

Howard, K. I., Moras, K., Brill, P. L., Martinovich, Z., & Lutz, W. (1996). Evaluation of psychotherapy: Efficacy, effectiveness, and patient progress. *American Psychologist, 51*, 1059–1064.

Hyman, R. B., Feldman, H. R., Harris, R. B., Levin, R. F., & Malloy, G. B. (1989). The effects of relaxation training on clinical symptoms: A meta-analysis. *Nursing Research, 38*, 216–220.

Ilardi, S. S., & Craighead, W. E. (1994). The role of non-specific factors in cognitive-behavior therapy for depression. *Clinical Psychology: Science and Practice, 1*, 138–156.

Ilardi, S. S., Craighead, W. E., & Evans, D. D. (1997). Modeling relapse in unipolar depression: Effects of dysfunctional cognitions and personality disorders. *Journal of Consulting and Clinical Psychology, 65*, 381–391.

Imber, S. D., Pilknois, P. A., Sotsky, S. M., Elkin, I., Watkins, J. T., Collins, J. F., Shea, M. T., Leber, W. R., & Glass, D. R. (1990). Mode-specific effects among three treatments for depression. *Journal of Consulting and Clinical Psychology, 58*, 352–359.

Jacobson, N. S., & Christensen, A. (1996). Studying the effectiveness of psychotherapy: How well can clinical trials do the job? *American Psychologist, 51*, 1031–1039.

Jacobson, N. S., Dobson, K. S., Truax, P. A., Addis, M. E., Koerner, K., Gollan, J. K., Gortner, E., & Prince, S. E. (1996). A component analysis of cognitive-behavioral treatment for depression. *Journal of Consulting and Clinical Psychology, 64*, 295–304.

Jacobson, N. S., Follette, W. C., Revenstorf, D., Baucom, D. H., Hahlweg, K., & Margolin, G. (1984). Variability in outcome and clinical significance of behavioral marital therapy: A re-analysis of outcome data. *Journal of Consulting and Clinical Psychology, 52*, 497–504.

Jacobson, N. S., Roberts, L. J., Berns, S. B., & McGlinchey, J. B. (1999). Methods for defining and determining the clinical significance of treatment effects: Description, application, and alternatives. *Journal of Consulting and Clinical Psychology, 67*, 300–307.

Jacobson, N. S., & Truax, P. (1991). Clinical significance: A statistical approach to defining meaningful change in psychotherapy research. *Journal of Consulting and Clinical Psychology, 59*, 12–19.

Jarrett, R. B., Kraft, D., Doyle, J., Foster, B. M., Eaves, G. G., & Silver, P. C. (2001). Preventing recurrent depression using cognitive therapy with and without a continuation phase—A randomized clinical trial. *Archives of General Psychiatry, 58*, 381–388.

Jorm, A. F. (1989). Modifiability of trait anxiety and neuroticism: A meta-analysis of the literature. *Australian and New Zealand Journal of Psychiatry, 23*, 21–29.

Kadera, S. W., Lambert, M. J., & Andrews, A. A. (1996). How much therapy is really enough? A session-by-session analysis of the psychotherapy dose-effect relationship. *Psychotherapy: Research and Practice, 5*, 1–21.

Karasu, T. B. (1986). The specificity versus nonspecificity dilemma: Toward identifying therapeutic change agents. *American Journal of Psychiatry, 143*, 687–695.

Kazantzis, N., Deane, F. P., & Ronan, K. R. (2000). Homework assignments in cognitive and behavioral therapy: A meta-analysis. *Clinical Psychology: Science and Practice*, 7, 189–202.

Kazdin, A. E. (1977). Assessing the clinical or applied importance of behavior change through social validation. *Behavior Modification, 1*, 427–452.

Kazdin, A. E. (1998). *Research design in clinical psychology* (3rd ed.). Boston: Allyn & Bacon.

Kazdin, A. E., & Bass, D. (1989). Power to detect differences between alternative treatments in comparative psychotherapy outcome research. *Journal of Consulting and Clinical Psychology, 57*, 138–147.

Kellner, R. (1975). Psychotherapy in psychosomatic disorders. A survey of controlled studies. *Archives of General Psychiatry, 32*, 1021–1028.

Kendall, P. C. (1999). Clinical Significance. *Journal of Consulting and Clinical Psychology, 67*, 283–284.

Kendall, P. C., Marrs-Garcia, A., Nath, S. R., & Sheldrick, R. C. (1999). Normative comparisons for the evaluation of clinical significance. *Journal of Consulting and Clinical Psychology, 67*, 285–299.

Kirsch, I. (1996). Hypnotic enhancement of cognitive-behavioral weight loss treatments: Another meta-reanalysis. *Journal of Consulting and Clinical Psychology, 64*, 517–519.

Kirsch, I., Montgomery, G., & Sapirstein, G. (1995). Hypnosis as an adjunct to cognitive-behavioral psychotherapy: A meta-analysis. *Journal of Consulting and Clinical Psychology, 63*, 214–220.

Kopta, S. M., Howard, K. I., Lowry, J. L., & Beutler, L. E. (1994). Patterns of symptomatic recovery in psychotherapy. *Journal of Consulting and Clinical Psychology, 62*, 1009–1016.

Krupnick, J. L., Sotsky, S. M., Elkin, I., Simmens, S., Moyer, J., Watkins, J., & Pilkonis, P. A. (1996). The role of the therapeutic alliance in psychotherapy and pharmacotherapy outcome: Findings in the National Institute of Mental Health treatment of depression collaborative research program. *Journal of Consulting and Clinical Psychology, 64*, 532–539.

Laessle, R. G., Zoettl, C., & Pirke, K. M. (1987). Meta-analysis of treatment studies for bulimia. *International Journal of Eating Disorders, 6*, 647–653.

Lambert, M. J. (1979). Characteristics of patients and the relationship to outcome in brief psychotherapy. *Psychiatric Clinics of North America, 2*, 111–123.

Lambert, M. J. (1983). Introduction to assessment of psychotherapy outcome: Historical perspective and current issues. In M. J. Lambert, E. R. Christensen, & S. S. DeJulio (Eds.), *The assessment of psychotherapy outcome.* New York: John Wiley & Sons.

Lambert, M. J. (1992). Psychotherapy outcome research: Implications for integrative and eclectic therapists. In J. C. Norcross & M. R. Goldfried (Eds.), *Handbook of psychotherapy integration* (pp. 94–129). New York: Basic Books.

Lambert, M. J. (2001). Psychotherapy outcome and quality improvement: Introduction to the special section on patient-focused research. *Journal of Consulting and Clinical Psychology, 69*, 147–149.

Lambert, M. J., & Bergin, A. E. (1973). Psychotherapeutic outcomes and issues related to behavioral and humanistic approaches. *Cornell Journal of Social Relations, 8*, 47–61.

Lambert, M. J., & Bergin, A. E. (1994). The effectiveness of psychotherapy. In A. E. Bergin & S. L. Garfield (Eds.), *Handbook of psychotherapy and behavior change* (4th ed.). (pp. 143–189). New York: John Wiley & Sons.

Lambert, M. J., Bergin, A. E., & Collins, J. L. (1977). Therapist-induced deterioration in psychotherapy. In A. S. Gurman, & A. M. Razin (Eds.), *Effective psychotherapy: A handbook of research* (pp. 452–481). New York: Pergamon.

Lambert, M. J., DeJulio, S. S., & Stein, D. M. (1978). Therapist interpersonal skills: Process, outcome, methodological considerations, and recommendations for future research. *Psychological Bulletin, 85*, 467–489.

Lambert, M. J., Hansen, N. B., & Finch, A. E. (2001). Patient-focused research: Using patient outcome data to enhance treatment effects. *Journal of Consulting and Clinical Psychology, 69*, 159–172.

Lambert, M. J., Hatch, D. R., Kingston, M. D., & Edwards, B. C. (1986). Zung, Beck, and Hamilton Rating Scales as measures of treatment outcome: A meta-analytic comparison. *Journal of Consulting and Clinical Psychology, 54*, 54–59.

Lambert, M. J., Shapiro, D. A., & Bergin, A. E. (1986). The effectiveness of psychotherapy. In S. L. Garfield & A. E. Bergin (Eds.), *Handbook of psychotherapy and behavior change* (3rd ed.) (pp. 157–211). New York: John Wiley & Sons.

Lambert, M. J., Whipple, J. L., Smart, D. W., Vermeersch, D. A., Nielsen, S. L., & Hawkins, E. J. (2001). The effects of providing therapists with feedback on patient progress during psychotherapy: Are outcomes enhanced? *Psychotherapy Research, 11*, 49–68.

Lambert, M. J., Whipple, J. L., Vermeersch, D. A., Smart, D. W., Hawkins, E. J., Nielsen, S. L., & Goates, M. (2002). Enhancing psychotherapy outcomes via providing feedback on client progress: A replication. *Clinical Psychology and Psychotherapy, 9*, 91–103.

Landman, J. T., & Dawes, R. M. (1982). Smith and Glass' conclusions stand up under scrutiny. *American Psychologist, 37*, 504–516.

Lang, P. J., & Lazovik, A. D. (1963). Experimental desensitization of a phobia. *Journal of Abnormal and Social Psychology, 66*, 519–525.

Leichsenring, F. (2001). Comparative effects of short-term psychodynamic psychotherapy and cognitive-behavioral therapy in depression: A meta-analytic approach. *Clinical Psychology Review, 21*, 401–419.

Lewandowski, L. M., Gebing, T. A., Anthony, J. L., & O'Brien, W. H. (1997). Meta-analysis of cognitive-behavioral treatment studies for bulimia. *Clinical Psychology Review, 17*, 703–718.

Lichtenstein, E., Glasgow, R. E., Lando, H. A., Ossip-Klein, D. J., et al. (1996). Telephone counseling for smoking cessation: Rationales and meta-analytic review of evidence. *Health Education Research, 11*, 243–257.

Lick, J. (1973). Statistical vs. clinical significance in research on the outcome of psychotherapy. *International Journal of Mental Health, 2*, 26–37.

Linden, W., & Chambers, L. (1994). Clinical effectiveness of non-drug treatment for hypertension: A meta-analysis. *Annals of Behavioral Medicine, 16*, 35–45.

Lipsey, M. W., & Wilson, D. B. (1993). The efficacy of psychological, educational, and behavioral treatment: Confirmation from meta-analysis. *American Psychologist, 48*, 1181–1209.

Luborsky, L., & DeRubeis, R. J. (1984). The use of psychotherapy treatment manuals—a small revolution in psychotherapy research style. *Clinical Psychology Review, 4*, 5–14.

Luborsky, L., Diguer, L., Seligman, D. A., Rosenthal, R., Krause, E. D., Johnson, S., Halperin, G., Bishop, M., Berman, J. S., & Schweizer, E. (1999). The researcher's own therapy allegiances: A "wild card" in comparisons of treatment efficacy. *Clinical Psychology: Science and Practice, 6*, 95–106.

Luborsky, L., McClellan, A. T., Woody, G. E., O'Brien, C. P., & Auerbach, A. (1985). Therapist success and its determinants. *Archives of General Psychiatry, 42*, 602–611.

Luborsky, L., Singer, J., & Luborsky, L. (1975). Comparative studies of psychotherapy. *Archives of General Psychiatry, 32*, 995–1008.

Lueger, R. J., Howard, K. I., Martinovich, Z., Lutz, W., Anderson, E. E., & Grissom, G. (2001). Assessing treatment progress of individual patients using expected treatment response models. *Journal of Consulting and Clinical Psychology, 69*, 150–158.

Lunnen, K., M., & Ogles, B. M. (1998). A multi-perspective, multivariable evaluation of reliable change. *Journal of Consulting and Clinical Psychology, 66*, 400–410.

Lyons, L. C., & Woods, P. J. (1991). The efficacy of rational-emotive therapy: A quantitative review. *Clinical Psychology Review, 11*, 357–369.

Mahrer, A. R. (1999). Embarrassing problems for the field of psychotherapy. *Journal of Clinical Psychology, 55*, 1147–1156.

Maling, M. S., Gurtman, M. B., & Howard, K. I. (1995). The response of interpersonal problems to varying doses of psychotherapy. *Psychotherapy Research, 5*, 63–75.

Malone, M. D., & Strube, M. J. (1988). Meta-analysis of non-medical treatments for chronic pain. *Pain, 34*, 231–244.

Marrs, R. W. (1995). A meta-analysis of bibliotherapy studies. *American Journal of Community Psychology, 23*, 843–870.

Martin, D. J., Garske, J. P., & Davis, M. K. (2000). Relation of the therapeutic alliance with outcome and other variables: A meta-analytic review. *Journal of Consulting and Clinical Psychology, 68*, 438–450.

Matt, G. E., & Navarro, A. M. (1997). What meta-analyses have and have not taught us about psychotherapy effects: A review and future directions. *Clinical Psychology Review, 17*, 1–32.

Mattick, R. P., Andrews, G., Hadzi-Pavlovic, D., & Christensen, H. (1990). Treatment of panic and agoraphobia. *The Journal of Nervous and Mental Disease, 178*, 567–573.

McDermut, W., Miller, I. W., & Brown, R. A. (2001). The efficacy of group psychotherapy for depression: A meta-analysis and review of the empirical research. *Clinical Psychology: Science and Practice, 8*, 98–116.

McNeilly, C. L., & Howard, K. I. (1991). The effects of psychotherapy: A reevaluation based on dosage. *Psychotherapy Research, 1*, 74–78.

McRoberts, C. H., Burlingame, G. M., & Hoag, M. J. (1998). Comparative efficacy of individual and group psychotherapy: A meta-analytic perspective. *Group Dynamics: Theory, Research, and Practice, 59*, 101–111.

Meltzoff, J., & Kornreich, M. (1970). *Research in psychotherapy.* New York: Atherton.

Meyer, F., & Schulte, D. (2002). Zur Validität der beurteilung des therapieefolgs durch therapeuten [The validity of therapists' ratings of therapy outcome]. *Zeitschrift für Klinische Psychalogie und Psychotherapie, 31*, 53–61.

Meyer, T. J., & Mark, M. M. (1995). Effects of psychosocial interventions with adult cancer patients: A meta-analysis of randomized experiments. *Health Psychology, 14*, 101–108.

Miller, R. C., & Berman, J. S. (1983). The efficacy of cognitive behavior therapies: A quantitative review of the research evidence. *Psychological Bulletin, 94*, 39–53.

Mitchell, J. E., & Raymond, N. C. (1992). Cognitive-behavioral therapy in treatment of bulimia nervosa. In K. A. Halmi & et. al (Eds.), *Psychobiology and treatment of anorexia nervosa and bulimia nervosa.* (pp. 307–327). Washington, DC: American Psychiatric Press.

Mohr, D. C. (1995). Negative outcome in psychotherapy: A critical review. *Clinical Psychology: Science and Practice, 2*, 1–27.

Mohr, D. C. (1999). Treatment of depression in multiple sclerosis: Review and meta-analysis. *Clinical Psychology: Science and Practice, 6*, 1–9.

Mohr, D. C., Beutler, L. E., Engle, D., Shoham-Salomon, V., et al. (1990). Identification of patients at risk for nonresponse and negative outcome in psychotherapy. *Journal of Consulting and Clinical Psychology, 58*, 622–628.

Morin, C. M., Culbert, J. P., & Schwartz, S. M. (1994). Nonpharmacological interventions for insomnia: A meta-analysis of treatment efficacy. *American Journal of Psychiatry, 151*, 1172–1180.

Mumford, E., Schlesinger, H. J., Glass, G. V., Patrick, C., & Cuerdon, T. (1984). A new look at evidence about reduced cost of medical utilization following mental health treatment. *Journal of Psychotherapy Practice and Research, 7*, 68–86.

Munoz, R. F., Hollon, S. D., McGrath, E., Rehm, L. P., et al. (1994). On the AHCPR Depression in Primary Care guidelines: Further considerations for practitioners. *American Psychologist, 49*, 42–61.

Murtagh, D.R.R., & Greenwood, K. M. (1995). Identifying effective psychological treatments for insomnia: A meta-analysis. *Journal of Consulting and Clinical Psychology, 63*, 79–89.

Najavits, L. M., & Gunderson, J. G. (1995). Better than expected: Improvements in borderline personality disorder in a 3-year prospective outcome study. *Comprehensive Psychiatry, 36*, 296–302.

Najavits, L. M., & Weiss, R. D. (1994). Variations in therapist effectiveness in the treatment of patients with substance use disorders: An empirical review. *Addiction, 89*, 679–688.

Nicholson, R. A., & Berman, J. S. (1983). Is follow-up necessary in evaluating psychotherapy? *Psychological Bulletin, 93*, 261–278.

Nietzel, M. T., & Fisher, S. G. (1981). Effectiveness of professional and paraprofessional helpers: A comment on Durlak. *Psychological Bulletin, 89*, 555–565.

Nietzel, M. T., Russell, R. L., Hemmings, K. A., & Gretter, M. L. (1987). Clinical significance of psychotherapy for unipolar depression: A meta-analytic approach to social comparison. *Journal of Consulting and Clinical Psychology, 55,* 156–161.

Oei, T. P. S., & Shuttlewood, G. J. (1996). Specific and nonspecific factors in psychotherapy: A case of cognitive therapy for depression. *Clinical Psychology Review, 16,* 83–103.

Ogles, B. M., Anderson, T., & Lunnen, K. M. (1999). The contribution of models and techniques to therapeutic efficacy: Contradictions between professional trends and clinical research. In M. A. Hubble, B. L. Duncan, & S. E. Miller (Eds.), *The heart and soul of change: What works in therapy* (pp. 201–225). Washington, DC: American Psychological Association.

Ogles, B. M., Lambert, M. J., & Sawyer, J. D. (1995). Clinical significance of the National Institute of Mental Health Treatment of Depression Collaborative Research Program data. *Journal of Consulting and Clinical Psychology, 63,* 321–326.

Ogles, B. M., Lambert, M. J., Weight, D. G., & Payne, I. R. (1990). Agoraphobia outcome measurement: A review and meta-analysis. *Psychological Assessment, 2,* 317–325.

Ogles, B. M., Lunnen, K. M., & Bonesteel, K. (2001). Clinical significance: History, definitions, and applications. *Clinical Psychology Review, 21,* 421–446.

Orlinsky, D. E., Grawe, K., & Parks, B. K. (1994). Process and outcome in psychotherapy: Noch einmal. In A. E. Bergin & S. L. Garfield (Eds.), *Handbook of psychotherapy and behavior change* (4th ed.) (pp. 270–376). New York: John Wiley & Sons.

Orlinsky, D. E., & Howard, K. I. (1980). Gender and psychotherapeutic outcome. In A. M. Brodsky & R. T. Hare-Mustin (Eds.), *Women and psychotherapy* (pp. 3–34). New York: Guilford Press.

Parloff, M. R. (1986). Placebo controls in psychotherapy research: A sine qua non or a placebo for research problems? *Journal of Consulting and Clinical Psychology, 54,* 79–87.

Patterson, C. H. (1984). Empathy, warmth, and genuineness in psychotherapy: A review of reviews. *Psychotherapy, 21,* 431–438.

Prendergast, M. L., Urada, D., & Podus, D. (2001). Meta-analysis of HIV risk-reduction interventions within drug abuse treatment programs. *Journal of Consulting and Clinical Psychology, 69,* 389–405.

Prioleau, L., Murdock, M., & Brody, N. (1983). An analysis of psychotherapy versus placebo studies. *The Behavioral and Brain Sciences, 6,* 275–310.

Procedures, Task Force on Promotion and Dissemination of Psychological Procedures (1995). Training in and dissemination of empirically-validated psychological treatments. *The Clinical Psychologist, 48,* 3–23.

Project Match Research Group (1998). Therapist effects in three treatments for alcohol problems. *Psychotherapy Research, 8,* 455–474.

Quality Assurance Project. (1982). A treatment outline for agoraphobia. *Australian and New Zealand Journal of Psychiatry, 16,* 25–33.

Quality Assurance Project. (1983). A treatment outline for depressive disorders. *Australian and New Zealand Journal of Psychiatry, 17,* 129–146.

Quality Assurance Project. (1984). Treatment outlines for the management of schizophrenia. *Australian and New Zealand Journal of Psychiatry, 18,* 19–38.

Quality Assurance Project. (1985a). Treatment outlines for the management of anxiety states. *Australian and New Zealand Journal of Psychiatry, 19,* 138–151.

Quality Assurance Project. (1985b). Treatment outlines for the management of obsessive compulsive disorders. *Australian and New Zealand Journal of Psychiatry, 19,* 240–253.

Quitkin, F. M., McGrath, P. J., Stewart, J. W., Taylor, B. P., & Klein, D. F. (1996). Can the effects of antidepressants be observed in the first two weeks of treatment? *Neuropsychopharmacology, 15,* 390–394.

Rachman, S. J., & Wilson, G. T. (1980). *The effects of psychological therapy* (2nd ed.). New York: Pergamon.

Ray, J. W., & Shadish, W. R. (1996). How interchangeable are different estimators of effect size? *Journal of Consulting and Clinical Psychology, 64,* 1316–1325.

Reynolds, C. F., Frank, E., Perel, J. M., Imber, S. D., Cornes, C., Miller, M. D., Mazumdar, S., Houck, P. R., Dew, M. A., Stack, J. A., Pollock, B. G., & Kupfer, D. J. (1999). Nortriptyline and interpersonal psychotherapy as maintenance therapies for recurrent major depression. *Journal of the American Medical Association, 281,* 39–45.

Richard, M., & Kordy, H. (2001). Early treatment response: Conceptualization, predictive validity and application management. Unpublished manuscript. Center for Psychotherapy, Stuttgart, Germany.

Robinson, L. A., Berman, J. S., & Neimeyer, R. A. (1990). Psychotherapy for the treatment of depression: A comprehensive review of controlled outcome research. *Psychological Bulletin, 108,* 30–49.

Rosenthal, D., & Frank, J. D. (1956). Psychotherapy and the placebo effect. *Psychological Bulletin, 53,* 294–302.

Rosenthal, R., & Rubin, D. B. (1982). Comparing effect sizes of independent studies. *Psychological Bulletin, 92,* 500–504.

Rosenzweig, S. (1936). Some implicit common factors in diverse methods of psychotherapy. *American Journal of Orthopsychiatry, 6,* 412–415.

Rousaville, B. J., O'Malley, S., Foley, S., & Weissman, M. M. (1988). Role of manual-guided training in the conduct and efficacy of interpersonal psychotherapy for depression. *Journal of Consulting and Clinical Psychology, 56*, 681–688.

Safran, J. D., & Muran, J. C. (2000). *Negotiating the therapeutic alliance: A relational treatment guide.* New York: Guilford Press.

Salvio, M. A., Beutler, L. E., Wood, J. M., & Engle, D. (1992). The strength of the therapeutic alliance in three treatments for depression. *Psychotherapy Research, 2*, 31–36.

Scogin, F., & McElreath, L. (1994). Efficacy of psychosocial treatments for geriatric depression: A quantitative review. *Journal of Consulting & Clinical Psychology, 62*, 69–73.

Scogin, F., Bynum, J., Stephens, G., & Calhoon, S. (1990). Efficacy of self-administered treatment programs: Meta-analytic review. *Professional Psychology: Research and Practice, 21*, 42–47.

Scogin, F., Floyd, M., Jamison, C., Ackerson, J., et al. (1996). Negative outcomes: What is the evidence on self-administered treatments? *Journal of Consulting and Clinical Psychology, 64*, 1086–1089.

Seligman, M. E. P. (1995). The effectiveness of psychotherapy: The *Consumer Reports* study. *American Psychologist, 50*, 965–974.

Seligman, M. E. P. (1996). Science as an ally of practice. *American Psychologist, 51*, 1072–1079.

Shadish, W. R., Matt, G. E., Navarro, A. M., Siegle, G., Crits-Cristoph, P., Hazelrigg, M. D., Jorm, A. F., Lyons, L. C., Nietzel, M. T., Prout, H. T., Robinson, L., Smith, M. L., Svartberg, M., & Weiss, B. (1997). Evidence that therapy works in clinically representative conditions. *Journal of Consulting and Clinical Psychology, 65*, 355–365.

Shadish, W. R., Montgomery, L. M., Wilson, P., Wilson, M. R., et al. (1993). Effects of family and marital psychotherapies: A meta-analysis. *Journal of Consulting and Clinical Psychology, 61*, 992–1002.

Shadish, W. R., Navarro, A. M., Matt, G. E., & Phillips, G. (2000). The effects of psychological therapies under clinically representative conditions: A meta-analysis. *Psychological Bulletin, 126*, 512–529.

Shadish, W. R., Ragsdale, K., Glaser, R. R., & Montgomery, L. M. (1995). The efficacy and effectiveness of marital and family therapy: A perspective from meta-analysis. *Journal of Marital and Family Therapy, 21*, 345–360.

Shadish, W. R., & Sweeney, R. B. (1991). Mediators and moderators in meta-analysis: There's a reason we don't let dodo birds tell us which psychotherapies should have prizes. *Journal of Consulting & Clinical Psychology, 59*, 883–893.

Shapiro, D. A., Barkham, M., Rees, A., Hardy, G., Reynolds, S., & Startup, M. (1994). Effects of treatment duration and severity of depression on the effectiveness of cognitive behavioral and psychodynamic-interpersonal psychotherapy. *Journal of Consulting and Clinical Psychology, 62*, 522–534.

Shapiro, D. A., & Shapiro, D. (1982). Meta-analysis of comparative therapy outcome studies: A replication and refinement. *Psychological Bulletin, 92*, 581–604.

Shapiro, D. A., & Shapiro, D. (1983). Comparative therapy outcome research: Methodological implications of meta-analysis. *Journal of Consulting and Clinical Psychology, 51*, 42–53.

Sharpe, D. (1997). Of apples and oranges, file drawers and garbage: Why validity issues in meta-analysis will not go away. *Clinical Psychology Review, 17*, 881–901.

Shepherd, M. (1984). What price psychotherapy? *British Medical Journal, 288*, 809–810.

Sherman, J. J. (1998). Effects of psychotherapeutic treatments for PTSD: A meta-analysis of controlled clinical trials. *Journal of Traumatic Stress, 11*, 413–435.

Shoham, V., & Rohrbaugh, M. J. (1999). Beyond allegiance to comparative outcome studies. *Clinical Psychology: Science and Practice, 6*, 120–123.

Shoham-Salomon, V., & Rosenthal, R. (1987). Paradoxical interventions: A meta-analysis. *Journal of Consulting and Clinical Psychology, 55*, 22–28.

Sloane, R. B., Staples, F. R., Cristol, A. H., Yorkston, N. J., & Whipple, K. (1975). *Short-term analytically oriented psychotherapy vs. behavior therapy.* Cambridge, MA: Harvard University Press.

Smith, M. L., & Glass, G. V. (1977). Meta-analysis of psychotherapy outcome studies. *American Psychologist, 32*, 752–760.

Smith, M. L., Glass, G. V., & Miller, T. I. (1980). *The benefits of psychotherapy.* Baltimore, MD: Johns Hopkins University Press.

Speer, D. C., & Newman, F. L. (1996). Mental health services outcome evaluation. *Clinical Psychology: Science and Practice, 3*, 105–129.

Stanton, M. D., & Shadish, W. R. (1997). Outcome, attrition, and family-couples treatment for drug abuse: A meta-analysis and review of the controlled, comparative studies. *Psychological Bulletin, 122*, 170–191.

Stein, D. M. (1980). *The comparative effectiveness of paraprofessional therapists.* M. J. Lambert (Chair). Society for Psychotherapy Research. Pacific Grove, CA.

Stein, D. M. & Lambert, M. J. (1984). On the relationship between therapist experience and psychotherapy outcome. *Clinical Psychology Review, 4*, 1–16.

Stein, D. M., & Lambert, M. J. (1995). Graduate training in psychotherapy: Are therapy outcomes enhanced? *Journal of Consulting and Clinical Psychology, 63*, 182–196.

Steinbrueck, S. M., Maxwell, S. E., & Howard, G. S. (1983). A meta-analysis of psychotherapy and drug therapy in the treatment of unipolar depression with adults. *Journal of Consulting and Clinical Psychology, 51*, 856–863.

Stiles, W. B., Shapiro, D. A., & Elliott, R. K. (1986). "Are all psychotherapies equivalent?" *American Psychologist, 41*, 165–180.

Strupp, H. H. (1980a). Success and failure in time-limited psychotherapy: A systematic comparison of two cases—comparison 1. *Archives of General Psychiatry, 37*, 595–603.

Strupp, H. H. (1980b). Success and failure in time-limited psychotherapy: A systematic comparison of two cases—comparison 2. *Archives of General Psychiatry, 37*, 708–716.

Strupp, H. H. (1980c). Success and failure in time-limited psychotherapy: A systematic comparison of two cases—comparison 3. *Archives of General Psychiatry, 37*, 947–954.

Strupp, H. H. (1980d). Success and failure in time-limited psychotherapy: With special reference to the performance of a lay counselor. *Archives of General Psychiatry, 37*, 831–841.

Stuart, S., & Bowers, W. A. (1995). Cognitive therapy with inpatients: Review and meta-analysis. *Journal of Cognitive Psychotherapy, 9*, 85–92.

Svartberg, M., & Stiles, T. C. (1991). Comparative effects of short-term psychodynamic psychotherapy: A meta-analysis. *Journal of Consulting and Clinical Psychology, 59*, 704–714.

Tang, T. Z., & DeRubeis, R. J. (1999). Sudden gains and critical sessions in cognitive-behavioral therapy for depression. *Journal of Consulting and Clinical Psychology, 67*, 894–904.

Taylor, S. (1996). Meta-analysis of cognitive-behavioral treatment for social phobia. *Journal of Behavior Therapy and Experimental Psychiatry, 27*, 1–9.

Telch, M. J., Lucas, J. A., Schmidt, N. B., Hanna, H. H., Jaimez, T. L., & Lucas, R. A. (1993). Group cognitive-behavioral treatments of panic disorder. *Behavior Research and Therapy, 31*, 279–287.

Thase, M. E., Greenhouse, J. B., Frank, E., Reynolds, C. F. I., Pilkonis, P. A., Hurley, K., Grochocinski, V., & Kupfer, D. J. (1997). Treatment of major depression with psychotherapy or psychotherapy-pharmacotherapy combinations. *Archives of General Psychiatry, 54*, 1009–1015.

Thompson, M. G., Thompson, L., & Gallagher-Thompson, D. (1995). Linear and nonlinear changes in mood between psychotherapy sessions: Implications for treatment outcome and relapse risk. *Psychotherapy Research, 5*, 327–336.

Tichenor, V., & Hill, C. E. (1989). A comparison of six measures of working alliance. *Psychotherapy, 26*, 195–199.

Tillitski, C. J. (1990). A meta-analysis of estimated effect sizes for group versus individual versus control treatments. *International Journal of Group Psychotherapy, 40*, 215–224.

Tonigan, J. S., Toscova, R., & Miller, W. R. (1995). Meta-analysis of the literature on Alcoholics Anonymous: Sample and study characteristics moderate findings. *Journal of Studies on Alcohol, 57*, 65–72.

Trull, T. J., Nietzel, M. T., & Main, A. (1988). The use of meta-analysis to assess the clinical significance of behavior therapy for agoraphobia. *Behavior Therapy, 19*, 527–538.

Tuschen-Caffier, B., Pook, M., & Frank, M. (2001). Evaluation of manual-based cognitive-behavioral therapy for bulimia nervosa in a service setting. *Behavior Research and Therapy, 39*, 299–308.

van Balkom, A.J.L.M., Bakker, A., Spinhoven, P., Blaauw, B.M.J.W., Smeenk, S., & Ruesink, B. (1997). A meta-analysis of the treatment of panic disorder with or without agoraphobia: A comparison of psychopharmacological, cognitive-behavioral, and combination treatments. *Journal of Nervous & Mental Disease, 185*, 510–516.

van Balkom, A.J.L.M., van Oppen, P., Vermeulen, A.W.A., & van Dyck, R. (1994). A meta-analysis on the treatment of obsessive compulsive disorder: A comparison of antidepressants, behavior, and cognitive therapy. *Clinical Psychology Review, 14*, 359–381.

Viswesvaran, C., & Schmidt, F. L. (1992). A meta-analytic comparison of the effectiveness of smoking cessation methods. *Journal of Applied Psychology, 77*, 554–561.

Wade, W. A., Treat, T. A., & Stuart, G. L. (1998). Transporting an empirically supported treatment for panic disorder to a service clinic setting: A benchmarking strategy. *Journal of Consulting and Clinical Psychology, 66*, 231–239.

Walters, G. D. (2000). Behavioral self-control training for problem drinkers: A meta-analysis of randomized control studies. *Behavior Therapy, 31*, 135–149.

Wampold, B. E. (2001). *The great psychotherapy debate: Models, methods, and findings.* Mahwah, NJ: Erlbaum.

Wampold, B. E., Mondin, G. W., Moody, M., Stich, F., Benson, K., & Ahn, H. (1997). A meta-analysis of outcome studies comparing bona fide psychotherapies: Empiricially, "all must have prizes." *Psychological Bulletin, 122*, 203–215.

Weinberger, J. (1995). Common factors aren't so common: The common factors dilemma. *Clinical Psychology: Science and Practice, 2*, 45–69.

Weisz, J. R., Weiss, B., Alicke, M. D., & Klots, M. L. (1987). Effectiveness of psychotherapy with children and adolescents: A meta-analysis for clinicians. *Journal of Consulting and Clinical Psychology, 55*, 542–549.

Weisz, J. R., Weiss, B., & Donenberg, G. R. (1992). The lab versus the clinic: Effects of child and adolescent psychotherapy. *American Psychologist, 47*, 1578–1585.

Whittal, M. L., Agras, W. S., & Gould, R. A. (1999). Bulimia Nervosa: A meta-analysis of psychosocial and pharmacological treatments. *Behavior Therapy, 30,* 117–135.

Wierzbicki, M., & Pekarik, G. (1993). A meta-analysis of psychotherapy dropout. *Professional Psychology: Research and Practice, 24,* 190–195.

Wilkins, W. (1984). Psychotherapy: The powerful placebo. *Journal of Consulting and Clinical Psychology, 52,* 570–573.

Wilson, G. T. (1998). Manual-based treatment and clinical practice. *Clinical Psychology: Science and Practice, 5,* 363–375.

Wolf, W. M. (1978). Social validity: The case for subjective measurement or how applied behavior analysis is finding its heart. *Journal of Applied Behavior Analysis, 11,* 203–214.

CHAPTER 6

THE INFLUENCE OF CLIENT VARIABLES ON PSYCHOTHERAPY

JOHN F. CLARKIN
New York Hospital, Cornell Medical Center
KENNETH N. LEVY
City University of New York

INTRODUCTION

Controversy about the effectiveness of psychotherapy has a long history. In 1952, British experimental psychologist, Hans Eysenck, caused a furor when he proclaimed that the application of psychotherapy was no more beneficial than the absence of treatment. In his report, Eysenck (1952) summarized the results of 24 reports of psychoanalytic and eclectic psychotherapies with more than 7,000 neurotic clients treated in naturalistic settings compared with two control groups. Eysenck found that the more intensive the therapy, the worse the results. In fact, Eysenck's data suggested that clients in psychoanalytic treatment had significantly worse cure rates than clients who received no treatment.

It has been more than 40 years since Eysenck rocked the treatment community with his claims that psychotherapy did not work. Despite the use of seriously flawed research methodology and a polemic tone, Eysenck's article was extremely important to the field and challenged clinical psychologists to pay more systematic attention to the results of their efforts and has spurred a great deal of empirical research.

Thanks in large part to researchers' responses to Eysenck's charge, we now know, generally speaking, that psychotherapy does indeed help people (Lambert, Shapiro, & Bergin, 1986; Smith, Glass, & Miller, 1980; Chapter 5 in this volume). Numerous studies and subsequent meta-analyses have demonstrated that any number of specific psychotherapeutic approaches, either alone or, in some cases, in combination with pharmacological approaches, are more effective than credible alternative psychological interventions containing nonspecific factors serving as "psychological placebos" (Barlow, 1996).

Contemporary researchers increasingly agree that psychotherapy works; nevertheless, psychotherapy research is at a critical period. A confluence of pressures both inside (e.g., evidence-supported treatment movement) and outside the profession (e.g., practice guidelines, managed care, legislation, National Alliance for the Mentally Ill) make it incumbent upon clinical psychologists to become better informed about the usefulness of psychotherapy. There has been a shift toward focusing research efforts on more precise questions, such as: Given a client's diagnosis, which treatment is recommended? What treatments have shown efficacy in empirical trials? Does the therapy produce results beyond symptom change? Do the changes achieved during the course of treatment endure with time? How does length of treatment affect the nature of long-term outcome? Which treatments that show efficacy in clinical trials have demonstrated similar effectiveness in local treatment settings?

The issue of client variables is an abstract way of stating the obvious: no two clients begin psychotherapy in the same condition. Every client is unique in terms of range and severity of problems, developmental history and achievements, interpersonal skills, intellectual acumen, state of pain, and desire for change. Many characteristics of the client may potentially influence the therapeutic venture. At the same time, the clients[1] behavior in therapy will be influenced by the characteristics and behavior of the individual therapist, for the therapeutic process is basically an interpersonal phenomenon. With a deceptively simple wisdom, Jerome Frank (1973) pointed out long ago that psychotherapy is an encounter between a demoralized client and a therapist whose goal is to energize the other. These straightforward truths lead us to the more refined questions: Which client and therapist characteristics interact most saliently and forcefully to produce symptom decline? Which of these interactions lead to improved social and work adjustment?

Comparative outcome studies of psychotherapy are costly and time consuming, and for the most part have not yielded clear evidence of the superiority of specific psychotherapies for specific disorders. Recent psychotherapy research has focused on the client's "diagnosis" and the techniques of therapy while ignoring the idiosyncratic aspects of the client that are even more salient in predicting change and guiding treatment decisions. However, large-scale studies comparing different forms of treatment for different disorders have revealed few differences in outcome based on technique. For example, recent examinations of psychotherapy outcome and process in the Treatment of Depression Collaborative Research Program (TDCRP) suggested that outcome is better predicted by client characteristics than by the effects of particular kinds of interventions (Ablon & Jones, 1999; Blatt, Quinlan, Pilkonis, & Shea, 1995; Zuroff et al., 2000). Reviewers (Bergin & Lambert, 1979; Frank, 1979) have suggested that the largest proportion of variance in therapy outcome is accounted for by the personal characteristics and qualities of the client. As much as 40% of client improvement in psychotherapy can be attributed to client variables and extratherapeutic influences (Lambert, 1992). These findings suggest that the study of client variables may have much to offer for our understanding of psychotherapy's effectiveness. Identification of premorbid clinical and personality characteristics predictive of outcome might help clinicians guide treatment choices and revise treatment methods based on the needs of different types of clients.

This chapter highlights the client attributes and characteristics that profoundly shape and influence therapeutic process and outcome. We review a number of relevant conceptual and methodological issues related to the influence of client variables on therapy selection, processes, and outcome. This chapter builds on the previous editions of this chapter (Garfield, 1994; Garfield & Bergin, 1986). Garfield's (1994) last review emphasized client variables in isolation, whereas we think the field is currently emphasizing client variables in interaction with both therapist and treatment variables. We emphasize client variables as mediators and moderators of psychotherapy process and outcome. Throughout this review we emphasize the interaction of client characteristics and the growing relationship with the therapist. This interaction is such that any research focused exclusively on client variables is (falsely, in our minds) assuming that the therapist reaction does not influence the client variable in question. As research in this area becomes more sophisticated, the interaction of client characteristics with therapist response will likely become the focus of clinical concern and research interest.

The previous chapter emphasized specific client variables of social class, personality, diagnosis, age, sex, intelligence, and length of disturbance. In this chapter, we review more current constructs relating to the client such as interpersonal relatedness and preparation for change. Since the previous edition (Garfield, 1994), psychotherapy research data by client diagnosis has grown considerably. Although this orientation has its strengths and weaknesses, the accumulation of data organized and investigated by client diagnosis and related treatment is so prominent in the field that it necessitates some review in this chapter. Garfield (1994) mentioned the influence of socioeconomic variables and ethnicity, but there has been a major accumulation of data on the psychotherapeutic influence on clients, with a diversity of ethnicity and socioeconomic levels, and we emphasize findings in this area.

The Range of Client Characteristics

The number of client variables with potential for informing the process and outcome of psychotherapy is virtually limitless. Everything from genome and brain chemistry to demographic variables and environmental conditions to personality traits, to problem area/diagnosis is arguably related to psychotherapy and its ingredients. Client characteristics can be external to the individual (e.g., social support) or intimate aspects of the individual (e.g., intelligence). Client characteristics can be invariant (e.g., gender, ethnic membership), relatively stable (e.g., SES, personality traits), or quite variable (e.g., motivation for change). Client variables can be psychological in nature such as personality traits, or they can be part of the individuals' biological system (e.g., state of REM sleep characteristics). Over the years the type of client variables investigated has apparently shifted from stable demographic variables to a broader range of variables, with increasing emphasis on the interaction of client variables with treatment variables as provided by the therapist.

The presence of an almost limitless number of client variables forces the reviewer (and clinician) to select those variables that have proven most relevant to essential aspects of the therapy enterprise. With the advantage of a growing body of information on the key processes and outcome of psychotherapy research, we have elected to focus on the specific client variables that relate to the matching of client and psychotherapy, process of psychotherapy, and therapy outcome.

Not only are there different types and sources of client variables, but these variables function in different ways in relation to psychotherapy process and outcome. Client variables can be conceptualized as static predictors of response to treatment. Thus, the clients' gender or ethnic membership can be examined as a predictor of treatment process or outcome. A client variable can be seen as a moderator or mediator of change (Holmbeck, 1998). A moderator variable affects the relationship between the predictor variable and a dependent variable, and the value or level of the moderator variable makes a differential impact on the dependent variable. In contrast, a mediator variable is a mechanism through which the independent variable affects the dependent variable. Thus, the independent variable influences the mediator, which, in turn, influences the outcome or dependent variable. Finally, a client variable can be conceptualized as a prescriptive variable, that is, one that prescribes a certain treatment as opposed to competing treatments. For example, in the evidence-based treatment movement, the client variable of diagnosis is seen as a prescription for certain psychotherapies.

Characteristics of Those Who Seek Therapy

Those Who Seek Therapy

Who is the psychotherapy client? What are the characteristics of individuals who request or receive psychotherapy in contrast to those who do not? Our examination of client variables and psychotherapy matching, process, and outcome should not be limited to the client variables describing only those who undergo psychotherapy. However, knowledge of those who obtain psychotherapy does help define the limits of the current research information on client variables and psychotherapy.

In the general population, those who report emotional distress (Veroff, Kulka, & Douvan, 1981; Ware, Manning, Duan, Wells, & Newhouse, 1984), exhibit psychological symptoms (Boyd, 1986; Yokopenic, Clark, & Aneshensel, 1983), and consider their mental health to be poor (Leaf et al., 1985) are most inclined to seek professional mental health care. Women are more likely than men to seek both informal support and professional help (Butler, Giordano, & Neren, 1985; Horwitz, 1977; Kessler, Brown, & Broman, 1981). Age is also related to help-seeking behavior. The elderly are more reluctant than younger individuals to seek help from mental health professionals, and they rely more readily on general medical practitioners and the clergy (Leaf, Bruce, Tischler, & Holzer, 1987; Waxman, Carner, & Klein, 1984). Those elderly who sought assistance, as compared to those who did not, had poor psychological well-being, more physical health problems, a higher level of stressful events, and greater deficits in social support (Phillips & Murrell, 1994).

Stress is related to seeking the services of mental health professionals, though in a somewhat complicated manner. Not everyone who experiences stress seeks mental health services. Those seeking assistance may experience the impact of the stressors more intensely (Goodman, Sewell, & Jampol, 1984) and are less likely to have strong social support from friends and relatives (Birkel & Reappucci, 1983).

Howard and colleagues (Howard et al., 1996) have summarized patterns of mental health service utilization using data from the Epidemiologic Catchment Area (ECA) survey and the National Comorbidity Survey (NCS). Both studies indicated that about 30% of adults will experience a diagnosable mental condition in any given year, and the majority of these individuals (from 56 to 60%) will have more than one disorder. What is striking is that in the ECA survey, more than 70% of those with a mental disorder received no services, and only 13% obtained treatment from a mental health professional. This would indicate that the vast majority of data we have on clients and its relationship to psychotherapy is based on information from a very small percentage of the individuals who actually need intervention.

Early Termination

Early termination or attrition from psychotherapy is an issue that has important clinical implications. From the clinician's point of view, those individuals who drop out from treatment prematurely are not taking advantage of an important resource in their lives. If the early termination can be predicted, the initiation and course of therapy can potentially be modified in order to motivate the client for concentrated work toward change and a reduction in premature dropout.

Most studies have suggested that age is not important in psychotherapy retention (DuBrin & Zastowny, 1988; Gunderson et al., 1989; Sledge, Moras, Hartley, & Levine, 1990). In contrast, several other variables seem to be important. In a multisite study of panic disorder, the client variables of lower household income and negative attitudes toward the treatment offered were independently associated with attrition (Grilo et al., 1998). Similarly, it was found that for clients suffering from obsessive-compulsive disorder, strong incongruent treatment expectations predicted attrition (Hansen, Hoogduin, Schaap, & de Haan, 1992).

Organista, Munoz, and Gonzalez (1994) and Miranda, Azocar, Organista, Dwyer, and Arean (under review) evaluated the benefits of a group cognitive/behavioral treatment for depression in clients with low income and the majority of whom were from Latino or African-American minority groups. The dropout rate was higher in this low-income minority population (40 to 60%) than in the NIMH multisite depression study (Elkin, Shea et al., 1989). Importantly, Miranda and colleagues found that adding case management services significantly reduced the dropout rate. Significant improvement in depression was reported in both studies, but on average the clients remained in the depressed range even with treatment according to their self-report questionnaire information.

Clients with a personality disorder diagnosis have been found to be at high risk for premature dropout, whether in inpatient settings (Chiesa, Drahorad, & Longo, 2000) or outpatient treatment settings (Gunderson et al., 1989; Shea et al., 1990; Skodol, Buckley, & Charles, 1983). The dropout rates vary from 42% (Gunderson et al., 1989) to 67% (Skodol, Buckley, & Charles, 1983). Given the dropout rate, the question becomes one of understanding the operative variables. Clarkin and colleagues (Smith, Koenigsberg, Yeomans, Clarkin, & Selzer, 1995; Yeomans et al., 1994) analyzed factors associated with attrition from psychotherapy for clients diagnosed with borderline personality disorder. They found that younger clients and those with high initial hostility were more likely to withdraw early from treatment. In a subset of clients, those who showed a predominance of narcissistic themes in their responses on the Rorschach test at the beginning of treatment were more likely to drop out of treatment, whereas clients who continued in treatment showed a predominance of rapprochement themes (Horner & Diamond, 1996). Hilsenroth, Handler, Toman, and Padawer (1995), using the Minnestoa Multiphasic Personality Inventory-2 and the Rorschach, examined 97 clients who prematurely terminated psychotherapy and 81 clients who completed at least six months of treatment. They found that Rorschach variables of interpersonal relatedness, psychological resources, and level of psychopathology significantly predicted premature termination. Beckham (1989) found that an initial negative impression of the therapist by the client predicted early dropout from psychotherapy.

There is a sharp contrast between the number of clients who terminate therapy after one session and the attention clinicians give to recommending no treatment for a particular client. With rare exceptions (see Frances & Clarkin, 1981) there has been no research attention given a recommendation of no treatment by the professional assessor/therapist following the assessment of clients as the optimal course of action.[2] This discrepancy implies that clinicians almost uniformly recommend treatments to those who seek help, while clients often decide after evaluation that pursuing treatment is not needed or indicated.

Summary

The epidemiological data suggest that only a minority of individuals who need mental health services as indicated by their diagnostic status actually seek assistance from the professionally trained practitioners. If clinicians wish to seek out the many who need psychological assistance but do not seek it, they must make contact with those professionals in the community who come into contact with troubled individuals, for example, physicians, religious leaders, school systems, and divorce lawyers.

If the individual does seek assistance, he or she is almost automatically placed in therapy, with little clinician attention to those who might handle their difficulties on their own or with watchful followup. However, many clients, after only one or a few contacts with the mental health system, decide that they can do without assistance. The development of a sharper distinction between those who do leave early and those who follow through on attempts to seek out professional assistance deserves more investigative attention. Among those variables that appear most important are negative attitudes toward the therapist or psychosocial treatment in general. In addition, there is an important clinical need to attend to client reasons for prematurely foregoing professional assistance from which they could potentially derive some important benefits. Given the large number of clients who leave treatment prematurely, study in this area should be given high priority.

Process and Outcome

Problem Area/Diagnosis and Severity

From a common-sense point of view, all psychotherapy should be targeted to the nature of the client's difficulty, problem, and psychopathology (depending on one's conceptualization of the problem area). There should be an inherent match between the clients' problem area and the therapeutic interventions that are constructed to alleviate or change that difficulty, problem area, and/or diagnostic entity.

Diagnosis as the Prescriptive Client Variable

Following the articulation of DSM-III in 1980 (APA, 1980), this diagnostic template and its successors have taken center stage in the description of pathology for reimbursement purposes, as well as in planning and guiding psychotherapy research as funded by the National Institute of Mental Health (NIMH). Many cogent arguments can be made for the use of alternatives to a categorical diagnosis, such as dimensional scores on symptom and trait measures. However, the DSM system has guided therapy research, and thus we are accumulating a body of information based on the client variable of diagnosis as defined by the four successive diagnostic manuals.

DSM-IV (APA, 1994) defines a mental disorder as a behavioral or psychological syndrome or pattern that an individual experiences or exhibits as clinically significant because it is associated with distress (e.g., a symptom) or disability (e.g., impairment in one or more areas of functioning) or with an increased risk of suffering death, pain, disability, or loss of function. In order to facilitate a systematic evaluation of the client with reference to mental disorders, general medical conditions, psychosocial and environmental problems, and level of functioning, the DSM-IV is a multiaxial system: Axis I—symptom disorders, Axis II—personality disorders, Axis III—general medical conditions, Axis IV—psychosocial and environment problems, and Axis V—a rating of the client's overall level of functioning. In actual practice, most psychotherapy research is focused on the Axis I condition, with little research on the Axis II personality disorders. As described later in this chapter, Axis II (personality disorders), IV (psychosocial and environmental problems), and V (overall functioning, related to severity of the illness and impact on functioning) are often empirically related to process and outcome of therapy.

Much has been written about the advantages and disadvantages of the DSM diagnostic system. The DSM system has been criticized for its promotion of the medical model to the detriment of a biopsychosocial understanding of conditions and their treatments, for its way of defining a mental disorder, for the proliferation of diagnoses across editions, and for its self-proclaimed atheoretical stance (Nathan, 1998). The conscious meanings of behaviors that are not considered in the DSM criteria are actually most relevant to treatment planning and its execution (Wakefield, 1998).

The use of DSM-IV as a guide for psychotherapy outcome research is a mixed blessing. For diagnoses that are closely tied to behaviors, such as alcohol and substance abuse, the diagnosis is tantamount to a description of a problem that is a target for treatment. In contrast, for diagnoses such as depression, there are many routes to such a feeling state, and the behaviors that are related to it are often complex and idiosyncratic. From a research point of view, there are problems with selecting a diagnostically "homogeneous" sample and an appropriate comparison group in order to investigate the impact of a given intervention. Clients selected solely by the diagnostic system for a specific disorder are not truly "homogeneous" from many points of view. First of all, two clients may actually obtain the same diagnosis but have very few common symptoms since DSM-IV is polythetic in nature. Second, most clients have more than one diagnosable condition or disorder. To use a common clinical situation, two clients may exhibit enough criteria to meet the diagnosis for major depressive disorder, but one client also has one or more Axis II personality disorders and the second client has none. Finally, clients with the same diagnosis at best have the same symptoms on either Axis I or Axis II, but other client variables can be quite heterogeneous. For example, two clients may have exactly the same symptoms that qualify for a major depressive disorder but one is married with a successful career and the other is unmarried with a poor or absent work history.

Thus, the movement to publicize lists of single DSM diagnoses with empirically supported or validated treatments (Chambless et al., 1998) can be extremely oversimplified and potentially misleading. The lists provide a simplistic algorithm for matching a client with a single diagnosis to a treatment for that diagnosis. Such an approach totally ignores the clinical reality that no two clients with the same single diagnosis are truly alike, and these differences are often relevant to treatment planning. Nondiagnostic client variables are totally ignored in this simplistic approach.

We do not review here the extensive research on psychotherapy outcome by the client variable of DSM diagnosis, for this research is extensively covered by other authors in the following chapters in this *Handbook*. Rather, we provide a review of the salient client diagnoses and problem areas that are related to treatment outcome studies. There have been a number of reviews of client diagnoses as a characteristic or condition of the client which provides a target for particular types of treatments. The reviews of this literature are growing, including reviews for government and practitioners (e.g., Roth & Fonagy, 1996), the generation of treatment guidelines by researchers (Beutler, Clarkin, & Bongar, 2000), independent institutes such as the Cochrane Institute, guilds such as the American Psychiatric Association, and the recent excellent review by the British Psychological Society Centers for Outcomes Research and Effectiveness for the UK Department of Health (2001). The British review includes the Cochrane reviews in its purview and provides an up-to-date summary for client diagnoses and problem areas including depression, anxiety disorders, eating disorders, somatic complaints, personality disorders, and deliberate self-harm.

Nondiagnostic Client Variables Related to Specific Diagnoses

With the growing list of psychotherapies that have shown efficacy in the treatment of a specific diagnosis as compared to a no-treatment control, some attention has been given to the nondiagnostic client characteristics that are related to the process and outcome in these studies. This information is most abundant as related to depression and substance abuse.

For example, Whisman (1993) has reviewed the mediators and moderators of change in the cognitive treatment of depression. Certain key client variables related to the depressive condition have been found to be mediators of treatment response; that is, they mediate the influence of independent variables on the dependent variables in the treatment. The strongest support for mediation was found for attributional style and to a lesser extent for dysfunctional attitudes. There is also evidence that certain client characteristics have a moderating influence on cognitive treatments. Sociodemographic characteristics are typically related to outcome (Dobson, 1989; Jarrett, Eaves, Grannemann, & Rush, 1991), whereas intelligence is not (Haaga, DeRubeis, Stewart, & Beck, 1991). Client-learned resourcefulness was related to outcome in one study but not replicated in three other studies (Beckham, 1989; Jarrett, Giles, Guillon, & Rush, 1991; Kavanagh & Wilson, 1989). A positive outcome from CT was observed in those clients who exhibited a positive expectation of help (Gaston, Marmar, Gallagher, & Thompson, 1989), a strong commitment to treatment (Marmar, Gaston, Gallagher, & Thompson 1989), a strong endorsement of the cognitive conceptualization of depression, and a willingness to learn new coping strategies and complete homework assignments.

Thase et al. (1997) have taken the research on client variables to new levels by investigating how the sleep profiles of patients with recurrent major depressive disorder are influenced by interpersonal therapy. Those clients with abnormal sleep profiles had significantly poorer clinical outcomes than those with normal sleep profiles. In addition, 75% of those clients who did not respond to IPT manifested remission during subsequent pharmacotherapy.

Severity of Symptoms

Previous reviews of general outcome research have concluded that severity of symptoms is related to poor treatment response (Beckham, 1989; Beutler & Hamblin, 1986; Garfield, 1994; Hoberman, Lewinsohn, & Tilson, 1988; Lambert & Anderson, 1996; Luborsky, Crits-Christoph, Mintz, & Auerbach, 1988). For example, random regression models were used to examine the role of depression severity in the NIMH Treatment of Depression Collaborative Research Program (TDCRP) (Elkin et al., 1995). In this large *N*, multisite study, the initial severity of depression and the impairment in functioning significantly predicted differential treatment response. There were no differential treatment responses with the less severely ill clients, but among those who were more severely depressed and incapacitated, medication played a more significant role in combination with psychosocial treatment.

In a study of 117 depressed clients stratified for depression severity (Shapiro et al., 1994), clients were treated in either cognitive behavioral or psychodynamic interpersonal therapy for either 8 or 16 sessions. On most measures of outcome, both treatments were equally effective across the severity of depression levels. However, those with more severe depression improved substantially more with the 16- in contrast to the 8-session treatment duration.

Similarly, in the treatment of clients with addictions, those with less severe symptoms demonstrated the best treatment response (McLellan, Luborsky, Woody, Druley, & O'Brien, 1983). The six-month treatment outcome for 649 clients who were dependent on opiates, alcohol, and/or cocaine was examined across 22 treatment settings (McLellan et al., 1994). Greater substance use at followup, regardless of the abused substance, was predicted by a greater severity of the alcohol and drug use problem at admission to treatment. The severity of the problem, not the number of services, was the sole predictor of this outcome. In addition, better social adjustment outcome at followup was negatively related to more severe psychiatric problems, employment difficulties, and family problems at admission.

Functional Impairment

For conceptual clarity and assessment focus, it is important to distinguish between the severity of the symptoms, the major focus of Axis I diagnoses, and the functional impairment that either results from or preceded the symptoms and provides the context for the arousal of symptoms. Functional impairment is addressed in DSM-IV on the axis related to overall level of functioning. Two individuals can have a depression of minor severity or major severity, in the context of previous high-level functioning (productive work, satisfying interpersonal relations) or previous low-level functioning.

In general, level of functional impairment is negatively correlated with prognosis across disorders such as depression (Gitlin, Swendsen, Heller, & Hammen, 1995; Kocsis et al., 1988; Sotsky et al., 1991), bulimia nervosa (Fahy & Russell, 1993), obsessive compulsive disorder (Keijsers, Hoogduin, & Schaap, 1994) and chemical dependency (McLellan, Woody, Luborsky, O'Brien, & Druley, 1983). In the treatment of depressed individuals, the best predictor of response to interpersonal psychotherapy (IPT) was emotional health prior to the initiation of treatment (Rounsaville, Weissman, & Prusoff, 1981). Luborsky and colleagues (Luborsky, 1962; Luborsky et al., 1980) found a significant positive correlation between psychological health as rated on the Health-Sickness Rating Scale (HSRS) and treatment outcome. In a study of 59 clients treated for 12 weeks with brief focal psychodynamic therapy, clients who had shown the highest level of adaptive functioning before therapy demonstrated the most improvement (Free, Green, Grace, Chernus, & Whitman, 1985).

In yet another post-hoc analysis of client predictors of treatment outcome for the NIMH study of the treatment of depression, Sotsky et al. (1991) examined the treatment of 239 outpatients with major depressive disorder in a 16-week treatment. Six client characteristics predicted outcome across all treatments (interpersonal psychotherapy, cognitive behavioral therapy, medication and clinical management, or placebo and clinical management), and this included client dysfunction (social and cognitive), expectation of improvement, and three aspects of the symptoms (endogenous depression, double depression, and duration of current episode). In addition to these six client characteristics which predicted across the treatments, there were some significant client predictors of a good match with a particular treatment. These authors reported on four such significant matches. Low social dysfunction was a predictor of superior response to IPT. Low cognitive dysfunction predicted response to CBT and to imipramine. High work dysfunction predicted the response to imipramine, and finally, high depression severity and impairment of function predicted response to imipramine and to interpersonal psychotherapy. These findings suggest that the focus of the intervention relates to outcome (e.g., low social dysfunction responses to IPT, which focuses on social interactions) and that the severity of the condition (symptoms and functioning) calls for a combination of medication and psychotherapy.

Comorbidity

The pervasive use of DSM-III and its successors in psychotherapy research has fostered examination of the so-called comorbid conditions as they relate to the psychotherapy process and the outcome of a specific symptom-based disorder (see Kendall & Clarkin, 1992). With the distinction since DSM-III (APA, 1980) between symptom conditions (Axis I) and personality disorders (Axis II), an empirical literature has accumulated concerning the influence of the personality disorders in the treatment of symptom conditions.

Personality Disorder and Depression. Most studies of major depressive disorder that have included clients with comorbid personality disorders have found poorer outcomes associated with co-occurrence of any personality disorder (Burns & Nolen-Hoeksema, 1992; Diguer, Barber, & Luborsky, 1993; Fiorot, Boswell, & Murray, 1990; Greenberg, Craighead, Evans, & Craighead, 1995; Hardy et al., 1995; Shea et al., 1990; Thompson, Gallagher, & Czirr, 1988). The importance of personality disorder, as a client variable, is also suggested by the fact that studies show the reported frequency of personality disorder diagnosis within a depressed population ranges from 24% (Hardy et al., 1995) to 87% (Friedman, Aronoff, Clarkin, Corn, & Hurt, 1983).

Burns and Nolen-Hoeksema (1992) conducted a naturalistic trial of cognitive behavioral therapy for depressed clients and found that borderline personality disorder, in particular, was related to poorer outcome. The diagnosis of a personality disorder was related to treatment outcome in the TDCRP study (Shea et al., 1990). Seventy-four percent of the depressed sample in the TDCRP study had a comorbid personality disorder. Clients with personality disorders had significantly worse outcome in social functioning than clients without personality disorders, and they were more likely to have residual symptoms of depression at termination.

In a study of 25 clients with major depression treated with 16 sessions of supportive-expressive dynamic therapy, clients with personality disorders showed poorer outcome compared to those without personality disorders (Diguer, Barber, & Luborsky, 1993). Hardy et al. (1995), in a randomized controlled trial of 114 depressed outpatients seen in either brief psychodynamic interpersonal therapy (BPI) or cognitive behavioral therapy (CBT), found that the presence of a cluster C (anxious-fearful) personality disorder reduced the effectiveness of BPI, but not CBT. Finally, others (Fiorot, Boswell, & Murray, 1990; Thompson, Gallagher, & Czirr, 1988) have reported that treatment trials with depressed elderly outpatients using behavioral, dynamic, or eclectic therapies have poorer outcomes for clients with a comorbid personality disorder.

In a review of 27 different studies, McDermut & Zimmerman (1998) concluded that depressed individuals without a comorbid personality disorder responded differently to treatment than depressed individuals with a personality disorder, the latter being more likely to not recover and to remain more symptomatic after treatment. This difference between those symptomatic individuals with and without personality disorder has direct relevance to both the need for an initial assessment and treatment planning (Clarkin & Abrams, 1998). Clearly, the evidence to date suggests that personality disorder, particularly borderline personality disorder, is a prevalent and powerful client characteristic that moderates outcome in depressed individuals (Wells, Burnam, Rogers, Hays, & Camp, 1992). Individuals diagnosed with borderline personality disorder (BPD) or obsessive compulsive personality disorder (OCD) have relatively high levels of negative outcome (Mohr, 1995).

Personality Disorder as a Moderator of Outcome in Anxiety Disorders. In a sample of 13 outpatients with social phobia, Turner (1987) found that personality disorder diagnosis predicted differential outcome. Schizotypal, borderline, and avoidant personality disorders were related to poor outcome, whereas histrionic and dependent personality disorders were related to better outcome. Clients with dependent personality disorders specifically responded better when in-vivo exposure was controlled by the therapist. Studies of anxiety disorders with comorbid avoidant personality disorder have found conflicting results (Brown, Heimberg, & Juster, 1995; Chambless, Tran, & Glass, 1997; Turner, 1987). The presence of a personality disorder has been found to be an obstacle to the treatment of obsessive-compulsive disorder (AuBuchon & Malatesta, 1994; Cottraux, Messy, Marks, Mollard, & Bouvard, 1993; Jenike, 1990). AuBuchon and Malatesta (1994) found that obsessive-compulsive clients with comorbid personality disorders responded less well to comprehensive behavior therapy than those without personality disorders. Hermesh, Shahar, and Munitz (1987) found that all eight of their borderline clients failed to comply with behavioral or pharmacological treatments for OCD. Similarly, Jenike, Baer, Moinichiello, and Carey (1986) found that only 7% of clients with schizotypal personality disorder responded to behavioral treatment, compared to 90% of clients without.

Personality disorder and eating disorders. A number of studies suggest that a comorbid personality disorder also has deleterious effects on the treatment outcome of eating disorders. Rossiter, Agras, Telch, and Schneider (1993) found that eating-disordered patients with comorbid personality disorders have poor outcome in comparison to eating-disordered patients without personality disorders. Cooper and colleagues (Coker, Vize, Wade, & Cooper, 1993; Cooper, Coker, & Fleming, 1994) found that comorbid personality disorder resulted in poor outcome in the treatment of eating disorders. Wilfley et al. (2000), in a randomized controlled study (group cognitive behavioral therapy versus group interpersonal psychotherapy) of 162 outpatients, found that the presence of any Axis II psychopathology did not predict treatment outcome. However, the presence of Cluster B personality disorders did predict poor outcome at one year following treatment. The association found between Axis II disorders and baseline eating-related psychopathology also suggested that this symptomatology may be more severe when occurring in the context of a personality disorder. This may be because individuals with personality disorders are often likely to have experiences (e.g., affective instability, social isolation) that trigger binge episodes. This line of reasoning would suggest that binge eating disorder clients with Cluster B personality disorders may require a specialized treatment that addresses cognitive and affective instability.

History of sexual abuse. Gleaves and Eberenz (1993), in a review of 464 women, assessed the history of sexual abuse in bulimic women who failed to engage in CBT treatment. Approximately 71% of the women who failed to respond to treatment reported a history of sexual abuse. The researchers propose that treatment should address both the eating disorder and the posttraumatic condition, if symptoms and histories of the trauma arise during treatment sessions in individuals failing to respond to CBT. Therefore, although CBT has consistently and convincingly been found to be effective in treating bulimia nervosa, certain client characteristics limit effective outcome.

Summary

Use of the DSM diagnostic system to guide psychotherapy research has had both negative and positive effects. The emphasis on client diagnosis has resulted in the lack of attention to other salient client variables (Pilkonis & Krause, 1999). In contrast, a benefit of the DSM multiaxial system is the inclusion of separate diagnostic axes, including one for personality disorders, which have resulted in the accumulation of data on the client variable of personality/personality disorder in the treatment of common symptom disorders. This research has demonstrated across a number of symptom disorders that the treatment effects for the symptoms are attenuated for those clients with co-occurring personality pathology in contrast to those without. This is an important finding that should influence treatment planning and future research efforts aimed at discovering more effective ways of treating those with concurrent symptoms and personality difficulties. At the very least, therapists should assess for both symptoms and personality disorders in their clinical evaluations. When an Axis II personality disorder is present, they should plan treatment for more modest gains, anticipate and address potential early patient dropout, and plan for disruptions in the treatment adherence and alliance. Many of the treatment manuals for symptom disorders such as anxiety and depression give insufficient information on approaches to patients with personality disorders who will present unique and difficult challenges in the treatment.

Sociodemographic Variables

Age

The usual approach to the influence of age on psychotherapy is to assess the relationship in a treated group of adults with a limited age range. It would appear that age is not important in either therapy retention (Berrigan & Garfield, 1981; Dubrin & Zastowny, 1988; Gunderson et al., 1989; Sledge, Moras, Hartley, & Levine, 1990) or treatment outcome (MacDonald, 1994; Smith, Glass, & Miller, 1980). One possible exception is the finding that younger age is associated with poor retention and outcome in the treatment of substance abuse disorders (Agosti, Nunes, & Ocepeck-Welikson, 1996). This latter finding may be due to the relationship between age and the natural course of substance abuse.

A different approach that is currently receiving more attention is to regard the client's age as an important variable in gauging the focus and nature of intervention. This approach is based on the notion that age is related to the psychological and biological nature of the organism, and thus to the expression or manifestation of the disorder in question. For example, clinicians intervene with children and adolescents in treatments that are structured differently from those for adults.

A meta-analysis of 17 empirical studies of the treatment of depressed elderly (Scogin & McElreath, 1994) indicated that psychosocial interventions are quite effective, with a mean effect size of treatment versus no treatment or placebo of .78. This figure compares well with the mean effect size for psychosocial treatments for depression in nonelderly adults. Interpersonal psychotherapy, in particular, has been shown to be effective with the elderly in both the acute and maintenance treatment of depression in the elderly (Frank et al., 1993; Reynolds, Frank, Houck, & Mazumdar, 1997; Reynolds et al., 1999). Thompson, Gallagher, and Breckenridge (1987) have provided empirical support for the effectiveness of cognitive behavioral therapies delivered in the individual format for depression in older adults. In comparing cognitive, behavioral, and brief psychodynamic treatments for depression in ambulatory elderly, this research group found comparable remission rates across treatment types and no difference in stability of effects for over two years (Gallagher-Thompson, Hanley-Peterson, & Thompson, 1990; Thompson, Gallagher, & Breckenridge, 1987). Although the majority of clients achieved remission, a subgroup of clients who did not respond to initial treatment, remained depressed at followup one and two years later despite continued treatment.

Cognitive behavioral treatments are also effective when delivered in a group format (Arean et al., 1993; Beutler et al., 1987; Steuer et al., 1984). Kemp, Corgiat, and Gill (1992) found that cognitive behavioral group therapy was effective in reducing depressive symptoms in older clients who had the presence or absence of disabling chronic illness. In contrast, however, those with disabling physical illnesses did not show continued decline in depression following group treatment, while those without disabling illnesses continued to improve.

Socioeconomic Status

In general, demographic characteristics and socioeconomic status (SES) have been found to be related to continuation in psychotherapy. Early studies (Berrigan & Garfield, 1981; Dodd, 1970; Fiester & Rudestam, 1975) found a positive relationship between higher social status and length of stay in treatment. For example, Armbuster and Fallon (1994) found lower SES to be associated with premature termination among general psychotherapy clients. In the treatment of substance use, a shorter length of stay was associated with lower educational background (Agosti, Nunes, & Ocepeck-Welikson, 1996; Epstein, McCrady, Miller, & Steinberg, 1994; McCusker, 1995). These results are not always consistent, however, and one can also find other studies in which SES was not related to terminating or remaining in treatment (e.g., MacDonald, 1994; Sledge, Moras, Hartley, & Levine, 1990).

Gender

Prior reviews make the generalization that there is usually no gender difference in premature termination from therapy or any gender effects in psychotherapy outcomes (Garfield, 1994; Greenspan & Kulish, 1985; Petry, Tennen, & Affleck, 2000; Sledge, Moras, Hartley, & Levine, 1990). In contrast to gender effects in general, gender might make a substantial difference with disorders that have a prevalence rate that is related to gender, such as depression. The prevalence of depression is about twofold in females in comparison to males (Kessler, McGonagle, Swartz, Blazer, & Nelson, 1993; Weissman & Klerman, 1977). In addition, the cause of depression may be different in females in contrast to males (Cyranowski, Frank, Young, & Shear, 2000; Nolen-Hoeksema, 1987). Despite the differences in prevalence and causes, with few exceptions, sex has been unrelated to outcome in the treatment of depression (e.g., Hollon et al., 1992; Paykel et al., 1999; Sotsky et al., 1991). Unfortunately, studies are rarely designed specifically to study this issue, and occasionally there is an exception to the lack of difference due to gender. For example, Thase, Frank, Kornstein, and Yonkers (2000) found across studies that women who were manifesting more severe depression did better in interpersonal therapy than they did in cognitive therapy. This result suggests that the search for gender differences in interaction with treatment is worth pursuing in future research.

There has been some attention to same-sex pairing between client and therapist, with some finding same-gender pairing providing greater client satisfaction and retention in treatment (Fujino, Okazaki, & Young, 1994) and others showing preference for opposite-gender matches (Willer & Miller, 1978). One large study (Flaskerud & Liu, 1991) found that client-therapist gender similarity had little effect on outcome. These inconsistent results suggest that the more sophisticated methods may reveal some advantage to matching and that further testing for matching within specific problem areas may reveal optimal matches.

Race

Several early studies found that ethnic minority clients attended significantly fewer sessions than Caucasian clients (Greenspan & Kulish, 1985; Salzman, Shader, Scott, & Binstock, 1970; Sue, McKinney, Allen, & Hall, 1974). However, other studies found no relation between race and premature termination (Sledge, Moras, Hartley, & Levine, 1990). Well-controlled research by Jones (1978; Jones & Zoppel, 1982) found that race-related client and therapist variables (e.g., race matching between therapist and client) were not decisive in therapy outcome. African-American and Caucasian clients benefited equally, and no differences were found between racially matched or mismatched therapist-client dyads. Lerner (1972) investigated the effects of treatment on severely disturbed and predominantly lower class African-American and Caucasian clients seen by Caucasian therapists. The vast majority of clients improved, and there was no evidence of racial differences in outcome. In addition, she found that low-income clients, regardless of race, showed more improvement in therapy when seen by therapists holding egalitarian attitudes toward low-income people in general than did clients not seen by therapist holding such attitudes. Ross (1983), using the same measure of therapist attitude, found that low-income African-American clients remained in therapy longer when seen by therapists with egalitarian attitudes. Within such a context, as the client communicates both verbally and nonverbally, the therapist allows himself or herself to empathize with the client's emotional position and develop an involving intersubjective perspective with the client. Thus, Lerner (1972) and Ross's (1983) research on the impact of therapist attitudes on treatment outcome found that egalitarian atmosphere is an important variable in work with lower-class clients. The studies by Lerner and Jones represent some of the most detailed and rigorous treatment studies involving African-American clients.

Occasionally, race-based differences are found and suggest the need for continued research. For example, Rosenheck, Fontana, and Cottrol (1995) found that African-American veterans with post-traumatic stress disorder were more likely to drop out of therapy and were less likely to benefit from treatment than their Caucasian counterparts. Unfortunately, these researchers did not study therapist ethnic group identification.

Various writers note how therapists talk of "properly managing" the initial sessions with clients of color (Griffith & Jones, 1979; Jenkins, 1997; Sue & Zane, 1987). Griffith and Jones (1979) have suggested that effective work with African-American clients, especially when the therapist is Caucasian, involves working quickly to establish a therapeutic alliance. Jenkins (1997) points out that it is important to emphasize the quality of the therapist-client relationship as fundamental to positive change, especially when working with ethnic minority clients. Sue and Zane (1987) note the importance of the therapist's establishing his or her "credibility" early on with the ethnic minority client. Gibbs (1985) suggests that African-American clients, mindful of racism, initially tend to take an interpersonal orientation in the therapy situation. That is, they are particularly sensitive to the process going on between themselves and their therapists. Sue and Zane (1987) contend that ethnic-minority clients come to believe in the credibility of therapists through two factors: ascribed and achieved status. Ascribed status is the position or role that one is assigned by others, usually based on factors such as age, expertise, and sex. Achieved credibility refers more directly to therapists' skills. Through the actions of therapists, clients come to have faith, trust, confidence, or hope. Unfortunately, the clinical wisdom offered for maximizing treatment benefits is seldom studied and remains largely untested.

In addition to the questions relating to the race/cultural background of therapist and patient, there are potential research questions concerning the relationship between race and the nature, features, expression of the problem area, or diagnostic issues faced by the client. For example, the presence of eating disorders in Caucasian and African-American women has been found to manifest a different pattern of pathology (Pike,

Dohm, Stiegel-Moore, Wilfley, & Fairburn, 2001). In both groups, eating disorders are associated with decrements in functioning, but the two groups differ on aspects of the eating disorder, including binge frequency, restraint, treatment–seeking behavior, and personal concerns about eating, body weight, and shape. Although these differences suggest that differential actions by therapists might result in different outcomes, there is, as yet, no evidence that outcomes vary because of these differences.

Summary

The influence of client demographic variables on outcome is mixed and inconsistent, possibly for many reasons. Attitudes toward age, gender, and race change with the times, and both patients and therapists will be influenced by the cultural atmosphere. The client's age, gender, ethnicity, and education are fixed variables to which the therapist must accommodate and adjust. There has been a growing recognition of the need in the field for training therapists in this accommodation process, and this ability is probably learned more directly from supervisors than from therapeutic manuals.

Demographic variables may be less important in themselves and are rather a marker for other related issues. For example, age is a marker for many aspects of clients' lives that are relevant to treatment planning. Age correlates with the development of the biological organism that unfolds during childhood to adolescence and declines during old age. Age correlates with the developmental and psychological tasks that an individual faces over a life span. Adolescents are establishing their own identity and making moves toward independence from the family of origin. Young adults are seeking intimate partners and beginning work careers. Middle-age adults are facing the tasks of satisfaction in intimacy and raising children. Advancing age brings issues of health, loss of loved ones, and diminishing activities.

Our society is attentive to issues of ethnic and cultural diversity. It is commonly taught now that the clinician must be attentive to the ethnic and cultural aspects of the client in order to form a fruitful therapeutic relationship. This orientation can be taken to an extreme form by calling for replication of all psychotherapy studies by diagnosis (EST literature) with all ethnic groups (Hall, 2001). This argument would be more convincing if there were signs that ethnic differences had a significant influence on treatment outcome or that ethnic variables were related to the nature of the conditions being treated.

The most fruitful areas of future research involve those in which the nature and manifestations of the problem area or diagnosis are related to the demographic characteristics of the clients. The two best examples are those reviewed in this section relating to depression and eating disorders. The prevalence rate and the experience of depression are related to gender. Race may have an influence on the pattern of eating disorders. Future research is needed to examine not only the treatment prognosis but also the issue of prescriptive treatments for depression as related to gender.

Personality Variables

Under the heading of diagnosis, we have previously considered the influence of personality disorders as defined in DSM on psychotherapy. Most reviewers consider the personality disorders to be an extreme of personality traits, with continuity between normality and disorders. In this section, we consider other personality traits as they influence the therapeutic encounter.

Expectancies

There is a history of research relating client expectancies and therapy process and outcome (Frank, 1973). Paul and Shannon's (1966) work on systematic desensitization) found that a positive expectancy condition yielded a better outcome than a no-treatment control. Frank (1961) considered the clients' confidence in his or her therapist and treatment to be the critical determinant of outcome. Client expectations of treatment were related to treatment duration (Lorr & McNair, 1964), attrition rates (Overall & Aronson, 1963), and outcome (Lennard & Bernstein, 1960). Gaston, Marmar, Gallagher, and Thompson (1989) found better outcomes for cognitive therapy clients who expected the treatment to work.

Client expectancies have a strong relationship to duration of treatment (Jenkins, Fuqua, & Blum, 1986) but an inconsistent relationship to treatment outcome (Beutler, Wakefield, & Williams, 1994). In a study of brief ambulatory psychotherapy (Joyce & Piper, 1998), client expectancies were associated strongly with the treatment alliance but only moderately related to treatment outcome. In the same study, client expectancy and a measure of quality of object relations combined in an additive fashion to relate to both alliance and outcome.

There is evidence that client expectancies and "difficulty" are related to therapist behavior

(Foley, O'Malley, Rounsaville, Prusoff, & Weissman, 1987) in delivering a manualized IPT treatment. Client difficulty as demonstrated in the therapy sessions was related to therapists' and supervisors' judgments of therapist performance; that is, therapists were seen as performing more poorly when clients were more difficult. Clients' pretreatment negative expectations about the outcome of therapy were associated with client difficulty, whereas level of presenting symptomatology was not.

Preparation for Change

A number of constructs describe the client's own preparation for behavioral, attitudinal, and emotional change as it intersects with help-seeking behavior.

Readiness to change. When the client makes a decision to seek therapy as a means of dealing with difficulties, to what extent is the client motivated to do what is necessary for change? Prior to coming for therapy, what efforts has the client made to make changes in order to overcome his or her difficulties? These basic questions have been examined extensively in relation to the issue of terminating the habitual and harmful behavior of smoking.

DiClemente and Prochaska (1982) described and assessed the frequency of 10 change processes in individuals who smoke. From this data set these investigators (Prochaska & DiClemente, 1983) described a series of five stages in the cessation of smoking: (1) precontemplation in which people are not intent on taking action, (2) contemplation in which people intend to take action, (3) preparation in which people intend to take immediate action, and finally (4) an action stage in which individuals make specific modifications in their behavior and (5) maintenance in which individuals take steps to avoid relapse to the undesired behaviors.

Addiction severity and frequency of smoking per day were significantly lower among those in the preparation stage than those in the precontemplation or contemplation stage (Crittendon, Manfredi, Lacey, Warnecke, & Parsons, 1994; DiClemente et al., 1991). During an intervention study, clients in the preparation stage made greater use of the intervention (as predicted) than did precontemplators or contemplators (DiClemente et al., 1991). In yet another study (Farkas et al., 1996), clients in the preparation stage were more likely to have stopped smoking one to two years later compared to clients in the contemplation or precontemplation stages.

The stages of change have been applied to seven different systems of psychotherapy (Prochaska & DiClemente, 1983, 1984, 1985). The dropout rate from treatment for a variety of disorders such as substance abuse, smoking, obesity, and medication treatment for hypertension and HIV/AIDS has been related to stages of change (Medeiros, Prochaska, & Prochaska, in press; Prochaska, Norcross, Fowler, Follick, & Abrams, 1992). Stage-related variables were more powerful than demographic variables, type and severity of problems, and other client variables. Furthermore, this group has made the prediction that the amount of change during treatment and following treatment is significantly related to the stage of change at the beginning of treatment (Prochaska, DiClemente, & Norcross, 1992). A clinical corollary or principle stated by this group is that the treatment should be matched to the client's stage of change and that a mismatch between client stage and therapist strategies will result in resistance.

In a large clinical trial, four treatments were compared for 739 smokers (Prochaska, DiClemente, Velicer, & Rossi, 1993). The four treatments included a home-based cessation program, a stage-matched individual treatment, an expert system computer report plus manualized treatment, and finally counselors plus computer and manualized treatment. At 18 months the stage-based and matched programs were superior to the other treatments. Results are not always consistent, however. For example, Ziedonis and Trudeau (1997) evaluated stage of change among a large group of community mental health center clients with schizophrenia spectrum diagnoses and substance use disorders. Their results did not support the validity of the predictions concerning stage of change and involvement in substance abuse treatment or its outcomes. It appears that the stage strategy often is predictive and can be used to design interventions, but the majority of research is on habit disorders and must be investigated in other client problem areas.

Ego Strength

An important factor known to affect treatment outcome is clients' ego strength (Kernberg et al., 1972; Sexton, Fornes, Kruger, Grendahl, & Kolseth, 1990; Sohlberg & Norring, 1989). Ego strength is defined as the presence of positive personality assets that enable an individual to tolerate and overcome his or her anxieties and to acquire new, more adequate defenses. According to Brown (1979, p. 184), "Ego-strength is also the client's capacity to hold on to his own identity despite psychic pain, distress, turmoil and conflict between opposing internal forces as well as the demands of reality." Consistent with these definitions, research has shown that those scoring high on ego strength measures are rated as better adjusted psychologically and show a greater capacity to cope with the stressors and problems in their life situations (Graham, 1990). Ego strength and similar concepts have also been generally found to be related to treatment outcome (Conte, Plutchik, Picard, & Karasu, 1991; Kernberg et al., 1972; Sexton, Fornes, Kruger, Grendahl, & Kolseth, 1990; Sohlberg & Norring, 1989). In the Menninger Psychotherapy Project, Kernberg et al. (1972) found a significant relationship between ego strength and outcome in psychoanalytically oriented psychotherapy ($R[df = 41] = .35$, $p < .05$). Exceptions to these findings include studies by Luborsky et al. (1980) and Endicott and Endicott (1964), both of whom found that the Barron's Ego Strength Scale was not significantly related to outcome. In addition, in the Columbia Psychoanalytic Center Project, clinical appraisals of ego strength were not significantly related to outcome (Weber, Bachrach, & Solomon, 1985). Whether ego strength influences particular aspects of the therapy process (i.e., formation of the therapeutic alliance and ability to obtain insight) or exerts direct effects on outcome is in need of further exploration.

Psychological Mindedness

McCallum and Piper (1996) have reviewed the client construct of psychological mindedness, in terms of its definition, assessment, and relationship to outcome. Psychological mindedness (PM) refers to a person's ability to understand people and their problems in psychological terms. From a psychodynamic perspective, PM refers to the ability to identify components of intrapsychic conflict. There are self-report measures of psychological mindedness, including a subscale of the CPI, a self-consciousness scale (Fenigstein, Scheier, & Buss, 1975), and clinical interviews, including the psychological-mindedness assessment procedure developed by these authors.

Baer, Dunbar, Hamilton, and Beutler (1980) factor analyzed therapist ratings of process items and found that a patient's demonstration of higher levels of insight and self-disclosure was related to treatment outcome. The Psychotherapy Research Project of the Menninger Foundation failed to find any significant relationships between ratings of psychological mindedness and outcome. In a comparative outcome study, Piper, Debbane, Bienvenu, and Garant (1984) found that psychological mindedness was significantly related and directly correlated with client outcomes in a short-term group therapy but was not predictive of outcome in the other three forms of therapy studied (long-term individual therapy, long-term group therapy, and short-term individual). In a controlled trial of an interpretive form of short-term group therapy, PM was directly related to remaining and working in groups but not to deriving benefit from them (Piper, McCallum, & Azim, 1992). In a day treatment trial, however, PM was directly related to both working and benefiting. The authors hypothesize that clients with higher levels of PM are better able to work and benefit in interpretive therapy in which internal conflicts are explored repeatedly, and, conversely, clients with lower levels of PM are better able to work and benefit in supportive therapy in which internal conflicts are not explored.

ANALYTIC-INTROJECTIVE DISTINCTION. Blatt et al. (1994) found that in long-term treatment, clients who were predominantly introjective (perfectionistic and self-critical) had generally better outcomes than clients who were predominantly anaclitic (concerned with abandonment and loss). In using the perfectionism subscale of the Dysfunctional Attitude Scale (DAS) as an analogue for introjective style, it was found that pretreatment perfectionism had a significant negative impact on therapeutic outcome across treatment conditions (Blatt, Quinlan, Pilkonis, & Shea, 1995). The distinction between anaclitic and introjective clients was also applied to a further analysis of data from the Menninger Psychotherapy Research Project (MPRP). Findings indicated that anaclitic and introjective clients are differentially responsive to psychotherapy and psychoanalysis. Anaclitic clients had significantly greater improvement in psychotherapy than they did in psychoanalysis. In contrast, introjective clients had significantly greater improvement in psychoanalysis than in psychotherapy.

Interpersonal Variables

Interpersonal Relatedness

One of the most frequently studied client factors is the client's quality of relating in interpersonal relationships (Luborsky, Barber, & Beutler, 1993). Interpersonal relatedness has been conceptualized in a variety of ways by a number of investigators from different theoretical orientations. Some investigators have assessed the history of interpersonal relationships, whereas other investigators have examined interpersonal functioning in current close relationships or have assessed clients' perceptions, beliefs, and wishes about relationships. Others have looked at how the client relates to the therapist during the therapy.

A number of investigators have demonstrated significant relationships between the pattern of a client's pretherapy interpersonal relationships and the therapeutic alliance established during treatment (Luborsky, McLellan, Woody, O'Brien, & Auerbach, 1985; Marmar, Weiss, & Gaston, 1989; Piper, Azim, Joyce, & McCallum, 1991). The findings in this area are somewhat mixed. Piper et al. (1991) found that the greater the disturbance between a client and his or her partner, the better the alliance established with the therapist. Those clients who were emotionally needier established longer term relationships, compared with those participants who did not seem to have such needs and stopped treatment prematurely. In addition, disturbance with one's partner is but one aspect of problems in interpersonal relationships, thus turning the client more toward an important positive alliance with the therapist. In contrast, in an uncontrolled followup study of 84 clients treated with individual psychoanalytic psychotherapy, the capacity to be related was significantly predictive of positive outcome (Clementel-Jones, Malan, & Trauer, 1990). These findings are also consistent with those of Alpher, Perfetto, Henry, and Strupp (1990), who found a significant positive relationship between clinician ratings based on clinical interviews of clients' capacity to engage in short-term dynamic psychotherapy and clinical outcome as assessed on the Rorschach test. Moras and Strupp (1982) also found that good pretreatment interpersonal functioning predicted a good alliance, but they did not find that poor interpersonal functioning predicted a poor alliance. On the other hand, consistent with Piper's findings, Walters, Solomon, and Walden (1982) report that clients who remained in treatment were more poorly adjusted than those who terminated prematurely.

It is plausible that clients with disturbed interpersonal functioning are nevertheless so dependent and needy of interpersonal relationships that they continue to stay in therapy despite problems expressing their needs and difficulties in their personal relationships. Correspondingly, those who drop out prematurely may do so because they have lower needs for closeness and intimacy, regardless of whether or not they have better overall interpersonal relationships or are better at denying interpersonal conflicts. Along these lines, in a 15-month followup assessment of clients at a long-term psychoanalytically oriented treatment facility, Blatt, Ford et al. (1994) found that those clients who made substantial clinical progress (defined as less frequent or less severe clinical symptoms and more intact social behavior) had produced more disrupted and malevolent interpersonal interactions on the Rorschach in their initial intake assessment. The authors suggested that clients who are more open about their disturbed interpersonal relationships are more likely to enter actively into therapy and to gain most from the treatment process.

Quality of Object Relations

Interpersonal relatedness has also been conceptualized in terms of the quality of object relations. Quality of object relations refers to a person's lifelong pattern of relationships and their characteristic way of interpreting social information. The quality of object relations is believed to be a dimension ranging from immature to mature levels of relatedness. In a comparative psychotherapy study, the therapist's rating of quality of object relations was directly related to favorable process and outcome in an interpretive form of short-term individual therapy (Piper, de Carufel, & Szkrumelak, 1985). In a controlled trial of interpretive, short-term individual therapy, quality of object relations was directly related to the therapeutic alliance and favorable outcome (Piper et al., 1991). These findings are consistent with those reported by Horowitz, Marmar, Weiss, DeWitt, and Rosenbaum (1984) in a study of brief individual therapy. In addition, in a controlled trial of intensive day treatment, which involved an integrated set of interpretive and supportive forms of group therapy, quality of object relations was directly related to remaining in and benefiting from treatment (Piper, Joyce, Azim, & Rosie, 1994). The authors conclude that clients with higher levels of Quality of Object Relations are better able to tolerate, work with, and benefit from the more demanding aspects of interpretive therapy, and, conversely, clients with lower levels of quality of object relations are better able to work with and benefit from the more gratifying aspects of supportive therapy.

Attachment Patterns

Since psychotherapy involves the creation and use of a relationship between two or more individuals (i.e., client and therapist, client, spouse/family and therapist), it is plausible that the clients' history of attachments to others and the quality of these attachments will have a predictive effect on the process and outcome of treatment. Following the seminal work by Bowlby (1969, 1980, 1988) and Ainsworth (1964) on the attachment between infants and their mothers, the construct of attachment has been examined in relation to adult behavior. The attachment behaviors of infant to the caregiver under situations of stress may be analogously related to the situation of a client in distress seeking a help-giving relationship with a therapist. The nature of attachment or attachment styles has been described as secure, anxious-ambivalent, anxious-avoidant, and disorganized (Bowlby, 1988).

In a treatment study of clients diagnosed with borderline personality disorder, those clients classified with the Adult Attachment Interview (AAI) as insecure-dismissive evidenced the best response to intervention compared to other attachment groups (Fonagy et al., 1996). In a naturalistic treatment study of outpatients with a variety of Axis I disorders (e.g., affective, anxiety, substance abuse), Meyer, Pilkonis, Proietti, Heape, and Egan (2001) rated attachment prototypes following an interview using a procedure described by one of the authors (Pilkonis, 1988). It was found that secure attachment style in contrast to various insecure attachments was associated with fewer symptoms prior to the initiation of treatment and with greater improvement following treatment.

Since both attachment style and quality of object refer to relationships with others in the client's life rather than with the current therapist, these constructs may have effects on the treatment process and/or outcome through more immediate mechanisms, including client expectancies and elicitation of helpful versus harmful responses from the therapist (Meyer et al., 2001). There is evidence that this might be the case. Individuals characterized by secure attachment perceive themselves to be competent in relationships and expect a positive response from others (Bartholomew, 1997; Bartholomew & Horowitz, 1991; Griffin & Bartholomew, 1994). Dozier (1990) found that dismissing patients are often resistant to treatment, have difficulty asking for help and retreat from the help that is offered. Dismissing individuals often become disorganized when they are confronted with emotional issues in therapy (Dozier, Lomax, & Tyrrell, 1996).

Satterfeld and Lyddon (1998) found that security of attachment was related to positive scores on the goals subscale of the Working Alliance Inventory (WAI; Horvath & Greenberg, 1986). Eames and Roth (2000) found that patient attachment orientation was related to the development of a therapeutic alliance during the early stages of therapy. Attachment status was also related to the frequency of therapeutic ruptures. Security of attachment was related to higher therapist-rated alliance, and fearful avoidance was related to lower levels of alliance. Interestingly, the preoccupied attachment dimension was related to low alliance at the beginning of treatment but higher alliance toward the end of treatment. These findings, taken together, suggest that anxiety about attachment and avoidance of intimacy may act to impede the development of a therapeutic alliance. However, regardless of high levels of anxiety about relationships, the strong drive of highly preoccupied individuals for intimacy might enable them to develop a better alliance as therapy continues. Surprisingly, Eames and Roth (2000) also found that dismissing attachment was related to positive changes in alliance during the course of therapy. Malinckrodt, Gantt, and Coble (1995) also found a subgroup of patients they called reluctant, who reported good alliances on the WAI but endorsed an unwillingness to participate in the self-revealing tasks of psychotherapy on the Client Attachment to Therapist Scale. These authors suggested that the reluctant cluster might correspond to the dismissing category.

Patient attachment may also influence alliance by influencing therapist response. Dolan, Arnkoff, and Glass (1993) found evidence to suggest that therapist and client attachment styles were interdependent and that ratings of working alliance were contingent on perceptions of therapist-client differences. Hardy, Stiles, Barkham, and Startup (1998) examined responses to patient attachment patterns and found that therapists tended to adopt more affective and relationship-oriented interventions in response to clients with overinvolved-preoccupied interpersonal styles and used more cognitive interventions with patients characterized as underinvolved-dismissing.

Patients in treatment with therapists who were dissimilar from them on the hyperactivating/deactivating dimension of attachment on the Adult Attachment Interview (AAI) showed better therapeutic outcomes and stronger therapeutic alliances (Dozier, Cue, & Barnett, 1994; Tyrell, Dozier, Teague, & Fallot, 1999). Clinicians classified as secure/autonomous on the AAI tended to challenge the patient's interpersonal style (whether deactivating or hyperactivating), while clinicians classified as insecure on the AAI were more likely to complement the patients' interpersonal style (Dozier et al., 1994; Tyrell, Dozier, Teague, & Fallot, 1999). Patients treated by clinicians classified as secure on the AAI have the best outcomes when the clinician is at the opposite side of the secure/autonomous continuum from the patient's AAI classification (e.g., the patient is rated Preoccupied on AAI, and the therapist is rated on the dismissing end of the autonomous category (F1, F2) (Dozier et al., 1994).

Diamond and colleagues (Diamond et al., 1999) reported findings from two clients with borderline personality disorder treated in Kernberg's transference-focused psychotherapy (Clarkin, Yeomans, & Kernberg, 1999) by the same therapist. Both clients progressed from insecure to secure states of mind regarding attachment with one year of treatment. However, consistent with previous research (Eames & Roth, 2000; Dolan, Arnkoff, & Glass, 1993; Dozier et al., 1994; Mallinckrodt, Gantt, & Coble, 1995; Tyrell et al., 1999), each patient interacted and affected the therapist in very different ways, and the therapist responded to each patient very differently. The therapist was engaged and active in the treatment of the client initially classified as preoccupied, whereas the same therapist was much less engaged, often felt dismissed, and developed a much weaker therapeutic bond with the other client.

In-Therapy Behavior

In many studies, clients' characteristics are measured with paper and pencil assessment instruments or are determined through semistructured interviews. A more direct test of clients' characteristics is to assess the clients' behavior during the therapy itself, such as their contribution to the therapeutic alliance and involvement in the treatment process.

CLIENT PARTICIPATION. Gomes-Schwartz (1978) analyzed process ratings from taped segments of therapy sessions and found that the feature most consistently predicting outcome was client willingness and ability to become actively involved in the therapy. In addition, O'Malley, Suh, and Strupp (1983) found that client involvement correlated significantly with all measures of outcome in the Vanderbilt Psychotherapy Outcome Study. Nelson and Borkovec (1989) found that canonical correlations of participation correlated with change on pre-post outcome measures.

THERAPEUTIC ALLIANCE. Client characteristics such as the ability to form an alliance with the therapist and initial functioning also proved important in predicting treatment outcome. Research has indicated that the clients' contribution to the therapeutic alliance is related to therapy outcome (Horowitz, Marmar, Weiss, DeWitt, & Rosenbaum, 1984; Marziali, Marmar & Krupnick, 1981). Krupnick et al. (1996) found that mean therapeutic alliance, assessed in the third, ninth, and fifteenth sessions, was significantly related to outcome across treatment groups. This relationship was determined primarily by the contributions of the client rather than by the therapist to the therapeutic alliance. Using the Vanderbilt Psychotherapy Process Scale (VPPS), Windholz and Silberschatz (1988) found that the clients' involvement in the relationship and the therapist-offered relationship were significantly correlated with the therapist's rating of outcome in a brief psychodynamic therapy.

With 86 clients manifesting anxiety, depression and personality disorders, alliance significantly predicted subsequent change in depression when prior change in depression during the treatment was partialed out (Barber, Connolly, Crits-Christoph, Gladis, & Siqueland, 2000). The authors suggest that their design and findings advance the research question in this area from whether therapeutic alliance during the first few weeks of psychotherapy predicts outcome to the question of the nature of the intertwined and sequential relationship between alliance and clients' improvement.

Summary: Interpersonal Behavior

Psychotherapy involves an interpersonal process between client and therapist. The clients' past interpersonal relationships and current ability to form a positive and fruitful relationship with the therapist are, on the face of it, quite relevant to the continuation and success of the therapy. This situation is, in some ways, a dilemma, in that many symptomatic individuals with disorders needing treatment are the same ones who have troubled interpersonal relations that may disrupt the therapeutic venture. Research support for the importance of these variables is abundant in the literature despite differing operationalizations and diverse treatment methods. Therapists must be experts in fostering relationships with individuals who have difficulty doing so.

Search for a Set of Client Characteristics

It is quite plausible that single-client variables will not prove to be as important to the treatment process and outcome as a set of interrelated client variables. Several teams of researchers have searched in different ways to find sets of client variables that have implications for outcome.

Client Variables across Problem Areas/Diagnoses

One of the most systematic and concerted efforts to isolate a set of specific client variables and demonstrate their influence on the course and outcome of treatment has been the work of Beutler and his colleagues. Beutler, Clarkin, and Bongar (2000) have recently documented the steps in identifying salient client characteristics that are potentially related to treatment process and outcome. First, comprehensive reviews of treatment studies were utilized to describe client characteristics (Beutler, 1979; Beutler & Berren, 1995; Beutler & Clarkin, 1990; Beutler, Consoli, & Williams, 1995; Beutler, Goodrich, Fisher, & Williams, 1999; Beutler, Wakefield, & Williams, 1994; Gaw & Beutler, 1995). Second, based on an extensive list of client variables, an attempt was made to extract the more trait-like characteristics that might have an enduring impact on the treatment process and outcome across time. This was followed by an attempt to relate these trait-like client variables to differential aspects of the pharmacological and psychosocial treatments employed. Since this chapter focuses almost entirely on client variables, we will provide an examination of treatment modifiers that were isolated to optimally match the client and treatment interactions. The interested reader can pursue a more complex analysis in Beutler, Clarkin, and Bongar (2000) as well as in Chapter 7 of this volume. Finally, Beutler and colleagues developed methods for assessing the client variables and conducted a predictive validity study using these client variables to predict treatment outcome (Beutler, Moleiro, Malik, & Harwood, 2000).

The six client variables identified and selected for investigation out of a large number of potential candidates included: (1) client functional impairment, (2) subjective distress, (3) social support, (4) problem complexity/chronicity, (5) client reactance/resistance, and (6) coping styles. These variables relate to the client's problems and psychopathology (complexity/chronicity, functional impairment), to the characteristic ways in which the individual responds to difficulty (subjective distress, reactance/resistance, coping styles), and to the nature of the client's interpersonal context (social support).

Two client variables—functional impairment and complexity/chronicity of problems—relate directly to the client's problems, illness, and/or psychopathology. Complexity may be defined as comorbidity (i.e., coexisting diagnosable symptom or Axis I disorders and/or coexisting Axis II or personality pathology) and the duration of the difficulties (i.e., the chronicity, frequency, and extent of recurrence). There is evidence that greater problem complexity calls for more complex and broadband treatment. For example, situation-specific problems, as opposed to chronic and recurrent problems, have been found to be more responsive to behavioral treatments. This seems to be true for those with mixed somatic symptoms (LaCroix, Clarke, Bock, & Doxey, 1986), alcohol abuse (Sheppard, Smith, & Rosenbaum, 1988), eating disorders (Edwin, Anderson, & Rosell, 1988), and chronic back pain (Trief & Yuan, 1983). On the other hand, there is little evidence of the superiority of more complex, conflict-focused interventions for clients with more complex difficulties.

Functional impairment is the observed or rated degree of impairment in daily functioning. The literature is often unclear concerning the cause and effect or even the temporal relationship between symptomatic status and functional impairment, although it is often assumed that symptom status leads to various degrees of functional impairment. Even among medical diseases, however, the degree of functional impairment may vary substantially, even in individuals with the same medical pathology or psychiatric condition. Reviews indicate that level of functional impairment is negatively correlated with prognosis across disorders such as depression (Gitlin, Swendsen, & Heller, 1995; Kocsis et al., 1988; Sotsky et al., 1991), bulimia nervosa (Fahy & Russell, 1993), obsessive-compulsive disorder (Keijsers, Hoogduin, & Schaap, 1994), and chemical dependency (McLellan, Woody, Luborsky, O'Brien, & Druley, 1983). If one regards disturbed object relations (Joyce & Piper, 1996) and comorbid personality disorders among substance abusers (Woody et al., 1984) as indications of functional impairment, these have been found to relate negatively to psychodynamic treatment outcome.

Three client variables—subjective distress, reactance/resistance, and coping styles—describe the way the individual deals with problems and symptoms and thus might be important client variables predicting psychotherapy outcome. Subjective distress refers to the client's internal state rather than objective behavior or performance, and clinically it is assumed that this internal state would have motivational properties. There is modest support for the assumption that subjective distress is motivational. There is also support for the assumption that psychosocial treatment has its greatest effects on those clients with moderate to high levels of subjective distress (Klerman, Dimascio, Weissman, Prusoff, & Paykel, 1974; Lambert & Bergin, 1983; McLean & Taylor, 1992). In the NIMH Collaborative Study of Depression, those clients with the most severe distress were most effectively treated by IPT, whereas IPT and CBT worked well for those with mild and moderate distress (Elkin, 1994; Elkin, Gibbons, Shea, & Shaw, 1996; Imber et al., 1990).

Since psychotherapy is a situation in which the client can potentially learn from the therapist, the client's receptivity to information, direction, advice, and interpretation from the therapist may be crucial to treatment success. Reactance is a construct defined by describing the behavior of an individual who responds in oppositional ways to perceived loss of choice (Brehm, 1966, 1976; Brehm & Brehm, 1981). Reactance theory is a thoughtful discussion of instances in which thoughts and behavior are free and unimpeded as compared to instances of reactance in which an aversive motivational state occurs and autonomous behavior is threatened. Brehm (1976) suggested that reactance might occur in psychotherapy in instances where the client attempts to avoid the influence of the therapist. Psychodynamic therapy has often been conceptualized as an effort to understand and interpret the resistance of the client. Others in a more cognitive and behavioral tradition have suggested that reactance can not only be dealt with, but also utilized in the therapeutic encounter (Tennen & Affleck, 1991; Tennen, Eron, & Rohrbaugh, 1985; Tennen, Rohrbaugh, Press, & White, 1981) to enhance outcome. Reactance and resistance involve a number of client behaviors and attitudes that describe a range of behaviors from simple noncompliance to delayed compliance to oppositional behavior in the face of the therapist's authority. It is quite likely that therapeutic impasses as defined by Safran and Muran (2000) often involve instances that could be conceptualized as reactance between client and therapist, thus stimulating the investigation of how to manage and/or utilize these situations.

Client resistance has been shown to be associated with poor prognosis with psychotherapy (Bischoff & Tracey, 1995; Miller, Benefield, & Tonigan, 1993; Stoolmiller, Duncan, Bank, & Patterson, 1993). A direct approach to these situations is that of Shoham-Salomon, Avner, and Neeman (1989). Reactance was measured as a pretreatment variable by the client's content-filtered tone of voice. In a treatment utilizing paradoxical interventions, those with higher pretreatment reactance benefited more from the therapy than those with lower reactance scores. A self-report measure of reactance (Dowd, Milne, & Wise, 1991) was significantly correlated with traits such as dominance, independence, autonomy, denial, self-sufficiency, lack of tolerance, and lack of conformity. In yet another study (Shoham, Bootzin, Rohrbaugh, & Urry, 1996), the role of reactance and treatment for insomnia was examined. It was found that paradoxical interventions were more effective for the high-reactance clients than for the low-reactance clients and that progressive muscle relaxation treatment was more effective for low-reactance clients.

Beutler and colleagues define coping style as the conscious and unconscious behaviors that are designed to enhance the individual's ability to avoid the negative effects of anxiety and to adapt to the environment. There is a body of literature that grossly divides coping styles into those that are externalizing (e.g., impulsivity, projection, sociopathic behavior) and those that are internalizing (e.g., obsessiveness, inhibition, inner directedness, and restraint). Clients at varying levels of externalizing and internalizing respond differently to various treatments. For example, among alcoholic subjects, individuals high and low on externalization/impulsivity responded differently to behavioral and interpersonal treatments. The externalizing clients did better when treated with behavioral treatments, and the introspective ones did better with an interpersonal therapy. Similarly, Longabaugh et al. (1994) found that alcoholics who were externalizing responded better to cognitive behavioral treatment than they did to relationship enhancement therapy. These results were not replicated in the large-scale Project MATCH (1997), which we described elsewhere in this chapter. Among a group of outpatients, cognitive therapy was more effective than interpersonal therapy among clients who were externalizing, and interpersonal therapy was most effective for the internalizing clients (Barber & Muenz, 1996).

Although the clients' social support is in some ways external to the client, it also seems clear that clients play a major role developing (or destroying) a social support network composed of friendships, work, and other relationships. Social support is a summary statement about the interpersonal context within which the individual operates and has been found to be a potent variable in treatment outcome. Social support has been measured as both the objective presence of others in the environment and the subjective sense that support is available. There is ample evidence that social support, especially the subjective sense of support, provides a buffer against relapse and improves prognosis (George, Blazer, & Hughes, 1989; Hooley & Teasdale, 1989; Longabaugh, Beattie, Noel, Stout, & Malloy, 1993; Moos, 1990; Zlotknick, Shea, Pilkonis, Elkin, & Ryan, 1996).

Sets of Client Variables and Generalized Anxiety Disorder

Borkovec (Borkovec & Miranda, 1999) has examined client variables in relationship to the successful treatment of individuals with generalized anxiety disorder (GAD). Given the presence of GAD, these researchers have studied client characteristics relevant to the disorder itself, including attention, thought, imagery, emotional psychophysiology, and their interactions. For example, at the physiological level, GAD is characterized by autonomic inflexibility due to a deficiency in parasympathetic tone. Thought content characterized by worry reduces parasympathetic tone. In addition, threatening words generate a defensive response in these clients, serving as an unconditional stimulus that leads to an orientation to associated conditional stimuli. At the level of interpersonal behavior, these clients have been found to be different from controls in their attachment-related childhood memories. On the Inventory of Interpersonal Problems (IIP), a self-report measure of areas of interpersonal difficulties, there are three different subtypes: (1) overly nurturant and intrusive in their interpersonal relations, (2) socially avoidant and unassertive, and (3) dominant and hostile. The authors point out that all of these client variables are relevant for differential treatment planning with GAD individuals.

Aptitude by Treatment Interaction Research

Reviews of psychotherapy research (Kopta, Lueger, Saunders, & Howard, 1999) often conclude that there is no evidence supporting the attractive notion that the individual client should be matched to a particular treatment tailored to that client's difficulties and other characteristics. However, the counterargument is that most psychotherapy studies lack sufficient power to examine potential matches between client and psychotherapy. In addition, clinicians work on the assumption that clients should be matched to particular psychotherapies and aspects of psychotherapy and therefore miss important relationships. The research corollary of the clinical attempt to guide treatment selection on the basis of client variables is a design that assesses the interactions of the treatment type or condition with the client variables, so-called aptitude by treatment interaction (ATI) research (Cronbach, 1975).

Smith and Sechrest (1991) have emphasized the design requirements for a fruitful exploration of appropriately matching clients according to certain aptitudes with specific treatments. They warn that ATIs may be infrequent, undependable, and difficult to detect. The treatment of alcohol and drug addictions has drawn a number of attempts to specify ATIs.

Probably one of the most extensive attempts to match client to treatment was done in Project MATCH, involving individuals with alcoholism who were treated with one of three treatments (Connors et al., 2000). For outpatients, ratings of alliance were positively predicted by client age, motivational readiness to change, socialization, and level of perceived social support. Client educational level, level of depression, and meaning seeking were negatively related to alliance. Among aftercare clients, alliance was positively predicted by readiness to change, socialization, and social support, and negatively predicted by level of depression. However, of the variables manifesting positive relationships with alliance, only a few were significant predictors in multiple regression equations. For outpatients, client age and motivational readiness to change were positive predictors, whereas education was a negative predictor of ratings of alliance.

In reference to matching clients to treatments as related to outcome (Project MATCH

Research Group, 1997b), 11 client attributes were examined. Alcohol-dependent outpatients, high in anger and treated in motivational enhancement therapy, had better post-treatment drinking behavior than an analogous group treated with Cognitive Behavioral Coping Skills Therapy (CBT). Aftercare clients high in alcohol dependence had better post-treatment outcomes in Twelve-Step Facilitation Therapy, and low-dependent clients did better in CBT.

A less developed, yet ambitious, project has been reported by Beutler, Moleiro, Malik, and Harwood (2000) to test the effects of a Prescribed Therapy against competing therapies for a mixed group of clients with substance abuse and depression. The prescriptive treatment focused on tailoring the treatment to four salient client characteristics (described earlier in this chapter): level of functional impairment, internalized or externalized coping, level of reactance, and level of distress. The prescripted treatment matched treatment and therapist characteristics to each of these four client variables: level of functional impairment modified the intensity of treatment, coping was matched to focus on meaning or behavior; reactance was matched with therapist directiveness; and distress was matched to therapist support or arousal techniques. A hierarchical analysis suggested that the fit of client and therapist across the three treatment conditions made a modest contribution to predictive power at the end of treatment and a large contribution at the end of a six-month followup period. Much more work is needed, but this research was generated by the plausible yet infrequently researched notion that the therapist should adapt to client variables. This approach is creative and refreshing as compared to the dominant research theme today of matching the client on only the diagnosis variable to treatments conceptualized in terms of theory and school of psychotherapy.

Summary

The ATI design has been used infrequently, despite its design benefits. One of the reasons might be that theoretical models may not be sufficient to use ATIs, inasmuch as the basic research on the pathology must be done first. Also, they require the time and expense related to gather information on a large number of clients. The finding of the ATI research to date has been relatively disappointing, and Project Match is a prime example. The model of the addiction pathology may have been limited, and therefore the client variables chosen were not central to the pathology itself. Further research is needed before abandoning more complete study of client variables and their contribution to outcomes within this paradigm.

Conclusions and Implications

1. The field of psychotherapy research has crystallized around the randomized clinical trial for clients "homogeneous" for a particular DSM-IV diagnosis. This research, furthered by NIMH and its funding, has been characterized as a Food and Drug Administration approach (Pilkonis & Krause, 1999), with its goal of establishing the evidence of treatment safety and efficacy in at least two clinical trials. This approach fosters internal validity and provides little consideration of clinical significance. The focus is on treatments, with little attention to patients, therapists, or individual differences. The yield of this orientation is group outcomes reflected in group mean scores, with no attention to mediators and moderators of outcome. This research concentration has led to the "empirically validated treatment" movement, which argues that the matching of the client variable of diagnosis with a particular treatment should be preferred in clinical practice and should be included in the training of clinical psychologists.

In contrast, we argue that it is precisely this kind of oversimplification that leads to the gap in understanding and information exchange between researchers and practitioners. Everyday clinical reality is one in which the diagnosis is only one of many client variables that must be considered in planning a treatment intervention. Nondiagnostic client characteristics may be more useful predictors of psychotherapy outcome than DSM-based diagnoses. The diagnostic categories allow for too much heterogeneity in personality traits to serve as useful predictors or matching variables. Psychotherapy research designs should, therefore, stress the interaction between client diagnosis and other salient client characteristics with intervention strategies.

2. If one abandons the simplistic notion that assessment of client diagnosis alone provides a clear road to treatment, one is faced with an overwhelming number of client variables to consider. It is impossible to adequately research all these variables in either post-hoc analysis of treatment studies focused on the brief treatment of symptom diagnostic constellation, or in planned prospective studies of nondiagnostic client variables. This review is an attempt to bring some order and perspective on the client variables that have shown promise thus far. The field has progressed from an early focus on client demographic variables to a focus on personality traits/disorders, especially those that are related to the nature of the disorder itself.

3. Single-client variables do not operate alone, as the individual client is a complex integrated person. Thus, research focused on a constellation of salient variables will be likely to show the greatest impact on treatment process and outcome. The work of Beutler and colleagues, Piper and colleagues, and Borkovec are exemplary in this regard.

4. Unfortunately, most of the research on nondiagnostic client variables involves a post-hoc analysis of the impact of various client variables on the outcome of interest. The examination by Sotsky and colleagues of the multisite NIMH collaborative depression study is an example of this type of investigation. It is interesting to contrast this approach with the theory-driven approach of Blatt and colleagues to the same data set. Although both approaches are informative, the field will be likely to make more progress if the latter direction with theory-guided inquiries is used. A further methodological progression is to investigate either individual or sets of nondiagnostic client variables in a prospective study. The work of Shoham-Salomon and the MATCH studies are prime examples. The most creative approach to date is to articulate areas of client variability that are likely to have the most powerful effect on treatment process and outcome, and to match the therapist behavior, regardless of school of psychotherapy, to the needs of the client (Beutler, Moleiro, Malik, & Harwood, 2000). It is in this work that the focus on client variables in interaction with therapist variables rather than looking at isolated variables is brought center stage and hopefully will result in more progress.

5. Currently, a major research concern is to extend efficacy research that is conducted on highly selected clients at research centers with carefully selected therapists to research that evaluates the effectiveness of specific therapeutic approaches to a more heterogeneous group of clients in the local community treated by community therapists. We agree that the central question of the generalizability of results from the somewhat pristine circumstances to the more heterogeneous community setting is a crucial one. An essential issue in this transfer has to do with client variables. In an efficacy study, efforts are made to limit and control client and therapist variability. Studies that are aimed at generalizing results will enhance the likelihood of improving outcomes for clients.

6. Most reviews of client variables in relationship to psychotherapy process and outcome are pessimistic because of the inconsistent and less than clear relationships described in the literature (Garfield, 1994; Petry, Tennen, & Affleck, 2000). Such reviews, including this one, must come to terms with this inconsistency in results. There have been a number of plausible problems in past approaches to client variables:

First, as emphatically stated by Smith and Sechrest (1991), a number of design issues must be addressed in order to provide a research setting in which client aptitude by treatment interactions can be detected, including sufficient numbers of subjects, a clear and theoretically sound articulation of mechanisms of change, and a strong treatment that is of sufficient duration and intensity to bring about change.

Second, pretreatment client variables have a plausible impact on the therapy, but as soon as therapy begins, the client variables are in a dynamic and ever changing context of therapist variables and behavior. There is a growing awareness and articulation of the inherent interactive nature of psychotherapy such that pretreatment client variables will have only a modest and often inconsistent relationship with therapy process and outcome. The therapist's responsiveness to client variables and behavior will determine the statistical relationship of the client variable to outcome (Stiles, Honos-Webb, & Surko, 1998).

Third, client variables can function in different ways. Most of the research has attempted to isolate single-client variables that have a prognostic relationship to therapy process or outcome. Often, reviews are tallies of which studies are positive and which ones are negative on a single-client variable. Often they are post-hoc client variables of convenience rather than theoretically driven explorations. There is often no clear rationale as to whether the client variable is a mediator or moderator. These variables are treated as mediators or moderators based on their characteristics, for example, gender or age.

It is important to determine, both theoretically and statistically, whether a particular client variable operates as a mediator, a moderator, or both (see Whisman, 1993). Mediating variables are not independent of moderator variables, and vice versa. Whisman also points out that the degree of mediation for a particular variable may be contingent on the level of a given moderator. James and Brett (1984) called this model "moderated mediation." Moderated mediation may be one reason previous research has often found contradictory results in regard to the relationship of client variables to outcome.

To the extent that a mediating variable is also a moderated variable, it becomes a prescriptive variable. For example, in the NIMH treatment of depression study, severity of illness is not only a prognostic variable but becomes a prescriptive variable because the most severely depressed clients responded to IPT and medication plus clinical management. Furthermore, the work of Borkovec implies that diagnosis is a prescriptive variable but only to the extent that it is moderated by important client variables related and specific to the diagnosis under question.

The individualized and more general characteristics of the clients who come for psychotherapy are central to the clinical enterprise of psychotherapy practice and the research investigation of psychotherapy. The focus of psychotherapy is on the clients' problem and diagnosis. Diagnosis is a statement based on common elements among many individuals, whereas an individual client's problem approaches a statement about the specific difficulties that are woven into the fabric of an individual's life at one point in time. Client characteristics are central to motivation for and the nature of participation in psychotherapy. Motivation for change and participation in treatment is individualized in the interaction between a particular therapist and a particular client. Client characteristics that are relevant to interpersonal processes are paramount in understanding the road to treatment outcome. The progress of psychotherapy and its research will depend directly on our efforts to further the exploration, understanding, and measurement of clients who seek our assistance with the difficulties they face.

FOOTNOTES

1. The words *client*, *patient*, and *consumer* are used differently by various professional groups. In this chapter, we use the convention of *client*, even though psychotherapy is now planned, paid for, and researched according to a DSM diagnosis inferring patient status. We would point out that all three terms infer a relationship with another: a client is under the protection of or receiving professional advice from an advisor; a patient is suffering from an illness and receives care from a doctor; and a consumer buys services from his or her insurance plan and a managed care provider.

2. Managed care is very interested in identifying individuals who, in their minds, do not need therapy. The concept of medical necessity is employed to limit the payment for therapy. We have found no research on the use of the concept of medical necessity.

REFERENCES

Ablon, J. S., & Jones, E. E. (1999). Psychotherapy process in the National Institute of Mental Health Treatment of Depression Collaborative Research Program. *Journal of Consulting and Clinical Psychology, 67(1)*, 64–75.

Agosti, V., Nunes, E., & Ocepeck-Welikson, K. (1996). Client factors related to early attrition from an outclient cocaine research clinic. *American Journal of Drug and Alcohol Abuse, 22*, 29–39.

Ainsworth, M. (1964). Patterns of attachment behavior shown by the infant in interaction with his mother. *Merrill-Palmer Quarterly, 10*, 51–58.

Alpher, V. S., Perfetto, Henry, W. P., & Strupp, H. H. (1990). Dynamic factors in client assessment and prediction of change in short-term dynamic psychotherapy. *Psychotherapy, 27*, 350–361.

American Psychiatric Association. (1980). *Diagnostic and Statistical Manual of Mental Disorders* (3rd ed.). Washington, DC: American Psychiatric Association.

American Psychiatric Association. (1994). *Diagnostic and Statistical Manual of Mental Disorders* (4th ed.). Washington, DC: American Psychiatric Association.

Arean, P. A., Perri, M. G., Nezu, A. M., Schein, R. L., Christopher, F., & Joseph, T. X. (1993). Comparative effectiveness of social problem-solving therapy and reminiscence therapy as treatments for depression in older adults. *Journal of Consulting and Clinical Psychology, 61*, 1003–1010.

Armbruster, P., & Fallon, T. (1994). Clinical, sociodemographic, and systems risk factors for attrition in a children's mental health clinic. *American Journal of Orthopsychiatry, 64*, 577–585.

AuBuchon, P. G., & Malatesta, V. J. (1994). Obsessive compulsive patients with comorbid personality disorder: associated problems and response to a comprehensive behavior therapy. *Journal of Clinical Psychiatry, 55*, 448–453.

Baer, P. E., Dunbar, P. W., Hamilton, J. E., & Beutler, L. E. (1980). Therapists' perceptions of the psychotherapeutic process: Development of a psychotherapy process inventory. *Psychological Reports, 46*, 563–570.

Barber, J. P., Connolly, M. B., Crits-Christoph, P., Gladis, L., & Siqueland, L. (2000). Alliance predicts clients' outcome beyond in-treatment change in symptoms. *Journal of Consulting and Clinical Psychology, 68*, 1027–1032.

Barber, J. P., & Muenz, L. R. (1996). The role of avoidance and obsessiveness in matching patients to cognitive and interpersonal psychotherapy: Empirical findings from the treatment for depression collaborative research program. *Journal of Consulting and Clinical Psychology, 64*, 951–958.

Barlow, D. H. (1996). The effectiveness of psychotherapy: Science and policy. *Clinical Psychology: Science and Practice, 3*, 236–240.

Bartholomew, K. (1997). Adult attachment processes: Individual and couple perspectives. *British Journal of Medical Psychology, 70*, 249–263.

Bartholomew, K., & Horowitz, L. M. (1991). Attachment styles among young adults: A test of a four-category model. *Journal of Personality and Social Psychology, 61*, 226–244.

Beckham, E. E. (1989). Improvement after evaluation in psychotherapy of depression: Evidence of a placebo effect? *Journal of Clinical Psychology, 45*, 945–950.

Bergin, A. E., & Lambert, M. J. (1979). Counseling the researcher. *Counseling Psychologist, 8(3)*, 53–56.

Berrigan, L. P., & Garfield, S. L. (1981). Relationship of missed psychotherapy appointments to premature termination and social class. *The British Journal of Clinical Psychology, 20*, 239–242.

Beutler, L. E. (1979). Toward specific psychological therapies for specific conditions. *Journal of Consulting and Clinical Psychology, 47*, 882–897.

Beutler, L. E., & Berren, M. R. (1995). *Integrative assessment of adult personality.* New York: Guilford Press.

Beutler, L. E. & Clarkin, J. F. (1990). *Systematic treatment selection: Toward targeted therapeutic interventions.* New York: Brunner/Mazel.

Beutler, L. E., Clarkin, J. F., & Bongar, B. (2000). *Guidelines for the systematic treatment of the depressed client.* New York: Oxford University Press.

Beutler, L. E., Consoli, A. J., & Williams, R. E. (1995). Integrative and eclectic therapies in practice. In B., Bongar & L. E. Beutler (Eds.), *Comprehensive textbook of psychotherapy: Theory and practice* (pp. 274–292). New York: Oxford University Press.

Beutler, L. E., Goodrich, G., Fisher, D., & Williams, O. B. (1999). Use of psychological tests/intstruments for treatment planning. In M. E. Maruish (Ed.), *The use of psychological tests for treatment planning and outcome assessment* (2nd ed.) (pp. 81–113). Hillsdale, NJ: Lawrence Erlbaum.

Beutler, L. E. & Hamblin, D. L. (1986). Individualized outcome measures of internal change: Methodological considerations. *Journal of Consulting and Clinical Psychology, 54*, 48–53.

Beutler, L. E., Moleiro, C., Malik, M., & Harwood, T. M. (2000, June). The UC Santa Barbara Study of fitting therapy to patients: First results. A paper presented at the annual meeting of the Society for Psychotherapy Research Chicago, IL.

Beutler, L. E., Scogin, F., Kirkish, P., Schretlen, D., Corbishley, A., Hamblin, D., Meredith, K., Potten, R., Bamford, C. R., & Levenson, A. I. (1987). Group cognitive therapy and alprazolam in the treatment of depression in older adults. *Journal of Consulting and Clinical Psychology, 55*, 550–556.

Beutler, L. E., Wakefield, P., & Williams, R. E. (1994). Use of psychological tests/instruments for treatment planning. In M., Maruish (Ed.), *Use of psychological testing for treatment planning and outcome assessment* (pp. 55–74). Chicago: Lawrence Erlbaum.

Birkel, R. C., & Reppucci, N. D. (1983). Social networks, information-seeking, and the utilization of services. *American Journal of Community Psychology, 11*, 185–205.

Bischoff, M. M., & Tracey, T. J. G. (1995). Client resistance as predicted by therapist behavior: A study of sequential dependence. *Journal of Counseling Psychology, 42*, 487–495.

Blatt, S. J., Ford, R. Q., Berman, W. H., Jr., Cook, B., Cramer, P., & Robins, C. E. (1994). *Therapeutic change: An object relations perspective.* New York: Plenum Press.

Blatt, S. J., Quinlan, D. M., Pilkonis, P. A., & Shea, M. T. (1995). Impact of perfectionism and need for approval on the brief treatment of depression: The National Institute of Mental Health Treatment of Depression Collaborative Research Program revisited. *Journal of Consulting and Clinical Psychology, 63*, 125–132.

Borkovec, T. D., & Miranda, J. (1999). Between-group psychotherapy outcome research and basic science. *Journal of Clinical Psychology, 55*, 147–158.

Bowlby, J. (1969). Disruption of affectional bonds and its effects on behavior. *Canada's Mental Health Supplement, 59*, 12.

Bowlby, J. (1980). By ethology out of psycho-analysis: An experiment in interbreeding. *Animal Behaviour, 28*, 649–656.

Bowlby, J. (1988). A secure base: *Parent-child attachment and healthy human development* (p. 205). New York: Basic Books.

Boyd, J. H. (1986). Use of mental health services for the treatment of panic disorder. *American Journal of Psychiatry, 143*, 1569–1574.

Brehm, J. W. (1966). *A theory of psychological reactance.* New York: Academic Press.

Brehm, S. S. (1976). *The application of social psychology to clinical practice.* Washington, DC: Hemisphere Press.

Brehm, S. S., & Brehm, J. W. (1981). *Psychological reactance: A theory of freedom and control.* New York: Academic Press.

Brown, E. J., Heimberg, R. G., & Juster, H. R. (1995). Social phobia subtype and avoidant personality disorder: Effect on severity of social phobia, impairment, and outcome of cognitive behavioral treatment. *Behavior Therapy, 26,* 467–486.

Brown, J. A. (1979). Ego identity states and personality variables. *Dissertation Abstracts International, 40,* 1879–1880.

Burns, D. D., & Nolen-Hoeksema, S. (1992). Therapeutic empathy and recovery from depression in cognitive) behavioral therapy: A structural equation model. *Journal of Consulting and Clinical Psychology, 60,* 441–449.

Butler, T., Giordano, S., & Neren, S. (1985). Gender and sex-role attributes as predictors of utilization of natural support systems during personal stress events. *Sex Roles, 13,* 515–524.

Chambless, D. L., Baker, M. J., Baucom, D. H., Beutler, L. E., Calhoun, K. S., Crits-Christoph, P., Daiuto, A., DeRubeis, R., Detweiler, J., Haaga, D. A. F., Johnson, S., McCury, S., Mueser, K. T., Pope, K. S., Sanderson, W. C., Shoham, V., Stickle, T., Williams, D. A., & Woody, S. R. (1998). Update on empirically validated therapies: II. *The Clinical Psychologist, 51,* 3–16.

Chambless, D. L., Tran, G. Q., & Glass, C. R. (1997). Predictors of response to cognitive-behavioral group therapy for social phobia. *Journal of Anxiety Disorders, 11,* 221–240.

Chiesa, M., Drahorad, C., & Longo, S. (2000). Early termination of treatment in personality disorder treated in a psychotherapy hospital. *British Journal of Psychiatry, 177,* 107–111.

Clarkin, J. F., & Abrams, R. (1998). Management of personality disorders in the context of mood and anxiety disorders. In A. J. Rush (Ed.), *Mood and anxiety disorders* (pp. 224–235). Philadelphia: Williams & Wilkins.

Clarkin, J. F., Yeomans, F. E., & Kernberg, O. F. (1999). *Psychotherapy for borderline personality.* New York: John Wiley & Sons.

Clementel-Jones, C., Malan, D., & Trauer, T. (1990). A retrospective follow-up study of 84 clients treated with individual psychoanalytic psychotherapy: Outcome and predictive factors. *British Journal of Psychotherapy, 6,* 363–376.

Coker, S., Vize, C., Wade, T., & Cooper, P. J. (1993). Patients with bulimia nervosa who fail to engage in cognitive behavior therapy. *International Journal of Eating Disorders, 13,* 35–40.

Connors, G. J., DiClemente, C. C., Dermen, K. H., Kadden, R., Carroll, K. M., & Frone, M. R. (2000). *Journal of Studies on Alcohol, 61,* 139–149.

Conte, H., Plutchik, R., Picard, S., & Karasu, T. (1991). Can personality traits predict psychotherapy outcome? *Comprehensive Psychiatry, 32,* 66–72.

Cooper, P. J., Coker, S., & Fleming, C. (1994). Self-help for bulimia nervosa: A preliminary report. *International Journal of Eating Disorders, 16,* 401–404.

Cottraux, J., Messy, P., Marks, I. M., Mollard, E., & Bouvard, (1993). Predictive factors in the treatment of obsessive-compulsive disorders with fluvoxamine and/or behaviour therapy. *Behavioural Psychotherapy, 21,* 45–50.

Crittendon, K. S., Manfredi, C., Lacey, L., Warnecke, R., & Parsons, J. (1994). Measuring readiness and motivation to quit smoking among women in public health clinics. *Addictive Behaviors, 19,* 497–507.

Cronbach, L. J. (1975). Beyond the two disciplines of scientific psychology. *American Psychologist, 30,* 116–127.

Cyranowski, J. M., Frank, E., Young, E., & Shear, M. K. (2000). Adolescent onset of the gender differences in lifetime rates of major depression: A theoretical model. *Archives of General Psychiatry, 57,* 21–27.

Diamond, D., Clarkin, J., Levine, H., Levy, K., Foelsch, P., & Yeomans, F. (1999). Attachment theory and borderline personality disorder: A preliminary report. *Psychoanalytic Inquiry, 19,* 831–884.

DiClemente, C. C., & Prochaska, J. O. (1982). Self-change and therapy change of smoking behavior: A comparison of processes of change of cessation and maintenance. *Addictive Behaviors, 7,* 133–142.

DiClemente, C. C., Prochaska, J. O., Fairhurst, S. K., Velicer, W. F., Velasques, M. M., & Rossi, J. S. (1991). The process of smoking cessation: An analysis of precontemplation, contemplation, and preparation stages of change. *Journal of Consulting and Clinical Psychology, 59,* 295–304.

Diguer, L., Barber, J. P., & Luborsky, L. (1993). Three concomitants: personality disorders, psychiatric severity and outcome of dynamic psychotherapy of major depression. *American Journal of Psychiatry, 150,* 1246–1248.

Dobson, K. S. (1989). A meta-analysis of the efficacy of cognitive therapy for depression. *Journal of Consulting and Clinical Psychology, 57,* 414–419.

Dodd, J. A. (1970). A retrospective analysis of variables related to duration of treatment in a university clinic. *Journal of Nervous and Mental Disease, 151,* 75–85.

Dolan, R. T. Arnkoff, D. B. & Glass, C. R. (1993). Client attachment style and the psychotherapist's interpersonal stance. *Psychotherapy, 30,* 408–412.

Dowd, E. T., Milne, C. R., & Wise, S. L. (1991). The Therapeutic Reactance Scale: A measure of psychological reactance. *Journal of Counseling and Development, 69,* 541–545.

Dozier, M. (1990). Attachment organization and treatment use for adults with serious psychopathological disorders. *Development and Psychopathology, 2,* 47–60.

Dozier, M., Cue, K., & Barnett, L. (1994). Clinicians as caregivers: Role of attachment organization in treatment. *Journal of Consulting and Clinical Psychology, 62,* 793–800.

Dozier, M., Lomax, L., & Tyrrell, C. (1996). Psychotherapy's challenge for adults using deactivating attachment strategies. Manuscript, University of Delaware.

Dubrin, J. R., & Zastowny, T. R. (1988). Predicting early attention from psychotherapy: An analysis of a large private practice cohort. *Psychotherapy, 25,* 393–408.

Eames, V., & Roth, A. (2000). Patient attachment orientation and the early working alliance—A study of patient and therapist reports of alliance quality and ruptures. *Psychotherapy Research, 10,* 421–434.

Edwin, D., Andersen, A. E., & Rosell, F. (1988). Outcome prediction of MMPI in subtypes of anorexia nervosa. *Psychosomatics, 29,* 273–282.

Elkin, I. (1994). The NIMH treatment of depression collaborative research program: Where we began and where we are. In A. E. Bergin & S. L. Garfield (Eds.), *Handbook of psychotherapy and behavior change* (4th ed.) (pp. 114–139). New York: John Wiley & Sons.

Elkin, I., Gibbons, R. D., Shea, M. T., & Shaw, B. F. (1996). Science is not a trial (but it can sometimes be a tribulation). *Journal of Consulting and Clinical Psychology, 64,* 92–103.

Elkin, I., Gibbons, R. D., Shea, M. T., Sotsky, S., Watkins, J., & Pilkonis, P. (1995). Initial severity and differential treatment outcome in the National Institute of Mental Health Treatment of Depression Collaborative Research Program. *Journal of Consulting and Clinical Psychology, 63,* 841–846.

Elkin, I., Shea, T., Watkins, J. T., Imber, S. D., Sotsky, S. M., et al. (1989). National Institute of Mental Health Treatment of Depression Collaborative Research Program: General effectiveness of treatments. *Archives of General Psychiatry, 46,* 971–982.

Endicott, N. A., & Endicott, J. (1964). The relationship between Rorschach Flexor and Extensor M responses and the MMPI. *Journal of Clinical Psychology, 20,* 388–389.

Epstein, E. E., McCrady, B. S., Miller, K. J., & Steinberg, M. (1994). Attrition from conjoint alcoholism treatment: Do dropouts differ from completers? *Journal of Substance Abuse, 6,* 249–265.

Eysenck, H. J. (1952). The effects of psychotherapy: An evaluation. *Journal of Consulting Psychology, 16,* 319–324.

Fahy, T. A., & Russell, G. F. M. (1993). Outcome and prognostic variables in bulimia nervosa. *International Journal of Eating Disorders, 14,* 135–145.

Farkas, A. J., Pierce, J. P., Zhu, S., Rosbrook, B., Gilpin, E. A., Berry, C., & Kaplan, R. M. (1996). Addiction versus stages of change models in predicting smoking cessation. *Addiction, 91,* 1271–1280.

Fenigstein, A., Scheier, M. F., & Buss, A. H. (1975). Public and private self-consciousness: Assessment and theory. *Journal of Consulting and Clinical Psychology, 43,* 522–527.

Fiester, A. R., & Rudestam, K. E. (1975). A multivariate analysis of early dropout process. *Journal of Consulting and Clinical Psychology, 43,* 528–535.

Fiorot, M., Boswell, P., & Murray, E. J. (1990). Personality and response to psychotherapy in depressed elderly women. *Behavior, Health, & Aging, 1,* 51–63.

Flaskerud, J. H., & Liu, P. Y. (1991). Effects of an Asian client-therapist language, ethnicity and gender match on utilization and outcome of therapy. *Community Mental Health Journal, 27,* 31–42.

Foley, S. H., O'Malley, S., Rounsaville, B., Prusoff, B. A., & Weissman, M. M. (1987). The relationship of client difficulty to therapist performance in interpersonal psychotherapy of depression. *Journal of Affective Disorders 12,* 207–217.

Fonagy, P., Leigh, T., Steele, M., Steele, H., Kennedy, R., Mattoon, G., Target, M., & Gerber, A. (1996). The relation of attachment status, psychiatric classification, and response to psychotherapy. *Journal of Consulting and Clinical Psychology, 64,* 22–31.

Frances, A., & Clarkin, J. F. (1981). No treatment as the prescription of choice. *Archives of General Psychiatry, 38,* 542–545.

Frank, E., Frank, N., Cornes, C., Imber, S. D., et al. (1993). Interpersonal psychotherapy in the treatment of late-life depression. In G. L. Klerman & M. M. Weissman (Eds.), *New applications of interpersonal psychotherapy* (pp. 167–198). Washington, DC: American Psychiatric Press.

Frank, J. D. (1971). Therapeutic factors in psychotherapy. *American Journal of Psychotherapy, 25,* 350–361.

Frank, J. D. (1973). *Persuasion and healing: A comparative study of psychotherapy* (Rev. Ed.). Baltimore, MD: Johns Hopkins University Press.

Frank, J. D. (1979). The present status of outcome studies. *Journal of Consulting and Clinical Psychology, 47(2),* 310–316.

Free, N. K., Green, B. L., Grace, M. C., Chernus, L. A., & Whitman, R. M. (1985). Empathy and outcome in brief focal dynamic therapy. *American Journal of Psychiatry, 142,* 917–921.

Friedman, R. C., Aronoff, Clarkin, J. F., Corn, R., & Hurt, S. W. (1983). Primary and secondary affective disorders in adolescents and young adults. *Acta Psychiatrica Scandinavica, 67,* 226–235.

Fujino, D. C., Okazaki, S., & Young, K. (1994). Asian-American women in the mental health system: An examination of ethnic and gender match between therapist and client. Special issue: Asian-American mental health. *Journal of Community Psychology, 22,* 164–176.

Gallagher-Thompson, D., Hanley-Peterson, P., & Thompson, L. W. (1990). Maintenance of gains versus relapse following brief psychotherapy for depression. *Journal of Consulting and Clinical Psychology, 58*, 371–374.

Garfield, S. L. (1994). Research on client variables in psychotherapy. In S. L. Garfield & A. E. Bergin (Eds.), *Handbook of psychotherapy and behavior change* (4th ed.) (pp. 72–113). New York: John Wiley & Sons.

Garfield, S. L., & Bergin, A. E. (Eds.) (1986). *Handbook of psychotherapy and behavior change* (3rd ed.). New York: John Wiley & Sons.

Gaston, L., Marmar, C., R., Gallagher, D., & Thompson, L. W. (1989). Impact of confirming patient expectations of change processes in behavioral, cognitive, and brief dynamic psychotherapy. *Psychotherapy: Theory, Research, Practice, Training, 26*, 296–302.

Gaw, K. F., & Beutler, L. E. (1995). Integrating treatment recommendations. In L. E. Beutler and M. Berren (Eds.), *Integrative assessment of adult personality* (pp. 280–319). New York: Guilford Press.

George, L. K., Blazer, D. G., & Hughes, D. C. (1989). Social support and the outcome of major depression. *British Journal of Psychiatry, 154*, 478–485.

Gibbs, J. T. (1985). City girls: Psychosocial adjustment of urban Black adolescent females. *SAGE: A Scholarly Journal on Black Women, 2*, 28–36.

Gitlin, M. J., Swendsen, J., Heller, T. L., & Hammen, C. (1995). Relapse and impairment in bipolar disorder. *American Journal of Psychiatry, 152*, 1635–1640.

Gleaves, D. H., & Eberenz, K. P. (1993). Eating disorders and additional psychopathology in women: The role of prior sexual abuse. *Journal of Child Sexual Abuse, 2*, 71–80.

Gomes-Schwartz, B. (1978). Effective ingredients in psychotherapy: Prediction of outcome from process variables. *Journal of Consulting and Clinical Psychology, 46*, 1023–1035.

Goodman, S. H., Sewell, D. R., & Jampol, R. C. (1984). On going to the counselor: Contributions of life stress and social supports to the decision to seek psychological counseling. *Journal of Counseling Psychology, 31*, 306–313.

Graham, J. R. (1990). *MMPI-2: Assessing personality and psychopathology*, (pp. 335). New York: Oxford University Press.

Greenberg, M. D., Craighead, W. E., Evans, D. D., & Craighead, L. W. (1995). An investigation of the effects of comorbid Axis II pathology on outcome of inpatient treatment for unipolar depression. *Journal of Psychopathology and Behavioral Assessment, 17*, 305–321.

Greenspan, M., & Kulish, N. M. (1985). Factors in premature termination in long term psychotherapy. *Psychotherapy, 22*, 75–82.

Griffin, D. W., & Bartholomew, K. (1994). The metaphysics of measurement: The case of adult attachment. In K. Bartholomew & D. Perlman (Eds.), Attachment processes in adulthood. *Advances in personal relationships, 5*, 17–52. Bristol, PA: Jessica Kingsley Publishers.

Griffith, M. S., & Jones, E. E. (1979). Race and psychotherapy: Changing perspectives. In J. H. Masserman (Ed.). *Current psychiatric therapies, 18.* New York: Grune & Stratton.

Grilo, C. M., Money, R., Barlow, D. H., Goddard, A. W., Gorman, J. M., Hofmann, S. G., Papp, L. A., Shear, M. K., & Woods, S. W. (1998). Pretreatment client factors predicting attrition from a multicenter randomized controlled treatment study for panic disorder. *Comprehensive Psychiatry, 39(6)*, 323–331.

Gunderson, J. G., Frank, A. F., Ronningstam, E. F., Wachter, S., Lynch, V. J., & Wolf, P. J. (1989). Early discontinuance of borderline clients from psychotherapy. *Journal of Nervous and Mental Disease, 177(1)*, 38–42.

Haaga, D. A., DeRubeis, R. J., Stewart, B. L., & Beck, A. T. (1991). Relationship of intelligence with cognitive therapy outcome. *Behavior Research and Therapy, 29*, 277–281.

Hall, G. C. Nagayama. (2001). Psychotherapy research with ethnic minorities: Empirical, ethical, and conceptual issues. *Journal of Consulting and Clinical Psychology, 69*, 502–510.

Hansen, A. M., Hoogduin, C. A., Schaap, C., & de Haan, E. (1992). Do drop-outs differ from successfully treated obsessive-compulsives? *Behaviour Research and Therapy, 30(5)*, 547–550.

Hardy, G. E., Barkham, M., Shapiro, D. A., Stiles, W. B., Rees, A., & Reynolds, S. (1995). Impact of Cluster C personality disorders on outcomes of contrasting brief psychotherapies for depression. *Journal of Consulting and Clinical Psychology, 63*, 997–1003.

Hardy, G. E., Stiles, W. B., Barkham, M., & Startup, M. (1998). Therapist responsiveness to client interpersonal styles during time-limited treatments for depression. *Journal of Consulting and Clinical Psychology, 66*, 304–312.

Hermesh, H., Shahar, A., & Munitz, H. (1987). Obsessive-compulsive disorder and borderline personality disorder. *American Journal of Psychiatry, 144*, 120–121.

Hilsenroth, M. J., Handler, L., Toman, Karen, M., & Padawer, J. R. (1995). Rorschach and MMPI-2 indices of early psychotherapy termination. *Journal of Consulting and Clinical Psychology, 63*, 956–965.

Hoberman, H. M., Lewinsohn, P. M., & Tilson, M. (1988). Group treatment of depression: Individual predictors of outcome. *Journal of Consulting and Clinical Psychology, 56*, 393–398.

Hollon, S. D., DeRubeis, R. J., Evans, M. D., Wiemer, M. J., Garvey, M. J., Grove, W. M., & Tuason, V. B. (1992). Cognitive therapy and pharmacotherapy for depression: Singly and in combination. *Archives of General Psychiatry, 49*, 774–781.

Holmbeck, G. N. (1998). Toward terminological, conceptual, and statistical clarity in the study of mediators and moderators: Examples from the child-clinical and pediatric psychology literature. In A. E. Kazdin (Ed.), *Methodological issues and strategies in clinical research* (2nd ed.). Washington, DC: American Psychological Association.

Hooley, J. M., & Teasdale, J. D. (1989). Predictors of relapse in unipolar depressives: Expressed emotion, marital distress, and perceived criticism. *Journal of Abnormal Psychology, 98*, 229–235.

Horner, M. S., & Diamond, D. (1996). Object relations development and psychotherapy dropout in borderline outpatients. *Psychoanalytic Psychology, 13(2)*, 205–223.

Horowitz, M. J., Marmar, C. M., Weiss, D. S., DeWitt, K. N., & Rosenbaum, R. (1984). Brief psychotherapy of bereavement reactions. *Archives of General Psychiatry, 41*, 438–448.

Horvath, A. O., & Greenberg, L. S. (1986). The development of the Working Alliance Inventory. In L. S. Greenberg & W. M. Pinsof (Eds.), *The psychotherapeutic process: A research handbook* (529–556). Guilford clinical psychology and psychotherapy series. New York: Guilford Press.

Horwitz, A. (1977). The pathways into psychiatric treatment: Some differences between men and women. *Journal of Health and Social Behavior, 18*, 169–178.

Howard, K. I., Cornille, T. A., Lyons, J. S., Vessey, J. T., Lueger, R. J., & Saunders, S. M. (1996). Patterns of mental health service utilization. *Archives of General Psychiatry, 53*, 696–703.

Imber, S. D., Pilkonis, P. A., Sotsky, S. M., Elkin, I., Watkins, J. T., Collins, J. F., Shea, M. T., Leber, W. R., & Glass, D. R. (1990). Mode-specific effects among three treatments for depression. *Journal of Consulting and Clinical Psychology, 58*, 352–359.

James, L. R., & Brett, J. M. (1984). Mediators, moderators, and tests for mediation. *Journal of Applied Psychology, 69*, 307–321.

Jarrett, R. B., Eaves, G. G., Grannemann, B. D., & Rush, A. J. (1991). Clinical, cognitive, and demographic predictors of response to cognitive therapy for depression: A preliminary report. *Psychiatry Research, 37*, 245–260.

Jarrett, R. B., Giles, D. E., Gullion, C. M., & Rush, A. J. (1991). Does learned resourcefulness predict response to cognitive therapy in depressed outpatients? *Journal of Affective Disorders, 23*, 223–229.

Jenike, M. A. (1990). Approaches to the patient with treatment-refractory obsessive compulsive disorder. *Journal of Clinical Psychiatry, 51*, 15–21.

Jenike, M. A., Baer, L., Minichello, W., & Carey, R. J. (1986). Coexistent obsessive-compulsive disorder and schizotypal personality disorder: A poor prognostic indicator. *Archives of General Psychiatry, 43*, 296.

Jenkins, A. H. (1997). The empathic context in psychotherapy with people of color. In A. C. Bohart & L. S. Greenberg (Eds.), *Empathy reconsidered: New directions in psychotherapy* (pp. 321–340). Washington, DC: American Psychological Association.

Jenkins, S. J., Fuqua, D. R., & Blum, C. R. (1986). Factors related to duration of counseling in a university counseling center. *Psychological Reports, 58*, 467–472.

Jones, E. E. (1978). Effects of race on psychotherapy process and outcome: An exploratory investigation. *Psychotherapy: Theory, Research and Practice, 15*, 226–236.

Jones, E. E., & Zoppel, C. L. (1982). Impact of client and therapist gender on psychotherapy process and outcome. *Journal of Consulting and Clinical Psychology, 50*, 259–272.

Joyce, A. S., & Piper, W. E. (1996). Dimensions and predictors of patient response to interpretation. *Psychiatry, 59*, 65–81.

Joyce, A. S., & Piper, W. E. (1998). Expectancy, the therapeutic alliance, and treatment outcome in short-term individual psychotherapy. *Journal of Psychotherapy Practice and Research*, 7, 236–248.

Kavanagh, D. J., & Wilson, P. H. (1989). Prediction of outcome with group cognitive therapy for depression. *Behaviour Research and Therapy, 27*, 333–343.

Keijsers, G. P. J., Hoogduin, C. A. L., & Schaap, C. P. D. R. (1994). Predictors of treatment outcome in the behavioral treatment of obsessive-compulsive disorder. *British Journal of Psychiatry, 165*, 781–786.

Kemp, B. J., Corgiat, M., & Gill, C. (1992). Effects of brief cognitive-behavioral group psychotherapy with older persons with and without disabling illness. *Behavior Health and Aging, 2*, 21–28.

Kendall, P., & Clarkin, J. F. (1992). Special Section: Comorbidity and treatment planning. *Journal of Consulting and Clinical Psychology, 60(6)*, 833–904.

Kernberg, O. F., Burstein, E., Coyne, L., Applebaum, A., Horowitz, L., & Voth, H. (1972). Psychotherapy and psychoanalysis: Final report of the Menninger Foundation's psychotherapy research project. *Bulletin of the Menninger Clinic, 36*, 1–275.

Kessler, R. C., Brown, R. L., & Broman, C. L. (1981). Sex differences in psychiatric help-seeking: Evidence from four large-scale surveys. *Journal of Health and Social Behavior, 22*, 49–64.

Kessler, R. C., McGonagle, K. A., Swartz, M., Blazer, D. G., & Nelson, C. B. (1993). Sex and depression in the National Co-morbidity survey. I: Lifetime prevalence, chronicity and recurrence. *Journal of Affective Disorders, 29*, 85–96.

Klerman, G. L., DiMascio, A., Weissman, M., Prusoff, B., & Paykel, E. S. (1974). Treatment of depression by drugs and psychotherapy. *American Journal of Psychiatry, 131*, 186–191.

Kocsis, J. H., Frances, A. J., & Voss, C. (1988). Imipramine treatment of chronic depression. *Archives of General Psychiatry, 45*, 253–257.

Kocsis, J. H., Frances, A. J., Voss, C., Mason, B. J., et al. (1988). Imipramine and social-vocational adjustment in chronic depression. *American Journal of Psychiatry, 145*, 997–999.

Kopta, S. M., Lueger, R. J., Saunders, S. M., & Howard, K. I. (1999). Individual psychotherapy outcome and process research: Challenges leading to greater turmoil. In J. T. Spence, J. M. Darley, & D. J. Foss (Eds.), *Annual Review of Psychology, 50* (pp. 441–471). Palo Alto, CA: Annual Reviews.

Krupnick, J. L., Sotsky, S. M., Simmens, S., Moyer, J., Elkin, I., Watkins, J., & Pilkonis, P. A. (1996). The role of the therapeutic alliance in psychotherapy and pharmacotherapy outcome: Findings in the National Institute of Mental Health treatment of depression collaborative research program. *Journal of Consulting and Clinical Psychology, 64*, 532–539.

LaCroix, J. M., Clarke, M. A., Bock, J. C., & Doxey, N. (1986). Predictors of biofeedback and relaxation success in multiple-pain patients: Negative findings. *International Journal of Rehabilitation Research, 9*, 376–378.

Lambert, M. J. (1992). Psychotherapy outcome research: Implications for integrative and eclectic therapists. In J. C. Norcross & M. R. Goldfried (Eds.), *Handbook of psychotherapy integration* (pp. 94–129). New York: Basic Books.

Lambert, M. J., & Anderson, E. M. (1996). Assessment for the time-limited psychotherapies. In L. J. Dickstein, M. B. Riba, & J. M. Oldham (Eds.), *Review of Psychiatry, 15* (pp. 23–42). Washington, DC: American Psychiatric Press.

Lambert, M. J., & Bergin, A. E. (1983). Therapist characteristics and their contribution to psychotherapy outcome. In C. E. Walker (Ed.), *The handbook of clinical psychology, 1*, (pp. 205–241). Homewood, IL: Dow Jones-Irwin.

Lambert, M. J., Shapiro, D. A. & Bergin, A. E. (1986). The effectiveness of psychotherapy. In S. L. Garfield & A. E. Bergin (Eds.), *Handbook of Psychotherapy and Behavior Change* (3rd ed) (pp. 157–211). New York: John Wiley & Sons.

Leaf, P. J., Bruce, M. L., Tischler, G. L., & Holzer, C. E. (1987). The relationship between demographic factors and attitudes toward mental health services. *Journal of Community Psychology, 15*, 275–284.

Leaf, P. J., Livingston, M. M., Tischler, G. L., Weissman, M. M., Holzer, C. E., & Myers, J. K. (1985). Contact with health professionals for the treatment of psychiatric and emotional problems. *Medical Care, 23*, 1322–1337.

Lennard, H. L., & Bernstein, A. (1960). *The anatomy of psychotherapy: Systems of communication and expectation.* New York: Columbia University Press.

Leon, S. C., Kopta, S. M., Howard, K. I., & Lutz, W. (1999). Predicting clients' responses to psychotherapy: Are some more predictable than others? *Journal of Consulting and Clinical Psychology, 67(5)*, 698–704.

Lerner, B. (1972). *Therapy in the ghetto.* Baltimore, MD: Johns Hopkins University Press.

Longabaugh, R., Beattie, M., Noel, N., Stout, R., & Malloy, P. (1993). The effect of social investment on treatment outcome. *Journal of Studies on Alcohol, 54*, 465–478.

Longabaugh, R., Rubin, A., Malloy, P., Beattie, M., Clifford, P. R., & Noel, N. (1994). Drinking outcomes of alcohol abusers diagnosed as antisocial personality disorder. *Alcoholism: Clinical and Experimental Research, 18*, 778–785.

Lorr, M., & McNair, D. M. (1964). Correlates of length of psychotherapy. *Journal of Clinical Psychology, 20*, 497–504.

Luborsky, L. (1962). Clinicians' judgments of mental health: A proposed scale. *Archives of General Psychiatry*, 7, 407–417.

Luborsky, L., Barber, J. P., & Beutler, L. (1993). Introduction to Special Section: A briefing on curative factors in dynamic psychotherapy. *Journal of Consulting and Clinical Psychology, 61*, 539–541.

Luborsky, L., Crits-Christoph, P., Mintz, J., & Auerbach, A. (1988). *Who will benefit from psychotherapy? Predicting therapeutic outcomes.* New York: Basic Books.

Luborsky, L., McLellan, A. T., Woody, G. E., O'Brien, C. P., & Auerbach, A. (1985). Therapist success and its determinants. *Archives of General Psychiatry, 42*, 602–611.

Luborsky, L., Mintz, J., Auerbach, A., Christoph, P., Bachrach, H., Todd, T., Johnson, M., Cohen, M., & O'Brien, P. (1980). Predicting the outcome of psychotherapy: Findings of the Penn Psychotherapy Project. *Archives of General Psychiatry, 37*, 471–481.

MacDonald, A. J. (1994). Brief therapy in adult psychiatry. *Journal of Family Therapy, 16*, 415–426.

Mallinckrodt, B., Coble, H. M., & Gantt, D. C. (1995). Working alliance, attachment memories, and social competencies of women in brief therapy. *Journal of Counseling Psychology, 42*, 79–84.

Mallinckrodt, B., Gantt, D., & Coble, H. (1995). Attachment patterns in the psychotherapy relationship: Development of a client attachment to therapist scale. *Journal of Counseling Psychology, 42*, 307–317.

Marmar, C. R., Gaston, L., Gallagher, D., & Thompson, L. W. (1989). Alliance and outcome in late-life depression. *Journal of Nervous and Mental Disease, 177,* 464–472.

Marmar, C. R., Weiss, D. S., & Gaston, L. (1989). Toward the validation of the California Therapeutic Alliance Rating System. *Psychological Assessment, 1,* 46–52.

Marmor, J. (1975). *Psychiatrists and their clients: A national study of private office practice.* Washington, DC: Joint Information Service of the American Psychiatric Association and the National Association for Mental Health.

Marziali, E., Marmar, C., & Krupnick, J. (1981). Therapeutic alliance scales: Development and relationship to psychotherapy outcome. *American Journal of Psychiatry, 138,* 361–364.

McCallum, M., & Piper, W. E. (1996). Psychological mindedness. *Psychiatry, 59,* 48–64.

McCusker, J. (1995). Outcomes of a 21-day drug detoxification program: Retention, transfer to further treatment, and HIV risk reduction. *American Journal of Drug and Alcohol Abuse, 21,* 1–16.

McDermut, W., & Zimmerman, M. (1998). The effect of personality disorders on outcome in the treatment of depression. In A. J. Rush (Ed.), *Mood & anxiety disorders* (pp. 321–338). Philadelphia: Williams & Wilkins.

McLean, P. D., & Taylor, S. (1992). Severity of unipolar depression and choice of treatment. *Behavior Research and Therapy, 30,* 443–451.

McLellan, A. T., Alterman, A. I., Metzger, D. S., Grissom, G. R., Woody, G. E., Luborsky, L., & O'Brien, C. P. (1994). Similarity of outcome predictors across opiate, cocaine, and alcohol treatments: Role of treatment services. *Journal of Consulting and Clinical Psychology, 62(6),* 1141–1158.

McLellan, A. T., Luborsky, L., Woody, G. E., Druley, K. A., & O'Brien, C. P. (1983). Predicting response to alcohol and drug abuse treatments: Role of psychiatry severity. *Archives of General Psychiatry, 40,* 620–625.

McLellan, A. T., Woody, G. E., Luborsky, L., O'Brien, C. P., & Druley, K. A. (1983). Increased effectiveness of substance abuse treatment: A prospective study of patient-treatment "matching." *Journal of Nervous and Mental Disease, 171,* 597–605.

Medeiros, M. E., Prochaska, J. O., & Prochaska, J. M. (in press). Predicting termination and continuation status in psychotherapy using the transtheoretical model. *Psychotherapy: Theory, research, practice, training.*

Meyer, B., Pilkonis, P. A., Proietti, J. M., Heape, C. L., & Egan, M. (2001). Adult attachment styles, personality disorders, and response to treatment. *Journal of Personality Disorders, 15,* 371–389.

Miller, W. R., Benefield, G., & Tonigan, J. S. (1993). Enhancing motivation for change in problem drinking: A controlled comparison of two therapist styles. *Journal of Consulting and Clinical Psychology, 61,* 455–461.

Miranda, J., Azocar, F., Organista, K. C., Dwyer, E., & Arean, P. (under review). Treatment of depression in disadvantaged medical patients.

Mohr, D. E. (1995). Negative outcome in psychotherapy: A critical review. *Clinical Psychology, Science and Practice, 2,* 1–27.

Moos, R. H. (1990). Depressed outpatients' life contexts, amount of treatment and treatment outcome. *Journal of Nervous and Mental Disease, 178,* 105–112.

Moras, K., & Strupp, H. (1982). Pretherapy interpersonal relations, client's alliance, and outcome in brief therapy. *Archives of General Psychiatry, 39,* 405–409.

Nathan, P. E. (1998). The DSM-IV and its antecedents: Enhancing syndromal diagnosis (pp. 3–27). In J. W. Barron (Ed.), *Making diagnosis meaningful.* Washington, DC: American Psychological Association.

Nelson, R. A., & Borkovec, T. D. (1989). Relationship of client participation to psychotherapy. *Journal of Behavior Therapy and Experimental Psychiatry, 20,* 155–162.

Nolen-Hoeksema, S. (1987). Sex differences in unipolar depression: Evidence and theory. *Psychological Bulletin, 101,* 259–282.

O'Malley, S. S., Suh, C. S., & Strupp, H. H. (1983). The Vanderbilt Psychotherapy Process Scale: A report on the scale development and a process-outcome study. *Journal of Consulting and Clinical Psychology, 51,* 581–586.

Organista, K. C., Munoz, R. F., & Gonzalez, G. (1994). Cognitive-behavioral therapy for depression in low-income and minority medial outpatients: Description of a program and exploratory analyses. *Cognitive Therapy Research, 18,* 241–259.

Overall, B., & Aronson, H. (1963). Expectations of psychotherapy in patients of lower socioeconomic class. *American Journal of Orthopsychiatry, 33,* 421–430.

Paul, G. L., & Shannon, D. T. (1966). Treatment of anxiety through systematic desensitization in therapy groups. *Journal of Abnormal Psychology, 71,* 124–135.

Paykel, E. S., Scott, J., Teasdale, J. D., Johnson, A. L., Garland, A., Moore, R., Jenaway, A., Cornwall, P. L., Hayhurst, H., Abbott, R., & Pope, M. (1999). Prevention of relapse of residual depression by cognitive therapy. *Archives of General Psychiatry, 56,* 829–835.

Petry, N. M., Tennen, H., & Affleck, G. (2000). Stalking the elusive client variable in psychotherapy research. In C. R. Snyder & R. E. Ingram (Eds.), *Handbook of psychological change: Psychotherapy processes and practices for the 21st century* (pp. 88–108). New York: John Wiley & Sons.

Phillips, M. A., & Murrell, S. A. (1994). Impact of psychological and physical health, stressful events, and social support on subsequent mental health help seeking among older adults. *Journal of Consulting and Clinical Psychology, 62(2)*, 270–275.

Pike, K. M., Dohm, F. A., Striegel-Moore, R. H., Wilfley, D. E., & Fairburn, C. G. (2001). A comparison of black and white women with binge eating disorder. *American Journal of Psychiatry, 158(9)*, 1455–1460.

Pilkonis, P. A. (1988). Personality prototypes among depressives: Themes of dependency and autonomy. *Journal of Personality Disorders, 2*, 144–152.

Pilkonis, P. A., & Krause, M. S. (1999). Summary: Paradigms for psychotherapy outcome research. *Journal of Clinical Psychology, 55(2)*, 201–205.

Piper, W. E., Azim, H. F. A., Joyce, A. S., & McCallum, M. (1991). Transference interpretations, therapeutic alliance, and outcome in short-term individual psychotherapy. *Archives of General Psychiatry, 48*, 946–953.

Piper, W. E., Azim, H. F. A., Joyce, A. S., & McCallum, M., Nixon, G. W. H., & Siegal, P. S. (1991). Quality of object relations versus interpersonal functioning as predictors of therapeutic alliance and psychotherapy outcome. *Journal of Nervous and Mental Disease, 179*, 432–438.

Piper, W. E., Debbane, E. G., Bienvenu, J. P., & Garant, J. (1984). A comparative study of four forms of psychotherapy. *Journal of Consulting and Clinical Psychology, 52*, 268–279.

Piper, W. E., de Carufel, F. L., & Szkrumelak, N. (1985). Patient predictors of process and outcome in short-term individual psychotherapy. *Journal of Nervous Mental Disorder, 173*, 726–773.

Piper, W. E., Joyce, A. S., Azim, H. F. A., & Rosie, J. S. (1994). Patient characteristics and success in day treatment. *Journal of Nervous and Mental Disease, 182*, 381–386.

Piper, W. E., McCallum, M., & Azim, H. F. A. (1992). *Adaptation to loss through short-term group psychotherapy.* New York: Guilford Press.

Prochaska, J. O., & DiClemente, C. C. (1983). Stages and process of self-change of smoking: Toward an integrative model of change. *Journal of Consulting and Clinical Psychology, 51*, 390–395.

Prochaska, J. O., & DiClemente, C. C. (1984). *The transtheoretical approach: Crossing traditional boundaries of change.* Homewood, IL: DowJones/Irwin.

Prochaska, J. O., & DiClemente, C. C. (1985). Common processes of change in smoking, weight control, and psychological distress. In S. Shiffman & T. Wills (Eds.), *Coping and substance abuse.* New York: Academic Press.

Prochaska, J. O., DiClemente, C. C., & Norcross, J. C. (1992). In search of how people change: Applications to addictive behaviors. *American Psychologist, 47*, 1102–1114.

Prochaska, J. O., DiClemente, C. C., Velicer, W. F., & Rossi, J. S. (1993). Standardized, individualized, interactive and personalized self-help programs for smoking cessation. *Health Psychology, 12*, 399–405.

Prochaska, J. O., Norcross, J. C., Fowler, J., Follick, M., & Abrams, D. B. (1992). Attendance and outcome in a work-site weight control program: Processes and stages of change as process and predictor variables. *Addictive Behavior, 17*, 35–45.

Project MATCH Research Group (1997a). Project MATCH secondary a priori hypotheses. *Addiction, 92*, 1671–1698.

Project MATCH Research Group (1997b). Matching alcoholism treatments to client heterogeneity: Project MATCH posttreatment drinking outcomes. *Journal of Studies in Alcoholism, 58*, 7–29.

Reynolds, C. F., Frank, E., Houck, P., & Mazumdar, S. (1997). Which elderly clients with remitted depression remain well with continued interpersonal psychotherapy after discontinuation of antidepressant medication? *American Journal of Psychiatry, 154(7)*, 958–962.

Reynolds, C. F., Frank, E., Perel, J., Imber, S., Cornes, C., Miller, M., Mazumdar, S, et al. (1999). Nortriptyline and interpersonal psychotherapy as maintenance therapies for recurrent major depression. *Journal of the American Medical Association, 281*, 39–45.

Rosenheck, R., Fontana, A., & Cottrol, C. (1995). Effect of clinician-veteran racial pairing in the treatment of posttraumatic stress disorder. *American Journal of Psychiatry, 152*, 555–563.

Ross, S. A. (1983). Variables associated with dropping out of therapy. *Dissertation Abstracts International, 44*, 616.

Rossiter, E. M., Agras, W. S., Telch, C. F., & Schneider, J. A. (1993). Cluster B personality disorder characteristics predict outcome in the treatment of bulimia nervosa. *International Journal of Eating Disorders, 13*, 349–357.

Roth, A., & Fonagy, P. (1996). *What works for whom? A critical review of psychotherapy research.* New York: Guilford Press.

Rounsaville, B. J., Weissman, M. M., & Prusoff, B. A. (1981). Psychotherapy with depressed outpatients. Client and process variables as predictors of outcome. *British Journal of Psychiatry, 138*, 67–74.

Safran, J. D., & Muran, J. C. (2000). *Negotiating the therapeutic alliance: A relational treatment guide.* New York: Guilford Press.

Salzman, C., Shader, R. I., Scott, D. A., & Binstock, W. (1970). Interviewer anger and patient dropout in walk-in-clinic. *Comprehensive Psychiatry, 11*, 267–273.

Satterfield, W. A., & Lyddon, W. J. (1998). Client attachment and the working alliance. *Counseling Psychology Quarterly, 11*, 407–415.

Scogin, F., & McElreath, L. (1994). Efficacy of psychosocial treatments for geriatric depression: A quantitative review. *Journal of Consulting and Clinical Psychology, 62*, 69–74.

Sexton, H., Fornes, G., Kruger, M. B., Grendahl, G., & Kolseth, M. (1990). Handicraft or interactional groups: A comparative outcome study of neurotic inclients. *Acta Psychiatrica Scandanavia, 82*, 339–343.

Shapiro, D. A., Barkham, M., Rees, A., Hardy, G. E., Reynolds, S., & Startup, M. (1994). Effects of treatment duration and severity of depression on the effectiveness of cognitive-behavioral and psychodynamic-interpersonal psychotherapy. *Journal of Consulting and Clinical Psychology, 62*, 522–534.

Shea, M. T., Pilkonis, P. A., Beckham, E., Collins, J. F., Elkin, I., Sotsky, S. M., & Docherty, J. P. (1990). Personality disorders and treatment outcome in the NIMH Treatment of Depression Collaborative Research Program. *American Journal of Psychiatry, 147*, 711–718.

Sheppard, D., Smith, G. T., & Rosenbaum, G. (1988). Use of MMPI subtypes in predicting completion of a residential alcoholism treatment program. *Journal of Consulting and Clinical Psychology, 56*, 590–596.

Shoham, V., Bootzin, R. R., Rohrbaugh, M., & Urry, H. (1996). Paradoxical versus relaxation treatment for insomnia: The moderating role of reactance. *Sleep Research, 24a*, 365.

Shoham-Salomon, V., Avner, R., & Neeman, R. (1989). You're changed if you do and changed if you don't: Mechanisms underlying paradoxical interventions. *Journal of Consulting and Clinical Psychology, 57*, 590–598.

Skodol, A. E., Buckley, P., & Charles, E. (1983). Is there a characteristic pattern to the treatment history of clinic outpatients with borderline personality? *Journal of Nervous and Mental Disease, 171(7)*, 405–410.

Sledge, W. H., Moras, K., Hartley, D., & Levine, M. (1990). Effect of time-limited psychotherapy on client dropout rates. *American Journal of Psychiatry, 147*, 1341–1347.

Smith, B., & Sechrest, L. (1991). Treatment of Aptitude X treatment interactions. *Journal of Consulting and Clinical Psychology, 59*, 233–244.

Smith, M. L., Glass, G. V., & Miller, T. I. (1980). *The benefits of psychotherapy.* Baltimore, MD: Johns Hopkins University Press.

Smith, T. E., Koenigsberg, H. W., Yeomans, F. E., Clarkin, J. F., & Selzer, M. A. (1995). Predictors of dropout in psychodynamic psychotherapy of borderline personality disorder. *Journal of Psychotherapy Practice and Research, 4*, 205–213.

Sohlberg, S., & Norring, C. (1989). Ego functioning predict first-year status in adults with anorexia nervosa and bulima nervosa. *Acta Psychiatrica Scandanavia, 80*, 325–333.

Sotsky, S. M., Glass, D. R., Shea, M. T., Pilkonis, P. A., Collins, J. F., Elkin, I., Watkins, J. T., Imber, S. D., Leber, W. R., Moyer, J., & Oliveri, M. E. (1991). Client predictors of response to psychotherapy and pharmacotherapy: Findings in the NIMH Treatment of Depression Collaborative Research Program. *American Journal of Psychiatry, 148(8)*, 997–1008.

Steuer, J. L., Mintz, J., Hamamen, C. L., et al. (1984). Cognitive-behavioral and psychodynamic group psychotherapy in treatment of geriatric depression. *Journal of Consulting and Clinical Psychology, 52*, 180–189.

Stiles, W. B., Honos-Webb, L., & Surko, M. (1998). Responsiveness in psychotherapy. *Clinical Psychology: Science and Practice, 5(4)*, 439–458.

Stoolmiller, M., Duncan, T., Bank, L., & Patterson, G. R. (1993). Some problems and solutions in the study of change: Significant patterns in client resistance. *Journal of Consulting and Clinical Psychology, 61*, 920–928.

Sue, S., McKinney, H., Allen, D., & Hall, J. (1974). Delivery of community mental health services to black and white clients. *Journal of Consulting and Clinical Psychology, 42*, 794–801.

Sue, S., & Zane, N. (1987). The role of culture and cultural techniques in psychotherapy: A critique and reformulation. *American Psychologist, 42*, 37–45.

Tennen, H., & Affleck, G. (1991). Paradox-based treatments. In C. R., Snyder & D. R. Forsyth (Eds.), *Handbook of social and clinical psychology: The health perspective* (pp. 624–643). Elmsford, NY: Pergamon Press.

Tennen, H., Eron, J. B., & Rohrbaugh, M. (1985). Paradox in context. In G. Weeks (Ed.), *Promoting change through paradoxical interventions* (pp. 187–214). Homewood, IL: Dorsey Press.

Tennen, H., Rohrbaugh, M., Press, S., & White, L. (1981). Reactance theory and therapeutic paradox: A compliance-defiance model. *Psychotherapy: Theory, Research and Practice, 18*, 14–22.

Thase, M. E., Buysse, D. J., Frank, E., Cherry, C. R., Cornes, C. L., Mallinger, A. G., & Kupfer, D. J. (1997). Which depressed clients will respond to interpersonal psychotherapy? The role of abnormal EEG sleep profiles. *American Journal of Psychiatry, 154*, 502–509.

Thase, M. E., Frank, E., Kornstein, S., & Yonkers, K. A. (2000). Gender differences in response to treatments of depression. In E. Frank (Ed.), *Gender and its effects on psychopathology* (pp. 103–129). Washington, DC: American Psychiatric Press.

Thompson, L. W., Gallagher, D., & Breckenridge, J. S. (1987). Comparative effectiveness of psychotherapies for depressed elders. *Journal of Consulting and Clinical Psychology, 55*, 385–390.

Thompson, L. W., Gallagher, D., & Czirr, R. (1988). Personality disorder and outcome in the treatment of late-life depression. *Journal of Geriatric Psychiatry, 21(2)*, 133–146.

Trief, P. M., & Yuan, H. A. (1983). The use of the MMPI in a chronic back pain rehabilitation program. *Journal of Clinical Psychology, 39*, 46–53.

Turner, R. M. (1987). The effects of personality disorder diagnosis on the outcome of social anxiety symptom reduction. *Journal of Personality Disorders, 1*, 136–143.

Tyrrell, C. L., Dozier, M., Teague, G. B., & Fallot, R. D. (1999). Effective treatment relationships for persons with serious psychiatric disorders: The importance of attachment states of mind. *Journal of Consulting and Clinical Psychology, 67*, 725–733.

UK Department of Health (2001). *Treatment choices in psychological therapies and counselling* (Ref. 23044). London: Department of Health Publications.

Veroff, J., Kulka, R. A., & Douvan, E. (1981). *Mental health in America: Patterns of help-seking from 1957 to 1976*. New York: Basic Books.

Wakefield, J. C. (1998). Meaning and melancholia: Why the DSM-IV cannot (entirely) ignore the patient's intentional system. In J. W. Barron (Ed.), *Making diagnosis meaningful* (pp. 29–72). Washington, DC: American Psychological Association.

Walters, G. D., Solomon, G. S., & Walden, V. R. (1982). Use of the MMPl in predicting psychotherapeutic persistence in groups in male and female outpatients. *Journal of Clinical Psychology, 38*, 80–83.

Ware, J. E., Manning, W. G., Duan, N., Wells, K. B., & Newhouse, J. P. (1984). Health status and the use of outclient mental health services. *American Psychologist, 39*, 1090–1100.

Waxman, H. M., Carner, E. A., & Klein, M. (1984). Underutilization of mental health professionals by community elderly. *The Gerontologist, 24*, 23–30.

Weber, J. J., Bachrach, H. M., & Solomon, M. (1985). Factors associated with the outcome of psychoanalysis: Report of the Columbia Psychoanalytic Center Research Project: II. *International Review of Psycho-Analysis, 12*, 127–141.

Weissman, M. M., & Klerman, G. L. (1977). Sex differences and the epidemiology of depression. *Archives of General Psychiatry, 34*, 98–111.

Wells, K. B., Burnam, A., Rogers, W., Hays, R., & Camp, P. (1992). The course of depression in adult outpatients. *Archives of General Psychiatry, 49*, 788–794.

Whisman, M. A. (1993). Mediators and moderators of change in cognitive therapy of depression. *Psychological Bulletin, 114(2)*, 248–265.

Wilfley, D. E., Friedman, M. A., Zoler Dounchis, J., Stein, R. I., Welch, R. R., Friedman, M. A., & Ball, S. A. (2000). Comorbid psychopathology in binge eating disorder: Relation to eating disorder severity at baseline and following treatment. *Journal of Consulting and Clinical Psychology, 68(4)*, 641–649.

Willer, B., & Miller, G. H. (1978). On the relationship of client satisfaction to client characteristics and outcome of treatment. *Journal of Clinical Psychology, 34*, 157–160.

Windholz, M. J., & Silbershatz, G. (1988). Vanderbilt psychotherapy process scale: A replication with adult outpatients. *Journal of Consulting and Clinical Psychology, 56*, 56–60.

Woody, G. E., McLellan, A. T., Luborsky, L., O'Brien, C. P., Blaine, J., Fox, S., Herman, I., & Beck, A. T. (1984). Severity of psychiatric symptoms as a predictor of benefits from psychotherapy: The Veterans Administration-Penn Study. *American Journal of Psychiatry, 141*, 1172–1177.

Yeomans, F. E., Gutfreund, J., Selzer, M. A., Clarkin, J. F., Hull, J. W., & Smith, T. E. (1994). Factors related to drop-outs by borderline patients: Treatment contract and therapeutic alliance. *Journal of Psychotherapy Practice and Research, 3(1)*, 16–24.

Yokopenic, P. A., Clark, V. A., & Aneshensel, C. S. (1983). Depression, problem recognition, and professional consultation. *Journal of Nervous and Mental Disease, 171*, 15–23.

Ziedonis, D. M., & Trudeau, K. (1997). Motivation to quit using substances among individuals with schizophrenia: Implications for a motivation-based treatment model. *Schizophrenia Bulletin, 23*, 229–238.

Zlotnick, C., Shea, M. T., Pilkonis, P., Elkin, I., & Ryan, C. (1996). Gender dysfunctional attitudes, social support, life events, and depressive symptoms over naturalistic follow-up. *American Journal of Psychiatry, 153*, 1021–1027.

Zuroff, D. C., Blatt, S. J., Sotsky, S. M., Krupnick, J. L., Martin, D. J., Sanislow, C. A., & Simmens, S. (2000). Relation of therapeutic alliance and perfectionism to outcome in brief outpatient treatment of depression. *Journal of Consulting and Clinical Psychology, 68(1)*, 114–124.

CHAPTER 7

THERAPIST VARIABLES

LARRY E. BEUTLER
MARY MALIK
SHABIA ALIMOHAMED
T. MARK HARWOOD
HANI TALEBI
SHARON NOBLE
EUNICE WONG
University of California, Santa Barbara

When research on psychotherapy began, discrete therapist characteristics were considered to be very important to gaining an understanding of psychotherapy outcomes. Over the past two decades, the emphasis on randomized clinical trials and specific therapy models has resulted in decreasing attention given to discrete therapist factors (Bergin, 1997; Beutler, 1997; Strupp & Anderson, 1997). Manual-driven treatments, randomized clinical trials (RCT) methodologies, and arguments between the merits of efficacy and effectiveness (Jacobson & Christensen, 1996; Nathan, Stuart, & Dolan, 2000) have left little room for attending to therapist qualities such as personality, beliefs, culture, and demographics that are not directly affected by training.

In efficacy research, the focus is on maximizing the power of treatments. Thus, efforts are made to control the influences of therapist factors by constructing treatment manuals that can be applied in the same way to all patients within a particular diagnostic group, regardless of any particular clinician. This research gives scant attention to any curative role that might be attributed to therapist factors that are independent of the treatment model and procedures. This research paradigm has been favored among funding agencies for nearly 20 years (Nathan, Stuart, & Dolan, 2000).

In contrast, effectiveness research models are more concerned with the value of usual rather than optimal treatments and with generalization of findings than with treatment consistency. Thus, they are generally applied to less restrictively defined patient populations, and they address both aspects of the treatment setting and the level of care. However, they, too, ignore the idiosyncratic and unique contributions of therapists, viewing treatments as entities that are separate from those who deliver them.

Emerging research methods are aimed at blurring efficacy and effectiveness models, but even this development has done little to reduce the infatuation with diagnostic groupings and manualized treatments of the past two decades. In the values of the past 20 years, clear conceptual distinctions are made between the influence of the therapist and the influence of the treatment itself; the former are sources of error, and the latter are "specific effects."

Despite the concerted effort to control, reduce, or eliminate the effects of both therapist variability and extradiagnostic patient variables, research has not been able to escape the need to recognize either the roles of the clinician (Blatt, Sanislow, Zuroff, & Pilkonis, 1996; Crits-Christoph, Baranackie, Kurcias et al., 1991; Luborsky et al., 1986; Luborsky, McLellan, Diguer, Woody, & Seligman, 1997; Strupp & Anderson, 1997) or the reciprocal influence of patient and therapist qualities on one another (Beutler, Clarkin, & Bongar, 2000). Variability among therapists and among patient responses to standardized treatments continues to be the rule rather than the exception (Crits-Christoph, Baranackie et al., 1991;

Howard, Krause, & Lyons, 1993). Noting such variability, Teyber and McClure (2000) have emphasized the importance of maintaining a relational or ATI (aptitude by treatment interaction) perspective when inspecting the role of therapist factors—remembering that focusing on discrete therapist variables may detract us from the more important influences of therapist, intervention, and patient fit with one another.

Advancement in psychotherapy research requires looking beyond the therapy model and the patient's diagnosis. We urge consideration of what works with whom, under what conditions. In the hope both of stemming the trend of focusing on variables that are assumed to be unidirectional rather than relational, and of drawing attention to promising areas where research attention may (or should) be renewed, in the following pages we will summarize some of the more important aspects of therapists that contribute to or promise to contribute to psychotherapy outcome.

OVERVIEW

In the fourth edition of this *Handbook*, Beutler, Machado, and Neufeldt (1994) classified therapist variables into four quadrants, representing two intersecting dimensions. The range of responses along the first of the two dimensions established the identity of qualities that vary from being extratherapy *"traits"* to therapy-specific *"states."* That is, one end of this dimension defined the degree to which the identified therapist variable was employed, developed, or defined specifically in order to further one's role as a psychotherapist (i.e., states). The other end reflected an enduring quality that was manifested in the therapist's extratherapy life and was incidental to therapy process (i.e., traits).

The second dimension established a distinction between objective and subjective qualities. Unfortunately, the terms used to define this second dimension in the earlier *Handbook* were sometimes confused with the means for measuring the variables within it. Thus, in order to clarify this distinction in the present review, the two categories of this dimension will be re-labeled *observable* and *inferred.* Observable qualities are comprised of those that are capable of being identified by procedures that are independent of the therapist. In other words, therapist variables in this class can be checked, observed, and verified directly through means other than simply asking the therapist (e.g., by using records, collateral reports). They include qualities like biological sex, age, and interventions used. In contrast, inferred qualities are comprised of hypothetical constructs whose identification relies on inferential processes. The qualities in this category include aspects of personality and relationship quality, as well as those whose presence is knowable only by therapist self-reports (e.g., gender attitudes, religious beliefs, theoretical alliance). To say that some of these qualities can only be inferred is not to discount the possibility that they are genetic, congenital, or indwelling.

Method and Limits of Review

The biggest difference between the current and the previous renditions of this chapter is not embodied in the labels used to cluster the therapist qualities, but in the methods by which the data from extant literature were analyzed. For the current review, we have employed meta-analytic procedures, wherever possible, relying heavily on the methods outlined by Rosenthal (1984) and by Hedges and Olkin (1985). We applied these concepts with the software developed by Shadish, Robinson, and Lu (1999). Like the previous review, the studies included have been restricted to those that: (1) were conducted on clinical populations and problems and (2) included direct measures of outcome. Thus, studies of psychotherapy processes that are measured without benefit of reliable outcome measures were excluded from our analysis. Similarly, studies using analogue designs, employing nonclinician therapists, nonpatient populations, or some contrived equivalent to the psychotherapy environment or relationship were excluded from the analysis undertaken here.

Our objective in this chapter was to compare the most recent published (or presented) findings to those reached in earlier reviews in order to determine how knowledge about the therapist is unfolding over time. After extracting a set of hypotheses from the third and fourth editions of this *Handbook*,[1] we initiated a review of contemporary and recent literature. We established a time boundary by which to direct our review, working backward from September 2000. We first looked for studies that included one or more therapist predictors or independent variables and that were published or presented in a major professional meeting during and after 1990. In those instances in which a critical mass of studies (n = 6) was not available during this decade, we extended the search limits to 1980. Thus, our discussion of the literature is based on a review of research during the past 10 or 20 years, depending on what point we were able to identify a sufficient number of studies to conduct a meta-analysis. It is notable, however, that there were several areas in which an insufficient number of studies were obtained in spite of these efforts. In these instances, the variables were reviewed without the benefit of meta-analytic findings. In a few cases, we were forced to exclude qualities previously considered, for lack of available studies during the 20-year period of our review.

Once a critical mass of studies was identified, we coded the relevant therapist variables, made summary judgments about the nature of the therapy (e.g., symptom focused, insight-oriented, etc.), rated the type of study (e.g., quasi-experimental, experimental, naturalistic) as defined by Kazdin (1998), and rated qualities of the patient and the presenting problem. We also recorded all relevant statistics and identified the dependent variables for each study. Outcome measures were classified as either symptom-specific or global, and a marker variable was selected to reflect one or both of these dimensions. In selecting the marker variables, we gave the most reliable and widely used measures priority over study-specific and face valid measures.

Following this procedure, we selected from one to four effect sizes for each study, depending on availability. The first effect size (ES1) was an endpoint estimate of change in a target symptom or problem. The second (ES2) was a reflection of a general or global measure of change—a broadband measure of change—at the end of treatment. The third (ES3) and fourth (ES4) were extracted if measures of these two types, respectively, were taken during a post-treatment followup period. These designations are used throughout this chapter to indicate these four types of outcomes. In each case, the effect sizes are reported as correlations *(r)*. Their significance is determined by whether the confidence interval (95%) includes a value of zero *(ns)*. Correlations can be translated to *d* values (see Beutler, Machado, & Neufeldt, 1994) but provide a more discriminating estimate of effects when the variables in question are continuous.

Our search for appropriate studies included several databases. First, we scoured all previous editions of the *Handbook of Psychotherapy and Behavior Change* in order both to define potential variables of interest and to establish a baseline set of hypotheses. Some studies in the most recent edition of the *Handbook* (Garfield & Bergin, 1994) fell within our defined temporal limits, and these studies were included in the meta-analysis. We also reviewed other major chapters and theoretical articles that were available to us, and then we conducted several separate computer searches based on words and synonyms that we found in these previous reviews. We also reviewed the tables of contents of recent journals in the field in order to find relevant research that had been missed using the prior methods. Approximately 35% of the studies we found on therapist qualities did not include data in a form that allowed the computation of effect sizes, but the result of our efforts was a collection of 141 studies that were subjected to meta-analyses, from which we extracted 327 effect sizes. The number of studies used to analyze various therapist qualities varied from 6 to 29. When fewer than six studies were available, the effect sizes were not collapsed across studies.

Therapist variables inevitably overlap with those discussed in chapters devoted to client and therapy process. This fact attests to the difficulty of clearly assigning ownership to these variables and qualities. For example, we have included some variables that some might consider to be independent of the therapist altogether, such as research on specific techniques and procedures as well as on the differences between using a manual and following one's own judgment. These areas have been included because we believe that neither the intervention used nor the decision to apply a manualized treatment can and should be disembodied from the person of the therapist (see Anderson & Strupp, 1996; Strupp & Anderson, 1997). By erring on the side of being over inclusive in our selection of therapist variables for this review, we hoped to obtain the most complete picture of therapist characteristics that exert treatment effects.

Hypotheses

Beutler, Machado, and Neufeldt (1994) drew a variety of conclusions regarding the variables represented in the four quadrants of the typography used here. Restated here, they represent the baseline against which we will compare current studies.

I. *Observable Traits* There is little evidence for the unidirectional effects of discrete observable traits (e.g., age, sex, ethnicity) on clinical outcomes. However, relational or ATI aspects of fitting observed traits to an aspect of treatment is generally related to some outcomes, most notably to reduced treatment dropout.

II. *Observable States* Therapist training, experience, skill, and other observable state variables are inconsistent correlates of outcome but may emerge as relating to treatment outcome as their confounding contributors are reduced. Among observable states, relational behaviors, as reflected in the circumplex model, are promising. However, therapist interventions are among the most powerful and widely researched of variables, but all families of interventions are not equally effective with all types of patients, and therapy manuals seem to increase the benefit of the treatment used. Within these families of interventions, certain cross-cutting classes of interventions, such as level of therapist directiveness, insight versus behavior change focus, and therapist self-disclosure are promising variables when they are selectively applied to patients who present with different traits and interpersonal styles. Patient qualities, such as the level of development, object formation and differentiation, coping style, and resistance levels, are promising and potential moderators of various therapist-offered interventions.

III. *Inferred Traits* With few exceptions, inferred therapist traits have not been directly or unidirectionally related to treatment outcome. To the degree that these traits are related to patient change, it is because of relational aspects that are reflected in patient-therapist similarity.

IV. *Inferred States* Inferred therapist states like the therapeutic relationship are consistently related to outcomes, but a causal relationship is yet to be established. Relationships among aspects of the therapist's theoretical beliefs and orientation with outcomes, however, are difficult to relate to specific changes. Only those beliefs related to behavioral theories seem to be related to treatment outcome.

Beutler, Machado, and Neufeldt (1994) observed that these conclusions were consistent with those presented in previous versions of the *Handbook.* However, they also noted significant improvement in the rigor entailed in the research methodologies used and observed that several areas of investigation had gone out of vogue either because of their poor showing or because research interests had simply shifted to other areas.

REVIEW

Observable Traits

Observable traits are enduring characteristics of therapists that transcend the psychotherapy relationship. These include demographic characteristics such as sex, age, and race. Social status has occasionally been included as a separate dimension, but because it is confounded with the other demographics, it is excluded from separate consideration in this chapter.

Therapist Sex

In contrast to the term *gender, sex* has come to be regarded as a biologically defined variable (Beutler, Brown, Crothers, Booker, & Seabrook, 1996). That is, it is subject to external definition, independent of self-report. Gender is a more complex concept and refers specifically to self-perceptions and subjective experiences that cannot be defined apart from therapist self-report. Gay, Lesbian, and Bisexual (GLB) perspectives are good examples. Some might be inclined to cluster GLB qualities as observable traits, given that they are partially defined by sexual behavior. However, a GLB designation implies much more than an observable behavior. It includes self-perceptions, world views, and interpersonal response patterns that earn a place for gender under the category of "inferred traits." By identifying gender as inferred, we do not mean to imply that the associated beliefs and views are somehow less real than others. Neither do we mean that the associated sexual attractions are not biologically determined. Indeed, there is much debate about the biological bases of attitudes and beliefs that are associated with GLB lifestyles. What we do intend is to represent the view that GLB is more than a cluster of sexual acts, just as being heterosexual is a designation that supersedes specific sexual acts. GLB is a viewpoint and a way of being.

It should also be recognized that even one's biological assignment is not a simple dichotomy of male and female (Bancroft, 1989). Sexual assignment is a complex function of genotype and brain androgenization, but for most people and in most circumstances, it is relatively easy and accurate to define male and female sex. Using this dichotomy, Bowman, Scogin, Floyd, and McKendree-Smith (2001) have summarized the effects of therapist sex on treatment outcome using meta-analytic procedures. Combining the results of 58 studies, the authors found a significant but small effect size favoring female therapists (d = .04). Though significant, the authors acknowledge the small effect size and observe that outcome did not differ as a function of patient sex. Moreover, the analyses failed to support the suggestion of Beutler, Machado, and Neufeldt (1994) that a relational or ATI fit between patient and therapist sex may reduce dropout rates (*d* = .01, *ns*).

In our review, we identified 10 studies (Table 7.1) that have been published since 1990 and that included a comparison of the effect of therapist sex on dropout and benefit. Only one of these studies (Krippner & Hutchinson, 1990) found a significant main effect of sex on outcome (ES1*(r)* =.12 favoring female therapists), and only one (Sue, Fujino, Hu, Takeuchi, & Zane, 1991) found a significant effect of sexual similarity and some type of outcome. The 23 available effect sizes were variable, ranging from 0 to .28. The (weighted) mean effect size for therapist sex, as a unidirectional variable, was .01 *(ns)*. A similar value was obtained for the mean effect size of patient-therapist sexual similarity *(ns)*. These findings fail to confirm a role of therapist sex or sexual fit as a contributor to outcome, including dropout, a conclusion that is similar to that of Bowman (1993). If any conclusion is warranted, it is that contemporary (recent) research has demonstrated even less of a predictable relationship between therapist sex and outcome than previously reported.[2]

Therapist Age

Research on therapist age and ageism curiously omits the inclusion of systematic measures of treatment outcome, relying instead on evidence that psychotherapy processes differ among older and younger therapists. The weak relationships that characterize the findings from research in this area can partially be attributed to the inevitable effect of confounding variables that is inherent to this type of research methodology. Under the best of circumstances, for example, therapist age is at least partially confounded with level of experience. It may also be confounded with therapist theoretical orientation, assuming that the most preferred theoretical orientations have changed as different cohorts of therapists pass through ever changing training programs. Age is seldom the primary focus of investigation in these studies. It is a post-hoc variable that is considered when an investigator has fully explored the primary objectives of the study and wishes to extract as much from the data as possible. It may not be surprising, therefore, that therapist age has not proven to be a very robust variable in research. There are no meta-analytic reviews devoted to the topic of therapist age, and most general reviews either ignore this variable altogether or conclude that it is of limited value in predicting outcomes (Atkinson & Schein, 1986; Sexton & Whiston, 1991).

We found only one contemporary study published between 1990 and 2000 that systematically included therapist age as a predictor variable (Barber & Muenz, 1996). This study found no relationship of age or age similarity with outcome (ES = .00). Research from the previous decade uncovered several studies that suggested the presence of a modest interaction effect of patient and therapist age on treatment benefit (e.g., Luborsky, Mintz, et al., 1980; Morgan, Luborsky, Crits-Christoph, Curtis, & Soloman, 1982), however. For example, Dembo, Ikle, and Ciarlo (1983) found that young adult clients (aged 18 to 30) whose therapists were of similar age experienced less distress and social isolation after treatment than clients whose therapists' ages were discrepant by 10 or more years (older or younger). Indeed, Beck (1988) found that therapists who were more than 10 years *younger* than their clients obtained the poorest outcomes of all levels of patient therapist age similarity. This latter study is noteworthy because it included quite large samples (*N* = 250 therapists and *N* = 1,500 patients) in which both therapist and patient ages extended along a considerable range. This methodological feature distinguishes this study from those conducted in university counseling centers and other agencies in which there is considerable age restriction.

We did not subject these studies to meta-analysis because they did not achieve what we considered to be a critical mass (*N* = 10). Qualitatively, in our review of these findings, we conclude that there is little contemporary research to suggest that therapist age or the age similarity of patient and therapist contributes significantly and meaningfully to treatment outcomes.

Therapist Race

Virtually no research, either recently or in years past, has been initiated in order to compare outcomes as a direct effect of therapist race or ethnicity, independently of that of the patient. Most research is relational in nature and assumes that mutuality is or may be improved when therapist and patient share certain ethnic experiences. These shared perspectives can be assumed to reflect systematic training to enhance cultural sensitivity (Valdez, 2000) or can be derived from the presence of a shared cultural background. Unfortunately, however, there is still a dearth of empirical evidence to support these hypotheses. Nonetheless, belief in the importance of a shared cultural perspective, underwrites the use of measures of

TABLE 7.1 Therapist Sex

Study	*N*	Diagnosis	Treatments	Measures	Outcome Effects	ES *[r]*
Fiorentine & Hillhouse, 1999	302	Substance abuse	Counseling	Therapist sex break-down not provided	Significant effect of gender match on abstinence (abstinence = no days of drug use over a six-month period)	ES1 = .15
Gottheil, Sterling, Weinstein, & Kurtz, 1994	634	Cocaine use	Individual psycho-therapy (not manualized)	Therapist sex: Male (*N*=3) Female (*N*=5)	No significant effect of gender on dropout (dropout = failure to return after intake)	ES2 = .002
					No significant effect of gender match on dropout (dropout = failure to return after intake)	ES2 = .09
Hampson & Beavers, 1996	434 (families)	Child or adolescent school/behavior problems; marital problems; family problems; problems with one parent	Family therapy	Female therapists conducted 69% of sessions	No significant effect of gender on therapist evaluation of degree to which family achieved therapy goals	ES2 = .01
Krippner & Hutchinson, 1990	288	Mixed depression/ anxiety (training clinic; clients with homicidal/suicidal ideation excluded)	Intake interview	Therapist sex: Male (*N*=11) Female (*N*=10)	Significant effect of female therapist gender on State-Trait Anxiety (STAI) scores;	ES1 = .12
					No significant effect of gender match on STAI scores	ES1 = 0[a]
Orme & Boswell, 1991	721	Mixed	Individual psycho-therapy	Therapist sex breakdown not provided	No significant effect of gender on attendance at intake	ES2 = 0[a]
					No significant effect of gender match on intake attendance	ES2 = 0[a]

Sterling, Gottheil, Weinstein, & Serota, 1998	967	Cocaine use	12 weeks of individual psychotherapy (one 60-minute session per week), intensive group psychotherapy (three 60-minute sessions per week), or both (one 60-minute individual session and one 60-minute group session per week)	Therapist sex: Male (*N*=6) Female (*N*=4)	No significant effect of gender on dropout (dropout = failure to return after intake)	ES2 = .04
					No significant effect of gender match on dropout	ES2 = .04
					No significant effect of gender on treatment length	ES2 = 0[a]
					No significant effect of gender match on length of treatment	ES2 = .06
					No significant effect of gender match on drug use (Addiction Severity Index [ASI] drug composite)	ES1 = –.08
					No significant effect of gender match on psychological state (ASI psychological composite)	ES2 = .08
Sue, Fujino, Hu, Takeuchi, & Zane, 1991	13,439	Mixed	N/A	Therapist sex breakdown not provided	Positive effect of gender match on lack of dropout (dropout = failure to return after first session)	ES2 = .045
					Positive effect of gender match on length of treatment	ES2 = .023
					Positive effect of gender match on Global Assessment Scale (GAS) outcomes	ES2 = .001
Talley, J. E., 1992	72	Mixed	"Very brief" individual psychotherapy	Therapist sex: Male (*N*=4) Female (*N*=8)	No significant effect of gender on multivariate outcome (Beck Depression Inventory, Zung Self-Rating Depression Scale, Zung Self-Rating Anxiety Scale)	ES1 = 0[a]
Wagner, Kilcrease-Fleming, Fowler, & Kazelskis, 1993	30	Sexual abuse	Individual psychotherapy	Therapist sex: Male (*N*=10) Female (*N*=7)	No significant effect of therapist gender on Child's Depression Inventory scores	ES1 = .24
					No significant effect of therapist gender on Piers-Harris Children's Self-Concept scale	ES2 = .28
Zlotnick, Elkin, & Shea, 1998	203	MDD	CBT/interpersonal therapy/imiprimine/PBO	Therapist sex: Male (*N*=20) Female (*N*=7)	No significant effect of therapist gender on Hamilton Rating Scale for Depression scores (HRSD)	ES1 = .12
					No significant effect of gender match on HRSD scores	ES1 = .14

[a] Effect size of zero used for results described merely as "not significant" with no other information provided or with direction of effect not specified.

"multicultural competence" in counseling and psychotherapy (e.g., Worthington, Mobley, Franks, & Tan, 2000).

The hypothesis that racial/ethnic similarity or sensitivity is a positive predictor of treatment benefit has been widely accepted, but this acceptance is based more on the basis of political exigencies and face validity than on empirical efforts to demonstrate its predictive validity. Contemporary scientific literature (e.g., Sexton & Whiston, 1991), as well as older studies (e.g., Atkinson, 1983; 1985; Atkinson & Schein, 1986), produce equivocal findings, at best, regarding the relationship of client-therapist ethnic similarity and treatment outcome. Whatever small advantages might be attributable to ethnic similarity are not consistent across ethnic groups and are thereby a very weak basis for definitive conclusions.

As in 1994 (Beutler, Machado, & Neufeldt, 1994), controlled assignment (quasi-experimental) studies still remain curiously absent in the literature on therapist ethnicity. In the designs used, the differences among various ethnic groups are confounded by failing either to differentiate among African-American, Hispanic, Asian, and other groups (e.g., Neimeyer & Gonzales, 1983) or an adequate number of ethnically identified therapists (e.g., Proctor & Rosen, 1981) to justify the analyses.

We found 11 papers, published between 1990 and 2000 (see Table 7.2), that reported data on ethnic/racial matching of patients and therapists that were suitable for meta-analysis. Ten of these reported improvement data, and four reported dropout data. Five improvement studies (Hosch et al., 1995; Ricker, Nystul, & Waldo, 1999; Snowden, Hu, & Jerrell, 1995; Sue et al., 1991; Yeh, Eastman, & Cheung, 1994) and three dropout studies (Sterling, Gottheil, Weinstein, & Serota, 1998; Sue et al., 1991; Yeh et al., 1994) produced evidence of a significant effect of patient-therapist ethnic similarity. These studies indicated that ethnic match, particularly among Asian-Americans (Snowden et al., 1995) and Mexican-Americans (Sue et al., 1991), was conducive to improvement.

Although the effect sizes ranged from 0 to .28, the mean (weighted) effect size *(r)* was .02 and was significant ($p < .05$). Moreover, the test of homogeneity indicated a great deal of intratest variability ($Q = 21.07$; $p < .05$), a finding that suggests the presence of unidentified moderators of treatment effects. The small size of this effect casts doubt on the value of ethnic similarity as a predictor of treatment effects, even calling into question the promising relationship noted by Beutler, Machado, and Neufeldt (1994). Nevertheless, it does raise the need to look to patient and therapist cultural beliefs and other such factors as moderators of treatment effects. For example, attitudinal factors may account for the observation that Asian-Americans (e.g., Fujino, Okazaki, & Young, 1994; Sue et al., 1991) and Latinos (e.g., Sue et al., 1991) may be more susceptible to ethnic fit with their therapists than African-Americans (also see Beck, 1988), and the impact of language match remains relatively unexplored (e.g., Snowden et al., 1995).

Future research should also note and adjust to the possibility that the strength of effect of racial/ethnic similarity may be attenuated if these undisclosed moderating variables are, in fact, masking a relationship between racial similarity and dropout. That is, premature termination and treatment benefit are likely to be confounded. Specifically, the high dropout rates among those patients who are mismatched with their therapists make these individuals unavailable for outcome assessment. If one can assume (and that assumption appears tenuous) that those who drop out of treatment are also likely to have poor outcomes, then it may well be that racial mismatching has an undisclosed negative effect on treatment outcomes.

Observable States

Professional Discipline and Amount of Training

The most frequently researched and controversial of the variables within the domain of therapist observable states include type of professional training (professional discipline), amount of training, skill in facilitating therapeutic processes (Alberts & Edelstein, 1990; Thompson, 1986), and level of experience (Guest & Beutler, 1988; Tracey, Hays, Malone, & Herman, 1988). However, few reviews have found meaningful direct effects of these qualities and characteristics on outcome.

One of the most interesting but, surprisingly, still under-researched areas pertains to the professional discipline of the therapist. In most research studies, the type and amount of training are confounded. The meta-analysis by Smith, Glass, and Miller (1980) remains the only comprehensive review, to our knowledge, that included a systematic inspection of outcomes as a function of the type as well as the amount of training. They obtained results slightly favoring psychologists ($r = .28$) over psychiatrists.

TABLE 7.2 Therapist Race/Ethnic Match

Study	*N*	Diagnosis	Treatments	Measures	Outcome Effects	ES *[r]*
Outcome as assessed by specific symptom improvement or global improvement						
Crits-Christoph, Siqueland et al., 1999	487	Cocaine dependence	Cognitive Therapy (CT) + Group Drug Counseling (GDC); Individual Drug Counseling (IDC) + GDC; Supportive Expressive Therapy + GDC; GDC alone	N/A	No significant effect of ethnic match on Addiction Severity Index (ASI) drug use composite scores	ES1 = 0[a]
Fiorentine & Hillhouse, 1999	356	Substance abuse	Counseling	Therapist ethnicity not provided	No significant effect of ethnic match on abstinence (abstinence = no days of drug use over a six-month period)	ES1 = .07
Hampson & Beavers, 1996	434 (families)	Child or adolescent school/behavior problems Marital problems Family problems Problems with one parent	Family therapy (not manualized)	Therapist ethnicity 93% European-American	No significant effect of ethnic match on outcome (therapist evaluation of degree to which family achieved therapy goals)	ES2 = 0[a]
Hosch et al., 1995	193	Schizophrenia	Psychotherapy and medication (individual psychotherapy)	Therapist ethnicity Hispanic/other	Significant effect of ethnic match on adherence to medication regime Significant effect of language match on adherence	ES2 = .14 ES2 = –.18
Ricker, Nystul, & Waldo, 1999	51	Mixed	Individual psychotherapy (six sessions)	Therapist ethnicity not provided	Significant effect of ethnic match on SCL-90 Global Severity Index (GSI) scores	ES2 = .28

(continues)

TABLE 7.2 (*Continued*)

Study	*N*	Diagnosis	Treatments	Measures	Outcome Effects	ES *[r]*
Rosenheck, Fontana, & Cottrol, 1995	4726	Post-traumatic stress disorder (PTSD)	Individual or group psychotherapy	Therapist ethnicity African-European-American	No significant effect of ethnic match on PTSD symptom reduction (clinician-rated improvement based on a 5-point Likert scale)	ES1 = .02
					No significant effect of ethnic match on global psychiatric severity	ES2 = –.06
Snowden, Hu, & Jerrell, 1995	26,943	Schizophrenia (35%) Adjustment reaction (19%)	N/A	Therapist ethnicity European-American (60%), Hispanic (15%), African-American (9%), Asian American (14%)	Significant effect of ethnic match on decreased use of emergency room	ES2 ≥ .01
					Significant effect of language match on decreased use of emergency room	ES2 ≥ .02
Sterling et al., 1998	967	Cocaine use	Individual therapy, intensive group therapy, or both	Therapist ethnicity African-American (*N*=6), European-American (*N*=4)	No significant effect of ethnic match on ASI drug composite	ES1 = –.05
					No significant effect of ethnic match on ASI psychological composite	ES2 = –.04
Sue, Fujino, Hu, Takeuchi, & Zane, 1991	13,439	Mixed	N/A	Therapist ethnicity Asian/African/Mexican/European-American	Effect of ethnic match on Global Assessment Scale (GAS) outcomes	ES2 = .01
Yeh, Eastman, & Cheung, 1994	4616	Mixed	N/A	Therapist ethnicity Asian/African/Mexican/European-American	Effect of ethnic match on GAS outcomes	ES2 = .03

Outcome as assessed by dropout or length of treatment						
Gottheil et al., 1994	634	Cocaine use	Individual psychotherapy	Therapist ethnicity African-American (*N*=5), European-American (*N*=3)	No significant effect of ethnic match on dropout (dropout = failure to return after intake)	ES2 = –.06
Sterling et al., 1998	967	Cocaine use	Individual therapy, intensive group therapy, or both	Therapist ethnicity African-American (*N*=6), European-American (*N*=4)	No significant effect of ethnic match on dropout (dropout = failure to return after intake)	ES2 = .05
					No significant effect of ethnic match on length of treatment	ES2 = .00
Sue, Fujino, Hu, Takeuchi, & Zane, 1991	13,439	Mixed	N/A	Therapist ethnicity Asian/African/ Mexican/ European-American	Effect of ethnic match on dropout (dropout = failure to return after first session)	ES2 = .17
					Significant effect of ethnic match on treatment length	ES2 = .05
Yeh, Eastman, & Cheung, 1994	4616	Mixed	N/A	Therapist ethnicity Asian/African/ Mexican/ European-American	Significant effect of ethnic match on dropout for adolescents (dropout = failure to return after first session)	ES2 = .18
					Effect of ethnic match on dropout	ES2 = .10

[a] Effect size of zero used for results described merely as "not significant" with no other information provided or with direction of effect not specified.

The results of individual studies of therapist training and experience have produced a mixture of findings. One study undertaken by the *Consumer Reports* (1995; Howard, Krause, Caburnay, & Noel, 2001; Seligman, 1995) has received a great deal of attention. This study was based on a survey of 22,000 readers of the magazine. Readers were asked to indicate whether they had ever sought or received mental health treatment from any of a variety of professionals. From this large readership pool, 7,000 completed the survey, and 4,100 of these reported that they had sought psychotherapy. Respondents were asked to rate the severity of their problems at the time they sought treatment and again at the end. A very similar percentage of those seeing psychologists and those seeing psychiatrists indicated that they had improved on this scale. Those who saw social workers, however, rated their improvement somewhat higher, whereas those who saw marriage and family counselors reported somewhat less benefit than those seeing psychologists or psychiatrists.

Similarly, using a more tightly controlled design among samples of psychiatrists, psychiatry residents, family practice residents, and medical students, Propst, Paris, and Rosberger (1994) found an effect favoring those trained in mental health professions, an effect that was most observable among psychiatry versus family practice residents. The effect size was a modest *(r)* .14—significant but not very powerful.

Blatt, Sanislow, Zuroff, and Pilkonis (1996) inspected the personal background characteristics of 24 psychiatrists and psychologists who saw patients in the Treatment of Depression Collaborative Research Project (TDCRP). Although they did not directly compare professionals from different backgrounds, they did compare those that did and did not rely on medication in their practices, an indirect index of professional affiliation. They found that the most effective treatments were offered by those who did not prescribe medication and who maintained a psychological rather than a biological orientation to depression and its treatment. A modestly strong effect size was obtained ($r = .48$).

These findings parallel other evidence that has addressed the efficiency and effectiveness of recognizing and treating specific clinical disorders, like Major Depression, by mental health practitioners and primary care providers. Wells and Sturm (1996) found that primary care providers were quite inaccurate in identifying depression and were less effective than mental health practitioners in treating it. Similarly, Lave, Frank, Schulberg, and Kamlet (1998) found that mental health experts cost more, but they outperformed primary care providers when treating depressed patients. Moreover, Barlow, Burlingame, Harding and Behrman (1997) found that professionally trained therapists were more focused than their nonprofessionally trained counterparts and that this focus was related to reduced symptoms (*rs* range from .20 to .26).

On the other hand, an emerging body of evidence suggests that the use of professional therapists may be contraindicated under certain circumstances. For example, among those who have been subjected to traumatic stress, working with professional grief counselors may slow progress and even encourage the development of protracted symptoms of anxiety and stress (Bisson & Deahl, 1994; Bisson, Jenkins, Alexander, & Bannister, 1997; Carlier, Lamberts, van Uchlen, & Gersons, 1998; Gist, Lubin, & Redburn, 1998). Professional therapists may be most useful among that subgroup of trauma victims who fail to respond to family and extant social support systems.

Assuming that the foregoing observation is the exception rather than the rule and that it is desirable to have some specific mental health training when working with most types of problems, it is difficult to define the amount of such training that is most beneficial. Thus, a meta-analytic review by Bowman et al. (2001) found a nonsignificant and small effect size among professional, nonprofessional, and graduate student therapists ($d = .08$), but the confounding of training and experience in these classifications makes it difficult to trust these conclusions. After all, a computer can deliver an effective treatment almost as well as a trained practitioner (Jacobs et al., 2001). But it is difficult to define the meaning of "training" for a computer.

These confounds and other problems associated with the declining attention to therapist variables have been discussed in a series of articles by leading theorists (Bergin, 1997; Beutler, 1997; Lambert & Okiishi, 1997; Luborsky et al., 1997; Strupp & Anderson, 1997). They conclude that different research paradigms or models may be necessary in order to understand therapist effects, including questions about how training and experience affect treatment outcomes.

Beutler (1997) has pointed out that the effects of training can only be understood if we know the content of training. It is not sufficient to simply note its presence. This conclusion is consistent with evidence that training that is directed by specific, manualized concepts and tasks tend to produce enhanced results over non-specified and general training (Shaw & Dobson, 1987; Shaw, Olmsted et al., 1999; Luborsky, Crits-Christoph, & McClellan et al., 1986; Luborsky, Diguer, Seligman et al., 1999). Beutler suggests that these findings may indicate that the definition of training is insensitive to important distinctions and variations among training programs and experiences. Thus, rather than using academic degree to represent amount of training received, researchers might be better advised to assess training in terms of the amount of time spent in studying treatment specific concepts and practices. Such a definition would allow one to separate the effects of type of training from the amount of training and clinical experience.

Four studies published in the past decade have attempted this task of disentangling the effects of amount and type of training (Bein et al., 2000; Pekarik, 1994; Steinhelber, Patterson, Cliffe, & LeGoullon, 1984; Stolk & Perlesz, 1990) by providing therapists with specific, additional training in the use of particular types of therapy. The effect sizes among these studies varied from (r) –.09 to .48. No clear pattern of effects were observable, and because of the limited number of studies, we did not assess the mean effect size for significance.

In one of the more noteworthy studies, Bein et al. (2000) assessed the effect of specific training in time-limited psychodynamic therapy. Comparisons of clinicians who did and did not have systematic training in this manualized version of psychodynamic therapy, but who were otherwise comparable on dimensions of experience, failed to yield a significant or meaningful difference.

In contrast, both Pekarik (1994) and Steinhelber et al. (1984) found that positive effects accrued to patients who were treated by therapists with specialized training or supervision. Though significant, the effect sizes associated with therapist training were uniformly small in these studies ($r < .10$), and Stolk and Perlesz (1990) found a negative relationship between the provision of enhanced training and subsequent patient satisfaction at the end of a five-month period. Overall, these findings tend to cast doubt on the validity of the suggestion that specific training in psychotherapy, even when unconfounded with general experience, may be related to therapeutic success or skill.

Professional Experience

Summarizing contemporary research on therapist experience, Christensen and Jacobson (1994) conclude that the evidence for the value of accruing professional experience is weak at best. They suggest that training doctoral-level psychotherapists is not justified by this literature. Although the negativity of this conclusion may be consistent with much of the available research, reviews of this topic, including meta-analytic reviews of research (e.g. Crits-Christoph et al., 1991; Stein & Lambert, 1995), have not always drawn such dour conclusions.

In an effort to disentangle these results, we found and evaluated four studies that quite effectively separated therapist experience level from various aspects of training. Interestingly, these studies generally support the role of therapist experience, though they do so to a greater or lesser degree (rs from –.19 to .48). Blatt et al. (1996) found the strongest positive relationship ($r = .48$) between experience level and outcome among those using the same, structured, and manualized treatments. Similarly, Propst, et al. (1994) found that experienced therapists produced more positive outcomes than inexperienced ones, across professional disciplines, looking both at the end of treatment and at followup. However, in this latter case, the effect sizes were less than .10, a striking difference from Blatt et al. In still another twist on these findings, Luborsky et al. (1997) found that some therapists are only effective with a particular type of patient, whereas others are effective with a wide variety of patients, partially dependent on the therapist's level of experience. Though significant, the effect sizes associated with these relationships were variable across these studies and were generally relatively small ($rs < .15$).

Although not falling within the temporal limits imposed on our meta-analysis, a re-analysis of the Multi-Center Collaborative Study for the Treatment of Panic Disorder (Hupert, Bufka et al., in press) revealed stronger effects of therapist experience than found by either Blatt et al. (1996) or Luborsky et al. (1997). An important contribution of this recent study was the separate consideration of measures of the levels of therapist experience in conducting psychotherapy and levels of training. The authors report effect sizes as high as (r) .72, indicating that general therapist experience in conducting psychotherapy was associated with decreases in patient anxiety levels and panic. Interestingly, however, they did not find that the amount of time spent conducting cognitive therapy was more advantageous to outcomes than simply the amount of general psychotherapy experience ($r = .20$). Such findings suggest that what is relevant about experience may be general clinical contact rather than the development of specific proficiencies. More research of this type may yield promising directions for study.

Interpersonal Psychotherapy Style

Interpersonal psychotherapeutic styles take different forms, ranging from patterns of dominance and positivity to various verbal and nonverbal styles. In this section, we consider three varieties that have generated a modicum of research (see Table 7.3). These include patterns of reciprocal interaction, as best typified by the circumplex model of interactions as applied to psychotherapy by Kiesler (1988), Benjamin (1974), and Constanino (2000); patterns of verbal expression (Elliott, Barker, Caskey, & Pistrang, 1982); and combinations of verbal and nonverbal behaviors.

Reciprocal Interactive Styles. Although therapist verbal and other interpersonal styles are usually conceptualized as exerting a unidirectional effect in much research, their relational and reciprocating influences have received more research attention. While interpersonal styles are relatively domain-specific and relatively stable across particular therapists and psychotherapy models (e.g., Hardy & Shapiro, 1985), they are reactive to patient responses and differences (Fairbanks, McGuire, & Harris, 1982; Stiles, Shapiro, & Firth-Cozens, 1989). Thus, interpersonal styles may be related to lexical qualities of therapist language, but they are more closely linked to interactive processes that affect therapist intentions (Elliott, 1985).

The circumplex model of communication identifies the presence of reciprocating friendly-to-unfriendly and dominant-to-submissive. These reciprocal concepts have been applied to predicting the development of good therapeutic relationships (Kiesler & Watkins, 1989; Kivlighan, McGovern, & Corazzini, 1984; Reandeau & Wampold, 1991), to evaluating theory-relevant changes during psychotherapy (Henry, Schacht & Strupp, 1990), and to assessing therapist-client compatibility (Henry & Strupp, 1991; Rudy, McLemore, & Gorsuch, 1985).

"Friendly behaviors," a concept under which we have also included research on "positive therapist behaviors" (Table 7.3), has been quite consistently associated with good outcomes (e.g., Beyebach & Carranza, 1997; Coady, 1991; Henry, Schacht, & Strupp, 1990; Najavits & Strupp, 1994; Thompson & Hill, 1993). Friendly behaviors are generally reciprocated by patient positive responses in these studies, and at least moderate levels of patient-therapist similarity in the friendly-unfriendly dimension and dissimilarity in the dominance-submissive dimension are associated with aspects of outcomes (Andrews, 1990; Rudy, McClemore, & Gorsuch, 1985; Tracey, 1986). Particularly strong ($r = .52$) effect sizes were obtained by Henry, Shacht, and Strupp (1990) for both therapist positivity (friendliness begets positivity) and dominance-submission as a reciprocating predictor. They found that poor outcome client-therapist dyads were distinguished from good outcome dyads by a pattern of low therapist positivity/friendliness, by high levels of therapist hostility, and by reciprocal, client self-criticism (a dominance-submission pattern).

A similar pattern was found by Andrews (1990), who explored compatibility between therapist and patient styles in three types of client-therapist dyads. One set of dyads was characterized by complementary patterns of communication (i.e., reciprocity on the control axis and correspondence on the friendly axis); another was characterized by acomplementarity (i.e., complementary on only one of the two axes); and still another was characterized by anticomplementarity (i.e., correspondence on the dominance axis and reciprocity on the friendly axis). As expected, those dyads that were characterized by complementarity were more likely to improve than those with anticomplementary stylistic behaviors ($r = .53$).

Such findings as the foregoing suggest that interpersonally compatible styles among therapists and clients may be indicative of whether or not psychotherapy will proceed in a positive direction. In an interesting contrast to this latter finding, Miller, Benefield, and Tonigan (1993) found that confrontational (unfriendly) styles were positively related to a decrease in drinking among alcohol-abusing patients one year after treatment. Unfriendly therapist behaviors also resulted in a lower level of efficiency in patient communication.

Although this literature has not grown substantially in the past decade, the available studies continue to be promising. Among the eight studies obtained for the current review, effect sizes (r) varied from near zero to .54 (Coady, 1991), with a mean effect size of .08. These results are nonsignificant and only suggestive of their being styles of communication that tend to draw out reciprocal and complementary responses from

TABLE 7.3 Therapeutic Style

Study	*N*	Diagnosis	Treatments	Outcome Effects	Effect Size *[r]*
Reciprocal Interpersonal Style					
Andrews, 1990	45	Mildly to moderately neurotic. None showing severe psychopathology or organic involvement	Combination of dynamic, cognitive behavioral, relationship-oriented support, and eclectically derived methods Sessions: 10–16, $M = 11.5$	Positive effect of patient-therapist anticomplementarity on positive change in patient outcome at post-test	ES2 = .53
Beyebach & Carranza, 1997	32	Marital, relational, academic achievement problems, depression, psychosomatic complaints	Individual solution-focused psychotherapy at private brief therapy center Groups: early dropout ($M = 1.7$ sessions); continuation ($M = 5.6$ sessions)	Positive effect of positive (vs. negative) therapist behaviors on continuation (vs. dropout)	ES2 = .49
Coady, 1991	9	"Well-functioning psychiatric outpatients"	Psychodynamic psychotherapy	Significant positive effect of positive therapist behavior (as measured by SASB) on overall outcome at post-test	ES2 = .54
Henry, Schacht, & Strupp, 1990	14	DSM-III Axis 1 & II, significant interpersonal problems	Time-limited dynamic psychotherapy Session: 25, weekly	Significant positive effect of positive therapist behavior (as measured by SASB) on change in introject at post-treatment Significant positive effect of positive therapist behavior (as measured by SASB) on positive change in symptomatic distress	ES1 = .52 ES2 = .52
Miller, Benefield & Tonigan, 1993	42	Problem drinkers	Drinker's Check-up with directive-confrontational counseling or with client-centered counseling Sessions: two motivational check-ups	Positive effect of positive therapist behaviors (low confrontation) on improved drinking composite scores at 12-month followup	ES3 = .65

(continues)

TABLE 7.3 (Continued)

Study	N	Diagnosis	Treatments	Outcome Effects	Effect Size *[r]*
Najavits & Strupp, 1994	80	NIMH Diagnostic Interview Schedule Axis 1 (87%), Axis II (67%); SCL-90-R—GSI < 1 SD of normative mean	Time-limited dynamic psychotherapy Therapist groups based on client outcome and treatment length: "more-effective" and "less effective" Sessions: 25, weekly	Significant positive effect of positive (vs. negative) therapist behaviors on positive ratings of therapist effectiveness at post-treatment	ES2 = .31
Rudy, McLemore, & Gorsuch, 1985	42	None stated	Advanced doctoral students delivered dynamic psychotherapy Sessions: M = 25, R = 6–80	Positive effect of positive therapist nonverbal interpersonal style (measured by SASB) on client-rated positive change at post-treatment	ES2 = .46
Thompson & Hill, 1993	24	Unassertive in interpersonal interaction. SCL-90-R—GSI M = 49.46 SD = 7.86	Advanced graduate student therapists delivered behavioral, humanistic and psychoanalytic psychotherapy Sessions: 6	Positive effect of positive (vs. negative) therapist behavior on positive change in global outcome at post-treatment	ES2 = .16
Verbal Styles					
Holzer et al., 1997	20	DSM-II nonpsychotic	Psychodynamic therapists in two groups: "most successful" (MS) & "least successful" (LS) Sessions: MS M = 61 weeks; LS M = 43 weeks	Positive effect of use of emotion words on improvement in global outcome scores at post-test	ES2 = .48
Tracey, 1986	33	Appropriate for time-limited therapy (not psychotic, able to form rapid affective bonds, able to tolerate loss)	Time-limited psychotherapy	Positive effect of therapist topic determination (TD) on improvement in global scores at post-treatment (therapist TD vs. Client TD, Dyad TD)	ES2 = .79

Nonverbal Styles					
Coady, 1991	9	"Well-functioning psychiatric outpatients"	Psychodynamic psychotherapy	Significant positive effect of positive therapist behavior (as measured by SASB) on overall outcome at post-test	ES2 = .54
Rudy, McLemore, & Gorsuch, 1985	42	None reported	Advanced doctoral students delivered dynamic psychotherapy Sessions: M = 25, R = 6–80	Positive effect of positive therapist nonverbal interpersonal style (measured by SASB) on patient-rated positive change at post-treatment	ES2 = .46
Combined Verbal and Nonverbal Styles					
Bennun & Schindler, 1988	35	Behavioral avoidance	Cognitive behavioral individual therapy with exposure and cognitive interventions Sessions: weekly, M = 12, SD = 3	Positive effect of therapist combined verbal and nonverbal style on improvement in patient symptom-specific scores at post-treatment	ES1 = .60
				Significant positive effect of combined therapist verbal and nonverbal style on patient-rated positive global outcome	ES2 = .83

ES1: Target measure at post-treatment.
ES2: Global measure at post-treatment.
ES3: Target measure at followup.
ES4: Global measure at followup.

patients. Complementary and positive interactive styles may be more conducive to therapeutic work than their counterparts.

VERBAL PATTERNS OF INTERACTION IN PSYCHOTHERAPY. Relevant verbal patterns of interaction that are used in psychotherapy include both noncontent (e.g., the number of words and sentences used) and content (i.e., topical) aspects of communication. Although studies of noncontent aspects of speech generated a plethora of research in the early days of the discipline, only a few studies of general therapist activity level have survived as a relevant area of contemporary research. Holzer et al. (1997) found that the use of emotion-laden words correlated with subsequent outcomes, and Tracey (1986) reported that the introduction of topics by the therapist is strongly associated with outcomes ($r = .79$). He compared two matched pairs of continuing and prematurely terminated client-therapist dyads in a planned, short-term therapy format. Although therapist initiation of topic was an important factor in retention, so was the emergence of agreement. High proportions of client-therapist topic agreement, regardless of who initiated the topic, were associated both with continuance in therapy and with the amount of benefit achieved. These findings were then cross validated on a larger sample of therapist-client dyads and in a different setting. Naturalistic studies have confirmed and extended the importance of therapist verbal activity levels (Horn-George & Anchor, 1982) and topic initiation (Horvath & Greenberg, 1986) in aspects of treatment process and session outcomes. Such findings suggest that a subtle pattern of collaboration and tacit agreement exists between patient and therapist in successful treatment, which may be particularly implicated in the development of the therapeutic relationship.

Though still promising, and in spite of some interesting findings, research on reciprocal verbal patterns is fading from view and from research interest, like many others that we have noted. Over the past two decades, it has failed to generate a sufficient number of independent studies to allow meta-analytic consideration.

PATTERNS OF MULTICHANNEL AND NONVERBAL COMMUNICATION. When people are attempting to conceal emotional states, discrepancies tend to appear between their verbal and nonverbal communication styles. Voice tone, body posture, and proxemic presentations tend to "leak" the information that is not disclosed in speech content (Babad, Bernieri, & Rosenthal, 1989; Ekman & Davidson, 1994). Among therapists, it is often thought that such discrepancies between content and noncontent aspects of speech can serve to identify hidden client emotional states (Fridlund, 1994). Indeed, it appears that speech sounds in which content has been filtered out and written communication that contains content but no speech sounds provide reliable, though often different, types of information about a patient to an observer or therapist. Comparisons of content-filtered speech samples and written transcripts provides a methodology by which to study channel incongruence. This methodology suggests that both content-laden and content-filtered speech can convey intense emotional states, although the noncontent aspects of language may be judged to be more accurate in a therapeutic environment (Mohr, Shoham-Salomon, Engle, & Beutler, 1991). Bernieri, Blanck, Rosenthal, Vannicelli, and Yerrell (1991) found that the degree of judged correspondence between content and noncontent channels of communication was higher among therapists when speaking *about* clients than when speaking *to* them. Correspondingly, therapists were rated as less helpful and more dishonest in the latter case.

Unfortunately, there have been few studies of nonverbal or combined nonverbal and verbal interaction patterns on actual clinical outcomes. An exception is the work of Bennun and Schindler (1988) who found that therapist verbal activity level was positively associated with treatment benefit among phobic patients in cognitive therapy (rs from .60 to .83; $p < .05$). Although these findings are generally consistent with older studies and suggest that correspondence between verbal and nonverbal qualities of communication facilitates psychological treatment, this research area is disappearing from view and has failed to generate a significant body of research in the past two decades.

Treatment Methods

MANUAL-GUIDED TREATMENT. Research on treatment methods and manuals has reaped the benefits that have accrued from the decline of research on the therapist as a variable in psychotherapy. Were it not for the fact that some neglected therapist states and traits may be forgotten but important predictors of treatment outcome, one might be disposed to believe that there is justice in this turn of the screw. For nearly three decades, what the therapist actually did was ignored, and what we knew about the effects of psychotherapy was restricted to self-reports, from which comparisons were made among different "theories." In these comparisons, the validity and reliability of self-reported procedures suffered in the face of the influence of uncontrolled and idiosyncratic influences exerted by the therapist's personal predilections and proclivities. Indeed, the gradual recognition of the uncontrolled influences exerted by the therapist him- or herself gave birth to treatment manuals. These manuals were originally viewed as a way of standardizing and controlling the processes of treatment in research studies so that therapy factors could be detected and extracted from the "noise" of therapist and patient factors (Nathan, Stuart, & Dolan, 2000). Standardization of treatment also provided a way of both improving training in psychotherapy and identifying ways to refine treatments in order to improve their effects.

Unfortunately, standardizing the treatment has not eliminated the influence of the individual therapist on outcomes (Luborsky, Crits-Christoph, McLellan 1985; Luborsky, McLellan, Diguer et al., 1997). Despite the controversies that surround them (e.g., Castonguay, Schut, Constantino, & Halperin, 1999; Chambless & Hollon, 1998; Davison, 1998; Newman & Castonguay, 1999; Weisz, Hawley, Pilkonis, Woody, & Follette, 2000), treatment manuals proliferate, and their use in clinical training has grown. No fewer than 12 separate lists of manualized treatments have been identified as being empirically supported. These lists have included three Division 12 task force reports (e.g., Chambless, Baker et al., 1998; Chambless, Sanderson et al., 1996; Task Force on Promotion and Dissemination of Psychological Procedures, 1995) and an associated book (Nathan & Gorman, 1998); the reports of a special working group on child and adolescent treatments (Spirito, 1999); three general reviews by independent groups and authors (e.g., Dobson & Craig, 1998; Kendall & Chambless, 1998; Seligman, 1993); a comprehensive review commissioned by the British government (Roth & Fonagy, 1996); and three reviews of special populations (Gatz, Fiske, Fox, KasKie, & Kasl-Godley, 1998; Read, Kahler, & Stevenson, 2001; Wilson & Gil, 1996). These lists are overlapping, and because they excluded both treatment models that have not been researched and those that have received little or no support, the lists do not nearly represent the total number of manuals available.

Drawing from just eight of these lists, Chambless and Ollendick (2001) observed that 108 different manualized treatments have been identified, all meeting specific criteria of empirical support for work with adults. They identified 37 additional manuals for working with children and adolescents. These 145 manuals, however, offered treatment for only 51 of the 397 available diagnostic and problem groups. Few psychotherapy training programs can actually introduce students to more than one or two of these manualized treatments, and, given the time required for training, it is difficult to imagine how students or professionals could learn enough of them to be of general value in practice.

Some (e.g., Addis, 1997; Barlow, 1994; Laidlaw, 2001; Waltz, Addis, Koerner, & Jacobson, 1993) view treatments as being robust and transferable across populations and settings by the use of manuals. Others (e.g., Beutler, 2000; Strupp & Anderson, 1997), however, argue that extant manuals may be too rigid to be usefully applied in most clinical settings, and they suggest that therapists may find that they stifle creativity. Several studies bear on this latter point. For example, Addis and Krasnow (2000) found that many therapists' attitudes toward manuals were very negative; Strupp and Anderson (1997) found that the most effective psychotherapists in controlled studies departed from manualized directives; and Henry and colleagues (Henry, Schacht et al., 1993; Henry, Strupp, Butler, Schacht, & Binder, 1993) found that therapist interpersonal skills were negatively correlated with the ability to learn a manual. Correlational data has even demonstrated that high levels of adherence to specific models or procedures of psychotherapy may actually interfere with the development of a good working relationship (Henry et al., 1993) and with good outcomes (Castonguay, Goldfried, Wiser, Raue, & Hayes, 1996). Allowing therapists flexibility may enhance outcomes as much as following structured treatments. For example, the mere process of providing therapists with feedback about the progress of their patients may result in adjustments to treatment that improve the results, even when therapists do not have an explicit manual (e.g., Lambert, Whipple et al., 2001).

Although the use of manuals reduces the variable efficacy of the procedures used and may enhance the positive effects of therapist experience (e.g., Crits-Christoph et al., 1991), there is still a great deal of variation in how a given manual is applied and used. The structure and form of how a given manual is applied vary as a function of the setting and population on which it is practiced (Malik, Alimohamed, Holaway, & Beutler, 2000). These variations leave many questions unanswered about the nature of "optimal" compliance, how to best maintain therapist adherence to these criteria over time, and how to optimize manual flexibility without falling prey to unbridled creativity (e.g., Addis, 1997; Beutler, 2000; Caspar, in press; Henry et al., 1993a). Most important, there is little evidence that the use of treatment manuals actually improves treatment outcomes.

For example, a meta-analysis of 90 studies revealed that naturalistically applied psychotherapy was as effective as using structured manuals. Both in clinically representative and nonrepresentative samples of patients, the two kinds of treatment produced similar levels of improvement that increased as a function of time in treatment (Shadish, Matt, Navarro, & Phillips, 2000). The authors concluded that many of the differences that have been observed among naturalistic and research studies might be the result of differences in patient severity and complexity rather than a weakness of naturalistic treatment per se. A mega-analysis of 302 meta-analyses of various forms of psychotherapy and psychoeducation (Lipsey & Wilson, 1993) also found very similar outcomes between highly structured research treatments and the usual treatments applied in naturalistic settings. Collectively, the consistency of these results suggests that, while the use of manuals reduces outcome variability, few mean differences in outcomes accrue as a function of using treatment manuals in clinically relevant samples.

During the last decade, three well-controlled studies have been conducted on the effects of manualized versus nonmanualized treatments. Comparing an individualized cognitive therapy to a manualized cognitive therapy, Emmelkamp, Bouman, and Blaauw (1994) found a modest, mean negative effect of manualization of treatment on both symptom and general functioning scores at both treatment's end and followup (with *rs* ranging from –.11 to –.33). In contrast, Schulte, Kunzel, Pepping, and Schulte-Bahrenberg (1992) found small positive effects of manualization on treatment ($r = .12$). To complete the picture, the previously reviewed study by Bein et al. (2000), based on the Vanderbilt II project, compared the effects of therapists before and after learning a manualized treatment. They found largely nonsignificant differences between the two conditions ($r = .02$).

Such findings as the foregoing do not speak well for the value of treatment manuals as a means of improving treatment effects, but the variability of such findings suggests that moderating (ATI) variables may influence the effectiveness of manual guided treatment. Multon, Kivlighan, and Gold (1996) trained therapists in the use of short-term dynamic therapy, using a manual, and compared the effectiveness of novice and experienced therapists. They concluded that those who know the least are able to benefit from manualized training the most.

Supervision. Supervision of psychotherapy cases has been the major method of ensuring that therapists develop proficiency and skill. Unfortunately, studies relating supervision to outcome are sparse, and in most studies, the nature of supervision is relatively unspecified. In one study that actually included patient outcomes, Steinhelber, Patterson, Cliffe, and LaGoullon (1984) found no relationship between amount of supervision and changes on the Global Assessment Scale (GAS) over the course of therapy. Interestingly, the authors noted that improved GAS ratings were positively correlated with the degree to which the theoretical orientations of the therapist and supervisor corresponded. This relational view of supervision was also studied by Dodenhoff (1981), who found that the trainee's attraction to the supervisor was correlated with the degree to which supervisors rated the trainee as successful. Apparently, supervisors tend to rate highly the performance of those who agree with them.

Adherence/compliance and skill/competence. A review of research on therapist proficiency suggests the value of differentiating between *specific competence*, a concept that is often referred to as either compliance or adherence, and *general competence*, a measure of the skillfulness one exercises when applying treatment procedures. These two concepts—compliance and skill—are not highly intercorrelated (Barber, Crits-Christoph, & Luborsky, 1996), and a therapist may exhibit specific competence without being judged as highly skilled in the application of treatment. Skillfulness, in turn, may be specific either to a particular patient group or to a particular type of therapy, or it may be general and cut across therapy procedures or patient types. Within these limits, competence is closely related to the smoothness and seamlessness of delivering treatment, regardless of whether or not one is using a manual.

Using this distinction, Barber, Crits-Christoph, and Luborsky (1996) found no relationship between treatment outcome and either the general or specific competence of applying supportive techniques. However, skillfulness in delivering expressive techniques was related to changes in patient depression. These findings suggest that therapist skillfulness is not ubiquitous and that some skills may be more important to outcome than others.

Four significant studies have been conducted on the relationship of adherence to a manual and treatment outcome (Barber, Crits-Christoph, & Luborsky, 1996; Bein et al., 2000; Feeley, DeRubeis, & Gelfand, 1999; Kendall & Chu, 2000). Although all of these studies report significant effects arising from adhering to a manualized treatment, our analysis of these findings reveals that the effect sizes are modest and of limited clinical utility (*rs* from .02 to .39). Notably, in this analysis, the higher effect sizes tended to cluster among general or global outcome measures (ES2) as opposed to targeted and symptom-specific ones (ES1). This variability suggests that compliance with a specified treatment may have more of a general than a specific effect. Collectively, moreover, the effects obtained in these studies suggest that there is a modest to small relationship between the degree to which a therapist complies with structured treatment and outcomes. This conclusion must be tempered by the observation (Henry, Strupp et al., 1993) that compliance with a treatment manual may be achieved at the cost of qualities that enhance the treatment relationship. The most effective therapists tend to depart from treatment manuals in applying treatment (Strupp & Anderson, 1997).

Compared to studies of adherence and compliance, more variable treatment effects are noted for therapist skillfulness. We inspected six studies of this construct and their resulting nine effect sizes for ES1 (targeted, post-treatment effect), ES2 (global post-treatment effect), and ES4 (global followup effect). Four studies (Barlow, Burlingame et al., 1997; Harkness, 1997; O'Malley, Foley et al., 1988; Stolk & Perlesz, 1990) reported a positive relationship of therapist skill with outcome. The effect size (*r*) values ranged from .26 (Barlow et al., 1997) to .64 (O'Malley, Foley et al., 1988), indicating a relatively strong effect, with a very strong effect in some cases. Two other studies (Castonguay, Goldfried et al., 1996; Svartberg & Stiles, 1994) found a negative relationship between skill or competency and outcomes. The absolute values of the three effect sizes associated with these studies were also relatively large and variable, ranging from .26 (Castonguay et al., 1996) to .57 (Svartberg & Stiles, 1994). Collectively, the (weighted) mean effect size for all six of these studies was a nonsignificant (*r*) .07.

In a very interesting effort to systematically control type of supervision, Harkness (1997) trained supervisors in two conditions of supervisory intervention. These supervisory models included a client-focused method of supervision, which focused on skill building, and a model of process supervision that provided the trainee with empathy much as would be expected of a therapist in therapy. Depressed patients rated the skillfulness of their own therapists on a weekly basis. The results emphasized that both supervisor empathy and skill training were related to patient-derived benefits. Trainees were most satisfied with skill-building advice, but the author concluded that skill building in the absence of attention to empathic attunement was doomed to be ineffective.

Though not providing data to support its inclusion in our meta-analytic review, Bryant, Simons, and Thase (1999) give some insight into the way therapist skillfulness might affect outcomes. They demonstrated that therapist skill was a predictor of patient compliance with cognitive therapy homework assignments. In turn, homework compliance was associated with improved outcomes among depressed patients.

In contrast to these latter findings, Castonguay, Goldfried et al. (1996) explored the effects of therapist adherence with the requirements of cognitive therapy (CT) among medicated and nonmedicated patients. The competence of the clinician to maintain a focus on the interpersonal consequences of behavior was a predictor of poor outcome on measures of depression ($r = -.44$) as well as on a more general measure of improvement ($r = -.26$). The authors suggested that poor outcomes resulted when therapists attempted to correct problems in the relationship by becoming overly focused on CT procedures. Similarly, Svartberg and Stiles (1994) found a negative relationship between the level of skill in applying short-term anxiety-provoking psychotherapy and outcome ($r = -.57$). In spite of its size, because of the small sample ($N = 13$), this finding was not significant and must be interpreted with caution.

Classes of Interventions

Interventions are the techniques and procedures used to initiate change in psychotherapy. These interventions are typically developed from a formal theory of psychopathology or symptom development, but unlike the theory, interventions can be directly observed. The spawning theories serve both to construct the techniques that are used in a treatment and to define which ones are appropriate and inappropriate. This leads to some interesting contradictions. For example, among the empirically supported treatments (e.g., Chambless, Baker et al., 1998; Nathan & Gorman, 1998), are those that actually proscribe the use of effective interventions because they derive from other, incompatible theories. Thus, although a treatment model may be empirically supported, this does not tell us the standing or influence of each component part. Although specific techniques comprise what we think of as treatment, there is an uncertain relationship between the effects of the specific procedures used and the effectiveness of the whole treatment package.

For example, Jacobson et al. (1996) found that the specific procedures of cognitive analysis and change added nothing to treatment benefit beyond that attributable to increasing the patient's social activities. There were no differences in outcomes when a complete protocol of cognitive therapy (CT) was compared with the same treatment, absent all but the behavioral activation procedures. The findings suggest that theories tend to overrate the importance of specific techniques, based on the assumed validity of the theoretical model from which these techniques arise. This conclusion is further supported by a meta-analysis that compared whole treatment packages with the same treatment, minus a theoretically important procedure or element (Ahn & Wampold, 2001).

The observation that individual techniques are relatively weak contributors to outcomes has led some investigators to hypothesize that different techniques are interchangeable. It is not a specific technique that is important, but rather the use of a cluster or family of related techniques. In pursuing this possibility, most authors have become persuaded to believe that these clusters of effective procedures may not best be identified within the confines of any single theory (see Lampropoulos, 2000a, 2000b, 2001; Norcross & Newman, 1992). Thus, these authors have turned to research methodologies, rather than theoretical constructs, to define effective procedures. As a result of these efforts, a relatively large body of empirical research has accumulated on the effects of using techniques that fall within various clusters and families of techniques. Generally, these families of techniques have been identified through a more or less systematic analysis of previous research findings (e.g., Beutler, 1983; Beutler & Clarkin, 1990; Beutler, Clarkin, & Bongar, 2000; Goldfried, 1981; Norcross & Goldfried, 1992; Prochaska, 1984). For example, Beutler, Clarkin, and Bongar (2000) reviewed a large body of research on depression and chemical abuse, and employed reliability analysis to group-specific techniques into four groups or families. Each family of intervention was represented as a continuous dimension, the ends of which constituted contrasting types of interventions. These four broad classes of interventions and the associated dimensional representations included: (1) A dimension of therapist-led to patient-self-directed procedures, (2) a dimension of insight-focused to symptom-focused and skill-building interventions, (3) a dimension of emotion-focused (abreactive) to task-focused or supportive interventions, and (4) a dimension of high- to low-treatment intensity.

Because of their relative reliability and independence from specific theoretical frameworks, we have adopted this classification system as a method of organizing our review of research on therapy interventions. Where the volume of literature permits, we will separately consider some of the more specific interventions within each general class of intervention. We will also consider one set of techniques (therapist self-disclosure) independently of this classification system because it is not clearly or consistently related to any one class of demand characteristics and goals. Because it has generated a modest amount of attention in recent years (e.g., Beutler, Machado, & Neufeldt, 1994; Watkins, 1990), it is inserted here for consideration and comparison.

Therapist Directiveness vs. Patient Self-Direction. Psychotherapists vary widely in the degree to which they assume the role of guide and teacher in moving clients to change behavior and feelings (Malik, Alimohamed et al., 2000). Even so, models of psychotherapy generally urge the therapist to adopt either an evocative (nondirective, facilitating) or a directive stance with patients. Behavioral, cognitive, and other "action-oriented" theories tend to emphasize the use of interventions that place the therapist in the role of teacher and guide. In contrast, relationship-oriented theories and nonaction models urge therapists to adopt roles in which the patient directs therapeutic movement.

Therapist-directed interventions have been studied both as a general class of procedures that reflect the interpersonal stance of the therapist and as specific techniques. In the first case, therapist directiveness is studied as a global feature or style of the therapist. In the second case, it is studied as a procedure selected by the therapist to address specific kinds of issues. An example of a specific technique that has generated an emerging body of research is the use of homework assignments. In the following paragraphs, we have considered both of these levels of specificity (see Table 7.4).

1. *General therapist directiveness* has been most frequently measured as a correlate of treatment outcome. In their meta-analytic review of 19 studies of short-term psychodynamic psychotherapy in comparison to alternative treatments, Svartberg and Stiles (1991) found that a global measure of therapist directiveness was negatively related to therapeutic benefit ($r = -.45$). On the other hand, a variety of studies are not included in this latter review (e.g., Lafferty, Beutler, & Crago, 1989), as well as some later controlled trials of directive and nondirective treatments (e.g., Beutler, Clarkin, & Bongar, 2000; Borkovec & Costello, 1993), in which outcomes favor directive interventions. Beutler, Machado, and Neufeldt (1994) concluded their review by suggesting that a positive relationship exists between therapist directiveness and beneficial outcomes.

We identified 15 studies (from 1990 to 2000) of the unidirectional effect of therapist directiveness (Table 7.4). The studies were nearly equally divided between two methodologies. Seven of the studies applied a controlled trial methodology (e.g., Borkovec & Costello, 1993; Boudewyns & Hyer, 1990; Klausner et al., 1998; McLean & Hakstian, 1990; Miller, Benefield, & Tonigan, 1993; O'Malley, Jaffe et al., 1992; Shapiro et al., 1995). For example, Borkovec and Costello (1993) report a randomized clinical trial (RCT) of nondirective and directive (cognitive) therapy to patients with generalized anxiety disorder (GAD). Anxiety symptoms responded better to the directive interventions.

The other methodology used was the computation of a post-hoc correlation of some measure of therapy process (therapist directiveness) and outcome (e.g., Al-Kubaisey et al., 1992; Beutler et al., 1991; Kaminer, Burleson et al., 1998; Karno, Beutler, & Harwood, 2002; Shaw et al., 1999; Stiles & Shapiro, 1994; Tracey, 1986; Verwaaijen & Van Acker, 1993), even though most of these correlational analyses were embedded within an RCT methodology. While prospective, RCT methods are considered to be more powerful for detecting causal effects; when compared to post-hoc correlations, no notable differences were found in the distribution or size of the effects across studies. Ten of the 15 studies produced significant effects favoring directive interventions, and two produced both negative and positive relationships, depending on the measure. The size of the effects was mixed, ranging from *(r)* –.17 to .79 with a weighted average of .06 *(ns)*. The strikingly large variability of effect sizes suggested (Howard, Krause, & Lyons, 1993) the presence of one or more moderating variables. Adopting the perspective of Luborsky and colleagues (Luborsky et al., 1980), that the influence of any therapy procedure is dependent on patient factors, we inspected the literature for moderating factors.

Addressing this latter point, Beutler, Moleiro, and Talebi (in press) identified 20 studies that investigated therapist directiveness as a relational ATI concept. Eighty percent of these studies found that patient resistance level was a significant moderator of the effects of therapist directiveness. This finding is consistent with other reviews of the same topic (e.g., Beutler, Clarkin, & Bongar, 2000; Beutler, Goodrich, Fisher, & Williams, 1999), all of which have suggested that therapist directiveness is both an indicator of treatment prognosis and a variable that is best adapted to the level of patient receptiveness. A cross-validation of this hypothesis on a mixed diagnostic, multisite sample of 284 depressed and chemically abusing patients revealed that patients with high levels of resistance benefited more from a nondirective treatment, whereas those who were independently judged to be nondefensive benefited more from directive therapeutic procedures (Beutler, Clarkin, & Bongar, 2000). This finding was supportive of previous observations not included in our meta-analysis (e.g., Beutler, Engle et al., 1991; Beutler, Mohr, Grawe et al., 1991; Shoham-Salomon, Avner, & Neeman, 1989; Shoham-Salomon & Hannah, 1991). Collectively, these data suggest consistent evidence that the effects of therapist directiveness are moderated by the level of

Table 7.4 Directiveness vs. Nondirectiveness

Study	*N*	Diagnosis	Treatments	Outcome Effects	Effect Size (*r*)
General Directiveness					
Al-Kubaisy et al., 1992	99	ICD-10 agoraphobia, social or specific phobia	Clinician-accompanied exposure + self-exposure (Ee); self-exposure (e); self-relaxation w/out exposure (r) Sessions: All groups: six 60-min, 14 weeks 90-min/day homework; Ee additionally get 9 hours of E. Patients provided with homework guidelines	Significant positive effect of directiveness on improvement in phobic symptoms at post-treatment and 14-week followup (Ee vs. e, r) Significant positive effect of directiveness on improvement in global symptoms at post-treatment and 14-week followup (Ee vs. e, r)	ES1 = .26 ES3 = .32 ES2 = .31 ES4 = .42
Beutler et al., 1991	63	DSM-III Major Depressive Disorder; Hamilton Rating Scale for Depression ≥ 16	Group cognitive behavior therapy (CT); focused expressive group psychotherapy (FEP) supportive, self-directed therapy (S/SD). Sessions: 20+, S/SD 30-min/week phone + selected readings *Manualized*	Significant negative effect of directiveness and positive change in depression scores at post-treatment and followup (CT, FEP vs. S/SD) Negative effect of directiveness on positive change in global symptom distress scores at post-treatment (CT, FEP vs. S/SD) Positive effect of directiveness on improvement in global symptom distress scores at followup (CT, FEP vs. S/SD)	ES1 = –.13 ES3 = –.03 ES2 = –.05 ES4 = .05
Borkovec & Costello, 1993	55	DSM-III principal diagnoses Generalized Anxiety Disorder	Nondirective (ND); applied relaxation (AR); cognitive behavioral therapy (CBT) Sessions: 2/week, 6 weeks; 2/last 3 wks. 1st 4 sessions 90 mins, others 1 hr *Manualized*	Positive effect of directiveness on improvement in anxiety scores at post-treatment and six-month followup (CBT, AR vs. ND) Positive effect of directiveness on improvement in trait anxiety scores at post-treatment and six-month followup (CBT, AR vs. ND)	ES1 = .41 ES3 = .27 ES1 = .29 ES3 = .15
Boudewyns & Hyer, 1990	38	DSM-III-R Post-Traumatic Stress Disorder	Augusta War Trauma Project Direct therapeutic exposure (DTE; implosive flooding); individual counseling treatment. (C) Sessions: minimum 10 50-min/week, 20-week inpatient program	Negative relationship between directiveness and physiological arousal at treatment end (DTE vs. conventional therapy; DTE group shows less physiological response to exposure stimuli at post-treatment) Positive effect of directiveness on global adjustment at 3-month followup (DTE vs. conventional therapy)	ES1 = –.05 ES4 = .48

Kaminer, Burleson, Blitz, Sussman, & Rounsaville, 1998	32	DSM-III-R psychoactive substance abuse disorders	Cognitive behavioral therapy (CBT); interactional therapy (IT) Sessions: 12 90-min/week *Manualized*	Significant positive effect of directiveness on reduction in substance use at 3-month followup (CBT vs. IT)	ES3 = .40
Karno, Beutler, & Harwood, 2002	47	Alcohol use as primary problem; Michigan Alcoholism Screening Test ≥ 6	Family systems therapy (FST), cognitive behavioral therapy (CBT)	Significant positive relationship between directiveness and reduction in alcohol use at post-treatment (CBT vs. FST)	ES1 = .27
Klausner et al., 1998	13	Major Depressive Disorder (SADS) Residual depressive symptoms 77% on medication	Goal focused group psychotherapy (GFGP); reminiscence therapy (RT) Sessions: 11 60-min/week	Significant positive effect of directiveness on positive change in depressed mood at post-treatment (GFGP vs. RT)	ES1 = .63
McLean & Hakstian, 1990	121	Minnesota Multiphasic Personality Inventory Depression scale ≥ 25 for men, ≥ 29.5 women, Beck Depression Inventory ≥ 23; Depression Adjective Checklist ≥ 14	Behavior therapy (B), relaxation training (R), nondirective psychotherapy (ND); drug therapy (D; amitriptyline 150 mg/day) Sessions: 10 weekly	Negative effect of directiveness on positive change in depression scores at $2^1/_4$-year followup (B, R, vs. ND)	ES3 = –.02
Miller, Benefield, & Tonigan, 1993	42	Problem drinkers	Drinker's Check-up with directive-confrontational counseling or with client-centered counseling Sessions: 2 motivational check-ups	Negative effect of directiveness on positive change in drinking composite scores at 12-month followup directive-confrontational vs. client-centered counseling)	ES3 = –.17
O'Malley, Jaffe et al., 1992	97	DSM-III alcohol dependence	Naltrexone (50 mg/day) or placebo, with coping skills or supportive therapy. Sessions: 12 weekly *Manualized*	Positive effect of more directiveness on improvement in alcohol-related outcome (coping skills/relapse prevention vs. supportive therapy)	ES1 = .03
Shapiro et al., 1995	104	DSM-III Major Depressive Episode, Present State Examination Index of Definition ≥ 5	Cognitive behavioral therapy (CB); psychodynamic interpersonal psychotherapy (PI) 16- or 8-session duration Sessions: 1 hr/week	Positive effect of directiveness on maintenance of gains at 12-month followup (CB vs. PI)	ES3 = .11

(continues)

TABLE 7.4 (Continued)

Study	*N*	Diagnosis	Treatments	Outcome Effects	Effect Size (*r*)
Shaw et al., 1999	36	Research Diagnostic Criteria: Major Depression; HRSD-17 $\geq$ 14	NIMH TDCRP Cognitive behavioral therapy (CBT) Sessions: minimum 12 in 15 weeks *Manualized*	Significant positive effect of directiveness (as session structure) on positive change in depression scores at post-treatment (pretreatment depression severity and adherence controlled)	ES1 = .44
				No effect of therapist directiveness (as session structure) on psychiatric symptom distress scores at post-treatment (pretreatment depression severity and adherence controlled)	ES2 = 0[a]
Stiles & Shapiro, 1994	39	Present State Examination Index of Definition Category System: depression (77%), anxiety disorders	Psychodynamic interpersonal therapy (PI); cognitive behavioral therapy (CB) Groups: 8 sessions each of PI & CB counterbalanced order (PI-CB or CB-PI) Sessions: 16 weekly	Positive effect of directiveness on rate of change in depression scores at end-point (CB Questions, General Advisement vs. PI Interpretation, Exploratory Reflections)	ES1 = .01
				Positive effect of directiveness on rate of change in global symptom distress scores at end-point (CB Questions, General Advisement vs. PI Interpretation, Exploratory Reflections)	ES2 = .15
Tracey, 1986	33	Appropriate for time-limited therapy (not psychotic, able to form rapid affective bonds, able to tolerate loss)	Time-limited psychotherapy	Positive effect of directiveness on improved global symptom scores at post-treatment (therapist topic determination vs. client, dyad topic determination)	ES2 = .79
Verwaaijen & Van Acker, 1993	13	Families of conduct-disordered (DSM-III) female adolescents at risk of institutionalization	Family therapy	Positive effect of therapist directiveness on symptom-specific improvement at post-treatment (therapist "direct influence" and "structuring therapy" vs. client-directed activities)	ES1 = .32
				Negative effect of therapist directiveness on global outcome scores at post-treatment (i.e., greater directiveness results in positive change)	ES2 = −.14

Homework					
De Araujo, Ito, & Marks, 1996	46	DSM-III-R Obsessive-Compulsive Disorder	Behavioral therapy: Ritual Prevention (ERP) or ERP + imaginal exposure Sessions: 9 weeks, 60 mins ERP, 30 mins ERP + imaginal exposure Homework: 90-min/day exposure	Significant positive effect of homework compliance at week 1 on symptom-specific improvement at post-treatment and followup	ES1 = .32 ES3 = .62
				Significant positive effect of homework compliance at week 1 on global improvement at post-treatment and followup	ES2 = .51 ES4 = .66
Kazdin & Mascitelli, 1982	90	Deficits in assertiveness and social skills	Rehearsal, rehearsal + self-instructions, rehearsal + homework practice, rehearsal + self-instruction + homework, wait list	Positive effect of homework on symptom-specific improvement at post-treatment (homework vs. no homework groups)	ES1 = .26
Leung & Heimberg, 1996	91	DSM-III-R Social Phobia, ADIS-R ≥ 4	Cognitive behavioral group therapy. Six-person groups, 12 2.5 hours/week group sessions	Positive effect of homework compliance on improved social anxiety symptom scores at post-treatment	ES1 = .24
Neimeyer & Feixas, 1990	63	Research Diagnostic Criteria: unipolar depression; Beck Depression Inventory (BDI) ≥ 16	Group cognitive therapy with and without homework 10 90-min/week sessions	Significant positive effect of homework compliance on positive change in depression symptoms at post-treatment (pretreatment depression scores controlled)	ES1 = .27
				Significant positive effect of homework compliance on positive change in depression symptoms at followup (pretreatment depression not controlled)	ES3 = .11
Vaughan et al., 1994	36	DSM-III-R Post-Traumatic Stress Disorder	3 CBT therapies: Eye-Movement Desensitization (EMD); Image Habituation Training (IHT) and Applied Muscle Relaxation (AMR) Sessions: 3–5 in 2–3 weeks Homework in IHT & AMR but not EMD	Significant negative effect of homework condition on reduction in flashbacks and nightmares and avoidance at post-treatment and followup (IHT, AMR vs. EMD)	ES1 = –.29
				Significant improvement in no-homework EMD group only	ES3 = –.19

ES1: Target measure at post-treatment.

ES2: Global measure at post-treatment.

ES3: Target measure at followup.

ES4: Global measure at follow-up.

[a] Results presented as not significant and without directional information.

patient resistance traits. This possibility deserves further research attention.

2. *Homework assignments* are an important aspect of many treatments and provide an example of one way in which therapists direct and guide treatment. Burns and Spangler (2000) used structural equation modeling (SEM) to inspect four hypothetical relationships between homework compliance and therapy outcome among depressed patients. Systematically applying statistical controls for a variety of patient and treatment factors, they found a significant correlation between homework compliance and treatment outcome. This study has been criticized because of the way that causal relations were inferred (Kazantizis, in press), but the conclusion that there is a causal link between homework compliance and treatment benefit has been supported by others (e.g., Addis & Jacobson, 2000; Bryant, Simons, & Thase, 1999; Kazdin & Mascitelli, 1982; Leung & Heimberg, 1996). A meta-analysis of homework by Kazantizis, Deane, and Ronan (2000) found an effect size *(r)* of .36 in favor of treatments that gave homework assignments, with a lesser but still significant effect size relating outcome to patient compliance with homework ($r = .22$).

Table 7.4 identifies five studies published in the last decade that inspected the relationship between homework compliance and treatment response in a way that could be subjected to effect size analysis. Five of these studies found a significant effect favoring compliance on various aspects of outcome. The effect sizes ranged from *(r)* –.29 (Vaughan et al., 1994) to .66 (De Araujo, Ito, & Marks, 1996). Collectively, the small sample of studies and the (weighted) mean ES of .10 *(ns)* failed to confirm the importance of homework assignments. Nonetheless, the studies reviewed included indications that patient factors may mediate the effects of homework on treatment benefit. Addis and Jacobson (2000), for example, found that patient acceptance of the therapist's rationale for using homework independently contributed to outcome over and above that contributed by simple compliance. If true, this latter finding again suggests that resistance tendencies may be overtly implicated in homework compliance and may thereby constitute a moderator of the effects of this aspect of directiveness.

Insight-Oriented versus Symptom-Oriented Interventions. Another procedure that has been implicated, by various theoretical models, as a contributor to treatment outcome is the degree to which therapists emphasize the achievement of insight as an avenue to change. They seek to foster change by uncovering events of the past that are thought to have provoked the maladaptive symptoms. Thus, they draw attention to recurrent patterns and themes in a patient's life and the expression of unrecognized (disowned) emotions. Once motives and patterns are identified, therapists attempt to enhance recognition that remote events, impulses, and feelings produced current problems and symptoms. They interpret meanings and motives, they give meanings to the presence of transference attachments, and they identify the patient's defenses against awareness.

In contrast, symptom-focused methods include altering reinforcement contingencies, modifying symptom-contingent thoughts, and changing an evoking environment. These latter interventions apply to contemporary events and evoking stimuli. Some aspect of overt behavior change is encouraged on the part of the patient.

In this section, we consider the relative importance of two subclasses of procedures: those that are used to enhance insight and those that attempt to evoke direct change of symptoms or to enhance skill levels (see Table 7.5). As in the previous section, the relative value of these insight and direct change interventions will be inspected at two levels. One level will involve a general comparison of whole treatment models, contrasting those that focus on insight with those that focus on direct change. At a more specific level, we will consider studies that have investigated the specific effects of interpretations, a class of insight-oriented technique that has received a good deal of research attention.

1. *Insight and symptom-focused models* have been compared in 21 studies since 1990 (Table 7.5). As with studies of resistance, some studies involved a direct comparison of two treatment models within a random assignment methodology (e.g., Barber & Muenz, 1996; Barkham et al., 1999; Beutler, Engle et al., 1991). Others have sought understanding by the post-hoc application of some continuous measure of an assumed dimension that extends from insight to direct change (Borkovec & Costello, 1993; Karno et al., 2002).

As noted in Table 7.5, the results of these comparisons were mixed. The preponderance of studies demonstrated that insight focus was related to improvement (a positive ES), although a substantial minority of ($n = 6$) studies found a

TABLE 7.5 Symptom vs. Insight-Oriented Interventions

Study	*N*	Diagnosis	Treatments	Outcome Effects	Effect Size (*r*)
Symptom vs. Insight Focus					
Barber & Muenz, 1996	84	NIMH TDCRP data. Research Diagnostic Criteria: Major Depression; HRSD-17 ≥ 14; personality disorders (avoidant and obsessive)	Cognitive therapy (CT), interpersonal therapy (IPT) Groups: depressed-avoidant; depressed-obsessive	Negative effect of symptom-focus on positive change in depression scores at post-treatment for more obsessive patients (CT vs. IPT)	ES1 = .15
Barkham, Shapiro, Hardy, & Rees, 1999	116	Subsyndromal depression	Cognitive behavioral therapy (CB); psychodynamic interpersonal therapy (PI) Session time frames: immediate or delayed treatment *Manualized*	Positive effect of symptom focus on positive change in depression scores at post-treatment (CB vs. PI) Significant positive effect of symptom-focus on positive change depression scores at 1-year followup (CB vs. PI)	ES1 = .07 ES3 = .27
Beutler et al., 1991	63	DSM-III Major Depressive Disorder; HRSD ≥ 16	Group cognitive behavior therapy (CBT); focused expressive group psychotherapy (FEP) supportive, self-directed therapy (S/SD) Sessions: 20+, S/SD 30-min phone sessions + selected readings *Manualized*	Negative effect of symptom-focus on positive change in depression scores at post-treatment and followup (CT & FEP > S/SD) Negative effect of symptom-focus on improvement in global symptom distress scores at post-treatment (CT, FEP vs. S/SD) Positive effect of symptom-focus on improvement in global symptom distress scores at followup (CT, FEP vs. S/SD)	ES1 = –.13 ES3 = –.03 ES2 = –.05 ES4 = .05
Bond & Bunce, 2000	65	Occupational stress	Acceptance & Commitment therapy (ACT), Innovation Promotion Program (IPP) *Manualized*	Negative effect of symptom-focus on improvement in global health at post-treatment and 13-week followup (IPP vs. ACT)	ES2 = –.37 ES4 = –.35

(continues)

TABLE 7.5 *(Continued)*

Study	*N*	Diagnosis	Treatments	Outcome Effects	Effect Size *(r)*
Borkovec & Costello, 1993	55	DSM-III principal diagnoses Generalized Anxiety Disorder (GAD)	Cognitive behavioral therapy CBT); applied relaxation (AR); nondirective (ND) Sessions: 12 2/wk; 2/last 3 wks. 1st 4 90-min., balance 1 hr *Manualized*	Positive effect of symptom-focus on reduction in anxiety scores at post-treatment and 6-month followup (CBT, AR > ND) Positive relationship between symptom-focus and reduction in trait anxiety at post-treatment and 6-month followup (CBT, AR > ND)	ES1 = .41 ES3 = .27 ES1 = .29 ES3 = .15
Crits-Christoph et al., 1999	487	DSM-IV cocaine and other substance abuse; Axis 1 disorders	4 groups: Group drug (GDC); individual drug + GDC (IDC/GDC); cognitive therapy + GDC (CT/GDC); supportive expressive therapy + GDC (SE/GDC) Sessions: 36 weeks *Manualized*	Significant positive relationship between symptom focus and positive change in drug use at 12-months post-baseline followup (IDC/GDC, CT/GDC vs. SE/GDC, GDC)	ES3 = .03
Imber et al., 1990	239	Research Diagnostic Criteria: Major Depression, present for previous 2 weeks. Pre-therapy sample HRSD-17 scores: $M = 19.5$, $SD = 4.4$	NIMH TDCRP Cognitive behavioral therapy (CBT), interpersonal psychotherapy (IPT); imipramine + clinical management (IMI-CM); placebo + CM (PLA-CM) Sessions: 16–20, $M = 13$ *Manualized*	Positive effect of symptom focus on improvement in global symptoms at post-treatment (CBT vs. IPT)	ES2 = .06
Kaminer et al., 1998	32	DSM-III-R psychoactive substance abuse disorders	Cognitive behavioral therapy (CBT); interactional therapy (IT) *Manualized*	Significant positive effect of symptom focus on positive change in substance use at 3-month followup (CBT vs. IT)	ES3 = .40
Karno et al., 2002	47	Alcohol use primary problem; Michigan Alcoholism Screening Test ≥ 6	Family systems therapy (FST); cognitive behavioral therapy (CBT)	Significant positive effect of symptom focus on positive change in alcohol use at post-treatment (CBT vs. FST)	ES1 = .27

Klausner et al., 1998	13	Major Depressive Disorder (SADS); residual depressive symptoms 77% on medication	Goal focused group psychotherapy (GFGP), reminiscence therapy (RT) Sessions: 11 60-min/week	Significant positive effect of symptom focus on improvement in depressed mood at post-treatment (GFGP vs. RT)	ES1 = .63
McLean & Hakstian, 1990	121	MMPI Depression scale ≥ 25 for men, ≥ 29.5 women; BDI ≥ 23; Depression Adjective Checklist ≥ 14	Behavior therapy (B), relaxation training (R), nondirective psychotherapy (ND); drug therapy (D; amitriptyline 150 mg/day) Sessions: 10 weekly	Negative effect of greater symptom-focus on positive change in depression at 2¼ year followup (B, R vs. ND)	ES3 = −.02
O'Malley, Jaffe, et al., 1992	97	DSM-III-R alcohol dependence	Naltrexone (50 mg/d) or placebo, with coping skills or supportive therapy 12 weekly psychotherapy sessions *Manualized*	Positive effect of symptom-focus on positive change in alcohol use (coping skills/relapse prevention vs. supportive therapy)	ES1 = .03
Piper, Joyce, McCallum, & Azim, 1998	144	DSM-III-R Major Depression, Dysthymia, personality disorders. 73% with previous psychiatric treatment	Short-term interpretative and supportive therapy Sessions: 20 50-min/week Interpretations $M = 11$ ($R = 3–23$); transference interpretations $M = 4$ (R = 0–14) *Manualized*	Positive effect of symptom-focus on positive change in depression scores at post-treatment (supportive vs. interpretive therapy)	ES1 = .14
				Positive effect of symptom-focus on positive change in global symptomatic distress at post-treatment (supportive vs. interpretive therapy)	ES2 = .07
Piper, McCallum, Joyce, Azim, & Ogrodniczuk, 1999	144	DSM-III-R Major Depression, Dysthymia; personality disorders. 73% with previous psychiatric treatment	Short-term interpretative and supportive therapy Sessions: 20 50-min/week *Manualized*	Significant positive effect of symptom-focus on average symptom-specific clinical improvement at 12-month followup (supportive vs. interpretive therapy)	ES3 = .05
				Significant positive effect of symptom-focus on clinical improvement in global distress scores at 12-month followup (supportive vs. interpretive therapy)	ES4 = .04

(continues)

TABLE 7.5 *(Continued)*

Study	*N*	Diagnosis	Treatments	Outcome Effects	Effect Size (*r*)
Reynolds et al., 1996	117	DSM-III-R Major Depression, retarded depression BDI ≥ 16	Cognitive behavioral (CB) or psychodynamic-interpersonal therapy (PI) in 16 or 8 sessions Peer supervision	Negative effect of symptom focus on positive change in depressed mood at end point (CBT vs. PI)	ES1 = –.26
Rohsenow, Monti, Martin, Michalec, & Abrams, 2000	108	DSM-III-R Cocaine Dependence	Cocaine-specific coping skills training (CST); meditation-relaxation training (MRT; control). Both with private substance abuse treatment Sessions: Up to 8, 45-min. 3–5 times/week *Manualized*	Significant positive effect of symptom-focus on positive change in cocaine use at 9-month followup (CST vs. MRT)	ES3 = .16
Rossello & Bernal, 1999	71	DSM-III Major Depression, Dysthymia	Cognitive behavioral therapy (CBT); interpersonal therapy (IPT); wait list (WL) 12 60-min/week sessions *Manualized*	Negative effect of symptom-focus on positive change in depression scores at post-treatment (CBT vs. IPT) Positive effect of symptom-focus on improvement in depression scores at followup (CBT vs. IPT)	ES1 = –.17 ES3 = .28
Shapiro et al., 1995	104	DSM-III Major Depressive Episode, Present State Examination Index of Definition ≥ 5	Cognitive behavioral therapy (CB); psychodynamic interpersonal psychotherapy (PI) 16- or 8-session duration Sessions: 1 hr/week	Positive effect of symptom-focus on maintenance of gains at 12-month followup (CB vs. PI)	ES3 = .11
Shea et al., 1992	239	Research Diagnostic Criteria: Major Depression; HRSD-17 ≥ 14	NIMH TDCRP data Cognitive behavioral therapy (CBT), interpersonal psychotherapy (IPT); imipramine + clinical management (IMI-CM); Placebo + CM (PLA-CM) Sessions: 16–20, *M* = 13 *Manualized*	Positive effect of symptom-focus on maintenance of gains (absence of relapse for treatment responders) at 18-month followup (CBT vs. IPT)	ES3 = .06

Stiles & Shapiro, 1994	39	Present State Examination Index of Definition Category System: depression (77%), anxiety disorders	Psychodynamic interpersonal therapy (PI); Cognitive-behavioral therapy (CB) Groups: 8 sessions each of PI & CB in counterbalanced order (PI-CB or CB-PI) Sessions: 16, weekly	Negative effect of symptom focus on positive change in depression scores at end point (CB Questions, General Advisement vs. PI Interpretation, Exploratory Reflections) Positive effect of symptom-focus on positive change in global symptom distress scores at end point (CB Questions, General Advisement vs. PI Interpretation, Exploratory Reflections)	ES1 = –.13 ES2 = .02
Verwaaijen & Van Acker, 1993	13	Families of conduct disordered (DSM-III) female adolescents at risk of institutionalization	Family therapy	Positive effect of symptom-focus on positive family change (therapist "direct influence" and "structuring therapy" vs. "stimulation of insight") Positive effect of symptom focus on positive estimates of treatment success (therapist "direct influence" and "structuring therapy" vs. "stimulation of insight")	ES1 = .22 ES2 = .29
Therapeutic Interpretations					
Connoly et al., 1999	29	DSM-III Major Depression, with concurrent Axis 1 and/or Axis II diagnoses	Brief supportive-expressive psychotherapy (SE) Sessions: 16, weekly	Negative effect of transference interpretations on positive change in depression scores at post-treatment (pretreatment depression scores and quality of interpersonal relationships controlled)	ES1 = –.22
Diemer, Lobell, Vivino, & Hill, 1996	25	SCL-90 – GSI >40 <70, minimum 1 dream and 1 troubling event per week	Therapy for interpersonal problems Sessions: 12 50-min/week with 2 sessions each of dream interpretation, event interpretation & unstructured sessions	Positive effect of increased interpretation on insight at post-session (dream, event interpretation vs. unstructured session)	ES2 = .01

(continues)

TABLE 7.5 (Continued)

Study	*N*	Diagnosis	Treatments	Outcome Effects	Effect Size (*r*)
Hill et al., 2000	14	GSI score T > 50 < 80, troubling dreams, recent loss; Impact of Events Scale > 1.0	Brief structured therapy focused on dreams OR loss (Therapists with humanistic/ experiential, psychodynamic, cognitive-behavioral orientations)	Negative relationship between therapist interpretation and symptomatic improvement associated with loss at post-treatment Positive effect of therapist interpretation on improved global symptom distress scores at post-treatment	ES1 = –.13 ES2 = .20
Hoglend, 1996	15	DSM-III Axis I & II, 73% moderate/serious breaks in career. GAS *M*=57, R = 48–69	Brief dynamic psychotherapy, with & w/out transference interpretations Sessions: 9–53, weekly. *M* = 26.5	No effect of interpretation on symptom-specific change at 4-year followup Significant negative effect of high-frequency transference interpretations on dynamic (vs. symptomatic) change at 4-year followup	ES3 = 0[a] ES4 = –.55
McCullough et al., 1991	16	DSM-III long-standing Axis II personality disorders	Brief psychotherapy interventions: patient-therapist and patient-significant-other interpretations Sessions: 50-min/week. *R* = 27–53; modal treatment 40 sessions	Positive effect of interpretation on positive (mostly) symptom-specific change at post-treatment	ES1 = .10
Milbrath et al., 1999	20	Stress response syndrome, pathological grief response to bereavement	Dynamic psychotherapy Sessions: 12, weekly *Manualized*	Significant positive effect of defense interpretations on global functioning at 5-month followup (pretreatment symptom level controlled)	ES4 = .48
Ogrodniczuk, Piper, Joyce, & McCallum, 2000	40	DSM-III-R Axis I (67% depression) & II (60% borderline, 44% paranoid)	Interpretive form of time-limited dynamic psychotherapy Sessions: 20 50-min/week Interpretations *M* = 14.4, transference interpretations (TIs) *M* = 3.7	Low QOR patients Significant negative effect of TIs on positive change in defensive style and family functioning at post-treatment	ES2 = –.40

Piper, Azim, Joyce, & McCallum, 1991	64	DSM-III Axis I (27% affective disorders, 25% adjustment disorder) & II (14% dependent)	Short-term time limited psycho-therapy 20 50-min/week sessions (M = 18.8 R = 11–22) *Manualized*	Hi QOR patients: Significant negative effect of proportion of transference interpretations (PTIs) on symptom-specific improvement at post-treatment	ES1 = –.17
				Significant negative effect of PTIs on global improvement at post-treatment	ES2 = –.34
Piper et al., 1998	144	DSM-III-R Major Depression, Dysthymia, personality disorders. 73% with previous psychiatric treatment	Short-term interpretative and supportive therapy Sessions: 20 50-min/week Interpretations M = 11 R = 3–23); transference interpretations M = 4 (R = 0–14) *Manualized*	Negative effect of interpretation on positive change in depression scores at post-treatment (interpretive vs. supportive therapy)	ES1 = –.14
				Negative effect of interpretation on positive change in global symptom distress scores at post-treatment (interpretive vs. supportive therapy)	ES2 = –.07
Piper et al., 1999	144	DSM-III-R Major Depression, Dysthymia; personality disorders. 73% with previous psychiatric treatment	Short-term interpretative and supportive therapy Sessions: 20 50-min/week *Manualized*	Negative effect of interpretation on average symptom-specific clinical improvement at 12-month followup (interpretive vs. supportive therapy)	ES3 = –.05
				Negative effect of interpretation on clinical improvement in global distress scores at 12-month followup (interpretive vs. supportive therapy)	ES4 = –.04

ES1: Target measure at post-treatment.

ES2: Global measure at post-treatment.

ES3: Target measure at followup.

ES4: Global measure at followup.

[a] Results presented as not significant and without directional information.

negative relationship between the degree of symptomatic (behavioral) focus and measures of improvement (e.g., Beutler et al., 1991; Bond & Bunce, 2000; McLean & Hakstian, 1990; Reynolds et al., 1996; Rosello & Bernal, 1999; Stiles & Shapiro, 1994). These latter findings indicated that improvement was relatively lower when direct efforts to change patient symptoms were applied than when insight-oriented procedures were applied. The failure of symptom-focused interventions to show a superiority to insight-oriented interventions is surprising, but the range of effects was also notable. Mean effect sizes of .03 *(ns)* and .04 *(ns)* were obtained for specific and global measures, respectively, indicating that the use of insight versus symptomatic treatments did not yield reliable differences.

These findings lend support to the oft-noted dodo bird verdict (e.g., Lambert & Bergin, 1992; Luborsky, Rosenthal et al., in press; Wampold, 2001; Wampold et al., 1997)—that all treatments are equivalent to one another. However, the salience of the dodo bird conclusion is tempered by methodological factors (Beutler, in press) and the variability of observed effects (Howard, Krause, & Lyons, 1993). These considerations raise the need to search for moderating variables that differentially affect the power of insight and symptom-focused treatments.

Indeed, a relatively large body of research has identified moderating patient variables that differentially empower insight and symptom-focused approaches. Beutler, Harwood, Alimohamed, and Malik (2002), for example, found 19 studies on the moderating effects of patient coping style, 80% of which supported the conclusion that this personality characteristic is differentially impacted by therapy type. Specifically, these authors concluded that patients who are self-reflective, introverted, and/or introspective tend to benefit from insight-oriented procedures, whereas patients who are impulsive, aggressive, and undercontrolled are responsive to symptom-focused procedures. This latter conclusion is supported by a wide variety of studies and measures (e.g., Beutler, Clarkin, & Bongar, 2000; Barber & Muenz, 1996; Beutler, Engle et al., 1991; Beutler, Machado, Engle, & Mohr, 1993; Beutler, Mohr, Grawe et al., 1991). In their analysis, Beutler, Harwood, and colleagues found only three studies (Crits-Christoph, Siqueland, Blaine et al., 1999; Project Match Research Group, 1997; Rohsenow, Monti, Martin et al., 2000) that failed to find the expected effect. Interestingly, these three studies were all large-scale, multisite investigations, suggesting that site factors may occlude these interaction effects. Only one multisite study found the expected interaction effect of patient and treatment (Beutler, Clarkin, & Bongar, 2000).

2. *Therapeutic interpretations* represent a specific, insight-focused procedure, whose relationship to outcome has been investigated widely. The nature of the interpretations studied, however, ranges from identifying symptoms and providing diagnostic labels that invoke "illness" as an explanation of problems (e.g., Klerman, Weissman, Rounsaville, & Chevron, 1984) to explanations of the patient's problems (e.g., Flowers & Booraem, 1990) to labeling unconscious wishes and needs (e.g., Caspar, 1995; Luborsky, 1996). Theoretical formulations, based on psychodynamic formulations, viewed interpretations as the primary method of facilitating change. Indeed, some research has suggested that when interpretations are consistent with the formulation of the problem developed by the patient and therapist, they tend to evoke improvement (e.g., Crits-Christoph, Cooper, & Luborsky, 1988).

Our review (Table 7.5) of the most recent decade of research uncovered 10 studies of the effects of various forms of interpretation on treatment outcome. Surprisingly, only four of these studies found that the number of interpretations used was related to some aspect of benefit (Diemer, Lobell et al., 1996; Hill et al., 2000; McCullough et al., 1991; Milbrath et al., 1999). The results, as one can see from the table, are very inconsistent. The mean effect size was nonsignificant ($r = .07$).

Once again, an inspection of individual studies reveals evidence of several moderating variables and a relatively strong ATI relational effect. For example, interpretive procedures worked best among those patients who had good interpersonal relationship skills, including good object relationships (Connolly, Crits-Christoph, Shappell et al., 1999; Ogrodniczuk, Piper, Joyce, & McCallum, 2000; Piper, McCallum, Joyce et al., 1999). Interestingly, even these latter findings are not entirely consistent, and several studies have found a negative relationship between quality of object relationships and outcome (e.g., Joyce & Piper, 1996; Piper, Azim, Joyce, & McCallum, 1991).

Fine nuances of interpretations may account for the wide variations of effects. For example, there is evidence that historical interpretations work somewhat better than motivational ones (Flowers & Booraem, 1990) and that addressing topics of interpersonal loss works better than interpretations of dreams (Hill, Zack, Wonnell et al., 2000). These findings suggest the presence of multiple relational or ATI dimensions that determine the effects of insight-oriented interventions. The exact nature of these moderators still remains a mystery.

Emotive versus supportive interventions. In recent years, there has been renewed emphasis on the role of emotional arousal in psychotherapy. Major reviews (e.g., Beutler, Booker, & Peerson, 1998; Greenberg, Elliott, & Lietaer, 1994; Orlinsky, Grawe, & Parks, 1994) conclude that interventions that provoke emotional arousal will increase positive outcomes, especially if applied early in the treatment. Beutler, Clarkin, and Bongar (2000) reached a similar conclusion from their review of literature and confirmed this relationship in an independent cross-validation of this relationship among 284 depressed and chemical-abusing patients in a multitude of treatments.

The interventions to which research has been directed include a variety of experiential procedures (e.g., Mahrer, 1996; Safran & Greenberg, 1991), focusing on procedures for working with dreams (Gendlin, 1986, 1996), and various cognitive and psychodynamic procedures that specifically focus on emotionally charged material (e.g., Castonguay, Goldfried, Wiser et al., 1996; Gaston, Piper, Debbane, Bienvenu, & Garant, 1994). Greenberg, Elliott, and Lietaer (1994) undertook a meta-analysis of studies that had used such methods and determined that the average effect size was *(d)* 1.26. This is a strong effect, but its meaning must be attenuated somewhat by the fact that this effect size was based on pre-post comparisons rather than on direct comparisons to a control or alternative treatment group. The pre-post method tends to produce inflated estimates of effect (Lipsey & Wilson, 1993; Rosenthal, 1984). However, the authors did include a comparison of 15 studies in which the effect size was based on a comparison of the emotion-enhancing treatment with a control or no-treatment group. The result was similar to the first analysis, producing an effect size *(d)* of 1.30, though it is not entirely clear whether this effect size was based on the difference between pre-post ES scores or on pre-post differences directly. The former would be expected to produce smaller effect sizes.

Our review identified 20 studies published between 1990 and 2000, in which the authors either explored the relationship of pre- or in-therapy arousal level and outcome or compared emotionally focused and nonemotionally focused interventions (Table 7.6). Sixteen of these studies provided some direct measure of in-session arousal (presumed to have been provoked by the therapy), which was then correlated with subsequent improvement. No clear pattern emerged. Although most of the studies found a positive relationship between in-session arousal and subsequent improvement either at the end of treatment or at followup, many produced mixed findings (e.g., Beutler et al., 1991; Boudewyns & Hyer, 1990; Castonguay et al., 1996; Hill et al., 2000; Marks et al., 1998), suggesting an undisclosed time or measurement effect.

To clarify the causal nature of the relationship between arousal and benefit, we identified nine studies that compared an emotionally enhancing or emotionally focused therapy with a therapy that attempted to directly reduce patient arousal (Table 7.6). The findings of these latter studies were again mixed, with no clear pattern emerging as to the relationship between emotional arousal and outcome.

Our analysis produced a consistently lower effect size than previous meta-analytic reviews. None of our effect sizes approximated those reported by Greenberg, Elliott, and Lietaer (1994). The reason for this difference is unclear, but one possibility may be that the use of emotional-arousing interventions has declined in recent years, with the corresponding ascendance of behavioral and cognitive interventions, producing a restricted range of effects and thus lowering the correlation. In support of this possibility, one can note from Table 7.6 that most studies of cathartic therapies, when contrasted with those in which the emotional focus merely recognized and acknowledged affect, produced somewhat higher effect sizes.

Moreover, the methodologies of the studies considered in our analysis do not address the questions of whether therapies that attempt to induce arousal do so effectively or whether outcome follows or precedes such induction. Several related studies do bear on these questions, however. These studies provide at least modest support for the conclusion that those treatments that specifically attempt to magnify and increase emotional experience actually evoke higher states of emotional experience (Beutler, Kim, Davison, Karno, & Fisher, 1996; Malik, Alimohamed, Holaway, & Beutler, 2000) and that they subsequently achieve better outcomes than interventions that do not seek to increase emotional intensity (Bond & Bunce, 2000;

TABLE 7.6 Emotion Focus vs. Supportive Interventions

Study	*N*	Diagnosis	Treatments	Outcome Effects	Effect Size (*r*)
Arousal Level					
Al-Kubaisy et al., 1992	99	ICD-10 agoraphobia, social or specific phobia	Clinician-accompanied exposure + self-exposure *(Ee)*; self-exposure *(e)*; self-relaxation w/out exposure *(r)*	Positive effect of in-session arousal on reduction in phobic symptom scores at post-treatment and 14-week followup (Ee, e vs. r)	ES1 = .14 ES3 = .23
			Sessions: All groups: 6 60-min, 14 weeks 90-min/day homework; *Ee* additionally get 9 hours of *E*	Positive effect of in-session arousal on global improvement at post-treatment and 14-week followup (Ee, e vs. r)	ES2 = .32 ES4 = .55
Arntz & van den Hout, 1996	54	DSM-III-R Panic Disorder with/without mild agoraphobia	Cognitive therapy (CT); Applied relaxation + in vivo exposure (AR) Sessions: 12, 1 hour/week *Manualized*	Significant negative effect of in-session arousal on positive change in panic frequency at post-treatment (AR vs. CT; initial panic severity controlled)	ES1 = –.39
				Negative effect of in-session arousal on positive change in panic frequency at 6-month followup (AR vs. CT; initial panic severity controlled)	ES3 = –.20
Beutler et al., 1991	63	DSM-III Major Depression; Hamilton Rating Scale for Depression (HRSD) ≥ 16	Group cognitive behavior therapy (CBT); focused expressive group psychotherapy (FEP); supportive, self-directed therapy (S/SD) Sessions: 20+, S/SD 30-min phone sessions + selected readings *Manualized*	Negative effect of in-session arousal on positive change in depression scores at post-treatment (FEP vs. CT, S/SD)	ES1 = –.14
				Positive effect of in-session arousal on positive change in global symptom distress scores at post-treatment (FEP vs. CT, S/SD)	ES2 = .09
				Positive effect of in-session arousal on positive change in depression scores at followup (FEP vs. CT, S/SD)	ES3 = .01
				Negative effect of in-session arousal on positive change in global symptom distress scores at followup (FEP vs. CT, S/SD)	ES4 = –.11

Boudewyns & Hyer, 1990	38	DSM-III-R Post-Traumatic Stress Disorder	Augusta War Trauma Project Direct Therapeutic Exposure (DTE; implosive flooding); individual counseling treatment (C) Sessions: minimum 10 50-min/week, 20-week inpatient program	Negative relationship between in-session arousal and physiological response to stimuli at treatment end (DTE vs. conventional therapy; DTE group shows less physiological response to exposure stimuli at post-treatment)	ES1 = –.05
				Positive effect of in-session arousal on global adjustment at 3-month followup (DTE vs. conventional therapy)	ES4 = .48
Burgess, Gill, & Marks, 1998	170	Recurrent nightmares	Self-exposure; self-relaxation. 4-week trial *Manualized*	Positive effect of in-session arousal on positive change in # of nightmares at post-treatment (exposure vs. relaxation)	ES1 = .43
				Positive effect of in-session arousal on positive change in # of nightmares at 6-month followup (exposure vs. relaxation)	ES3 = .31
				Positive effect of in-session arousal on positive partner-rating of patient well-being at 6-month followup (exposure vs. relaxation)	ES4 = .35
Castonguay et al., 1996	30	Research Diagnostic Criteria: Major Depression; BDI ≥ 20; HRSD ≥ 14 (moderately-severely depressed)	Cognitive therapy; cognitive therapy w. imipramine (2-300 mg/day) Sessions: cognitive: M = 15.4; with IMI: M = 14.4 + weekly drug management *Manualized*	Negative effect of in-session arousal (level of experiencing) on positive change in depression scores at post-treatment	ES1 = –.32
				Positive effect of in-session arousal (level of experiencing) on improvement in global functioning scores at post-treatment	ES2 = .20
Crits-Christoph et al., 1999	487	DSM-IV cocaine and other substance abuse; Axis 1 disorders	4 groups: Group drug (GDC); individual drug + GDC (IDC/GDC); cognitive therapy + GDC (CT/GDC); supportive expressive therapy + GDC (SE/GDC) Sessions: 36 weeks *Manualized*	Positive effect of in-session arousal on positive change in drug use composite scores at 12-month followup (SE/GDC vs. CT/GDC, IDC/GDC, GDC)	ES3 = .03

(*continues*)

Table 7.6 *(Continued)*

Study	*N*	Diagnosis	Treatments	Outcome Effects	Effect Size *(r)*
Hill et al., 2000	14	GSI score T > 50 < 80, troubling dreams, recent loss; Impact of Events Scale > 1.0	Brief structured therapy focused on dreams OR loss. Therapists with humanistic/ experiential psycho-dynamic, cognitive behavioral orientations	Negative effect of in-session arousal on positive symptomatic change associated with loss at post-treatment (loss vs.dream-interpretation focus)	ES1 = –.13
				Positive effect of in-session arousal on improvement in global symptom distress scores at post-treatment (loss vs. dream-interpretation focus)	ES2 = .20
Marks, Lovell, Noshirvani, Livanou, & Thrasher, 1998	77	DSM-III-R Post Traumatic Stress Disorder	Prolonged exposure (E; imaginal and live); cognitive restructuring (C), exposure + cognitive restructuring (EC), relaxation (R) Sessions: 10 90-min/week; EC: 10 105-min/week *Manualized*	No effect of in-session arousal on PTSD symptomology at post-treatment (E, EC vs. C, R)	ES1 = 0[a]
				Significant positive effect of in-session arousal on improvement in overall functioning scores at post-treatment and 3-month followup (E, EC vs. C, R)	ES2 = .12 ES4 = .31
				Significant positive effect of in-session arousal on improvement in PTSD-related symptom scores at 3-month followup (E, EC vs. C, R)	ES3 = .23
Miller, Benefield, & Tonigan, 1993	42	Problem drinkers	Drinker's Check-up with directive-confrontational counseling or with client-centered counseling Sessions: 2 motivational check-ups	Negative effect of in-session arousal on positive change in drinking composite at 12-month followup (directive-confrontational vs. client-centered counseling)	ES3 = –.17

Piper et al., 1998	144	DSM-III-R Major Depression, Dysthymia, personality disorders 73% with previous psychiatric treatment	Short-term interpretative and supportive therapy Sessions: 20 50-min/week Interpretations $M = 11$ ($R = 3–23$); transference interpretations $M = 4$ ($R = 0–14$) *Manualized*	Negative effect of in-session arousal on positive change in depression scores at post-treatment (interpretive vs. supportive therapy)	ES1 = –.14
				Negative effect of in-session arousal on improvement in global symptom distress scores at post-treatment (interpretive vs. supportive therapy)	ES2 = –.07
Piper et al., 1999	144	DSM-III-R Major Depression, Dysthymia, personality disorders 73% with previous psychiatric treatment	Short-term interpretative and supportive therapy Sessions: 20 50-min/week *Manualized*	Negative effect of in-session arousal on average symptom-specific clinical improvement at 12-month followup (interpretive vs. supportive therapy)	ES3 = –.05
				Negative effect of in-session arousal on clinical improvement in global symptomatic distress at 12-month follow-up (interpretive vs. supportive therapy)	ES4 = –.04
Schmidt et al., 2000	77	DSM-IV Panic Disorder with/without agoraphobia 32% with other anxiety disorders. 54% on psychotropic medications	Cognitive behavior therapy (CBT); CBT + breathing retraining (CBT-BR); wait list 12 120-min/week sessions + homework *Manualized*	Positive effect of in-session arousal on improved end-state functioning scores (CBT vs. CBT-BR)	ES2 = .19
Shapiro et al., 1995	104	DSM-III Major Depressive Episode, Present State Examination Index of Definition ≥ 5	Cognitive behavioral therapy (CB); psychodynamic interpersonal psychotherapy (PI) 16- or 8-session duration Sessions: 1 hr/week	Negative effect of in-session arousal on maintenance of gains at 12-month followup (PI vs. CB)	ES3 = –.11

(continues)

Table 7.6 *(Continued)*

Study	*N*	Diagnosis	Treatments	Outcome Effects	Effect Size *(r)*
Sitharthan, Sitharthan, Hough, & Kavanagh, 1997	42	Moderate alcohol dependence	Modified cue exposure (CE); cognitive behavior therapy (CBT) Six 90-min/week sessions *Manualized*	Significant positive effect of in-session arousal on positive change in overall alcohol use at 6-month followup (CE vs. CBT)	ES3 = .28
Vaughan et al., 1994	36	DSM-III-R Post Traumatic Stress Disorder (PTSD)	3 CBT therapies: Eye-Movement Desensitization (EMD); Image Habituation Training (IHT) and Applied Muscle Relaxation (AMR). 3–5 sessions in 2–3 weeks	Positive effect of greater in-session arousal on improvement in PTSD-related symptom scores at post-treatment and 3-month followup (EMD, IHT vs. AMR)	ES1 = .15 ES3 = .07
Emotion vs. Non-Emotion Focus					
Al-Kubaisy et al., 1992	99	ICD-10 agoraphobia, social or specific phobia	Clinician-accompanied exposure (E) + Self-exposure (Ee); Self-exposure *(e)*; Self-relaxation w/out exposure *(r)* All groups: 6 60-min. sessions, 14 weeks 90-min/day self-exposure homework; Ee additionally get 9 hours of E	Positive effect of emotion focus on improvement in phobic symptom scores at post-treatment and 14-week followup (Ee, e vs. r) Positive effect of emotion focus on improved global symptom scores at post-treatment and 14-week followup (Ee, e vs. r)	ES1 = .14 ES3 = .23 ES2 = .32 ES4 = .55
Beutler et al., 1991	63	DSM-III Major Depression; Hamilton Rating Scale for Depression (HRSD) ≥ 16	Group cognitive behavior therapy (CBT); focused expressive group psychotherapy (FEP) supportive, self-directed therapy (S/SD) Sessions: 20+, S/SD 30-min phone sessions + selected readings *Manualized*	Negative effect of emotion focus on positive change in depression scores at post-treatment (FEP vs. CT) Positive effect of emotion focus on improvement in global symptom distress scores at post-treatment (FEP vs. CT) Positive effect of emotion focus on positive change in depression scores at followup (FEP vs. CT) Negative effect of emotion focus on improvement in global symptom distress scores at followup (FEP vs. CT)	ES1 = –.19 ES2 = .35 ES3 = .09 ES4 = –.45

Bond & Bunce, 2000	65	Occupational stress	Acceptance & Commitment Therapy (ACT; emotion focus), Innovation Promotion Program (IPP; problem focus) *Manualized*	Significant positive effect of emotion focus on improvement in global outcome at post-treatment and followup (ACT vs. IPP)	ES2 = .37 ES4 = .35
Borkovec & Costello, 1993	55	DSM-III principal diagnoses Generalized Anxiety Disorder (GAD)	Nondirective (ND); applied relaxation (AR); cognitive behavioral therapy (CBT) Sessions: 12, 2/week; 2 sessions in last 3 weeks. 1st 4 sessions 90-min, rest, 1 hr *Manualized*	Negative effect of emotion focus on positive change in anxiety scores at post-treatment and 6-month followup (ND vs. CBT, AR) Negative effect of emotion focus on positive change in trait anxiety scores at post-treatment and 6-month followup (ND vs. CBT, AR)	ES1 = –.41 ES3 = –.27 ES1 = –.29 ES3 = –.15
Holzer, Pokorny, Kachele, & Luborsky, 1997	20	DSM-II nonpsychotic	Psychodynamic therapists in 2 groups: "most successful" (MS) & "least successful" (LS) Sessions: MS M = 61 weeks; LS M = 43 weeks	Positive effect of emotion focus on improved global functioning composite scores at post-test	ES2 = .48
Piper et al., 1998	144	DSM-III-R Major Depression, Dysthymia, personality disorders 73% with previous psychiatric treatment	Short-term interpretative and supportive therapy Sessions: 20 50-min/week Interpretations M = 11 (R = 3–23); transference interpretations M = 4 (R = 0–14) *Manualized*	Negative effect of emotion focus on positive change in depression scores at post-treatment (interpretive vs. supportive therapy) Negative effect of emotion focus on positive change in global symptom distress scores at post-treatment (interpretive vs. supportive therapy)	ES1 = –.14 ES2 = –.07

(continues)

Table 7.6 *(Continued)*

Study	N	Diagnosis	Treatments	Outcome Effects	Effect Size (r)
Piper et al., 1999	144	DSM-III-R Major Depression, Dysthymia; personality disorders 73% with previous psychiatric treatment	Short-term interpretative and supportive therapy Sessions: 20 50-min/week *Manualized*	Negative effect of emotion focus on average symptom-specific clinical improvement at 12-month followup (interpretive vs. supportive therapy)	ES3 = –.05
				Negative effect of emotion focus on average clinical improvement in global symptomatic distress at 12-month follow-up (interpretive vs. supportive therapy)	ES3 = –.04
Shea et al., 1992	239	Research Diagnostic Criteria: Major Depression; HRSD-17 ≥ 14	NIMH TDCRP data Cognitive behavioral therapy (CBT), interpersonal psychotherapy (IPT); imipramine + clinical management (IMI-CM); placebo + CM (PLA-CM) Sessions: 16–20, M = 13 *Manualized*	Negative effect of emotion focus on maintenance of gains at 18-month followup (IPT vs. CBT)	ES3 = –.06
Vaughan et al., 1994	36	DSM-III-R Post Traumatic Stress Disorder	3 CBT therapies: Eye-Movement Desensitization (EMD); Image Habituation Training (IHT) and Applied Muscle Relaxation (AMR) Sessions: 3–5 in 2–3 weeks	Positive effect of emotion focus on improvement in PTSD-related symptom scores at post-treatment and 3-month followup (EMD, IHT vs. AMR)	ES1 = .15 ES3 = .07

ES1: Target measure at post-treatment.
ES2: Global measure at post-treatment.
ES3: Target measure at followup.
ES4: Global measure at followup.
[a] Results presented as not significant and without directional information.

Vaughn et al., 1994). On the other hand, among comparative studies that include therapies that merely address but do not directly attempt to magnify emotional experience (e.g., Client-Centered Therapy), the emotional tone is more restricted, and the relationships of arousal to outcome is less clear (Borkovec & Costello, 1993; Stiles, Agnew-Davies, Hardy, Barkham, & Shapiro, 1998).

Several studies of emotion-focused interventions have attempted to identify and evaluate moderating factors that may impact treatment effects. These moderators are sought in the form of either an ATI quality of the patient or by the type of outcome assessed. For example, Gaston, Piper, Debbane, Bienvenu, and Garant (1994) found that the impact of exploratory (emotion-focused) and supportive (nonemotion-focused) interventions was a complex function of the length of treatment and the quality of the working alliance. Only in long-term therapy (approximately two years), and among patients who had good working alliances with their therapists, did exploratory interventions produce better outcomes than supportive interventions. When patients had poor relationships with their therapists, supportive interventions were more effective than exploratory interventions. These findings support the hypothesis that effective therapy consists of a pattern of tears and repairs in the emotional attachment between therapy and patient (Horvath, 1995; Safran, Muran, & Samstang, 1994).

Other relational and interactive factors have also been noted to affect outcomes. For example, Beutler et al. (1996) determined that the effect of an emotional enhancing therapy was most noticeable among those patients whose initial levels of distress were low, and Hardy, Stiles, Barkham, and Startup (1998) found that patients who were intensely involved in their problems became involved in therapy earlier than those who were underinvolved. The former group subsequently experienced greater benefits than the latter, and these effects were associated with levels of emotional intensity.

In a still different permutation of effects, Hill, Zack, Wonnell et al. (2000) compared treatments among patients with either troubling dreams or recent losses. The effectiveness of experiential dream work or insight work varied as a function of the type of problem presented. Insight procedures were most effective among patients who had experienced a recent loss. Dream work increased emotional arousal and benefit among those who had troubling dreams.

TREATMENT INTENSITY. In the world of clinical practice, it is conventional to adjust the level of care (treatment length, frequency of sessions, and treatment setting) to the patient's level of impairment and risk of being harmful to self and others. Howard and colleagues (Howard, Moras et al., 1996; Kopta, Howard, Lowry, & Beutler, 1994; Sperry, Brill et al., 1996) suggest that the relationship between amount of treatment benefit and the intensity (number or spacing of sessions) of the treatment is best described by a negatively accelerating curve. Even though this curvilinear relationship is the most frequently observed, there is evidence that it may be relatively fragile (e.g., Hilsenroth, Ackerman, & Blagys, 2001). Many factors affect the relationship between treatment dose and response. The chronicity and reactivity of the symptoms addressed (e.g., Howard, Moras et al., 1996), the type of problem presented (e.g., Shapiro et al., 1994), the type of treatment, and even the method of evaluating outcomes (e.g., Kadera, Lambert, & Andrews, 1996) can change the shape or course of the relationship.

In a recent comprehensive review of the moderating influence of patient impairment on the intensity of treatment effects, Beutler, Harwood, Alimohamed, and Malik (2002) found modest support for increasing the frequency or length of treatment among highly impaired patients. Our review of nonpharmacological methods of increasing treatment intensity (Table 7.7) identified five studies on which effect sizes could be computed. Although the mean effect size was significant ($r = .11$), the heterogeneity estimate was also significant ($Q = 22.89$; $p < .05$), suggesting the presence of a patient modifier.

Only one study (Reynolds et al., 1996) in our analysis found a negative relationship between the number of sessions and the rate of change. A critical issue in this and other studies in this line of research, however, is the failure to address the confound between impairment and attendance at treatment sessions. If impairment level interferes with treatment attendance, then one is better advised to correlate *planned* treatment length with outcomes rather than actual attendance (e.g., Shapiro et al., 1995). Unfortunately, with the insufficient number of studies of this type we do not have a clear picture of the relationship between treatment intensity and outcomes among patients whose level of impairment varies.

Although the intensity of treatment seems to be partially dictated by the problem severity (e.g., Beutler, Kim, Davison, Karno, & Fisher, 1996), it

TABLE 7.7 Intensity of Treatment

Study	N	Diagnosis	Treatments	Outcome Effects	Effect Size (r)
Avants et al., 1999	237	DSM-III-R Cocaine Dependence/Abuse	Day Treatment Program (DT); Enhanced Standard Care (EC; cognitive behavioral, physical health, vocational skills, community resources groups). Daily methadone for all patients Sessions: over 12 weeks. Methadone up to 85 mg/day; DT 5 hours/day 5 days/week, M=10.7 weeks; EC 2 hour/week, M=10.9 weeks *Manualized*	No effect of greater intensity of treatment on drug use outcome at post-treatment or followup (DT vs. EC)	ES1 = 0[a] ES3 = 0[a]
Hampson & Beavers, 1996	434	Child/adolescent behavior, marriage, family problems	Family therapy Sessions: "5 or less" and "6 or more" client groups	Positive effect of greater number of sessions on positive change in goal attainment at post-treatment (≤ 5 vs. ≥ 6 sessions)	ES1 = .55
Hoglend, 1993	45	DSM-III personality disorders, Dysthymia, Major Depression, adjustment, anxiety disorders	Dynamic psychotherapy Sessions: 9–53 *Manualized*	Significant positive effect of treatment length on positive dynamic change at 4-year followup (≥ 30 sessions, show improved problem-solving capacity, self-esteem, interpersonal functioning)	ES4 = .35
Reynolds et al., 1996	117	DSM-III-R Major Depression, retarded depression, Beck Depression Inventory > 16	Cognitive behavioral (CB) or psychodynamic-interpersonal therapy (PI) in 16 or 8 sessions Peer supervision	Negative effect of number of sessions on rate of change in depressive mood at post-treatment (16 vs. 8 session treatment)	ES1 = –.37
Shapiro et al., 1995	104	DSM-III Major Depressive Episode; Present State Examination Index of Definition ≥ 5	Cognitive behavioral therapy (CB); psychodynamic-interpersonal psychotherapy (PI) 16- or 8-session duration Sessions: 1 hr/week	Positive effect of treatment length on maintenance of gains at 1-year followup (16 vs. 8 sessions)	ES3 = .19

ES1: Target measure at post-treatment.

ES2: Global measure at post-treatment.

ES3: Target measure at followup.

ES4: Global measure at followup.

[a] Results presented as not significant and without directional information.

is not always clear how best to adjust the intensity or nature of treatment as a function of problem severity and impairment. Different methods of analyzing the Treatment of Depression Collaborative Research Program (TDCRP) data, for example, have produced different answers to this question. Elkin et al. (1989) reported no differences in the psychotherapy responses as a function of patient depressive severity. In contrast, Sotsky et al. (1991) found that interpersonal psychotherapy (IPT) was more effective than cognitive therapy among patients who had relatively high levels of cognitive dysfunction and role impairments. The method of analyzing these data accounts for the differences.

Shapiro et al. (1994) compared two types of interventions as applied within two time frames (8 or 16 weeks) and found that when patient impairment was relatively high, longer term treatment was most effective. However, when patient impairment was relatively low, the intensity of treatment had no significant effect on outcome. Unfortunately, in this study, the effect of intensifying treatments did not survive a one-year followup analysis (Shapiro et al., 1995).

Using a still different method of identifying treatment intensity (chronicity, comorbidity, family impairment), Beutler, Clarkin, and Bongar (2000) also found that patients with moderate and high levels of social and interpersonal impairment were more disposed to benefit when treated with intensive treatment. In this case, intensive treatments consisted of adding psychoactive medication, increasing the number of sessions of treatment, or adding group and family therapy. Similarly, Joyce and Piper (1996) found that the better the patient's ability to establish relationships with others, the more likely they were to benefit from insight-oriented treatments, which may be, in turn, assumed to be more intensive than symptomatic treatments.

The relationship of treatment intensity to outcome is not consistent, however. Some studies have found that adding antidepressants to supportive psychotherapy, a method that is designed to be more intensive than psychotherapy alone, increases the effectiveness of treatment among the more depressed and dysfunctional patients (e.g., Beutler, Clarkin, & Bongar, 2000). Other studies, however, have found just the opposite relationship. In these studies, the addition of medication has been found to be most beneficial among the least impaired patients (e.g., Schulberg, Pilkonis, & Houck, 1998). Some of these inconsistencies can be attributed to method factors that confound the relationship between impairment level and treatment intensity (e.g., Shadish et al., 2000). It is also possible that adding medication to psychotherapy does not increase the experienced intensity of the psychosocial treatment.

Self-Disclosure. Another aspect of therapist intervention has generated research, but this dimension does not easily fit into the foregoing scheme. That is, it is not readily apparent whether therapist self-disclosure is a directive procedure, one that is symptom or insight focused, or one that raises or lowers emotional intensity. Indeed, like many specific techniques, it may be designed to do all of these things at different times and by different therapists. Thus, it is considered here within a separate category, which is to acknowledge it as an emerging and potentially important area of research, albeit one that has not yet accumulated a critical mass of studies that meet our criteria of rigor.

The self-disclosure literature, including research from the 1970s, was reviewed by Watkins (1990). Although Watkins concludes that self-disclosure is an important skill to develop, it is clear from his review that precious little research has attended to effects on outcomes. The most frequently cited dependent variable was some aspect of patient satisfaction or an estimate of the "effectiveness" of the therapist's response.

Among outcome studies, the best available study over the past two decades continues to be Barrett and Berman (2001). In this study, self-disclosure was systematically controlled, and the effects indicated that it was associated with lowered distress (r = .33). The two other studies on this topic were based on a single sample and also found positive effects, although not as strong as those by Barrett and Berman (2001). Piper et al. (1998) studied self-disclosure within the context of an RCT comparison of supportive and interpretive therapies, finding a generally positive effect on subsequent depression and distress scores (r = .14). This finding was confirmed on specific measures of clinical improvement (Piper et al., 1999; *r's* from .04 to .05).

The results indicate a statistically significant, but clinically weak, effect of therapist self-disclosure, although the variability of effect sizes might suggest the role of methodological rigor as a mediator of how strong the relationship between self-disclosure and outcome might be.

Inferred Traits

Inferred traits include personality and coping patterns, therapist level of emotional well-being, values and beliefs, and cultural attitudes. Research in this area has frequently attended to defining ways in which patient and therapist qualities interact, producing patterns of fit and mismatch. However, patient and therapist qualities are frequently difficult to disentangle. Therapist traits frequently affect how the therapist perceives and responds to the patient, and this may, in turn, affect how the patient responds. Thus, if there is some bias in how patients are diagnosed (Garb, 1998), then identifying therapists who work especially well with some diagnostic groups may be impeded. The need for careful controls and assurance of independence of constructs in conducting research in this area are necessary.

At the same time, it is clear that inferred therapist traits interact with various patient attributes (e.g., Kaplan & Garfinkel, 1999) and that some relational aspects of patient-therapist correspondence (similarity or dissimilarity) may affect patient response to treatment. For example, Herman (1998) found that correspondence between patient and therapist on the Structural Profile Inventory (SPI; Lazarus, 1989), a 35-item inventory designed to illuminate patients' modality functioning for use in multimodal therapy, facilitated outcome.

Unfortunately, research on therapist traits and patient-therapist matching on these dimensions lost favor once federal funding agencies turned their attention to the study of manualized treatments and the use of randomized trials methods. As a result, in recent years, very few outcome studies have been published on the nature of the therapist, allowing little in the way of conclusions. In most instances, we were unable to generate a critical mass of appropriate studies published in the last two decades to support a meta-analytic review.

General Personality and Coping Patterns

The therapist's personality has been posited as influential to patient outcome, and a wide array of personality dimensions have been suggested as potentially relevant. However, many of these personality dimensions overlap, creating difficulties for researchers interested in exploring this area. Further hampering this research is the fact that extant personality measures are usually very general in nature and not constructed for the purpose of examining the effects of therapist personality on patient outcome (Najavits et al., 1995). Because of these and numerous other difficulties, therapist personality continues to be a relatively neglected and fading area of outcome research despite the longstanding attention to this variable by theorists.

Although some early attempts to correlate omnibus personality dimensions with outcome yielded promising findings, subsequent efforts to cross-validate these findings were often disappointing (Beutler, Machado, & Neufeldt, 1994). For example, Antonuccio, Lewinsohn, and Steinmetz (1982) correlated a variety of therapist characteristics to outcome, through post-hoc analyses, in a study involving more than 100 depressed patients. Patients were randomly assigned to a homogenous type of therapy, with both the skill levels and the experience of the therapists carefully controlled. However, none of the therapist personality traits was found to be significantly related to treatment efficacy. Such disappointing findings probably have contributed to the general decline of interest in this area of research.

More specific measures of personality dimensions, though not widely researched, do suggest some promising effects that deserve notation. Berry and Sipps (1991), for example, found that personality similarity on the targeted dimensions of the Myers-Briggs Type indicator was predictive of premature termination. Although the actual effect size was small ($r = .13$), it suggested that the more similar the patient and therapist's personality, the higher the probability that the client would drop out of treatment. Thus, differences rather than similarity were positive indicators.

In contrast, Herman (1998) found the opposite effect on treatment benefits. Personality similarity was a positive predictor of subsequent benefit. The effect was relatively large ($r = .79$). Collectively, the results of these two studies are difficult to understand. They are precisely opposite one another and do not thereby lend much support to the conventional wisdom that has assumed that similarity increases the attachment and participation in treatment (e.g., Beutler & Clarkin, 1990). Conclusions about the effects of therapist general personality similarity and outcome are not possible at this time, and research has decreased significantly since the first edition of this *Handbook* (Bergin & Garfield, 1971).

Dominance

Research that has examined specific therapist qualities derived from the theoretical literature has fared slightly better than research taking a more global, omnibus approach. For example, dogmatism and dominance are related theoretical constructs and are thought to exert a negative influence on outcome because of their negative effect on therapist flexibility. To test this hypothesis, Henry, Schacht, and Strupp (1990) conducted a post-hoc analysis of 14 therapist-patient dyads and confirmed that poor outcomes were associated with therapists who had internalized dogmatic and controlling introjects.

According to Washton and Stone-Washton (1990), a low desire to control the patient is one of the primary characteristics of the ideal therapist. This may be especially true when the therapist is treating ethnically diverse patients. The ethnic fit of patient and therapist may be moderated by the level of therapist dominance. For example, Hall and Maloney (1983) found that, among Anglos and Latinos, therapists with high-dominance needs tended to work better with clients from their own culture, whereas those with low-dominance needs worked better with those from other cultures. Thus, Latino patients earned either better or worse outcomes than Anglos, depending on therapist dominance.

Locus of Control, Conceptual Level, and Coping Style

Although previous research found in the *Handbook of Psychotherapy and Behavior Change* (Beutler, Machado, & Neufeldt, 1994) has reported promising relationships between therapist locus of perceived control and conceptual level or style, little research of these areas has been done within the past 20 years. Possibly related to dominance and openness, locus of perceived control, as a concept in cognitive psychology, has received a great deal of attention in the psychotherapy research literature. However, this attention has in the main been directed toward patients and not toward efforts to understand psychotherapists. When research into locus of control and therapists has been conducted, it has typically involved naturalistic designs and post-hoc analyses that do not have the benefit of prospectively driven hypotheses. For example, Hunt et al. (1985) investigated therapist and client similarity on the conceptual level (abstract attributions), finding a significant but small effect on outcome as a function of conceptual similarity. This finding is generally consistent with the conclusions of the earlier *Handbook* review (Beutler, Machado, & Neufeldt, 1994). Though interesting, no substantial conclusions are yet warranted because of the low level of interest in these concepts.

Emotional Well-Being

Beutler, Machado, and Neufeldt (1994), in the earlier edition of this volume, concluded that therapist emotional well-being and freedom from distress were positively correlated with treatment benefits. This conclusion was based on a review of 15 empirical studies that were published between 1968 and 1991. Most of these studies were simple correlational analyses, but they consistently found a positive relationship between measures of therapist well-being and subsequent treatment benefit.

We identified nine studies of therapist emotional well-being (Table 7.8) that were susceptible to analysis of effect size. As in the earlier review, these studies were based on naturalistic and correlational designs. The effect sizes ranged from 0 (Antonuccio, Lewinsohn, & Steinmetz, 1982) to .71 (McCarthy & Frieze, 1999). Notably, however, all of the effect sizes were in the same direction, suggesting a positive relationship of well-being and patient benefit, and the mean (weighted) effect size was both positive and significant ($r = .12, p < .05$). As an example, Luborsky et al. (1985) used a general measure of well-being and three well-defined but distinctive therapies and reliable outcome measures, finding moderate effect sizes of *(r)* .41 and .33 for end of treatment and followup, respectively. This finding was similar to an earlier study by the same group (Luborsky, Mintz et al., 1980), which obtained an effect size *(r)* of .34, and compared favorably to other studies in this series.

The findings cut across types of outcomes. McGuff, Gitlin, and Enderlin (1996) found that self-reported therapist confidence during the first session of treatment was associated with patient attendance; McCarthy and Frieze (1999) found that measures of therapist burnout were negatively associated with self-reported outcome; and Williams and Chambless (1990) found that clients who judged their therapist to have high levels of self-confidence were among the most likely to improve. Therapist well-being may also be moderated by patient well-being. Talley, Strupp, and Morey (1990), for example, found that therapist self-concept affected outcome only when both patients and therapists shared a high level of esteem.

Perhaps the most important observation that can be made from these findings is that high

TABLE 7.8 Emotional Well-Being

Study	N	Diagnosis	Treatments	Outcome Effects	Effect Size (r)
Antonuccio, Lewinsohn, & Steinmetz, 1982	106	Mixed diagnoses (unipolar depression, a psychiatric syndrome, or no diagnosis)	Cognitive behavioral group	Effect of self-confidence on depression scores at post-treatment did not attain statistical significance. No directional information provided	ES1 = 0[a]
Greenspan & Kulish, 1985	718	Mixed diagnoses	Individual psychotherapy (psychoanalytic therapy)	Positive effect of therapist's personal therapy on client retention. Therapists with a history of personal therapy evidenced lower rates of premature client termination than therapists with no history of personal therapy	ES2 = .10
McGuff, Gitlin, & Enderlin, 1996	84	Mixed diagnoses	Individual psychotherapy	Positive effect of therapist confidence at first session on client-rated effectiveness of therapy	ES2 = .42
				Positive effect of therapist confidence at first session on client attendance in treatment	ES1 = .32
McCarthy & Frieze, 1999	131	Mixed diagnoses	Mixed group and individually administered treatment (eclectic, client-centered, behavioral, cognitive and psychoanalytic psychotherapies)	Positive effect of emotional well-being on client-rated therapy quality	ES2 = .71
Lafferty, Beutler, & Crago, 1989	60	Mixed diagnoses (anxiety disorder, affective disorder, adjustment disorder, and no psychiatric diagnosis)	Individual psychotherapy (psycho-dynamic, eclectic, client-centered, and behavioral therapies)	Positive effect of emotional well-being on global severity of distress at post-treatment	ES2 = .17
Luborsky, McLellan, Woody, O'Brien, & Auerbach, 1985	110	Methadone hydrochloride-maintained, drug-dependent	Individual psychotherapy (supportive-expressive psychotherapy, cognitive-behavioral psychotherapy, and drug counseling)	Positive effect of emotional well-being on global general symptomatology at 7-month followup	ES4 = .41
				Positive effect of emotional well-being on addiction severity scores at 7-month followup	ES3 = .33
Luborsky, Mintz, Auerbach, Crits-Christoph, Bachrach, Todd, Johnson, Cohen, & O'Brien, 1980	73	Mixed diagnoses (Nonpsychotic)	Individual psychoanalytically oriented psychotherapy	Positive effect of emotional well-being on "Residual Rated Benefits," a composite rating by therapists and patients of how much benefit each patient received from treatment	ES2 = .34
Wiggins & Giles, 1984	32	N/A	Individual psychotherapy	Positive effect of emotional well being on one-month post-treatment self-esteem scores	ES1 = .59
Williams & Chambless, 1990	33	Agoraphobia with panic attacks	10 sessions of individually tailored in vivo exposure	Positive effect of self-confidence on reduction of "fearful situations" scores at post-treatment	ES1 = .39

ES1: Target measure at post-treatment.
ES2: Global measure at post-treatment.
ES3: Target measure at followup.
ES4: Global measure at followup.
[a] Results presented as not significant and without directional information.

levels of therapist well-being cannot be assumed to be present among therapists in research studies. It may indeed be a hidden moderator of many contradictory or inconsistent therapy findings. It should be remembered that psychotherapists are frequent consumers of mental health treatment. Norcross, Geller, and Kurzawa (2000) report that from 3% to 7% of psychotherapists' case loads are other psychotherapists. Accordingly, it is surprising that explorations of this variable have generally lost favor over the past few years.

Although the latter conclusion is suggestive, the studies reported here do not support the existence of a causal relationship between therapist well-being and benefit. One avenue for inferring the presence of such a relationship has traditionally been a correlation between the amount of personal therapy received by a therapist and the amount of benefit achieved by these therapists' patients (Clark, 1986; Greenberg & Staller, 1981). This avenue of determining a relationship between emotional well-being and clinical effectiveness has been fraught with problems because no direct relationship exists between amount of therapy received and end-point emotional well-being. Therapists who receive psychotherapy may initially be more disturbed and distressed than those who don't seek such treatment, a disparity that may not be eradicated by any amount of personal psychotherapy. Even if they are not, however, other factors besides emotional well-being go into the process of electing to enter psychotherapy. Guy, Stark, and Poelstra (1988) found that those therapists who were likely to seek therapy were dominantly psychoanalytic in orientation, and Norcross and Prochaska (1986) found that these therapists were more inclined to self-inspection and self-blame than those who did not seek personal therapy.

In terms of treatment effects, some suggestion is also offered that personal therapy for therapists can be associated with iatrogenic effects on therapists' effectiveness (Buckley, Karasu, & Charles, 1981), although most older reviews of this literature have failed to find consistent relationships. Research conducted during the last decade has not clarified the role of personal therapy. We found only one relevant study (McDevitt, 1987) that determined that personal therapy enhanced therapists' recognition of their own countertransference tendencies. Unfortunately, this study did not report findings on patient outcomes among therapists who received personal therapy. Thus, we conclude that there is no persuasive evidence for a positive relationship between the act of receiving personal psychotherapy and treatment outcome. One may seek personal psychotherapy because of a correlated group of features, including personal openness, desire to avoid professional burnout, motivation, distress, life stress, sensitivity, and faith in treatment.

Values, Attitudes, and Beliefs

Because therapists are regarded as agents of change and because the focus of these change efforts is predominantly on the attitudes, beliefs, and lifestyles of patients, many of whom are distressed and potentially victimized, society has expressed great concern that the therapist will exert unwarranted or unwanted influence on some patients. Many researchers have conceptualized psychotherapy as a process in which the therapist's values are a primary ingredient. Frank and Frank (1991) indicated that the past 20 years of research continues predominantly to support the earlier view (Frank, 1973) that psychotherapy is a process of interpersonal persuasion in which therapist values, beliefs, and optimism serve to overcome demoralization, instill hope, and provide a believable meaning of life for patients.

General values and attitudes. A substantial literature on values and psychotherapy accumulated during the 1970s and 1980s (e.g., Beutler, 1981; Kelly, 1990; Richards & Bergin, 2000; Shafranske, 1996), but this line of research has lost popularity over the past two decades. Unfortunately, the number of available studies precludes testing effect sizes in a summary analysis. Moreover, methodological problems continue to affect this area of research, and consensus has yet to be achieved even on what constitutes a "value." Although better instruments are emerging for assessing the array of potential values among therapists (Jensen & Bergin, 1988), there is still little agreement as to what constitutes a "value" and very limited data has been collected on outcomes in psychotherapy that are related to values. Indeed, little progress has been made in determining what values are important to the practice of psychotherapy or how values should be integrated into psychotherapeutic practice (Bergin, 1991).

Typically, when significant effects are obtained in this area of research, the effect sizes are variable and often small. The limited research during the late 1980s and early 1990s has continued to show the presence of a general shift in patient values and beliefs toward those of their therapists (e.g., Arizmendi et al., 1985; Beutler et al., 1983; Hamblin, Beutler, Scogin, & Corbishley, 1993; Kelly & Strupp, 1992). However, several studies have demonstrated that initial patient-therapist dissimilarity on some values is positively related with good outcome (e.g., Arizemendi et al., 1985; Beutler et al., 1983). Our computations reflect this inconsistency and reveal values (*r*) that range widely from .01 (Williams & Chambless, 1990) to .84 (Arizmendi et al., 1985).

Several researchers have attempted to explain the inconsistency of these results (cf. Beutler, 1981; Beutler & Bergan, 1991; Kelly & Strupp, 1992). Williams and Chambless (1990) suggest that the contradictions may reflect the moderating influence of the therapists' attitudes, at least as perceived by the patient. Several others (e.g., Beutler, 1983; Tjelviet, 1986) also note these differences and conclude that regardless of the direction of relationship, the result simply underlines the probability that persuasion and conversion are more appropriate metaphors than the metaphor of "healing" when discussing psychotherapy outcomes. Regardless of the explanation, the limited evidence available at present suggests that therapeutic improvement is associated with value changes. Both patient and therapist values are now more explicitly identified and identifiable, and are discussed in treatment more frequently than former traditions would allow. Nonetheless, the paucity and inconsistency of the results over the past decade have failed either to shed further light on the role of therapist values on psychotherapy outcome or to demonstrate that therapist values can be used to enhance the efficiency of outcome predictions.

Religious Beliefs. Traditionally, there has been at least mild antagonism between psychotherapy and religion (e.g., Bergin, 1980, 1983 vs. Ellis, 1980, 1981). Over the years, however, it has become more apparent that psychotherapy is not and cannot be value-free. For a time, attention was directed increasingly on the role of patient and therapist religion on the treatment process and outcome (e.g., Bergin, 1991; Bergin & Jensen, 1990; Shafranske & Malony, 1990). Interestingly, however, the interest stirred in this domain during the 1980s had largely disappeared by 2000.

Bergin (1991) summarized the research of two decades ending in 1990 and rejected the view that religion has a negative impact on one's mental health. He concluded that people who are intrinsically religious may even be more open to change than those who are either nonreligious or extrinsically religious. After reviewing a single decade (1984–1994) of research on the role of religion on psychotherapy preferences, Worthington, Kurusu, McCullough, and Sandage (1996) concluded that "religious clients" in the United States, especially those who identify themselves as "Christian," tend to prefer therapists who share their religious beliefs, whereas non-Christian, religious patients have no particular preference for therapists of various religions. Moreover, regardless of patients' religious preferences, disclosure of a therapist's religious affiliation alters what things are discussed and revealed in psychotherapy.

Related research during this period revealed that both nonreligious and religious therapists were able to provide effective treatment to Christian patients, regardless of these preferences, as long as the therapists were able to provide religion-congruent interventions (Propst, Ostrom, Watkins, Deant, & Mashburn, 1992). Perhaps this finding reflects some common values that cut across religious affiliations (Jensen & Bergin, 1988; Worthington et al., 1996). Indeed, some evidence exists for the presence of a core set of religious beliefs that affect religious patients' expectations for psychotherapy in a relatively consistent and positive way (Keating & Fretz, 1990; Shafranske, & Malony, 1990). However, differences in values may also interfere with the development of the treatment relationship. For example, Worthington et al. (1996) found that the more fundamental one's Christian identification and the more literally one interprets the Bible, the more particular and critical the patient is about the therapist's behavior, expecting and wanting more religious ceremony (e.g., prayer, use of scripture, biblical quotes) to be a part of psychotherapy.

Unfortunately, the relative decline of research in the area of religion and treatment outcome during the past decade prevents us from achieving an understanding about how religious influences may be changing in psychotherapy. Moreover, outcome research on therapist religion has been and remains "embarrassingly sparse" (Worthington et al., 1996; p. 477)—so much so that a meta-analytic comparison was not possible. The limited evidence to date is not sufficient to conclude that unique outcomes accrue with religiously oriented therapy or that therapist religion has anything to add to the effectiveness of psychological interventions among religious people, beyond facilitating positive expectations. At the same time, a growing body of literature on theory and technique has evolved which provides prime targets for new research (Miller, 1999; Richards & Bergin 2000a, 2000b; Shafranske, 1996).

Translating these theoretical concepts into research has resulted in mixed findings. Project Match (Project Match Research Group, 1997) assessed therapist religious background factors but found no relationship of these behaviors to post-treatment alcohol use among patients. Martinez (1991), on the other hand, evaluated the religious similarity of patient and therapist and found a negative relationship with outcome, a finding that was reported in several earlier studies (Beutler, 1981).

Cultural Attitudes

Gender and Ageism. Gender research has gained salience in the past two decades. Perceptions of sex and cultural role attitudes (ethnic attitudes, ageism, etc.) and behaviors have been linked to aspects of personality and treatment expectation. In spite of this interest, little research has utilized actual outcome measures and representative samples. A special issue of *In Session*, edited by Campos and Goldfried (2001), on the Gay, Lesbian, and Bisexual (GLB) client, for example, included both an article on cognitive behavioral therapy (CBT; Safran & Rogers, 2001) and a more general article on treatment issues (Dworkin, 2001), but both of these reports relied on case descriptions and neither reported any outcome measures or studies. Partly in response to the omissions in the literature, Goldfried (Rabasca, 2000) has started a group (AFFIRM) comprised of psychologists who share a common interest in the problems experienced by GLB, their relatives and friends, with an agenda of initiating and encouraging research on issues that will bring this disenfranchised group into the psychological mainstream.

Contemporary research has demonstrated the presence of systematic bias among psychotherapists against GLB patients. Though not assessed on psychotherapy outcome, evidence does suggest the presence of diagnostic biases (e.g., Lilling & Friedman, 1995) that exaggerate the degree of pathology among GLB patients and heightened tendencies among psychotherapists to attribute blame and responsibility to these patients (Hayes & Erkis, 2000). However, these are not consistent or uniform findings, and several studies have failed to find evidence of systematic distortions of perceptions and judgments among samples of clinicians (e.g., Crawford, McLeod, Zamboni, & Jordan, 1999; Danziger & Welfel, 2000; Liddle, 1995). Some studies have even found a reverse bias in which clients with nonheterosexual preferences are seen in a more positive light than heterosexual patients (Glenn & Russell, 1986).

Although the relationship is not consistent regarding a systematic and replicable bias against patients with nonheterosexual preferences, it is clear that the therapist's ability to present a helpful image to patients depends on his or her attitudes and beliefs about the Gay, Lesbian, and Bisexual lifestyles. Homophobic and conflicted attitudes affect therapist perceptions of responsibility (Hayes & Erkis, 2000), clinical judgments (Crawford, McLeod, Zamboni, & Jordan, 1999), and willingness to work with nonheterosexual patients (Wisch & Mahalik, 1999). The impeding effects of these attitudinal biases on the part of therapists may become magnified when the patient is HIV positive. Hayes and Erkis (2000) determined that therapists were more likely to blame HIV positive patients for personal problems, to be less empathic, to be less motivated to provide treatment, and to attribute more severe problems to patients whom they believed had become infected through sexual contact or drug abuse rather than through a blood transfusion.

Conversely, evidence (Wisch & Mahalik, 1999) suggests that therapist acceptance of various gender views is associated both with comfort in working with nonheterosexual patients, reducing the level of overattributing psychopathology, and improving the prognostic expectations for these patients. Unfortunately, without supporting research on treatment outcomes, it is impossible to determine whether these views translate to effectiveness. Only a very small number of studies have actually related these cultural biases to clinical outcomes (the criteria for inclusion in our meta-analysis).

For example, Liddle (1996, 1997) surveyed GLB clients, comparing their reported responses to psychotherapy to the reports of heterosexual individuals. He found that nonheterosexual respondents had seen a greater number of therapists and had received a larger number of psychotherapy sessions than heterosexual individuals. Therapists who used procedures that were dismissive of nonheterosexual views were judged by patients to be unhelpful, while therapists who had been independently determined to be affirming of gay lifestyles were judged to have been more helpful than nongay affirming therapists.

Among heterosexual therapists, Liddle found that females were rated more effective than males, and those therapists (of either sex) who conveyed a lack of understanding of gay issues were judged to have had a negative impact on the patient's commitment to and retention in psychotherapy. This latter finding is reminiscent of that of an older study by Brooks (1981) who found that lesbian clients who reported having achieved poor results in psychotherapy frequently indicated that their previous therapist had been a heterosexual male, compared with those who benefitted from their previous therapy.

The picture is only slightly clearer with respect to ageist bias among clinicians. The available evidence, limited as it is, suggests that therapists hold a negative and stereotypic view of older patients (Danziger & Welfel, 2000; Ivey, Wieling, & Harris, 2000), although this view may be moderated by level of clinician experience in working with older patients (Meeks, 1990). Again, however, outcome data are lacking.

Although there is some evidence of a systematic (if not consistent) gender, ageist, or cultural bias among psychotherapists, little is known about the effects of these "-isms" on treatment outcomes. While we were unable to define a critical mass of studies for meta-analytic comparison, we believe that, conservatively, it is likely that therapist ageist and sexist attitudes affect the ability to develop working relationships and, concomitantly, restrict the availability of treatment resources for those who are the objects of therapist bias. It is likely that the significance of therapist attitudes extends far beyond the limited context of gender and age bias. Evidence suggests that such male-gender stereotypic attitudes as control of emotions, power drive, competition, work over family choices, and sexual dominance are related to the emergence of patient attributes such as hostility, anxiety, paranoia, and psychoticism, whether or not the patient is heterosexual or nonheterosexual (e.g., Tokar, Fischer, Schaub, & Moradi, 2000).

Another indication of the importance of therapist attitudes is found in research which suggests that therapists identifying themselves as "feminist" in orientation may be better able to establish a good working relationship than can nonfeminst therapists, regardless of the patient's gender preferences (Cantor, 1991), and therapists who hold nontraditional views of sexual roles may promote more change and satisfaction among female clients than those who hold traditional gender views (e.g., Banikiotes & Merluzzi, 1981; Hart, 1981).

Ethnicity. In a previous section, we have reviewed the status of research on therapist race. Though inseparable from race, therapist ethnicity is a more complex concept than race (Beutler, Brown et al., 1996). Ethnicity is generally conceptualized as a distal marker of attitudes toward race, identification with culture, and various value systems (e.g., Sue et al., 1994). For example, if patients and therapists of similar ethnic background tend to persist longer in treatment, it is probably because they share certain value and belief perspectives that make the relationship more compatible. It must be noted, however, that this same collection of compatibility factors may come into play to temper or underestimate the degree to which ethnic similarity is associated with treatment improvement.

Given that therapists hold personal beliefs and values that may affect their ability to establish a positive working alliance with their clients, it is relevant to question how such attitudes influence treatment outcome with ethnic minorities. Gray-Little and Kaplan (2000) note that both practical and conceptual limitations plague research specifically relevant to therapy with ethnic minority groups. An obvious practical obstacle has been the infrequent utilization of mental health services by these populations and the associated lack of presence in psychotherapy research trials. These authors point to the dilemma of the investigator faced with data on a small number of ethnic minorities. Does one eliminate minority data if it is discrepant, collapse it with majority group data if not obviously discrepant, or revert to excluding minorities from research altogether, so as to eliminate such a predicament from the outset? Conceptual difficulties include problems inherent in attempting to define and measure race and ethnicity.

Much of the literature on therapist attitudes in working with members of ethnic minority groups is in the form of surveys and analogue studies; few outcome studies exist. Out of the five (Malgady, Rogler, & Constantino, 1990 report two studies) outcome studies that we identified, three pertain to outcome associated with therapist cultural sensitivity training (Evans, Acosta, Yamamoto, & Skilbeck, 1984; Thompson, Worthington, & Atkinson, 1994; Wade & Bernstein, 1991), and two specifically examine the use of a culturally sensitive treatment (Malgady, Rogler, & Costantino, 1990). However, the effect sizes are consistent and relatively high (Table 7.9), ranging from *(r)* .12 (Thompson, Worthington,

TABLE 7.9 Therapist Cultural Attitudes: Ethnicity

Study	N	Diagnosis	Treatments	Outcome Effects	Effect Size
Evans, Acosta, Yamamoto, & Skilbeck, 1984	171	Mixed diagnoses (transient situational disturbances, psychoses, and neuroses)	Individual psychotherapy	Positive effect of therapist cultural orientation training on client satisfaction with therapy at followup	ES4 = .12
Malgady, Rogler, & Costantino, 1990	210	Mixed symptomatology (anxiety symptoms, conduct problems, poor social judgment, and low self-esteem)	Group intervention (Puerto Rican cuentos modeling therapy compared with art/play therapy and a no-treatment, discussion-oriented control group)	Positive effect of adapted cuentos versus control treatment on anxiety at post-treatment	ES1 = .37
				Positive effect of adapted cuentos versus control treatment on anxiety at 1-year followup (N = 178)	ES3 = .22
Malgady, Rogler, & Costantino, 1990	90	Mixed symptomatology (anxiety symptoms, conduct problems, poor social judgment, and low self-esteem)	Group intervention (18 weekly 90-min Hero/Heroine therapy sessions compared with 8 monthly attention control discussion sessions)	Positive effect of Hero/Heroine intervention on anxiety at post-treatment	ES1 = .19
Thompson, Worthington, & Atkinson, 1994	100	NA	Client-centered psychotherapy (one 35–45-minute session)	Positive effect of cultural content orientation on client willingness to self-refer	ES2 = .12
Wade & Bernstein, 1991	80	Presenting problems include personal issues and vocational concerns	Brief individual psychotherapy (up to 3 sessions)	Positive effect of cultural sensitivity training on client satisfaction with counseling	ES2 = .71

ES1: Target measure at post-treatment.

ES2: Global measure at post-treatment.

ES3: Target measure at followup.

ES4: Global measure at followup.

[a] Results presented as not significant and without directional information.

& Atkinson, 1994) to *(r)* .71 (Wade & Bernstein, 1991). Though the number is small, the (weighted) average is significant ($r = .13$, $p < .05$).

Inferred States

Therapeutic Relationship

The quality of the therapeutic relationship can be assessed from the perspective of the therapist, the patient, or an independent observer. Indeed, these perspectives often give different pictures of the therapeutic alliance (e.g., Ogrodniczuk, Piper, Joyce, & McCallum, 2000). Yet, the quality of the therapist relationship from all of these perspectives has been one of the most widely accepted and consistently supported correlates of therapeutic change (Andrews, 2000; Lambert, 1992). Accordingly, it is one of the variables defined in earlier editions of this volume as among the stronger predictors of treatment outcome (e.g., Orlinsky et al., 1994; Beutler, Machado, & Neufeldt, 1994).

Meta-analyses of the relationship between therapeutic relationship and outcome have produced moderate effect size values, ranging from *(r)* .11 (Stevens, Hynan, & Allen, 2000) to .26 *(r)* (Horvath & Symonds, 1991). Martin, Garske, and Davis (2000) compared the correlations between relationship and outcome as a function of the type of relationship measure used. The mean correlation, an estimate of effect size, was *(r)* .23, based on 58 studies, which was quite consistent with the findings of Horvath and Symonds who reviewed only 24 studies. The correlations obtained by Martin et al., however, varied from .17 for the California Psychotherapy Alliance Scale (CALPAS), (Gaston, 1991) to .29 for the Penn Therapeutic Alliance Scales (Luborsky et al., 1983). Collectively, these findings suggest that, though significant, less than 10% of the variation in outcomes can be accounted for by relationship quality. The exact contribution of relationship may be dependent on how it is measured, however. These studies also suggest that the construct of the working or therapeutic alliance is still in need of further definition and refinement.

We identified 28 studies, published between 1990 and September 2000, that related a measure of the therapeutic alliance to a general measure of symptom change and 12 studies that related the alliance to a target symptom change measure. We obtained weighted mean relationships that were consistent with previous meta-analyses, with a mean effect size *(r)* of .22 ($p < .05$) when assessed against the general outcome measure and *(r)* of .17 ($p < .05$) for the targeted measure (Table 7.10). The results added further support to our conclusion that the therapeutic relationship is modestly related to treatment outcomes.

The collection of meta-analytic findings over the past 10 years indicates that relationship quality accounts for a far more modest proportion of the variance in outcome than the 30% suggested by Lambert (1992) based on visual inspection and unsystematic analytic procedures, and certainly less than the 80% estimated by Andrews (2000). We note, moreover, that the effect sizes reported in Table 7.10 are variable, ranging from near zero ($r = .04$) to *(r)* .78. The higher values tend to be obtained among patients with diffuse and subjective problems, such as depression, general anxiety, and self-esteem problems.

It is commonly assumed that good relationships cause or produce good outcomes, but our review does little to establish the validity of this assumption. Indeed, this assumption cannot be justified on the basis of the methods currently used. Only indirect evidence is available to support this causal assumption. For example, there is evidence that the size of the correlation between relationship quality and outcome increases with time in treatment (e.g., Saunders, 2000; Stiles, Agnew-Davies, Hardy, Barkham, & Shapiro, 1998). This suggests that initial symptom change may serve to enhance the quality of the relationship, rather than vice versa. This causal chain has also been supported by Tang and DeRubeis (1999) who used statistical modeling to compare various causal explanations of the relationship of alliance outcome in cognitive therapy. They concluded that early cognitive change tended to produce early improvement and that this improvement, in turn, contributed to the strength of the therapeutic relationship.

On the other hand, the strength of the therapeutic alliance cannot be attributed solely to the *consequences* of early symptomatic change. The correlation between early symptom change and relationship quality is not a universal observation (e.g., Barber, Luborsky, Gallop et al., 2001; Stevens, Hynan, & Allen, 2000). Barber and colleagues (Barber, Luborsky et al., 2001), for example, found that, while drug abuse treatments did not differ in overall effects, they did differ in how closely the quality of the therapeutic relationship correlated with outcome. Interestingly, among cognitive therapies, a strong therapeutic alliance was actually associated with *increased* dropout rates.

On a more positive note, one of the most persuasive sources of evidence for the independent and

TABLE 7.10 Therapeutic Relationship/Alliance

Study	N	Diagnosis	Treatments	Outcome Effects	Effect Size (r)
Bachelor, 1991	46	Mixed diagnoses (interpersonal problems, personality disorders, psychoneuroses, marital problems)	Individual psychotherapy	Positive effect of working alliance on composite symptom specific measure at post-treatment	ES1 = .59
				Positive effect of working alliance on global functioning at post-treatment	ES2 = .69
Barber et al., 1999	85	Cocaine dependence	Individual psychotherapy (supportive-expressive therapy, time-limited psychodynamic, and cognitive therapy)	Positive effect of working alliance at sessions 2 and 5 on depression scores at post-treatment	ES1 = .04
				Positive effect of working alliance at session 2 on global functioning at post-treatment	ES2 = .09
Barber, Connolly, Crits-Cristoph, Gladis, & Siqueland, 2000	84	Mixed diagnoses (Chronic Depression, Generalized Anxiety Disorder, Avoidant, Obsessive-Compulsive, or Personality Disorder)	Psychodynamically oriented individual psychotherapy	Positive effect of working alliance at sessions 2, 5, and 10 on depression scores at post-treatment	ES1 = .30
Bernal, Bonilla, Padilla-Cotto, & Perez-Prado, 1998	79	Mixed diagnoses	Mixed individual psychotherapy	Positive effect of working alliance on effectiveness factor (controlling for initial symptom severity) at post-treatment	ES1 = .56
Castonguay, Goldfried, Wiser, Raue, & Hayes, 1996	30	Major Depressive Disorder	Individual cognitive therapy	Positive effect of working alliance on depression scores at post-treatment	ES1 = .59
				Positive effect of working alliance on global functioning at post-treatment	ES2 = .45
Eltz, Shirk, & Sarlin, 1995	38	Mixed diagnoses (major depression, dysthymia, and conduct disorder)	Psychodynamically-oriented individual psychotherapy	Positive effect of alliance on self-rated global functioning at post-treatment	ES2 = .54

(continues)

TABLE 7.10 (Continued)

Study	N	Diagnosis	Treatments	Outcome Effects	Effect Size (r)
Frank and Gunderson, 1990	143	Schizophrenia (both DSM-II and DSM-III standards)	Individual psychotherapy (reality adaptive supportive and exploratory insight oriented therapies)	Positive effect of working alliance on global functioning at 2-year post-treatment	ES2 = .33
Gaston, Marmar, Gallagher, & Thompson, 1991	54	Current episode of Major Depressive Disorder	Mixed treatment (behavior, cognitive, and brief dynamic therapies)	Positive effect of working alliance at session 5 on depression scores at post-treatment	ES1 = .42
Gaston, Piper, Debbane, Bienvenu, & Garant, 1994	17	Mixed diagnoses (interpersonal difficulties, anxiety, depression, and low self-esteem)	Analytically oriented individual psychotherapy (according to Malan's 1976 guidelines)	Positive effect of working alliance on depression scores at 6-month post-treatment	ES1 = .44
				Positive effect of working alliance on global functioning at 6-month post-treatment	ES2 = .13
Gaston et al., 1994	15	Mixed diagnoses (interpersonal difficulties, anxiety, depression, and low self-esteem)	Analytically oriented individual psychotherapy (according to Malan's 1976 guidelines)	Positive effect of working alliance on depression scores at 2-year post-treatment	ES1 = .15
				Positive effect of working alliance on global functioning at 2-year post-treatment	ES2 = .27
Gaston, Thompson, Gallagher, Cournoyer, & Gagnon, 1998	91	Major Depressive Disorder	Individual psychotherapy (behavioral, cognitive, or brief dynamic therapy)	Positive effect of working alliance on depression scores at post-treatment	ES1 = .30
Hilliard, Henry, & Strupp, 2000	50	Mixed diagnoses (87% Axis I Diagnoses and 67% Axis II diagnoses)	Individual short-term dynamic psychotherapy	Positive effect of working alliance on symptom specific improvement at post-treatment	ES1 = .48
				Positive effect of working alliance on global functioning at post-treatment	ES2 = .07

Joyce & Piper, 1998	64	Mixed diagnoses (affective, impulse control, or anxiety disorders; dependent or avoidant disorders)	Dynamically oriented time-limited individual therapy	Positive effect of working alliance on symptom-specific dysfunction measures at post-treatment	ES1 = .31
				Positive effect of working alliance on individualized objectives (global) at post-treatment	ES2 = .45
Kazdin, 2000	144	Mixed diagnoses (Conduct Disorder, Attention-Deficit/Hyperactivity Disorder, Oppositional Defiant Disorder, Major Depressive Disorder)	Cognitive problem-solving, skills training for children and parent management training for parents	Positive effect of working alliance on parent satisfaction with symptom specific treatment measure at post-treatment	ES1 = .62
Keijsers, Hoogduin, & Schaap, 1994	40	Obsessive-Compulsive Disorder	Individual in vivo exposure and response prevention	Positive effect of working alliance on reduction of compulsive fear at post-treatment	ES1 = .03
				Positive effect of working alliance on global functioning at post-treatment	ES2 = .24
Luborsky, McLellan, Diguer, Woody, & Seligman, 1997	110	Opiate-Addiction (methadone-maintained)	Individual psychotherapy (supportive-expressive dynamic psychotherapy plus drug counseling, cognitive behavioral therapy plus drug counseling, or drug counseling alone)	Positive effect of working alliance on composite symptom specific treatment measure at post-treatment	ES1 = .58
Mallinckrodt, 1993	61	Mixed diagnoses	Individual psychotherapy	Positive effect of working alliance on symptom specific composite treatment measures at post-treatment	ES1 = .77
Mallinckrodt, 1996	34	Mixed diagnoses	Individual psychotherapy	Positive effect of working alliance on symptom specific measure at post-treatment	ES1 = .36
Patton, Kivlighan, & Multon, 1997	16	Mixed diagnoses (interpersonal problems or anxiety)	Psychoanalytically oriented individual psychotherapy	Positive effect of working alliance on symptom specific measures of clinical distress at post-treatment	ES1 = .48

(continues)

Table 7.10 *(Continued)*

Study	*N*	Diagnosis	Treatments	Outcome Effects	Effect Size (*r*)
Piper, Azim, Joyce & McCallum, 1991	64	Mixed diagnoses (Affective, Adjustment, Impulse Control, or Anxiety Disorders)	Dynamically oriented individual Psychotherapy	Positive effect of working alliance on composite symptom-specific dysfunction measures at post-treatment	ES1 = .61
				Positive effect of working alliance on individualized objectives (global) at post-treatment	ES2 = .72
Piper, Azim, Joyce, McCallum, Nixon, & Siegel, 1991	64	Mixed diagnoses (Affective, Adjustment, Impulse Control, or Anxiety Disorders)	Dynamically oriented individual psychotherapy	Positive effect of working alliance on general symptom-specific measures at post-treatment	ES1 = .38
	64			Positive effect of working alliance on individualized objectives (global) at post-treatment	ES2 = .52
	62			Positive effect of working alliance on general symptom specific measures at followup	ES3 = .43
	49			Positive effect of working alliance on individualized objectives (global) at followup	ES4 = .31
Piper, Boroto, Joyce, McCallum, & Azim, 1995	31	Mixed diagnoses	Dynamically oriented individual psychotherapy	Positive effect of working alliance on measure of quality of object relations at post-treatment	ES1 = .44
Saunders, 2000	114	Mixed (Depressive, Anxiety, Adjustment, or Personality Disorder Diagnosis)	Psychodynamically oriented individual psychotherapy	Positive effect of working alliance on composite measure of symptom specific distress at post-treatment	ES1 = .24

Sexton, 1993	34	Mixed diagnoses (Anxiety or Depressive Disorder)	Multimodal group therapy	Positive effect of alliance on composite measure of symptom specific improvement	ES1 = .42
Stiles, Agnew-Davies, Hardy, Barkham, & Shapiro, 1998	72	Depression	Individual psychotherapy (time-limited psychodynamic-interpersonal and cognitive behavioral therapies)	Positive effect of working alliance on depression scores at post-treatment	ES1 = .23
				Positive effect of working alliance on global general symptomatology scores at post-treatment	ES2 = .19
				Positive effect of working alliance on depression scores at 1-year followup	ES3 = .18
				Positive effect of working alliance on global general symptomatology scores at 1-year followup	ES4 = .20
Svartberg & Stiles, 1994	13	Mixed diagnoses (psycho-sexual dysfunction, social phobia, OCD, Major Depression, Adjustment Disorder)	Individual psychoanalytically oriented anxiety provoking therapy	Positive effect of working alliance on symptom-specific distress at post-treatment	ES1 = .51
				Positive effect of working alliance on global severity of distress at post-treatment	ES2 = .23
Williams & Chambless, 1990	33	Agoraphobia with panic attacks	10 sessions of individually tailored in vivo exposure	Positive effect of working alliance on reduction of "fearful situations" scores at post-treatment	ES1 = .30
Zuroff et al., 2000	149	Mixed diagnoses (nonbipolar, nonpsychotic major depressive disorders)	Two forms of individual psycho-therapy (interpersonal therapy and CBT) compared with imipramine plus clinical management	Positive effect of working alliance on composite measure of symptom-specific distress at post-treatment	ES1 = .34

ES1 = Post-treatment symptom specific effect size.

ES2 = Post-treatment global effect size.

ES3 = Follow-up symptom specific effect size.

ES4 = Follow-up global effect size.

causal impact of relationship factors on outcome is found in that body of research that correlates early relationship quality with distal outcomes. These studies quite consistently show that the quality of the therapeutic relationship during early sessions, before symptom change has occurred, successfully predicts long-term treatment benefits (e.g., Bachelor, 1991; Stiles, Agnew-Davies, Hardy, Barkham, & Shapiro, 1998; Svartberg, Seltzer, Choi, & Stiles, 2001; Weerasekera, Linder, Greenberg, & Watson, 2001).

An even more persuasive demonstration of this relationship is found in studies that have statistically controlled the effect of early symptom change while assessing the relationship between the quality of the early alliance and distal outcome. These studies have consistently found that the therapeutic relationship is correlated with outcome over and above that which can be attributed to early improvement itself (Barber, Luborsky et al., 1999; Gaston, Marmar, Gallagher, & Thompson, 1991).

Another indication of this causal link is derived from evidence that the size of the relationship-outcome correlation is responsive to variations in patient and treatment qualities. One might think that the quality of the therapeutic relationship would be influenced by variations in patient abilities to attach and form relationships and that this ability would, in turn, be affected by the interventions used. Both patient attachment ability and the appropriateness of the therapeutic technique should be reflected in outcomes. Indeed, the size of the relationship between therapeutic alliance and outcome has been found to be relational, depending on both patient receptivity and the use of particular techniques (Gaston, Thompson, Gallagher, Cournoyer, & Gagnon, 1998; Piper, Boroto, Joyce, McCallum, & Azim, 1995), as our theories would predict. Among some patients and in some treatment procedures, techniques themselves are sufficient to predict outcome, but among other patients and treatment models, the alliance adds independent power to these predictions (e.g., Barber, Luborsky et al., 2001).

We can conclude that the patient-therapist relationship accounts for a significant but still relatively small percentage of the variance in outcome in most instances, with more general and diffuse indices of change being more responsive to relationship factors than more specific ones. The therapeutic relationship probably accounts for somewhere between 7% (Horvath & Symonds, 1991) and 17% (our analysis) of the variance in outcomes. In spite of these positive findings, it still remains uncertain as to the causal nature of this relationship and the degree to which either therapy procedures, the fit of patient and therapist, and change itself facilitates the development of relationship qualities.

Theoretical Orientation

One's theoretical orientation is associated with a variety of specific techniques, but the correspondence between the treatment model used and the techniques employed is probably much weaker than one might think. The treatment model used by a clinician, whether or not governed by a manual largely represents his or her philosophy and beliefs about what induces and maintains change. Treatment manuals were designed to eliminate the variations that characterized different therapists, and the several efforts to define treatments that are empirically supported tacitly assume that a good deal of similarity exists among treatments that are governed by the same guiding philosophy (e.g., cognitive therapy, psychodynamic therapy). But evidence continues to accumulate indicating that there is substantial therapist variability within any given application of a theoretical model or manual (e.g., Crits-Christoph, Barancackie et al., 1991; Malik, Alimohamed, Holloway, & Beutler, 2000; Najavits & Weiss, 1994). Cognitive therapy is arguably the best defined theoretical model and should be the most consistent across different applications, as well as the most clearly distinct from insight-oriented procedures. In order to determine the degree of comparability among different cognitive therapy manuals as well as the distinctiveness of applications of these manuals compared to other treatments, Malik, Alimohamed et al. (2000) compared three manualized renditions of cognitive therapy, both with each other and with a variety of alternative, manualized treatment models. Malik et al. determined that while there were certain similarities among the three cognitive therapies, there were also very substantial differences among them. When compared to other psychotherapies, some applications of cognitive therapy could not even be distinguished from psychodynamic and experiential therapies in the degree to which they focused on insight versus symptom change. Collectively, these findings emphasize that the way even a highly structured and manualized therapy is conducted is heavily dependent on the unique contributions of the therapist's particular belief systems and theories.

The review of the meta-analyses and associated effect sizes that represent the effects of 35 different theoretical models (Table 7.11), compared to a no-treatment or placebo treatment by Beutler, Machado, and Neufeldt (1994), revealed effect sizes *(d)* that ranged from .14 to 1.82 and averaged .82 (translates to r = .41). This latter value is very consistent with the original value reported by Smith and Glass (1977). An additional meta-analysis (Wampold, Mondin et al., 1997) found that, among 295 effects, comparisons of psychotherapies to no-treatment controls yielded a mean effect size *(d)* of .82 (r = .40), which was exactly that reported by Beutler, Machado, and Neufeldt (1994). Lower effect sizes were noted when comparing psychotherapies to placebo controls (d = .48; r = .22). This latter analysis did not separate the different models of psychotherapy, after first testing and confirming the thesis that there were no differences among them.

A systematic mega-analysis of meta-analyses by Lipsey and Wilson (1993), in which 302 separate meta-analyses were summarized, reported that the overall mean effect size of treatment was *(d)* .47 (r = .31). The lower value, when compared to either the later Wampold et al. data or the report of Beutler, Machado, and Neufeldt, may be attributed both to the wide range of studies compared, which included both educational programs and school-based interventions and psychotherapeutic ones, and to the failure to distinguish between a no-treatment and a placebo control condition. The authors also noted that between-group comparisons obtain smaller differences than single-group (pre-post) studies (the mean differences were *[d]* .46 and .76, respectively), which may have been another factor that limited the effect size estimates in this mega-review. The fact that the use of a specific model of treatment produced significantly higher effect sizes than placebo (*ds* of .48 and .67; translates to *rs* of .22 and .33) testifies to the value of having a specific belief and associated method (Table 7.11).

Although all of the foregoing indicates how important the therapist's beliefs and philosophy are, it is also noteworthy that the differences among various theoretical models have frequently been disappointing (e.g., Wampold, 2001), as have comparisons between therapies that have added or subtracted a theoretically important component from the comprehensive treatment. (Contrast the meta-analyses by Ahn & Wampold, 2001, with those of Lyons & Woods, 1991.) These observations, as well as the low effect sizes attributable to the various classes of interventions reviewed earlier, reinforce the conclusion that the effectiveness of treatment may be more closely related to the particular beliefs and values that are passed from the therapist to the patient during treatment than of a more specific effect of the techniques used.

This latter hypothesis has received some support from a limited body of evidence, indicating that compatibility between a patient's beliefs and the therapist's therapeutic orientation may account for the effect of specific treatment models. For example, Steinhelber, Patterson, Cliffe, and LaGoullon (1984) found a relationship between Global Assessment Scale (GAS) changes over the course of therapy, among patients in a training clinic, and the degree of correspondence between the therapist/trainee's and the supervisor's theoretical orientations.

The distinctive effects of the therapist's peculiar theoretical beliefs, and even patient-therapist belief compatibility, while significant, remain quite small. For example, in a meta-analysis that included therapist-defined theoretical orientation, Bowman et al. (in press) found a significant but small effect size based on 14 studies favoring behavior therapy over psychodynamic therapy (d = .10; r = .06). As one can determine by computing the common variances from the effect sizes reported in Table 7.11, the model of therapy adopted and used by a therapist accounts for less than 10% of the observed differences in outcomes (Lambert, 1992; Wampold, 2001). The effect sizes associated with various models of psychotherapy range widely but are as high or higher than the effect sizes that have been found to describe the therapeutic relationship (also see Beutler, in press).

CONCLUSIONS

This review was intended both to assess the relative importance of various therapist factors in determining psychotherapy outcome and to compare contemporary findings with those noted in earlier editions of this *Handbook*. However, the strongest impression with which we are left at the conclusion of this review is that over the last two decades, there has been a precipitous decline of interest in researching areas that are not associated with specific effects of treatment and its implementation. Observable and inferred traits of the therapist have seen the greatest decline in research interest, even though several factors

TABLE 7.11 Summary of Effect Sizes Associated with Different Therapist Orientations

Reference (No. of Studies)	Therapist Orientation	*Effect Size r*
Smith, Glass, & Miller, 1980	**Psychodynamic (475)**	.33
	Dynamic eclectic	.41
	Adlerian	.30
	Hypnotherapy	.68
	Client-centered	.30
	Gestalt	.31
	Rational-emotive	.33
	Transactional analysis	.33
	Reality therapy	.07
	Systematic desens.	.47
	Implosive	.33
	Behavior modification	.35
	Cognitive behavioral	.50
	Eclectic behavioral	.42
	Vocational personal	.32
Shapiro & Shapiro, 1982	**Behavioral (214)**	.48
	Self-control	.46
	Biofeedback	.42
	Covert behavioral	.61
	Flooding	.50
	Relaxation	.42
	Systematic desens.	.45
	Reinforcement	.45
	Modeling	.59
	Cognitive	.46
	Dynamic/humanistic	.20
	Therapeutic philosophy/orientation	
Wampold et al, 1997	Psychotherapy vs. no Tx	.41
Lipsey & Wilson, 1993		.31
Wampold et al, 1997	Psychotherapy vs. placebo	.22
Lipsey & Wilson, 1993		.22
Lipsey & Wilson, 1993	Psychotherapy vs. drug Tx	.14–.36
Wampold, 2001; Wampold et al., 1997	Difference among psychotherapies	ns
Miller & Berman, 1983	Behavior Tx vs. other	.10
	Behavior Tx vs. no Tx	.51
Lyons & Woods, 1991	RET vs. other	.63
	RET vs. no Tx	.63
Brown, 1987	Range for all Tx	.13–.68

within these clusters of variables have, over the years, been viewed as being very promising predictors of treatment outcome.

For example, recent research is noticeably sparse, or even absent, on the effect of therapist personality, well-being, personal values, and religious viewpoints on outcomes. Interest has also waned in the areas of therapist race/ethnicity, age, and sex. However, these latter variables may eventually be resurrected in a changed form. For example, interest in age effects is being translated into a concern with ageism, and interest in race is shifting to interest in culture. Indeed, most of the concerns that have traditionally been associated with therapist demographics are shifting their focus to a list of "-isms," denoting a shift from biologically identified variables to attitudinal and philosophical correlates of these biological identifiers.

This shift of interest parallels a corollary change of societal values more generally. Unfortunately, psychotherapy outcome research is not leading the way in these new directions but is instead following. A plethora of writings have emerged on sexism, ageism, gender attitudes, racism, and other -isms in psychotherapy, and research is growing in how many of these -isms affect people and cultures. But psychotherapy outcome research is still lacking on most of these reconstructed variables. To the degree that it has addressed these broadened views of gender, ethnicity, and the like, it has focused more on patient preferences and attitudes that arise in response to the therapist's efforts than on actual outcomes. Many assumptions are made about the importance of ethnic, gender, and cultural factors to outcomes, even to the point of advocating that special therapies be built around these concepts. But these assumptions and admonitions are not accompanied by actual research evidence to show that these treatments might actually work. Notably lacking in the literature we reviewed were outcome studies of feminist therapy, ethnically congruent therapy, GLB groups, and, less so, age-compatible therapy.

We look forward to being able to identify ethnic attitudes that affect therapy outcome more directly than racial identity; age-related viewpoints that impact change more than mere years of survival; and gender perspectives that can replace biological sex as an outcome predictor. But that day is not yet here, and we urge researchers to accelerate its arrival.

A no less insidious effect of this shift of focus concerns the fate of the variables that are increasingly being studied and those that are increasingly being neglected. Often, in this changing world, the fear is that the subject of research may be more frequently determined by funding patterns and political agenda than by true promise for improving psychotherapy. As a notable example, consider the increase of research over the past 10 years on specific models of treatment for various diagnostic groups. This movement is at least partially driven by the availability of research grants in these areas.

Repeatedly in our review, we have been faced with the observation of widely varied effect sizes, opposite relationships between variables and outcomes among different studies, and weak effect sizes. We have also repeatedly been confronted with research evidence that patient, environmental, and measurement moderators are present that must come to be understood in order to be able to differentially predict and control therapeutic outcomes. Thus, throughout the four clusters of therapist variables around which this review has been organized, the theme of identifying patient-therapy and patient-therapist interactions is pervasive.

I. *Observable Traits.* Our review supports previous reviews in suggesting that therapist sex, age, and race are poor predictors of outcome. Both our analysis and previous meta-analyses (e.g., Bowman et al., in press) have obtained very small ($r < .05$) effect sizes. However, we continue to be struck by evidence that the effects of therapist traits on outcomes cannot be adequately judged without inspecting aspects of patient functioning and the correspondence between patient and therapist qualities. Even as biological traits fade in importance, the need to inspect patient-therapist compatibility on the new attitudinal definitions of ethnicity, culture, and age becomes all the more important.

II. *Observable States.* Research in these areas is waning or shifting to other areas. This is surprising in view of some interesting, if not consistent, effects. Although therapist training, skill, experience, and style are weak contributors to outcome, estimates of effect sizes are variable, ranging from (r) .08 (Bowman et al., in press) to .72 (Hupert, Bufka, Barlow et al., 2001). Our results are most consistent with the lower figures ($r = .07$, *ns*), but the variability of these relationships begs for attention.

The lion's share of research attention on therapist observable states is being directed to the interventions and techniques selected and used by the therapist. Classes of similar interventions have been identified and evaluated for effects, but there is very little support for the view that any one class is particularly effective. Estimates of effects, based on meta-analyses, vary from moderately negative to moderately positive (e.g., Kazantizis, Deane, & Ronan, 2000). Our own analyses reveals more modest effects than this, with most intervention classes being poorly correlated with outcomes (*rs* from 0 to .11). However, evidence is accumulating on the role of patient moderators in determining the effectiveness of interventions. It seems quite likely that all procedures have an effect when used on a compatible patient, but this effect averages to near zero when patient factors are not considered.

Because the field has been so preoccupied with finding a treatment or cluster of procedures that work across patient groups, a good deal of work remains to be done to identify the patient factors that determine compatibility. We believe that the most productive research of the next decade will be in the service of identifying what patient qualities indicate the selection of different procedures and techniques in different settings.

III. *Inferred Traits.* Research on therapist personality, well-being, and personal values is sparse but has produced some interesting findings. Our analysis revealed a significant, though modest, effect size associated with therapist well-being and cultural attitudes (*r's* of .12 and .13). Unfortunately, most of these topics are becoming less productive in spite of their promising nature. Although interest in the cultural beliefs of the therapist and in GLB attitudes in psychotherapy has captured some attention, these latter topics have yet to be widely studied within the context of psychotherapy outcome. Equally promising effects have been noted with respect to a variety of attitudes and values, especially when research considers the relative similarity or difference between those of the therapist and patient. The findings suggest that such differences are motivating and often encourage therapeutic change to occur. We believe that this line of research remains promising and should certainly be emphasized in coming years.

IV. *Inferred States.* Two clusters of variables compete for attention among inferred states. Although the importance of these two variables was noted in previous reviews, the intensity of the competition seems to have increased. One variable is the therapist's model of treatment. The other is the therapist's contribution to the therapeutic relationship and, concomitantly, the effect of the relationship on outcome. Both clusters of variables are promising, and each has accumulated a body of research to support its value.

Research suggests moderately strong effect sizes for relationship qualities, averaging in the neighborhood of .22 (Martin, Garske, & Davis, 2000). Research on the factors that contribute to a working relationship and the impact of this relationship on outcome has been productive, as these latter results would suggest. Although the causal role of relationship is still unproven, there can be no doubt that relationship quality is one of the stronger correlates of outcome. It is more difficult to extract a single estimate to indicate the strength of the effect associated with the therapist's theoretical orientation or model. However, our analysis has reported (Table 7.11) values that average in the mid-.30s for different models. The effects of these models, relative to placebos or no treatments, are somewhat more modest but are at least equivalent to those attributable to the therapeutic alliance.

Much has been accomplished through the emphasis given to testing and comparing different psychotherapy models, identifying those that work for different groups, and studying their clinical utility. This research has produced new models of treatment and demonstrated that different problems can be very effectively treated by psychosocial interventions. However, when one looks at the relationship between the effect sizes associated with various classes of procedure and those associated with global models, one may conclude that the amount of energy devoted to uncovering uniquely effective procedures within therapeutic models is misplaced. Classes of procedures do not have uniform effects, and the influence of the therapist's therapeutic model cannot be accounted for by the more modest effects of specific procedures.

We conclude that the tendency to pit relationship factors against technical ones, or common factors against specific ones, or the dodo bird against "empirically supported treatments," must be replaced by a more integrative and synergistic perspective. Judging from the effect sizes reported here, even taken together, the therapeutic relationship and one's therapy model contribute to a small part of the predicted and predictable variance. Patient moderating variables are repeatedly implicated by research, and the need to integrate patient, therapist, procedural, and relationship factors is the major priority for future research.

With these observations, we await the next decade of research. We continue to note that research methods are improving, that measures are more targeted and useful, and that investigators are more sophisticated in the questions they pose and the methods they use. We applaud these changes and look forward to what they might yet produce.

Acknowledgments

The authors would like to thank Ms. Lauren Brookman and Mr. Francisco Rocco for their assistance with this chapter.

Footnotes

1. The meta-analyses reported for this chapter were based only on published or in press studies. In a comparison of published and unpublished effect sizes, Lipsey and Wilson (1993) found that the effect sizes were larger in published than in unpublished papers. They attribute this difference to biases in the

publishing and review processes. This is clearly a possibility, but we believe that it is equally likely that unpublished studies remain unpublished as much because of methodological weaknesses as because of the size of the treatment differences. Since information on which to base methodological ratings of unpublished studies is extremely varied and inconsistent, we have taken the more cautious course of relying only on published works.

2. On all tables, ES1 = End of treatment, specific measure; ES2 = End of treatment, global measure; ES3 = Followup, specific measure; ES4 = Followup, global measure.

REFERENCES

Addis, M. E. (1997). Evaluating the treatment manual as a means of disseminating empircally validated psychotherapies. *Clinical Psychology: Science and Practice, 4*, 1–11.

Addis, M. E., & Jacobson, N. S. (2000). A closer look at the treatment rationale and homework compliance in cognitive behavioral therapy for depression. *Cognitive Therapy and Research, 24*, 313–326.

Addis, M. E., & Krasnow, A. D. (2000). A national survey of practicing psychologists' attitudes toward psychotherapy treatment manuals. *Journal of Consulting and Clinical Psychology, 68*, 1–9.

Ahn, H., & Wampold, B. E. (2001). Where o where are the specific ingredients? A meta-analysis of component studies in counseling and psychotherapy. *Journal of Counseling Psychology, 48*, 251–257.

Alberts, G., & Edelstein, B. (1990). Therapist training: A critical review of skill training studies. *Clinical Psychology Review, 10*, 497–511.

Al-Kubaisy, T., Marks, I. M., Logsdail, S., Marks, M. P., Lovell, K., Sungur, M., & Araya, R. (1992). Role of exposure homework in phobia reduction: A controlled study. *Behavior Therapy, 23*, 599–621.

Anderson, T., & Strupp, H. H. (1996). The ecology of psychotherapy research. *Journal of Consulting and Clinical Psychology, 64*, 776–782.

Andrews, H. B. (2000). The myth of the scientist-practitioner: A reply to R. King (1998) and N. King and Ollendick (1998). *Australian Psychologist, 35*, 60–63.

Andrews, J.D.W. (1990). Interpersonal self-confirmation and challenge in psychotherapy. *Psychotherapy, 27*, 485–504.

Antonuccio, D. O., Lewinsohn, P. M., & Steinmetz, J. L. (1982). Identification of therapist differences in a group treatment for depression. *Journal of Consulting and Clinical Psychology, 50*, 433–435.

Arizmendi, T. G., Beutler, L. E., Shanfield, S. B., Crago, M. & Hagaman, R. (1985). Client-therapist value similarity and psychotherapy outcome: A microscopic analysis. *Psychotherapy, 22*, 16–21.

Atkinson, D., & Schein, S. (1986). Similarity in counseling. *The Counseling Psychologist, 14*, 319–354.

Atkinson, D. R. (1985). A meta-review of research on cross-cultural counseling and psychotherapy. *Journal of Multicultural Counseling and Development, 13*, 138–153.

Atkinson, D. (1983). Ethnic similarity and counseling psychology. *The Counseling Psychologist, 11*, 79–92.

Babad, E. Y., Bernieri, F., & Rosenthal, R. (1989). Nonverbal communication and leakage in the behavior of biased and unbiased teachers. *Journal of Personality and Social Psychology, 56*, 89–94.

Bachelor, A. (1991). Comparison and relationship to outcome of diverse dimensions of the helping alliance as seen by client and therapist. *Psychotherapy, 28*, 534–549.

Bancroft, J. (1989). *Human sexuality and its problems* (2nd ed.). Singapore: Longman Singapore Publishers.

Banikiotes, P. G., & Merluzzi, T. V. (1981). Impact of counselor gender and counselor sex role orientation on perceived counselor characteristics. *Journal of Counseling Psychology, 28*, 342–348.

Barber, J. P., Connolly, M., Crits-Christoph, P., Gladis, L., & Siqueland, L. (2000). Alliance predicts patients' outcome beyond in-treatment change in symptoms. *Journal of Consulting & Clinical Psychology, 68(6)*, 1027–1032.

Barber, J. P., Crits-Christoph, P., & Luborsky, L. (1996). Effects of therapist adherence and competence on patient outcome in brief dynamic therapy. *Journal of Consulting and Clinical Psychology, 64(3)*, 619–622.

Barber, J. P., & Muenz, L. R. (1996). The role of avoidance and obsessiveness in matching patients to cognitive and interpersonal psychotherapy: Empirical findings from the Treatment of Depression Collaborative Research Program. *Journal of Consulting and Clinical Psychology, 64(5)*, 951–958.

Barber, J. P., Luborsky, L., Crits-Christoph, P., Thase, M. E., Weiss, R., Frank, A., Onken, L., & Gallop, R. (1999). Therapeutic alliance as a predictor of outcome in treatment of cocaine abuse. *Psychotherapy Research, 9*, 54–73.

Barber, J. P., Luborsky, L., Gallop, R., Crits-Christoph, P., Frank, A., Weiss, R. D., Thase, M. E., Connolly, M. B., Gladis, M., Foltz, C., & Siqueland, L. (2001). Therapeutic alliance as a predictor of outcome and retention in the National Institute on Drug Abuse Collaborative Cocaine Treatment Study. *Journal of Consulting and Clinical Psychology, 69*, 119–124.

Barkham, M., Shapiro, D. A., Hardy, G. E., & Rees, A. (1999). Psychotherapy in two-plus-one sessions: Outcomes of a randomized controlled trial of cognitive-behavioral and psychodynamic-interpersonal therapy for subsyndromal depression. *Journal of Consulting and Clinical Psychology, 67(2)*, 201–211.

Barlow, D. H. (1994). Psychological interventions in the era of managed competition. *Clinical Psychology: Science and Practice, 1*, 109–122.

Barlow, D. H., Burlingame, G. M., Harding, J. A., & Behrman, J. (1997). Therapeutic focusing in time-limited group psychotherapy. *Group Dynamics: Theory, Research, and Practice, 1(3)*, 254–266.

Barlow, D. H., Gorman, J. M., Shear, M. K., & Woods, S. W. (2000). Cognitive-behavioral therapy, imipramine, or their combination for panic disorder: A randomized controlled trial. *Journal of the American Medical Association, 283*, 2529–2536.

Barrett, M. S., & Berman, J. (2001). Is psychotherapy more effective when therapists disclose information about themselves? *Journal of Consulting and Clinical Psychology, 69*, 597–603.

Beck, D. F. (1988). *Counselor characteristics: How they affect outcomes.* Milwaukee, WI: Family Service of America.

Bein, E., Anderson, T., Strupp, H. H., Henry, W., Schacht, T. E., Binder, J. L., & Butler, S. F. (2000). The effects of training in time-limited dynamic psychotherapy: Changes in therapeutic outcome. *Psychotherapy Research, 10(2)*, 119–132.

Benjamin, L. S. (1974). Structural analysis of social behavior. *Psychological Review, 81*, 392–445.

Bennun, I., & Schindler, L. (1988). Therapist and patient factors in the behavioural treatment of phobic patients. *British Journal of Clinical Psychology, 27*, 145–150.

Bergin, A. E. (1980). Psychotherapy and religious values. *Journal of Consulting and Clinical Psychology, 48*, 95–105.

Bergin, A. E. (1983). Religiosity and mental health: a critical reevaluation and meta-analysis. *Professional Psychology: Research and Practice, 14*, 170–184.

Bergin, A. E. (1991). Values and religious issues in psychotherapy and mental health. *American Psychologist, 46*, 394–403.

Bergin, A. E. (1997). Neglect of the therapist and human dimensions of change: A commentary. *Clinical Psychology: Science and Practice, 4*, 83–89.

Bergin, A. E., & Garfield, S. L. (Eds.)(1971). *Handbook of psychotherapy and behavior change.* New York: John Wiley & Sons.

Bergin, A. E., & Garfield, S. L. (Eds)(1994). *Handbook of psychotherapy and behavior change.* (4th ed). New York: John Wiley and Sons.

Bergin, A. E., & Jensen, J. P. (1990). Religiosity of psychotherapists: A national survey. *Psychotherapy, 27*, 3–7.

Bernal, G., Bonilla, J., Padilla-Cotto, L., & Perez-Prado, E. M. (1998). Factors associated to outcome in psychotherapy: An effectiveness study in Puerto Rico. *Journal of Clinical Psychology, 54(3)*, 329–342.

Bernieri, F., Blanck, P. D., Rosenthal, R., Vannicelli, M., & Yerrell, P. H. (1991). Verbal-nonverbal congruency and affect in therapists' speech in speaking to and about patients. Unpublished manuscript. Oregon State University, Corvallis.

Berry, W. G., & Sipps, G. J. (1991). Interactive effects of counselor-client similarity and client self-esteem on termination type and number of sessions. *Journal of Counseling Psychology, 38*, 120–125.

Beutler, L. E. (1979). Values, beliefs, religion, and the persuasive influence of psychotherapy. *Psychotherapy: Theory, Research, and Practice, 16*, 432–440.

Beutler, L. E. (1981). Convergence in counseling and psychotherapy: A current look. *Clinical Psychology Review, 1*, 79–109.

Beutler, L. E. (1983). *Eclectic psychotheapy: A systematic approach.* New York: Pergamon Press.

Beutler, L. E. (1997). The psychotherapist as a neglected variable in psychotherapy: An illustration by reference to the role of therapist experience and training. *Clinical Psychology: Science and Practice, 4*, 44–52.

Beutler, L. E. (2000). David and Goliath: When psychotherapy research meets health care delivery systems. *American Psychologist, 55*, 997–1007.

Beutler, L. E. (in press). The dodo bird really is extinct. *Clinical Psychology: Science and Practice.*

Beutler, L. E., Booker, K., & Peerson, S. (1998). Experiential Treatments: Humanistic, Client-Centered, and Gestalt Approaches. In P. Salkovskis (Ed.), *Comprehensive Clinical Psychology (vol. 6, pp. 163–182.* Oxford, U.K.: Pergamon Press.

Beutler, L. E., Brown, M. T., Crothers, L., Booker, K., & Seabrook, M. K. (1996). The dilemma of factitious demographic distinctions in psychological research. *Journal of Consulting and Clinical Psychology, 64*, 892–902.

Beutler, L. E., & Clarkin, J. F. (1990). *Systematic treatment selection.* New York: Brunner/Mazel.

Beutler, L. E., Clarkin, J. F., & Bongar, B. (2000). *Guidelines for the systematic treatment of the depressed patient.* New York: Oxford University Press.

Beutler, L. E., Engle, D., Mohr, D., Daldrup, R. J., Bergan, J., Meredith, K., & Merry, W. (1991). Predictors of differential and selfdirected psychotherapeutic procedures. *Journal of Consulting and Clinical Psychology, 59*, 333–340.

Beutler, L. E., Goodrich, G., Fisher, D., & Williams, O. B. (1999). *Use of psychological tests/instruments for treatment planning.* In M. E. Maruish (Ed.), The use of psychological tests for treatment planning and outcome assessment (2nd ed.)(pp. 81–113). Hillsdale, NJ: Lawrence Erlbaum.

Beutler, L. E., & Harwood, T. M. (2000). *Prescriptive psychotherapy.* New York: Oxford University Press.

Beutler, L. E., Harwood, T. M., Alimohamed, S., & Malik, M. (2002). Functional impairment and coping style. In J. Norcross (Ed), *Psychotherapy relationships that work: Therapist contributions and responsiveness to patient needs* (pp. 145–170). New York: Oxford University Press.

Beutler, L. E., Kim, E. J., Davison, E., Karno, M., & Fisher, D. (1996). Research contributions to improving managed health care outcomes. *Psychotherapy, 33*, 197–206.

Beutler, L. E., Machado, P.P.P., Engle, D., & Mohr, D. (1993). Differential patient X treatment maintenance of treatment effects among cognitive, experiential, and self-directed psychotherapies. *Journal of Psychotherapy Integration, 3*, 15–32.

Beutler, L. E., Machado, P.P.P., & Neufeldt, S. (1994). Therapist variables. In S. L. Garfield & A. E. Bergin (Eds.), *Handbook of psychotherapy and behavior change* (4th ed.) (pp. 259–269). New York: John Wiley & Sons.

Beutler, L. E., Mohr, D. C., Grawe, K., Engle, D., & MacDonald, R. (1991). Looking for differential effects: Cross-cultural predictors of differential psychotherapy efficacy. *Journal of Psychotherapy Integration, 1*, 121–142.

Beutler, L. E., Moleiro, C., Malik, M., & Harwood, T. M. (2000, June). *The UC Santa Barbara Study of fitting therapy to patients: First results.* A paper presented at the annual meeting of the Society for Psychotherapy Research (international), Chicago, IL.

Beutler, L. E., Moleiro, C., & Talebi, H. (in press). Resistance. In J. Norcross (Ed.), *Psychotherapy relationships that work: Therapists' relational contributors to effective psychotherapy.* New York: Oxford University Press.

Beyebach, M., & Carranza, V. E. (1997). Therapeutic interaction and dropout: Measuring relational communication in solution-focused therapy. *Journal of Family Therapy, 19*, 173–212.

Bisson, J. I., & Deahl, M. P. (1994). Psychological debriefing and prevention of post traumatic stress: More research is needed. *British Journal of Psychiatry, 165*, 717–720.

Bisson, J. I., Jenkins, P. L., Alexander, J., & Bannister, C. (1997). A randomised controlled trial of psychological debriefing for victims of acute harm. *British Journal of Psychiatry, 171*, 78–81.

Blatt, S. J., Sanislow, C. A., Zuroff, D. C., & Pilkonis, P. A. (1996). Characteristics of effective therapists: Further analyses of data from the National Institute of mental Health Treatment of Depression Collaborative Research Program. *Journal of Consulting and Clinical Psychology, 64*, 1276–1284.

Bond, F. W., & Bunce, D. (2000). Mediators of change in emotion-focused and problem-focused worksite stress management interventions. *Journal of Occupational Health Psychology, 5(1)*, 156–163.

Borkovec, T. D., & Costello, E. (1993). Efficacy of applied relaxation and cognitive-behavioral therapy in the treatment of generalized anxiety disorder. *Journal of Consulting and Clinical Psychology, 61(4)*, 611–619.

Boudewyns, P. A., & Hyer, L. (1990). Physiological response to combat memories and preliminary treatment outcome in Vietnam veteran PTSD patients treated with direct therapeutic exposure. *Behavior Therapy, 21(1)*, 63–87.

Bowman, D. G. (1993). Effects of therapist sex on the outcome of therapy. *Psychotherapy, 30*, 678–684.

Bowman, D. G., Scogin, F., Floyd, M., & McKendree-Smith, N. (2001). Effect of therapist sex on outcome of psychotherapy: A meta-analysis. *Psychotherapy, 38*, 142–148.

Brooks, V. R. (1981). Sex and sexual orientation as variables in therapist's biases and therapy outcomes. *Clinical Social Work Journal, 9*, 198–210.

Bryant, M. J., Simons, A. D., & Thase, M. E. (1999). Therapist skill and patient variables in homework compliance: Controlling an uncontrolled variable in cognitive therapy outcome research. *Cognitive Therapy and Research, 23*, 381–399.

Buckley, P., Karasu, T. B., & Charles, E. (1981). Psychotherapists view their personal therapy. *Psychotherapy: Theory, Research and Practice, 18*, 299–305.

Burns, D. O., & Spangler, D. L. (2000). Does psychotherapy homework lead to improvements in depression in cognitive-behavioral therapy or does improvement lead to increased homework compliance? *Journal of Consulting and Clinical Psychology, 68*, 46–56.

Campos, P. E., & Goldfried, M. R. (2001). Introduction: Perspectives on therapy with gay, lesbian, and Bisexual clients. *In session, 57*, 609–614.

Cantor, D. W. (1991). Women as therapists: What we already know. In D. W. Cantor (Ed.), *Women as therapists: A multitheoretical casebook* (pp. 3–19). New York: Springer Publishing Co.

Carlier, I.V.E., Lamberts, R. G., van Uchlen, A. J., & Gersons, B.P.R. (1998). Disaster related post-traumatic stress in police officers: A field study of the impact of debriefing. *Stress Medicine, 14*, 143–148.

Caspar, F. (1995). *Plan analysis: Toward optimizing psychotherapy.* Seattle, WA: Hogrefe & Huber Publishers.

Caspar, F. (Ed.)(in press). *The inner processes of psychotherapists: Innovations in clinical training.* New York: Oxford University Press.

Castonguay, L. G., Goldfried, M. R., Wiser, S., Raue, P. J., & Hayes, A. M. (1996). Predicting the effect of cognitive therapy for depression: A study of unique and common factors. *Journal of Consulting and Clinical Psychology, 64*, 497–504.

Castonguay, L. G., Schut, A. J., Constantino, M. J., & Halperin, G. S. (1999). Assessing the role of treatment manuals: Have they become necessary but nonsufficient ingredients of change? *Clinical Psychology: Science and Practice, 6*, 449–455.

Chambless, D. L., Baker, M. J., Baucom, D. H., Beutler, L. E., Calhoun, K. S., Crits-Christoph, P., Daiuto, A., DeRubeis, R., Detweiler, J., Haaga, D. A. F., Johnson, S. B., McCurry, S., Mueser, K. T., Pope, K. S., Sanderson, W. C., Shoham, V., Stickle, T., Williams, D. A., & Woody, S. R.

(1998). Update on empirically validated therapies, II. *The Clinical Psychologist, 51*, 3–16.

Chambless, D. L., & Hollon, S. D. (1998). Defining empirically supported therapies. *Journal of Consulting and Clinical Psychology, 66*, 7–18.

Chambless, D. L., & Ollendick, T. H. (2001). Empirically supported psychological interventions: Controversies and evidence. *Annual Review of Psychology, 52*, 685–716.

Chambless, D. L., Sanderson, W. C., Shoham, V., Johnson, S. B., Pope, K. S., Crits-Christoph, P., Baker, M., Johnson, B., Woody, S. R., Sue, S., Beutler, L. E., Williams, D. A., & McCurry, S. (1996). An update on empirically validated therapies. *The Clinical Psychologist, 49(2)*, 5–14.

Chevron, E. S., & Rounsaville, B. J. (1983). Evaluating the clinical skills of psychotherapists. *Archives of General Psychiatry, 40*, 1129–1132.

Christensen, A., & Jacobson, N. S. (1994). Who (or what) can do psychotherapy: The status and challenge of nonprofessional therapies. *Psychological Science, 5*, 8–14.

Clark, M. M. (1986). Personal therapy: A review of empirical research. *Professional Psychology, 17*, 541–543.

Coady, N. F. (1991). The association between client and therapist interpersonal processes and outcomes in psychodynamic psychotherapy. *Research on Social Work Practice, 1* (2), 122–138.

Connolly, M. B., Crits-Christoph, P., Shappell, S., Barber, J. P., Luborsky, L., & Shaffer, C. (1999). Relation of transference interpretations to outcome in the early sessions of brief supportive-expressive psychotherapy. *Psychotherapy Research, 9(4)*, 485–495.

Constantino, M. J. (2000). Interpersonal process in psychotherapy through the lens of structural analysis of social behavior. *Applied and Preventive Psychology, 9*, 153–172.

Consumer Reports (1995, November). Mental health: Does therapy help? Pp. 734–739.

Crawford, I., McLeod, A., Zamboni, B. D., & Jordan, M. B. (1999). Psychologists' attitudes toward gay and lesbian parenting. *Professional Psychology: Research and Practice, 30*, 394–401.

Crits-Christoph, P., Barancackie, K., Kurcias, J. S., Beck, A. T., Carroll, K., Perry, K., Luborsky, L., McLellan, A. T., Woody, G. E., Tompson, L., Gallagher, D., & Zitrin, C. (1991). Meta-analysis of therapist effects in psychotherapy outcome studies. *Psychotherapy Research, 1*, 81–91.

Crits-Christoph, P., Cooper, A., & Luborsky, L. (1988). The accuracy of therapists' interpretations and the outcome of dynamic psychotherapy. *Journal of Consulting and Clinical Psychology, 56*, 490–495.

Crits-Christoph, P., Siqueland, L., Blaine, J., Frank, A., Luborsky, L., Onken, L. S., Muenz, L. R., Thase, M. E., Weiss, R. D., Gastfried, D. R., Woody, G. E., Barber, J. P., Butler, S. F., Daley, D., Salloum, I., Bishop, S., Najavits, L. M., Lis, J., Mercer, D., Griffin, M. L., Morals, K., & Beck, A. (1999). Psychosocial treatments for cocaine dependence. *Archives of General Psychiatry, 56*, 493–502.

Danziger, P. R., & Welfel, E. R. (2000). Age, gender and health bias in counselors: An empirical analysis. *Journal of Mental Health Counseling, 22*, 135–149.

Davison, G. C. (1998). Being bolder with the Boulder model: The challenge of education and training in empirically supported treatments. *Journal of Consulting and Clinical Psychology, 66*, 163–167.

De Araujo, L. A., Ito, L. M., & Marks, I. M. (1996). Early compliance and other factors predicting outcome of exposure for obsessive-compulsive disorder. *British Journal of Psychiatry, 169(6)*, 747–752.

Dembo, R., Ikle, D. N., & Ciarlo, J. A. (1983). The influence of client-clinician demographic match on client treatment outcomes. *Journal of Psychiatric Treatment and Evaluation, 5*, 45–53.

Diemer, R. A., Lobell, L. K., Vivino, B. L., & Hill, C. E. (1996). Comparison of dream interpretation, event interpretation and unstructured sessions in brief therapy. *Journal of Counseling Psychology, 43(1)*, 99–112.

Dobson, K. S., & Craig, K. D. (Eds.)(1998). *Empirically supported therapies.* Thousand Oaks, CA: Sage Publications.

Dodenhoff, J. T. (1981). Interpersonal attraction and direct-indirect supervisor influence as predictors of counselor trainee effectiveness. *Journal of Counseling Psychology, 28*, 47–52.

Dworkin, S. H. (2001). Treating the bisexual client. *In session, 57*, 671–680.

Ekman, P., & Davidson, R. J. (1994). *The nature of emotion: Fundamental questions.* New York: Oxford University Press.

Elkin, I., Shea, T., Watkins, J. T., Imber, S. D., Sotsky, S. M., Collins, J. F., Glass, D. R., Pilkonis, P. A., Leber, W. R., Docherty, J. P., Feister, S. J., & Parloff, M. B. (1989). National Institute of Mental Health treatment of depression collaborative research program. *Archives of General Psychiatry, 46*, 971–982.

Elliott, R. (1985). Helpful and nonhelpful events in brief counseling interviews: An empirical taxonomy. *Journal of Counseling Psychology, 32*, 307–322.

Elliott, R., Barker, C. B., Caskey, N., & Pistrang, N. (1982). Differential helpfulness of counselor verbal response modes. *Journal of Counseling Psychology, 29*, 354–361.

Ellis, A. (1980). Psychotherapy and atheist values: A response to A. E. Bergin's "Psychotherapy and religious values." *Journal of Consulting and Clinical Psychology, 48*, 635–639.

Ellis, A. (1981). Science, religiosity, and rational emotive psychology. *Psychotherapy: Theory, Research and Practice, 18*, 155–158.

Eltz, M. J., Shirk, S. R., & Sarlin, N. (1995). Alliance formation and treatment outcome among maltreated adolescents. *Child Abuse and Neglect, 19(4)*, 419–431.

Emmelkamp, P. M., Bouman, T. K., & Blaauw, E. (1994). Individualized versus standardized therapy: A comparative evaluation with obsessive-compulsive patients. *Clinical Psychology and Psychotherapy, 1* (2), 95–100.

Evans, L. A., Acosta, F. X., Yamamoto, J., & Skilbeck, W. M. (1984). Orienting psychotherapists to better serve low income and minority patients. *Journal of Clinical Psychology, 40*, 90–96.

Fairbanks, L. A., McGuire, M. T., & Harris, C. J. (1982). Nonverbal interaction of patients and therapists during psychiatric interviews. *Journal of Abnormal Psychology, 91*, 109–119.

Feeley, M., DeRubeis, R. J., & Gelfand, L. A. (1999). The temporal relation of adherence and alliance to symptom change in cognitive therapy for depression. *Journal of Consulting and Clinical Psychology, 67(4)*, 578–582.

Fiorentine, R., & Hillhouse, M. P. (1999). Drug treatment effectiveness and client-counselor empathy. *Journal of Drug Issues, 29*, 59–74.

Flowers, J. V., & Booraem, C. D. (1990). The frequency and effect on outcome of different types of interpretation in psychodynamic and cognitive-behavioral group psychotherapy. *International Journal of Group Psychotherapy, 40*, 203–214.

Frank, A. F., & Gunderson, J. G. (1990). The role of the therapeutic alliance in the treatment of schizophrenia: Relationship to course and outcome. *Archives of General Psychiatry, 47(3)*, 228–236.

Frank, J. D. (1973). *Persuasion and healing: A comparative study of psychotherapy* (rev. ed.). Baltimore: The Johns Hopkins University Press.

Frank, J. D., & Frank, J. B. (1991). *Persuasion and Healing*, 3rd ed., Baltimore: The Johns Hopkins University Press.

Fridlund, A. J. (1994). *Human facial expression: An evolutionary view.* New York: Academic Press.

Fujino, D. C., Okazaki, S., & Young, K. (1994). Asian-American women in the mental health system: An examination of ethnic and gender match between therapist and client. *Journal of Community Psychology, 22*, 164–176.

Garb, H. N. (1998). *Studying the clinician.* Washington, DC: American Psychological Association Press.

Gaston, L. (1991). Reliability and criterion-related validity of the Calfornia Psychotherapy Alliance Scales–Patient Version. *Psychological Assessment, 3*, 68–74.

Gaston, L., Marmar, C. R., Gallagher, D., & Thompson, L. W. (1991). Alliance prediction of outcome beyond in-treatment symptomatic change as psychotherapy processes. *Psychotherapy Research, 1*, 104–113.

Gaston, L., Piper, W. E., Debbane, E. G., Bienvenu, J., & Garant, J. (1994). Alliance and technique for predicting outcome in short- and long-term analytic psychotherapy. *Psychotherapy Research, 4(2)*, 121–135.

Gaston, L., Thompson, L., Gallagher, D., Cournoyer, L., & Gagnon, R. (1998). Alliance, technique, and their interactions in predicting outcome of behavioral cognitive and brief dynamic therapy. *Psychotherapy Research, 8*, 190–209.

Gatz, M., Fiske, A., Fox, L. S., Kaskie, B., & Kasl-Godley, J. E. (1998). Empirically validated psychological treatments for older adults. *Journal of Mental Health and Aging, 41*, 9–46.

Gendlin, E. T. (1986). *Let your body interpret your dreams.* Wilmette, IL: Chiron Publications.

Gendlin, E. T. (1996). *Focusing-oriented psychotherapy.* New York: Guilford Press.

Gist, R. Lubin, B., & Redburn, B. G. (1998). Psychosocial, ecological, and community perspectives on disaster response. *Journal of Personal and Interpersonal Loss, 3*, 25–51.

Glenn, A. A., & Russell, R. K. (1986). Heterosexual bias among counselor trainees. *Counselor Education and Supervision, 25*, 222–229.

Goldfried, M. R. (Ed.)(1981). *Converging themes in psychotherapy.* New York: Springer Publishing Co.

Gottheil, E., Sterling, R. C., Weinstein, S. P., & Kurtz, J. W. (1994). Therapist/patient matching and early treatment dropout. *The Journal of Addictive Diseases, 13*, 169–176.

Gray-Little, B. & Kaplan, D. (2000). Race and ethnicity in psychotherapy research. In C. R. Snyder & R. E. Ingram (Eds.), *Handbook of psychological change: Psychotherapy processes and practices for the 21st* century (pp. 591–613). New York: John Wiley & Sons, Inc.

Greenberg, L. S., Elliott, R. K., & Lietaer, G. (1994). Research on experiential psychotherapies. In A. E. Bergin & S. L. Garfield (Eds.), *Handbook of psychotherapy and behavior change* (4th ed., pp. 509–542). New York: John Wiley & Sons.

Greenberg, R. P., & Staller, J. (1981). Personal therapy for therapists. *American Journal of Psychiatry, 138*, 1467–1471.

Greenspan, M., & Kulish, N. M. (1985). Factors in premature termination in long-term psychotherapy. *Psychotherapy, 22*, 75–82.

Guest, P. D., & Beutler, L. E. (1988). The impact of psychotherapy supervision on therapist orientation and values. *Journal of Consulting and Clinical Psychology, 56*, 653–658.

Guild, M. (1969). Therapeutic effectiveness of analyzed and unanalyzed therapists. Unpublished doctoral dissertation, St. John's University, New York.

Guy, J. D., Stark, M. J., & Poelstra, P. L. (1988). Personal therapy for psychotherapists before and after entering professional practice. *Professional Psychology: Research and Practice, 19*, 474–476.

Hall, G. C. N., & Malony, H. N. (1983). Cultural control in psychotherapy with minority clients. *Psychotherapy: Theory, Research and Practice, 20,* 131–142.

Hamblin, D. L., Beutler, L. E., Scogin, F., & Corbishley, A. (1993). Patient responsiveness to therapist values and outcome in group cognitive therapy. *Psychotherapy Research, 3,* 36–46.

Hampson, R. B., & Beavers, W. R. (1996). Measuring family therapy outcome in a clinical setting: Families that do better or do worse in therapy. *Family Process, 35,* 347–361.

Hardy, G. E., & Shapiro, D. A. (1985). Therapist response modes in prescriptive vs. exploratory psychotherapy. *British Journal of Clinical Psychology, 24,* 235–245.

Hardy, G. E., Stiles, W. B., Barkham, M., & Startup, M. (1998). Therapist responsiveness to client interpersonal styles during time-limited treatments for depression. *Journal of Consulting & Clinical Psychology, 66,* 304–312.

Harkness, D. (1997). Testing interactional social work theory: A panel analysis of supervised practice and outcomes. *Clinical Supervisor, 15(1),* 33–50.

Hart, L. E. (1981). An investigation of the effect of male therapists' views of women on the process and outcome of therapy with women. *Dissertation Abstracts International, 42,* 2529B.

Hayes, J. A., & Erkis, A. J. (2000). Therapist homophobia, client sexual orientation, and source of client HIV infection as predictors of therapist reactions to clients with HIV. *Journal of Counseling Psychology, 47,* 71–78.

Hedges, L. V., & Olkin, I. (1985). *Statistical methods for meta-analysis.* New York: Academic Press.

Henry, W. P., Schacht, T. E., & Strupp, H. H. (1990). Patient and therapist introject, interpersonal process, and differential psychotherapy outcome. *Journal of Consulting and Clinical Psychology, 58,* 768–774.

Henry, W. P., Schacht, T. E., Strupp, H. H., Butler, S. F., & Binder, J. L. (1993). Effects of training in time-limited dynamic psychotherapy: Mediators of therapists' responses to training. *Journal of Consulting and Clinical Psychology, 61,* 441–447.

Henry, W. P., & Strupp, H. H. (1991). Vanderbilt University: The Vanderbilt Center for Psychotherapy Research. In L. E. Beutler and M. Crago (Eds.), *Psychotherapy research: An international review of programatic studies* (pp. 166–174). Washington, DC: American Psychological Association.

Henry, W. P., Strupp, H. H., Butler, S. F., Schacht, T. E., & Binder, J. L. (1993). Effects of training in time-limited dynamic psychotherapy: Changes in therapist behavior. *Journal of Consulting and Clinical Psychology, 61,* 434–440.

Herman, S. M. (1998). The relationship between therapist-client modality similarity and psychotherapy outcome. *Journal of Psychotherapy Practice and Research, 7,* 56–64.

Hill, C. E., Zack, J. S., Wonnell, T. L., Hoffman, M. A., Rochlen, A. B., Goldberg, J. L., Nakayama, E. Y., Heaton, K. J., Kelley, F. A., Eiche, K., Tomlinson, M. J., & Hess, S. (2000). Structured brief therapy with a focus on dreams or loss for clients with troubling dreams and recent loss. *Journal of Counseling Psychology, 47(1),* 90–101.

Hilliard, R. B., Henry, W. P., & Strupp, H. H. (2000). An interpersonal model of psychotherapy: Linking patient and therapist developmental history, therapeutic process, and types of outcome. *Journal of Consulting and Clinical Psychology, 68(1),* 125–133.

Hilsenroth, M. J., Ackerman, S. J., & Blagys, M. D. (2001). Evaluating the phase model of change during short-term psychodynamic psychotherapy. *Psychotherapy Research, 11,* 29–47.

Holzer, M., Pokorny, D., Kachele, H., & Luborsky, L. (1997). The verbalization of emotions in the therapeutic dialogue – A correlate of therapeutic outcome? *Psychotherapy Research, 7(3),* 261–273.

Horn-George, J. B., & Anchor, K. N. (1982). Perceptions of the psychotherapy relationship in long- versus short-term therapy. *Professional Psychology, 13,* 483–491.

Horvath, A. O. (1995). The therapeutic relationship: From transference to alliance. *Psychotherapy in Practice, 1,* 7–17.

Horvath, A. O., & Greenberg, L. (1986). The development of the Working Alliance Inventory. In L. S. Greenberg, & W. M. Pinsof (Eds.), *The psychotherapeutic process.* New York: Guilford Press.

Horvath, A. O., & Symonds, B. D. (1991). Relation between working alliance and outcome in psychotherapy: A meta-analysis. *Journal of Counseling Psychology, 38,* 139–149.

Hosch, H. M., Barrientos, G. A., Fierro, C., Ramirez, J. I., Pelaez, M. P., Cedillos, A. M., Meyer, L. D., & Perez, Y. (1995). Predicting adherence to medications by Hispanics with schizophrenia. *Hispanic Journal of Behavioral Sciences, 17,* 320–333.

Howard, K. I., Krause, M. S., Caburnay, C. A., & Noel, S. B. (2001). Syzygy, science, and psychotherapy: The *Consumer Reports* study. *Journal of Clinical Psychology, 57,* 865–874.

Howard, K. I., Krause, M. S., & Lyons, J. (1993). When clinical trials fail: A guide for disaggregation. In L. S. Onken & J. D. Blaine (Eds.), *Behavioral treatments for drug abuse and dependence* (pp. 291–302) (NIDA Research Monograph No. 137). Washington, DC: National Institute of Drug Abuse.

Howard, K. I., Moras, K., Brill, P. L., Martinovitch, Z., & Lutz, W. (1996). Evaluation of psychotherapy: Efficacy, effectiveness, and patient progress. *American Psychologist, 51,* 1059–1064.

Hunt, D. D., Carr, J. E., Dagadakis, C. S., & Walker, E. A. (1985). Cognitive match as a predictor of psychotherapy outcome. *Psychotherapy, 22,* 718–721.

Hupert, J. D., Bufka, L. F., Barlow, D. H., Gorman, J. M., Shear, M. K., & Woods, S. W. (2001). Therapists, therapist variables, and CBT outcome for panic disorder: Results from a multicenter trial. *Journal of Consulting and Clinical Psychology, 69,* 747–755.

Ivey, D. C., Wieling, E., & Harris, S. M. (2000). Save the young—the elderly have lived their lives: Ageism in marriage and family therapy. *Family Process, 39,* 163–175.

Jacobs, M. K., Christensen, A., Snibbe, J. R., Dolezal-Wood, S., Huber, A., & Polterok, A. (2001). A comparison of computer-based versus traditional individual psychotherapy. *Professional Psychology: Research and Practice, 32,* 92–96.

Jacobson, N. S., & Christensen, A. (1996). Studying the effectiveness of psychotherapy: How well can clinical trials do the job? *American Psychologist, 51,* 1031–1039.

Jacobson, N. S., Dobson, K. S., Truax, P. A., Addis, M. E., Koerner, K., Gollan, J. K., Gortner, E., & Prince, S. E. (1996). A component analysis of cognitive-behavioral treatment for depression. *Journal of Consulting and Clinical Psychology, 64,* 295–304.

Jensen, J. P., & Bergin, A. E. (1988). Mental health values of professional therapists: A national interdisciplinary survey. *Professional Psychology: Research and Practice, 19,* 290–297.

Joyce, A. S., & Piper, W. E. (1996). Interpretive work in short-term individual psychotherapy: An analysis using hierarchical linear modeling. *Journal of Consulting and Clinical Psychology, 64,* 505–512.

Joyce, A. S., & Piper, W. E. (1998). Expectancy, the therapeutic alliance, and treatment outcome in short-term individual psychotherapy. *Journal of Psychotherapy Practice and Research, 7(3),* 236–248.

Junkert-Tress, B., Schnierda, U., Haftkamp, N., Schmitz, N., & Tress, W. (2001). Effects of short-term dynamic psychotherapy for neurotic, somatoform, and personality disorders: A prospective 1-year follow-up study. *Psychotherapy Research, 11,* 187–200.

Kadera, S. W., Lambert, M. J., & Andrews, A. A. (1996). How much therapy is enough? A session-by-session analysis of the psychotherapy dose-effect relationship. *Journal of Psychotherapy Practice and Research, 5,* 132–151.

Kaminer, Y., Burleson, J. A., Blitz, C., Sussman, J., & Rounsaville, B. J. (1998). Psychotherapies for adolescent substance abusers: A pilot study. *Journal of Nervous & Mental Disease, 186,* 684–690.

Kaplan, A. S., & Garfinkel, P. E. (1999). Difficulties in treating patients with eating disorders: A review of patient and clinician variables. *Canadian Journal of Psychiatry, 44,* 665–670.

Karno, M., Beutler, L. E., & Harwood, T. M. (2002). Interactions between psychotherapy process and patient attributes that predict alcohol treatment effectiveness: A preliminary report. *Addictive Behaviors, 27,* 779–797.

Kazantizis, N., Deane, F. P., & Ronan, K. R. (2000). Homework assignments in cognitive and behavioral therapy: A meta-analysis. *Clinical Psychology: Science and Practice, 7,* 189–202.

Kazantzis, N., Ronan, K., & Deane, F. P. (in press). Concluding causation from correlation: Comment on Burns and Spangler. *Journal of Consulting and Clinical Psychology, 69,* 1079–1083.

Kazdin, A. E. (1998). *Research design in clinical psychology* (3rd ed.). New York: Allyn & Bacon.

Kazdin, A. E. (2000). Perceived barriers to treatment participation and treatment acceptability among antisocial children and their families. *Journal of Child and Family Studies, 9(2),* 157–174.

Kazdin, A. E., & Mascitelli, S. (1982). Covert and overt rehearsal and homework practice in developing assertiveness. *Journal of Consulting and Clinical Psychology, 50,* 250–258.

Keating, A. M., & Fretz, B. R. (1990). Christians' anticipations about counselors in response to counselor descriptions. *Journal of Counseling Psychology, 37,* 293–296.

Keijsers, G., Hoogduin, C., & Schaap, C. (1994). Predictors of treatment outcome in the behavioural treatment of obsessive-compulsive disorder. *British Journal of Psychiatry, 165(6),* 781–786.

Kelly, T. A. (1990). The role of values in psychotherapy: A critical review of process and outcome effects. *Clinical Psychology Review, 10,* 171–186.

Kelly, T. A., & Strupp, H. H. (1992). Patient and therapist values in psychotherapy: Perceived changes, conversion, similarity, and outcome. *Journal of Consulting and Clinical Psychology, 60,* 34–40.

Kendall, P. C., & Chambless, D. L. (Eds.)(1998). Empirically supported psychological therapies. *Journal of Consulting and Clinical Psychology, 66,* 3–167.

Kendall, P. C., & Chu, B. C. (2000). Retrospective self-reports of therapist flexibility in a manual-based treatment for youths with anxiety disorders. *Journal of Clinical Child Psychology, 29(2),* 209–220.

Kernberg, O. (1973). Psychotherapy and psychoanalysis: Final report of the Menninger Foundation's psychotherapy research project. *International Journal of Psychiatric Medicine, 11,* 62–77.

Kiesler, D. J. (1988). *Therapeutic meta-communications: Therapist impact disclosure as feedback in psychotherapy.* Palo Alto, CA: Consulting Psychologists Press.

Kiesler, D. J., & Watkins, L. M. (1989). Interpersonal complementarity and the therapeutic alliance: A study of relationship in psychotherapy. *Psychotherapy, 26,* 183–194.

Kivlighan, D. M., Jr., McGovern, T. V., & Corazzini, J. G. (1984). Effects of content and timing of structuring interventions on group therapy process and outcome. *Journal of Counseling Psychology, 31*, 363–370.

Klausner, E. J., Clarkin, J. F., Spielman, L., Pupo, C., Abrams, R., & Alexopoulos, G. S. (1998). Late-life depression and functional disability: The role of goal-focused group psychotherapy. *International Journal of Geriatric Psychiatry, 13*, 707–716.

Klerman, G. L., Weissman, M. M., Rounsaville, B. J., & Chevron, E. S. (1984). *Interpersonal psychotherapy of depression.* New York: Basic Books, Inc.

Kopta, S. M., Howard, K. I., Lowry, J. L., & Beutler, L. E. (1994). Patterns of symptomatic recovery in time-unlimited psychotherapy. *Journal of Consulting and Clinical Psychology, 62*, 1009–1016.

Krippner, K. M., & Hutchinson, R. L. (1990). Effects of a brief intake interview on clients' anxiety and depression: Follow-up. *International Journal of Short-Term Psychotherapy, 5*, 121–130.

Lafferty, P., Beutler, L. E., & Crago, M. (1989). Differences between more and less effective psychotherapists: A study of select therapist variables. *Journal of Consulting and Clinical Psychology, 57*, 76–80.

Laidlaw, K. (2001). An empirical review of cognitive therapy for late life depression: Does research evidence suggest adaptations are necessary for cognitive therapy with older adults? *Clinical Psychology and Psychotherapy, 8*, 1–14.

Lambert, M. J. (1992). Psychotherapy outcome research: Implications for integrative and eclectic therapists. In J. C. Norcross & M. R. Goldfried (Eds.), *Handbook of Psychotherapy Integration* (pp. 94–129). New York: Basic Books.

Lambert, M. J., & Bergin, A. E. (1992). Achievements and limitations of psychotherapy research. In Donald K. Freedheim, Herbert J. Freudenberger, et al. (Eds.), *History of psychotherapy: A century of change.* Washington, DC: American Psychological Association.

Lambert, M. J., & Bergin, A. E. (1994). The effectiveness of psychotherapy. In A. E. Bergin & S. L. Garfield (Eds.), *Handbook of psychotherapy and behavior change* (4th ed.) (pp. 143–189). New York: John Wiley & Sons.

Lambert, M. J., DeJulio, S. S., & Stein, D. M. (1978). Therapist interpersonal skills: Process, outcome, methodological considerations, and recommendations for future research. *Psychological Bulletin, 85*, 467–489.

Lambert, M. J., & Okiishi, J. C. (1997). The effects of the individual psychotherapist and implications for future research. *Clinical Psychology: Science and Practice, 4*, 66–75.

Lambert, M. J., Whipple, J. L., Smart, D. W., Vermeersch, D. A., Nielsen, S. L., & Hawkins, E. J. (2001). The effects of providing therapists with feedback on patient progress during psychotherapy: Are outcomes enhanced? *Psychotherapy Research, 11*, 49–68.

Lampropoulos, G. K. (2000a). Evolving psychotherapy integration: Eclectic selection and prescriptive applications of common factors in therapy. *Psychotherapy, 37*, 285–297.

Lampropoulos, G. K. (2000b). Definitional research issues in the common factors approach to psychotherapy integration: Misconceptions, clarifications, and proposals. *Journal of Psychotherapy Integration, 10*, 415–438.

Lampropoulos, G. K. (2001). Bridging technical eclecticism and theoretical integration: Assimilative integration. *Journal of Psychotherapy Integration, 11*, 5–19.

Lave, J. R., Frank, R. G., Schulberg, H. C., & Kamlet, M. S. (1998). Cost-effectiveness of treatment for major depression in primary care practice. *Archives of General Psychiatry, 55*, 645–651.

Lazarus, A. A. (1989). *The practice of multi-modal therapy* (updated edition). Baltimore, MD: Johns Hopkins University Press.

Leung, A. W., & Heimberg, R. G. (1996). Homework compliance, perceptions of control, and outcome of cognitive-behavioral treatment of social phobia. *Behavior Research and Therapy, 34*, 423–432.

Liddle, B. J. (1995). Sexual orientation bias among advanced graduate students of counseling and counseling psychology. *Counselor Education & Supervision, 34*, 321–331.

Liddle, B. J. (1996). Therapist sexual orientation, gender, and counseling practices as they relate to ratings on helpfulness by gay and lesbian clients. *Journal of Counseling Psychology, 43*, 394–401.

Liddle, B. J. (1997). Gay and lesbian clients' selection of therapists and utilization of therapy. *Psychotherapy, 34*, 11–18.

Lilling, A. H., & Friedman, R. C. (1995). Bias towards gay patients by psychoanalytic clinicians: An empirical investigation. *Archives of Sexual Behavior, 24*, 563–571.

Lipsey, M. W., & Wilson, D. B. (1993). The efficacy of psychological, educational, and behavioral treatment: Confirmation from meta-analyses. *American Psychologist, 48*, 1181–1209.

Luborsky, L. (1996). *The symptom-context method: Symptoms as opportunities in psychotherapy.* Washington, DC: American Psychological Association Press.

Luborsky, L. (1997). The core conflictual relationship theme: A basic case formulation method. In Tracy D. Eells (Ed.), *Handbook of psychotherapy case formulation.* New York: Guilford Press.

Luborsky, L., Crits-Christoph, P., Alexander, L., Margolis, M., & Cohen, M. (1983). Two helping alliance methods for predicting outcomes of psychotherapy: A counting signs vs. a global rating method. *Journal of Nervous and Mental Disease, 171*, 480–490.

Luborsky, L., Crits-Christoph, P., McLellan, T., Woody, G., Piper, W., Imber, S., & Liberman, B. (1986). Do therapists vary much in their success? Findings from four outcome studies. *American Journal of Orthopsychiatry, 56*, 501–512.

Luborsky, L., Diguer, L., Seligman, D. A., Rosenthal, R., Krause, E. D., Johnson, S., Halperin, G., Bishop, M., Berman, J. S., & Schweizer, E. (1999). The researcher's own therapy allegiances: A "wild card" in comparisons of treatment efficacy. *Clinical Psychology: Science & Practice, 6*, 95–106.

Luborsky, L., McLellan, A. T., Diguer, L., Woody, G., & Seligman, D. A. (1997). The psychotherapist matters: Comparison of outcomes across twenty-two therapists and seven patient samples. *Clinical Psychology: Science and Practice, 4*, 53–63.

Luborsky, L, McLellan, A. T., Woody, G. E., O'Brien, C. P., & Auerbach, A. (1985). Therapist success and its determinants. *Archives of General Psychiatry, 42*, 602–611.

Luborsky, L., Mintz, J., Auerbach, A., Crits-Christoph, P., Bachrach, H., Todd, T., Johnson, M., Cohen, M., & O'Brien, C. P. (1980). Predicting the outcome of psychotherapy: Findings of the Penn Psychotherapy Project. *Archives of General Psychiatry, 37*, 471–481.

Luborsky, L., Rosenthal, R., Diguer, L., Andrusyna, T. P., Berman, J. S., Levitt, J. T., Seligman, D. A., & Krause, E. D. (in press). The dodo bird verdict is alive and well–mostly. *Clinical Psychology: Science and Practice.*

Lyons, L. C., & Woods, P. J. (1991). The efficacy of rational-emotive therapy: A quantitative review of the outcome research. *Clinical Psychology Review, 11(4)*, 357–369.

Mahrer, A. R. (1996). *The complete guide to experiential psychotherapy.* New York: John Wiley & Sons.

Malik, M., Alimohamed, S., Holaway, R., & Beutler, L. E. (2000, June). Are all cognitive therapies alike? Validation of the TPRS. Paper presented at the annual meeting of the Society for Psychotherapy Research, Chicago, IL.

Mallinckrodt, B. (1993). Session impact, working alliance, and treatment outcome in brief counseling. *Journal of Counseling Psychology, 40(1)*, 25–32.

Mallinckrodt, B. (1996). Change in working alliance, social support, and psychological symptoms in brief therapy. *Journal of Counseling Psychology, 43(4)*, 448–455.

Marks, I., Lovell, K., Noshirvani, H., Livanou, M., & Thrasher, S. (1998). Treatment of posttraumatic stress disorder by exposure and/or cognitive restructuring. *Archives of General Psychiatry, 55*, 317–325.

Martin, D. J., Garske,, J. P., & Davis, M. K. (2000). Relation of the therapeutic alliance with outcome and other variables: A meta-analytic review. *Journal of Consulting and Clinical Psychology, 68*, 438–450.

Martinez, F. I. (1991). Therapist-client convergence and similarity of religious values: Their effect on client improvement. *Journal of Psychology and Christianity, 10*, 137–143.

McCarthy, W. C., & Frieze, I. H. (1999). Negative aspects of therapy: Client perceptions of therapists' social influence, burnout, and quality of care. *Journal of Social Issues, 55*, 33–50.

McCullough, L., Winston, A., Farber, B. A., Porter, F., Pollack, J., Vingiano, W., Laikin, M., & Trujillo, M. (1991). The relationship of patient-therapist interaction to outcome in brief psychotherapy. *Psychotherapy, 28(4)*, 525–533.

McDevitt, J. W. (1987). Therapists' personal therapy and professional self-awareness. *Psychotherapy, 24*, 693–703.

McGuff, R., Gitlin, D., & Enderlin, M. (1996). Clients' and therapists' confidence and attendance at planned individual therapy sessions. *Psychological Reports, 79*, 537–538.

McLean, P. D., & Hakstian, A. R. (1990). Relative endurance of unipolar depression treatment effects: Longitudinal follow-up. *Journal of Consulting and Clinical Psychology, 58*, 482–488.

Meeks, S. (1990). Age bias in the diagnostic decision-making behavior of clinicians. *Professional Psychology: Research and Practice, 21*, 279–284.

Milbrath, C., Bond, M., Cooper, S., Znoj, H. J., Horowitz, M. J., & Perry, J. C. (1999). Sequential consequences of therapists' interventions. *Journal of Psychotherapy Practice and Research, 8(1)*, 40–54.

Miller, W. R. (Ed.) (1999). *Integrating spirituality into treatment: Resources for practitioners.* Washington, DC: American Psychological Press.

Miller, W. R., Benefield, R. G., & Tonigan, J. S. (1993). Enhancing motivation for change in problem drinking: A controlled comparison of two therapist styles. *Journal of Consulting and Clinical Psychology, 61*, 455–461.

Mohr, D. C., Shoham-Salomon, V., Engle, D., & Beutler, L. E. (1991). The expression of anger in psychotherapy for depression: Its role and measurement. *Psychotherapy Research, 1*, 125–135.

Morgan, R., Luborsky, L., Crits-Christoph, P., Curtis, H., & Solomon, J. (1982). Predicting the outcomes of psychotherapy by the Penn Helping Alliance Rating Method. *Archives of General Psychiatry, 39*, 397–402.

Multon, K. D., Kivlighan, D. M., & Gold, P. B. (1996). Changes in counselor adherence over the course of training. *Journal of Counseling Psychology, 43*, 356–363.

Najavits, L. M., Griffin, M. L., Luborsky, L., Frank, A., Weiss, R. D., Liese, B. S., Thompson, H., Nakayama, E., Siqueland, L., Daley, D., & Onken, L. S. (1995). Therapist's emotional reactions to substance abusers: A new questionnaire and initial findings. *Psychotherapy: Theory, Research and Practice, 32*, 669–677.

Najavits, L. M., & Strupp, H. H. (1994). Differences in the effectiveness of psychodynamic therapists: A process-outcome study. *Psychotherapy, 31(1)*, 114–123.

Najavits, L. M., & Weiss, R. D. (1994). Variations in therapist effectiveness in the treatment of patients with substance use disorders: An empirical review. *Addiction, 89*, 679–688.

Nathan, P. E., & Gorman, J. M. (Eds.). (1998). *A guide to treatments that work.* New York: Oxford University Press.

Nathan, P. E., Stuart, S. P., & Dolan, S. L. (2000). Research on psychotherapy efficacy and effectiveness: Between Scylla and Charybdis? *Psychological Bulletin, 126*, 964–981.

Neimeyer, G. J., & Gonzales, M. (1983). Duration, satisfaction, and perceived effectiveness of cross-cultural counseling. *Journal of Counseling Psychology, 30*, 91–95.

Neimeyer, R. A., & Feixas, G. (1990). The role of homework and skill acquisition in the outcome of group cognitive therapy for depression. *Behavior Therapy, 21*, 281–292.

Newman, M. G., & Castonguay, L. G. (1999). Contemporary challenges and new directions in psychotherapy: An introduction. *In Session, 55*, 1321–1323.

Norcross, J. C., Geller, J. D., & Kurzawa, E. K. (2000). Conducting psychotherapy with psychotherapists: I. Prevalence, patients, and problems. *Psychotherapy, 37*, 199–205.

Norcross, J. C., & Goldfried, M. R. (Eds.) (1992). *Handbook of psychotherapy integration.* New York: Basic Books.

Norcross, J. C., & Newman, C. F. (1992). Psychotherapy integration: Setting the context. In J. C. Norcross & M. R. Goldfried (Eds.), *Psychotherapy integration* (pp. 3–45). New York: Basic Books.

Norcross, J. C., & Prochaska, J. O. (1986). Psychotherapist heal thyself—II. The self-initiated and therapy-facilitated change of psychological distress. *Psychotherapy, 23*, 345–356.

Ogrodniczuk, J. S., Piper, W. E., Joyce, A. S., & McCallum, M. (2000). Different perspectives of the therapeutic alliance and therapist technique in 2 forms of dynamically oriented psychotherapy. *Canadian Journal of Psychiatry, 45*, 452–458.

O'Malley, S. S., Foley, S. H., Rounsaville, B. J., Watkins, J. T., Stotsky, S., M., Imber, S. D., & Elkin, I. (1988). Therapist competence and patient outcome in interpersonal psychotherapy of depression. *Journal of Consulting and Clinical Psychology, 56*, 496–501.

O'Malley, S. S., Jaffe, A. J., Chang, G., Schottenfeld, R. S., Meyer, R. E., & Rounsaville, B. (1992). Naltrexone and coping skills therapy for alcohol dependence. *Archives of General Psychiatry, 49*, 881–887.

Orlinsky, D. E., Grawe, K., & Parks, B. K. (1994). Process and outcome in psychotherapy—Noch Einmal. In A. E. Bergin & S. L. Garfield (Eds.), *Handbook of Psychotherapy and Behavior Change* (4th ed.) (pp. 270–376). New York: John Wiley & Sons.

Orme, D. R., & Boswell, D. (1991). The pre-intake drop-out at a community mental health center. *Community Mental Health Journal, 27*, 375–379.

Patterson, G. R., & Forgatch, M. S. (1985). Therapist behavior as a determinant for client noncompliance: A paradox for the behavior modifier. *Journal of Consulting and Clinical Psychology, 53*, 846–851.

Patton, M. J., Kivlighan, D. M., & Multon, K. D. (1997). The Missouri Psychoanalytic Counseling Research Project: Relation of changes in counseling process to client outcomes. *Journal of Counseling Psychology, 44(2)*, 189–208.

Pekarik, G. (1994). Effects of brief therapy training on practicing psychotherapists and their clients. *Community Mental Health Journal, 30(2)*, 135–144.

Piper, W. E., Azim, H. F., Joyce, A. S., & McCallum, M. (1991). Transference interpretations, therapeutic alliance, and outcome in short-term individual psychotherapy. *Archives of General Psychiatry, 48(10)*, 946–953.

Piper, W. E., Azim, H. F., Joyce, A. S., McCallum, M., Nixon, G., & Segal, P. S. (1991). Quality of object relations versus interpersonal functioning as predictors of therapeutic alliance and psychotherapy outcome. *Journal of Nervous and Mental Disease, 179(7)*, 432–438.

Piper, W. E., Boroto, D. R., Joyce, A. S., McCallum, M., & Azim, H. F. A. (1995). Pattern of alliance and outcome in short-term individual psychotherapy. *Psychotherapy, 32*, 639–647.

Piper, W. E., Joyce, A. S., Azim, H. F., & McCallum, M. (1998). Interpretive and supportive forms of psychotherapy and patient personality variables. *Journal of Consulting and Clinical Psychology, 66(3)*, 558–567.

Piper, W., McCallum, M., Joyce, A. S., Azim, H. F., & Ogrodniczuk, J. S. (1999). Follow-up findings for interpretive and supportive forms of psychotherapy and patient personality variables. *Journal of Consulting & Clinical Psychology, 67(2)*, 267–273.

Prochaska, J. O. (1984). *Systems of psychotherapy: A transtheoretical analysis* (2nd ed.). Homewood, IL: Dorsey Press.

Proctor, E. K., & Rosen, A. (1981). Expectations and preferences for counselor race and their relation to intermediate treatment outcomes. *Journal of Counseling Psychology, 28*, 40–46.

Project Match Research Group. (1997). Matching alcoholism treatments to client heterogeneity: Project Match posttreatment drinking outcomes. *Journal of Studies in Alcoholism, 58*, 7–29.

Propst, L. R., Ostrom, R., Watkins, P., Deant, T., & Mashburn, D. (1992). Comparative efficacy of religious and nonreligious cognitive-behavioral therapy for the treatment of clinical depression in religious individuals. *Journal of Consulting and Clinical Psychology, 60,* 94–103.

Propst, A., Paris, J., & Rosberger, Z. (1994). Do therapist experience, diagnosis and functional level predict outcome in short-term psychotherapy. *Canadian Journal of Psychiatry, 39(3),* 168–176.

Rabasca, L. (2000, June). Family ties: Psychologists unite in support of their gay relatives. *APA Monitor, 31(6),* 38–39.

Read, J. P., Kahler, C. W., & Stevenson, J. F. (2001). Bridging the gap between alcoholism treatment research and practice: Identifying what works and why. *Professional Psychology: Research and Practice, 32,* 227–238.

Reandeau, S. G., & Wampold, B. E. (1991). Relationship of power and involvement of working alliance: A multiple-case sequential analysis of brief therapy. *Journal of Counseling Psychology, 38,* 107–114.

Reynolds, S., Stiles, W., Barkham, M., Shapiro, D. A., Hardy, G. E., & Rees, A. (1996). Acceleration of changes in session impact during contrasting time-limited psychotherapies. *Journal of Consulting and Clinical Psychology, 64(3),* 577–586.

Richards, P. S., & Bergin, A. E. (2000a). Toward religious and spiritual competency for mental health professional. In P. S. Richards & A. E. Bergin (Eds.), *Handbook of psychotherapy and religious diversity* (pp. 3–26). Washington, DC: American Psychological Association Press.

Richards, P. S., & Bergin, A. E. (Eds.) (2000b). *Handbook of psychotherapy and religious diversity.* Washington, DC: American Psychological Association Press.

Ricker, M., Nystul, M., & Waldo, M. (1999). Counselors' and clients' ethnic similarity and therapeutic alliance in time-limited outcomes of counseling. *Psychological Reports, 84,* 674–676.

Rohsenow, D. J., Monti, P. M., Martin, R. A., Michalec, E., & Abrams, D. B. (2000). Brief coping skills treatment for cocaine abuse: 12-month substance use outcomes. *Journal of Consulting and Clinical Psychology, 68(3),* 515–520.

Rosenheck, R., Fontana, A., & Cottrol, C. (1995). Effect of clinician-veteran racial pairing in the treatment of posttraumatic stress disorder. *American Journal of Psychiatry, 152,* 555–563.

Rosenthal, R. (1984). *Meta-analytic procedures for social research.* Beverly Hills, CA: Sage Press.

Rossello, J., & Bernal, G. (1999). The efficacy of cognitive-behavioral and interpersonal treatments for depression in Puerto Rican adolescents. *Journal of Consulting and Clinical Psychology, 67(5),* 734–745.

Roth, A., & Fonagy, P. (1996). *What works for whom? A critical review of psychotherapy research.* New York: Guilford Press.

Rounsaville, B. J., O'Malley, S. S., Foley, S. H., & Weissman, M. M. (1988). Role of manual-guided training in the conduct and efficacy of interpersonal psychotherapy for depression. *Journal of Consulting and Clinical Psychology, 56,* 681–688.

Rudy, J. P., McLemore, C. W., & Gorsuch, R. L. (1985). Interpersonal behavior and therapeutic progress: Therapists and clients rate themselves and each other. *Psychiatry, 48,* 264–281.

Safran, J. D., & Greenberg, L. S. (1991). *Emotion, psychotherapy, & change.* New York: Guilford Publications.

Safran, J., Muran, J. C., & Samstang, L. W. (1994). Resolving therapeutic alliance ruptures: A task analytic investigation. In A. Horvath & L. S. Greenberg (Eds.), *The working alliance: Theory, reseach, and practice* (pp. 225–255). New York: John Wiley & Sons.

Safran, S. A., & Rogers, T. (2001). Cognitive-Behavioral Therapy with gay, lesbian, and bisexual clients. *In session, 57,* 629–644.

Saunders, S. M. (2000). Examining the relationship between the therapeutic bond and the phases of treatment outcome. *Psychotherapy: Theory, Research, Practice, & Training, 37(3),* 206–218.

Schulberg, H. C., Katon, W., Simon, G. E., & Rush, A. J. (1998). Treating major depression in primary care practice: An update of the Agency for Health Care Policy and Research practice guidelines. *Archives of General Psychiatry, 55,* 1121–1127.

Schulberg, H. C., Pilkonis, P. A., & Houck, P. (1998). The severity of Major Depression and choice of treatment in primary care practice. *Journal of Consulting and Clinical Psychology, 66,* 932–938.

Schulte, D., Kunzel, R., Pepping, G., & Schulte-Bahrenberg, T. (1992). Tailor-made versus standardized therapy of phobic patients. *Advanced Behavior Research and Therapy, 14,* 67–92.

Seligman, M.E.P. (1993). *What you can change and what you can't.* New York: Alfred A. Knopf.

Seligman, M.E.P. (1995). The effectiveness of psychotherapy: The *Consumer Reports* study. *American Psychologist, 50,* 965–974.

Sexton, H. (1993). Exploring a psychotherapeutic change sequence: Relating process to intersessional and posttreatment outcome. *Journal of Consulting and Clinical Psychology, 61(1),* 128–136.

Sexton, T. L., & Whiston, S. C. (1991). A review of the empirical basis for counseling: Implications for practice and training. *Counselor Education and Supervision, 30,* 330–354.

Shadish, W. R., Matt, G. E., Navarro, A. M., & Phillips, G. (2000). The effects of psychological therapies under clinically representative conditions: A meta-analysis. *Psychological Bulletin, 126,* 512–529.

Shadish, W. R., Robinson, L., & Lu, C. (1999). *A computer program for effect size calculation.* Saint Paul, MN: Assessment Systems Corp.

Shafranske, E. P. (Ed.) (1996). *Religion and the clinical practice of psychology.* Washington, DC: American Psychological Association.

Shafranske, E. P., & Malony, H. N. (1990). Clinical psychologists' religious and spiritual orientations and their practice of psychotherapy. *Psychotherapy, 27,* 72–78.

Shapiro, D. A., Barkham, M., Rees, A., Hardy, G. E., Reynolds, S., & Startup, M.. (1994). Effects of treatment duration and severity of depression on the effectiveness of cognitive-behavioral and psychodynamic-interpersonal psychotherapy. *Journal of Consulting and Clinical Psychology, 62,* 522–534.

Shapiro, D. A., Rees, A., Barkham, M., Hardy, G., Reynolds, S., & Startup, M. (1995). Effects of treatment duration and severity of depression on the maintenance of gains after cognitive-behavioral and psychodynamic-interpersonal therapy. *Journal of Consulting and Clinical Psychology, 63,* 378–387.

Shaw, B. F., & Dobson, K. S. (1987). The use of treatment manuals in cognitive therapy: Experience and issues. *Journal of Consulting and Clinical Psychology, 56,* 673–680.

Shaw, B. F., Olmsted, M., Dobson, K. S., Sotsky, S. M., Elkin, I., Yamaguchi, J., Vallis, T. M., Lowery, A., Watkins, J. T., & Imber, S. D. (1999). Therapist competence ratings in relation to clinical outcome in cognitive therapy of depression. *Journal of Consulting and Clinical Psychology, 67,* 837–846.

Shoham-Salomon, V., Avner, R., & Neeman, K. (1989). "You are changed if you do and changed if you don't": Mechanisms underlying paradoxical interventions. *Journal of Consulting and Clinical Psychology, 57,* 590–598.

Shoham-Salomon, V., & Hannah, M. T. (1991). Client-treatment interactions in the study of differential change processes. *Journal of Consulting and Clinical Psychology, 59,* 217–225.

Smith, M. L., & Glass, G. V. (1977). Meta-analysis of psychotherapy outcome studies. *American Psychologist, 32(9),* 752–760.

Smith, M. L., Glass, G. V., & Miller, T. I. (1980). The benefits of psychotherapy. Baltimore: Johns Hopkins University Press.

Snowden, L. R., Hu, T.-W., & Jerrell, J. M. (1995). Emergency care avoidance: Ethnic matching and participation in minority-serving programs. *Community Mental Health Journal, 31,* 463–473.

Sotsky, S. M., Glass, D. R., Shea, T. M., Pilkonis, P. A., Collins, J. F., Elkin, I., Watkins, J. T., Imber, S. D., Leber, W. R., Moyer, J., & Oliveri, M. E. (1991). Patient predictors of response to psychotherapy and pharmacotherapy: Findings in the NIMH Treatment of Depression Collaborative Research Program. *American Journal of Psychiatry, 148,* 997–1008.

Sperry, L., Brill, P. L., Howard, K. I., & Grissom, G. R. (1996). *Treatment outcomes in psychotherapy and psychiatric interventions.* New York: Brunner/Mazel.

Spirito, A.. (Ed.) (1999). Empirically supported treatments in pediatric psychology. *Journal of Pediatric Psychology, 24,* 87–174.

Stein, D. M., & Lambert, M. J. (1995). Graduate training in psychotherapy: Are therapy outcomes enhanced? *Journal of Consulting and Clinical Psychology, 63,* 182–196.

Steinhelber, J., Patterson, V., Cliffe, K., & LaGoullon, M. (1984). An investigation of some relationships between psychotherapy supervision and patient change. *Journal of Clinical Psychology, 40,* 1346–1353.

Sterling, R. C., Gottheil, E., Weinstein, S. P., & Serota, R. (1998). Therapist/patient race and sex matching: Treatment retention and 9-month follow-up outcome. *Addiction, 93,* 1043–1050.

Stevens, S. E., Hynan, M. T., & Allen, M. (2000). A meta-analysis of common factor and specific treatment effects across the outcome domains of the phase model of psychotherapy. *Clinical Psychology: Science & Practice, 7(3),* 273–290.

Stiles, W. B., Agnew-Davies, R., Hardy, G. E., Barkham, M., & Shapiro, D. A. (1998). Relations of the alliance with psychotherapy outcome: Findings in the second Sheffield Psychotherapy Project. *Journal of Consulting and Clinical Psychology, 66(5),* 791–802.

Stiles, W. B., & Shapiro, D. A. (1994). Disabuse of the drug metaphor: Psychotherapy process-outcome correlations. *Journal of Consulting and Clinical Psychology, 62(5),* 942–948.

Stiles, W. B., Shapiro, D. A., & Firth-Cozens, J. (1989). Therapist differences in the use of verbal response mode forms and intents. *Psychotherapy, 26,* 314–322.

Strupp, H. H., & Anderson, T. (1997). On the limitations of therapy manuals. *Clinical Psychology: Science and Practice, 4,* 76–82.

Strupp, H. H., & Hadley, S. M. (1977). A tripartite model of mental health and therapeutic outcomes. *American Psychologist, 32,* 187–196.

Sue, S., Fujino, D. C., Hu, L.-T., Takeuchi, D. T., & Zane, N.W.S. (1991). Community mental health services for ethnic minority groups: A test of the cultural responsiveness hypothesis. *Journal of Consulting and Clinical Psychology, 59,* 533–540.

Svartberg, M., Seltzer, M. H., Choi, K., & Stiles, T. C. (2001). Cognitive change before, during, and after short-term dynamic and nondirective psychotherapies: A preliminary growth modeling study. *Psychotherapy Research, 11,* 201–219.

Svartberg, M., & Stiles, T. C. (1991). Comparative effects of short-term psychodynamic psychotherapy: A meta-analysis. *Journal of Consulting and Clinical Psychology, 59,* 704–714.

Svartberg, M., & Stiles, T. C. (1994). Therapeutic alliance, therapist competence, and client change in short-term anxiety-provoking psychotherapy. *Psychotherapy Research, 4(1),* 20–33.

Talley, J. E. (1992). *The predictors of successful very brief psychotherapy.* Springfield, IL: Charles C. Thomas, Publisher.

Talley, P. F., Strupp, H. H., & Morey, L. C. (1990). Matchmaking in psychotherapy: Patient-therapist dimensions and their impact on outcome. *Journal of Consulting and Clinical Psychology, 58*, 182–188.

Tang, T. Z., & DeRubeis, R. J. (1999). Sudden gains and critical sessions in cognitive-behavioral therapy for depression. *Journal of Consulting and Clinical Psychology, 67(6)*, 894–904.

Task Force on Promotion and Dissemination of Psychological Procedures (1995). Training in and dissemination of empirically validated psychological treatments: Report and recommendations. *The Clinical Psychologist, 48(1)*, 3–23.

Teyber, E., & McClure, F. (2000). Therapist variables. In C. R. Snyder & R. E. Ingram (Eds.), *Handbook of psychological change* (pp. 62–87). New York: John Wiley & Sons.

Thompson, A. P. (1986). Changes in counseling skills during graduate and undergraduate study. *Journal of Counseling Psychology, 33*, 65–72.

Thompson, B. J., & Hill, C. E. (1993). Client perceptions of therapist competence. *Psychotherapy Research, 3(2)*, 124–130.

Thompson, S. C., & Wierson, M. (2000). Enhancing perceived control in psychotherapy. In C. R. Snyder & R. E. Ingram (Eds.), *Handbook of psychological change: Psychotherapy processes & practices for the 21st* century (pp. 177–197). New York: John Wiley & Sons.

Thompson, C. E., Worthington, R., & Atkinson, D. R. (1994). Counselor content orientation, counselor race, and Black women's cultural mistrust and self-disclosures. *Journal of Counseling Psychology, 41*, 155–161.

Tjelveit, A. C. (1986). The ethics of value conversion in psychotherapy: Appropriate and inappropriate therapist influence on client values. *Clinical Psychology Review, 6*, 515–537.

Tokar, D. M., Fischer, A. R., Schaub, M., & Moradi, B. (2000). Masculine gender roles and counseling-related variables: Links with and mediation by personality. *Journal of Counseling Psychology, 47*, 380–393.

Tracey, T. J. (1986). Interactional correlates of premature termination. *Journal of Consulting and Clinical Psychology, 54(6)*, 784–788.

Tracey, T. J., & Hays, K. (1989). Therapist conplementarity as a function of experience and client stimuli. *Psychotherapy, 26*, 462–468.

Tracey, T. J., Hays, K. A., Malone, J., & Herman, B. (1988). Changes in counselor response as a function of experience. *Journal of Counseling Psychology, 35*, 119–126.

Valdez, J. N. (2000). Psychotherapy with bicultural Hispanic clients. *Psychotherapy, 37*, 240–246.

Vaughan, K., Armstrong, M. S., Gold, R., O'Connor, N., Jenneke, W., & Tarrier, N. (1994). A trial of eye-movement desensitization compared to image habituation training and applied muscle relaxation in posttraumatic stress disorder. *Journal of Behavior Therapy and Experimental Psychiatry, 25(4)*, 283–291.

Verwaaijen, A. A. G., & Van Acker, J. C. A. (1993). Family treatments for adolescents at risk of placement II: Treatment process and outcome. *Family Therapy, 20(2)*, 103–132.

Wade, P., & Bernstein, B. L. (1991). Culture sensitivity training and counselor's race: Effects on Black female client's perceptions and attrition. *Journal of Counseling Psychology, 38*, 9–15.

Wagner, W. G., Kilcrease-Fleming, D., Fowler, W. E., & Kazelskis, R. (1993). Brief-term counseling with sexually abused girls: The impact of sex of counselor on clients' therapeutic involvement, self-concept, and depression. *Journal of Counseling Psychology, 40*, 490–500.

Waltz, J., Addis, M. E., Koerner, K., & Jacobson, N. S. (1993). Testing the integrity of a psychotherapy protocol: Assessment of adherence and competence. *Journal of Consulting and Clinical Psychology, 61*, 620–630.

Wampold, B. E. (2001). *The great psychotherapy debate: Models, methods, and findings.* Hillsdale, NJ: Erlbaum Associates.

Wampold, B. E., Mondin, G. W., Moody, M., Stich, F., Benson, K., & Ahn, H. (1997). A meta-analysis of outcome studies comparing bona fide psychotherapies: Empirically, "all must have prizes." *Psychological Bulletin, 122*, 203–215.

Washton, A., & Stone-Washton, N. (1990). Abstinence and relapse in cocaine addicts. *Journal of Psychoactive Drugs, 22*, 135–147.

Watkins, C. E., Jr. (1990). The effects of counselor self-disclosure: A research review. *The Counseling Psychologist, 18*, 477–500.

Weerasekera, P., Linder, B., Greenberg, L., & Watson, J. (2001). The working alliance in client-centered and process-experiential therapy of depression. *Psychotherapy Research, 11*, 221–233.

Weisz, J. R., Hawley, K. M., Pilkonis, P. A., Woody, S. R., & Follette, W. C. (2000). Stressing the (other) three Rs in the search for empirically supported treatments: Review procedures, research quality, relevance to practice and the public interest. *Clinical Psychology: Science and Practice, 7*, 243–258.

Wells, K. B., & Sturm, R. (1996). Informing the policy process: From efficacy to effectiveness data on pharmacotherapy. *Journal of Consulting and Clinical Psychology, 64*, 638–645.

Wiggins, J. D., & Giles, T. A. (1984). The relationship between counselors' and students' self-esteem as related to counseling outcomes. *School Counselor, 32*, 18–22.

Williams, K. E., & Chambless, D. L. (1990). The relationship between therapist characteristics and outcome of in vivo exposure treatment for agoraphobia. *Behavior Therapy, 21*, 111–116.

Wilson, J. J., & Gil, K. M. (1996). The efficacy of psychological and pharmacological interventions for the treatment of chronic disease-related and non-disease-related pain. *Clinical Psychology Review, 16*, 573–597.

Wisch, A. F., & Mahalik, J. R. (1999). Male therapists' clinical bias: Influence of client gender roles and therapist gender role conflict. *Journal of Counseling Psychology, 46*, 51–60.

Worthington, E. L., Kurusu, T. A., McCullough, M. E., & Sandage, S. J. (1996). Empirical research on religion and psychotherapeutic processes and outcomes: A 10-year review and research prospectus. *Psychological Bulletin, 119*, 448–487.

Worthington, R. L., Mobley, M., Franks, R. D., & Tan, J. A. (2000). Multicultrual counseling competencies: Verbal content, counselor attributions, and social desirability. *Journal of Counseling Psychology, 47*, 460–468.

Yeh, M., Eastman, K., & Cheung, M. K. (1994). Children and adolescents in community health centers: Does the ethnicity or the language of the therapist matter? *Journal of Community Psychology, 22*, 153–163.

Zlotnick, C., Elkin, I., & Shea, M. T. (1998). Does the gender of a patient or the gender of a therapist affect the treatment of patients with major depression? *Journal of Consulting and Clinical Psychology, 66*, 655–659.

Zuroff, D. C., Blatt, S. J., Sotsky, S. M., Krupnick, J. L., Martin, D. J., Sanislow, C. A., & Simmens, S. (2000). Relation of therapeutic alliance and perfectionism to outcome in brief outpatient treatment of depression. *Journal of Consulting and Clinical Psychology, 68(1)*, 114–124.

CHAPTER 8

FIFTY YEARS OF PSYCHOTHERAPY PROCESS-OUTCOME RESEARCH: CONTINUITY AND CHANGE

DAVID E. ORLINSKY
University of Chicago
MICHAEL HELGE RØNNESTAD
University of Oslo
ULRIKE WILLUTZKI
Ruhr-University Bochum

HISTORICAL BACKGROUND

Research on the relations of the psychotherapeutic process to patient outcomes has acquired what must seem a venerable history by now, since the first true process-outcome studies were conducted as long as 50 years ago (e.g., Bartlett, 1950; Blau, 1950; Boun, 1951; Conrad, 1952; Garfield & Kurz, 1952; Haimowitz & Haimowitz, 1952; Heine, 1950; Mensh & Golden, 1951; Miles, Barrabee, & Finesinger, 1951; Page, 1953; Roshal, 1953; Thorley & Craske, 1950). This early efflorescence of studies marked the culmination of a lengthy preparatory period, extending from the late 1920s to the early 1950s, which Orlinsky and Russell (1994) described as the initial phase of psychotherapy research, when the main concern of researchers was to establish a role for scientific research.[1]

The emergence of process-outcome studies as a specific field within psychotherapy research depended on the prior development of systematic outcome research, on one hand, and objective process research, on the other. Bergin (1971) dated the first efforts at systematic outcome research to the 1920s (Huddleston, 1927; Matz, 1929) and 1930s (Alexander, 1937; Carmichael & Masserman, 1939; Curran, 1937; Fenichel, 1930; Hyman, 1936; Jones, 1936; Kessel & Hyman, 1933; Landis, 1937; Luff & Garrod, 1935; Masserman & Carmichael, 1938; Neutstatter, 1935; Ross, 1936; Schilder, 1939; Yaskin, 1936), but Eysenck's (1952) critical challenge to the field provided the impetus in developing modern outcome studies.

The modern study of psychotherapeutic processes has two distinct sources. One was the development of electronic recording of therapy sessions, beginning as early as the 1930s (Lasswell, 1935, 1936, 1937) and the 1940s (Bernard, 1943; Covner, 1942, 1944; Porter, 1943a, 1943b; Rogers, 1942a, 1942b). Previously, the events of therapy were available only as summarized by therapists in selective and impressionistic case histories, usually written for didactic or disputatious reasons. Freud himself noted that while "It is our task to give information on the subject [of psychoanalytic therapy] to . . . impartial persons . . . it is to be regretted that we cannot let them be present as an audience at a treatment of this kind. . . . For good or ill, therefore, [they] must be content with our information" (1926/1959, p. 185). However, by the early 1950s the advantage of audio recording of therapy for research purposes was recognized even in psychoanalytic circles (e.g., Brody, Newman, & Redlich, 1951; Gill, Newman, & Redlich, 1954; Redlich, Dollard, & Newman, 1950), as it had already been by client-centered therapists (Rogers, 1942a, 1942b; Rogers & Dymond, 1954).[2] As Auld and

Murray noted (1955, p. 377), the "sound recording of interviews . . . made a common set of data available to scientists, a set that can be preserved and studied, as many times as necessary" and to which the objective techniques of content analysis could be applied (Auld & Murray, 1955; Berelson, 1952; Marsden, 1965, 1971).

A second approach to the study of process evolved in the 1960s among researchers who emphasized the importance of having an experiential perspective on the events of therapy (Meyer, Borgatta, & Fanshel, 1964; Orlinsky & Howard, 1966, 1967; Snyder, 1961; Strupp, Fox, & Lessler, 1966). Rather than rely exclusively on nonparticipant-observers' analyses of recordings, these investigators adapted psychometric methods that had been previously developed to quantify and compare subjective perceptions and judgments (e.g., Thurstone & Chave, 1929), such as rating scales and questionnaires, to objectively study the subjective experiences of patients and therapists themselves. This approach evolved partly as a reaction against the positivistic ideology that dominated psychological research in the United States during the 1950s.

In retrospect, however, it seems clear that those who sought to objectify the experiences of patients and therapists as participant-observers as well as those who relied on nonparticipant observers to gain an objective view of therapeutic process had as their common aim a "search for scientific rigor," which was the main concern of the second historical phase of psychotherapy research that lasted roughly from 1955 to 1970 (Orlinsky & Russell, 1994). The aspirations and achievements of that period were codified in an extraordinary synopsis by Meltzoff and Kornreich (1970) and in specific areas of psychotherapy research by the authors of this *Handbook*'s first edition (Bergin & Garfield, 1971). The state of the art in process research was marked by Kiesler's (1973) influential review and collation of process research methods, and in outcome research by Waskow and Parloff's (1975) NIMH-sponsored authoritative review of outcome research methods.

A third historical phase of psychotherapy research (c. 1970–1985) can be described as one of "expansion, differentiation, and organization," marked in large part by "the coalescence of a research mainstream committed to a program of objective, quantitative—and, where possible, experimental—studies" (Orlinsky & Russell, 1994, p. 196). The experimental approach was exemplified early on by the comparative outcome studies of DiLoreto (1971) and Sloane, Staples, Cristol, Yorkston, and Whipple (1975) and culminated in the design of the well-known NIMH-sponsored multisite comparative trial of treatments for depression (Elkin et al., 1985). The research activities and results of this period are summarized in the third edition of this *Handbook* (Garfield & Bergin, 1986), in Lambert's reviews of outcome findings (1979; Lambert, Christensen, & DeJulio, 1983), and in Gurman and Razin's (1977) thoughtful anthology on effective therapy.

A singular achievement of this period with respect to outcome research was the application of meta-analysis to demonstrate the effectiveness of psychotherapies (Smith, Glass, & Miller, 1980; Shapiro & Shapiro, 1982), answering in positive terms Eysenck's (1952) question about the effectiveness of psychotherapies. This new methodology led many researchers subsequently to routinely examine and report effect size as well as the statistical significance, assessing the magnitude as well as the likelihood of their findings. The previous edition of this chapter, and other chapters both in the previous and present editions of the *Handbook*, also report effect size data as a way to facilitate the integration of findings from diverse studies.[3]

A major development in the area of process research was the revival of interest in the therapeutic relationship, which was inspired by Bordin's (1979) application of the psychoanalytic "working alliance" concept. This produced an outpouring of research (e.g., Horvath & Greenberg, 1994), which continues to the present day and is comparable to that generated in the previous period by Rogers's (1957) formulation concerning the necessary and sufficient conditions of therapeutic change (Truax & Mitchell, 1971).

Another innovation in the area of process research that has proven remarkably fruitful was the introduction by Rice and Greenberg (1984) of the "task-analytic" method for intensive analysis of therapy sessions, in which the markers for therapeutically significant events are defined in ways that allow the development and impact of those events to be tracked and rated. The compendium edited by Greenberg and Pinsof (1986a) also helped to advance process studies by updating Kiesler's (1973) earlier volume with a collection of more recently developed research methods.

The fourth phase in the history of psychotherapy research, starting in about 1985, is more difficult to characterize because we are still so close to it, or are perhaps still in it. The accomplishments of the first 10 years of this period in various research areas were summarized by authors of the *Handbook*'s fourth edition (Bergin & Garfield, 1994), and the accomplishments of more recent years by the authors of the present edition. Research developments in this period were also presented in collections organized by specific theoretical perspectives (e.g., Dahl, Kächele, & Thomä, 1988; Lietaer, Rombauts & Van Balen, 1990; Miller, Luborsky, Barber, & Docherty, 1993), by treatment modality (Beck & Lewis, 2000), and by geographical area (Beutler & Crago, 1991). Overall, this latest phase may be described somewhat paradoxically as one of consolidation, standardization, and elaboration, yet also of fundamental critique, innovation, and controversy.

An aspect of *consolidation* was the publication of final reports and retrospective summaries of several long-term projects (following that of Frank, Hoehn-Saric, Imber, Liberman, & Stone, 1978, e.g., Luborsky, 2000; Luborsky, Crits-Christoph, Mintz, & Auerbach, 1988; Luborsky & Crits-Christoph, 1990; Strupp, 1993; Wallerstein, 1986), although perhaps none with as much varied and continuing impact as the NIMH Treatment of Depression Collaborative Research Program (Elkin, 1994). Drawing inspiration in part from that landmark project, there was considerable *standardization* of research practice, including the use of randomized clinical trials with patients of specific diagnostic categories, with therapists trained in accordance with treatment "manuals" to provide specific interventions, and with adherence checks to ensure that those interventions were delivered as specified. Moreover, there has been a substantial *elaboration* of data analytic techniques beyond the familiar variance and regression analysis methods to include even more sophisticated statistical procedures (e.g., hierarchical linear modeling).

At the same time, fundamental criticisms of mainstream research methods have been advanced both with respect to the assessment of patient outcomes and the study of therapeutic processes. For example, a major *critique* of group comparison research designs and an alternative individualized approach to outcome measurement was strongly advanced by Howard and colleagues (e.g., Howard, Krause, & Vessey, 1994; Howard, Moras, Brill, Martinovich, & Lutz, 1996; Howard, Orlinsky, & Lueger, 1995; Krause, Howard, & Lutz, 1998; Lutz, Martinovich, & Howard, 1999; Lyons, Howard, O'Mahoney, & Lish, 1997; Sperry, Brill, Howard, & Grissom, 1996). Critiques and efforts to reformulate research goals and methods in the study of therapeutic processes can also be found in discussions by prominent researchers (e.g., Elliott & Anderson, 1994; Greenberg, 1994; Hill, 1994a; Stiles, Shapiro, & Harpet, 1994).

Notable among the *innovations* in this period has been the developments and progressively greater acceptance of qualitative research (e.g., Bachelor, 1995; Hill, Nutt-Williams, Heaton, Thompson, & Rhodes, 1996; Jennings & Skovholt, 1999; Knox, Hess, Petersen, & Hill, 1997; Rasmussen & Angus, 1996; Rennie, 1994a, 1994b; Rhodes, Hill, Thompson, & Elliott, 1994; Skovholt & Rønnestad, 1992, 1995; Stiles, 1999; Stiles et al., 1990; Stiles, Shankland, Wright, & Field, 1997a) and new approaches to the analysis of narrative and interviews (e.g., Breuer, 1996; Flick, 1999; Frommer & Rennie, 2001; Lamnek, 1995; Mayring, 1999; Toukmanian & Rennie, 1992). Some common approaches to the qualitative study of psychotherapy are "grounded theory" methodology (Glaser & Strauss, 1967; Strauss & Corbin, 1990), comprehensive process analysis (Elliott, 1989), the phenomenological approach of Giorgi (1985), and the consensual qualitative method (Hill, Thompson, & Williams, 1997). Moreover, at least two major research journals have devoted special sections or issues to this methodology—the *Journal of Counseling Psychology* (Hill, 1994b) and, more recently, *Psychotherapy Research* (Elliott, 1999).

The possibilities and problems of grounding psychotherapeutic practice on accumulated research knowledge were also addressed in a systematic way by Beutler and Clarkin (1990) and Grawe (1997; Grawe, Donati & Bernauer, 1994), as well as in collections offered by Aveline and Shapiro (1995) and Talley, Butler, and Strupp (1994). However, the greatest *controversy* in this area has been stirred by the 1995 report of the Task Force on Promotion and Dissemination of Psychological Procedures appointed by the Division of Clinical Psychology of the American Psychological Association (1995; Chambless et al., 1996). This effort to help "clinical psychology . . . survive in this heyday of biological psychiatry," despite its lack of "the enormous promotional budgets and sale staff of pharmaceutical companies" (Task Force, 1995, p. 3), has been expounded and expanded, praised and defended by many, for example, in *Clinical Psychology: Science and Practice* (1996, vol. 3) and the *Journal of Consulting and Clinical Psychology* (Kendall & Chambless, 1998) and much criticized by others (e.g., Bohart, O'Hara, & Leitner, 1998; Henry, 1998; Wampold, 1997, 2001) as well-intentioned but premature, partial, and misguided.

It is far beyond the scope of this work to enter that controversy (a balanced summary of which was provided by Elliott, 1998), except to note that in restricting the scope of its survey to controlled clinical trials of manualized treatments for specifically diagnosed disorders, the Task Force peremptorily excluded the significant body of well-replicated results that has accumulated in 50 years of process-outcome research. Although the Task Force authors "suggest that psychologists hold an advantage in being the primary scientists in the psychotherapy field" (p. 3.), ignoring large amounts of evidence hardly seems like model scientific behavior. Moreover, although explicitly seeking to counter the influence of biological psychiatry, the Task Force authors themselves succumb to that influence by modeling their criteria on FDA drug approval criteria and giving other evidence of being "deeply imbedded in a medical model of psychotherapy" (Wampold, 2001, p. 19).

The controversy over empirically supported treatments in the United States has to be understood within the broader context of the managed care revolution that has intensified the traditional competition between psychiatry, psychology, and other mental health disciplines for professional jurisdiction (Abbott, 1988) and scarce economic resources. Psychiatry has been beset by pressures from resource managers and from the pharmaceutical industry to rely on pharmacological treatments and to minimize the amount of time spent with patients. With rare exceptions, academic psychiatry in America has virtually withdrawn from the provision of formal psychotherapies, and training in psychotherapies is not generally given to residents (Luhrmann, 2000). Without a major industry deeply invested in their work, the professions of psychology, social work, and counseling have been forced to defend their contributions in the healthcare system by demonstrating their effectiveness in the provision of short-term treatments, both in themselves and often in comparison to pharmacological methods too. Further reflecting the relevance of economic factors for psychotherapy practice and research is a heightened concern with cost-effectiveness and cost-benefit analysis in outcome assessment (e.g., Miller & Magruder, 1999; Yates, 1994).

Fortunately, American readers should soon have available the report of another Task Force (Norcross, 2001, 2002), created by the APA Division of Psychotherapy, whose aim was "to extend and counterbalance extant efforts to promulgate treatment guidelines based solely upon lists of empirically supported treatments," whose "dual aims are to identify elements of effective therapy relationships and to determine efficacious methods of customizing psychotherapy to the individual patient." And, of course, the discussion of empirically supported or validated treatments is not just an American phenomenon. The issue has also been explored and positions have been adopted in Germany (e.g., Reinecker & Fiedler, 1997; Strauss & Kächele, 1998), the United Kingdom (e.g., Aveline, Shapiro, Parry, & Freeman, 1995; Parry, 1999), and elsewhere. In Norway, for example, the Norwegian Psychological Association recently completed the formulation of alternative treatment guidelines for the treatment of depression (Norsk Psykologforening, 2002) in order to counter the efficacy-driven, randomized trial-based guidelines that the Norwegian Health Authorities had issued along the lines proposed by the Swedish Psychiatric Association, which had been modeled on the guidelines published by the American Psychiatric Association (American Psychiatric Association, 1993, 1994).

Readers who believe that valid scientific knowledge regarding the effectiveness of psychotherapies can *only* come from controlled clinical trials of manualized treatments for specifically diagnosed disorders will undoubtedly be disappointed in this chapter. Experimental designs are not well suited to the kind of questions most often studied in process-outcome research. Although process-outcome questions can be included in order to enrich the information yield of controlled clinical trials, as in the NIMH study of depression (Elkin, 1994), the process-outcome aspects of such studies are not themselves experimental in nature. No one to our knowledge has yet designed a study that would randomly assign specific categories of patients either to warm and empathic therapists or to insensitive and indifferent therapists, nor would such a study be approved as ethical by an institutional review board. Lest we be misunderstood, we wish to state explicitly that we do favor using the results of psychotherapy research to improve the effectiveness of therapeutic processes and their wise and efficient application in clinical practice. Our argument, rather, is against the promulgation of any one method as the "gold standard" in psychotherapy research and for the notion that a genuinely scientific understanding of psychotherapy demands the judicious and critical integration of results arrived at by varied methods. The accumulated findings of a half century's process-outcome research constitutes a large part of that knowledge and should also be part of that understanding.

PSYCHOTHERAPY PROCESS AND OUTCOME

Conceptual clarity about the meaning of the psychotherapy process and outcome is essential to fostering the development and use of process-outcome research. In a previous version of this chapter, the following general definition of psychotherapy was proposed in order "to set boundaries on the field of inquiry without excluding any of the specific practices, findings, or perspectives that have been significant in clinical work" (Orlinsky & Howard, 1978, p. 284.): "Psychotherapy is (1) a relation among persons, engaged in by (2) one or more individuals defined as needing special assistance to (3) improve their functioning as persons, together with (4) one or more individuals defined as able to render such special help." It was noted that "part (1) broaches the matter of therapeutic process in the broadest terms, and part (3) suggests the terms in which [to] deal with therapeutic outcome."

From our current perspective, we would amplify part 1 (defining "therapeutic process in the broadest terms") by denoting specific happenings and events observed in therapy, including (primarily) the *actions, experiences, and relatedness of patient and therapist in therapy sessions* when they are physically together, and (secondarily) the *actions and experiences of the participants specifically referring to one another that occur outside of therapy sessions* when they are not physically together. The latter may include actions by patients such as carrying out "homework" assignments, and experiences such as an imagined dialogue with the therapist. Relations between co-patients and co-therapists would also be included when therapy involves more than one patient and/or more than one therapist, along with characteristics of the total group. This definition is meant to include everything that transpires between and within the participants when they are actually or virtually in each other's presence (corresponding to what we describe below as "treatment process" as distinct from "change process").

We would also clarify the notion of "functioning as persons," meaning here the person *qua* person—that is, the person as a whole, in relation to his or her self, his or her own life and fate as an organism, his or her standing as the member of a social and moral community and as a participant in a valued and meaningful cultural tradition. In this context we would expand on the definition of psychotherapy offered by Frank and Frank (1991, p. 1):

> Attempts to relieve suffering and disability are usually labeled treatment, and every society trains some of its members to apply this form of influence. Treatment typically involves a personal relationship between healer and sufferer. Certain types of therapy rely primarily on the healer's ability to mobilize healing forces in the sufferer by psychological means. These forms of treatment may be generically termed psychotherapy.

Even this historically and culturally inclusive definition is not sufficiently broad, since its authors focus like good physicians on "suffering and disability," and define psychotherapy as a component of the larger category of "treatment." Without doubt, psychotherapy is a form of treatment "by psychological means," and psychotherapeutic practice in modern societies has evolved largely in the context of healthcare institutions as a "mental health" service. Nevertheless, the ways in which psychotherapy is actually utilized in our society suggest (Orlinsky, 1989) that therapy also is, or can be, (1) a form of remedial or higher education in the social-emotional sphere of functioning (what in the nineteenth century might have been termed "moral education"), (2) a nonviolent form of social control for deviant behavior (a substitute or adjunct form of "correctional" influence for those who offend against others or themselves), and (3) a facilitator of meaningful personal orientation and philosophy of life (or "spiritual" development, for those whom Maimonides might have found "perplexed" or Durkheim "anomic"). Many who seek psychotherapy in fact do not qualify for a diagnosable form of suffering or disability. Some are constrained to do so as a result of having transgressed against a basic social norm (e.g., marital infidelity, to avoid divorce) or against a legal norm (e.g., youthful delinquency, to avoid prison or as a condition of parole). Many more do so because they are unhappy with their lives, their relationships, and their selves. Thus, "functioning as persons" ought to include terms such as deviance and deficient well-being in addition to suffering and disability.

With regard to the second and fourth parts of the definition given in 1978, the special nature of the assistance that patients require and therapists are "defined as able to render" should be emphasized. We all need help some of the time, and, in our society, the norms of friendship and family relations allow us to expect help and require us to offer help in turn (e.g., Pilisuk & Parks, 1986). In contemporary society, the psychotherapies are predominantly (and for pragmatic reasons, quite legitimately) viewed as psychological treatments for emotional, behavioral, or mental disorders. However, from another point of view, the psychotherapies can also be seen as representing the refinement and professionalization of personal helping skills, which may be sought when individuals' normal social networks fail (e.g., in crises), or become insubstantial (e.g., in rapidly changing or highly mobile societies), or when the level of expertise in helping skills that is needed exceeds that available in normal social networks. This form of personal help is offered in modern urban societies, *as* a professional service, *by* persons whose expertise in helping skills has been formally recognized by training institutes, licensing bodies, and professional reputation, *to* persons whose need for well-being, disabilities, transgressions, or suffering (often though not always meeting standard diagnostic criteria) are genuine "mental health" concerns.

Aspects of Process

Several important variations have become attached to the meaning of the term *process* which, unless clearly recognized, are likely to cause confusion. Four areas of variability deserve special attention: (1) the question of observational perspective; (2) the focus on treatment process versus change process; (3) the analysis of temporal and causal sequences; and (4) multiple levels of description.

Observational perspectives. Therapeutic processes are naturally observed and also can be assessed for research purposes by the participants themselves, that is, by patients and therapists. The most common way of having patients and therapists generate research data is through the use of postsession questionnaires and rating scales (e.g., Addis & Jacobson, 2000; Barrett-Lennard, 1986; Orlinsky & Howard, 1975; Stiles & Snow, 1984), although techniques such as interpersonal process recall have been used as well (e.g., Elliott, 1984, 1986; Hill, 1989). Therapeutic processes may also be observed and assessed by nonparticipants (persons who do not directly interact with the patient and therapist) based on recordings, videotapes, or other records made of therapy sessions (e.g., Benjamin, Foster, Roberto, & Estroff, 1986; Dürr & Hahlweg, 1996; Klein, Mathieu-Coughlan, & Kiesler, 1986; Luborsky et al., 1988; Stiles, 1999; Suh, Strupp, & O'Malley, 1986; Znoj, Grawe, & Jeger, 2000). In their efforts to compare internally reliable assessments of the same substantive variable (e.g., therapist empathy) made by patients, therapists, and nonparticipant-observers, process researchers have been forced to recognize that these may not be very highly correlated and may produce divergent findings in relation to other process or outcome variables (e.g., Hilliard, Henry, & Strupp, 2000). The fact that reliability and validity of assessments can nevertheless be established *within* observational perspectives implies that the meaning of process from a patient's perspective, though not unrelated, is not necessarily the same as the meaning of process from a therapist's perspective, nor is each the same as what process means to external observers. By analyzing process-outcome studies in this respect, the previous editions of this chapter demonstrated that readers should look carefully at the perspectives from which process and outcome were assessed before inferring that results from any specific combination of process-by-outcome observational perspectives hold as well for any other combination of perspectives.

Treatment process and change process. Some investigators use the term *process* to refer to processes of change through which clients or patients are hypothesized to improve. These change processes tend to be viewed as occurring within the patient, often but by no means exclusively or even mainly during therapy sessions. For example, Carl Rogers's (1961) "process equation of psychotherapy" refers to the process "in the client" and focuses on change occurring in aspects of the client's psychological functioning (e.g., manner of experiencing, construal of meaning, relationship to problems, manner of relating). The therapist's behavior during sessions was not viewed as part of this therapeutic process, but rather as therapist-offered "conditions" creating an interpersonal environment more or less facilitative of "the patient's process."

The influential "change events" paradigm of process research proposed by Rice and Greenberg (1984; Greenberg, 1991) follows this tradition, though with a broader clinical conception of client change events. Yet another example of identifying the term *process* with patient change is found in the concept of therapeutic alliance formulated by researchers at the Menninger Foundation (Frieswyk, Colson, & Allen, 1984), who stipulated that this should include "the extent to which the patient makes active use of the treatment as a resource for constructive change" (Frieswyk et al., 1986, p. 36).

Other researchers use the term *process* primarily to refer to the events—all of the events—that occur as part of therapy sessions, without *a priori* distinctions between neutral and specifically helpful or hindering events. Various well-known schemes of process assessment exemplify this approach (e.g., Bastine, Fiedler, & Kommer, 1989; Benjamin, Foster, Roberto, & Estroff, 1986; Czogalik, 1991; Elliott, 1984; Hill, 1986; Kächele, 1992; Stiles, 1986). These schemes focus on the actions, perceptions, intentions, thoughts, and feelings of the patient and therapist, as well as the relationship between them, which are generally viewed as occurring inside therapy sessions. This more pragmatic and descriptive approach to process analysis tends to be taken when investigators do not have strong *a priori* hypotheses about the sources of change in psychotherapy, and it is basically the position that has been taken in this chapter.

Drawing a potentially misleading metaphor (Stiles & Shapiro, 1989) from the field of pharmacology, treatment processes sometimes have been described as including both inert and active ingredients (e.g., Frank, Hoehn-Saric, Imber, Liberman, & Stone, 1978; Gomes-Schwartz, 1978). Active ingredients are conceived as having a demonstrable causal relation to change processes and, through these change processes, to outcome. Researchers who assess the relation of outcome to explicitly stipulated change processes are, in effect, attempting to validate clinically derived hypotheses. On the other hand, researchers who assess the relation of outcome to various treatment processes are taking a more empirical path to discovering the effective aspects of psychotherapy. (In both cases, researchers should heed the methodological caution offered by Stiles, 1988.) Both strategies seem legitimate, and researchers should of course be free to do what best suits them, but at least there will be less confusion if we use specifically qualified phrases such as *treatment process* and *change process.*

TEMPORAL AND CAUSAL SEQUENCES. Confusion can also arise from discrepancies in how researchers construe the sense of sequence implied by the idea of process. Sequence may be understood descriptively as temporal succession, or logically as causal consequence. Temporal succession is the more general meaning, since simple temporal succession does not imply cause and effect, whereas causal sequences do imply some passage of time. Both meanings may be used in considering either treatment processes or change processes.

Researchers have faced a dilemma in this regard. Although psychotherapy occurs in real time, temporal analyses of therapeutic processes generally require costly longitudinal research designs and typically demand Herculean efforts involving vast amounts of data. Some notable attempts have been made by a few researchers (e.g., Labov & Fanshel, 1977; Pittenger, Hockett, & Danehy, 1960; Scheflen, 1973), but their studies generally have focused on fairly circumscribed segments of treatment (for an exception to this rule, see Czogalik, 1991; Czogalik & Russell, 1994, 1995). On the other hand, although cross-sectional research designs may permit causal inferences and produce more manageable amounts of data, they promote a synchronic causal analysis of therapy process in which temporal sequences are left unspecified. Consequently, those wishing to specify how the results of such research ought to be implemented in real-time practice typically have been forced to rely on clinical intuition rather than on a solid research base. One new development documented in this chapter that offers hope in this regard is the application of statistical methods to determine growth curves and change trajectories in process variables over the course of treatment (see the later section on Temporal Patterns).

MULTIPLE LEVELS OF DESCRIPTION. Finally, the venerable problem of units of measurement or levels of description in process research must be addressed (Russell & Staszewski, 1988). As Greenberg noted, "the unit chosen, be it word, phrase, utterance, problem area, initial period of therapy, and so on, will depend on the constructions of interest and on the questions being asked by a particular study" (1986, p. 715). Over the past four decades, process studies have focused on virtually all descriptive levels, although for reasons of economy and accessibility rather more on the microscopic end of the spectrum. Wide variations in descriptive levels have stretched to the limit whatever meaning *process* retains as a simple, unqualified term. Comparing microanalyses of actions or utterances (e.g., Bänninger-Huber, 1992; Bänninger-Huber & Widmer, 1999) to macroanalyses of treatment phases (e.g., Howard, Lueger, Maling, & Martinovich, 1993) is not so much like comparing apples to oranges as it is amoebas to elephants. Greenberg and Pinsof (1986b) referred to the macro-micro distinction of scale in outcome variables made by researchers as "big O" versus "little o," but did not similarly dramatize distinctions of scale in process variables as "big P" versus "little p." In fact, this would be far too simple. Greenberg (1986) proposed distinguishing four levels of description—content (utterance), speech act, episode, and relationship—but even these cover only a portion of the spectrum of units studied by process researchers. Elliott (1991) subsequently proposed six unit levels. This chapter in the fourth edition of the *Handbook* distinguished nine temporal spans or levels of process (see Table 8.1). As these are essentially heuristic distinctions, the number of levels actually used in any given case is largely a matter of practical convenience.

The point here is simply that the familiar term *process* signifies many different things in the psychotherapy research literature, and careful readers must therefore be attentive to subtle but important variations of meaning. In addition to noting the specific content aspect of process under study, it never hurts to ask the following questions: Is treatment process or change process the actual topic? Is process understood mainly in temporal or in causal terms? At what descriptive levels, from micro to meta, were process variables assessed? And from whose perspective were the observations made?

Aspects of Outcome

The concept of *outcome* has also been subject to an accumulation of divergent meanings. Two areas of variant usage have already been noted in the discussion of process: observational perspective and level of analysis.

Observational perspective. Strupp, Hadley, and Gomes-Schwartz (1977) established that definitions and criteria of outcome differ according to whether assessments are made by the patient, the therapist, an expert nonparticipant, or interested laypersons, such as the patient's family. Like process, outcome has a different, yet valid, meaning in each perspective, which can be shown by disaggregating perspectives for outcome as well as process in the tabulation of findings (e.g., Lambert, Salzer, & Bickman, 1998; Park & Elkin, 2001). Again, the analysis and separate tabulation of process-outcome findings by observational perspective in previous editions of this chapter should caution readers not to assume an equivalence of results as judged by patient, therapist, or outside rater.

Level of analysis. Level of analysis presents a more difficult problem, particularly at the microscopic end of the hierarchy. Some investigators view the immediate consequences of a therapeutic intervention as outcome events despite the fact that they occur within the session, for example, patient insight following a therapist's interpretation, or expressive behavior indicating softening of internal conflict after the use of a Gestalt two-chair technique, or increase in self-efficacy expectation regarding a specific situation after behavioral rehearsal by role-playing. Against this we have long argued that, as a practical matter, evidence of outcome ought to be observed *outside* the patient-therapist relationship (Orlinsky & Howard, 1978). Of what value is a treatment that proceeds well in itself but changes little in the patient's ongoing life or personality? We agree with Greenberg and Pinsof (1986b) that it is crucial to distinguish between little o's and big O's, but we believe these distinctions only apply at level 3 and higher (see Table 8.1). Thus, we view changes made by patients *inside* therapy as a distinct aspect of process, which we refer to as in-session impacts (level 2). However, this does not mean that outcome can only be evaluated at the termination of treatment or at specified followup times. In principle, immediate outcomes or micro-outcomes (levels 3 and 4) can be meaningfully assessed after any session—first, fifth, or fifteenth—or intermittently over the course of treatment, as is often done in research on cognitive behavioral therapy (e.g., DeRubeis & Feeley, 1990; Fennell & Teasdale, 1987; Michalak & Schulte, 2002).

Evaluative versus descriptive assessment. Some researchers do not limit outcome to clinical improvement or deterioration, but refer instead to any type of serial dependency in treatment. The confusion between descriptive and evaluative consequences arises particularly at the more microscopic levels of analysis. For example, Czogalik (Personal communication, 1992) remarked that time-series analyses of serial dependency between patient and therapist utterances in his data show that therapist self-disclosures do have

TABLE 8.1 Levels of Analysis for Psychotherapeutic Process and Outcome

Timeframe	Timescale	Process Focus	Outcome Focus
Level 1: Liminal	Split-seconds	*Micromomentary processes* (gaze shifts; facial expressions)	None
Level 2: Momentary	Large fractions to small multiples of minutes	*Moment-by-moment processes* (tactical moves, e.g., specific utterances; interactive turns)	*In-session impacts* (emergent helpful or hindering experiences, e.g., insight, catharsis)
Level 3: Situational	Large fractions to small multiples of hours	*Session processes* (strategic change events; rupture and repair of alliance; dynamics of whole sessions)	*Postsession outcome* (immediate improvements in mood, motivation, and cognition, e.g., resolution of "splitting")
Level 4: Daily	Large fractions to small multiples of days	*Session-sequential processes* (intersession experiences; use of homework assignments; very brief treatment episodes, e.g., emergency therapy)	*Micro-outcome* (enhancement of current functioning, e.g., boost in morale; communication skills; better handling of problem situations)
Level 5: Monthly	Large fractions to small multiples of months (weeks)	*Phase/short course processes* (formation and evolution of a therapeutic alliance; or whole short-term treatment episode, e.g., 12–26 weeks)	*Mini-outcome* (upgrading of week-to-week psychological state, e.g., symptom reduction, lessening of irrational cognitions)
Level 6: Seasonal	Large fractions to small multiples of years (months)	*Medium-course processes* (work on recurrent interpersonal, cognitive, and motivational conflicts; medium-term treatment episodes, e.g., 6–24 months)	*Meso-outcome* (change in personal adaptation, e.g., increase in self-ideal congruence, resolution of dysfunctional attitudes and cognitions)
Level 7: Perennial	Large fractions to small multiples of decades (years)	*Long course processes* (long-term treatment episodes, e.g., 2–7+ years)	*Macro-outcome* (personality change, e.g., methods of defense; removal of neurotic blocks to growth)
Level 8: Developmental	Life trajectory vectors and stage transitions	*Multitreatment processes* (sequential treatment episodes)	*Mega-outcome* (character change, e.g., modification of Axis-II personality disorder)
Level 9: Biographic	Life course	*Therapeutic career* (total treatment history)	*Meta-outcome* (retrospective view of life course as influenced by treatment experience)

significant effects on some patients, in contrast to our earlier report that therapist self-disclosure has little apparent effect on outcome (Orlinsky & Howard, 1986). Our response (aside from noting that the term *self-disclosure* has been variously defined) is that serially dependent responses to specific processes, even when they occur outside sessions, do not constitute clinical outcome unless they indicate some favorable or unfavorable change in the patient's condition.

There are multiple value criteria by which such judgments can be made. Patients' behaviors can be assessed as more or less effective, authentic, or benevolent toward self and others; their products, as more or less beautiful or creative; their persons, as more or less normal, noble, or spiritually fulfilled (Orlinsky, 1989, 2001). Since there are many possible criteria and points of view on outcome (e.g., Krause & Howard, 1976; Strupp, Hadley, & Gomes-Schwartz, 1977), one needs to decide which criteria and which viewpoints to assess, and to investigate rather than simply overlook discrepancies between them (Lambert, Salzer, & Bickman, 1998; Park & Elkin, 2001). From our point of view, outcome is a clinical concept signifying some degree of improvement or deterioration in the patient's condition, as judged from some observer's perspective by some value criterion (Orlinsky & Howard, 1980). For the sake of clarity, we proposed the term *output* to designate the whole spectrum of changes that may arise as a result of psychotherapy—whether in patients, therapists, their families and associates, or the organizations, institutions, and value patterns of their social milieu (Orlinsky & Howard, 1986).

Outcome Specificity. A development worthy of note is the trend toward assessment of outcome differentiated with respect to particular patient populations. In order to further increase communication and comparability, a panel of experts (Strupp, Horowitz, & Lambert, 1997) attempted to update Waskow and Parloff's (1975) "core battery" of outcome measures in a manner that focused specifically on separate disorders. Though valuable in many ways, this focus on disorders assumes that psychotherapy is just a psychiatric mental health treatment, and it disregards clients who may not meet diagnostic criteria but who nevertheless seek help in dealing with troubling problems of living by consulting psychotherapists, who evidently (Smith, Staudinger, & Baltes, 1994) do possess practical wisdom in these matters. Other researchers have sought specificity by differentiating between particular dimensions of outcome, for example, symptomatology, causal factors, and consequences of problems (e.g., Schulte, 1997). Greater specificity in tracking outcomes has also emerged in the study of dose-effect relations, where particular sets of symptoms or problem clusters are shown to remit after different amounts of treatment (see the later section on Temporal Patterns).

Cumulative Knowledge

The progress of process-outcome research can be traced in the previous editions of this *Handbook*, beginning with the method-oriented survey of Marsden (1971) who concluded three decades ago that "We now find ourselves possessed of a legion of findings badly in need of consolidation and integration" (p. 392). An effort has been made in subsequent editions to meet Marsden's request (Orlinsky, Grawe, & Parks, 1994; Orlinsky & Howard, 1978, 1986) by integrating the ever growing number of process-outcome findings into a coherent and clinically realistic conceptual scheme. Those findings, which had been extracted from hundreds of studies published between 1950 and 1992, numbered more than 2,300 at last count, and research in this area has flourished since then. In our search we have found 279 new studies that contained at least one, and often many, process-outcome findings. Our aim in this fifth edition of the *Handbook* is to provide readers with access to the process-outcome research literature for the years 1993–2001 and to consider how much, and how, these recent studies have advanced our knowledge and understanding of effective psychotherapy. To do this in a way that doesn't require readers to study those earlier chapters, we present two key features of earlier chapters as a baseline of cumulative knowledge. First is the conceptual framework known as the "Generic Model of Psychotherapy" (Orlinsky & Howard, 1987), which was developed in the 1986 edition of the chapter to sort therapy process variables into coherent categories. Then we present an overview of process-outcome research findings as summarized in the 1994 version of this chapter. This will provide a context for understanding the directions taken by recent studies of the relations between therapeutic processes and patient outcomes.

The Generic Model of Psychotherapy

The Generic Model of Psychotherapy distinguishes between psychotherapeutic process as a *system of action*, in the sense defined by Parsons and Shils (1954), and other larger surrounding systems which constitute its functional environment. The action system of psychotherapy consists of *interactions* over time that occur between persons vis-à-vis one another in the reciprocal roles of patient and therapist—as those interactions are experienced by the persons involved and as they may also happen to be observed by others.

Although the interactions of patient and therapist over time constitute the therapeutic process, the *persons* who are interacting in the roles of patient and therapist are actually themselves part of the functional environment of therapy. Each person is a separate self, each has a separate history, and each separately has roles in many other relationships in a life outside of psychotherapy.

It is customary to think of the patient and therapist as being "in" therapy, but it is really more accurate to think of therapy as operating "in" the context formed by the lives and personalities of those persons. Past and current events in the patient's life and personality clearly influence the interactions that take place in therapy, and of course the interactions that take place in therapy explicitly aim to exert a favorable influence on current and future events in the patient's life and personality.

Past and current events in the therapist's life and personality also influence the interactions that take place in therapy, though of course in ways that are expected to differ significantly from the patient. Moreover, the interactions that take place in therapy also exert some influence on current and future events in the therapist's life and personality. We refer to the latter as an *output* of therapy in order to preserve the traditional meaning of the term *outcome* as referring to the effects of therapy on the patient.

Another context or functional environment in which therapy takes place is constituted by the social institutions and cultural patterns of the community to which patient and therapist belong. The community's social institutions and organizations impose their influence on all the psychotherapy practices and cases that take place in it. These include the immediate *treatment setting* (e.g., university counseling center, community mental health clinic, inpatient psychiatric ward, or private office practice) and personnel in the treatment setting who interact regularly with patients and therapists (e.g., receptionists, supervisors); the wider *service delivery system* in which the treatment setting is located (e.g., managed care systems and health maintenance organizations or HMOs); *other social institutions* located within or outside the service delivery system (e.g., welfare agencies, law courts, patients' and therapists' families); and social, economic, and political *currents of change* affecting community life (e.g., holiday seasons, business recessions, national crises). Similarly, the community's cultural beliefs and values about normal personality, the appropriate forms of emotional experience and expression, communicative norms, the nature and causes of deviance (pathology), and the right and proper modes of helping, all exert a guiding influence on the therapeutic process, just as those beliefs and values in turn are affected over time by what articulate and influential members of the community experience in therapy—as patients and as therapists.

Thus, psychotherapy as a system of action is viewed as having both individual and collective contexts that influence therapeutic processes (as *inputs*) and, in turn, are influenced by therapeutic processes *outputs*, including patient *outcome*). Therapy has its most immediate impact on the individuals directly involved in the process. When considering research on the relation of therapeutic process to *outcome*, the focus clearly is on how the events of therapy influence current and future events in the patient's life and personality. Even so, it would be shortsighted to overlook the individual impact of therapy on therapists (e.g., Farber, 1983) and the aggregate long-term influence of psychotherapy on other institutions (e.g., Schlesinger, Mumford, Glass, Patrick, & Sharfstein, 1983) and on the community at large (e.g., Bellah, Madsen, Sullivan, Swidler, & Tipton, 1985; MacIntyre, 1981; Newman & Howard, 1986).

The psychotherapeutic action system itself, or therapeutic process, is understood broadly in the Generic Model as *treatment process* as defined above (rather than as *change process*). This definition includes all of the interactions experienced by patient and therapist, or observed by others, during therapy sessions (as well as their actions and experiences with respect to each other outside sessions). Which of all these constitute change process (the processes by which patients change for the better or for worse) is an empirical question that should eventually be answered, by process-outcome research.

The inherent complexity of psychotherapeutic process has led researchers to observe it from many aspects. Following the research literature, five process facets were recognized in the 1986 version of this chapter: the normative or organizational facet, familiarly referred to as the *therapeutic contract* (e.g., Menninger, 1958); the technical or procedural facet focusing on treatment tasks, called *therapeutic operations;* the specifically interpersonal facet of involvement between patient and therapist, generally known as the *therapeutic bond* (e.g., Bordin, 1979); the intrapersonal or reflexive facet of involvement, called *participant self-relatedness;* and the clinical or pragmatic facet of process, focusing on *in-session impacts*. By 1994, advances in the sequential analysis of temporal processes within and across sessions led to the recognition of a sixth process facet dealing with *sequential patterns*. The process facets of the Generic Model are summarized in Table 8.2 and are presented in greater detail with the listing of studies in Tables 8.4 through 8.32.

THERAPEUTIC CONTRACT. When people enter therapy, they do so by engaging in the social roles of patient or therapist, and their actions and experiences are shaped by and reflect the normative expectations associated with those roles, as understood and interpreted by each party. Norms defining the optimal interaction between patient and therapist that are presumed to promote favorable outcomes (i.e., what the ideal-type patient ought to do and what the ideal-type therapist ought to do) are defined by the *treatment model* advocated in the therapist's orientation. Therapists learn these norms and how to implement them in practice from their professional training and supervision. Persons who engage in the patient role generally learn what they are expected to do through direct participation, but many have a general idea based on popular culture (e.g., movies and television) or their participation in social circles where being in therapy is common and is often discussed (Kadushin, 1969). Two aspects of the therapeutic contract that have been studied by process-outcome researchers are *contractual provisions* (e.g., individual vs. group or couple or family therapy modality, schedule of

TABLE 8.2 Generic Model of Psychotherapy: Process Categories

1. Organizational Aspect of Therapy: *Therapeutic Contract*
The therapeutic contract defines the norms of the participants' roles as patient and therapist, and the therapeutic situation or frame, as determined by the therapist's treatment model (orientation). *Contractual provisions* include treatment goals, methods, manner, format, schedule, term, fees, and financial arrangements. *Contractual implementation* refers to actions by which those provisions are made effective (e.g., negotiation of goal consensus, repair of contractual lapses, etc.).

2. Technical Aspect of Therapy: *Therapeutic Operations*
The cycle of reciprocal role-specific behaviors performed by the participants in therapy: (1) the *patient's presentation* of problematic complaints and demonstration of characteristic thought, feeling, and behavior patterns; (2) the *therapist's construal* or expert understanding of these in terms of a clinical treatment model (e.g., as diagnostic evaluations and case formulations); (3) the *therapist's intervention* strategy and techniques based on the treatment model; and (4) the *patient's responsiveness* to those interventions (cooperation).

3. Interpersonal Aspect of Therapy: *Therapeutic Bond*
The quality of involvement between the particular persons who occupy the normatively specified roles of patient and therapist, as reflected in their *personal rapport* expressive attunement and affective attitude and in their *task-teamwork* reciprocal investment and task coordination.

4. Intrapersonal Aspect of Therapy: *Self-Relatedness*
Each participant's experience of self concurrent with enacting the roles of patient and the therapist and relating to one another as persons. Included are each person's self-awareness, self-construal, self-regulation, and self-esteem (typically rated jointly in terms of openness or defensiveness).

5. Clinical Aspect of Therapy: *In-Session Impacts*
Immediate positive or negative impacts on the participants of their interactions during the therapy session. *Patient impacts* may be positive ("therapeutic realizations") and/or negative ("harms")—for example, insight vs. confusion, relief vs. distress, encouragement vs. demoralization, self-efficacy vs. dependence. *Therapist impacts* may be positive ("returns") and/or negative ("costs") accruing from their work investment—for example, self-efficacy vs. frustration, professional growth vs. burnout.

6. Sequential Aspect of Process: *Temporal Patterns*
Distinctive characteristics and sequelae of events or moments in *session development* (e.g., facilitating moments); distinctive characteristics of periods or stages in the *treatment stage* (e.g., early vs. late sessions); or temporal aspects of the whole *treatment course* (e.g., total number of sessions).

sessions, financial arrangements) and *contractual implementation* (e.g., how faithfully and skillfully participants adhere to the norms).

Therapeutic operations. Therapeutic operations are the procedural tasks to which patients and therapists commit themselves in undertaking a therapeutic contract. Freud (1912b), for example, gave to patients the task of following "the fundamental rule of psycho-analysis" by free-associating and to analysis that of following its "necessary counterpart," the rule of evenly distributed attention or "giving equal notice to everything" (p. 112), as well as making timely, tactful, and accurate interpretations (Freud, 1937). The procedural facet of various treatment models was more elaborately formulated in later years in the form of treatment manuals (e.g., Beck, Rush, Shaw, & Emery, 1979; Klerman, Weissman, Rounsaville, & Chevron, 1984; Luborsky, 1984; Strupp & Binder, 1984). Viewed generically, such operations always involve some forms of *problem presentation, expert understanding, therapist intervention,* and *patient cooperation.* A way has to be provided for persons in the patient role to present their complaints and otherwise make their problematic experiences available to the therapist (problem presentation). Persons in the therapist role have to apply their professional skills and knowledge to assess and evaluate what their patients present (expert understanding) and, according to how that is understood (e.g., Witteman & Koele, 1999), to present some course of action for dealing with the problematic situation (therapist interventions). Finally, participation in a course of therapeutic action typically requires patients to become actively involved in some fashion (patient cooperation).

Therapeutic bond. As the patient and therapist negotiate a therapeutic contract and perform their respective therapeutic tasks, they also inevitably perceive and respond to each other simply as persons—that is, as persons with specific characteristics having no formal bearing on their roles in therapy (e.g., age, gender, ethnicity, cultural style, personal manner, and attractiveness). This informal and strictly interpersonal facet of the therapeutic relationship is the therapeutic bond, which may be strong or weak and relatively positive, negative, or neutral in character. The task-instrumental aspect of the therapeutic bond is reflected in the quality of *collaborative teamwork,* based on their *personal investment* (how deeply or superficially the participants engage in their roles) and on their *interactive coordination* (how well or poorly their actions combine). By contrast, the social-emotional aspect of the therapeutic bond is reflected in the quality of their *personal rapport,* based on their *expressive attunement* (how effectively and empathically they communicate) and on their respective *affective attitudes* (how strongly and how positively or negatively they feel toward each other). In therapy as elsewhere, little is likely to be accomplished by persons who don't work well together and neither understand nor like each other. When more than two or three participants are involved in therapy, the bond generalizes into a "group atmosphere" in which effective teamwork and cohesive morale are important factors (e.g., Bednar & Kaul, 1994).

Participant self-relatedness. The phrase *participant self-relatedness* refers to the reflexive aspect of the individual's experience while engaging in activities and relationships, an aspect that is recognized more clearly in terms such as self-awareness, self-control, and self-esteem. As part of every interaction, patient and therapist also experience and react to varying levels of internal arousal; they perceive and construe their own moods, desires, and intentions; they exercise varying degrees of self-control over their impulses; they experience fluctuating levels of self-efficacy; and so forth. The participants' states of self-relatedness constitute an integral part of the treatment process and may have an impact on other aspects of process and outcome, for example, on their receptivity to one another, or on their ability to assimilate what is happening during sessions. The observable or behavioral aspect of self-relatedness is typically expressed in a person's social demeanor or "face" (Goffman, 1956). Persons who are in close and sustained "face-to-face" contact typically register and respond to each other's state of self-relatedness at an intuitive and preconscious level, a phenomenon to which experiential therapists have drawn attention (e.g., Whitaker & Malone, 1953) and which Freud (1912b) for one described as "unconscious to unconscious" communication. Clinically relevant aspects of negative self-relatedness in therapy are generally regarded as defensiveness or constriction, whereas positive self-relatedness may be referred to as openness, centeredness, or psychological-mindedness.

In-session impacts. In-session impacts consist of clinically relevant consequences of therapeutic operations and relations as experienced by participants within the therapy session. Some researchers refer to these as little outcomes or "little o" (e.g., Greenberg & Pinsof, 1986b), but by our criteria outcome should be reflected in impacts made on patients in their activities and relations outside of therapy sessions and beyond the bounds of their roles as patients. Favorable in-session impacts on *patients* include such events as insight, catharsis, resolution of intrapersonal conflicts, experiences of self-efficacy in problem solving, and enhanced feelings of hope and determination to carry on (previously called "therapeutic realizations"). However, it is also important to note that patients may experience negative in-session impacts, such as confusion, embarrassment, or anxiety. Therapists, too, experience both positive and negative in-session impacts (e.g., Farber & Heifetz, 1981; Orlinsky et al., 1999) which, though generally of secondary interest to researchers, may become clinically important if they interfere with effective performance of the therapist role (e.g., through burnout).

Temporal patterns. The concept of process is inherently linked to time as well as to function. Until the late 1980s and early 1990s, the only temporal aspect of therapy that had been given much study by process-outcome researchers was the total duration of a course of therapy, measured either chronologically or by number of sessions. Growing statistical sophistication since then has enabled researchers to examine outcome as a function of patterns of sequential relations within sessions *(session development)*, as well as patterns extending across successive sessions *(treatment stage)* or a whole therapy episode *(treatment course)*. However, longer courses of treatment (e.g., 80 or more sessions) still for the most part require sampling or else intensive single-case quantitative analysis (e.g., Czogalik & Hettinger, 1987, 1988; Czogalik & Russell, 1994, 1995).

These six aspects of the psychotherapeutic process originated as categories for organizing our survey of process-outcome findings and will be used to do so again later in the present chapter, at which time each will be made more specific by reference to the variables included in it.

Nevertheless, although it is necessary to present and discuss them separately and sequentially in the text, it is essential theoretically to remember that the first five are conceived as concurrent facets of a complex phenomenon rather than as distinct steps or stages of process. They are functionally interconnected, and together they define the psychotherapeutic system as it unfolds over time.

The Generic Model of Psychotherapy holds that each form of therapy involves a particular configuration of these process facets; that there is always some therapeutic contract, which entails specific therapeutic operations, in the course of which the participants evolve a therapeutic bond of some kind and quality, and experience specific modes of self-relatedness, through which they attain some positive or negative in-session impacts; and, further, that these facets interact and over time develop together as a temporal pattern of events. To distinguish among the various species belonging to the genera of psychotherapies would require a description of how each process facet is configured and how the several process aspects are interrelated, which is beyond our present scope. However, it is plausible to suppose that different types of specific therapies may be best adapted and produce differential results for different types of patients and therapists, as has been suggested by a number of studies (e.g., Beutler & Clarkin, 1990; Beutler, Mohr, Grawe, Engle, & MacDonald, 1991; Grawe, 1989b, 1991; Rohrbaugh, Shoham, & Racioppo, 2002; Shoham & Rohrbaugh, 1995; Stiles, Shankland, Wright, & Field, 1997b).

The Generic Model also explicitly emphasizes the fact that the psychotherapeutic processes occur in a complex human environment constituted most immediately by the lives and personalities of the participants, and to a lesser extent by the significant others with whom their lives are intertwined, as well as by the social organizations and institutions and relevant cultural patterns of their community. To highlight these theoretical features of the Generic Model, some of the functional interrelations among process facets are illustrated in Figure 8.1, which also indicates some of their main connections to the individual and collective environment.

Arrows in the diagram should be understood as hypotheses about the interrelations of various process facets with one another and ultimately with outcome. For example, the participants' interpersonal behavior towards one another in therapy is determined jointly by their personal style and by their conceptions of their respective roles as patient and therapist. Their interpersonal behavior towards one another then jointly defines the character and strength of their therapeutic bond. So too does the progress of their therapeutic operations, which is reciprocally influenced in turn by the state of the therapeutic bond. The latter implies that the character and strength of the therapeutic bond at any point in time should

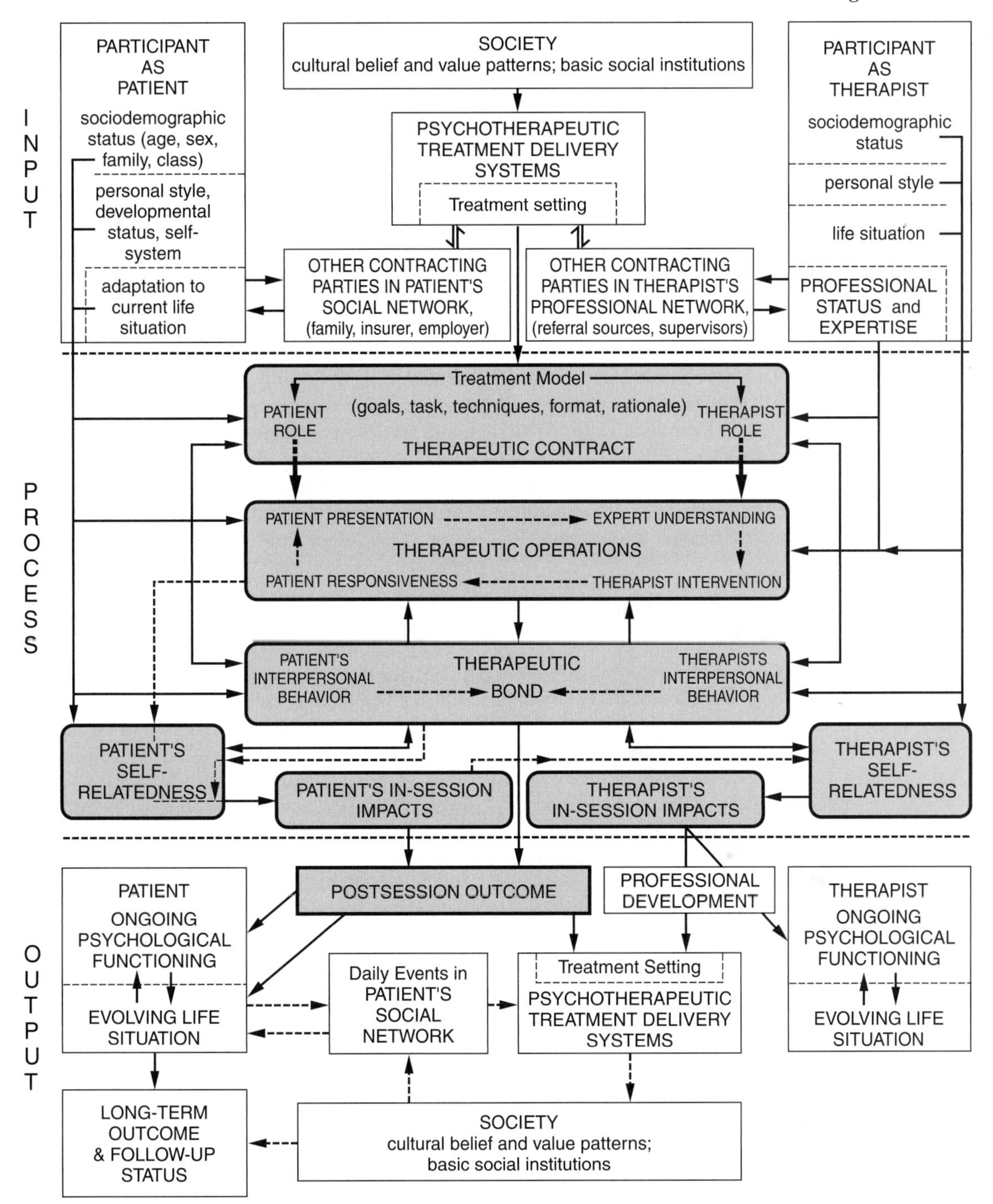

FIGURE 8.1 Generic model of psychotherapy: Integration of input, process, and output variables.

(together with other factors) influence how and what the patient presents to the therapist, how the therapist understands that presentation, what the therapist decides is an appropriate intervention, and how the patient responds to that intervention. The therapeutic bond also reciprocally influences the participants' self-relatedness in sessions and the patient's self-relatedness in particular functions as a filter to determine how much the patient's responses to the therapist's interventions are assimilated and realized as in-session impacts.

These and other hypotheses are described elsewhere (Orlinsky & Howard, 1987). Their systematic character and complexity should demonstrate that what was presented in the 1986 and 1994 versions of this chapter is more than a simple accounting of atomistically conceived "effective ingredients" in which each contributes separately to a final clinical outcome (Shapiro et al., 1994; Stiles & Shapiro, 1994). The value of the scheme as a conceptual model is indicated not only by its ability to synthesize the results of hundreds of process-outcome studies, but also by the hypotheses that have stimulated empirical studies (Ambühl, 1993; Foppa-Drew, 1989; Grawe, 1989a; Kolden, 1991, 1996; Kolden & Howard, 1992; Kolden et al., 2000; Saunders, 1998, 2000; Saunders, Howard, & Orlinsky, 1989) and have proven useful in theoretical discussions of the therapeutic process (Henry, 1996; Henry & Strupp, 1994) and therapy supervision (Rønnestad & Orlinsky, 2000).

Consistent Process-Outcome Findings: 1950–1992

By our count, a total of 2,354 separate process-outcome findings drawn from hundreds of studies was amassed in the four decades between 1950 and 1992. To understand this figure, one should take note of how we counted findings. A unitary finding was conceptualized as the assessed linkage of *one process variable measured from one observational perspective* with *an outcome variable measured from one observational perspective.* Our working assumption was that observational perspectives are relatively independent of one another—for example, that a patient's experience of therapist empathy *may* differ from the therapist's experience of empathy and that both of these *may* differ from ratings of therapist empathy made by external observers, and (on the other hand) that measures of patient outcome based on the patient's, therapist's, and independent judge's perspectives *may* differ from one another. This approach has served well in previous editions of this chapter. Whether and to what extent observations from different perspectives agree with respect to a particular variable remains an empirical question to be tested, rather than an assumption to be made, because the label placed on the variable in each case is nominally the same.

Viewed in another way, each variable was defined conceptually *and* methodologically with joint reference to its nominal content and the observational perspective from which it was assessed. If a process variable defined by a single concept (e.g., therapist empathy) was measured from two different observational perspectives (e.g., was rated by the patient and by an external judge), that would be counted as two variables. However, if two or more instruments were used to assess a variable from the same observational perspective (e.g., two patient-rated anxiety scales), they were viewed as equivalent and counted as one.

In our count of process-outcome findings, we noted the assessed relation between a specific process variable (as defined above) and a specific outcome variable (also as defined above), and we tabulated each finding no matter whether the association of the process variable and the outcome variable was determined to be significantly positive, significantly negative, or null (statistically nonsignificant). Typically, several process-outcome findings might be reported in a single study. The 2,354 findings noted for the period 1950–1992 were derived from nearly 500 studies. This vast accumulation reflected the emergence of a new stage in research-based knowledge about psychotherapy. More recent findings need to be viewed in the context of that cumulative body of knowledge. Accordingly, we first summarize the state of the field as described in the last edition of this *Handbook* using the categories of the Generic Model of Psychotherapy, with special emphasis on the most robustly consistent process-outcome findings.[4]

Therapeutic contract. In and of themselves, various *contractual provisions* showed no consistent relation to outcome (see Table 8.5). The record indicated that effective therapy can be conducted in different modalities (e.g., group vs. individual therapy), under different schedules (e.g., time-limited vs. unlimited treatment), and with varied term and fee arrangements. This lack of consistent relations between outcome and contractual provisions applies only to their study singly as main effects and does not rule out the possibility of significant interaction effects should combinations of contractual provisions be studied or should the effects of contractual provisions on outcome be studied in conjunction with other variables (e.g., type of patient population or level of patient impairment).

The record shows a different situation with regard to aspects of *contractual implementation* (see Table 8.7). Several variables met our criteria for consistency of findings, including *goal consensus* and *expectational clarity*, *patient role preparation*, *patient verbal activity, patient suitability for treatment,* and *therapist skill. Stability of treatment arrangements* and *therapist adherence to treatment model* showed promise for future research. The relations of patient suitability and therapist skill to outcome stand out as particularly robust, considering the consistency of findings across the various process perspectives from which they have been studied. Together the findings indicate that when an appropriately prepared patient who is viewed as suited to the form of treatment in question does become actively engaged in talking with a therapist who is seen as skillful, the result of therapy is likely to be regarded as beneficial.

THERAPEUTIC OPERATIONS. A larger number of findings is available with regard to several aspects of therapeutic operations. The *cognitive and behavioral processes* observable in the *patient's problem presentation* during sessions show a very high rate of significant positive association with outcome from every observational perspective that has been studied (see Table 8.9). Examples of such processes are the patients' ability to focus on issues of genuine concern, to sustain their focus on a topic, and to show action-oriented rather than state-oriented intentions. These processes probably reflect factors that are also related to judgments of the patient's suitability for treatment. Although the content of what patients talk about doesn't seem as important as the cognitive and behavioral processes they manifest, the evidence suggests that patients might do well to focus conversationally on their *life problems* and *core personal relationships.*

Findings on the complementary aspects of *therapists' expert understanding* are less consistent (see Table 8.11), but at least suggest that therapists can be helpful by focusing their interventions on *patient problems* and, with sufficient tact and caution, on *patients' affective responses* during sessions.

By contrast, the evidence is more decisive concerning modes of *therapist intervention* (see Table 8.13). *Experiential confrontation* (e.g., the Gestalt two-chair technique) appears to be a potent form of intervention across several process perspectives. *Interpretations* also appear to be a frequently beneficial intervention, at least when viewed from the patient's and rater's process perspectives (but, curiously, *not* the therapist's). Where *paradoxical intention* can be used appropriately, the evidence suggests that it is effectively related to outcome. Other therapist interventions and response modes (e.g., *exploration* and *clarification/reflection*) show a less consistent association with outcome.

Finally, process-outcome findings amply document the importance of *patient responsiveness* to therapist interventions (see Table 8.15). The evidence is especially strong with regard to *patient cooperation versus resistance* across three independent process perspectives but is also very consistent for *positive affective arousal.*

THERAPEUTIC BOND. The strongest evidence linking process to outcome concerns the therapeutic bond or alliance, reflecting more than 1,000 process-outcome findings. There are high rates of significant positive associations for large numbers of these findings across multiple process perspectives, both for the bond as a whole (see Table 8.17) and for its various constituent aspects. In the Generic Model, those aspects are defined as *personal role investment* and *interactive coordination,* viewed as complementary aspects of collaborative teamwork (see Tables 8.19 and 8.21), and *communicative attunement* and *mutual affirmation,* viewed as complementary aspects of personal rapport (see Tables 8.23 and 8.25). This finding is especially consistent when the bond is viewed from the patient's perspective.

PATIENT AND THERAPIST SELF-RELATEDNESS. Equally strong evidence links outcome to *patient openness versus defensiveness* (see Table 8.28). All observational perspectives on this process variable provide convincing evidence about its salience for outcome, which probably should be seen in conjunction with other patient variables, such as *patient suitability for treatment, patient cooperation* with therapist interventions, and *patient contribution to the bond.* Taken together, these variables document the critical importance of the patient's contribution to treatment, and by implication they also suggest how therapists can help patients make a constructive contribution to their own treatment.

IN-SESSION IMPACT. A consistent relation of *therapeutic realizations* (patients' positive in-session impacts) to outcome is evident from every process perspective except that of therapists (see Table 8.30). This lacuna in therapists' perceptiveness was particularly noticeable with respect to aspects of their own participation, such as the use of interpretive interventions and their own contributions to the therapeutic bond. Perhaps because therapists generally try their best with all their patients, they do not seem to discriminate the relatedness of these process factors to outcome.

SEQUENTIAL PATTERNS. The study of temporal factors in relation to outcome is at a very promising but early stage of development, except with respect to overall length of therapy. A large body of findings already indicates that longer *treatment duration* is very generally (though not linearly) associated with better outcome (see Table 8.32). Although positive effects can be documented for relatively brief episodes of psychotherapy, process-outcome research as well as followup outcome data suggest that patients often seek and generally benefit from additional care.

ROBUST PROCESS-OUTCOME FINDINGS. Cumulatively, based on replication of findings as a criterion, 11 types of process variables were found to be robustly linked to outcome, where significant associations were consistently found across multiple observational perspectives for both the process and outcome assessments (see Orlinsky, Grawe, & Parks, 1994, Tables 8.57 & 8.58). These are patient suitability, patient cooperativeness vs. resistance, global therapeutic bond (or group cohesion), patient contribution to the bond, patient interactive collaboration, patient expressiveness, patient affirmation of the therapist, reciprocal affirmation, patient openness vs. defensiveness, therapeutic realizations, and treatment duration.

Thus, the quality of the patient's participation in therapy appears to emerge as the most important determinant of outcome. The therapeutic bond, especially as perceived by the patient, is also importantly involved in mediating the process-outcome link. The therapist's contribution to helping the patient achieve a favorable outcome is made mainly through empathic, affirmative, collaborative, and self-congruent engagement with the patient, and through the timely and skillful application of potent interventions such as experiential confrontation, interpretation, and paradoxical intention.

These conclusions, reached in 1994, were based on the detailed analysis of hundreds of studies containing process-outcome findings, with respect to all observational perspectives on process in conjunction with all observational perspectives on outcome. By that time, more than 2,300 separate findings had been classified and conceptually integrated into a conceptual model that sought to meet the need expressed by Marsden (1971) in the first edition of this *Handbook:* "We now find ourselves possessed of a legion of findings badly in need of consolidation and integration" (p. 392). Since the last edition of the *Handbook*, this area of psychotherapy research has continued to flourish. Overall, 320 new publications appeared between 1993 and 2001 pertaining to process-outcome research, most of which were new studies that often each contained multiple process-outcome findings. The sheer volume and richness of this literature make a detailed and comprehensive analysis of findings practically unattainable. Our aim in this fifth edition of the *Handbook* is to provide readers instead with a conceptually organized introduction to the process-outcome research literature for these years, and to consider how much, and how, recent research has advanced our knowledge and understanding of effective psychotherapy.

CONTINUITY AND CHANGE: PROCESS-OUTCOME STUDIES, 1993–2001

To be included in our survey, a study had to report empirical relationships (positive, negative, or null) between actually measured process and actually measured outcome variables in actual cases of psychotherapy. Simply to set some boundary to our task and to be consistent with past practices in this chapter, these criteria led us to omit studies that used volunteer clients (unless they were shown to meet caseness criteria) or role-play therapists (unless they had been given some clinical training or supervision), as well as analogue studies in general (without meaning to impugn their potential value). We also excluded studies that simply stipulated a particular treatment in order to assess its efficacy or effectiveness but in which some aspect of the actual treatment process was not observed, or if observed (e.g., to assess treatment integrity) had not been related to assessments of outcome (for these, see the *Handbook*'s chapters on outcome research). Similarly, studies that examined the influence of patient or therapist characteristics on therapeutic processes but did not relate the process measures to outcome, were also excluded (e.g., Fonagy et al., 1996; Ford, Fisher, & Larson, 1997; Zlotnick, Elkin, & Shea, 1998). (For these and similar studies, see the *Handbook*'s chapters on patient and therapist variables.)

Unfortunately, our criteria this time, as in the past, led us to exclude a number of pure process studies. These are studies in which treatment processes were measured but were not related to outcome, either because outcomes were not assessed by our definition[5] or, if assessed (e.g., to demonstrate that the treatment was effective), had nevertheless not been examined in relation to measures of process. As a result, many interesting process studies that give valuable insights into the ways that therapy works have not been comprehensively reviewed in this *Handbook* for years. A few examples of such studies during the current period that were unfortunately excluded are those by Connolly et al. (1996); Goldfried, Raue, and Castonguay (1998); Greenberg, Ford, Alden, and Johnson (1993); and Honos-Webb, Stiles, Greenberg, and Goldman (1998). Readers interested in process research should also note the important special journal sections on process studies edited by Russell (1995) and by Greenberg and Newman (1996).

Two other types of research that often overlap with process research are not covered in this review. One consists of systematic single-case studies (see Jones, 1993), which can be highly revealing but difficult to weigh in relation to multisubject process-outcome studies. The other aspect of process research not included, in order to be consistent with past editions of this chapter, is purely qualitative research, which as noted earlier has grown in both volume and value during the last several years. On this subject, see Elliott (1989), Giorgi (1985), Hill, Thomspon, and Williams (1997), along with the qualitative studies already cited and others such as Hanna and Ritchie (1995), Varvin and Stiles (1999), Watson and Rennie (1994), and Werbart (1997a, 1997b).

Our strict inclusion criteria for process-outcome research nevertheless yielded a plethora of studies in the sources we examined. Likely English-language journals published in the United States, the United Kingdom, and Canada were systematically searched from January 1993 through December 2001, as were likely journals published in Germany and the Scandinavian countries. Relevant papers that may have been published elsewhere, often outside the notice of English readers, were also solicited from European colleagues to ensure optimal access to recent *process-outcome research*. To find relevant publications in the German-language area (Germany, Austria, and German-speaking Switzerland), close to 200 researchers working in clinical psychology, psychotherapy, psychosomatics, psychiatry, and medical psychology were sent a letter (by U.W.) requesting them to notify us of their relevant research. These people were mainly picked from the list of academic institutions and members in the German psychology registry (Hogrefe) as well as the membership rosters of the German Collegium for Psychosomatic Medicine (DKPM) and the Society of Psychotherapy Research (SPR). As a result, 294 papers and a number of references were sent to us from both German-language and international publications, although most of these did not meet our criteria for process-outcome findings. In addition, a number of German-language journals were systematically searched from 1993 through summer 2001, as listed in Table 8.3. In order to find relevant publications in the Nordic language area (Denmark, Finland, Norway, and Sweden), key informants were asked via e-mail (by M.H.R.) to provide lists of psychotherapy researchers. E-mails requesting psychotherapy process-outcome studies were sent to 41 people who returned 29 papers and numerous references, the majority of which did not satisfy our inclusion criteria. All papers received were written in English. Selected Nordic journals were systematically reviewed to ensure inclusion of research that satisfied our criteria, as listed in Table 8.3. We thank the following colleagues in the United Kingdom for advice concerning English journals that should be scanned (M. Aveline, E. Guthrie, F. Margison, T. Schröder, and D.A. Shapiro), and we offer apologies to colleagues everywhere whose work we inadvertently overlooked.

Table 8.3 summarizes the sources from which a rich harvest of studies was drawn for our review. Twenty-seven journals were systematically searched; 23 from January 1993 through the latest available issue in 2001, and 3 more for slightly shorter periods. Four journals yielded more than 20 studies meeting our criteria for process-outcome findings, and nine yielded 10 or more. The *Journal of Consulting and Clinical Psychology* was the single largest source during the years reviewed,[6] followed by *Psychotherapy Research*, *Behaviour Research and Therapy*, and the *Journal of Counseling Psychology*. Two of the eight journals yielding 10 or more studies are published in German, underlining the need to give access to them for researchers who do not read German.[7] Two more of the highest yielding journals are devoted primarily to behavioral research, which marks a welcome broadening of the sphere in which process-outcome research findings now appear. Overall, we accessed a total of 321 sources, including 279 articles and 42 empirical research reviews and meta-analyses, added to the process-outcome literature since the last edition of the *Handbook*.[8] More than a third of *all* the process-outcome studies published since 1950 have appeared in the nine years since our last review. We

TABLE 8.3 Sources of Studies Containing Process-Outcome Findings

Journal	Years	N
Searched Systematically:		
Journal of Consulting and Clinical Psychology	1993–2001[b]	79
Psychotherapy Research	1993–2001	36
Behaviour Research and Therapy	1993–2002[b]	23
Journal of Counseling Psychology	1993–2001	21
Psychotherapy	1993–2001	17
Z. für Klinische Psychologie → Z. für Klin. Psych. & Psychotherapie[a]	1993–2002[b]	16
Behavior Therapy	1993–1997	13
Clinical Psychology Science and Practice	1997–2001	11
Psychotherapie, Psychosomatik, Medizinische Psychologie	1993–2001[b]	10
British Journal of Psychiatry	1993–2001	9
Cognitive Therapy and Research	1993–2000	8
Journal of Clinical Psychology	1993–2001	7
Z. für Klinische Psychologie, Psychopathologie und Psychotherapie, Z. für Klin. Psych., Psychiatrie und Psychotherapie[a]	1992–2001[b]	5
British Journal of Clinical Psychology	1993–2001	5
British Journal of Medical Psychology	1993–2001	4
Verhaltenstherapie	1993–2001[b]	4
Clinical Psychology and Psychotherapy	1997–2001	3
Acta Psychiatrica Scandinavia	1996–2001	2
Archives of General Psychiatry	1993–2001	2
Other Sources	—	
Books and collections		21
Conference papers and dissertations		4
Other Journals: Two Process-Outcome Studies	as listed	6
Gesellschaft für wissenschaftliche Gesprächspsychotherapie-Zeitschrift (1995–1996); *J. of Psychotherapy Practice and Research* (1993); *Verhaltenstherapie und psychosoziale Praxis* (1999)		
Other Journals: One Process-Outcome Study	as listed	15
American J. of Psychotherapy (1993); *Group* (1997); *Gruppenpsychotherapie und Gruppendynamik* (2002[b]); *International J. of Group Psychotherapy* (1994); *International J. of Psychoanalysis* (2000); *J. of Clinical Child Psychology* (1997); *J. of Cognitive Psychotherapy* (1992); *J. of Constructivist Psychology* (2001); *J. of Nervous and Mental Disease* (1998); *J. of Personality Disorder* (1996); *Nordic J. of Psychiatry* (1997); *Psychological Bulletin* (1990); *Verhaltenstherapie und Verhaltensmedizin* (2000); *Verhaltenstherapie und Verhaltensmodifikation* (2000); *Z. für Psychosomatische Medizin und Psychotherapie* (2002[b]).		
Searched Systematically Journals: No Process-Outcome Studies		0
Canadian Psychology (1993–2001[b]); *The Counseling Psychologist* (1993–2001[b]); *J. Counseling & Development* (1993–2001[b]); *Nordisk Psykologi* (1993–2001); *Professional Psychology* (1993–2001); *Psychotherapeut* (1993–2001); *Scandinavian J. of Psychology* (1993–2001); *Tidsskrift for Norsk Psykologforening* (1993–2001).		

[a] Indicates change of journal's name.

[b] Final year not complete.

present this large body of recent research next, organized in terms of the process facets defined in the Generic Model of Psychotherapy.

Therapeutic Contract

Research relating outcome to the organizational facet of therapeutic process can be divided into findings concerning contractual provisions, which define the basic frame in which therapy occurs, and findings involving contractual implementation or the manner and extent to which provisions were carried out in practice.

Contractual Provisions

Contractual provisions stipulate where and when the treatment is to take place *(treatment context);* whether it is to be individual therapy or a form of therapy including more than one patient, for example, group or family therapy *(treatment modality);* how and how much the therapist is to

TABLE 8.4 Therapeutic Contract: Provisions

1. *Treatment Context: Setting* [Inpatient vs. Outpatient; Clinic vs. Home]
   Burns, Beadsmore, Bhat, Olive, & Mathers (1993)
   Burns, Raferty, Beadsmoore, McGuigan, & Dickson (1993)
   DeJong-Meyer, Hautzinger, Rudolf, Strauss, & Frick (1996a, 1996b)
   Hautzinger, DeJong-Meyer, Treiber, Rudolf, & Thien (1996)
   Hautzinger, DeJong-Meyer, Treiber, Rudolf, Thien, & Bailer (1996)
   Latimer, Newcomb, Winters, & Stinchfield (2000)
   Rychtarik et al. (2000)
   Sennekamp & Hautzinger (1994)
   Speer (1994)
   Von Rad, Senf, & Bräutigam (1998)
   — (meta-analyses/reviews) —
   Heimberg & Juster (1995)
   Stanley & Turner (1995)

2. *Treatment Modality: Collectivity* [Individual vs. Group or Family]
   Emanuels-Zuurveen & Emmelkamp (1996)
   Fals-Stewart, Birchler, & O'Farrell (1996)
   Flannery-Schroeder & Kendall (2000)
   Frettlöh & Kröner-Herwig (1999)
   Lucas & Telch (1993)
   McFarlane et al. (2000)
   Öst (1996) [group size]
   Scholing & Emmelkamp (1993, 1996)
   Shadish et al. (1993)
   Stangicr, Heidenreich, & Peitz (2001)
   Turner, Beidel, Cooley, Woody, & Messer (1994)
   Winter, Nieschalk, & Stoll (1996)
   Wlazlo, Schroeder-Hartwig, Münchau, Kaiser, & Hand (1992)
   — (meta-analyses/reviews) —
   Antonuccio, Thomas, & Danton (1997)
   Bretz, Heekerens, & Schmitz (1994)
   Forsyth & Corazzini (2000)
   Fuhriman & Burlingame (1994)
   Gould, Otto, Pollack, & Yap (1997)
   Hoag & Burlingame (1997)
   Jacobi, Dahme, & Rustenbach (1997)
   McDermut, Miller, & Brown (2001)
   Robinson, Berman, & Neimeyer (1990)

(continues)

TABLE 8.4 ***(Continued)***

3. Compensation: Fee
Sandell et al. (2000)

4. Time: Session Duration
Turner, Valtierra, Talken, Miller, & DeAnda (1996)

5. Time: Schedule [Session Frequency]
Avants, Margolin, Kosten, Rounsaville, & Schottenfeld (1998)
Goren (1993)
Kächele, Kordy, Richard, & Research Group TR-EAT (2001)
Rowe & Craske (1998)
Sandell et al. (2000)

6. Time: Term [Time-Limited vs. Unlimited]
James, Thorn, & Williams (1993)
Reynolds et al. (1996)
Smyrnios & Kirkby (1993)

7. Adjuncts: Use of Patient Self-Monitoring
Baker & Kirschenbaum (1993)
Cote, Gauthier, Laberge, Cormier, & Plamondon (1994)
Gould, Clum, & Shapiro (1993)
Grant & Cash (1995)
Treasure et al. (1996)
— (meta-analyses/reviews) —
Abramowitz (1996)
Kazantzis, Deane, & Ronan (2000)
Rowan & Andrasik (1996)
Stanley & Turner (1995)

8. Adjuncts: Third-Party Involvement [Parent; Partner]
Kendall (1994)
Lauth (1996)
Nauta, Scholing, Emmelkamp, & Minderaa (2001)
— (meta-analyses/reviews) —
Stanley & Turner (1995)

9. Adjuncts: Use of Maintenance/Booster Sessions
Jarrett et al. (1998)
McKay (1997)
McKay et al. (1997)
— (meta-analyses/reviews) —
Eyberg, Edwards, Boggs, & Foote (1998)
Weissman (1994)

10. Adjuncts: Progress Monitoring Feedback to Therapist
Lambert et al. (2001)

be paid *(compensation);* how long each session should last, how frequently they should occur and whether there should be a limited or unlimited number of sessions *(timing);* and so forth.

In contrast to past chapters, where no studies were found that examined the relation of outcome to *treatment setting,* 10 studies were found that did so during the current period, in addition to two meta-analysis or review papers (Table 8.4.1). These studies offered contrasts between therapy conducted in inpatient and outpatient settings, and between therapy conducted in clinic or home set-

TABLE 8.5 Therapeutic Contract—Findings on Contractual Provisions (1950–1992)

1. Therapeutic Collectivity: Dyad versus Group[a]			*Outcome*			
	Patient	Therapist	Rater	Score	Combined	Total
	– 0 +	– 0 +	– 0 +	– 0 +	– 0 +	– 0 +
Ind.> Grp.	0 2 2	0 4 1	1 4 1	1 12 2	0 0 0	2 22 6
2. Fees: Normal versus Reduced[b]				*Outcome*		
	Patient	Therapist	Rater	Score	Combined	Total
	– 0 +	– 0 +	– 0 +	– 0 +	– 0 +	– 0 +
Hi> Lo	0 4 0	0 3 1	0 0 0	0 1 2	0 1 0	0 9 3
3. Schedule of Sessions: Weekly versus Other[c]				*Outcome*		
	Patient	Therapist	Rater	Score	Combined	Total
	– 0 +	– 0 +	– 0 +	– 0 +	– 0 +	– 0 +
wk > other	2 3 2	0 2 1	0 2 0	2 10 1	0 0 0	4 17 4
4. Contractual Term: Time-Limited versus Unlimited[d]				*Outcome*		
	Patient	Therapist	Rater	Score	Combined	Total
	– 0 +	– 0 +	– 0 +	– 0 +	– 0 +	– 0 +
lim>unlim	0 1 2	0 1 0	0 0 0	3 3 2	0 0 0	3 5 4
5. Role Preparation for Patient[e]				*Outcome*		
	Patient	Therapist	Rater	Score	Combined	Total
Process	– 0 +	– 0 +	– 0 +	– 0 +	– 0 +	– 0 +
Prep>No	0 9 5	0 3 5	0 1 4	0 5 10	0 0 0	0 18 24

[a] + = outcome of individual therapy superior to group or other therapy modality; – = outcome of individual therapy inferior to group or other therapy modality.

[b] + = fee level positively associated with outcome; – = fee level negatively associated with outcome.

[c] + = outcome for once-weekly sessions superior to other schedules; – = outcome for once-weekly sessions inferior to other schedules.

[d] + = outcome of time-limited therapy superior to unlimited therapy; – = unlimited therapy superior to time-limited therapy.

[e] + = role preparation associated with positive outcome; – = role preparation associated with negative outcome.

tings. The results suggest that setting does not make a significant difference overall. The qualification to this statement is "other things being equal," although a number of interaction effects suggest otherwise and thus encourage further research. For example, in a study of depression, DeJong-Meyer, Hautzinger, Rudolf, Strauss, & Frick (1996a) reported that patients with endogenous depression profited more from an inpatient treatment than from a similar outpatient treatment, whereas patients with a diagnosis of unipolar nonendogenous depression profited more from outpatient treatment (Hautzinger, DeJong-Meyer, Treiber, Rudolf, & Thien, 1996). The difficulty of such research is that setting is readily confounded with other variables that need to be assessed—for example, patients' level of impairment and the differential dosage of therapy within equivalent treatment durations (inpatient settings typically providing more intensive therapeutic contact).

More thorough investigation has been devoted to the relation of outcome to *treatment modality* or "collectivity," that is, to the size and composition of the social unit in which therapy is conducted, from the one-patient/one-therapist dyad to forms involving several related patients (family therapy) or multiple unrelated and unacquainted patients (group therapy). Nineteen studies and four meta-analyses comparing group and individual therapy had accumulated by 1992 (Table 8.5.1), and since then another 13 studies have been added (Table 8.4.2). The fact that nine meta-analyses and reviews of findings were also published during this period indicates how great the interest has been in comparing treatment modalities. The general impression from the newer studies is much the same as from earlier research: overall there does not appear to be a consistent difference in effectiveness between individual and group therapy (also see the chapter on group research elsewhere in this volume). However, although most studies show no significant difference, group treatment fares better in some cases (Frettlöh & Kröner-Herwig, 1999; Wlazlo, Schroeder-Hartwig Münchau, Kaiser, & Hand, 1992), while in others patients profit more from individual therapy (Winter, Nieschalk, & Stoll, 1996). Moreover, long-cherished assumptions about what setting is good for which patient may not hold; for example, in the treatment of social anxiety where a group setting traditionally is assumed to offer the ideal learning context and is rarely compared to individual treatment, the study by Stangier, Heidenreich, & Peitz (2001) showed that individual treatment was clearly better at treatment termination and followup. It should also be kept in mind that none of these studies analyzed the specific healing factors of the group (e.g., those described by Yalom, 1970), which might be expected to show some additional advantages of group treatment.

The relation to outcome of how much and by whom therapists are paid for treatment was previously examined in nine studies (Table 8.5.2), most of which found it had no significant impact, and in this period just one study was found that investigated the effects of *compensation* (Table 8.4.3). Sandell et al. (2000) performed a series of path analyses on clients who had terminated psychoanalytic treatment, and they found that neither amount of money spent nor subsidization showed any direct relationship to outcome. In that study, financial variables exerted their influence by allowing patients more freedom of choice, typically enabling them to choose longer treatments. The authors noted that their findings do not support the psychoanalytic assumption that patients who pay their own fees are more motivated and take more responsibility for their share of treatment.

Contractual provisions about the timing of therapy sessions determine their length, frequency, and number.[9] There were only a few studies concerning any of these provisions in the current period: only one on *session duration* (Table 8.4.4), which seems hitherto not to have been studied at all; five on *session frequency* (Table 8.4.5), which join 14 previous studies (Table 8.5.3); and just three comparing *time-limited versus unlimited treatments* (Table 8.4.6), which add a bit to eight prior studies (Table 8.5.4). The verdict of those multiple studies is quite mixed, suggesting that whatever influence schedule provisions may have on outcome likely occurs through interaction with other variables (e.g., type of therapy and overall length of treatment). For example, the study of psychoanalytic treatment by Sandell et al. (2000) found that greater session frequency had a small negative effect in therapies of short duration, whereas there was an increasingly positive effect of increasing frequency the longer that treatments lasted, although the differences still did not appear before the three-year followup. Furthermore, given the popularity of time-limited treatments, it seems odd that relatively few studies have been done on differences in outcome between limited and unlimited formats controlling for the effects of treatment duration.

A few studies touched on each of several additional topics that can be considered as contractual provisions, typically in connection with behavioral treatments. Prominent among these was the inclusion of *patient self-monitoring* (Table 8.4.7) as a useful adjunct to or replacement for therapist contact, which was examined in five studies and in no less than four reviews.

Three studies and one review focused on the effects on treatment outcome of *involving a third party* (such as a parent of child patients or the partner of an adult patient) without necessarily redefining the treatment modality as family or marital therapy (Table 8.4.8).

Another modification of behavioral and cognitive behavioral treatment that was investigated in three studies and two reviews is the use of *"post-treatment" booster sessions* as an effective way to maintain or enhance the benefits derived from treatment, although this of course can also be viewed as extending the period of treatment (and the therapeutic relationship) with a reduced schedule of sessions (Table 8.4.9).

Finally, one study that seems to hold great promise for future practice, especially in the managed care setting (Table 8.4.10), showed that ongoing *monitoring of patient progress with feedback to therapists* can make a significant contribution to improving quality of care (Lambert et al., 2001).

One topic that previous studies had shown to be consequential but that has received no further attention is a contractual provision that bears directly on contractual implementation: the use of *preparatory role-induction* or orientation procedures (Table 8.5.5). More often than not, pretreatment orientation procedures enhanced outcome significantly, especially for first-time patients or patients to whom therapy is culturally unfamiliar, as well as for therapists having little experience with specific patient populations and cultures.

Contractual Implementation

Many more studies assessed the relation of outcome to how well the provisions of the therapeutic contract were carried out in practice. With respect to the *therapist role*, these studies focused primarily on the therapist's adherence to a specified treatment model or set of treatment goals, and the therapist's observed skillfulness or competence in conducting treatment (also see the chapter by Beutler et al. on therapist variables in this volume).

Six studies and one review examined outcome as a function of *therapist adherence* (Table 8.6.A1), a topic that had not yet received attention in the last edition. Although assessments of adherence or treatment fidelity are not new in psychotherapy research, relating those assessments to outcome was something of an innovation in the studies cited, with indications of a modest but positive association (Beutler et al., this volume). However, *therapist skillfulness* was already a topic of considerable interest by the late 1980s, with 22 studies cited in the last edition of this chapter (Table 8.7.1), and the trend continues with another 17 studies reported since 1993 (Table 8.6.A2). The earlier studies suggest that therapist competence, observed in practice, and adherence are both significantly and favorably related to outcome, although more recent results appear more mixed (Beutler et al., this volume).

Two other aspects of therapist role implementation drew less attention from researchers than they deserve. One is the amount and nature of the *therapist's verbal behavior* as a participant in the therapeutic dialogue. Five new studies (Table 8.6.A3) add to 19 previously cited with findings in this area (Table 8.7.2). The other aspect is the important issue of *repairing alliance ruptures*, which only one study examined in relation to outcome (Table 8.6.A4).

Studies of contractual implementation regarding the *patient role* include a focus on the patient's suitability for treatment (or, correlatively, the credibility of treatment with respect to the patient), the patient's expectations in treatment, the patient's verbal behavior as a participant in the therapeutic dialogue, the patient's compliance with homework assignments (where those are used), and the way that the patient terminates treatment.

Eleven publications (Table 8.6.B1) add new evidence to 22 previous studies (Table 8.7.3) linking outcome to the degree of fit between patient and treatment (i.e., *patient suitability and treatment credibility*,) a topic that most recently has been investigated mainly in the context of cognitive behavioral treatments. The overall impression is that positive judgments of suitability/credibility, usually made early in therapy, more often than not predict favorable outcome.

Another much studied and clearly related aspect of contractual implementation concerns the linkage of *patients' expectations* about treatment to outcome. Fourteen recent studies (Table 8.6.B2) produced evidence on this topic, which doubles the number of previous studies in this area (Table 8.7.4). In addition, one current and one slightly older review assess the accumulated findings in this area, which overlaps to some extent with questions about goal and task consensus studied as an element of the therapeutic alliance (see Table 8.20.3).

The relation of outcome to the *patient's verbal behavior* in therapy extends beyond the amount of talk to various qualities of conversation such as timing, initiative in bringing up topics, and verbalization of emotion. Five new publications from European investigators (Table 8.6.B3) add further knowledge beyond the eight studies cited in previous editions (Table 8.7.5). Generally, it has been found that patients who talk more tend to have better outcomes, but these recent studies follow more differentiated conceptualizations which suggest that this can be a rich area for researchers to explore.

The study of *homework compliance* in relation to outcome obviously is limited to the primarily cognitive behavioral treatments that use this method, and is a relatively recent development. Twelve new studies (Table 8.6.B4) can be added to three reported in the last edition (Burns & Nolen-Hoeksema, 1991; Persons, Burns, & Perloff, 1988; Worthington, 1986), along with other studies of "patient cooperation" listed under Therapeutic Operations (Table 8.14.A1). Homework assignments might also be considered as a type of intervention under that general heading, but since it mainly involves patient activity, we include it here and emphasize varying degrees of compliance as an aspect of patient role implementation.

The effect on outcome of how *termination* comes about (e.g., prematurely or at the expected

TABLE 8.6 Therapeutic Contract: Implementation

A. Therapist Implementation

1. *Therapist Adherence to Model/Goals*
   Barber, Crits-Christoph, & Luborsky (1996)
   Bright, Baker, & Neimeyer (1999)
   Dürr & Hahlweg (1996)
   Henggeler, Melton, Brondino, Scherer, & Hanley (1997)
   Huey, Henggeler, Brondino, & Pickrel (2000)
   Schulte-Bahrenberg & Schulte (1993)
   — (meta-analyses/reviews) —
   Durham & Allan (1993)

2. *Therapist Skill (Competence/Control) vs. Difficulties*
   Barber, Crits-Christoph, & Luborsky (1996)
   Bassler & Krauthauser (1996)
   Bright, Baker, & Neimeyer (1999)
   Dick, Grawe, Regli, & Heim (1999)
   Dreessen & Arntz (1999)
   Dürr & Hahlweg (1996)
   Eugster & Wampold (1996)
   Margraf, Barlow, Clark, & Telch (1993)
   Regli, Bieber, Mathier, & Grawe (2000)
   Ryle & Golynkina (2000)
   Schulte & Künzel (1995)
   Shaw et al. (1999)
   Smith & Grawe (2000)
   Smith, Regli, & Grawe (1999)
   Svartberg & Stiles (1994)
   Svartberg, Seltzer, & Stiles (1996, 1998)
   Willutzki, Hernandez-Bark, Davis, & Orlinsky (1997)

3. *Therapist Verbal Behavior* [Activity, Initiative]
   Anderson, Bein, Pinnell, & Strupp (1999)
   Eyssell, Zeising, & Stuhr (1992)
   Hölzer, Mergenthaler, Pokorny, Kächele, & Luborsky (1996)
   Hölzer, Pokorny, Kächele, & Luborsky (1997)
   Schulte & Künzel (1995)

4. *Therapist Repair of Alliance Rupture*
   — (meta-analyses/reviews) —
   Safran, Murran, Samstag, & Stevens (2002)

B. Patient Implementation

1. *Patient Suitability for Treatment* [Treatment Credibility]
   Addis & Jacobson (1996)
   Durham, Allan, & Hackett (1997)
   Hardy, Barkham, Shapiro, Reynolds, & Rees (1995)
   Hellström & Öst (1996)
   Margraf, Barlow, Clark, & Telch (1993)
   Öst, Stridh, & Wolf (1998)
   Priebe (1993)
   Priebe & Gruyters (1995)
   Safran, Segal, Vallis, Shaw, & Samstag (1993)
   Schoenberger, Kirsch, Gearan, Montgomery, & Pastyrnak (1997)
   Tarrier et al. (1999)

(continues)

TABLE 8.6 *(Continued)*

2. *Patient Expectations*
   Addis & Jacobson (2000)
   Anderson & Strupp (1996) [awareness of being in study]
   Archer, Forbes, Metcalfe, & Winter (2000)
   Clark et al. (1999)
   DeJong-Meyer, Hautzinger, Rudolf, Strauss, & Frick (1996b)
   Durham, Allan, & Hackett (1997)
   Feeston et al. (1997)
   Hautzinger et al. (1996)
   Ladouceur et al. (2000)
   Mueller & Pekarik (2000)
   Priebe & Gruyters (1995)
   Safren, Heimberg, & Juster (1997)
   Schoenberger, Kirsch, Gearan, Montgomery, & Pastyrnak (1997)
   Spanos et al. (1993)
   — (meta-analyses/reviews) —
   Arnkoff, Glass, & Shapiro (2002)
   Durham & Allan (1993)

3. *Patient Verbal Behavior* [Activity, Initiative]
   Fiedler, Albrecht, Rogge, & Schulte (1996)
   Hölzer, Mergenthaler, Pokorny, Kächele, & Luborsky (1996)
   Schulte & Künzel (1995)
   Stiles, Agnew-Davies, Hardy, Barkham, & Shapiro (1998)
   Strauss, Kröger, Hoffmann, & Burgmeier-Lohse (1994)

4. *Patient Homework Compliance*
   Addis & Jacobson (1996, 2000)
   Bryant, Simons, & Thase (1999)
   Burns & Spangler (1999)
   Edelman & Chambless (1993, 1995)
   Leung & Heimberg (1996)
   Margraf, Barlow, Clark, & Telch (1993)
   Peters, Plöhn, Buhk, & Dahme (1998)
   Schmidt & Woolaway-Bickel (2000)
   Startup & Edmonds (1994)
   Troop et al. (1996)
   — (meta-analyses/reviews) —
   Kazantzis, Deane, & Ronan (2000)

5. *Termination [Premature vs. Completed]*
   Tasca et al. (1999)

completion of treatment) was the subject of five previous studies (Table 8.7.6), to which only one was added in the recent period (Table 8.6.B5). In that study, patients in a partial hospitalization program who completed treatment had better outcomes, but the results of previous studies suggest that while proper handling of termination can be important, it is probably what happens in therapy prior to termination that has most impact.

Therapeutic Operations

Studies of the implementation of patient and therapist roles as defined in a Therapeutic Contract lead naturally to consideration of Therapeutic Operations, which comprise the technical "business" that patient and therapist contracted to conduct with one another. In the Generic Model of Psychotherapy, the events most relevant to this process facet are distinguished into four "moments" or steps, which occur more or less

Table 8.7 Therapeutic Contract—Findings on Contractual Implementation (1950–1992)

1. Therapist's Skillfulness[a] — *Outcome*

Process	Patient			Therapist			Rater			Score			Combined			Total		
	–	0	+	–	0	+	–	0	+	–	0	+	–	0	+	–	0	+
Patient	0	5	6	0	0	2	0	0	0	0	2	2	0	0	0	0	7	10
Therapist	0	0	0	0	0	2	0	0	0	0	0	0	0	0	0	0	0	2
Rater	0	1	2	0	0	2	0	3	5	0	0	0	0	1	3	0	5	12
Total	0	6	8	0	0	6	0	3	5	0	2	2	0	1	3	0	12	24

2. Therapist's Verbal Activity[b] — *Outcome*

Process	Patient			Therapist			Rater			Score			Combined			Total		
	–	0	+	–	0	+	–	0	+	–	0	+	–	0	+	–	0	+
Patient	1	1	0	0	1	0	0	0	0	0	0	0	0	0	2	1	2	2
Therapist	0	1	0	1	1	0	0	0	0	0	0	0	0	0	0	1	2	0
Rater	0	1	0	0	1	0	0	3	2	0	1	2	0	1	1	0	7	5
Index	0	1	2	0	2	2	0	0	0	1	5	1	0	0	1	1	8	6
Total	1	4	2	1	5	2	0	3	2	1	6	3	0	1	4	3	19	13

3. Patient's Suitability for Treatment[c] — *Outcome*

Process	Patient			Therapist			Rater			Score			Combined			Total		
	–	0	+	–	0	+	–	0	+	–	0	+	–	0	+	–	0	+
Patient	0	0	1	0	0	1	0	0	1	0	0	0	0	1	0	0	1	3
Therapist	0	4	2	0	2	7	0	1	3	0	2	6	0	0	0	0	9	18
Rater	0	0	0	0	0	1	0	1	4	0	2	1	0	0	0	0	3	6
Total	0	4	3	0	2	9	0	2	8	0	4	7	0	1	0	0	13	27

4. Patient Expectational Clarity/Goal Consensus[d] — *Outcome*

Process	Patient			Therapist			Rater			Score			Combined			Total		
	–	0	+	–	0	+	–	0	+	–	0	+	–	0	+	–	0	+
Patient	0	1	2	0	0	1	0	0	0	0	2	2	0	0	0	0	3	5
Therapist	0	1	0	1	2	0	0	0	1	0	2	0	0	0	0	1	5	1
Rater	0	0	1	0	0	1	0	3	1	0	1	1	0	0	0	0	4	4
Index	0	2	1	0	0	4	0	0	0	0	1	2	0	1	1	0	4	8
Total	0	4	4	1	2	6	0	3	2	0	6	5	0	1	1	1	16	18

5. Patient Verbal Activity[e] — *Outcome*

Process	Patient			Therapist			Rater			Score			Combined			Total		
	–	0	+	–	0	+	–	0	+	–	0	+	–	0	+	–	0	+
Patient	0	2	1	0	1	1	0	1	1	0	0	4	0	0	0	0	4	7

6. Termination Procedures[f] — *Outcome*

Process	Patient			Therapist			Rater			Score			Combined			Total		
	–	0	+	–	0	+	–	0	+	–	0	+	–	0	+	–	0	+
Therapist	0	0	0	0	1	2	0	2	0	0	1	2	0	0	0	0	4	4
Rater	0	0	0	0	0	0	0	4	0	0	2	0	0	0	0	0	6	0
Index	0	1	1	0	1	0	0	0	1	0	1	0	0	0	0	0	3	2
Total	0	1	1	0	2	2	0	6	1	0	4	2	0	0	0	0	13	6

[a] + = therapist skillfulness positively related to outcome; – = negatively related to outcome.

[b] + = therapist verbal activity positively related to outcome; – = negatively related to outcome.

[c] + = patient suitability for treatment associated with positive outcome, or patient unsuitability associated with negative outcome; – = patient suitability for treatment associated with negative outcome or patient unsuitability associated with positive outcome.

[d] + = patient expectations and clarity/contractual consensus associated with positive outcome; – = expectations and clarity/contractual associated with negative outcome.

[e] 1950–1986: + = patient verbal activity positively related to outcome; – = negatively related to outcome.

[f] + = mutual planned termination associated with positive outcome, or premature termination associated with negative outcome; – = mutual planned termination associated with negative outcome, or premature termination associated with positive outcome.

continuously and simultaneously as therapeutic transactions unfold. The four moments are patient presentation, therapist understanding, therapist intervention, and patient responsiveness (as explained earlier). Each is then differentiated more finely in terms of the particular process variables that researchers have studied in each area.

Patient Presentation

The person who participates in therapy in the role of patient (or client, counselee, analysand, etc.) is presumed, by virtue of that role, to present some sort of problem that becomes the therapist's job to understand and treat. The patient's presentation of that problem to the therapist occurs in various ways during sessions: in the topical focus of the patient's conversation, in the patient's behavior with the therapist, and in the cognitive and affective processes manifested in the patient's communications and interactions.

Several recent studies examined the relation of outcome to the topics on which patient presentations focused. In this respect, five studies from the Bernese team led by K. Grawe considered the patient's *focusing on problems* (Table 8.8.A1) with somewhat mixed results, although eight previous studies had suggested a moderately consistent, though not strong, association with favorable outcome (Table 8.9.1).

Another four studies examined outcome as a function of patients' *focusing on interpersonal patterns and attitudes* (Table 8.8.A2), some using Luborsky's well-known Core Conflictual Relationship Theme (CCRT) model (Luborsky & Crits-Christoph, 1990).

Two studies also focused on the impact of patients' *affective focus* by examining their verbalization of emotions in the therapeutic dialogue (Table 8.8.A3).

We note that there was no further research on the effects of the patient's *here-and-now focus* on issues in the therapeutic situation itself, a topic that six earlier studies had shown to be unpromising (Table 8.9.2).

The patient's presentation of therapeutically relevant "material" occurs through behavior as well as speech. Of prime relevance here is the extent to which patients *disclose* themselves in sessions or, conversely, conceal themselves via secrets and omissions, which was an issue explored in four pioneering studies (Table 8.8.B1). This issue is conceptually related to the question of patient role-engagement as an aspect of the Therapeutic Bond (Table 8.18.2).

Table 8.8. Therapeutic Operations: Patient Presentation

A. Presentation Focus

1. *Problem Focus*
   Dick (1999)
   Dick, Grawe, Regli, & Heim (1999)
   Regli, Bieber, Mathier, & Grawe (2000)
   Smith & Grawe (2000)
   Smith, Regli, & Grawe (1999)

2. *Interpersonal Focus [Attitudes; Patterns]*
   Clarke & Llewelyn (1994)
   Grenyer & Luborsky (1996)
   McMullen & Conway (1994, 1997)
   Strauss et al. (1995)

3. *Affect Focus*
   Hölzer, Pokorny, Kächele, & Luborsky (1997)
   Merten (2001)

B. Presentation Behavior

1. *Self-Disclosure vs. Secrets/Omissions*
   Hahn, Achter, & Shambaugh (2001)
   Hill, Thompson, Cogar, & Denman (1993)
   Stiles & Shapiro (1994)
   Tschuschke & Dies (1994)

2. *Transference Reactions*
   Gelso, Kivlighan, Wine, Jones, & Friedman (1997)
   Patton, Kivlighan, & Multon (1997)

3. *Family Interaction Quality [in Family Therapy]*
   Dürr & Hahlweg (1996)

C. Cognitive/Affective Processes

1. *Quality of Cognitive/Affective Processing*
   DeJong-Meyer et al. (1999)
   Hoppe (1993)
   Mergenthaler (1996)
   Schulte, Hartung, & Wilke (1997)
   Stiles, Shankland, Wright, & Field (1997)
   Znoj, Grawe, & Jeger (2000)

2. *Negative Attitudes*
   Greene & Blanchard (1994)
   Hatcher & Barends (1996)

The key psychoanalytic concept of *transference* also bears on the way patients present essential information through their behavior toward the therapist during sessions. Sophisticated empirical analyses of outcome in relation to transference behavior were reported in two publications from

TABLE 8.9 Therapeutic Operations—Findings on Patient Presentation (1950–1992)

1. Patient Focus on Life Problems[a] — *Outcome*

	Patient			Therapist			Rater			Score			Combined			Total		
Process	–	0	+	–	0	+	–	0	+	–	0	+	–	0	+	–	0	+
Patient	0	1	2	0	0	0	0	0	0	0	0	0	0	0	0	0	1	2
Therapist	0	0	0	0	1	0	0	0	1	0	0	0	0	0	0	0	1	1
Rater	0	1	0	0	0	0	0	1	1	0	0	2	0	0	1	0	2	4
Total	0	2	2	0	1	0	0	1	2	0	0	2	0	0	1	0	4	7

2. Patient Focus on Here-Now Involvement[b] — *Outcome*

	Patient			Therapist			Rater			Score			Combined			Total		
Process	–	0	+	–	0	+	–	0	+	–	0	+	–	0	+	–	0	+
Patient	0	1	0	0	0	1	0	0	0	0	0	0	0	0	0	0	1	1
Therapist	0	2	1	0	3	0	0	2	0	0	0	0	0	0	0	0	7	1
Rater	0	1	0	0	0	1	0	3	0	0	2	2	0	0	0	0	6	3
Total	0	4	1	0	3	2	0	5	0	0	2	2	0	0	0	0	14	5

3. Patient Cognitive and Behavioral Processing[c] — *Outcome*

	Patient			Therapist			Rater			Score			Combined			Total		
Process	–	0	+	–	0	+	–	0	+	–	0	+	–	0	+	–	0	+
Patient	0	0	1	0	0	1	0	0	0	0	0	1	0	0	1	0	0	4
Therapist	0	0	1	0	0	1	0	0	0	0	0	0	0	0	0	0	0	2
Rater	0	0	0	0	0	0	0	0	1	0	0	1	0	1	1	0	1	3
Index	0	0	0	0	0	0	0	0	2	0	0	2	1	0	0	1	0	4
Total	0	0	2	0	0	2	0	0	3	0	0	4	1	1	2	1	1	13

[a] + = patient focus on life problems associated with positive outcome; – = negatively related to outcome.

[b] + = patient focus on here-now involvement associated with positive outcome; – = negatively related to outcome.

[c] + = appropriate cognitive or behavioral processes associated with positive outcome, or inappropriate processes negatively related to outcome; – = appropriate cognitive or behavioral associated with negative outcome, or inappropriate processes positively related to outcome.

members of the Missouri Psychoanalytic Counseling Research Project (Table 8.8.B2).

Finally, one study of behavioral therapy with families of schizophrenic patients examined the relation of outcome to the varying quality of *interaction between family members* (Table 8.8.B3).

Another diverse but similarly valuable set of studies concerns the characteristics of *cognitive and affective processing* evident in the verbal and nonverbal aspects of patient presentations. Six recent studies, mainly by European researchers (Table 8.8.C1), add further evidence to eight earlier studies (Table 8.9.3) whose findings typically show a very consistent relationship with outcome. The studies in this area probe into the psychology of patient presentations and deserve to be followed up by future research. Another more specific variable that received attention in two other studies was the impact on outcome of patients' *negative attitudes* (Table 8.8.C2).

Therapist Expert Understanding

Studies that seek to relate outcome to therapists' expert understanding of what their patients present in treatment have focused mostly on the topics on which therapists focus rather than on cognitive and affective processes—which could probably be done with great profit, following the lead of Caspar (1997). Moreover, the studies in this area cover a wide range of topics so that only a few accumulate with respect to each.

Thus, two recent studies (Table 8.10.1) examine the therapist's *focus on patient affective processes*, adding to 10 earlier studies where the findings in relation to outcome (Table 8.11.1) were equivocal. Almost all the process observations were made from the external rater's perspective, including one study of cognitive behavioral therapy with children where therapist focus on affect was negatively related to outcome.

TABLE 8.10 Therapeutic Operations: Therapist Understanding

1. Focus on Patient Affective Process
Goldfried, Castonguay, Hayes, Drozd, & Shapiro (1997)
Hölzer, Pokorny, Kächele, & Luborsky (1997)

2. Focus on Patient Cognitive Process
Goldfried, Castonguay, Hayes, Drozd, & Shapiro (1997)
Hayes, Castonguay, & Goldfried (1996)
Hope, Heimberg, & Bruch (1995)

3. Focus on Patient Defensiveness/Resistance
Henggeler, Melton, Brondino, Scherer, & Hanley (1997)
Winston, Samstag, Winston, & Muran (1994)
— (meta-analyses/reviews) —
Beutler, Moleiro, & Talebi (2002)

4. Focus on Patient Development/Life History
Goldfried, Castonguay, Hayes, Drozd, & Shapiro (1997)
Hayes, Castonguay, & Goldfried (1996)
Hayes & Strauss (1998)

5. Focus on Patient Interpersonal Relations
Goldfried, Castonguay, Hayes, Drozd, & Shapiro (1997)
Hayes, Castonguay, & Goldfried (1996)
Strauss et al. (1995)
Wolfson et al. (1997)

6. Focus on Patient Problems
Dick (1999)
Feeley, DeRubeis, & Gelfant (1999)
Høglend & Piper (1995)

7. Focus on Patient Resources
Dick (1999)
Dick, Grawe, Regli, & Heim (1999)
Regli, Bieber, Mathier, & Grawe (2000)
Smith & Grawe (2000)
Smith, Regli, & Grawe (1999)

In a broader context of cognitive behavioral therapy, three studies also explored therapist *focusing on patient cognitive processes* in relation to outcome, one of which also involved a comparison with psychodynamic therapists (Table 8.10.2).

Two more salient areas of therapist focus in psychodynamic therapy are patients' resistances and patients' development or life history. Two studies and a major review of findings relative to outcome will be found regarding a *focus on defensiveness or resistances* (Table 8.10.3), and three other recent studies examine outcome in terms of the therapist's *focus on patient development* (Table 8.10.4).

Another four studies consider the effectiveness of therapist concentration on *patients' interpersonal relationships* (Table 8.10.5), joining eight studies cited in the last edition of this chapter (Table 8.11.2). Current interpersonal relationships are the main focus of the newer forms of interpersonal therapy (e.g., Klerman, Weissman, Rounsaville, & Chevron, 1984), but consideration of recurring patterns of relationship overlaps the life history focus noted above, as well as several studies of transference in the therapeutic relationship, important in psychodynamic treatments, that were cited in previous editions of this chapter. However, researchers have evidently lost interest in the therapist's *focus on here-and-now* transactions (Table 8.11.3), perhaps again because six prior studies failed to show much relation to outcome (although one study showed a negative impact of therapist here-and now focus in the context of *low* empathy and genuineness ratings of the therapist).

Finally, an interesting contrast is presented by therapist focus on patients' problems and therapist focus on patients' positive resources. Three recent studies examine the effectiveness of therapists' *focusing on patients' problems,* one in the context of cognitive therapy and another in a psychodynamic context (Table 8.10.6). These join eight previous studies (Table 8.11.4) that showed a mix of positive and null findings with outcome (but also two negative associations). These are complemented by five recent studies from the Bernese group on the effectiveness of therapists' *focusing on patients' resources* rather than their psychopathology or other deficits (Table 8.10.7), all of which show a significant association with positive outcomes. The latter approach is linked to Grawe's (1997, 1998) systematic integrative approach to psychological therapy.

Therapist Interventions

Therapist interventions or "techniques" are the formal and deliberate responses that therapists make to help resolve their patients' personal difficulties, based on their expert understanding of the patient's presentation and the recommendations of the treatment model they follow. As deliberate actions, interventions can be viewed more generally in terms of therapeutic strategies

TABLE 8.11 Therapeutic Operations—Findings on Therapist Understanding (1950–1992)

1. Therapist Focus: Patient Affect[a]

	Outcome					
	Patient	Therapist	Rater	Score	Combined	Total
Process	– 0 +	– 0 +	– 0 +	– 0 +	– 0 +	– 0 +
Therapist	0 0 0	0 0 1	0 0 0	0 0 0	0 0 0	0 0 1
Rater	0 1 0	1 2 0	1 0 4	0 3 3	0 1 1	2 7 8
Total	0 1 0	1 2 1	1 0 4	0 3 3	0 1 1	2 7 9

2. Therapist Focus: Core Interpersonal Relationships and Transference[b]

	Outcome					
	Patient	Therapist	Rater	Score	Combined	Total
Process	– 0 +	– 0 +	– 0 +	– 0 +	– 0 +	– 0 +
Therapist	0 0 0	0 1 0	0 2 0	0 2 0	0 0 0	0 5 0
Rater	0 1 1	0 1 1	1 4 3	1 2 3	0 2 2	2 10 10
Total	0 1 1	0 2 1	1 6 3	1 4 3	0 2 2	2 15 10

3. Therapist Focus: Here-Now Involvements[c]

	Outcome					
	Patient	Therapist	Rater	Score	Combined	Total
Process	– 0 +	– 0 +	– 0 +	– 0 +	– 0 +	– 0 +
Rater	1 1 0	1 1 0	0 1 0	1 3 1	0 1 0	3 7 1

4. Therapist Focus: Patient's Problems[d]

	Outcome					
	Patient	Therapist	Rater	Score	Combined	Total
Process	– 0 +	– 0 +	– 0 +	– 0 +	– 0 +	– 0 +
Patient	1 0 1	0 0 0	0 0 0	0 0 0	0 0 0	1 0 1
Therapist	0 0 0	1 0 1	0 3 0	0 1 2	0 0 0	1 4 3
Rater	0 0 0	0 0 0	0 2 2	0 1 3	0 0 1	0 3 6
Total	1 0 1	1 0 1	0 5 2	0 2 5	0 0 1	2 7 10

[a] + = therapist focus on patient affect associated with positive outcome; – = negatively related to outcome.

[b] + = therapist focus on interpersonal relationships and transference associated with positive outcome; – = negatively related to outcome.

[c] + = therapist focus on here-now involvements associated with positive outcome; – = negatively related to outcome.

[d] + = therapist focus on patient problems associated with positive outcome; – = negatively related to outcome.

(i.e., goals and steps taken to achieve them) and more specifically in terms of therapeutic tactics (i.e., moves made to implement strategic steps).

An impressive list of 16 studies and one review were focused on *therapeutic change strategies* during this review period (Table 8.12.A1), significantly augmenting the nine with mixed findings cited in the last edition (Table 8.13.1). Some of the recent studies relating outcome to therapeutic strategy reflect the continued work of teams led by K. Grawe in Berne and D. Schulte in Bochum, but these groups, working from a generally cognitive behavioral background, have now been joined by others drawing on psychodynamic perspectives (e.g., the groups of E. Jones in Berkeley, D. Kivlighan in Missouri, and R. Sandell in Sweden). This group of studies represents a healthy trend toward studying therapist interventions at a more inclusive and meaningful level, although they have so far shown rather mixed results.

At a more tactical level, the effectiveness of nine distinct types of intervention method was assessed by various researchers in this review period, although only with a few for each. Two studies whose authors ground their work in linguistic analyses evaluated the therapist's use of *questioning* as an intervention method (Table 8.12.B1).

Three other studies (Table 8.12.B2) focused on the use of *reflection and feedback*, for which 11 studies were cited in the last edition (Table

TABLE 8.12 Therapeutic Operations: Therapist Interventions

A. Intervention Strategy

1. Therapeutic Strategies

Ablon & Jones (1998)
DeJong-Meyer et al. (1999)
Dick, Grawe, Regli, & Heim (1999)
Dürr & Hahlweg (1996)
Eyssell, Zeising, & Stuhr (1992)
Jones & Pulos (1993)
Patton, Kivlighan, & Multon (1997)
Regli, Bieber, Mathier, & Grawe (2000)
Sandell et al. (2000)
Schmidtchen & Hennies (1996)
Schulte, Hartung, & Wilke (1997)
Smith & Grawe (2000)
Smith, Regli, & Grawe (1999)
Vogel & Schulte (1997)
Weissmark & Giacomo (1994)
Znoj, Grawe, & Jeger (2000)
— (meta-analyses/reviews) —
Schmidtchen (2001)

B. Intervention Methods

1. Questioning

Russell, Bryant, & Estrada (1996)
Stiles & Shapiro (1994)

2. Reflection/Feedback

Schmidtchen (2001)
Stiles & Shapiro (1994)
Tschuschke & Dies (1994, 1997)
— (meta-analyses/reviews) —
Claiborn, Goodyear, & Horner (2002)
Schmidtchen (2001)

3. Advice/Guidance/Prescription

Goren (1993)
Hayes & Strauss (1998)
Kolden (1996)
Stiles & Shapiro (1994)

4. Support

Dick (1999)
Dürr & Hahlweg (1996)
Gaston, Piper, Debbane, Bienvenu, & Garant (1994)
Gaston, Thompson, Gallagher, Cournoyer, & Gagnon (1998)
Hayes & Strauss (1998)

5. Evocative Exploration

Gaston, Piper, Debbane, Bienvenu, & Garant (1994)
Gaston, Thompson, Gallagher, Cournoyer, & Gagnon (1998)
Kolden (1996)
Schmidtchen & Hennies (1996)
Watson & Greenberg (1996)

6. Experiential Confrontation

Foa et al. (1999)
Greenberg & Hirscheimer (1994)
Hayes & Strauss (1998)
Jaycox, Foa, & Morral (1998)
Kolden (1996)
Paivio, Hall, Holowaty, Jellis, & Tran (2001)
Watson & Greenberg (1996)
— (meta-analyses/reviews) —
Abramowitz (1996)

7. Interpretation [Accuracy, Frequency]

Castonguay, Goldfried, Wiser, Raue, & Hayes (1996)
Connolly et al. (1999)
Høglend (1993, 1996b)
Høglend, Engelstad, Sørbye, Heyerdahl, & Amlo (1994)
Norville, Sampson, & Weiss (1996)
Piper, Joyce, McCallum, & Azim (1993)
Stiles & Shapiro (1994)
— (meta-analyses/reviews) —
Crits-Christoph & Connally (2002)

8. Activating Patient's Resources

Dick (1999)
Dick, Grawe, Regli, & Heim (1999)
Dürr & Hahlweg (1996)
Regli, Bieber, Mathier, & Grawe (2000)
Smith & Grawe (2000)
Smith, Regli & Grawe (1999)

9. Therapist Self-Disclosure

Barrett & Berman (2001)
Schmidtchen (2001)
Schmidtchen & Hennies (1996)
— (meta-analyses/reviews) —
Hill & Knox (2002)
Schmidtchen (2001)

TABLE 8.13 Therapeutic Operations—Findings on Therapist Interventions (1950–1992)

1. Change Strategies (Heuristics)[a] — *Outcome*

Process	Patient			Therapist			Rater			Score			Combined			Total		
	−	0	+	−	0	+	−	0	+	−	0	+	−	0	+	−	0	+
Therapist	0	1	2	0	0	3	0	2	0	0	2	0	0	0	0	0	5	5
Rater	0	0	0	0	0	0	0	1	1	0	2	1	0	3	3	0	6	5
Index	0	0	0	0	0	0	0	0	0	0	0	0	0	0	1	0	0	1
Total	0	1	2	0	0	3	0	3	1	0	4	1	0	3	4	0	11	11

2. Reflection/Clarification[b] — *Outcome*

Process	Patient			Therapist			Rater			Score			Combined			Total		
	−	0	+	−	0	+	−	0	+	−	0	+	−	0	+	−	0	+
Therapist	0	0	0	0	1	0	0	1	0	0	0	0	0	0	0	0	2	0
Rater	0	0	0	1	0	0	0	2	0	1	2	1	0	2	0	2	6	1
Index	2	0	0	0	0	0	0	0	0	1	0	0	0	0	0	3	0	0
Total	2	0	0	1	1	0	0	3	0	2	2	1	0	2	0	5	8	1

3. Support[c] — *Outcome*

Process	Patient			Therapist			Rater			Score			Combined			Total		
	−	0	+	−	0	+	−	0	+	−	0	+	−	0	+	−	0	+
Patient	0	3	1	0	2	0	0	1	1	0	0	0	0	0	0	0	6	2
Therapist	0	1	1	0	5	1	0	1	1	0	1	1	0	0	0	0	8	4
Rater	0	1	1	0	2	1	0	3	1	0	4	3	0	1	1	0	11	7
Total	0	5	3	0	9	2	0	5	3	0	5	4	0	1	1	0	25	13

4. Exploration[d] — *Outcome*

Process	Patient			Therapist			Rater			Score			Combined			Total		
	−	0	+	−	0	+	−	0	+	−	0	+	−	0	+	−	0	+
Patient	0	1	1	0	1	0	0	0	1	0	0	0	0	0	0	0	2	2
Therapist	0	1	0	1	1	0	0	0	1	0	0	2	0	0	0	1	2	3
Rater	0	6	1	0	2	4	0	6	3	0	5	3	0	1	0	0	20	11
Total	0	8	2	1	4	4	0	6	5	0	5	5	0	1	0	1	24	16

5. Experiential Confrontation[e] — *Outcome*

Process	Patient			Therapist			Rater			Score			Combined			Total		
	−	0	+	−	0	+	−	0	+	−	0	+	−	0	+	−	0	+
Patient	0	1	2	0	0	0	0	1	1	0	0	0	0	0	0	0	2	3
Therapist	0	0	0	0	0	2	0	0	0	0	0	0	0	0	0	0	0	2
Rater	0	0	2	0	0	0	0	0	0	0	2	5	0	0	0	0	2	7
Index	0	0	2	0	0	0	0	1	0	1	1	1	0	0	0	1	2	3
Total	0	1	6	0	0	2	0	2	1	1	3	6	0	0	0	1	6	15

6. Interpretation[f] — *Outcome*

Process	Patient			Therapist			Rater			Score			Combined			Total		
	−	0	+	−	0	+	−	0	+	−	0	+	−	0	+	−	0	+
Patient	0	0	5	0	1	0	0	0	0	0	0	0	0	0	0	0	1	5
Therapist	0	1	0	1	0	4	1	1	1	0	1	0	0	0	0	2	3	5
Rater	0	0	2	0	2	0	0	0	5	1	3	4	0	1	2	1	6	13
Index	0	0	0	0	0	0	0	0	0	0	1	1	0	0	0	0	1	1
Total	0	1	7	1	3	4	1	1	6	1	5	5	0	1	2	3	11	24

(continues)

TABLE 8.13 (Continued)

7. Therapist's Self-Disclosure[g]

	Outcome																	
	Patient			Therapist			Rater			Score			Combined			Total		
Process	–	0	+	–	0	+	–	0	+	–	0	+	–	0	+	–	0	+
Patient	0	1	0	0	1	0	0	1	0	0	0	0	0	1	1	0	4	1
Therapist	0	1	0	0	1	0	0	0	0	0	0	0	0	1	0	0	3	0
Rater	0	1	0	1	0	1	0	2	0	0	3	0	0	3	0	1	9	1
Index	0	0	0	0	0	0	0	0	0	0	0	1	0	0	0	0	0	1
Total	0	3	0	1	2	1	0	3	0	0	3	1	0	5	1	1	16	3

8. Paradoxical Intention[h]

	Outcome																	
	Patient			Therapist			Rater			Score			Combined			Total		
Process	–	0	+	–	0	+	–	0	+	–	0	+	–	0	+	–	0	+
Index	0	0	4	0	0	0	0	0	1	0	0	7	0	0	1	0	0	13

[a] + = suitable change strategy associated with positive outcome; – = negatively related to outcome; for example, see 1994 chapter, footnotes to Table 9.8.19.

[b] + = therapist use of reflection associated with positive outcome; – = negatively related to outcome.

[c] + = therapist use of support associated with positive outcome; – = negatively related to outcome.

[d] + = therapist use of exploration associated with positive outcome; – = negatively related to outcome.

[e] + = therapist use of experiential confrontation associated with positive outcome; – = negatively related to outcome.

[f] + = therapist use of interpretation associated with positive outcome; – = negatively related to outcome.

[g] + = therapist use of self-disclosure associated with positive outcome; – = negatively related to outcome; includes findings of Elliott, Barker, Caskey, & Pistrang (1982) inadvertently omitted from 1994 summary.

[h] + = therapist use of paradoxical intention associated with positive outcome; – = negatively related to outcome.

8.13.2), and for which two current reviews of findings are also available.

Four recent studies examined the impact of therapist *prescriptiveness, guidance, and advice* (Table 8.12.B3), adding new evidence to that provided by five previously cited but untabulated studies (Orlinsky, Grawe, & Parks, 1994, p. 308) which had suggested that this approach was generally unhelpful (except perhaps with highly disturbed patients who might be at risk with use of "uncovering" techniques).

Five more studies examined therapists' use of *support and encouragement* (Table 8.12.B4), generally sustaining the 21 previous studies that showed it to be a generally benign and occasionally potent but not consistently effective intervention (Table 8.13.3).

Another set of five recent studies (Table 8.12.B5) on therapists' use of *evocative exploration* joins 18 previous studies that had shown exploration (conceived more broadly) to be modestly and inconsistently related to outcome (Table 8.13.4).

The technique of *experiential confrontation* via focally guided imagination has been used both by process-experiential therapists (e.g., the Gestalt empty-chair intervention for dealing with "unfinished business") and by cognitive behavioral therapists (e.g., as an exposure method for dealing with post-traumatic distress), among others. Seven recent studies and one review of this intervention (Table 8.12.B6) contribute further evidence to 14 previous studies (Table 8.13.5) suggesting much more often than not that this is a therapeutically effective procedure (although one capable of producing negative effects with patients so disturbed as to require hospitalization).

The widely used psychodynamic method of *interpretation* continued to receive attention from researchers in seven studies during this period, as well as a current review of the effectiveness of relational interpretations (Table 8.12.B7). The confusion in this area requires correction. On the one hand, it is important to note that 24 previous studies (Table 8.13.6) have found the use of *interpretation in general* to be fairly consistently, and occasionally strongly, associated with positive therapeutic outcome. On the other hand, there is consistent evidence, cited in the review by Henry, Strupp, Schacht, and Gaston (1994) and confirmed by recent studies, that the use of *transference interpretations* specifically in brief psychotherapies is associated with negative therapeutic outcomes and ought to be avoided. The use of transference interpretation was developed as a way of dealing with transference resistances in the context of long-term psychoanalytic treatment (Freud, 1912a), and presupposes a long-standing positive alliance. Whatever its value may be in that context, its use as a technique in brief psychotherapies probably should be abandoned. Yet, interpretation as a more general mode of intervention can be helpful to patients, and the negative effects attributable to one specific application should not prevent its judicious use.

The point of the transference interpretation is to demonstrate clearly to the patient that his or her perceptions of the therapist in a particular circumstance are not accurate but represent instead a characteristic distortion, one that recurrently reproduces in contemporary adult emotional involvements an early core conflictual relationship. For this demonstration to be effective, the patient must have already internalized, as a basis for comparison with the current transference experience, a realistic image of the therapist as a reliable and perspicacious ally whose interpretations have generally been accurate, timely, tactful, and helpful. It is also essential to recognize the distinction that Freud (1912a) made between *unconscious* conflict-generated transferences and the more benign *preconscious* positive transference, which facilitates the patient's experiencing the therapist as a source of support. It is only *unconscious* transferences that need to be interpreted in therapy, initially as sources of resistance and eventually as important opportunities for change because they make "the patient's hidden and forgotten erotic impulses immediate and manifest" (p. 108) and so allow the patient's adult ego to reevaluate them and be reconciled with them. It is unlikely that such events can occur productively on the basis of a few sessions' contact between patient and therapist.

Six recent studies, mostly from the Bernese group, strike a more positive note by presenting evidence on the effectiveness of interventions designed to *activate patients' resources* (Table 8.12.B8), that is, the strengths that patients bring with them to therapy and can use to deal with their conflicts, deficits, or problems. Although most therapies seek to utilize the patient's potential for change, they typically do so without consistent and systematic emphasis, often focusing more explicitly on patients' problems and pathologies. Grawe (1997) suggested working with patients' resources as a general therapeutic strategy; studies of *resource activation* interventions suggest that these are generally related to positive outcome (e.g., Willutzki, Haas, & Neumann, 2000).

Three studies and two current reviews focus on the usefulness of *therapist self-disclosure* as a therapeutic technique (Table 8.12.B9). These join 10 previous studies that yielded more null than positive findings as well as one negative finding (Table 8.13.7), implying that therapist self-disclosure may occasionally be helpful for some patients but is not usually so. However, closer inspection has revealed an ambiguity in the definition of therapist self-disclosure that may be a source of misunderstanding. Some researchers define self-disclosure as therapists' statements of their own thoughts or feelings in the session in response to what a patient has presented; other investigators define it as therapists' statements that reveal facts about themselves and personal experiences in their own lives; still others may include both. The actual impact of this intervention on outcome will probably not be determined until these two senses of self-disclosure are clearly distinguished. In either case, it seems likely to be a technique best used on a limited basis and only with specifically receptive patients.

Finally, we found no further research on therapists' use of *paradoxical intention*, which 11 previous studies and 2 meta-analyses had shown to be most consistently related to positive outcomes with appropriate patients (Table 8.13.8), and with moderate to large effects. These findings ought not be lost to view simply because no recent work has added to them.

Patient Responsiveness

Researchers have studied patients' immediate reactions to therapist interventions alternately as matters of in-session behavior, cognitive response, and affective impact, all of which have shown a marked association with outcome.

Resistance to the therapist's intervention *versus cooperative involvement* in therapeutic work was assessed with regard to outcome in 18 recent studies of varied types of therapy in varied settings, and results specifically for client-centered therapy with children were appraised in a recent review (Table 8.14.A1). This adds an impressive array of evidence to the 24 previous studies in which patient cooperativeness more often than not was significantly and sometimes strongly related to positive outcome, especially when cooperativeness was assessed by the therapist and by external observers (Table 8.15.1).

TABLE 8.14 Therapeutic Operations: Patient Responsiveness

A. Behavior

1. Resistance vs. Cooperation in Therapeutic Work

Ablon & Jones (1999)
Araujo, Ito, & Marks (1996)
Dürr & Hahlweg (1996)
Edelman & Chambless (1993, 1995)
Fiedler, Vogt, Rogge, & Schulte (1994)
Hatcher & Barends (1996)
Hayes & Strauss (1998)
Jones & Pulos (1993)
Joyce & Piper (1996)
Michalak & Schulte (2002)
Nosper (1999)
Paivio, Hall, Holowaty, Jellis, & Tran (2001)
Patton, Kivlighan, & Multon (1997)
Schmidtchen, Acke, & Hennies (1995)
Seibel & Dowd (1999)
Strauss, Kröger, Hoffmann, & Burgmeier-Lohse (1994)
Westerman, Foote, & Winston (1995)
— (meta-analyses/reviews) —
Schmidtchen (2001)

B. Cognition

1. Self-Exploration

Eyssell, Zeising, & Stuhr (1992)
Schmidtchen, Acke, & Hennies (1995)
— (meta-analyses/reviews) —
Schmidtchen (2001)

2. Refocusing Attention

Woody, Chambless, & Glass (1997)

C. Affect

1. Total Affective Arousal

Burgoon et al. (1993)
Castonguay, Pincus, Agras, & Hines (1998)
Cummings, Slemon, & Hallberg (1993)
Dick, Grawe, Regli, & Heim (1999)
Foa, Riggs, Massie, & Yarczower (1995)
Jaycox, Foa, & Morral (1998)
Merten (2001)
Regli, Bieber, Mathier, & Grawe (2000)
Smith & Grawe (2000)
Smith, Regli & Grawe (1999)
— (meta-analyses/reviews) —
Abramowitz (1996)

2. Positive Affect

Merten (2001)
Nosper (1999)
Saunders (1998)
Schmidtchen, Acke, & Hennies (1995)
— (meta-analyses/reviews) —
Schmidtchen (2001)

3. Negative Affect

Ablon & Jones (1999)
Araujo, Ito, & Marks (1996)
Callahan (2000)
Eugster & Wampold (1996)
Hayes & Strauss (1998)
Jones & Pulos (1993)
Merten (2001)
Nosper (1999)
Saunders (1998)
Schmidtchen, Acke, & Hennies (1995)
Sexton (1993, 1996)
— (meta-analyses/reviews) —
Schmidtchen (2001)

In contrast to the concentration on resistance versus cooperativeness, only four studies examined the relation of patients' cognitive responses to outcome. Three of those and one review focused on *patient self-exploration* (Table 8.14.C1), which had been a concern in 35 previous studies (Table 8.15.2). The overall findings of those prior studies suggested that self-exploration more often than not appeared unrelated to outcome, although occasionally it was fairly strongly predictive of positive outcome and might also rarely be associated with negative outcome. Both recent studies of self-exploration were conducted in Germany in the context of client-centered therapy, which

TABLE 8.15 Therapeutic Operations—Findings on Patient Responsiveness (1950–1992)

1. Patient's Cooperation versus Resistance[a]

	Outcome																	
	Patient			Therapist			Rater			Score			Combined			Total		
Process	−	0	+	−	0	+	−	0	+	−	0	+	−	0	+	−	0	+
Patient	0	0	5	0	2	0	0	2	0	0	0	2	0	1	0	0	5	7
Therapist	0	3	4	0	2	5	0	0	2	0	1	5	0	0	0	0	6	16
Rater	0	0	1	0	0	2	0	2	3	0	2	2	0	0	2	0	4	10
Index	0	0	0	0	0	0	0	0	1	0	0	0	0	0	0	0	0	1
Total	0	3	10	0	4	7	0	4	6	0	3	9	0	1	2	0	15	34

2. Patient's Self-Exploration[b]

	Outcome																	
	Patient			Therapist			Rater			Score			Combined			Total		
Process	−	0	+	−	0	+	−	0	+	−	0	+	−	0	+	−	0	+
Patient	0	2	0	0	1	0	0	0	0	0	2	1	0	0	1	0	5	2
Therapist	0	0	1	0	0	2	0	2	0	0	2	0	0	0	0	0	4	3
Rater	0	12	2	0	6	8	0	11	1	2	15	8	0	0	0	2	44	19
Total	0	14	3	0	7	10	0	13	1	2	19	9	0	0	1	2	53	24

3. Patient's Total Affective Response[c]

	Outcome																	
	Patient			Therapist			Rater			Score			Combined			Total		
Process	−	0	+	−	0	+	−	0	+	−	0	+	−	0	+	−	0	+
Patient	0	1	2	0	2	0	0	0	0	0	0	0	0	0	0	0	3	2
Therapist	0	0	1	0	0	2	0	0	0	0	0	0	0	0	0	0	0	3
Rater	0	0	0	0	0	0	0	0	0	0	0	0	0	2	0	0	2	0
Total	0	1	3	0	2	2	0	0	0	0	0	0	0	2	0	0	5	5

4. Patient's Positive Affective Response[d]

	Outcome																	
	Patient			Therapist			Rater			Score			Combined			Total		
Process	−	0	+	−	0	+	−	0	+	−	0	+	−	0	+	−	0	+
Patient	0	0	2	0	0	1	0	0	0	0	0	0	0	0	0	0	0	3
Therapist	0	0	3	0	0	3	0	0	0	0	0	0	0	0	0	0	0	6
Total	0	0	5	0	0	4	0	0	0	0	0	0	0	0	0	0	0	9

5. Patient's Negative Affective Response[e]

	Outcome																	
	Patient			Therapist			Rater			Score			Combined			Total		
Process	−	0	+	−	0	+	−	0	+	−	0	+	−	0	+	−	0	+
Patient	2	2	0	0	2	1	0	0	0	0	0	1	0	1	0	2	5	2
Therapist	1	1	0	0	3	2	0	1	1	2	1	1	0	0	0	3	6	4
Rater	1	3	0	5	1	1	1	3	0	4	0	4	0	0	0	11	7	5
Index	0	0	0	0	0	0	0	0	0	0	0	0	0	0	1	0	0	1
Total	4	6	0	5	6	4	1	4	1	6	1	6	0	1	1	16	18	12

[a] + = patient cooperation associated with positive outcome, or patient resistance associated with negative outcome; – = patient cooperation associated with negative outcome, or associated with positive outcome.

[b] + = patient self-exploration associated with positive outcome; – = associated with negative outcome.

[c] + = patient total affective arousal associated with positive outcome; – = associated with negative outcome.

[d] + = patient positive affective arousal associated with positive outcome; – = associated with negative outcome.

[e] + = patient negative affective arousal associated with positive outcome; – = associated with negative outcome.

had emphasized its theoretical importance, and the decline in interest in self-exploration evident elsewhere probably reflects the lack of research involvement among client-centered therapists in recent years as compared to earlier times. As an interesting contrast, the third study of patients' cognitive responsiveness to interventions centered on the relation to outcome of their *refocusing attention from self* in a cognitive behavioral treatment of social phobia, showing a positive relationship to outcome (Table 8.14.B2).

Studies of patients' affective reactions to therapist interventions were more numerous and can be divided into those focusing on total affective arousal, positive affect, and negative affect. Ten publications and one review concerned patients' *total affective arousal* in response to therapist interventions (Table 8.14.C1), adding substance to the five previously reported, which had shown arousal per se to be associated with positive outcomes about half the time but not a factor in negative outcomes (Table 8.15.3). Interestingly, the recent studies were done largely in the context of cognitive behavioral therapies.

By contrast, the four studies relating outcome to patients' experiences of *positive affect* during sessions were more often conducted in the context of client-centered and psychodynamic treatments, together with one review of client-centered child therapy (Table 8.14.C2). Those join a surprisingly small number of previous studies (only three) that nevertheless showed a very consistent association between positive patient affect and outcome.

On the other hand, 12 recent studies and one review of patients' experiences of distressing or *negative affect* during sessions (Table 8.14.C3) join 20 studies cited in previous editions, where earlier findings presented a very mixed picture that may be clarified by recent studies (Table 8.15.5). Two-fifths of nearly 50 previous findings were significantly associated with outcome, either negatively or positively, suggesting that experiencing distressing and negative emotions during sessions has strong effects that can be for good or ill depending on how effectively therapists deal with them.

Therapeutic Bond

No area of process-outcome research has garnered more attention than has the therapeutic bond, both in terms of general alliance characteristics and more specific aspects of the patient-therapist relationship.

Global Bond Characteristics

Global relational quality is the dyadic equivalent of positive group cohesion, and an amazing total of 53 studies have examined its relation to outcome since 1992 (Table 8.16.1), at which time 56 previous studies had already been published with 132 separate findings (Table 8.17.1). Collectively, and from four current meta-analytic reviews, it is clear that *global alliance and group cohesion* are quite consistently (though not invariably) associated with positive outcome in psychotherapy. Indeed, few findings in this or related fields seem better documented. For example, Martin et al. (2000) conducted a meta-analysis of data from 79 studies (58 published, 21 unpublished), which "indicated that the overall relation of therapeutic alliance with outcome [in and of itself] is moderate, but consistent . . . [and that] . . . the relation of alliance and outcome does not appear to be influenced by other moderator variables, such as the type of outcome measure used in the study, the type of outcome rater, the time of alliance assessment, the type of alliance rater, the type of treatment provided, or the publication status of the study" (p. 438). This robust association almost assures researchers of a statistically significant finding, which (from a slightly cynical point of view) may be one reason we have such a rich array of studies at our disposal.

Patients' and therapists' respective overall contributions to the therapeutic bond have also received much attention in relation to outcome. Twelve recent studies (Table 8.16.2) conducted in contexts as varied as cognitive behavioral, interpersonal, psychodynamic, and integrative therapies, as well as individual and group treatment formats, examined the outcome impact of the *therapist's overall bond contribution*, joining 50 previous studies (Table 8.17.2). Those had shown a rather consistent association between positive outcomes and the therapist's contribution when the latter was rated by patients, but also more null findings and a few negative findings when the therapist's contribution was rated by external observers.

A more consistent association with positive outcomes was found in 20 previous studies of the *patient's overall bond contribution* (Table 8.17.3) viewed from all observational perspectives (although a handful of findings showing negative outcomes from the therapist's and external observer's perspectives occurred among the otherwise numerous positive outcome findings). These are joined by nine studies published since

TABLE 8.16 Therapeutic Bond: Global Bond

1. *Overall Relational Quality* [Total Alliance; Group Climate]

Ambühl (1993)
Barber, Connolly, Crits-Christoph, Gladis, & Siqueland (2000)
Barber et al. (1999)
Barber et al. (2001)
Bernal, Bonilla, Padilla-Cotto, & Pérez-Prado (1998)
Blatt, Sanislow, Zuroff, & Pilkonis (1996)
Brown & O'Leary (2000)
Carroll, Nich, & Rounsaville (1997)
Castonguay, Goldfried, Wiser, Raue, & Hayes (1996)
Castonguay, Pincus, Agras, & Hines (1998)
Connors, Carroll, DiClemente, Longabaugh, & Donavan (1997)
Cummings, Slemon, & Hallberg (1993)
Dazord, Gerin, Seulin, Duclos, & Amar (1997)
Dick (1999)
Dick, Grawe, Regli, & Heim (1999)
Durham, Allan, & Hackett (1997)
Eaton, Abeles, & Gutfreund (1993)
Eyssell, Zeising, & Stuhr (1992)
Feeley, DeRubeis, & Gelfant (1999)
Hatcher (1999)
Hatcher & Barends (1996)
Heppner, Cooper, Mulholland, & Wei (2001)
Hilliard, Henry, & Strupp (2000)
Hoffart & Sexton (2002)
Kendall & Southam-Gerow (1996)
Kivlighan & Shaughnessy (1995)
Kolden (1996)
Konzag, Fikentscher, & Bandemer-Greulich (2000a, 2000b)
Krupnick et al. (1994).
Lunnen & Ogles (1998)
MacKenzie & Tschuschke (1993)
Mallinckrodt (1993, 1996)
Margraf, Barlow, Clark, & Telch (1993)
Merten (2001)
Murran et al. (1995)
Paivio & Bahr (1998)
Paivio, Hall, Holowaty, Jellis, & Tran (2001)
Paivio & Patterson (1999)
Patton, Kivlighan, & Multon (1997)
Price & Jones (1998)
Raue, Goldfried, & Barkham (1997)
Regli, Bieber, Mathier, & Grawe (2000)
Rudolf & Manz (1993)
Saunders (2000)
Schauenburg, Sammet, Rabung, & Strack (2002)
Schmidtchen & Hennies (1996)
Smith & Grawe (2000)
Smith, Regli & Grawe (1999)
Svensson & Hansson (1999)
Tschuschke & Dies (1994)
Wilson et al. (1999)
— (meta-analyses/reviews) —
Burlingame, Fuhriman, & Johnson (2002)
Horvath & Bedi (2002)
Martin, Garske, & Davis (2000)
Schmidtchen (2001)

2. *Therapist's Overall Contribution to Bond Quality*

Blatt, Zuroff, Quinlan, & Pilkonis (1996)
Carroll, Nich, & Rounsaville (1997)
Keijsers, Hoogduin, & Schaap (1994)
Krupnick et al. (1996)
Ladouceur et al. (2000)
Marziali, Munroe-Blum, & McCleary (1999)
Paulson, Truscott, & Stuart (1999)
Sexton (1993, 1996)
Strauss, Kröger, Hoffmann, & Burgmeier-Lohse (1994)
Svartberg, Seltzer, & Stiles (1998)
Svartberg & Stiles (1994)
Tschacher, Baur, & Grawe (2000)

3. *Patient's Overall Contribution to Bond Quality*

Carroll, Nich, & Rounsaville (1997)
Dick, Grawe, Regli, & Heim (1999)
Eyssell, Zeising, & Stuhr (1992)
Gaston, Piper, Debbane, Bienvenu, & Garant (1994)
Gaston, Thompson, Gallagher, Cournoyer, & Gagnon (1998)
Krupnick, Sotsky et al. (1996)
Regli, Bieber, Mathier, & Grawe (2000)
Smith & Grawe (2000)
Smith, Regli, & Grawe (1999)

TABLE 8.17 Therapeutic Bond—Findings on Global Relational Quality (1950–1992)

1. Overall Quality of Bond/Alliance/Group Cohesion[a]

	Outcome																	
	Patient			Therapist			Rater			Score			Combined			Total		
Process	–	0	+	–	0	+	–	0	+	–	0	+	–	0	+	–	0	+
Patient	0	1	14	0	2	6	0	3	5	0	5	11	0	1	4	0	12	40
Therapist	0	3	6	0	2	8	0	1	2	0	6	3	0	0	1	0	12	20
Rater	0	1	5	0	3	3	0	2	6	1	5	7	0	1	3	1	12	24
Index	0	0	0	0	0	0	0	4	0	0	2	2	0	2	1	0	8	3
Total	0	5	25	0	7	17	0	10	13	1	18	23	0	4	9	1	44	87

2. Therapist's Overall Contribution to the Bond[b]

	Outcome																	
	Patient			Therapist			Rater			Score			Combined			Total		
Process	–	0	+	–	0	+	–	0	+	–	0	+	–	0	+	–	0	+
Patient	0	1	12	0	3	4	0	2	1	0	8	12	0	0	0	0	14	29
Therapist	0	1	1	1	0	5	0	1	0	0	2	1	0	0	0	1	4	7
Rater	0	6	3	1	3	6	0	7	0	3	11	10	0	0	1	4	27	20
Total	0	8	16	2	6	15	0	10	1	3	21	23	0	0	1	5	45	56

3. Patient's Overall Contribution to the Bond[c]

	Outcome																	
	Patient			Therapist			Rater			Score			Combined			Total		
Process	–	0	+	–	0	+	–	0	+	–	0	+	–	0	+	–	0	+
Patient	0	0	2	0	0	2	0	0	1	0	0	1	0	0	0	0	0	6
Therapist	0	1	3	0	1	4	1	1	1	1	0	2	0	0	1	2	3	11
Rater	0	3	2	1	1	6	0	2	4	2	5	8	0	0	0	3	11	20
Total	0	4	7	1	2	12	1	3	6	3	5	11	0	0	1	4	14	37

[a] + = good reciprocal bond associated with positive outcome, or poor bond associated with negative outcome; – = good reciprocal bond associated with negative outcome, or reciprocal bond associated with negative outcome.

[b] + = therapist's overall positive contribution to bond associated with positive outcome, or therapist's negative contribution to bond associated with negative outcome; – = therapist's overall positive contribution associated with negative outcome, or therapist's negative contribution associated with positive outcome.

[c] + = patient's overall positive contribution to bond associated with positive outcome, or patient's negative contribution to bond associated with negative outcome; – = patient's overall positive contribution associated with negative outcome, or patient's negative contribution associated with positive outcome.

1992 that also represent a range of therapeutic contexts (Table 8.16.3).

Global measures of the therapeutic bond, and of patients' and therapists' contributions to shaping its qualities, represent summary assessments that intuitively combine many specific aspects of relationship. Those aspects have also been studied separately in relation to outcome, and they are described in the Generic Model with respect to the instrumental or teamwork aspect of relationship (*personal role investment* and *interactive coordination*) and the social-emotional or personal rapport aspect of relationship (*expressive attunement* and *affective attitude*).

Personal Role Investment

This aspect of therapeutic teamwork concerns the level of personal engagement shown by the participants in their respective roles, that is, the motivation and credibility of their role enactment (e.g., Goffman, 1961).

Thirteen recent studies (Table 8.18.1) considered the relation of therapeutic outcome to *therapist role engagement and credibility*, adding evidence to 39 previous studies whose findings more often than not showed that patients of therapists who were viewed as positively engaged and credible helpers had better outcomes (Table 8.19.1).

Even more impressively, 28 studies (Table 8.18.2) of *patient role engagement and motivation* published since 1992 substantially broadened the 38 that were cited in previous editions of this chapter (Table 8.19.3). In those earlier studies, findings more often than not showed patients who experienced themselves as positively engaged and motivated help-seekers, and patients who were seen as such by their therapists also had better outcomes. When rated by external observers, however, there were more null than positive findings.

Unfortunately, the joint quality of reciprocal role investment between patient and therapist has only rarely been studied (Table 8.19.5) and was not studied at all during the current review period.

Interactive Coordination

To function well as a team, patients and therapists not only need to be committed to their work but

TABLE 8.18 Therapeutic Bond: Personal Role Investment

1. *Therapist Role Engagement/Credibility*
   - Dick (1999)
   - Dick, Grawe, Regli, & Heim (1999)
   - Eugster & Wampold (1996)
   - Eyssell, Zeising, & Stuhr (1992)
   - Hatcher (1999)
   - Heppner, Cooper, Mulholland, & Wei (2001)
   - Hoffart & Friis (2000)
   - Regli, Bieber, Mathier, & Grawe (2000)
   - Saunders (1998)
   - Smith & Grawe (2000)
   - Smith, Regli, & Grawe (1999)
   - Stiles, Agnew-Davies, Hardy, Barkham, & Shapiro (1998)
   - Strauss, Kröger, Hoffmann, & Burgmeier-Lohse (1994)
2. *Patient Role Engagement/Motivation*
   - Ablon & Jones (1999)
   - Baker & Kirschenbaum (1993)
   - Dazord, Gerin, Seulin, Duclos, & Amar (1997)
   - Dick (1999)
   - Dick, Grawe, Regli, & Heim (1999)
   - Eugster & Wampold (1996)
   - Geller & Farber (1993)
   - Goren (1993)
   - Hatcher (1999)
   - Hatcher & Barends (1996)
   - Henggeler, Melton, Brondino, Scherer, & Hanley (1997)
   - Keijsers, Hoogduin, & Schaap (1994)
   - Kendall & Southam-Gerow (1996)
   - Ladouceur et al. (2000)
   - MacKenzie & Tschuschke (1993)
   - Michalak & Schulte (2002)
   - Öst, Stridh, & Wolf (1998)
   - Regli, Bieber, Mathier, & Grawe (2000)
   - Ryle & Golynkina (2000)
   - Saunders (2000)
   - Schmidtchen, Acke, & Hennies (1995)
   - Sennekamp & Hautzinger (1994)
   - Smith & Grawe (2000)
   - Smith, Regli & Grawe (1999)
   - Strauss, Kröger, Hoffmann, & Burgmeier-Lohse (1994)
   - Tarrier et al. (1999)
   - Tarrier, Sommerfield, Pilgrim, & Faragher (2000)
   - Tschacher, Baur, & Grawe (2000)

TABLE 8.19 Therapeutic Bond—Findings on Personal Role Investment (1950–1992)

1. Therapist's Engagement versus Detachment[a] — *Outcome*

	Patient			Therapist			Rater			Score			Combined			Total		
Process	–	0	+	–	0	+	–	0	+	–	0	+	–	0	+	–	0	+
Patient	0	2	7	0	0	6	0	0	1	0	1	0	0	1	0	0	4	14
Therapist	0	2	0	0	2	2	0	0	0	0	3	0	0	0	0	0	7	2
Rater	0	0	1	0	0	1	0	0	0	0	4	3	0	1	0	0	5	5
Total	0	4	8	0	2	9	0	0	1	0	8	3	0	2	0	0	16	21

2. Therapist's Credibility (Sureness) versus Unsureness[b] — *Outcome*

	Patient			Therapist			Rater			Score			Combined			Total		
Process	–	0	+	–	0	+	–	0	+	–	0	+	–	0	+	–	0	+
Patient	0	3	3	0	1	1	0	0	3	0	3	1	0	0	0	0	7	8
Therapist	0	1	1	0	1	0	0	0	1	0	0	1	0	0	0	0	2	3
Rater	0	0	1	0	0	1	0	0	1	0	2	1	0	0	0	0	2	4
Index	0	0	0	0	0	0	0	0	0	0	0	0	0	0	1	0	0	1
Total	0	4	5	0	2	2	0	0	5	0	5	3	0	0	1	0	11	16

3. Patient's Role Engagement[c] — *Outcome*

	Patient			Therapist			Rater			Score			Combined			Total		
Process	–	0	+	–	0	+	–	0	+	–	0	+	–	0	+	–	0	+
Patient	0	1	8	0	1	3	0	1	0	0	3	1	0	0	1	0	6	13
Therapist	0	1	6	0	0	6	0	0	0	0	0	0	0	0	0	0	1	12
Rater	0	4	1	0	0	5	1	2	3	1	4	1	0	0	0	2	10	10
Total	0	6	15	0	1	14	1	3	3	1	7	2	0	0	1	2	17	35

4. Patient's Motivation[d] — *Outcome*

	Patient			Therapist			Rater			Score			Combined			Total		
Process	–	0	+	–	0	+	–	0	+	–	0	+	–	0	+	–	0	+
Patient	0	0	1	0	1	0	0	0	0	0	0	2	0	0	1	0	1	4
Therapist	0	3	3	0	1	6	0	1	0	1	1	0	0	0	0	1	6	9
Rater	0	1	0	0	1	0	0	0	1	0	3	0	0	1	0	0	6	1
Total	0	4	4	0	3	6	0	1	1	1	4	2	0	1	1	1	13	14

5. Reciprocal Role Investment[e] — *Outcome*

	Patient			Therapist			Rater			Score			Combined			Total		
Process	–	0	+	–	0	+	–	0	+	–	0	+	–	0	+	–	0	+
Patient	0	0	1	0	1	0	0	0	0	0	0	0	0	0	0	0	1	1
Therapist	0	0	0	0	0	0	0	0	0	0	0	0	0	0	0	0	0	0
Rater	0	0	0	0	0	0	0	0	2	0	0	0	0	0	0	0	0	2
Total	0	0	1	0	1	0	0	0	2	0	0	0	0	0	0	0	1	3

[a] + = therapist role engagement associated with positive outcome, or detachment associated with negative outcome; – = therapist role engagement associated with negative outcome, or detachment associated with positive outcome.

[b] + = therapist credibility associated with positive outcome, or unsureness associated with negative outcome; – = therapist credibility associated with negative outcome, or unsureness associated with positive outcome.

[c] + = patient role engagement associated with positive outcome; – = associated with negative outcome.

[d] + = patient motivation for therapy associated with positive outcome; – = associated with negative outcome.

[e] Three untabulated studies cited in Orlinsky, Grawe, & Parks (1994), p. 321.

TABLE 8.20 Therapeutic Bond: Interactive Coordination

1. *Therapist Collaborative versus Directiveness/Control*
   Fiedler, Albrecht, Rogge, & Schulte (1994)
   Fiedler, Vogt, Rogge, & Schulte (1994)
   Margraf, Barlow, Clark, & Telch (1993)
   Schulte, Hartung, & Wilke (1997)
   Schulte & Künzel (1995)
   Stiles, Agnew-Davies, Hardy, Barkham, & Shapiro (1998)
2. *Patient Collaborative versus Directiveness/Control*
   Schulte & Künzel (1995)
   Seibel & Dowd (1999)
   Strauss, Kröger, Hoffmann, & Burgmeier-Lohse (1994)
3. *Goal and Task Agreement*
   Hatcher (1999)
   Hatcher & Barends (1996)
   Henggeler, Melton, Brondino, Scherer, & Hanley (1997)
   Long (2001)
   Paivio & Bahr (1998)
   Quinn, Dotson, & Jordan (1997)
   Rector, Zuroff, & Segal (1999)
   Treasure et al. (1999)
   — (meta-analyses/reviews) —
   Tryon & Winograd (2002)
4. *Control Congruence*
   Lichtenberg et al. (1998)
   Westerman (1998)

must also be able to coordinate their efforts effectively, either as equal collaborators or in a directive leader-follower mode. *Therapists' collaborative versus directive* behavior was the focus of six recent studies (Table 8.20.1), largely from the Bochum group of D. Schulte. The results of these studies are mixed, leaving the impression that the focus of therapist directiveness and the treatment approach (e.g., exposure vs. cognitive therapy) have an impact on whether collaborative or directive therapist behavior is more helpful (Schulte, Hartung, & Wilke, 1997). These join 26 previous studies (Table 8.21.1) that contrasted therapist collaborativeness with either directiveness or permissiveness and also seemed to show very mixed findings (possibly due to theoretical unclarity; see Schulte & Künzel, 1995), though favorable outcomes were more likely with therapist collaborativeness as viewed from the patient's perspective.

Three recent studies by European colleagues (Table 8.20.2) also assessed the impact on outcome of *patients' collaborative versus controlling* behavior, adding to 21 prior studies whose findings more consistently indicated a better outcome for patients with a collaborative relational style (Table 8.21.2).

The impact on outcome of leadership coordination and control in the relationship was also examined in two recent studies (Table 8.20.4) with regard to the degree of *control congruence* between patient and therapist, thus shifting the level of analysis from individual behaviors to emergent relational properties. Eight other recent studies (Table 8.20.3) also focused at the relational level on the impact of patients' and therapists' *goal and task agreement* on outcome; a current review chapter found this alliance aspect a generally effective element of the therapeutic relationship.

Expressive Attunement

Besides more or less effective teamwork, another aspect of any relationship is the level of personal rapport between participants, which involves both the quality of their communication and their feelings towards one another. Questions of communication quality turn on how well persons express themselves and how much empathic understanding they show.

After Rogers (1957) theoretical paper on the effective conditions of personality change, a great deal of research focused on the impact of *therapists' empathic understanding*. As of 1992, 53 studies had presented more than 100 findings relating therapist empathy to outcome (Table 8.23.1), but over time the flow of studies has progressively diminished: 39 from 1958 through 1984, 14 from 1985 through 1992, and only 7 from 1993 through 2001 (Table 8.22.1). This trend may be due to relatively less research having been done on client-centered therapy (or at least process-outcome research; see Elliott, Greenberg, & Lietaer, this volume), and partly to a general acceptance of empathy as a factor in outcome, which has been clearly confirmed again in a current meta-analysis (Bohart et al., 2002).[10] However, studies tabulated in this chapter's last edition showed considerable variation across observational perspectives, with patient ratings and objective indices of therapist empathy most clearly associated with favorable outcomes, and therapist ratings of their own empathy by contrast hardly at all related to measures of patient outcome. Findings on therapist empathy were also considered in two current reviews (Table 8.22.1).

TABLE 8.21 Therapeutic Bond—Findings on Interactive Coordination (1950–1992)

1. Therapist Collaboration *(Cb)* versus Directiveness *(D)* or Permissiveness *(P)*[a]

	Outcome																	
	Patient			Therapist			Rater			Score			Combined			Total		
Process	–	0	+	–	0	+	–	0	+	–	0	+	–	0	+	–	0	+
Patient	0	1	3	0	1	2	1	0	1	0	1	1	0	0	0	1	3	7
Therapist	0	2	3	1	2	5	0	0	1	2	4	1	1	0	0	4	8	10
Rater	0	0	0	1	1	0	1	0	0	2	3	1	1	1	2	5	5	3
Total	0	3	6	2	4	7	2	0	2	4	8	3	2	1	2	10	16	20

2. Patient Collaboration *(Cb)* versus Dependence *(Dp)* or Controlling *(Cn)*[b]

	Outcome																	
	Patient			Therapist			Rater			Score			Combined			Total		
Process	–	0	+	–	0	+	–	0	+	–	0	+	–	0	+	–	0	+
Patient	0	1	5	0	1	2	0	0	1	0	1	0	0	0	1	0	3	9
Therapist	0	2	2	0	1	6	0	1	2	0	2	0	0	0	0	0	6	10
Rater	0	2	0	0	0	0	0	2	1	0	2	3	0	0	4	0	6	8
Total	0	5	7	0	2	8	0	3	4	0	5	3	0	0	5	0	15	27

[a] + = therapist collaboration associated with positive outcome, or therapist directiveness *(D)* or permissiveness *(P)* associated with negative outcome; – = therapist collaboration associated with negative outcome, or therapist directiveness *(D)* or permissiveness *(P)* associated with positive outcome.

[b] + = patient collaboration associated with positive outcome, or patient dependence *(Dp)* or controlling *(Cn)* associated with negative outcome; – = patient collaboration associated with negative outcome, or patient dependency *(Dp)* or controlling *(Cn)* associated with positive outcome.

TABLE 8.22 Therapeutic Bond: Expressive Attunement

1. *Therapist Empathic Understanding*
   Ablon & Jones (1999)
   Eyssell, Zeising, & Stuhr (1992)
   Fiedler, Albrecht, Rogge, & Schulte (1994)
   Konzag, Fikentscher, & Bandemer-Greulich (2000a, 2000b)
   Russell, Bryant, & Estrada (1996)
   Saunders (2000)
   Schmidtchen & Hennies (1996)
   — (meta-analyses/reviews) —
   Bohart, Elliott, Greenberg, & Watson (2002)
   Schmidtchen (2001)
2. *Patient Expressiveness*
   Ablon & Jones (1999)
   Stiles, Agnew-Davies, Hardy, Barkham, & Shapiro (1998)
3. *Patient Empathic Understanding*
   Hill, Thompson, Cogar, & Denman (1993)
   Schmidtchen, Acke, & Hennies (1995)
4. *Communicative Rapport*
   Piper, Boroto, Joyce, & McCallum (1995)

There were no recent studies of *therapist expressiveness* to add to the 11 cited in prior editions of this chapter (Table 8.23.2), and very few studies focused on the effects for outcome of the patient's side of communicative attunement.

Only two recent studies (Table 8.22.2) examined *patient expressiveness*, in contrast to 25 previous studies whose findings were tabulated in the last edition and showed patient expressiveness related to positive outcome more often than not, except from the patient's perspective (Table 8.23.3).[11]

Similarly, just two recent studies (Table 8.22.3) also examined the relation of outcome to the *patient's empathic understanding* in therapy, which join seven previous studies (Table 8.23.4). This scarcity of studies is less surprising, since patient empathy was never directly raised as an issue by theories of psychotherapy, and it was previously considered in only seven studies. Both therapist expressiveness and patient empathy will gain more attention from researchers if they view the therapeutic relationship as a resonating bidirectional communication system rather than a therapist-made environment exerting a unidirectional influence on the patient.

Communicative rapport was assessed from patients' and therapists' perspectives in one

TABLE 8.23 Therapeutic Bond—Findings on Expressive Attunement (1950–1992)

1. Therapist Empathic Understanding[a]

	Outcome																	
	Patient			Therapist			Rater			Score			Combined			Total		
Process	–	0	+	–	0	+	–	0	+	–	0	+	–	0	+	–	0	+
Patient	0	4	12	0	1	6	0	2	4	0	6	10	0	0	2	0	13	34
Therapist	0	4	1	0	3	3	0	3	0	0	5	0	0	0	0	0	15	4
Rater	0	7	1	0	6	2	0	3	1	0	8	15	0	0	0	0	21	19
Index	0	1	1	0	0	2	0	0	0	0	0	1	0	0	1	0	1	5
Total	0	16	15	0	10	13	0	8	5	0	19	26	0	0	3	0	53	62

2. Therapist Expressiveness[b]

	Outcome																	
	Patient			Therapist			Rater			Score			Combined			Total		
Process	–	0	+	–	0	+	–	0	+	–	0	+	–	0	+	–	0	+
Patient	0	1	0	0	1	0	0	0	0	0	0	0	0	1	0	0	3	0
Rater	0	0	1	0	0	1	0	1	0	0	2	3	0	2	0	0	5	5
Index	0	0	0	0	0	1	0	0	0	0	1	1	0	0	0	0	1	2
Total	0	1	1	0	1	2	0	1	0	0	3	4	0	3	0	0	9	7

3. Patient Expressiveness[c]

	Outcome																	
	Patient			Therapist			Rater			Score			Combined			Total		
Process	–	0	+	–	0	+	–	0	+	–	0	+	–	0	+	–	0	+
Patient	0	0	4	0	2	1	0	2	0	0	1	0	0	0	1	0	5	6
Therapist	0	2	0	0	0	5	0	0	1	0	1	0	0	0	0	0	3	6
Rater	0	2	4	1	2	3	0	2	1	1	2	7	0	1	2	2	9	17
Index	0	0	0	0	0	1	0	0	0	0	0	1	0	0	1	0	0	3
Total	0	4	8	1	4	10	0	4	2	1	4	8	0	1	4	2	17	32

4. Patient's Empathic Understanding[d]

	Outcome																	
	Patient			Therapist			Rater			Score			Combined			Total		
Process	–	0	+	–	0	+	–	0	+	–	0	+	–	0	+	–	0	+
Patient	0	0	0	0	0	0	0	0	1	0	0	1	0	0	1	0	0	3
Index	1	2	0	1	2	1	0	0	0	0	1	0	0	0	1	2	5	2
Total	1	2	0	1	2	1	0	0	1	0	1	1	0	0	2	2	5	5

5. Communicative Rapport[e]

	Outcome																	
	Patient			Therapist			Rater			Score			Combined			Total		
Process	–	0	+	–	0	+	–	0	+	–	0	+	–	0	+	–	0	+
Patient	0	0	2	0	0	1	0	1	1	0	0	1	0	0	0	0	1	5
Therapist	0	1	0	0	1	1	0	1	1	0	1	0	0	0	0	0	4	2
Rater	0	1	1	0	1	2	0	1	1	0	1	1	0	0	0	0	4	5
Index	0	2	6	0	2	6	0	0	0	0	3	2	0	0	0	0	7	14
Total	0	4	9	0	4	10	0	3	3	0	5	4	0	0	0	0	16	26

[a] + = therapist empathic attunement associated with positive outcome; – = therapist empathic attunement associated with negative outcome.

[b] + = therapist expressiveness associated with positive outcome; – = therapist expressiveness associated with negative outcome.

[c] + = patient expressiveness associated with positive outcome; – = patient expressiveness associated with negative outcome.

[d] + = patient attunement associated with positive outcome; – = patient attunement associated with negative outcome.

[e] + = reciprocal attunement associated with positive outcome; – = reciprocal attunement associated with negative outcome.

recent study which showed that both were positively related to measures of outcome (Table 8.22.4). Unfortunately, researchers' interest in this topic has diminished dramatically, with 17 studies done through 1984 and just two more from 1985 through 1992, despite the fact that the findings showed communicative rapport to be consistently and sometimes substantially related to positive outcomes (Table 8.23.5).

Affective Attitude

Personal rapport in a relationship is also manifested in the feelings that persons have towards one another (e.g., liking, warmth, trust vs. wariness, aloofness, resentment).

Therapist affirmation versus negation has been a major focus of process-outcome research since Rogers (1957) emphasized positive regard as a facilitator of growth and healing, with no less than 73 separate studies cited in past editions of this chapter and another 12 studies in the current period (Table 8.24.1). A clear majority of 154 findings from prior studies showed affirmative therapist behavior related to positive outcome, most notably when therapist affirmation was assessed from the patient's perspective (Table 8.25.1). A current review of the topic judges this to be a probably effective element of therapeutic relationships, but from the patient's perspective a more definite conclusion would be warranted (Table 8.24.1).

Patient affirmation versus negation toward the therapist was also considered with respect to outcome in 32 previous studies but only 4 recent ones (Table 8.24.2). That substantial body of earlier research showed that positive outcomes were consistently associated with affirmative patient feelings, whether those were assessed by the patients, the therapist, or outside observers (Table 8.25.2).

Some research has also focused on affective attitudes at a joint relational level, in terms of *reciprocal affective patterns* and more specifically in terms of mutual affirmation versus negation. Seven recent studies and one review (Table 8.24.3) add evidence to 19 previous studies in which nearly 80% of the findings showed that mutual affirmation in the therapeutic bond was associated with positive patient outcome (Table 8.25.3). This was most decisively so when reciprocal affect was assessed by independent observers and by patients.

TABLE 8.24 Therapeutic Bond: Affective Attitude

1. *Therapist Affirmation versus Negation*
   Archer, Forbes, Metcalfe, & Winter (2000)
   Dürr & Hahlweg (1996)
   Eugster & Wampold (1996)
   Hatcher & Barends (1996)
   Liddle (1996)
   Merten, Anstadt, Ullrich, Krause, & Buchheim (1996).
   Murran, Samstag, Jilton, Batchelder, & Winston (1997)
   Najavits & Strupp (1994)
   Quinn, Dotson, & Jordan (1997)
   Rector, Zuroff, & Segal (1999)
   Russell, Bryant, & Estrada (1996)
   Stiles, Agnew-Davies, Hardy, Barkham, & Shapiro (1998)
   — (meta-analyses/reviews) —
   Farber & Lane (2002)
2. *Patient Affirmation versus Negation*
   Ablon & Jones (1999)
   Kendall (1994)
   Merten, Anstadt, Ullrich, Krause, & Buchheim (1996)
   Murran, Samstag, Jilton, Batchelder, & Winston (1997)
3. *Reciprocal Affective Pattern*
   Anstadt, Merten, Ullrich, & Krause (1997)
   Merten (2001)
   Murran, Samstag, Jilton, Batchelder, & Winston (1997)
   Paivio & Bahr (1998)
   Saunders (1998)
   Saunders (2000)
   Tracey, Sherry, & Albright (1999)
   — (meta-analyses/reviews) —
   Binder & Strupp (1997)

Experiential Congruence

The Generic Model of Psychotherapy originated as a scheme for classifying process variables that researchers used in their studies rather than as a set of *a priori* categories. The model continued to evolve as researchers added new variables to their studies. For the most part, the major categories developed in 1986 have successfully assimilated the findings of later studies, but a new category for "temporal patterns" was introduced in the 1994 edition of this chapter because by then researchers had begun to study how process variables evolve over the course of treatment and were examining how those patterns of change related to outcome. A number of

TABLE 8.25 Therapeutic Bond—Findings on Affective Attitude (1950–1992)

1. Therapist Affirmation (versus Negativity) Toward Patient[a] — *Outcome*

	Patient			Therapist			Rater			Score			Combined			Total		
Process	–	0	+	–	0	+	–	0	+	–	0	+	–	0	+	–	0	+
Patient	1	4	14	1	2	12	0	1	5	0	12	9	0	1	1	2	20	41
Therapist	0	6	5	0	4	12	0	4	1	1	5	1	0	0	0	1	19	19
Rater	1	4	2	0	4	4	0	7	7	0	9	13	0	0	1	1	24	27
Total	2	14	21	1	10	28	0	12	13	1	26	23	0	1	2	4	63	87

2. Patient Affirmation (versus Negativity) Toward Therapist[b] — *Outcome*

	Patient			Therapist			Rater			Score			Combined			Total		
Process	–	0	+	–	0	+	–	0	+	–	0	+	–	0	+	–	0	+
Patient	0	3	6	1	2	5	0	0	2	0	3	3	0	0	0	1	8	16
Therapist	0	1	5	0	1	10	0	1	0	0	4	0	0	0	0	0	7	15
Rater	0	0	0	0	0	1	1	0	1	0	1	4	0	0	1	1	1	7
Index	0	0	0	0	0	0	0	0	0	0	0	0	0	0	3	0	0	3
Total	0	4	11	1	3	16	1	1	3	0	8	7	0	0	4	2	16	41

3. Mutual Affirmation (versus Negativity)[c] — *Outcome*

	Patient			Therapist			Rater			Score			Combined			Total		
Process	–	0	+	–	0	+	–	0	+	–	0	+	–	0	+	–	0	+
Patient	0	1	7	0	1	1	0	2	2	0	0	1	0	0	0	0	4	11
Therapist	0	0	0	0	1	1	0	0	0	0	1	0	0	0	0	0	2	1
Rater	0	0	3	0	0	0	0	0	3	0	1	3	0	0	1	0	1	10
Index	0	0	1	0	0	1	0	0	0	0	0	1	0	0	0	0	0	3
Total	0	1	11	0	2	3	0	2	5	0	2	5	0	0	1	0	7	25

[a] + = therapist warmth/acceptance associated with positive outcome, or therapist coldness/hostility associated with negative outcome; – = therapist warmth/acceptance associated with negative outcome, or therapist coldness/hostility associated with positive outcome.

[b] + = patient affirmation associated with positive outcome, or patient hostility associated with negative outcome; – = patient affirmation associated with negative outcome, or patient hostility associated with positive outcome.

[c] + = mutual affirmation associated with positive outcome; – = mutual affirmation associated with negative outcome.

minor additions and adjustments in the scheme of process facets will be found in this edition, but the most important of those was prompted by three studies that explore a new aspect of the therapeutic bond.

Cummings and her colleagues (Cummings, Hallberg, Martin, & Slemon, 1992; Cummings, Martin, Hallberg, & Slemon, 1992) first showed a positive relation between session effectiveness and the *congruence* between patients' and therapists' immediate postsession recall of what was most important in the session. More recently, Kivlighan and Arthur (2000) refined the operationalization of congruence and demonstrated its positive relation to post-treatment outcome. In addition, drawing inspiration from Peplinsky and Karst (1964), they examined the way that congruence evolved over the course of treatment and the relation of increasing congruence to favorable outcome (Table 8.26). The results suggest that the degree to which patient and therapist converge in how they experience their session—in other words, the degree to which they *experience the same relational reality*—is positively related to outcome. These studies introduce the experiential interior of the therapeutic relationship as a variable in process-outcome research and as a new Generic Model category, which has

TABLE 8.26 Therapeutic Bond: Experiential Congruence

Experiential Congruence
- Cummings, Hallberg, Martin, & Slemon (1992)
- Cummings, Martin, Hallberg, & Slemon (1992)
- Kivlighan & Arthur (2000)

only rarely been studied and then seemingly just as a process variable independent of outcome (e.g., Orlinsky & Howard, 1975).

Self-Relatedness

Process variables of self-relatedness assess aspects of the reflexive or "inner" psychological state of the participants during sessions. These variables have been studied in both patients and therapists and can be positive or negative with respect to therapeutic learning.

Patient Self-Relatedness

Fifteen recent studies examined various aspects of patients' self-relatedness. Most of the newer studies assessed positive aspects of self-relatedness, five of them focusing again on *patient openness* or genuineness (Table 8.27.A1), adding richly to 28 previous studies whose findings had shown a very consistent association between patient openness and positive outcome (Table 8.28.1).

Only one recent study investigated the relation of outcome to patient *"experiencing"* levels[12] during sessions (Table 8.27.A2), and curiously enough that study was conducted in an investigation of cognitive behavioral treatment. This variable, which was initially defined in the context of experiential client-centered therapy, was previously much studied with fairly positive though rather inconsistent findings (Table 8.28.2).

Three other studies focused on conceptually similar aspects of self-relatedness, such as the patient's *acceptance of feelings* (Table 8.27.A3), the patient's sense of *autonomy* or choicefulness (Table 8.27.A4), and the patient's level of *defensive maturity* (Table 8.27.A5).[13]

Four recent studies examined outcome in relation to an aspect of patient self-relatedness that is new to process-outcome research (Table 8.27.A6). This promising innovation considers outcome as a function of the patient's internalization of the therapeutic relationship as a basis for *modeled self-care*,[14] and seems definitely worth the attention of future investigators.

Two studies also focused innovatively on negative aspects of patient self-relatedness in relation to outcome—one on *defensive inhibition* (Table 8.27.B1) and the other on distressing (e.g., embarrassed) *self-consciousness* (Table 8.27.B2).

Therapist Self-Relatedness

Three aspects of therapist self-relatedness were topics of study in connection with outcome during the current period. Three recent studies and

TABLE 8.27 Self-Relatedness

A. Patient Positive Self-Relatedness

1. *Openness* [Genuineness]
   Ablon & Jones (1999)
   Ambühl (1993)
   Eugster & Wampold (1996)
   Fiedler, Albrecht, Rogge, & Schulte (1996)
   Kolden (1996)

2. *"Experiencing"*
   Castonguay, Goldfried, Wiser, Raue, & Hayes (1996)

3. *Acceptance of Feelings*
   Eyssell, Zeising, & Stuhr (1992)

4. *Felt Autonomy*
   Schulte & Künzel (1995)

5. *Defense Maturity*
   Winston, Samstag, Winston, & Muran (1994)

6. *Modeled Self-Care* [Internalization]
   Bassler & Krauthauser (1996)
   Geller & Farber (1993) [new var]
   Harrist, Quintana, Strupp, & Henry (1994).
   Knox, Goldberg, Woodhouse, & Hill (1999)

B. Patient Negative Self-Relatedness

1. *Defensive Inhibition*
   Saunders (1998)

2. *Self-Consciousness*
   Woody, Chambless, & Glass (1997)

C. Therapist Self-Relatedness

1. *Openness* [Genuineness, Self-Congruence]
   Eugster & Wampold (1996)
   Eyssell, Zeising, & Stuhr (1992)
   Schmidtchen & Hennies (1996)
   — (meta-analyses/reviews) —
   Klein, Kolden, Michels, & Chisholm-Stockard (2002)
   Schmidtchen (2001)

2. *Countertransference Management*
   Hayes, Riker, & Ingram (1997)
   — (meta-analyses/reviews) —
   Gelso & Hayes (2002)

3. *Self-Critical Reflectivity*
   Najavits & Strupp (1994)

TABLE 8.28 Findings on Participant Self-Relatedness (1950–1992)

1. Patient Openness versus Defensiveness[a]

	Outcome																	
	Patient			Therapist			Rater			Score			Combined			Total		
Process	–	0	+	–	0	+	–	0	+	–	0	+	–	0	+	–	0	+
Therapist	0	0	2	0	0	6	0	0	1	0	1	0	0	0	0	0	1	9
Rater	0	1	1	0	0	2	0	0	1	0	1	9	0	2	5	0	4	18
Index	0	0	0	0	0	0	0	0	0	0	0	0	0	1	2	0	1	2
Total	0	1	4	0	0	9	0	2	4	0	3	11	0	3	8	0	9	36

2. Patient's "Experiencing" (Articulation of Felt Meaning)[b]

	Outcome																	
	Patient			Therapist			Rater			Score			Combined			Total		
Process	–	0	+	–	0	+	–	0	+	–	0	+	–	0	+	–	0	+
Patient	0	0	1	0	0	0	0	0	0	0	0	0	0	0	1	0	0	2
Therapist	0	0	0	0	0	3	0	0	0	0	1	0	0	0	0	0	1	3
Rater	0	4	1	0	3	5	0	2	0	1	8	8	0	0	1	1	17	15
Total	0	4	2	0	3	8	0	2	0	1	9	8	0	0	2	1	18	20

3. Therapist Self-Congruence (Genuineness)[c]

	Outcome																	
	Patient			Therapist			Rater			Score			Combined			Total		
Process	–	0	+	–	0	+	–	0	+	–	0	+	–	0	+	–	0	+
Patient	0	3	4	0	2	1	0	1	0	0	7	5	0	1	1	0	14	11
Therapist	0	3	0	0	0	4	0	1	0	0	3	0	0	0	0	0	7	4
Rater	0	2	0	0	2	1	0	1	0	1	10	6	0	0	0	1	15	7
Index	0	0	1	0	0	0	0	0	0	0	0	0	0	0	0	0	0	1
Total	0	8	5	0	4	6	0	3	0	1	20	11	0	1	1	1	36	23

4. Therapist's Self-Acceptance and Assurance versus Self-Rejection and Control[d]

	Outcome																	
	Patient			Therapist			Rater			Score			Combined			Total		
Process	–	0	+	–	0	+	–	0	+	–	0	+	–	0	+	–	0	+
Therapist	0	2	1	1	1	1	0	0	0	0	2	1	0	0	0	1	5	3
Index	0	0	0	0	0	0	0	0	0	0	0	0	0	1	2	0	1	2
Total	0	2	1	1	1	1	0	0	0	0	2	1	0	1	2	1	6	5

[a] + = patient inner openness associated with positive outcome, or defensiveness negatively related to outcome; – = patient openness associated with negative outcome, or defensiveness associated with positive outcome.
[b] + = articulated felt meaning associated with positive outcome; – = articulated felt meaning negatively related to outcome.
[c] + = therapist genuineness associated with positive outcome; – = therapist genuineness negatively related to outcome.
[d] + = therapist self-acceptance associated with positive outcome, or therapist self-rejection and control associated with poor outcome; – = therapist self-rejection and control associated with positive outcome, or therapist self-acceptance associated with negative outcome.

two current reviews (Table 8.27.C1) examined the familiar variable of *therapist openness* (genuineness or self-congruence), joining 35 previous studies whose findings showed this to be only sometimes but not consistently related to positive outcome (Table 8.28.3).

Another study from a psychodynamic perspective examined outcome in relation to the therapist's *management of countertransference issues* in therapy, and a current study also reviews findings in that area (Table 8.27.C2).

Finally, one study examined the therapist's *self-critical reflectivity* with results suggesting that critical self-reflection may be a characteristic of effective therapists (Table 8.27.C3), which overlaps partly with two previous studies of therapist self-acceptance versus self-rejection that yielded mixed results (Table 8.28.4).

TABLE 8.29 In-Session Impacts

A. Patient Positive Impacts [Therapeutic Realizations]	
1. Global Positive Impact/Productivity	
Ablon & Jones (1999)	Kolden (1996)
Ambühl (1993)	Kolden et al. (2000)
Eugster & Wampold (1996)	Mallinckrodt (1993)
Hatcher & Barends (1996)	Stiles, Reynolds et al. (1994)
Henggeler, Melton, Brondino, Scherer, & Hanley (1997)	
2. Cognitive Shift	
Hayes & Strauss (1998)	Paulson, Truscott & Stuart (1999)
Hoffart & Sexton (2002)	Tang & DeRubeis (1999a)
Murran et al. (1995)	
3. Insight	
Archer, Forbes, Metcalfe, & Winter (2000)	Hoffart & Sexton (2002)
Cummings, Slemon, & Hallberg (1993)	Kivlighan, Multon, & Patton (2000)
Elliott & Wexler (1994)	O'Connor, Edelstein, Berry, & Weiss (1994)
Gelso, Kivlighan, Wine, Jones, & Friedman (1997)	Sexton (1993, 1996)
	Stiles, Reynolds et al. (1994)
4. Problem Resolution	
Greenberg & Hirscheimer (1994)	— (meta-analyses/reviews) —
Schmidtchen, Acke, & Hennies (1995)	Schmidtchen (2001)
Stiles, Reynolds et al. (1994)	Stiles (2002)
Watson & Greenberg (1996)	
5. Emotional Relief/Catharsis	
Araujo, Ito, & Marks (1996)	Paulson, Truscott, & Stuart (1999)
Archer, Forbes, Metcalfe, & Winter (2000)	
6. Morale (Support/Encouragment/Hope)	
Elliott & Wexler (1994)	Paulson, Truscott, & Stuart (1999)
Hoffart & Sexton (2002)	Stiles, Reynolds et al. (1994)
7. Stress Habituation	
Jaycox, Foa, & Morral (1998)	
8. Self-Efficacy/Personal Growth	
Cummings, Slemon, & Hallberg (1993)	
Tschacher, Baur, & Grawe (2000)	
B. Patient Negative Impacts [Harms]	
Elliot & Wexler (1994)	
Hatcher & Barends (1996)	
Sexton (1996)	
Stiles, Reynolds et al. (1994)	

In-Session Impacts

In-session impacts are immediate clinical changes (e.g., feeling better or feeling worse) that occur during a session in response to what is happening during the session. In principle, these changes occur for both participants in therapy, but in practice process-outcome research thus far has focused only on patients.[15] Although these impacts can be negative as well as positive (e.g., confusion rather

TABLE 8.30 Findings on In-Session Impacts (1950–1992)

Patient Positive Impacts (Therapeutic Realizations)[a]	Outcome																	
	Patient			Therapist			Rater			Score			Combined			Total		
Process	–	0	+	–	0	+	–	0	+	–	0	+	–	0	+	–	0	+
Patient	0	2	8	0	0	2	0	5	4	0	4	3	0	1	4	0	12	21
Therapist	0	4	1	0	1	1	0	1	1	0	2	2	0	0	1	0	8	6
Rater	0	1	3	0	0	5	0	1	1	0	3	5	0	0	5	0	5	19
Index	0	0	0	0	0	0	1	0	1	0	0	0	0	0	6	1	0	7
Total	0	7	12	0	1	8	1	7	7	0	9	10	0	1	16	1	25	53

[a] + = positive in-session impact associated with positive outcome, or negative in-session impact associated with negative outcome; – = negative in-session impact associated with positive outcome, or positive in-session impact associated with negative outcome.

than insight, or anxiety rather than assurance), researchers have mainly studied positive impacts (formerly called "therapeutic realizations").

As many as 28 recent studies assessed the relation of various types of in-session impact to outcome, and several studies weighed more than one kind of impact, joining 38 previous studies whose many findings showed a consistent association between therapeutic realizations and positive outcomes (Table 8.30).

Nine of the recent studies examined the *global positive impact* and rated productivity of sessions in relation to outcome (Table 8.29.A1), while others probed more specific impacts.

Five studies of cognitive therapy focused on the contribution to outcome of significant *cognitive shifts* during sessions (Table 8.29.A2).

Nine other recent studies assessed outcome in relation to the somewhat similar (but differently conceptualized) impact of *insight*, mainly in the context of psychodynamic and experiential therapy (Table 8.29.A3).

Four studies explored the association of outcome with *problem resolution* as conceptualized in experiential treatments, and two current reviews assessed findings, one with respect to patients' assimilation of problematic experiences and the other in the specific context of client-centered child therapy (Table 8.29.A4).

Emotional in-session impacts were also investigated in several recent studies. Three of those studies focused on *emotional relief or catharsis* (Table 8.29.A5); four explored the effects of *heightened morale* in terms of felt support, encouragement, and hope (Table 8.29.A6); and one assessed *stress habituation* during sessions of exposure therapy as related to improvement in posttraumatic stress disorder (Table 8.29.A7). On a more general level, two studies examined patients' in-session experiences of *self-efficacy and personal growth* (Table 8.29.A8).

Finally, four of the recent studies included measures of negative in-session impacts and assessed their association with patients' outcomes (Table 8.29.B).

Temporal Sequence

Temporal patterns in process variables have been analyzed at several levels in relation to outcome, as a function of time in the session, stage in therapy, and the whole course of treatment.

Session Development

Only three recent studies (Table 8.31.A) examined the sequential position or patterns of change in process events within single or adjacent therapy sessions, and these join only five previous studies (Table 8.32.1). The scarcity of these studies is disappointing in view of the technical interest of their methods and their ability to shed light on how process events evolve and transform into shorter- and longer-term outcome effects. It seems likely that many pure process studies could easily add interesting evidence on this level if they would assess postsession or intersession outcomes in their analyses.

Process Stage or Trajectory

In contrast to the scant attention paid to session development, 54 recent studies representing a wide range of treatment contexts focused on process stage or change trajectories in relation to outcome (Table 8.31.B), making it the most popular variable of process-outcome researchers along with global assessments of the alliance (Table 8.16.1). Three current review chapters also

TABLE 8.31 Temporal Patterns

A. Session Development

Burgoon et al. (1993)
Murran, Samstag, Jilton, Batchelder, & Winston (1997)
Tang & DeRubeis (1999a)

B. Process Stage or Trajectory

Addis & Jacobson (2000)
Blatt, Zuroff, Bondi, Sanislow, & Pilkonis (1998)
Bouchard et al. (1996)
Carroll et al. (1994)
Castonguay, Pincus, Agras, & Hines (1998)
Clark et al. (1994)
DeJong-Meyer et al. (1999)
Dürr & Hahlweg (1996)
Elliott & Wexler (1994)
Fiedler, Albrecht, Rogge, & Schulte (1994)
Fiedler, Vogt, Rogge, & Schulte (1994)
Gaston, Thompson, Gallagher, Cournoyer, & Gagnon (1998)
Gelso, Kivlighan, Wine, Jones, & Friedman (1997)
Hoffart & Sexton (2002)
Hölzer, Pokorny, Kächele, & Luborsky (1997)
Jones, Peveler, Hope, & Fairburn (1993)
Kendall et al. (1997)
Kivlighan & Arthur (2000)
Kivlighan & Shaughnessy (1995)
Leung & Heimberg (1996)
Mallinckrodt (1993, 1996)
Mergenthaler (1996)
Merten (2001)
Merten, Anstadt, Ullrich, Krause, & Buchheim (1996)
Murran, Samstag, Jilton, Batchelder, & Winston (1997)
Nosper (1999)
O'Connor, Edelstein, Berry, & Weiss (1994)
Paivio & Bahr (1998)
Paivio & Patterson (1999)
Patton, Kivlighan, & Multon (1997)
Piper, Boroto, Joyce, & McCallum (1995)
Priebe (1993)
Priebe & Gruyters (1995)
Rector, Bagby, Segal, Joffe, & Levitt (2000)
Regli, Bieber, Mathier, & Grawe (2000)
Rosner, Frick, Beutler, & Daldrup (1999)
Rudolf & Manz (1993)
Schauenburg, Sammet, Rabung, & Strack (2002)
Schauenburg, Sammet, & Strack (2002)
Schmidtchen, Acke, & Hennies (1995)
Schmidtchen & Hennies (1996)
Schulte, Hartung, & Wilke (1997)
Schulte & Künzel (1995)
Smith & Grawe (2000)
Smith, Regli, & Grawe (1999)
Startup & Edmonds (1994)
Strauss, Kröger, Hoffmann, & Burgmeier-Lohse (1994)
Tarrier & Humphreys (2000)
Tracey, Sherry, & Albright (1999)
Westerman (1998)
Wilson, Loeb et al. (1999)
Winston, Samstag, Winston, & Muran (1994)
Woody, Chambless, & Glass (1997)
Znoj, Grawe, & Jeger (2000)
— (meta-analyses/reviews) —
Prochaska & Norcross (2002)
Schmidtchen (2001)
Tang & DeRubeis (1999b)

C. Treatment Course

1. Dose Effects

Anderson & Lambert (2001)
Avants, Margolin, Kosten, Rounsaville, & Schottenfeld (1998)
Barkham et al. (1996)
DeJong-Meyer, Hautzinger, Rudolf, Strauss, & Frick (1996b)
Hautzinger et al. (1996)
Hilesenroth, Ackerman, & Blagys (2001)
Howard, Lueger, Maling, & Martinovich (1993)
Kadera, Lambert, & Andrews (1996)
Kopta, Howard, Lowry, & Beutler (1994)
Lichtenberg et al. (1998)
Lueger (1998)
Maling, Gurtman, & Howard (1995)
Penava, Otto, Maki, & Pollack (1998)
Reynolds et al. (1996)
Salzer, Bickman, & Lambert (1999)
Schauenburg, Sammet, & Strack (2002)
Shadish et al. (1993)
Svensson & Hansson (1999)
Warner et al. (2001)
Wilson, Mason, & Ewing (1997)

(continues)

TABLE 8.31 *(Continued)*

2. Treatment Duration

Archer, Forbes, Metcalfe, & Winter (2000)
Barkham, Rees et al. (1996)
Bassler, Krauthauser, & Hoffmann (1995)
Bernal, Bonilla, Padilla-Cotto, & Pérez-Prado (1998)
Borgart & Meermann (1999)
Bovasso, Eaton, & Armenian (1999)
Clark et al. (1999)
Durham et al. (1994)
Eaton, Abeles, & Gutfreund (1993)
Gaston, Piper, Debbane, Bienvenu, & Garant (1994)
Goren (1993)
Hellström, Fellenius, & Öst (1996)
Høglend (1993, 1996a, 1996b)
Høglend, Engelstad, Sørbye, Heyerdahl, & Amlo (1994)
Høglend & Piper (1997)
Houts, Berman, & Abramson (1994)
Kächele, Kordy, Richard, & Research Group TR-EAT (2001)
Latimer, Newcomb, Winters, & Stinchfield (2000)
McMullen & Conway (1994)
Nosper (1999)
Öst, Brandberg, & Alm (1997)
Power, Sharp, Swanson, & Simpson (2000)
Sandell, Blomberg et al. (2000)
Seikkula, Alakare, & Aaltonen (2001)
Shapiro, Barkham et al. (1994)
Shapiro et al. (1995).
Smyrnios & Kirkby (1993)
Snell, Mallinckrodt, Hill, & Lambert (2001)
Stephens, Roffman, & Curtin (2000)
Svartberg, Seltzer, & Stiles (1998)
Tarrier, Sommerfield, Pilgrim, & Faragher (2000)
— (meta-analyses/reviews) —
Elliott (2001)
Gould, Otto, Pollack, & Yap (1997)
Gurman (2001)
Jacobi, Dahme, & Rustenbach (1997)
McCullough & Andrews (2001)
McGinn & Sanderson (2001)
Messer (2001)
Rohrbaugh & Shoham (2001)

consider findings on the impact of treatment stage. Taken together, these add greatly to 29 previous studies that assessed outcome and stage of treatment, which consistently showed stage effects in relation to outcome (Table 8.32.2).

The popularity of this area may be due to researchers' growing use of statistical techniques such as growth curves and hierarchical linear equations to model change over time, but it nevertheless has produced an important conceptual advance, from a temporally decontextualized synchronic representation of therapeutic process (arrived at by averaging across randomly selected process segments) to a truer representation of process as patterns of change or trajectories across sequential time points. As a caution, however, one should note that temporal trajectories often are estimated as best-fit lines from observations made at relatively few time-points and that the statistical techniques used often require making assumptions that can impact their results. Nevertheless, this is clearly a significant development in the field[16]; the 54 recently published studies mark a major new focus of process-outcome research and reflect a trend that is likely to continue unabated.

Treatment Course

Two temporal aspects of whole treatment courses have been studied in relation to outcome—one fairly new and the other as old as psychotherapy research itself. The new area, launched by Howard et al. (1986), examines the effects of therapy as a function of variable dosage; the old area, dating to 1950 at least (Bartlett, 1950), examines the association between outcome and the total duration of treatment.

Nineteen studies during the current review period examined *dose-effect relationships* across a wide variety of treatments, settings, types of patients, and often using very large data sets (Table 8.31.C1). Using statistical techniques such as probit analysis and survival analysis, these investigations represent an important development that parallels and complements the study of process trajectories (mentioned above), which together serve to bring temporality fully into the domain of process-outcome research.

The traditional assessment of outcome as a function of overall treatment duration also continued during this review period with the addition of 31 recent studies (Table 8.31.C2) to the 97 pre-

TABLE 8.32 Findings on Temporal Patterns (1950–1992)

1. Session Development[a]												
	Outcome											
	Patient		Therapist		Rater		Score		Combined		Total	
Process	0	+	0	+	0	+	0	+	0	+	0	+
Rater	0	0	0	0	0	0	0	0	1	1	1	1
Index	1	2	3	0	3	1	0	1	0	5	7	9
Total	1	2	3	0	3	1	0	1	1	6	8	10

2. Stage of Treatment[b]												
	Outcome											
	Patient		Therapist		Rater		Score		Combined		Total	
Process	0	+	0	+	0	+	0	+	0	+	0	+
Stage	2	5	5	2	3	4	2	9	2	20	14	40

3. Treatment Duration[c]																		
	Outcome																	
	Patient			Therapist			Rater			Score			Combined			Total		
Process	–	0	+	–	0	+	–	0	+	–	0	+	–	0	+	–	0	+
Long>Short	0	15	16	2	13	33	1	7	20	3	14	30	0	1	1	6	50	100

[a] + = in-session sequential effects differentially associated with outcome; 0 = no significant association.

[b] + = stage of therapy differentially associated with outcome; 0 = no significant association.

[c] + = longer treatment duration associated with positive outcome; – = longer treatment duration associated with negative outcome.

vious studies that have examined this association. Moreover, a total of eight recent reviews assessed the numerous findings relating treatment duration to outcome in various treatment contexts. The findings of previous studies (Table 8.32.3) indicated more often than not that greater treatment duration was associated with better outcomes, but certainly not invariably so; in some cases, shorter treatment duration was associated with better outcomes.

Of particular note is a set of six reviews showing that changes achieved in rather limited times by treatments of diverse orientations are often impressive (Special Issue on Brief Therapy, 2001). However, comparisons between studies favoring brief therapies and others to the value of longer treatment durations are impeded by the qualitative differences in outcomes assessed. For example, Howard, Lueger, Maling, and Martinovich (1993) present evidence that changes in the patient occur in a qualitative stepwise way: initially, in the form of "remoralization" (i.e., a more hopeful, active stance and an improvement of well-being), followed by the reduction of symptomatology in a second stage of outcome, and by the reduction of the patient's vulnerabilities in a third stage. This phase model implies different outcome operationalizations for the different phases in therapy and contributes to a more detailed analysis of the impact of treatment duration on outcome. Further studies in this area can be expected to clarify what can be achieved with short treatment durations and what cannot be achieved without longer treatments.

Clearly, the impact of treatment duration on outcome must be produced by interaction with many other factors, and the relationship between treatment duration and outcome is not linear. The dosage studies show that a minimum exposure to therapy is needed and that diminishing gains are obtained beyond a certain point. It is also not hard to believe that, for patients receiving an appropriate treatment in which they are doing well, more is likely to be better (up to a point), whereas for patients not receiving an appropriate treatment, or receiving a treatment in which they are not doing well, less is likely to be better (or at least less bad). The studies in hand demonstrate these varied possibilities. Careful analysis of their findings should help to define the circumstances in which (and the extent to which) longer or shorter treatment durations may yield more desirable outcomes.

CONCLUDING COMMENTS

In 1994, the conclusion of this chapter noted that "the volume of process-outcome findings has more than doubled since the [1986] edition of this *Handbook*" and that "newly reported findings were drawn from 192 papers," which "reflects an astonishing rate of growth in the number and activity of researchers since 1985." A count of the studies cited for their process-outcome findings in the present edition totals 279 (in addition to 42 empirical reviews and meta-analyses)—nearly half again the number of studies cited in 1994. Over a third of all the process-outcome studies published since 1950 appeared in less than the past 10 years. Clearly, the rate of growth in the number and activity of researchers reporting process-outcome findings continues to be astonishing.

The accelerating expansion of process-outcome research that we have documented in this chapter has several major consequences. The first is clearly that this body of scientific work is too large and too informative to ignore. Those who continue to ignore it because the research designs of these studies usually are not randomized experimental trials (or for other reasons) assume the posture of scientific ostriches.[17] A responsible and realistic account of the results of psychotherapy research and their implications for practice cannot avoid considering the substantial and well-replicated findings of process-outcome studies.

Given the present development of the field, the detailed findings of these many studies are more difficult to present in summary tables than in past editions. That is because, in addition to their sheer numbers, the studies as a group have become ever more specialized and heterogeneous. Process-outcome findings now occur in studies of very specific yet different patient populations and types of disorder, using very specific yet different types of therapist and treatment procedures, and very specific yet different approaches to outcome assessment. Classifying and combining those findings would require a multidimensional scheme using several input variable categories from the Generic Model (appearing at the top of Figure 8.1), in addition to our current set of process variable categories and a methodical classification of findings by process and outcome observational perspectives. If successful, such a finely nuanced scheme would effectively organize the body of research findings to provide a detailed and complex answer to the well-known specificity question (Kiesler, 1966; Paul, 1967): What aspects of therapy and what kinds of therapy, provided how and by what kind of therapist, under what circumstances, for what kinds of patients with what kinds of problems, are likely to lead to what kinds of results? Though not enough is known yet to answer that question, we already know too much to neatly summarize compactly in a set of tables.

Another example of the increased complexity of research, and the "growing pains" associated with it, is the impact on outcome assessment made by the use of new statistical methods. Assessment of outcome was traditionally done at specific points in time, most typically at the termination of treatment and at one or more arbitrarily selected times afterward. These are recognized as termination outcome and followup outcome status, measured in terms of change from pretreatment status, either by statistical significance or clinical significance criteria (e.g., Jacobson & Revenstorf, 1988; Kazdin, 1977, 1994; Wolf, 1978). Another point at which the patient's status has been assessed, especially in studies that feature detailed analyses of in-session events, is the time following the session, or between sessions, as treatment continues. These are recognized as postsession outcomes or intersession outcomes. However, researchers have been quick to make use of newer statistical techniques (such as growth curves and hierarchical linear modeling[16]) that enable them to go beyond point estimates and calculations of difference to the projection of trajectories of change in patient functioning. Thus, outcome can be assessed as it unfolds during the course of treatment in the form of treatment outcome trajectories, and as it continues to unfold post-treatment by constructing followup outcome trajectories estimated from periodic measures of subsequent patient status. These strategies clearly represent an important advance, but they also introduce a new order of complexity. Among recent process-outcome studies one finds any one (or several) of five different outcome assessment strategies, which still need to be systematically related to one another. From micro to macro levels of focus (Table 8.1), these are: postsession (or intersession) status; treatment outcome trajectory; termination outcome status; followup outcome trajectory; and long-term followup status.

The limits imposed by the amount and complexity of recent studies make it impractical to analyze all of the specific findings of the studies we reviewed. However, we shall report our general impressions based on those studies, which are as follows. Overall, the findings of process-outcome studies published from 1993 through 2001 require no radical change in the conclusions reached previously on the basis of research from 1950 through 1992.[18] Some of those conclusions have been further strengthened by the addition of many new studies in familiar areas, such as the impact of the therapeutic bond and its specific facets on outcome. Knowledge in other areas has been further differentiated with respect to the initial and boundary conditions in which the conclusions hold true—for example, the use of interpretation in general being linked to positive outcomes but linked to negative outcomes when used with a specific focus on transference (patient-therapist relationship) issues in brief psychotherapies. Still other recent studies have led to the rapid filling in of gaps in knowledge, such as the impact of patterns of change in process measures over the course of treatment and the effects of dosage on various aspects of patients' functioning.

This seems to be something worth celebrating. Indeed, we would point out that this body of knowledge could easily be enlarged if researchers who are mainly interested in evaluating and comparing the outcomes of different treatments would routinely include some process measures (e.g., clients' perceptions of the therapeutic alliance at one or several points over the course of treatment), and if those researchers whose main interest is the intensive analysis of session processes would routinely include some outcome measures (e.g., ratings of clients' postsession or intersession functioning). The inclusion of standard, well-developed, convenient, and readily available measures of process and outcome would require little additional investment by researchers and would surely produce more informative and useful results.

The task of understanding and interpreting process-outcome research could also be made easier if authors and editors would ensure that published reports routinely included clear and adequate information about precisely what was done and found. Having analyzed almost 300 studies for this review, we may say that many of the studies we read were hard to understand, despite close and persistent attention. This was particularly true in the (not uncommon) case of studies published piecemeal in different journals, where the information needed to understand and assess reported findings is often unavailable. If researchers would like their work to be understood and appreciated by colleagues, we would recommend that the following information be provided as a *minimum:*[19] (1) *For patients:* inclusion and exclusion criteria, number of patients recruited, treatment and project attrition, number of patients for analysis; diagnosis and severity of problems; age, gender, marital/parental status, and socioeconomic/ethnic status. (2) *For therapists:* number of therapists, number of patients treated per therapist; profession, orientation, training, and experience; age, gender, marital/parental status, and socioeconomic/ethnic status. (3) *For treatments:* treatment modality (group vs. individual), therapeutic model/orientation (which may or may not be identical to primary orientation of therapist), treatment specification (manualization); treatment setting; session duration, session frequency, total number of sessions; information on supervision. (4) *For process and outcome measures:* focal content and observational perspective (who assesses what); assessment schedule (making clear which data were collected when); construction of variables from measures (how measurement information was configured and used in data analyses).

In sum, the findings of process-outcome research to date favor a complex but comprehensible view of therapy. Effective psychotherapy is clearly more than a set of technical procedures, but it is also more than a warm, supportive relationship. Both the common factors of relationship and specific therapeutic interventions have an impact on outcome. Moreover, beneath largely semantic differences, a number of basically similar interventions tend to be used in different, sometimes quite contrasting "treatment packages." (The fact that specific interventions as well as common factors tend to be shared by diverse treatment packages may help explain the *relative* comparability of their results.) Again, the results of process-outcome research suggest that psychotherapy is more than what the therapist does, intentionally or otherwise; it is, after all, the patient's experience. Yet what the therapist does in therapy clearly makes a difference in what a patient experiences and learns. Outcome appears to be best understood as a synergistic result of the patient's problems and resources, combined with the therapist's skills and limitations. Both relationship variables and intervention procedures, patient participation and therapist influences, contribute jointly and variously to shaping the outcome of therapy. Wise researchers will strive to balance the need for simplicity and control with a realistic respect for the complex integrity of the therapeutic process.

Author Note

D.E.O. dedicates this chapter to the memory of Kenneth I. Howard (1932–2000), co-author of this chapter in the 1978 and 1986 editions of the *Handbook*, and, as in the past, thanks Marcia Bourland for unfailing patience and support. For their help with work on this chapter, M.H.R. thanks Anne Helene Fraas Tveit, Marianne Sandhei, Ida Stubberud, and Wibeke Moger of Oslo, and U.W. thanks Tobias Teismann and Mine Gözütok of Bochum.

FOOTNOTES

1. Alternative perspectives to that of Orlinsky and Russell (1994) on the history of psychotherapy research can be found in Freedheim (1992), Part III (e.g., Strupp & Howard, 1992, and Hill and Corbett (1993).

2. A decade later, cinematic and video recording of therapy sessions added greatly to the richness of the raw data, although content analysis by investigators remained an essential aspect of this approach (e.g., Gottschalk & Auerbach, 1966).

3. The overwhelming volume of distinguishable process-outcome findings in the period under review—sometimes numbering close to 100 in a single study (e.g., Regli, Bieber, Mathier, & Grawe, 2000)—made it effectively impossible to extend that practice to the present chapter.

4. The widespread use of statistical meta-analysis in psychotherapy research as a method of integrating the results of quantitative findings has led to the devaluation of "box-score" tallies and to some extent has also distracted researchers' attention from the need for conceptual or theoretical integration of research findings. As valuable as their contribution has been, statistical meta-analyses focus on the quantitative size of effects but do not clarify their meaning. At the same time, the use of more limited tallies of findings do provide an estimate of the replicability of findings under varied conditions of observation with varied research subjects, and consistent replicability across such variations is an indicator of robustness. Replicability and robustness of findings are essential criteria in science, and this much may be shown by box-score tallies even if the separate question of effect size is not addressed.

5. Our standard for outcome requires assessment of a patient's experience and behavior *outside* of therapy. This would even include immediate postsession evaluations of session effects and the assessment of patient status between sessions while therapy is ongoing, but not the in-session impacts that some authors refer to as "little o" outcomes.

6. Special acknowledgment for the impressive volume and quality of process-outcome studies and other psychotherapy research is due to L. E. Beutler and his associate editors during much of the period under review.

7. The smaller number of studies in Nordic journals is attributable partly to the smaller number of researchers in this region and partly to the likelihood of their publishing in English-language journals.

8. Occasional citations are made to relevant publications from earlier years which had not been mentioned in previous editions of this chapter.

9. A related aspect of contractual implementation that previous studies had indicated had some effect on outcome, but that received no recent attention, is *timeliness in starting treatment* (versus delay, e.g., on a waiting list). Other studies relating outcome to temporal variables such as stage of treatment and overall treatment duration are discussed later in this chapter under Temporal Patterns.

10. Readers interested in the role of empathy in psychotherapy may also want to consult Bohart and Greenberg (1997).

11. Perhaps patients almost always see themselves as expressive, and therapists almost always see themselves as empathic, thereby reducing the sensitivity of their perspectives on those variables to variations in patient outcome.

12. Referring to the "experiencing" concept of Gendlin (1962), as developed for research by Klein, Mathieu-Coughlan, and Kiesler (1986).

13. Referring to Vaillant's (1971, 1977) concept of a hierarchy of defenses reflecting different levels of maturity.

14. See Orlinsky and Geller (1994) for theoretical and methodological background.

15. Future research might also focus on the in-session impacts of therapists, for there is reason to believe that positive and negative experiences in therapy impact the therapist's sense of current professional growth and that this sense of currently experienced growth reflects a renewal of the morale and motivation needed to practice therapy, a replenishment of the energy and refreshing of the acumen demanded by therapeutic work (Orlinsky et al., 1999, p. 212).

16. See, for example, Bryk and Raudenbush (1987) and the journal special sections edited by Gottman and Rushe (1993) and Hoyle (1994).

17. This is not intended as a criticism of randomized experimental designs, which have unique virtues and some important limitations, but rather of those who regard them as the only legitimate method for acquiring scientific knowledge.

18. Those conclusions, summarized under Cumulative Knowledge in the present chapter, were presented in Orlinsky, Grawe, and Parks (1994, especially Tables 8.57, 8.58, and related text).

19. This information can be offered as footnotes when multiple aspects of a study are presented in different publications.

References

Text References

Abbott, A. (1988). *The system of professions: An essay on the division of expert labor.* Chicago: University of Chicago Press.

Addis, M. E., & Jacobson, N. S. (2000). A closer look at the treatment rationale and homework compliance in cognitive-behavioral therapy for depression. *Cognitive Therapy and Research, 24,* 313–326.

Alexander, F. (1937). *Five year report of the Chicago Institute for Psychoanalysis, 1932–1937.* Chicago, IL: Chicago Institute for Psychoanalysis.

Ambühl, H. (1993). Was ist therapeutisch an Psychotherapie? Eine empirische Überprüfung der Annahmen im "Generic Model of Psychotherapy" [What is therapeutic about psychotherapy? An empirical test of the assumptions in the "Generic Model of Psychotherapy"]. *Zeitschrift für Klinische Psychologie, Psychopathologie, und Psychotherapie, 41,* 285–303.

American Psychiatric Association. (1993). Practice guidelines for major depressive disorder in adults. *American Journal of Psychiatry, 150,* 1–23.

American Psychiatric Association. (1994). Practice guideline for the treatment of patients with bipolar disorder. *American Journal of Psychiatry, 151,* 1–36.

Auld, F., & Murray, E. J. (1955). Content-analysis studies of psychotherapy. *Psychological Bulletin, 52(5),* 377–395.

Aveline, M., & Shapiro, D. A. (Eds.). (1995). *Research foundations for psychotherapy.* Chichester, England: John Wiley & Sons.

Aveline, M., Shapiro, D. A., Parry, G., & Freeman, C. (1995). Building research foundations for psychotherapy practice. In M. Aveline & D. A. Shapiro (Eds.), *Research foundations for psychotherapy.* Chichester, England: John Wiley & Sons.

Bachelor, A. (1995). Clients' perception of the therapeutic alliance: A qualitative analysis. *Journal of Counseling Psychology, 42(3)* 325–337.

Bänninger-Huber, E. (1992). Prototypical affective microsequences in psychotherapeutic interaction. *Psychotherapy Research, 2,* 291–306.

Bänninger-Huber, E., & Widmer, C. (1999). Affective relationship patterns and psychotherapeutic change. *Psychotherapy Research, 9,* 74–87.

Barrett-Lennard, G. T. (1986). The Relationship Inventory now: Issues and advances. In L. S. Greenberg & W. M. Pinsof (Eds.), *The psychotherapeutic process: A research handbook.* New York: Guilford Press.

Bartlett, M. R. (1950). A six-month follow-up of the effects of personal adjustment counseling of veterans. *Journal of Consulting Psychology, 14,* 393–394.

Bastine, R., Fiedler, P., & Kommer, D. (1989). Was ist therapeutisch an der Psychotherapie? Versuch einer Bestandsaufnahme und Systematisierung der psychotherapeutischen Prozessforschung [What is therapeutic in psychotherapy? A review and systematization of psychotherapy process research]. *Zeitschrift für Klinische Psychologie, 18,* 3–22.

Beck, A. P., & Lewis, C. M. (Eds.). (2000). *The process of group psychotherapy: Systems for analyzing change.* Washington, DC: American Psychological Association.

Beck, A. T., Rush, A. J., Shaw, B. F., & Emery, G. (1979). *Cognitive therapy of depression.* New York: Guilford Press.

Bednar, R. L., & Kaul, T. (1994). Experiential group research. In S. L. Garfield & A. E. Bergin (Eds.), *Handbook of psychotherapy and behavior change* (4th ed.). New York: John Wiley & Sons.

Bellah, R. N., Madsen, R., Sullivan, W. M., Swidler, A., & Tipton, S. M. (1985). *Habits of the heart: Individualism and commitment in American life.* Berkeley: University of California Press.

Benjamin, L. S., Foster, S. W., Roberto, L. G., & Estroff, S. E. (1986). Breaking the family code: Analyses of videotapes of family interactions by structural analysis of social behavior (SASB). In L. S. Greenberg & W. M. Pinsof (Eds.), *The psychotherapeutic process: A research handbook.* New York: Guilford Press.

Berelson, B. (1952). *Content analysis in communication research.* Glencoe, IL: Free Press.

Bergin, A. E. (1971). The evaluation of therapeutic outcomes. In A. E. Bergin & S. L. Garfield (Eds.), *Handbook of psychotherapy and behavior change* (1st ed.). New York: John Wiley & Sons.

Bergin, A. E., & Garfield, S. L. (Eds.). (1971). *Handbook of psychotherapy and behavior change* (1st ed.). New York: John Wiley & Sons.

Bergin, A. E., & Garfield, S. L. (Eds.). (1994). *Handbook of psychotherapy and behavior change* (4th ed.). New York: John Wiley & Sons.

Bernard, J. (1943). Studies in the phonographic recordings of verbal material: I. The use of phonographic recordings in counseling practice and research. II. A transcribing device. *Journal of Consulting Psychology, 6,* 105–113, 149–153.

Beutler, L. E., & Clarkin, J. F. (1990). *Systematic treatment selection.* New York: Brunner/Mazel.

Beutler, L. E., & Crago, M. (Eds.). (1991). *Psychotherapy research: An international review of programmatic research.* Washington, DC: American Psychological Association.

Beutler, L. E., Malik, M., Alimohamed, S., Harwood, T. M., Talebi, H., Noble, S., & Wong, E. (this volume). Therapist variables. In M. J. Lambert (Ed.), *Handbook of psychotherapy and behavior change* (5th ed.). New York: John Wiley & Sons.

Beutler, L. E., Mohr, D. C., Grawe, K., Engle, D., & MacDonald, R. (1991). Looking for differential treatment effects: Cross-cultural predictors of differential psychotherapy efficacy. *Journal of Psychotherapy Integration, 1,* 121–142.

Blau, T. H. (1950). Report on a method of predicting success in psychotherapy. *Journal of Clinical Psychology, 6,* 403–406.

Bohart, A., Elliott, R., Greenberg, G., & Watson, J. (2002). Empathy. In J. C. Norcross (Ed.), *Psychotherapy relationships that work: Therapist contributions and responsiveness to patient needs.* New York: Oxford University Press.

Bohart, A. C., & Greenberg, L. S. (Eds.). (1997). *Empathy reconsidered: New directions in psychotherapy.* Washington, DC: American Psychological Association.

Bohart, A. C., O'Hara, M., & Leitner, L. M. (1998). Empirically violated treatments: Disenfranchisement of humanistic and other psychotherapies. *Psychotherapy Research, 8,* 141–157.

Bordin, E. S. (1979). The generalizability of the psychoanalytic concept of the working alliance. *Psychotherapy: Theory, Research, and Practice, 16,* 252–260.

Boun, O. H. (1951). An investigation of therapeutic relationship in client-centered psychotherapy. Unpublished doctoral dissertation, University of Chicago.

Breuer, F. (1996). *Qualitative Psychologie. Grundlagen, Methoden und Anwendungen eines Forschungsstils.* [Qualitative psychology. Premises, methods and applications of a research style]. Opladen: Westdeutscher Verlag.

Brody, E. B., Newman, R., & Redlich, F. C. (1951). Sound recording: The problem of evidence in psychiatry, *Science, 113,* 379–380.

Bryk, A. S., & Raudenbush, S. W. (1987). Application of hierarchical linear models to assess change. *Psychological Bulletin, 101, (1),* 147–158.

Burns, D. D., & Nolen-Hoeksema, S. (1991). Coping styles, homework compliance, and the effectiveness of cognitive-behavioral therapy. *Journal of Consulting and Clinical Psychology, 59,* 305–311.

Carmichael, H. T., & Masserman, J. H. (1939). Results of treatment in a psychiatric outpatients' department. *Journal of the American Medical Association, 113,* 2292–2298.

Caspar, F. (1997). What goes on in a psychotherapist's mind? *Psychotherapy Research,* 7, 105–125.

Chambless, D. L., Sanderson, W. C. Shoham, V., Johnson, S. B., Pope, K. S., Crits-Christoph, P., Baker, M., Johnson, B., Woody, S. R., Sue, S., Beutler, L., Williams, D. A., & McCurry, S. (1996). An update on empirically validated therapies. *The Clinical Psychologist, 49,* 5–18.

Connolly, M. B., Crits-Christoph, P., Demorest, A., Azarian, K., Muenz, L., & Chittams, J. (1996). Varieties of transference patterns in psychotherapy. *Journal of Consulting and Clinical Psychology, 64,* 1213–1221.

Conrad, D. C. (1952). An empirical study of the concept of psychotherapeutic success. *Journal of Consulting Psychology, 16,* 92–97.

Covner, B. J. (1942). Studies in phonographic recordings of verbal material: I. The use of phonographic recordings in counseling practice and research. *Journal of Consulting Psychology, 6,* 105–113.

Covner, B. J. (1944). Studies in phonographic recordings of verbal material: III. The completeness and accuracy of counseling interview reports. *Journal of General Psychology, 30,* 181–203.

Cummings, A. L., Hallberg, E., Martin, J., & Slemon, A. G. (1992). Participants' memories for therapeutic events and ratings of session effectiveness. *Journal of Cognitive Psychotherapy, 6,* 113–124.

Cummings, A. L., Martin, J., Hallberg, E. T., & Slemon, A. G. (1992). Memory for therapeutic events, session effectiveness, and working alliance in short-term counseling. *Journal of Counseling Psychology, 39,* 306–312.

Curran, D. (1937). The problem of assessing psychiatric treatment. *Lancet, 11,* 1005–1009.

Czogalik, D. (1991). University of Ulm: Interactional processes in psychotherapy. In L. E. Beutler & M. Crago (Eds.), *Psychotherapy research: An international review of programmatic studies.* Washington, DC: American Psychological Association.

Czogalik, D. (1992). Personal communication to D. Orlinsky during presentation made at a meeting of the Society for Psychotherapy Research Chicago area group.

Czogalik, D., & Hettinger, R. (1987). The process of psychotherapeutic interaction: A single case study. In W. Huber (Ed.), *Progress in psychotherapy research.* Louvain-la-Neuve, Belgium: Presses Universitaires de Louvain.

Czogalik, D., & Hettinger, R. (1988). Mehrebenenanalyse der psychotherapeutischen Interaktion: Eine Verlaufsstudie am Einzelfall [Multilevel analysis of psychotherapeutic interaction: A process study of a single case]. *Zeitschrift für Klinische Psychologie, 17,* 31–45.

Czogalik, D., & Russell, R. L. (1994). Therapist structure of participation: An application of P-technique and chronographic analysis. *Psychotherapy Research, 4,* 75–94.

Czogalik, D., & Russell, R. L. (1995). Interactional structures of therapist and client participation in adult psychotherapy: P technique and chronography. *Journal of Consulting and Clinical Psychology, 63,* 28–36.

Dahl, H., Kächele, H., & Thomä, H. (Eds.). (1988). *Psychoanalytic process research strategies.* Berlin: Springer-Verlag.

DeJong-Meyer, R., Hautzinger, M., Rudolf, G.A.E., Strauss, W., & Frick, U. (1996a). Die Überprüfung der Wirksamkeit einer Kombination von Antidepressiva- und Verhaltenstherapie bei endogen depressiven Patienten: Varianzanalytische Ergebnisse zu den Haupt- und Nebenkriterien des Therapieerfolgs. [The effectiveness of antidepressants and cognitive-behavioral therapy combined in patients with endogenous depression: Results of analyses of variance regarding main and secondary outcome criteria]. *Zeitschrift für Klinische Psychologie, 25*, 93–109.

DeRubeis, R. J., & Feeley, M. (1990). Determinants of change in cognitive therapy for depression. *Cognitive Therapy & Research, 14*, 469–482.

DiLoreto, A. O. (1971). *Comparative psychotherapy: An experimental analysis.* Chicago: Aldine-Atherton.

Dürr, H., & Hahlweg, K. (1996). Familienbetreuung bei schizophrenen Patienten: Analyse des Therapieverlaufes [Process analysis of behavioral family management with schizophrenic patients]. *Zeitschrift für Klinische Psychologie, 25*, 33–46.

Elkin, I. (1994). The NIMH treatment of depression collaborative research program: Where we began and where we are. In S. L. Garfield & A. E. Bergin (Eds.), *Handbook of psychotherapy and behavior change* (4th ed.). New York: John Wiley & Sons.

Elkin, I., Parloff, M. B., Hadley, S. W., & Autry, J. H. (1985). NIMH Treatment of Depression Collaborative Research Program: Background and research plan. *Archives of General Psychiatry, 42*, 305–316.

Elliott, R. (1984). A discovery oriented approach to significant events in psychotherapy: Interpersonal process recall and comprehensive process analysis. In L. N. Rice & L. S. Greenberg (Eds.), *Patterns of change: Intensive analysis of psychotherapy process.* New York: Guilford Press.

Elliott, R. (1986). Interpersonal process recall (IPR) as a psychotherapy process research method. In L. S. Greenberg & W. M. Pinsof (Eds.), *The psychotherapeutic process: A research handbook.* New York: Guilford Press.

Elliott, R. (1989). Comprehensive process analysis: Understanding the change process in significant therapy events: In M. J. Packer & R. B. Addison (Eds.), *Entering the circle: Hermeneutic investigations in psychology.* Albany: State University of New York Press.

Elliott, R. (1991). Five dimensions of therapy process. *Psychotherapy Research, 1*, 92–103.

Elliott, R. (1998). Editor's introduction: A guide to the empirically supported treatments controversy. *Psychotherapy Research, 8*, 115–125.

Elliott, R. (Ed.). (1999). Special issue: Qualitative psychotherapy research. *Psychotherapy Research, 9(3)*, 251–257.

Elliott, R., & Anderson, C. (1994). Simplicity and complexity in psychotherapy research. In R. L. Russell (Ed.), *Reassessing psychotherapy research.* New York: Guilford Press.

Elliott, R., Barker, C. B., Caskey, N., & Pistrang, N. (1982). Differential helpfulness of counselor verbal response modes. *Journal of Counseling Psychology, 29*, 354–361.

Eysenck, H. J. (1952). The effects of psychotherapy: An evaluation. *Journal of Consulting Psychology, 16*, 319–324.

Farber, B. A. (1983). The effects of psychotherapeutic practice upon psychotherapists. *Psychotherapy: Theory, Research, and Practice, 20*, 174–182.

Farber, B. A., & Heifetz, L. J. (1981). The satisfactions and stresses of psychotherapeutic work: A factor analytic study. *Professional Psychology, 12*, 621–630.

Fenichel, O. (1930). *Ten years of the Berlin Psychoanalytic Institute, 1920–1930.* Cited in Bergin (1971).

Fennell, M. J., & Teasdale, J. D. (1987). Cognitive therapy for depression: Individual differences and the process of change. *Cognitive Therapy and Research, 11*, 253–271.

Flick, U. (1999). *Qualitative Forschung. Theorie, Methoden, Anwendung in Psychologie und Sozialwissenschaften.* [Qualitative research. Theory, methods and applications in psychology and social research]. Reinbek: Rowohlt.

Fonagy, P., Leigh, T., Steele, M., Steele, H., Kennedy, R., Mattoon, G., Target, M., & Gerber, A. (1996). The relation of attachment status, psychiatric classification, and response to psychotherapy. *Journal of Consulting and Clinical Psychology, 64*, 22–31.

Foppa-Drew, S. (1989). The empirical validity of the Generic Model on a single case level: A longitudinal correlational analysis of 47 cases. Paper presented at the 20th Annual Meeting of Society for Psychotherapy Research, Toronto.

Ford, J. D., Fisher, P., & Larson, L. (1997). Object relations as a predictor of treatment outcome with chronic posttraumatic stress disorder. *Journal of Consulting and Clinical Psychology, 65*, 547–559.

Frank, J. D., & Frank, J. B. (1991). *Persuasion and healing: A comparative study of psychotherapy* (3rd ed.). Baltimore, MD: Johns Hopkins University Press.

Frank, J. D., Hoehn-Saric, R., Imber, S. D., Liberman, B. L., & Stone, A. R. (1978). *Effective ingredients of successful psychotherapy.* New York: Brunner/Mazel.

Freedheim, D. K. (Ed.). (1992). *History of psychotherapy: A century of change.* Washington, DC: American Psychological Association.

Frettlöh, J., & Kröner-Herwig, B. (1999). Einzel- und Gruppentherapie in der Behandlung chronischer Schmerzen – Gibt es Effektivitätsunterschiede? [Individual versus group training in the treatment of chronic pain: Which is more efficacious?]. *Zeitschrift für Klinische Psychologie, 28*, 256–266.

Freud, S. (1912a). The dynamics of the transference. In J. Strachey (Ed.), *The standard edition of the complete psychological works of Sigmund Freud* (Vol. 12) (pp. 97–108). London: Hogarth Press, 1958.

Freud, S. (1912b). Recommendations to physicians practicing psycho-analysis. In J. Strachey (Ed.),

The standard edition of the complete psychological works of Sigmund Freud (Vol. 12) (pp. 109–120). London: Hogarth Press, 1958.

Freud, S. (1926). The question of lay analysis. In J. Strachey (Ed.), *The standard edition of the complete psychological works of Sigmund Freud* (Vol. 20) pp. 183–258. London: Hogarth Press, 1959.

Freud, S. (1937). Constructions in analysis. In J. Strachey (Ed.), *The standard edition of the complete psychological works of Sigmund Freud* (Vol. 23) pp. 257–269. London: Hogarth Press, 1959.

Frieswyk, S. H., Allen, J. G., Colson, D. B., Coyne, L., Gabbard, G. O., Horwitz, L., & Newsom, G. (1986). Therapeutic alliance: Its place as a process and outcome variable in dynamic psychotherapy research. *Journal of Consulting and Clinical Psychology, 54,* 32–38.

Frieswyk, S. H., Colson, D. B., & Allen, J. G. (1984). Conceptualizing the alliance from a psychoanalytic perspective. *Psychotherapy, 27,* 460–464.

Frommer, J., & Rennie, D. (Eds.). (2001). *Qualitative psychotherapy research: Methods and methodology.* Legnerich, Germany: Pabst Science Publishers.

Garfield, S. L., & Bergin, A. E. (Eds.). (1986). *Handbook of psychotherapy and behavior change* (3rd ed.). New York: John Wiley & Sons.

Garfield, S. L., & Kurz, M. (1952). Evaluation of treatment and related procedures in 1,216 cases referred to a mental hygiene clinic. *Psychiatric Quarterly, 26,* 414–424.

Gendlin, E. T. (1962). *Experiencing and the creation of meaning.* New York: Free Press of Glencoe.

Gill, M., Newman, R., & Redlich, F. C. (1954). *The initial interview in psychiatric practice.* New York: International Universities Press.

Giorgi, A. (1985). Sketch of a psychological phenomenological method. In A. Giorgi (Ed.), *Phenomenology and psychological research* (pp. 8–22). Pittsburgh, PA: Duquesne University Press.

Glaser, B., & Strauss, A. L. (1967). *The discovery of grounded theory: Strategies for qualitative research.* Hawthorne, NY: Aldine de Gruyter.

Goffman, E. (1956). The nature of deference and demeanor. *American Anthropologist, 58,* 473–502. [Also in E. Goffman, *Interaction ritual: Essays on face-to-face behavior.* Garden City, NY: Doubled Anchor, 1967.]

Goffman, E. (1961). Role distance. In E. Goffman, *Encounters: Two studies in the sociology of interaction.* Indianapolis, In: Bobbs-Merrill.

Goldfried, M. R., Raue, P. J., & Castonguay, L. G. (1998). The therapeutic focus in significant sessions of master therapists: A comparison of cognitive-behavioral and psychodynamic-interpersonal interventions. *Journal of Consulting and Clinical Psychology, 66,* 803–810.

Gomes-Schwartz, B. A. (1978). Effective ingredients in psychotherapy: Prediction of outcomes from process variables. *Journal of Consulting and Clinical Psychology, 46,* 1023–1035.

Gottman, J. M., & Rushe, R. H. (Eds.). (1993). Special section: The analysis of change. *Journal of Consulting and Clinical Psychology, 61,* 907–983.

Gottschalk, L. A., & Auerbach, A. H. (Eds.). (1966). *Methods of research in psychotherapy.* New York: Appleton-Century-Crofts.

Grawe, K. (1989a). A comparison of the intercorrelations between input, process, and outcome variables of the Generic Model for different forms of psychotherapy. Paper presented at the 20th Annual Meeting of Society for Psychotherapy Research, Toronto.

Grawe, K. (1989b). Von der psychotherapeutischen Outcomeforschung zur differentiellen Prozessanalyse [From psychotherapeutic outcome research to differential process analysis]. *Zeitschrift für Klinische Psychologie, 18,* 23–34.

Grawe, K. (1991). The Bernese Psychotherapy Research Program. In L. E. Beutler & M. Crago (Eds.), *Psychotherapy research: An international review of programmatic studies.* Washington, DC: American Psychological Association.

Grawe, K. (1997). Research-informed psychotherapy. *Psychotherapy Research, 7,* 1–19.

Grawe, K. (1998). *Psychologische therapie [Psychological therapy].* Göttingen: Verlag für Psychologie.

Grawe, K., Donati, R., & Bernauer, F. (1994). *Psychotherapie im Wandel—Vom der Konfession zur Profession.* Göttingen: Hogrefe. [Translated as: *Psychotherapy in transition: From faith to facts.* Seattle: Hogrefe, 1998.]

Greenberg, L. S. (1986). Research strategies. In L. S. Greenberg & W. M. Pinsof (Eds.), *The psychotherapeutic process: A research handbook.* New York: Guilford Press.

Greenberg, L. S. (1991). Research on the process of change. *Psychotherapy Research, 1,* 3–16.

Greenberg, L. S. (1994). The investigation of change: Its measurement and explanation. In R. L. Russell (Ed.), *Reassessing psychotherapy research.* New York: Guilford Press.

Greenberg, L. S., Ford, C. L., Alden, L. S., & Johnson, S. M. (1993). In session change in emotionally focused therapy for couples. *Journal of Consulting and Clinical Psychology, 61,* 78–84.

Greenberg, L. S., & Newman, F. L. (Eds.). (1996). Special section: Psychotherapy process research. *Journal of Consulting and Clinical Psychology, 64,* 435–512.

Greenberg, L. S., & Pinsof, W. M. (Eds.). (1986a). *The psychotherapeutic process: A research handbook.* New York: Guilford Press.

Greenberg, L. S., & Pinsof, W. M. (1986b). Process research: Current trends and perspectives. In L. S. Greenberg & W. M. Pinsof (Eds.), *The psychotherapeutic process: A research handbook.* New York: Guilford Press.

Gurman, A. S., & Razin, A. M. (Eds.). (1977). *Effective psychotherapy: A handbook of research.* Oxford: Pergamon Press.

Haimowitz, N. R., & Haimowitz, M. L. (1952). Personality changes in client centered therapy. In W. Wolff & J. A. Precher (Eds.), *Success in psychotherapy.* New York: Grune & Stratton.

Hanna, F. J., & Ritchie, M. H. (1995). Seeking the active ingredients of psychotherapeutic change: Within and outside the context of therapy. *Professional Psychology: Research and Practice, 26,* 176–183.

Hautzinger, M., DeJong-Meyer, R., Treiber, R., Rudolf, G.A.E., & Thein, U. (1996). Wirksamkeit kognitiver Verhaltenstherapie, Pharmakotherapie und deren Kombination bei nichtendogenen, unipolaren Depressionen [Efficacy of cognitive-behavioral therapy, pharmacotherapy, and the combination of both in non-melancholic, unipolar depression]. *Zeitschrift für Klinische Psychologie, 25,* 130–145.

Heine, R. W. (1950). An investigation of the relationship between change in personality from psychotherapy as reported in patients and the factors seen by patients as producing change. Unpublished doctoral dissertation, University of Chicago.

Henry, W. P. (1996). Structural analysis of social behavior as a common metric for programmatic psychopathology and psychotherapy research. *Journal of Consulting and Clinical Psychology, 64,* 1263–1275.

Henry, W. P. (1998). Science, politics, and the politics of science: The use and misuse of empirically validated treatment research. *Psychotherapy Research, 8,* 126–140.

Henry, W. P., & Strupp, H. H. (1994). The therapeutic alliance as interpersonal process. In A. O. Horvath & L. S. Greenberg (Eds.), *The working alliance: Theory, research and practice* (pp. 51–84). New York: John Wiley & Sons.

Henry, W. P., Strupp, H. H., Schact, T. E., & Gaston, L. (1994). Psychodynamic approaches. In S. L. Garfield & A. E. Bergin (Eds.), *Handbook of psychotherapy and behavior change* (4th ed.). New York: John Wiley & Sons.

Hill, C. E. (1986). An overview of the Hill counselor and client verbal response modes category systems. In L. S. Greenberg & W. M. Pinsof (Eds.), *The psychotherapeutic process: A research handbook.* New York: Guilford Press.

Hill, C. E. (1989). *Therapist techniques and client outcomes: Eight cases of brief psychotherapy.* Newbury Park, CA: Sage Publications.

Hill, C. E. (1994a). From an experimental to an exploratory naturalistic approach to studying psychotherapy process. In R. L. Russell (Ed.), *Reassessing psychotherapy research.* New York: Guilford Press.

Hill, C. E. (Ed.). (1994b). Special section: Qualitative research in counseling process and outcome. *Journal of Counseling Psychology, 41(4).*

Hill, C. E., & Corbett, M. M. (1993). A perspective on the history of process and outcome research in counseling psychology. *Journal of Counseling Psychology, 40,* 3–24.

Hill, C. E., Nutt-Williams, Heaton, K. J., Thompson, B. J., & Rhodes, R. (1996). Therapist retrospective recall of impasses in long-term psychotherapy: A qualitative analysis. *Journal of Counseling Psychology, 43(2),* 207–217.

Hill, C., Thompson, B. J., & Williams, E. N. (1997). A guide to conducting consensual qualitative research. *Counseling Psychologist, 25,* 517–572.

Hilliard, R. B., Henry, W. P., & Strupp, H. H. (2000). An interpersonal model of psychotherapy: Linking patient and therapist developmental history, therapeutic process, and types of outcome. *Journal of Consulting and Clinical Psychology, 68,* 125–133.

Honos-Webb, L., Stiles, W. B., Greenberg, L. S., & Goldman, R. (1998). Assimilation analysis of process-experiential psychotherapy: A comparison of two cases. *Psychotherapy Research, 8,* 264–286.

Horvath, A. O., & Greenberg, L. S. (Eds.). (1994). *The working alliance: Theory and research.* New York: John Wiley & Sons.

Howard, K. I., Kopta, S. M., Krause, M. S., & Orlinsky, D. E. (1986). The dose-effect relationship in psychotherapy. *American Psychologist, 41,* 159–164.

Howard, K. I., Krause, M. S., & Vessey, J. (1994). Analysis of clinical trial data: The problem of outcome overlap. *Psychotherapy, 31,* 302–307.

Howard, K. I., Lueger, R. J., Maling, M. S., & Martinovich, Z. (1993). A phase model of psychotherapy: Causal mediation of outcome. *Journal of Consulting and Clinical Psychology, 61,* 678–685.

Howard, K. I., Moras, K., Brill, P., Martinovich, Z., & Lutz, W. (1996). Evaluation of psychotherapy: efficacy, effectiveness, and patient progress. *American Psychologist, 51,* 1059–1064.

Howard, K. I., Orlinsky, D. E., & Lueger, R. J. (1995). The design of clinically relevant outcome research: Some considerations and an example. In M. Aveline & D. Shapiro (Eds.), *Research foundations of psychotherapy practice* (pp. 3–48). Chichester, England: John Wiley & Sons.

Hoyle, R. H. (Ed.). (1994). Special section: Structural equation modeling in clinical research. *Journal of Consulting and Clinical Psychology, 62,* 427–521.

Huddleston, J. H. (1927). Psychotherapy in two hundred cases of psychoneurosis. *Military Surgeon, 60,* 161–170.

Hyman, H. T. (1936). The value of psychoanalysis as a therapeutic procedure. *Journal of the American Medical Association, 107,* 326–329.

Jacobson, N. S., & Revenstorf, D. (1988). Statistics for assessing the clinical significance of psychotherapy techniques: Issues, problems, and new developments. *Behavioral Assessment, 10*, 133–145.

Jennings, L., & Skovholt, T. M. (1999). The cognitive, emotional, and relational characteristics of master therapists. *Journal of Counseling Psychology, 46*, 3–11.

Jones, E. (1936). *Report of the clinic work (London Clinic of Psychoanalysis): 1926–1936.* Cited in Bergin (1971).

Jones, E. E. (Ed.). (1993). Special section: Single-case research in psychotherapy. *Journal of Consulting and Clinical Psychology, 61*, 371–430.

Kächele, H. (1992). Narration and observation in psychotherapy research: Reporting on a 20 year long journey from qualitative case reports to quantitative studies on the psychoanalytic process. *Psychotherapy Research, 2*, 1–15.

Kadushin, C. (1969). *Why people go to psychiatrists.* New York: Atherton.

Kazdin, A. E. (1977). Assessing the clinical or applied importance of behavior change through social validation. *Behavior Modification, 1*, 427–452.

Kazdin, A. E. (1994). Methodology, design, and evaluation in psychotherapy research. In S. L. Garfield & A. E. Bergin (Eds.), *Handbook of psychotherapy and behavior change* (4th ed.). New York: John Wiley & Sons.

Kendall, P. C., & Chambless, D. L. (Eds.). (1998). Special section: Empirically supported psychological therapies. *Journal of Consulting and Clinical Psychology, 66*, 3–167.

Kessel, L., & Hyman, H. T. (1933). The value of psychoanalysis as a therapeutic procedure. *Journal of the American Medical Association, 101*, 1612–1615.

Kiesler, D. J. (1966). Some myths of psychotherapy research and the search for a paradigm. *Psychological Bulletin, 65*, 110–136.

Kiesler, D. J. (Ed.). (1973). *The process of psychotherapy: Empirical foundations and systems of analysis.* Chicago: Aldine.

Kivlighan, D. M., & Arthur, E. G. (2000). Convergence in client and counselor recall of important session events. *Journal of Counseling Psychology, 47*, 79–84.

Klein, J. H., Mathieu-Coughlan, P., & Kiesler, D. J. (1986). The experiencing scales. In L. S. Greenberg & W. M. Pinsof (Eds.), *The psychotherapeutic process: A research handbook.* New York: Guilford Press.

Klerman, G. L., Weissman, M. M., Rounsaville, B. J., & Chevron, E. S. (1984). *Interpersonal therapy of depression.* New York: Basic Books.

Knox, S. Hess, S. A. Petersen, D. A., & Hill, C. (1997). A qualitative analyses of client perceptions of the effects of helpful therapist self-disclosure in long-term therapy. *Journal of Counseling Psychology, 44, (3)*, 274–283.

Kolden, G. G. (1991). The Generic Model of Psychotherapy: An empirical investigation of process and outcome relationships. *Psychotherapy Research, 1*, 62–73.

Kolden, G. G. (1996). Change in early sessions of dynamic therapy: Universal processes and the Generic Model of Psychotherapy. *Journal of Consulting and Clinical Psychology, 64*, 489–496.

Kolden, G. G., & Howard, K. I. (1992). An empirical test of the generic model of psychotherapy: *Journal of Psychotherapy Practice and Research, 1*, 225–236.

Kolden, G. G., Strauman, T. J., Gittleman, M., Halverson, J. L., Heerey, E., & Schneider, K. L. (2000). The Therapeutic Realizations Scale-Revised (TRS-R): Psychometric characteristics and relationship to treatment process and outcome. *Journal of Clinical Psychology, 56*, 1207–1220.

Krause, M. S., & Howard, K. I. (1976). Program evaluation in the public interest: a new research methodology. *Community Mental Health Journal, 12*, 291–300.

Krause, M. S., Howard, K. I., & Lutz, W. (1998). Exploring individual change. *Journal of Consulting and Clinical Therapy, 66*, 838–845.

Labov, W., & Fanshel, D. (1977). *Therapeutic discourse: Psychotherapy as conversation.* New York: Academic Press.

Lambert, M. J. (1979). *The effects of psychotherapy.* Montreal: Eden Press.

Lambert, M. J., Christensen, E. R., & DeJulio, S. S. (1983). *The assessment of psychotherapy outcome.* New York: John Wiley & Sons.

Lambert, M. J., Whipple, J. L., Smart, D. W., Vermeersch, D. A., Nielsen, S. L., & Hawkins, E. J. (2001). The effects of providing therapists with feedback on patient progress during psychotherapy: Are outcomes enhanced? *Psychotherapy Research, 11*, 49–68.

Lambert, W., Salzer, M. S., & Bickman, L. (1998). Clinical outcome, consumer satisfaction, and ad hoc ratings of improvement in children's mental health. *Journal of Consulting and Clinical Therapy, 66*, 270–279.

Lamnek, S. (1995). *Qualitative Sozialforschung.* [Qualitative social research.] (2 vols.). München: PVU.

Landis, C. (1937). A statistical analysis of psychotherapeutic methods. In L. E. Hinsie (Ed.), *Concepts and problems of psychotherapy.* New York: Columbia University Press.

Lasswell, H. D. (1935). Verbal references and physiological changes during the psychoanalytic interview: A preliminary communication. *Psychoanalytic Review, 22*, 10–24.

Lasswell, H. D. (1936). Certain prognostic changes during trial (psychoanalytic) interviews. *Psychoanalytic Review, 23*, 241–247.

Lasswell, H. D. (1937). Veraenderungen an einer Versuchsperson waehrend einer Kurzen Folge von psychoanalytischen Interviews. *Imago, 23*, 375–380.

Lietaer, G., Rombauts, J., & Van Balen, R. (Eds.). (1990). *Client-centered and experiential psychotherapy in the nineties.* Leuven, Belgium: Leuven University Press.

Luborsky, L. (1984). *Principles of psychoanalytic psychotherapy: A manual for supportive-expressive treatment.* New York: Basic Books.

Luborsky, L. (2000). A pattern-setting therapeutic alliance study revisited. *Psychotherapy Research, 10,* 17–29.

Luborsky, L., & Crits-Christoph, P. (Eds.). (1990). *Understanding transference: The CCRT method.* New York: Basic Books.

Luborsky, L., Crits-Christoph, P., Mintz, J., & Auerbach, A. (1988). *Who will benefit from psychotherapy? Predicting therapeutic outcomes.* New York: Basic Books.

Luff, M. C., & Garrod, M. (1935). The after-results of psychotherapy in 500 adult cases. *British Medical Journal, 2,* 54–59.

Luhrmann, T. M. (2000). *Of two minds: The growing disorder in American psychiatry.* New York: Alfred A. Knopf.

Lutz, W.. Martinovich, Z., & Howard, K. I. (1999). Patient profiling: An application of random coefficient regression models to depicting the response of a patient to outpatient psychotherapy. *Journal of Consulting and Clinical Psychology, 67,* 529–538.

Lyons, J. S., Howard, K. I., O'Mahoney, M. T., & Lish, J. D. (1997). *The measurement and management of clinical outcomes in mental health.* New York: John Wiley & Sons.

MacIntyre, A. (1981). *After virtue: A study in moral theory* (Ch. 3). Notre Dame, IN: University of Notre Dame Press.

Marsden, G. (1965). Content-analysis studies of psychotherapy: 1954 through 1964. *Psychological Bulletin, 63,* 298–321.

Marsden, G. (1971). Content-analysis studies of psychotherapy: 1954 through 1968. In A. E. Bergin & S. L. Garfield (Eds.), *Handbook of psychotherapy and behavior change* (1st ed.). New York: John Wiley & Sons.

Martin, D. J., Garske, J. P., & Davis, K. M. (2000). Relation of the therapeutic alliance with outcome and other variables: A meta-analytic review. *Journal of Consulting and Clinical Psychology, 68,* 438–450.

Masserman, J. H., & Carmichael, H. T. (1938). Diagnosis and prognosis in psychiatry: With a follow-up study of the results of short-term general hospital therapy of psychiatric cases. *J. Mental Science, 84,* 893–946.

Matz, P. B. (1929). Outcome of hospital treatment of ex-service patients with nervous and mental disease in the U. S. *U. S. Veterans Bureau Medical Bulletin, 5,* 829–842.

Mayring, P. (1999). *Einführung in die qualitative Sozialforschung.* [Introduction to qualitative social research.] München: PVU.

Meltzoff, J., & Kornreich, M. (1970). *Research in psychotherapy.* New York: Atherton.

Menninger, K. (1958). *Theory of psychoanalytic technique.* New York: Basic Books.

Mensh, I., & Golden, J. (1951). Factors in psychotherapeutic success. *Journal of the Missouri State Medical Association, 48,* 180–184.

Meyer, H. J., Borgatta, E. F., & Fanshel, D. (1964). A study of the interview process: The caseworker-client relationship. *Genetic Psychology Monographs, 69,* 247–295.

Michalak, J., & Schulte, D. (2002). Zielkonflikte und Therapiemotivation. [Goal conflicts and therapy motivation]. *Zeitschrift für Klinische Psychologie und Psychotherapie,* in press.

Miles, H. W., Barrabee, E. L., & Finesinger, J. E. (1951). Evaluation of psychotherapy, with a follow-up of 62 cases of anxiety neuroses. *Psychosomatic Medicine, 13,* 83–105.

Miller, N. E., Luborsky, L., Barber, J. P., & Docherty, J. P. (Eds.). (1993). *Psychodynamic treatment research: A handbook for clinical practice.* New York: Basic Books.

Miller, N. E., & Magruder, K. M. (Eds.). (1999). *Cost-effectiveness of psychotherapy: A guide for practitioners, researchers, and policymakers.* New York: Oxford University Press.

Neutstatter, W. L. (1935). The results of fifty cases treated by psychotherapy. *Lancet, 1,* 796–799.

Newman, F. L., & Howard, K. I. (1986). Therapeutic effort, treatment outcome, and national health policy. *American Psychologist, 41,* 181–187.

Norcross, J. C. (Ed.) (2001). Empirically supported therapy relationships: Summary Report of the Division 29 Task Force. *Psychotherapy, 38(4)* pp. 345–497.

Norcross, J. C. (Ed.) (2002). *Psychotherapy relationships that work: Therapist contributions and responsiveness to patient needs.* New York: Oxford University Press.

Norsk Psykologforening (2002). Veileder i forståelse og behandling av affektive lidelser. Tidsskrift for Norsk Psykologforening, 39. (Norwegian Psychological Association. Guidelines for the understanding and treatment of affective disturbances. *Journal of the Norwegian Psychological Association,* in press.

Orlinsky, D. E. (1989). Researchers' images of psychotherapy: Their origins and influence on research. *Clinical Psychology Review, 9,* 413–442.

Orlinsky, D. E. (2001). Adding concepts of outcome to the Generic Model of Psychotherapy. Paper presented at 4th North American Society for Psychotherapy Research conference, Puerto Vallarta, Mexico.

Orlinsky, D. E., & Geller, J. D. (1994). Patients' representations of their therapists and therapy: A new research focus. In N. Miller, L. Luborsky, J. Barber, & J. Docherty (Eds.), *Psychodynamic treatment research.* New York: Basic Books.

Orlinsky, D. E., Grawe, K., & Parks, B. K. (1994). Process and outcome in psychotherapy—noch einmal. In S. L. Garfield & A. E. Bergin (Eds), *Handbook of psychotherapy and behavior change* (4th ed.). New York: John Wiley & Sons.

Orlinsky, D. E., & Howard, K. I. (1966). *Therapy Session Report*, Forms P(atient) & T(herapist). Chicago: Institute for Juvenile Research.

Orlinsky, D. E., & Howard, K. I. (1967). The good therapy hour: Experiential correlates of patients' and therapists' evaluations of therapy sessions. *Archives of General Psychiatry, 16*, 621–632.

Orlinsky, D. E., & Howard, K. I. (1975). *Varieties of psychotherapeutic experience: Multivariate analyses of patients' and therapists' reports.* New York: Teachers College Press.

Orlinsky, D. E., & Howard, K. I. (1978). The relation of process to outcome in psychotherapy. In S. L. Garfield & A. E. Bergin (Eds.), *Handbook of psychotherapy and behavior change* (2nd ed.). New York: John Wiley & Sons.

Orlinsky, D. E., & Howard, K. I. (1980). The relation of gender to psychotherapeutic outcome. In A. Brodsky & R. Hare-Mustin (Eds.), *Women in psychotherapy: An assessment of research and practice.* New York: Guilford Press.

Orlinsky, D. E., & Howard, K. I. (1986). Process and outcome in psychotherapy. In S. L. Garfield & A. E. Bergin (Eds.), *Handbook of psychotherapy and behavior change* (3rd ed.). New York: John Wiley & Sons.

Orlinsky, D. E., & Howard, K. I. (1987). A generic model of psychotherapy. *Journal of Integrative and Eclectic Psychotherapy, 6*, 6–27.

Orlinsky, D. E., Rønnestad, M. H., Ambühl, H., Willutzki, U., Botermans, J-F., Cierpka, M., Davis, J. D., & Davis, M. (1999). Psychotherapists' assessments of their development at different career levels. *Psychotherapy: Theory/Research/Practice/Training, 36*, 203–215.

Orlinsky, D. E., & Russell, R. L. (1994). Tradition and change in psychotherapy research. In R. L. Russell (Ed.), *Reassessing psychotherapy research.* New York: Guilford Press.

Page, A. H. (1953). An assessment of the predictive value of certain language measures in psychotherapeutic counseling. In W. U. Snyder (Ed.), *Group report of a program of research in psychotherapy.* State College, PA: Pennsylvania State University.

Park, S., & Elkin, I. (2001). Patterns of change in subjective well-being, coping ability, and depressive symptomatology from three perspectives: the client, the significant other, and the therapist. Paper presented at 4th North American Society for Psychotherapy Research conference, Puerto Vallarta, Mexico.

Parry, G. (1999). Psychotherapy services in the English National Health Service. In N. E. Miller & K. M. Magruder (Eds.), *Cost-effectiveness of psychotherapy* (pp. 317–326). New York: Oxford University Press.

Parsons, T., & Shils, E. A. (Eds.). (1954). *Toward a general theory of action.* Cambridge, MA: Harvard University Press.

Paul, G. L. (1967). Strategy of outcome research in psychotherapy. *Journal of Consulting Psychology, 31*, 109–118.

Peplinsky, H. B., & Karst, T. O. (1964). Convergence: A phenomenon in counseling and in psychotherapy. *American Psychologist, 19*, 333–338.

Persons, J. B., Burns, D. D., & Perloff, J. M. (1988). Predictors of dropout and outcome in cognitive therapy for depression in a private practice setting. *Cognitive Therapy & Research, 12*, 557–576.

Pilisuk, M, & Parks, S. H. (1986). *The healing web: Social networks and human survival.* Hanover, NH: University Press of New England.

Pittenger, R. E., Hockett, C. F., & Danehy, J. H. (1960). *The first five minutes.* Ithaca, NY: Paul Martineau.

Porter, E. H., Jr. (1943a). The development and evaluation of a measure of counseling interview procedure. I. The development. *Educational and Psychological Measurement, 3*, 105–126.

Porter, E. H., Jr. (1943b). The development and evaluation of a measure of counseling interview procedure. II. The evaluation. *Educational and Psychological Measurement, 3*, 215–238.

Rasmussen, B., & Angus, L. (1996). Metaphor in psychodynamic psychotherapy with borderline and non-borderline clients: A qualitative analysis. *Psychotherapy, 33(4)*, 521–530.

Redlich, F. C., Dollard, J., & Newman, R. (1950). High fidelity recording of psychotherapeutic interviews. *American Journal of Psychiatry, 107*, 42–48.

Regli, D., Bieber, K., Mathier, F., & Grawe, K. (2000). Beziehungsgestaltung und Aktivierung von Ressourcen in der Anfangsphase von Therapien [Realization of therapeutic bond and activation of resources in initial therapy sessions]. *Verhaltenstherapie und Verhaltensmedizin, 21*, 399–420.

Reinecker, H., & Fiedler, P. (Eds.). (1997). *Therapieplanung in der modernen Verhaltenstherapie.* [Therapy planning in modern behavior therapy]. Lengerich: Papst.

Rennie, D. L. (1994a). Clients' deference in psychotherapy. *Journal of Counseling Psychology, 41(4)*, 427–437.

Rennie, D. L. (1994b). Storytelling in psychotherapy: The client's subjective experience. *Psychotherapy, 31(2)*, 234–243.

Rhodes, R. H., Hill, C. E., Thompson, B. J., & Elliott, R. (1994). Client retrospective recall of resolved and unresolved misunderstandings events. *Journal of Counseling Psychology, 41(4)*, 473–483.

Rice, L. N., & Greenberg, L. S. (Eds.). (1984). *Patterns of change: Intensive analysis of psychotherapy process.* New York: Guilford Press.

Rice. L. N., & Kerr, G. P. (1986). Measures of client and therapist vocal quality. In L. S. Greenberg & W. M. Pinsof (Eds.), *The psychotherapeutic process: A research handbook.* New York: Guilford Press.

Rogers, C. R. (1942a). *Counseling and psychotherapy.* Boston: Houghton Mifflin.

Rogers, C. R. (1942b). The use of electrically recorded interviews in improving psychotherapeutic techniques. *American Journal of Orthopsychiatry, 12,* 429–434.

Rogers, C. R. (1957). The necessary and sufficient conditions of therapeutic personality change. *Journal of Consulting Psychology, 22,* 95–103.

Rogers, C. R. (1961). The process equation of psychotherapy. *American Journal of Psychotherapy, 15,* 27–45.

Rogers, C. R., & Dymond, R. F. (Eds.). (1954). *Psychotherapy and personality change.* Chicago: University of Chicago Press.

Rohrbaugh, M. J., Shoham, V., & Racioppo, M. W. (2002). Toward family-level attribute x treatment interaction (ATI) research. In H. Liddle, D. Santisteban, et al. (Eds.), *Family psychology intervention science.* Washington, DC: APA.

Rønnestad, M. H., & Orlinsky, D. E. (2000). Psykoterapiveiledning til besvaer: Nar veiledning hemmer og ikke fremmer faglig utvikling [Supervisory discontent: When supervision inhibits professional development], pp. 291–321. In A. Holte, G. H. Nielsen, & M. H. Rønnestad (Eds.), *Psykoterapi og psykoterapiveiledning.* Oslo, Norway: Gyldendal Akademisk.

Roshal, J.J.G. (1953). The type-token ratio as a measure of changes in behavior variability during psychotherapy. In W. U. Snyder (Ed.), *Group report of a program of research in psychotherapy.* State College: Pennsylvania State University.

Ross, T. A. (1936). *An enquiry into prognosis in the neuroses.* London: Cambridge University Press.

Russell, R. L. (Ed.). (1995). Special section: Multivariate process research. *Journal of Consulting and Clinical Psychology, 63,* 3–45.

Russell, R. L., & Staszewski, C. (1988). The unit problem: Some systematic distinctions and critical dilemmas for psychotherapy process research. *Psychotherapy, 25,* 191–200.

Sandell, R., Blomberg, J., Lazar, A., Carlsson, J., Broberg, J., & Schubert, J. (2000). Varieties of long-term outcome among patients in psychoanalysis and long-term psychotherapy: A review of findings in the Stockholm Outcome of Psychoanalysis and Psychotherapy Project (STOPP). *The International Journal of Psychoanalysis, 81(5),* 921–942.

Saunders, S. M. (1998). Clients' assessment of the affective environment of the psychotherapy sessions: Relationship to session quality and treatment effectiveness. *Journal of Clinical Psychology, 54,* 597–605.

Saunders, S. M. (2000). Examining the relationship between the therapeutic bond and the phases of treatment outcome. *Psychotherapy, 37,* 206–218.

Saunders, S. M., Howard, K. I., & Orlinsky, D. E. (1989). The Therapeutic Bond Scales: Psychometric characteristics and relationship to treatment effectiveness. *Psychological Assessment, 1,* 323–330.

Scheflen, A. E. (1973). *Communicational structure: Analysis of a psychotherapy transaction.* Bloomington: University of Indiana Press.

Schilder, P. (1939). Results and problems of group psychotherapy in severe neuroses. *Mental Hygiene, 23,* 87–98.

Schlesinger, H. J., Mumford, E., Glass, G. V., Patrick, C., & Sharfstein, S. (1983). Mental health treatment and medical care utilization in a fee-for-service system: Outpatient mental health treatment following the onset of a chronic disease. *American Journal of Public Health, 73,* 422–429.

Schulte, D. (1997). Dimensions of outcome measurement. In H. H. Strupp, L. M. Horowitz, & M. J. Lambert, *Measuring patient changes in mood, anxiety, and personality disorders: Toward a core battery.* Washington, DC: American Psychological Association.

Schulte, D., Hartung, J., & Wilke, F. (1997). Handlungskontrolle der Angstbewältigung. Was macht Reizkonfrontation so effektiv? [Action control in treatment of anxiety disorders. What makes exposure so effective?] *Zeitschrift für Klinische Psychologie, 26,* 118–128.

Schulte, D., & Künzel, R. (1995). Relevance and meaning of therapist's control. *Psychotherapy Research, 5,* 169–185.

Shapiro, D. A., Harper, H., Startup, M., Reynolds, R., Bird, D., & Suoka, A. (1994). The high-water mark of the drug metaphor: A meta-analytic critique of process-outcome research. In R. L. Russell (Ed.), *Reassessing psychotherapy research.* New York: Guilford Press.

Shapiro, D. A., & Shapiro, D. (1982). Meta-analysis of comparative therapy outcome studies: A replication and refinement. *psychological Bulletin, 92,* 581–604.

Shoham, V., & Rohrbaugh, M. J. (1995). Aptitude x treatment interaction (ATI) research: Sharpening the focus, widening the lens. In M. Aveline & D. Shapiro (Eds.), *Research foundations for psychotherapy practice* (pp. 73–95). Sussex, England: John Wiley & Sons.

Skovholt, T. M., & Rønnestad, M. H. (1992). Themes in therapist and counselor development. *Journal of Counseling and Development, 70,* 505–515.

Skovholt, T. M., & Rønnestad, M. H. (1995). *The evolving professional self: Stages and themes in counselor and therapist development.* West Sussex, England: John Wiley & Sons.

Sloane, R. B., Staples, F. R., Cristol, A. H., Yorkston, N. J., & Whipple, K. (1975). *Psychotherapy versus behavior therapy.* Cambridge, MA: Harvard University Press.

Smith, M. L., Glass, E. V., & Miller, T. I. (1980). *The benefits of psychotherapy.* Baltimore, MD: Johns Hopkins University Press.

Smith, U., Staudinger, U. M., & Baltes, P. B. (1994). Occupational settings facilitating wisdom-related knowledge: The sample case of clinical psychologists. *Journal of Consulting and Clinical Psychology, 62,* 989–999.

Snyder, W. U. (1961). *The psychotherapy relationship.* New York: Macmillan.

Special Issue on Brief Therapy (2001). *Clinical Psychology: Science and Practice, 8(1)* 1–97.

Sperry, L., Brill, P., Howard, K. I., & Grissom, G. (1996). *Treatment outcomes in psychotherapy and psychiatric interventions.* New York: Brunner/Mazel.

Stangier, U., Heidenreich, T., & Peitz, M. (2001). *Effektivität kognitiv-behavioraler Einzel-vs. Gruppentherapie bei sozialer Phobie: Ergebnisse eines 6-Monats-Follow-up.* [Efficiency of cognitive-behavioral individual vs. group therapy with patients with social phobia: Results for the 6-month follow-up]. Paper on the 19th Symposium of the Special Interest Group for Clinical Psychology and Psychotherapy of the German Psychological Association. Bern, May 25, 2001.

Stiles, W. B. (1986). Development of a taxonomy of verbal response modes. In L. S. Greenberg & W. M. Pinsof (Eds.), *The psychotherapeutic process: A research handbook.* New York: Guilford Press.

Stiles, W. B. (1988). Psychotherapy process-outcome correlations may be misleading. *Psychotherapy, 25,* 27–35.

Stiles, W. B. (1999). Signs and voices in psychotherapy. *Psychotherapy Research, 9,* 1–21.

Stiles, W. B., Elliott, R., Llewelyn, S. P., Firth-Cozens, J. A., Margison, F. R., Shapiro, D. A., & Hardy, G. (1990). Assimilation of problematic experiences by clients in psychotherapy. *Psychotherapy, 27,* 411–420.

Stiles, W. B., Shankland, M. C., Wright, J., & Field, S. D. (1997a). Dimensions of clients' initial presentation of problems in psychotherapy: The Early Assimilation Research Scale. *Psychotherapy Research, 7,* 155–171.

Stiles, W. B., Shankland, M. C., Wright, J., & Field, S. D. (1997b). Aptitude-treatment interactions based on clients' assimilation of their presenting problems. *Journal of Consulting and Clinical Psychology, 65,* 889–893.

Stiles, W. B., & Shapiro, D. A. (1989). Abuse of the drug metaphor in psychotherapy process-outcome research. *Clinical Psychology Review, 9,* 521–543.

Stiles, W. B., & Shapiro, D. A. (1994). Disabuse of the drug metaphor: Psychotherapy process-outcome research correlations. *Journal of Consulting and Clinical Psychology, 62,* 942–948.

Stiles, W. B., Shapiro, D. A., & Harper, H. (1994). Finding the way from process to outcome: Blind alleys and unmarked trails. In R. L. Russell (Ed.), *Reassessing psychotherapy research.* New York: Guilford Press.

Stiles, W. B., & Snow, J. S. (1984). Dimensions of psychotherapy session impact across sessions and across clients. *British Journal of Clinical Psychology, 23,* 59–63.

Strauss, A. L., & Corbin, J. (1990). *Basics of qualitative research.* Newbury Park, CA: Sage.

Strauss, B. M., & Kächele, H. (1998). The writing on the wall—Comments on the current discussion about empirically validated treatments in Germany. *Psychotherapy Research, 8,* 158–170.

Strupp, H. H. (1993). The Vanderbilt psychotherapy studies: Synopsis. *Journal of Consulting and Clinical Psychology, 61,* 431–433.

Strupp, H. H., & Binder, L. (1984). *Psychotherapy in a new key: A guide to time-limited dynamic psychotherapy.* New York: Basic Books.

Strupp, H. H., Fox, R. E., & Lessler, K. (1966). *Patients view their psychotherapy.* Baltimore, MD: Johns Hopkins University Press.

Strupp, H. H., Hadley, S. W., & Gomes-Schwartz, B. (1977). *Psychotherapy for better or worse: The problem of negative effects.* New York: Jason Aronson.

Strupp, H. H., Horowitz, L. M., & Lambert, M. J. (1997). *Measuring patient changes in mood, anxiety, and personality disorders: Toward a core battery.* Washington, DC: American Psychological Association.

Strupp, H. H., & Howard, K. I. (1992). A brief history of psychotherapy research. In D. K. Freedheim (Ed.), *History of psychotherapy: A century of change* (pp. 309–334). Washington, DC: American Psychological Association.

Suh, C. S., Strupp, H. H., & O'Malley, S. S. (1986). The Vanderbilt process measures: The psychotherapy process scales (VPPS) and the negative indicators scale (VNIS). In L. S. Greenberg & W. M. Pinsof (Eds.), *The psychotherapeutic process: A research handbook.* New York: Guilford Press.

Talley, F., Butler, S., & Strupp, H. H. (Eds.). (1994). *Research findings and clinical practice: Bridging the chasm.* New York: Basic Books.

Task Force on Promotion and Dissemination of Psychological Procedures. (1995). Training in and dissemination of empirically validated psychological treatments: Report and recommendations. *The Clinical Psychologist, 48,* 3–23.

Thorley, A. S., & Craske, N. (1950). Comparison and estimate of group and individual methods of treatment. *British Medical Journal, 1,* 97–100.

Thurstone, L. L., & Chave, E. J. (1929). *The measurement of attitude.* Chicago: University of Chicago Press.

Toukmanian, S. G., & Rennie, D. L. (Eds.). (1992). *Psychotherapy process research: Paradigmatic and narrative approaches.* Newbury Park, CA: Sage.

Truax, C. B., & Mitchell, K. M. (1971). Research on certain therapist interpersonal skills in relation to process and outcome. In A. E. Bergin & S. L. Garfield (Eds.), *Handbook of psychotherapy and behavior change* (1st ed.) (pp. 299–344). New York: John Wiley & Sons.

Vaillant, G. E. (1971). Theoretical hierarchy of adaptive ego-mechanisms. *Archives of General Psychiatry, 24,* 107–118.

Vaillant, G. E. (1977). *Adaptation to life.* New York: Little, Brown.

Varvin, S., & Stiles, W. B. (1999). Emergence of severe traumatic experiences: An assimilation analysis of psychoanalytic therapy with a political refugee. *Psychotherapy, 9(3),* 381–403.

Wallerstein, R. S. (1986). *Forty-two lives in treatment: A study of psychoanalysis and psychotherapy.* New York: Guilford Press.

Wampold, B. E. (1997). Methodological problems in identifying efficacious psychotherapies. *Psychotherapy Research,* 7, 21–43.

Wampold, B. E. (2001). *The great psychotherapy debate: Models, methods, and findings.* Mahwah, NJ: Lawrence Erlbaum Associates.

Waskow, I. E., & Parloff, M. B. (Eds.). (1975). *Psychotherapy change measures.* Rockville, MD: National Institute of Mental Health.

Watson, J. C., & Rennie, D. L. (1994). Qualitative analysis of clients' subjective experience of significant moments during the exploration of problematic reactions. *Journal of Counseling Psychology, 41(4),* 500–509.

Werbart, A. (1997a). Patterns of repetition and change in a psychoanalytically informed therapeutic environment for severely disturbed patients. Unpublished doctoral dissertation, Department of Psychology, Stockholm University, Sweden.

Werbart, A. (1997b). Separation, termination-process and long-term outcome in psychotherapy with severely disturbed patients. *Bulletin of the Menninger Clinic, 61,* 16–43.

Whitaker, C. W., & Malone, T. (1953). *The roots of psychotherapy.* New York: Blakiston.

Willutzki, U., Haas, H., & Neumann, B. (2000). Resource-oriented psychotherapy for clients suffering from social phobia: An overview of its effects and some impressions from the process. Paper at the 31st International Meeting of the Society for Psychotherapy Research. Chicago, USA: June 2000.

Winter, B., Nieschalk, M., & Stoll, W. (1996). Die Auswirkungen der Entspannungstherapie als Gruppen- und Einzelbehandlung bei chronischem Tinnitus. [The effects of relaxation therapy as individual and group treatment in management of chronic tinnitus]. *Psychotherapie, Psychosomatik, Medizinische Psychologie, 46,* 147–152.

Witteman, C., & Koele, P. (1999). Explaining treatment decisions. *Psychotherapy Research, 9,* 100–114.

Wlazlo, Z., Schroeder-Hartwig, K., Münchau, N., Kaiser, G., & Hand, I. (1992). Exposition in-vivo bei sozialen Ängsten und Defiziten [Exposure in vivo for social phobia and social skills deficits]. *Verhaltenstherapie, 2,* 23–39.

Wolf, M. M. (1978). Social validity: The case of subjective measurement or how applied behavior analysis is finding its heart. *Journal of Applied Behavior Analysis, 11,* 203–214.

Worthington, E. L. (1986). Client compliance with homework directive during counseling. *Journal of Counseling Psychology, 33,* 124–130.

Yalom, I. D. (1970). *The theory and practice of group psychotherapy.* New York: Basic Books.

Yaskin, J. C. (1936). The psychoneuroses and neuroses: a review of a hundred cases with special reference to treatment and results. *American Journal of Psychiatry, 93,* 107–125.

Yates, B. T. (1994). Toward the incorporation of costs, cost-effectiveness analysis, and cost-benefit analysis into clinical research. *Journal of Consulting and Clinical Psychology, 62,* 729–736.

Zlotnick, C., Elkin, I., & Shea, M. T. (1998). Does the gender of a patient or the gender of a therapist affect the treatment of patients with major depression? *Journal of Consulting and Clinical Psychology, 66,* 655–659.

Znoj, H. J., Grawe, K., & Jeger, P. (2000). Die differentielle Bedeutung des Handlungskontrollmodus für klärungs- und bewältigungsorientierte Therapien [Differential meaning of the role of action control in insight and action-oriented therapy]. *Zeitschrift für Klinische Psychologie und Psychotherapie, 29,* 53–59.

Table References

Ablon, J. S., & Jones, E. E. (1998). How expert clinicians' prototypes of an ideal treatment correlate with outcome in psychodynamic and cognitive-behavioral therapy. *Psychotherapy Research, 8,* 71–83.

Ablon, J. S., & Jones, E. E. (1999). Psychotherapy process in the National Institute of Mental Health Treatment of Depression Collaborative Research Program. *Journal of Consulting and Clinical Psychology, 67,* 64–75.

Abramowitz, J. S. (1996). Variants of exposure and response prevention in the treatment of obsessive-compulsive disorder: A meta-analysis. *Behavior Therapy, 27,* 583–600.

Addis, M. E., & Jacobson, N. S. (1996). Reasons for depression and the process and outcome of cognitive-behavioral psychotherapies. *Journal of Consulting and Clinical Psychology, 64,* 1417–1424.

Addis, M. E., & Jacobson, N. S. (2000). A closer look at the treatment rationale and homework compliance in cognitive-behavioral therapy for depression. *Cognitive Therapy and Research, 24,* 313–326.

Ambühl, H. (1993). Was ist therapeutisch an Psychotherapie? [What is therapeutic in psychotherapy?] *Zeitschrift für Klinische Psychologie, Psychopathologie und Psychotherapie, 41,* 285–303.

Anderson, E. M., & Lambert, M. J. (2001). A survival analysis of clinically significant change in outpatient psychotherapy. *Journal of Clinical Psychology, 57,* 875–888.

Anderson, T., Bein, E., Pinnell, B. J., & Strupp, H. H. (1999). Linguistic analysis of affective speech in psychotherapy: A case grammar approach. *Psychotherapy Research, 9,* 88–99.

Anderson, T., & Strupp, H. H. (1996). The ecology of psychotherapy research. *Journal of Consulting and Clinical Psychology, 64,* 776–782.

Anstadt, T., Merten, J., Ullrich, B., & Krause, R. (1997). Affective dyadic behavior, core conflictual relationship themes, and success of treatment. *Psychotherapy Research, 7,* 397–417.

Antonuccio, D. O., Thomas, M., & Danton, W. G. (1997). A cost-effectiveness analysis of cognitive behavior therapy and fluoxetine (Prozac) in the treatment of depression. *Behavior Therapy, 28,* 187–210.

Araujo, L. A., Ito, L. M., & Marks, M. (1996). Early compliance and other factors predicting outcome of exposure for obsessive-compulsive disorder. *British Journal of Psychiatry, 169,* 747–752.

Archer, R., Forbes, Y., Metcalfe, C., & Winter, D. (2000). An investigation of the effectiveness of a voluntary sector psychodynamic counselling service. *British Journal of Medical Psychology, 73,* 401–412.

Arnkoff, D. B., Glass, C. R., & Shapiro, S. J. (2002). Expectations and preferences. In J. C. Norcross (Ed.), *Psychotherapy relationships that work: Therapist contributions and responsiveness to patient needs.* New York: Oxford University Press.

Avants, S. K., Margolin, A., Kosten, T. R., Rounsaville, B. J., & Schottenfeld, R. S. (1998). When is less treatment better? The role of social anxiety in matching methadone patients to psychosocial treatments. *Journal of Consulting and Clinical Psychology, 66,* 791–802.

Baker, R. C., & Kirschenbaum, D. S. (1993). Self-monitoring may be necessary for successful weight control. *Behavior Therapy, 24,* 377–394.

Barber, J. P., Connolly, M. B., Crits-Christoph, P., Gladis, L., & Siqueland, L. (2000). Alliance predicts patients' outcome beyond in-treatment change in symptoms. *Journal of Consulting and Clinical Psychology, 68,* 1027–1032.

Barber, J. P., Crits-Christoph, P., & Luborsky, L. (1996). Effects of therapist adherence and competence on patient outcome in brief dynamic therapy. *Journal of Consulting and Clinical Psychology, 64,* 619–622.

Barber, J. P., Luborsky, L., Crits-Christoph, P., Thase, M. E., Weiss, R., Frank, A., Onken, L., & Gallop, R. (1999). Therapeutic alliance as a predictor of outcome in treatment of cocaine dependence. *Psychotherapy Research, 9,* 54–73.

Barber, J. P., Luborsky, L., Gallop, R., Crits-Christoph, P., Frank, A., Weiss, R. D., Thase, M. E., Connolly, M. B., Gladis, M., Foltz, C., & Siqueland, L. (2001). Therapeutic alliance as a predictor of outcome and retention in the National institute on Drug Abuse Collaborative Cocaine Treatment Study. *Journal of Consulting and Clinical Psychology, 69,* 119–124.

Barkham, M., Rees, A., Shapiro, D. A., Stiles, W. B., Agnew, R. M., Halstead, J., Culverwell, A., & Harrington, V.M.G. (1996). Outcomes of time-limited psychotherapy in applied settings: Replicating the second Sheffield Psychotherapy Project. *Journal of Consulting and Clinical Psychology, 64,* 1079–1085.

Barkham, M., Rees, A., Stiles, W. B., Shapiro, D. A., Hardy, G. E., & Reynolds, S. (1996). Dose-effect relations in time-limited psychotherapy for depression. *Journal of Consulting and Clinical Psychology, 64,* 927–935.

Barrett, M. S., & Berman, J. S. (2001). Is psychotherapy more effective when therapists disclose information about themselves? *Journal of Consulting and Clinical Psychology, 69,* 597–603

Bassler, M., & Krauthauser, H. (1996). Zur Evaluation des therapeutischen Prozesses von stationärer Psychotherapie mit der Repertory-Grid-Technik. [Evaluation of the therapeutic process in inpatient psychotherapy by means of repertory grid technique]. *Psychotherapie, Psychosomatik, Medizinische Psychologie, 46,* 29–37.

Bassler, M., Krauthauser, H., & Hoffmann, S. O. (1995). Welche Faktoren beeinflussen die Dauer stationärer Psychotherapie? [Which factors influence the duration of inpatient psychotherapy?] *Psychotherapie, Psychosomatik, Medizinische Psychologie, 45,* 167–175.

Bernal, G., Bonilla, J., Padilla-Cotto, L., & Pérez-Prado, E. M. (1998). Factors associated to outcome in psychotherapy: An effectiveness study in Puerto Rico. *Journal of Clinical Psychology, 54,* 329–342.

Beutler, L. E., Moleiro, C. M., & Talebi, H. (2002). Resistance. In J. C. Norcross (Ed.), *Psychotherapy relationships that work: Therapist contributions and responsiveness to patient needs.* New York: Oxford University Press.

Binder, J. L., & Strupp, H. H. (1997). "Negative process": A recurrently discovered and underestimated facet of therapeutic process and outcome in the individual psychotherapy of adults. *Clinical Psychology: Science and Practice, 4,* 121–139.

Blatt, S. J., Sanislow, C. A., III, Zuroff, D. C., & Pilkonis, P. A. (1996). Characteristics of effective therapists: Further analyses of data from the National Institute of Mental Health Treatment of Depression Collaborative Research Program. *Journal of Consulting and Clinical Psychology, 64,* 1276–1284.

Blatt, S. J., Zuroff, D. C., Bondi, C. M., Sanislow, C. A., & Pilkonis, P. A. (1998). When and how perfectionism impedes the brief treatment of depression: Further analyses of the National Institute of Mental Health Treatment of Depression Collaborative Research Program. *Journal of Consulting and Clinical Psychology, 66,* 423–428.

Blatt, S. J., Zuroff, D. C., Quinlan, D. M., & Pilkonis, P. A. (1996). Interpersonal factors in brief treatment of depression: Further analyses of the National Institute of Mental Health Treatment of Depression Collaborative Research Program. *Journal of Consulting and Clinical Psychology, 64,* 162–171.

Bohart, A., Elliott, R., Greenberg, G., & Watson, J. (2002). Empathy. In J. C. Norcross (Ed.), *Psychotherapy relationships that work: Therapist contributions and responsiveness to patient needs.* New York: Oxford University Press.

Borgart, E.-J., & Meermann, R. (1999). Bedingungsfaktoren unterschiedlicher Behandlungsdauer bei Angststörungen im Rahmen stationärer Verhaltenstherapie. [Influencing factors of different durations of behavioural therapy in in-patients with anxiety disorders]. *Psychotherapie, Psychosomatik, Medizinische Psychologie, 49,* 109–113.

Bouchard, S., Gauthier, J., Laberge, B., French, D., Pelletier, M.-H., & Godbout, C. (1996). Exposure versus cognitive restructuring in the treatment of panic disorder with agoraphobia. *Behaviour Research and Therapy, 34,* 213–224.

Bovasso, G. B., Eaton, W. W., & Armenian, H. K. (1999). The long-term outcomes of mental health treatment in a population-based study. *Journal of Consulting and Clinical Psychology, 67,* 529–538.

Bretz, H. J., Heekerens, H.-P., & Schmitz, B. (1994). Eine Metaanalyse zur Wirksamkeit von Gestalttherapie. [A meta-analysis of the evaluation research on gestalt therapy]. *Zeitschrift für Klinische Psychologie, Psychopathologie und Psychotherapie, 42,* 241–260.

Bright, J. I., Baker, K. D., & Neimeyer, R. A. (1999). Professional and paraprofessional group treatments for depression: A comparison of cognitive-behavioral and mutual support interventions. *Journal of Consulting and Clinical Psychology 67,* 491–501.

Brown, P. D., & O'Leary, K. D. (2000). Therapeutic alliance: Predicting continuance and success in group treatment for spouse abuse. *Journal of Consulting and Clinical Psychology, 68,* 340–345.

Bryant, M. J., Simons, A. D., & Thase, M. E. (1999). Therapist skill and patient variables in homework compliance: Controlling an uncontrolled variable in cognitive therapy outcome research. *Cognitive Therapy and Research, 23,* 381–399.

Burgoon, J. K., Beutler, L. E., LePoire, B. A., Engle, D., Bergan, J., Salvio, M., & Mohr, D. C. (1993). Nonverbal indices of arousal in group psychotherapy. *Psychotherapy, 30,* 635–645.

Burlingame, G., Fuhriman, A., & Johnson, J. (2002). Cohesion in group therapy. In J. C. Norcross (Ed.), *Psychotherapy relationships that work: Therapist contributions and responsiveness to patient needs.* New York: Oxford University Press.

Burns, D. D., & Spangler, D. L. (1999). Does psychotherapy homework lead to improvements in depression in cognitive-behavioral therapy or does improvement lead to increased homework compliance? *Journal of Consulting and Clinical Psychology, 68,* 46–56.

Burns, T., Beadsmore, A., Bhat, A. V., Oliver, A., & Mathers, C. (1993). A controlled trial of home-based acute psychiatric services. I: Clinical and social outcome. *British Journal of Psychiatry, 163,* 49–54.

Burns, T., Raferty, J., Beadsmoore, A., McGuigan, S., & Dickson, M. (1993). A controlled trial of home-based acute psychiatric services. II: Treatment patterns and costs. *British Journal of Psychiatry, 163,* 55–61.

Callahan, P. E. (2000). Indexing resistance in short-term dynamic psychotherapy (STDP): Change in breaks in eye contact during anxiety (BECAS). *Psychotherapy Research, 10,* 87–99.

Carroll, K. M., Nich, C., & Rounsaville, B. J. (1997). Contribution of the therapeutic alliance to outcome in active versus control psychotherapies. *Journal of Consulting and Clinical Psychology, 65,* 510–514.

Carroll, K. M, Rounsaville, B., Nich, C., Gordon, L. T., Wirtz, P. W., & Gawin, F. (1994). One-year follow-up of psychotherapy and pharmacotherapy for cocaine dependence. *Archives of General Psychiatry, 51,* 989–997.

Castonguay, L. G., Goldfried, M. R., Wiser, S., Raue, P. J., & Hayes, A. M. (1996). Predicting the effect of cognitive therapy for depression: A study of unique and common factors. *Journal of Consulting and Clinical Psychology, 64,* 497–504.

Castonguay, L. G., Pincus, A. L., Agras, W. S., & Hines, C. E. III. (1998). The role of emotion in group cognitive-behavioral therapy for binge eating disorder: When things have to feel worse before they get better. *Psychotherapy Research, 8,* 225–238.

Claiborn, C. D., Goodyear, R., & Horner, P. (2002). Feedback. In J. C. Norcross (Ed.), *Psychotherapy relationships that work: Therapist contributions and responsiveness to patient needs.* New York: Oxford University Press.

Clark, D. M., Salkovskis, P. M., Hackmann, A., Middleton, H., Anastasiades, P., & Gelder, M. (1994).

Comparison of cognitive therapy, applied relaxation and imipramine in the treatment of panic disorder. *British Journal of Psychiatry, 164*, 759–769.

Clark, D. M., Salkovskis, P. M., Hackmann, A., Wells, A., Ludgate, L., & Gelder, M. (1999). Brief cognitive therapy for panic disorder: A randomized controlled trial. *Journal of Consulting and Clinical Psychology, 67(4)*, 583–589.

Clarke, S., & Llewelyn, S. (1994). Personal constructs of survivors of childhood sexual abuse receiving cognitive analytic therapy. *British Journal of Medical Psychology, 67*, 273–289.

Connolly, M. B., Crits-Christoph, P., Shappell, S., Barber, J. P., Luborsky, L., & Shaffer, C. (1999). Relation of transference interpretations to outcome in the early sessions of brief supportive-expressive psychotherapy. *Psychotherapy Research, 9*, 485–495.

Connors, G. J., Carroll, K. M., DiClemente, C. C., Longabaugh, R., & Donavan, D. M. (1997). The therapeutic alliance and its relationship to alcoholism treatment participation and outcome. *Journal of Consulting and Clinical Psychology, 65*, 588–598.

Cote, G., Gauthier, J. G., Laberge, B., Cormier, H. J., & Plamondon, J. (1994). Reduced therapist contact in the cognitive-behavioral treatment of panic disorder. *Behavior Therapy, 25*, 123–145.

Crits-Christoph, P., & Connally, M. B. (2002). Relational interpretations. In J. C. Norcross (Ed.), *Psychotherapy relationships that work: Therapist contributions and responsiveness to patient needs.* New York: Oxford University Press.

Cummings, A. L., Hallberg, E., Martin, J., & Slemon, A. G. (1992). Participants' memories for therapeutic events and ratings of session effectiveness. *Journal of Cognitive Psychotherapy, 6*, 113–124.

Cummings, A. L., Martin, J., Hallberg, E., & Slemon, A. G. (1992). Memory for therapeutic events, session effectiveness, and working alliance in short-term counseling. *Journal of Counseling Psychology, 39*, 306–312.

Cummings, A. L., Slemon, A. G., & Hallberg, E. T. (1993). Session evaluation and recall of important events as a function of counselor experience. *Journal of Counseling Psychology, 40*, 156–165.

Dazord, A., Gerin, P., Seulin, C., Duclos, A., & Amar, A. (1997). Day-treatment evaluation: therapeutic outcome after a treatment in a psychiatric day-treatment center: Another look at the "outcome equivalence paradox." *Psychotherapy Research, 7*, 57–69.

DeJong-Meyer, R., Hautzinger, M., Rudolf, G. A. E., Strauss, W., & Frick, U. (1996a). Die Überprüfung der Wirksamkeit einer Kombination von Antidepressiva- und Verhaltenstherapie bei endogen depressiven Patienten: Varianzanalytische Ergebnisse zu den Haupt- und Nebenkriterien des Therapieerfolgs. [The effectiveness of antidepressants and cognitive-behavioral therapy combined in patients with endogenous depression: Results of analyses of variance regarding main and secondary outcome criteria]. *Zeitschrift für Klinische Psychologie, 25*, 93–109.

DeJong-Meyer, R., Hautzinger, M., Rudolf, G. A. E., Strauss, W., & Frick, U. (1996b). Prädiktions- und Verlaufsanalysen bei kombinierter psychologischer und medikamentöser Therapie endogen depressiver Patienten [Outcome prediction and longitudinal analyses of endogenously depressed patients treated with combined psychological and antidepressant therapies]. *Zeitschrift für Klinische Psychologie, 25*, 110–129.

DeJong-Meyer, R., Schmitz, S., Ehlker, M., Greis, S., Hinsken, U., Sonnen, B., & Dickhöver, N. (1999). Handlungsorientierte Interaktionsbeiträge in verschiedenen Therapien: Prozeβsteuerung und Erfolgsrelevanz [Action-orientated interaction in different therapeutic approaches: Process impact and outcome relevance]. *Zeitschrift für Klinische Psychologie, Psychiatrie und Psychotherapie, 47*, 172–190.

Dick, A. (1999). Die Beeinflussung von Glück und Wohlbefinden durch Psychotherapie. Unpublished doctoral dissertation, Faculty of Psychology, University of Berne: Berne, Switzerland.

Dick, A., Grawe, K., Regli, D., & Heim, P. (1999). Was soll ich tun, wenn . . .? Empirische Hinweise für die adaptive Feinsteuerung des Therapiegeschehens innerhalb einzelner Sitzungen. [What should I do when . . .? Empirical hints for the adaptive fine tuning of the therapy process within sessions] *Verhaltenstherapie und psychosoziale Praxis, 31*, 253–280.

Dreessen, L., & Arntz, A. (1999). Personality disorders have no excessively negative impact on therapist-rated therapy process in the cognitive and behavioural treatment of axis I anxiety disorders. *Clinical Psychology and Psychotherapy, 6*, 384–394.

Durham, R. C., & Allan, T. (1993). Psychological treatment of generalised anxiety disorder. *British Journal of Psychiatry, 163*, 19–26.

Durham, R. C., Allan, T., & Hackett, C. A. (1997). On predicting improvement and relapse in generalized anxiety disorder following psychotherapy. *British Journal of Clinical Psychology, 36*, 101–119.

Durham, R. C., Murphy, T., Allan, T., Richard, K., Treliving, L. R., & Fenton, G. W. (1994). Cognitive therapy, analytic psychotherapy and anxiety management training for generalized anxiety disorder. *British Journal of Psychiatry, 165*, 315–323.

Dürr, H., & Hahlweg, K. (1996). Familienbetreuung bei schizophrenen Patienten: Analyse des Therapieverlaufes [Process analysis of behavioral family management with schizophrenic patients]. *Zeitschrift für Klinische Psychologie, 25*, 33–46.

Eaton, T. T., Abeles, N., & Gutfreund, M. J. (1993). Negative indicators, therapeutic alliance, and therapy outcome. *Psychotherapy Research, 3,* 115–123.

Edelman, R. E., & Chambless, D. L. (1993). Compliance during sessions and homework in exposure-based treatment of agoraphobia. *Behaviour Research and Therapy, 31,* 767–773.

Edelman, R. E., & Chambless, D. L. (1995). Adherence during sessions and homework in cognitive-behavioral treatment of social phobia. *Behaviour Research and Therapy, 33,* 573–577.

Elliott, R. (2001). Contemporary brief experiential psychotherapy. *Clinical Psychology: Science and Practice, 8,* 38–50.

Elliott, R., & Wexler, M. M. (1994). Measuring the impact of sessions in process-experiential therapy of depression: The Session Impacts Scale. *Journal of Counseling Psychology, 41,* 166–174.

Emanuels-Zuurveen, L., & Emmelkamp, P.M.G. (1996). Individual behavioural-cognitive therapy v. marital therapy for depression in maritally distressed couples. *British Journal of Psychiatry, 169,* 181–188.

Eugster, S. L., & Wampold, B. E. (1996). Systematic effects of participant role on evaluation of the psychotherapy session. *Journal of Consulting and Clinical Psychology, 64,* 1020–1028.

Eyberg, S. M., Edwards, D., Boggs, S. R., & Foote, R. (1998). Maintaining the treatment effects of parent training: The role of booster sessions and other maintenance strategies. *Clinical Psychology: Science and Practice, 5,* 544–554.

Eyssell, D., Zeising, S., & Stuhr, U. (1992). Prozess-Erfolgsforschung am Beispiel klientenzentrierter Psychotherapie und psychodynamischer Kurzpsychotherapie. [Process-outcome-research: An example of client-centered and psychodynamic short psychotherapy]. *Zeitschrift für Klinische Psychologie, Psychopathologie und Psychotherapie, 40,* 58–78.

Fals-Stewart, W., Birchler, G. R., & O'Farrell, T. J. (1996). Behavioral couples therapy for male substance-abusing patients: Effects on relationship adjustment and drug-using behavior. *Journal of Consulting and Clinical Psychology, 64,* 959–972.

Farber, B. A., & Lane, J. S. (2002). Positive regard. In J. C. Norcross (Ed.), *Psychotherapy relationships that work: Therapist contributions and responsiveness to patient needs.* New York: Oxford University Press.

Feeley, M., DeRubeis, R. J., & Gelfant, L. A. (1999). The temporal relation to adherence and alliance to symptom change in cognitive therapy for depression. *Journal of Consulting and Clinical Psychology, 67(4),* 578–582.

Feeston, M. H., Ladouceur, R., Gagnon, F., Thibodeau, N., Rhéaume, J., Letarte, H., & Bujold, A. (1997). Cognitive-behavioral treatment of obsessive thoughts: A controlled study. *Journal of Consulting and Clinical Psychology, 65,* 405–413.

Fiedler, P., Albrecht, M., Rogge, K.-E., & Schulte, D. (1994). Wenn Verhaltenstherapeuten mit ihren phobischen Patienten über Ängste sprechen: Eine Episodenstudie zur prognostischen Relevanz therapeutischer Lenkung and Empathie [When behavior therapists and their phobic patients talk about anxiety: An episode analysis of the prognostic relevance of therapeutic directivity and empathy]. *Verhaltenstherapie, 4,* 243–253.

Fiedler, P., Albrecht, M., Rogge, K.-E., & Schulte, D. (1996). Untersuchungen zur Aufmerksamkeitsfluktuation bei Phobien. Eine Prozessanalyse der verhaltenstherapeutischen Angstbehandlung. [Attention and attentional bias in phobias. Process analysis of the behavioral treatment of anxiety disorders]. *Zeitschrift für Klinische Psychologie, 25,* 221–233.

Fiedler, P., Vogt, L., Rogge, K.-E., & Schulte, D. (1994). Die prognostische Relevanz der Autonomie-Entwicklung von Patienten in der verhaltenstherapeutischen Phobienbehandlung: Eine Prozeßanalyse mittels SASB. [The predictive value of autonomy for outcome of behavior therapy of phobias. A process analysis using SASB]. *Zeitschrift für Klinische Psychologie, 23,* 202–212.

Flannery-Schroeder, E. C., & Kendall, P. C. (2000). Group and individual cognitive-behavioral treatments for youth with anxiety disorders: A randomized clinical trial. *Cognitive Therapy and Research, 24,* 251–278.

Foa, E. B., Dancu, C. V., Hembree, E. A., Jaycox, L. H., Meadows, E. A., & Street, G. P. (1999). A comparison of exposure therapy, stress inoculation training, and their combination for reducing posttraumatic stress disorder in female assault victims. *Journal of Consulting and Clinical Psychology, 67,* 194–200.

Foa, E. B., Riggs, D. S., Massie, E. D., & Yarczower, M. (1995). The impact of fear activation and anger on the efficacy of exposure treatment for posttraumatic stress disorder. *Behavior Therapy, 26,* 487–499.

Forsyth, D. R., & Corazzini, J. G. (2000). Groups as change agents. In C. R. Snyder & R. E. Ingram (Eds.) *Handbook of psychological change: Psychotherapy processes and practices for the 21st Century* (pp. 309–336). New York: John Wiley & Sons.

Frettlöh, J., & Kröner-Herwig, B. (1999). Einzel- und Gruppentherapie in der Behandlung chronischer Schmerzen – Gibt as Effektivitätsunterschiede? [Individual versus group training in the treatment of chronic pain: Which is more efficacious?]. *Zeitschrift für Klinische Psychologie, 28,* 256–266.

Fuhriman, A., & Burlingame, G. M. (1994). Group psychotherapy: Research and practice. In A. Fuhriman & G. M. Burlingame (Eds.), *Handbook of group psychotherapy: An empirical and clinical synthesis* (pp. 3–40). New York: John Wiley & Sons.

Gaston, L., Piper, W. E., Debbane, E. G., Bienvenu, J-P., & Garant, J. (1994). Alliance and technique for predicting outcome in short- and long-term analytic psychotherapy. *Psychotherapy Research, 4,* 121–135.

Gaston, L., Thompson, L., Gallagher, D., Cournoyer, L-G., & Gagnon, R. (1998). Alliance, technique, and their interactions in predicting outcome of behavioral, cognitive, and brief psychodynamic therapy. *Psychotherapy Research, 8,* 190–209.

Geller, J. D., & Farber, B. A. (1993). Factors influencing the process of internalization in psychotherapy. *Psychotherapy Research, 3,* 166–180.

Gelso, C. J., & Hayes, J. A. (2002). Management of countertransference. In J. C. Norcross (Ed.), *Psychotherapy relationships that work: Therapist contributions and responsiveness to patient needs.* New York: Oxford University Press.

Gelso, C. J., Kivlighan, D. M., Wine, B., Jones, A., & Friedman, S. C. (1997). Transference, insight, and the course of Time-Limited Therapy. *Journal of Counseling Psychology, 44,* 209–217.

Goldfried, M. R., Castonguay, L. G., Hayes, A. M., Drozd, J. F., & Shapiro, D. A. (1997). A comparative analysis of the therapeutic focus in cognitive-behavioral and psychodynamic-interpersonal sessions. *Journal of Consulting and Clinical Psychology, 65,* 740–748.

Goren, S. S. (1993). The prediction of child psychotherapy outcome: Factors specific to treatment. *Psychotherapy, 30,* 152–158.

Gould, R. A., Clum, G. A., & Shapiro, D. (1993). The use of bibliotherapy in the treatment of panic: A preliminary investigation. *Behavior Therapy, 24,* 241–252.

Gould, R. A., Otto, M. W., Pollack, M. H., & Yap, L. (1997). Cognitive behavioral and pharmacological treatment of generalized anxiety disorder: A preliminary meta-analysis. *Behavior Therapy, 28,* 285–305.

Grant, J. R., & Cash, T. F. (1995). Cognitive-behavioral body image therapy: Comparative efficacy of group and modest-contact treatments. *Behavior Therapy, 26,* 69–84.

Greenberg, L. S., & Hirscheimer, K. (1994). Relating degree of resolution of unfinished business to outcome. Santa Fe, NM: North American Society for Psychotherapy Research. Cited in Greenberg, L., & Forester, F. (1996). Resolving unfinished business: The process of change. *Journal of Consulting and Clinical Psychology, 64,* 439–446.

Greene, B., & Blanchard, E. B. (1994). Cognitive therapy for irritable bowel syndrome. *Journal of Consulting and Clinical Psychology, 62,* 560–568.

Grenyer, B.F.S., & Luborsky, L. (1996). Dynamic change in psychotherapy: Mastery of interpersonal conflicts. *Journal of Consulting and Clinical Psychology, 64,* 411–416.

Gurman, A. S. (2001). Brief therapy and family/couple therapy: An essential redundancy. *Clinical Psychology: Science and Practice, 8,* 51–65.

Hahn, J. H., Achter, J. A., & Shambaugh, E. J. (2001). Client distress disclosure, characteristics at intake, and outcome in brief counseling. *Journal of Counseling Psychology, 48,* 203–211.

Hardy, G. E., Barkham, M., Shapiro, D. A., Reynolds, S., & Rees, A. (1995). Credibility and outcome in cognitive-behavioural and psychodynamic-interpersonal psychotherapy. *British Journal of Clinical Psychology, 34,* 555–569.

Harrist, R. S., Quintana, S. M., Strupp, H. H., & Henry, W. P. (1994). Internalization of interpersonal process in time-limited dynamic psychotherapy. *Psychotherapy, 31(1),* 49–57.

Hatcher, R. L. (1999). Therapists' views of treatment alliance and collaboration in therapy. *Psychotherapy Research, 9,* 405–423.

Hatcher, R. L., & Barends, A. W. (1996). Patients' view of the alliance in psychotherapy: Exploratory factor analysis of three alliance measures. *Journal of Consulting and Clinical Psychology, 64,* 1326–1336.

Hautzinger, M., DeJong-Meyer, R., Treiber, R., Rudolf, G.A.E., & Thien, U. (1996). Wirksamkeit kognitiver Verhaltenstherapie, Pharmakotherapie und deren Kombination bei nichtendogenen, unipolaren Depressionen [Efficacy of cognitive-behavioral therapy, pharmacotherapy, and the combination of both in non-melancholic, unipolar depression]. *Zeitschrift für Klinische Psychologie, 25,* 130–145.

Hautzinger, M., DeJong-Meyer, R., Treiber, R., Rudolf, G.A.E., Thien, U., & Bailer, M. (1996). Verlaufsanalysen und Prädiktoren des Therapieerfolgs bei psychologischer und pharmakologischer Therapie nicht-endogener Depressionen [Process analyses and prediction of treatment outcome of psychological and pharmacological therapy of non-endogenous unipolar depression]. *Zeitschrift für Klinische Psychologie, 25,* 146–154.

Hayes, A. M., Castonguay, L. G., & Goldfried, M. R. (1996). Effectiveness of targeting the vulnerability factors of depression in cognitive therapy. *Journal of Consulting and Clinical Psychology, 64,* 623–627.

Hayes, A. M., & Strauss, J. L. (1998). Dynamic systems theory as a paradigm for the study of change in psychotherapy: An application to cognitive therapy for depression. *Journal of Consulting and Clinical Psychology, 66,* 939–947.

Hayes, J. A., Riker, J. R., & Ingram, K. M. (1997). Countertransference behavior and management in brief counseling: A field study. *Psychotherapy Research, 7,* 145–153.

Heimberg, R. G., & Juster, H. R. (1995). Cognitive-behavioral treatments: Literature review. In R. G. Heimberg, M. R. Liebowitz, D. A. Hope, & F. R. Schneier (Eds.), *Social phobia. Diagnosis, Assessment and Treatment* (pp. 261–309). New York: Guilford Press.

Hellström, K., Fellenius, J., & Öst, L.-G. (1996). One versus five sessions of applied tension in the treatment of blood phobia. *Behaviour Research and Therapy, 34,* 101–112.

Hellström, K., & Öst, L.-G. (1996). Prediction of outcome in the treatment of specific phobia. A cross validation study. *Behaviour Research and Therapy, 34,* 403–411.

Henggeler, S. W., Melton, G. B., Brondino, M. J., Scherer, D. G., & Hanley, J. H. (1997). Multisystemic therapy with violent and chronic juvenile offenders and their families: The role of treatment fidelity in successful dissemination. *Journal of Consulting and Clinical Psychology, 65,* 821–833.

Heppner, P. P., Cooper, C., Mulholland, A., & Wei, M. (2001). A brief, multidimensional, problem-solving psychotherapy outcome measure. *Journal of Counseling Psychology, 48,* 330–343.

Hilesenroth, M. J., Ackerman, S. J., & Blagys, M. D. (2001). Evaluating the phase model of change during short-term psychodynamic psychotherapy. *Psychotherapy Research, 11,* 29–47.

Hill, C. E., & Knox, S. (2002). Self-disclosure. In J. C. Norcross (Ed.), *Psychotherapy relationships that work: Therapist contributions and responsiveness to patient needs.* New York: Oxford University Press.

Hill, C. E., Thompson, B. J., Cogar, M. C., & Denman, D. W., III. (1993). Beneath the surface of long-term therapy: Therapist and client report of their own and each other's covert processes. *Journal of Counseling Psychology, 40,* 278–287.

Hilliard, R. B., Henry, W. P., & Strupp, H. H. (2000). An interpersonal model of psychotherapy: Linking patient and therapist developmental history, therapeutic process, and types of outcome. *Journal of Consulting and Clinical Psychology, 68,* 125–133.

Hoag, M. J., & Burlingame, G. M. (1997). Evaluating the effectiveness of child and adolescent group treatment: A meta-analytic review. *Journal of Clinical Child Psychology, 26,* 234–246.

Hoffart, A., & Friis, S. (2000). Therapists' emotional reactions to anxious patients during integrated behavioral-psychodynamic treatment: A psychometric evaluation of a feeling word checklist. *Psychotherapy Research, 10,* 462–473.

Hoffart, A., & Sexton, H. (2002). The role of optimism in the process of schema-focused cognitive therapy of personality problems. *Behaviour Research and Therapy,* in press.

Høglend, P. (1993). Transference interpretations and long-term change after dynamic psychotherapy of brief to moderate length. *American Journal of Psychotherapy, 47,* 494–505.

Høglend, P. (1996a). Analyses of transference in patients with personality disorders. *Journal of Personality Disorder, 10,* 122–131.

Høglend, P. (1996b). Long-term effects of transference interpretations: comparing results from a quasi-experimental and a naturalistic long-term follow-up study of brief dynamic psychotherapy. *Acta Psychiatrica Scandinavia, 93,* 205–211.

Høglend, P., Engelstad, V., Sørbye, Ø., Heyerdahl, O., & Amlo, S. (1994). The role of insight in exploratory psychodynamic psychotherapy. *British Journal of Medical Psychology, 67,* 305–317.

Høglend, P., & Piper, W. E. (1995). Focal adherence in brief dynamic psychotherapy: A comparison of findings from two independent studies. *Psychotherapy, 32,* 618–628.

Høglend, P., & Piper, W. E. (1997). Treatment length and termination contracts in dynamic psychotherapy. A comparison of findings from two independent studies of brief dynamic psychotherapy. *Nordic Journal of Psychiatry, 51,* 37–42.

Hölzer, M., Mergenthaler, E., Pokorny, D., Kächele, H., & Luborsky, L. (1996). Vocabulary measures for the evaluation of therapy outcome: Re-studying transcripts from the Penn Psychotherapy Project. *Psychotherapy Research, 6,* 95–108.

Hölzer, M., Pokorny, D., Kächele, H., & Luborsky, L. (1997). The verbalization of emotions in the therapeutic dialogue—A correlate of therapeutic outcome? *Psychotherapy Research, 7,* 261–273.

Hope, D. S., Heimberg, R. G., & Bruch, M. A. (1995). Dismantling cognitive-behavioral group therapy for social phobia. *Behaviour Research and Therapy, 33,* 637–650.

Hoppe, F. (1993). Psychologische Wirkfaktoren der hypnotischen Schmerzlinderung: Eine Prozessstudie zur symptom- und problembezogenen Anwendung von Hypnose bei chronischen Schmerzpatienten. [Psychological mechanisms of hypnotic pain reduction: A study of the processes mediating the effects of symptom and problem-oriented hypnosis in chronic pain patients]. *Zeitschrift für Klinische Psychologie, 22,* 4, 420–440.

Horvath, A. O., & Bedi, R. P. (2002). The alliance. In J. C. Norcross (Ed.), *Psychotherapy relationships that work: Therapist contributions and responsiveness to patient needs.* New York: Oxford University Press.

Houts, A. C., Berman, J. S., & Abramson, H. (1994). Effectiveness of psychological and pharmacological treatments for nocturnal enuresis. *Journal of Consulting and Clinical Psychology, 62,* 737–745.

Howard, K. I., Lueger, R. J., Maling, M. S., & Martinovich, Z. (1993). A phase model of psychotherapy outcome: Causal mediation of change. *Journal of Consulting and Clinical Psychology, 61,* 678–685.

Huey, S. J., Henggeler, S. W., Brondino, M. J., & Pickrel, S. G. (2000). Mechanisms of change in multisystemic therapy: Reducing delinquent behavior through therapists adherence and improved family and peer functioning. *Journal of Consulting and Clinical Psychology, 68*, 451–467.

Jacobi, C., Dahme, B., & Rustenbach, S. (1997). Vergleich kontrollierter Psycho- und Pharmakotherapiestudien bei Bulimia und Anorexia Nervosa. [A comparison of controlled psychological and pharmacological treatment studies for bulimia and anorexia nervosa]. *Psychotherapie, Psychosomatik, Medizinische Psychologie, 47*, 346–364.

James, L. D., Thorn, B. E., & Williams, D. A. (1993). Goal specification in cognitive behavioral therapy for chronic headache pain. *Behavior Therapy, 24*, 305–320.

Jarrett, R. B., Basco, M. R., Risser, R., Ramana, J., Marwill, M., Kraft, D., & Rush, A. J. (1998). Is there a role for continuation phase cognitive therapy for depressed outpatients? *Journal of Consulting and Clinical Psychology, 66*, 1036–1040.

Jaycox, L. H., Foa, E. B., & Morral, A. R. (1998). Influence of emotional engagement and habituation on exposure therapy for PTSD. *Journal of Consulting and Clinical Psychology, 66*, 185–192.

Jones, E. E., & Pulos, S. M. (1993). Comparing the process in psychodynamic and cognitive-behavioral therapies. *Journal of Consulting and Clinical Psychology, 61*, 306–316.

Jones, R., Peveler, R. C., Hope, R. A., & Fairburn, C. G. (1993). Changes during treatment for bulimia nervosa: A comparison of three psychological treatments. *Behaviour Research and Therapy, 31*, 479–485.

Joyce, A. S., & Piper, W. E. (1996). Interpretive work in short-term individual psychotherapy: An analysis using hierarchical linear modeling. *Journal of Consulting and Clinical Psychology, 64*, 505–512.

Kächele, H., Kordy, H., Richard, M., & Research Group TR-EAT. (2001). Therapy amount and outcome of inpatient psychodynamic treatment of eating disorders in Germany: Data from a multicenter study. *Psychotherapy Research, 11*, 239–257.

Kadera, S. W., Lambert, M. J., & Andrews, A. A. (1996). A session-by-session analysis of the psychotherapy dose-effect relationship. *Journal of Psychotherapy Practice and Research, 5*, 132–151.

Kazantzis, N., Deane, F. P., & Ronan, K. R. (2000). Homework assignments in cognitive and behavioral therapy: A meta-analysis. *Clinical Psychology: Science and Practice*, 7, 189–202.

Keijsers, G.P.J., Hoogduin, C.A.L., & Schaap, C.P.D.R. (1994). Prognostic factors in the behavioral treatment of panic disorder with and without agoraphobia. *Behavior Therapy, 25*, 689–708.

Kendall, P. C. (1994). Treating anxiety disorders in children: Results of a randomized clinical trial. *Journal of Consulting and Clinical Psychology, 62*, 100–110.

Kendall, P. C., Flannery-Schroeder, E., Panichelli-Mindel, S. M., Southam-Gerow, M., Henin, A., & Warman, M. (1997). Therapy for youths with anxiety disorders: A second randomized clinical trial. *Journal of Consulting and Clinical Psychology, 65*, 366–380.

Kendall, P. C., & Southam-Gerow, M. A. (1996). Long-term follow-up of a cognitive-behavioral therapy for anxiety-disordered children. *Journal of Consulting and Clinical Psychology, 64*, 724–730.

Kivlighan, D. M., & Arthur, E. G. (2000). Convergence in client and counselor recall of important session events. *Journal of Counseling Psychology, 47*, 79–84.

Kivlighan, D. M., Multon, K. D., & Patton, M. J. (2000). Insight and symptom reduction in time-limited psychoanalytic counseling. *Journal of Counseling Psychology, 47*, 50–58.

Kivlighan, D. M., & Shaughnessy, P. (1995). Analysis of the development of the working alliance using hierarchical linear modelling. *Journal of Counseling Psychology, 42*, 338–349.

Klein, M. H., Kolden, G. G., Michels, J., & Chisholm-Stockard, S. (2002). Congruence/genuineness. In J. C. Norcross (Ed.), *Psychotherapy relationships that work: Therapist contributions and responsiveness to patient needs.* New York: Oxford University Press.

Knox, S., Goldberg, J. L., Woodhouse, S. S., & Hill, C. E. (1999). Clients' internal representations of their therapists. *Journal of Counseling Psychology, 46*, 244–256.

Kolden, G. G. (1996). Change in early sessions of dynamic therapy: Universal processes and the Generic Model of Psychotherapy. *Journal of Consulting and Clinical Psychology, 64*, 489–496.

Kolden, G. G., Strauman, T. J., Gittleman, M., Halverson, J. L., Heerey, E., & Schneider, K. L. (2000). The Therapeutic Realizations Scale-Revised (TRS-R): Psychometric characteristics and relationship to treatment process and outcome. *Journal of Clinical Psychology, 56*, 1207–1220.

Konzag, T.-A., Fikentscher, E., & Bandemer-Greulich, U. (2000a). Vernetzte Evaluierung von Prozess- und Ergebnisqualität in der stationären Psychotherapie. [A cross-linked evaluation of the quality of processes and results in in-patient psychotherapy—A practicability study]. *Psychotherapie, Psychosomatik, Medizinische Psychologie, 50*, 376–383.

Konzag, T.-A., Fikentscher, E., & Bandemer-Greulich, U. (2000b). Integrierte stationäre Psychotherapie bei schweren Persönlichkeitsstörungen. [Integrated in-patient psychotherapy for patients with severe personality disorders]. In W. Tress (Hrsg.), *Psychotherapeutische Medizin im Krankenhaus* (80–95). Frankfurt am Main: Verlag für Akademische Schriften.

Kopta, S. M., Howard, K. I., Lowry, J. L., & Beutler, L. E. (1994). Patterns of symptomatic recovery in psychotherapy. *Journal of Consulting and Clinical Psychology, 62*, 1009–1016.

Krupnick, J. L., Elkin, I., Collings, J., Simmens, S., Sotsky, S. M., Pilkonis, P. A., & Watkins, J. T. (1994). Therapeutic alliance and clinical outcome in the NIMH Treatment of Depression Collaborative Research Program: Preliminary findings. *Psychotherapy, 31(1)*, 28–35.

Krupnick, J. L., Sotsky, S. M., Simmens, S., Moyer, J., Elkin, I., Watkins, J., & Pilkonis, P. A. (1996). The role of therapeutic alliance in psychotherapy and pharmacotherapy outcome: Findings in the National Institute of Mental Health Treatment of Depression Collaborative Research Program. *Journal of Consulting and Clinical Psychology, 64*, 532–539.

Ladouceur, R., Dugas, M. J., Freeston, M. H., Léger, E., Gagnon, F., & Thibodeau, N. (2000). Efficacy of a cognitive-behavioral treatment for generalized anxiety disorder: Evaluation in a controlled clinical trial. *Journal of Consulting and Clinical Psychology, 68*, 957–964.

Lambert, M. J., Whipple, J. L, Smart, D. W., Vermeersch, D. A., Nielsen, S. L., & Hawkins, E. J. (2001). The effects of providing therapists with feedback on patient progress during psychotherapy: Are outcomes enhanced? *Psychotherapy Research, 11*, 49–68.

Latimer, W. W., Newcomb, M., Winters, K. C., & Stinchfield, R. D. (2000). Adolescent substance abuse treatment outcome: The role of substance abuse problem severity, psychosocial, and treatment factors. *Journal of Consulting and Clinical Psychology, 68*, 684–696.

Lauth, G. (1996). Effizienz eines metakognitiven-strategischen Trainings bei lern- und aufmerksamkeitsbeeinträchtigten Grundschülern. [Efficiency of a metacognitive-strategic training with learning and attention-deficit disordered children]. *Zeitschrift für Klinische Psychologie, 25(1)*, 21–32.

Leung, A. W., & Heimberg, R. G. (1996). Homework compliance, perceptions of control, and outcome of cognitive-behavioral treatment of social phobia. *Behaviour Research and Therapy, 34*, 423–432.

Lichtenberg, J. W., Wettersten, K. B., Mull, H., Moberly, R. L., Merkley, K. B., & Corey, A. T. (1998). Relationship formation and relational control as correlates of psychotherapy quality and outcome. *Journal of Counseling Psychology, 45*, 322–337.

Liddle, B. J. (1996). Therapist sexual orientation, gender, and counseling practices as they relate to ratings of helpfulness by gay and lesbian clients. *Journal of Counseling Psychology, 43*, 394–401.

Long, J. R. (2001). Goal agreement and early therapeutic change. *Psychotherapy, 38*, 219–232.

Lucas, R. A., & Telch, M. J. (1993). Group versus individual treatment of social phobia. Paper presented at the annual meeting of the Association for the Advancement of Behavior Therapy, Atlanta, GA.

Lueger, R. J. (1998). Using feedback on patient progress to predict the outcome of psychotherapy. *Journal of Clinical Psychology, 54*, 383–393.

Lunnen, K. M., & Ogles, B. M. (1998). A multiperspective, multivariable evaluation of reliable change. *Journal of Consulting and Clinical Psychology, 66*, 400–410.

MacKenzie, K. R., & Tschuschke, V. (1993). Relatedness, group work and outcome in long-term inpatient psychotherapy groups. *Journal of Psychotherapy Practice and Research, 2*, 147–156.

Maling, M. S., Gurtman, M. B., & Howard, K. I. (1995). The response of interpersonal problems to varying doses of psychotherapy. *Psychotherapy Research, 5*, 63–75.

Mallinckrodt, B. (1993). Session impact, working alliance, and treatment outcome in brief counseling. *Journal of Counseling Psychology, 40*, 25–32.

Mallinckrodt, B. (1996). Change in working alliance, social support, and psychological symptoms in brief therapy. *Journal of Counseling Psychology, 43*, 448–455.

Margraf, J., Barlow, D. H., Clark, D. M., & Telch, M. J. (1993). Psychological treatment of panic: Work in progress on outcome, active ingredients, and follow-up. *Behaviour Research and Therapy, 31*, 1–8.

Martin, D. J., Garske, J. P., & Davis, K. M. (2000). Relation of the therapeutic alliance with outcome and other variables: A meta-analytic review. *Journal of Consulting and Clinical Psychology, 68*, 438–450.

Marziali, E., Munroe-Blum, H., & McCleary, L. (1999). The effects of the therapeutic alliance on the outcomes of individual and group psychotherapy with borderline personality disorder. *Psychotherapy Research, 9*, 424–436.

McCullough, L., & Andrews, S. (2001). Assimilative Integration: Short-term dynamic psychotherapy for treating affect phobias. *Clinical Psychology: Science and Practice, 8*, 82–97.

McDermut, W., Miller, I. W., & Brown, R. A. (2001). The efficacy of group psychotherapy for depression: A meta-analysis and review of the empirical research. *Clinical Psychology: Science and Practice, 8*, 98–116.

McFarlane, W. R., Lukens, E., Link, B., Dushay, R., Deakins, S., Newmark, M., Dunne, E. J., Horen, B., & Toran, J. (2000). Multiple-family groups and psychoeducation in the treatment of schizophrenia. *Archives of General Psychiatry, 57*, 679–687.

McGinn, L. K., & Sanderson, W. C. (2001). What allows cognitive-behavioral therapy to be brief: Overview, efficacy and crucial factors facilitating brief treatment. *Clinical Psychology: Science and Practice, 8*, 23–37.

McKay, D. (1997). A maintenance program for obsessive-compulsive disorder using exposure with response prevention: 2-year follow-up. *Behaviour Research and Therapy, 35,* 367–369.

McKay, D., Todaro, J., Neziroglu, F., Campisi, T., Moritz, E. K., & Yaruyura-Tobias, J. A. (1997). Body dysmorphic disorder: A preliminary evaluation of treatment and maintenance using exposure with response prevention. *Behaviour Research and Therapy, 35,* 67–70.

McMullen, L. M., & Conway, J. B. (1994). Dominance and nurturance in the figurative expressions of psychotherapy clients. *Psychotherapy Research, 4,* 43–57.

McMullen, L. M., & Conway, J. B. (1997). Dominance and nurturance in the narratives told by clients in psychotherapy. *Psychotherapy Research, 7,* 83–98.

Mergenthaler, E. (1996). Emotion-abstraction patterns in verbatim protocols: A new way of describing psychotherapeutic processes. *Journal of Consulting and Clinical Psychology, 64,* 1306–1315.

Merten, J. (2001). *Beziehungsregulation in Psychotherapien. Maladaptive Beziehungsmuster und der therapeutische Prozess* [Alliance regulation in psychotherapy. Maladaptive alliance patterns and the therapeutic process]. Stuttgart: Kohlhammer.

Merten, J., Anstadt, T., Ullrich, B., Krause, R., & Buchheim, P. (1996). Emotional experience and facial behavior during the psychotherapeutic process and its relation to treatment outcome: A pilot study. *Psychotherapy Research, 6,* 198–212.

Messer, S. B. (2001). What makes brief psychodynamic therapy time efficient. *Clinical Psychology: Science and Practice, 8,* 5–22.

Michalak, J., & Schulte, D. (2002). Zielkonflikte und Therapiemotivation. [Goal conflicts and therapy motivation]. *Zeitschrift für Klinische Psychologie und Psychotherapie,* in press.

Mueller, M., & Pekarik, G. (2000). Treatment duration prediction: Client accuracy and its relationship to dropout, outcome, and satisfaction. *Psychotherapy, 37,* 117–123.

Murran, J. C., Gorman, B. S., Safran, J. D., Twinning, L., Samstag, L. W., & Winston, A. (1995). Linking in-session change to overall outcome in short-term cognitive therapy. *Journal of Consulting and Clinical Psychology, 63,* 651–657.

Murran, J. C., Samstag, L. W., Jilton, R., Batchelder, S., & Winston, A. (1997). Development of a suboutcome strategy to measure interpersonal process in psychotherapy from an observer perspective. *Journal of Clinical Psychology, 53,* 405–420.

Najavits, L. M., & Strupp, H. H. (1994). Differences in the effectiveness of psychodynamic therapists: A process-outcome study. *Psychotherapy, 31(1),* 114–123.

Nauta, M. H., Scholing, A., Emmelkamp, P.M.G., & Minderaa, R. B. (2001). Cognitive-behavioural therapy for anxiety disordered children in a clinical setting: Does additional cognitive parent training enhance treatment effectiveness? *Clinical Psychology and Psychotherapy, 8,* 330–340.

Norville, R., Sampson, H., & Weiss, J. (1996). Accurate interpretations and brief psychotherapy outcome. *Psychotherapy Research, 6,* 16–29.

Nosper, M. (1999). Der Erfolg psychosomatischer Rehabilitation in Abhängigkeit von der Behandlungsdauer. [Time required for symptomatic improvement in in-patient psychosomatic rehabilitation treatment]. *Psychotherapie, Psychosomatik, Medizinische Psychologie, 49,* 354–360.

O'Connor, L., Edelstein, S., Berry, J. W., & Weiss, J. (1994). Changes in the patient's level of insight in brief psychotherapy: Two pilot studies. *Psychotherapy, 31(3),* 533–544.

Öst, L.-G. (1996). One session group treatment of spider phobia. *Behaviour Research and Therapy, 34,* 707–715.

Öst, L.-G., Brandberg, M., & Alm, T. (1997). One versus five sessions of exposure in the treatment of flying phobia. *Behaviour Research and Therapy, 35,* 987–996.

Öst, L.-G., Stridh, B.-M., & Wolf, M. (1998). A clinical study of spider phobia: Prediction of outcome after self-help and therapist-directed treatments. *Behaviour Research and Therapy, 36,* 17–35.

Paivio, S. C., & Bahr, L. M. (1998). Interpersonal problems, working alliance, and outcome in short-term experiential therapy. *Psychotherapy Research, 8,* 392–407.

Paivio, S. C., Hall, I. E., Holowaty, K.A.M., Jellis, J. B., & Tran, N. (2001). Imaginal confrontation for resolving child abuse issues. *Psychotherapy Research, 11,* 433–453.

Paivio, S. C., & Patterson, L. A. (1999). Alliance development in therapy for resolving child abuse issues. *Psychotherapy, 36(4),* 343–353.

Patton, M. J., Kivlighan, D. M., Jr., & Multon, K. D. (1997). The Missouri Psychoanalytic Counseling Research Project: Relation of changes in counseling process to client outcomes. *Journal of Counseling Psychology, 44,* 189–208.

Paulson, B. L., Truscott, D., & Stuart, J. (1999). Clients' perceptions of helpful experiences in counseling. *Journal of Counseling Psychology, 46,* 317–324.

Penava, S. J., Otto, M. W., Maki, K. M., & Pollack, M. H. (1998). Rate of improvement during cognitive-behavioral group treatment for panic disorder. *Behaviour Research and Therapy, 36,* 665–673.

Peters, G., Plöhn, S., Buhk, H., & Dahme, B. (1998). Imaginative Schmerztherapie: Effekte imaginativer Transformationen and angenehmer Vorstellungen und der Einfluss der Selbstanwendung zu Hause auf den Behandlungserfolg bei chronischen Kopfschmerzen. [Psychological pain therapy by imaginative transformations vs. pleasant imagery with home practice]. *Zeitschrift für Klinische Psychologie, 27*, 30–40.

Piper, W. E., Boroto, D. R., Joyce, A. S., & McCallum, M. (1995). Pattern of alliance and outcome in short-term individual psychotherapy. *Psychotherapy, 32*, 639–647.

Piper, W. E., Joyce, A. S., McCallum, M., & Azim, F. A. (1993). Concentration and correspondence of transference interpretations in short-term psychotherapy. *Journal of Consulting and Clinical Psychology, 61*, 596–595.

Power, K. G., Sharp, D. M., Swanson, V., & Simpson, R. J. (2000). Therapist contact in cognitive behaviour therapy for panic disorder and agoraphobia in primary care. *Clinical Psychology and Psychotherapy, 7*, 37–47.

Price, P., & Jones, E. E. (1998). Examining the alliance using the Psychotherapy Process Q-Set. *Psychotherapy, 35(3)*, 392–404.

Priebe, S. (1993). Ist die Bewertung einer stationären Behandlung durch depressive Patienten für den Verlauf bedeutsam? [Is depressive in-patients' assessment of treatment predictive of symptom change?] *Verhaltenstherapie, 3*, 208–212.

Priebe, S., & Gruyters, T. (1995). The importance of the first three days: Predictors of treatment outcome in depressed in-patients. *British Journal of Clinical Psychology, 34*, 229–236.

Prochaska, J. O., & Norcross, J. C. (2002). Stages of change. In J. C. Norcross (Ed.), *Psychotherapy relationships that work: Therapist contributions and responsiveness to patient needs.* New York: Oxford University Press.

Quinn, W. H., Dotson, D., & Jordan, K. (1997). Dimensions of therapeutic alliance and their associations with outcome in family therapy. *Psychotherapy Research, 7*, 429–438.

Raue, P. J., Goldfried, M. R., & Barkham, M. (1997). The therapeutic alliance in psychodynamic-interpersonal and cognitive-behavioral therapy. *Journal of Consulting and Clinical Psychology, 65*, 582–587.

Rector, N. A., Bagby, R. M., Segal, Z. V., Joffe, R. T., & Levitt, A. (2000). Self-criticism and dependency in depressed patients treated with cognitive therapy or pharmacotherapy. *Cognitive Therapy and Research, 24*, 571–584.

Rector, N. A., Zuroff, D. C., & Segal, Z. V. (1999). Cognitive change and the therapeutic alliance: The role of technical and nontechnical factors in cognitive therapy. *Psychotherapy, 36(4)*, 320–328.

Regli, D., Bieber, K., Mathier, F., & Grawe, K. (2000). Beziehungsgestaltung und Aktivierung von Ressourcen in der Anfangsphase von Therapien [Realization of therapeutic bond and activation of resources in initial therapy sessions]. *Verhaltenstherapie und Verhaltensmedizin, 21*, 399–420.

Reynolds, S., Stiles, W. B., Barkham, M., Shapiro, D. A., Hardy, G. E., & Rees, A. (1996). Acceleration of changes in session impact during contrasting time-limited psychotherapies. *Journal of Consulting and Clinical Psychology, 64*, 577–586.

Robinson, L. A., Berman, J. S., & Neimeyer, R. A. (1990). Psychotherapy for the treatment of depression: A comprehensive review of controlled outcome research. *Psychological Bulletin, 108*, 30–49.

Rohrbaugh, M. J., & Shoham, V. (2001). Brief therapy based on interrupting ironic processes: The Palo Alto model. *Clinical Psychology: Science and Practice, 8*, 66–81.

Rosner, R., Frick, U., Beutler, L. E., & Daldrup, R. (1999). Depressionsverläufe in unterschiedlichen Psychotherapieformen—Modellierung durch hierarchische lineare Modelle (HLM). [Course of depression in different psychotherapies—an application of hierarchical linear models]. *Zeitschrift für Klinische Psychologie, 28*, 112–120.

Rowan, A. B., & Andrasik, F. (1996). Efficacy and cost-effectiveness of minimal therapist contact treatments of chronic headaches: A review. *Behavior Therapy, 27*, 207–234.

Rowe, M. K., & Craske, M. G. (1998). Effects of an expanding-spaced vs. massed exposure schedule on fear reduction and return of fear. *Behaviour Research and Therapy, 36*, 701–717.

Rudolf, G., & Manz, R. (1993). Zur prognostischen Bedeutung der therapeutischen Arbeitsbeziehung aus der Perspektive von Patienten und Therapeuten. [The prognostic relevance of a working alliance as seen by patients and therapists]. *Psychotherapie, Psychosomatik, Medizinische Psychologie, 43*, 193–199.

Russell, R. L., Bryant, F. B., & Estrada, A. U. (1996). Confirmatory P-technique analyses of therapist discourse: High- versus low-quality child therapy sessions. *Journal of Consulting and Clinical Psychology, 64*, 1366–1376.

Rychtarik, R. G., Connors, J. J., Whitney, R. B., McGillicuddy, N. B., Fitterling, J. M., & Wirtz, P. W. (2000). Treatment settings for persons with alcoholism: Evidence for matching clients to inpatient versus outpatient care. *Journal of Consulting and Clinical Psychology, 68*, 277–289.

Ryle, A., & Golynkina, K. (2000). Effectiveness of time-limited cognitive analytic therapy of borderline personality disorder: Factors associated with outcome. *British Journal of Medical Psychology, 73*, 197–210.

Safran, J. D., Murran, J. C., Samstag, L. W., & Stevens, C. L. (2002). Repair of alliance ruptures. In J. C. Norcross (Ed.), *Psychotherapy relationships that work: Therapist contributions and responsiveness to patient needs.* New York: Oxford University Press.

Safran, J. D., Segal, Z. V., Vallis, T. M., Shaw, B. F., & Samstag, L. W. (1993). Assessing patient suitability for short-term cognitive therapy with an interpersonal focus. *Cognitive Therapy and Research, 17,* 23–38.

Safren, S. A., Heimberg, R. G., & Juster, H. R. (1997). Clients' expectancies and their relationship to pretreatment symptomatology and outcome of cognitive-behavioral group treatment for social phobia. *Journal of Consulting and Clinical Psychology, 65,* 694–698.

Salzer, M. S., Bickman, L., & Lambert, E. W. (1999). Dose-effect relationship in children's psychotherapy services. *Journal of Consulting and Clinical Psychology, 67,* 228–238.

Sandell, R., Blomberg, J., Lazar, A., Carlsson, J., Broberg, J., & Schubert, J. (2000). Varieties of long-term outcome among patients in psychoanalysis and long-term psychotherapy: A review of findings in the Stockholm Outcome of Psychoanalysis and Psychotherapy Project (STOPP). *The International Journal of Psychoanalysis, 81(5),* 921–942.

Saunders, S. M. (1998). Clients' assessment of the affective environment of the psychotherapy session: Relationship to session quality and treatment effectiveness. *Journal of Clinical Psychology, 55,* 597–605.

Saunders, S. M. (2000). Examining the relationship between the therapeutic bond and the phases of treatment outcome. *Psychotherapy, 37,* 206–218.

Schauenburg, H., Sammet, I., Rabung, S., & Strack, M. (2002). Wie wirkt die Gruppenkohäsion in der stationären Therapie depressiver Patienten? [What effect does group cohesion have in inpatient therapy of depressive patients?] *Gruppenpsychotherapie und Gruppendynamik,* in press.

Schauenburg, H., Sammet, I., & Strack, M. (2002). Verlauf der Symptombelastung und Vorhersage des Behandlungserfolgs in der stationären Psychotherapie? [Process of symptomatology and prediction of outcome in in-patient psychotherapy?] *Zeitschrift für Psychosomatische Medizin und Psychotherapie,* in press.

Schmidt, N. B., & Woolaway-Bickel, K. (2000). The effects of treatment compliance on outcome in cognitive-behavioral therapy for panic disorder: Quality versus quantity. *Journal of Consulting and Clinical Psychology, 68,* 13–18.

Schmidtchen, S. (2001). Neue Forschungsergebnisse zu Prozessen und Ergebnissen der klientenzentrierten Kinderspieltherapie. [New research results on the process and outcome of client-centered play therapy for children.] In C. Boeck-Singelmann, T. Hensel & C. Monden-Engelhordt (Eds.), *Personzentrierte Psychotherapie mit Kindern und Jugendlichen* (pp. 153–194). [Person-centered psychotherapy with children and adolescents.] Göttingen: Hogrefe.

Schmidtchen, S., Acke, H., & Hennies, S. (1995). Heilende Kräfte im kindlichen Spiel! Prozeβ–analyse des Klientenverhaltens in der Kinderspieltherapie [Healing forces in children's play! Process analysis of client behavior in child play therapy]. *Gesellschaft für wissenschaftliche Gesprächspsychotherapie-Zeitschrift, 99,* 15–23.

Schmidtchen, S., & Hennies, S. (1996). Wider den Non-Direktivitätsmythos. Hin zu einer differentiellen Psychotherapie! Empirische Analyse des Therapeutenverhaltens in erfolgreichen Kinderspieltherapien [Against the myth of non-directiveness. Towards a differential psychotherapy! Empirical analysis of therapist behavior in successful child play therapy]. *Gesellschaft für wissenschaftliche Gesprächspsychotherapie-Zeitschrift, 104,* 14–24.

Schoenberger, N. E., Kirsch, I., Gearan, P., Montgomery, G., & Pastyrnak, S. L. (1997). Hypnotic enhancement of a cognitive behavioral treatment for public speaking anxiety. *Behavior Therapy, 28,* 127–140.

Scholing, A., & Emmelkamp, P.M.G. (1993). Exposure with and without cognitive therapy for generalized social phobia: Effects of individual and group treatment. *Behaviour Research and Therapy, 31,* 667–681.

Scholing, A., & Emmelkamp, P.M.G. (1996). Treatment of generalized social phobia: Results at long-term follow-up. *Behaviour Research and Therapy, 34,* 447–452.

Schulte, D., Hartung, J., & Wilke, F. (1997). Handlungskontrolle der Angstbewältigung. Was macht Reizkonfrontation so effektiv? [Action control in treatment of anxiety disorders. What makes exposure so effective?] *Zeitschrift für Klinische Psychologie, 26,* 118–128.

Schulte, D., & Künzel, R. (1995). Relevance and meaning of therapist's control. *Psychotherapy Research, 5,* 169–185.

Schulte-Bahrenberg, T., & Schulte, D. (1993). Change of psychotherapy goals as a process of resignation. *Psychotherapy Research, 3,* 153–165.

Seibel, C. A., & Dowd, E. T. (1999). Reactance and therapeutic noncompliance. *Cognitive Therapy and Research, 23,* 373–279.

Seikkula, J., Alakare, B., & Aaltonen, J. (2001). Open dialogue in psychosis II: A comparison of good and poor outcome cases. *Journal of Constructivist Psychology, 14,* 267–284.

Sennekamp, W., & Hautzinger, M. (1994). Haben "optimistische" Depressive eine bessere Heilungschance als "pessimistische"? Eine Untersuchung zum Zusammenhang von Erfolgserwartung und Behandlungsergebnissen bei unipolar depressiven Patienten [Have "optimistic" depressives a better outcome than "pessimistic" depressives? Correlation between expectation and treatment outcome in unipolar depressive patients]. *Verhaltenstherapie, 4,* 238–242.

Sexton, H. (1993). Exploring a psychotherapeutic change sequence: Relating process to intersessional and posttreatment outcome. *Journal of Consulting and Clinical Psychology, 61*, 128–136.

Sexton, H. (1996). Process, life events, and symptomatic change in brief eclectic psychotherapy. *Journal of Consulting and Clinical Psychology, 64*, 1358–1365.

Shadish, W. R., Montgomery, L. M., Wilson, P., Wilson, M. R., Bright, I., & Okwumabua, T. (1993). Effects of family and marital psychotherapies: A meta-analysis. *Journal of Consulting and Clinical Psychology, 61*, 992–1002.

Shapiro, D. A., Barkham, M., Rees, A., Hardy, G. E., Reynolds, S., & Startup, M. (1994). Effects of treatment duration and severity of depression on the effectiveness of cognitive-behavioral and psychodynamic-interpersonal psychotherapy. *Journal of Consulting and Clinical Psychology, 62*, 522–534.

Shapiro, D. A., Rees, A., Barkham, M., Hardy, G. E., Reynolds, S., & Startup, M. (1995). Effects of treatment duration and severity of depression on the maintenance of gains after cognitive-behavioral and psychodynamic-interpersonal psychotherapy. *Journal of Consulting and Clinical Psychology, 63*, 378–387.

Shaw, B. F., Elkin, I., Yamaguchi, J., Olmsted, M., Vallis, T. M., Dobson, K. S., Lowery, A., Sotsky, S. M., & Watkins, J. T. (1999). Therapist competence ratings in relation to clinical outcome in cognitive therapy of depression. *Journal of Consulting and Clinical Psychology, 67*, 837–846.

Smith, E., & Grawe, K. (2000). Die Rolle der Therapiebeziehung im therapeutischen Prozess. Gefahren und Chancen [The role of therapeutic bond in the therapeutic process]. *Verhaltenstherapie und Verhaltensmodifikation, 21*, 421–438.

Smith, E., Regli, D., & Grawe, K. (1999). Wenn Therapie wehtut. Wie können Therapeuten zu fruchtbaren Problemaktualisierungen beitragen? [When therapy hurts. How can therapists contribute to productive problem actualization?] *Verhaltenstherapie und psychosoziale Praxis, 31, 31*, 227–252.

Smyrnios, K. X., & Kirkby, R. J. (1993). Long-term comparison of brief versus unlimited psychodynamic treatments with children and their parents. *Journal of Consulting and Clinical Psychology, 61*, 1020–1027.

Snell, M. N., Mallinckrodt, B., Hill, R. D., & Lambert, M. J. (2001). Predicting counseling center clients' response to counseling: A 1-year follow-up. *Journal of Counseling Psychology, 48*, 463–473.

Spanos, N. P., Liddy, S. J., Scott, H., Garrard, J. S., Tirabasso, A., & Hayward, A. (1993). Hypnotic suggestion and placebo for the treatment of chronic headache in a university volunteer sample. *Cognitive Therapy and Research, 17*, 191–205.

Speer, D. C. (1994). Can treatment research inform decision makers? Nonexperimental method issues and examples among older outpatients. *Journal of Consulting and Clinical Psychology, 62*, 560–568.

Stangier, U., Heidenreich, T., & Peitz, M. (2001). *Effektivität kognitiv-behavioraler Einzel- vs. Gruppentherapie bei sozialer Phobie: Ergebnisse eines 6-Monats-Follow-up.* [Efficiency of cognitive-behavioral individual vs. group therapy with patients with social phobia: Results for the 6-month follow-up]. Paper on the 19th Symposium of the Special Interest Group for Clinical Psychology and Psychotherapy of the German Psychological Association. Bern, May 25, 2001.

Stanley, M. A., & Turner, S. M. (1995). Current status of pharmacological and behavioral treatment of obsessive-compulsive disorder. *Behavior Therapy, 26*, 163–186.

Startup, M., & Edmonds, J. (1994). Compliance with homework assignments in cognitive-behavioral psychotherapy for depression: Relation to outcome and methods of enhancement: *Cognitive Therapy and Research, 18*, 567–579.

Stephens, R. S., Roffman, R. A., & Curtin, L. (2000). Comparison of extended versus brief treatments for marijuana use. *Journal of Consulting and Clinical Psychology, 68*, 898–908.

Stiles, W. B. (2002). Assimilation of problematic experiences. In J. C. Norcross (Ed.), *Psychotherapy relationships that work: Therapist contributions and responsiveness to patient needs.* New York: Oxford University Press.

Stiles, W. B., Agnew-Davies, R., Hardy, G. E., Barkham, M., & Shapiro, D. A. (1998). Relations of the alliance with psychotherapy outcome: Findings in the second Sheffield Psychotherapy Project. *Journal of Consulting and Clinical Psychology, 66*, 791–802.

Stiles, W. B., Reynolds, S., Hardy, G. E., Rees, A., Barkham, M., & Shapiro, D. A. (1994). Evaluation and description of psychotherapy sessions by clients using the Session Evaluation Questionnaire and the Session Impact Scale. *Journal of Counseling Psychology, 41(2)*, 175–185.

Stiles, W. B., Shankland, M. C., Wright, J., & Field, S. D. (1997). Aptitude-treatment interactions based on clients' assimilation of their presenting problems. *Journal of Consulting and Clinical Psychology, 65*, 889–893.

Stiles, W. B., & Shapiro, D. A. (1994). Disabuse of the drug metaphor: Psychotherapy process-outcome correlations. *Journal of Consulting and Clinical Psychology, 62*, 942–948.

Strauss, B., Dauert, E., Gladewitz, J., Kaak, A., Kieselbach, S., Lammert, K., & Struck, D. (1995). Anwendung der Methode des Zentralen Beziehungskonfliktthemas (ZBKT) in einer Untersuchung zum Prozess und Ergebnis stationärer Langzeitgruppenpsychotherapie. [Application of the core conflictual relationship theme method (CCRT) in a study of the process and outcome of inpatient long-term group psychotherapy]. *Psychotherapie, Psychosomatik, Medizinische Psychologie, 45*, 342–350.

Strauss, B., Kröger, U., Hoffmann, K., & Burgmeier-Lohse, M. (1994). Prozessmerkmale des Indikations- und Abschlussgespräches in stationärer Psychotherapie: Indikatoren für den Behandlungserfolg? [Process features of the indication and termination sessions in in-patient psychotherapy: Indicators for therapy outcome?] *Zeitschrift für Klinische Psychologie, Psychopathologie und Psychotherapie, 42*, 157–175.

Svartberg, M., Seltzer, M. H., & Stiles, T. C. (1996). Self-concept improvement during and after short-term anxiety-provoking psychotherapy: A preliminary growth curve study. *Psychotherapy Research, 6*, 43–55.

Svartberg, M., Seltzer, M. E., & Stiles, T. C. (1998). The effects of common and specific factors in short-term anxiety-provoking psychotherapy. *Journal of Nervous and Mental Disease, 186*, 691–696.

Svartberg, M., & Stiles, T. C. (1994). Therapeutic alliance, therapist competence, and client change in short-term anxiety-provoking psychotherapy. *Psychotherapy Research, 4*, 20–33.

Svensson, B., & Hansson, L. (1999). Therapeutic alliance in cognitive therapy for schizophrenic and other long-term mentally ill patients: Development and relationship to outcome in an inpatient treatment programme. *Acta Psychiatrica Scandinavia, 99*, 281–287.

Tang, T. Z., & DeRubies, R. J. (1999a). Sudden gains and critical sessions in cognitive-behavioral therapy for depression. *Journal of Consulting and Clinical Psychology, 67(4)*, 894–904.

Tang, T. Z., & DeRubeis, R. J. (1999b). Reconsidering rapid early response in cognitive behavioral therapy for depression. *Clinical Psychology: Science and Practice, 6*, 283–288.

Tarrier, N., & Humphreys, L. (2000). Subjective improvement in PTSD patients with treatment by imaginal exposure or cognitive therapy: Session by session changes. *British Journal of Clinical Psychology, 39*, 27–34.

Tarrier, N., Pilgrim, H., Sommerfield, C., Faragher, B., Reynolds, M., Graham, E., & Barrowclough, C. (1999). A randomized trial of cognitive therapy and imaginal exposure in the treatment of chronic posttraumatic stress disorder. *Journal of Consulting and Clinical Psychology, 67*, 13–18.

Tarrier, N., Sommerfield, C., Pilgrim, H., & Faragher, B. (2000). Factors associated with outcome in cognitive-behavioral treatment of post-traumatic stress disorder. *Behaviour Research and Therapy, 38*, 191–202.

Tasca, G. A., Balfour, L., Bissada, H., Busby, K., Conrad, G., Cameron, P., Colletta, S., Potvin-Kent, M., & Turpin, P. (1999). Treatment completion and outcome in a partial hospitalization program: Interactions among patient variables. *Psychotherapy Research, 9*, 232–247.

Tracey, T.J.G., Sherry, P., & Albright, J. M. (1999). The interpersonal process of cognitive-behavioral therapy: An examination of complementarity over the course of treatment. *Journal of Counseling Psychology, 46*, 80–91.

Treasure, J. L., Katzman, M., Schmidt, U., Troop, N., Todd, G., & de Silva, P. (1999). Engagement and outcome in the treatment of bulimia nervosa: First phase of a sequential design comparing motivation enhancement therapy and cognitive behavioural therapy. *Behaviour Research and Therapy, 37*, 405–418.

Treasure, J., Schmidt, U., Troop, N., Tiller, J., Todd, G., & Turnbull, S. (1996). Sequential treatment for bulimia nervosa incorporating a self-care manual. *British Journal of Psychiatry, 168*, 94–98.

Troop, N., Schmidt, U., Tiller, J., Todd, G., Keilen, M., & Treasure, J. (1996). Compliance with a self-care manual for bulimia nervosa: Predictors and outcome. *British Journal of Clinical Psychology, 35*, 435–438.

Tryon, G. S., & Winograd, G. (2002). Goal consensus and collaboration. In J. C. Norcross (Ed.), *Psychotherapy relationships that work: Therapist contributions and responsiveness to patient needs.* New York: Oxford University Press.

Tschacher, W., Baur, N., & Grawe, K. (2000). Temporal interaction of process variables in psychotherapy. *Psychotherapy Research, 10*, 296–308.

Tschuschke, V., & Dies, R. (1994). Intensive analysis of therapeutic factors and outcome in long-term inpatient groups. *International Journal of Group Psychotherapy, 44*, 185–208.

Tschuschke, V., & Dies, R. R. (1997). The contribution of feedback to outcome in long-term group psychotherapy. *Group, 21*, 3–15.

Turner, P. R., Valtierra, M., Talken, T. R., Miller, V. I., & DeAnda, J. R. (1996). Effect of session length on treatment outcome for college students in brief therapy. *Journal of Counseling Psychology, 43*, 228–232.

Turner, S. M., Beidel, D. C., Cooley, M. R., Woody, S. R., & Messer, S. C. (1994). A multicomponent behavioural treatment for social phobia: Social effectiveness training. *Behaviour Research and Therapy, 32*, 381–190.

Vogel, G., & Schulte, D. (1997). Methoden- und verlaufsorientierte Strategien von Psychotherapeuten. [Method-oriented strategies and process-oriented strategies of psychotherapists.] *Zeitschrift für Klinische Psychologie, 26*, 38–49.

Von Rad, M., Senf, W., & Bräutigam, W. (1998). Psychotherapie und Psychoanalyse in der Krankenversorgung: Ergebnisse des Heidelberger Katamnese-Projektes. [Final results of the Heidelberg long-term psychotherapy follow-up project]. *Psychotherapie, Psychosomatik, Medizinische Psychologie, 48*, 88–100.

Warner, L. K., Herron, W. G., Javier, R. A., Patalano, F., Sisenwein, F., & Primavera, L. H. (2001). A comparison of dose-response curves in cognitive-behavioral and psychodynamic psychotherapies. *Journal of Clinical Psychology, 57*, 63–73.

Watson, J. C., & Greenberg, L. S. (1996). Pathways to change in the psychotherapy of depression: Relating process to session change and outcome. *Psychotherapy, 33*, 262–274.

Weissman, M. M. (1994). Psychotherapy in the maintenance treatment of depression. *British Journal of Psychiatry, 165* (supplement 26), 42–50.

Weissmark, M. S., & Giacomo, D. A. (1994). A therapeutic index: Measuring therapeutic actions in psychotherapy. *Journal of Consulting and Clinical Psychology, 62*, 315–323.

Westerman, M. A. (1998). Curvilinear trajectory in patient coordination over the course of short-term psychotherapy. *Psychotherapy, 35(2)*, 206–219.

Westerman, M. A., Foote, J. P., & Winston, A. (1995). Change in coordination across phases of psychotherapy and outcome: Two mechanisms for the role played by patients contribution to the alliance. *Journal of Consulting and Clinical Psychology, 63*, 672–675.

Willutzki, U., Hernandez-Bark, G., Davis, J., & Orlinsky, D. (1997). Client outcome as a function of therapists' difficulties and coping strategies in the course of psychotherapy: Initial results. Paper presented at the 28th Annual Meeting of the Society of Psychotherapy Research. Geilo (Norway), June 25–29, 1997.

Wilson, G. T., Loeb, K. L., Walsh, B. T., Labouvie, E., Petkova, E., Liu, X., & Waternaux, C. (1999). Psychological versus pharmacological treatments of bulimia nervosa: Predictors and processes of change. *Journal of Consulting and Clinical Psychology, 67*, 451–459.

Wilson, S. B., Mason, T. W., & Ewing, M.J.M. (1997). Evaluating the impact of receiving university-based counseling services on student retention. *Journal of Counseling Psychology, 44*, 316–320.

Winston, B., Samstag, L. W., Winston, A., & Muran, J. C. (1994). Patient defense/therapist intervention. *Psychotherapy, 31*, 478–490.

Winter, B., Nieschalk, M., & Stoll, W. (1996). Die Auswirkungen der Entspannungstherapie als Gruppen- und Einzelbehandlung bei chronischem Tinnitus. [The effects of relaxation therapy as individual and group treatment in management of chronic tinnitus]. *Psychotherapie, Psychosomatik, Medizinische Psychologie, 46*, 147–152.

Wlazlo, Z., Schroeder-Hartwig, K., Münchau, N., Kaiser, G., & Hand, I. (1992). Exposition in-vivo bei sozialen Ängsten und Defiziten [Exposure in vivo for social phobia and social skills deficits]. *Verhaltenstherapie, 2*, 23–39.

Wolfson, L., Miller, M., Houck, P., Ehrenpreis, L., Stack, J. A., Frank, E., Cornes, C., Mazumdar, S., Kupfer, D. J., & Reynolds III, C. F. (1997). Foci of interpersonal psychotherapy (IPT) in depressed elders: Clinical and outcome correlates in a combined IPT/nortriptyline protocol. *Psychotherapy Research, 7*, 45–55.

Woody, S. R., Chambless, D. L., & Glass, C. R. (1997). Self-focused attention in the treatment of social phobia. *Behaviour Research and Therapy, 35*, 117–129.

Znoj, H. J., Grawe, K., & Jeger, P. (2000). Die differentielle Bedeutung des Handlungskontrollmodus für klärungs- und bewältigungsorientierte Therapien [Differential meaning of the role of action control in insight and action-oriented therapy]. *Zeitschrift für Klinische Psychologie und Psychotherapie, 29*, 53–59.

Section 3

Major Approaches

CHAPTER 9

BEHAVIOR THERAPY WITH ADULTS

PAUL M. G. EMMELKAMP
University of Amsterdam

This chapter provides an overview of the current status of behavior therapy with adult disorders. Emphasis throughout is on the application of behavioral procedures on clinical patients. Since separate chapters in this volume are devoted to health psychology, behavior therapy with children, and (behavioral) marital therapy for marital distress, these topics will not be dealt with in this chapter. Cognitive interventions are covered only insofar as they are contrasted with behavioral procedures or form an integral part of cognitive behavioral procedures. For a more detailed discussion of cognitive therapy, the reader is referred to Chapter 10 by Hollon and Beck in this volume. As an aside, to separate procedures that are purely behavioral from procedures that are purely cognitive is rather artificial. Most cognitive procedures have clear behavioral techniques in them, and though less obvious, most behavioral procedures also contain cognitive elements.

The research on behavior therapy with adults has proliferated to such an extent that it is impossible to provide a comprehensive review of the whole area in one chapter. In the last decade, significant progress has been made in a number of areas, although the development of effective treatments has advanced in an uneven fashion. Therefore, the scope of this chapter is limited to those disorders for which the behavioral approach has been most influential. This chapter reviews the state-of-the-art of current behavioral procedures for anxiety disorders, depression, substance abuse, sexual dysfunctions, personality disorders, and schizoprenia. Since controlled studies of the behavioral treatment of paraphilias has hardly been reported in the last decade, this subject is not reviewed. It is hoped that the chapter provides a fair evaluation of the progress that has been achieved in behavior therapy, particularly in the last decade.

ANXIETY DISORDERS

In this section, the principles of behavioral treatment strategies for simple phobia, panic disorder with agoraphobia, social phobia, obsessive-compulsive disorder, generalized anxiety disorder, and post-traumatic stress disorder will be presented, followed by a review of empirical findings on their effectiveness.

Exposure therapy consists of exposing patients to situations they fear. Exposure can be carried out in two ways: (1) in imagination, in which patients must imagine themselves to be in a fearful situation or (2) in vivo, in which patients are actually exposed to this situation. The treatment is based on the notion that anxiety subsides through a process of habituation after a person has been exposed to a fearful situation for a prolonged period of time, without trying to escape. Considerable evidence exists, both on subjective and physiological measures, that this is indeed the case (Craske, 1999). Exposure in vivo is usually more effective than exposure in imagination (for a review, see Emmelkamp, 1994). Other important variables in exposure treatments are the degree of anxiety and the duration of exposure trials. Exposure tasks can be ordered hierarchically from low anxiety to high anxiety (gradual exposure), or patients can be confronted with the most difficult situation from the start (flooding). Exposure can be either self-controlled (i.e., patients decide for themselves when to enter a more difficult situation) or controlled by the therapist. The most successful programs are those carried out in vivo, during a long uninterrupted period of time (prolonged), in which escape and avoidance of the situation are prevented (Emmelkamp, 1994).

If anxious patients escape the situation that they fear, anxiety usually will subside. This escape behavior, however, will reinforce the anxiety and hence lead to further avoidance and escape behavior in the future. Therefore, in exposure programs it is often necessary to deal with this escape behavior by response prevention, which means that the patients are no longer allowed to perform escape behavior. Response prevention is an essential part of treatment with obsessive-compulsive disorder, but also plays a part in the treatment of social phobia and agoraphobia.

Massed exposure sessions are held more frequently than *spaced exposure* sessions. In agoraphobia, specific phobias, and obsessive-compulsive disorder, massed exposure was generally more or as effective as spaced exposure in reducing avoidance behavior and self-reported anxiety. As for the expanding-spaced exposure (ESE) sessions, in which the intertrial interval doubles between sessions, research showed that the ESE sessions led to no clear return of fear, whereas a massed condition (four exposure trials within one day) did lead to return of fear one month after the end of treatment (van Hout & Emmelkamp, 2002).

The Process of Exposure

Exposure is usually explained in terms of habituation. Habituation refers to a decline in fear responses, particularly the physiological responses, over repeated exposures to fear-provoking stimuli. The classical habituation theory predicts that habituation would not occur if (baseline) arousal was high. Then, arousal would further increase and lead to *sensitization* (i.e., increase in fear responses after repeated exposures to fear-provoking stimuli). However, the literature revealed that a reduction instead of a further increase in psychophysiological and subjective anxiety could be expected, for instance, during exposure to high fear-provoking stimuli (e.g., flooding therapy). Recent habituation theories have been extended to accommodate these findings. These dual-process theories describe complex interactions between habituation and sensitization, in which habituation can eventually occur after exposure to high fear-provoking stimuli (van Hout & Emmelkamp, 2002).

Several studies have provided supportive evidence for the role of habituation in exposure therapy, self-reported fear, and physiological arousal showing a declining trend across exposures, consistent with habituation (e.g., van Hout, Emmelkamp, & Scholing, 1994).

Cognitive Change Models

The success of exposure in vivo has also been explained by the acquisition of fresh, disconfirmatory evidence, which weakens the catastrophic cognitions. From this perspective, exposure is viewed as a critical intervention through which catastrophic cognitions may be tested. This is in line with cognitive behavioral therapy (CBT) based on the perceived danger theory according to Beck and colleagues. Within this model, exposure (i.e., behavioral experiments) is generally regarded as a necessity for testing the validity of dysfunctional thoughts next to other strategies such as Socratic questioning of probabilities.

Several process studies have been performed looking into the cognitive processes of exposure in vivo. In these process studies, thoughts are generally collected by means of in vivo assessment (e.g., thoughts are reported into a tape recorder) during exposure, or by using thought-listings (i.e., free report of all thoughts on paper) directly following exposure. In general, inconsistent findings are reported in these process studies designed to measure the relationship between cognitive change and improvement during in vivo exposure in phobic patients (van Hout & Emmelkamp, 2002).

More consistent results were found in a process study using a short self-report questionnaire to measure the frequency of thoughts during exposure in vivo. Results showed that cognitive change (decrease in frequency of negative self-statements) was achieved by exposure to in vivo therapy. However, cognitive change per se was not related to a positive treatment outcome. The results suggested that the magnitude of the frequency ratings of negative self-statements at the start, during, and at the end of exposure therapy was the most critical factor. The most improved patients reported overall less negative thoughts (e.g., van Hout, Emmelkamp, & Scholing, 1994).

Clinicians hold that cognitive avoidance during exposure is detrimental to its effects. Distraction is one of the safety measures used by phobic patients with a disorder. As predicted by the emotional processing theory of Foa and Kozak (1986), a number of studies have shown that distraction during exposure inhibits habituation, but results are inconclusive (Craske, 1999; Kamphuis & Telch, 2000; Mohlman & Zinbarg, 2000; Penfold & Page, 1999). The results of these studies are difficult to interpret because of the different populations studied and distracters used.

Specific Phobia

With specific phobia, the treatment of choice is usually exposure in vivo (Craske, 1999; Emmelkamp, 1994). Craske (1999) summarized 10 controlled studies that reported clinically significant change. In some of these studies, applied relaxation or modeling was added to exposure. After a mean of five hours of therapy, over 75% of the patients were rated as clinically improved. One three-hour session of prolonged exposure in vivo was as effective as five one-hour sessions (Öst, Alm, Brandberg, & Breitholz, 2001).

Two recent analogue studies suggest that adding cognitive threat appraisal to exposure may enhance emotional processing of fear cues (Kamphuis & Telch, 2000; Mohlman & Zinbarg, 2000). Nevertheless, in controlled outcome studies, there is no consistent evidence that cognitive techniques potentiate the effects derived from exposure (Emmelkamp & Felten, 1985; Getka & Glass, 1992; Ladouceur, 1983; Marshall, 1985). Two studies compared exposure in vivo and cognitive therapy with claustrophobic subjects (Booth & Rachman, 1992; Öst et al., 2001). Exposure in vivo and cognitive therapy were found to be equally effective.

Although the use of relaxation during exposure is not recommended, occasionally reports appear suggesting that relaxation may have beneficial effects (e.g., McGlynn, Moore, Lawyer, & Karg, 1999). Taken together, these studies suggest that pre-exposure relaxation training can reduce arousal and fear during in vivo exposure. But what is the clinical relevance of this finding? For example, subjects in the McGlynn et al. (1999) study received life relaxation training for *six* consecutive days before they underwent one session of exposure in vivo consisting of six four-minute exposure trials. Although the subjects who had received relaxation training experienced (slightly less) fear during exposure (less than a 1-point difference on a 0–10 Subjective Units of Discomfort Scale), this did not result in significantly better results on the behavioral avoidance test. Clinically, it might be therapeutically wise to spend the time that would have been devoted to relaxation to prolonged exposure in vivo instead.

Blood Phobia

Although prolonged exposure in vivo seems to be the treatment of choice for most specific phobias, in blood phobia additional measures may be required, given the unusual pattern of physiological responses. Instead of an increase in heart rate and respiration as typically seen in phobics, blood phobics show bradycardia and a decrease in blood pressure, which may result in fainting. In such cases, adding applied tension to exposure in vivo may be therapeutically wise. With applied tension, patients are taught to tense their muscles when exposed to a series of slides of wound injuries and blood. In later sessions, patients have to donate blood and observe open-heart or lung surgery. Patients learn to recognize the earliest sign of a drop in blood pressure and to apply the tension technique to reverse it. Öst, Fellenius, and Sterner (1991) found that exposure plus applied tension was more effective than exposure to blood stimuli alone.

Virtual Reality Exposure

There is now some evidence that exposure can be conducted using virtual reality technology. Virtual reality (VR) integrates real-time computer graphics, body tracking devices, visual displays, and other sensory inputs to immerse individuals in a computer-generated virtual environment. VR exposure has several advantages over exposure in vivo. The treatment can be conducted in the therapist's office; the therapist and patient do not have to go outside to do the exposure exercises in real phobic situations. Hence, treatment may be more cost-effective than therapist-assisted exposure in vivo. Furthermore, VR treatment can also be applied on patients who are too anxious to undergo real-life exposure in vivo.

A few case studies have been reported demonstrating the effectiveness of exposure provided by virtual reality. In a study on college students with fear of heights, seven weekly sessions of virtual reality exposure, conducted with an expensive laboratorium computer, was found to be more effective than a no-treatment control (Rothbaum, Hodges et al., 1995). Emmelkamp, Bruynzeel, Drost, and van der Mast (2001) evaluated the effectiveness of two sessions of low-budget VR versus two sessions of exposure in vivo in a within-group design in individuals suffering from acrophobia. VR exposure was found to be at least as effective as exposure in vivo on anxiety and avoidance. However, VR exposure as first treatment was already so effective that a ceiling effect occurred, thus diminishing the potential effects of exposure in vivo. The aims of a study by Emmelkamp, Krijn et al. (2002) was to compare the effectiveness of exposure in vivo versus VR exposure in a between-group design with acrophobic patients. In order to enhance the comparability of exposure environments, the locations used in the exposure in vivo program were exactly reproduced in virtual worlds that were used in VR exposure. In previous studies of VR exposure, the VR worlds were not identical to the situations used in real-life exposure. VR exposure was found to be as effective as exposure in vivo on anxiety and avoidance and on attitudes toward heights. VR exposure showed the same improvement on the Behavioral Avoidance Test (BAT) as exposure in vivo, thus demonstrating that results of VR exposure were not restricted to self-report, but were also reflected in a reduction of actual avoidance behavior. Moreover, the six-month followup data revealed that patients were able to maintain their gains. In another controlled study, Rothbaum, Hodges et al. (2000) found a combination of anxiety management and VR exposure to be as effective as a combination of anxiety management and exposure in vivo in subjects with fear of flying. It should be noted, however, that the situations used in the VR condition were rather different from the actual exposure used in the in vivo condition. Taken together, the results of these studies show considerable evidence that VR exposure is an effective treatment for patients with acrophobia.

Pharmacotherapy

A few studies in the 1970s investigated whether benzodiazepines combined with exposure in vivo would enhance the effectiveness of exposure in vivo alone in patients with specific phobia, but results were inconclusive (Craske, 1999). More recently, the high-potency benzodiazepine alprazolam was found to increase rather than decrease anxiety in flight phobics. A combination of exposure in vivo plus alprazolam was less effective than treatment by exposure alone (Wilhelm & Roth, 1997). Given the high success rate of exposure in vivo, a combination with pharmacotherapy is not recommended.

Panic Disorder and Agoraphobia

Panic disorder is characterized by recurrent panic attacks, which are discrete periods of intense fear and discomfort that often occur unexpectedly. Panic attacks are accompanied by a number of symptoms, such as shortness of breath, dizziness, palpitations, trembling, sweating, choking, abdominal distress, depersonalization or derealization, fear of dying, or fear of going crazy. Panic disorder often leads to extensive avoidance behavior, since these patients fear being in places or situations from which it is difficult to escape, or in which there is no help at hand in case of a panic attack.

Exposure in vivo is well documented in numerous randomized controlled clinical trials (see reviews and meta-analyses by Chambless & Gillis, 1993; Clum, Clum, & Surls, 1993; Cox, Swinson, Morrison, & Lee, 1993; Emmelkamp, 1994; Mattick, Andrews, Hadzi-Pavlovic, & Christensen, 1990; van Balkom, Bakker et al., 1997; and van Balkom, Nauta, & Bakker, 1995). The results of these reviews and meta-analyses are usually consistent, indicating that exposure in vivo has a substantial effect size for phobic symptoms; results with respect to panic attacks are inconclusive.

Although prolonged exposure has been found to be superior to short exposure, this does not mean that having the opportunity to escape during exposure in vivo has detrimental effects as once thought (Craske, 1999). A treatment procedure whereby patients are allowed to escape the situation but have to reenter it again and again is as effective as prolonged exposure in vivo (Emmelkamp, 1982). This form of treatment can be conducted as a self-help program (Emmelkamp, 1982) and can be done through a self-help book or a computer (Gosh & Marks, 1987). Ferguss, Cox, and Wickwire (1995) investigated the value of exposure therapy delivered by phone. Subjects were agoraphobics living in rural areas in Ontario. Eight weekly telephone sessions of approximately an hour were held. The therapist never saw the patients. Nevertheless, results revealed that treatment so delivered was effective and more so than a waiting list control group. Results were maintained at a six-month followup.

Although exposure therapies can be conducted as self-help programs either with instructions by a live therapist, by a computer, or by phone, there is some evidence that therapist guidance may lead to superior results. Williams and Zane (1989) compared exposure in which the therapist was quite active in guiding agoraphobics in how to perform therapeutic tasks with an exposure condition with less therapist involvement. Guided mastery treatment was found to be superior. However, in a more recent study, guided mastery was not found to be more effective than exposure with less therapist involvement (Zane & Williams, 1993).

Exposure in vivo leads not only to a reduction of anxiety and avoidance, but also to a reduction of panic attacks (e.g. Lelliott, Marks,

Monteiro, Tsakiris, & Noshirvani, 1987; Michelson, Mavissakalian, & Marchione, 1985; Telch Agras, Tayloor, Roth, & Gallen, 1985) and a reduction of negative self-statements (van Hout, Emmelkamp, & Scholing, 1994; van den Hout & Emmelkamp, 2001). The largest reduction in negative self-statements within an exposure session was found when the patient correctly predicted the anxiety he or she would experience during that session (van Hout & Emmelkamp, 1994).

The results of exposure therapy with agoraphobics are long-lasting. Followup reports ranging from four to nine years after treatment have been published. Generally, improvements brought about by the treatment were maintained (Bakker, van Balkom, Spinhoven, Blaauw, & van Dyck, 1998; Gould, Otto, & Pollack, 1995). For example, in 10 studies reviewed by O'Sullivan and Marks (1990), 76% of the patients were rated as improved or much improved at followup. In the longest followup period to date, of 93 patients treated with exposure in vivo, 68% were still in remission at seven-year followup (Fava, Zielezny, Savron, & Grandi, 1995).

Exposure In Vivo versus Cognitive Therapy

A number of studies with agoraphobics have shown that exposure in vivo is superior to cognitive therapy consisting of insight into irrational beliefs (RET) and training of incompatible positive self-statements (SIT) (Emmelkamp et al., 1978; Emmelkamp et al., 1986; Emmelkamp & Mersch, 1982). Current cognitive behavioral approaches focus more directly on the panic attacks than is the case in RET and self-instructional training. A number of cognitively oriented researchers have stressed psychological factors in accounting for panic attacks (Clark, 1986; Ehlers & Margraf, 1989). In these models, it is assumed that patients misinterpret bodily sensations as a sign of a serious physical danger (e.g., a heart attack). The common element is that patients are likely to mislabel such bodily sensations and attribute them to a threatening disease and as a result may panic. Central to the cognitive conceptualization of panic is the interpretation of bodily sensations as dangerous. A positive feedback loop between physiological arousal and anxiety is postulated that leads to an ascending "spiral" ending in the full-blown panic attack.

Those formulations of panic have led to a renewed interest in the treatment of panic by cognitive and behavioral methods. The cognitive therapy of Clark and colleagues consists of explanation and discussion of the way hyperventilation induces panic, breathing exercises, interoceptive exposure, and relabeling of bodily symptoms. This package produced a substantial and rapid reduction in panic attack frequency in two studies with a small number of patients (Clark, Salkovskis, & Chalkley, 1985; Salkovskis, James, & Clark, 1986). However, both studies lacked a formal control group. Clark, Salkovskis et al. (1994) compared the cognitive therapy for panic with applied relaxation and drug treatment (imipramine). All three treatments were found to be effective in reducing panic, anxiety, and avoidance. The cognitive therapy was found to be superior to the other two treatments on 12 out of 17 measures. Patients treated with imipramine relapsed significantly more than patients treated with cognitive therapy. At a 15-month followup, 80% of cognitive therapy patients, 47% of applied relaxation patients, and 50% of imipramine patients were panic free. Beck, Stanley, Baldwin, Deagle, and Averill (1994) found cognitive therapy more effective than relaxation and a minimal contact control condition in panic patients with mild or moderate agoraphobia. However, a substantial number of patients (68%) who had received relaxation therapy appeared to be treatment responders at the post-test, somewhat less than the 82% responders in the cognitive therapy condition.

Van den Hout, van Oppen et al. (1994) evaluated the effects of cognitive therapy and exposure in vivo in patients with panic disorder and agoraphobia. Half of the patients received four sessions of cognitive therapy, followed by eight sessions of cognitive therapy plus exposure. In the other condition, the first four sessions consisted of supportive therapy in order to control for therapist attention. As expected, cognitive therapy led to a reduction of panic attacks, whereas panic was not affected by supportive therapy. However, on all other measures, that is, the Fear Questionnaire, Behavioral Avoidance Test, Beck Depression Inventory, and measures of fear of fear and state and trait anxiety, improvement commenced *after* exposure in vivo began. Thus, although cognitive therapy led to a reduction of panic attacks, it did not automatically lead to an abandonment of the agoraphobic avoidance behavior. Also, Rijken, Kraaimaat, de Ruiter, and Garssen (1992), Williams and Falbo (1996), and Burke, Drummond, and Johnston (1997) did not find a combination therapy more effective than exposure alone in agoraphobic patients.

Williams and Falbo (1996) found exposure in vivo superior to cognitive therapy on several measures of phobia and panic-related cognitions. In contrast, two studies found cognitive therapy as effective as exposure in vivo (Bouchard et al., 1996; Hoffart, 1998). However, in both studies exposure in vivo was an essential component of cognitive therapy, which makes the results difficult to interpret. In the Hoffart study, patients in cognitive therapy had to complete a behavioral task each day, which they had to perform alone. Also, in the Bouchard et al. study, behavioral experiments (exposure in vivo) formed an essential element of the cognitive therapy.

There is now considerable evidence that the degree of agoraphobic disability has a significant bearing on panic treatment effectiveness. In the study of Williams and Falbo (1996), 94% of low-agoraphobia subjects were free of panic after treatment, while only 52% of the high-agoraphobia subjects became panic free. As noted by the authors, the findings suggest that when panic treatment research excludes people with severe agoraphobic avoidance, as it has routinely done, an overtly positive estimate of panic treatment effectiveness can result.

Taken together, there is convincing evidence that cognitive therapy dealing with misinterpretations of bodily sensations is highly effective in reducing panic attacks. However, this does not necessarily lead to a reduction of the avoidance behavior in severe agoraphobic patients. A combination of cognitive therapy and exposure in vivo is not more effective than exposure in vivo alone. Furthermore, the role that cognitions play in cognitive therapy remains unclear (Oei, Llamas, & Devilly, 1999). Given this state of affairs, cognitive therapy (without exposure in vivo) cannot be recommended for panic patients with severe agoraphobia.

Exposure to Interoceptive Stimuli

Griez and van den Hout (1986) hypothesized that repeated exposure to an interoceptive cue by means of CO_2 inhalation would lead to anxiety reduction in panic patients. In two studies (Griez & van den Hout, 1986; van den Hout, Molen, Griez, Lousberg, & Nansen, 1987), CO_2-induced subjective anxiety in patients was found to decrease as the number of CO_2-induced exposures to interoceptive anxiety symptoms increased.

Barlow, Craske, Cerny, & Klosko (1989) evaluated the effects of a comprehensive package consisting of exposure to interoceptive stimuli, imaginal exposure, breathing retraining, and cognitive restructuring. This package was found to be more effective than applied relaxation and no-treatment. In a second study from the same group (Klosko, Barlow, Toussinari, & Cerny, 1990), this package was found to be more effective than alprazolam and placebo. However, in a recent large multicenter trial (Barlow, Gorman, Shear, & Woods, 2000), this package was found to be as effective as imipramine, and both active treatments were more effective than placebo. A combined treatment of CBT and imipramine was not significantly superior to CBT plus placebo. Six months after treatment discontinuation in the intent to treat analysis the response rates were 39% for CBT alone, 19.7% for imipramine alone, 13% for placebo, and 26.3% for CBT combined with imipramine.

A number of studies investigated the effects of various components of a cognitive behavioral treatment package. Craske, Rowe, Lewin, and Noriega-Dimitri (1997) compared two treatments: (1) CIE, which consisted of cognitive restructuring, interoceptive exposure, and in vivo exposure to agoraphobic situations, and (2) CBE, which consisted of cognitive restructuring, breathing retraining, and in vivo exposure to agoraphobic situations. Results indicated that interoceptive exposure was more effective than breathing retraining. Similarly, Schmidt et al. (2000) compared CBT with and without breathing retraining. Results revealed that breathing retraining added little to other components of the CBT intervention.

Applied Relaxation

In *applied relaxation* (Öst, 1988) patients learn to recognize the first signs of anxiety and subsequently learn to cope with anxiety instead of being overwhelmed by it. In the first phase of treatment, patients monitor the first signs of anxiety and situations in which anxiety occurs as homework assignments. In the second stage, patients are trained in progressive relaxation. In the third stage, patients learn to relax on the command "RELAX" (cue-controlled relaxation). The fourth phase of treatment aims at generalizing relaxation to daily life situations, for example, when the patient is in a meeting, driving, or writing. In the last sessions, patients are exposed to fear-provoking situations and have to apply their relaxation skills. In panic disorder, the purpose of applied relaxation is to teach the patient to observe the very first signs of a panic attack (small bodily sensation) and to apply the relaxation technique to cope with these symptoms before they have developed into a full-blown panic attack. When patients have learned to relax, they have to apply this in vivo in panic situations.

Applied relaxation has also been evaluated with panic patients. In a study by Öst (1988), applied relaxation proved to be superior to progressive relaxation and led to clinically meaningful changes not only in reducing panic attacks but also on measures of general anxiety and depression. However, applied relaxation was found to be less effective than cognitive therapy (Clark et al., 1994) and a package consisting of exposure to introceptive stimuli, imaginal exposure, and cognitive restructuring (Barlow et al., 1989).

Öst, Westling, and Hellstrom (1993) investigated the relative effectiveness of exposure in vivo, cognitive therapy, and applied relaxation in patients with panic disorder and agoraphobia. All patients received instructions for exposure as homework assignments. Results showed that all three treatments were about equally effective. On some measures there was a slight superiority of applied relaxation. Results were maintained up to one-year followup. It is unclear what the additional effects of the various treatments are, given the well-documented effectiveness of self-exposure in vivo alone.

Öst and Westling (1995) investigated the relative effectiveness of cognitive therapy with applied relaxation in patients with panic disorder with mild or no agoraphobic avoidance. Both treatments were found to be equally effective. The percentages of panic-free patients for cognitive therapy and applied relaxation, respectively, were 74% and 65% after 12 sessions and 89% and 82% at one-year followup. Results generalized to symptoms of generalized anxiety and depression. Interestingly, both cognitive therapy and applied relaxation resulted in improvements on a measure of cognitive misinterpretation.

Arntz and van den Hout (1996) also compared cognitive therapy and applied relaxation in patients with panic disorder with no or mild agoraphobic avoidance. In contrast to the results of Öst and Westling (1995), results revealed that cognitive therapy was more effective than applied relaxation in reducing the number of panic attacks. At the end of treatment, 77.8% of patients in the cognitive therapy condition were panic free, in contrast to 50% of patients in the applied relaxation condition. Both treatments were clearly more effective than a wait list control group. Here, only 27.7% were panic free.

CBT: Effects on Comorbid Conditions

Many panic disorder-patients have one or more additional anxiety disorders or a mood disorder (e.g., Brown, Antony, & Barlow, 1995). There is some evidence that successful treatment of the panic disorder also results in improvement in comorbid disorders (Brown et al., 1995; Tsao, Lewin, & Craske, 1998). However, although Brown et al. (1995) found a significant decrease in the rate of comorbidity immediately after treatment, the rates of comorbidity at two-year followup returned to pretreatment levels, with the exception of generalized anxiety disorder (GAD). Further research is needed to clarify the degree to which treatment responses are symptom specific.

CBT: The Role of the Therapist

There is some evidece that cognitive behavior therapy can be applied with reduced therapist contact (Cote, Gauthier, Laberge, & Cormier, 1994) or can be conducted by competent nurse-therapists (Kingdon, Tyrer, Seivewright, Ferguson, & Murphy, 1996). Results with respect to the efficacy of bibliotherapy are inconclusive (e.g., Febbraro, Clum, Roodman & Wright, 1999; Gould & Clum, 1995). Although the results of these studies are encouraging, more controlled studies are needed before recommendations for clinical practice can be made.

Spouse-Aided Therapy

In anxiety disorders, two different formats of spouse-aided therapy can be distinguished. In *partner-assisted exposure*, the partner accompanies the patient to each treatment session. The couple receives a treatment rationale in which the focus is on exposing the patient to phobic situations. The partner can assist in making a hierarchy consisting of gradually more difficult exposure tasks. At each session, the patients are given a number of exposure homework assignments. The role of the partner is to stimulate the patient to do these exercises, to help in confronting the phobic situations, to accompany the patient if necessary, and to reinforce the patient in mastering these exposure exercises successfully. Thus, treatment focuses on the phobia. Relationship problems, if any, are not discussed.

Other spouse-aided approaches in anxiety disorders have focused on interpersonal difficulties thought to maintain agoraphobic symptoms. These approaches include *communication training* and *partner-assisted problem solving* directed either at phobia-related conflicts or at general life stresses and problems.

In contrast to expectations derived from general systems theory, there is no evidence that exposure therapy of the patient with agoraphobia has adverse effects on the relationship or the partners' symptoms. The controlled studies in this area concur that the relationship remains stable or improves slightly, with no exacerbation of symptoms in the partner of the patient. Thus, the system-theoretic conceptualization of anxiety disorders being a symptom of more serious marital problems is not supported by the empirical evidence (Emmelkamp & Gerlsma, 1994).

Studies investigating the effects of spouse-aided therapy in individuals with agoraphobia led to conflicting results. Most studies have evaluated the effects of partner-assisted exposure. In two studies (Cobb, Mathews, Childs-Clarke, & Blowers, 1984; Emmelkamp et al., 1992) spouse-aided exposure therapy was found to be no more effective than treatment of the patient alone. In contrast, one study (Cerny, Barlow, Craske, & Himadi, 1987) found superiority for the spouse-aided exposure condition, when compared to a non-spouse group on measures of agoraphobia. However, this study has a number of methodological problems which make the results difficult to interpret. Taken together, the results of studies that have been conducted so far indicate that there is no need to include the spouse in the exposure treatment of agoraphobics.

The results of studies that evaluated the efficacy of interpersonal skills training interventions are rather mixed, so no general conclusions are allowed. Treatment focusing on general life stress rather than on relationship difficulties was found to be less effective than exposure by the patient alone. In contrast, studies that focused on relationship issues in addition to exposure led to slightly better results, especially at followup. Notably, this was also the case in couples that were not maritally distressed. Given the finding that criticism of the spouse may be related to relapse at followup, this may require specific attention to communication training in couples with a critical partner (Emmelkamp & Vedel, 2002).

CBT Compared to Other Psychotherapies

Few studies have evaluated the effects of psychotherapies other than cognitive behavior therapy in patients with panic disorder with or without agoraphobia. Van den Hout, et al. (1994) found cognitive therapy more effective than supportive psychotherapy in reducing panic attacks. Furthermore, Craske, Maidenberg, and Bystritsky (1995) found a cognitive behavior therapy package more effective than nondirective psychotherapy. In both studies, treatment involved only four sessions. Hoffart and Martinsen (1990) compared two inpatient programs in agoraphobics: (1) psychodynamic therapy and (2) exposure plus psychodynamic therapy. Only the integrated therapy resulted in stable improvements. Given a number of methodological problems, including lack of randomization and lack of behavioral measures, the results are difficult to interpret.

Teusch, Böhme, and Gatspar (1997) compared two inpatient programs: (1) exposure in vivo and (2) exposure in vivo plus client-centered therapy. Both treatment formats led to significant reductions in panic, avoidance, and depressive symptoms. The combined treatment was superior to client-centered therapy on readiness to expose oneself actively to phobic situations at discharge and at six-month followup, reduction in agoraphobia at three-month followup, and general anxiety at six-month followup. Unfortunately, a behavioral measure was not included. Moreover, all patients received "psychogymnastics," occupational therapy, and creative therapy concurrently, which makes the results of this study difficult to interpret. Finally, an exposure-only condition was not included in the design, thus precluding conclusions with respect to the additive effect of client-centered therapy to exposure in vivo.

Two studies compared cognitive therapy with another psychotherapy in patients with panic disorder without severe agoraphobia. Beck, Sokol, Clark, Berschick, and Wright (1992) compared cognitive therapy with client-centered supportive therapy. After eight weeks, 71% of the patients in the cognitive therapy condition were panic free in contrast to 25% of the patients who had received nondirective therapy. Shear, Pilkonis, Cloitre, and Leon (1994) compared cognitive therapy with nonprescriptive treatment in patients with panic disorder. This nonprescriptive treatment included psychodynamic elements. In this study, cognitive therapy was not found to be superior to nonprescriptive treatment.

In sum, few controlled studies support the effects of other psychotherapies than cognitive behavioral therapy for panic disorder with or without agoraphobia. Unfortunately, due to methodological problems (e.g., few sessions, concurrent inpatient treatment, lack of randomization), results with respect to the effects of alternative psychotherapies are inconclusive.

CBT Compared with Pharmacotherapy

Many studies have been reported that have investigated the relative contribution of cognitive behavioral procedures and psychopharmaca, which would be difficult to discuss in any detail. Therefore, the emphasis will be on recent meta-analyses. CBT is generally as effective or more effective than psychopharmaca (Chambless & Gillis, 1993; Clum et al., 1993; Gould et al., 1995; van Balkom et al., 1995, 1997). Although two meta-analyses found no evidence that psychopharmaca enhance the effects of exposure or CBT (Gould et al., 1995; van Balkom et al., 1995), a recent meta-analysis suggests that the combination of antidepressants with exposure in vivo is the most effective treatment for panic disorder (Bakker et al., 1998).

Combined treatment of alprazolam and exposure or CBT results in poorer maintenance of remission of panic disorder than CBT alone (Marks et al., 1993; Otto, Pollack, & Sabatino, 1996; Spiegel & Bruce, 1997) but can facilitate discontinuation of alprazolam therapy in patients who have been treated with alprazolam only (Bruce, Spiegel, Gregg, & Nuzzarello, 1995). Furthermore, pretreatment attrition and dropout rates are lower in CBT than in pharmacotherapy (Gould et al., 1995; Hofmann et al., 1998), which renders the results of studies comparing CBT and pharmacotherapy difficult to interpret.

Prognostic Factors

Most predictor variables (demographics, severity, expectancy and motivation) have not consistently been found to be predictive of outcome (Steketee & Shapiro, 1995). A number of sudies have investigated whether comorbid depression affected exposure in vivo and panic management, but results are equivocal (Mennin & Heimberg, 2000). There is no evidence that moderate depressed mood affects treatment outcome. The results with respect to the impact of major depression on treatment outcome are inconclusive.

Comorbid personality disorders are also common in panic disorder and agoraphobia, the avoidant and dependent personality disorders being most frequently found (van Velzen & Emmelkamp, 1999). Although some personality *traits* have been found to be associated with poorer outcome (Mennin & Heimberg, 2000; van Velzen & Emmelkamp, 1996), there is no evidence that the presence of personality *disorders* per se results in poorer outcome when personality disorder diagnosis is formally established with a structured interview (Dreessen & Arntz, 1998).

Although there appears to be little evidence, if any, that the relationships of couples where one is diagnosed as agorophobic are distressed or that the partner of the agoraphobic is likely to have a disorder, there is some evidence that the quality of the marital relationship may affect the outcome of exposure in vivo (Emmelkamp & Gerlsma, 1994). However, the results of studies on this topic are inconclusive. In a study by Chambless and Steketee (1999), higher hostility of family members as assessed by the Camberwell interview was related to poorer outcome, but this finding has not been replicated.

Social Phobia

Empirical Results of Behavioral and Cognitive Treatment Strategies

A social phobia is characterized by a marked and persistent fear of possible scrutiny by other people. Patients with this disorder are often inclined to avoid situations in which they could be criticized, which usually leads to significant interference in social relationships and occupational functioning (DSM-IV, 1994). The last decades have demonstrated a gradual shift in the strategies used to treat this disorder. In the 1970s, treatments for social anxiety or social failure (at that time social phobia was not acknowledged as a separate anxiety disorder) consisted largely of social skills training, whereas some studies used systematic desensitization or flooding. In the last decade, studies on treatment outcome with social phobics concentrated on exposure in vivo, social skills training, cognitive strategies, and treatments in which cognitive and behavioral strategies were integrated. Several reviews, including three meta-analyses, have been published about the efficacy of (cognitive) behavioral treatments for social phobia (e.g., Feske & Chambless, 1995; Gould, Buckminster, Otto, Pollack, and Yap, 1997; Taylor, 1996), and the main results will be shortly summarized here.

Gradual exposure in vivo has been studied extensively for social phobics, both on its own and in combination with other strategies (Emmelkamp, 1994; Scholing & Emmelkamp, 1993a). It was found to be highly effective and well applicable in clinical practice, in both group and individual treatments. In meta-analyses on treatments for social phobia, it appeared that the mean improvement in exposure in vivo treatments (without addition of other ingredients) was about one standard deviation (Feske & Chambless, 1995; Taylor, 1996), which in psychotherapy outcome research is considered to be a large effect size.

The effectiveness of cognitive procedures is divergent. In two studies that included a pure cognitive condition, it appeared that for patients with a generalized social phobia cognitive therapy was as effective as exposure in vivo, but these treatments were conducted in groups (Emmelkamp & Felten, 1985; Mattick, Andrews, Hadzi-Pavlovic, 1989). In a study by Hope, Heimberg, and Bruch (1995), however, 70% of patients treated with exposure were rated as clinically improved, in contrast to only 36% of patients treated with cognitive behavioral group therapy. For patients with a more specific social phobia (e.g., fear of writing, blushing, trembling, or sweating) exposure in vivo seems indispensable, and it is doubtful whether cognitive strategies do have additional value (Scholing & Emmelkamp, 1993b).

Social skills training has also been shown to be an effective treatment (e.g., Mersch, Jansen, & Arntz, 1995). In view of the fact that inadequate social skills seem less important in the etiology and maintenance of social fears than was once thought, questions about the effective ingredients of the treatment have been raised. It is possible that skills training is useful mainly in enhancing patients' self-confidence. In addition, the effects of social skills training, when conducted in groups (as is usually the case), can be explained in terms of in vivo exposure, both in the group sessions and in homework assignments.

Several studies have compared single treatments (e.g., only exposure in vivo) with combined treatments (e.g., cognitive therapy with exposure in vivo). The results suggest that there is little reason to prefer a combined treatment to a single treatment, provided that the single treatment consists of exposure in vivo (Feske & Chambless, 1995; Mersch, Jansen, & Arntz, 1995).

Matching Patient to Treatment

In accordance with the reported heterogeneity of social phobics, several attempts have been made to divide patients into more homogeneous subgroups and to match treatment strategies to specific patient characteristics. The research strategy usually includes the following design. Patients are divided into two groups, showing different response patterns (e.g., behavioral reactors low in social skills, cognitive reactors, or physiological reactors). Within each group, half of the patients receive a consonant treatment, matching the reactor type (e.g. relaxation in the case of physiological reactors; social skills training in the case of behavioral reactors; and cognitive therapy in the case of cognitive reactors), whereas the other half receive a treatment that does not fit the response pattern. In all, it appears that both matched and standardized treatments led to improvement and that they were equally effective (Jerremalm, Jansson, & Öst, 1986; Mersch et al., 1991; Öst et al., 1981).

Cognitive Behavior Therapy versus Other Psychotherapies

Cottraux et al. (1997) compared the efficacy of cognitive behavior therapy and supportive psychotherapy. After six weeks, cognitive therapy was more effective than supportive therapy, but patients in the cognitive therapy condition had received more therapy hours (eight sessions of one hour) than patients in the supportive therapy (three sessions of 30 minutes), which makes the results difficult to interpret. Heimberg, Dodge, and Hope (1990) compared cognitive therapy with a supportive therapy. At six-months followup, 81% of patients in the cognitive therapy condition were rated as improved, in contrast to 47% who had received supportive therapy.

Group Treatment versus Individual Treatment

It can be expected that, especially for social phobia, group treatments have clear advantages over individual treatments. Group treatment provides a continuous exposure to a group, which for many social phobics is one of the most anxiety-provoking situations. However, only two studies have directly compared group and individual treatments for social phobics (Scholing & Emmelkamp, 1993a, 1996; Wlazlo et al., 1990), and both of them did not find overall differences in effectiveness between the treatment modalities.

Cognitive Behavior Therapy versus Pharmacotherapy

Heimberg et al. (1998) compared cognitive behavioral group therapy (CBGT) with the MAO phenelzine. At the end of the active treatment phase, 75% of the CBGT patients, 77% of phenelzine patients, 41% of placebo patients, and

35% of the control group patients were classified as treatment responders. Six months after the treatment had been finished, however, CBGT patients had maintained their gains, whereas 50% of the phenelzine patients had relapsed. Turner, Beidel, and Jacob (1994) found exposure (flooding) to be more effective than atenolol on behavioral measures and a composite index.

Predictors of Outcome

Some studies have examined variables predicting treatment outcome. Thus far, the only variable that has been proven consistently predictive is a decrease in fear of negative evaluation (Feske & Chambless, 1995) or change in the frequency of negative self-statements (Scholing & Emmelkamp, 1999), but one could argue that this is in fact an outcome variable instead of a predictor. Neither personality disorder (Mersch, Jansen, & Arntz, 1995; van Velzen, Emmelkamp, & Scholing, 1997) nor comorbid anxiety or mood disorder (van Velzen, Emmelkamp, & Scholing, 1997) did predict outcome of CBT.

Long-Term Results

As far as long-term followup data are available, the results of CBT appeared to be stable at 14 months (Mersch, Emmelkamp, & Lips, 1991) and at 18-months followup, both in generalized social phobics (Scholing & Emmelkamp, 1996a) and in specific social phobics (Scholing & Emmelkamp, 1996b). Furthermore, Turner, Beidel, and Cooley-Quille (1995) reported that treatment gains were maintained two years after treatment with a broad-spectrum treatment for social phobia. For individual patients the results are divergent. Scholing and Emmelkamp (1996a) found that between the post-test and the 18-months followup, 58% of the patients still functioned at their post-test level, 20% had relapsed, and 22% had further improved.

Concluding Remarks

Considering the clinical relevance of the data, it must be concluded that the improvements in social phobia following CBT are encouraging but that many patients still report substantial fear at the end of treatment. On the basis of the empirical findings, treatments for social phobia should at least include a considerable amount of in vivo exposure. Although a pure exposure treatment is highly effective for a number of social phobics, it seems plausible that an integrated package will be applicable for a larger group of patients. In that view, it is not surprising that there is a trend toward development of integrated treatments consisting of different strategies (e.g., Turner, Beidel, & Jacob, 1994). The other strategies may be particularly useful to motivate patients to enter the fear-provoking situations, for example, by providing them with skills they can use when they are in danger of getting too anxious.

GENERALIZED ANXIETY DISORDER

In recent years, a number of studies have been conducted that investigated the effectiveness of behavioral and cognitive procedures on patients with generalized anxiety disorder (GAD). Although exposure procedures are effective when anxiety is triggered by external stimuli, avoidance is less obvious in GAD. Therefore, the emphasis is on reducing the excessive psychophysiological activation characteristic of GAD by means of relaxation procedures and on changing the worrying by cognitive techniques. Although biofeedback may also lead to reduced arousal levels and reduction in Trait-Anxiety (Rice, Blanchard & Purcell, 1993), there is no evidence that biofeedback deserves a special status, since other forms of relaxation training tend to yield comparable clinical effects (Emmelkamp, 1990).

Relaxation forms an essential ingredient in anxiety management training and in applied relaxation. In both procedures, patients are trained to recognize the physiological cues of tension and to apply relaxation whenever tension is perceived. Anxiety management includes additional procedures for reducing anxiety symptoms, such as distraction, controlling upsetting thoughts, and panic management. Both anxiety management (Butler, Gelder, Hibbert, Cullington, & Kilmes, 1987; Jannoun, Oppenheimer, & Gelder, 1982; Tarrier & Main, 1986) and applied relaxation (Barlow, Rapee, & Brown, 1992; Borkovec & Costello, 1993; Öst & Breitholz, 2000) have been found to be effective in GAD.

Behavior Therapy versus Cognitive Therapy

The cognitive treatment for generalized anxiety is to a large extent based on research that demonstrates the association between GAD and cognitions (Wells, 1999). This has led to the development of treatment approaches that directly challenge cognitions and beliefs associated with anxiety. Earlier studies focused on changing self-statements, but results were meager

(Emmelkamp, 1994). More recently, a number of studies have evaluated more comprehensive cognitive approaches based on Beck and Emery (1985). In five studies, applied relaxation (Barlow, Rapee, & Brown, 1992; Borkovec & Costello, 1993; Öst & Breitholz, 2000) and anxiety management training (Lindsay, Crino, & Andrews, 1997; White, Keenan & Brooks, 1992) were found to be as effective as cognitive therapy. In contrast, Butler, Fennell, Robson, and Gelder (1991) found a slight superiority of cognitive therapy over behavior therapy consisting of relaxation, exposure in vivo, and reengagement in pleasurable and rewarding activities. The results of two other studies are inconclusive. Durham and Turvey (1987) found cognitive therapy superior to anxiety management but only at followup. Durham et al. (1994) found cognitive therapy to be significantly more effective than psychodynamic psychotherapy but not more effective than anxiety management. However, fewer patients were rated as clinically improved after anxiety management training than after cognitive therapy. The results of this study are difficult to interpret since cognitive therapy and psychodynamic psychotherapy were delivered by experienced therapists at weekly intervals over six months, whereas anxiety management training was delivered at fortnightly intervals by inexperienced registrars in psychiatry.

Concluding Remarks

Results of studies into behavior therapy and cognitive therapy with GAD patients are promising but less so than in simple phobia, social phobia, or panic disorder. A recent meta-analysis reported an overall effect size for CBT of .70, only slightly higher than the effect size for pharmacotherapy (.60) (Gould, Otto, Pollack, & Yap, 1997). Craske (1999) reviewed seven studies, which reported the clinical significance of the improvements achieved and found that 57% of the GAD patients improved and 47% achieved high end state functioning. Many patients remained symptomatic. Furthermore, although a cognitive behavioral package has been found to be more effective than nondirective therapy (Borkovec & Costello, 1993; Borkovec et al., 1987), other studies (Blowers, Cobb, & Matthews, 1987; Stanley, Beck, & Glassco, 1996) found nondirective therapy at least as effective as CBT. Thus, further studies are needed to investigate which are the essential ingredients for successful treatment of GAD.

Obsessive-Compulsive Disorder

Obsessions are experienced as senseless or repugnant thoughts, which the patient attempts to ignore or suppress. Compulsions are repetitive, apparently purposeful behaviors that are intentionally produced and performed according to certain rules or in a stereotyped fashion. Compulsions serve to neutralize or to prevent discomfort and/or anxiety. Rituals or compulsions usually accompany obsessions. The majority of obsessive-compulsive patients have obsessions as well as compulsions. Generally, obsessions are anxiety inducing, and the performance of compulsions leads to anxiety reduction. Obsessive-compulsive patients not only try to neutralize discomfort or anxiety with compulsions, but also try to avoid stimuli that might provoke discomfort or anxiety. In a number of patients, neutralizing thoughts (cognitive rituals) serve the same function as rituals, that is, undoing the expected harmful effects of the obsession.

Exposure In Vivo and Response Prevention

Obsessive-compulsive problems are among the most difficult problems to treat, yet it is in this area that behavioral research has made significant advances. Exposure in vivo and response prevention are effective with a substantial number of obsessive-compulsive patients (van Oppen & Emmelkamp, 1997). With this treatment, patients are exposed to stimuli that trigger obsessions and urges to ritualize but are prevented from performing the rituals. For a description of exposure in vivo and response prevention, the reader is referred to Emmelkamp, Bouman, & Scholing (1993).

Research over the past decades has determined what the essential ingredients of successful treatment are (Emmelkamp, 1994). There is no need to elicit high anxiety during treatment since gradual exposure in vivo is as effective as flooding in vivo. As gradual exposure evokes less tension and is easier for the patient to carry out by her/himself, it is to be preferred to flooding. Although some hold that adding imaginal exposure may enhance treatment effectiveness, the result of a recent controlled study does not support this contention (De Araujo, Ito, Marks, & Deale, 1995). Both exposure to distressing stimuli and response prevention of the ritual are essential components (Abramowitz, 1997; Emmelkamp,

1994). Exposure led to more anxiety reduction but less improvement of rituals, while the reverse was found for response prevention. Furthermore, although results of a meta-analysis suggest that exposure in vivo carried out by the patient him/herself and response prevention in his or her natural environment is slightly less effective than therapist-controlled exposure (Abramowitz, 1998), results of controlled studies found therapist-controlled and self-controlled exposure equally effective (Emmelkamp, 1994).

Generally, treatment with exposure in vivo and response prevention results in considerable clinical improvement. Exposure in vivo plus response prevention is more effective than relaxation control (Marks, 1997) and anxiety management (Lindsay, Crino, & Andrews, 1997). A recent meta-analysis showed that at the end of treatment, patients' functioning was more comparable to individuals from the general population than to individuals with untreated obsessive-compulsive disorder (OCD) (Abramowitz, 1998). Positive results of exposure in vivo and response prevention were not restricted to patients treated in experimental studies, but generalized to OCD patients treated in clinical settings (Franklin, Abramowitz, Kozak, Levitt, & Foa, 2000).

Although treatment by exposure and response prevention was originally applied when the patient was hospitalized, treatment can also be administered by the patient in his natural environment. Admission to a hospital is not necessary for most OCD patients, as the same results can be achieved if the treatment is provided in their own environment (van den Hout et al., 1988). Exposure in vivo and response prevention have successfully been applied in a group format (e.g., van Noppen, Pato, Marsland, & Rasmussen, 1998). Fals-Stewart, Marks, and Schafer (1993), however, found individual behavior therapy to result in faster reduction in obsessive-compulsive symptoms than group treatment.

There is some evidence that exposure and response prevention can be administered by phone. Bachofen et al. (1999) evaluated the effects of a computer program which was designed to assist OCD patients in carrying out self-exposure and response prevention. Patients used a touch-tone telephone to access computer-driven interviews via an Interactive Voice Response system. This program resulted in statistically and clinically significant improvement in OCD symptomatology. However, nearly half of the patients dropped out of the study.

Family members are often involved in the rituals of OCD patients, and this often results in a heavy burden (Amir, Freshman, & Foa, 2000). Although a substantial number of patients have relationship problems, there is no evidence that involving the patient's partner in the treatment is more effective than treating the patient on his/her own (Emmelkamp, de Haan, & Hoogduin, 1990).

The positive results of exposure and response prevention are not restricted to improvements in anxiety, avoidance, compulsions, obsessions, and depressed mood. Although treatment is not directed at cognitions, exposure and response prevention also results in significant changes in obsessional beliefs and intrusions (Emmelkamp, van Oppen, & van Balkom, 2000). In addition, McKay, Neziroglu, Todaro, & Yaryura-Tobias (1996) found treatment to result in significant changes in some comorbid personality disorders (PDs) but not in obsessive-compulsive PD. Finally, psychoanalysts hold that obsessive-compulsive disorder is associated with inadequate defense mechanisms. But even here some evidence suggests that successful behavior therapy results in a significant increase in the use of more adaptive defense mechanisms (Albucher, Abelson, & Nesse, 1998).

Improvements are also reflected in biological measures. Peter, Tabrizian, and Hand (2000) found that cholesterol levels decreased significantly from pre- to post-treatment. Furthermore, there is evidence that successful treatment leads to significant improvement in right caudate glucose metabolic activity as assessed with brain imaging techniques (Brody et al., 1998; Schwartz, Stoessel, Baxter, Martin, & Phelps, 1996).

Individualized Treatment

Emmelkamp, Bouman, and Blaauw (1994) studied whether treatment based on a functional analysis would be better than a standardized exposure/response prevention program. Obsessive-compulsive patients were randomly assigned to two conditions. In one condition, the patients were treated with the standardized behavioral program of exposure in vivo and response prevention. The other treatment program was individually tailored to the needs of the patient. Therefore, four to five interviews were held with all patients by an experienced behavior therapist in order to enable him to make a functional analysis and a treatment plan based on this analysis. Neither on obsessive-compulsive complaints nor on depression and general psychopathology were the treatments found to be differentially effective. Exposure in vivo plus response prevention was as effective as treatment that included other techniques and focused on other targets than just the obsessive-compulsive behavior. Thus, at least in the short term, the results of an individually tailored treatment were comparable to the results of a standardized behavioral package. Of course, long-term followup results are needed in order to make more definite claims for either a standardized treatment package or a broader multimodal treatment approach for obsessive-compulsives.

Exposure versus Cognitive Therapy

A number of studies have compared the effectiveness of exposure in vivo plus response prevention and cognitive therapy. Various cognitive procedures have been evaluated: self-instruction training, Rational Emotive Therapy (RET), and cognitive therapy along the lines of Beck and Emery. Self-instruction training did not prove to increase the effectiveness of exposure in vivo and response prevention (Emmelkamp, Van der Helm, van Zanten, & Plochg, 1980). A number of patients did, in fact, not benefit at all from adding positive self-statements during the training with exposure in vivo. As a number of patients with obsessive-compulsive problems are characterized by an excessive inclination to talk about and doubt themselves, it is doubtful whether self-instruction training is the most suitable cognitive therapy for these problems. This form of cognitive therapy appears to affect the cognitive functions superficially, while the deeper cognitive structures are left untouched.

Emmelkamp, Visser, and Hoekstra (1988) studied the value of rationally challenging irrational thoughts, along the lines of Rational Emotive Therapy (RET), in OCD patients. The results showed that, in relation to obsessive-compulsive behavior, RET was as effective as exposure in vivo. In contrast, Emmelkamp and Beens (1991) found that RET did not enhance the effects of exposure in vivo. In the studies on RET, cognitive therapy was provided "pure"; that is, patients were not instructed to change their behavior.

To date, only one controlled study (van Oppen, de Haan, van Balkom, & Spinhoven, 1995) has been reported in which cognitive therapy along the lines of Beck and Emery was compared with exposure in vivo plus response prevention. Both cognitive therapy and exposure in vivo led to statistically as well as clinically significant improvement. Multivariate significant interaction effects on the obsessive-compulsive measures and on the generalized measures suggested a greater efficacy of cognitive therapy in comparison to exposure in vivo. Furthermore, the differences in effect size and in the percentage of recovered patients suggest that cognitive therapy might be superior to exposure in vivo. Significantly more patients were rated as reliably changed or as "recovered" in the cognitive therapy condition.

The slightly more favorable results of cognitive therapy in the van Oppen et al. (1995) study, as compared to the results of cognitive therapy as applied in the studies by Emmelkamp and his colleagues (1988; 1991), might be related to the inclusion of behavioral experiments in the cognitive therapy of van Oppen et al. (1995). Jones and Menzies (1998) investigated specific cognitive interventions directed at decreasing danger-related expectancies concerning contamination in obsessive-compulsive patients. Treatment did not involve exposure and response prevention or behavioral experiments. Although this specific form of cognitive therapy was more effective than no-treatment control, it has not yet been compared to the gold standard exposure in vivo and response prevention.

Exposure versus Pharmacotherapy

Over the last 20 years, a number of controlled studies have been carried out on the effect of drugs, which concentrate on the disrupted serotenergic neurotransmission: clomipramine, fluvoxamine, and fluoxetine. Two studies focused on the question of whether a combination of clomipramine and behavior therapy (exposure in vivo and response prevention) was more effective than behavior therapy on its own or clomipramine on its own. Behavior therapy proved to be more effective than clomipramine. In Marks et al.'s study (1980), clomipramine improved the effect of behavior therapy to some extent, but in a later study Marks et al. (1988) showed that after 3.5 months, the combination of clomipramine and behavior therapy was not more effective than behavior therapy on its own. On six-year followup of the patients of the Marks et al. (1980) study, clomipramine was no longer more effective than placebo (O'Sullivan, Noshirvani, Marks, Monteiro, & Lelliot, 1991). Van Balkom et al. (1998) compared cognitive behavior therapy, a combination of cognitive therapy and fluvoxamine, and a combination of behavior therapy and fluvoxamine. Results revealed that cognitive and behavior therapy were no less effective than the combined treatment approaches. More recently, Hohagen et al. (1998) found behavior therapy plus fluvoxamine not to be more effective than behavior therapy plus placebo on compulsions. On obsessions, however, fluvoxamine was more effective than placebo. In severely depressed patients, the fluvoxamine-behavior therapy combination was superior to the placebo-behavior therapy combination.

In three recent meta-analyses (van Balkom et al., 1994; Cox et al., 1993; Kobak, Greist, Jefferson, Katzelnick, & Henry, 1998) and a review by Stanley and Turner (1995), the effects of various treatments for obsessive-compulsive disorder were compared. In the van Balkom et al. meta-analysis, behavior therapy was superior to serotenergic antidepressants and other antidepressants on self-ratings, with effect sizes of 1.46, 0.95, and 0.48, respectively. Adding serotenergic antidepressants did not enhance the effectiveness of behavior therapy more than adding placebo, the latter combination being the most effective (effect sizes for behavior therapy plus antidepressant: 1.56; for behavior therapy plus placebo: 1.69). On assessor ratings, no differences between behavior therapy and serotenergic antidepressants were found. Assessors apparently rated the patients treated with serotonergic antidepressants as more improved than the patients themselves did (effect sizes assessor rating: 1.63; self-rating: 0.95). Also in an earlier meta-analysis (Christensen, Hadzi-Pavlovic, Andrews, & Mattick, 1987), effect sizes were higher for clinician-rated measures, and these measures were used more frequently in drug trials than in behavioral treatment. In the meta-analysis of Kobak, Greist, Jefferson, Katzelnick, & Henry (1998), exposure in vivo and response prevention was found to be superior to treatment with serotonin reuptake inhibitors (STIs).

Stopping the antidepressant medication usually results in a relapse, in contrast to stopping exposure and response prevention (Marks, 1997). Thus, exposure and response prevention appears to be cost-effective and is the first choice of treatment for OCD (Expert Consensus Panel for Obsessive-Compulsive Disorder, 1997). However, antidepressant medication may be a useful adjunct to exposure and response prevention when OCD is accompanied by severe comorbid depression.

Long-Term Results and Relapse Prevention

Although a substantial number of followup studies on the long-term effects of exposure and response prevention have been reported, these reports do not usually provide information with respect to the number of patients who relapsed. The general picture is that 70 to 80% of obsessive-compulsive patients who completed trials of exposure therapy are improved up to six years (Foa & Kozak, 1996; Marks, 1997).

A cognitive behavioral model of the relapse process in obsessive-compulsive patients proposed by Emmelkamp et al. (1992) assumes that individuals freely make a choice to give in to the urge to ritualize. Although patients may have become symptom free, sooner or later they will be confronted with stressful situations that pose a threat to their sense of control. Such stressful situations may involve undergoing major stressors like a loss of job, divorce, or death, but also consist of an accumulation of daily hassles with which a patient is unable to cope. The model assumes that important roles are played by a number of mediating factors: play coping styles of the patient, social support, and expressed emotion of significant others. In the model it is supposed that the more stress an individual experiences, the less coping skills he or she has, the more he/she lacks an adequate social support system, and the more he/she is exposed to high levels of expressed emotion, the more likely he/she will relapse. Some support for this relapse prevention model was found (Emmelkamp et al., 1992). Several programs have now been developed to prevent relapse in OCD patients, and the first results are encouraging (Hiss, Foa, & Kozak, 1995; McKay, 1997).

Prognostic Factors

Few robust prognostic factors have been found: most predictor variables (e.g., demographic variables, severity and type of OCD problem, anxiety, and depression) were not consistently associated with outcome across studies (e.g., Castle, Deale, Marks, & Cutts, 1994; de Haan et al., 1997; Keijsers, Hoogduin, & Schaap, 1994; Steketee, Eisen, Dyck, Warshaw, & Rasmussen, 2000; Steketee & Shapiro, 1995). Thus, the literature is inconclusive about whether pretreatment depression, anxiety, severity, and type of obsessive-compulsive problem (checkers vs. washers) predict outcome.

Other variables, however, may affect treatment outcome. There is some evidence that perceived Expressed Emotion predicts poor outcome at post-test (Chambless & Steketee, 1999) and two-year followup (Emmelkamp, Kloek, & Blaauw, 1994). Sahoo, Gillis, and Misra (1999) found conditionability (delayed habituation) to be associated with poor therapeutic outcome with exposure and response prevention.

OCD is often associated with personality disorders (PDs), especially the avoidant, dependent, histrionic, and obsessive-compulsive PDs (van Velzen and Emmelkamp, 1999). Results with respect to comorbid PDs as predictors of outcome are inconclusive (Dreessen, Hoekstra, & Arntz, 1997; van Velzen & Emmelkamp, 1996). Finally, Blaauw and Emmelkamp (1994) found that the therapeutic relationship affected outcome, but this variable has not been studied extensively.

Post-Traumatic Stress

War Trauma

Six controlled studies have been published on the behavioral treatment of war trauma. Treatment consisting of relaxation and imaginal exposure resulted in significant reduction of symptoms associated with post-traumatic stress disorder (PTSD) and was significantly more effective than no-treatment in a study by Keane, Fairbank, Caddell, and Zimering (1989). Both Cooper and Clum (1989) and Boudewyns, Hyer, Woods, Harrision, and McCronie (1990) found imaginal exposure (flooding) to be more effective than conventional therapy. Glynn et al. (1999) found that 18 sessions of exposure therapy and cognitive restructuring resulted in significant reduction of PTSD symptomatology up to three-months followup, and were more effective than wait list control. Given the fact that associated interpersonal difficulties have not improved with exposure treatment, Glynn et al. also investigated whether Behavioral Family Therapy (BFT) would have additive benefits subsequent to exposure therapy. Unfortunately, BFT did not lead to enhanced outcome. Many families dropped out during this phase of the therapy.

Eye-movement desensitization and reprocessing (EMDR) is a controversial treatment that entails imaginal exposure to traumatic images, while saccadic eye movements are induced by tracking a therapist's finger as it is moved rapidly from side to side. EMDR is believed to restore the disrupted physiological balance between excitatory and inhibitory systems in the brain produced by exposure to trauma (Shapiro, 1999). Devilly, Spence, and Rapee (1998) found hardly any improvement with EMDR in war veterans at six-months followup. Macklin et al. (2000) found that EMDR resulted in only modest improvements immediately after treatment and that these improvements were lost at five-year followup.

Rape and Assault Trauma

Two behavioral and cognitive behavioral treatments are now widely applied in the treatment of rape victims: stress management/stress inoculation training (SIT) and exposure. Stress management was found to be effective in studies by Veronen and Kilpatrick (1983), Frank et al. (1988), Resick et al. (1988), and Foa, Rothbaum, Riggs, and Murdock, (1991). In the last-named study, exposure, SIT, and supportive counseling were compared. At followup, the percentages of women who no longer met criteria for PTSD were 55% in the exposure condition, 50% in the SIT condition, and 45% in the supportive counseling condition. These differences failed to reach statistical significance.

In the largest study reported to date, Foa et al. (1999) randomly assigned 96 women across conditions of exposure, stress inoculation training (SIT), combination treatment (exposure plus SIT), and wait list control. Treatment consisted of nine sessions. Sixty-nine women were victims of sexual assault, and 27 were victims of nonsexual assault. Results corroborated the results of the Foa et al. (1991) study. All active treatments were superior to the waiting list control condition. Exposure was consistently superior on four of the seven indices of treatment outcome. Combination treatment was not found to be superior to exposure alone on any of the outcome measures. Exposure yielded the greatest number of participants achieving good end-state functioning at one-year followup (52% for exposure, 42% for SIT, and 36% for the combined approach).

Other Traumas

In an uncontrolled study, Hickling and Blanchard (1997) evaluated the effects of a cognitive behavioral program on 10 individuals who had been involved in a motor vehicle accident. Treatment consisted of relaxation training, exposure therapy, and cognitive restructuring. At three-months followup, seven out of eight patients with full PTSD had initially improved to non-PTSD. In a controlled study in patients suffering from PTSD following a motor vehicle accident, a similar cognitive behavioral therapy package was found more effective than wait list control (Fecteau & Nicki, 1999).

Two studies have compared cognitive therapy and exposure in victims of PTSD resulting from a variety of traumas. Tarrier et al. (1999) found imaginal exposure to be as effective as cognitive therapy. Marks, Lovell, Noshirvani, Livanou, and Trasher (1998) compared exposure, cognitive therapy, and a combined cognitive-exposure treatment with relaxation control. All three active treatments were more effective than relaxation control up to six-months followup. Combining cognitive therapy with exposure did not result in added value above exposure alone or cognitive therapy alone. Exposure yielded the greatest number of participants achieving good end-state functioning (53% for exposure, 32% for cognitive restructuring, 32% for the combined approach, and 15% for relaxation). In an earlier study by the same research group, there was a slight superiority on phobic avoidance for in vivo exposure over imaginal exposure (Richards, Lovell, & Marks, 1994). At post-treatment and at one-year followup, no patients met criteria for PTSD.

Results comparing EMDR and other psychological interventions are inconclusive. Although a recent meta-analysis (van Etten & Taylor, 1998) found that cognitive behavior therapy and EMDR were about equally effective, few controlled studies have directly compared these methods. Vaughan et al. (1994) found EMDR as effective as imaginal exposure and applied relaxation. Patients in all three conditions had a significantly better outcome on the PTSD symptoms of avoidance and hyperarousal than wait list controls. However, Devilly and Spence (1999) found that cognitive behavior therapy (consisting of relaxation, exposure, and cognitive therapy) both statistically and clinically was more effective in reducing PTSD symptomatology up to three-months followup. Furthermore, dismantling studies have questioned the theoretical rationale of EMDR, since eye movements appear to be unnecessary for improvement (Cahill, Carrigan, & Frueh, 1999; Devilly et al., 1998; Lohr, Tolin, & Lilienfeld, 1998).

Acute Stress Disorder

A number of studies have evaluated whether prophylactic treatment of subjects with acute stress disorder can prevent PTSD. In recent rape victims, Foa, Hearst-Ikeda, and Perry (1995) found that four sessions consisting of relaxation, cognitive restructuring, imaginal exposure, and in vivo exposure resulted in significantly fewer PTSD cases in the treatment group than in the no-treatment control group two months after the assault. However, no differences were found six-months later. Bryant, Harvey, Dang, Sackville, and Basten (1998) identified trauma survivors who were at risk of developing chronic post-traumatic stress disorder. All subjects fulfilled the DSM-IV criteria for acute stress disorder. Treatment started within two weeks after the trauma and lasted five sessions. Cognitive behavior therapy, consisting primarily of exposure and cognitive restructuring, was found to be more effective than supportive counseling. Immediately after treatment, 8% of CBT subjects and 83% of supportive counseling subjects met criteria for PTSD. At six-months followup the figures were 17% and 67%, respectively. In a following study, Bryant, Sackville, Dang, Moulds, and Guthrie (1999) found prolonged exposure with or without anxiety management to be more effective in terms of preventing full PTSD than supportive counseling. Six months after treatment, only 15% of the prolonged exposure subjects, 20% of the prolonged exposure and anxiety management subjects, and 67% of the supportive counseling subjects met the criteria for PTSD. The authors suggested that prolonged exposure was the most critical component.

Concluding Remarks

Results of studies of EMDR are mixed, and many studies suffer from methodological flaws, which preclude the drawing of firm conclusions. Although stress inoculation training has been found to be effective, it should be noted that research into stress inoculation has been limited to female (sexual) assault victims. Exposure has been found to be effective in a number of controlled studies across a variety of different traumas and appears to be the treatment of choice. There is no evidence that a combination of cognitive therapy and exposure enhances the effects of exposure.

Depression

A number of controlled outcome studies of the effectiveness of cognitive behavioral interventions for depression have been reported. Before embarking on the task of reviewing these studies, a brief discussion of the major behavioral models of depression that have led to various treatment approaches is provided.

Behavioral Models

Operant Model

The operant conditioning model is based on the assumption that depressive symptoms result from too low a rate of response-contingent reinforcement and that depression will be ameliorated when the rate of reinforcement for adaptive behavior is increased (Lewinsohn, 1975; Lewinsohn & Hoberman, 1982). According to Lewinsohn, when behavior decreases due to nonreinforcement, the other symptoms of depression such as low energy and low self-esteem will follow more or less automatically. Treatment approaches that are suggested by this formulation of depression include (1) reengagement of the depressed individual in constructive and rewarding activities and (2) training in social skills to enhance the individual's capacity to receive social reinforcements resulting from social interactions. It has been suggested (e.g., Lewinsohn & Hoberman, 1982) that lack of social skill could be one of the antecedent conditions producing a low rate of positive reinforcement. Indeed, a number of studies have shown depressed individuals to be less socially skillful than controls. However, an association between depressed mood and (lack of) social skills does not necessarily imply a causal relationship. Only prospective studies can answer the question of the direction of causality between depression on the one hand and social skills on the other. Results of most longitudinal studies investigating this issue were not consistent with the hypothesis that social skill deficits function as an antecedent to depression (Segrin, 2000). Although it has been consistently found that daily mood ratings correlate with rate of pleasant activities (e.g., Lewinsohn & Hoberman, 1982), this finding does not necessarily imply that increasing pleasant-activity rate will improve mood. Biglan and Craker (1982) studied this issue and found that such increases in pleasant activities did not produce improvements in mood, thus challenging one of the basic assumptions of Lewinsohn's theory of depression.

Several researchers have stressed the co-occurrence of depression and marital distress (e.g., Beach, 2001). Depressed persons are characterized by an aversive interpersonal style to which others respond with negativity and rejection. A lower proportion of positive verbal behavior and a higher proportion of negative verbal and nonverbal behavior have characterized the interaction of depressed individuals with their partner. A substantial number of depressed patients presenting for treatment also experience marital distress, whereas in approximately half of the couples who have marital problems at least one of the spouses is depressed. These data suggest that depression and marital distress are closely linked. Furthermore, marital distress is an important precursor of depressive symptoms. In addition, persons who, after being treated for depression, return to distressed marriages are more likely to experience relapse. When patients are asked about the sequence of depression and marital distress, most patients hold that marital distress preceded the depressive episode (Emmelkamp & Vedel, 2002). Results of the studies discussed above suggest that it might be important to enroll the partner in the treatment of depressed patients. A number of behavior therapists have used behavioral marital therapy consisting of training in communication skills as a therapeutic approach. Furthermore, Nezu (1987) developed training in problem-solving skills, based on the idea that depression results from deficits in problem-solving skills.

Self-Control Model

Rehm (1977) has proposed a self-control model of depression that provides a framework for integrating the cognitive and behavioral models. Rehm acknowledges the importance of reinforcement in the development of depression, but he holds that the reinforcement can be self-generated rather than derived from environmental sources. In Rehm's view the depressed mood and the low rate of behavior, and other characteristics of depressed individuals, are the result of negative self-evaluations, lack of self-reinforcement, and high rates of self-punishment. In Rehm's most recent view (Rehm, Mehta, & Dodrill, 2001), depression involves (1) selective attention to negative events to the relative exclusion of positive events; (2) selective attention to the immediate as opposed to the long-term outcomes of behavior; (3) stringent, perfectionistic self-evaluative standards; (4) depressive attributions for successes and failures; (5) insufficient contingent self-reward; and (6) excessive self-administered punishment. Thus, contributions from cognitive theories about depression are now integrated in the self-control model of depression. Several studies have been conducted to test Rehm's hypotheses about the role of self-reinforcement in depression, but results are inconclusive. Results of studies investigating the interaction between external reinforcement than self-reinforcement showed that subjects exhibiting a lower frequency of self-reinforcement than individuals exhibiting a higher frequency of self-reinforcement were characterized by depressed mood. Thus, there is some evidence that reinforcement reduction in the environment may lead to depressed mood for those individuals who engage in a low frequency of self-reinforcement (Rehm et al., 2001).

Cognitive Behavioral Interventions

The major cognitive and behavioral approaches differ with respect to the role that they ascribe to the various factors in the etiology and functioning of depression, which leads to different emphases in the various therapeutic procedures based on these models. Cognitive therapies focus on changing patients' depressogenic cognitions and hence their depressed affect and behavior. Cognitive therapy aims to help patients identify the assumptions and schemas that support patterns of stereotypical negative thinking and to change specific errors in thinking (Hollon & Beck, this volume). Behavioral approaches attempt to change the maladaptive behavior in order to increase positive reinforcement, which can be done by increasing activity level, enhancing social or relationship skills, and training in problem solving. Within behavior models of depression, cognitions are seen as the consequence of depression, and hence it is assumed that these faulty cognitions will change as a result of the behavioral treatment. Self-control therapy aims to change deficits in self-control behavior: self-monitoring, self-evaluation, and self-reinforcement.

Increasing Pleasant Activities

Lewinsohn (1975) has suggested increasing pleasant activities by means of homework assignments as one way of increasing positive reinforcement to the depressed person. Several studies have investigated whether this approach on its own could be successful in improving depression. Typically, activities that are rated as enjoyable but not engaged in during the last few weeks are given as homework assignments. Activities that appear to be relatively easy are chosen first, while more difficult tasks are assigned in later sessions. Although all studies (Gardner & Oei, 1981; Wilson, 1982; Wilson, Goldin, & Charbonneau-Powis, 1983; Zeiss, Lewinsohn, & Munoz, 1979) found this behavioral approach to result in improvement of depression, the question is whether this improvement is due to the increase in pleasant activities per se or to "nonspecific" variables. In the study of Wilson et al. (1983), improvement of depression was not related to an increase of pleasant activities. Furthermore, Zeiss et al. (1979) found that cognitive therapy and social skills training led to increases similar to the condition that had received instructions to increase the rate of pleasant activities. These findings cast doubt on the validity of Lewinsohn's behavioral theory of depression.

Social Skills Training

Sanchez, Lewinsohn, and Larson (1980) contrasted group assertion training and group psychotherapy and found that at post-treatment, assertiveness training was slightly more effective than group psychotherapy on measures of assertiveness and depression. The difference in outcome between the treatment formats reached acceptable levels of statistical significance at one-month followup. Zeiss et al. (1979) also included a social skills training condition in their comprehensive study and found this treatment to be as effective as cognitive therapy and task assignments. On most measures of social skills, patients were found to have improved at the end of therapy. However, none of these effects could be directly attributed to the social skills training, since patients receiving this training did not show more improvement than patients receiving a different treatment modality. A relatively weak mode of assertion training was used—covert modeling—which does not seem to be particularly suited for clinical populations. Rehm, Fuchs, Roth, Kornblith, and Ramono (1979) compared assertiveness training with training in self-control and found that assertiveness training resulted in more improvement on measures of social skills. However, the self-control therapy resulted in the largest reduction in depressed mood. In the Hersen, Bellack, Himmelhoch, and Thase (1984) study, four treatments were compared: (1) social skills training plus placebo, (2) social skills training plus amitriptyline, (3) amitriptyline, and (4) psychotherapy plus placebo. Social skills plus placebo yielded the best clinical results in depression but failed to reach acceptable levels of statistical significance. In general, all four treatment formats were about equally effective. Bellack, Hersen, and Himmelhoch (1983) analyzed behavioral measures of the social skills of these patients and found that patients receiving social skills were, after treatment, more similar to normal controls on these measures than patients from the other two groups. Finally, in adolescents, social skills training led to an improvement of mood in males but not in females (Reed, 1994).

In sum, although a number of studies have shown that social skills training leads to increased assertiveness and improved social performance, the relationship between improved social performance and reduction in depressed mood remains unclear. The studies conducted so far did not show that social skills training per se was related to reduction of depression.

Self-Control Therapies

A number of studies by Rehm and colleagues have evaluated the effectiveness of a self-control therapeutic package and its individual components. The self-control program developed by Fuchs and Rehm (1977) consists of six weeks of training in self-monitoring, self-evaluation, and self-reinforcement. Subjects were given log forms on which to monitor each day's positive activities (self-monitoring). During the self-evaluation phase of the program, the importance of setting realistic goals in evaluating oneself accurately was stressed. Subjects had to choose subgoals that were concrete and attainable and to rate their accomplished behavior toward those goals. Finally, subjects were instructed to self-administer rewards contingent on accomplishment of a behavioral subgoal (self-reinforcement). Treatment was conducted in a group format. This program was found to be slightly more effective than other group psychotherapies and no-treatment control on some measures of depression, but most of these differences were not maintained at followup (for review, see Emmelkamp, 1994). One study found that a 12-week self-control therapy program accelerated the improvement of a standard treatment for depression (van den Hout, Arntz, & Kunkels, 1995). Taking the "self-control" studies together, there is some evidence that this program may help deal with mild to moderate depression, although the therapeutic processes are not yet well understood. Apart from the van den Hout et al. (1995) study, not one study has included clinically depressed patients; all other studies treated volunteers. Since all self-control treatments have been conducted in a group format, it cannot be ruled out that "nonspecific" group processes were more influential in affecting outcome than the self-control procedures.

Problem Solving

There is now a large body of literature (e.g., Lyubomirsky & Nolen-Hoeksema, 1995) that demonstrates a relation between depression and a deficit in problem solving. There is some evidence that training in problem solving leads to improved mood in depressed individuals. In this treatment, the following phases can be distinguished: problem orientation, problem definition and formulation, generation of alternative solutions, decision making, and solution implementation and verification. Nezu and Perri (1989), using a dismantling research methodology, found the total problem-solving package more effective than an abbreviated version of problem solving. Arean, Perri, and Nezu (1993) compared the effectiveness of problem-solving therapy in comparison with a life review treatment condition in older adults. Both treatments were conducted in groups and were found to be more effective than no-treatment control. Problem solving was superior to the life review therapy on the Hamilton Rating Scale for Depression but not on the BDI. Although the results are encouraging, further comparative studies are needed before more definite statements can be made with respect to the clinical value of this treatment.

Spouse-Aided Therapy

Two forms of spouse-aided therapy have been evaluated. In cases with co-occurring depression and marital discord, conjoint *behavioral marital therapy* may be applied. In this therapy, the emphasis is not only on the mood disorder, but also on the communication between the partners. Generally, the earlier phase of therapy deals with problems associated with depression that could hinder a successful application of marital therapy. Examples of such problems are complicated grief or a low-activity level in the depressed patient. Later on, the focus of the therapy is shifted to training both spouses in communication skills. To date, three controlled studies have shown that *conjoint behavioral marital therapy* in depressed, maritally distressed couples may be a good alternative to individual cognitive behavior therapy (Beach & O'Leary, 1992; Emanuels-Zuurveen & Emmelkamp, 1996; Jacobson, Dobson, Fruzetti, Schmaling, & Saluski, 1991). These studies suggest that with depressed, maritally distressed couples, behavioral marital therapy seems to have an exclusive effect on the marital relationship, which is not found in individual cognitive behavior therapy, while it is as effective as cognitive therapy in reducing depressed mood. Not surprisingly, behavioral marital therapy was hardly effective with depressed patients who did not experience marital problems.

Partner-assisted cognitive behavior therapy for depression was developed by Emanuels-Zuurveen and Emmelkamp (1997) for depressed nonmaritally distressed couples and is based on Lewinsohn's and Beck's individual therapy of depression. During spouse-aided therapy, partners join all sessions. Treatment focuses on the depression and on ways both partners can deal more adequately with depression-related situations rather than on the marital relationship per se. Therefore, spouses are involved in devising reinforcing activities, stimulating the patient to engage in rewarding activities and participate in role-playing. Spouses are also asked to attend to the dysfunctional thoughts of the patient and to discuss these thoughts with both patient and therapist. In addition, partners are actively involved in designing behavioral experiments to test (irrational) beliefs and are encouraged to take part in challenging the patient's assumptions. The results of partner-assisted cognitive behavior therapy were comparable to those of individual cognitive behavior therapy (Emanuels-Zuurveen & Emmelkamp, 1997). Both treatments led to statistically significant improvement on depressed mood, behavioral activity, and dysfunctional cognitions. However, none of the treatment formats affected relationship variables, which comes as no surprise, since couples were not maritally distressed prior to treatment. Thus, partner-assisted cognitive behavior therapy was as effective as individual cognitive behavior therapy.

Morbid Grief

When depression is caused by grief, alternative (behavioral) procedures may be indicated. Ramsay (1979) treated patients with pathological grief with a kind of imaginal prolonged exposure to bereavement cues and found this treatment to be effective in an uncontrolled series of 23 cases. Two controlled studies that investigated the value of exposure in morbid grief have been reported (Mawson, Marks, Ramm, & Stern, 1981; Sireling, Cohen, & Marks, 1988). In both studies, imaginal exposure (guided mourning) was found to be slightly superior to a treatment with anti-exposure instructions. Patients who had received anti-exposure instructions and who had been encouraged to undertake new activities and not to think about the loss (but to think about the future rather than to dwell on the past) improved markedly despite the continued avoidance of bereavement cues.

More recently, a number of other interventions have been developed to address the suffering of individuals who experience the loss of a loved one, and these interventions were reviewed by Kato and Mann (1999). Few studies led to clinically significant changes. As far as behavioral procedures are concerned, there is some evidence that trying to increase social activities may even have harmful effects. Other cognitive behavioral procedures such as cognitive restructuring, trauma desensitization, and behavioral skills training had no effect. An important flaw in the bereavement studies is that "stage of bereavement" has not been taken into account in the interventions used.

Behavioral Therapy versus Cognitive Therapy

A number of studies have evaluated the relative efficacy of cognitive therapy with various forms of behavior therapy. All studies (Boelens, 1990; Comas-Diaz, 1981; Scogin, Jamison, & Gochneaur, 1989; Thompson, Gallagher, & Steinmetz Breckenbridge, 1987; Wilson et al., 1983) found both forms of treatment more effective than no-treatment control or routine psychiatric treatment (Boelens, 1990; De Jong, Henrich, & Ferstl, 1981; Miller, Norman, Keitner, Bishop, & Dow, 1989). In none of these studies was one treatment (cognitive or behavioral) superior to the other. Similar results were reported by Gardner and Oei (1981), Zeiss et al. (1979), and Rokke, Tomhave, and Jocic, (1999), but in the last-named study patients were allowed to choose their treatment; thus, treatment allocation was not randomized. Also, in a recent meta-analysis, behavior therapy was found to be as effective as cognitive therapy (Gloaguen, Cottraux, Cucherat, & Blackburn, 1998). Since a variety of depressed patients were involved in these studies (i.e., outpatients, inpatients, geriatric patients, and low-socioeconomic Puerto Rican women) and the results were quite consistent across these populations, the finding that both treatments were equally effective is quite robust.

Boelens (1990) compared behavior therapy, cognitive therapy, and a combination of these methods and found no evidence that the combined procedure enhanced the effects of each treatment on its own. In a similar vein, Jacobson et al. (1996) compared complete cognitive behavioral therapy, behavioral activation alone, and behavioral activitation with automatic thought modification. CBT was no more effective than behavioral activation alone or behavioral activitation with thought modification, at post-test, or at the two-year followup (Gortner, Gollan, Dobson, & Jacobson, 1998).

A question of some interest is whether cognitive therapy and behavior therapy have differential effects on cognitive and behavioral variables. Although a number of studies were designed to show that these treatments have specific effects on relevant targets, the results are rather negative. Generally, relevant behavioral and cognitive variables are changed as much by cognitive therapy as by behavior therapy (e.g., Boelens, 1990; De Jong et al., 1981; Jacobson et al., 1996; Thompson et al., 1987; Zeiss et al., 1979). Thus, there is no evidence that each treatment modality selectively influenced the specific target behaviors. Similarly, in the NIMH study comparing interpersonal psychotherapy, cognitive behavior therapy, and imipramine, hardly any mode-specific difference was found (Imber et al., 1990).

In sum, behavioral programs have shown statistically and clinically significant results in reduction of depression, change of thinking patterns, and improved social performance. Most studies were unable to show, however, that the target behavior directly addressed in the treatment modality was selectively affected. Rather, the effects of behavioral programs were "nonspecific," changing both behavioral and cognitive components, thus precluding conclusions with respect to the therapeutic processes responsible for the improvement.

One major problem in interpreting the results of cognitive therapy for depression concerns the behavioral components included in the "cognitive" package. Beck's cognitive therapy seeks to uncover dysfunctional depressogenic cognitions and to correct these cognitions by systematic "reality testing." Actually, this particular treatment approach is an amalgam of cognitive and behavioral interventions, including behavioral task assignments and assertiveness training. Very few studies used a "pure" cognitive condition (e.g., Boelens, 1990). Thus, it is questionable whether the positive effects of cognitive therapy should be ascribed to the cognitive elements of treatment, to the behavioral elements of treatments, or to nonspecific variables.

Various pharmacological interventions have long been established as the standard of treatment for major depression. Although a number of studies have compared the effects of drug treatment with cognitive therapy (e.g., DeRubeis, Gelfand, Tang, & Simons, 1999), relatively few studies have compared behavioral procedures with drug treatment. Hersen et al. (1984) found social skills training as effective as amitriptyline but no evidence that a combination of drug and social skills training was superior. McLean & Hakstian (1979, 1990) found behavior therapy more effective than amitriptilyne. Boelens et al. (1990), De Jong et al. (1981), and Miller et al. (1989) all found behavior therapy somewhat more effective than routine psychiatric treatment which included the prescription of drugs, usually tricyclic antidepressants.

It is generally assumed that treatment is effective only to the degree that it addresses a patient's specific problems and compensates for the deficit. Thus, social skills training is supposed to be the most effective with patients lacking in social skills, and cognitive therapy is supposed to be the most effective with patients characterized by dysfunctional cognitions. However, as reviewed by Rude and Rehm (1991), this is often not the case. In fact, a number of studies show an advantage for high-functioning subjects. There is a trend showing that assertive and well social functioning depressed patients react better to behavioral procedures, while patients with less maladaptive beliefs profit more from cognitive therapy.

Concluding Remarks

There is now increased evidence that cognitive and behavioral approaches are effective in alleviating depression in mildly to moderately depressed individuals, but no single approach has been found to be consistently superior. Unfortunately, long-term followup studies are relatively rare. Only a few studies have addressed the issue of maintenance of treatment effects. Generally, results are disappointing (Emmelkamp, 1994). In a recent study (Gortner et al., 1998), almost half of the patients who recovered by the end of treatment had suffered a relapse two years later. The principal finding of the present review is that a variety of cognitive behavioral procedures are successful in improving depression, but one cannot conclude that the specific components of treatment were responsible for improvement. This finding suggests that common elements in these treatment are responsible for the improvements achieved. Such common elements are a clear rationale, highly structured therapy, homework assignments, and the training in skills (either cognitive or behavioral) that the patients can utilize in handling his or her problems.

Sexual Dysfunctions

The next section involves a review of studies on treatment of sexual dysfunctions; controlled studies are discussed for male and female dysfunctions, respectively. According to DSM-IV, female sexual arousal disorder can be differentiated into "lifelong" versus "acquired" and into "generalized" versus "situational." A lifelong arousal disorder (orgasmic dysfunction) is defined as the condition in which a female has never experienced orgasm. Other female sexual dysfunctions include the sexual pain disorders vaginismus and dyspareunia. The male sexual arousal disorder is called male erectile disorder and can also be specified according to type (lifelong versus acquired and generalized versus situational). Other male dysfunctions are the male orgasmic disorder and premature ejaculation. Both males and females may suffer from a sexual desire disorder (hypoactive sexual desire disorder or sexual aversion disorder). Patients with inhibited sexual desire report a lack of desire in engaging in sexual activities or even aversion of sex. Problems of sexual desire are often not differentiated from other sexual complaints, which inhibits the generalizability of findings across patients.

Male Erectile Disorders

Exposure Programs

Based on the notion that erectile failure is associated with (performance) anxiety, a number of controlled studies have been reported that investigated the effectiveness of systematic desensitization (SD). Results of SD were no better than standard advice as far as performance was concerned (Kockott, Dittmar, & Nusselt, 1975), better than relaxation (Auerbach & Killman, 1977), and as effective as a Masters and Johnson program (Everaerd & Dekker, 1985; Mathews et al., 1976). Takefman and Brender (1984) attempted to investigate elements of the Masters and Johnson package. Half of the couples received a ban on sexual intercourse, whereas the other half received skills training in communication of sexual preferences. Both groups improved on erectile ability, but the minimal intervention provided, and the lack of a control group, make the results difficult to interpret.

Cognitive Therapy

Since psychogenic erectile failure has been assumed to be caused by performance anxiety, some have argued that dealing with such cognitions is a necessary prerequisite for successful treatment (e.g., Bach, Brown, & Barlow, 1999; Bancroft, 1997; Rosen, Leiblum, & Spector, 1994). Munjack et al. (1984) found some evidence that Rational Emotive Therapy (RET) was effective in reducing sexual anxiety and improving sexual intercourse. However, at followup six to nine months after the end of treatment, most men had fallen back. Everaerd and Dekker (1985) found RET to be as effective as sex therapy at post-test, but at followup the RET group was shown to be superior. Given the very high attrition rate from RET, results are difficult to interpret. Dekker, Dronkers, and Stafleu (1985) investigated the effects of a comprehensive program, focusing on irrational cognitions, sexual behavior, and social functioning. The treatment program consisted of RET, masturbation exercises (in the form of homework assignments), and social skills training. Treatment was conducted in groups. In two studies (Dekker et al., 1985; Everaerd, Dekker et al., 1982) this program led to improved sexual functioning of men with partners. In the Dekker et al. (1985) study, treatment was ineffective for men without a partner. If the primary problem was inhibited sexual desire, treatment was also found to be ineffective. Men who have never had sexual partners, or are not able to maintain a sexual relationship, may have comorbid interpersonal problems. For such partnerless men, interpersonal problems may be a better target for treatment than the sexual dysfunction per se.

Interpersonal Problems

Stravinsky et al. (1997) investigated (in single men) whether treatment focusing on the sexual dysfunction alone would be as effective as a treatment focusing on interpersonal problems or a combined approach in which both the sexual dysfunction and the interpersonal problems were dealt with. All three treatments were conducted in small groups, and all treatments were found to be more effective than no-treatment control. As far as sexual dysfunction was concerned, no differences between groups were found up to one-year followup. Nearly 80% of the patients who had received treatment focusing on the interpersonal problems no longer met the DSM-III-R criteria for sexual dysfunction at one-year followup, in contrast to 40% of patients receiving sex therapy only. The results of this study suggest that at least in a number of (single) men, sexual dysfunction may be the result of social anxiety.

Concluding Remarks

Summarizing the results of the psychological studies of erectile failure, we can draw a few conclusions. When averaging across studies, sex therapy results in improvements in about two-thirds of dysfunctional males. Gradual exposure in vivo to sexual situations as involved in Masters and Johnson's approach is an important element of treatment for male dysfunction. Whether the addition of masturbation exercises or cognitive restructuring would enhance treatment of a "conventional" Masters and Johnson program has not yet been investigated in controlled studies.

Surprisingly, findings from research into hormonal and physiological causes of male erectile disorders (Ackerman & Carey, 1995) on the one hand and findings from laboratory studies into cognitive and attentional factors on the other hand (Everaerd et al., 1999) have not led to a reconceptualization of cognitive behavioral sex therapy for men with erectile failure. Similarly, the finding that erectile dysfunction is often related to depressed affect (e.g., Araujo, Durante, Feldman, Goldstein, & McKinlay, 1998; Meisler & Carey, 1991; Mitchell, DiBartolo, Brown, & Barlow, 1998) has also not yet been taken into account in the treatment of erectile dysfunction.

Treatment for male sexual dysfunctions is now highly medicalized. A number of medical and surgical approaches (prostheses, intracorporal injection, constriction rings or vacuum pump devices, and oral medication) are now widely used in the treatment of erectile dysfunction. However, well-controlled studies of the long-term efficacy, impact on the partner, and effect on self-esteem of the male are lacking (Rosen & Leiblum, 1995). For example, although auto-injection may be effective, it is unacceptable for many couples and leads to high dropout rates. Comparisons of medical and behavioral approaches have not been reported.

Disorders in Ejaculation

Patients rarely refer themselves to treatment for retarded ejaculation, so no controlled studies have been reported for this type of problem. Premature ejaculation, on the other hand, is much more prevalent in clinical settings. Behavioral treatment for ejaculation disorder is based on the pause technique of Semans (1956). The patient is required to masturbate, and ejaculation has to be prevented by stopping the stimulation by the partner (or the patient himself) as the male feels that ejaculation is imminent. This sequence has to be repeated several times and also has to be practiced during intercourse (female superior position). This procedure can be expanded with sensate focus, the squeeze technique in which the partner squeezes the frenulum of the penis, thus preventing ejaculation, and with communication skills. Although four studies report favorable results using a combination of these techniques, a number of methodological problems preclude more definite conclusions about the effectiveness of this approach (O'Donohue, Swingen, Dopke, & Regev, 1999; St. Lawrence & Madakasira, 1992). There is also some evidence that very few men still profit from such a therapy at followup three years later (DeAmicis, Goldberg, LoPiccolo, Friedman, & Davies, 1985; Metz, Pryor, Nesvacil, Abuzzahab, & Koznar, 1997) or six years later (Hawton Catalan, Martin, & Fagg, 1986).

One of the problems associated with the studies in this area is that no differentiation is made between the etiological causes of premature ejaculation. Most behavior therapists once held that premature ejaculation in nearly all cases was caused by psychological factors. However, there are now good grounds to differentiate between biogenic and psychogenic premature ejaculation (e.g. Metz et al., 1997). Studies taking into account the etiology of the ejaculation disorder and matching medical interventions and psychological therapy to the biogenic and psychogenic nature of the ejaculation disorder are clearly needed. Furthermore, the combination of behavior therapy and pharmacotherapy is another area in which controlled studies are warranted (Balon, 1996).

Female Arousal Disorder and Inhibited Female Orgasm

Most studies in this area do not adequately define their sample in terms of female arousal or orgasmic disorder and hence will be discussed together. Moreover, given the fact that sexual desire disorder is relatively new, and most studies were conducted before 1990, information with respect to the sexual desire disorder is lacking in most reports.

Exposure Programs

Many articles have reported the effects of systematic desensitization in the treatment of female sexual dysfunctions and were reviewed in earlier editions of this *Handbook* (Emmelkamp, 1986, 1994) and by O'Donohue, Dopke, and Swingen (1997). Summarizing the results of studies that investigated the effects of systematic desensitization on female sexual dysfunctions, we can make the following conclusions. There is considerable evidence that systematic desensitization leads to anxiety reduction, but there is no evidence that systematic desensitization is more effective in reducing anxiety than other approaches such as sex education by means of a videotape, a Masters and Johnson program, or masturbation training. Unfortunately, a number of studies did not provide sufficient information to evaluate whether systematic desensitization leads to improved orgasmic functioning. When orgasmic functioning was evaluated, results of systematic desensitization were generally poor.

A number of studies have evaluated the effects of a Masters and Johnson program with dysfunctional women, generally resulting in enhanced sexual functioning. There is no evidence that testosterone enhances improvement. Furthermore, diazepam influences the effects of this sex therapy program negatively.

Masturbation Training

One question addressed by researchers is whether treatment of the couple is a necessary prerequisite for successful treatment. In contrast with Masters and Johnson, the idea behind masturbation training is that the woman herself is primarily responsible for the dysfunction and can do something about it. In this treatment, a graded series of exercises are used to enhance acceptance of the body and feeling of pleasure, eventually resulting in an orgasm by means of self-stimulation. Libman et al. (1984) compared this program applied to the dysfunctional woman only with couple sex therapy. There was some evidence that involvement of the partner enhanced treatment outcome. A number of other controlled studies have been conducted investigating the value of self-stimulation exercises in dealing with female orgasmic dysfunctions. Although a number of authors claim superior results with masturbation training in "preorgasmic groups" without any involvement of the partner (reviewed by Baucom, Shoham, Mueser, Diatuo, & Stickel, 1998; O'Donohue et al., 1997) closer scrutiny of the original data shows that this treatment does not generalize well to orgasms during intercourse (Hurlbert & Apt, 1995; Wakefield, 1987).

Hurlbert and Apt (1995) compared masturbation training and the coital alignment technique in 36 women who participated with their partner in a sexual enrichment workshop. The coital alignment technique (Eichel, Eichel, & Kule, 1988) is directed to full body contact during intercourse and alignment of the female genitalia to permit maximum stimulation throughout intercourse. Both groups also received assertiveness training exercises to enhance sexual communication skills and sensate focus exercises. Both conditions resulted in significant improvements in the number of orgasms experienced in partner-related activities, orgasm consistency in sexual intercourse, and orgasm strength. Women who received training in the coital alignment technique yielded a 56% increase in orgasm during sexual intercourse, whereas those women who received masturbation training yielded a 27% increase in orgasm during sexual intercourse. On other measures, the coital alignment technique was also more effective than masturbation training. However, it is questionable whether the results can be generalized to a clinically dysfunctional population.

In sum, when anxiety reduction is the therapeutic target, both desensitization procedures and a Masters and Johnson program have been shown to be effective. However, anxiety reduction hardly affected orgasmic capacity. Other methods that focus more directly on reaching orgasm (e.g., masturbation training and coital alignment technique) seem to be more effective in dealing with this target, at least with primary orgasmic failure, but not all clients accept this treatment approach. The greatest gains in terms of orgasm with partner can be expected with the coital alignment technique. Generally, results of sex therapy are more negative for secondary or situational orgasmic dysfunction (McCabe & Delaney, 1992). Whether the partner should be involved in sex therapy should not be dependent on the attitude of the therapist but on the wishes of the patient. If the goal of therapy is to experience orgasm with the partner, the partner should be involved in the therapy in one way or another (e.g., minimally by means of homework assignments). Unfortunately, most studies investigating the effects of masturbation training did not assess sexual anxiety, precluding conclusions with respect to anxiety reduction.

Vaginismus and Dyspareunia

Vaginismus is defined as recurrent or persistent involuntary spasm of the musculature of the vagina that interferes with coitus. Few studies have evaluated the outcome of sex therapy in females with vaginismus. Although some report rather positive results of an adapted Masters and Johnson program (Hawton & Catalan, 1990; Hawton, Catalan, Martin, & Fagg, 1986), results of the study of Clement and Schmidt (1983) were less positive. Whereas immediately after therapy penetration was no longer a problem in two-thirds of their patients, penetration re-occurred as a problem at subsequent followups. Furthermore, improvement with respect to penetration did not necessarily lead to enhanced sexual satisfaction. Controlled studies in this area are still lacking. Reissing, Binik, and Khalifé (1999) have cast serious doubts about the current conceptualization of vaginismus. They hold that women currently assessed as vaginismic can be better understood as suffering from either a vaginal penetration phobia or genital pain disorder.

Dyspareunia, defined as genital pain related to sexual intercourse, may result from vaginismus, lack of lubrication, or a variety of physical factors (Meana & Binnik, 1994). Although in cases of organic pathology medical or surgical interventions are needed, these interventions on their own (without additional sex therapy) generally do not result in successful intercourse (Rosen & Leiblum, 1995). Controlled studies of the effects of sex therapy with dyspareunia are lacking, which is surprising given the high prevalence of this disorder.

Behavioral Marital Therapy and Sex Therapy

Relationship factors are a major area of focus in current conceptualizations of sexual dysfunctions (Simkins-Bullock, Wildman, Bullock, & Sugrue, 1992). Couples' pretreatment communication level and females' sexual interest have been found to be related to treatment outcome in dysfunctional men (Hawton, Catalan, & Fagg, 1992). Pretreatment marital distress is also related to outcome (Baucom et al., 1998). A number of studies evaluated the differential effectiveness of a modified Masters and Johnson program and marital therapy, but results are inconclusive (for review, see Emmelkamp, 1994). Although some studies suggest that marital distress can be managed by focusing on the sexual problems, other studies indicate that treatment of the sexual problems will be enhanced by marital therapy. The results of studies into the additional value of marital therapy beyond sex therapy are difficult to interpret, owing to heterogeneity of dysfunctions included in the samples, differences in samples studied, and different measures used to assess marital distress.

Concluding Comment

A number of controlled studies have shown the short-term effectiveness of the behavioral sex therapies, but generally results are less substantial than originally claimed by Masters and Johnson. Few studies evaluated the long-term effectiveness of sex therapy. Masters and Johnson (1970) reported a followup of their patients up to five years after treatment and found results of treatment maintained. Other followup studies are less optimistic about the improvements achieved (reviewed by Emmelkamp, 1994; see also DeAmicis et al., 1985; Milan, Kilmann, & Boland 1988; Sarwer & Durlak, 1997). Assertions concerning the long-term efficacy of sex therapy do not seem to be warranted, given the high rate of attrition during treatment, the relatively high divorce rate, the limited participation in the followup studies, and the high number of patients receiving additional treatment in-between post-test and followup in a number of studies. Moreover, the effectiveness of sex therapy may be restricted to compliant couples without comorbid psychological problems and without too much marital distress (Hawton, 1995). Further research into prognostic variables is needed before more definitive conclusions are warranted.

Whether intensive treatment for sexual dysfunctions is justified remains questionable. There is some evidence (LoPicolo, Heiman, Hogan, & Roberts, 1985) that treatment with one therapist is as effective as treatment with two therapists as advocated by Masters and Johnson. In addition, in contrast to Masters and Johnson, who treated patients in daily sessions over a two-week period, most therapies are now conducted on a weekly basis. Finally, bibliotherapy may also be of value to a substantial number of patients with sexual dysfunctions, especially when bibliotherapy is combined with minimal intervention. In a recent meta-analysis, bibliotherapy resulted in an effect size of 0.68. Apart from the cost-effectiveness, bibliotherapy may have additional advantages by enhancing feelings of self-efficacy and problem-solving potential (van Lankveld, 1998).

Most studies reported were conducted in specialized sex clinics. Catalan, Hawton, and Day (1990) reported that of the 200 referrals for sex therapy, fewer than 40% entered treatment. Given the high dropout rate from sex therapy in such centers, it is questionable whether the results of treatment of individuals and couples treated in these clinics may be generalized to patients with sexual dysfunctions in mental health settings.

It was surprising, and slightly astonishing, to see that research on the effects of psychological treatment of sexual dysfunctions has apparently come to a stand-still. In doing literature searches in this area, only a few controlled studies were found in the past eight years, in contrast to earlier reviews of this area (Emmelkamp, 1986, 1994) when a number of controlled studies were reported from groups around the world. The lack of recent controlled outcome studies can hardly be attributed to the fact that the effects of sex therapies have been well established by well-controlled outcome studies. Actually, there are still few methodologically sound studies in this area (see O'Donohue et al., 1997, 1999 for methodological criticism).

Given the rise of medical interventions in this area, some researchers may have become disappointed in the effects of sex therapy. Hormonal therapy, vacuum devices, penile prosthetic devices, injections of papaverine and prostaglandin E, and certain drugs (e.g., yohimbine, viagra, antidepressants) all have been claimed to be of value (e.g., Balon, 1996; Carey & Johnson, 1996; McConaghy, 1996). However, such physical interventions are not the panacea for all sexual dysfunctions. Psychologists should continue to stress the biopsychosocial nature of sexual disorders and remain alert to a further medicalization of sexual dysfunctions. There is a clear need for studies investigating the effects of psychological therapies versus such medical interventions and combinations (e.g., Hartmann & Langer, 1993).

A number of researchers in this area have withdrawn to their laboratories to conduct basic research into sexual dysfunctions or have moved into other areas. Unfortunately, the results of these laboratory studies have not yet led to improved treatment programs. As an example, performance anxiety is generally held to be a main feature of sexual dysfunctions. However, laboratory research has not clearly demonstrated the negative effects of anxiety on sexual arousal. In contrast, a few studies indicate that anxiety actually may enhance sexual responses (e.g., Laan, 1994; Rowland, Cooper, & Heiman, 1995). As shown by a study of Palace (1995), an arousal-evoking film (danger situation) led to significant increases in both subjective and physiological sexual arousal in sexually dysfunctional women, which was further enhanced by the effects of false feedback. Unfortunately, this research has had little impact on the current practice of sex therapy.

Alcohol Abuse

Alcohol dependence is characterized by either tolerance (need for markedly increased amounts of alcohol to achieve the desired effect) or alcohol withdrawal symptoms after cessation or reduction in drinking. Considerable evidence supports a two-dimensional model of alcohol dependence, in which the dimensions differ on severity, psychopathology, and premorbid risk factors. Type A alcoholism is characterized by less severe alcohol dependence, less psychosocial impairment, later age of onset, lower heritability, fewer childhood risk factors, and less impulsive/antisocial behavior patterns than Type B (Ball, Jaffe, Crouse-Artus, Rounsaville, & O'Malley, 2000). These types are yet to receive much empirical attention in outcome research.

Aversive conditioning has long been used in the treatment of alcoholism, but interest has waned in the last decades. In recent years, the interest of clinicians and researchers has moved away from aversive conditioning methods to alternative cognitive behavioral methods.

Motivational Interviewing

Motivational interviewing is one of the most popular behavioral methods in the addiction field, although one might wonder what is exactly behavioral in this procedure. Motivational interviewing was developed by Miller (1983, 1996) and tries to influence the expectations and behavior of the substance abuser. This is achieved by an empathetic therapist who tries to help the patients to reach their own decisions with respect to the pros and cons of substance abuse by giving advice, clarification, and feedback. Thus, rather than being coercive or confrontational, the therapist helps the patient to become aware of the necessity for behavioral change and to convey the patient's responsibility in choosing whether and how to make changes. Motivational interviewing was found to be more effective than directive confrontational counseling (Miller, Benefield, & Tonigan, 1993). Although motivational interviewing originally was intended to be a prelude to treatment, it might also be used as a stand-alone treatment. Motivational interviewing has now been evaluated in a number of controlled studies either as "appetizer" or as stand-alone treatment. As far as enhancement of motivation and prevention of dropout is concerned, this procedure is more effective than other treatments, but only in less severely dependent drinkers (Noonan & Moyers, 1997). As stand-alone treatment, it was found to be as effective as cognitive behavior therapy and the 12-step approach.

Controlled Drinking

Although 25 years ago there was a near consensus that total abstinence was the only viable treatment goal, more recently the results of a number of studies have suggested that a substantial number of problem drinkers can learn and maintain a pattern of moderate and nonproblem drinking. Proponents of the abstinence goal for alcoholics hold that alcoholism is more or less an irreversible disease, as illustrated by the Alcoholics Anonymous insistence that its members are but "one drink away from a drunk." In the United States, controlled drinking has been a controversial issue, leading to unjustified accusations by supporters of the abstinence-oriented approach (Pendery, Maltzman, & West, 1982) of unscientific conduct of Sobell and Sobell (1984), pioneers of the controlled drinking program. There is now considerable evidence, however, that a substantial number of problem drinkers can drink without problems, even when the treatment focuses on total abstinence.

Controlled-drinking treatment programs typically involve self-monitoring of drinking, training in drinking rate control (e.g., expanding the time frame between drinks), goal setting, functional analysis of drinking behavior, including identifying high-risk situations, and instructions about alternatives to alcohol abuse.

A series of studies have evaluated this particular approach, and there is some evidence that this program is at least as effective as more traditional abstinence-oriented programs. Most controlled-drinking clients achieved moderation of alcohol use, and most abstinence-oriented clients failed to abstain but nonetheless moderated their drinking (Emmelkamp, 1994; Marlatt, Larimer, Baer, & Quigley, 1993; Miller, Leckman, Delaney, & Tinkom, 1992). More recently, Walters (2000) included 17 studies in a meta-analysis and found that behavioral self-control programs were more effective than no-treatment and at least as effective as abstinence-oriented programs, especially at followups of one year or longer. The followup findings are rather important because the proponents of the abstinence-oriented approach hold that the effects of controlled drinking programs are temporary. In addition, this meta-analysis does not support claims that abstinence-oriented programs achieve superior results to controlled-drinking programs in alcohol-dependent subjects rather than in problem drinkers. The proponents of the abstinence-oriented approach have further argued that the studies of controlled drinking have been conducted in academic centers not involving real clinical alcohol abusers. Walters (2000) meta-analyzed the results of 8 clinically representative studies, but this did not lead to different conclusions than those based on all 17 studies. Thus, there is considerable evidence that controlled-drinking may be a viable alternative for abstinence in a substantial number of patients. Further research is needed to investigate for which patients abstinence-oriented programs are better suited than controlled-drinking programs and vice versa.

Coping Skills Training and Relapse Prevention

Based on cognitive social learning theory, a number of cognitive behavioral treatments have been devised, including self-management programs, social skills training, cognitive restructuring, and problem solving. A central feature of these various methods is the development of coping skills to enable the patient to stop or control his/her drinking. These approaches are at least partly based on the assumption that alcoholism or problem drinking is a habitual, maladaptive way of coping with stress. Indeed, there is considerable evidence that relapse among alcoholics is related to high levels of stress, lack of coping resources (Moser & Annis, 1995), poor social support, and low self-efficacy (e.g., Miller, Westerberg, Harris, & Tonigan, 1996; Noone, Dua, & Markham, 1999). Even minor stressors and (lack of) social support were found to be related to craving in substance abuse patients (Ames & Roitzsch, 2000).

A clear advantage of cognitive behavioral programs is that they attempt to teach coping skills to deal with stressful events that occur after the end of treatment, although the emphasis placed on relapse prevention varies across the various programs. These programs have their roots in the seminal work of Marlatt (1996). Exposure to a heavy drinking model is likely to increase the risk of relapse and maintenance of heavy drinking. Marlat and Gordon (1980) reported that for alcoholics, 23% of relapses involved social pressure situations such as being offered a drink, and in another 29% of the cases, frustrating situations in which the individual was unable to express anger preceded drinking behavior. These findings suggest that social skills training may be a useful treatment procedure. Previous controlled studies on the effects of social skills training with alcoholics were reviewed in the earlier editions of this *Handbook* (Emmelkamp, 1986, 1994). The controlled studies in this area clearly showed beneficial effects of social skills training with previous drinkers. It was concluded that social skills training might be an important ingredient in multimodal treatment programs for socially anxious alcoholics who lack the necessary social skills.

Other techniques that are directed at relapse prevention include self-monitoring of substance abuse, identification of high-risk situations for relapse, strategies for coping with craving, and training in problem solving to deal with future lapses. Such multimodal relapse prevention programs were found to be more effective than no-treatment (Chaney, O'Leary, & Marlatt, 1978; O'Farrell, Choquette, Cutter, Brown, & McCourt, 1993). However, the results of comparative evaluations with other interventions, that is, interactional group therapy (Ito, Donovan, & Hall, 1988; Kadden, Cooney, Getter, & Litt, 1989) and supportive therapy (O'Malley et al., 1996) are inconclusive.

In a meta-analysis by Irvin, Bowers, Dunn, and Wang (1999), relapse prevention in substance abuse disorders resulted in a rather modest effect size (0.25) that tended to decrease over time. Relapse prevention was most effective in alcohol use disorders in contrast to drug use and smoking. Furthermore, relapse prevention was found to have more effect on psychosocial functioning than on alcohol use.

Although coping skills training has been found to be effective in a number of studies, it is unclear which components in the treatment package are responsible for the results achieved. Further studies are needed to determine which of the various components included in the treatment package (e.g., self-monitoring, the identification of high-risk situations, strategies for coping with craving, and training in problem solving) are the necessary ingredients for successful therapeutic outcome and prevention of relapse and which components are redundant. As noted by Miller, Andrews, Wilbourne, and Bennett (1998), there is much stronger support for the behavioral coping strategies than for cognitive restructuring.

Another area of interest is whether adjunctive medication may enhance the effects of coping skills training. There is some evidence that anti-craving drugs such as Naltrexone (a long-acting opioid antagonist) and Acamprosate (a drug acting on the inhibitory GABA system) attenuate drinking behavior in alcohol-dependent patients (Anton et al., 1999; O'Brien, 1996; O'Malley et al., 1996).

Treatment Matching

It has been hypothesized that drinking outcomes will be better if clients receive individualized treatment that addresses their specific needs. A number of studies have been conducted into treatment matching of alcoholics.

Kadden et al. (1989) randomly assigned alcoholics who had been treated as impatients to either a coping skills training or an interaction group therapy aftercare program. The group-administered coping skills training included problem solving, interpersonal skills, relaxation, and skills for coping with negative moods and urges to drink. Although both treatment formats were found to be equally effective, coping skills training was found to be more effective for subjects higher in sociopathy or psychopathology (Type B alcoholics). Interactional therapy was more effective for subjects lower in sociopathy. Nearly identical results were found at two-year followup (Cooney, Kadden, Litt, & Getter, 1991). In a study by Litt, Babor, Del Boca, Kadden, and Cooney (1992), Type B alcoholics also had better outcomes with coping skills than with interactional therapy, whereas the reverse was true for Type A's. The results of this study are consistent with the view that treatment should be matched to the patients' needs rather than providing uniform treatment to all alcoholics.

In the largest multicenter psychotherapy trial ever conducted, Project MATCH investigated which patient characteristics were related to beneficial outcomes in three different treatment programs. Two related randomized clinical trials were conducted, one with outpatients (N = 952) and the other with aftercare patients who had received inpatient or day hospital treatment (N = 774). Patients were followed up to three years after treatment (Project MATCH, 1998). Patients in both RCTs received either (1) 12 sessions of cognitive behavior therapy, (2) 12 sessions of 12-step enhancement therapy, or (3) four sessions of motivational enhancement therapy. All three conditions resulted in significant and sustained improvement on a range of alcohol-related outcome variables. All three types of interventions were equally effective. Unfortunately, very few significant matching predictors were found. The major results of the MATCH project are summarized in two publications (Project MATCH research group, 1997a, 1998). The predictor variables with the most compelling theoretical justification and strongest empirical support were designated "primary a priori matching variables." Less supported but promising matching variables were designated "secondary a priori matching variables." Only one out of ten primary variables (severity of psychiatric problem) was consistently related to outcome across the various time periods related to matching but not at three-years followup. Patients with low psychiatric severity as measured by the Addiction Severity Index had fewer abstinent days after CBT than after 12-step enhancement therapy, but only in the outpatient sample. Contrary to prediction, no significant differences were found among the three treatments for patients with moderate to severe psychological problems.

As for the secondary hypotheses (Project MATCH research group, 1997b), in the outpatient sample but not in the aftercare sample, hostility predicted better drinking outcome in the motivational enhancement therapy than in the CBT condition. Furthermore, 12-step enhancement therapy led to superior results in high alcohol-dependent patients; low-dependent patients did better in CBT but only in the aftercare sample.

Finally, Thevos, Roberts, Thomas, and Randall (2000) investigated social phobia and outcome in the MATCH study. It was hypothesized that social phobic alcoholics treated with CBT would have better drinking outcomes than social phobic alcoholics treated with Twelve-Step Facilitation Therapy (TSF). This hypothesis was partly supported. CBT was superior to TSF only in female social phobic alcoholics and only in the outpatient arm. No matching effects were noted in the aftercare arm.

In sum, despite the millions of dollars invested in the largest multicenter study ever, we still know little, if anything, with respect to treatment matching. No matching effect was observed in one arm of the study that was also present in the other arm. The major value of this mammoth project (which some have compared with the *Titanic!*) is not the finding on matching it was designed for, but the fact that a four-session motivational enhancement therapy was as effective as 12 sessions of CBT or 12-step enhancement therapy. Thus, the MATCH study provides us with arguments for a stepped care model in the treatment of alcohol dependence. Why not start with four sessions of motivational enhancement and provide one of the more intensive treatments only for those patients who did not benefit from the motivational enhancement treatment? Furthermore, the overall effectiveness of the 12-step enhancement therapy in the MATCH project comes as a surprise given the rather limited effectiveness of AA-approaches in randomized controlled studies (Kownacki & Shadish, 1999). Only one other study compared the effectiveness of 12-step treatment with cognitive behavior therapy (Crosby, Finney, & Moos, 1997); both treatments were found to be about equally effective and as effective as a combination of both approaches. Results are difficult to interpret since patients were not randomly assigned to the treatment conditions.

Communication Training and Spouse-Aided Therapy

Spouse-aided interventions with alcohol-dependent patients were once regarded as most appropriate for only a subset of clients with severe marital or family problems. These clients were presumed to be in an "alcoholic relationship" with a specific pathological marital structure and in need of distinct treatment interventions. Research now points in the direction of also involving a significant other across a broader spectrum of clients.

Within a behavioral framework, drinking is assumed to have a negative effect on communication between partners and marital satisfaction, and has also been linked to other marital issues like domestic violence and sexual dysfunction. Research has differentiated families of alcoholics from healthier control families in that the former typically manifest poor communication, organization, problem solving, conflict management, and affect regulation processes. However, comparing alcoholic couples to nonalcoholic but distressed couples revealed that the latter group was characterized by similar dysfunctional processes as the former. Alcoholic couples do differ from nonalcoholic couples in that they report more domestic violence. Even in nonalcoholic couples, more drinking is associated with increased violence. There is some evidence that specific behaviors of the spouse can function either as a cue or reinforcer for drinking or drug-taking behavior.

Communication Training

Following the earlier work of Azrin and his colleagues (e.g., Hunt & Azrin, 1973) in which behavioral family therapy was included in broad spectrum treatment programs, Monti et al. (1990) evaluated the effects of communication training more directly. Seventy-three hospitalized male alcoholics received, in addition to standard treatment, (1) cognitive behavioral mood management training, (2) individual communication training, or (3) communication training with a family member or close friend participating. The two communication skills groups included training in effective communication skills in general and in alcohol-specific situations. Cognitive behavioral mood management was designed to cope with negative emotions and desires to drink using cognitive restructuring, relaxation training, and stimulus control. Both communication training conditions were found to be significantly more effective than the cognitive behavioral mood management training. All three groups improved significantly in coping skills and showed reduced anxiety in both general and alcohol-specific situations. In additional analyses (Rohsenow et al., 1991), the two communication conditions were combined. The results of these analyses revealed that the level of initial skills deficit did not predict benefit from skills training. Anxious patients benefited as much as less anxious patients in communication training. The more cognitively oriented mood management training only benefited alcoholics who had higher education and were less anxious.

Longabaugh, Wirtz, Beattie, Noel, and Stout (1995) investigated the relationship between patient characteristics and differential emphasis on relationship enhancement. They compared various treatment conditions with more or less focus on relationship enhancement. A brief exposure to relationship enhancement with an emphasis on increasing the patient's own coping skills was found to be the treatment of choice both in the least problematic couples and in highly problematic relationships. On the other hand, extended relationship enhancement therapy was found to be most effective with patients who were either highly invested in unsupportive relationships or less invested in highly supportive relationships. When there were no relationship difficulties, relationship enhancement was probably ineffective since it focused on a nonexisting problem; when the relationship is too problematic, relationship enhancement is futile. If replicated, the results may provide important clinical guidelines for making matching predictions for the needed doses of relationship enhancement in a cognitive behavioral program.

Spouse-Aided Therapy

In general, behavioral couple treatment for alcohol use disorders focuses on self-control and coping skills to facilitate and maintain abstinence, improving spouse coping with drinking-related situations, improving relationship functioning in general, and improving functioning within other social systems in which the couple is currently involved. The degree of emphasis on each of these four domains and the techniques used to target these domains varies across different treatment protocols. Two well-known protocols are the ones used in the Harvard Counseling for Alcoholics' Marriages (CALM) project by Timothy O'Farrell and the Alcohol Behavioral Couple Treatment (ABCT) protocol used by Barbara McCrady (McCrady, Stout, Noel, Abrams, & Nelson, 1991). The main differences between these two protocols are that O'Farrell's treatment is designed to be used conjointly or subsequent to a treatment focusing on cessation of drinking, whereas the treatment developed by McCrady is designed as a stand-alone treatment. Also, part of the CALM treatment is delivered in a group format, whereas McCrady's treatment is delivered during individual couple sessions.

Some techniques often used in these treatments are the sobriety or Antabuse contract to reduce conflict and distrust between the couple, identifying high-risk situations and teaching both partners alternative skills to cope with these situations, as well as improving communication between the partners by using role-playing to reduce conflict, enhance marital satisfaction, and reduce the chance of relapse.

O'Farrell, Cutter, and Floyd (1985) found 10 sessions of BMT significantly more effective than an interactional couples therapy group and no-treatment control, particularly on marital adjustment. Further evidence showing the greater effectiveness of BMT over individual therapy was provided by O'Farrell et al. (1996). O'Farrell, Kleinke, and Cutter (1998) hypothesized that sexual impotence is caused by both prolonged heavy drinking and relationship conflict, and they expected that BMT would restore sexual functioning more than individual counseling would. This hypothesis was not, however, supported by the results of their study.

Domestic violence and marital violence are common in alcohol-dependent populations. Although the therapy did not focus on violence, BMT reduced the occurrence of domestic violence considerably (O'Farrell & Murphy, 1995). In successfully treated couples, in which the patient was no longer dependent on alcohol, the risk of domestic violence was not greater than that in the community at large.

McCrady et al. (1991) found that behavioral marital therapy was more effective than spouse-aided therapy focusing on the alcohol problem only, in terms of both drinking behavior and marital satisfaction. In a later study, McCrady, Epstein, and Hirsch (1996) compared 15 sessions of BMT as sole treatment with BMT plus AA involvement and BMT plus relapse prevention; all treatments were found to be about equally effective. In a related study on the same sample, Raytek, McCrady, Epstein, and Hirsch (1999) found that experienced therapists developed better therapeutic alliances in BMT than less experienced therapists (advanced graduate students in clinical psychology). The quality of the therapeutic alliance and the therapists' competence was found to be related to number of sessions attended and dropout of treatment: couples were more compliant and less inclined to prematurely stop the intervention with more experienced therapists.

A study by Sobell, Sobell, and Leo (2000) is of some interest. In their spouse-aided CBT program, half of the spouses were encouraged to provide social support and were trained in how to cope with a lapse on the part of their partner, while the other half of the spouses did not receive such instructions. Both treatment programs were found to be equally effective until one-year followup. Marital stability was found to be positively related to success of treatment. In studies of the natural recovery of alcohol abusers, social support, especially from a spouse, was significantly related to successfully changing the drinking behavior. Finally, there is some evidence that restoring marital satisfaction and reducing conflicts reduce the chance for relapse (Emmelkamp & Vedel, 2002).

Engaging clients in treatment is a serious problem in the addiction field. A number of interventions have been claimed to be successful in assisting partners or concerned significant others to motivate the alcoholic individual to change his/her drinking behavior and to undergo treatment. A recent study (Miller, Meyers, & Tonigan, 1999) compared the effectiveness of three unilateral strategies: (1) encouragement of involvement in the 12-step program of AA, (2) confrontational family meetings, and (3) community reinforcement and family treatment (CRAFT). In the last-named approach, participants were trained to raise the awareness of the alcohol problem using motivational interviewing, reinforce nondrinking, enhance communication skills, plan competing activities, and deal with high-risk situations. The CRAFT program was the most successful of the three strategies in engaging alcoholic individuals in treatment.

Cue Exposure

Siegel (1983) suggested that drug cues may serve as conditioned stimuli for a compensatory response (opposite in direction to the unconditioned drug effect) that compensates for the impending unconditioned drug response. In alcoholics, this compensatory response would probably be an aversive state and could be interpreted as craving. Since Siegel's study, many addiction theories have assumed that craving plays a central role in the acquisition and maintenance of drug dependence and in relapse (Tiffany & Conklin, 2000). Based on these theories, cue exposure programs have been developed.

After the pioneering work of Rankin, Hodgson, and Stockwell (1983) looking into the effects of cue exposure in alcoholics, there is now substantial evidence in favor of cue exposure as (part of) a cognitive behavioral intervention for alcohol problems. Cue-exposure treatment, involving exposing patients to the sight and smell of alcohol during the treatment sessions and response prevention of drinking afterward, has resulted in changes in drinking behavior in problem drinkers (Drummond & Glautier, 1994; Monti & Rohsenow, 1999). Furthermore, increased physiological reactivity in the presence of alcohol cues has been associated with decreased time to relapse following cue exposure treatment (Drummond & Glautier, 1994; Rohsenow et al., 1994).

However, it is questionable whether exposure to the sight and smell of alcohol alone provides functional exposure. Laberg and Ellertsen (1987) showed that exposure to alcohol per se did not elicit craving. Increased autonomic arousal and craving were found only in subjects given alcohol and exposed to more available alcohol. Similarly, Sitharthan, Sitharthan, Hough, and Kavanaugh (1997) found that an exposure program consisting of sight and smell cues and small priming doses of alcohol in a supervised setting was effective in problem drinkers. Further studies directly comparing alcohol-related cues with priming doses of alcohol as cues in the cue exposure program are needed.

Cue exposure can be understood in terms of both classical and operant conditioning. Although it is usually explained in terms of habituation, it is likely that cognitive factors (e.g., self-efficacy and outcome expectancies) are also involved. Cue exposure makes the patient aware that an urge to continue drinking can be weakened and may enhance self-efficacy in naturally occurring risk situations (Staiger, Greeley, & Wallace, 1999). However, cue exposure may be less effective when the risk situation is dissimilar to the exposure situation (Monti & Rohsenow, 1999).

The relevance of the craving model for alcohol dependence is still being investigated. Ames and Roitzch (2000) found that 64% of an inpatient sample did not experience craving. A recent meta-analysis on substance abusers revealed that alcoholics had a significantly smaller craving effect size compared to cigarette smokers, cocaine addicts, and heroin addicts (Carter & Tiffany, 1999).

Comorbidity

Considerable evidence has been collected showing that a substantial number of alcohol-dependent patients also fulfill the criteria for an anxiety disorder, most often panic disorder (Kushner, Abrams, & Brochardt, 2000). Given the fact that having a comorbid panic disorder enhanced the probability of relapse in treated alcoholics (Tomasson & Vaglum, 1996), it is tempting to assume that dual treatments focusing on both the alcohol dependence and the panic disorder might be profitable for these patients. Bowen, D'Arcy, Keegan, and Stenhilsel (2000) evaluated whether a cognitive behavioral treatment for panic disorder would enhance the effects of the regular alcoholism program in alcohol-dependent inpatients with comorbid panic disorder. Unfortunately, the addition of 12 hours of CBT directed at panic and agoraphobia led to enhanced outcome on neither drinking measures nor mood and anxiety symptoms.

Depression is highly prevalent among individuals with alcohol dependence. Given the finding that depressed mood is often an important trigger of relapse (Marlatt, 1996), Brown, Evans, Miller, Burgess, and Mueller (1997) investigated whether CBT focusing on depression could enhance the effects of routine alcohol treatment and prevent relapse. At 6-months followup, 47% of the patients who had been treated for their depression as well as for the alcohol problem were completely abstinent as compared to 13% of the control patients, who had received the standard alcohol treatment plus relaxation.

The co-occurrence of alcohol abuse and personality disorders has been established in epidemiological and clinical studies. Although the presence of a personality disorder may predict relapse (Verheul, van den Brink, & Hartgers, 1998), the influence of personality disorders on the effects of specific behavioral programs has not been investigated.

Drug Abuse

Motivational interviewing was found to be a useful adjunct to methadone treatment in drug abusers (Saunders, Wilkinson, & Phillips, 1995). Drug abusers (N = 122) received either motivational interviewing or psychoeducation. At six-months followup the patients who had received motivational interviewing experienced less relapse than the patients in the control condition.

Coping Skills Training and Relapse Prevention

Coping skills training has also been used for patients with drug abuse, primarily in order to prevent relapse. In cocaine-dependent patients, relapse prevention based on cognitive behavioral principles was found to be more effective than interpersonal psychotherapy and clinical management (Carroll, Rounsaville, & Gawin, 1991; Carroll et al., 1994a). In the studies by Carroll and colleagues, the superiority of relapse prevention was significant only for the more severe cocaine users. Furthermore, cocaine-dependent patients with a comorbid depressive disorder treated with cognitive behavior therapy had better outcomes than patients without a depressive disorder (Carroll, Nich, & Rounsaville, 1995). In a more recent study on cocaine abusers who were also alcohol dependent, relapse prevention was found to be superior to clinical management but not to a 12-step enhancement program. No differences were found between relapse prevention and the 12-step enhancement program for either alcohol abuse or cocaine abuse (see Carroll, Nich, Ball, McCance, and Rounsaville, 1998).

In a study of cocaine abusers by Wells, Peterson, Gainey, Hawkins, and Catalano (1994), relapse prevention was not found to be more effective than a 12-step recovery support group: both treatments led to a considerable reduction in cocaine use at the six-month followup. However, the 12-step patients showed significantly greater increases than the relapse prevention patients in alcohol use from 12 weeks to the six-month followup. Although in the McKay et al. (1997) study, group counseling based on the 12-step enhancement proved to be superior in terms of total abstinence, relapse prevention resulted in less relapse than the counseling group. Furthermore, relapse prevention fared better in limiting the extent of cocaine use in the patients still using.

Relapse prevention in marijuana users led to rather disappointing results: only 15% of the patients were abstinent at one-year followup (Stephens, Roffman, & Simpson (1994).

Contingency Management and Community Reinforcement Approach

Contingency management, based on operant conditioning, is particularly useful for drug abusers. In contingency management the program's tangible reinforcers (vouchers) are provided when the desired behavior is shown; they are withheld when the desired behavior does not occur. In these programs, various target behaviors have been used (e.g., drug abstinence, medication compliance, or attendance at therapy sessions). Contingency management procedures have been found to be effective in cocaine-dependent patients (Higgins & Wong, 1998), opioid dependent patients (e.g., Bickel, Amass, Higgins, Badger, and Esch, 1997; Gruber, Chutuape, & Stitzer, 2000; Silverman et al., 1996b; Stitzer, Iguchi, & Felch, 1992) and have also led to a reduced use of marijuana (Petry, 2000).

It is not the delivery of the reinforcer per se but the *contingent* delivery of reinforcer that is effective. Stitzer et al. (1992) evaluated methadone take-home privileges as a reward for decreased illicit drug use and found take-home privileges that were contingent on drug-free urines more beneficial than noncontingent take-home privileges. Similarly, Silverman et al., in a study of cocaine-abusing patients (1996a), found that contingent delivery of reinforcers based on drug-free urine screens resulted in a 42% abstinence rate (at least 10 weeks), whereas that was only the case for 17% of the yoked control patients, who received the reinforcers noncontingently.

Although contingency management procedures have been found to be effective across various drug abusers, most effects have been demonstrated immediately after treatment. Higgins et al. (1995) found that most of the results of contingency management were not maintained until followup. Thus, there is a clear need for long-term followup studies in this area. Furthermore, contingency management is usually embedded in the Community Reinforcement Approach (Azrin, 1976). In this individualized treatment, the therapist systematically alters the drug user's environment so that reinforcement density from nondrug sources is relatively high during sobriety and low during drug use (Higgins & Wong, 1998). The Community Reinforcement Approach involves an amalgam of techniques, including training in social skills and/or drug refusal skills, cognitive behavioral marital therapy, procedures to support medication compliance, and vocational counseling for the unemployed. Higgins et al. (1995) found the Community Reinforcement Approach plus contingent vouchers treatment to result in slightly better results at followup than the Community Reinforcement Approach alone, but this was not corroborated in the urinalysis results.

A comprehensive behavioral program, evaluated by Azrin et al. (1994), was an extension of the Community Reinforcement Approach and consisted of (1) stimulus control procedures to eliminate stimuli that were predecessors of drug use and to increase activities incompatible with drug use, (2) urge control procedures to interrupt internal stimuli associated with drug use, and (3) social control procedures, wherein abstinence was assisted through significant others. In addition, a number of other procedures could be used, including specific social skills training, relationship enhancement, problem solving training, and vocational counseling, if needed. The effects of this behavioral program were compared with those of a nonbehavioral group program. The behavioral program was clearly superior to the nonbehavioral treatment, in terms of both reduction of cocaine use (assessed with urinalysis) and depressed mood.

Cue Exposure

Relatively few studies have evaluated the effects of cue exposure on illicit drug users (e.g., Childress et al., 1993; Powell, Bradley, & Gray 1993). Although these studies show that cue exposure results in statistically significant decreases in (subjective) craving in opiate addicts, the *clinical* relevance of cue exposure as a treatment for drug addicts and its long-term effects has still to be investigated.

Spouse-Aided Therapy

Fals-Stewart, Birchler, and O'Farrell (1996) and Fals-Stewart et al. (2000) investigated the value of behavioral couples therapy in male drug abusers. The addition of behavioral couples therapy to individual behavioral therapy enhanced the effects of individual behavioral therapy as sole treatment. Results were stable until one-year followup. More couples in the individual behavioral therapy showed significant deterioration than couples who had received spouse-aided therapy at one-year followup.

Matching

Matching has received relatively little attention in the area of illicit drug abuse. However, a few studies have investigated the influence of prognostic variables on treatment outcome. There is substantial evidence that severity of the cocaine addiction is related to dropout of treatment and less effective treatment outcome (Alterman, McKay, Mulvaney, & McLellan, 1996; Carroll et al., 1991; Carroll, Power, Bryant, & Rounsaville, 1993). Bad outcome is further predicted by current alcohol dependence (Carroll et al., 1993, 1994b) and higher psychiatric symptom severity at intake as assessed by the Addiction Severity Index (Carroll et al., 1991, 1993). Good outcome is predicted by self-efficacy and commitment to abstinence (McKay et al., 1997).

SCHIZOPHRENIA

Schizophrenia is a severe illness marked by positive symptoms (hallucinations and delusions) and negative symptoms (emotional withdrawal and poor social functioning). In the early days of behavior therapy, the emphasis was on the application of operant conditioning with psychiatric inpatients. In the tradition of operant conditioning, token economies were devised for chronic psychiatric inpatients (Paul & Lentz, 1977). The increased evidence that biological factors are involved in schizophrenia led the behavior therapists to lose interest in this disorder. More recently, however, it has been recognized that schizophrenia does not belong solely to the domain of biological psychiatry. Many schizophrenics do not take their medication after discharge or do not respond to it, even to the newer antipsychotics. Furthermore, medication alone is inadequate in treating problems in social functioning. Although such medication is important in managing the acute phase of the disorder, their main impact is on positive symptoms like hallucinations and delusions rather than on the negative symptoms as interpersonal deficits and social withdrawal. Many schizophrenics on adequate dosages of medication still experience considerable problems in social functioning. Thus, there is a clear need for alternative approaches that may be effective in remedying the problems left untouched by medication.

Zubin and Spring (1977) formulated a diathesis stress model for understanding schizophrenia in which it is assumed that some individuals are born with a biological vulnerability for developing schizophrenia. Only if the individual does not have the biological capacity to deal with stress will the illness develop or will relapses occur. An inability to cope in the social environment is thought to be a significant source of stress and to contribute to an exacerbation of symptoms (psychotic episode). If the model is correct, coping skills training (to deal more adequately with stressors) could have something to offer to such patients. Four types of interventions have been developed to teach the patient or his family how to deal more adequately with stress: social skills training, family education, cognitive behavior therapy, and cognitive rehabilitation. In the last decade, these types of interventions have been empirically evaluated in a number of controlled studies.

Social Skills Training

Many schizophrenics are characterized by deficits in social functioning that begin in childhood. Even when the positive psychotic symptoms react favorably to medication, most schizophrenics will still exhibit severe social skills deficits. In social skills training (SST), patients are trained in basic skills, such as conversation skills and assertiveness, in order to respond to stressors more adequately and thus reduce the stress. SST aims to improve the quality of life by increasing the individual's social competence. Improving the social competence is an important goal because it is an important predictor of the course and outcome of schizophrenia (Strauss & Carpenter, 1977). SST with schizophrenics is usually conducted in small groups and consists of structured training of interpersonal competencies by means of instruction, modeling, behavior rehearsal, in vivo exercises in the community, and feedback. Of recent interest is the transfer of learned skills to a variety of situations in the natural environment. Other innovations in these programs involve medication self-management, recreational skills, and training in social problem solving, in addition to training in basic conversation skills and assertiveness. Studies evaluating the effects of SST training with schizophrenics have been reviewed by Dilk and Bond (1996), Heinssen, Liberman, and Kopelowicz (2000), and Penn and Mueser (1996). Generally, SST led to significant improvements in social skills on role-play tests, but not on psychopathology. However, in the studies conducted in hospital settings, treatment results hardly generalized to novel situations. More recently, these programs have been adapted for use in short-term inpatient programs directed at community reentry and in day treatments.

The UCLA Social and Independent Living Skills training modules are highly structured educational training modules that teach patients a broad range of skills in community functioning, including symptom management, basic conversation skills, and medication management. Another recent development is more intensive, longer-term skills projects. In recent studies reviewed by Heinssen et al. (2000), weekly training varied from 150 to 720 minutes, followed by less intensive training (60 to 90 minutes each week) during a prolonged followup period. The improvements achieved were maintained up to two years after treatment (Liberman et al., 1998). Although brief SST was minimally superior to control interventions, there is some evidence that more intensive SST is more effective than supportive psychotherapy (Marder et al., 1996) and occupational therapy (Liberman et al., 1998) on social adjustmnent and independent living skills. Furthermore, schizophrenics with cognitive deficits, as evidenced by poorer performance on neurocognitive tests, may have significant deficits in skill acquisition (Kopelowicz, Liberman, Mintz, & Zarate, 1996).

Family Intervention

Since schizophrenia usually develops in late adolescence or early adulthood, the family of origin is often the patient's most important social network. There is now increasing evidence that high expressed emotion (EE) by family members of the patient, including high criticism, hostility, and overinvolvement, is probably stressful for schizophrenics. As shown by Tarrier and Barrowclough (1990), schizophrenics living with family members characterized by high levels of EE are two times as likely to relapse as are patients not living in high EE households. Given this state of affairs, it is not surprising that family intervention programs have been designed to change relatives from high to low EE.

In contrast to social skills training which focuses on improving patients' coping efforts, the behavioral family training programs are designed to improve the relatives' coping efforts and to reduce negative affect toward the patient. The best known programs are those of Falloon, Boyd, and McGill (1984) in the United States, consisting of an educational program, communication training, and problem-solving training, and those of Tarrier and his colleagues in the UK. This program also involves an educational program, coping skills training, and problem solving. Dixon, Adams, and Lucksted (2000), Lehman and Steinwachs (1998), and Penn and Mueser (1996) have reviewed the effects of these programs. The main conclusions of these reviews are as follows.

There is substantial evidence that behavioral family intervention combined with maintenance neuroleptic medication is effective in reducing the relapse rate of schizophrenics in the first year of discharge; relapse can be forestalled, but not prevented; behavioral interventions are superior to routine care and educational programs alone; interventions need to be long term, at least nine months; reduction in relapse is associated with change in the relatives' EE levels from high to low (Tarrier et al., 1994); family interventions are associated with reduced family burden. Thus, the results on the effects of behaviorally oriented family intervention are highly encouraging.

Cognitive Rehabilitation

Schizophrenics are characterized by attentional deficits and deficits in social perception and can hardly be distinguished on neuropsychological tests from individuals with brain injury. Impairments in neurocognitive functioning are believed to underlie the problems in social perception and social skills. It has been argued that training that focuses on cognitive functioning deficits and social perception should be included in behavioral programs. In the studies on social skills training and behavioral family therapy, variations in the cognitive deficits of patients have been neglected. Presumably, behavioral approaches have to be modified for patients with severe cognitive deficits.

Brenner et al. (1995) designed a treatment program (Integrated Psychological Therapy), in which cognitive function training was combined with social skills training. Integrated Psychological Therapy resulted in improved cognitive functioning and reduced psychopathology (Brenner et al., 1995). Spaulding, Reed, Sullivan, Richardson, and Weiler (1999) investigated whether Integrated Psychological Therapy would enhance patients' responses to standard psychiatric rehabilitation. Cognitive rehabilitation enhanced improvement in social competence, in contrast to supportive therapy, which did not result in any additional benefit. Another form of cognitive rehabilitation was investigated by Velligan et al. (2000). In their cognitive adaptation training, patients were trained in compensatory strategies to bypass neurocognitive impairments. Compensatory strategies include the use of signs, labels, and electronic devices designed to cue and sequence appropriate behaviors. Outpatients with schizophrenia who received cognitive adaptation training did better than those in the control condition, in terms of adaptive functioning and reduction of psychopathology. In other studies, more limited cognitive rehabilitation (attentional training) resulted in marginal improvements only (Benedict et al., 1994; Kern, Green, Goldstein, 1995).

Studies that investigate whether the addition of cognitive functioning training enhances the effects of social skills training programs are now needed.

Cognitive Behavior Therapy

Over the last decade, behavior therapy procedures for schizophrenia have also included cognitive approaches. Cognitive behavior therapy for schizophrenia has been developed in the United Kingdom. Although there are some differences between various programs, most programs seek to reduce the stresses of individuals with schizophrenia, strengthen adaptive coping skills, and focus directly on the patient's psychotic symptoms, but psychotic beliefs are not directly confronted. The emphasis is on gently challenging the patient's underlying cognitive assumptions and reality testing. The therapy usually includes a number of behavioral strategies such as relaxation, anxiety management, problem solving, and activity planning.

In controlled studies with patients with acute psychosis, this intervention was more effective than other therapies (Drury et al., 1996a, 1996b). At nine-month followup, 95% of the CBT group and 44% of the control group reported no or only minor hallucinations or delusions. However, at five-year followup most differences between groups had disappeared (Dickerson, 2000). Hallucinations and delusions were still significantly less in the CBT group as compared to the other condition. Haddock et al. (1999), who also studied patients with acute psychosis, failed to replicate the results of this study.

In the program developed by Tarrier and colleagues, the emphasis is on coping strategy enhancement (CSE) in chronic schizophrenic patients. This program was supported in two controlled studies (Tarrier et al., 1993, 1998). In the Tarrier et al. (1998) study, 33% of the CSE patients, 14% of the patients who received supportive counseling, and 11% of the 28 patients in the routine care group had a 50% reduction in positive symptoms, but this differential result was not maintained at one-year followup (Tarrier et al., 1999). Another controlled study into CBT was reported by Garety et al. (1997). The CBT group was superior to the standard care group on the Brief Psychiatric Rating Scale up to 18-months followup: 65% in the CBT condition showed a reliable clinical improvement compared with 18% for the control group (Kuipers et al., 1998). Finally, Sensky et al. (2000) compared CBT with nondirective therapy, with an equal amount of sessions spaced at similar intervals. Patients were medication refractory schizophrenic patients. At the end of treatment, there were no significant differences between the two interventions. At 9-month followup, however, the CBT condition was clearly superior to the nonspecific condition. The results achieved are impressive and clinically relevant. CBT resulted in a reduction on the Schizophrenia Scale of the Comprehensive Psychiatric Rating Scale (CPRS) from 10.7 at pretest to 4.0 at followup. In addition, a substantial reduction was achieved on negative symptoms. Turkington and Kingdon (2000) also compared cognitive behavior therapy with nondirective therapy in routine clinical care. Cognitive behavior therapy was superior to nondirective therapy.

Although the results of these studies are very promising, they should be qualified. In the controlled studies discussed above, a number of patients were excluded because of a variety of cognitive deficits, manifested exclusively in negative symptoms, medication noncompliance, or substance abuse. Therefore, the patients who are the most ill may be unable to benefit from this approach (Dickerson, 2000).

PERSONALITY DISORDERS

Personality disorders (PDs) have been neglected in the behavioral literature until recently. In the 1960s and 1970s, hardly any study on behavior therapy referred to PD. At this time, PD had a vague psychodynamic connotation, and behavior therapists were inclined to ignore this part of the patient's problems. Since the introduction of DSM-III (APA, 1987) in which the PDs were described atheoretically, many behavior therapists increasingly acknowledged that a number of patients were actually suffering from a PD or had one or more PDs as a comorbid condition. For example, in Foa and Emmelkamp's (1983) volume on failures in behavior therapy, a number of contributors admitted, albeit reluctantly, that personality problems could impede the success of behavior therapy in a number of disorders or could lead to dropping out of treatment. PDs are now conceptualized as maladaptive behavioral interaction patterns, and the etiology is interpreted in terms of social learning processes. Although clinical behavior therapists have gradually accepted the concept of PD, this concept was still not acceptable in some academic circles (Pretzer, 1994).

Given this state of affairs, it is not surprising that research into the behavioral and cognitive therapy of PDs is just beginning. Very few outcome studies have been conducted, which evaluate the effects of behavior therapy in patients with PD, most of which were uncontrolled. In the few controlled studies that have been conducted, encouraging results have been achieved with behavior therapy in chronically suicidal borderline patients and in patients with avoidant personality disorder.

Avoidant Personality Disorder

Most studies have been conducted with patients with avoidant PD (Alden, 1989; Cappe & Alden, 1986; Stravinsky, Marks & Jule, 1982). The results of these studies show that various behavioral strategies (exposure and social skills training) are more effective than no-treatment control. However, results are usually modest to moderate. Renneberg, Goldstein, Phillips and Chambless (1999), in an uncontrolled study, found that results were maintained up to one-year followup. Alden (1989) found that skills training did not enhance the effects of exposure in vivo. However, Alden and Capreol (1993) found that interpersonal profiles might be related to outcome. Patients who had interpersonal problems related to distrustful and angry behavior benefited from the graduated exposure procedure but not from social skills training, whereas patients who experienced interpersonal problems related to being coerced and controlled by others benefited equally from exposure and social skills training.

Borderline Personality Disorder

Two controlled studies have evaluated the effects of behavior therapy in patients with borderline personality disorder. Liberman and Eckman (1981) compared behavior therapy with insight-oriented psychotherapy in patients who had made repeated suicide attempts. Behavior therapy was found to be more effective than psychodynamic psychotherapy. Linehan, Armstrong, Suarez, Allmon, and Heard (1991) compared dialectical behavior therapy with care as usual. One year of behavior therapy led to less attrition, less parasuicidal behavior, and fewer days of hospitalization than the control condition. Dialectical behavior therapy has also been successfully applied in an inpatient setting (Bohus et al., 2000), but this study did not include adequate controls.

Concluding Remarks

Very few controlled studies have been reported evaluating the effects of behavior therapy with PD, but the results found are encouraging. The studies have been limited to avoidant personality disorder and borderline personality disorder. Although now and then case studies are reported evaluating the contribution of behavior therapy in other personality disorders (e.g., Persons & Bertagnolli, 1994; Turkat & Maisto, 1995; Turner & Hersen, 1991), controlled studies are needed before conclusions with respect to the beneficial effects of behavior therapy with respect to the other personality disorders can be made.

SUMMARY AND CONCLUSIONS

Research on behavioral-based treatments for anxiety disorders has clearly and consistently shown the positive effects of interventions. The effects of exposure in vivo are now well established for agoraphobia, simple phobia, social phobia, and obsessive-compulsive disorders. Studies of the behavioral and cognitive treatment of depression represent one of the more exciting areas of clinical research. The progression of research in this area has advanced our knowledge, but a number of important issues remain. For example, we have no idea why cognitive therapy, behavioral interventions, IPT, and pharmacotherapy work equally well with depressed patients, although various researchers provide various theoretical explanations. Unfortunately, to date there is no evidence that either cognitive or behavioral theories explain the improvements achieved with these various treatment procedures.

In the area of substance abuse, the interest has moved away from aversive procedures into multifaceted self-control programs. One of the promising areas for future research is relapse prevention. The results of studies that investigated coping skills programs to prevent relapse look promising. Another new area that looks promising is spouse-aided therapy.

Behavioral techniques for sexual dysfunctions have hardly been investigated in the last decade. Evidence is emerging that casts doubt on the long-term usefulness of these approaches. Apparently, some researchers may have become disappointed in the effects of sex therapy, given the rise of medical interventions in this area. Psychologists should continue to stress the biopsychosocial nature of sexual disorders and remain alert to further medicalization of sexual dysfunctions. There is a clear need for studies investigating the effects of psychological therapies versus such medical interventions and their combination. An area that deserves further study is the treatment of paraphilias. Very few controlled studies have been published since an earlier review (Emmelkamp, 1994), and progress in this area has been minimal.

Although behavior therapists have been very productive in evaluating the efficacy of various techniques, relatively little attention has been devoted to the therapeutic process. It is, however, becoming increasingly clear that the quality of the therapeutic relationship may be influential in determining the success or failure of behavioral therapies, although well-controlled studies in this area are rare. It is a common misconception that behavior therapists are "unempathic" and apply only techniques.

Studies evaluating the outcome of behavioral techniques whose effects have already been established for the "average" patient are not likely to produce new knowledge. Studies investigating conditions leading to success or failure of these techniques are highly needed. The therapeutic relationship seems to be one area where future research efforts are needed. Presumably, the results of such research programs may eventually lead to preventing failure in a substantial number of cases.

Author Note

Thanks are due to Ellen Vedel and Wiljo van Hout for the assistance in preparing this chapter.

References

Abramowitz, J. S. (1997). Variants of exposure and response prevention in the treatment of obsessive-compulsive disorder: A meta-analysis. *Behavior Therapy, 27,* 583–600.

Abramowitz, J. S. (1998). Does cognitive-behavioral therapy cure obsessive-compulsive disorder? A meta-analytic evaluation of clinical significance. *Behavior Therapy, 29,* 339–355.

Ackerman, M. D., & Carey, M. P. (1995). Psychology's role in the assessment of erectile dysfunction: Historical precedents, current knowledge, and methods. *Journal of Consulting and Clinical Psychology, 63,* 862–876.

Albucher, R. C., Abelson, J. L., & Nesse, R. M. (1998). Defense mechanism changes in successfully treated patients with obsessive-compulsive disorder. *American Journal of Psychiatry, 155,* 558–559.

Alden, L. (1989). Short-term structured treatment for avoidant personality disorder. *Journal of Consulting and Clinical Psychology, 56,* 756–764.

Alden, L., & Capreol, M. J. (1993). Avoidant personality disorder: Interpersonal problems as predictors of treatment response. *Behavior Therapy, 24,* 357–376.

Alterman, A. I., McKay, J. R., Mulvaney, F. D., & McLellan, A. T. (1996). Prediction of attrition from day hospital treatment in lower socioeconomic cocaine-dependent men. *Drug and Alcohol Dependence, 40,* 227–233.

American Psychiatric Association. (1994). *DSM-IV: Diagnostic statistical manual of mental disorder* (4th ed.). Washington, DC: Author.

Ames, S. C., & Roitzsch, J. C. (2000). The impact of minor stressful life events and social support on cravings: A study of inpatients receiving treatment for substance dependence. *Addictive Behaviors, 25,* 539–547.

Amir, N., Freshman, M., & Foa, E. B. (2000). Family distress and involvement in relatives of obsessive-compulsive disorder patients. *Journal of Anxiety Disorders, 14,* 209–217.

Anton, R. F., Moak, D. H., Waid, R., Latham, P. K., Malcolm, R. J., & Dias, J. K. (1999). Naltrexone and cognitive behavioral therapy for the treatment of outpatient alcoholics: Results of a placebo-controlled trial. *American Journal of Psychiatry, 156,* 1758–1764.

Araujo, A. B., Durante, R., Feldman, H. A., Goldstein, I., & McKinlay, J. B. (1998). The relationship between depressive symptoms and male erectile dysfunction: Cross-sectional results from the Massachusetts Male Aging Study. *Psychosomatic Medicine, 60,* 458–465.

Arean, P. A., Perri, M. G., & Nezu, A. M. (1993). Comparative effectiveness of social problem-solving therapy and reminiscence therapy as treatment for depression in older adults. *Journal of Consulting and Clinical Psychology, 61,* 1003–1010.

Arntz, A., & van den Hout, M. (1996). Psychological treatment of panic disorder without agoraphobia: Cognitive therapy versus applied relaxation. *Behaviour Research and Therapy, 34,* 113–121.

Auerbach, R., & Killman, P. R. (1977). The effects of group systematic desensitization on secondary erectile failure. *Behavior Therapy, 8,* 330–339.

Azrin, N. H. (1976). Improvements in the community reinforcement approach to alcoholism. *Behaviour Research and Therapy, 14,* 339–348.

Azrin, N. H., McMahon, P. T., Donahue, B., Besalel, V. A., Lapinski, K. J., Kogan, E. S., Acierno, R. E., & Galloway, E. (1994). Behavior therapy for drug abuse: A controlled treatment outcome study. *Behaviour Research and Therapy, 32,* 857–866.

Bach, A. K., Brown, T. A., & Barlow, D. H. (1999). The effects of false negative feedback on efficacy expectancies and sexual arousal in sexually functional men. *Behavior Therapy, 30,* 79–95.

Bachofen, M., Nakagawa, A., Marks, I. M., Park, J. M., Greist, J. H., Baer, L., Wenzel, K. W., Parkin, J. R., & Dottl, S. L. (1999). *Journal of Clinical Psychiatry, 60,* 545–549.

Baker, A. L., & Wilson, P. H. (1985). Cognitive-behavior therapy for depression: The effects of booster sessions on relapse. *Behavior Therapy, 16,* 335–344.

Bakker, A., van Balkom, A.J.L.M., Spinhoven, P., Blaauw, B.M.W.J., & van Dyck, R. (1998). Follow-up on the treatment of panic disorder with or without agoraphobia: A Quantitative review. *Journal of Nervous and Mental Disease, 186,* 414–419.

Ball, S. A., Jaffe, A. J., Crouse-Artus, M. S., Rounsaville, B. J., & O'Malley, S. S. (2000). Multidimensional subtypes and treatment outcome in first-time DWI offenders. *Addictive Behaviors, 25,* 167–181.

Balon, R. (1996). Antidepressants in the treatment of premature ejaculation. *Journal of Sex and Marital Therapy, 22,* 85–96.

Bancroft, J. (1997). Sexual problems. In D. M. Clark & C. G. Fairburn (Eds.), *Science and practice of cognitive behaviour therapy* (pp. 243–257). Oxford: Oxford University Press.

Barlow, D. H., Craske, M., Cerny, J., & Klosko, J. (1989). Behavioral treatment of panic disorder. *Behavior Therapy, 20,* 261–282.

Barlow, D. H., Gorman, J. M., Shear, M. K., & Woods, S. W. (2000). Cognitive-behavioral therapy, imipramine, or their combination for panic disorder: A randomized controlled trial. *Journal of the American Medical Association, 283,* 2529–2536.

Barlow, D. H., Rapee, R. M., & Brown, T. A. (1992). Behavioral treatment of generalized anxiety disorder. *Behavior Therapy, 23,* 551–570.

Baucom, D. H., Shoham, V., Mueser, K. T., Daiuto, A. D., & Stickle, T. R. (1998). Empirically supported couple and family interventions for marital distress and adult mental health problems. *Journal of Consulting and Clinical Psychology, 66,* 53–88.

Beach, S.R.H. (2001). *Marital and family processes in depression.* Washington, DC: American Psychological Association.

Beach, S.R.H., & O'Leary, K. D. (1992). Treating depression in the context of marital discord: Outcome and predictors of response for marital therapy versus cognitive therapy. *Behavior Therapy, 23,* 507–528.

Beck, A. T., & Emery, G. (1985). *Anxiety disorders and phobias: A cognitive perspective.* New York: Basic Books.

Beck, A. T., Sokol, L., Clark, D. A., Berschick, R., & Wright, F. (1992). A cross-over study of focused cognitive therapy for panic disorder. *American Journal of Psychiatry, 149,* 778–783.

Beck, J. G., Stanley, M. A., Baldwin, L. E., Deagle, E. A., & Averill, P. M. (1994). Comparison of cognitive therapy and relaxation training for panic disorder. *Journal of Consulting and Clinical Psychology, 62,* 818–826.

Bellack, A. S., Hersen, M., & Himmelhoch, J. M. (1983). A comparison of social-skills training, pharmacotherapy and psychotherapy for depression. *Behavior Research and Therapy, 21,* 101–108.

Benedict, R.H.B., Harris, A. E., Markow, T., McCormick, J. A., Nuechterlein, K. H., & Asarnow, R. F. (1994). Effects of attention training on information processing in schizophrenia. *Schizophrenia Bulletin, 20,* 537–546.

Bickel, W. K., Amass, L., Higgins, S. T., Badger, G. J., & Esch, R. A. (1997). Effects of adding behavioral treatment to opioid detoxification with buprenorphine. *Journal of Consulting and Clinical Psychology, 65,* 803–810.

Biglan, A., & Craker, D. (1982). Effects of pleasant-activities manipulation on depression. *Journal of Consulting and Clinical Psychology, 50,* 436–438.

Blaauw, E., & Emmelkamp, P.M.G. (1994). The therapeutic relationship: A study on the value of the Therapist Client Rating Scale. *Behavioural and Cognitive Psychotherapy, 22,* 25–35.

Blowers, C., Cobb, J., & Mathews, A. (1987). Generalized anxiety: A controlled treatment study. *Behaviour Research and Therapy, 25,* 493–502.

Boelens, W. (1990). Cognitieve en gedragstherapie bij depressie. Dissertation, University of Groningen.

Bohus, M., Haaf, B., & Stiglmayr, C. (2000). Evaluation of inpatient dialectical-behavioral therapy for borderline personality disorder—a prospective study. *Behaviour Research & Therapy, 38,* 875–887

Booth, R., & Rachman, S. (1992). The reduction of claustrophobia—I. *Behaviour Research and Therapy, 23,* 207–221.

Borkovec, T. D., & Costello, E. (1993). Efficacy of applied relaxation and cognitive-behavioral therapy in the treatment of generalized anxiety disorder. *Journal of Consulting and Clinical Psychology, 61,* 611–619.

Borkovec, T. D., Mathews, A. M., Chambers, A., Ebrahimi, S., Lytle, R., & Nelson, R. (1987). Effects of relaxation training with cognitive or nondirective therapy and the role of relaxation-induced anxiety in the treatment of generalized anxiety. *Journal of Consulting and Clinical Psychology, 55,* 883–888.

Bouchard, S., Gauthier, J., Laberge, B., French, D., Pelletier, M., & Godbout, D. (1996). Exposure versus cognitive restructuring in the treatment of panic disorder with agoraphobia. *Behaviour Research and Therapy, 34,* 213–224.

Boudewyns, P. A., Hyer, L., Woods, M. G., Harrison, W. R., & McCronie, E. (1990). PTSD among Vietnam veterans: An early look at treatment outcome using direct therapeutic exposure. *Journal of Traumatic Stress, 3,* 359–368.

Bowen, R. C., D'Arcy, C., Keegan, D., & Stenhilsel, van A. (2000). A controlled trial of cognitive behavioral treatment of panic in alcoholic inpatients with comorbid panic disorder. *Addictive Behaviors, 25,* 593–597.

Brenner, H. D., Roder, V., Hodel, B. M., Kienzie, N., Reed, D., & Liberman, R. P. (1995). *Integrated psychological therapy for schizophrenic patients.* Bern: Hogrefe & Huber.

Brody, A. L., Saxena, S., Schwartz, J. M., Stoessel, P. W., Maidment, K., Phelps, M. E., & Baxter, L. R. (1998). FDG-PET predictors of response to behavioral therapy and pharmacotherapy in obsessive-compulsive disorder. *Psychiatry Research: Neuroimaging, 84,* 1–6.

Brown, R. A., Evans, D. M., Miller, I. W., Burgess, E. S., & Mueller, T. I. (1997). Cognitive-behavioral treatment for depression in alcoholism. *Journal of Consulting and Clinical Psychology, 65,* 715–726.

Brown, T. A., Antony, M. M., & Barlow, D. H. (1995). Diagnostic co-morbidity in panic disorder: Effect on treatment outcome and course of comorbid diagnoses following treatment. *Journal of Consulting and Clinical Psychology, 63,* 408–418.

Bruce, T. J., Spiegel, D. A., Gregg, S. F., & Nuzzarello, A. (1995). Predictors of alprazolam discontinuation with and without cognitive behavior therapy in panic disorder. *American Journal of Psychiatry, 152,* 1156–1160.

Bryant, R. A., Harvey, A. G., Dang, S. T., Sackville, T., & Basten, C. (1998). Treatment of acute stress disorder: A comparison of cognitive-behavioral therapy and supportive counseling. *Journal of Consulting and Clinical Psychology, 66,* 862–866.

Bryant, R. A., Sackville, T., Dang, S. T., Moulds, M., & Guthrie, R. (1999). Treating acute stress disorder: An evaluation of cognitive behavior therapy and supportive counseling techniques. *American Journal of Psychiatry, 156,* 1780–1768.

Burke, M., Drummond, L. M., & Johnston, D. W. (1997). Treatment choice for agoraphobic women: Exposure or cognitive therapy? *British Journal of Clinical Psychology, 36,* 409–420.

Butler, G., Fennell, M., Robson, P., & Gelder, M. (1991). Comparison of behavior therapy and cognitive behavior therapy in the treatment of generalized anxiety disorder. *Journal of Consulting and Clinical Psychology, 59,* 167–175.

Butler, G., Gelder, M., Hibbert, G., Cullington, A., & Klimes, I. (1987). Anxiety management: Developing effective strategies. *Behaviour Research and Therapy, 25,* 517–522.

Cahill, S. P., Carrigan, M. H., & Frueh, B. C. (1999). Does EMDR work? *Journal of Anxiety Disorders, 13,* 5–33.

Cappe, R., & Alden, L. E. (1986). A comparison of treatment strategies for clients functionally impaired by extreme shyness and social avoidance. *Journal of Consulting and Clinical Psychology, 54,* 796–801.

Carey, M. P., & Johnson, B. T. (1996). Effectiveness of yohimbine in the treatment of erectile disorders: Four meta-analytic integrations. *Archieves of Sexual Behavior, 25,* 341–360.

Carroll, K. M., Nich, C., & Rounsaville, B. J. (1995). Differential symptom reduction in depressed cocaine abusers treated with psychotherapy and pharmacotherapy. *Journal of Nervous and Mental Disease, 183,* 251–259.

Carroll, K. M., Nich, C., Ball, S. A., McCance, E., & Rounsaville, B. J. (1998). Treatment of cocaine and alcohol dependence with psychotherapy and disulfiram. *Addiction, 93,* 713–727.

Carroll, K. M., Power, M. D., Bryant, K., & Rounsaville, B. J. (1993). One-year follow-up of treatment seeking cocaine abusers: Psychopathology and dependence severity as predictors of outcome. *Journal of Nervous and Mental Disease, 181,* 71–79.

Carroll, K. M., Rounsaville, B. J., & Gawin, F. H. (1991). A comparative trial of psychotherapies for ambulatory cocaine abusers: Relapse prevention and interpersonal psychotherapy. *American Journal of Drug and Alcohol Abuse, 17,* 229–247.

Carroll, K. M., Rounsaville, B. J., Gordon, L. T., Nich, C., Jatlow, P., Bisinghini, R. M., & Gawin, F. (1994a). Psychotherapy and pharmacotherapy for ambulatory cocaine abusers. *Archives of General Psychiatry, 51,* 177–187.

Carroll, K. M., Rounsaville, B. J., Nick, C., Gordon, L. T., Wirtz, P. W., & Gawin, F. (1994b). One-year follow-up of psychotherapy and pharmacotherapy for cocaine dependence: Delayed emergence of psychotherapy effects. *Archives of General Psychiatry, 51,* 989–997.

Carter, B. L., & Tiffany, S. T. (1999). Meta-analysis of cue-reactivity in addiction research. *Addiction, 94,* 327–340.

Castle, D. J., Deale, A., Marks, I. M., & Cutts, F. (1994). Obsessive-compulsive disorder: Prediction of outcome from behavioural psychotherapy. *Acta Psychiatrica Scandinavia, 89,* 393–398.

Catalan, M., Hawton, K., & Day, A. (1990). Couples referred to a sexual dysfunction clinic: Psychological and physical morbidity. *British Journal of Psychiatry, 156,* 61–67.

Cerny, J. A., Barlow, D. M., Craske, M. G., & Himadi, W. G. (1987). Couples treatment of agoraphobia: A two-year follow-up. *Behavior Therapy, 18,* 401–415.

Chambless, D. L., & Gillis, M. M. (1993). Cognitive therapy of anxiety disorders. *Journal of Consulting and Clinical Psychology, 61,* 248–260.

Chambless, D. L., & Steketee, G. (1999). Expressed emotion and behavior therapy outcome: A prospective study with obsessive-compulsive and agoraphobic outpatients. *Journal of Consulting and Clinical Psychology, 67,* 658–665.

Chaney, E. F., O'Leary, M. R., & Marlatt, G. A. (1978). Skill training with problem drinkers. *Journal of Consulting and Clinical Psychology, 46,* 1092–1104.

Childress, A. R., Hole, A. V., Ehrman, R. N., Robbins, S. J., McLellan, A. T., & O'Brien, C. P. (1993). Cue reactivity and cue reactivity interventions in drug dependence. In L. S. Onken, J. D. Blaine, &

J. J. Boren (Eds.), *Behavioral treatment for drug abuse and dependence.* Rockville, MD: National Institute on Drug Abuse.

Christensen, H., Hadzi-Pavlovic, D., Andrews, G., & Mattick, R. (1987). Behavior therapy and tricyclic medication in the treatment of obsessive-compulsive disorder: A quantitative review. *Journal of Consulting and Clinical Psychology, 55,* 701–711.

Clark, D. M. (1986). A cognitive approach to panic. *Behavior Research and Therapy, 24,* 461–470.

Clark, D. M. (1991). Cognitive therapy for panic disorder. Paper presented at the NIH Consensus Development Conference on Treatment of Panic Disorder, September 1991, Washington, DC.

Clark, D. M., Salkovskis, P. M., & Chalkley, A. J. (1985). Respiratory control as a treatment for panic attacks. *Journal of Behavior Therapy and Experimental Psychiatry, 16,* 23–30.

Clark, D. M., Salkovskis, P. M., Hackman, A., Middleton, H., Anastasiades, P., & Gelder, M. (1994). A comparison of cognitive therapy, applied relaxation and imipramine in the treatment of panic disorder. *British Journal of Psychiatry, 164,* 759–769.

Clement, U., & Schmidt, G. (1983). Long-term results and limitations of outcome. In G. Arentewicz & G. Schmidt (Eds.), *The treatment of sexual disorders: Concepts and techniques of couple therapy.* (pp. 123–146). New York: Basic Books.

Clum, G. A., Clum, G., & Surls, R. (1993). A meta-analysis of treatments for panic disorder. *Journal of Consulting and Clinical Psychology, 61,* 317–326.

Cobb, J. P., Mathews, A. A., Childs-Clarke, A., & Blowers, C. M. (1984). The spouse as co-therapist in the treatment of agoraphobia. *British Journal of Psychiatry, 144,* 282–287.

Comas-Diaz, L. (1981). Effects of cognitive and behavioral group treatment on the depressive symptomatology of Puerto Rican women. *Journal of Consulting and Clinical Psychology, 49,* 627–632.

Cooney, N. L., Kadden, R. M., Litt, M. D., & Getter, H. (1991). Matching alcoholics to coping skills or interactional therapies. Two-year follow-up results. *Journal of Consulting and Clinical Psychology, 59,* 598–601.

Cooper, N. A., & Clum, G. A. (1989). Imaginal flooding as a supplementary treatment for PTSD in combat veterans. A controlled study. *Behavior Therapy, 20,* 381–391.

Cote, G., Gauthier, J. G., Laberge, B., & Cormier, H. J. (1994). Reduced therapist contact in the cognitive behavioral treatment of panic disorder. *Behavior Therapy, 25,* 123–145.

Cottraux, J., Messy, P., Marks, I., & Mollard, E. (1993). Predictive factors in the treatment of obsessive-compulsive disorders with fluvoxamine and/or behaviour therapy. *Behavioural Psychotherapy, 21,* 45–50.

Cottraux, J., Note, I., Albuisson, E., Yao, S. N., Note, B., Mollard, E., Bonasse, F., Jalenques, I., Guerin, J., & Coudert, A. J. (1997). Cognitive behavior therapy versus supportive therapy in social phobia: A randomized controlled trial. *Psychotherapy and Psychosomatics, 69,* 137–146.

Cox, B. J., Swinson, R. P., Morrison, B., & Lee, P. S. (1993). Clomipramine, fluoxetine, and behaviour therapy in the treatment of obsessive-compulsive disorder: A meta-analysis. *Journal of Behavior Therapy and Experimental Psychiatry, 24,* 149–153.

Craske, M. G. (1999). *Anxiety disorders. Psychological approaches to theory and treatment.* Boulder, Co: Westview Press.

Craske, M. G., Maidenberg, E., Bystritsky, A. (1995). Brief cognitive-behavioral versus nondirective therapy for panic disorder. *Journal of Behavior Therapy and Experimental Psychiatry, 26,* 113–120.

Craske, M. G., Rowe, M., Lewin, M., & Noriega-Dimitri, R. (1997). Interoceptive exposure versus breathing retraining within cognitive-behavioural therapy for panic disorder with agoraphobia. *Journal of Clinical Psychology, 36,* 85–99.

Crosby Quimette, P., Finney, J. W., & Moos, R. H. (1997). Twelve-step and cognitive-behavioral treatment for substance abuse: A comparison of treatment effectiveness. *Journal of Consulting and Clinical Psychology, 65,* 230–240.

De Amicis, L. A., Goldberg, D. C., LoPiccolo, J., Friedman, J. M., & Davies, L. (1985). Clinical follow-up of couples treated for sexual dysfunction. *Archives of Sexual Behavior, 14,* 467–489.

De Araujo, L. A., Ito, L. M., Marks, I. M., & Deale, A. (1995). Does imagined exposure to the consequences of not ritualising enhance live exposure for OCD? A controlled study. *British Journal of Psychiatry, 167,* 65–70.

de Haan, E., van Oppen, P., van Balkom, A., Spinhoven, P., Hoogduin, K., & van Dyck, R. (1997). Prediction of outcome and early vs. late improvement in OCD patients treated with cognitive behaviour therapy and pharmacotherapy. *Acta Psychiatrica Scandinavica, 96,* 354–361.

De Jong, R., Henrich, G., & Ferstl, R. (1981). A behavioral treatment program for neurotic depression. *Behavioural Analysis and Modifications, 4,* 275–287.

Dekker, J., Dronkers, J., & Stafleu, J. (1985). Treatment of sexual dysfunctions in male-only groups: Predicting outcome. *Journal of Sex and Marital Therapy, 11,* 80–90.

DeRubeis, R. J., Gelfand, L. A., Tang, T. Z., & Simons, A. D. (1999). Medications versus cognitive behavior therapy for severely depressed outpatients: Mega-analysis of four randomized comparisons. *American Journal of Psychiatry, 156,* 1007–1013.

Devilly, G. J., & Spence, S. H. (1999). The relative efficacy and treatment distress of EMDR and a cognitive-behavior trauma treatment protocol in the amelioration of posttraumatic stress disorder. *Journal of Anxiety Disorders, 13,* 131–157.

Devilly, G. J., Spence, S. H., & Rapee, S. H. (1998). Statistical and reliable change with eye movement desensitization and reprocessing: Treating trauma within a veteran population. *Behavior Therapy, 29,* 435–455.

Dickerson, F. B. (2000). Cognitive behavioral psychotherapy for schizophrenia: a review of recent empirical studies. *Schizophrenia Research, 43,* 71–90.

Dilk, M. N., & Bond, G. R. (1996). Meta-analytic evaluation of skills training research for individuals with severe mental illness. *Journal of Consulting and Clinical Psychology, 64,* 1337–1346.

Dixon, L., Adams, C., & Lucksted, A. (2000). Update on family psychoeducation for schizophrenia. *Schizophrenia Bulletin, 26,* 5–20.

Dreessen, L., & Arntz, A. (1998). The impact of personality disorders on treatment outcome of anxiety disorders: Best-evidence synthesis. *Behaviour Research and Therapy, 36,* 483–504.

Dreessen, L., Hoekstra, R., & Arntz, A. (1997). Personality disorders do not influence the results of cognitive and behavior therapy for obsessive compulsive disorder. *Journal of Anxiety Disorders, 11,* 503–521.

Drummond, D. C., & Glautier, S. (1994). A controlled trial of cue exposure treatment in alcohol dependence. *Journal of Consulting and Clinical Psychology, 62,* 809–817.

Drury, V., Birchwood, M., Cochrane, R., & MacMillan, F. (1996a). Cognitive therapy and recovery from acute psychosis: A controlled trial. I. Impact on psychotic symptoms. *British Journal of Psychiatry, 169,* 593–601.

Drury, V., Birchwood, M., Cochrane, R., & MacMillan, F. (1996b). Cognitive therapy and recovery from acute psychosis: A controlled trial. II. Impact on recovery time. *British Journal of Psychiatry, 169,* 602–607.

Durham, R. C., Murphy, T., Allan, T., Richard, K., Treliving, L. R., & Fenton, G. W. (1994). Cognitive therapy, analytic psychotherapy and anxiety management training for generalised anxiety disorder. *British Journal of Psychiatry, 165,* 315–323.

Durham, R. C., & Turvey, A. A. (1987). Cognitive therapy vs behaviour therapy in the treatment of chronic general anxiety. *Behavior Research and Therapy, 25,* 229–234.

Ehlers, A., & Margraf, J. (1989). The psychophysiological model of panic attacks. In P.M.G. Emmelkamp, W. Everaerd, F. Kraaimaat, & M. van Son (Eds.), *Fresh perspectives on anxiety* (pp. 1–29). Amsterdam: Swets.

Eichel, E. W., Eichel, J. D., & Kule, S. (1988). The technique of coital alignment and its relation to female orgasmic response and simultaneous orgasm. *Journal of Sex and Marital Therapy, 14,* 129–141.

Emanuels-Zuurveen, L., & Emmelkamp, P.M.G. (1996). Individual behavioral-cognitive therapy vs. marital therapy for depression in martially distressed couples. *British Journal of Psychiatry, 169,* 181–188.

Emanuels-Zuurveen, L., & Emmelkamp, P.M.G. (1997). Spouse-aided therapy with depressed patients. *Behavior Modification, 21,* 62–77.

Emmelkamp, P.M.G. (1982). *Phobic and obsessive-compulsive disorders: Theory, research and practice.* New York: Plenum.

Emmelkamp, P.M.G. (1986). Behavior therapy. In S. Garfield & A. Bergin (Eds.), *Handbook of psychotherapy and behavior change* (3rd ed.) (pp. 385–442). New York: John Wiley & Sons.

Emmelkamp, P.M.G. (1990). Anxiety and fear. In A. S. Bellack, M. Hersen, & A. E. Kazdin (Eds.), *International handbook of behavior modification and therapy* (2nd ed.) (pp. 283–306). New York: Plenum.

Emmelkamp, P.M.G. (1994). Behavior therapy with adults. In Bergin & S. Garfield (Eds.), *Handbook of psychotherapy and behavior change* (4th ed.). New York: John Wiley & Sons.

Emmelkamp, P.M.G., & Beens, H. (1991). Cognitive therapy with obsessive-compulsive disorder: A comparative evaluation. *Behaviour Research and Therapy, 29,* 293–300.

Emmelkamp, P. M. G., Bouman, T., & Blaauw, E. (1994). Individualized versus standardized therapy: A comparative evaluation with obsessive-compulsive patients. *Clinical Psychology & Psychotherapy, 1,* 95–100.

Emmelkamp, P.M.G., Bouman, T. K., & Scholing, A. (1993). *Anxiety disorders: A practitioner's guide.* Chichester: John Wiley & Sons.

Emmelkamp, P. M. G., Brilman, E., Kuiper, H., & Mersch, P. P. A. (1986). Agoraphobia: A comparison of self-instructional training, rational emotive therapy and exposure in vivo. *Behavior Modification, 10,* 37–53.

Emmelkamp, P.M.G., Bruynzeel, M., Drost, L., & van der Mast, C.A.P.G. (2001). Virtual reality exposure in acrophobia: A comparison with exposure in vivo. *CyberPsychology and Behavior, 4,* 335–339.

Emmelkamp, P.M.G., de Haan, E., & Hoogduin, C.A.L. (1990). Marital adjustment and obsessive-compulsive disorder. *British Journal of Psychiatry, 156,* 55–60.

Emmelkamp. P.M.G., & Felten, M. (1985). The process of exposure in vivo: cognitive and physiological changes during treatment of acrophobia. *Behaviour Research and Therapy, 23,* 219–223.

Emmelkamp, P.M.G., & Gerlsma, C. (1994). Marital functioning and the anxiety disorders. *Behavior Therapy, 25,* 407–429.

Emmelkamp, P.M.G., Kloek, J., & Blaauw, E. (1994). Obsessive-compulsive disorder. In P. Wilson (Ed.), *Relapse prevention* (pp. 213–234). New York: Guilford Press.

Emmelkamp, P.M.G., Krijn, M., Hulsbosch, L., de Vries, S., Schuemie, M. J., & van der Mast, C.A.P.G. (2002). Virtual reality treatment versus exposure in vivo: A comparative evaluation in acrophobia. *Behaviour Research and Therapy* (in press).

Emmelkamp, P. M. G., Kuipers, A., & Eggeraat, J. (1978). Cognitive modification versus prolonged exposure in vivo: A comparison with agoraphobics. *Behaviour Research and Therapy, 16,* 33–41.

Emmelkamp, P. M. G., & Mersch, P. P. A. (1982). Cognition and exposure in vivo in the treatment of agoraphobia: Short-term and delayed effects. *Cognitive Therapy and Research, 6,* 77–90.

Emmelkamp, P.M.G., Van der Helm, M., van Zanten, B., & Plochg, I. (1980). Contributions of self-instructional training to the effectiveness of exposure in vivo. A comparison with obsessive-compulsive patients. *Behaviour Research and Therapy, 18,* 61–66.

Emmelkamp, P.M.G., Van Dyck, R., Bitter, M., Heins, R., Onstein, E. J., & Eisen, B. (1992). Spouse-aided therapy with agoraphobics. *British Journal of Psychiatry, 160,* 51–56.

Emmelkamp, P.M.G., van Oppen, P., & van Balkom, A. (2000). Cognitive changes in patients with obsessive-compulsive rituals treated with exposure in vivo and response prevention. In R. Frost & G. Steketee (Eds.), *Obsessive compulsive beliefs* Amsterdam: Elsevier (in press).

Emmelkamp, P.M.G., & Vedel, E. (2002). Spouse-aided therapy. In M. Hersen & W. Sledge (Eds.), *The Encyclopedia of psychotherapy.* New York: Academic Press.

Emmelkamp, P.M.G., Visser, S., & Hoekstra, R. J. (1988). Cognitive therapy vs exposure in vivo in the treatment of obsessive-compulsives. *Cognitive Therapy and Research, 12,* 103–144.

Everaerd, W.T.A.M., & Dekker, J. (1985). Treatment of male sexual dysfunction: Sex therapy compared with systematic desensitization and rational emotive therapy. *Behaviour Research and Therapy, 23,* 13–24.

Everaerd, W.T.A.M., Dekker, J., Dronkers, J., Van der Rhee, K., Stafleu, J., & Wisselius, G. (1982). Treatment of homosexual and heterosexual dysfunction in male-only groups of mixed sexual orientation. *Archives of Sexual Behavior, 11,* 1–10.

Everaerd, W., Laan, E., & Spiering, M. (2000). Male sexuality. In L. Szuchman & F. Muscarella (Eds.), *Psychological perspectives on human sexuality* (pp. 60–100). New York: Wiley.

Expert Consensus Panel (1997). The Expert Consensus Guideline series: Treatment of obsessive-compulsive disorder. *Journal of Clinical Psychiatry, 58* (supplement 4).

Falloon, I.R.H., Boyd, J. L., & McGill, C. (1984). *Family care of schizophrenia.* New York: Guilford Press.

Fals-Stewart, W., Birchler, G. R., & O'Farrell, T. J. (1996). Behavioral couples therapy for male substance-abusing patients: Effects on relationship adjustment and drug-using behavior. *Journal of Consulting and Clinical Psychology, 64,* 959–972.

Fals-Stewart, W., Marks, A. P., & Schafer, J. (1993). A comparison of behavioral group therapy and individual behavior therapy in treating obsessive-compulsive disorder. *Journal of Nervous and Mental Disease, 181,* 189–193.

Fals-Stewart, W., O'Farrell, T. J., Feehan, M., Birchler, G. R., Tiller, S., & McFarlin, S. K. (2000). Behavioral couples therapy versus individual-based treatment for male substance-abusing patients: An evaluation of significant individual change and comparison of improvement rates. *Journal of Substance Abuse Treatment, 18,* 249–254.

Fava, G. A., Zielezny, M., Savron, G., & Grandi, S. (1995). Long-term effects of behavioural treatment for panic disorder with agoraphobia. *British Journal of Psychiatry, 166,* 87–92.

Febbraro, G.A.R., Clum, G. A., Roodman, A. A., & Wright, J. H. (1999). The limits of bibliotherapy: A study on the differential effectiveness of self-administered interventions in individuals with panic attacks. *Behavior Therapy, 30,* 209–222.

Fecteau, G., & Nicki, R. (1999). Cognitive behavioural treatment of post traumatic stress disorder after motor vehicle accident. *Behavioural and Cognitive Psychotherapy, 27,* 201–214.

Ferguss, K. D., Cox, B. J., Wickwire, K. (1995). Efficacy of telephone-administered behavioural therapy for panic disorder with agoraphobia. *Behaviour Research and Therapy, 31,* 465–470.

Feske, U., & Chambless, D. L. (1995). Cognitive-behavioral versus exposure only treatment for social phobia: A meta-analysis. *Behavior Therapy, 26,* 695–720.

Foa, E. B., Dancu, C. V., Hembree, E. A., Jaycox, L. H., Meadows, E. A., & Street, G. P. (1999). A comparison of exposure therapy, stress inoculation training, and their combination for reducing posttraumatic stress disorder in female assault victims. *Journal of Consulting and Clinical Psychology, 67,* 194–200.

Foa, E. B., & Emmelkamp, P.M.G. (Eds.). (1983). *Failures in behavior therapy.* New York: John Wiley & Sons.

Foa, E. B., Hearst-Ikeda, D., & Perry, K. J. (1995). Evaluation of a brief cognitive-behavioral program for the prevention of chronic PTSD in recent assault victims. *Journal of Consulting and Clinical Psychology, 63,* 948–955.

Foa, E. B., & Kozak, M. J. (1986). Emotional processing of fear: Exposure to corrective information. *Psychological Bulletin, 99,* 20–35.

Foa, E. B., & Kozak, M. J. (1996). Psychological treatment for obsessive-compulsive disorder. In M. R. Mavissakalian & R. F. Prien (Eds.), *Long-term treatments of anxiety disorders* (pp. 285–309). Washington, DC: American Psychiatric Association Press.

Foa, E. B., Rothbaum, B. O., Riggs, D. S., & Murdock, T. B. (1991). Treatment of posttraumatic stress disorder in rape victims: A comparison between cognitive-behavioral procedures and counseling. *Journal of Consulting and Clinical Psychology, 59,* 715–723.

Frank, E., Anderson, B., Stewart, B. D., Dancu, C., Hughes, C., & West, D. (1988). Efficacy of cognitive behavior therapy and systematic desensitization in the treatment of rape trauma. *Behavior Therapy, 19,* 403–420.

Franklin, M. E., Abramowitz, J. S., Kozak, M. J., Levitt, J. T., & Foa, E. B. (2000). Effectiveness of exposure and ritual prevention for obsessive-compulsive disorder: Randomized compared with nonrandomized samples. *Journal of Consulting and Clinical Psychology, 68,* 594–602.

Fuchs, C. Z., & Rehm, L. P. (1977). A self-control behavior therapy program for depression. *Journal of Consulting and Clinical Psychology, 45,* 206–215.

Gallagher-Thompson, D., Hanley-Peterson, P., & Thompson, L. W. (1990). Maintenance of gains versus relapse following brief psychotherapy for depression. *Journal of Consulting and Clinical Psychology, 58,* 371–374.

Gardner, P., & Oei, T. S. (1981). Depression of self-esteem: An investigation that used behavioral and cognitive approaches to the treatment of clinically depressed clients. *Journal of Clinical Psychology, 37,* 128–135.

Garety, P., Fowler, D., Kuipers, E., Freeman, D., Dunn, G., Bebbington, P., Hadley, C., & Jones, S. (1997). London-East Anglia randomised controlled trial of cognitive-behavioural therapy for psychosis. II. Predictors of outcome. *British Journal of Psychiatry, 171,* 420–426.

Getka, E. J., & Glass, C. R. (1992). Behavioral and cognitive-behavioral approaches to the reduction of dental anxiety. *Behavior Therapy, 18,* 3–16.

Gloaguen, V., Cottraux, J., Cucherat, M., & Blackburn, I. M. (1998). A meta-analysis of the effects of cognitive therapy in depressed patients. *Journal of Affective Disorders, 49,* 59–72.

Glynn, S. M., Eth, S., Randolph, E. T., Foy, D. W., & Urbaitis, M., et al. (1999). A test of behavioral family therapy to augment exposure for combat-related posttraumatic stress disorder. *Journal of Consulting and Clinical Psychology, 67,* 243–251.

Gortner, E. T., Gollan, J. K., Dobson, K. S., & Jacobson, N. S. (1998). Cognitive-behavioral treatment for depression: Relapse prevention. *Journal of Consulting and Clinical Psychology, 66,* 377–384.

Gosh, A., Marks, I. M., & Carr, A. C. (1987). Therapist contact and outcome of self-exposure treatment for phobias. *British Journal of Psychiatry, 152,* 234.

Gould, R. A., Buckminster, S., Pollack, M. H., Otto, M. W., & Yap, L. (1997). Cognitive-behavioral and pharmacological treatment for social phobia: A meta-analysis. *Clinical Psychology, Science and Practice, 4,* 291–306.

Gould, R. A., & Clum, G. A. (1995). Self-help plus minimal therapist contact in the treatment of panic disorder. A replication and extension. *Behavior Therapy, 26,* 533–546.

Gould, R. A., Otto, M. W., & Pollack, M. H. (1995). A meta-analysis of treatment outcome for panic disorder. *Clinical Psychology Review, 15,* 819–844.

Gould, R. A., Otto, M. W., Pollack, M. H., & Yap, L. (1997). Cognitive-behavioral and pharmacological treatment of generalized anxiety disorder: A preliminary meta-analysis. *Behavior Therapy, 28,* 285–305.

Griez, E., & van den Hout, M. A. (1986). CO_2 inhalation in the treatment of panic attacks. *Behaviour Research and Therapy, 24,* 145–150.

Gruber, K., Chutuape, M. A., & Stitzer, M. L. (2000). Reinforcement-based intensive outpatient treatment for inner city opiate abusers: a short-term evaluation. *Drug and Alcohol Dependence, 57,* 211–223.

Haddock, G., Tarrier, N., Morrison, A. P., Hopkins, R., Drake, R., & Lewis, S. (1999). A pilot study evaluating the effectiveness of individual inpatient cognitive-behavioural therapy in early psychosis. *Social Psychiatry and Psychiatric Epidemiology, 34,* 254–258.

Hartmann, U., & Langer, D. (1993). Combination of psychosexual therapy and intrapenile injections in the treatment of erectile dysfunctions: Rationale and predictors of outcome. *Journal of Sex Education and Therapy.*

Hawton, K. (1995). Treatment of sexual dysfunctions by sex therapy and other approaches. *British Journal of Psychiatry, 17,* 307–314.

Hawton, K., & Catalan, J. (1990). Sex therapy for vaginismus: Characteristics of couples and treatment outcome. *Sexual and Marital Therapy, 5,* 39–48.

Hawton, K., Catalan, J., & Fagg, J. (1992). Sex therapy for erectile dysfunction: Characteristics of couples, treatment outcome, and prognostic factors. *Archives of Sexual Behavior, 21,* 161–176.

Hawton, K., Catalan, J., Martin, P., & Fagg, J. (1986). Long-term outcome of sex therapy. *Behaviour Research and Therapy, 24,* 665–675.

Heiman, J. R., & LoPiccolo, J. (1983). Clinical outcome of sex therapy: Effects of daily vs. weekly treatment. *Archives of General Psychiatry, 40,* 443–449.

Heimberg, R. G., Dodge, C. S., & Hope, D. A. (1990). Cognitive behavioral treatment of social phobia: Comparison to a credible placebo control. *Cognitive Therapy and Research, 14,* 1–23.

Heimberg, R. G., Liebowitz, M. R., Hope, D. A., Schneier, F. R., Holt, C. S., et al. (1998). Cognitive behavioral group therapy vs. phenelzine therapy for social phobia. *Archives of General Psychiatry, 55,* 1133–1141.

Heinssen, R., Liberman, R. P., & Kopelowicz, A. (2000). Psychosocial skills training for schizophrenia: Lessons from the laboratory. *Schizophrenia Bulletin, 26,* 21–45.

Hersen, M., Bellack, A. S., Himmelhoch, J. M., & Thase, M. E. (1984). Effects of social skill training, amitriptyline, and psychotherapy in unipolar depressed women. *Behavior Therapy, 15,* 21–40.

Hickling, E. J., & Blanchard, E. B. (1997). The private practice psychologist and manual-based treatments: Post-traumatic stress disorder secondary to motor vehicle accidents. *Behaviour Research and Therapy, 35,* 191–203.

Higgins, S. T., Budney, A. J., Bickel, W. K., Foerg, F. E., Ogden, D., & Badger, G. J. (1995). Outpatient behavioral treatment for cocaine dependence: One year outcome. *Experimental and Clinical Psychopharmacology, 3*, 205–212.

Higgins, S. T., & Wong, C. J. (1998). Treating cocaine abuse: What does research tell us. In S. T. Higgins & J. L. Katz (Eds.), *Cocaine abuse: Behavior, pharmacology, and clinical applications.* New York: Academic Press.

Hiss, H., Foa, E. B., & Kozak, M. J. (1995). Relapse prevention program for treatment of obsessive-compulsive disorder. *Journal of Consulting and Clinical Psychology, 62*, 801–808.

Hoffart A. (1998). Cognitive and guided mastery therapy of agoraphobia: Long-term outcome and mechanisms of change. *Cognitive Theory & Research, 22*,195–207.

Hoffart, A., & Martinsen, E. W. (1990). Exposure-based integrated vs. pure psychodynamic treatment of agoraphobic inpatients. *Psychotherapy, 27*, 210–218.

Hofmann, G., Barlow, D. H., Papp, L. A., Detweiler, M. F., Ray, S. E., Shear, M. K., Wods, S. W., & Gorman, J. M. (1998). Pretreatment attrition in a comparative treatment outcome study on panic disorder. *American Journal of Psychiatry, 155*, 43–47.

Hohagen, F., Winkelmann, G., Rasche-Reuchle, H., Hand, I., Koenig, A., Muenschau, N., Hiss, H., Geiger-Kabisch, C., Kaeppler, C., Schramm, P., Rey, E., Aldenhoff, J., & Berger, M. (1998). Combination of behavior therapy with fluvoxamine in comparison with behaviour therapy and placebo: Results of a multicentre study. *British Journal of Psychiatry, 173*, 71–78.

Hope, D. A., Heimberg, R. G., & Bruch, M. A. (1995). Dismantling cognitive-behavioral group therapy for social phobia. *Behaviour Research and Therapy, 33*, 637–650.

Hunt, G. M., & Azrin, N. H. (1973). A community-reinforcement approach to alcoholism. *Behaviour Research and Therapy, 11*, 91–104.

Hurlbert, D. F., & Apt, C. (1995). The coital alignment technique and directed masturbation: A comparative study on female orgasm. *Journal of Sex and Marital Therapy, 21*, 21–29.

Imber, S. D., Pilkonis, P. A., Sotsky, S. M., Elkin, I., Watkins, J. T., Collins, J. F., Shea, M. T., Leber, W. R., & Glass, D. R. (1990). Mode-specific effects among three treatments for depression. *Journal of Consulting and Clinical Psychology, 58*, 352–359.

Irvin, J. E., Bowers, C. A., Dunn, M. E., & Wang, M. C. (1999). Efficacy of relapse prevention: A meta-analytic review. *Journal of Consulting and Clinical Psychology, 67*, 563–570.

Ito, J. R., Donovan, D. M., & Hall, J. J. (1988). Relapse prevention in alcohol aftercare: Effects on drinking outcome, change process, and aftercare attendance. *British Journal of Addiction, 83*, 171–181.

Jacobson, N. S., Dobson, K., Fruzetti, A. E., Schmaling, K. B., & Salusky, S. (1991). Marital therapy as a treatment for depression. *Journal of Consulting and Clinical Psychology, 59*, 547–557.

Jacobson, N. S., Dobson, K., Truax, P. A., Addis, M. E., Koerner, K., Gollan, J. K., Gortner, E., & Prince, S. E. (1996). A component analysis of cognitive-behavioral treatment for depression. *Journal of Consulting and Clinical Psychology, 64*, 295–304.

Jannoun, L., Oppenheimer, C., & Gelder, M. (1982). A self-help treatment program for anxiety state patients. *Behavior Therapy, 13*, 103–111.

Jerremalm, A., Jansson, L., & Öst, L. G. (1986). Cognitive and physiological reactivity and the effects of different behavioural methods in the treatment of social phobia. *Behaviour Research and Therapy, 24*, 171–180.

Jones, M. K., & Menzies, R. G. (1998). Danger ideation reduction therapy (DIRT) for obsessive-compulsive washers: A controlled trial. *Behaviour Research and Therapy, 36*, 959–970.

Kadden, R. M., Cooney, N. L., Getter, H., & Litt, M. D. (1989). Matching alcoholics to coping skills or interactional therapies: Posttreatment results. *Journal of Consulting and Clinical Psychology, 57*, 698–704.

Kamphuis, J. H., & Telch, M. J. (2000). Effects of distraction and guided threat reappraisal on fear reduction during exposure-based treatments for specific fears. *Behaviour Research and Therapy, 38*, 1163–1181.

Kato, P. M., & Mann, T. (1999). A synthesis of psychological interventions for the bereaved. *Clinical Psychology Review, 19*, 275–296.

Keane, T. M., Fairbank, J. A., Caddell, J. M., & Zimering, R. T. (1989). Implosive (flooding) therapy reduces symptoms of PTSD in Vietnam combat veterans. *Behavior Therapy, 20*, 245–260.

Keijsers, G.P.J., Hoogduin, C.A.L., & Schaap, C.P.D.R. (1994). Predictors of treatment outcome in the behavioural treatment of obsessive-compulsive disorder. *British Journal of Psychiatry, 165*, 781–786.

Kern, R. S., Green, M. F., & Goldstein, M. J. (1995). Modification of performance on the span of apprehension, a putative marker of vulnerability to schizophrenia. *Journal of Abnormal Psychology, 104*, 385–389.

Kingdon, D., Tyrer, P., Seivewright, N., Ferguson, B., & Murphy, S. (1996). The Nottingham study of neurotic disorders: Influence of cognitive therapists on outcome. *British Journal of Psychiatry, 169*, 93–97.

Klosko, J. S., Barlow, D. H., Toussinari, R. B., & Cerny, J. A. (1990). A comparison of alprazolam and behavior therapy in the treatment of panic disorder. *Journal of Consulting and Clinical Psychology, 58*, 805–810.

Kobak, K. A., Greist, J. H., Jefferson, J. W., Katzelnick, D. J., & Henry, J. (1998). Behavioral versus pharmacological treatments of obsessive compulsive disorder: A meta-analysis. *Psychopharmacology, 136*, 205–216.

Kockott, G., Dittmar, F., & Nusselt, L. (1975). Systematic desensitization and erectile impotence: A controlled study. *Archives of Sexual Behavior, 4,* 493–500.

Kopelowicz, A., Liberman, R. P., Mintz, J., & Zarate, R. (1996). Comparison of efficacy of social skills training for deficit and nondeficit negative symptoms in schizophrenia. *American Journal of Psychiatry, 154,* 424–425.

Kownacki, R. J., & Shadish, W. R. (1999). Does Alcoholic Anonymous work? The results from a meta-analysis of controlled experiments. *Substance Use and Misuse, 34,* 1897–1916.

Kuipers, E., Fowler, D., Garety, P., Chisholm, D., Freeman, D., Dunn, G., Bebbington, P., & Hadley, C. (1998). London-East Anglia randomised controlled trial of cognitive-behavioural therapy for psychosis. III. Follow-up and economic evaluation at 18 months. *British Journal of Psychiatry, 173,* 61–68.

Kuriansky, J. B., Sharpe, L., & O'Connor, D. (1982). The treatment of anorgasmia: Long-term effectiveness of a short-term behavioral group therapy. *Journal of Sex and Marital Therapy, 8,* 29–43.

Kushner, M. G., Abrams, K., & Brochardt, C. (2000). The relationship between anxiety disorders and alcohol use disorders: A review of major perspectives and findings. *Clinical Psychology Review, 20,* 149–171.

Laan, E. (1994). *Determinants of sexual arousal in women.* Ph.D. thesis, University of Amsterdam.

Laberg, J. C., & Ellertsen, B. (1987). Psychophysiological indicators of craving in alcoholics: Effects of cue exposure. *British Journal of Addiction, 82,* 1341–1348.

Ladouceur, R. L. (1983). Participant modeling with or without cognitive treatment for phobias. *Journal of Consulting and Clinical Psychology, 51,* 942–944.

Lehman, A. F., & Steinwachs, D. M. (1998). Translating research into practice: The Schizophrenia Patient Outcomes Research Team (PORT) treatment recommendations. *Schizophrenia Bulletin, 24,* 1–10.

Lelliott, P. T., Marks, I. M., Monteiro, W. O., Tsakiris, F., & Noshirvani, H. (1987). Agoraphobia 5 years after imipramine and exposure: Outcome and prediction. *Journal of Nervous and Mental Disease, 175,* 599–605.

Lewinsohn, P. M. (1975). The behavioral study and treatment of depression. In M. Hersen, R. M. Eisler, & P. M. Miller (Eds.), *Progress in behavior modification* (Vol. 1, pp. 19–65). New York: Academic Press.

Lewinsohn, P. M., & Hoberman, H. M. (1982). Depression. In A. S. Bellack, M. Hersen, & A. E. Kazdin (Eds.), *International handbook of behavior modification and therapy* (pp. 397–431). New York: Plenum.

Liberman, R. P., & Eckman, T. (1981). Behavior therapy vs insight-oriented therapy for repeated suicide attempters. *Archives of General Psychiatry, 38,* 1126–1130.

Liberman, R. P., Wallace, C. J., Blackwell, G., Kopelowicz, A., Vaccaro, J. V., & Mintz, J. (1998). Skills training versus psychosocial occupational therapy for persons with persistent schizophrenia. *American Journal of Psychiatry, 155,* 1087–1091.

Libman, E., Fichten, C. S., Brender, W., Burstein, R., Cohen, J., & Binik, I. (1984). A comparison of three therapeutic formats in the treatment of secondary orgasmic dysfunctions. *Journal of Sex and Marital Therapy, 10,* 147–159.

Lindsay, M., Crino, R., & Andrews, G. (1997). Controlled trial of exposure and response prevention in obsessive-compulsive disorder. *British Journal of Psychiatry, 171,* 135–139.

Linehan, M. M., Amstrong, H. E., Suarez, A., Allmon, D. J., & Heard, H. L. (1991). Cognitive-behavioral treatment of chronically suicidal borderline patients. *Archives of General Psychiatry, 48,* 1060–1064.

Litt, M. D., Babor, T. F., Del Boca, F. K., Kadden, R. M., & Cooney, N. L. (1992). Types of alcoholics, II: Application of an empirically derived typology to treatment matching. *Archives of General Psychiatry, 49,* 609–614.

Lohr, J. M., Tolin, D. F., & Lilienfeld, S. O. (1998). Efficacy of eye movement desensitization and reprocessing: Implications for behavior therapy. *Behavior Therapy, 29,* 123–156.

Longabaugh, R., Wirtz, P. W., Beattie, M. C., Noel, N., & Stout, R. (1995). Matching treatment focus to patient social investment and support: 18 month follow-up results. *Journal of Consulting and Clinical Psychology, 63,* 296–307.

LoPiccolo, J., Heiman, J. R., Hogan, D. R., & Roberts, C. W. (1985). Effectiveness of single therapist versus cotherapy teams in sex therapy. *Journal of Consulting and Clinical Psychology, 53,* 287–294.

Lyubomirsky, S., & Nolen-Hoeksema, S. (1995). Effects of self-focused rumination on negative thinking and interpersonal problem-solving. *Journal of Personality and Social Psychology, 69,* 176–190.

Macklin, M. L., Metzger, L. J., Lasko, N. B., Berry, N. J., Orr, S. P., & Pitman, R. K. (2000). Five-year follow-up study of eye movement desensitization and reprocessing therapy for combat-related posttraumatic stress disorder. *Comprehensive Psychiatry, 41,* 24–27.

Marder, S. R., Wirshing, W. C., Mintz, J., McKenzie, J., Johnston, K., Eckman, T. A., Lebell, M., Zimmerman, K., & Liberman, R. P. (1996). Two-year outcome of social skills training and group psychotherapy for outpatients with schizophrenia. *American Journal of Psychiatry, 153,* 1585–1592.

Marks, I. M. (1997). Behaviour therapy for obsessive-compulsive disorder: A decade of progress. *Canadian Journal of Psychiatry, 42,* 1021–1027.

Marks, I. M., Lelliott, P., Basoglu, M., Noshirvani, H., Monteiro, W., Cohen, D., & Kasvikis, Y. (1988). Clomipramine, self-exposure and therapist-aided exposure for obsessive-compulsive rituals. *British Journal of Psychiatry, 152,* 522–534.

Marks, I. M., Lovell, K., Noshirvani, H., Livanou, M., & Trasher, S. (1998). Treatment of posttraumatic stress disorder by exposure and/or cognitive restructuring. *Archives of General Psychiatry, 55,* 317–325.

Marks, I. M., Stern, R. S., Mawson, D., Cobb, J., & McDonald, R. (1980). Clomipramine and exposure for obsessive-compulsive rituals: I. *British Journal of Psychiatry, 136,* 1–25.

Marks, I. M., Swinson, R. P., Basoglu, M., Kuch, K., Noshirvani, H., O'Sullivan, G., Leliott, P., Kirby, M., McNamee, G., Sengun, S., & Wickwire, K. (1993). Alprazolam and exposure alone and combined in panic disorder with agoraphobia. *British Journal of Psychiatry, 162,* 776–787.

Marlatt, G. A. (1996). Taxonomy of high-risk situations for alcohol relapse: Evolution and development of a cognitive-behavioral model. *Addiction, 91 (Supplement).* S37–S49.

Marlatt, G. A., & Gordon, J. R. (1980). Determinants of relapse: Implications for the maintenance of behavior change. In P. Davidson (Ed.), *Behavioral medicine, changing health lifestyles.* New York: Brunner/Mazel.

Marlatt, G. A., Larimer, M. E., Baer, J. S., & Quigley, L. A. (1993). Harm reduction for alcohol problems: Moving beyond the controlled drinking controversy. *Behavior Therapy, 24,* 461–504.

Marshall, W. L. (1985). Variable exposure in flooding. *Behaviour Research and Therapy, 23,* 117.

Masters, W. H., & Johnson, V. E. (1970). *Human sexual inadequacy.* Boston: Little, Brown.

Mathews, A. M., Bancroft, J., Whitehead, A., Hackman, A., Julier, D., Bancroft, J., Gath, D., & Show, P. (1976). The behavioural treatment of sexual inadequacy: A comparative study. *Behaviour Research and Therapy, 14,* 427–436.

Mattick, R. P., Andrews, G., Hadzi-Pavlovic, D., & Christensen, H. (1990). Treatment of panic and agoraphobia: An integrative review. *Journal of Nervous and Mental Disease, 178,* 567–576.

Mawson, D., Marks, I., Ramm, E., & Stern, R. S. (1981). Guided mourning for morbid grief: A controlled study. *British Journal of Psychiatry, 138,* 185–193.

McCabe, M. P., & Delaney, S. M. (1992). A evaluation of therapeutic programs for the treatment of secondary inorgasmia in women. *Archives of Sexual Behavior, 21,* 69–89.

McConaghy, N. (1996). Treatment of sexual dysfunctions. In V. B. Van Hasselt & M. Hersen (Eds.), *Sourcebook of psychological treatment manuals for adult disorders* (pp. 333–373). New York: Plenum.

McCrady, B. S., Epstein, E. E., & Hirsch, L. S. (1996). Issues in the implementation of a randomized clinical trial that includes Alcoholics Anonymous: Studying AA-related behaviors during treatment. *Journal of Studies on Alcohol, 57,* 604–612.

McCrady, B. S., Stout, R., Noel, N., Abrams, D., & Nelson, H. F. (1991). Effectiveness of 3 types of spouse-involved behavioral alcoholism-treatment. *British Journal of Addiction, 86,* 1415–1424.

McGlynn, F. D., Moore, P. M., Lawyer, S., & Karg, R. (1999). Relaxation training inhibits fear and arousal during in vivo exposure to phobia-cue stimuli. *Journal of Behavior Therapy and Experimental Psychiatry, 30,* 155–168.

McKay, D. (1997). A maintenance program for obsessive-compulsive disorder using exposure with response prevention: 2-year follow-up. *Behaviour Research and Therapy, 35,* 367–369.

McKay, D., Neziroglu, F., Todaro, J., & Yaryura-Tobias, J. A. (1996). Changes in personality disorders following behavior therapy for obsessive-compulsive disorder. *Journal of Anxiety Disorders, 10,* 47–57.

McKay, J. R., Alterman, A. I., Cacciola, J. S., Rutherford, M. J., O'Brien, C. P., & Koppenhaver, J. (1997). Group counseling versus individualized relapse prevention aftercare following intensive outpatient treatment for cocaine dependence: Initial results. *Journal of Consulting and Clinical Psychology, 65,* 778–788.

McLean, P. D., & Hakstian, A. R. (1979). Clinical depression: Comparative efficacy of outpatient treatment. *Journal of Consulting and Clinical Psychology, 47,* 818–836.

McLean, P. D., & Hakstian, A. R. (1990). Relative endurance of unipolar depression treatment effects: Longitudinal follow-up. *Journal of Consulting and Clinical Psychology, 58,* 482–488.

Meana, M., & Binnik, Y. M. (1994). Painful coitus: A review of female dyspareunia. *Journal of Nervous and Mental Disease, 182,* 264–272.

Meisler, A. W., & Carey, M. P. (1991). Negative affect and male sexual arousal. *Archives of Sexual Behavior, 20,* 541–554.

Mennin, D. S., & Heimberg, R. G. (2000). The impact of comorbid mood and personality disorders in the cognitive-behavioral treatment of panic disorder. *Clinical Psychology Review, 20,* 339–357.

Mersch, P.P.A., Emmelkamp, P.M.G., & Lips, C. (1991). Social phobia: Individual response patterns and the long-term effects of behavioral and cognitive interventions. A follow-up study. *Behaviour Research and Therapy, 29,* 357–362.

Mersch, P. P., Jansen, M., & Arntz, A. (1995). Social phobia and personality disorder: Severity of complaints and treatment effectiveness. *Journal of Personality Disorders, 9,* 143–159.

Metz, M. E., Pryor, J. L., Nesvacil, L. B., Abuzzahab, F. S., & Koznar, J. (1997). Premature ejaculation: A psychophysiological review. *Journal of Sex and Marital Therapy, 23,* 3–23.

Michelson, L., Mavissakalian, M., & Marchione, K. (1985). Cognitive and behavioural treatments of agoraphobia: Clinical, behavioural, and psychophysiological outcomes. *Journal of Consulting and Clinical Psychology, 53,* 913–925.

Milan, R. J., Kilmann, P. R., & Boland, J. P. (1988). Treatment outcome of secondary orgasmic dysfunction: A two to six year follow-up. *Archives of Sexual Behavior, 17,* 463–480.

Miller, I. W., Norman, W. H., Keitner, G. I., Bishop, S. B., & Dow, M. G. (1989). Cognitive-behavioral treatment of depressed inpatients. *Behavior Therapy, 20,* 25–47.

Miller, P. J., Westerberg, V. S., Harris, R. J., & Tonigan, J. S. (1996). What predicts relapse? Prospective testing of antecedent models. *Addiction, 91,* 155–171.

Miller, W. R. (1983). Motivational interviewing with problem drinkers. *Behavioural Psychotherapy, 11,* 441–448.

Miller, W. R. (1996). Motivational interviewing: Research, practice and puzzles. *Addictive Behaviors, 21,* 835–842.

Miller, W. R., Andrews, N. R., Wilbourne, P., & Bennett, M. E. (1998). A wealth of alternatives. In Miller, W. R., & Heather, N. (Eds.), *Treating addictive behaviors* (2nd ed.) (pp. 203–216).

Miller, W. R., Benefield, G., & Tonigan, J. S. (1993). Enhancing motivation for change in problem drinking: A controlled comparison of two therapist styles. *Journal of Consulting and Clinical Psychology, 61,* 455–461.

Miller, W. R., Leckman, A. L., Delaney, H. D., & Tinkcom, M. (1992). Long-term follow-up of behavioral self-control training. *Journal of Studies on Alcohol, 53,* 249–261.

Miller, W. R., Meyers, R. J., & Tonigan, J. S. (1999). Engaging the unmotivated in treatment for alcohol problems: A comparison of three strategies for intervention through family members. *Journal of Consulting and Clinical Psychology, 67,* 688–697.

Mitchell, W. B., DiBartolo, P. M., Brown, T. A., & Barlow, D. H. (1998). Effects of positive and negative mood on sexual arousal in sexually functional males. *Archives of Sexual Behavior, 27,* 197–207.

Mohlman, J., & Zinbarg, R. E. (2000). What kind of attention is necessary for fear reduction? An empirical test of the emotional processing model. *Behavior Therapy, 31,* 113–133.

Monti, P. M., Abrams, D. B., Binkoff, J. A., Zwick, W. R., Liepman, M. R., Nirenberg, T. D., & Rohsenow, D. J. (1990). Communication skills training, communication skills training with family and cognitive-behavioral mood management training for alcoholics. *Journal of Studies on Alcohol, 51,* 263–270.

Monti, P., & Rohsenow, D. J. (1999). Coping skills training and cue exposure therapy in the treatment of alcoholism. *Alcohol Research and Health, 23,* 107–115.

Moser, A., & Annis, H. (1995). The role in coping in relapse crisis outcome: A prospective study of treated alcoholics. *Addiction, 91,* 1101–1114.

Munjack, D. J., Schlaks, A., Sanchez, V. C., Usigli, R., Zulueta, A., & Leonard, M. (1984). Rational emotive therapy in the treatment of erectile failure: An initial study. *Journal of Sex and Marital Therapy, 10,* 170–175.

Nezu, A. H. (1987). A problem-solving formulation of depression: A literature review and proposal of a pluralistic model. *Clinical Psychology Review, 7,* 121–144.

Nezu, A. H., & Perri, M. G. (1989). Social problem-solving therapy for unipolar depression: An initial dismantling investigation. *Journal of Consulting and Clinical Psychology, 57,* 408–413.

Noonan, W., & Moyers, T. (1997). Motivational interviewing. *Journal of Substance Misuse, 2,* 8–16.

Noone, M. N., Dua, J., & Markham, R. (1999). Stress, cognitive factors, and coping resources as predictors of relapse in alcoholics. *Addictive Behaviors, 24,* 687–693.

O'Brien, C. P. (1996). Recent developments in the pharmacotherapy of substance abuse. *Journal of Consulting and Clinical Psychology, 64,* 677–686.

O'Donohue, W. T., Dopke, C., & Swingen, D. N. (1997). Psychotherapy for female sexual dysfunction. *Clinical Psychology Review, 17,* 537–566.

O'Donohue, W. T., Swingen, D. N., Dopke, C. A., & Regev, L. G. (1999). Psychotherapy for male sexual dysfunction: A review. *Clinical Psychology Review, 19,* 591–630.

Oei, T.P.S., Llamas, M., & Devilly, G. J. (1999). The efficacy and cognitive proceses of cognitive behaviour therapy in the treatment of panic disorder with agoraphobia. *Behavioural and Cognitive Psychotherapy, 27,* 63–88.

O'Farrell, T. J., Choquette, K. A., Cutter, H.S.G., Brown, E. D., & McCourt, W. F. (1993). Behavioral marital therapy with and without additional couples relapse prevention sessions for alcoholics and their wives. *Journal of Studies on Alcohol, 54,* 652–666.

O'Farrell, T. J., Cutter, H.S.G., & Floyd, F. J. (1985). Evaluating behavioral marital therapy for male alcoholics: Effects on marital adjustment and communication from before to after therapy. *Behavior Therapy, 16,* 147–167.

O'Farrell, T. J., Kleinke, C., & Cutter, H.S.G. (1998). Sexual adjustment of male alcoholics: Changes from before to after receiving alcoholism counseling with and without marital therapy. *Addictive Behaviors, 23,* 419–425.

O'Farrell, T. J., & Murphy, C. M. (1995). Marital violence before and after alcoholism treatment. *Journal of Consulting and Clinical psychology, 63,* 256–262.

O'Malley, S. S., Jaffe, A. J., Chang, G., Rode, S., Schottenfeld, R. S., Meyer, R. E., & Rounsaville, B. J. (1996). Six month follow-up of naltrexone and coping skills therapy for alcohol dependence. *Archives of General Psychiatry, 53,* 217–224.

Öst, L. G. (1988). Applied relaxation vs. progressive relaxation in the treatment of panic disorder. *Behaviour Research and Therapy, 26,* 13–22.

Öst, L. G., Alm, T., Brandberg, M., & Breitholz, E. (2001). One vs. five sessions of exposure and five sessions of cognitive therapy in the treatment of claustrophobia. *Behaviour Research and Therapy, 39*, 167–183.

Öst, L. G., & Breitholz, E. (2000). Applied relaxation vs. cognitive therapy in the treatment of generalized anxiety disorder. *Behaviour Research and Therapy, 38*, 777–790.

Öst, L. G., Fellenius, J., & Sterner, K. (1991). Applied tension, exposure in vivo, and tension-only in the treatment of blood phobia. *Behaviuor Research and Therapy, 29*, 561–574.

Öst, L. G., Jerremalm, A., & Johansson, J. (1981). Individual response patterns and the effect of different behavioral methods in the treatment of social phobia. *Behaviour Research and Therapy, 19*, 1–16.

Öst, L. G., & Westling, B. E. (1995). Applied relaxation vs. cognitive therapy in the treatment of panic disorder. *Behaviour Research and Therapy, 33*, 145–158.

Öst, L. G., Westling, B. E., & Hellstrom, B. (1993). Applied relaxation, exposure in vivo and cognitive methods in the treatment of panic disorder with agoraphobia. *Behaviour Research and Therapy, 31*, 383–394.

O'Sullivan, G., Noshirvani, H., Marks, I., Monteiro, W., & Lelliott, P. (1991). Six years follow-up after exposure and clomipramine therapy for obsessive-compulsive disorder. *Journal of Clinical Psychiatry, 52*, 150–155.

Otto, M. W., Pollack, M. H., & Sabatino, S. A. (1996). Maintenance of remission following cognitive behavior therapy for panic disorder. Possible deleterious effects of concurrent medication treatment. *Behavior Therapy, 27*, 473–482.

Paul, G. L., & Lentz, R. J. (1977). *Psychosocial treatment of chronic mental patients: Milieu versus social-learning programs.* Cambridge, MA: Harvard University Press.

Pendery, M. L., Maltzman, I. M., & West, L. J. (1982). Controlled drinking by alcoholics?: New findings and a reevaluation of a major affirmative study. *Science, 217*, 169–175.

Penfold, K., & Page, A. C. (1999). The effect of distraction on within-session anxiety reduction during brief in vivo exposure for mild blood-injection fears. *Behavior Therapy, 30*, 607–621.

Penn, D., & Mueser, K. T. (1996). Research update on the psychosocial treatment of schizophrenia. *American Journal of Psychiatry, 153*, 607–617.

Persons, J. B., & Bertagnolli, A. (1994). Cognitive-behavioural treatment of multiple-problem patients: Application to personality disorders. *Clinical Psychology and Psychotherapy, 1*, 279–285.

Peter, H, Tabrizian, S., & Hand, I. (2000). Serum cholesterol level in patients with obsessive-compulsive disorder during treatment with behavior therapy and SSRI or placebo. *International Journal of Psychiatry in Medicine, 30*, 27–39.

Petry, N. M. (2000). A comprehensive guide to the application of contingency management procedures in clinical settings. *Drug and Alcohol Dependence, 58*, 9–25.

Powell, T., Bradley, B., & Gray, J. (1993). Subjective craving for opiates: Evaluation of a cue-exposure protocol for use with detoxified opiate addicts. *British Journal of Clinical Psychology, 32*, 39–53.

Pretzer, J. (1994). Cognitive therapy of personality disorders: The state of the art. *Clinical Psychology and Psychotherapy, 1*, 257–266.

Project MATCH research group (1997a). Matching alcoholism treatments to client heterogeneity: Project MATCH posttreatment drinking outcomes. *Journal of Studies on Alcohol, 58*, 7–29.

Project MATCH research group (1997b). Project MATCH secondary a priori hypotheses. *Addiction, 92*, 1671–1698.

Project MATCH research group (1998). Matching alcoholism treatments to client heterogeneity: Project MATCH three-year drinking outcomes. *Journal of Studies on Alcohol, 58*, 7–29.

Ramsay, R. (1979). Bereavement. In D. Sjöden et al. (Eds.), *Trends in behavior therapy.* New York: Academic Press.

Rankin, H., Hodgson, R., & Stockwell, T. (1983). Cue exposure and response prevention with alcoholics: A controlled trial. *Behaviour Research and Therapy, 21*, 435–446.

Raytek, H. S., McCrady, B. S., Epstein, E. E., & Hirsch, L. S. (1999). Therapeutic alliance and retention of couples in conjoint alcoholism treatment. *Addictive Behaviors, 24*, 317–330.

Reed, M. K. (1994). Social skills training to reduce depression in adolescents. *Adolescence, 29*, 293–302.

Rehm, L. P. (1977). A self-control model of depression. *Behavior Therapy, 8*, 787–804.

Rehm, L. P., Fuchs, C. Z., Roth, D. M., Kornblith, S. J., & Ramono, J. M. (1979). A comparison of self-control and assertion skills treatment of depression. *Behavior Therapy, 10*, 429–442.

Rehm, L. P., Mehta, P., & Dodrill, C. L. (2001). Depression. In M. Hersen & V. B. van Hasselt (Eds.), *Advanced Abnormal Psychology* (2nd ed.) (pp 307–324). New York: Kluwer Academic/Plenum.

Reissing, E. D., Binik, Y. M., & Khalifé, S. (1999). Does vaginismus exist? A critical review of the literature. *Journal of Nervous and Mental Disease, 187*, 261–274.

Renneberg, B., Goldstein, A., Phillips, D., & Chambless, D. L. (1990). Intensive behavioral group treatment of avoidant personality disorder. *Behavior Therapy, 21*, 363–377.

Resick, P. A., Jordan, C. G., Girelli, S. A., Kotsis-Hutter, C., & Marhoefer-Dvorak, S. (1988). A comparative outcome study of behavioral group therapy for sexual assaults victims. *Behavior Therapy, 19*, 385–401.

Rice, K. M., Blanchard, E. B., & Purcell, M. (1993). Biofeedback treatments of generalized anxiety disorder: Preliminary results. *Biofeedback and Self-Regulation, 18,* 93–105.

Richards, D. A., Lovell, K., & Marks, I. M. (1994). Post-traumatic stress disorder: Evaluation of a behavioural treatment programme. *Journal of Traumatic Stress,* 7, 669–680.

Rijken, H., Kraaimaat, F., de Ruiter, C., & Garssen, B. (1992). A follow-up study on short-term treatment of agoraphobia. *Behaviour Research and Therapy, 30,* 63–66.

Rohsenow, D. J., Monti, P. M., Binkoff, J. A., Leipman, M. R., Nirenberg, T. D., & Abrams, D. B. (1991). Patient-treatment matching for alcoholic men in communication skills versus cognitive-behavioral mood management training. *Addictive Behaviors, 16,* 63–69.

Rohsenow, D. J., Monti, P. M., Rubonis, A. V., Sirota, A. D., Niaura, R. S., Colby, S. M., Wunschel, S. M., & Abrams, D. B. (1994). Cue reactivity as a predictor of drinking among male alcoholics. *Journal of Consulting and Clinical Psychology, 62,* 620–626.

Rokke, P. D., Tomhave, J. A., & Jocic, Z. (1999). The role of client choice and target selection in self-management therapy for depression in older adults. *Psychology & Aging, 14,* 155–169.

Rosen, R. C., & Leiblum, S. R. (1995). Treatment of sexual disorders in the 1990s: An integrated approach. *Journal of Consulting and Clinical Psychology, 63,* 877–890.

Rosen, R. C., Leiblum, S. R., & Spector, I. (1994). Psychologically based treatment for male erectile disorder: A cognitive interpersonal model. *Journal of Sex and Marital Therapy, 20,* 67–85.

Rothbaum, B. O., Hodges, L., Kooper, R. Opdyke, D., Williford, J., & North, M. M. (1995). Effectiveness of virtual graded exposure in the treatment of acrophobia. *American Journal of Psychiatry, 152,* 626–628.

Rothbaum, B. O., Hodges, L., Smith, S., Lee, J. H., & Price, L. (2000). A controlled study of virtual reality exposure therapy for the fear of flying. *Journal of Consulting and Clinical Psychology, 68,* 1020–1026.

Rowland, D. L., Cooper, S. E., & Heiman, J. R. (1995). A preliminary investigation of affective and cognitive response to erotic stimulation in men before and after sex therapy. *Journal of Sex and Marital Therapy, 21,* 3–20.

Rude, S. S., & Rehm, L. P. (1991). Response to treatments for depression: The role of initial status on targeted cognitive and behavioral skills. *Clinical Psychology Review, 11,* 493–514.

Sahoo, D., Gillis, J. S., & Misra, S. K. (1999). Conditionability trait as a predictor of response to behavior therapy in obsessive-compulsive neurosis. *Social Science International, 15,* 68–76.

Salkovskis, P. M., Jomes, D.R.G., & Clark, D. M. (1986). Respiratory control in the treatment of panic attacks: Replication and extension with concurrent measurement of behaviour and pCO_2. *British Journal of Psychiatry, 148,* 526–532.

Sanchez, V. C., Lewinsohn, P. M., & Larson, D. W. (1980). Assertion training: Effectiveness in the treatment of depression. *Journal of Clinical Psychology, 36,* 526–529.

Sarwer, D. B., & Durlak, J. A. (1997). A field trial of the effectiveness of behavioral treatment for sexual dysfunctions. *Journal of Sex and Marital Therapy, 23,* 87–97.

Saunders, J. B., Wilkinson, C., & Phillips, M. (1995). The impact of a brief motivational intervention with opiate users attending a methadone program. *Addiction, 90,* 415–424.

Schmidt, N. B., Woolaway-Bickel, K., Trakowski, J., Santiago, H., Storey, J., Koselka, M., & Cook, J. (2000). Dismantling cognitive-behavioral treatment for panic disorder: Questioning the utility of breathing retraining. *Journal of Consulting and Clinical Psychology, 68,* 417–424.

Scholing, A., & Emmelkamp, P.M.G. (1993a). Cognitive and behavioral treatments of fear of blushing, sweating or trembling. *Behaviour Research and Therapy, 31,* 155–170.

Scholing, A., & Emmelkamp, P.M.G. (1993b). Exposure with and without cognitive therapy for generalized social phobia: Effects of individual and group treatment. *Behaviour Research and Therapy, 31,* 667–681.

Scholing, A., & Emmelkamp, P.M.G. (1996a). Treatment of generalized social phobia: Results at long-term follow-up. *Behaviour Research and Therapy, 34,* 447–452.

Scholing, A., & Emmelkamp, P.M.G. (1996b). Treatment of fear of blushing, sweating, or trembling: Results at long-term follow-up. *Behavior Modification, 20,* 338–356.

Scholing, A., & Emmelkamp, P.M.G. (1999). Prediction of treatment outcome in social phobia: A cross-validation. *Behaviour Research and Therapy, 37,* 659–670.

Schwartz, J. M., Stoessel, P. W., Baxter, L. R., Martin, K. M., Phelps, M. E. (1996). Systematic changes in cerebral glucose metabolic rate after successful behavior modification treatment of obsessive-compulsive disorder. *Archives of General Psychiatry, 53,* 109–113.

Scogin, F., Jamison, C., & Gochneaur, K. (1989). Comparative efficacy of cognitive and behavioral bibliotherapy for mildly and moderately depressed adults. *Journal of Consulting and Clinical Psychology, 57,* 403–407.

Segrin, C. (2000). Social skills deficits associated with depression. *Clinical Psychology Review, 20,* 379–403.

Semans, J. H. (1956). Premature ejaculation: A new approach. *Southern Medical Journal, 49,* 353–357.

Sensky, T., Turkington, D., Kingdon, D., Scott, J. L., Scott, J., Siddle, R., O'Carroll, M., & Barnes, T.R.E. (2000). A randomized controlled trial of cognitive-behavioral therapy for persistent symptoms in schizophrenia resistant to medication. *Archives of General Psychiatry, 57*, 165–172.

Shapiro, F. (1999). Eye movement desensitization and Reprocessing (EMDR) and the anxiety disorders: Clinical and research implications of an integrated psychotherapy treatment. *Journal of Anxiety Disorders, 13*, 35–67.

Shear, M. K., Pilkonis, P. A., Cloitre, M., & Leon, A. C. (1994). Cognitive behavioral treatment compared with nonprescriptive treatment of panic disorder. *Archives of General Psychiatry, 53*, 395–401.

Siegel, S. (1983). Classical conditioning, drug tolerance, and drug dependence. In R. G. Smart, F. B. Glaser, Y. Israel, H. Kalant, R. E. Popham, & W. Schmidt (Eds.), *Research advances in alcohol and drug problems.* (Vol. 7, pp. 207–246). New York: Plenum.

Silverman, K., Higgins, S. T., Brooner, R. K., Montoya, I. D., Cone, E. J., Schuster, C. R., & Preston, K. L. (1996a). Sustained cocaine abstinence in methadone maintenance patients through voucher-based reinforcement therapy. *Archives of General Psychiatry, 53*, 409–415.

Silverman, K., Wong, G. J., Higgins, S. T., Brooner, R. K., Montoya, I. D., Contoreggi, C., Umbricht-Schneiter, A., Schuster, C. R., & Preston, K. L. (1996b). Increasing opiate abstinence through voucher-based reinforcement therapy. *Drug and Alcohol Dependence, 41*, 157–165.

Simkins-Bullock, J., Wildman, B. G., Bullock, W. A., & Sugrue, D. P. (1992). Etiological attributions, responsibility attributions, and marital adjustment in erectile dysfunction patients. *Journal of Sex and Marital Therapy, 18*, 83–103.

Sireling, L., Cohen, D., & Marks, I. (1988). Guided mourning for morbid grief: A controlled replication. *Behavior Therapy, 19*, 121–132.

Sitharthan, T., Sitharthan, G., Hough, M., & Kavanagh, D. J. (1997). Cue-exposure in moderation drinking: A comparison with cognitive-behavior therapy. *Journal of Consulting and Clinical Psychology, 65*, 878–882.

Sobell, M. B., & Sobell, L. C. (1984). The aftermath of heresy: A response to Pendery et al.'s (1982). critique of "individualized behavior therapy for alcoholics." *Behavior Research and Therapy, 22*, 413–440.

Sobell, M. B., Sobell, L. C., & Leo, G. I. (2000). Does enhanced social support improve outcomes for problem drinkers in guided self-change treatment? *Journal of Behavior Therapy and Experimental Psychiatry, 31*, 41–54.

Spaulding, W. D., Reed, D., Sullivan, M., Richardson, C., & Weiler, M. (1999). Effects of cognitive treatment in psychiatric rehabilitation. *Schizophrenia Bulletin, 25*, 657–676.

Spiegel, D. A., & Bruce, T. J. (1997). Benzodiazepines and exposure-based cognitive behavior therapies for panic disorder: Conclusions from combined treatment trials. *American Journal of Psychiatry, 154*, 773–781.

St. Lawrence, J. S., & Madakasira, S. (1992). Evaluation and treatment of premature ejaculation: A critical review. *International Journal of Psychiatry in Medicine, 22*, 77–97.

Staiger, P. K., Greeley, J. D., & Wallace, S. D. (1999). Alcohol exposure therapy: generalisation and changes in responsivity. *Drug and Alcohol Dependence, 57*, 29–40.

Stanley, M. A., Beck, J. G., & Glassco, J. D. (1996). Treatment of generalized anxiety in older adults: A preliminary comparison of cognitive-behavioral and supportive approaches. *Behavior Therapy, 27*, 565–581.

Stanley, M. A., & Turner, S. M. (1995). Current status of pharmacological and behavioral treatment of obsessive-compulsive disorder. *Behavior Therapy, 26*, 163–186.

Steketee, G., Eisen, J., Dyck, I., Warshaw, M., & Rasmussen, S. (2000). Predictors of course in obsessive-compulsive disorder. *Psychiatry Research, 89*, 229–238.

Steketee, G., & Shapiro, L. J. (1995). Predicting behavioral treatment outcome for agoraphobia and obsessive-compulsive disorder. *Clinical Psychology Review, 15*, 317–346.

Stephens, R. S., Roffman, R. A., & Simpson, E. E. (1994). Treating adult marijuana dependence: A test of the relapse prevention model. *Journal of Consulting and Clinical Psychology, 62*, 92–99.

Stitzer, M. L., Iguchi, M. Y., & Felch, L. J. (1992). Contingency take-home incentive: Effects on drug use of methadone maintenance patients. *Journal of Consulting and Clinical Psychology, 60*, 972–934.

Strauss, J. S., & Carpenter, W. T. (1977). Prediction of outcome in schizophrenia. *Archives of General Psychiatry, 34*, 158–163.

Stravinsky, A., Gaudette, G., Lesage, A., Arbel, N., Petit, P., Clerc, D., Fabian, J., Lamontagne, Y., Langlois, R., Lipp, O., & Sidoun, P. (1997). The treatment of sexually dysfunctional men without partners: A controlled study of three behavioural group approaches. *British Journal of Psychiatry, 170*, 338–344.

Stravinsky, A., Lesage, A., Marcouiller, M., & Elie, R. (1989). A test of the therapeutic mechanism in social skills training with avoidant personality disorder. *Journal of Nervous and Mental Disease, 177*, 739–744.

Stravinsky, A., Marks, I. M., & Jule, W. (1982). Social skills problems in neurotic outpatients. *Archives of General Psychiatry, 39*, 1378–1385.

Takefman, J., & Brender, W. (1984). An analysis of the effectiveness of two components in the treatment of erectile dysfunction. *Archives of Sexual Behavior, 13*, 321–340.

Tarrier, N., & Barrowclough, C. (1990). Family interventions for schizophrenia. *Behavior Modification, 14*, 408–440.

Tarrier, N., Barrowclough, C., Vaughy, C., Bamrah, J. S., Porceddu, K., Watts, S., & Freeman, H. L. (1994). Community management of schizophrenia: A two-year follow-up of a behavioral intervention with families. *British Journal of Psychiatry, 154*, 625–628.

Tarrier, N., Beckett, R., Harwood, S., Baker, A., Yusupoff, L., & Ugarteburu, I. (1993). A trial of two cognitive-behavioural methods of treating drug-resistant residual psychotic symptoms in schizophrenic patients: I. Outcome. *British Journal of Psychiatry, 162*, 524–532.

Tarrier, N., & Main, C. J. (1986). Applied relaxation training for generalised anxiety and panic attacks. *British Journal of Psychiatry, 149*, 330–336.

Tarrier, N., Pilgrim, H., Sommerfield, C., Farager, B., Reynolds, M., Graham, E., & Barrowcloughgh, C. (1999). A randomized trial of cognitive therapy and imaginal exposure in the treatment of chronic posttraumatic stress disorder. *Journal of Consulting and Clinical Psychology, 67*, 13–18.

Tarrier, N., Yusupoff, L., Kinney, C., McCarthy, E., Gledhill, A., Haddock, G., & Morris, J. (1998). Randomised controlled trial of intensive cognitive behaviour therapy for patients with chronic schizophrenia. *British Medical Journal, 317*, 303–307.

Taylor, S. (1996). Meta-analysis of cognitive-behavioral treatment for social phobia. *Journal of Behavior Therapy and Experimental Psychiatry, 27*, 1–9.

Telch, M. J., Agras, W. S., Tayloor, C. B., Roth, W. T., & Gallen, C. C. (1985). Combined pharmacological and behavioral treatment for agoraphobia. *Behaviour Research and Therapy, 23*, 325–335.

Teusch, L., Böhme, H., & Gastpar, M. (1997). The benefit of an insight-oriented and experiential approach on panic and agoraphobia symptoms. *Psychotherapy and Psychosomatics, 66*, 293–301.

Thevos, A. K., Roberts, J. S., Thomas, S. E., & Randall, C. L. (2000). Cognitive behavioral therapy delays relapse in female socially phobic alcoholics. *Addictive Behaviors, 25*, 333–345.

Thompson, L. W., Gallagher, D., & Steinmetz Breckenridge, J. S. (1987). Comparative effectiveness of psychotherapies for depressed elders. *Journal of Consulting and Clinical Psychology, 55*, 385–390.

Tiffany, S. T., & Conklin, C. A. (2000). A cognitive processing model of alcohol craving and compulsive alcohol use. *Addiction, 95, Supplement*, S145–S153.

Tomasson, J., & Vaglum, P. (1996). Psychopathology and alcohol consumption among treatment seeking alcoholics: A prospective study. *Addiction, 91*, 1019–1030.

Tsao, J.C.I., Lewin, M. R., & Craske, M. G. (1998). The effects of cognitive-behavior therapy for panic disorder on comorbid conditions. *Journal of Anxiety Disorders, 12*, 357–371.

Turkat, I. D., & Maisto, S. A. (1995). Personality disorders: Application of the experimental method to the formulation and modification of personality disorders. In D. H. Barlow (Ed.), *Clinical handbook of psychological disorders*. New York: Guilford Press.

Turkington, D., & Kingdon, D. (2000). Cognitive-behavioural techniques for general psychiatrists in the management of patients with psychosis. *British Journal of Psychiatry, 177*, 101–106.

Turner, S. M., Beidel, D. C., & Cooley-Quille, M. R. (1995). Two-year follow-up of social phobics treated with Social Effectiveness Therapy. *Behaviour Research and Therapy, 33*, 553–555.

Turner, S. M., Beidel, D. C., & Jacob, R. G. (1994). Social phobia: A comparison of behavior therapy and atenolol. *Journal of Consulting and Clinical Psychology, 62*, 350–358.

Turner, S. M., & Hersen, M. (1991). Disorders of social behavior: A behavioral approach. In S. M. Turner, K. S. Calhoun, & H. E. Adams (Eds.), *Handbook of clinical behavior therapy*. New York: John Wiley & Sons.

van Balkom, A.J.L.M., Bakker, A., Spinhoven, P., Blaauw, B.M.J.W., Smeenk, S., & Ruesink, B. (1997). A meta-analysis of the treatment of panic disorder with or without agoraphobia: A comparison of psychopharmacological, cognitive-behavioral, and combination treatments. *Journal of Nervous and Mental Disease, 185*, 510–516.

van Balkom, A.J.L.M., de Haan, E., van Oppen, P., Spinhoven, P., Hoogduin, K.A.L., & van Dyck, R. (1998). Cognitive and behavioral therapies alone versus in combination with fluvoxamine in the treatment of obsessive-compulsive disorder. *Journal of Nervous and Mental Disease, 186*, 492–499.

van Balkom, A.J.L.M., Nauta, M.C.E., & Bakker, A. (1995). Meta-analysis on the treatment of panic disorder with agoraphobia: Review and re-examination. *Clinical Psychology and Psychotherapy, 2*, 1–14.

van Balkom, A.J.L.M., van Oppen, P., Vermeulen, A.W.A., Nauta, M.C.E., Vorst, H.C.M., & van Dyck, R. (1994). A meta-analysis on the treatment of obsessive-compulsive disorder: A comparison of antidepressants, behavior and cognitive therapy. *Clinical Psychology Review, 14*, 359–381.

van den Hout, J. H., Arntz, A., & Kunkels, F. H. (1995). Efficacy of a self-control program in a psychiatric day-treatment center. *Acta Psychiatrica Scandinavia, 92*, 25–29.

van de Hout, M., Emmelkamp, P. M. G., Kraaykamp, J., & Griez, E. (1988). Behavioural treatment of obsessive-compulsives: Inpatient versus outpatient. *Behaviour Research and Therapy, 26*, 331–332.

van den Hout, M. A., Molen, M. van der, Griez, E., Lousberg, H., & Nansen, A. (1987). Reduction of CO_2-induced anxiety in patients with panic attacks afer repeated CO_2-exposure. *American Journal of Psychiatry, 144*, 788–791.

van Etten, M. L., & Taylor, S. (1998). Comparative efficacy of treatments for post-traumatic stress disorder. A meta-analysis. *Clinical Psychology and Psychotherapy, 5*, 126–144.

van Hout, W.J.P.J., & Emmelkamp, P.M.G. (2002). Exposure in vivo. In M. Hersen & W. Sledge (Eds.), *The Encyclopedia of Psychotherapy.* New York: Academic Press.

van Hout, W.J.P.J., Emmelkamp, P.M.G., & Scholing, A. (1994). The role of negative self-statements in agoraphobic situations: A process study of eight panic disorder patients with agoraphobia. *Behavior Modification, 18,* 389–410.

van Lankveld, J.J.D.M. (1998). Bibliotherapy in the treatment of sexual dysfunctions: A meta-analysis. *Journal of Consulting and Clinical Psychology, 66,* 702–632.

van Noppen, B. L., Pato, M. T., Marsland, R., & Rasmussen, S. A. (1998). A time-limited behavioral group treatment of obsessive-compulsive disorder. *Journal of Psychotherapy Practice and Research,* 7, 272–280.

van Oppen, P., de Haan, E., van Balkom, A.J.L.M., & Spinhoven, P. (1995). Cognitive therapy and exposure in vivo in the treatment of obsessive-compulsive disorder. *Behaviour Research and Therapy, 33,* 379–390.

van Oppen, P., & Emmelkamp, P.M.G. (1997). Behaviour and cognitive therapy for obsessive-compulsive disorder. In J. A. den Boer & H.G.M. Westenberg (Eds.), *Focus on obsessive-compulsive spectrum disorders.* (pp. 185–204). Amsterdam: Synthesis Publishers.

van Velzen, C.J.M., & Emmelkamp, P.M.G. (1996). The assessment of personality disorders: implications for cognitive and behavior therapy. *Behaviour Research and Therapy, 34,* 655–668.

van Velzen, C.J.M., & Emmelkamp, P.M.G. (1999). The relationship between anxiety disorders and personality disorders. In J. Derksen, C. Maffei, & H. Groen (Eds.), *Treatment of personality disorders* (pp. 129–153). New York: Plenum.

van Velzen, C.J.M., Emmelkamp, P.M.G., & Scholing, A. (1997). The impact of personality disorders on behavioural treatment outcome for social phobia. *Behaviour Research and Therapy, 35,* 889–900.

Vaughan, K., Armstrong, M. S., Gold, R., O'Connor, N., Jenneke, W., & Tarrier, N. (1994). A trial of eye movement desensitization compared to image habituation training and applied muscle relaxation in post-traumatic stress disorder. *Journal of Behavior Therapy and Experimental Psychiatry, 25,* 283–291.

Velligan, D. I., Bow-Thomas, C. C., Huntzinger, C., Ritch, J., Ledbetter, N., Prihoda, T. J., & Miller, A. L. (2000). Randomized controlled trial of the use of compensatory strategies to enhance adaptive functioning in outpatients with schizophrenia. *American Journal of Psychiatry, 157,* 1317–1328.

Verheul, R., van den Brink, W., & Hartgers, C. (1998). Personality disorders predict relapse in alcoholic patients. *Additive Behaviors, 23,* 869–882.

Veronen, L. J., & Kilpatrick, D. G. (1983). Stress management for rape victims. In D. Meichenbaum & M. E. Jaremko (Eds.), *Stress reduction and prevention.* New York: Plenum.

Wakefield, J. C. (1987). The semantics of success: Do masturbation exercises lead to partner orgasm? *Journal of Sex and Marital Therapy, 13,* 3–14.

Walters, G. D. (2000). Behavioral self-control training for problem drinkers: A meta-analysis of randomized control studies. *Behavior Therapy, 31,* 135–149.

Wells, A. (1999). A cognitive model of generalized anxiety disorder. *Behavior Modification, 23,* 526–555.

Wells, E. A., Peterson, P. L., Gainey, R. R., Hawkins, J. D., & Catalano, R. F. (1994). Outpatient treatment for cocaine abuse: A controlled comparison of relapse prevention and twelve-step approaches. *American Journal of Drug and Alcohol Abuse, 20,* 1–17.

White, J., Keenan, M., & Brooks, N. (1992). Stress control: A controlled comparative investigation of large group therapy for generalized anxiety disorder. *Behavioural Psychotherapy, 20,* 97–114.

Whitehead, A., Mathews, A., & Ramage, M. (1987). The treatment of sexually unresponsive women: A comparative evaluation. *Behaviour Research and Therapy, 25,* 195–205.

Wilhelm, F. H., & Roth, W. T. (1997). Acute and delayed effects of alprazolam on flight phobics during exposure. *Behaviour Research and Therapy, 35,* 831–841.

Williams, S. L., & Falbo, J. (1996). Cognitive and performance-based treatments for panic attacks in people with varying degrees of agoraphobic disability. *Behaviour Research and Therapy, 34,* 253–264.

Williams, S. L., & Zane, G. (1989). Guided mastery and stimulus exposure treatment for severe performance anxiety in agoraphobics. *Behaviour Research and Therapy, 27,* 237–245.

Wilson, P. H. (1982). Combined pharmacological and behavioral treatment of depression. *Behaviour Research and Therapy, 20,* 173–184.

Wilson, P. H., Goldin, J. C., & Charbonneau-Powis, M. (1983). Comparative efficacy of behavioral and cognitive treatments of depression. *Cognitive Therapy and Research,* 7, 111–124.

Wlazlo, Z., Schroeder-Hartwich, K., Hand, I., Kaiser, G., & Munchau, N. (1990). Exposure in vivo versus social skills training for social phobia: Long-term outcome and differential effects. *Behaviour Research & Therapy, 28,* 181–193.

Zane, G., & Williams, S. L. (1993). Performance-related anxiety in agoraphobia: Treatment procedures and cognitive mechanisms of change. *Behavior Therapy, 24,* 625–643.

Zeiss, A. M., Lewinsohn, P. M., & Munoz, R. F. (1979). Nonspecific improvement effects in depression using interpersonal skills training, pleasant activity schedules, or cognitive training. *Journal of Consulting and Clinical Psychology, 47,* 427–439.

Zubin, J., & Spring, B. (1977). Vulnerability: A new view of schizophrenia. *Journal of Abnormal Psychology, 86,* 103–126.

CHAPTER 10

COGNITIVE AND COGNITIVE BEHAVIORAL THERAPIES

STEVEN D. HOLLON
Vanderbilt University
AARON T. BECK
University of Pennsylvania

Few approaches have generated as much interest over the last quarter century as the cognitive and cognitive behavioral interventions. Based on the notion that thinking plays a role in the etiology and maintenance of at least some disorders, these interventions seek to reduce distress and enhance adaptive coping by changing maladaptive beliefs and providing new information-processing skills. The various approaches differ somewhat in the extent to which they emphasize cognitive mechanisms to the exclusion of more behavioral ones, but these differences are subtle and many professionals in the field have come to refer to these various interventions under the general rubric of cognitive behavior therapy (CBT).

Although early enthusiasm for these approaches sometimes outstripped their empirical support, there has been a veritable explosion of controlled clinical trials dealing with a diverse array of fully clinical populations over the last 15 years. For the most part, CBT has fared well in these trials, typically proving superior to minimal treatment (and nonspecific controls) and at least equal or superior to alternative psychosocial or pharmacological approaches, across adults (DeRubeis & Crits-Christoph, 1998) and children and adolescents (Kazdin & Weisz, 1998). Particularly exciting are indications that CBT may produce changes that endure beyond the end of treatment. This can be said for few other interventions. For example, as effective as medications are for many disorders, there is no evidence that they are anything more than palliative; that is, they suppress symptoms so long as they are taken but do nothing to alter underlying risk. CBT, on the other hand, may actually be curative; that is, there is evidence that CBT can reduce risk so that patients need not stay in treatment forever or that disorders can actually be prevented so that they are never expressed (Hollon, DeRubeis, & Seligman, 1992).

All cognitive interventions attempt to produce change by influencing thinking. Nonetheless, there is considerable variation with respect to both process and procedure. Those interventions that were developed by more dynamically trained theorists tend to emphasize the role of meaning. For example, in rational emotive therapy (RET; Ellis, 1962), patients are taught to examine the rationality of their beliefs and to adopt a more stoic philosophy. Similarly, in cognitive therapy (CT; Beck, 1991), patients are encouraged to treat their beliefs as hypotheses to be tested, and they are trained to run behavioral experiments to test the accuracy of their beliefs.

Conversely, those interventions that were developed by more behaviorally oriented theorists tend to conceptualize cognition in a more concrete fashion and often emphasize more peripheral mechanisms of change. Examples include stress inoculation training (SIT; Meichenbaum, 1985) or problem-solving training (PST; D'Zurilla & Goldfried, 1971) that seek to use modeling and repetition to compensate for perceived deficits in cognitive skills. Similarly, some cognitive behavioral approaches to the treatment of panic and the anxiety disorders still rely heavily on repeated exposure in the service of extinction or habituation. Other approaches like relapse prevention (RP; Marlatt & Gordon, 1985) or dialectic behavior therapy (DBT; Linehan, 1993) have incorporated cognitive elements into largely behavioral programs for specific disorders (addiction and borderline personality disorder, respectively).

It is not yet clear that these variations in theory and procedure have important implications for either treatment or prevention. What is clear is that the various cognitive behavioral interventions have performed well in a number of controlled trials with a diverse array of populations. The current review examines research on the cognitive behavioral therapies. First, we summarize findings as they relate to the treatment of depression and anxiety-based disorders, including post-tramatic stress. This is followed by a review of outcome research on eating disorders followed by an analysis of outcome in problems presented by children and adolescents. We then turn our attention to substance abuse problems, followed by a brief look at research on personality disorders, schizophrenia, behavioral medicine, and marital distress. Within research on these disorders we examine both the efficacy and underlying mechanisms of action.

Depression and the Prevention of Relapse

No disorder has received more attention from cognitive behavioral theorists than depression. Work in this area has played an integral role in the development of cognitive theory and has given rise to a number of discriminable interventions. These include cognitive therapy (Beck, Rush, Shaw, & Emery, 1979), later efforts to incorporate cognitive principles into largely behavioral interventions (Lewinsohn, Munoz, Youngren, & Zeiss, 1986), and recent efforts to integrate these approaches with more interpersonal and dynamic precepts (McCullough, 2000). All show the widespread impact of cognitive theory on current practice. The resultant interventions have generally done well in controlled trials. The cognitive behavioral interventions (along with interpersonal psychotherapy) and medications are recognized as being effective in the treatment of depression (American Psychiatric Association, 2000). The bulk of the empirical work on fully clinical populations has focused on cognitive therapy (CT), but other related approaches have been tested as well.

Cognitive Therapy

According to cognitive theory, people who are depressed hold unrealistically negative views about themselves, their worlds, and their futures (the negative cognitive triad) and fall prey to systematic distortions in information processing that leave them unable to correct these maladaptive beliefs (Beck, 1991). Their thoughts are filled with negative ruminations that seem to arise unbidden (automatic thoughts) and that are organized in accordance with certain underlying themes that put them at risk for future depressions (core beliefs and dysfunctional attitudes). These maladaptive beliefs and information-processing proclivities are part of an integrated knowledge structure (schema) that influences both what can be remembered and the way judgments are formed. These schemata are latent predispositions that can lie dormant for years before being activated, typically by some kind of stressful (or symbolic) life event.

In cognitive therapy, patients are taught to systematically evaluate their beliefs and information-processing proclivities in the service of becoming less depressed and reducing subsequent risk (Beck et al., 1979). The approach relies heavily on the process of empirical disconfirmation; patients are taught to treat their beliefs as hypotheses and to gather additional information and conduct behavioral experiments to test their accuracy. In essence, patients are encouraged to act like scientists, withholding judgment about the validity of their beliefs until they have been examined in a systematic fashion. The approach has been modified in recent years to more effectively deal with the kinds of stable core beliefs that give rise to maladaptive interpersonal behavioral propensities that are the hallmarks of long-standing personality disorders (Beck, Freeman, & Associates, 1990).

Is CT effective? CT typically has fared well in comparison to alternative interventions with respect to the reduction of acute distress. Most quantitative reviews find CT superior to no-treatment or nonspecific treatment controls and at least as effective as alternative psychosocial or pharmacological interventions (Dobson, 1989; Gloaguen, Cottraux, Cucherat, & Blackburn, 1998). Effect sizes tend to be large relative to minimal treatment controls, and most patients show a good response, with about half of all outpatients showing a complete remission. Other studies suggest that its efficacy may extend to inpatient samples (Bowers, 1990; Miller, Norman, Keitner, Bishop, & Dow, 1989; Thase, Bowler, & Harden, 1991) and to patients with bipolar disorder (Lam et al., 2000), although the latter work is still relatively new.

Although CT is clearly effective in the treatment of depression, questions remain regarding how it compares to medications in the treatment of more severely depressed patients. Quantitative reviews suggest a modest advantage for CT over medications, but that advantage is largely based on early studies that implemented medication treatment in a less than optimal fashion (Hollon & Shelton, 2001). For example, medications were withdrawn prior to the end of active treatment in one study (Rush, Beck, Kovacs, & Hollon, 1977) and, in a second study, response to medication in a general practice setting was so poor as to raise questions about the adequacy of implementation (Blackburn, Bishop, Glen, Whalley, & Christie, 1981). Subsequent studies that did a more adequate job of implementing medication treatment typically found no advantage for CT over drugs in terms of acute response (the psychiatric sample in Blackburn et al., 1981; Hollon, DeRubeis, Evans et al., 1992; Murphy, Simons, Wetzel, & Lustman, 1984).

None of these studies was placebo-controlled; inclusion of such a comparison can help determine whether medication treatment was adequately implemented (Jacobson & Hollon, 1996a). The National Institute of Mental Health's Treatment of Depression Collaborative Research Project was the first study to include such a comparison, and while either medication treatment or interpersonal psychotherapy (IPT) was superior to placebo in the treatment of more severely depressed outpatients, CT was not (Elkin et al., 1995). No differences were observed among less severely depressed outpatients. These findings led many to conclude that, although CT might be effective in the treatment of less severe depressions, medications (or perhaps IPT) were to be preferred in the treatment of more severely depressed patients (American Psychiatric Association, 2000).

These findings were not robust across research sites, however. CT performed as well as pharmacotherapy at the site that had the most experience in its implementation and less well at two other sites that were less experienced in its use (Jacobson & Hollon, 1996b). Moreover, the finding of poorer response to CT among more severely depressed outpatients was not consistent with other studies already in the literature. DeRubeis and colleagues conducted an analysis combining data from several studies in which they compared response to drugs and CT among more severely depressed patients in these trials (DeRubeis, Gelfand, Tang, & Simons, 1999). As shown in Figure 10.1, only the NIMH study showed any advantage for drugs over CT among such patients; across the studies sampled, differences between the two conditions were virtually nonexistent.

Subsequent placebo-controlled trials have supported the notion of comparable efficacy, although with a caveat. Jarrett and colleagues found CT as effective as medication treatment

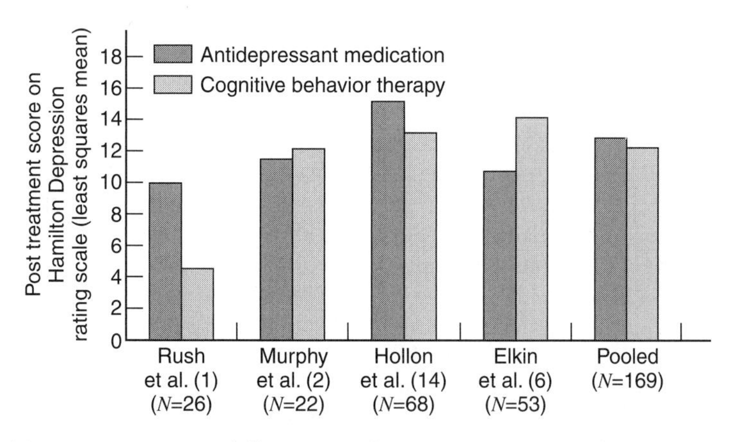

FIGURE 10.1 Treatment response following medication or cognitive therapy for severe depression: Mega-analysis of four randomized comparisons. From "Medication versus cognitive behavior therapy for severely depressed outpatients: Mega-analysis of four randomized comparisons" by R. J. DeRubeis et al., 1999, *American Journal of Psychiatry, 156*, p. 1010. Copyright 1999 by the American Psychiatric Association. Reprinted by permission.

with a monoamine oxidase inhibitor and superior to pill-placebo in the treatment of atypical depression (Jarrett et al., 1999). A recently completed but as yet unpublished replication of the NIMH study has demonstrated that either CT or medications were superior to pill-placebo and comparable to one another in the treatment of more severely depressed outpatients (DeRubeis, Hollon, Amsterdam, & Shelton, 2001). The caveat mentioned earlier is that there was a site-by-treatment interaction reminiscent of what was found in the NIMH study. CT was better than medications at the site with the more experienced cognitive therapists (Pennsylvania) but less effective than medications at the site where the cognitive therapists were less experienced (Vanderbilt). Therapists at the latter site were provided with ongoing supervision from the Beck Institute and improved both their rated competence and patient outcomes over the course of the study. Obviously, other factors varied across sites and could have accounted for the differences that were found.

It has long been known that allegiance effects predict differential response in controlled trials; much of the early advantage for cognitive therapy over other interventions disappeared when investigator allegiance was taken into account (Robinson, Berman, & Neimeyer, 1990). It seems possible that differential expertise and competence account for the major portion of allegiance effects (Hollon, 1999). Allegiance effects have gotten smaller over time as comparative studies have incorporated investigators with competing allegiances into the larger research teams (Gaffan, Tsaousis, & Kemp-Wheeler, 1995). Pressumably those sites in the NIMH study and our own study with more experienced cognitive therapists performed better relative to medications than did those sites with less experienced providers, just as earlier trials with less adequate medication treatment tended to produce advantages for CT. Moreover, continued training and supervision can enhance the performance of less experienced cognitive therapists (as indicated in our unpublished study); only minimal ongoing supervision was provided during the NIMH study (Elkin et al., 1989). Such additional training is most likely to be necessary with more difficult patients. More competent therapists also appear to produce better results in medication treatment; the kind of training and supervision provided in well-run clinical trials appears to improve the quality of the outcomes observed (Hollon, 1996). It seems reasonable to conclude that CT is about as effective as medications regardless of severity, at least among nonpsychotic patients. Nevertheless, additional placebo-controlled trials are desirable, particularly those that address the issue of training and supervision in a systematic fashion.

Does CT prevent symptom return? Depression is a chronic episodic disorder; even patients who have been successfully treated appear to be at considerable risk for future episodes. Although pharmacotherapy suppresses the reemergence of symptoms so long as it is continued, there is no indication that it does anything to reduce underlying risk (Hollon & Shelton, 2001). Current pharmacological practice is moving in the direction of maintaining medications indefinitely for patients with a history of recurrence (APA, 2000). There are indications that continuation CT can prevent the return of symptoms following initial response (see, for example, Jarrett et al., 2001). Session frequency typically is reduced to no more than monthly contacts, and effects are most pronounced for patients with a history of early onset or unstable remission during acute treatment.

Even more exciting are indications that CT may have an enduring effect that extends beyond the end of treatment. Patients treated to remission with CT are about half as likely to experience a depressive relapse following treatment termination as patients treated to remission with medications (see Hollon & Shelton, 2001, for a review). The NIMH study is the sole exception in the literature, and even in that study such nonsignificant differences as were observed favored CT over the other active interventions (Shea et al., 1992). As shown in Figure 10.2, Evans and colleagues found that patients treated with CT did as well following treatment termination as patients who continued on active medications (Evans et al., 1992). We replicated this finding in our as yet unpublished comparison of CT versus medications in the treatment of more severely depressed patients. In that study, patients treated to remission with CT were considerably less likely to relapse following treatment termination than patients treated to remission with medications and no more likely to relapse than patients who continued on medications (Hollon, DeRubeis, Shelton, & Amsterdam, 2001).

Two recent studies suggest that adding CT to medications following the initial response can not only reduce the level of residual symptoms, but also protect against subsequent symptom return follow-

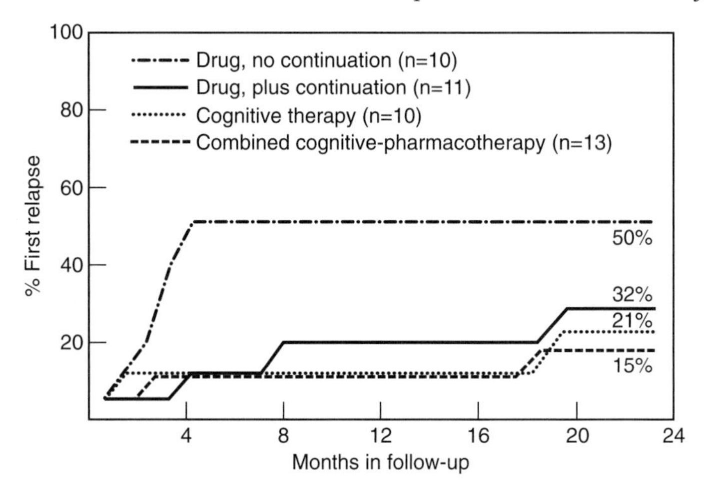

FIGURE 10.2 Relapse after successful treatment. From "Differential relapse following cognitive therapy and pharmacotherapy for depression" by M. D. Evans et al., 1992, Archives of General Psychiatry, 49, p. 805. Copyright 1992 by the American Medical Association. Reprinted by permission.

ing treatment termination (Fava, Rafanelli, Grandi, Conti, & Belluardo, 1998; Paykel et al., 1999). Moreover, unlike the other studies in this literature, Fava and colleagues extended medication treatment long enough to protect patients from relapse. What was observed in that study was likely an enduring effect for prior CT with respect to the prevention of recurrence. Preventing relapse (the return of symptoms associated with the treated episode) is impressive because it suggests that CT has an enduring effect; preventing recurrence (the onset of a wholly new episode) is even more impressive because it suggests that CT can change the course of the underlying disorder. Medication may be the current standard of treatment, but it is largely palliative; it works only as long as it is continued or maintained. CT, on the other hand, may actually be curative. There are even indications that CT can prevent initial onset in persons at risk with no prior history of depression (Seligman, Schulman, DeRubeis, & Hollon, 1999).

Finally, Teasdale, Segal, and Williams (1995) have developed a mindfulness-based cognitive therapy (MBCT) that draws on strategies from dialectic behavior therapy (acceptance and meditation) to help teach patients to distance themselves from their depressive ruminations. In this approach, patients are trained to focus not so much on the content of thinking as on its process. Rather than examine the accuracy of their beliefs, they are encouraged to be aware of their occurrence without responding to them in an affective fashion. In a recent trial, MBCT was shown to have an enduring effect that reduced risk for relapse among patients first treated to remission with medications (Teasdale et al., 2000). Given that this training can be provided in an economical group format and that meditation has gained widespread acceptance in the popular culture, MBCT is likely to receive an enthusiastic response in the field.

COMBINED TREATMENT WITH CT AND DRUGS. Combining CT with medication appears to produce only a modest increment in efficacy of about 10 to 15%, large enough to be of interest clinically but not large enough to be detected in the smaller studies that comprise the bulk of the literature (Hollon & Shelton, 2001). However, effects of that magnitude are large enough to be of value if robust, and there are indications that combined treatment retains any of the specific advantages associated with either single modality. Medications sometimes work faster than CT (especially for more severe and chronic patients) and depend less on the skill of the therapist. At the same time, CT's enduring effect appears to be robust regardless of whether it is provided with medications or without during acute treatment (Evans et al., 1992) or added after medications have been used to bring patients to remission (Fava et al., 1998; Paykel et al., 1999). Thus, there may be reasons to prefer combined (or sequential) treatment, particularly for patients who have complex or chronic problems or an elevated risk for recurrence.

A recent trial with a newly developed cognitive behavioral intervention suggests that the combination of drugs and psychotherapy may be particularly effective in the treatment of chronic depression. The newly developed intervention, called a Cognitive Behavioral Analysis System for Psychotherapy (CBASP), represents an innovative blend of cognitive, behavioral, dynamic, and interpersonal components. It is predicated on the notion that patients with chronic depression have a particular difficulty learning from experience in problematic interpersonal relationships (McCullough, 2000). In that trial, patients provided with combined treatment did considerably better than patients provided with either single modality alone (Keller et al., 2000). In fact, the pattern of response was wholly consistent with an additive model; patients in combined treatment showed the same early gains as patients treated with medications alone, but also showed later gains uniquely associated with the cognitive behavioral intervention. Overall, gains produced by combined treatment relative to either single modality were considerably larger than those found in earlier studies. Whether this enhanced response for combined treatment was unique to CBASP or a more general reflection of the special needs of chronic patients remains to be seen, but the study is likely to generate renewed interest in combined treatment in general and CBASP in particular.

Who benefits from CT? There are few clear indications that specific types of patients do better or worse in CT than in other types of interventions, at least among nonpsychotic patients. That is, few patient characteristics have yet been found that are of use in selecting one treatment over another (prescription). As previously described, the suggestion from the NIMH study that more severely depressed outpatients do less well in CT than in pharmacotherapy was not robust across sites (Elkin et al., 1989) and has not been replicated in other studies (e.g., DeRubeis et al., 1999). Similarly, neither endogenicity nor melancholia predicted differential response in any of the studies previously reviewed. Rude and Rehm (1991) found little evidence that degree of cognitive dysfunction predicted differential response, and McKnight and colleagues reported that dexamethasone nonsuppression did not predict differential response to CT versus medications in a controlled trial (McKnight, Nelson-Gray, & Barnhill, 1992).

Nonetheless, it would be premature to conclude that such prescriptive indices do not exist. For a variety of reasons, it is simply more difficult to detect moderation than it is to detect a main effect for treatment (Smith & Sechrest, 1991). The appropriate designs are more complex, prescriptive indices need to be carefully assessed, and larger samples are required to generate adequate statistical power. Because few of the existing studies were designed with such considerations in mind, it is possible that such indices may be detected in more methodologically adequate trials.

One of the better examples of research of this kind also illustrates the pitfalls of relying on clinical judgment alone to match patients to treatments. In a reanalysis of the NIMH study data, Barber and Muenz (1996) found that avoidant patients did better in CT than in IPT (especially if married), whereas obsessive patients did better in IPT than in CT. Casual clinical inference would have predicted the opposite pattern based on perceived similarities between the respective treatments and interpersonal style. These findings provide support for a "theory of opposites" in the sense that patients seem to need what they don't have from their therapist. Earlier analyses based on data from that same NIMH study indicated that low social dysfunction predicted superior response to IPT, whereas low cognitive dysfunction predicted superior response to cognitive therapy (Sotsky et al., 1991).

The recent APA guideline on the treatment of depression suggests that cognitive therapy may be particularly effective in the treatment of patients with personality disorder (APA, 2000). Although that may ultimately prove to be true (particularly for the newer schema-focused modifications), the claim itself was based on a misinterpretation of the existing literature. Most egregious was the misreading of data reported by Shea and colleagues on the impact of differential treatment on patients with personality disorders in the NIMH study (Shea et al., 1990). Personality disorder predicted poorer response to treatment in either medication treatment or IPT but not in CT. However, it was not that patients with personality disorders did better in CT than in the other conditions; rather, it was that patients without personality disorders did worse. Errors of this kind abound in the literature with respect to efforts to identify predictors of differential response.

Most studies suggest that chronicity and comorbidity predict poorer response to treatment but not necessarily differential response. Patients with depression superimposed on underlying personality disorders often take months or even years to show a full response, rather than the several weeks shown by patients free of such complications. Not being married also appears to predict poor response, although the reasons remain unclear (see, for example, Sotsky et al., 1991). A recent but as yet unpublished study suggests that post-traumatic stress disorder (PTSD) is a nonspecific negative prognostic index, whereas generalized anxiety disorder (GAD) predicts differential response. Anxious patients do better on medications than in CT, whereas nonanxious patients show the opposite pattern (DeRubeis et al., 2001). Patients with atypical depressions appear to be particularly vulnerable to relapse, as do patients with histories of early onset or chronic dysthymia or residual symptoms at remission (Hollon, DeRubeis, Shelton, & Amsterdam, 2001). Whether any of the relationships between patient characteristics and outcome will survive replication remains to be seen. However, it is easier to predict who is at risk for relapse (and either kept on medication or provided with a course of CT for its enduring effects) than it is to identify patient characteristics that predict differential response during acute treatment.

What are CT's active ingredients? Cognitive theory assumes that change is brought about in CT by virtue of efforts to examine the accuracy of existing beliefs; nonspecific aspects of the therapeutic relationship are seen as playing a secondary role (Beck et al., 1979). Measures have been developed to assess adherence to those components of treatment specified by theory (Hill, O'Grady, & Elkin, 1992), as well as to assess the competence with which CT is implemented (Shaw & Dobson, 1988). An effort to relate the quality of execution of treatment components to treatment response in the NIMH study was somewhat disappointing, with competence showing only a modest relation to outcome after controlling for adherence and nonspecific facilitative conditions (Shaw et al., 1999). Studies by DeRubeis and colleagues have been somewhat more promising. In those trials, adherence to CT early in treatment predicted subsequent response, whereas the rated quality of the therapeutic alliance appeared to be more a consequence of symptom change than a cause (see, for example, Feeley, DeRubeis, & Gelfand, 1999). In those studies, the extent to which the therapist structured the session and used concrete cognitive and behavioral techniques best predicted subsequent response. Moreover, Burns and Spangler (2000) have shown that homework compliance appears to mediate subsequent response and not vice versa; that is, patients who do more homework subsequently get better, not that getting better leads to doing more homework. Thus, the existing literature, sparse though it is, is largely consistent with the notion that cognitive therapy produces change in depression largely through processes specified by the theory.

Does CT work by changing cognition? Cognitive theory also suggests that change in beliefs is the primary mechanism of change in CT. However, although thinking typically becomes less negative across the course of therapy, comparative trials typically find that pharmacotherapy or other interventions can produce as much change in cognition as does CT (e.g., Imber et al., 1990; Simons, Garfield, & Murphy, 1984). Such findings are sometimes interpreted as indicating that cognition is merely epiphenomenal, but specificity of change is not particularly informative with respect to mediation (Hollon, DeRubeis, & Evans, 1987). However, differential covariation is informative; studies that have examined the relation between change in beliefs (particularly expectations) and subsequent change in depression have found stronger relations in CT than in pharmacotherapy (see, for example, DeRubeis et al., 1990). Such a pattern is consistent with the notion that cognitive change mediates subsequent change in depression in CT.

Theory further suggests that, although the disconfirmation of negative expectations is central to the reduction of existing distress, it is the modification of underlying propensities such as attributional styles that is critical to the prevention of future episodes (see, for example, Abramson, Metalsky, & Alloy, 1989). Consistent with these predictions, Hollon and colleagues found that CT produced greater change in attributional styles than did pharmacotherapy and that change in attributional styles appeared to mediate CT's relapse preventive effect (Hollon, Evans, & DeRubeis, 1990). Teasdale and colleagues have also reported that change in underlying propensities like attributional style predicts subsequent relapse (Teasdale et al., 2001). However, in their trial, it was becoming less extreme and more even-handed that was beneficial, not simply becoming less negative. That is, patients who became unrealistically positive were also at greater risk, a pattern that we replicated in our most recent study (DeRubeis & Hollon, personal communication). These findings, along with those just reported with respect to expectancy change, are consistent with the notion that different aspects of cognitive change mediate different aspects of response to CT.

Finally, Tang and DeRubeis (1999) have observed that many patients treated with CT show "sudden gains" following a single session that accounts for the bulk of the change they show across the course of treatment. These "sudden gains" occur at different times for different patients, but tend to be preceded by cognitive change and followed by improved ratings of the therapeutic alliance. In effect, it's as if the patient suddenly "understands" that it is their thinking that is unduly negative, rather than their personalities or even their life situations. Once they come to this realization, they seem to do a better job of managing their own affect and behavior. Patients who show "sudden gains" tend to get better faster and to stay better longer than do patients who show a more gradual pattern of response. This work, combined with the process studies just described, suggests that patients are most likely to respond when they do their homework and their therapists focus on specific cognitive behavioral strategies in a structured fashion. However, change within the client is just as likely to emerge in an unpredictable fashion as it is to arise in a gradual and cumulative way.

Other Cognitive Behavioral Approaches

Several approaches to the treatment of depression incorporate cognitive components into largely behavioral frameworks. For example, Lewinsohn and colleagues developed a psychoeducational approach for the prevention and treatment of depression that incorporates cognitive strategies into a more conventional behavioral framework (Lewinsohn et al., 1986). Initial trials in adult samples were supportive (Lewinsohn, Hoberman, & Clarke, 1989), and a recent meta-analysis suggests that the magnitude of its effect approaches that produced by individual CBT (Cuijpers, 1998). However, it has rarely been applied in fully clinical populations, although it has been used extensively in the prevention and treatment of depression in children and adolescents, as discussed in a later section.

Self-control therapy (SCT) seeks to remedy perceived deficits in self-regulatory skills (Rehm, 1977). Early trials in adult populations were generally supportive but typically lacked clinical realism, and the approach has not been widely adopted in clinical practice (see Hollon & Beck, 1994, for a review). As with Lewinsohn's approach, much of its recent success has come in the treatment of depression in children and adolescents.

Finally, problem-solving therapy (PST), which seeks to improve coping capacity, also has done well in controlled trials in recruited adult populations (see, for example, Nezu & Perri, 1989). However, once again, these studies lacked clinical realism. In more clinically relevant studies, PST was effective in the treatment of suicidal adolescents (Lerner & Clum, 1990) and reduced depression and hopelessness among patients with a history of repeated suicide attempts (Salkovskis, Atha, & Storer, 1990). A recent trial in England found that a simpfied version of PST was as effective as medication and superior to a placebo control in a primary care sample (Mynors-Wallis, Gath, Lloyd-Thomas, & Tomlison, 1995). This latter work will likely lead to a resurgence of interest in this approach, especially in primary care settings.

Summary

There can be little doubt that cognitive behavioral interventions are effective in the treatment of depression. In particular, CT has been tested extensively in clinical populations and appears to be as effective as medications with respect to the reduction of acute distress and quite possibly is longer lasting. In a chronic recurrent disorder like depression, evidence of a preventive effect is most exciting. MBCT, though based on limited evidence, also appears to have an enduring effect, and CBASP appears to enhance the efficacy of medications in the treatment of chronic depression. Further research on these treatments is needed. Other more behavioral versions of CBT have fared well in more limited trials and, as discussed in a subsequent section, show real promise in the prevention and treatment of depression among children and adolescents.

Panic and the Anxiety Disorders

Some of the most exciting work in the last 15 years has been done in the treatment of panic and the anxiety disorders. Earlier studies in this area lacked clinical realism and largely focused on problems like assertion difficulties or evaluation anxiety. However, by the time of our last review, sophisticated theoretical models had been proposed, and a number of methodologically elegant studies had been conducted with actual clinical populations (Hollon & Beck, 1994). If anything, this trend has accelerated in the intervening years, and powerful cognitive behavioral interventions exist for many (but not all) of the anxiety disorders.

Catastrophic Cognitions in Panic and Agoraphobia

Few disorders have undergone so complete a reconceptualization in the last 15 years as panic disorder and agoraphobia. Behavior theory viewed panic as a conditioned response to external cues to be extinguished via exposure, whereas biological models viewed it as a spontaneous discharge of the neural centers mediating stress response and treated it with medications (see Hollon & Beck, 1994). More recent cognitive models have emphasized the role of catastrophic cognitions. According to these models, people panic when they misinterpret benign bodily sensations as signs of impending physical or mental catastrophe (Beck & Emery, 1985; Clark, 1986). Therefore, it is more important that patients test the accuracy of their beliefs than that they necessarily expose themselves to problematic situations.

Cognitive behavioral interventions based on this model have been shown to be both specific and effective in the treatment of panic disorder (DeRubeis & Crits-Christoph, 1998). Historically, more behaviorally oriented theorists like Barlow have emphasized repeated exposure to interioceptive cues and incorporated a broader range of coping strategies like relaxation training within an approach called panic control treatment (PCT; Barlow & Cerny, 1988). Conversely, cognitively oriented theorists like Clark have focused on the disconfirmation of the catastrophic beliefs and tend to discourage the use of strategies that function like safety behaviors (CT; Clark & Salkovskis, 1991). However, these differences are subtle at best, and many in the field have come to think of them as equivalent interventions (DeRubeis & Crits-Christoph, 1998).

Early studies of the cognitive interventions were unimpressive but typically tested generic treatments that did not focus explicitly on catastrophic misinterpretations (see Hollon & Beck, 1994, for a review). Interventions focused specifically on catastrophic misinterpretations have been considerably more successful. Barlow and Lehman (1996) reviewed a dozen trials conducted through the mid-1990s and found that PCT or CT eliminated panic in up to 80% of treated patients and typically was superior to various no-treatment or credible psychotherapy controls. Reviewing an overlapping set of studies, DeRubeis and Crits-Christoph (1998) concluded that CBT was both efficacious and specific in the treatment of panic disorder, with most studies showing it to be superior to minimal treatment controls or alternative interventions. There were only two exceptions. The first was a study by Black and colleagues in which substantial modifications were made to the cognitive intervention (Black, Wesner, Bowers, & Gabel, 1993). The second was a study by Shear and colleagues in which critical elements of CBT were provided to patients in the control condition (Shear, Pilkonis, Claitre, & Lean, 1994).

Two studies illustrate the efficacy of the cognitive behavioral interventions. In one of the more impressive studies in the literature, Clark and colleagues found CT focused on catastrophic misinterpretations to be superior to either imipramine pharmacotherapy or applied relaxation in a sample of patients with panic disorder (Clark et al., 1994). Differences between the active treatments are shown in Figure 10.3. Moreover, all three active treatments were superior to a wait list control. Nearly 90% of the patients treated with CT were panic-free after three months of treatment versus only about 50% of the patients treated with the other interventions. Virtually none of the patients assigned to the wait list control were panic free. CT also produced greater change in catastrophic cognitions than did the other conditions (as well as anxiety and avoidance). Medications were continued for six months and then withdrawn, with patients in the psychosocial conditions receiving only a limited number of booster sessions between months three and six. All patients were then followed across the next nine months. During the followup period, only 5% of the patients previously treated with focused CT relapsed, compared with 40% of patients treated with medications. Consistent with theory, patients with the least catastrophic cognitions at the end of treatment were less likely to replase following treatment termination. This enduring effect for CT has been replicated in other trials, although patients treated with more purely behavioral interventions sometimes also show continued gains (Arntz & Van den Hout, 1996; Öst & Westling, 1995).

The other illustrative study was a particularly impressive multisite comparison of drugs and

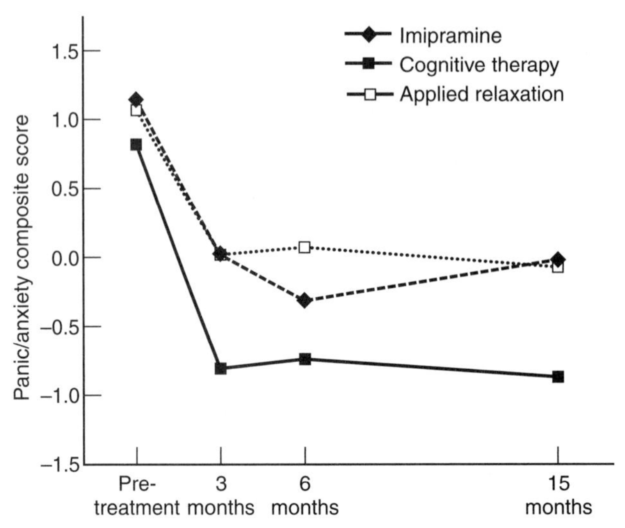

FIGURE 10.3 Cognitive therapy versus applied relaxation or medication in the treatment of panic disorder. From "A comparison of cognitive therapy, applied relaxation and imipramine in the treatment of panic disorder" by D. M. Clark et al., 1994, *British Journal of Psychiatry, 164*, p. 766. Copyright 1994 by the British Royal Society of Psychiatry. Reprinted by permission.

CBT conducted by Barlow and colleagues (Barlow, Gorman, Shear, & Woods, 2000). In that study, 312 panic-disordered patients (with or without mild agoraphobia) were randomly assigned to three months of weekly acute treatment followed by six months of monthly maintenance treatment with either CBT or imipramine pharmacotherapy, alone or in combination, or a pill-placebo control. The study also included a fifth condition in which CBT was combined with a pill-placebo. Each single modality was superior to pill-placebo, with combined treatment somewhat better still by the end of maintenance treatment. Imipramine produced higher quality response among treatment completers, but CBT was more enduring. Only 4% of the patients who responded to CBT had a relapse following treatment termination versus 25% of the responders to imipramine. Curiously, adding medications undermined the long-term durability of CBT. Patients in the combined condition showed the highest rate of relapse, whereas patients treated with CBT plus placebo were no more likely to relapse than patients treated with CBT alone.

Several studies suggest that CBT can be used to facilitate discontinuation from high-potency benzodiazepines. These medications are efficacious in the suppression of panic symptoms but tend to provoke rebound panic attacks when discontinued. Using an extremely slow withdrawal, Otto and colleagues found that 76% of patients were able to taper off drugs compared to only 25% of controls (Otto et al., 1993). Similarly, Bruce and colleagues pooled data across two trials and found that exposure to CBT facilitated discontinuation from alprazolam in over 75% of treated patients relative to only 30% of controls (Bruce, Spiegel, & Hegel, 1999). Although there is some controversy as to whether patients should be started on alprazolam in the first place, it does appear that CBT can help them discontinue this medication without again becoming symptomatic.

Many of these studies have systematically excluded patients with more severe agoraphobic avoidance. A recent study by Williams and Falbo (1996) that included patients with a wide range of agoraphobic avoidance suggests a note of caution. In that study, cognitive therapy with or without exposure-based treatment was superior to a wait list control in reducing panic frequency, but the likelihood of becoming panic-free was strongly related to degree of agoraphobic avoidance (94% for patients with low avoidance versus 52% for patients with high avoidance). Similarly, Bouchard and colleagues found lower rates of end-state functioning for group CBT or exposure treatment than is typically reported in the literature in a sample of patients with at least some agoraphobic avoidance (Bouchard et al., 1996).

Finally, Clark and colleagues have shown that a brief version of cognitive therapy can be highly effective in the treatment of panic disorder (Clark et al., 1999). In this study, extensive use was made of between-session self-study modules to reduce treatment time from the normal 12 to 15 sessions to about 6.5 hours of therapist time, including booster sessions. Both full and brief CT were superior to a wait list control on all measures but did not differ from each other. This suggests that CT can be markedly reduced in duration in a manner that may suit third-party payers and still produce beneficial effects.

Hypochondriasis and Concerns about Illness

Hypochondriasis is common in medical settings and is generally considered difficult to manage. Such patients believe they have a physical illness and take little comfort from medical reassurance. The disorder has rarely been studied empirically, and it has long been thought to be largely impervious to treatment. However, a cognitive model of hypochondriasis has been developed that provides a promising basis for intervention (Warwick & Salkovskis, 1990). This model suggests that the central feature of the disorder is an enduring tendency to misinterpret innocuous physical signs and symptoms as evidence of serious illness. These misinterpretations lead to considerable anxiety and repeated efforts to seek reassurance. The model is similar to the one developed by Clark and colleagues for panic, with the primary difference being the imminence of the concerns. Panic disorder typically involves threats that could happen within the next several minutes, like having a heart attack, whereas hypochondriasis typically involves dangers that are more likely to occur over a period of months or years, like developing cancer.

As might be expected, treatment for hypochondriasis is patterned closely after CT for panic. Patients are provided with a rationale that suggests that the problem lies not so much with their health as with their health anxiety. They are encouraged to identify and challenge the evidence for their misinterpretations of sensations as symptoms and are helped to construct more realistic interpretations. Behavioral experiments are used to induce innocuous "symptoms" via deliberate body focusing and to prevent repeated body checking and reassurance seeking. Homework assignments are given after each session, and patients are encouraged to keep a daily record of negative thoughts and rational responses.

This approach has been tested in two studies with clinical populations. In the first, Warwick and colleagues found CT superior to a wait list control after four months of treatment; gains were essentially maintained at a three-month followup (Warwick, Clark, Cobb, & Salkovskis, 1996). Patients went from spending over 50% of their time worried about their health to less than 15%, and disease conviction dropped from nearly 70% to under 10%. In a subsequent trial, CT was again compared to a wait list control, as well as a behavioral stress management condition (Clark et al., 1998). As shown in Figure 10.4, both active treatments were superior to the wait list control, with cognitive behavior therapy somewhat better than the behavioral intervention over the course of acute treatment. These studies suggest that CT is a promising intervention for the treatment of hypochondriasis. Whether it will prove to be specific remains to be seen, but in a disorder that has been thought to be refractory to treatment for so long this is progress indeed.

Generalized Anxiety Disorder and the Primacy of Worry

Generalized anxiety disorder (GAD) has long presented a problem for behavior theory, since the pervasive arousal traditionally thought to be the hallmark of the disorder often has no clear external referent (Hollon & Beck, 1994). Behavioral interventions like exposure plus response prevention are of little use in GAD, since there are no clear external stimuli to target. With the recent emphasis on chronic and pervasive apprehension and worry, the core features of the disorder are now seen as being even more cognitive (Brown, Barlow, & Liebowitz, 1994). Benzodiazepines provide some relief and are widely prescribed, but can induce dependence and lose potency with prolonged use; antidepressants are less problematic but do nothing to reduce future risk. More traditional forms of psychotherapy have long been touted but rarely tested.

Interventions that incorporate cognitive aspects may be particularly effective in the treatment of generalized anxiety disorder. According to cognitive theory, chronic and diffuse states of anxious arousal are largely the product of a systematic tendency to overestimate the presence of danger across situations or to underestimate one's ability to cope with those risks that are present (Beck & Emery, 1985). According to this theory, any intervention that reduces the unrealistic perception of danger or enhances the

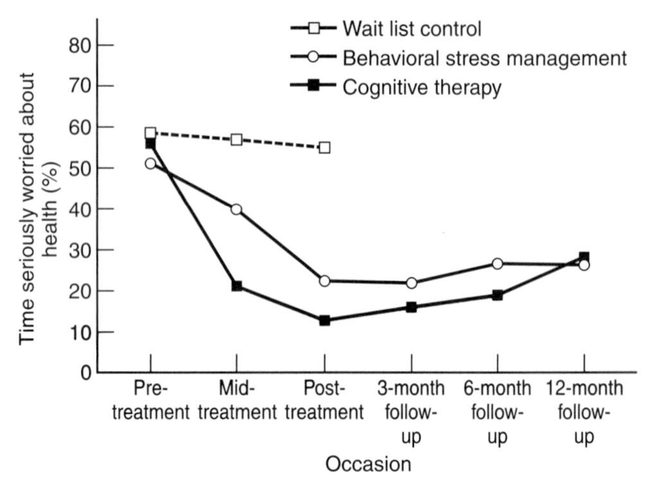

FIGURE 10.4 Cognitive therapy in the treatment of hypochondriasis: Time spent seriously worried about health as a function of treatment. From "Two psychological treatments for hypochondriasis" by D. M. Clark et al., 1998, *British Journal of Psychiatry, 173,* p. 224. Copyright 1998 by the British Royal Society of Psychiatry. Reprinted by permission.

perception of one's ability to cope with threat should reduce distress.

Current cognitive behavioral approaches to GAD typically combine relaxation training or meditation with cognitive restructuring to bring the process of worry under control (Barlow & Lehman, 1996). CBT has been found to be superior to minimal treatment and nonspecific controls in a number of studies (see Borkovec & Ruscio, 2001, for a review) and more effective than dynamic psychotherapy in the one study in which it has been compared (Durham et al., 1994). Few studies have found differences between CBT and more purely cognitive or behavioral interventions with respect to acute treatment, and treatment gains typically have been maintained across extended followups (Borkovec & Ruscio, 2001). CBT also has fared well in direct comparisons to medications (typically minor tranquilizers). In several trials, CBT has been either more effective or longer lasting than drugs in the treatment of GAD (see Hollon & Beck, 1994, for a review).

Although CBT has rarely been superior to behavior therapy alone with respect to acute treatment, differences favoring the more cognitive interventions have sometimes emerged over extended followup periods (e.g., Borkovec & Costello, 1993; Durham et al., 1994). This suggests that the inclusion of cognitive strategies may enhance the efficacy of behavior therapy with respect to the maintenance of treatment gains. With the change in emphasis in the disorder from arousal to worry, Ladouceur and colleagues have dropped relaxation training entirely to focus more intensively on purely cognitive targets like intolerance of uncertainty and cognitive avoidance (Ladouceur et al., 1999). A recent controlled treatment trial found this more purely cognitive intervention to be superior to a delayed treatment control; 77% of all participants treated with CT no longer met criteria for GAD following treatment (Ladouceur et al., 2000). It remains to be seen how this approach will compare to more typical cognitive behavioral interventions that incorporate relaxation training, but there are indications that incorporating cognitive components into treatment may facilitate the maintenance of gains.

Interpersonal Anxiety and Social Phobia

Social phobia involves an undue fear of evaluation by others and the accompanying desire to avoid situations in which such scrutiny is anticipated. According to cognitive theory, persons with social phobia have an underlying belief that they are defective or inadequate in some way that will be exposed in social situations, leading to ridicule or censure from others (Beck & Emery, 1985). More purely behavioral approaches have focused on deficits in social skills or the inhibiting effect of conditioned anxiety, whereas biological approaches have capitalized on the serendiptous effects of the monoamine oxidase inhibitors (see Hollon & Beck, 1994).

A number of studies have shown that cognitive restructuring facilitates the maintenance of gains produced by exposure to social situations and that this combination may be a particularly powerful intervention for social phobia (see Barlow & Lehman, 1996, for a review). Heimberg and colleagues have done some of the most exemplary work in the literature, developing a cognitive behavioral group treatment (CBGT) that proved superior to supportive therapy and for which gains were maintained across a five-year followup (Heimberg et al., 1993). Heimberg and colleagues found phenelzine or CBGT superior to either pill-placebo or educational-supportive group therapy in the treatment of social phobia (Heimberg et al., 1998). In this study, 133 patients from two sites were treated for 12 weeks in one of four treatment conditions. Responders to the two active treatments were then provided with an additional six months of maintenance treatment and were subsequently tracked over a six-month followup period. As shown in Figure 10.5, patients treated with phenelzine showed more rapid response by six weeks, but rates of response were comparable between the two active treatments by week 12 and superior to either control condition. Moreover, and even more importantly, 50% of the patients treated with phenelzine relapsed following treatment termination compared to only 17% of the patients treated with CBGT (Liebowitz et al., 1999). These findings parallel those found with depression and panic disorder and suggest that CBGT is as effective as medication in the treatment of social phobia and quite possibly is longer lasting.

Clark and colleagues have suggested that patients with social phobia focus undue attention on their image of themselves in social situations and engage in safety behaviors (strategies designed to protect them from feared consequences) that tend to retard learning in such situations (Wells et al., 1995). In essence, they attend selectively to images of themselves that are unduly negative and less flattering than they actually appear to others. Clark and colleagues videotaped patients engaging in various feared behaviors, both with and without safety behaviors, and then invited patients to watch both tapes and rate themselves on various characteristics. Patients typically find that they appear more competent when they don't engage in safety behaviors than when they do and that their internal images are considerably more negative and self-derogatory than they actually come across. Moreover, patients show greater change in beliefs and greater reductions in anxiety when they drop their safety behaviors in exposure situations. Clark and colleagues have argued that targeting self-focused attention and encouraging patients to drop their safety behaviors during exposure can facilitate their capacity to learn from experience and hasten their response to treatment.

Simple Phobias and the Perception of Danger

Simple phobias involve an intense fear of certain objects or situations and a corresponding desire

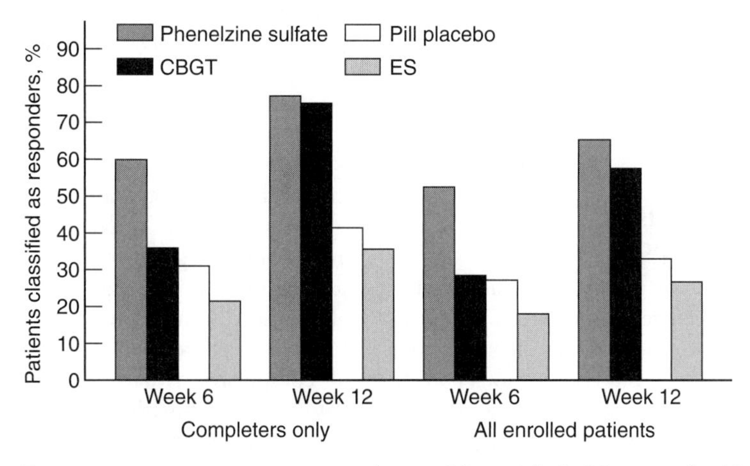

FIGURE 10.5 Response to treatment among patients with social phobia treated with medications or cognitive behavioral group therapy. From "Cognitive behavioral group therapy vs. phenelzine therapy for social phobia: 12-week outcome" by Heimberg et al., 1998, *Archives of General Psychiatry, 55,* p. 1137. Copyright 1998 by the American Medical Association. Reprinted by permission.

to avoid being in their presence. Simple phobias typically involve fears of bodily harm or danger and can be distinguished from social phobias, which involve concerns about being evaluated negatively by others. According to cognitive theory, individuals with simple phobias perceive greater danger or risk in the feared situation than do other people (Beck & Emery, 1985). Such individuals have a "dual belief system"; they can recognize that their fears are unwarranted when not in the phobic situation, but, as they approach the feared object, they are overwhelmed by thoughts of impending danger and visual or somatic images consistent with those beliefs. By way of contrast, behavior theory suggests that phobias are established via traumatic conditioning and maintained by avoidance behaviors that protect them from extinction. Behavioral interventions such as systematic desensitization or exposure plus response prevention are clearly effective and are currently considered the standard for treatment (see Hollon & Beck, 1994, for a review).

Recent studies suggest that brief cognitive behavioral interventions focused on reducing unwarranted concerns also can be effective in the treatment of specific phobias. For example, Thorpe and Salkovskis (1997) found that a brief one-session intervention focused on cognitive restructuring reduced spider-relevant threat beliefs and associated distress. Similarly, Thom and colleagues found that a single session of cognitive behavior therapy combining stress inoculation training with imaginal exposure was superior to control conditions and more enduring than medications in the treatment of dental anxiety (Thom, Sartory, & Hohren, 2000). These studies suggest that CBT may be effective in the treatment of specific phobias; how it compares with more purely behavioral intervention remains to be determined.

Obsessive-Compulsive Disorder and Personal Responsibility

According to cognitive theory, obsessions typically involve the recurrent perception that one has placed oneself or others at risk through some action (or failure to act), and compulsions consist of attempts to undo this risk through some type of subsequent action. From a cognitive perspective, the issue of personal responsibility looms large; it is this theme that is believed to most distinguish obsessive-compulsive disorder (OCD) from the other anxiety disorders with their more generic perceptions of danger. Salkovskis (1999) has described how this propensity to assign responsibility to oneself can motivate neutralizing and other counterproductive strategies and details the ways in which examining the implications of these beliefs can facilitate the therapeutic process.

Behavior theory views OCD as a product of traumatic conditioning and subsequent negative reinforcement; exposure plus response prevention has been shown to be an effective form of treatment (see Hollon & Beck, 1994, for a review). However, although behavioral interventions appear to reduce compulsive behaviors, they are less effective with ruminations and appear to be of little use with patients who are free of compulsions (Salkovskis & Westbrook, 1989). Conversely, the serotonin reuptake inhibitors have been shown to provide symptomatic relief, but treatment gains are rarely maintained once medications are discontinued, and many find the associated sexual side effects disconcerting (Abramowitz, 1997).

Until recent years, tests of CBT have been few and not particularly powerful (see Hollon & Beck, 1994, for a review). Two recent studies have compared conventional CBT to exposure plus response prevention in the treatment of patients with compulsive rituals with somewhat differing results. Van Oppen and colleagues found the two interventions largely comparable, although there were some modest indications of an advantage for CBT (van Oppen et al., 1995). In that trial, 39% of the CBT patients showed full recovery, compared to only 17% of the patients treated with exposure. Conversely, McLean and colleagues found CBT to be marginally less effective than exposure plus response prevention in the group treatment of OCD, although both treatments were superior to a delayed treatment control (McLean et al., 2001). It is not clear why outcomes differed between these trials, although McLean and colleagues have a clear allegiance to the more behavioral approach.

Freeston and colleagues have described a more compelling test of CBT that included exposure to obsessive thoughts, response prevention of neutralizing strategies, cognitive restructuring, and relapse prevention in a sample of patients free of compulsive rituals (Freeston et al., 1997). Patients treated with CBT showed considerably greater change than did patients assigned to a wait list control; in turn, these latter patients showed benefit when subsequently provided with treatment. Over two-thirds of the sample who had treatment showed clinically significant change, as did over three-quarters of those who completed treatment. Treatment gains were largely maintained across a six-month followup, although some slippage was noted. These findings suggest that CBT can be used in the treatment of OCD; how it compares to more purely behavioral approaches, or whether it can enhance or prolong its effects, remains to be determined (also see Emmelkamp, this volume).

Post-traumatic Stress Disorder

Exposure to traumatic events outside the range of normal human experience can produce a clinical syndrome known as post-traumatic stress disorder (PTSD). Although PTSD shares the symptoms of increased arousal and persistent avoidance with the phobic disorders, other symptoms, such as flashbacks and intrusive recollections or affective constriction and a sense of interpersonal detachment, are relatively distinct (Foa & Meadows, 1997). Both exposure to memories for the event and anxiety management programs like stress inoculation training (SIT) have been widely used. Anxiety management programs typically combine behavioral strategies like relaxation training and controlled breathing with more cognitive strategies like positive imagery and some limited cognitive restructuring. Recent theoretical formulations have emphasized the role of exaggerated concerns of danger and unwarranted beliefs about diminished personal worth and have focused on more cognitive strategies that target those beliefs (Ehlers & Clark, 2000; Foa & Rothbaum, 1997).

Early studies typically found SIT effective in the treatment of PTSD but not more so than exposure alone (see Hollon & Beck, 1994, for a review). Resick and colleagues completed one of those early trials and then developed a more cognitively oriented approach called cognitive processing therapy that targets specific maladaptive beliefs related to safety, trust, and self-esteem (Resick & Schnicke, 1992). In this approach, patients are encouraged to write down detailed descriptions of the traumatic event and then read it back to the therapist as a form of exposure, and the implications of the exposure are then discussed. Cognitive processing therapy is currently being compared to exposure therapy alone in an ongoing trial that suggests that both may be highly effective in ameliorating PTSD (see Foa, 2000, for a description).

Foa, the other major contributor to this literature, is more behaviorally oriented. Her research group has completed a recent study comparing SIT with prolonged exposure, both alone and in combination (Foa et al., 1999). Although all three conditions were superior to a wait list control, combined treatment did not improve on prolonged exposure alone. In fact, as can be seen in Figure 10.6, combined treatment was no more effective than SIT, and each was somewhat less effective than prolonged exposure alone, although differences were significant only on measures of depression and anxiety. Foa (2000) reported that a yet to be published study suggests that augmenting exposure therapy with cognitive restructuring was less efficient than simply conducting exposure therapy alone.

Two studies have compared exposure versus cognitive restructuring in the treatment of patients

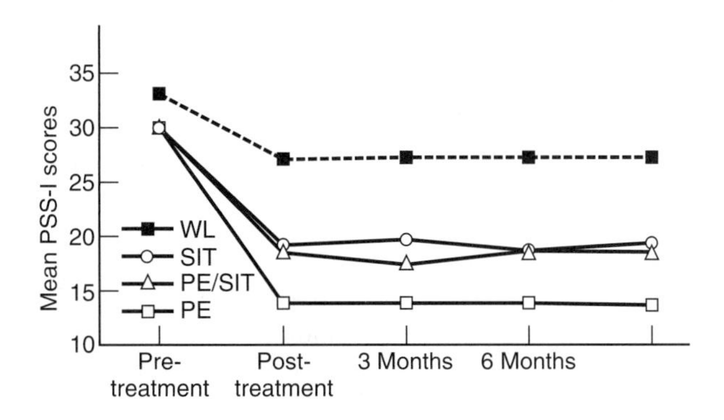

FIGURE 10.6 Prolonged exposure and stress inoculation training alone and in combination in the treatment of posttraumatic stress disorder. From "A comparison of exposure therapy, stress inoculation training, and their combination for reducing posttraumatic stress disorder in female assault victims" by Foa et al., 1999, *Journal of Consulting and Clinical Psychology*, *67*, p. 199. Copyright 1999 by the American Psychological Association. Reprinted by permission.

with mixed traumas. In the first, Marks and colleagues found that both prolonged exposure and cognitive therapy, alone or in combination, improved symptoms of PTSD more than relaxation training (Marks, Lovell, Noshirvani, Livanou, & Thrasher, 1998). However, there was no indication that adding cognitive restructuring enhanced the efficacy of exposure therapy. In fact, the group that received only the latter intervention seemed to maintain its gains better over a six-month followup. In the second study, Tarrier and colleagues found imaginal exposure and cognitive therapy comparably effective in the treatment of mixed traumas (Tarrier et al., 1999). Devilly and Spence (1998) found the combination of prolonged exposure plus stress inoculation training superior to eye movement and desensitization reprocessing (EMDR) in a sample of patients with mixed trauma. Finally, recent studies suggest that a brief course of cognitive behavior therapy can prevent the onset of PTSD in either assault (Foa, Hearst-Ikeda, & Perry, 1995) or accident victims (Bryant, Harvey, Dang, Sackville, & Basten, 1998). These findings are especially encouraging in light of indications that simple debriefing strategies may actually have adverse long-term consequences (Mayou, Ehlers, & Hobbs, 2000).

It appears that the cognitive behavioral interventions, particularly those that include some type of exposure, are effective in the treatment of PTSD. What remains unclear is whether these approaches are as effective as prolonged exposure alone (Foa, 2000). The fact that three different studies by two different groups suggest that adding cognitive components reduces the efficacy of prolonged exposure is cause for concern (Foa et al., 1999; Foa, 2000; Marks et al., 1998). At the same time, both of the groups responsible for those studies are best known for their expertise with behavioral interventions; groups with greater proficiency with cognitive approaches like those headed by Resick or Tarrier typically find comparable effects between methods. This suggests that allegiance, perhaps operating through the mechanism of differential competence, has played a role in the reduced effectiveness of CT.

In a recent theoretical article, Ehlers and Clark (2000) suggest that PTSD becomes persistent when individuals process trauma in a way that leads to a sense of serious current threat. The emphasis on the model is on the term "current." As the authors describe, the paradox of PTSD from a cognitive perspective is that memories for prior events create a state of anxiety, which usually implies impending threat. This sense of current threat is seen as a consequence of the combination of excessively negative appraisals of the implications of the trauma and a disturbance of autobiographical memory characterized by poor elaboration and perceptual priming. This model differs from earlier cognitive formulations by virtue of specifying more fully the processes contributing to the maintenance of distress and addressing the idiosyncratic nature of the appraisals made by different individuals. As such, it represents an evolution in cognitive theory that may well guide the development of the next generation of cognitive interventions. Prolonged exposure may prove to be the most effective treatment for PTSD and simple conditioning the most parsimonious explanation. However, given the impact of this group's theoretical contributions to the treatment of other anxiety disorders, it will be interesting to see if their more sophisticated cognitive model can be used to inform the treatment process.

Summary

CBT appears to be paticularly effective in the treatment of several of the anxiety disorders, including panic, GAD, social phobia, and possibly hypochondrias. Recent studies suggest that these interventions have an enduring effect that extends beyond the end of treatment. More purely behavioral interventions based on exposure remain the standard of treatment for OCD and PTSD. Although sophisticated cognitive models have been articulated and may hold considerable promise, they have not yet been tested. The various cognitive and behavioral models have emerged as some of the most compelling theoretical explanations for the various anxiety disorders, and interventions based on these models have been clearly established as among the most effective and likely to produce long-lasting benefits. Whether more cognitively oriented theories can enhance the efficacy and explanatory power of conditioning-based exposure models for disorders like OCD and PTSD remains to be determined, but that clearly has been the case for several other anxiety disorders.

Eating Disorders and Obesity

The eating disorders represent a diagnostic group in which CBT has met with mixed success.

Aberrant beliefs about food and weight appear to play a particularly important role in these disorders, and therefore these disorders are especially amenable to treatment with CBT. Controlled clinical trials suggest that CBT is specifically effective in the treatment of bulimia nervosa (Wilson & Agras, 2001). Less has been done in the treatment of anorexia nervosa, although a sophisticated clinical approach has been proposed. CBT appears to be effective in the treatment of binge eating disorder, but not more so than traditional behavioral weight loss programs. CBT appears to slow the process of weight regain following treatment for obesity but does not prevent weight gain altogether.

Treatment of Bulimia and Mechanisms of Change

Bulimia nervosa is a disorder characterized by a chaotic eating pattern that consists of extreme dieting punctuated by episodes of binge eating and subsequent efforts to purge, typically via vomiting, laxative abuse, or fasting (Fairburn, 1981). Self-esteem is often poor, and associated psychopathology is common, particularly affective distress and substance abuse. Initially thought to be refractory to treatment, recent studies have made it clear that the disorder is quite responsive to a number of different interventions, including both CBT and certain antidepressants (Wilson & Agras, 2001).

Cognitive theory states that overvalued ideas concerning body weight and shape and unrealistic beliefs about what one should and should not eat, which are often driven by underlying doubts about one's self-worth and attractiveness to others, play a major role in the etiology and maintenance of bulimia (Fairburn, 1981). According to this view, these beliefs lead the individual to engage in excessive dietary restraint, which then puts the individual (most are female) at risk for loss of control binge eating, particularly under conditions of stress. Once a binge has occurred, the bulimic individual typically engages in some form of purge behavior in an effort to avoid gaining weight. A more purely behavioral model holds that binge behaviors are reinforced by the reduction in anxiety produced by the subsequent purge, whereas a biological model suggests that bulimia is a consequence of an excessive craving for carbohydrates produced by a deficit in central serotonin regulation (see Hollon & Beck, 1994).

Therapies based on cognitive theory typically incorporate both behavioral and cognitive components, with the behavioral emphasized in the early sessions and the cognitive coming increasingly into play as treatment proceeds. Behavioral components focus on establishing more regular eating patterns (including the prohibition of restrictive dieting and purge behaviors), whereas cognitive strategies are used to identify and change beliefs regarding food, weight, and body image, with attention to relapse prevention in later sessions. CBT is clearly effective in the treatment of bulimia (Compas, Haaga, Keefe, Leitenberg, & Williams, 1998). It has been found to be superior to wait list or minimal treatment controls in numerous comparisons and has typically equaled or exceeded alternative interventions (including both behavior therapy and pharmacotherapy) in direct comparisons. Across these studies, nearly 80% of all patients treated for bulimia have shown a reduction in binge and purge behaviors, and nearly 60% have become abstinent with regard to those symptoms (Wilson & Agras, 2001). Treatment is generally well tolerated and change well maintained following treatment termination.

A major study conducted in the early 1990s found that both CBT and behavior therapy were superior to IPT in reducing bulimic symptoms by the end of active treatment, but that treatment gains were better maintained following CBT than behavior therapy (Fairburn, Jones, Peveler, Hope, & O'Connor, 1993). Moreover, patients treated with IPT continued to improve following termination such that differences no longer favored CBT across an extended followup (Fairburn et al., 1995). This led to a subsequent multisite study in which CBT was again compared to IPT (Agras, Walsh, Fairburn, Wilson, & Kraemer, 2000). As shown in Figure 10.7, cognitive behavior therapy produced higher rates of recovery (absence of symptoms) and remission (symptomatic improvement) than did IPT. Patients treated with IPT again showed modest gains after termination, but treatment gains were largely maintained following CBT, and differences were still apparent one year after treatment termination (although no longer significant). Findings from these studies (among others) have led many to conclude that CBT works faster than IPT and is more enduring than behavior therapy (or medications) and therefore to be preferred in the treatment of bulimia (Wilson & Agras, 2001).

Cognitive behavior therapy also has fared well in comparisons to pharmacotherapy (Whittal, Agras, & Gould, 1999). For example, Agras

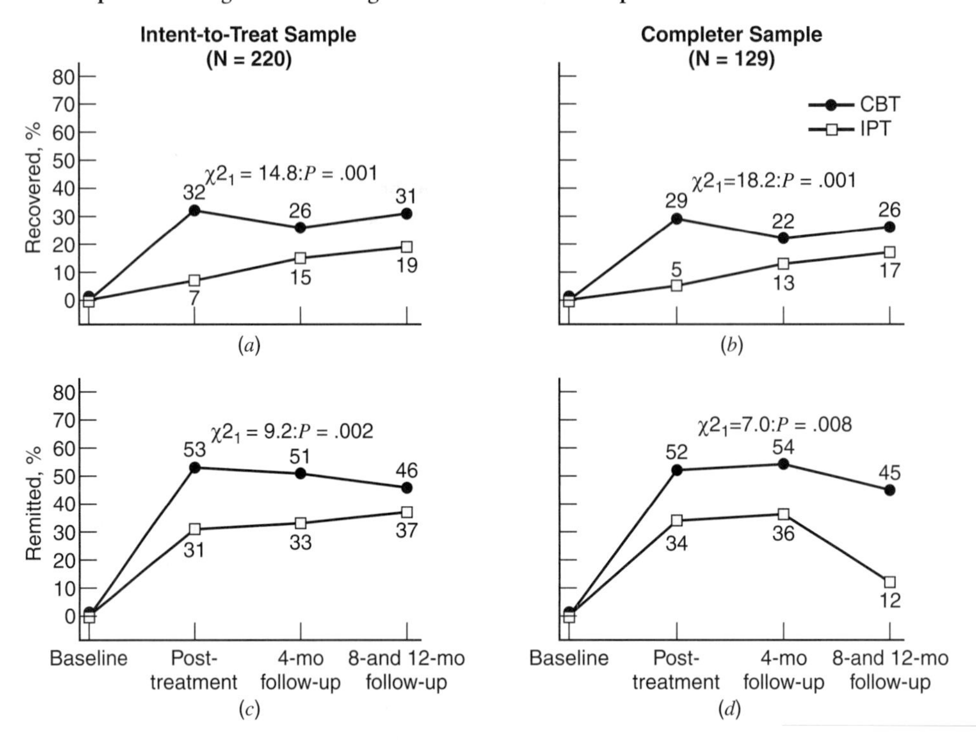

FIGURE 10.7 Rates of recovery and remission following treatment for bulimia nervosa. From "A multicenter comparison of cognitive-behavioral therapy and interpersonal psychotherapy for bulimia nervosa" by Agras et al., 2000, *Archives of General Psychiatry, 57*, p. 464. Copyright 2000 by the American Medical Association. Reprinted by permission.

and colleagues found that CBT with or without medications was superior to medication alone and lasted longer (Agras et al., 1992). Similarly, Leitenberg and colleagues found CBT to be superior to medications with respect to the reduction of bulimic symptoms and found no indication that adding medications did anything to enhance the effects of CBT (Leitenberg et al., 1994). Walsh and colleagues did find a modest advantage for CBT plus medications over CBT plus pill-placebo, but this difference was not significant (Walsh et al., 1997). These studies suggest that CBT is both more effective and more enduring than medications in the treatment of bulimia. Medications appear to work via the suppression of appetite. Thus, they make it easier to diet and do little to change problematic beliefs regarding food and weight.

Thus, it appears clear that CBT is effective in the treatment of bulimia nervosa. Most patients will respond to relatively brief courses of treatment, and many will become symptom-free. Treatment gains are better maintained than in either more purely behavioral or pharmacological approaches, and there are indications that the approach may work through mechanisms targeted by theory and implicated in the basic etiology of the disorder.

Anorexia Nervosa and the Aesthetics of Self-Denial

Anorexia nervosa involves a pervasive pattern of self-starvation, often to the point that weight loss becomes life threatening (Wilson, Vitousek, & Loeb, 2000). Anorexia shares the same misguided beliefs about food and weight found in bulimia nervosa, but also involves the notion that exercising control over physiological desires is consistent with a higher ascetic ideal (Garner & Bemis, 1982). Treatment is complicated not only by the rigidity of the beliefs regarding the consequences of becoming fat, but also by the sense of accomplishment that accompanies the pursuit of thinness.

In a recent theoretical monograph, Vitousek and colleagues describe a cognitive approach to enhancing motivation for change in treatment-resistant anorexic patients (Vitousek, Watson, & Wilson, 1998). They encourage clinicians to recognize that their clients really do want to be thin and see its pursuit as a means of providing meaning and order to their lives. Giving up this pursuit can be as difficult as asking a young mother to give up her child. Although parenting is often arduous and demanding, it also provides moments of satisfaction and joy and an overall sense that one is doing something worthwhile with her life. Vitousek and colleagues recommend first examining the functional utility of weight loss in a Socratic fashion that makes explicit use of experimental strategies and then exploring the personal values and sense of ascetic ideal that underlie the pursuit of thinness. Throughout, the importance of thinness is examined in relation to other life goals, and considerable attention is paid to underlying concerns about self-worth and interpersonal relationships.

This approach remains largely untested. The few trials that have been conducted have shown no great benefit for conventional CBT in the treatment of restricting anorexics (see Hollon & Beck, 1994). However, these studies typically have not addressed the importance of thinness as a life goal and the role its pursuit plays in the maintenance of self-esteem. Treasure and colleagues found that cognitive analytic therapy was as effective as behavior therapy in maintaining patients in outpatient treatment without resorting to hospitalization, but used an approach that did not fully deal with the motivational aspects of the pursuit of thinness (Treasure, Todd, Brolly, Nehmed, & Denman, 1995). Thus, although a coherent cognitive approach to the treatment of anorexia nervosa has been articulated, it has yet to be adequately tested. Whether this approach will improve on the limited success afforded by existing treatments remains to be determined, but careful tests of treatment efficacy would be a welcome addition to the treatment literature.

Binge Eating Disorder and the Absence of Constraint

Binge eating is a newly recognized disorder that involves excessive food intake and loss of control eating in the absence of restrictive dieting or efforts to purge. Dietary restriction appears to play little role in binge eating disorder. Obese binge eaters show less dietary restriction than patients with bulimia nervosa, diet no more than their obese counterparts who do not binge, and show no exacerbation in binge episodes when they do restrict caloric intake during weight loss treatment (Wilson & Agras, 2001).

Although this is a relatively newly articulated disorder, several studies suggest that CBT can be effective in its treatment (see, for example, Wilfley et al., 1993). At the same time, preliminary evidence suggests that CBT is no more effective than traditional behavioral weight loss treatment (Agras et al., 1994; Marcus, Wing, & Fairburn, 1995). This has led some to conclude that such behavioral weight loss programs are to be preferred, since they reduce both weight and binge eating and are more widely available than CBT (Gladis et al., 1998). Whether that will continue to be the case as more sophisticated models of the disorder are developed remains to be seen, but for now it appears that although CBT is effective, it may be less cost-effective than more traditional behavioral alternatives.

Obesity and the Impermanence of Weight Loss

There is considerable controversy as to whether it is possible to produce lasting weight loss through purely psychosocial means in people who are obese (Brownell & Rodin, 1994). Many obese individuals will lose weight in standard behavioral programs (Perri & Fuller, 1995), but the majority will regain most of the weight lost within a few years of treatment termination (Jeffery et al., 2000). Extending the length of treatment appears to increase weight loss, and building in post-treatment contacts appears to slow the process of weight regain, but these strategies may simply forestall the inevitable weight gains that follow interventions (Perri, 1998). Given that an obsessive preoccupation with weight loss can lead to demoralization and the development of pathological eating habits, some investigators have suggested that dieting be discouraged altogether (Garner & Wooley, 1991). However, even modest weight loss on the order of 5 to 10% appears to confer significant health benefits if the weight is not regained (Wing & Jeffrey, 1995).

Several strategies have been tried. Initial efforts to extend the benefits of behavioral weight loss programs by adding cognitive components provided little benefit, but more recent efforts have met with somewhat more success (see Hollon & Beck, 1994). For example, Perri and colleagues found that extended therapy with PST led to better maintenance of weight loss than standard behavior therapy (Perri et al., 2001). Similarly, Sbrocco and colleagues found that training in decision making regarding food choices was less effective than standard behavior therapy by the end of treatment, but led to continued weight loss (and hence better maintenance) across an extended followup (Sbrocco, Nedegaard, Stone, & Lewis, 1999). Whether these approaches will improve the maintenance of weight loss remains to be seen, but they do appear to be somewhat promising.

Cooper and Fairburn (2001) have suggested that the primary problem in the weight loss literature is that it has failed to take into account the cognitive factors that lead to weight regain. They suggest that too many patients set unrealistic goals that are hard to meet and as a consequence abandon efforts that have produced more modest levels of weight loss. They recommend adopting an individualized approach that helps patients accept more limited weight loss goals and describe specific strategies for maintaining losses that have already been achieved. Whether this approach will improve upon existing interventions remains to be seen, but it is clear that the major problem in the field remains the inability of most patients to sustain the weight loss that they do achieve.

Summary

CBT is clearly the treatment of choice for bulimia nervosa; it is more effective than IPT or more traditional interventions and more enduring than either behavior therapy or medications. Anorexia nervosa remains problematic; although a sophisticated approach has been described, it has yet to be adequately tested. CBT appears to be effective in the treatment of binge eating disorder, but not more so than more cost-effective and widely available behavioral weight loss programs. Finally, including cognitive strategies in behavior treatment of obesity appears to slow but not prevent the process of weight regain. It remains to be seen whether recently articulated models of these latter disorders will lead to the kind of innovations that have proved so successful in the treatment of bulimia nervosa.

Child and Adolescent Disorders

Disorders of childhood and adolescence are often divided into undercontrolled (or externalizing) versus overcontrolled (or internalizing) disorders (Kazdin & Weisz, 1998). Undercontrolled disorders typically involve behaviors that are problematic to others, such as aggression or hyperactivity, whereas overcontrolled disorders tend to involve more private distress. At the time of our last review, most of the work in this area had focused on the undercontrolled disorders, which appear to involve deficits in cognitive mediation and were generally treated with skills training approaches like PST and self-instructional training (Hollon & Beck, 1994). The overcontrolled disorders, which are presumed to involve distortions in existing beliefs, have been the subject of considerable attention over the last few years (Kendall, 1993). We start with a review of that work and then conclude with a review of work in the treatment of undercontrolled disorders.

Depression in Children and Adolescents

A number of studies have suggested that a variety of cognitive behavioral interventions are effective in the treatment of children and adolescents (Curry, 2001). Some approaches emphasize behavioral components like activity scheduling and skills training to a greater extent (particularly for younger children), whereas others are more likely to include specific attention to the identification and modification of negative beliefs (particularly with adolescents). Many also include affect management skills such as relaxation training and impulse control techniques.

The bulk of the studies done with preadolescent children have been conducted in school-based settings with samples selected on the basis of self-reported (but not diagnosed) depression (Curry, 2001). In most instances, CBT has proved superior to minimal treatment or control conditions (including school counseling) and at least comparable to more purely behavioral interventions. There was also evidence of sustained response. For example, Weisz and colleagues found that elementary school children trained to use behavioral strategies to change negative situations and cognitive strategies to buffer their own reactions to those situations improved more than controls. Moreover, these changes were sustained through a nine-month followup (Weisz, Thurber, Sweeney, Proffitt, & LeGagnoux, 1997). On the whole, these studies suggest that CBT is effective in reducing depressive symptoms in school-age children and that this may be a lasting effect that goes beyond the simple provision of attention.

The majority of the studies in adolescent populations have been conducted in clinical settings with participants who had a diagnosable disorder; most have found CBT effective in the treatment of adolescent depression (Curry, 2001;

but see Vostanis, Feehan, Grattan, & Bickerton, 1996, for an exception). For example, Lewinsohn and colleagues developed a structured group intervention called the Adolescent Coping with Depression Course (CWD-A) that was superior to a wait list control in a pair of studies (Clarke, Rohde, Lewinsohn, Hops, & Seeley, 1999; Lewinsohn, Clarke, Hops, & Andrews, 1990). Little was gained in either study by adding a group for parents. Comparisons to alternative interventions have been somewhat more mixed. Wood and colleagues found CBT superior to relaxation training in an adolescent sample (Wood, Harrington, & Moore, 1996). On the other hand, Rossello and Bernal (1999) found that IPT had a greater impact on self-esteem and social adaptation (but not depression) in a sample of Puerto Rican adolescents.

In perhaps the most clinically representative study in this literature, Brent and colleagues found CBT superior to either systematic behavioral family therapy or nondirective supportive therapy in the treatment of depressed suicidal adolescents in an outpatient setting (Brent, Kolko, Birmaher, Baugher, & Bridge, 1997). Results are shown in Figure 10.8. In that study, Beck's cognitive therapy was adapted to place additional emphasis on the exploration of issues of autonomy and the acquisition of problem-solving and affect regulation skills. Patients who entered the study via clinic referral were less likely to respond than were participants who responded to an advertisement (Brent, Kolko, Birmaher, Baugher, & Bridge, 1998), and the presence of comorbid disorders and family problems predicted need for subsequent treatment (Brent, Kolko et al., 1999). There was little indication that CBT had an enduring effect, since there were no differences in long-term outcome at a two-year followup (Birmaher et al., 2000).

On the whole, it appears that the CBT is effective in the treatment of depression in children and adolescents. There appears to be little basis for preferring CBT to more purely behavioral strategies, although both hold up well relative to other interventions. More structured strategies that emphasize behavioral and relatively concrete cognitive components appear better suited to the treatment of preadolescent children in school-based settings, whereas interventions for depressed adolescents more directly parallel those that are used for adults. What is surprising is the relative lack of advantage conferred by involving parents in treatment (see studies by Lewinsohn and colleagues or Brent and colleagues). Whether this reflects something unique to adolescents or a lack of integration of family models remains to be seen.

Finally, there are indications that CBT can be used to prevent the onset of depression in children and adolescents who are not currently in episode. Clarke and colleagues completed two studies that found that a modified version of the "Coping with Depression" course reduced the frequency of diagnosable depression in at-risk adolescents (Clarke et al., 1995; Clarke et al., 2001). Similarly, an intervention based on CT prevented depressive onset in preadolescent children (Jaycox, Reivich, Gillham, & Seligman, 1994). These studies suggest that CBT can prevent the onset of depression in a portion of persons at risk.

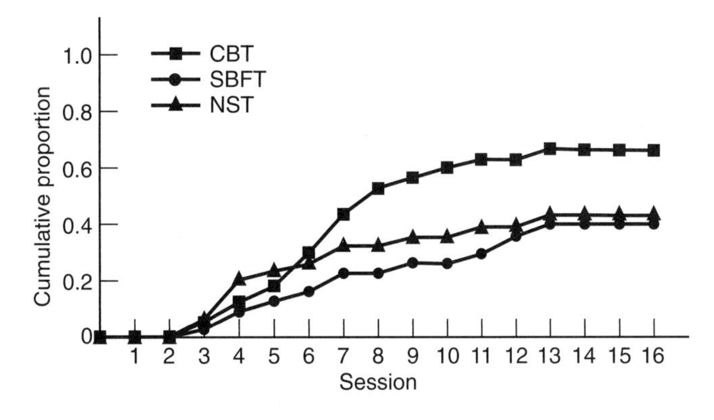

FIGURE 10.8 Time to sustained remission as a function of treatment among depressed adolescents. From "A clinical psychotherapy trial for adolescent depression comparing cognitive, family, and supportive therapy" by D. A. Brent et al., 1997, *Archives of General Psychiatry, 54*, p. 883. Copyright 1997 by the American Medical Association. Reprinted by permission.

Treatment of Anxiety Disorders in Children and Adolescents

The last decade has seen some particularly promising work in the treatment of anxiety disorders in children and adolescents (Kazdin & Weisz, 1998). For example, Kendall and colleagues have developed an approach that combines cognitive restructuring with behavioral exposure and relaxation training to help children and adolescents deal with their fears (Kendall, 1993). Empirical trials with this approach have been quite encouraging. In an initial trial, children aged 9 to 13 who met diagnostic criteria for overanxious disorder, separation anxiety, or avoidant disorder showed considerable improvement across 16 weeks of treatment, whereas those assigned to a wait list control showed little change (Kendall, 1994). Nearly two-thirds of the participants no longer met diagnostic criteria at the end of treatment, and gains were largely maintained across the next several years (Kendall & Southam-Gerow, 1996). As shown in Figure 10.9, Kendall and colleagues essentially replicated these findings in a second randomized trial (Kendall et al., 1997), and Barrett and colleagues have done the same in a study conducted in Australia (Barrett, Dadds, & Rapee, 1996). In the Australian study, adding anxiety management training for the parents enhanced the efficacy of CBT on some measures, and treatment gains again were well maintained over time; 85% of the treated children no longer met criteria for anxiety disorders six years after treatment (Barrett, Duffy, Dadds, & Rapee, 2001).

CBT also appears to be effective when provided in a group context. Barrett (1998) found group CBT superior to a wait list control in 7 to 14 year olds (75% no longer met criteria for anxiety disorder in the treated group versus 25% of the controls). This finding was replicated in a second study in which treatment gains were maintained through a 12-month followup (Silverman et al., 1999). Two studies found no differences between group and individual CBT (Cobham, Dadds, & Spence, 1998; Flannery-Schroeder & Kendall, 2000), with the latter trial finding both modalities superior to a wait list control. There are even indications that early intervention child- and family-focused groups based on CBT principles can prevent the onset of anxiety-related problems in children (Dadds, Spence, Holland, Barrett, & Laurens, 1997). In that study, applying CBT in a preventive fashion reduced rates of onset of anxiety problems relative to a monitoring only control (54% versus 16%), with differences

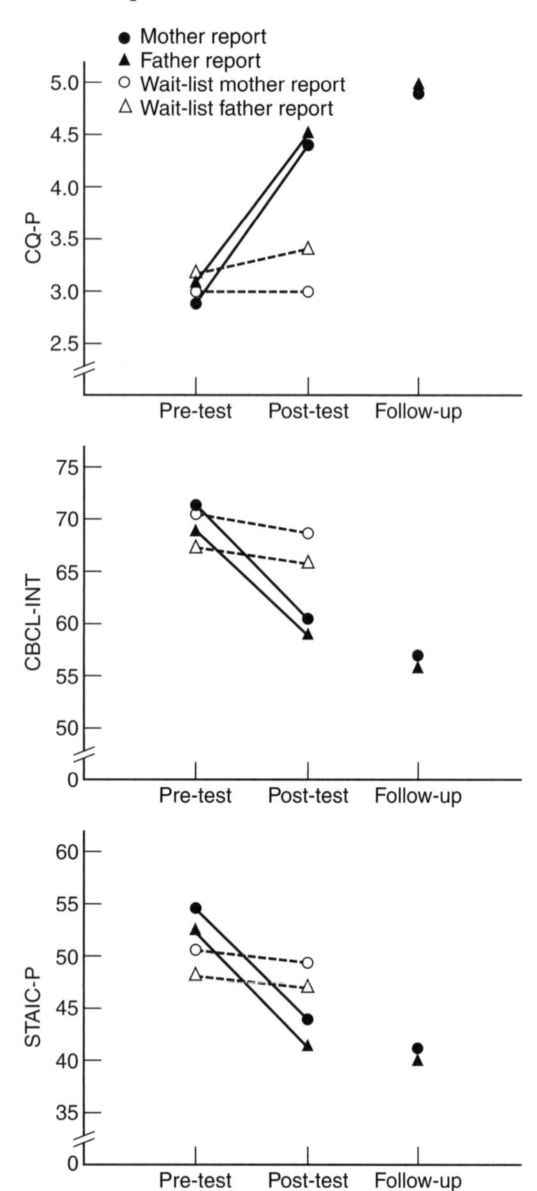

FIGURE 10.9 Parent reports of response to treatment among anxious youths. From "Therapy for youths with anxiety disorders: A second randomized clinical trial" by P. C. Kendall et al., 1997, *Journal of Consulting and Clinical Psychology, 65*, p. 375. Copyright 1997 by the American Psychological Association. Reprinted by permission.

in risk maintained across a 24-month followup (Dadds et al., 1999).

On the whole, this is an impressive series of studies. Each has focused on cases (or onsets) serious enough to warrant formal diagnoses, and comorbid cases have often been included. Efforts have been made to assess the clinical significance of the change produced (most participants no longer meet diagnostic criteria after treatment), and extended followups indicate that the changes produced are largely stable over time. It remains unclear how this intervention compares to other alternative forms of treatment, but no other intervention has been subjected to such rigorous evaluation in fully clinical populations. The approach clearly is efficacious; the only question is whether that efficacy is specific. It is of interest that reductions in anxious self-talk appear to mediate the changes produced by treatment (Treadwell & Kendall, 1996).

CBT also appears to be effective in the treatment of other childhood anxiety disorders (King & Ollendick, 1997). For example, Silverman and colleagues found CBT to be as effective as contingency management in reducing simple phobias, although treatment gains were largely matched by an educational support control (Silverman et al., 1999). King and colleagues found exposure-based CBT more effective than a wait list control in getting school-refusing children back to school and reducing their distress (King et al., 1998). Last and colleagues also found exposure-based CBT effective in getting phobic children to return to school, but not more so than an education-support control (Last, Hansen, & Franco, 1998). Whether CBT adds to the efficacy of exposure alone remains to be seen, but it clearly appears to be effective in the treatment of specific phobias and school refusal.

Aggression and Conduct Disorder

CBT has long been used in the treatment of aggression and conduct disorder, particularly strategies like stress-inoculation or problem-solving training that helped interrupt "thoughtless" responses to perceived provocation (see Hollon & Beck, 1994, for a review). Early studies with aggressive or conduct-disordered children that emphasized these approaches were largely successful, though not necessarily more so than more purely behavioral interventions.

Perhaps the most impressive work in this literature comes from a series of studies conducted by Kazdin and colleagues involving the application of PST to prepubertal children hospitalized for severe conduct disorder. In these studies, PST (including a self-instructional component) was consistently superior to relationship therapy or an attention placebo (Kazdin, Bass, Siegel, & Thomas, 1989; Kazdin, Esveldt-Dawson, French, & Unis, 1987a, 1987b) and comparable to parent management training (Kazdin et al., 1987a; Kazdin, Siegel, & Bass, 1992). The combination of PST plus parent management training was the most effective treatment group (Kazdin et al., 1992). As shown in Figure 10.10, PST produced decrements in aggressive behaviors and increments in prosocial behaviors that were both generalized and sustained following termination of treatment.

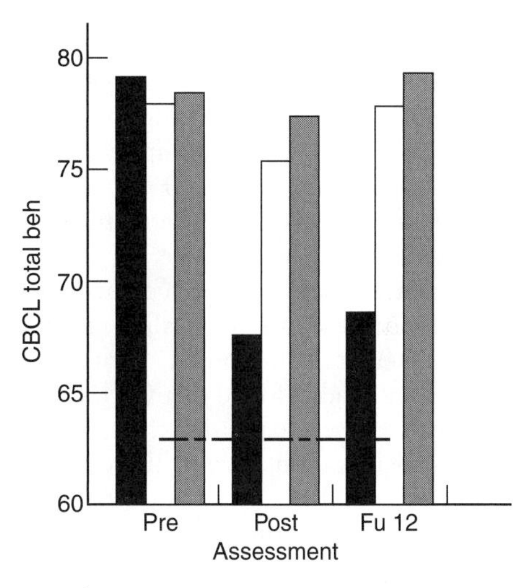

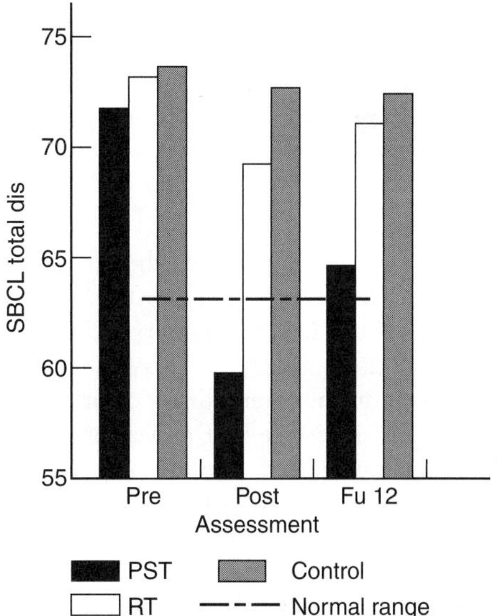

FIGURE 10.10 Behavior problems and school disability as a function of treatment for conduct disorder. From "Problem-solving skills training and relationship therapy in the treatment of antisocial child behavior" by A. E. Kazdin et al., 1987, *Journal of Consulting and Clinical Psychology, 55*, p. 83. Copyright 1987 by the American Psychological Association. Reprinted by permission.

Impulsivity and Attention Deficit Hyperactivity Disorder

CBT also has been applied to the treatment of impulsivity and attention deficit disorder, with mixed success. From a cognitive perspective, these children lack the capacity to inhibit their own behavior such that they respond too rapidly to external events and fail to anticipate negative consequences or engage in planful problem solving (Kendall & Braswell, 1985). The goal of cognitive training is to help them learn to think before they act. Numerous studies have shown that self-instructional training combined with modeling and faded rehearsal can be used to teach impulsive children to engage in more reflective problem solving and improve task performance (see Hollon & Beck, 1994). However, gains often did not generalize beyond the training tasks or were not stable over time.

It is even less clear that such cognitive behavioral training produces clinically meaningful change in children diagnosed with ADHD. Although some studies found that CBT enhanced performance on specific training tasks, others did not, and generalization beyond those tasks was rare (see Abikoff, 1985, for a review). Furthermore, direct comparisons typically found that CBT was less effective than, and did little to enhance the efficacy of, stimulant medications (Hinshaw, Henker, & Whalen, 1984). As a consequence, CBT has failed to supplant more purely behavioral interventions as the primary adjunct to medication treatment of ADHD.

Summary

CBT shows great promise in the treatment of internalizing disorders such as depression and anxiety. As with adults, these interventions appear to be efficacious and quite possibly enduring. With respect to the externalizing disorders, skills training approaches like PST appear promising in the treatment of aggression and conduct disorder, especially when used as part of a multifaceted program. Although self-instructional training is somewhat effective in the treatment of subclinical impulsivity, its utility in treatment of diagnosable ADHD has yet to be demonstrated.

Substance Abuse and the Prevention of Relapse

As in obesity, it is easier to produce change than it is to maintain it with respect to substance abuse. Cognitive theorists interested in the area have emphasized the development of procedures designed to prevent relapse following successful treatment (Brownell, Marlatt, Lichtenstein, & Wilson, 1986). In particular, Marlatt and colleagues' approach to relapse prevention appears to hold real theoretical promise (Marlatt & Gordon, 1985). However, despite generating considerable enthusiasm in the field, the empirical evidence speaking to its efficacy is at best mixed and inconsistent across the various substance abuse domains.

Relapse Prevention and Matching to Treatment in Alcohol Abuse

Historically, few areas of research have been as heavily politicized as the treatment of alcohol abuse. Strong competing models exist, and disputes over their implications and the proper interpretation of empirical trials have spilled into the popular press (Marlatt, 1983). A traditional disease model suggests that alcoholism is a progressive disorder and that abstinence is the only viable option for the true addict. Conversely, social learning theory suggests that self-regulatory skills can be acquired at any time and that insistence on abstinence undermines efforts at self-control and increases risk for relapse.

The rancor in the field has largely settled down, due in part to a growing acceptance of the principle of harm avoidance, the adoption of strategies that reduce or minimize harm associated with ongoing pattern of substance use (Marlatt, Larimer, Baer, & Quigley, 1993). For example, a recent practice guideline notes that patients often prefer to moderate substance use rather than to abstain altogether and that for many this is a realistic goal (American Psychiatric Association, 1995). The guideline notes that several different types of CBT, including cognitive therapy, relapse prevention, and motivational interviewing, can all contribute to the reduction in drinking behavior and the minimization of harm.

Relapse prevention (RP) uses cognitive behavioral strategies to help patients avoid "loss of control" drinking (Marlatt & Gordon, 1985). The strategies used include discussing ambivalence, identifying emotional and environmental cues, exploring the decision chain leading to the resumption of substance use, and learning from brief "lapses" how to limit intake without drinking to excess. The empirical data supporting these interventions are promising but somewhat inconsistent. Although it does appear to reduce the severity of relapses when they do occur, it does produce a lower rate of abstinence than other types of treatment (Carroll, 1996). The general consensus appears to be that many individuals can benefit from this approach, but that some patients, particularly those with the most severe and chronic problems or consequent cognitive impairment, may do best with abstinence. Recent work by Marlatt and colleagues has focused on reducing the instigation of heavy drinking patterns in at-risk college students with considerable success. Even a brief single-session motivational interview appears to reduce subsequent abuse patterns in at-risk college students (Marlatt et al., 1998).

The success of the various cognitive behavioral interventions and the indications that different patients responded to different interventions served as the impetus for the largest and most ambitious study of psychotherapy to date. Project MATCH was designed to test whether matching patients to different interventions could be used to improve treatment efficacy (Project MATCH Research Group, 1997). In that trial, a total of 1,726 patients with varying degrees of alcohol problems were randomly assigned to 12 sessions each of CBT or 12-step facilitation or four sessions of motivational enhancement therapy based on motivational interviewing. Although patients in all three conditions showed improvement over time, there were few differences between the conditions and little evidence for the several matching hypotheses that had motivated the study. In particular, there was no evidence that CBT was superior to either of the other two approaches for patients with more severe psychiatric symptoms or for patients with psychopathic character traits, as had been suggested in earlier studies.

Given the size and expense of the trial, many in the field have been disappointed in the relatively meager yield, and some have been reluctant to conclude that any of the interventions were particularly effective. At the least, Project MATCH provided no basis for arguing that CBT was more effective than the more traditional 12-step approach, a lack of differences echoed in a recent naturalistic comparison between the two approaches (Ouimette, Finney, & Moos, 1997). At the same time, a recent study suggested that less impaired patients do better with CBT than with supportive therapy, whereas patients with higher levels of craving and poorer cognitive functioning derive greater benefit from naltrexone than placebo (Jaffe et al., 1996). Clearly, more needs to be done in this regard, but it is doubtful that anything as big and expensive (or as uncontrolled) as Project MATCH will be attempted in the near future.

Treatment of Drug Abuse

Similarly, indications for the use of CBT in the treatment of drug abuse also are mixed. Early studies suggested that either CT or supportive-expressive psychotherapy could enhance the efficacy of routine drug counseling among patients with opioid dependence maintained on methadone, particularly for patients with more severe psychiatric symptoms (see Hollon & Beck, 1994, for a review). During this same period, work was also underway examining the efficacy of relapse prevention (RP) adapted to emphasize abstinence as an explicit goal in the treatment of cocaine abuse (Carroll, 1996). In those studies, RP typically was more effective among patients with more severe patterns of abuse, whereas desipramine pharmacotherapy had only a short-lived effect that dissipated before the end of treatment (see, for example, Carroll, Rounsaville, Gordon, et al., 1994). Moreover, as shown in Figure 10.11, there was evidence that patients treated with RP (but not medications) continued to improve following treatment termination (Carroll, Rounsaville, Nich et al., 1994).

These studies set the stage for a large multisite collaborative study sponsored by the National Institute on Drug Abuse in the treatment of cocaine addition (Crits-Christoph et al., 1999). In that trial, 487 patients were randomly assigned to one of four manual-guided treatments: individual drug counseling plus group drug counseling (GDC), cognitive therapy plus GDC, supportive-expressive psychotherapy plus GDC, or GDC alone. CT in that trial represented a refined version of the approach in which an emphasis was placed on identifying and testing both the specific thoughts associated with actual drug-taking behaviors and the underlying beliefs presumed to increase risk (Beck, Wright, & Newman, 1992). As shown in Figure 10.12, the results indicated that patients who received a combination of individual drug counseling plus GDC did better in terms of reducing drug abuse than did patients in any other condition, including the two psychotherapy combinations, which did not do better than GDC alone. There was no indication that patients with more severe psychiatric symptoms did better in either psychotherapy or that those patients with antisocial traits did better in CT than in supportive-expressive psychotherapy.

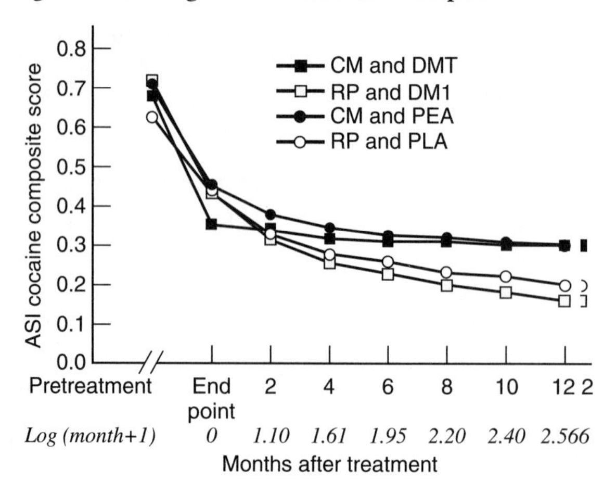

Cocaine Use Across Time by Psychotherapy

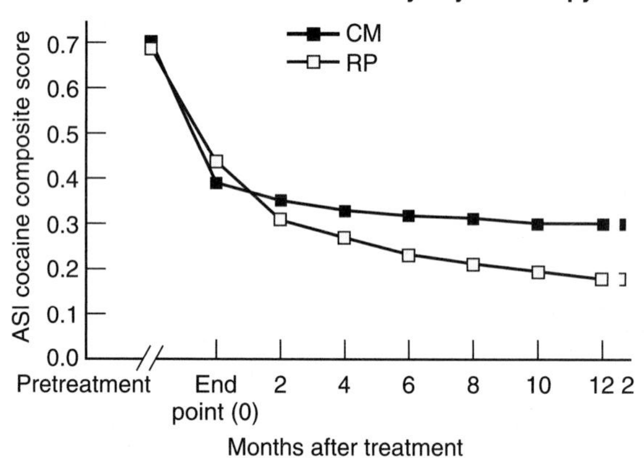

Cocaine Use Across Time by Pharmacotherapy

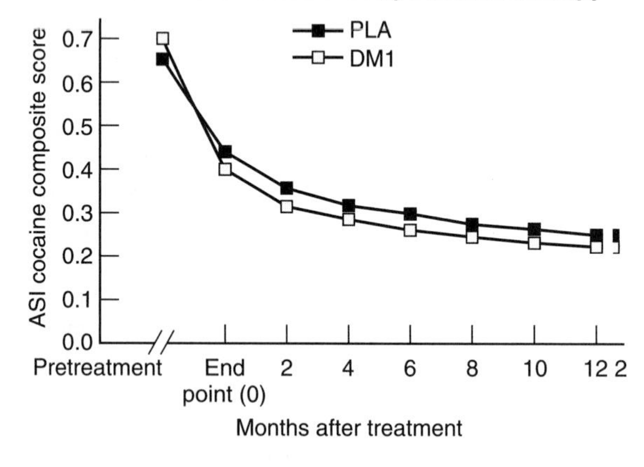

FIGURE 10.11 Cocaine use across time as a function of treatment. From "One-year follow-up of psychotherapy and pharmacotherapy for cocaine dependence: Delayed emergence of psychotherapy effects" by K. M. Carroll et al., 1994, *Archives of General Psychiatry, 51*, p. 995. Copyright 1994 by the American Medical Association. Reprinted by permission.

Exactly why the two psychotherapies fared so poorly relative to how they had done in earlier trials remains unclear, although the authors speculate that adding individual drug counseling to GDC may have given them a tougher standard against which to compete. Similarly, it is not clear why none of the matching hypotheses suggested by earlier trials bore out, although the results were

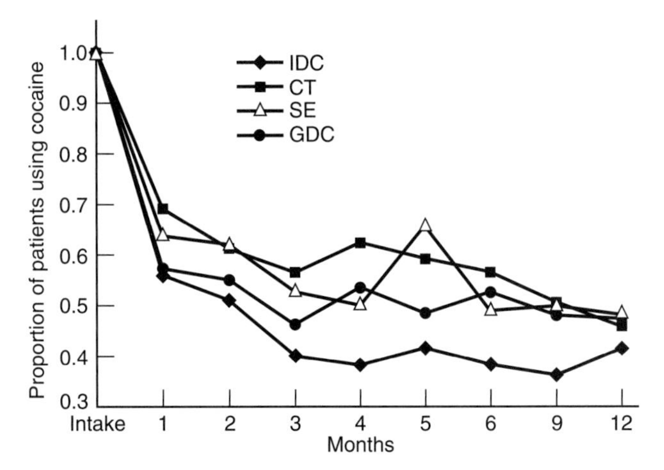

FIGURE 10.12 Proportion of patients in each treatment condition who reported any cocaine use in the past 30 days. From "Psychosocial treatments for cocaine dependence: National Institute on Drug Abuse Collaborative Cocaine Treatment Study" by P. Crits-Christoph et al., 1999, *Archives of General Psychiatry, 56*, p. 499. Copyright 1999 by the American Medical Association. Reprinted by permission.

quite similar to what happened in the treatment of alcoholism (Project MATCH Research Group, 1997). It is possible that the therapists' relative lack of experience working with drug abuse populations may have worked against the two psychotherapy conditions. Although well trained in their respective modalities, the cognitive and supportive-expressive therapists had less experience working with patients who abused substances than did the therapists in the individual drug counseling condition. In that regard, it is of interest that experienced drug counselors provided training in CBT produced higher rates of abstinence in their clients than were achieved in a 12-step facilitation group with cocaine-abusing patients (Maude-Griffin et al., 1998). It is also possible that some other type of cognitive behavioral intervention would have performed better, although another recent study found no advantage for RP over a more conventional 12-step approach (Wells, Peterson, Gainey, Hawkins, & Catalano, 1994). Clearly, more work needs to be done in this area, but for now the best that can be said is that outcomes using CBT are decidedly mixed.

Smoking Cessation and Subsequent Relapse

Multicomponent behavior therapy programs that include cognitive components have long been known to be effective in reducing smoking behavior (Compas et al., 1998). These programs typically are successful in helping participants stop smoking, although many resume within several months of treatment termination. Moreover, there is little indication that any of the components, including the cognitive ones, are essential to their success (see Hollon & Beck, 1994). Nonetheless, the consensus seems to be that RP and other cognitive behavioral strategies can help reduce risk of relapse following smoking cessation (Law & Tang, 1995). In particular, these interventions appear to prolong the duration of treatment effects and reduce the severity of relapses when they do occur (Carroll, 1996).

Much of the work in recent years has focused on the use of cognitive behavioral strategies in the treatment of smokers with a history of affective distress. Hall and colleagues found that a cognitive behavioral intervention adapted from the treatment for depression that emphasized scheduling pleasant events and restructuring negative beliefs enhanced the efficacy of nicotine gum among participants with a history of depression (Hall, Munoz, & Reus, 1994). The authors essentially replicated this effect in a study that also found nortriptyline effective in reducing smoking rates (Hall et al., 1998). Finally, Brown and colleagues have shown that adding CBT for depression (the original intervention) improved abstinence rates even further over CBT adapted for smoking cessation among patients with a history of depression (Brown et al., 2001). These findings suggest that while standard multicomponent behavior therapy may represent the current standard in the reduction of smoking behaviors, CBT targeted at both smoking and depression may be partcularly useful for participants with a history of affective distress.

Summary

It remains unclear just how effective CBT (including relapse prevention) is in the treatment of substance abuse. It typically outperforms minimal treatment controls, but it has a more inconsistent record relative to attention placebos and rarely exceeds alternative interventions. It does appear to enhance the durability of treatment effects and to reduce the severity of relapses when they do occur, but it does less to reduce the risk of their occurrence than other interventions. Evidence for its efficacy in the treatment of alcoholism is no better than mixed, although it may facilitate controlled drinking in patients with less severe patterns and forestall problems in at-risk young adults. Evidence of its efficacy in the treatment of drug abuse also is inconsistent; therapists may require expertise with addicted clients as well as the intervention. It remains unclear whether cognitive strategies contribute to the success of multicomponent packages in the treatment of smoking, although they do appear to reduce risk for relapse among smokers who are also depressed. On the whole, cognitive behavioral strategies (including relapse prevention) appear to have some promise, but the results of trials to date have been inconsistent and inconclusive.

Dialectic Behavior Therapy and the Treatment of Personality Disorders

Few treatment innovations have generated as much interest in recent years as dialectic behavior therapy (DBT; Linehan, 1993). DBT is a cognitive behavioral intervention originally developed to treat chronically suicidal individuals who often were found to have borderline personality disorder. Patients with borderline personality disorder are notoriously difficult to treat, and their frequent suicide attempts and self-injurious behaviors (referred to as parasuicidal behaviors) make them stressful clients with whom to work. These patients tend to relate to others in an unpredictable and affectively labile fashion, and their inability to tolerate strong states of negative affect is seen as being the central deficit in the disorder.

The primary focus in DBT is on reducing instances of parasuicidal behavior, followed by attention to behaviors that interfere with the progress of therapy and that undermine the quality of life. DBT combines a variety of cognitive and behavioral techniques with acceptance strategies adapted from Zen teaching within a problem-oriented framework to accomplish these goals, including behavioral skills training, contingency management, cognitive modification, and exposure to emotional cues. Instances of parasuicidal behavior are exhaustively explored, with an emphasis on identifying alternative strategies that could have been adopted to deal with the problems or situations that triggered their occurrence. In addition, an effort is made to help patients learn to manage emotional distress rather than simply reducing or avoiding it.

As shown in Figure 10.13, Linehan and colleagues found that DBT reduced the frequency of parasuicidal behaviors and number of days hospitalized in a sample of borderline patients relative to "treatment as usual" in the community (Linehan, Armstrong, Suarez, Allmon, & Heard, 1991). Patients assigned to DBT also were more likely to complete treatment, which included both individual and group sessions. Depression, hopelessness, and suicidal ideation also decreased over time, although differences between the groups were not significant. Patients treated with DBT reported less anger and showed better social and overall adjustment (Linehan, Tutek, Heard, & Armstrong, 1994). These differences were largely maintained at a one-year followup (Linehan, Heard, & Armstrong, 1993).

Efforts to replicate this study have been few, though encouraging. Linehan and colleagues found that DBT reduced substance use and improved social and overall adjustment relative to "treatment as usual" in a sample of drug-dependent women with borderline personality disorder (Linehan et al., 1999). This same group is reported to have replicated their earlier finding of superiority of DBT over alternative treatment as conducted by experts in the community. This still unpublished study, as well as several other ongoing trials involving other research groups working with a variety of different populations in a variety of different sites, is reported in Koerner and Linehan (2000). It would be premature to state that DBT is empirically supported (there are as yet no replications by independent research groups in the literature), but work to date has been promising and further support may be close at hand.

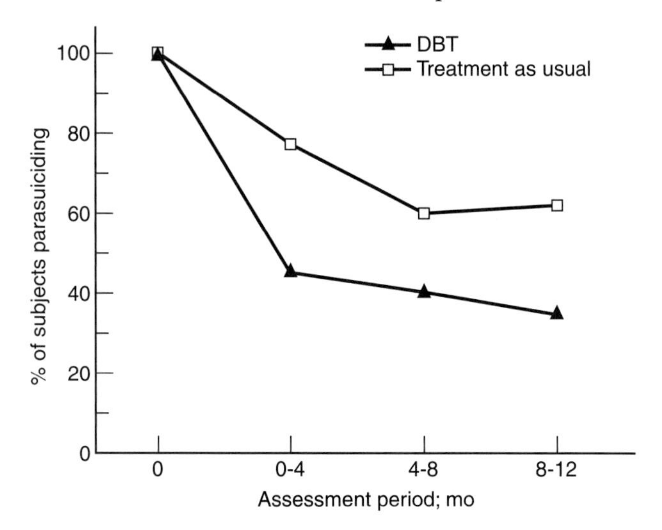

FIGURE 10.13 Proportion of subjects with parasuicide as a function of treatment. From "Cognitive-behavioral treatment of chronically parasuicidal borderline patients" by M. M. Linehan et al., 1991, *Archives of General Psychiatry, 48*, p. 1062. Copyright 1991 by the American Medical Association. Reprinted by permission.

Considerable efforts have been made in adapting CT for use with borderline personality-disordered patients (Layden, Newman, Freeman, & Morse, 1993) and other personality disorders (Beck, Freeman, & Associates, 1990). One trial is currently underway with borderline patients with the hope that it will lead to modifications of treatment for patients with comorbid personality disorders who have other primary disorders. The essence of the modified approach is to link the compensatory behavioral strategies that patients characteristically overuse to the distorted views they hold about themselves and others and the misguided rules they have adopted to deal with life. For example, dependent patients believe that they are weak and must depend on others, whereas paranoid patients believe that others are malevolent and therefore cannot be trusted. These beliefs can be tested; even laying out the linkages involved can help explain characteristic patterns of behavior that appear self-defeating and hard to understand (J.S. Beck, 1998).

SCHIZOPHRENIA AND DELUSIONAL THINKING

Delusions have traditionally been regarded as being impervious to logic or empirical disconfirmation. Nonetheless, a recent series of studies suggest that CBT can be used directly to address delusions and hallucinations in medicated patients (Rector & Beck, 2000). These approaches have a long history but have only recently begun to receive renewed empirical attention, mostly from investigators in Great Britain (Haddock et al., 1998).

Implicit in these approaches is the notion that delusions represent an attempt to make sense out of troublesome or puzzling experiences and that the schizophrenic patient is not wholly impervious to reason or evidence (Beck & Rector, 2000). Efforts to directly confront the implausibility of the beliefs appear to be less effective than a more gentle approach that examines the context in which the beliefs developed and the quality of the evidence that provides their support. Tarrier and colleagues found that a cognitive behavioral intervention that incorporated the strategies just described was superior to generic problem-solving training and that each was superior to the wait list control, even though the patients were medicated and diagnosed with chronic schizophrenia (Tarrier et al., 1993). Patients in the focused CBT condition evidenced a 50% reduction in delusions and hallucinations by the end of treatment relative to a 25% reduction in the patients treated with generic problem solving. In a subsequent trial, adding CBT to routine care was more effective than adding supportive counseling, with each superior to routine care alone in chronic medicated patients (Tarrier et al., 1998). Treatment

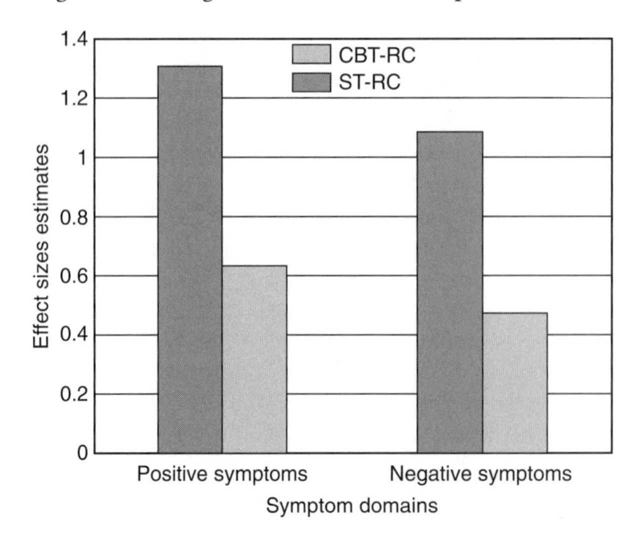

FIGURE 10.14 Cognitive behavioral therapy versus supportive therapy in medicated schizophrenic patients: Differential effects on positive and negative symptoms. From "Cognitive behavioral therapy for schizophrenia: An empirical review" by N. A. Rector and A. T. Beck, 2001, *Journal of Nervous and Mental Disorders*, 189, p. 285. Copyright 2001 by Lippincott Williams & Wilkins. Reprinted by permission.

gains were essentially maintained over an extended followup (Tarrier et al., 2000).

Working independently, a second research group based in London found that the addition of CBT produced similar reductions in delusional thinking and other aspects of pathology when added to routine care in the treatment of medicated patients with chronic schizophrenia (Garety, Kuipers, Fowler, Chamberlein, & Dunn, 1994). These results were essentially replicated in a larger trial with a chronic, medicated population, with the addition of CBT producing greater benefit than routine care alone (Kuipers et al., 1997). In this latter study, the incremental benefits associated with the addition of CBT were maintained through a nine-month followup (Kuipers et al., 1998).

As is true of other disorders, the gains produced by CBT are better maintained than those produced by other interventions. For example, Sensky and colleagues found that a nonspecific "befriending" therapy produced as much change as CBT among chronic medicated patients across nine months of active treatment. However, "befriended" patients deteriorated following the end of active treatment, whereas patients treated with CBT continued to improve across a 12-month post-treatment followup (Sensky et al., 2000). Similarly, Pinto and colleagues found that CBT not only maintained advantages found at post-treatment over supportive therapy in medicated patients with respect to positive symptoms, but also showed continued improvement with respect to negative symptoms across a 12-month post-treatment followup (Pinto, La Pia, Mannella, Domenico, & DeSimone, 1999).

The work just described has focused on treating residual symptoms in chronic medicated patients. Drury and colleagues found that the addition of CBT shortened the time to recovery among acutely ill inpatients (Drury, Birchwood, Cochrane, & MacMillan, 1996). In their trial, 65% of patients treated with the addition of CBT achieved full symptomatic recovery by 12 weeks compared to 40% of patients receiving routine care; mean recovery time and time in hospital were both reduced by about 50%. Though as yet unreplicated, this work suggests that CBT may have a role to play in the treatment of acutely ill patients.

A recent meta-analysis of the studies just described found that adding CBT to routine care, including medication, was associated with a between-group effect size of .91 relative to adding supportive therapy (Rector & Beck, 2001). As shown in Figure 10.14, this advantage was apparent with respect to both positive and negative symptoms, despite the fact that many of the patients were already being treated with atypical neuroleptics. There were also indications that CBT reduced levels of depression, a common correlate of schizophrenia that is associated with increased risk for relapse and suicide.

This work represents one of the most exciting developments with CBT in the last decade. Although no one would suggest that schizophrenic patients should not be medicated, such patients often show residual symptoms both positive and especially negative that need to be addressed. Moreover, indications that CBT might speed the course of recovery are most welcome indeed. It remains unclear whether CBT can reduce risk for relapse, but it does appear to have a more enduring effect than other adjunctive interventions to which it has been compared. The studies suggest that CBT may have a role to play in the treatment of schizophrenia.

Behavioral Medicine

CBT has been adopted widely in the field of behavioral medicine. Approaches that enhance the acquisition of cognitive skills have been most prominent in this domain, with SIT and self-instructional training serving as a model for many of the specific programs (Turk, Meichenbaum, & Genest, 1983). Unlike patients who have psychopathological disorders, the typical medical patient is not apt to have entrenched maladaptive beliefs or problematic information-processing styles that need to be changed. In most instances, the task in this literature has been to help people who are relatively well adjusted deal with negative life events that sometimes fall outside the range of everyday human experience.

Preparation for Noxious Medical Procedures

One of the classic applications of this approach has been to help people prepare for and cope with a variety of noxious medical procedures. For example, Kendall and colleagues found SIT superior to a variety of control conditions in terms of reducing anxiety and enhancing adjustment to surgery during cardiac catheterization (Kendall et al., 1979). Peterson and Shigetomi (1981) found that self-statement training reduced surgical fears in young children, and Kaplan and colleagues found that self-instructional training reduced distress during sigmoidoscopy exams (Kaplan, Atkins, & Lenhard, 1982). Elliott and Olson (1983) found stress-management procedures helpful in managing children's distress during painful treatment for burns, and Jay and Elliot (1990) reported that SIT reduced parents' distress when their children had to undergo painful medical procedures. Numerous studies have found that cognitive behavioral stress-management procedures help both adults and children cope with painful dental procedures (see, for example, Getka & Glass, 1992). Hener and colleagues found that CBT facilitated psychosocial adjustment to home peritoneal kidney dialysis wherein patients who do not comply with their medication regime face hospitalization and possible death (Hener, Weisenberg, & Har-Even, 1996). These and other studies suggest that stress-management techniques modeled on SIT can help people cope with noxious medical procedures.

Coping with Cancer

Closely related to the applications just discussed are efforts to use CBT to mitigate the more negative aspects of cancer treatment. For example, Jay and colleagues found that SIT reduced distress in children undergoing painful bone marrow aspirations and lumbar punctures (e.g., Jay, Elliott, Katz, & Siegel, 1987). CBT also has been used to enhance adjustment to the disease itself. For example, Fawzy and colleagues found that a brief cognitive behavioral intervention that included PST and anxiety management strategies improved coping skills and reduced affective distress and led to better preservation of immune system functioning (Fawzy, Cousins et al., 1990; Fawzy, Kemeny et al., 1990). Moreover, as shown in Figure 10.15, patients treated with cognitive behavior therapy were more likely to be free from recurrence and more likely to survive a subsequent six-year followup (Fawzy et al., 1993). Such programs are important not only because of their potential to reduce distress and contribute to the overall quality of life, but because they can have an indirect effect on the disease process itself by virtue of enhancing immune system functions. This effect may not be specific to CBT, but it does appear to be a benefit of even brief exposure with this approach (Fawzy, Fawzy, Arndt, & Pasnau, 1995).

Prevention and Treatment of HIV Infection and AIDS

CBT has been used both to reduce risk for HIV infection (see Kelly & Murphy, 1992) and to reduce distress following notification of HIV status (see Hollon & Beck, 1994). In an interesting series of studies, Antoni and colleagues found that an extensive program of CBT not only protected participants against distress following notification, but also produced better preservation of immune system functioning among those participants who proved to be infected (Antoni et al., 1991). Subsequent studies have replicated this effect in persons

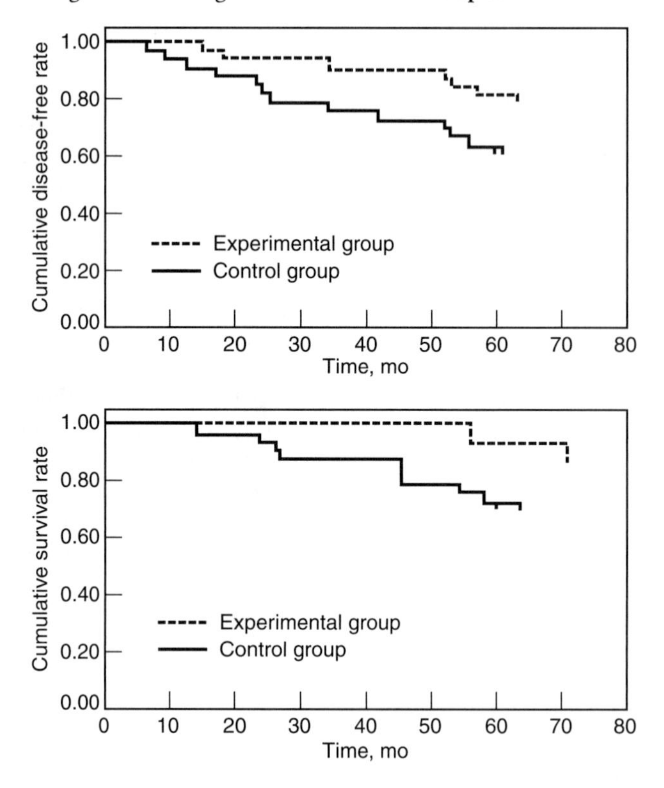

FIGURE 10.15 Time to recurrence and time to death as a function of treatment. From "Malignant melanoma: Effects of an early structured psychiatric intervention, coping, and affective state on recurrence and survival 6 years later" by Fawzy et al., 1993, *Archives of General Psychiatry, 50,* p. 684. Copyright 1993 by the American Medical Association. Reprinted by permission.

with chronic HIV infection (Lutgendorf et al., 1997) and have shown that reductions in distress mediate better preservation of immune system functions over time (Antoni et al., 2000). Figure 10.16 presents the delayed effects of cognitive behavioral stress management (CBSM) on immune system functioning from that later study.

It would be premature to conclude that such effects are specific to the cognitive behavior therapy; in fact, one study found that CBT was less effective than either IPT or medications in reducing distress among HIV seropositive patients (Markowitz et al., 1998). However, it does appear that the cognitive behavioral interventions can both reduce high-risk behaviors and enhance adaptation following notification of HIV status. Indications that they might also help preserve immune system functioning are particularly exciting.

Chronic Pain

CBT also appears to be effective in the treatment of chronic pain, although questions remain as to how it compares with more purely operant behavioral approaches (Morely, Eccleston, & Williams, 1999). Unlike operant approaches, which focus exclusively on the modification of pain behaviors, CBT also attends to the interpretative and affective aspects of the pain experience. Most of these programs are modeled after SIT and combine training in relaxation and behavioral coping skills with cognitive restructuring and self-statement modification. Numerous studies have found such interventions superior to control conditions in the treatment of chronic pain associated with a number of diverse disorders (see Compas et al., 1998, for a review). These include rheumatic disease (Parker et al., 1995), irritable bowel syndrome (Greene & Blanchard, 1994; Payne & Blanchard, 1995), and recurrent abdominal pain in children (Sanders et al., 1989). Considerable work has been done with respect to low back pain. CBT appears to be about as effective as more purely operant approaches and may enhance their efficacy when added in combination (Kole-Snijders et al., 1999).

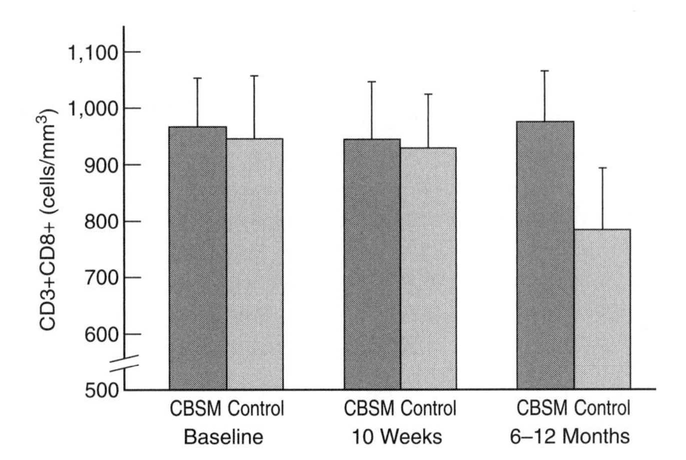

FIGURE 10.16 Delayed effects of treatment on immune system functioning in HIV+ patients. From "Cognitive-behavioral stress management intervention effects on anxiety, 24-hr urinary norepinephrine output, and t-cytotoxic/suppressor cells over time among symptomatic HIV-infected gay men" by Antoni et al., 2000, *Journal of Consulting and Clinical Psychology, 68*, p. 39. Copyright 2000 by the American Psychological Association. Reprinted by permission.

Tension and Migraine Headaches

CBT is clearly effective in the treatment of tension headaches, although it is less clear that it is effective with migraines (Blanchard, 1992). CBT is modeled after SIT and typically includes training in attentional redeployment, cognitive restructuring, and verbal self-instruction in combination with more purely behavioral techniques. With respect to tension headaches, CBT has proved superior to minimal-treatment or nonspecific controls and at least as effective as, and likely to enhance the efficacy of, more purely behavioral interventions (see, for example, Blanchard, Applebaum, Radnitz, Michultka, et al., 1990). In the one study in which they have been compared, CBT was superior to amitriptyline pharmacotherapy (Holroyd, Nash, Pingel, Cordingley, & Jerome, 1991). Gains appear to be well maintained following CBT, something that has not been the case for the pharmacological approaches (Blanchard, 1992). The evidence is not so clear that cognitive behavioral interventions are effective in the treatment of migraine headaches. Early studies failed to find CBT interventions superior to even minimal-treatment controls, and later studies tended to find that the addition of cognitive components did little to enhance the efficacy of more purely behavioral interventions (e.g., Blanchard, Appelbaum, Radnitz, Morrill, et al., 1990). Thus, although CBT appears to be effective in the treatment of tension headaches, there is little indication that it adds to the effectiveness of more purely behavioral interventions in the treatment of migraine headaches (Holroyd & Penzien, 1994).

Summary

CBT appears to be effective in the treatment of a variety of medical disorders, particularly those approaches like SIT, PST, and self-instructional training that aid in the acquisition of cognitive skills. These approaches appear to facilitate coping with noxious medical procedures and may help enhance the quality of life and improve immune system functioning for people with cancer. They appear to reduce risk for HIV infection and help preserve immune system functioning in those who are infected. They ameliorate chronic pain and help prevent headache pain, at least with respect to tension headaches. Questions of specificity remain, particularly with respect to the more purely behavioral interventions. Although the cognitive strategies incorporated in these approaches are less sophisticated than those applied to other psychiatric disorders, they appear to be adequate to meet the pragmatic needs of patients in medical settings.

MARITAL DISTRESS

A cognitive theory of marital distress suggests that the way in which partners interpret one another's behaviors and the expectations they hold play an important role in determining how they behave toward one another and their satisfaction with their relationship (Baucom, Epstein, Sayers, & Sher, 1989). According to this theory, any intervention that systematically changes maladaptive beliefs regarding the partner's behaviors or the more general standards to which the partner is held should lead to a reduction in marital distress (Baucom & Epstein, 1990; Beck, 1988).

Numerous studies have shown that cognitive and cognitive behavioral approaches are superior to minimal treatment controls in the treatment of marital distress (see Baucom, Shoham, Mueser, Daiuto, & Stickle, 1998, for a recent review; and Sexton et al., this volume). One recent study has even shown that a brief weekend program of CBT can prevent subsequent marital problems (Kaiser, Hahlweg, Fehm-Wolfsdorf, & Groth, 1998). However, it is not clear that the addition of cognitive components does anything to enhance the efficacy of more purely behavioral interventions, and findings with respect to the maintenance of gains are similarly mixed (e.g., Halford, Sanders, & Behrens, 1993).

At the same time, questions can be raised about the implementation of CBT in these trials. Many studies have presented the cognitive and behavioral components in a sequential fashion rather than as a truly integrated approach. Such a strategy may not do justice to the complex interrelations between cognition, affect, and behavior that underlie relational issues and does not adequately represent the sophistication of current clinical practice (see Hollon & Beck, 1994). Subsequent trials should integrate these components in a more clinically sophisticated fashion and use experienced therapists to ensure that the respective interventions are adequately implemented.

Conclusions and Recommendations

Cognitive and cognitive behavioral interventions appear to be effective in the treatment of a variety of clinical disorders. In the previous edition of this book, we noted that there had been a veritable explosion of high-quality controlled studies across a number of different disorders (Hollon & Beck, 1994). This trend has continued over the ensuing years, and CBT is one of the interventions receiving the most consistent empirical support in the treatment of adult psychiatric populations (DeRubeis & Crits-Christoph, 1998), children and adolescents (Kazdin & Weisz, 1998), and behavioral medicine (Compas et al., 1998). With regard to the specific areas of disorder, the following conclusions can be drawn:

1. CT appears to be at least as effective as alternative interventions in the treatment of outpatient depression and reduces risk following treatment termination. It appears to be a useful adjunct to medications in the treatment of inpatient populations and bipolar disorder, although work with this latter population is still quite preliminary. Its active ingredients and mechanisms of change remain unclear, although they may work via changing beliefs and associated behaviors. Other cognitive behavioral approaches have shown promise in the treatment of children and adolescents but have not been extensively evaluated in adult clinical populations.

2. Some of the most dramatic breakthroughs in the last two decades have come in the treatment of anxiety disorders. CBT appears to be particularly effective in the treatment of panic, GAD, social phobia, and possibly hypochondriasis, and like depression there are indications that these interventions have an enduring effect that lasts beyond the end of treatment. More purely behavioral interventions based on exposure remain the standard of treatment for OCD and PTSD, as well as simple phobia, but sophisticated cognitive models have been proposed that hold considerable promise. Within each disorder some theorists emphasize cognitive mechanisms, whereas others focus on more behavioral processes like extinction and habituation. Treatment strategies vary somewhat as a function of emphasis. Whether this distinction influences outcomes remains unclear, but approaches based on each do well relative to other types of treatments.

3. CBT has become the standard of treatment for bulimia nervosa, being more effective than IPT and longer lasting than either behavior therapy or medications. Anorexia nervosa still remains problematic; a sophisticated cognitive model has been proposed but has not yet been adequately tested. CBT appears to be effective in the treatment of binge eating disorder but less cost-effective than widely available behavioral weight loss programs. Including cognitive components appears to slow but not prevent the process of weight gain following behavior therapy for obesity. More sophisticated cognitive models have been articulated for these latter disorders but not yet tested.

4. CBT shows great promise in the treatment of internalizing disorders in children and

adolescents. It appears to be at least as effective as alternative interventions in the treatment of depression and anxiety and to have an enduring effect that makes it ideal for studies of prevention. With repect to the externalizing disorders the picture is more mixed. Skills training approaches like PST have value in the treatment of aggression and conduct disorder, but despite the apparent success of self-instructional training in the treatment of impulsivity in nonclinical samples, medication and behavior modification remain the treatments of choice for ADHD.

5. It remains unclear just how effective CBT is in the treatment of substance abuse. Evidence for the efficacy of relapse prevention and related approaches in the treatment of alcoholism has been inconsistent, although it does appear to reduce risk for less severe problem drinkers and young adults who have not yet established a stable drinking pattern. Similarly, studies differ with respect to whether CBT can match or enhance the efficacy of standard drug counseling for opioid or cocaine abuse. Successful treatment may require expertise with the addiction as well as the intervention. Finally, it remains unclear whether cognitive strategies add to the efficacy of multicomponent treatment packages for the reduction of smoking, although they appear to reduce risk for relapse among smokers who are also depressed.

6. Sophisticated models have been developed to guide the treatment of the personality disorders. DBT has been shown to reduce parasuicidal behavior among patients with borderline personality disorder. Given how difficult these patients are to treat, it is not surprising that this approach has generated great interest in the field. Considerable effort has gone into adapting CT for use in the treatment of personality disorders, but it has yet to be evaluated empirically.

7. One of the most exciting developments over the last decade has been the emerging evidence that CBT can be used to reduce belief in delusions and speed the course of recovery in patients with schizophrenia who are maintained on medications. The bulk of this work has been done in Great Britain and has already spurred considerable interest in other parts of the world.

8. CBT appears to be useful in the management of a number of medical disorders, particularly those approaches like SIT that provide training in specific coping skills. These interventions can be used to help patients tolerate noxious medical procedures, prevent high-risk behaviors, preserve immune system functioning, and reduce chronic pain. The cognitive components of these interventions rarely need to be as sophisticated as those required for dealing with psychiatric patients, but the beneficial effects of these interventions are well established.

9. Little new work has been done in the area of marital discord. This is disappointing since misperceptions so clearly play a role in the maintenance of such distress. Although sophisticated models have been expressed, studies in the empirical literature typically have implemented cognitive strategies in a mechanistic fashion and failed to integrate them with more purely behavioral components. More clinically sophisticated empirical work remains to be done.

CBT appears to be effective for a broad range of clinical and medical disorders. Negative findings are few and often may be a consequence of a failure to implement the approach in an adequate manner. Whereas early studies often provided less than fully representative interventions to nonclinical populations, there is now a large number of well-controlled trials in fully clinical populations. In most instances, these interventions have been found to be at least as effective as, and sometimes superior to, more purely behavioral or pharmacological interventions. Comparisons with dynamic or humanistic therapies have been few, but also generally supportive. Moreover, there are numerous indications that the cognitive and cognitive behavioral interventions may produce more lasting change than other interventions, particularly medication treatment.

Important issues remain. For many disorders, the extent to which the underlying mechanisms of change are cognitive in nature remains unclear. Different theorists emphasize different mechanisms and adjust their interventions accordingly. For example, Clark and colleagues at the Maudsley focus on putting patients in situations that test their worst fears, whereas theorists like Barlow or Foa are more likely to rely on multiple exposures in the service of habituation. Similarly, Beck and colleagues spend more time mapping out the belief systems (cognitive conceptualizations) of their patients than do theorists like Jacobson or Linehan. Whether these differences in theory and implementation influence the quality or nature of the outcomes produced remains to be seen, but they are apparent, even if somewhat subtle.

Some types of CBT have received more empirical attention than have others. RET remains the least adequately tested of all the major approaches, although it has generally performed well in studies in which it has been adequately implemented (Hollon & Beck, 1994). CT has fared well in a number of different patient populations, including depression, panic and the anxiety disorder, and more recently schizophrenia. Somewhat more behaviorally oriented versions of CBT have done well with panic and the anxiety disorders, as well as bulimia, and DBT has done well with patients with borderline personality disorder. SIT appears to be well established in the treatment of a variety of medical and stress-related disorders, whereas PST appears to be of use in the treatment of children and adolescents with externalizing disorders. Whether any of these approaches will prove superior to the others with any of these populations remains to be seen, but each appears to be effective in the treatment of at least some of these disorders.

Although important questions remain, it appears that the cognitive and cognitive behavioral interventions are effective in the treatment of a broad range of disorders. The growth in the quality and quantity of the empirical support for these approaches over the last 15 years truly has been impressive. In most instances, those studies have suggested that these approaches are at least as effective as the best available alternatives for a number of disorders. Moreover, there are indications that they may produce an enduring effect rarely shared by other approaches. Although questions of moderation and mediation need to be resolved, it appears that the cognitive and cognitive behavioral interventions have fully come of age.

REFERENCES

Abikoff, H. (1985). Efficacy of cognitive training interventions in hyperactive children: A critical review. *Clinical Psychology Review, 5*, 479–512.

Abramowitz, J. S. (1997). Effectiveness of psychological and pharmacological treatments for obsessive-compulsive disorder: A quantitative review. *Journal of Consulting and Clinical Psychology, 65*, 44–52.

Abramson, L. Y., Metalsky, G. I., & Alloy, L. B. (1989). Hopelessness depression: A theory-based subtype of depression. *Psychological Review, 96*, 358–372.

Agras, W. S., Rossiter, E. M., Arnow, B., Schneider, J. A., Telch, C. F., Raeburn, S. D., Bruse, B., Perl, M., & Koran, L. M. (1992). Pharmacological and cognitive-behavioral treatment for bulimia nervosa: A controlled comparison. *American Journal of Psychiatry, 149*, 82–87.

Agras, W. S., Telch, C. F., Arnow, B., Eldredge, K., Wilfley, D., Raeburn, S. D., Henderson, J., & Marnell, M. (1994). Weight loss, cognitive-behavioral, and desipramine treatments in binge eating disorder: An additive design. *Behavior Therapy, 25*, 209–224.

Agras, W. S., Walsh, T., Fairburn, C. G., Wilson, G. T., & Kraemer, H. C. (2000). A multicenter comparison of cognitive-behavioral therapy and interpersonal psychotherapy for bulimia nervosa. *Archives of General Psychiatry, 57*, 459–466.

American Psychiatric Association (1995). Practice guideline for the treatment of patients with substance use disorders: Alcohol, cocaine, opioids. *American Journal of Psychiatry, 152 (Suppl.)*, 1–59.

American Psychiatric Association (2000). Practice guideline for the treatment of patients with major depressive disorder (revision). *American Journal of Psychiatry, 157 (Suppl. 4)*, 1–45.

Antoni, M. H., Baggett, L., Ironson, G., LaPerriere, A., August, S., Klimas, N., Schneiderman, N., Fletcher, M. A. (1991). Cognitive-behavioral stress management intervention buffers distress responses and immunologic changes following notification of HIV-1 seropositivity. *Journal of Consulting and Clinical Psychology, 59*, 906–915.

Antoni, M. H., Cruess, D. G., Cruess, S., Lutgendorf, S., Kumar, M., Ironson, G., Klimas, K., Fletcher, M. A., & Schneiderman, N. (2000). Cognitive-behavioral stress management intervention effects on anxiety, 24-hr urinary norepinephrine output, and T-cytotoxic/suppressor cells over time among symptomatic HIV-infected gay men. *Journal of Consulting and Clinical Psychology, 68*, 31–45.

Arntz, A., & Van den Hout, M. (1996). Psychological treatments of panic disorder without agoraphobia: Cognitive therapy versus applied relaxation. *Behaviour Research and Therapy, 34*, 113–121.

Barber, J. P., & Muenz, L. R. (1996). The role of avoidance and obsessiveness in matching patients to cognitive and interpersonal psychotherapy: Empirical findings from the Treatment for Depression Collaborative Research Program. *Journal of Consulting and Clinical Psychology, 64*, 951–958.

Barlow, D. H., & Cerny, J. A. (1988). *Psychological treatment of panic.* New York: Guilford Press.

Barlow, D. H., Gorman, J. M., Shear, M. K., & Woods, S. W. (2000). Cognitive-behavioral therapy, imipramine, or their combination for panic disorder: A randomized controlled trial. *JAMA, 283*, 2529–2536.

Barlow, D. H., & Lehman, C. L. (1996). Advances in the psychosocial treatment of anxiety disorders. *Archives of General Psychiatry, 53*, 727–735.

Barrett, P. M. (1998). An evaluation of cognitive-behavioral group treatments for childhood anxiety disorders. *Journal of Clinical Child Psychology, 27,* 459–468.

Barrett, P. M., Dadds, M. R., & Rapee, R. M. (1996). Family treatment of childhood anxiety: A controlled trial. *Journal of Consulting and Clinical Psychology, 64,* 333–342.

Barrett, P. M., Duffy, A. L., Dadds, M. R., & Rapee, R. M. (2001). Cognitive-behavioral treatment of anxiety disorders in children: Long-term (6-year) follow-up. *Journal of Consulting and Clinical Psychology, 69,* 135–141.

Baucom, D. H., & Epstein, N. (1990). *Cognitive-behavioral marital therapy.* New York: Brunner/Mazel.

Baucom, D. H., Epstein, N., Sayers, S., & Sher, T. G. (1989). The role of cognitions in marital relationships: Definitional, methodological, and conceptual issues. *Journal of Consulting and Clinical Psychology, 57,* 31–38.

Baucom, D. H., Shoham, V., Mueser, K. T., Daiuto, A. D., & Stickle, T. R. (1998). Empirically supported couple and family interventions for marital distress and adult mental health problems. *Journal of Consulting and Clinical Psychology, 66,* 53–88.

Beck, A. T. (1988). *Love is never enough.* New York: Harper & Row.

Beck, A. T. (1991). Cognitive therapy: A 30-year retrospective. *American Psychologist, 46,* 368–375.

Beck, A. T., & Emery, G. (1985). *Anxiety disorders and phobias: A cognitive perspective.* New York: Basic Books.

Beck, A. T., Freeman, A., & Associates (1990). *Cognitive therapy of personality disorders.* New York: Guilford Press.

Beck, A. T., & Rector, N. A. (2000). Cognitive therapy of schizophrenia: A new therapy for the new millennium. *American Journal of Psychotherapy, 54,* 291–300.

Beck, A. T., Rush, A. J., Shaw, B. F., & Emery, G. (1979). *Cognitive therapy of depression.* New York: Guilford Press.

Beck, A. T., Wright, F. D., & Newman, C. F. (1992). Cocaine abuse. In A. Freeman & F. M. Dattilio (Eds.), *Comprehensive casebook of cognitive therapy* (pp. 185–192). New York: Plenum Press.

Beck, J. S. (1998). Complex cognitive therapy treatment for personality disorder patients. *Bulletin of the Menninger Clinic, 62,* 170–194.

Birmaher, B., Brent, D. A., Kolko, D. J., Baugher, M., Bridge, J., Holder, D., Iyengar, S., & Ulloa, R. E. (2000). Clinical outcome after short-term psychotherapy for adolescents with major depressive disorder. *Archives of General Psychiatry, 57,* 29–36.

Black, D. W., Wesner, R., Bowers, W., & Gabel, J. (1993). A comparison of fluvoxamine, cognitive therapy, and placebo in the treatment of panic disorder. *Archives of General Psychiatry, 50,* 44–50.

Blackburn, I. M., Bishop, S., Glen, A.I.M., Whalley, L. J., & Christie, J. E. (1981). The efficacy of cognitive therapy in depression: A treatment trial using cognitive therapy and pharmacotherapy, each alone and in combination. *British Journal of Psychiatry, 139,* 181–189.

Blanchard, E. B. (1992). Psychological treatment of benign headache disorders. *Journal of Consulting and Clinical Psychology, 60,* 537–551.

Blanchard, E. B., Appelbaum, K. A., Radnitz, C. L., Michultka, D., Morrill, B., Kirsch, C., Hillhouse, J., Evans, D. D., Guarmieri, P., Attanasio, V., Andrasik, F., Jaccard, J., & Dentinger, M. P. (1990). Placebo-controlled evaluation of abbreviated progressive muscle relaxation and of relaxation combined with cognitive therapy in the treatment of tension headache. *Journal of Consulting and Clinical Psychology, 58,* 210–215.

Blanchard, E. B., Appelbaum, K. A., Radnitz, C. L., Morrill, B., Michultka, D., Kirsch, C., Guarnieri, P., Hillhouse, J., Evans, D. D., Jaccard, J., & Barron, K. D. (1990). A controlled evaluation of thermal biofeedback and thermal biofeedback combined with cognitive therapy in the treatment of vascular headache. *Journal of Consulting and Clinical Psychology, 58,* 216–224.

Borkovec, T. D., & Costello, E. (1993). Efficacy of applied relaxation and cognitive behavioral therapy in the treatment of generalized anxiety disorder. *Journal of Consulting and Clinical Psychology, 61,* 611–619.

Borkovec, T. D., & Ruscio, A. M. (2001). Psychotherapy for generalized anxiety disorder. *Journal of Clinical Psychiatry, 62 (Suppl. 11),* 37–42.

Bouchard, S., Gauthier, J., LaBerge, B., French, D., Pelletier, M.-H., & Godbout, C. (1996). Exposure versus cognitive restructuring in the treatment of panic disorder with agoraphobia. *Behaviour Research and Therapy, 34,* 213–224.

Bowers, W. A. (1990). Treatment of depressed inpatients: Cognitive therapy plus medication, relaxation plus medication, and medication alone. *British Journal of Psychiatry, 156,* 73–78.

Brent, D. A., Holder, D., Kolko, K. J., Birmaher, B., Baugher, M., Roth, C., Iyengar, S., & Johnson, B. A. (1997). A clinical psychotherapy trial for adolescent depression comparing cognitive, family, and supportive treatments. *Archives of General Psychiatry, 54,* 877–885.

Brent, D. A., Kolko, K. J., Birmaher, B., Baugher, M., & Bridge, J. (1999). A clinical trial for adolescent depression: Predictors of additional treatment in the acute and follow-up phases of the trial. *Journal of the American Academy of Child and Adolescent Psychiatry, 38,* 263–270.

Brent, D. A., Kolko, D. J., Birmaher, B., Baugher, M., Bridge, J., Roth, C., & Holder, D. (1998). Predictors of treatment efficacy in a clinical trial of three psychosocial treatments for adolescent depression. *Journal of the American Academy of Child and Adolescent Psychiatry, 37,* 906–914.

Brown, R. A., Kahler, C. W., Niaura, R., Abrams, D. B., Sales, S. D., Ramsey, S. E., Goldstein, M. G., Burgess, E. S., & Miller, I. W. (2001). Cognitive-behavioral treatment for depression in smoking cessation. *Journal of Consulting and Clinical Psychology, 69*, 471–480.

Brown, T. A., Barlow, D. H., & Liebowitz, M. R. (1994). The empirical basis of generalized anxiety disorder. *American Journal of Psychiatry, 15*, 1272–1280.

Brownell, K. D., Marlatt, G. A., Lichtenstein, E., & Wilson, G. T. (1986). Understanding and preventing relapse. *American Psychologist, 41*, 765–782.

Brownell, K. D., & Rodin, J. (1994). The dieting maelstrom: Is it possible and advisable to lose weight? *American Psychologist, 49*, 781–791.

Bruce, T. J., Spiegel, D. A., & Hegel, M. T. (1999). Cognitive-behavioral therapy helps prevent relapse and recurrence of panic disorder following alprazolam discontinuation: A long-term follow-up of the Peoria and Dartmouth studies. *Journal of Consulting and Clinical Psychology, 67*, 151–156.

Bryant, R. A., Harvey, A. G., Dang, S. T., Sackville, T., & Basten, C. (1998). Treatment of acute stress disorder: A comparison of cognitive-behavioral therapy and supportive counseling. *Journal of Consulting and Clinical Psychology, 66*, 862–866.

Burns, D. D., & Spangler, D. L. (2000). Does psychotherapy homework lead to improvements in depression in cognitive-behavioral therapy or does improvement lead to increased homework compliance? *Journal of Consulting and Clinical Psychology, 68*, 46–56.

Carroll, K. M. (1996). Relapse prevention as a psychosocial treatment: A review of controlled clinical trials. *Experimental and Clinical Psychopharmacology, 4*, 46–54.

Carroll, K. M., Rounsaville, B. J., Gordon, L. T., Nich, C., Jatlow, P., Bisighini, R. M., & Gawin, F. H. (1994). Psychotherapy and pharmacotherapy for ambulatory cocaine abusers. *Archives of General Psychiatry, 51*, 177–187.

Carroll, K. M., Rounsaville, B. J., Nich, C., Gordon, L. T., Wirtz, P. W., & Gawin, F. (1994). One-year follow-up of psychotherapy and pharmacotherapy for cocaine dependence: Delayed emergence of psychotherapy effects. *Archives of General Psychiatry, 51*, 989–997.

Clark, D. M. (1986). A cognitive approach to panic. *Behavior Research and Therapy, 24*, 461–470.

Clark, D. M., & Salkovskis, P. M. (1991). *Cognitive therapy with panic and hypochondriasis.* New York: Pergamon Press.

Clark, D. M., Salkovskis, P. M., Hackmann, A., Middleton, H., Anastasiades, P., & Gelder, M. (1994). A comparison of cognitive therapy, applied relaxation and imipramine in the treatment of panic disorder. *British Journal of Psychiatry, 164*, 759–769.

Clark, D. M., Salkovskis, P. M., Hackmann, A., Wells, A., Fennell, M., Ludgate, J., Ahmad, S., Richards, H. C., & Gelder, M. (1998). Two psychological treatments for hypochondrias: A randomised controlled trial. *British Journal of Psychiatry, 173*, 218–225.

Clark, D. M., Salkovskis, P. M., Hackmann, A., Wells, A., Ludgate, J., & Gelder, M. (1999). Brief cognitive therapy for panic disorder: A randomized controlled trial. *Journal of Consulting and Clinical Psychology, 67*, 583–589.

Clarke, G. N., Hawkins, W., Murphy, M., Sheeber, L. B., Lewinsohn, P. M., & Seeley, J. (1995). Targeted prevention of unipolar depressive disorder in an at-risk sample of high school adolescents: A randomized trial of a group cognitive intervention. *Journal of the American Academy of Child and Adolescent Psychiatry, 34*, 312–321.

Clarke, G. N., Hornbrook, M. C., Lynch, F., Polen, M., Gale, J., Beardslee, W. R., O'Connor, E., & Seeley, J. (2001). A randomized trial of a group cognitive intervention for preventing depression in adolescent offspring of depressed parents. *Archives of General Psychiatry, 58*, 1127–1134.

Clarke, G. N., Rohde, P., Lewinsohn, P. M., Hops, H., Seeley, J. R. (1999). Cognitive-behavioral treatment of adolescent depression: Efficacy of acute group treatment and booster sessions. *Journal of the American Academy of Child and Adolescent Psychiatry, 38*, 272–279.

Cobham, V. E., Dadds, M. R., & Spence, S. H. (1998). The role of parental anxiety in the treatment of childhood anxiety. *Journal of Consulting and Clinical Psychology, 66*, 893–905.

Compas, B. E., Haaga, D.A.F., Keefe, F. J., Leitenberg, H., & Williams, D. A. (1998). Sampling of empirically supported psychological treatments from health psychology: Smoking, chronic pain, cancer, and bulimia nervosa. *Journal of Consulting and Clinical Psychology, 66*, 89–112.

Cooper, Z., & Fairburn, C. G. (2001). A new cognitive behavioural approach to the treatment of obesity. *Behaviour Research and Therapy, 39*, 499–511.

Crits-Christoph, P., Siqueland, L., Blaine, J., Frank, A., Luborsky, L., Onken, L. S., Muenz, L. R., Thase, M. E., Weiss, R. D., Gastfiend, D. R., Woody, G. E., Barber, J. P., Butler, S. F., Daley, D., Salloum, I., Bishop, S., Najavits, L. M., Lis, J., Mercer, D., Griffin, M. L., Moras, K., & Beck, A. T. (1999). Psychosocial treatments of cocaine dependence: National Institute on Drug Abuse Collaborative Cocaine Treatment Study. *Archives of General Psychiatry, 56*, 493–502.

Cuijpers, P. (1998). A psychoeducational approach to the treatment of depression: A meta-analysis of Lewinsohn's "Coping with Depression" course. *Behavior Therapy, 29*, 521–533.

Curry, J. F. (2001). Specific psychotherapies for childhood and adolescent depression. *Biological Psychiatry, 49,* 1091–1100.

Dadds, M. R., Holland, D. E., Laurens, K. R., Mullins, M., Barrett, P. M., & Spence, S. H. (1999). Early intervention and prevention of anxiety disorders in children: Results at 2-year follow-up. *Journal of Consulting and Clinical Psychology, 67,* 145–150.

Dadds, M. R., Spence, S. H., Holland, D., Barrett, P. M., & Laurens, K. (1997). Early intervention and prevention of anxiety disorders: A controlled trial. *Journal of Consulting and Clinical Psychology, 65,* 627–635.

DeRubeis, R. J., & Crits-Christoph, P. (1998). Empirically supported individual and group psychological treatments for adult mental disorders. *Journal of Consulting and Clinical Psychology, 66,* 37–52.

DeRubeis, R. J., Evans, M. D., Hollon, S. D., Garvey, M. J., Grove, W. M., & Tuason, V. B. (1990). How does cognitive therapy work? Cognitive change and symptom change in cognitive therapy and pharmacotherapy for depression. *Journal of Consulting and Clinical Psychology, 58,* 862–869.

DeRubeis, R. J., Gelfand, L. A., Tang, T. Z., & Simons, A. D. (1999). Medication versus cognitive behavior therapy for severely depressed outpatients: Mega-analysis of four randomized comparisons. *American Journal of Psychiatry, 156,* 1007–1013.

DeRubeis, R. J., Hollon, S. D., Amsterdam, J., & Shelton, R. C. (2001, July). Acute effects of cognitive therapy, pharmacotherapy, and placebo in severely depressed outpatients. In D. M. Clark (Chair), *Cognitive therapy versus medications in the treatment of severely depressed outpatients: Acute response and the prevention of relapse.* Symposium conducted at the meeting of the World Congress of Behavioral and Cognitive Therapy, Vancouver, Canada.

Devilly, G. J., & Spence, S. H. (1998). The relative efficacy and treatment distress of EMDR and a cognitive-behavior trauma protocol in the amelioration of posttraumatic stress disorder. *Journal of Anxiety Disorder, 13,* 131–157.

Dobson, K. S. (1989). A meta-analysis of the efficacy of cognitive therapy for depression. *Journal of Consulting and Clinical Psychology, 57,* 414–419.

Drury, V., Birchwood, M., Cochrane, R., & MacMillan, F. (1996). Cognitive therapy and recovery from acute psychosis: A controlled trial, I: Impact on psychotic symptoms. *British Journal of Psychiatry, 169,* 593–601.

Durham, R. C., Murphy, T., Allan, T., et al. (1994). Cognitive therapy, analytic psychotherapy and anxiety management for generalized anxiety disorder. *British Journal of Psychiatry, 165,* 315–323.

D'Zurilla, T. J., & Goldfried, M. R. (1971). Problem-solving and behavior modification. *Journal of Abnormal Psychology, 78,* 107–126.

Ehlers, A., & Clark, D. M. (2000). A cognitive model of posttraumatic stress disorder. *Behaviour Research and Therapy, 38,* 319–345.

Elkin, I., Gibbons, R. D., Shea, T., Sotsky, S. M., Watkins, J. T., Pilkonis, P. A., & Hedeker, D. (1995). Initial severity and differential treatment outcome in the National Institute of Mental Health Treatment of Depression Collaborative Research Program. *Journal of Consulting and Clinical Psychology, 63,* 841–847.

Elkin, I., Shea, M. T., Watkins, J. T., Imber, S. D., Sotsky, S. M., Collins, J. F., Glass, D. R., Pilkonis, P. A., Leber, W. R., Docherty, J. P., Fiester, S. J., & Parloff, M. B. (1989). NIMH Treatment of Depression Collaborative Research Program: I. General effectiveness of treatments. *Archives of General Psychiatry, 46,* 971–982.

Elliott, C. H., & Olson, R. A. (1983). The management of children's behavioral distress in response to painful medical treatment for burn injuries. *Behavior Research and Therapy, 21,* 675–683.

Ellis, A. (1962). *Reason and emotion in psychotherapy.* New York: Lyle Stuart.

Evans, M. D., Hollon, S. D., DeRubeis, R. J., Piasecki, J. M., Grove, W. M., Garvey, M. J., & Tuason, V. B. (1992). Differential relapse following cognitive therapy and pharmacotherapy for depression. *Archives of General Psychiatry, 49,* 802–808.

Fairburn, C. G. (1981). A cognitive behavioral approach to the treatment of bulimia. *Psychological Medicine, 11,* 707–711.

Fairburn, C. G., Jones, R., Peveler, R. C., Hope, R. A., & O'Connor, M. (1993). Psychotherapy and bulimia nervosa: Long-term effects of interpersonal psychotherapy, behavior therapy and cognitive-behavior therapy. *Archives of General Psychiatry, 50,* 419–428.

Fairburn, C. G., Norman, P. A., Welch, S. L., O'Connor, M. E., Doll, H. A., & Peveler, R. C. (1995). A prospective study of outcome in bulimia nervosa and the long-term effects of three psychological treatments. *Archives of General Psychiatry, 52,* 304–312.

Fava, G. A., Rafanelli, C., Grandi, S., Conti, S., & Belluardo, P. (1998). Prevention of recurrent depression with cognitive behavioral therapy. *Archives of General Psychiatry, 55,* 816–820.

Fawzy, F. I., Cousins, N., Fawzy, N. S., Kemeny, M. E., Elashoff, R., & Morton, D. (1990). A structured psychiatric intervention for cancer patients: I. Changes over time in methods of coping and affective disturbance. *Archives of General Psychiatry, 47,* 720–725.

Fawzy, F. I., Fawzy, N. W., Arndt, L. A., & Pasnau, R. O. (1995). Critical review of psychosocial interventions in cancer care. *Archives of General Psychiatry, 52,* 100–113.

Fawzy, F. I., Fawzy, N. S., Hyun, C. S., Elashoff, R., Guthrie, D., Fahey, J. L., & Morton, D. (1993).

Malignant melanoma: Effects of an early structured psychiatric intervention, coping, and affective state on recurrence and survival 6 years later. *Archives of General Psychiatry, 50,* 681–689.

Fawzy, F. I., Kemeny, M. E., Fawzy, N. S., Elashoff, R., Morton, D., Cousins, N., & Fahey, J. L. (1990). A structured psychiatric intervention for cancer patients: II. Changes over time in immunological measures. *Archives of General Psychiatry, 47,* 729–735.

Feeley, M., DeRubeis, R. J., & Gelfand, L. A. (1999). The temporal relation of adherence and alliance to symptom change in cognitive therapy for depression. *Journal of Consulting and Clinical Psychology, 67,* 578–582.

Flannery-Schroeder, E. C., & Kendall, P. C. (2000). Group and individual cognitive-behavioral treatments for youth with anxiety disorders: A randomized clinical trial. *Cognitive Therapy and Research, 24,* 251–278.

Foa, E. B. (2000). Psychosocial treatment of posttraumatic stress disorder. *Journal of Clinical Psychiatry, 61* (Suppl. 5), 43–48.

Foa, E. B., Dancu, C. V., Hembree, E. A., Jaycox, L. H., Meadows, E. A., & Street, G. P. (1999). Comparison of exposure therapy, stress inoculation training, and their combination for reducing posttraumatic stress disorder in female assault victims. *Journal of Consulting and Clinical Psychology, 67,* 194–200.

Foa, E. B., Hearst-Ikeda, D., & Perry, K. J. (1995). Evaluation of a brief cognitive-behavioral program for the prevention of chronic PTSD in recent assault victims. *Journal of Consulting and Clinical Psychology, 63,* 948–955.

Foa, E. B., & Meadows, E. A. (1997). Psychosocial treatments for PTSD: A critical review. *Annual Review of Psychology, 48,* 449–480.

Foa, E. B., & Rothbaum, B. O. (1997). *Treating the trauma of rape.* New York: Guilford Press.

Freeston, M. H., Ladouceur, R., Gagnon, F., Thibodeau, N., Rheaume, J., Letarte, H., & Bujold, A. (1997). Cognitive-behavioral treatment of obsessive thoughts: A controlled study. *Journal of Consulting and Clinical Psychology, 65,* 405–413.

Gaffan, E. A., Tsaousis, I., & Kemp-Wheeler, S. M. (1995). Researcher alliance and meta-analysis: The case of cognitive therapy for depression. *Journal of Consulting and Clinical Psychology, 63,* 966–980.

Garety, P., Kuipers, L., Fowler, D., Chamberlein, F., & Dunn, G. (1994). Cognitive behavioural therapy for drug resistant psychosis. *British Journal of Medical Psychology, 67,* 259–271.

Garner, D. M., & Bemis, K. M. (1982). A cognitive-behavioral approach to anorexia nervosa. *Cognitive Therapy and Research, 6,* 123–150.

Garner, D. M., & Wooley, S. C. (1991). Confronting the failure of behavioral and dietary treatments for obesity. *Clinical Psychology Review, 11,* 729–780.

Getka, E. J., & Glass, C. R. (1992). Behavioral and cognitive-behavioral approaches to the reduction of dental anxiety. *Behavior Therapy, 23,* 433–448.

Gladis, M. M., Wadden, T. A., Vogt, R., Foster, G., Kuehnel, R. H., & Bartlett, S. J. (1998). Behavioral treatment of obese binge eaters: Do they need different care? *Journal of Psychosomatic Research, 17,* 336–345.

Gloaguen, V., Cottraux, J., Cucherat, M., & Blackburn, I.-M. (1998). A meta-analysis of the effects of cognitive therapy in depressed patients. *Journal of Affective Disorders, 49,* 59–72.

Greene, B., & Blanchard, E. B. (1994). Cognitive therapy for irritable bowl syndrome. *Journal of Consulting and Clinical Psychology, 62,* 576–582.

Haddock, G., Tarrier, N., Spaulding, W., Yusupoff, L., Kinney, C., & McCarthy, E. (1998). Individual cognitive-behavior therapy in the treatment of hallucinations and delusions: A review. *Clinical Psychology Review, 18,* 821–838.

Halford, K. W., Sanders, M. R., & Behrens, B. C. (1993). A comparison of the generalization of behavioral marital therapy and enhanced behavioral marital therapy. *Journal of Consulting and Clinical Psychology, 61,* 51–60.

Hall, S. M., Munoz, R. F., & Reus, V. I. (1994). Cognitive-behavioral intervention increases abstinence rates for depressive-history smokers. *Journal of Consulting and Clinical Psychology, 62,* 141–146.

Hall, S. M., Reus, V. I., Munoz, R. F., Sees, K. L., Humfleet, G., Hartz, D. T., Frederick, S., & Triffleman, E. (1998). Nortriptyline and cognitive-behavioral therapy in the treatment of cigarette smoking. *Archives of General Psychiatry, 55,* 683–690.

Heimberg, R. G., Liebowitz, M. R., Hope, D. A., Schneier, F. R., Holt, C. S., Welkowitz, L. A., Juster, H. R., Campeas, R., Bruch, M. A., Cloitre, M., Fallon, B., & Klein, D. F. (1998). Cognitive behavioral group therapy vs. phenelzine therapy for social phobia: 12-week outcome. *Archives of General Psychiatry, 55,* 1133–1141.

Heimberg, R. G., Salzman, D. G., Holt, C. S., et al. (1993). Cognitive-behavioral group treatment for social phobia: Effectiveness at five-year follow-up. *Cognitive Therapy and Research, 17,* 325–339.

Hener, T., Weisenberg, M., & Har-Even, D. (1996). Supportive versus cognitive-behavioral intervention programs in achieving adjustment to home peritoneal kidney dialysis. *Journal of Consulting and Clinical Psychology, 64,* 731–741.

Hill, C. E., O'Grady, K. E., & Elkin, I. (1992). Applying the Collaborative Study Psychotherapy Rating Scale to rate therapist adherence in cognitive-behavior therapy, interpersonal psychotherapy, and clinical management. *Journal of Consulting and Clinical Psychology, 60,* 73–79.

Hinshaw, S. P., Henker, B., & Whalen, C. K. (1984). Cognitive-behavioral and pharmacologic interventions for hyperactive boys: Comparative and combined effects. *Journal of Consulting and Clinical Psychology, 52,* 739–749.

Hollon, S. D. (1996). The efficacy and effectiveness of psychotherapy relative to medications. *American Psychologist, 51,* 1025–1030.

Hollon, S. D. (1999). Allegiance effects in treatment research: A commentary. *Clinical Psychology: Science and Practice, 6,* 107–112.

Hollon, S. D., & Beck, A. T. (1994). Cognitive and cognitive-behavioral therapies. In S. L. Garfield & A. E. Bergin (Eds.), *Handbook of psychotherapy and behavior change* (4th ed.) (pp. 428–466). New York: John Wiley & Sons.

Hollon, S. D., DeRubeis, R. J., & Evans, M. D. (1987). Causal mediation of change in treatment for depression: Discriminating between nonspecificity and noncausality. *Psychological Bulletin, 102,* 139–149.

Hollon, S. D., DeRubeis, R. J., Evans, M. D., Wiemer, M. J., Garvey, M. J., Grove, W. M., & Tuason, V. B. (1992). Cognitive therapy and pharmacotherapy for depression: Singly and in combination. *Archives of General Psychiatry, 49,* 774–781.

Hollon, S. D., DeRubeis, R. J., & Seligman, M.E.P. (1992). Cognitive therapy and the prevention of depression. *Applied and Preventive Psychology, 1,* 89–95.

Hollon, S. D., DeRubeis, R. J., Shelton, R. C., & Amsterdam, J. (2001, July). Cognitive therapy and the prevention of relapse in severely depressed outpatients. In D. M. Clark (Chair), *Cognitive therapy versus medications in the treatment of severely depressed outpatients: Acute response and the prevention of relapse.* Symposium conducted at the meeting of the World Congress of Behavioral and Cognitive Therapy, Vancouver, Canada.

Hollon, S. D., Evans, M. D., & DeRubeis, R. J. (1990). Cognitive mediation of relapse prevention following treatment for depression: Implications of differential risk. In R. E. Ingram (Ed.), *Psychological aspects of depression* (pp. 117–136). New York: Plenum Press.

Hollon, S. D., & Shelton, R. C. (2001). Treatment guidelines for major depressive disorder. *Behavior Therapy, 32,* 235–258.

Holroyd, K. A., Nash, J. M., Pingel, J. D., Cordingley, G. E., & Jerome, A. (1991). A comparison of pharmacological (Amitriptyline HCL) and nonpharmacological (cognitive-behavioral) therapies for chronic tension headaches. *Journal of Consulting and Clinical Psychology, 59,* 387–393.

Holroyd, K. A., & Penzien, D. B. (1994). Psychosocial interventions in the management of recurrent headache disorders: I. Overview and effectiveness. *Behavioral Medicine, 20,* 53–63.

Imber, S. D., Pilkonis, P. A., Sotsky, S. M., Elkin, I., Watkins, J. T., Collins, J. F., Shea, M. T., Leber, W. R., & Glass, D. R. (1990). Mode-specific effects among three treatments for depression. *Journal of Consulting and Clinical Psychology, 58,* 352–359.

Jacobson, N. S., & Hollon, S. D. (1996a). Cognitive-behavior therapy versus pharmacotherapy: Now that the jury's returned its verdict, it's time to present the rest of the evidence. *Journal of Consulting and Clinical Psychology, 64,* 74–80.

Jacobson, N. S., & Hollon, S. D. (1996b). Prospects for future comparisons between drugs and psychotherapy: Lessons from the CBT-versus-pharmacotherapy exchange. *Journal of Consulting and Clinical Psychology, 64,* 104–108.

Jaffe, A. J., Rounsaville, B. J., Change, G., Schottenfeld, R. S., Meyer, R. E., & O'Malley, S. S. (1996). Naltrexone, relapse prevention, and supportive therapy with alcoholics: An analysis of patient treatment matching. *Journal of Consulting and Clinical Psychology, 64,* 1044–1053.

Jarrett, R. B., Kraft, D., Doyle, J., Foster, B. M., Eaves, G. G., & Silver, P. C. (2001). Preventing recurrent depression using cognitive therapy with and without a continuation phase: A randomized clinical trial. *Archives of General Psychiatry, 58,* 381–388.

Jarrett, R. B., Schaffer, M., McIntire, D., Witt-Browder, A., Kraft, D., & Risser, R. C. (1999). Treatment of atypical depression with cognitive therapy or phenelzine: A double-blind, placebo-controlled trial. *Archives of General Psychiatry, 56,* 431–437.

Jay, S. M., & Elliott, C. H. (1990). A stress inoculation program for parents whose children are undergoing painful medical procedures. *Journal of Consulting and Clinical Psychology, 58,* 799–804.

Jay, S. M., Elliott, C. H., Katz, E., & Siegel, S. E. (1987). Cognitive behavioral and pharmacological interventions for children's distress during painful medical procedures. *Journal of Consulting and Clinical Psychology, 55,* 860–865.

Jaycox, L. H., Reivich, K. J., Gillham, J., & Seligman, M.E.P. (1994). Prevention of depressive symptoms in school children. *Behaviour Research and Therapy, 32,* 801–816.

Jeffery, R. W., Drewnowski, A., Epstein, L. H., Stunkard, A. J., Wilson, G. W., Wing, R. R., & Hill, D. R. (2000). Long-term maintenance of weight loss: Current status. *Health Psychology, 19 (Suppl.),* 5–16.

Kaiser, A., Hahlweg, K., Fehm-Wolfsdorf, G., & Groth, T. (1998). The efficacy of a compact psychoeducational group training program for married couples. *Journal of Consulting and Clinical Psychology, 66,* 753–760.

Kaplan, R. M., Atkins, C. J., & Lenhard, L. (1982). Coping with a stressful sigmoidoscopy: Evaluation of cognitive and relaxation preparations. *Journal of Behavioral Medicine, 5*, 67–82.

Kazdin, A. E., Bass, D., Siegel, T., & Thomas, C. (1989). Cognitive-behavioral therapy and relationship therapy in the treatment of children referred for antisocial behavior. *Journal of Consulting and Clinical Psychology, 57*, 522–535.

Kazdin, A. E., Esveldt-Dawson, K., French, N. H., & Unis, A. S. (1987a). Problem-solving skills training and relationship therapy in the treatment of antisocial child behavior. *Journal of Consulting and Clinical Psychology, 55*, 76–85.

Kazdin, A. E., Esveldt-Dawson, K., French, N. H., & Unis, A. S. (1987b). Effects of parent management training and problem-solving skills training combined in the treatment of antisocial child behavior. *Journal of the American Academy of Child and Adolescent Psychiatry, 26*, 416–424.

Kazdin, A. E., Siegel, T. C., & Bass, D. (1992). Cognitive problem-solving skills training and parent management training in the treatment of antisocial behavior in children. *Journal of Consulting and Clinical Psychology, 60*, 733–747.

Kazdin, A. E., & Weisz, J. R. (1998). Identifying and developing empirically supported child and adolescent treatments. *Journal of Consulting and Clinical Psychology, 66*, 19–36.

Keller, M. B., McCullough, J. P., Klein, D. N., Arnow, B., Dunner, D. L., Gelenberg, A. J., Markowitz, J. C., Nemeroff, C. B., Russell, J. M., Thase, M. E., Trivedi, M. H., & Zajecka, J. (2000). A comparison of nefazodone, the cognitive behavioral-analysis system of psychotherapy, and their combination for the treatment of chronic depression. *New England Journal of Medicine, 342*, 1462–1470.

Kelly, J. A., & Murphy, D. A. (1992). Psychological interventions with AIDS and HIV: Prevention and treatment. *Journal of Consulting and Clinical Psychology, 60*, 576–585.

Kendall, P. C. (1993). Cognitive-behavioral therapies with youth: Guiding theory, current status, and emerging developments. *Journal of Consulting and Clinical Psychology, 61*, 235–247.

Kendall, P. C. (1994). Treating anxiety disorders in children: Results of a randomized clinical trial. *Journal of Consulting and Clinical Psychology, 62*, 100–110.

Kendall, P. C., & Braswell, L. B. (1985). *Cognitive-behavioral modification with impulsive children.* New York: Guilford Press.

Kendall, P. C., Flannery-Schroeder, E., Panichilli-Mindel, S. M., Southam-Gerow, M., Henin, A., & Warman, M. (1997). Therapy for youths with anxiety disorders: A second randomized clinical trial. *Journal of Consulting and Clinical Psychology, 65*, 366–380.

Kendall, P. C., & Southam-Gerow, M. A. (1996). Long-term follow-up of a cognitive-behavioral therapy for anxiety-disorder youth. *Journal of Consulting and Clinical Psychology, 64*, 724–730.

Kendall, P. C., Williams, L., Pechacek, T. F., Graham, L. E., Shissalak, C., & Herzoff, N. (1979). Cognitive-behavioral and patient education interventions in cardiac catheterization procedures. *Journal of Consulting and Clinical Psychology, 47*, 49–58.

King, N. J., & Ollendick, T. H. (1997). Treatment of childhood phobias. *Journal of Child Psychology and Psychiatry and Allied Disciplines, 38*, 389–400.

King, N. J., Tonge, B. J., Heyne, D., Prichard, M., Rollings, S., Young, D., Myerson, N., & Ollendick, T. H. (1998). Cognitive-behavioral treatment of school refusing children: A controlled evaluation. *Journal of the American Academy of Child and Adolescent Psychiatry, 37*, 395–403.

Koerner, K., & Linehan, M. M. (2000). Research on dialectical behavior therapy for patients with borderline personality disorder. *Psychiatric Clinics of North America, 23*, 151–167.

Kole-Snijders, A.M.J., Vlaeyen, J.W.S., Goossens, M.E.J.B., Rutten-van Molken, M.P.M.H., Heuts, P.H.T.G., van Breukelen, G., & van Eek, H. (1999). Chronic low-back pain: What does cognitive coping skills training add to operant behavioral treatment? Results of a randomized clinical trial. *Journal of Consulting and Clinical Psychology, 67*, 931–944.

Kuipers, E., Fowler, D., Garety, P., Chisholm, D., Freeman, D., Dunn, G., Bebbington, P., & Hadley, C. (1998). London-East Anglia randomised controlled trial of cognitive behaviour therapy for psychosis: III. Follow-up and economic evaluation at 18 months. *British Journal of Psychiatry, 173*, 61–68.

Kuipers, E., Garety, P., Fowler, D., Dunn, G., Bebbington, P., Freeman, D., & Hadley, C. (1997). The London-East Anglia randomised controlled trial of cognitive behaviour therapy for psychosis: Effects of the treatment phase. *British Journal of Psychiatry, 171*, 319–325.

Ladouceur, R., Dugas, M. J., Freeston, M. H., Leger, E., Gagnon, F., & Thibodeau, N. (2000). Efficacy of a cognitive-behavioral treatment for generalized anxiety disorder: Evaluation in a controlled clinical trial. *Journal of Consulting and Clinical Psychology, 68*, 957–964.

Ladouceur, R., Dugas, M. J., Freeston, M. H., Rheaume, J., Blais, F., Gagnon, F., Thibodeau, N., & Boisvert, J.-M. (1999). Specificity of generalized anxiety disorder symptoms and processes. *Behavior Therapy, 30*, 191–207.

Lam, D. H., Bright, J., Jones, S., Hayward, P., Schuck, N., Chisholm, D., & Sham, P. (2000). Cognitive therapy for bipolar illness—A pilot study of relapse prevention. *Cognitive Therapy and Research, 24*, 503–520.

Last, C. G., Hansen, C., & Franco, N. (1998). Cognitive-behavioral treatment of school phobia.

Journal of the American Academy of Child and Adolescent Psychiatry, 37, 404–411.

Law, M., & Tang, J. L. (1995). An analysis of the effectiveness of interventions intended to help people stop smoking. *Archives of Internal Medicine, 155*, 1933–1941.

Layden, M. A., Newman, C. F., Freeman, A., & Morse, S. B. (1993). *Cognitive therapy of borderline personality disorder.* Needham Heights, MA: Allyn & Bacon.

Leitenberg, H., Rosen, J. C., Wolf, J., Vara, L. S., Detzer, M., & Srebnik, D. (1994). Comparison of cognitive behavior therapy and desipramine in the treatment of bulimia nervosa. *Behaviour Research and Therapy, 32*, 37–45.

Lerner, M. S., & Clum, G. A. (1990). Treatment of suicide ideators: A problem-solving approach. *Behavior Therapy, 21*, 403–411.

Lewinsohn, P. M., Clarke, G. N., Hops, H., & Andrews, J. (1990). Cognitive-behavioral treatment for depressed adolescents. *Behavior Therapy, 21*, 385–401.

Lewinsohn, P. M., Hoberman, H. M., & Clarke, G. N. (1989). The Coping with Depression Course: Review and future directions. *Canadian Journal of Behavioural Science, 21*, 470–493.

Lewinsohn, P. M., Munoz, R. F., Youngren, M. A., & Zeiss, A. M. (1986). *Control your depression.* Englewood Cliffs, NJ: Prentice-Hall.

Liebowitz, M. R., Heimberg, R. G., Schneier, F. R., et al. (1999). Cognitive-behavioral group therapy versus phenelzine in social phobia: Long-term outcome. *Depression and Anxiety, 10*, 89–98.

Linehan, M. M. (1993). *Cognitive-behavioral treatment of borderline personality disorder.* New York: Guilford Press.

Linehan, M. M., Armstrong, H. E., Suarez, A., Allmon, D., & Heard, H. L. (1991). Cognitive-behavioral treatment of chronically parasuicidal borderline patients. *Archives of General Psychiatry, 48*, 1060–1064.

Linehan, M. M., Heard, H. L., & Armstrong, H. E. (1993). Naturalistic follow-up of a behavioral treatment for chronically parasuicidal borderline patients. *Archives of General Psychiatry, 50*, 971–974.

Linehan, M. M., Schmidt, H., Dimeff, L. A., Craft, J. C., Kanter, J., & Comtois, K. A. (1999). Dialectical behavior therapy for patients with borderline personality disorder and drug-dependence. *American Journal on Addictions, 8*, 279–292.

Linehan, M. M., Tutek, D. A., Heard, H. L., & Armstrong, H. E. (1994). Interpersonal outcome of cognitive behavioral treatment for chronically suicidal borderline patients. *American Journal of Psychiatry, 151*, 1771–1776.

Lutgendorf, S., Antoni, M., Ironson, G., Klimas, N., Kumar, M., Starr, K., McCabe, P., Cleven, K., Fletcher, M. A., & Schneiderman, N. (1997). Cognitive behavioral stress management decreases dysphoric mood and herpes simplex virus-Type 2 antibody titers in symptomatic HIV-seropositive gay men. *Journal of Consulting and Clinical Psychology, 65*, 31–43.

Marcus, M. D., Wing, R. R., & Fairburn, C. G. (1995). Cognitive treatment of binge eating vs. behavioral weight control in the treatment of binge eating disorder. *Annals of Behavioral Medicine, 17*, S090.

Markowitz, J. C., Kocsis, J. H., Fishman, B., Spielman, L. A., Jacobsberg, L. B., Frances, A. J., Klerman, G. L., & Perry, S. W. (1998). Treatment of depressive symptoms in human immunodeficiency virus-positive patients. *Archives of General Psychiatry, 55*, 452–457.

Marks, I., Lovell, K., Noshirvani, H., Livanou, M., & Thrasher, S. (1998). Treatment of posttraumatic stress disorder by exposure and/or cognitive restructuring: A controlled study. *Archives of General Psychiatry, 55*, 317–325.

Marlatt, G. A. (1983). The controlled-drinking controversy: A commentary. *American Psychologist, 38*, 1097–1110.

Marlatt, G. A., Baer, J. S., Kivlahan, D. R., Dimeff, L. A., Larimer, M. E., Quigley, L. A., Somers, J. M., & Williams, E. (1998). Screening and brief intervention for high-risk college student drinkers: Results from a 2-year follow-up assessment. *Journal of Consulting and Clinical Psychology, 66*, 604–615.

Marlatt, A., & Gordon, J. (1985). *Relapse prevention: Maintenance strategies in the treatment of addictive behaviors.* New York: Guilford Press.

Marlatt, A., Larimer, M. E., Baer, J. S., & Quigley, L. A. (1993). Harm reduction for alcohol problems: Moving beyond the controlled drinking controversy. *Behavior Therapy, 24*, 461–504.

Maude-Griffin, P. M., Hohenstein, J. M., Humfleet, G. L., Reilly, P. M., Tusel, D. J., & Hall, S. M. (1998). Superior efficacy of cognitive-behavioral therapy for urban crack cocaine abusers: Main and matching effects. *Journal of Consulting and Clinical Psychology, 66*, 832–837.

Mayou, R. A., Ehlers, A., & Hobbs, M. (2000). Psychological debriefing for road traffic accident victims. *British Journal of Psychiatry, 176*, 589–593.

McCullough, J. P. (2000). *Treatment for chronic depression: Cognitive behavioral analysis system of psychotherapy.* New York: Guilford Press.

McKnight, D. L., Nelson-Gray, R. O., & Barnhill, J. (1992). Dexamethasone suppression test and response to cognitive therapy and antidepressant medication. *Behavior Therapy, 23*, 99–111.

McLean, P. D., Whittal, M. L., Thordarson, D. S., Taylor, S., Sochting, I., Koch, W. J., Paterson, R., & Anderson, K. W. (2001). Cognitive versus behavior therapy in the group treatment of obsessive-compulsive disorder. *Journal of Consulting and Clinical Psychology, 69*, 205–214.

Meichenbaum, D. (1985). *Stress inoculation training.* New York: Pergamon.

Miller, I. W., Norman, W. H., Keitner, G. I., Bishop, S. B., & Dow, M. G. (1989). Cognitive-behavioral treatment of depressed inpatients. *Behavior Therapy, 20,* 25–47.

Morely, S., Eccleston, C., & Williams, A. (1999). Systematic review and meta-analysis of randomized controlled trials of cognitive behaviour therapy and behaviour therapy for chronic pain in adults, excluding headache. *Pain, 80,* 1–13.

Murphy, G. E., Simons, A. D., Wetzel, R. D., & Lustman, P. J. (1984). Cognitive therapy and pharmacotherapy, singly and together, in the treatment of depression. *Archives of General Psychiatry, 41,* 33–41.

Mynors-Wallis, L. M., Gath, D. H., Lloyd-Thomas, A. R., & Tomlinson, D. (1995). Randomised controlled trial comparing problem solving treatment with amitriptyline and placebo for major depression in primary care. *British Medical Journal, 310,* 441–445.

Nezu, A. M., & Perri, M. G. (1989). Social problem-solving therapy for unipolar depression: An initial dismantling investigation. *Journal of Consulting and Clinical Psychology, 57,* 408–413.

Öst, L. G., & Westling, B. E. (1995). Applied relaxation vs. cognitive behavior therapy in the treatment of panic disorder. *Behaviour Research and Therapy, 33,* 145–158.

Otto, M. W., Pollack, M. H., Sachs, G. S., Reiter, S. R., Meltzer-Brody, S., & Rosenbaum, J. F. (1993). Discontinuation of benzodiazepine treatment: Efficacy of cognitive-behavioral therapy for patients with panic disorder. *American Journal of Psychiatry, 150,* 1485–1490.

Ouimette, P. C., Finney, J. W., & Moos, R. H. (1997). Twelve-step and cognitive-behavioral treatment for substance abuse: A comparison of treatment effectiveness. *Journal of Consulting and Clinical Psychology, 65,* 230–240.

Parker, J. C., Smart, K. L., Buckelew, S. P., Stucky-Ropp, R. C., Hewett, J. E., Johnson, J. C., Wright, G. E., Irvin, W. S., & Walker, S. E. (1995). Effects of stress management on clinical outcomes in rheumatoid arthritis. *Arthritis and Rheumatism, 38,* 1807–1818.

Paykel, E. S., Scott, J., Teasdale, J. D., Johnson, A. L., Garland, A., Moore, R., Jenaway, A., Cornwall, P. L., Hayhurst, H., Abbott, R., & Pope, M. (1999). Prevention of relapse in residual depression by cognitive therapy. *Archives of General Psychiatry, 56,* 829–835.

Payne, A., & Blanchard, E. B. (1995). A controlled comparison of cognitive therapy and self-help support groups in the treatment of irritable bowel syndrome. *Journal of Consulting and Clinical Psychology, 63,* 779–786.

Perri, M. G. (1998). The maintenance of treatment effects in the long-term management of obesity. *Clinical Psychology: Science and Practice, 5,* 526–543.

Perri, M. G., & Fuller, P. R. (1995). Success and failure in the treatment of obesity: Where do we go from here? *Medicine, Exercise, Nutrition, & Health, 4,* 255–272.

Perri, M. G., Nezu, A. M., McKelvey, W. F., Shermer, R. L., Renjilian, D. A., & Viegener, B. J. (2001). Relapse prevention training and problem-solving therapy in the long-term management of obesity. *Journal of Consulting and Clinical Psychology, 69,* 722–726.

Peterson, L., & Shigetomi, C. (1981). The use of coping techniques in minimizing anxiety in hospitalized children. *Behavior Therapy, 12,* 1–14.

Pinto, A., La Pia, S., Mannella, R., Domenico, G., & DeSimone, L. (1999). Cognitive-behavioral therapy and clozapine for clients with treatment-refractory schizophrenia. *Psychiatric Services, 50,* 901–904.

Project MATCH Research Group. (1997). Matching alcoholism treatments to client heterogeneity: Project MATCH posttreatment drinking outcomes. *Journal of Studies on Alcohol, 58,* 7–29.

Rector, N. A., & Beck, A. T. (2001). Cognitive behavioral therapy for schizophrenia: An empirical review. *Journal of Nervous and Mental Disorders, 189,* 278–287.

Rehm, L. P. (1977). A self-control model of depression. *Behavior Therapy, 8,* 787–804.

Resick, P. A., & Schnicke, M. K. (1992). Cognitive processing therapy for sexual assault victims. *Journal of Consulting and Clinical Psychology, 60,* 748–756.

Robinson, L. A., Berman, J. S., & Neimeyer, R. A. (1990). Psychotherapy for the treatment of depression: A comprehensive review of controlled outcome research. *Psychological Bulletin, 108,* 30–49.

Rossello, J., & Bernal, G. (1999). The efficacy of cognitive-behavioral and interpersonal treatments for depression in Puerto Rican adolescents. *Journal of Consulting and Clinical Psychology, 67,* 734–745.

Rude, S. S., & Rehm, L. P. (1991). Response to treatments for depression: The role of initial status on targeted cognitive and behavioral skills. *Clinical Psychology Review, 11,* 493–514.

Rush, A. J., Beck, A. T., Kovacs, M., & Hollon, S. D. (1977). Comparative efficacy of cognitive therapy and pharmacotherapy in the treatment of depressed outpatients. *Cognitive Therapy and Research, 1,* 17–38.

Salkovskis, P. M. (1999). Understanding and treating obsessive-compulsive disorder. *Behaviour Research and Therapy, 37 (Suppl. 1),* S29–S52.

Salkovskis, P. M., Atha, C., & Storer, D. (1990). Cognitive-behavioural problem solving in the treatment of patients who repeatedly attempt suicide: A controlled trial. *British Journal of Psychiatry, 157,* 871–876.

Salkovskis, P. M., & Westbrook, D. (1989). Behaviour therapy and obsessional ruminations: Can failure be turned into success? *Behaviour Research and Therapy, 27,* 149–160.

Sanders, M. R., Rebgetz, M., Morrison, M. I, Bor, W., Gordon, A., Dadds, M., & Shepherd, R. (1989). Cognitive-behavioral treatment of recurrent nonspecific abdominal pain in children: An analysis of generalization, maintenance, and side effects. *Journal of Consulting and Clinical Psychology, 57,* 294–300.

Sbrocco, T., Nedegaard, R. C., Stone, J. M., & Lewis, E. L. (1999). Behavioral choice treatment promotes continuing weight loss: Preliminary results of a cognitive-behaivoral decision-based treatment for obesity. *Journal of Consulting and Clinical Psychology, 67,* 260–266.

Seligman, M. E. P., Schulman, P., DeRubeis, R. J., & Hollon, S. D. (1999). The prevention of depression and anxiety. *Prevention and Treatment, 2,* Article 8. Available on the World Wide Web: http://journals.apa.org/prevention/volume2/pre002008a.html.

Sensky, T., Turkington, D., Kingdon, D., Scott, J. L., Scott, J., Siddle, R., O'Carroll, M., & Barnes, T.R.E. (2000). Cognitive-behavioural treatment for persistent symptoms in schizophrenia. *Archives of General Psychiatry, 57,* 165–173.

Shaw, B. F., & Dobson, K. S. (1988). Competency judgments in the training and evaluation of psychotherapists. *Journal of Consulting and Clinical Psychology, 56,* 666–672.

Shaw, B. F., Elkin, I., Yamaguchi, J., Olmsted, M., Vallis, T. M., Dobson, K. S., Lowery, A., Sotsky, S. M., Watkins, J. T., & Imber, S. D. (1999). Therapist competence ratings in relation to clinical outcome in cognitive therapy of depression. *Journal of Consulting and Clinical Psychology, 67,* 837–846.

Shea, M. T., Elkin, I., Imber, S. D., Sotsky, S. M., Watkins, J. T., Collins, J. F., Pilkonis, P. A., Beckham, E., Glass, D. R., Dolan, R. T., & Parloff, M. B. (1992). Course of depressive symptoms over follow-up: Findings from the National Institute of Mental Health Treatment of Depression Collaborative Research Program. *Archives of General Psychiatry, 49,* 782–787.

Shea, M. T., Pilkonis, P. A., Beckham, E., Collins, J. F., Elkin, I., Sotsky, S. M., & Docherty, J. P. (1990). Personality disorders and treatment outcome in the NIMH Treatment of Depression Collaborative Research Program. *American Journal of Psychiatry, 147,* 711–718.

Shear, M. K., Pilkonis, P. A., Claitre, M., & Lean, A. C. (1994). Cognitive behavioral treatment compared with nonprescriptive treatments of panic disorder. *Archives of General Psychiatry, 51,* 395–401.

Silverman, W. K., Kurtines, W. M., Ginsburg, G. S., Weems, C. F., Lumpkin, P. W., & Carmichael, D. H. (1999). Treating anxiety disorders in children with group cognitive-behavioral therapy: A randomized clinical trial. *Journal of Consulting and Clinical Psychology, 67,* 995–1003.

Silverman, W. K., Kurtines, W. M., Ginsberg, G. S., Weems, C. F., Rabian, B., & Serafini, L. T. (1999). Contingency management, self-control, and education support in the treatment of childhood phobic disorders: A randomized clinical trial. *Journal of Consulting and Clinical Psychology, 67,* 675–687.

Simons, A. D., Garfield, S. L., & Murphy, G. E. (1984). The process of change in cognitive therapy and pharmacotherapy for depression. *Archives of General Psychiatry, 41,* 45–51.

Smith, B., & Sechrest, L. (1991). Treatment of apptitude X treatment interactions. *Journal of Consulting and Clinical Psychology, 59,* 233–244.

Sotsky, S. M., Glass, D. R., Shea, M. T., Pilkonis, P. A., Collins, J. F., Elkin, I., Watkins, J. T., Imber, S. D., Leber, W. R., Moyer, J., & Oliveri, M. E. (1991). Patient predictors of response to psychotherapy and pharmacotherapy: Findings in the NIMH Treatment of Depression Collaborative Research Program. *American Journal of Psychiatry, 148,* 997–1008.

Tang, T. Z., & DeRubeis, R. J. (1999). Sudden gains and critical sessions in cognitive-behavioral therapy for depression. *Journal of Consulting and Clinical Psychology, 67,* 894–904.

Tarrier, N., Beckett, R., Harwood, S., Baker, A., Yusupoff, L., & Ugarteburu, I. (1993). A trial of two cognitive-behavioural methods of treating drug-resistant residual psychotic symptoms in schizophrenic patients: I. Outcome. *British Journal of Psychiatry, 162,* 524–532.

Tarrier, N., Kinney, C., McCarthy, E., Humphreys, L., Wittkowski, A., & Morris, J. (2000). Two-year follow-up of cognitive-behavioral therapy and supportive counseling in the treatment of persistent symptoms in chronic schizophrenia. *Journal of Consulting and Clinical Psychology, 68,* 917–922.

Tarrier, N., Pilgrim, H., Sommerfield, C., Faragher, B., Reynolds, M., Graham, E., & Barrowclough, C. (1999). A randomized trial of cognitive therapy and imaginal exposure in the treatment of chronic posttraumatic stress disorder. *Journal of Consulting and Clinical Psychology, 67,* 13–18.

Tarrier, N., Yusupoff, L., Kinney, C., McCarthy, E., Gledhill, A., Haddock, G., & Morris, J. (1998). A randomised controlled trial of intensive cognitive behaviour therapy for chronic schizophrenia. *British Medical Journal, 317,* 303–307.

Teasdale, J. D., Scott, J., Moore, R. G., Hayhurst, H., Pope, M., & Paykel, E. S. (2001). How does cognitive therapy prevent relapse in residual depression? Evidence from a controlled trial. *Journal of Consulting and Clinical Psychology, 69,* 347–357.

Teasdale, J. D., Segal, Z., & Williams, J.M.G. (1995). How does cognitive therapy prevent depressive relapse and why should attentional control (mindfulness) training help? *Behaviour Research and Therapy, 33*, 25–39.

Teasdale, J. D., Segal, Z., Williams, J.M.G., Ridgeway, V. A., Soulsby, J. M., & Lau, M. A. (2000). Prevention of relapse/recurrence in major depression by mindfulness-based cognitive therapy. *Journal of Consulting and Clinical Psychology, 68*, 615–623.

Thase, M. E., Bowler, K., & Harden, T. (1991). Cognitive behavior therapy of endogenous depression: Part 2: Preliminary findings in 16 unmedicated inpatients. *Behavior Therapy, 22*, 469–477.

Thom, A., Sartory, G., & Hohren, P. (2000). Comparison between one-session psychological treatment and benzodiazepine in dental phobia. *Journal of Consulting and Clinical Psychology, 68*, 378–387.

Thorpe, S. J., & Salkovskis, P. M. (1997). The effect of one-session treatment for spider phobia on attentional bias and beliefs. *British Journal of Clinical Psychology, 36*, 225–241.

Treadwell, K.R.H., & Kendall, P. C. (1996). Self-talk in anxiety-disordered youth: States of mind, content specificity, and treatment outcome. *Journal of Consulting and Clinical Psychology, 64*, 941–950.

Treasure, J., Todd, G., Brolly, J., Nehmed, A., & Denman, F. (1995). A pilot study of a randomised trial of cognitive analytic therapy vs. educational behavioral therapy for adult anorexia nervosa. *Behaviour Research and Therapy, 33*, 363–367.

Turk, D. C., Meichenbaum, D., & Genest, M. (1983). *Pain and behavioral medicine: A cognitive-behavioral perspective.* New York: Plenum.

van Oppen, P., de Haan, E., van Balkom, A., Spinhoven, P., Hoogduin, K., & van Dyck, R. (1995). Cognitive therapy and exposure in vivo in the treatment of obsessive compulsive disorder. *Behaviour Research and Therapy, 33*, 379–390.

Vitousek, K., Watson, S., & Wilson, G. T. (1998). Enhancing motivation for change in treatment-resistant eating disorders. *Clinical Psychology Review, 18*, 391–420.

Vostanis, P., Feehan, C., Grattan, E., & Bickerton, W. L. (1996). Treatment for children and adolescents with depression. *Clinical Child Psychology and Psychiatry, 1*, 199–212.

Walsh, B. T., Wilson, G. T., Loeb, K. L., Devlin, M. J., Pike, K. M., Roose, S. P., Fleiss, J., & Waternaux, C. (1997). Medication and psychotherapy in the treatment of bulimia nervosa. *American Journal of Psychiatry, 154*, 523–531.

Warwick, H.M.C., Clark, D. M., Cobb, A. M., & Salkovskis, P. M. (1996). A controlled trial of cognitive-behavioural treatment of hypochondriasis. *British Journal of Psychiatry, 169*, 189–195.

Warwick, H.M.C., & Salkovskis, P. M. (1990). Hypochondriasis. *Behaviour Research and Therapy, 28*, 105–117.

Weisz, J. R., Thurber, C. A., Sweeney, L., Proffitt, V. D., & LeGagnoux, G. L. (1997). Brief treatment of mild to moderate child depression using primary and secondary control enhancement training. *Journal of Consulting and Clinical Psychology, 65*, 703–707.

Wells, A., Clark, D. M., Salkovskis, P., Ludgate, J., Hackmann, A., & Gelder, M. (1995). Social phobia: The role of in-situation safety behaviours in maintaining anxiety and negative beliefs. *Behavior Therapy, 26*, 153–161.

Wells, E. A., Peterson, P. L., Gainey, R. R., Hawkins, J. D., & Catalano, R. F. (1994). Outpatient treatment for cocaine abuse: A controlled comparison of relapse prevention and twelve-step approaches. *American Journal of Drug and Alcohol Abuse, 20*, 1–17.

Whittal, M. L., Agras, W. S., & Gould, R. A. (1999). Bulimia nervosa: A meta-analysis of psychosocial and psychopharmacologic treatments. *Behavior Therapy, 30*, 117–135.

Wilfley, D. E., Agras, W. S., Telch, C. F., Rossiter, E. M., Schneider, J. A., Cole, A. G., Sifford, L., & Raeburn, S. D. (1993). Group cognitive-behavioral therapy and group interpersonal psychotherapy for the non-purging bulimic individual: A controlled comparison. *Journal of Consulting and Clinical Psychology, 61*, 296–305.

Williams, S. L., & Falbo, J. (1996). Cognitive and performance-based treatments for panic attacks in people with varying degrees of agoraphobic disability. *Behaviour Research and Therapy, 34*, 253–264.

Wilson, G. T., & Agras, W. S. (2001). Practice guidelines for eating disorders. *Behavior Therapy, 32*, 219–234.

Wilson, G. T., Vitousek, K. M., & Loeb, K. L. (2000). Stepped care treatment for eating disorders. *Journal of Consulting and Clinical Psychology, 68*, 564–572.

Wing, R. R., & Jeffery, R. W. (1995). Effect of modest weight loss on changes in cardiovascular risk factors: Are there differences between men and women or between weight loss and maintenance? *International Journal of Obesity, 19*, 67–73.

Wood, A., Harrington, R., & Moore, A. (1996). Controlled trial of a brief cognitive-behavioral intervention in adolescent patients with depressive disorders. *Journal of Child Psychology and Psychiatry, 37*, 737–746.

CHAPTER 11

RESEARCH ON EXPERIENTIAL PSYCHOTHERAPIES

ROBERT ELLIOTT
University of Toledo
LESLIE S. GREENBERG
York University, Canada
GERMAIN LIETAER
Catholic University of Leuven, Belgium

This review covers approaches to psychotherapy generally referred to as "experiential." Experiential therapies are part of the tradition of humanistic psychology (see Cain & Seeman, 2001; Schneider, Bugental, & Fraser, 2001), with the major subapproaches being the client-centered (or person-centered; e.g., Rogers, 1961), Gestalt (e.g., Perls, Hefferline, & Goodman, 1951), and existential (e.g., Yalom, 1980). Other influential experiential approaches have been psychodrama (Moreno & Moreno, 1959), a cluster of emotion-focused expressive approaches (Daldrup, Beutler, Engle, & Greenberg, 1988; Mahrer, 1983; Pierce, Nichols, & DuBrin, 1983), body-oriented therapies (Kepner, 1993), and experiential-interpersonal views of such authors as van Kessel and Lietaer (1998), Yalom (1995), and Schmid (1995). Originally designated as humanistic or third-force therapies, these therapies have recently begun to be grouped together under the experiential umbrella (Greenberg, Elliott, & Lietaer, 1994; Greenberg, Watson, & Lietaer, 1998).

The process-experiential (PE) approach is one current expression of the contemporary humanistic-experiential tradition in psychotherapy that has attracted a substantial research base. It integrates client-centered and Gestalt therapy traditions into an emotion-focused approach that emphasizes both the relationship and the process of reflection on aroused emotions to create new meaning (Greenberg, Rice, & Elliott, 1993). Other current expressions include Gendlin's (1996) focusing-oriented approach, emphasizing the creation of new meaning by focusing on bodily felt referents; dialogical Gestalt therapy (Hycner & Jacobs, 1995; Yontef, 1998); and integrative forms of person-centered/experiential psychotherapy (Finke, 1994; Lietaer & Van Kalmthout, 1995; Mearns & Thorne, 2000). In practice, these contemporary approaches strive to maintain a creative tension between the client-centered emphasis on creating a genuinely empathic and prizing therapeutic relationship (Barrett-Lennard, 1998; Biermann-Ratjen, Eckert, & Schwartz, 1995; Rogers, 1961), and a more active, task-focused process-directive style of engagement that promotes deeper experiencing (Gendlin, 1996; Perls et al., 1951).

Although these approaches vary somewhat in technique and conception, they nevertheless share a number of distinctive theoretical assumptions. Most important among these assumptions is that they view human nature as inherently trustworthy, growth-oriented, and guided by choice. Human beings are viewed as oriented toward growth and full development of their potentialities.

The first and most central characteristic of experiential psychotherapy is its focus on promoting in-therapy *experiencing*. Methods that stimulate emotional experience are used within the context of an empathic facilitative relationship. Commitment to a *phenomenological* approach flows directly from this central interest in experiencing. People are viewed as meaning-creating, symbolizing agents, whose subjective experience is an essential aspect of their humanness. In addition, the experiential-humanistic view of functioning emphasizes the operation of an integrative, formative tendency, oriented toward survival, growth, and the creation of meaning. Moreover, all experientially oriented theorists are united by the general principle that people are wiser than their intellect alone. In an experiencing organism, consciousness is seen as being at the peak of a pyramid of nonconscious organismic functioning. In addition, experiments in directed awareness help focus and concentrate attention on unformed experience and intensify its vividness. Of central importance is the idea that tacit experiencing is an important guide to conscious experience, fundamentally adaptive, and potentially available to awareness.

Because of their view of tacit experiencing, experiential therapists agree that it is disrespectful and disempowering for therapists to act as experts on the content of their clients' inner experience ("content directiveness"). Continuing key points of contention within experiential camps, however, are (a) whether minor content-directive interventions can be used, as long as they are tentative and respectful, and also (b) the degree to which therapists should act as process experts by suggesting ways clients can work more productively on particular types of problems ("process directiveness"). All experiential therapies are process-directive to a certain extent, but PE, Gestalt, and emotional-focused therapy for couples are more process-directive, whereas client-centered (CC) and so-called supportive or nondirective therapies are less process directive.

In addition, almost all experiential therapies view the therapeutic relationship as potentially curative. Internal tacit experiencing is most readily available to awareness when the person turns his or her attention internally within the context of a supportive interpersonal relationship. Interpersonal safety and support are thus regarded as key elements in enhancing the amount of attention available for self-awareness and exploration. Experiential approaches also are consistently *person-centered.* This involves genuine concern and respect for each person. The person is seen holistically, not as a symptom-driven case or as best characterized by a diagnosis. Each person's subjective experience is of central importance to the humanist, and, in an effort to grasp this experience, the therapist attempts to empathically enter into the other person's world in a special way that goes beyond the subject-object dichotomy. Being allowed to share another person's world is considered a special privilege requiring a special kind of relationship. All experiential approaches dispute the psychoanalytic claim that the relationship between the client and the therapist can be reduced to an unconscious repetition of previous attachments. Rather, they generally share the view that a real relationship with the therapist provides the client with a new, emotionally validating experience.

In this chapter, we review research published since our previous review (Greenberg et al., 1994), which covered research published between 1978 and 1992, plus earlier research on experiential therapy outcome that has become available. A key element of the chapter is a meta-analysis of over 125 experiential therapy outcome studies. In addition, we carry previous reviews of this literature further by applying criteria promulgated by the Society of Clinical Psychology (Division 12, American Psychological Association) for designating psychotherapies as empirically supported (Task Force on Promotion and Dissemination of Psychological Procedures, 1995). We realize that these criteria are controversial (e.g., Bohart, O'Hara, & Leitner, 1998; Wampold, 1997; Elliott, 1998), even in their most recent and polished version (Chambless & Hollon, 1998). Nevertheless, we will use the Chambless-Hollon criteria here because they are widely recognized.

Because of space limitations and the increasing amount and range of research, this survey is not exhaustive. In particular, we have not reviewed research on the therapeutic bond, helping and hindering processes, child psychotherapy, and measurement construction of research (but see Cain & Seeman, 2001, for reviews of many of these topics). In addition, we have chosen not to review research on the growing number of integrative approaches, such as empathic-psychodynamic approaches (the conversational-interpersonal model investigated by Shapiro and colleagues, such as Shapiro et al., 1994), motivational interviewing (Project MATCH Research Group, 1997), and acceptance and commitment therapy (Hayes, Strosahl, & Wilson, 1999).

As Greenberg et al. (1998) note, additional programmatic empirical research on experiential therapy is still needed, but clear progress has taken place in the last 10 years, including research on specific populations. Especially noteworthy are three recently published major handbooks of humanistic and experiential psychotherapy that cover research done in the experiential tradition, including research methods for getting at subjective experience (Cain & Seeman, 2001; Greenberg et al., 1998; Schneider et al., 2001). Additional information, including research bibliographies and research protocols, is available on the Internet at www.experiential-researchers.org.

ARE EXPERIENTIAL THERAPIES EFFECTIVE?: A META-ANALYSIS

In both North America and Europe, economic pressure on mental health services and scientific-political trends toward treatment standardization have led to calls for certain therapies to be officially recognized as effective, reimbursed by insurance, and actively promoted in training programs at the expense of other therapies (Meyer, Richter, Grawe, von Schulenburg, & Schulte, 1991; Task Force on Promotion and Dissemination of Psychological Procedures, 1995). These reports were not kind to experiential therapies and attempted to enshrine preconceptions about the supposed ineffectiveness of experiential therapies as both scientific fact and healthcare policy.

Understandably, experiential-humanistic therapists (e.g., Bohart, O'Hara, & Leitner, 1998; Schneider, 1998) responded to these challenges with some alarm. They challenged the assumptions and methods used in the current research literature and in current attempts to institute criteria for designating certain therapies as effective. Strangely, the argument from research evidence has been relatively neglected in this controversy. In fact, a substantial body of research data supports the effectiveness of experiential therapies. Furthermore, this body of research is continuing to grow rapidly.

We report here the latest of a continuing series of meta-analytic reviews of research on the effectiveness of experiential therapies, substantially updating earlier reports (Elliott, 1996, 2002; Greenberg et al., 1994). The present analysis triples the number of studies analyzed in Greenberg et al.'s (1994) original review, from 35 to 111; the added studies are summarized in Table 11.1. In attempting to be as complete as possible, we have added a substantial number of German studies, as well as many older and more recent studies as we could obtain. At this point, the analysis includes pre-post effect size data from 127 experiential therapy samples in 112 studies (involving a total of 6,569 clients). In terms of controlled studies, there are 42 comparisons (from 37 studies, involving 1,149 clients) with wait list or no-treatment conditions; 74 comparisons (55 studies, 1,375 clients) between experiential and nonexperiential therapies; and 5 comparisons between different experiential therapies (5 studies, 164 clients).

Of the pre-post therapy samples reviewed, 52 investigated client-centered (CC) therapy in a relatively pure form, while 11 studied "nondirective" therapy with minor directive (e.g., relaxation training or education) elements. Eighteen studies examined task-focused, integrative process-experiential (PE) therapies; 10 studies evaluated the closely related emotionally focused therapy (EFT) for couples; 10 dealt with Gestalt therapy, 11 with encounter/sensitivity groups (generally in marathon formats) and another 15 looked at the outcome of various other experiential/humanistic therapies (e.g., focusing-oriented, psychodrama, or integrative). Ten of the studies reviewed were published prior to 1970, 19 came from the 1970s, and 31 from the 1980s. However, more than half (67) have appeared since 1990. These studies offer evidence for a revival of outcome research on experiential therapies. The average treatment length was 22 sessions (SD: 22.5, range 2–124); the average number of clients studied was 51.7 (SD: 142.5; range 6–1,426). Across the whole sample, researcher theoretical allegiances were most commonly pro-experiential (71%), although this breakdown varies across analyses.

For each study, characteristics of the treatments, clients, therapists, or the studies were rated in order to estimate the contribution of these features to effect size. For example, a "process-directiveness" variable was coded, with PE, Gestalt, emotion-focused, and "other" experiential therapies coded as more process-directive ("2"), and CC and supportive-nondirective therapies coded as less process directive ("1").

Standardized pre-post differences *(d)* were used for effect size (ES) calculations using standard estimation procedures (Smith, Glass, & Miller, 1980) and D/STAT (Johnson, 1989). ESs were calculated for each subscale of each outcome measure used, and then averaged across subscales within measures for each of three assessment periods: post-therapy, early followup (less than a year), and late followup (a year or longer). For *pre-post effect sizes*, measured effects were first averaged for each treatment condition and then across the three assessment periods to yield an overall value for each treatment in each study. In addition, standard corrections for small sample bias and sample-size weighting formulas (Hunter & Schmidt, 1990) were applied to these ESs in order to obtain more precise estimates of overall

TABLE 11.1 Outcome Research on Humanistic-Experiential Therapies: Pre-Post Effect Sizes

Study	Treatment[a] (length)	Population (*n* of completers)	Type of Measure[b]	Mean Change ES[c]
1. Client-Centered: (*n:* 52; mES: .91; 1994: 13 samples; mES: 1.15)				
Baehr (1954)	CC Inpatient Program (variable)	Hospitalized (66)	SSy	Post: .64
Barrett-Lennard (1962)	CC Individual (33)	Mixed outpatient (36)	SSy, Adj	Post: .77
Beck et al. (1992)	CC Individual (8)	Panic (15)	SSy, CSy	Post: 1.32
Boeck-Singelmann et al. (1992)	CC Individual w/ 2 therapists (13)	Mixed outpatient (immediate + delayed = 53)	Imp, Scm	Immed. Post: .59 Delay Post: .99
Borkovec & Costello (1993)	Nondirective (12)	Generalized Anxiety (18)	CSy, SSy, Exp	Post: 1.18 FU6mo: 1.72 FU12mo: 1.50
Braaten (1989)	CC Group (14)	Volunteer Professionals (25)	SSy, Exp (25)	Post: .36 FU10mo: .20
DiLoreto (1971)	CC (10)	Minor (20)	Ssy, Csy, PC	Post: .36 FU: .57
Dircks et al. (1982)	CC Group (11)	Cancer (30)	Imp	Post: .91
Eckert & Biermann-Ratjen (1990)	CC Group in Inpatient Setting (50)	Mixed Severe (nonpsychotic) (117)	PC, Scm, Adj	Post: .18
Eckert & Wuchner (1996)	CC Inpatient Program (100 days)	1. Borderline (14) 2. Schizophrenia (13) 3. Depression (16)	CSy	1. Post: 1.71 FU: 2.08 2. FU: .59 3. FU: 1.00
Engel-Sittenfeld et al. (1980)	CC (15)	Chronic sleep problems (6)	Csy, Phy	Post: .14 FU6mo: .22
Eymael (1987)	CC (16)	Neurotic, Psycho-somatic (14)	Imp	FU7mo: 2.20
Fife (1978)	Individual CC (8)	Parents of children with leukemia (8)	Rel	Post: .26
Fleming & Thornton (1980)	Group CC (16)	Depression (9)	SSy, Adj, Scm	Post: 2.26 FU: 2.72
Gallagher (1953)	CC (mdn: 5.5)	Mixed Students (41)	SSy, PC	Post: .29
Grawe et al. (1990)	CC (m:32)	Interpersonal problems (15)	Adj, CSy, Exp, PC, Scm, SSy, TC	Post: .79 FU6mo: .83 FU12mo: .96
Greenberg & Watson (1998) "York I"	CC (16)	Depression (17)	Ssy, Scm, Adj, TC	Post: 1.85 FU6mo: 1.85
Greenberg et al. (2001) "York II"	CC (18)	Depression (19)	SSy, Adj, Scm	Post: 1.09
Haimovitz & Haimowitz (1952)	Invidual or Group CC (max: 38)	Mixed outpatient (56)	PC	Post: .56 FU1yr: .84
Holden et al. (1989)	Rogerian (9)	Postpartum depression (60)	CSy, SSy	Post(2): .76
King et al. (2000)	CC (7)	Depression in Primary Care (1. 3-way RCT: 62; 2. 2-way RCT: 107; 3. Pref trial: 52)	SSy, Adj, Cost	1. FU2mo: .85 FU10mo: .91 2. FU2mo: 1.13 FU10: 1.21 3. FU2mo: 1.00 FU10mo: .95

(continues)

TABLE 11.1 *(Continued)*

Study	Treatment[a] (length)	Population (*n* of completers)	Type of Measure[b]	Mean Change ES[c]
Lietaer (1989)	CC(50)	Neurotic (33)	Imp	Post: 1.92
Meyer (1981)	CC (19)	Psychosomat. (Immediate + Delayed: 33)	CSy, PC, Scm	Post(3): .59 FU3mo(3): .66 FU9mo(3): .84 FU12yr(1): 1.22
Muench (1947)	Nondirective (various)	Mixed outpatient (12)	Adj, Exp, PC	Post: .97
Raskin (1949, 1952)	CC (6)	Mixed outpatient (10)	Exp, Adj, Scm	Post: 1.27
Rudolph et al. (1980)	CC (m:11)	Neurotic (149)	Imp	Post: 1.15
Schmidtchen et al. (1993)	CC Play Therapy (30)	Children	CSy	Post: 2.08 FU6mo: 2.55
Schwab (1995)	Intensive + Weekly Group CC (1. Immed.: 34 hrs.; 2. Delayed: 22)	Lonely (1.40; 2. 21)	Adj	1. Post: .53 FU4mo: .61 2. Post: .61 FU4mo: .68
Shaw (1977)	Group Nondirective (8)	Depression (8)	CSy, SSy	Post: .93
Shlien et al. (1962)	CC (1. Time unlimited: 37; 2. Time limited: 18)	Mixed outpatient (1. 30; 2. 20)	Scm	1. Post: .50 FU: .50 2. Post: .64 FU: .64
Speierer (1979)	CC (26)	Neurotic (87)	PC, Imp	Post: 1.67 FU16mo: 2.48
Speierer (2000)	CC w/ inpatient rehabilitation	Alcoholics (37)	Scm	Post: .29
Tarrier et al. (1998, 2000)	Supportive counseling (20)	Chronic schizophrenia (23)	CSy, SSy, Adj, Scm, Imp	Post: .13 FU12mo: .09 FU24mo: .62
Teusch (1990)	CC inpatient program (12 wk)	Schizophrenic (high-functioning) (73)	Imp	Post: 1.54
Teusch & Böhme (1991)	CC inpatient program (12 wk)	Agoraphobia w/ Panic (29)	CSy, PC	FU12mo: 1.32
Teusch, Böhme, & Gastpar (1997)	CC inpatient program (12 wk)	Panic w/ agoraphobia (20)	CSy, PC	Post: .70 FU6mo: .96 FU1yr: 1.04
Teusch, Finke, & Böhme (1999); Böhme, Finke, & Teusch (1999)	CC inpatient program (12 wk)	Mixed inpatient (385)	CSy, PC	Post: .80 FU1yr: .96
Tscheulin (1995, 1996)	CC inpatient program (~75 days)	Mixed inpatient (1. 1426; 2. 632; 3. 92; 4. 156)	SSy, Scm, PC	1. Post: .63 2. Post: .74 3. Post: .60 FU18mo: .46 4. Post: .74 FU18mo: .82
2. Supportive/Nondirective plus Minor Directive: (*n* 11; mES: .84; 1994: 5 samples; mES: 1.15)				
Beutler et al. (1991)	Supportive/ Self-directed (readings) (20)	Depressed (20)	CSy, SSy	Post: 1.22 FU3mo: 2.22 FU10mo: 1.19
Borkovec et al. (1987)	Nondirective + Relaxation (12)	Generalized Anxiety (14)	CSy, SSy	Post: .92

(continues)

TABLE 11.1 *(Continued)*

Study	Treatment[a] (length)	Population (*n* of completers)	Type of Measure[b]	Mean Change ES[c]
Borkovec & Mathews (1988)	Nondirective + Relaxation (12)	Gen. Anx. + Panic (10)	CSy, SSy	Post: 1.17 FU6mo: .93 FU12mo: 1.06
Brent et al. (1997); Kolko et al. (2000)	Nondirective Supportive (16)	Depressed adolescents (23)	CSy, SSy, Adj, Scm, Rel	Post: .62 FU24mo: .82
Edelman et al. (1999)	Supportive Therapy Group (12)	Recently diagnosed breast cancer (24)	CSy, Adj, Scm	Post: .19 FU4mo: .19
Gruen (1975)	Supportive (m: 17)	Heart attack inpatients (34)	CSy, SSy, PC	Post: .40 FU4mo: .66
Lerner & Clum (1990)	Supportive (10)	Suicidal students (9)	Adj, Ssy	Post: .68 FU3mo: .67
Propst et al. (1992)	Pastoral Counseling (religious content) (18)	Depressed Religious (10)	Adj, CSy, SSy	Post: 1.35 FU3mo: 1.57 FU24mo: 1.80
Salts & Zonker (1983)	Unstructured Group (8)	Divorced (21)	Scm, Ssy	Post(2): .41
Schefft & Kanfer (1987)	Group CC + readings (9)	Shyness (21)	Ind, SSy, Scm, PC	Post: .93 FU2mo: .93
Shear et al. (1994)	Nonprescriptive (information) (15)	Panic (21)	CSy, SSy, Adj	Post: .91 FU6mo: 1.17
3. Process-Experiential (Marker-guided): (*n:* 18; mES: 1.26; 1994: 6 samples; mES: 1.39)				
Clarke (1993)	Meaning Creation (8)	Childhood sexual abuse (9)	Exp, Sim, Adj	—[d]
Clarke & Greenberg (1986)	Experiential 2-Chair (2)	Decisional Conflicts (16)	Adj	Post: 1.14
Elliott et al. (1998)	PE (16)	Crime-related PTSD (6)	SSy, EXP	Post: .82 Post 6mo: .93
Gibson (1998)	Feminist PE (12)	Depression (6)	SSy, CSy, Adj	Post: .50
Goldman et al. (1996)	Relating without Violence Program (36)	Domestic violence perpetrators (48)	Ssy	Post: 1.60
Greenberg & Watson (1998) "York I"	PE (16)	Depression (17)	SSy, Scm, Adj, TC	Post: 2.49 FU6mo: 1.88
Greenberg et al. (2001) "York II"	PE (18)	Depression (19)	SSy, Adj, Scm	Post: 1.79
Greenberg & Webster (1982)	Experiential 2-Chair (6 max)	Decisional conflicts (31)	Adj, SSy	Post: 2.07 FU1mo: 2.16
Jackson & Elliott (1990)	PE (16)	Depression (15)	Adj, CSy, Exp, Scm, SSy, TC	Post: 1.36 FU6mo: 2.05 FU18mo: 1.80
Lowenstein (1985)	CC + Evoc Unfolding (5)	Interpersonal plus anxiety (12)	Scm, SSy, TC	Post: .94
Mestel & Votsmeier-Röhr (2000)	Integrative Experiential Inpatient Program (6 weeks)	Depression (412)	SSy, Adj, Exp	Post: 1.11 FU22mo: .98
Paivio & Greenberg (1995)	Empty Chair (12)	Unresolved relationship issues (15)	SSy, Adj, TC, Rel, Scm	Post: 1.65 FU4mo: 1.57

(continues)

TABLE 11.1 *(Continued)*

Study	Treatment[a] (length)	Population (*n* of completers)	Type of Measure[b]	Mean Change ES[c]
Paivio & Nieuwenhuis (2001)	Individual EFT (20)	Adults abused as children (Immed. + delayed: 32)	Ind, SSy, Adj, Rel, Scm, Imp	Post: 1.53 FU9mo: 1.45
Sachse (1995)	Goal-oriented CC (33)	Psychosomatic (29)	SSy, Adj, Scm, PC	Post: 1.52
Souliere (1995)	Empty Chair (2)	Unresolved relationship issues (20)	Ind, Exp, Scm, Rel	Post: 1.52
Toukmanian & Grech (1991)	Perceptual Processing Experiential (10)	Interpersonal problems (18)	Scm Exp	Post: .70
Watson et al. (2001)	Process Experiential (15)	Depression (33)	SSy, Adj, Scm, PC	Post: .90
Wolfus & Bierman (1996)	Relating Without Violence Program (36)	Domestic violence perpetrators (55)	Scm, PC	Post: .96
4. Gestalt Therapy: (*n:* 10; mES: 1.23; 1994: 3 samples; mES: 1.27)				
Beutler et al. (1984)	Gestalt group (3)	Mixed inpatients (39)	Adj, SSy	Post(2): .78 FU13mo(1): 1.09
Beutler et al. (1991)	Gestalt group (20)	Depressed (22)	CSy, SSy	Post: 1.18 FU3mo: 1.89 FU10mo: 1.87
Cross et al. (1982)	Gestalt/TA (12)	Mixed (15)	Adj, Exp, TC	Post: 1.22 FU4mo: 1.23 FU1yr: 1.26
Felton & Davidson (1973)	Gestalt Educational Program, w/ group counseling (semester)	Under-achieving high school students (61)	Scm	Post: .94
Greenberg et al. (1978)	Gestalt/TA Weekend Marathon group	Mixed, mostly neurotic (24)	Adj, Scm	Post: .73
Jessee & Guerney (1981)	Gestalt Relationship Enhancement Group (12)	Marital distress (18)	Rel	Post: 3.05
Johnson (1977); Johnson & Smith (1997)	Gestalt Two-Chair (5)	Snake phobia (8)	CSy, Adj	Post: 2.55
Little (1986)	Gestalt Parent Group (10)	Parents of "problematic children" (10)	Rel	Post: .87
Serok et al. (1984)	Intensive Gestalt Group (48)	Inpatients with schizophrenia (7)	Imp	—[d]
Serok & Zemet (1983)	Gestalt Group (10)	Inpatients w/ schizophrenia (9)	PC	Post: .54
Tyson & Range (1987)	Group Gestalt Empty-Chair Dialogues (4)	Mild depression (11)	SSy, PC	Post: .56 FU7wk: .88
Yalom et al. (1977)	Gestalt Weekend Marathon Group	Mixed neurotic (23)	Exp	FU2mo: .23

(continues)

TABLE 11.1 *(Continued)*

Study	Treatment[a] (length)	Population (*n* of completers)	Type of Measure[b]	Mean Change ES[c]
5. Emotionally Focused Therapy for Couples: (*n:* 10; mES: 1.40; 1994: 4 samples; mES: 2.21)				
Dandeneau & Johnson (1994)	EFT Couples (6)	Normal/mildly distressed (12)	Rel, Ind	Post: .98 FU3mo: 1.77
Dessaulles (1991)	EFT Couples (15)	Depression (6)	Rel	Post: .80
Goldman & Greenberg (1992)	EFT Couples (10)	Marital distress (14)	Rel, Ind	Post: 2.51 FU4mo: 1.52
Gordon-Walker et al. (1998)	EFT Couples (10)	Parents of chronically-ill children (16)	Rel	Post: 1.90 FU3mo: .90
James (1991)	EFT Couples (12)	Moderate marital distress (14)	Rel, Ind	Post: 1.73 FU4mo: 1.26
Johnson & Greenberg (1985a, 1985b)	EFT Couples (8)	Marital distress (1. Immed.: 15; 2. Delayed: 14)	Rel, Ind	1. Post: 2.47 FU2mo: 2.96 2. Post: 1.27 Fu2mo: 2.62
Johnson & Talitman (1997)	EFT Couples (12)	Marital distress (34)	Rel	Post: 1.35
Johnson et al. (1998)	Emotionally Focused Family Therapy (10)	Families with bulimic adolescents (9)	Ssy	Post: .67
MacPhee et al. (1995)	EFT Couples (10)	Female inhibited sexual desire (25)	SSy, Adj, Rel	Post: .57 FU: .49
6. Other Experiential (focusing-oriented, emotive, psychodrama, or integrative): (*n:* 15; mES: .86; 1994: 5 samples; mES: 1.02)				
Bierenbaum et al. (1976)	Emotive(9)	Neurotic students (41)	Exp, SSy, Ind	Post: 1.09
Beutler & Mitchell (1981)	Experiential	Mixed outpatient (20)	Imp	—[d]
Dahl & Waal (1983)	Primal Therapy (1 yr)	Chronic neurotic (13)	CSy, Ind	FU2yr: 1.10
de Vries et al. (1997)	Experiential + Existential (18)	Cancer (in active progression) (35)	SSy, Scm, Phy	Post: .13
Durak et al. (1997)	Supplemental Focusing Training (5)	Outpatient clients in various therapies (17)	Exp	Post: .62
Holstein (1990)	Focusing + Cog. Behav. Group (20)	Weight problems (7)	Phy	Post: .38 FU3mo: .66
James (1991)	EFT Couples + Relationship Enhancement (12)	Moderate marital distress (14)	Rel, Ind	Post: 2.63 FU4mo: 1.82
Katonah (1991)	Focusing (6)	Cancer (in remission) (12)	PC, SSy	Post: .50 FU6mo: 1.03
Mulder et al. (1994)	Experiential Group Therapy	HIV-positive gay men (13)	SSy, Adj, Exp, Rel, Phy	—[d]
Nichols (1974)	Emotive (9)	Neurotic students (21)	Exp, SSy, Ind	Post: 1.28 FU2mo: 1.73
Pierce et al. (1983)	Emotive (>6 mo)	Mixed Private Practice (97)	CSy, Scm, Ind, PC	Post: 1.37
Ragsdale et al. (1996)	Adventure/ Psychodrama (26 days)	Chronic PTSD	CSy, Adj	Post: .41
Rezaeian et al. (1997)	Intensive Psychodrama (60)	Depressed males (18)	Scm	Post: 1.51

(continues)

TABLE 11.1 *(Continued)*

Study	Treatment[a] (length)	Population (*n* of completers)	Type of Measure[b]	Mean Change ES[c]
Sherman (1987)	Reminiscence + Focusing Group (10)	Community Elderly (35)	Exp, Scm, PC	FU3mo: .40
Snijders et al. (2002)	Integrative CC Day Treatment Program	Personality disorders (72)	SSy, Adj, PC	Post: .57 FU6mo: .95
Spiegel et al. (1981, 1989)	Supportive-Existential Group (50)	Women with metastatic breast cancer	Imp, Phy	—[d]
Tschuschke & Anbeh (2000)	Psychodrama (12)	Mixed outpatients (72)	Ind, SSy, Adj	Post(early): .44
Tyson & Range (1987)	Active Expression Group (4)	Mild depression (11)	SSy, PC	Post: .38 FU7wk: .04
Van der Pompe et al. (1997)	Experiential-Existential Group (13)	Metastatic breast cancer (11)	Phy	—[d]
7. Encounter/Growth/Marathon Groups: (*n:* 11; mES: .69)				
Bruhn (1978)	CC Marathon Group (2.5 days)	Neurotic (78)	Scm	FU1mo: .26 FU6mo: .50
Foulds (1970)	Experiential-Gestalt Growth Group (9 4-hr)	Normal college students (19)	Exp	Post: .82
Foulds et al. (1970)	Weekend Marathon Group	Normal college students (16)	Scm	Post: 1.18
Foulds (1971a)	Experiential-Gestalt Growth Group (8 × 4.5 hr)	Normal college students (15)	Exp	Post: .59
Foulds (1971b)	Experiential-Gestalt Growth Group (8 × 4.5 hr)	Normal college students (29)	Exp	Post: .80
Foulds & Guinan (1973)	Gestalt Marathon Group (2 weekends)	Normal college students (30)	Scm	Post: .98
Foulds et al. (1974a)	Weekend Marathon Group	Normal college students (15)	Adj	Post: .75
Foulds et al. (1974b)	Experiential-Gestalt Weekend Marathon Group	Normal college students (18)	PC	Post: .24
Monti et al. (1980)	Sensitivity Training Group (20)	Mixed inpatients (23)	PC	Post(3): .02 FU6mo(3): .40
Pomrehn et al. (1986)	CC Group Marathon (2.5 days)	Neurotic (87)	Imp, Scm, Exp	FU1mo: .50 FU12mo: 1.22
Westermann et al. (1983)	CC Group Marathon (2.5 days)	Neurotic (164)	Imp, Scm, PC	FU1mo(4): .47 FU6mo(1): 1.32

[a] Individual treatment unless otherwise noted; number of sessions given in parentheses; CC: Client-Centered Therapy; PE: Process-Experiential Therapy; EFT: Emotionally Focused Therapy.

[b] Adj: social adjustment or interpersonal problems measures; CSy: clinician ratings of symptoms; Exp: measures of experiential functioning; Imp: estimates based on improvement ratings or percent recovered; PC: measures of personality and coping style; Rel: measures of relationship quality (e.g., marital); Scm: schematic/self image measures; SSy: self ratings of symptoms; Ind: Target complaint or individualized problem measures; Phy: health, physical status.

[c] ESs for multiple outcome measures were first averaged within instruments (e.g., 8 scales of Freiberg Personality Inventory), then across instruments for each treatment group and each assessment period. FU: Follow-up (followed by time period in months or years; e.g., 3mo = 3 months).

[d] Pre-post ES could not be calculated from data provided.

effect. Analyses of *controlled and comparative effect sizes* compared mean overall pre-post effects between control or comparative treatment conditions, with positive values assigned where the experiential treatment showed a larger amount of change. Finally, *equivalence analyses* (Rogers, Howard, & Vessey, 1993) were carried out for key comparisons, using .4 SD as the minimum clinically interesting difference, as previously proposed by Elliott, Stiles, and Shapiro (1993).

Total Pre-Post Change in Experiential Therapies

Table 11.1 summarizes pre-post effects for all studies for which such data could be calculated. Overall unweighted results are given in Table 11.2. The average pre-post effect, across the 127 treatment groups and assessment periods, was .99. The data clearly indicate that clients maintained or perhaps even increased their post-treatment gains over the post-therapy period, with the largest effects obtained at early followup. Weighting effects by sample size produced a somewhat smaller ES of .86 SD. This smaller weighted effect primarily reflects the contribution of large German studies with relatively small ESs, in particular two reported by Tscheulin (1995, 1996), with samples of 1,426 and 632, respectively.

Controlled Research on the Effectiveness of Experiential Therapies

Pre-post effects do not tell us, of course, whether clients in experiential therapies fared better than untreated clients, thus making it difficult to infer that therapy was responsible for changes made by clients. These effects are generally larger than control group comparisons (Lipsey & Wilson, 1993). Therefore, we examined control-referenced effect sizes (differences between pre-post ESs) in the 42 treated groups in which experiential treatments were compared to wait list or no treatment controls (see Table 11.3). The unweighted mean-controlled effect size for these

TABLE 11.2 Summary of Overall Pre-Post Change, Controlled and Comparative Effect Sizes

	n	*m*	SD
Pre-Post Change ES (mean *d*)			
By Assessment Point:			
Post	114	.97	.61
Early Followup (1–11mos.)	53	1.16	.72
Late Followup (12 mos)	33	1.04	.52
Overall (mES):			
Unweighted	127	.99	.58
Weighted by *n*	6,569[a]	.86	.42
Controlled ES (vs. untreated clients)[b]			
Unweighted mean difference	42	.89	.71
Experiential mean pre-post ES	40	1.02	.63
Control mean pre-post ES	40	.11	.49
Weighted mean difference	1,149[a]	+.78	.57
Comparative ES (vs. other treatments)[b]			
Unweighted mean difference	74	+.04	.56
Experiential mean pre-post ES	69	1.00	.66
Comparative treatment mean pre-post ES	69	1.00	.73
Weighted mean difference	1,375[a]	+.01	.44
Comparative ES (more vs. less process-directive experiential)			
Unweighted	5	.48	.26
Weighted by *n*	164[a]	.45	.25

Note. Where indicated, number of clients in humanistic treatment conditions used as weighting variable (corrects for small sample bias).

[a] Total number of clients in studies combined.

[b] Mean difference in change ESs for conditions compared, except where these are unavailable; positive values indicate pro-humanistic therapy results.

TABLE 11.3 Controlled Outcome Research on Experiential Therapies

Study	Experiential Treatment	Control Condition	Mean Difference in Effect Size
1. Client-Centered: (*n:* 11; m ES: .78)			
Boeck-Singelmann et al. (1992)	CC (1. Immed.; 2. Delayed)	Wait list	1: +1.51 2: + 1.14
Braaten (1989)	CC Group	No-treatment	+1.19
DiLoreto (1971)	CC	No treatment + No contact	+.31
Dircks et al. (1982)	CC Group	No treatment	+.27
Eymael (1987)	CC	Wait list	+2.20
Meyer (1981)	CC	Wait list	+.56
Rudolph et al. (1980)	CC	Wait list	+.30
Schwab (1995)	CC Group (1. Immed.; 2. Delayed)	Wait list	1: +.42 2: +.51
Shaw (1977)	Nondirective	Wait list	+.25
2. Supportive/Nondirective plus Minor Directive: (3 samples; m ES: .43)			
Gruen (1975)	Supportive-Experiential	No treatment	+.53
Propst et al. (1992)	Pastoral Counseling	Wait list	+.55
Salts & Zonker (1983)	Unstructured Group	Wait list	+.23
3. Process-Experiential/Emotion-Focused: (*n:* 3; m ES: .89)			
Clarke & Greenberg (1986)	Experiential Two-Chair	Wait list	+.96
Paivio & Nieuwenhuis (2001)	Individual EFT	Wait list	+1.43
Wolfus & Bierman (1996)	Relating Without Violence Program	No treatment	+.33
4. Gestalt Therapy: (*n:* 3; m ES: .64)			
Johnson (1977)	Gestalt Two-Chair	No treatment	+1.05
Little (1986)	Gestalt Parent Group	Treatment early terminators	+.84
Tyson & Range (1987)	Group Gestalt Empty-Chair Dialogues	No treatment	+.10
5. Emotionally Focused Therapy for Couples: (*n:* 6; m ES: 1.93)			
Dandeneau & Johnson (1994)	EFT Couples	Wait list	+1.51
Goldman & Greenberg (1992)	EFT Couples	Wait list	+2.14
Gordon-Walker et al. (1996)	EFT Couples	Wait list	+1.47
James (1991)	EFT Couples	Wait list	+.85
Johnson & Greenberg (1985a & 1985b)	EFT Couples (1. Immed.; 2. Delay)	Wait list	1: +3.28 2: +2.51

(continues)

TABLE 11.3 *(Continued)*

Study	Experiential Treatment	Control Condition	Mean Difference in Effect Size
6. Other Experiential: (*n:* 7; m ES: .68)			
James (1991)	EFT Couples + Relationship Enhancement	Wait list	+1.58
Katonah (1991)	Focusing	Wait list	+1.57
Mulder et al. (1994, 1995)	Experiential Group Therapy w/ HIV	Wait list/ No treatment	+1.04[a]
Ragsdale et al. (1996)	Adventure/Psychodrama	Wait list	+.59
Sherman (1987)	Focusing	No treatment	+.27
Tyson & Range (1987)	Active Expression Group	No treatment	–.41
van der Pompe et al. (1997)	Experiential-Existential Group w/ breast cancer (*n*=11)	Wait list	+.17
7. Encounter/Growth/Marathon Groups: (*n:* 9; m ES: .75)			
Foulds (1970)	Experiential-Gestalt Growth Group	No treatment	+.65
Foulds et al. (1970)	Weekend Marathon	No treatment	+1.36
Foulds (1971a)	Experiential-Gestalt Growth Group	No treatment	+.48
Foulds (1971b)	Experiential-Gestalt Growth Group	No treatment	+.75
Foulds & Guinan (1973)	Gestalt Marathon	No treatment	+1.02
Foulds et al. (1974a)	Weekend Marathon	No treatment	+.65
Foulds et al. (1974b)	Experiential-Gestalt Weekend Marathon	No treatment	+.23
Pomrehn et al. (1986)	CC Group Marathon	Wait list	+.61
Westermann et al. (1983)	CC Group Marathon	Wait list	+1.07

Note. Effect size values given are differences in change effect sizes (averaged across measures and assessment periods). Abbreviations: CC: Client-Centered Therapy; PrExp: Process Experiential Therapy; ND+: Nondirective plus minor directive; EFT: Emotionally Focused Therapy (for couples).

[a] Based on combined sample of reportedly equivalent experiential and cognitive treatments.

studies (Table 11.2) was also large, .89, a value quite comparable to the mean pre-post effect of .99. In fact, the average pre-post effect in the 39 untreated conditions was .11, indicating that there was little or no improvement in the untreated clients in these studies; clients in 5 of the 42 untreated groups showed a clinically significant level of average deterioration (negative effect sizes of –.40 or larger). The fact that the controlled effects corroborated the pre-post effects also supports the validity of using pre-post effects, making it possible to draw on a much larger sample of studies. Finally, as with pre-post effects, weighting by sample size produced a comparable, though slightly smaller, mean effect of .78.

Comparative Outcome Research on Experiential vs. Nonexperiential Therapies

Though impressive, the pre-post and controlled effect-size analyses reported so far do not address the issue of comparative treatment effectiveness, which is central to the current controversy about the effectiveness of experiential therapies. For this, we analyzed 74 comparisons between experiential and nonexperiential therapies, summarized in Table 11.4. Five studies compared different experiential therapies (e.g., Greenberg & Watson, 1998) and were therefore not included in these analyses. The average unweighted difference in pre-post effects between experiential and nonexperiential therapies (Table 11.2) was +.04,

TABLE 11.4 Comparative Outcome Research on Experiential Therapies

Study	Experiential Treatment	Comparison Treatment	Mean Difference in Effect Size
1. Client-Centered: (*n:* 28; m comparative ES: –.04)			
Beck et al. (1992)	CC	Focused Cognitive Therapy	–.95
Borkovec et al. (1993)	Nondirective	Cognitive Therapy	–.36
Borkovec et al. (1993)	Nondirective	Applied Relaxation	–.99
DiLoreto (1971)	CC	Systematic Desensitization	–.03
DiLoreto (1971)	CC	Rational Emotive Therapy	+.06
Eckert & Biermann-Ratjen (1990)	CC	Psychodynamic Inpatient Group	.00[a]
Engel-Sittenfeld et al. (1980)	Individual CC	Group Autogenic Training	–.14
Engel-Sittenfeld et al. (1980)	Individual CC	Individual Biofeedback	–.23
Eymael (1987)	CC	Behavior Therapy	–.53
Fife (1978)	CC	Behavior Therapy	+.25
Fleming & Thornton (1980)	Nondirective Group	Cognitive Therapy	+.50
Fleming & Thornton (1980)	Nondirective Group	Coping Skills Training	+.50
Grawe et al. (1990)	CC	Behavior Therapy (Broad-Band & Individualized)	–.08
Grawe et al. (1990)	CC	Group Behavior Therapy	–.22
Greenberg & Watson (1998) "York I"	CC	PrExp	–.33
Greenberg et al. (2001) "York II"	CC	PrExp	–.71
King et al. (2000) (1. 3-way trial; 2. 2-way trial; 3. Preference trial)	CC	CBT	1: –.19 2: –.16 3: –.08
King et al. (2000)	CC	Treatment as Usual (primary care physician)	+.10
Meyer (1981)	CC	Short-term Dynamic Therapy	+.44
Shaw (1977)	Nondirective	Cognitive Therapy	–1.15
Shaw (1977)	Nondirective	Behavioral Therapy	–.22
Shlien et al. (1962)	CC	Adlerian Therapy	.00[a]
Schmidtchen et al. (1993)	CC Play therapy	Pedagogical Support Group	+1.47
Tarrier et al. (1998, 2000)	Supportive counseling + routine care	Cognitive Behavioral Therapy + Routine care	+.08
Tarrier et al. (1998, 2000)	Supportive counseling + routine care	Routine care	+.31
Teusch et al. (1997)	CC program	CCT plus behavioral exposure	–.37
2. Supportive/Nondirective plus Minor Directive: (*n:* 13; m ES: –.32)			
Beutler et al. (1991)	Supportive/Self-directed (bibliotherapy)	Cognitive Therapy Group	+.06
Beutler et al. (1991)	Supportive/Self-directed (ND+)	Focused Expressive Group	+.11
Borkovec et al. (1987)	Nondirective + Relaxation	Cognitive Therapy/Relaxation	–.68
Borkovec & Mathews (1988)	Nondirective + Relaxation	Cognitive Therapy/Relaxation	–.50
Borkovec & Mathews (1988)	Nondirective + Relaxation	Desensitization/Relaxation	+.02

(continues)

Table 11.4 *(Continued)*

Study	Experiential Treatment	Comparison Treatment	Mean Difference in Effect Size
Brent et al. (1997); Kolko et al. (2000)	Nondirective Supportive + Information	Cognitive Behavioral Therapy	–.13
Brent et al. (1997); Kolko et al. (2000)	Nondirective Supportive + Information	Systemic Behavior Family Therapy	–.08
Edelman et al. (1999)	Supportive Therapy Group	Cognitive Behavioral Therapy Group	–.12
Lerner & Clum (1990)	Supportive	Behavioral Problem-Solving Group	–1.42
Propst et al. (1992)	Pastoral Counseling	Cognitive Therapy (nonreligious or religious)	+.09
Salts & Zonker (1983)	Unstructured Group	Social Skills Training Group	–.31
Schefft & Kanfer (1987)	Group CC + readings	Cognitive Behavioral Therapy	–.72
Schefft & Kanfer (1987)	Group CC + readings	Cognitive Behavioral plus Structured Process Therapy	–.68
Shear et al. (1994)	Nonprescriptive	Cognitive Behavioral Therapy	+.25
3. Process-Experiential/Emotion-Focused (Individual): (*n:* 6; m ES: +.55)			
Clarke (1993)	Meaning creation + empty chair	Cognitive Therapy	+.76
Clarke & Greenberg (1986)	PrExp	Behavioral Problem-Solving Treatment	+.57
Greenberg & Watson (1998) "York I"	PrExp	CC	+.33
Greenberg et al. (2001) "York II"	PrExp	CC	+.71
Paivio & Greenberg (1995)	PrExp	Psychoeducational Group	+1.24
Souliere (1995)	Empty-Chair Dialogue	Cognitive Restructuring	+.11
Toukmanian & Grech (1991)	PrExp	Self-Help/Psycho-educational Groups	+.55
Watson et al. (2001)	PrExp	Cognitive behavioral	+.11
4. Gestalt Therapy: (*n:* 11; m ES: –.07)			
Beutler et al. (1984)	Gestalt Group	Inpatient treatment as usual (w/out group)	–.41
Beutler et al. (1984)	Gestalt Group	Process-Supportive (Psychodynamic) Group	–.55
Beutler et al. (1984)	Gestalt Group	Behavior Therapy Group	–.17
Beutler et al. (1991)	Focused Expressive Group	Cognitive Therapy Group	+.17
Beutler et al. (1991)	Focused Expressive Group	Supportive/Self-directed (ND+)	–.11
Cross et al. (1982)	Gestalt	Behavior Therapy	–.45
Felton & Davidson (1973)	Gestalt Educational Program	Standard school program	+1.16
Jessee & Guerney (1981)	Gestalt Couples Group	Relationship Enhancement	–.36
Johnson & Smith (1997)	Gestalt Two Chair	Systematic Desensitization	+.10

(continues)

TABLE 11.4 *(Continued)*

Study	Experiential Treatment	Comparison Treatment	Mean Difference in Effect Size
Serok, Rabin, & Spitz (1984)	Intensive Gestalt Group w/ Schizophrenia	Inpatient treatment as usual	+.90
Serok & Zemet (1983)	Additional Gestalt Group	Inpatient treatment as usual	+.35
Tyson & Range (1987)	Group Gestalt Empty-Chair	Theater workshop	+.51
Tyson & Range (1987)	Group Gestalt Empty-Chair	Active Expression Group (= Other experiential)	−.34
Yalom et al. (1977)	Gestalt Marathon Group	Meditation/Tai Chi	+.06
5. Emotionally Focused Therapy for Couples: (*n:* 5; m ES: +.89)			
Dandeneau & Johnson (1994)	EFT	Cognitive Therapy	+.70
Dessaulles (1991)	EFT	Antidepressant medication	+1.49
Goldman & Greenberg (1992)	EFT	Structural-Systemic Therapy	−.02
James (1991)	EFT	EFT + Relationship Enhancement	−.73
Johnson & Greenberg (1985a)	EFT	Marital Problem-Solving Therapy	+1.47
6. Other Experiential: (*n:* 12; m ES: +.18)			
Beutler & Mitchell (1981)	Experiential Group	Analytic Group	+.82
Holstein (1990)	CB Group + Focusing	Cognitive Behavioral Weight Loss Group	+.14
Monti et al. (1980)	Sensitivity Training Group	Social Skills Training group	−.34
Mulder et al. (1994)	Experiential Group w/ HIV	Cognitive Behavioral Group	.00[a]
Nichols (1974)	Cathartic	Dynamic Therapy	+1.16
Rezaeian et al. (1997)	Intensive Psychodrama	TAU	+.74
Rezaeian et al. (1997)	Intensive Psychodrama	TAU + Intensive Psychodrama	−.16
Sherman (1987)	Reminiscence + Focusing Group	Traditional Reminiscence group	+.10
Spiegel et al. (1981, 1989)	Existential Support Group + TAU	TAU	+.50
Tschuschke & Anbeh (2000)	Psychodrama	Group analysis	.00
Tschuschke & Anbeh (2000)	Psychodrama	Eclectic/Integrative Group	+.04
Tyson & Range (1987)	Active Expression Group	Theater workshop	−.85

Note. Multiple treatments for a given study listed separately. Effect sizes are differences in change effect sizes (averaged across measures and assessment periods). Types of experiential treatment correspond to main headings in Table 11.1. Abbreviations: CC: Client-Centered Therapy; EFT Emotionally Focused Therapy (for couples); ND+: Nondirective plus minor directive; PrExp: Process-Experiential Therapy; Other: Other or unspecified experiential treatment; TAU: treatment-as-usual.

[a] Based on reported equivalence.

TABLE 11.5 Equivalence Analysis: Comparisons between Treatments

	n	mES	SD_{ES}	$t(0)$	$t(1.41)$	Result
Experiential vs. Nonexperiental therapies	74	+.04	.56	+.61	−5.5**	Equivalent
Experiential vs. CB therapies	46	−.11	.51	−1.49	+3.88*	Equivalent
Experiential vs. non-CB therapies	28	+.29	.57	+2.65*	−1.03	Better
CC/Nondirective-supportive vs. CB	32	−.25	.45	−3.11**	+1.96+	Trivially different
Pure CC vs. CB	20	−.19	.44	−1.94+	+2.15*	Trivially different
Process-Directive vs. CB	14	+.20	.51	+1.43	−1.49	Equivocal
More vs. less Process-Directive	5	+.48	.26	+4.07*	−.60	Better
Allegiance-Controlled Comparisons						
Experiential vs. CB	46	−.05	.43	−.74	+5.65**	Equivalent
Experiential vs. non-CB therapies	28	+.08	.50	+.81	−3.45**	Equivalent
CC/ND+ vs. CB	32	−.03	.42	−.37	+4.97**	Equivalent
CC(pure) vs. CB	20	−.03	.43	−.32	−3.89**	Equivalent
Process-Directive vs. CB	14	−.09	.44	−.76	+2.65*	Equivalent
More vs. less Process-Directive	5	+.01	.22	+.08	−3.90*	Equivalent

+ p <.10; * p <.05; ** p <.01

Note: mES: mean comparative effect size (difference between therapies); SD_D: standard deviation for the comparative effect sizes; *t(0)*: usual one-group *t* value against a zero-difference null hypothesis; *t(|.4|)*: equivalence *t* value against a ± .4 SD difference null hypothesis. "Result" refers to the interpretation of the results of the equivalence testing: "Equivalent": significantly less than ± .4 SD criterion but not significantly greater than zero; "equivocal" neither significantly different nor equivalent); "Worse/Better": humanistic shows poorer or better outcome (significantly different from zero but not significantly different from ± .4 SD criterion); "Trivially different": both significantly different from zero and significantly less than ± .4 SD criterion.

indicating no overall difference. Once again, weighting by sample size produced comparable results. In 45 (60%) of the comparisons, clients in experiential and nonexperiential therapies were within ±.4 SD of each other. However, there is also heterogeneity in comparative effect sizes, as evidenced by 13 comparisons in which clients in the nonexperiential treatments did substantially better (comparative effect size < −.4 SD) than clients in experiential therapies, while experientially treated clients did substantially better (> .4 SD) in the remaining 16 comparisons.

Applying equivalence analysis to this and other treatment comparisons makes it possible to "prove the null hypothesis" of equivalence between experiential and nonexperiential therapies. These analyses are summarized in Table 11.5, with equivalence analyses given in the *t(0)*, *t(.4)*, and Result columns. In the case of the overall comparison between experiential and nonexperiential therapies, the obtained zero-order difference is significantly less than ±.4 SD, the predetermined minimum substantive difference criterion (t [.4] = 5.5; n = 74; p < .001). In other words, on the basis of this sample, it can be concluded that experiential and nonexperiential treatments are, in general, *equivalent* in their effectiveness.

Cognitive Behavioral (CB) vs. Experiential Therapies. A significant center of controversy involves assumptions shared by many academic or CB-oriented psychologists that experiential therapies are inferior to cognitive behavioral treatments. The comparative studies analyzed here did not exclusively use CB treatments (only 46 out of 74 comparisons). Therefore, it can be argued that the effects of the CB treatments were watered down by the inclusion of comparisons involving other types of therapy (i.e., psychodynamic, psychoeducational, and "treatment as usual").

In order to clarify this issue, we undertook a series of subsidiary equivalence analyses (see Table 11.5). These analyses indicated that, for the subsample of 28 studies analyzed here, experiential therapies showed larger pre-post effects than non-CB therapies. On the other hand, the 46 studies comparing experiential to CB therapies revealed a mean difference of −.11, which was clinically *equivalent* (i.e., statistically significantly less than the ±.4 minimum difference but not significantly different from zero). Thus, these data support the claim that experiential therapies in general are equivalent to CB therapies in effectiveness.

Nevertheless, in light of recent controversies in Germany over government recognition of *Gesprächspsychotherapie* (the German version of CC therapy) as a valid treatment, more precise analyses are required. Specifically, it is important to address claims by Grawe, Donati, and Bernauer (1994) that client-centered therapy is less effective than cognitive behavior therapy, based on their meta-analysis of 10 comparative treatment studies. In fact, when the focus is further narrowed to the 32 studies comparing CC or nondirective/supportive therapies to CB treatments, a "trivial" statistical superiority for CB appeared (comparative ES: –.25); this effect is *both* significantly greater than zero and significantly less than the .4 SD criterion difference. The same result occurred for the subsample of 20 comparisons between pure CC and CB treatments (mean comparative ES: –.19).

On the other hand, when "process-directive" experiential therapies (i.e., process-experiential, emotionally focused therapy for couples, Gestalt, and focusing) are lumped together, the mean difference between them and CB favors the experiential therapies (+.20), but the difference is equivocal (neither significantly different nor equivalent). In fact, in the five studies (Greenberg, Goldman, & Angus, 2001; Greenberg & Watson, 1998; James, 1991; Tyson & Range, 1987; Watson, Gordon, Stermac, Kalogerakos & Steckley, 2001) in which more versus less process-directive experiential therapies were compared directly, the mean comparative effect size significantly favored the process-directive therapies (+.48; $t(0) = 4.07$; $p < .05$).

In spite of the clinically trivial superiority of CB treatments to the less process-directive experiential therapies, it appears likely that the significant differences found may reflect method factors, in particular, researcher allegiance effects (Luborsky et al., 1999). Therefore, we ran additional analyses statistically controlling for researcher allegiance, by removing variance in comparative ESs due to this variable. When this was done (see Table 11.5, bottom), all of the treatment comparisons were zero-order and statistically equivalent: The allegiance-corrected mean comparative effect sizes were significantly less than the .4 criterion, and not significantly greater than zero.

Method, Client, and Treatment Moderators of Study Outcome

Outcome effect sizes can potentially be affected by a variety of factors, including research method (type of measure, size of sample, regional origin of the research, year of study, and researcher theoretical allegiance), client problem, and treatment characteristics (modality, setting, length, therapist experience). These factors are also likely to be confounded with differences between various forms of experiential therapy. As Table 11.6 indicates, most of these potential moderators show little or no relation to effect size.

METHOD FACTORS. In terms of research design features, *researcher theoretical allegiance* showed no association with pre-post effect size but turned out to be a very strong predictor of comparative ES ($r = -.59$; $p < .01$). In other words, proponents of experiential treatments typically produced substantial, positive comparative effects, while advocates of nonexperiential approaches typically found experiential treatments to be less effective than other approaches, and researchers whose allegiance was neutral, mixed, or indeterminate typically obtained no difference results. As noted earlier, when researcher allegiance was controlled for, differences between experiential and other therapies disappeared. (These allegiance effects are likely to include differential effort by trainers, supervisors, and therapists.) In addition, researcher theoretical allegiance may also play a role in studies using no-treatment or wait list controls ($r = -.30$). We also found that experiential therapies show significantly larger effects when compared to wait list as opposed to no-treatment controls ($r = .39$), which is possible because wait-listed clients refrained from seeking treatment while they were waiting for therapy to begin. Finally, as in previous measure-level meta-analyses, we found large differences among different types of outcome measure ($n = 480$ effects; 11 categories; $\eta = .53$; $F = 18.2$; $p < .001$), with individualized and clinician-rated measures showing the largest effects and measures of personality/coping style, cost, and health status the smallest.

CLIENT FACTORS. Regarding client factors, we expected that clients with less severe or emotion-focused problems (e.g., depression) would show greater change in experiential therapies than clients with more severe or cognitive/behavior-based problems (e.g., schizophrenia, habit disorders). We found that client problem made a

Table 11.6 Predictor Analyses: Correlations

	Pre-post ES (n = 127)	Controlled ES (n = 42)	Comparative ES[a] (n = 74)
Year of Publication	.12	.19	–.02
Regional origin (North America: 1; German-speaking: 2)	–.13	–.13	.04
Sample size (n of clients)	–.08	–.14	–.05
Researcher allegiance (pro: 1; neutral: 2; con: 3)	–.08	–.30+	–.59**
Type of control group (no treatment: 1; wait list: 2)	—	.39*	—
Setting (outpatient: 1; inpatient: 2)	–.18*	–.16	–.05
Client age (adolescent, college: 1; adult: 2; old adults (>50): 3	.07	.16	.10
Client problem/disorder (nonlinear correlation ε, 9 categories)	.44**	.58*	.38
Therapist experience level	–.18	–.04	–.04
Therapy length (n of sessions)	–.01	–.19	.16
Therapy modality (nonlinear correlation ε, 5 categories)	.44**	.71**	.33+
Process-directiveness vs. client-centered/nondirective (CC, nondirective: 1; PE, Gestalt, EFT, other: 2)	.23*	.25	.34**

+ p <.1; * p <.05; ** p <.01

[a] Comparisons between experiential and nonexperiential therapies.

difference for pre-post and controlled effects, but not for comparative effects (see Table 11.6). As in our previous reviews, the largest effects were obtained for specific relationship problems, while the smallest effects were generally obtained for habit disorders, severe disorders, and physical problems (e.g., cancer).

Treatment factors. Degree of process directiveness proved to be the most consistent predictor of effect size across all three types of studies. As implied in the equivalence analyses described earlier, process-directive therapies such as PE and EFT had larger effects than CC or nondirective-supportive therapies, at least in pre-post and comparative treatment analyses. Similarly, treatment modality also predicted pre-post and controlled effect sizes, reflecting the consistently strong results with Greenberg and Johnson's (1988) EFT for couples.

Another recent meta-analysis of 30 controlled outcome studies of experiential-humanistic therapies was carried out by Anderson and Levitt (2000). They reported preliminary results somewhat lower than those reported here (mean-weighted, controlled effect size of .50 vs. .79). Because of multiple methods differences between their analysis and ours, and because they did not report pre-post and comparative effect sizes, it is difficult to interpret the discrepancy in results. Nevertheless, the body of available evidence analyzed here strongly supports the effectiveness of experiential-humanistic therapies.

Outcome for Different Client Problems: Differential Treatment Effects

Investigation of treatments for specific client presenting problems or disorders has blossomed during the period since our last review. In particular, experiential treatments have been found to be effective with depression, anxiety, and trauma, as well as to have possible physical health benefits and applicability to clients with severe problems, including schizophrenia. In this section, we summarize recent studies, relate them to our meta-analysis, and evaluate the status of experiential therapies as empirically supported treatments for specific client problems.

Anxiety

RECENT STUDIES. Teusch and colleagues have investigated the effect of CC therapy on anxiety (Teusch, Böhme, & Gastpar, 1997; see also Teusch, Finke, & Böhme, 1999). In this study, clients were randomly assigned to pure CC therapy or to CC plus additional behavioral exposure. In the first study (Teusch et al., 1997), 40 clients with severe panic and agoraphobia were admitted to an inpatient anxiety treatment program. Most of the clients had been treated by pharmacological means unsuccessfully. CC and behavioral agoraphobia manuals were used. The clients were examined for panic, anxiety, agoraphobia, and depressive symptoms on admission, at discharge and at 3-, 6-, and 12-month followup. Both CC treatment and a combination with exposure treatment reduced panic, avoidance, and depressive symptoms significantly. At post-treatment, the combined treatment was superior in clients' coping actively with anxiety and improving agoraphobic symptoms. However, at 1-year followup, the difference between treatments was no longer statistically significant in the reduction of anxiety and depressive symptoms.

In another study of clients with panic disorder, Shear, Pilkonis, Cloitre, and Leon (1994) compared what they referred to as "nonprescriptive" therapy (information about panic, plus reflective listening) to CB therapy, using a variety of measures. Although the researchers had intended the experiential therapy treatment as a relationship control, overall pre-post change was slightly larger for clients in nonprescriptive therapy (comparative ES: +.24; not statistically significant). (Similar no-difference results were also reported earlier by Grawe, 1976.)

Johnson and Smith (1997) randomly assigned 23 snake-phobic participants to one of three groups: Gestalt empty-chair dialogue, systematic desensitization, and no therapy control. Following treatment, measures were taken of clients' avoidance behavior and their subjective experience. Both empty-chair dialogue clients and those treated with desensitization were significantly less phobic than those given no therapy. No other group differences were found. The authors concluded that this provided evidence for the efficacy of the Gestalt empty-chair dialogue in the treatment of simple phobia.

On the other hand, two studies by cognitive therapy researchers showed substantial superiority for CB treatments over experiential treatments in clients with anxiety disorders. First, Beck, Sokol, Clark, Berchick, and Wright (1992) used a brief (eight half-hour sessions) individual CC treatment as a relationship control in a study of cognitive therapy of panic. Although the 15 clients in CC therapy showed substantial pre-post change on the symptom measures used (overall ES: 1.32), clients in cognitive therapy showed significantly more change (comparative ES: –.77). Second, Borkovec and Costello (1993) compared 12-session nondirective, applied relaxation, and CB treatment in 55 clients with generalized anxiety, using a variety of symptom measures. Once again, there was substantial pre-post change (overall ES: 1.47), but clients in the two other treatments showed significantly greater change (comparative ES: –.99 for applied relaxation and –.36 for CB therapy). (A very recent study, Barrowclough et al., 2001, reports similar results for elderly adults treated with CB therapy vs. person-centered counseling.)

Meta-analysis and analysis of extent of empirical support. The meta-analysis data set contains eight studies of anxiety disorders, primarily panic and generalized anxiety, treated with CC or nondirective-supportive therapies (Beck et al., 1992; Borkovec & Costello, 1993; Borkovec & Mathews, 1988; Borkovec et al., 1987; Johnson & Smith, 1997; Teusch & Böhme, 1991; Shear et al., 1994; Teusch et al., 1997). The mean pre-post effect size for the experiential therapies in these studies was 1.30 (SD: .52), a large effect. On the other hand, for the nine treatment comparisons between experiential and nonexperiential treatments, the mean comparative effect size was –.38 (SD: .44). This is a moderate and statistically significant ($t = -2.6$; $p < .05$) finding in favor of the nonexperiential treatments; all were some form of CB therapy, and all but two were conducted by CB adherents.

Applying the Chambless and Hollon (1998) criteria, we find four of the eight comparative effects favoring the nonexperiential treatments (Beck et al., 1992; Borkovec & Costello, 1993; Borkovec & Mathews, 1988; Borkovec et al., 1987). However, only one of these studies deals with panic (Beck et al., 1992), while the three on generalized anxiety disorder all emanate from Borkovec and colleagues. In other words, the requirement for replication across independent research settings is not satisfied for particular kinds of anxiety disorder. On the other hand, if more relaxed criteria for empirical support are met, such as those proposed by Elliott (2000), the very strong pre-post effects can be used to provide evidence of effectiveness.

A useful integration of these two kinds of data might run as follows: the large pre-post effects (>.90) obtained in almost all of the studies analyzed suggest that experiential treatments are *possibly efficacious* (Chambless & Hollon, 1998) in treating anxiety, while also suggesting that CB therapies may be somewhat *more specific and efficacious*. This apparent moderate CB advantage has two possible explanations: On the one hand, it is likely to be due to researcher allegiance effects; when researcher allegiance is controlled for, the difference is no longer statistically significant (ES: –.18). On the other hand, it is also possible that anxiety disorders may respond somewhat better to CB therapies. In our clinical experience, clients with significant anxiety often appear desperate for expert guidance, a situation that experiential therapists may need to address more directly, either by exploring the issue with clients or by adding content directive elements to their therapy, such as providing information about the role of trauma or emotional processes in panic attacks (e.g., Wolfe & Sigl, 1998).

Trauma and Abuse

Recent studies. Gestalt and psychodramatic treatments have been employed to treat the sequelae of trauma in several studies. Paivio and Greenberg (1995) studied a 12-session PE therapy emphasizing empty-chair work for clients with unfinished business with significant others, contrasting it with a psychoeducational comparison treatment.

In a study of childhood attachment injury based on this model, Paivio and Greenberg (1995) randomly assigned 34 clients with unresolved feelings related to a significant other to either experiential therapy using a Gestalt empty-chair dialogue intervention or a psychoeducation group (Paivio & Greenberg, 1995). Treatment outcomes were evaluated before and after the treatment period in each condition and at four months and one year after the experiential therapy. Outcome instruments targeted general symptoms, interpersonal distress, target complaints, unfinished business resolution, and perceptions of self and other in the unfinished relationship. Results indicated that experiential therapy achieved clinically meaningful, stable gains for most clients and significantly greater improvement than the psychoeducational group on all outcome measures (mean comparative effect size: +1.24).

Subsequently, Paivio and Nieuwenhuis (2001) compared a 20-session emotion-focused therapy (EFT) of adults with unresolved issues of childhood abuse with a wait list control. EFT clients showed significantly greater improvements than wait-listed clients in multiple domains of disturbance, including general and PTSD symptoms, global interpersonal problems, self-affiliation, target complaints, and resolution of issues with abusive others. Overall pre-post controlled effect sizes were substantial (+1.43). Clinically significant change on at least one dimension occurred for 100% of clients in treatment, as compared with 36% of wait list clients.

Ragsdale, Cox, Finn, and Eisler (1996) tested 24 participants of a psychodrama-based inpatient post-traumatic stress disorder (PTSD) treatment program both immediately before and following completion of treatment. Responses were compared to a treatment/wait list comparison group composed of 24 clients awaiting entry into the program. All treatment and wait list comparison group participants received weekly PTSD outpatient group therapy. Significant improvements were found in the inpatient treatment group in areas of hopelessness, feelings of guilt and shame, loneliness, and emotional expressiveness. Other indices of psychological functioning, including interpersonal skills, gender role stress, anxiety, anger, and PTSD symptoms, did not change significantly in response to treatment. No positive changes in any area of psychological function occurred in the treatment/wait list comparison group.

Two recent small-scale studies also provided support for the effectiveness of experiential treatments of trauma: First, Clarke (1993) carried out a pilot study comparing an experiential treatment to a cognitive treatment with sexual abuse survivors. The eight-session experiential therapy combined meaning creation with empty-chair work, depending on the client's initial level of arousal (if high, then meaning creation; if blocked, then empty-chair work). Although the sample consisted of only nine clients in each treatment condition, clients in the experiential treatment did much better than clients in the CB treatment (mean comparative ES: +.76). Second, Elliott, Davis, and Slatick (1998) reported pilot outcome data on six clients with crime-related PTSD seen for 16 sessions of PE therapy. These clients evidenced substantial pre-post improvement on both general and PTSD symptoms.

Meta-analysis and analysis of extent of empirical support. The meta-analysis data set contains six studies of trauma and abuse (Clarke,

1993; Elliott et al., 1998; Paivio & Greenberg, 1995; Paivio & Nieuwenhuis, 2001; Ragsdale et al., 1996; Souliere, 1995), all involving process-directive experiential therapies. The mean pre-post effect size for these therapies was 1.15 (SD: .46), a large effect. Two of these studies (Paivio & Niewenhuis, 2001; Ragsdale et al., 1996) used wait list control groups (mean-controlled ES: +.99; SD: .58), while three (Clarke, 1993; Paivio & Greenberg, 1995; Souliere, 1995) used active treatment comparison conditions (mean comparative ES: +.69; SD: .56). The three controlled or comparative studies whose effects favored PE therapy by a statistically significant degree involved two independent research settings (Clarke; Paivio/Greenberg), thus fulfilling the Chambless and Hollon's (1998) criteria for an efficacious and specific treatment.

Depression

Recent studies. In the York I Depression study, Greenberg and Watson (1998) compared the effectiveness of PE therapy with one of its components, CC therapy, in the treatment of 34 adults suffering from major depression. The CC treatment emphasized the establishment and maintenance of the Rogerian relationship conditions and empathic responding. The experiential treatment consisted of the CC conditions, plus the use of specific process-directive Gestalt and experiential interventions at client markers indicating particular cognitive-affective problems. Treatments showed no difference in reducing depressive symptoms at termination and at six-month followup. The experiential treatment, however, had superior effects at midtreatment on depression and at termination on the total level of symptoms, self-esteem, and reduction of interpersonal problems (mean overall comparative effect size for PE vs. CC: +.33). The addition of specific active interventions at appropriate points in the treatment of depression appeared to hasten and enhance improvement.

Watson and Greenberg (1996) identified a pathway from in-session process and task resolution to postsession change and final outcome in the treatment of depression. Clients' degree of problem resolution correlated significantly with depth of client experiencing, and sustained resolution over treatment resulted in better outcome. Clients' task-specific postsession change scores correlated significantly with change in depression post-therapy and six months later, indicating that postsession change is related to reduction in symptoms. The two treatments also were compared on client process and outcome. The PE group showed significantly higher levels of experiencing, vocal quality and expressive stance, and greater problem resolution than the CC group in two of three PE interventions studied.

Weerasekera, Linder, Greenberg, and Watson (2001) examined the development of the working alliance in experiential therapy of depression. Results revealed that the alliance-outcome relation varied with alliance dimension (goal, task, or bond), outcome measure (symptom improvement vs. self esteem, relational problems), and when in-treatment alliance was measured. Analyses revealed that early alliance scores predicted outcome independently of early mood changes. Although no treatment group differences were found for bond and goal alliance, the PE group displayed higher task alliance scores in the midphase of therapy. The level of pre-treatment depression did not affect alliance formation.

In the York II depression study, Greenberg, Goldman, and Angus (2001) replicated the York I study by comparing the effects of CC and PE on 38 clients with major depressive disorder; they obtained a comparative effect size of +.71 in favor of PE therapy. They then combined the York I and II samples to increase power of detecting differences between treatment groups. Statistically significant differences among treatments were found on all indices of change for the combined sample. This provided evidence that the addition of PE interventions to the basic CC relationship conditions improves outcome.

In another recent study, Watson, Gordon, Stermac, Kalogerakos, and Steckley (2001) carried out a randomized clinical trial study comparing PE and CB therapies in the treatment of major depression. Sixty-six clients participated in 16 sessions of psychotherapy once a week. Results indicated that there were no significant differences between groups (comparative ES: +.11). Both treatments were effective in improving clients' level of depression, self-esteem, general symptom distress and dysfunctional attitudes. However, there were significant differences between groups with respect to two subscales of the Inventory of Interpersonal Problems: Clients in PE therapy were significantly more self-assertive and less overly accommodating at the end of treatment than clients in CB therapy. At the end of treatment, clients in both groups developed significantly more emotional reflection for solving distressing problems.

In a large, complex study involving three different substudies, King et al. (2000) compared CB and CC therapies to treatment as usual (primarily medication) for depressed clients seen in naturalistic primary care situations in the UK. One substudy (n = 62) was a three-way randomized clinical trial (RCT) comparing all three conditions; another substudy (n = 107) was a two-way RCT comparing CB to CC therapies; while the third substudy (n = 52) was a two-way preference trial in which clients were allowed to choose either CB or CC therapy. Measures included self-reports of symptoms and social adjustment measures, as well as estimates of cost, administered pre-therapy and two and ten months later. CC clients received an average of seven sessions. For CC therapy, overall pre-post effects varied from .88 (three-way RCT) to 1.17 (two-way RCT). Treatment comparisons found few if any differences between the three treatments: comparative ES for CC therapy vs. treatment as usual: +.10; comparative ESs for CB therapy: –.08 to –.19.

Brent et al. (1997) and Kolko, Brent, Baugher, Bridge, and Birmaher (2000) carried out a comparison between a nondirective-supportive therapy and two different CB treatments (individual and behavioral-systemic family therapy) with depressed adolescents, intending the nondirective therapy as a relational control condition. Using a wide variety of measures, they found a moderate degree of change over the course of therapy and followups (overall ES: .72) in the experiential therapy. The first report of this study (Brent et al., 1997) proclaimed the superiority of individual CB therapy on symptom measures; however, subsequent reports (e.g., Kolko et al., 2000), using 24-month followup data and a broader range of measures, including measures of cognitive and family functioning, produced overall no-difference findings (comparative ES: –.13).

Mestel and Votsmeier-Röhr (2000) reported on the results of a six-week integrative process-experiential inpatient program involving a large, naturalistic German sample of 412 moderately to severely depressed patients. Using measures of symptoms, interpersonal problems, and quality of self-relationship administered at pre-treatment, at discharge, and at 22-month followup, they obtained an overall pre-post effect of 1.05.

Rezaeian, Mazumdar, and Sen (1997) examined the effectiveness of psychodrama in changing the attitudes of 54 depressed male Iranian clients. Participants were divided into three treatment groups of 18 clients each: a psychodrama group, a conventional psychiatric treatment group, and a combination therapy. Measures of depression and personal attitudes toward family, sexual matters, and so on were administered before and 24 weeks after treatment. The psychodrama group therapy was more effective than the conventional psychiatric treatment in changing the attitudes of the participants. The combination of both psychodrama group therapy and conventional psychiatric treatment, however, turned out to be the best treatment. Nevertheless, the results from the combination of both psychodrama group therapy and conventional psychiatric therapy did not differ significantly from the psychodrama group therapy alone.

Meta-analysis and analysis of extent of empirical support. The meta-analysis data set contains 24 study samples of depressed clients, most commonly CC (nine samples) or PE (six samples). The mean pre-post effect size across these 23 samples is large (1.18; SD: .55). In contrast to the rest of the data set, the four controlled comparisons with no treatment or wait list controls indicate only a weak effect for therapy (mean-controlled ES: .12; SD: .39), including the only negative-controlled effect (Tyson & Range, 1987) in the data set, apparently an outlier involving a nonclinical sample. The 16 comparisons with nonexperiential therapies support an equivalence conclusion (mean comparative ES: –.02; SD: .69; $t(.4)= 2.23$, $p < .05$). In fact, substantial positive and negative comparative results are perfectly balanced (positive: 3; negative: 4; neutral: 9). Four of the comparisons between more and less process-directive experiential treatments involved depressed clients (mean comparative ES: +.41; SD: 25). It is worth noting, however, that in comparisons with nonexperiential therapies for depression, more process-directive therapies (ES: +.16; SD: .74) did not produce significantly better results than less process-directive therapies (ES: –.15; SD: .66; $t = –.89$; n.s.).

Given the balanced nature of the comparative effects, Chambless and Hollon's (1998) equivalence criterion is most relevant. In fact, both of the studies with large enough samples (> 25 per group; King et al., 2000; Watson et al., 2001) reported no-difference results for clients seen in experiential therapies as compared to CB therapy. In addition, when Greenberg, Goldman, and Angus (2001) combined data from the two York depression studies, they found that clients seen in PE therapy had a significantly better outcome than clients in another active treatment (CC therapy), thus adding support from a third study. Finally, the four comparisons between different experiential therapies (three significant differences involving two independent research settings) provide support for process-directive experiential therapies as specific and efficacious (Chambless & Hollon, 1998).

Treatment of Anger and Aggression

Wolfus and Bierman (1996) evaluated an integrative, PE treatment program, "Relating without Violence" (RWV), which was designed to ameliorate psychological and emotional factors believed to contribute to domestic violence and to strengthen conflict resolution skills in perpetrators of domestic violence. Participants were 57 perpetrators who participated in RWV, 20 perpetrators who did not, and 24 offenders with no history of violence. The group of offenders who participated in RWV showed statistically significant changes over and above the changes exhibited by the two comparison groups, demonstrating that RWV was effective in achieving its main objectives: it changed the way offenders who had committed domestic violence dealt with violence within the confines of the institution, and it resulted in the modification of personality traits associated with aggressive behavior. RWV led to a decrease in the use of destructive responses to conflict, both physical and psychological; reduced irritability and readiness for anger; and reduced defensiveness. The reduction in defensiveness, in particular, meant that program participants became less suspicious that other people meant them harm and became less likely to hold themselves in a constant state of readiness to counterattack in response to any perceived threats of emotional pain. The overall pre-post effect appears to be .96, with a comparative effect of +.33. However, the authors appear to have reported only scales on which there were significant differences; such selective reporting makes these values somewhat questionable.

A subsequent study (Goldman, Bierman, & Wolfus, 1996) examined changes in expressing anger for 48 RWV participants in groups. Results showed that before RWV the participants frequently experienced intense angry feelings which they expressed with little provocation in aggressive behavior directed toward others. The men's anger was initially higher than 90% of men in general. After participating in RWV, the men's experience and expression of anger declined significantly, and they were within the normal range for men (overall pre-post effect: 1.6, again based on selective reporting of data).

Serok and Levi (1993) assessed the efficacy of Gestalt therapy for a group of nine hard-core criminals as compared with nine hard-core criminals who met together but were not given Gestalt therapy. Participants were tested in prison before and after intervention using an instrument to measure internal locus of control and degree of assumption of personal responsibility. The findings in these areas, in addition to the observations of the prison's social worker, confirmed the effectiveness of the Gestalt therapy.

Though somewhat weak, these data involve a client population which in the past has not been considered appropriate for experiential therapy. The fact that some positive evidence has emerged suggests the need for further research on experiential approaches to working with clients with anger and aggression problems.

Schizophrenia and Severe, Chronic Dysfunction

Surprisingly, more than 30 years after the early disappointment of the Wisconsin Study (Rogers, Gendlin, Kiesler, & Truax, 1967) on the impact of CC therapy with clients diagnosed with schizophrenia, recent research in Europe has begun to provide support for the effectiveness of CC and other experiential therapies with clients suffering from severe, chronic difficulties, including schizophrenia and borderline personality processes.

Naturalistic Effectiveness Studies. Most of these studies are uncontrolled, naturalistic studies, some with large samples of clients treated in inpatient settings for 75 to 100 days (Teusch, 1990; Teusch et al., 1999; Tscheulin, 1995), and others in outpatient or day treatment settings (Snijders, Huijsman, de Groot, Maas, & de Greef, 2002; Tschuschke & Anbeh, 2000). Teusch and Tscheulin and their colleagues have, for example, provided reports that cover many hundreds of patients treated in inpatient settings in programs based on CC principles, often with adjunctive art, movement or occupational therapy, as well as 12-step programs and occasional medication. These studies are classic effectiveness studies that document the value of inpatient CC treatment program in real-world settings. For example, Tscheulin (1995) reported results for four mixed inpatient samples of clients, two followed to discharge (n = 1,426 and 632), and two followed over 18 months postdischarge (n = 92 and 156). Overall pre-post effect sizes varied from .53 to .78. Teusch and colleagues (1999) reported extensive test results for 248 clients with chronic, severe problems (overall pre-post ES: .88). Given the severity and chronicity of these clients difficulties, these effect sizes appear to be quite impressive, although the use of nonspecific client groups makes them difficult to interpret.

SCHIZOPHRENIA. Three studies involve treatment of clients diagnosed with schizophrenia (Eckert & Wuchner, 1996; Tarrier et al., 1998, 2000; Teusch, 1990). Eckert and Wuchner (1996) followed the treatment of 13 schizophrenia patients in a 100-day inpatient program based on CC principles (pre-post ES: .59), while Teusch evaluated 73 high-functioning schizophrenia patients in a similar 12-week inpatient program (ES: 1.54). In the only RCT in this area, Tarrier and colleagues (1998, 2000) used an additive design to study the incremental effects of CC supportive counseling and CB training on top of treatment as usual. CC treatment was intended as a relational control condition. Initial reports (Tarrier et al., 1998) on post-treatment outcome favored the cognitive therapy; however, this situation was completely reversed at 24-month followup, at which time the CC therapy was substantially better than CB (Tarrier et al., 2000) (overall comparative ES: +.08 vs. CB; +.31 vs. routine care). The mean pre-post ES for these three studies is .80.

SEVERE PERSONALITY DISORDERS. There are also two recent studies involving treatment of borderline and other severe personality disorders in addition to samples of clients with schizophrenia and severe depression, Eckert and Wuchner (1996) also reported large effects for a CC inpatient program used to treat clients with borderline personality disorder diagnoses (overall pre-post effect: 1.9). In addition, Snijders and others (2002) used an integrative experiential day treatment program to treat 72 clients with severe personality disorders (overall pre-post ES: .76).

META-ANALYSIS AND ANALYSIS OF EXTENT OF EMPIRICAL SUPPORT. The meta-analysis data set contains 15 studies of therapy with severely dysfunctional clients seen in inpatient or day treatment/aftercare settings, including the domestic violence offenders described in the previous section. The mean pre-post effect size is .85 (SD: .50), a large effect. In addition, there are 10 comparative studies (mean comparative ES: .02; SD: .42). Given the combination of large pre-post effects with zero-order comparative effects, there appears to be enough evidence to indicate that experiential therapies are possibly efficacious (Chambless & Hollon, 1998) and deserving of further investigation in the treatment of severe, chronic problems, including schizophrenia and borderline personality disorder.

Health-Related Problems

CANCER. Three studies have examined the effects of experiential-existential group therapies for people living with cancer. Spiegel, Bloom, and Yalom (1981; see also Spiegel, Bloom, Kraemer, & Gottheil, 1989) compared a supportive-existential group for women with metastatic breast cancer to treatment as usual. They showed that women in the supportive-existential group showed better improvement on psychological distress measures and substantially longer survival times (means of 31 vs. 11 months). In a later study, van der Pompe, Duivenvoorden, Antoni, Visser, and Heijnen (1997) randomly assigned patients who had been treated for early-stage breast cancer and were diagnosed with either positive axillary lymph nodes or distant metastases to either a 13-week experiential existential group psychotherapy (EEGP) program or a waiting list control (WLC) condition. Endocrine and immune measures were obtained before and after the intervention period. After the 13 weeks of treatment, clients in the EEGP group showed improvements on many measures (e.g., lower levels of plasma cortisol, percentages of natural killer cells). Importantly, this was only found in those breast cancer patients presenting relatively high endocrine and immune baseline levels, suggesting that the patients' profile with regard to endocrine and immune function at the start of a program can have an important effect. If replicated on a larger scale, these results might be relevant for the treatment of physical symptoms related to breast cancer.

However, in another study with patients with cancer, de Vries et al. (1997) examined the effect of experiential therapy on tumor progression in 35 patients in advanced stages of cancer, who were no longer amenable to regular medical treatment. Patients were offered 12 sessions of individual experiential-existential counseling, each session lasting 1.5 to 2 hours. In addition, every two weeks, patients participated in supportive group therapy sessions. Results show that in 5 out of 35 patients, tumor growth became stationary during or immediately following therapy. In four patients, this stationary period lasted three to nine months, and in one patient the period lasted two years. Natural killer cell activity, self-reported loneliness, depression, purpose in life, and locus of control showed no change from pre- to post-intervention (overall mean effect: .13).

Finally, Edelman, Bell, and Kidman (1999) also compared a 12-session supportive therapy group with a CB therapy group for patients with recently diagnosed breast cancer. Clients changed relatively little in either treatment (overall pre-post ES: .19; comparative ES: –.12).

HIV. Mulder, Emmelkamp, Antoni, Mulder, and associates (1994) examined the effectiveness of a CB group therapy and an experiential group psychotherapy program for 39 asymptomatic HIV-infected homosexual men. Both therapies consisted of 17 sessions over a 15-week period. Both psychosocial interventions decreased distress significantly, as compared with a waiting-list control group. The authors reported no significant changes in the intervention groups as compared with the control group in coping styles, social support, and emotional expression. CB and experiential therapies did not differ from each other in their effects on psychological distress or on the other psychosocial variables. In another analysis of the same sample, Mulder, Antoni, Emmelkamp, Veugelers, and associates (1995) examined the effects of CB group therapy and experiential group therapy on decline of immune functioning from pre-intervention to 24-month post-test with 26 HIV-infected homosexual men. No differences in the rate of decline of CD4 cells or T cell responses between the CB and experiential condition were found. T cell functioning increased in the combined treatment sample and did so to a greater extent than in control patients. However, there were no significant changes in CD4 cell count from pre- to post-intervention. Patients who showed larger decreases in psychological distress, however, showed a smaller decline in CD4 cell counts. Thus, this study provided some initial, tentative indication that experiential therapy groups may be helpful for persons living with HIV.

Other medical problems. Jacobi (1995) evaluated the effectiveness of Guided Imagery and Music (GIM) as a music-centered experiential therapy for persons with rheumatoid arthritis. It was hypothesized that therapeutically induced arousal of affect would facilitate the resolution of conflicting emotions and reduce reported pain and psychological distress. Twenty-seven patients receiving treatment in an outpatient clinic of a teaching hospital received individual sessions in GIM. Data were collected at entry, at the sixth GIM treatment session, and at two- and eight-week followup sessions. There were significant improvements in the level of psychological distress (e.g., SCL-90-R) and behavioral functioning (e.g., 50-foot walking speed).

Sachse (1995) applied goal-oriented CC therapy (similar to PE) to 29 clients with psychosomatic problems using a variety of measures. He found that clients with psychosomatic problems had difficulty exploring their emotions and other internal experiences, which necessitated longer treatment (mean 33 sessions). The first half of the treatment had to be devoted to helping clients learn how to access and describe their experiences. Once this was accomplished, however, these clients were quite able to benefit from experiential therapy. Pre-post effects were large (ES: 1.52).

Meta-analysis and analysis of extent of empirical support. The meta-analysis data set contains seven studies of clients with health-related problems seen in experiential therapies. The mean pre-post effect size is .59 (SD: .50), a medium effect, which is consistent with the generally smaller effects found with measures of physical functioning. In addition, there are five comparative studies (mean comparative ES: +.01; SD: .28) and five controlled studies (mean controlled ES: .70; SD: .57). Given the existence of these studies, there appears to be enough evidence to indicate that experiential therapies are possibly efficacious (Chambless & Hollon, 1998) and therefore deserving of further investigation as adjunctive treatments with physical problems such as cancer (see also Dircks, Grimm, Tausch, & Wittern, 1982; Katonah, 1991), HIV, psychosomatic problems (see also Meyer, 1981), and eating disorders (see also Holstein, 1990).

Research on Generic Therapeutic Processes

The central task in experiential therapy is the deepening of experience. An associated but not identical general task is increasing access to emotions and emotional arousal. These two overlapping but distinct generic client processes have received a fair amount of attention over this review period. As will become clear from the following review, it appears that it is helpful to promote deeper experiencing and emotional processing (general tasks) in experiential therapy. Deeper emotional processing involves both higher emotional arousal and reflection on the aroused experience (Greenberg, Korman, & Paivio, 2002). In addition to these generic processes, specific therapeutic tasks and the microprocesses involved in resolving these tasks have been studied. The specific tasks, though engaging clients in specific micro-level processes of change unique to each task, all seem to involve deeper emotional experience and processing. Research has also continued on two other general therapist processes: empathy and response modes (types of therapist speech act). Both empathy and more specific process-directive forms of intervention have been found to be useful in promoting the general client processes of experiencing and emotional processing. Research on the generic client and therapist processes will be reviewed first, followed by research on specific tasks.

Experiencing and Levels of Processing

The Experiencing Scales (Klein, Mathieu, Gendlin, & Kiesler, 1969; Klein, Mathieu-Coughlan, & Kiesler, 1986) measure the degree to which clients or therapists are fully engaged in their experience. Scores range from a 1, in which individuals narrate their experience in a detached manner and do not represent themselves as agents in their own narratives, to a 3, representing a simple, reactive emotional response to a specific situation, through a score of 4 in which a person focuses on feelings. At level 6, readily accessible feelings and meanings are synthesized to solve problems, and at level 7, clients are fully engaged in their momentary experience in a free-flowing, open, focused manner. Research on depth of experiencing in therapy has found a consistent relationship between depth of experiencing and outcome, especially in CC therapy (Bohart et al., 1996; Hendricks, 2002; Klein et al., 1986).

Greenberg, Watson, and Goldman (1998) argued that increases in depth of experiencing in successful brief treatments produce emotional problem-solving specific to core issues rather than overall change in level of functioning, as initially formulated by Rogers (1961). They further argued that previous failures to find a clear linear increase in experiencing over time in successful treatments (e.g.. Rogers et al., 1967) may have been due to the failure of these previous studies to rate experiencing on meaningful therapeutic episodes. Taking a perspective that change occurs in key events, they contended that taking experiencing measurements from random samples across therapy is not meaningful because random sampling misses important events. They proposed that resolution of key emotional issues is best measured by an increase in depth of experiencing on core themes and should relate to outcome.

Goldman and Greenberg (2001), therefore, identified segments in which clients were addressing core therapeutic themes, and found that increases across treatment in experiencing on these core themes predicted outcome on a range of measures). They found that increase in on-theme depth of experiencing, from early to late in therapy, was superior to the working alliance in predicting outcome. Higher experiencing while narrating traumatic events has also been correlated with better immune response (Lutgendorf, Antoni, Kumar, & Schneiderman, 1994).

In a recent study of *therapist* experiencing, Adams and Greenberg (1996), building on Goldman's study, found that the level of client experiencing to which therapist interventions referred predicted subsequent client level of psychotherapeutic experiencing and outcome. Therapists' interventions oriented toward internal client experience were found to exert an immediate influence in shifting clients from external to internal experience. Significant correlations between proportion of therapist-initiated client shifts from external to internal process and residual gain scores on the outcome measures were also found. Thus, within the context of experiential psychotherapy for depression, the level of client experience at which therapists aim their interventions can exert an immediate influence on client depth of experiencing and is related to reduced symptoms and increased self-esteem.

Level of client processing. Level of client cognitive-affective processing is a process closely related to client experiencing. In programs of research by Toukmanian (e.g., 1986, 1992), Sachse (see Sachse & Elliott, 2002) and Takens (2001), levels of client perceptual processing (LCPP) and client processing modes (PM) in therapy were studied. The LCPP scale consists of seven categories, each measuring a particular pattern of cognitive-affective processing (Toukmanian, 1986). The seven categories code client statements, from shallow to deep levels, as follows: undifferentiated statements, elaborations, differentiation with external focus, differentiation with analytic focus, differentiation with internal focus, reevaluation, and, finally, integration. The PM scale similarly measures levels of linguistic processing related to explication of meaning. Clients who gain more from treatment have been shown to be more likely to engage in more complex mental operations such as internally differentiating and integrating, and reevaluating (Stinckens, 2001; Toukmanian, 1992, Toukmanian & Grech, 1991), while clients with the greatest in-therapy gains in perceptual-processing tended to have greater pre-treatment to post-treatment gains on the measures of self-concept and perceptual congruence (Day, 1994).

Emotional Arousal Expression and Processing

Empirical evidence for the key role of emotion in therapy is growing. Recent process research has consistently demonstrated a relationship between in-session emotional activation and outcome in various therapies (Beutler, Clarkin, & Bongar 2000; Iwakabe, Rogan, & Stalikas, 2000; Jones & Pulos, 1993). For example, Korman (1998) has shown that emotion-focused, PE therapy of depression, when successful, led to significant changes in clients' emotional states. This research used the Emotion Episode (EE) method (Greenberg & Korman, 1993; Korman, 1998) to identify in-session episodes in which clients talk about their emotions. Clients with better outcomes showed significantly more changes in their emotions from early to late sessions than did clients with poorer outcomes.

Another source of evidence on the role of affective experience in psychotherapy comes from research on the expression of emotion. Mahrer and colleagues have shown that certain types of "good moments" in therapy (Mahrer et al., 1987) are characterized by emotional expression. Fitzpatrick, Peternelli, Stalikas, and Iwakabe (1999) studied two sessions conducted by Rogers (and six by Ellis) and found that good moments of therapy had significantly higher emotional involvement than a control sample of therapy segments, as measured by the Experiencing Scale and the Strength of Feeling Scale—Revised.

In terms of the measurement of emotional arousal, Burgoon, Le-Poire, Beutler, Engle, and colleagues (1993) found that both general and specific aspects of emotional arousal can be reliably rated from nonverbal behaviors. Vocal tension, nervous vocalizations and laughter, random body movement, and vocal expressiveness were all associated with higher global arousal. (Machado, Beutler, and Greenberg, 1999, also found that training in emotionally focused methods increases therapists' affect sensitivity to these sorts of emotion cues.)

Emotion has also been found to be important in resolving interpersonal problems. Research on the relationship between emotional arousal and the resolution of unfinished business with a significant other has shown that emotional arousal is significantly related to outcome (Greenberg & Foerster, 1996; Greenberg & Malcolm, 2002; Hirscheimer, 1996; Paivio & Greenberg, 1995). In addition, Raphael, Middleton, Martinek, and Misso (1993) concluded from reviews of the bereavement outcome literature that controlled studies offer general support for the beneficial effects of treatments that promote emotional expression in bereavement. Some studies, however, failed to demonstrate superior outcome for treatment over controls.

Furthermore, couples who showed higher levels of emotional experiencing accompanying a softening in the blaming partners' stance in therapy were found to interact more affiliatively and ended therapy more satisfied than couples who showed lower emotional experiencing (Greenberg, Ford, Alden, & Johnson, 1993). A similar effect of the expression of underlying emotion has been found in resolving family conflict in structural family therapy (Diamond & Liddle, 1996).

Although research suggests that the expression and arousal of emotion can contribute to change, this may be true only for some people with some types of concerns (cf. Pierce, Nichols, & DuBrin, 1983). For example, Rosner, Beutler, and Daldrup (2000) compared the role of emotional arousal and vicarious emotional experience in cognitive group therapy (CGT) and focused expressive psychotherapy (FEP; a manualized form of Gestalt therapy), two treatments with opposite process assumptions about the desirability of expressing emotions. Although the types of emotions generally experienced by CGT clients and FEP clients did not differ significantly overall, differences in arousal were found in group members who were either active or primarily observed during sessions (i.e., that actively participating clients in the FEP group expressed more emotion than those in the CGT group), while this was not true for the observing group members.

In spite of these promising indications of the importance of emotional involvement in therapy, the actual relationships between emotion, cognition, and somatic processes remain unclear. Arousal and expression of emotion alone may be inadequate in promoting change. For example, venting has not been found to be effective in reducing distress (Bushman, Baumeister, & Stack, 1999; Kennedy-Moore & Watson, 1999). Several theorists have concluded that discharge works best when combined with some form of cognitive processing, suggesting that therapeutic change is a function of a dual cognitive-affective process (Bohart, 1980; Greenberg & Safran, 1987; Mecheril & Kemmler, 1994). For example, expressing anger reduces hostile feelings only if it leads to coping with the stimulus—that is, only if it leads to changing the environment or one's perception of it. This points to the need for processing aroused emotion in order to make sense of it by symbolizing it in awareness and by clarifying its sources. Making sense of emotion in new ways also helps to break cycles of maladaptive automatic emotions.

Pos (1999) found that increase in depth of experiencing on Emotion Episodes across therapy predicted outcome in the treatment of depression, while Warwar and Greenberg (2000) showed that good outcome clients showed both higher emotional arousal and deeper levels on the Experiencing scale during Emotion Episodes. This indicated that emotional arousal, plus making sense of this arousal to solve problems (level six on the Experiencing scale), distinguished good and poor outcomes. Mergenthaler (1996) also found that emotional tone plus the use of more abstract words distinguished good and poor cases of dynamic and experiential therapy, again demonstrating that it is both emotion *and* reflection on emotion that is important to the change process. He demonstrated that an in-session emotion cycle (relaxation, increase in arousal, arousal plus reflection, more abstract reflection alone, and back to relaxation) is associated with good outcome. Stalikas and Fitzpatrick (1995) showed that in-session change was related to both higher levels of reflection and strength of feeling. These studies indicate that to be transformed, and transformative, emotion needs to be both aroused and reflected on.

Thus, the empirical literature on emotion in experiential psychotherapy suggests that therapies successfully targeting clients' emotional experience are associated with changes over treatment in clients' in-session emotional experiences. The type of emotional expression investigated, however, affects the outcomes found. Emotional arousal and expression in specific circumstances, and with certain types of individuals and problems, are related to constructive change in physical and mental health. The evidence also indicates that certain types of therapeutically facilitated emotional awareness and arousal, when expressed in supportive relational contexts and in conjunction with some sort of conscious cognitive processing of the emotional experience, is important for therapeutic change for many clients and problems.

Therapist Empathy

EMPATHY AND OUTCOME. Empathy has long been considered to be central to the change process in experiential-humanistic therapies (e.g., Barrett-Lennard, 1981; Rogers, 1975). In a recent meta-analysis of the general association between therapist empathy and client outcome, Bohart, Elliott, Greenberg, and Watson (2002) found a medium effect size (weighted, corrected r) of .30. This effect size is on the same order of magnitude as previous analyses of the relationship between therapeutic alliance and outcome (e.g., Horvath & Symmonds, 1991). Interestingly, only six of the existing studies involve experiential therapies, and the average association of empathy to outcome in these studies was .25, a value in the same range as the overall sample value. Clearly, empathy does not appear to be differentially effective in experiential therapies (and there was even a suggestion that it might be *more* important in cognitive behavioral therapies).

Further evidence for the effects of empathy on outcome comes from research on the outcome of CC therapy, analyzed in our meta-analysis (see also Elliott, 2002; Greenberg & Watson, 1998). Although the therapist in CC therapy intends to provide unconditional positive regard and congruence as well as empathy, the only obvious "technique" in classical client-centered therapy is therapist empathy; successful CC treatment therefore provides indirect evidence of the effects of empathy. Nevertheless, empathy is probably better conceived of as a "climate" variable created by both therapist and client together rather than as a variable unilaterally "provided" by the therapist.

EMPATHY: EXPERIENCE AND BEHAVIOR. Greenberg and Rosenberg (2000) qualitatively analyzed therapist reports of their experience of empathy based on tape-assisted process recall. Although the therapists reported occasionally feeling a little of what the client was feeling, this was not the predominant experience of being empathic. Rather, understanding, imagining, sensing, and thinking were the predominant processes involved in the therapist's experience of empathy. Taylor (1996) also explored psychotherapists' experiences of empathy with their clients in order to understand the characteristics and meanings of such experiences. Phenomenological analysis of interview texts of retrospective accounts of empathy in this study resulted in four major interrelated themes: Letting Go (of expectations), Connecting (with the client's experience), Being Responsible and Responsive (to the client), and Danger (of misunderstanding).

Vanaerschot (1999), in an intensive study of the characteristics of client and therapist-perceived change events, found that 82% of these events, taken from three long-term psychotherapies (two client-centered/experiential, one psychodynamic), contained high to medium (referred to as "varying") degrees of empathic attunement, while only 18% of the events had minimal empathic attunement. Client perception of empathy in these events was also found not to be dependent on the therapist response mode of reflection of feelings. Furthermore, the client-perceived helping processes that distinguished the high attunement events were insight into oneself, having the opportunity to and risking talking about personal issues, and searching together (Vanaerschot, 1997b).

Brodley (1994, 2001) recently provided some clues about what makes empathic responses effective. She selected therapist responses from her own and Rogers' tapes based on strong confirming responses by the client (e.g., "That's exactly it"). In her own sessions, she found that words for emotional components (like "tense," "hurt," and "furious") were used in only 31% of the therapist speech units, whereas words or phrases that refer to complex meanings (e.g., "feeling ignored") were used in 59% of the speech units. In the case material of Rogers, the proportion of both types of targets was lower, but the proportion between the two was similar. Furthermore, for both therapists, 55 to 66% of speech units contained brief and relatively common figures of speech (e.g., "part of you has been torn away"), which make the reflections more lively and personal, while 80 to 84% of their responses reflected the client's agency, either in relation to the outside world (two-thirds) or in relation to self (one-third).

Therapist Response Modes

An archive of 140 therapy session transcripts of Carl Rogers (Lietaer & Brodley, 1998) has provided a rich basis for studies on his response modes (e.g., Farber, Brink, & Raskin, 1996), and has proved useful for questioning assumptions about client-centered practice, especially its supposed nondirectiveness. A number of investigators have found that responses stemming from the therapist's frame of reference—feedback, confrontation, interpretation, and personal self-disclosure—are much more pronounced in Rogers' later demonstration sessions. There were 2 to 4% of responses from the therapist's frame of reference in the Chicago therapies, versus an average of about 10% in the later demonstration sessions (Brodley, 1994: Gundrum, Lietaer et al., 1999; Merry, 1996). These data show that the older Rogers became freer in "the use of self" and that his "content directivity" became a bit more pronounced. Gazzola and Stalikas (1997) also investigated qualitative differences between interpretations leading to different in-session client change events in six sessions conducted by Carl Rogers. Results indicated that significant in-session therapeutic phenomena were preceded by interpretations and that qualitative differences exist between interpretations that precede change events and those that do not. This investigation indicated that not only are interpretations used in CC therapy, but they are also efficient in producing in-session client change.

Stinckens (2001) compared the response profile of Rogers with the profile of a sample of neo-client-centered/experiential therapists and a sample of PE therapists, all working with the internal critic. The two comparison groups, in contrast to Rogers, used many more open exploratory questions (18% versus 1%) and much less reflection of *expressed* feelings (25% versus 63%). The rate of process directives (e.g., proposing that the client turn attention inside or speak to the empty chair) was quite high in the PE sessions in which chair dialogue was being used (23%), low but visible in the neo-client-centered/experiential sessions (5%) and almost nonexistent in Rogers' sessions. Similar differences are found when Rogers was compared to Perls in their interviews with Gloria (Missiaen, Wollants, Lietaer, & Gundrum, 2000). Leijssen et al. (2000) compared four therapists when they were doing client-centered therapy versus when they were doing focusing training: Although process directives were much higher in the focusing training sessions (16% versus 2%), content-directive responses (interpretation, feedback, confrontation) were much lower (3% versus 17%). Some studies have also shown that a variety of response modes such as exploratory reflections, open exploratory questions, and interpersonal responses (feedback, confrontation, and here-and-now disclosure of the therapist) are used in client-centered and experiential therapy (Davis, 1995; Lietaer & Dierick, 1996). All these findings show that a variety of response profiles occur within the experiential family of therapies; even within the same therapist large variations in style are often found.

Finally, a few studies have shown differences between experiential and other approaches. Vanaerschot (1997a) found a higher rate of reflection of expressed feelings and narrative aspects in experiential therapy than in psychodynamic therapy, while Vansteenwegen (1997) reported a greater focus on feelings of the individual partners in experiential couples therapy than in treatment with a communication therapist, who focused on the here-and-now interaction of the couple. Using a postsession therapist intervention-style questionnaire, Lietaer and Dierick (1999) compared three samples of experiential group therapists (client-centered, Gestalt, and psychodrama) with a sample of behavior group therapists and a sample of psychoanalytic group therapists. Although the three experiential suborientations were highly similar on the dimensions "Facilitating experiential exploration," "Meaning attribution," and "Personal presence," large differences were found on "Executive function," with psychodramatists and Gestalt therapists being more structuring and using more procedures. The psychoanalytic group was lowest on all dimensions except for "Meaning attribution" and highest on the subscale "Psychodynamic interpretation." Behavior therapists were lowest on the subscale "Psychodynamic interpretation" and highest on the subscale "Direction, advice, procedures."

These studies on response modes show that, besides some similarities, some striking differences between orientations are observed. An empathic moment-by-moment focus on the experiencing self of the client seems always to be more salient in experiential forms of therapy than in other approaches.

Research on Specific Therapeutic Tasks

In addition to the general therapeutic processes reviewed in the previous section, research has continued on several key experiential tasks, each characterized by a particular client sign of readiness (marker), a sequence of therapist actions and client in-session microprocesses, and definition of successful resolution (Greenberg et al., 1994).

Focusing on an Unclear or Painful Felt Sense

Focusing is a method devised to deepen client experiencing. In focusing (Gendlin, 1996), the therapist encourages the client to imagine an internal psychological "space" in which he or she feels things and then helps the client explore and symbolize experiences that are either unclear or painful. The full focusing procedure consists of six steps, each with its own markers or indicators, but the most common marker is the immediate presence of an unclear internal feeling ("felt sense"). Focusing is also sometimes used when the client is experiencing immediate painful feelings or is having trouble finding an internal focus. Recent studies have been done in Japan, North America, and Europe on factors that enhance the effectiveness of focusing. For example, Morikawa (1997) factor analyzed questionnaires from focusing sessions, finding that "clearing a space," "finding a right distance," and having a listener refer to their experiencing each helped clients focus. Iberg (1996) found that clients reported an increased impact of sessions in which therapists used focusing-type questions.

In the most extensive research program to date on focusing, Leijssen (1996) investigated whether focusing enhanced client-centered therapy. In an initial study, she took sessions with explicitly positive and negative evaluations by client or therapist and found that 75% of positive sessions contained focusing steps and only 33% of negative sessions contained focusing. In a second study (Leijssen, 1996), eight clients who successfully terminated therapy in less than 20 sessions were studied: Prominent use of focusing occurred in all eight cases; almost every session acquired an intense experience-oriented character in which the client discovered aspects of the problem which had remained hitherto out of reach. It is believed that all of these clients achieved contact with their bodily felt experience without being flooded by it. Leijssen (1996) also investigated whether long-term clients deemed to be stagnating in their therapy could be taught to focus and to increase experiencing level. Of the four clients studied, she found that the two clients who returned to their previous levels of experiencing after Focusing training both expressed unhappiness with their regular therapists and wished to continue with the Focusing trainer. For clients with low levels of experiencing, it appears that clients don't easily learn the skill. Thus, for focusing to take place and to be sustained, continued process direction is required (Leijssen, Lietaer, Stevens, & Wels, 2000).

Two-Chair Dialogue for Conflict Splits

This therapeutic task is most clearly manifested when clients present verbal statements of "splits," indicating that an experienced conflict between the two aspects of self. In general, resolution has been found to involve microprocesses such as deeper experiencing of feelings and needs and softening of an internal critical voice (Greenberg, 1979, 1983). Recent research on this task has continued to provide support for and elaboration of models of resolution, while also placing more focus on understanding self-critical processes. Mackay (1996) provided some empirical support for Greenberg's (1983) three-stage model of successful two-chair work, consisting of Opposition (conflict), Merging (softening and mutual understanding), and Integration (negotiation of mutually satisfying compromises). Moderate support was found for the model, but adding a Pre-opposition stage (for people who experienced a substantial interruption of contact) was also suggested. McKee (1995) found that clients engaged in two-chair dialogue tended to use significantly more focused (inwardly exploring) and emotional (distorted by overflow of emotion) vocal qualities than clients receiving empathic reflection. Furthermore, these clients also used significantly less externalizing (lecturing) and limited (emotionally restricted) vocal qualities.

Turning to self-criticism processes, Sicoli and Halberg (1998) investigated novice client performance using the Gestalt two-chair technique. The presence of "wants and needs" was found to be significantly greater overall for sessions in which the critic softened, compared to sessions with no softening. Similarly, Whelton and Greenberg (2000) found that high contempt and low resilience in response to the critic related to depression proneness.

In the most extensive study on conflict splits to date, Stinckens (2001) analyzed 75 episodes in which an inner critic was clearly present. She found that therapists use five strategies in working with the inner critic: (1) identifying it; (2) putting it at a distance; (3) empathically attuning to it; (4) shifting attention to organismic experiencing; and (5) integrating different parts of the self. In general, identifying the inner critic and shifting attention to organismic experiencing were most frequently used. Rogers typically made extensive use of the strategy of identifying the critic but avoided empathizing with it. In contrast to Rogers, contemporary client-centered/experiential psychotherapists were more likely to empathize with the critic (18% versus 2%). Process-experiential therapists working with the two-chair technique more frequently used the strategy of integrating parts of self and avoided putting the critic at a distance. In addition, Stinckens (2001) carried out more intensive analyses of a smaller number of critic episodes, finding that a variety of strategies were used flexibly in relation to the specific type of inner critic (e.g., rigid versus mild) in order to facilitate constructive change.

Empty-Chair Dialogue for Unfinished Business

This task, drawn from Gestalt therapy, addresses a class of processing difficulties in which schematic emotion memories of significant others continue to trigger the reexperiencing of unresolved emotional reactions. Thus, when one thinks of the other person, bad feelings ensue. This task involves reexperiencing the unresolved feelings in the safety of the therapeutic environment. The purpose of the intervention is to allow the person to express feelings fully to the imagined significant other (such as an alcoholic parent) in an empty chair. This helps remobilize the client's suppressed needs and the sense of entitlement to those needs, thereby empowering the client to separate appropriately from the other person. This occurs by either achieving a better understanding of the other or holding the other accountable for wrong done to the self (Greenberg & Foerster, 1996). Outcome research on the use of empathy and chair work for unfinished relationships (Paivio & Greenberg, 1995) were reviewed earlier in the section on trauma and abuse.

Process Research. O'Leary and Nieuwstraten (1999) explored the identification and exploration of "unfinished business" in Gestalt reminiscence therapy with seven older adults (all over 65 years old). Results showed that the initial expression of unfinished business by older adults is often in nonpersonal language and that the task of the therapist is to assist them in both personalizing the issue and exploring and finishing it.

A refined model of the microprocesses involved in change (developed by a task-analytic research program) was validated by comparing successful and unsuccessful resolution of unfinished business (Greenberg & Foerster, 1996). Four performance components—intense expression of feeling, expression of need, shift in representation of other, and self-validation or understanding of the other—were found to discriminate between resolution and nonresolution performances. McMain (1996) related changes in self-other schemas to psychotherapy outcome in the treatment of unfinished business. Measures of self-other schemas were based on ratings of clients' performances while engaged in an imaginary dialogue with a targeted significant other. The results indicated that successful outcome was predicted by change in the representation of the self. Specifically, increases in self-autonomy, self-affiliation, and positive responses of self in relation to the significant other were each predictive of treatment outcome at post-therapy and at four-month followup. Change in the representation of the other failed to predict treatment outcome. Using the same sample, Paivio and Bahr (1998) found that interpersonal problems at the beginning of treatment predicted alliance.

Greenberg and Malcolm (2002) demonstrated that clients who resolved their unfinished business with a significant other in a manner consistent with the model enjoyed significantly greater improvement in symptom distress, interpersonal problems, affiliation toward self, degree of unfinished business, and change in target complaints. This suggests that the components of resolution capture a clinically important process that relates to outcome. More specifically, a significantly greater number of clients in the resolved group were found to express intense emotions. In addition, almost all clients in the resolution group experienced the mobilization of an interpersonal need and a shift in their view of the other, while no clients in the unresolved group experienced a shift in their view of the other. These results provide evidence of the importance of emotional arousal in this task and showed that those clients who identified and expressed previously unmet interpersonal needs, and experienced a shift in their view of the other, changed more than those who did not engage in these processes. Finally, in a study of childhood maltreatment, Paivio, Hall, Holowaty, Jellis, and Tran (2001) found that high and low engagers in imaginal confrontations in empty-chair dialogue, differed significantly in their outcomes. High engagers achieved significantly greater resolution of issues with abusive and neglectful others, and reduced discomfort on current abuse-related target complaints.

The preceding studies, in combination, provide substantial evidence that degree of client engagement in expression of emotions and unmet needs during empty-chair work predicts successful resolution of unfinished issues with significant others.

Evocative Unfolding of Problematic Reactions

This task, identified in the context of CC therapy (Rice, 1974; Rice & Saperia, 1984), addresses a class of schematic processing difficulties that control interactions with other people and situations. The problematic reaction point (PRP) marker for this event consists of three identifiable features: a particular incident; a reaction on the part of the client; and an indication that the client views his or her own reaction as puzzling, inappropriate, or otherwise problematic. Watson and Rennie (1994) used the tape-assisted process recall to obtain clients' reports of their subjective experiences during the exploration of problematic reactions and found that clients alternated between two primary activities: symbolic representation of their experience and reflexive self-examination.

In addition, Watson (1996) found that resolution sessions, in contrast to nonresolution sessions, were characterized by high levels of referential activity (Bucci, 1993), which occurred when clients described a problematic situation and then immediately differentiated an emotional reaction. In these sessions, clients also reported a change in mood immediately following vivid descriptions of the problematic situation. These two studies highlight both the role that vivid description can play in promoting clients' emotional arousal during sessions and the role of self-reflection in the change process. These findings validate the proposition that vividly re-evoking the situation, and clients' subsequent differentiation of their subjective experience, are both necessary but different aspects of productive therapy process, and in particular are important steps in resolving problematic reactions (Greenberg et al., 1993; Rice & Saperia, 1984).

Creation of Meaning in Emotional Crises

Consistent with the interests of existential therapists, meaning creation events occur when a client seeks to understand the meaning of an emotional experience or crisis (Clarke, 1989, 1991). This task involves the linguistic symbolization of emotional experience when high emotional arousal is present. Clarke (1996) conducted a study to determine which client performance components distinguish successful from unsuccessful creation of meaning episodes. The test of the performance model revealed that it contained four steps that distinguished between successful and unsuccessful creation of meaning. These steps involved symbolization of the challenge to a cherished belief, the emotional reaction to that challenge, a hypothesis as to the origin of the belief, and an evaluation of the present tenability of the belief. The change processes involved in successful creation of meaning were demonstrated to include a cognitive and emotional dimension. The end result of creation of meaning—the change in a particular belief or the emotion attached to that belief—is similar to the result sought by cognitive interventions.

Body Work

Body work involves awareness and modification of breathing patterns (and sometimes therapeutic massage); it is a little-researched task in experiential therapy. Holmes, Morris, Clance, and Putney (1996) investigated the relationship between the use of Breath work and therapeutic changes in levels of distress associated with self-identified problems, death anxiety, self-esteem, and sense of affiliation with others. Two treatments were compared involving 24 adult clients, with one group participating in a combination of experientially oriented psychotherapy plus six monthly sessions of Breath work; the second group participated only in experientially oriented psychotherapy. The psychotherapy plus Breath work condition showed significant reductions in death anxiety and increase in self-esteem compared to the therapy alone condition.

Hershbell (1998) interviewed 11 adults in an advanced Gestalt therapy training program about their experience with Gestalt body-oriented interventions. The interventions included attention to breathing, therapist observation and mirroring of gestures and posture, directed awareness of a client's embodied sensations, and working with "I statements" that verbally expressed the observed bodily phenomena. Clients indicated that the methods heightened self-knowledge and contributed to the emergence of a new perspective for the future. The methods were experienced on several dimensions, most often as physical sensations, emotions and cognitions, and, less frequently, spiritually, intuitively, or as an energy phenomenon. These studies offer some support for the benefits of body-oriented methods in psychotherapy.

Intensive Process Research

Experiential-humanistic therapies have a long tradition of intensive process research. In this section, we review a few of the studies from the review period.

Client Agency. Rennie (2000) analyzed the opening moments of dialogue between a client and her therapist, making use of the client's commentary given during a tape-assisted process recall interview of the interaction. Even in this brief space of time, the client was found to have exerted conscious control over the therapy process. Such control is understood to be an expression of the client reflexivity, defined both as self-awareness and as agency within that self-awareness. This expression of agency complements Rennie's (1994) earlier finding of the prevalence of client deference in therapy. Bolger's (1999) qualitative analysis of the experience of emotional pain revealed that the experience of brokenness lies at the heart of emotional pain and that allowing the brokenness and staying with it with an increased sense of agency led to transformation of the sense of self (Greenberg & Bolger, 2001).

Narrative processes. Research on the construction of meaning in experiential therapy has been developed by investigators of narrative processes in therapy. Grafanaki and McLeod (1999) analyzed narrative processes in the construction of helpful and hindering events in experiential psychotherapy. Three main categories emerged from analysis of this material: therapist as audience, negotiation of a new story line, and co-construction of the story of therapy. A comparison of narrative processes occurring during helpful and hindering events revealed that helpful events were characterized by the experience of a sense of "flow" between participants, which facilitated the storytelling process. Results suggest that existing narrative approaches to therapy have not given enough attention to the role of the client-therapist relationship in enabling the client to construct a life narrative.

Levitt, Korman, and Angus (2000) found that in a good outcome dyad in the therapy of depression, metaphors of "being burdened" were transformed into metaphors of "unloading the burden" over the course of the therapy, while there was no transformation evident in the poor-outcome dyad. The good-outcome therapy tended to have a higher level of experiencing when discussing burden metaphors, in comparison with the poor-outcome therapy. Furthermore, in the exploration of metaphoric expressions, the successful dyad had more narrative sequences involving internal experiences.

Angus and colleagues' studies of narrative sequences have revealed interesting patterns associated with good outcomes in experiential therapies (Angus, Levitt, & Hardtke, 1999; Lewin, 2000). Using log-linear narrative-sequence analyses, Angus et al. (1999) found that perceptual process CC (Toukmanian, 1992), PE, and psychodynamic therapy dyads differed significantly from one another in terms of both the number of identified narrative sequences and the type of narrative sequences (external, internal, reflexive). More specifically, in the psychodynamic therapy sessions a pattern of reflexive (40%) and external (54%) narrative sequences predominated, with therapist and client engaged in a process of meaning construction (reflexive) linked to the client's descriptions of past and current episodic memories (external). In contrast, the PE therapy dyad evidenced a pattern of internal (29%) and reflexive (46%) narrative sequences, in which the client and therapist engaged in a process of identifying and differentiating emotional experiences (internal) and then generating new understandings of those experiences (reflexive) during the therapy hour. As compared to the other two dyads, the proportion of Internal narrative sequences was three times higher in PE therapy sessions than in the perceptual processing CC sessions and five times higher than in the Psychodynamic sessions. The primary goal of PE psychotherapy is to assist clients in developing more differentiated and functional emotion schemes. The evidence from these analyses indicates that this goal is achieved by an alternating focus on client exploration of experiential states (internal narrative modes/sequences), followed by meaning-making inquiries (reflexive narrative modes/sequences) in which new feelings, beliefs, and attitudes are contextualized and understood.

For its part, the perceptual processing CC therapy dyad revealed a pattern of consecutive reflexive narrative sequences (54%) occurring across topic segments in which clients and therapist engaged in extended reflexive analyses of both life events (external, 36%), and to a lesser extent emotional experiences (internal, 19%). The chaining of the reflective narrative sequences appeared to facilitate an extended client inquiry into core self-related issues in which automatic processing patterns were identified and challenged.

The Narrative Processes Coding System (NPCS; Angus et al., 1999) has also used to identify shifts in reflexive/meaning-making, internal/emotion-focused and external/event descriptions in therapy sessions (Lewin, 2000). Using this method, good-outcome experiential therapists were found to be twice as likely to shift clients to emotion-focused and reflexive narrative modes than poor-outcome experiential therapists. In addition, good-outcome depressed clients initiated more shifts to emotion-focused and reflexive discourse than poor-outcome clients. Depressed clients, who achieved good outcomes in brief experiential therapy, were found to spend significantly more time engaged in reflexive and emotion-focused discourse than were poor-outcome clients. These findings provide empirical support for the importance of emotion and reflexive processes in the treatment of depression.

Assimilation of Problematic Experiences. The assimilation model is a recent attempt at developing a stage model of how change occurs in successful therapy, one that lends itself to intensive, narrative case study research. According to this model, therapeutic progress consists of the successive assimilation of problematic experiences into the client's schemata. The Assimilation of Problematic Experiences Scale (APES; see Honos-Webb, Stiles, Greenberg, & Goldman, 1998; Honos-Webb, Surko, Stiles, & Greenberg, 1999) is a 0 to 7, fully anchored rating scale of the degree of assimilation of a particular problematic experience, from Level 0, Warded Off, through Level 7, Mastery.

Honos-Webb, Stiles, Greenberg, and Goldman (1998) applied the assimilation model to two cases of process-experiential psychotherapy, one with good outcome and one with relatively poor outcome. Qualitative analysis of the successful client's transcripts suggested that assimilation occurred over time in at least three problematic experiences. Analysis of three themes in the less successful therapy indicated that the client made progress but that assimilation was blocked at two levels of the assimilation sequence. In a further qualitative assimilation analysis of the successful case, the researchers excerpted 43 relevant passages tracking two major themes and rated each passage on the APES (Honos-Webb, Surko, Stiles, & Greenberg, 1999). Ratings by independent raters who used a marker-based APES manual were highly correlated with the investigators' consensus ratings. APES ratings tended to increase across sessions, as expected in successful therapy. In this study, the client's dominant "superwoman" voice was shown to assimilate a voice of need and weakness, while her dominant "good-girl" voice assimilated a voice of rebellion and assertiveness, yielding a more complex and flexible community of voices within the self. This was interpreted as supporting an emerging formulation of the self as a "community of voices," leading to a reformulation of the goal of therapy as facilitating diversity and tolerance among the different self-aspects or voices.

CONCLUSIONS

EXPERIENTIAL THERAPIES AS EMPIRICALLY SUPPORTED TREATMENTS. In contrast to our previous review (Greenberg et al., 1994), we have emphasized outcome research in this summary. This is not because we favor outcome research over process research, but rather because the political nature of the current historical moment requires the collection, integration, and dissemination of information about the large body of accumulated evidence, in the face of numerous challenges to experiential-humanistic therapies in several countries, including the United States, United Kingdom, Germany, the Netherlands, and Australia (to mention only those with which we are most familiar).

At the same time, there is much more solid evidence for the efficacy and effectiveness of these therapies than at our last review. The data on experiential therapy outcome research has grown rapidly, with half of the existing studies appearing in the past 10 years. This has allowed us to pursue more sophisticated strategies than in our previous reviews, including equivalence analyses, weighting of effect sizes, controls for researcher allegiance, and analysis of bodies of evidence on specific client problems. These analyses go a long way toward meeting the demands implicit in the criteria put forward by the APA Division 12 Task Force and others (e.g., Chambless & Hollon, 1998; Meyer, Richter, Grawe, von Schulenburg, & Schulte, 1991; Nathan, 1996; Roth & Fonagy, 1996).

In fact, we have argued that for some classes of client problems, the existing research is now more than sufficient to warrant a positive valuation of experiential therapy in four important areas: depression, anxiety disorders, trauma, and marital problems, even using the strict version put forward by Chambless and Hollon (1998; the successor to the APA Division 12 Criteria). First, for depression, experiential therapies have been researched extensively, to the point where the claim of empirical support as "efficacious" (based on equivalence to established treatments or superiority to another active treatment in two or more independent research settings) can be supported for experiential therapies in general and for PE therapy in particular (see Greenberg et al., 2001; King et al., 2000; Watson et al., 2001). In addition, the PE therapy suborientation warrants the claim of empirical support as "specific and efficacious" (based on superiority to another treatment or equivalence to an established treatment in two or more research settings; see Greenberg et al., 2000; Watson et al., 2001).

Second, for anxiety disorders, the existing evidence is mixed but sufficient to warrant a verdict of "possibly efficacious." (At least one study shows "equivalence" to an established treatment; see Borkovec & Mathews, 1988 and Shear et al., 1994.) However, the available evidence on treatment of panic and generalized anxiety also suggests that experiential therapies may be less efficacious than CB therapies. Although this may reflect researcher allegiance effects, the possibility may also be cause for concern among experiential therapists treating these disorders.

Third, for helping clients deal with the sequelae of traumatic and abusive events, the evidence we reviewed points to a conclusion that PE therapies are "specific and efficacious" treatments (see Clarke, 1993; Paivio & Greenberg, 1995; Paivio & Nieuwenhuis, 2001; Souliere, 1995). The existing data do not speak directly to the efficacy of CC therapy with these problems, and so it is not yet known the extent to which the active, process-directive elements of PE therapy are important elements of work with trauma and abuse survivors.

Fourth, while individual therapy is emphasized here, emotionally focused therapy (EFT) for couples (e.g., Greenberg & Johnson, 1988; Johnson & Greenberg, 1985a) continues to gain research support as an experiential treatment for marital distress. Now, with 10 pre-post studies (mean ES: 1.40), six controlled studies (mean ES:

1.93), and five comparative outcome studies (mean ES: +.89), EFT has the best track record of any experiential therapy and was moved from "probably efficacious" to "efficacious and possibly specific" in a recent review (Baucom, Mueser, Shoham, & Daiuto, 1998) using the Chambless-Hollon criteria.

CONTINUING DIFFERENTIATION OF KEY EXPERIENTIAL PROCESSES. The review period also saw continuing work on such central therapeutic processes as experiencing, emotional arousal and expression, and empathy. In particular, recent research supports the idea that although deeper emotional experiencing and emotional arousal are important in therapy, researchers need to focus on these processes not in general but rather during key therapeutic episodes and in relation to important client content themes. As for emotional arousal, the evidence suggests that it is not sheer emotional experiencing and expression by itself that is therapeutic; rather, *what is critical is emotional expression in conjunction with reflective processing.* Thus, the therapist works with the client to construct or reconstruct a meaning perspective on the emotional experience. We have also noted the reemergence of the previously moribund area of therapist empathy in the form of a book (Bohart & Greenberg, 1997) and a meta-analysis of the general psychotherapy literature (Bohart et al., 2002), as well as interesting new work on the nature of empathy. The meta-analysis suggested that empathy is an "empirically supported relational element" of psychotherapy in general. As to therapist response modes, recent research has shown that empathic reflection is no longer the only key therapist response, but that a variety of more process-directive therapist responses have come to be used in a flexible way within a broadly conceived empathic-experiential therapy process. At the same time, process research has continued on important therapeutic tasks, including empty-chair work, two-chair work, evocative unfolding, meaning creation, and focusing. This research is building on previous research-informed task models, providing confirmation in some cases, and clarification and differentation in others. Clearer links between process and outcome have been identified.

PROMISING EMERGING AREAS. Beyond the client problems that have now been shown to be "efficacious" or "efficacious and specific," and the key therapeutic processes that are gathering empirical support and clarification, we uncovered several promising areas worthy of further study. Even at this time, however, using the Chambless and Hollon (1998) criteria, there is enough evidence to designate most of these promising new approaches as "possibly efficacious." Part of what is so interesting about these areas is that none of them falls within the axis of depression-anxiety-trauma-interpersonal difficulties that have traditionally been seen as the purview of experiential-humanistic therapies. First, based on a small number of naturalistic studies, experiential treatments for problems related to anger and aggression (especially domestic violence) have gained some support (e.g., Wolfus & Bierman, 1996). Second, experiential therapies have emerged as viable alternatives for problems of severe client dysfunction, including schizophrenia (see Tarrier et al, 1998; Teusch, 1990) and severe personality disorders (see Eckert & Wuchner, 1996; Snijders et al., 2002; Tscheulin, 1996). Third, multiple studies—mostly naturalistic—now exist on various health-related problems, including cancer (e.g., Edelman et al., 1999), HIV (e.g., Mulder et al., 1994), and psychosomatic problems (e.g., Sachse, 1995). In other words, experiential therapies show promise as possibly efficacious treatments for a variety of problems of pressing societal significance, touching on areas of criminal justice, severe and persistant mental illness, and the healthcare system.

THE PROCESS-DIRECTIVENESS ISSUE. As we have shown in the meta-analysis, process-directive experiential therapies such as PE, Gestalt, and emotion-focused therapy for couples appear to have somewhat larger effect sizes and to do better when pitted against CB and nondirective (CC and supportive-nondirective) therapies. Although we tend to take these results as indicating a slight superiority for process directive over nondirective experiential therapies, we are aware that it is also possible that researcher allegiance effects are once again operating, since much of the current pro-experiential therapy research has been carried out by PE and emotionally focused therapy researchers, while much of the research on less directive therapies such as CC therapy has been conducted by CB-oriented researchers looking for "relational controls."

In spite of our own theoretical "reviewer allegiance" to the process-directive therapies, we continue to find ourselves impressed by the robustness of the client-centered (or person-centered, as it is commonly called today) approach to therapy. Time and time again, nonexperiential therapy researchers have been surprised by the long-term effectiveness of CC and nondirective-supportive therapies, even when these were intended as control groups (two recent examples: Kolko et al., 2000; Tarrier et al., 2000). After more than 50 years, it appears unwise to dismiss Rogers' original vision of the optimal therapeutic relationship and its healing power.

Recommendations for research. Although the field of experiential therapy research has made signal progress during the past 10 years, more research is needed. It is essential to clarify the parameters of client response in well-researched areas such as depression, for example, by studying depressed adolescents (e.g., Brent et al., 1997) or by trying to optimize treatments (e.g., comparing more vs. less process-directive therapies). Experiential therapy research has achieved momentum, and it is essential that this momentum be maintained. Experiential therapists and others looking for resources to help them begin doing research may find it useful to check out the following website for measures, research bibliographies, protocols, and criteria: www.experiential-researchers.org.

Second, we have outlined some promising client problem areas that warrant development as substantial areas of research, including severe client problems, anger and aggression, and health-related problems.

Third, research on health outcomes and costs is needed. The initial evidence suggests that health consequences are a neglected but important topic for outcome research. Furthermore, if experiential therapists continue to seek funding and training support from government and private insurance, cost research is needed to justify the investment of "other people's money." The recent study of King and colleagues (2000) documenting the cost of CC versus cognitive behavior therapy for treating depression in primary care settings is a good start in this direction, but much more, and more sophisticated, research are needed.

Fourth, elaboration of emotion theory (e.g., Greenberg, Korman, & Paivio, 2002) has led to greater appreciation of how emotion is expressed in the human brain, as part of a dynamic, three-way interaction between brain processes, behavior, and experience. Such a systemic view is nonreductionist and entirely consistent with humanistic principles. Following from this, over the next 10 years, we hope to see brain scanning methods applied to studying change in clients in experiential therapies.

Fifth, in order to remain in the research arena, experiential therapists need not simply attack previous attempts to develop criteria for designating experiential therapies as "empirically supported," but need to develop alternative criteria that are more appropriate to the assumptions and goals of experiential therapies (Bohart et al., 1998; Elliott, 2000; McLeod, 2001) and to the well-being of their clients.

Practical training implications. We conclude with the proposition that the neglect of experiential therapies in many training programs is no longer warranted. Experiential therapies should generally be offered in graduate programs and internships, especially as treatments for depression and trauma, relationship problems, and possibly for other client problems as well. In training programs that have emphasized CB therapy to the exclusion of other approaches, the evidence is now strong enough for us to recommend that experiential-humanistic therapies should be considered empirically supported treatments. In fact, the student's education as psychologist is incomplete without a greater emphasis on such training.

Acknowledgment

We acknowledge the contributions of the many colleagues who sent us information on their research; we ask them to continue sending omitted or new studies. In addition, we thank Julia von Starck for translation assistance; and Robert Janner and Deanna House for bibliographic assistance.

References

Adams, K. E., & Greenberg, L. S. (June, 1996). Therapists' influence on depressed clients' therapeutic experiencing and outcome. Forty-third Annual Convention for the Society for Psychotherapy Research, St. Amelia Island, FL.

Anderson, A., & Levitt, H. (June, 2000). Evaluating outcomes of experiential psychotherapy: A quantitative review. Paper presented at meeting of Society for Psychotherapy Research, Chicago, IL.

Angus, L., Levitt, H., & Hardtke, K. (1999). The Narrative Processes Coding System: Research applications and implications for psychotherapy practice. *Journal of Clinical Psychology, 55*, 1255–1270.

*Baehr, G. O. (1954). The comparative effectiveness of individual psychotherapy, group psychother-

* Indicates studies included in meta-analysis

apy, and a combination of these methods. *Journal of Consulting Psychology, 18*, 179–183.

*Barrett-Lennard, G. T. (1962). Dimensions of therapist response as causal factors in therapeutic change. *Psychological Monographs, 76(43)*, 1–36.

Barrett-Lennard, G. T. (1981). The empathy cycle: Refinement of a nuclear concept. *Journal of Counseling Psychology, 28*, 91–100.

Barrett-Lennard, G. T. (1998). *Carl Rogers' helping system: Journey and substance.* London, UK: Sage Publications.

Barrowclough, C., Kind, P., Colville, J., Russell, E., Burns, A., & Tarrier, N. (2001). A randomized trial of the effectiveness of cognitive-behavioral therapy and supportive couseling for anxiety symptoms in older adults. *Journal of Consulting and Clinical Psychology, 69*, 756–762.

Baucom, D. H., Mueser, K. T., Shoham, V., & Daiuto, A. D. (1998). Empirically supported couple and family interventions for marital distress and adult mental health problems. *Journal of Consulting and Clinical Psychology, 66*, 53–88.

*Beck, A. T., Sokol, L., Clark, D. A., Berchick, R., & Wright, F. (1992). A crossover study of focused cognitive therapy for panic disorder. *American Journal of Psychiatry, 149*, 778–783.

Beutler, L. E., Clarkin, J. F., & Bongar, B. (2000). *Guidelines for the systematic treatment of the depressed patient.* New York: Oxford University Press.

*Beutler, L. E., Engle, D., Mohr, D., Daldrup, R. J., Bergan, J., Meredith, K., & Merry, W. (1991). Predictors of differential response to cognitive, experiential, and self-directed psychotherapeutic procedures. *Journal of Consulting and Clinical Psychology, 59*, 333–340.

*Beutler, L. E., Frank, M., Schieber, S. C., Calver, S., & Gaines, J. (1984). Comparative effects of group psychotherapies in a short-term inpatient setting: An experience with deterioration effects. *Psychiatry, 47*, 66–76.

*Beutler, L. E., & Mitchell, R. (1981). Differential psychotherapy outcome among depressed and impulsive patients as a function of analytic and experiential treatment procedures. *Psychiatry, 44*, 297–306.

*Bierenbaum, H., Nichols, M. P., & Schwartz, A. J. (1976). Effects of varying session length and frequency in brief emotive psychotherapy. *Journal of Consulting and Clinical Psychology, 44*, 790–798.

Biermann-Ratjen, E.-M., Eckert, J., & Schwartz, H.-J. (1995). *Gesprächspsychotherapie. Verändern durch Verstehen* (7th rev. ed.). Stuttgart: Kohlhammer.

*Boeck-Singelmann, C., Schwab, R., & Tönnies, S. (1992). Klientenzentrierte Psychotherapie in Form von Teamtherapie. In M. Behr, U. Esser, F. Petermann, W. M. Pfeiffer, & R. Tausch (Eds.), *Personzentrierte Psychologie & Psychotherapie* (pp. 9–23). Köln: GwG-Verlag. [Cited in S. Tönnies. (1994). *Selbst-kommunikation: Empirische Befunde zu Diagnostik und Therapie.* Heidelberg, Germany: Roland Asanger.]

Bohart, A. (1980). Toward a cognitive theory of catharsis. *Psychotherapy: Theory, Research and Practice, 17*, 192–201.

Bohart, A. C., et al. (1996). Experiencing, knowing, and change. In R. Hutterer, G. Pawlowsky, P. F. Schmid, & R. Stipsits (Eds.), *Client-centered and experiential psychotherapy. A paradigm in motion* (pp. 199–211). Frankfurt am Main: Peter Lang.

Bohart, A. C., Elliott, R., Greenberg, L. S., & Watson, J. C. (2002). Empathy redux: The efficacy of therapist empathy. In J. Norcross (Ed.), *Psychotherapy relationships that work.* New York: Oxford University Press.

Bohart, A., & Greenberg, L. (Eds.) (1997). *Empathy Reconsidered: New Directions in Theory Research & Practice.* Washington, DC: APA Press.

Bohart, A. C., O'Hara, M., & Leitner, L. M. (1998). Empirically violated treatments: Disenfranchisement of humanistic and other psychotherapies. *Psychotherapy Research, 8*, 141–157.

*Böhme, H., Finke, J., & Teusch, L. (1999). Effekte stationärer Gesprächspsychotherapie bei verschiedenen Krankheitsbildern: 1-Jahres-Katamnese [Effects of inpatient client-centered psychotherapy on several disorders]. *Psychotherapie Psychosomatik Medizinische Psychologie, 48*, 20–29. [used for CGI ratings]

Bolger, E. (1999). Grounded theory analysis of emotional pain. *Psychotherapy Research, 99*, 342–362.

*Borkovec, R., & Costello, E. (1993). Efficacy of applied relaxation and cognitive-behavioral therapy in the treatment of generalized anxiety disorder. *Journal of Consulting and Clinical Psychology, 61*, 611–619.

*Borkovec, T. D., & Mathews, A. (1988). Treatment of nonphobic anxiety disorders: A comparison of nondirective, cognitive, and coping desensitization therapy. *Journal of Consulting and Clinical Psychology, 56*, 877–884.

*Borkovec, T. D., Mathews, A. M., Chambers, A., Ebrahimi, S., Lytle, R., & Nelson, R. (1987). The effects of relaxation training with cognitive or nondirective therapy and the role of relaxation-induced anxiety in the treatment of generalized anxiety. *Journal of Consulting and Clinical Psychology, 55*, 883–888.

*Braaten, L. J. (1989). The effects of person-centered group therapy. *Person-Centered Review, 4*, 183–209.

*Brent, D. A., Holder, D., Kolko, D., Birmaher, B., Baugher, M., Roth, C., & Johnson, B. (1997). A clinical psychotherapy trial for adolescent depression comparing cognitive, family, and supportive treatment. *Archives of General Psychitary, 54*, 877–885.

Brodley, B. T. (1994). Some observations of Carl Rogers' behavior in therapy interviews. *The Person-Centered Journal, 1(2)*, 37–47.

Brodley, B. T. (2001). Observations of empathic understanding in a client-centered practice. In S. Haugh & T. Merry (Eds.), *Empathy* (pp. 16–37). Llangarron, Ross-on-Wye: PCCS Books.

*Bruhn, M. (1978). *Kurz- and längerfristige Auswirkungen personenzentrierter Gesprächsgruppen (Encounter) bei Klienten einer psychotherapeutischen Beratungsstelle.* Unveröff. Diss., Universität Hamburg. [Cited in S. Tönnies. (1994). *Selbst-kommunikation: Empirische Befunde zu Diagnostik und Therapie.* Heidelberg, Germany: Roland Asanger.]

Bucci, W. (1993). Primary process analogue: The referential activity (RA) measure. In N. E. Miller, *Psychodynamic treatment research: A handbook for clinical practice* (pp. 387–406). New York: Basic Books.

Burgoon, J. K., Le Poire, B. A., Beutler, L. E., Engle, D., et al. (1993). Nonverbal indices of arousal in group psychotherapy. *Psychotherapy: Theory, Research, Practice, Training, 30,* 635–645.

Bushman, B. J., Baumeister, R. F., & Stack, A. D. (1999). Catharsis, aggression, and persuasive influence: Self-fulfilling or self-defeating prophecies? *Journal of Personality and Social Psychology, 76,* 367–376.

Cain, D., & Seeman, J. (Eds.) (2001). *Humanistic psychotherapies: Handbook of research and practice.* Washington, DC: APA Publications.

Chambless, D. L., & Hollon, S. D. (1998). Defining empirically supported therapies. *Journal of Consulting and Clinical Psychology, 66,* 7–18.

Clarke, K. M. (1989). Creation of meaning: An emotional processing task in psychotherapy. *Psychotherapy, 26,* 139–148

Clarke, K. M. (1991). A performance model of the creation of meaning event. *Psychotherapy, 28,* 395–401.

Clarke, K. M. (1993). Creation of meaning in incest survivors. *Journal of Cognitive Psychotherapy, 7,* 195–203.

Clarke, K. M. (1996). Change processes in a creation of meaning event. *Journal of Consulting and Clinical Psychology, 64,* 465–470.

*Clarke, K. M., & Greenberg, L. S. (1986). Differential effects of the gestalt two-chair intervention and problem solving in resolving decisional conflict. *Journal of Counseling Psychology, 33,* 11–15.

Cohen, J. (1988). *Statistical power analysis for the behavioral sciences* (2nd ed.). Hillsdale, NJ: Erlbaum.

*Cross, D. G., Sheehan, P. W., & Khan, J. A. (1982). Short- and long-term follow-up of clients receiving insight-oriented therapy and behavior therapy. *Journal of Consulting and Clinical Psychology, 50,* 103–112.

Cummings, A. L. (1999). Experiential interventions for clients with genital herpes. *Canadian Journal of Counselling, 33,* 142–156.

*Dahl, A. A., & Waal, H. (1983). An outcome study of primal therapy. *Psychotherapy and Psychosomatics, 39,* 1554–1564.

Daldrup, R., Beutler, L., Engle, D., & Greenberg, L. (1988). *Focused expressive therapy: Freeing the overcontrolled patient.* London: Cassell.

*Dandeneau, M., & Johnson, S. (1994). Facilitating intimacy: A comparative outcome study of emotionally focused and cognitive interventions. *Journal of Marital and Family Therapy, 20,* 17–33.

Davis, K. L. (1995). The role of therapist actions in process-experiential therapy. *Dissertation Abstracts International, 56,* 519B.

Day, S. (1994). *Self-concept, schematic processing and change in Perceptual Processing Experiential Therapy.* Unpublished MA thesis, York University.

*Dessaulles, A. (1991). *The treatment of clinical depression in the context of marital distress.* Unpublished doctoral dissertation, University of Ottawa. [information taken from Johnson, S. M., Hunsley, J., Greenberg, L., & Schindler, D. (1999). Emotionally focused couples therapy: Status and challenges. *Clinical Psychology: Science and Practice, 6,* 67–79.]

*de Vries, M. J., Schilder, J. M., Mulder, C. L., Vrancken, A.M.E., Remie, M. E., & Garssen, B. (1997). Phase II Study of psychotherapeutic intervention in advanced cancer. *Psycho-Oncology, 6,* 129–137.

Diamond, G., & Liddle, H. A. (1996). Resolving a therapeutic impasse between parents and adolescents in multidimensional family therapy. *Journal of Consulting and Clinical Psychology, 64,* 481–488.

*DiLoreto, A. (1971). *Comparative psychotherapy: An experimental analysis.* Chicago: Aldine-Atherton.

*Dircks, P., Grimm, F., Tausch, A-M., & Wittern, J-O. (1982). Förderung der seelischen Lebensqualität von Krebspatienten durch personenzentrierte Gruppengespräche. *Zeitschrift für Klinische Psychologie, 9,* 241–251.

*Durak, G. M., Bernstein, R., & Gendlin, E. T. (1997). Effects of focusing training on therapy process and outcome. *Focusing Folio, 15(2),* 7–14.

*Eckert, J., & Biermann-Ratjen, E. M. (1990). Client-centered therapy versus psychoanalytic psychotherapy: Reflections following a comparative study. In G. Lietaer, J. Rombauts, & R. Van Balen (Eds.), *Client-centered and experiential psychotherapy in the nineties* (pp. 457–468). Leuven, Belgium: Leuven University Press.

*Eckert, J., & Wuchner, M. (1996). Long-term development of borderline personality disorder. In R. Hutterer, G. Pawlowsky, P. E. Schmid, & R. Stipsits (Eds.), *Client-centered and experiential psychotherapy. A paradigm in motion* (pp. 213–233). Frankfuram main: Peter Lang.

*Edelman, S., Bell, D. R., & Kidman, A. D. (1999). Group CBT versus supportive therapy with patients who have primary breast cancer. *Journal of Cognitive Psychotherapy, 13,* 189–202.

Elliott, R. (1996). Are client-centered/experiential therapies effective? A meta-analysis of outcome research. In U. Esser, H. Pabst, & G-W Speierer (Eds.), *The power of the Person-Centered-Approach: New challenges-perspectives-answers* (pp. 125–138). Köln, Germany: GwG Verlag.

Elliott, R. (1998). Editor's introduction: A guide to the empirically-supported treatments controversy. *Psychotherapy Research, 8,* 115–125.

Elliott, R. (September 2000). *Proposed criteria for demonstrating empirical support for humanistic and other therapies: Working draft.* Available on Internet: http://experiential-researchers.org/methodology/humanist.html

Elliott, R. (2002). Research on the effectiveness of humanistic therapies: A meta-analysis. In D. Cain & J. Seeman (Eds.), *Humanistic psychotherapies: Handbook of research and practice* (pp. 57–81). Washington, DC: APA.

*Elliott, R., Davis, K., & Slatick, E. (1998). Process-experiential therapy for post-traumatic stress difficulties. In L. Greenberg, G. Lietaer, & J. Watson (Eds.), *Handbook of experiential psychotherapy* (pp. 249–271). New York: Guilford Press.

Elliott, R., Stiles, W. B., & Shapiro, D. A. (1993). "Are some psychotherapies more equivalent than others?" In T. R. Giles (Ed.), *Handbook of effective psychotherapy* (pp. 455–479). New York: Plenum Press.

*Elliott, R., Wagner, J., Nathan-Montano, E., Urman, M., Slatick, E., Jersak, H., & Gutiérrez, C. (April 1999). Outcome of process experiential therapy in a naturalistic treatment protocol. Poster Presented at Medical College of Ohio Annual Symposium on Research in Psychiatry, Toledo, Ohio.

*Ends, E. J., & Page, C.W.A. (1957). A study of three types of group psychotherapy with hospitalized male inebriates. *Quarterly Journal of Studies in Alcohol, 8,* 263–277.

*Ends, E. J., & Page, C.W.A. (1959). Group psychotherapy and concomitant psychological change. *Psychological Monographs, 73,* Whole No. 480, 1–31.

*Engel-Sittenfeld, P., Engel, R. R., Huber, H. P., Zangel, K. (1980). Wirkmechanismen psychologischer Therapieverfahren bei der Behandlung chronischer Schlafstörungen. *Zeitschrift für Klinische Psychologie, 9,* 34–52.

*Eymael, J. (1987). *Gedragstherapie en client-centered therapie vergeleken* [Behavior therapy and client-centered therapy compared]. Leuven, Belgium: Acco.

Farber, B. A., Brink, D. C., & Raskin, P. M. (Eds.). (1996). *The psychotherapy of Carl Rogers. Cases and commentary.* New York: Guilford Press.

*Felton, G. S., & Davidson, H. R. (1973). Group counseling can work in the classroom. *Academic Therapy, 8,* 461–468.

*Fife, B. L. (1978). Reducing parental overprotection of the leukemic child. *Social Science and Medicine, 12,* 117–122.

Finke, J. (1994). *Empathie und Interaktion: Methodik und Praxis der Gesprächspsychotherapie.* Stuttgart: Thieme.

Fitzpatrick, M., Peternelli, L., Stalikas, A., & Iwakabe, S. (1999). Client involvement and occurrence of in-session therapeutic phenomena. *Canadian Journal of Counselling, 33,* 179–191.

*Fleming, B. M., & Thornton, F. (1980). Coping skills training as a component in the short-term treatment of depression. *Journal of Consulting and Clinical Psychology, 48,* 652–654.

*Foulds, M. L. (1970). Effects of a personal growth group on a measure of self-actualization. *Journal of Humanistic Psychology, 10,* 33–38.

*Foulds, M. L. (1971a). Changes in locus of internal-external control: A growth group experience. *Comparative Group Studies, 1,* 293–300.

*Foulds, M. L. (1971b). Measured changes in self-actualization as a result of a growth group experience. *Psychotherapy: Theory, Research and Practice, 8,* 338–341.

*Foulds, M. L., Girona, R., & Guinan, J. F. (1970). Changes of ratings of self and others as a result of a marathon group. *Comparative Group Studies, 1,* 349–355.

*Foulds, M. L., & Guinan, J. F. (1973). Marathon group: Changes in ratings of self and others. *Psychotherapy: Theory, Research and Practice, 10,* 30–32.

*Foulds, M. L., Guinan, J. F., & Hannigan, P. (1974a). Marathon group: Changes in scores on the California Psychological Inventory. *Journal of College Student Personnel, 14,* 474–479.

*Foulds, M. L., Guinan, J. F., & Warehime, R. G. (1974b). Marathon group: changes in perceived locus of control. *Journal of College Student Personnel, 14,* 8–11.

*Gallagher, J. J. (1953). MMPI changes concommitant with client-centered therapy. *Journal of Consulting Psychology, 17,* 334–338.

Gazzola, N., & Stalikas, A. (1997). An investigation of counselor interpretations in client-centered therapy. *Journal of Psychotherapy Integration, 7,* 313–327.

Gendlin, G. T. (1996). *Focusing-oriented psychotherapy: A manual of the experiential method.* New York: Guilford Press.

*Gibson, C. (1998). *Women-centered therapy for depression.* Unpublished dissertation. Department of Psychology, University of Toledo.

*Goldman, A., & Greenberg, L. (1992). Comparison of integrated systemic and emotionally focused approaches to couples therapy. *Journal of Consulting and Clinical Psychology, 60,* 962–969.

*Goldman, R., Bierman, R., & Wolfus, B. (June, 1996). *Relationing without violence (RWV): A treatment program for incarcerated male batterers.* Poster session presented at the Society for Psychotherapy Research, St. Amelia Island, FL.

Goldman, R., & Greenberg, L. S. (2001). Change in thematic depth of experience and outcome in experimental psychotherapy. Unpublished manuscript.

*Gordon-Walker, J., Johnson, S., Manion, I., & Cloutier, P. (1996). An emotionally focused marital intervention for couples with chronically ill children. *Journal of Consulting and Clinical Psychology, 64,* 1029–1036.

Grafanaki, S., & McLeod, J. (1999). Narrative processes in the construction of helpful and hindering events in experiential psychotherapy. *Psychotherapy Research, 9,* 289–303.

Grawe, K. (1976). *Differentielle Psychotherapie: I.* Bern: Huber.

*Grawe, K., Caspar, F., & Ambühl, H. (1990). Differentielle Psychotherapieforschung: Vier Therapieformen im Vergleich. *Zeitschrift für Klinische Psychologie, 19,* 287–376.

Grawe, K., Donati, R., & Bernauer, F. (1994). *Psychotherapie im Wandel: Von der Konfession zur Profession.* Göttingen, Germany: Hogrefe.

*Greenberg, H., Seeman, J., Cassius. (1978). Changes in marathon therapy. *Psychotherapy: Theory, Research and Practice, 15,* 61–67.

Greenberg, L. S. (1979). Resolving splits: The two-chair technique. *Psychotherapy: Theory, Research and Practice, 16,* 310–318.

Greenberg, L. S. (1983). Toward a task analysis of conflict resolution in Gestalt Therapy. *Psychotherapy: Theory, Research and Practice, 20,* 190–201.

Greenberg, L. S., & Bolger, L. (2001). An emotion focused approach to the over-regulation of emotion and emotional pain. *In Session, 57(2),* 197–212.

Greenberg, L. S. Elliott, R., & Lietaer, G. (1994). Research on humanistic and experiential psychotherapies. In A. E. Bergin & S. L. Garfield (Eds.). *Handbook of psychotherapy and behavior change* (4th ed.) (pp. 509–539). New York: John Wiley & Sons.

Greenberg, L. S., & Foerster, F. (1996). Resolving unfinished business: The process of change. *Journal of Consulting and Clinical Psychology, 64,* 439–446.

Greenberg, L. S., Ford, C. L., Alden, L. S., & Johnson, S. M. (1993). In-session change in emotionally focused therapy. *Journal of Consulting and Clinical Psychology, 61,* 78–84.

*Greenberg, L. S., Goldman, R., & Angus, L. (2001). The York II psychotherapy study on experiential therapy of depression. Unpublished manuscript, York University.

Greenberg, L. S., & Johnson, S. M. (1988). *Emotionally focused therapy for couples.* New York: Guilford Press.

Greenberg, L. S., & Korman, L. (1993). Assimilating emotion into psychotherapy integration. *Journal of Psychotherapy Integration, 3,* 249–265.

Greenberg, L., Korman, L., & Paivio, S. (2002). Emotion in humanistic therapy. In D. Cain & J. Seeman (Eds.), *Humanistic psychotherapies: Handbook of research and practice* (pp. 499–530). Washington, DC: APA Press.

Greenberg, L. S., & Malcolm, W. (2002). Resolving unfinished business: Relating process to outcome. *Journal of Consulting and Clinical Psychology, 70,* 406–416.

Greenberg, L. S., Rice, L. N., & Elliott, R. (1993). *Facilitating emotional change: The moment-by-moment process.* New York: Guilford Press.

Greenberg, L. S., & Rosenberg, R. (June, 2000). *Varieties of emotional experience.* Paper presented at the International Conference of Client Centered and Experiential psychotherapy. Chicago, Illinois.

Greenberg, L. S., & Safran, J. D. (1987). *Emotion in psychotherapy.* New York: Guilford Press.

Greenberg, L. S., & Watson, J. (1998). Experiential therapy of depression: Differential effects of client-centered relationship conditions and process experiential interventions. *Psychotherapy Research, 8,* 210–224.

Greenberg, L. S., Watson, J., & Goldman, R. (1998). Process-experiential therapy of depression. In L. S. Greenberg, J. C. Watson, & G. Lietaer (Eds.), *Handbook of experiential psychotherapy* (pp. 227–248), New York: Guilford Press.

Greenberg, L. S., Watson, J., & Lietaer, G. (1998). *Handbook of experiential psychotherapy.* New York: Guilford Press.

*Greenberg, L. S., & Webster, M. (1982). Resolving decisional conflict by means of two-chair dialogue and empathic reflection at a split in counseling. *Journal of Counseling Psychology, 29,* 468–477.

*Gruen, W. (1975). Effects of brief psychotherapy during the hospitalization period on the recovery process in heart attacks. *Journal of Consulting and Clinical Psychology, 43,* 223–232.

Gundrum, M., Lietaer, G., & Van Hees-Matthyssen, C. (1999). Carl Rogers' responses in the 17th session with Miss Mun: comments from a process-experiential and psychoanalytic perspective. *British Journal of Guidance & Counselling, 27(4),* 462–482.

*Haimovitz, N. R., & Haimowitz, M. L. (1952). Personality changes in client-centered therapy. In W. Wolff & J. A. Precher, *Success in psychotherapy* (pp. 63–93). New York: Grune & Stratton.

Hayes, S. C., Strosahl, K. D., & Wilson, K. G. (1999). *Acceptance and commitment therapy: An experiential approach to behavior change.* New York: Guilford Press.

Hendricks, M. N. (2002). Focusing-Oriented/Experiential Psychotherapy. In D. Cain & J. Seeman (Eds.), *Humanistic psychotherapies: Handbook of research and practice* (pp. 221–252). Washington, DC: APA.

Hershbell, A. S. (1998). Client experience of gestalt body-awareness interventions. *Dissertation Abstracts International, 59*, 2419B.

Hirscheimer, K. (1996). *Development and verification of a measure of unfinished business.* Master's thesis, Department of Psychology, York University.

*Holden, J. M., Sagovsky, R., & Cox, J. L. (1989). Counselling in a general practice setting: Controlled study of health visitor intervention in treatment of postnatal depression. *British Medical Journal, 298*, 223–226.

Holmes, S. W., Morris, R., Clance, P. R., & Putney, R. T. (1996). Holotropic breathwork: An experiential approach to psychotherapy. *Psychotherapy: Theory, Research, Practice, Training, 33*, 114–120.

*Holstein, B. E. (August, 1990). The use of focusing in combination with a cognitive behavioral weight loss program. Paper presented at American Psychological Association meeting, Boston, MA.

Honos-Webb, L., Stiles, W. B., Greenberg, L. S., & Goldman, R. (1998). Assimilation analysis of process-experiential psychotherapy: A comparison of two cases. *Psychotherapy Research, 8*, 264–286.

Honos-Webb, L., Surko, M., Stiles, W. B., & Greenberg, L. S. (1999). Assimilation of voices in psychotherapy: The case of Jan. *Journal of Counseling Psychology, 46*, 448–460.

Horvath, A. O., & Symonds, B. D. (1991). Relation between working alliance and outcome in psychotherapy: A meta-analysis. *Journal of Counseling Psychology, 38*, 139–149.

Hunter, J. E., & Schmidt, F. L. (1990). *Methods of meta-analysis.* Newbury Park, CA: Sage.

Hycner, R., & Jacobs, L. M. (1995). *The healing relationship in Gestalt therapy: A dialogical/self psychology approach.* Highland, NY: Gestalt Journal Press.

Iberg, J. R. (1996). Using statistical experiments with post-session client questionnaires as a student-centered approach to teaching the effects of therapist activities in psychotherapy. In A Hutterer, R., Pawlowsky, G., Schmid, P. F., & Stipsits, R. (Eds.). *Client-centered and experiential psychotherapy. A paradigm in motion* (pp. 255–271). Frankfurt am Main: Peter Lang.

Iwakabe, S., Rogan, K., & Stalikas, A. (2000). The relationship between client emotional expressions, therapist interventions, and the working alliance: An exploration of eight emotional expression events. *Journal of Psychotherapy Integration, 10*, 375–401.

*Jackson, L., & Elliott, R. (June, 1990). Is experiential therapy effective in treating depression?: Initial outcome data. Paper presented at Society for Psychotherapy Research, Wintergreen, VA.

Jacobi, E. M. (1995). The efficacy of the bonny method of Guided Imagery and Music as experiential therapy in the primary care of persons with rheumatoid arthritis. *Dissertation Abstracts International, 56*, 1110B.

*James, P. S. (1991). Effects of a communication training component added to an emotionally focused couples therapy. *Journal of Marital and Family Therapy, 17*, 263–275.

*Jessee, R. E., & Guerney, B. G. (1981). A comparison of gestalt and relationship enhancement treatments with married couples. *American Journal of Family Therapy, 9*, 31–41.

Johnson, B. T. (1989). *D/STAT: Software for the meta-analytic review of research literatures.* Hillsdale, NJ: Erlbaum.

*Johnson, S., & Greenberg, L. S. (1985a). Differential effects of experiential and problem solving interventions in resolving marital conflict. *Journal of Consulting and Clinical Psychology, 53*, 175–184.

*Johnson, S., & Greenberg, L. (1985b). Emotionally focused couples therapy: An outcome study. *Journal of Marital and Family Therapy, 11*, 313–317.

*Johnson, S. M., Maddeaux, C., & Blouin, J. (1998). Emotionally focused family therapy for bulimia: Changing attachment patterns. *Psychotherapy, 35*, 238–247.

*Johnson, S. M., & Talitman, E. (1997). Predictors of outcome in emotionally focused marital therapy. *Journal of Marital and Family Therapy, 23*, 135–152.

*Johnson, W. R. (1977). The use of a snake phobia paradigm and nonverbal behavior change in assessing treatment outcome: "The empty chair" versus systematic desensitization (Doctoral dissertation, Georgia State University, 1976). *Dissertation Abstracts International, 37*, 4146B. (University Microfilms No. 77-2933)

*Johnson, W. R., & Smith, E.W.L. (1997). Gestalt empty-chair dialogue versus systematic desensitization in the treatment of a phobia. *Gestalt Review, 1*, 150–162.

Jones, E. E., & Pulos, S. M. (1993). Comparing the process in psychodynamic and cognitive-behavioral therapies. *Journal of Consulting and Clinical Psychology, 61*, 306–316.

*Katonah, D. G. (1991). *Focusing and cancer: A psychological tool as an adjunct treatment for adaptive recovery.* Unpublished dissertation, Illinois School of Professional Psychology, Chicago, IL. [available online at: www.focusing.org/adjunct_treatment.html]

Kennedy-Moore, E., & Watson, J. C. (1999). *Expressing emotion: Myths, realities, and therapeutic strategies.* New York: Guilford Press.

Kepner, J. (1993). *Body process. Working with the body in psychotherapy.* San Francisco: Jossey-Bass.

*King, M., Sibbald, B., Ward, E., Bower, P., Lloyd, M., Gabbay, M., & Byford, S. (2000). Randomised controlled trial of non-directive counselling, cognitive-behavior therapy and usual general practitioner care in the management of depression as well as mixed anxiety and depression in primary care [Monograph]. *Health Technology Assessment, 4(19),* 1–84.

Klein, M. H., Mathieu, P. L., Gendlin, E. T., & Kiesler, D. J. (1969). *The Experiencing Scale: A research and training manual* (Vol 1.). Madison, WI: Wisconsin Psychiatric Institute.

Klein, M. H., Mathieu-Coughlan, P., & Kiesler, D. J. (1986). The Experiencing Scales. In L. Greenberg & W. Pinsof (Eds.), *The psychotherapeutic process* (pp. 21–71). New York: Guilford Press.

*Kolko, D. J., Brent, D. A., Baugher, M., Bridge, J., & Birmaher, B. (2000). Cognitive and family therapies for adolescent depression: Treatment specificity, mediation, and moderation. *Journal of Consulting and Clinical Psychology, 68,* 603–614.

Korman, L. M. (1998). Changes in clients' emotion episodes in therapy. (Doctoral dissertation, York University). *Dissertation Abstracts International, 59(5),* 2422B.

Leijssen, M. (1996). Characteristics of a healing inner relationship. In R. Hutterer, G. Pawlowsky, P. F. Schmid, & R. Stipsits (Eds.), *Client-centered and experiential psychotherapy: A paradigm in motion* (pp. 427–438). Frankfurt am Main, Germany: Peter Lang.

Leijssen, M., Lietaer, G., Stevens, I., & Wels, G. (2000). Focusing training for stagnating clients: An analysis of four cases. In J. Marques-Teixeira & S. Antunes (Eds.), *Client-centered and experiential psychotherapy* (pp. 207–224). Linda a Velha, Portugal: Vale & Vale.

*Lerner, M. S., & Clum, G. A. (1990). Treatment of suicide ideators: A problem-solving approach. *Behavior Therapy, 21,* 403–411.

Levitt, H., & Angus. L. (1999). Psychotherapy process measure research and the evaluation of psychotherapy orientation: A narrative analysis. *Journal of Psychotherapy Integration, 9,* 279–300.

Levitt, H., Korman, Y., & Angus, L. (2000). A metaphor analysis in treatments of depression: Metaphor as a marker of change. *Counselling Psychology Quarterly, 2,* 1–11.

Lewin, J. (2000). *Both sides of the coin: Comparative analyses of narrative process patterns in poor and good outcome dyads engaged in brief experiential psychotherapy for depression.* Unpublished Master's thesis. York University, Toronto, Canada.

Lietaer, G. (1989). The working alliance in client-centered therapy: Reflections on findings with post-session questionnaires. In H. Vertommen, G. Cluckers, & G. Lietaer (Eds.), *De relatie in therapie* [The relationship in therapy] (pp. 207–235). Leuven, Belgium: Leuven University Press.

Lietaer, G., & Brodley, B. (1998). *Cases and demonstration sessions of Carl Rogers: Bibliographical survey of empirical studies and clinical reflections.* Unpublished manuscript, Katholieke Universiteit Leuven.

Lietaer, G., & Dierick, P. (1996). Client-centered group psychotherapy in dialogue with other orientations: Commonality and specificity. In R. Hutterer, G. Pawlowsky, P. F. Schmid, & R. Stipsits (Eds.), *Client-centered and experiential psychotherapy. A paradigm in motion* (pp. 562–583). Frankfurt am Main: Peter Lang.

Lietaer, G., & Dierick, P. (1999). Interventies van groepspsychotherapeuten. In W. Trijsburg, S. Colijn, E. Collumbien, & G. Lietaer (Eds.), *Handboek Integratieve Psychotherapie. Inventarisatie en perspectief* (pp. V 1.1 1–19). Leusden: De Tijdstroom.

Lietaer, G., & Van Kalmthout, M. (Eds.). (1995). *Praktijkboek gesprekstherapie. Psychopathologie en experiëntiële procesbevordering.* Leusden: De Tijdstroom.

Lipsey, M. W., & Wilson, D. B. (1993). The efficacy of psychological, educational, and behavioral treatment: Confirmation from meta-analysis. *American Psychologist, 48,* 1181–1209.

*Little, L. F. (1986). Gestalt therapy with parents when a child is presented as the problem. *Family Relations, 35,* 489–496.

*Lowenstein, J. (1985). *A test of a performance model of problematic reactions and an examination of differential client performances in therapy.* Unpublished thesis, Department of Psychology, York University.

Luborsky, L., Diguer, L., Seligman, D. A., Rosenthal, R., Krause, E. D., Johnson, S., Halperin, G., Bishop, M., Berman, J. S., & Schweizer, E. (1999). The researcher's own therapy allegiances: A "wild card" in comparisons of treatment efficacy. *Clinical Psychology: Science and Practice, 6,* 95–106.

Lutgendorf, S. K., Antoni, M. H., Kumar, M., & Schneiderman, N. (1994). Changes in cognitive coping strategies predict EBV-antibody titre change following a stressor disclosure induction. *Journal of Psychosomatic Research, 38,* 63–78.

Machado, P.P.P., Beutler, L. E., & Greenberg, L. S. (1999). Emotion recognition in psychotherapy: Impact of therapist level of experience and emotional awareness. *Journal of Clinical Psychology, 55,* 39–57.

Mackay, B. (1996). The Gestalt two-chair technique: How it relates to theory. *Dissertation Abstracts International, 57,* 2158B.

*MacPhee, D. C., Johnson, S. M., & Van der Veer, M. D. (1995). Low sexual desire in women: The effects of marital therapy. *Journal of Sex and Marital Therapy, 21,* 159–182.

Mahrer, A. R. (1983). *Experiential psychotherapy: Basic practices.* New York: Brunner/Mazel.

Mahrer, A. R., Dessaulles, A., Nadler, W. P., Gervaize, P. A., & Sterner, I. (1987). Good and very good moments in psychotherapy: content, distribution, and facilitation. *Psychotherapy: Theory, Research, Practice, Training, 24,* 7–14.

McKee, S. (1995). *Voice quality and depth of perceptual processing of depressed clients engaged in two types of experiential therapy.* MA thesis, York University.

McLeod, J. (2001). *Qualitative research in counselling and psychotherapy.* London, UK: Sage.

McMain, S. (1996). Relating changes in self-other schemas to psychotherapy outcome. *Dissertation Abstracts International, 56*, 5775B.

Mearns, D., & Thorne, B. (2000). *Person-centred therapy today: New frontiers in theory and practice.* London: Sage.

Mecheril, P., & Kemmler, L. (1994). Der sprachliche Umgang mit Emotionen in der klientenzentrierten Gesprächspsychotherapie. *Jahrbuch für Personzentrierte Psychologie und Psychotherapie, 4*, 125–144.

Mergenthaler, E. (1996). Emotion-abstraction patterns in verbatim protocols: A New Way of Describing Psychotherapeutic Processes. *Journal of Consulting and Clinical Psychology, 64*, 1306–1315.

Merry, T. (1996). An analysis of ten demonstration interviews by Carl Rogers: Implications for the training of client-centered counsellors. In R. Hutterer, G. Pawlowsky, P. F. Schmid, & R. Stipsits (Eds.), *Client-centered and experiential psychotherapy. A paradigm in motion* (pp. 273–283). Frankfurt am Main: Peter Lang.

*Mestel, R., & Votsmeier-Röhr, A. (June, 2000). Longterm follow-up study of depressive patients receiving experiential psychotherapy in an inpatient setting. Paper presented at meeting of Society for Psychotherapy Research, Chicago, IL.

*Meyer, A. E. (Ed.). (1981). The Hamburg Short Psychotherapy Comparison Experiment. *Psychotherapy and Psychosomatics, 35*, 81–207.

Meyer, A. E., Richter, R., Grawe, K., von Schulenburg, J.-M., & Schulte, B. (1991). *Forschungsgutachten zu Fragen eines Psychotherapeutengesetzes.* Hamburg, Universitätskrankenhaus Eppendorf.

Missiaen, C., Wollants, G., Lietaer, G., & Gundrum, M. (2000). Gloria-Rogers en Gloria-Perls onder experiëntieel vergrootglas. *Gestalt. Tijdschrift voor Gestalttherapie, 7(7)*, 19–76.

*Monti, P. M., Curran, J. P., Corriveau, D. P., DeLancey, A. L., & Hagerman, S. M. (1980). Effects of social skills training groups and sensitivity training groups with psychiatric patients. *Journal of Consulting and Clinical Psychology, 48*, 241–248.

Moreno, J. L., & Moreno, Z. T. (1959). *Foundations of psychotherapy.* Beacon, NY: Beacon House.

Morikawa, Y. (1997). Making practical the focusing manner of experiencing in everyday life: A consideration of factor analysis. *Journal of Japanese Clinical Psychology, 15*, 58–65.

*Muench, G. A. (1947). *An evaluation of non-directive psychotherapy: By means of the Rorschach and other indices.* Stanford, CA: Stanford University Press.

*Mulder, C. L., Antoni, M. H., Emmelkamp, P.M.G., Veugelers, P. J., Sandfort, T.G.M., van de Vijver, F.A.J.R., & de Vries, M. J. (1995). Psychosocial group intervention and the rate of decline of immunological parameters in asymptomatic HIV-infected homosexual men. *Psychotherapy-and-Psychosomatics. 63*, 185–192.

*Mulder, C. L., Emmelkamp, P.M.G., Antoni, M. H., Mulder, J. W., Sandfort, T.G.M., & de Vries, M. J. (1994). Cognitive-behavioral and experiential group psychotherapy for HIV-infected homosexual men: A comparative study. *Psychosomatic Medicine, 56*, 423–431.

Nathan, P. E. (1996). Validated forms of psychotherapy may lead to better-validated psychotherapy. *Clinical Psychology: Science and Practice, 3*, 251–255.

*Nichols, M. P. (1974). Outcome of brief cathartic psychotherapy. *Journal of Consulting and Clinical Psychology, 42*, 403–410.

O'Leary, E., & Nieuwstraten, I. M. (1999). Unfinished business in gestalt reminiscence therapy: A discourse analytic study. *Counselling Psychology Quarterly, 12*, 395–411.

Paivio, S. C., & Bahr, L. M. (1998). Interpersonal problems, working alliance, and outcome in short-term experiential therapy. *Psychotherapy Research, 8*, 392–407.

*Paivio, S. C., & Greenberg, L. S. (1995). Resolving "unfinished business": Efficacy of experiential therapy using empty chair dialogue. *Journal of Consulting and Clinical Psychology, 63*, 419–425.

Paivio, S. C., Hall, I. E., Holowaty, K.A.M., Jellis, J. B., & Tran, N. (2001). Imaginal confrontation for resolving child abuse issues. *Psychotherapy Research, 11*, 433–453.

*Paivio, S. C., & Nieuwenhuis, J. A. (2001). Efficacy of emotion focused therapy for adult survivors of child abuse: A preliminary study. *Journal of Traumatic Stress, 14*, 115–133.

Perls, F. S., Hefferline, R. F., & Goodman, P. (1951). *Gestalt Therapy.* New York: Julian Press.

Pierce, R. A., Nichols, M. P., & DuBrin, J. R. (1983). *Emotional expression in psychotherapy.* New York: Gardner Press.

*Pomrehn, G., Tausch, R., & Tönnies, S. (1986). Personzentrierte Gruppenpsychotherapie: Prozesse und Auswirkungen nach 1 Jahr bei 87 Klienten. *Zeitschrift für Personenzentrierte Psychologie und Psychotherapie, 5*, 19–31.

Pos, A. E. (1999). *Depth of experiencing during emotion episodes and its relationship to core themes and outcome.* Unpublished Master's thesis, York University, Toronto.

Project MATCH Research Group. (1997). Matching alcoholism treatments to client heterogeneity: Project MATCH posttreatment drinking outcomes. *Journal of Studies on Alcohol, 58*, 7–29.

Propst, L. R., Ostrom, R., Watkins, P., Dean, T., & Mashburn, D. (1992). Comparitive efficacy of religious and nonreligious cognitive-behavioral therapy for the treatment of clinical depression in religious individuals. *Journal of Consulting and Clinical Psychology, 60*, 94–103.

*Ragsdale, K. G., Cox, R. D., Finn, P., & Eisler, R. M. (1996). Effectiveness of short-term specialized inpatient treatment for war-related posttraumatic stress disorder: A role for adventure-based counseling and psychodrama. *Journal of Traumatic Stress, 9*, 269–283.

Raphael, B., Middleton, W., Martinek, N., & Misso, V. (1993). Counseling and therapy of the bereaved. In M. S. Stroebe & W. Stroebe (Eds.), *Handbook of bereavement: Theory, research, and intervention* (pp. 427–453). New York: Cambridge University Press.

*Raskin, N. J. (1949). An analysis of six parallel studies of the therapeutic process. *Journal of Consulting Psychology, 13*, 206–220.

*Raskin, N. J. (1952). An objective study of the locus-of-evaluation factor in psychotherapy. In W. Wolff & J. A. Precher, *Success in psychotherapy* (pp. 143–162). New York: Grune & Stratton.

Rennie, D. L. (1994). Client's deference in psychotherapy. *Journal of Counseling Psychology, 41*, 427–437.

Rennie, D. L. (2000). Aspects of the client's conscious control of the psychotherapeutic process. *Journal of Psychotherapy Integration, 10*, 151–167.

*Rezaeian, M. P, Mazumdar, D.P.S., & Sen, A. K. (1997). The effectiveness of psychodrama in changing the attitudes among depressed patients. *Journal of Personality and Clinical Studies, 13*, 19–23.

Rice, L. N. (1974). The evocative function of the therapist. In D. Wexler & L. N. Rice (Eds.), *Innovations in client-centered therapy* (pp. 289–311). New York: John Wiley & Sons.

Rice, L. N., & Saperia, E. P. (1984). Task analysis and the resolution of problematic reactions. In L. N. Rice & L. S. Greenberg (Eds.), *Patterns of change* (pp. 29–66). New York: Guilford Press.

Rogers, C. R. (1961). *On becoming a person.* Boston: Houghton Mifflin.

Rogers, C. R. (1975). Empathic: An unappreciated way of being. *Counseling Psychologist, 5(2)*, 2–10.

Rogers, C. R., & Dymond, R. F. (Eds.) (1954). *Psychotherapy and personality change.* Chicago: University of Chicago Press.

Rogers, C. R., Gendlin, E. T., Kiesler, D. J., & Truax, C. B. (1967). *The therapeutic relationship and its impact.* Madison: University of Wisconsin Press.

Rogers, J. L., Howard, K. L., & Vessey, J. T. (1993). Using significance tests to evaluate equivalence between two experimental groups. *Psychological Bulletin, 113*, 553–565.

Rosner, R., Beutler, L. E., & Daldrup, R. (2000). Vicarious emotional experience and emotional expression in group psychotherapy. *Journal of Clinical Psychology, 56*, 1–10.

Roth, A., & Fonagy, P. (1996). *What works for whom?: A critical review of psychotherapy research.* New York: Guilford Press.

Rudolph, J., Langer, I., & Tausch, R. (1980). Prüfung der psychischen Auswirkungen und Bedingungen von personenzentrierter Einzel-Psychotherapie. *Zeitschrift für Klinisiche Psychologie, 9*, 23–33.

*Sachse, R. (1995). Zielorientierte Gesprächspsychotherapie: Effektive psychotherapeutische Strategien bei Klienten und Klientinnen mit psychosomatischen Magen-Darm-Erkrankungen. In J. Eckert (Ed.), *Forschung zur Klientenzentrierten Psychotherapie* (pp. 27–49). Köln, Germany: GwG-Verlag.

Sachse, R., & Elliott, R. (2002). Process-outcome research in client-centered and experiential therapies. In D. Cain & J. Seeman, *Humanistic psychotherapies: Handbook of research and practice* (pp. 83–116). Washington, DC: APA Publications.

*Salts, C. J., & Zonker, C. E. (1983). Effects of divorce counseling groups on adjustment and self concept. *Journal of Divorce, 6*, 55–67.

*Schefft, B. K., & Kanfer, F. H. (1987). The utility of a process model in therapy: A comparative study of treatment effects. *Behavior Therapy, 18*, 113–134.

Schmid, P. F. (1995). *Personale Begegnung. Der personzentrierte Ansatz in Psychotherapie, Beratung, Gruppenarbeit und Seelsorge.* (2nd rev. ed.). Würzburg: Echter.

*Schmidtchen, S., Hennies, S., & Acke, H. (1993). Zwei Fliegen mit einer Klappe? Evaluation der Hypothese eines zweifachen Wirksamheitanspruches der klientenzentrierten Spieltherapie. *Psychologie in Erziehung und Unterricht, 40*, 34–42.

Schneider, K. J. (1998). Toward a science of the heart: Romanticism and the revival of psychology. *American Psychologist, 53*, 277–289.

Schneider, K. J., Bugental, J.F.T., & Fraser, J. F. (Eds.) (2001). *Handbook of humanistic psychology.* Thousand Oaks, CA: Sage.

*Schwab, R. (1995). Zur Prozessforschung in der gesprächspsychotherapeutische Gruppentherapie: Überlegungen im Anschluss an empirische Ergebnisse aus Gruppen mit Einsamen. In J. Eckert (Ed.), *Forschung zur Klientenzentrierten Psychotherapie* (pp. 151–165). Köln, Germany: GwG-Verlag.

Serok, S., & Levi, N. (1993). Application of Gestalt therapy with long-term prison inmates in Israel. *Gestalt Journal, 16:* 105–127.

*Serok, S., Rabin, C., & Spitz, Y. (1984). Intensive Gestalt group therapy with schizophrenics. *International Journal of Group Psychotherapy, 34*, 431–450.

*Serok, S., & Zemet, R. M. (1983). An experiment of Gestalt group therapy with hospitalized schizophrenics. *Psychotherapy: Theory, Research & Practice, 20*, 417–424.

Shapiro, D. A., Barkham, M., Rees, A., Hardy, G. E., Reynolds, S., & Startup, M. (1994). Effects of treatment duration and severity of depression on the effectiveness of cognitive-behavioral and psychodynamic-interpersonal psychotherapy. *Journal of Consulting and Clinical Psychology, 62*, 522–534.

*Shaw, B. F. (1977). Comparison of cognitive therapy and behavior therapy in the treatment of depression. *Journal of Consulting and Clinical Psychology, 45*, 543–551.

*Shear, K. M., Pilkonis, P. A., Cloitre, M., & Leon, A. C. (1994). Cognitive behavioral treatment compared with nonprescriptive treatment of panic disorder. *Archives of General Psychiatry, 51*, 395–401.

*Sherman, E. (1987). Reminiscence groups for community elderly. *The Gerontologist, 27*, 569–572.

*Shlien, J. M., Mosak, H. H., & Dreikurs, R. (1962). Effect of time limits: A comparison of two psychotherapies. *Journal of Counseling Psychology, 9*, 31–34.

Sicoli, L. A., & Hallberg, E. T. (1998). An analysis of client performance in the two-chair method. *Canadian Journal of Counselling, 32*, 151–162.

Smith, M. L., Glass, G. V., & Miller, T. I. (1980). *The benefits of psychotherapy*. Baltimore, MD: Johns Hopkins University Press.

*Snijders, J. A., Huijsman, A. M., de Groot, M. H., Maas, J. J., & de Greef, A. (2002). Psychotherapeutische deeltijdbehandeling van persoonlijkheidsstoornissen: psychodiagnostische feedback, werkzaamheid en cliëntensatisfactie [Personality disorders in psychotherapeutic daytreatment: Psychological test feedback, effects and client satisfaction.]. *Tijdschrift voor Psychiatrie, 44*, 71–81.

*Souliere, M. (1995). The differential effects of the empty chair dialogue and cognitive restructuring on the resolution of lingering angry feelings. (Doctoral dissertation, University of Ottawa, 1994). *Dissertation Abstracts International, 56*, 2342B. (University Microfilms No. AAT NN95979)

*Speierer, G. W. (1979). Ergebnisse der ambulanten Gesprächspsychotherapie. *Fortschritte der Medizin, 97*, 1527–1533.

*Speierer, G. W. (2000). Alkoholpatientinnen: Psychopathologie, Begleitssymptome, Indikationsstellung, Therapieziele and Behandlungseffekte aus der Sicht der Gesprächspsychotherapie. In G. W. Speierer (Ed.), *Neue Ergebnisse der ambulanten und stationären Gesprächspsychotherapie* (pp. 31–48). Köln, Germany: GwG-Verlag.

*Spiegel, D., Bloom, J. R., Kraemer, H. C., & Gottheil, E. (1989, October 14). Effect of psychosocial treatment on survival of patients with metastatic breast cancer. *The Lancet, 2(8668)*, 888–891.

*Spiegel, D., Bloom, J. R., & Yalom, I. (1981). Group support for patients with metastatic cancer. *Archives of General Psychiatry, 38*, 527–533.

Stalikas, A., & Fitzpatrick, M. (1995). Client good moments. An intensive analysis of a single session. *Canadian Journal of Counselling, 29*, 160–175.

Stinckens, N. (2001). *Werken met de innerlijke criticus, Gerichte empirische verkenning vanuit een cliëntgericht-experiëntiële microtheorie*. Unpublished doctoral dissertation, Katholieke Universiteit Leuven.

Takens, R. J. (2001). *Een vreemde nabij. Enkele aspekten van de psychotherapeutische relatie onderzocht*. Unpublished doctoral dissertation, Vrije Universiteit Amsterdam.

*Tarrier, N., Kinney, C., McCarthy, E., Humphreys, L., Wittkowski, A., & Morris, J. (2000). Two-year follow-up of cognitive-behavioral therapy and supportive counseling in the treatment of persistent symptoms in chronic schizophrenia. *Journal of Consulting and Clinical Psychology, 68*, 917–922.

*Tarrier, N., Yusupoff, L., Kinney, C., McCarthy, E., Gledhill, A., & Morris, J. (1998). A randomised controlled trial of intensive cognitive behaviour therapy for chronic schizophrenia. *British Medical Journal, 317*, 303–307.

Task Force on Promotion and Dissemination of Psychological Procedures. (1995). Training in and dissemination of empirically-validated psychological treatments: Report and recommendations. *The Clinical Psychologist, 48*, 3–23.

Taylor, B. (1996). Psychotherapists' experiences of empathy: A phenomenological inquiry. *Dissertation Abstracts International, 56(8)*, 4594B.

*Teusch, L. (1990). Positive effects and limitations of client-centered therapy with schizophrenic patients. In G. Lietaer, J. Rombauts, & R. Van Balen (Eds.), *Client-centered and experiential psychotherapy in the nineties* (pp. 637–644). Leuven, Belgium: Leuven University Press.

*Teusch, L., & Böhme, H. (1991). Results of a one-year follow up of patients with agoraphobia and/or panic disorder treated with an inpatient therapy program with client-centered basis. *Psychotherapie-Psychosomatik Medizinische Psychologie, 41*, 68–76.

*Teusch, L., Böhme, H., & Gastpar, M. (1997). The benefit of an insight-oriented and experiential approach on panic and agoraphobia symptoms. *Psychotherapy and Psychosomatics, 66*, 293–301.

*Teusch, L, Finke, J., & Böhme, H. (1999). Wirkeffekte der stationären störungsspezifischen Gesprächspsychotherapie (GPT) [Effects of inpatient disorder-specific client-centered therapy]. In J. Finke, L. Teusch, H. Böhme, & M. Gastpar, *Arbeitgruppe Gesprächspsychotherapie—Forschung* [Report of a working group on client-centered therapy] (part 4). Essen, Germany: Rheinische Klinken Essen.

Toukmanian, S. G. (1986). A measure of client perceptual processing. In L. Greenberg & W. Pinsof (Eds.), *The psychotherapeutic process* (pp. 107–130). New York: Guilford Press.

Toukmanian, S. G. (1992). Studying the client's perceptual process and their outcomes in psychotherapy.

In S. G. Toukmanian & D. L. Rennie (Eds.), *Psychotherapy process research: Paradigmatic and narrative approaches.* Newbury Park, CA: Sage.

Toukmanian, S. G., & Grech, T. (1991). *Changes in cognitive complexity in the context of perceptual-processing experiential therapy.* Department of Psychology Report No. 194, York University.

*Tscheulin, D. (Ed.) (1995). *Qualitätssicherung an der Hochgrat-Klinik Wolfsried.* Wurzberg, Germany: Hochgrat-Klinik Wolfsried-Reisach GmbH.

*Tscheulin, D. (Ed.) (1996). *Zwischenbericht zur Effektqualitätssicherung an der Hochgrat-Klinik Wolfsried.* Wurzberg, Germany: Hochgrat-Klinik Wolfsried-Reisach GmbH.

*Tschuschke, V., & Anbeh, T. (2000). Early Treatment effects of long-term outpatient group therapies. First preliminary results. *Group Analysis 33(3)*, 397–411.

*Tyson, G. M., & Range, L. M. (1987). Gestalt dialogues as a treatment for mild depression: Time works just as well. *Journal of Clinical Psychology, 43*, 227–231.

*van der Pompe, G., Duivenvoorden, H. J., Antoni, M. H., Visser, A., & Heijnen, C. J. (1997). Effectiveness of a short-term group psychotherapy program on endocrine and immune function in breast cancer patients: An exploratory study. *Journal of Psychosomatic Research, 42*, 453–466.

van Kessel, W., & Lietaer, G. (1998). Interpersonal processes. In L. Greenberg, G. Lietaer, & J. Watson (Eds.), *Handbook of experiential psychotherapy* (pp. 155–177). New York: Guilford Press.

Vanaerschot, G. (1997a). *Plaats en betekenis van de empathische interactie in belevingsgerichte psychotherapie. Theoretische en empirische exploratie.* Unpublished doctoral dissertation, K. U. Leuven.

Vanaerschot, G. (1997b). Empathic resonance as a source of experience. In A. C. Bohart & L. S. Greenberg (Eds.), *Empathy reconsidered. New directions in psychotherapy* (pp. 141–165). Washington, DC.: American Psychological Association.

Vanaerschot, G. (1999). De empathische interactie in de praktijk. *Tijdschrift Cliëntgerichte Psychotherapie, 37(1)*, 5–20.

Vansteenwegen, A. (1997). Do marital therapists do what they say they do? A comparison between experiential and communication couples therapy. *Sexual and Marital Therapy, 12*, 35–43.

Wampold, B. E. (1997). Methodological problems in identifying efficacious psychotherapies. *Psychotherapy Research, 7*, 21–43.

Warwar, N., & Greenberg, L. (2000). Catharsis is not enough: Changes in emotional processing related to psychotherapy outcome. Paper presented at the International Society for Psychotherapy Research Annual Meeting. June, Indian Hills, Chicago.

Watson, J. C. (1996). The relationship between vivid description, emotional arousal, and in-session resolution of problematic reactions. *Journal of Consulting and Clinical Psychology, 64*, 459–464.

*Watson, J. C., Gordon, L., Stermac, L., Kalogerakos, F., & Steckley P. (2001). *Comparing the effectiveness of process-experiential with cognitive-behavioral psychotherapy in the treatment of depression.* Unpublished manuscript, University of Toronto, Toronto, CA.

Watson, J. C., & Greenberg, L. S. (1996). Pathways to change in the psychotherapy of depression: Relating process to session change and outcome. *Psychotherapy: Theory, Research, Practice, Training, 33:* 262–274.

Watson, J. C., & Rennie, D. (1994). Qualitative analysis of clients' subjective experience of significant moments during the exploration of problematic reactions. *Journal of Counseling Psychology, 41*, 500–509.

Weerasekera, P., Linder, B., Greenberg, L., & Watson, J. (2001). The working alliance in client-centered and process-experiential therapy of depression. *Psychotherapy Research, 11:* 221–233.

*Westermann, B., Schwab, R., & Tausch, R. (1983). Auswirkungen und Prozesse personzentrierter Gruppenpsychotherapie bei 164 Klienten einer Psychotherapeutischen Beratungsstelle. *Zeitschrift für Klinische Psychologie, 12*, 273–292.

Whelton, W., & Greenberg, L. (2000, June). Self-contempt and self-resilience in the self-criticism of persons vulnerable to depression. Paper presented at meeting of Society for Psychotherapy Research, Chicago, IL.

Wolfe, B., & Sigl, P. (1998). Experiential psychotherapy of the anxiety disorders. In L. S. Greenberg, J. C. Watson, & G. Lietaer (Eds.), *Handbook of experiential psychotherapy* (pp. 272–294). New York: Guilford Press.

*Wolfus, B., & Bierman, R. (1996). An evaluation of a group treatment program for incarcerated male batterers. *International Journal of Offender Therapy and Comparative Criminology, 40*, 318–333.

Yalom, I. D. (1980). *Existential psychotherapy.* New York: Basic Books.

Yalom, I. D. (1995). *The theory and practice of group psychotherapy* (rev. ed.). New York: Basic Books.

*Yalom, I. D., Bond, G., Bloch, S., Zimmerman, E., & Friedman, L. (1977). The impact of a weekend group experience on individual therapy. *Archives of General Psychiatry, 34*, 399–415.

Yontef, G. (1998). Dialogic gestalt therapy. In L. S. Greenberg, J. C. Watson, & G. Lietaer (Eds.), *Handbook of experiential psychotherapy* (pp. 82–102). New York: Guilford Press.

Section 4

Research on Applications in Special Groups and Settings

CHAPTER 12

PSYCHOTHERAPY FOR CHILDREN AND ADOLESCENTS

ALAN E. KAZDIN
Yale University

Psychotherapy for children and adolescents has made remarkable gains within the past two decades. There are now well over 1,500 controlled trials of therapy (Kazdin, 2000b). Reviews consistently conclude that treatment is effective for a range of clinical problems (Weisz, Weiss, Han, Granger, & Morton, 1995). The recent identification of evidence-based treatments for many childhood problems underscores the achievements (e.g., Christopherson & Mortweet, 2001; Kazdin & Weisz, in press; Lonigan & Elbert, 1998). There is, of course, another side that places these advances in perspective. There are now hundreds of psychotherapies for children. A recent count documented over 550, but the count could not be fixed as "new" treatments continue to emerge (Kazdin, 2000d). The vast majority of treatments in use have not been studied empirically. For those that have been studied, it is not at all clear why they work and for whom. Thus, there is much to do to identify and develop effective interventions for children and adolescents.

This chapter focuses on the scope of the clinical problems that children experience, special challenges raised by providing treatment to children, current status of the evidence, and limitations of current therapy research.[1] Evidence-based treatments are discussed at some length, and specific techniques are illustrated to convey more concretely the exemplary research that has been completed and is currently underway. The neglect of critical questions about therapy and the very limited progress in understanding how therapy works, among other issues, are highlighted. A model is offered to direct future researchers to address major lacunae in current research.

CLINICAL PROBLEMS IN CHILDHOOD AND ADOLESCENCE

The need for interventions stems in part from the scope of clinical dysfunctions that children and adolescents experience. For purpose of presentation, the dysfunctions are grouped into three categories: psychiatric disorders, problem and at-risk behaviors, and delinquency.

Psychiatric Disorders

Mental disorders refer to patterns of behavior that are associated with distress, impairment, or significantly increased risk of suffering, death, pain, disability, or an important loss of freedom (American Psychiatric Association, 1994). The range of psychological dysfunctions or disorders that individuals can experience is enumerated in various diagnostic systems, such as the *Diagnostic and Statistical Manual of Mental Disorders* (DSM-IV; APA, 1994) and the *International Classification of Diseases* (ICD-10; World Health Organization [WHO], 1992). The DSM is the dominant system in use (Maser, Kaelber, & Weise, 1991) and recognizes several disorders that arise in infancy, childhood, or adolescence. These disorders are grouped into 10 categories and highlighted in Table 12.1. Several disorders not included in the table can arise over the life span and hence are not unique to childhood and adolescence. Major examples include Schizophrenia, Anxiety, Mood, Eating, Substance-Related, Sexual and Gender Identity Disorders, and Adjustment Disorders.

Table 12.2 includes five categories that represent broader domains of dysfunction. These

TABLE 12.1 Categories of Major Disorders First Evident in Infancy, Childhood, or Adolescence

Mental Retardation: Significant subaverage general intellectual functioning (Intelligence Quotient [IQ] of approximately < 70) associated with deficits or impairments in adaptive behavior (e.g., communication, self-care, social skills, and functional academic or work skills). Onset is before the age of 18. Degrees of severity are distinguished based on intellectual impairment and adaptive functioning.

Learning Disorders: Achievement that is substantially below normative levels, based on the individual's age, schooling, and level of intelligence. Separate disorders are distinguished based on the domain of dysfunction and include disorders of reading, mathematics, and written expression.

Motor Skills Disorder: Marked impairment in the development of motor coordination that interferes with academic achievement or activities of daily living and that cannot be traced to a general medical condition.

Communication Disorders: Impairment in the use of language that is substantially below normative levels of performance. The impairment interferes with daily functioning (e.g., at school). Separate disorders are distinguished and include disorders of expressive language, mixed receptive-expressive language, phonological (use of speech sounds) disorders, and stuttering.

Pervasive Developmental Disorders: Severe and pervasive impairment in several areas of development, including social interactions, language and communication, and play (stereotyped behaviors, interests, and activities). These are usually evident in the first years of life. Separate disorders are distinguished based on the scope of impairment and time of onset and include autistic disorder, Rett's, Asperger's, and childhood disintegrative disorders.

Attention-Deficit and Disruptive Behavior Disorders: Behaviors associated with inattention, impulsivity, overactivity, oppositionality and disobedience, provocative, aggressive, and antisocial behavior. Separate disorders are distinguished, including attention-deficit/hyperactivity, conduct, and oppositional defiant disorders.

Feeding and Eating Disorders of Infancy or Early Childhood: Persistent eating and feeding disturbances such as eating nonnutritive substances (pica), repeated regurgitation and rechewing of food (rumination disorder), and persistent failure to eat adequately, resulting in significant failure to gain weight or weight loss (feeding disorder of infancy or early childhood).

Tic Disorders: Sudden, rapid, and recurrent stereotyped motor movement or vocalizations. Separate disorders are distinguished based on scope of the tics (e.g., motor, vocal) and their duration and include Tourette's, chronic motor or vocal, and transient tic disorders.

Elimination Disorders: Dysfunction related to urination or defecation in which these functions appear to be uncontrolled and beyond the age in which control has usually been established. Two disorders, enuresis and encopresis, are distinguished and require the absence of medical condition in which these symptoms would emerge.

Other Disorders of Infancy, Childhood, or Adolescence: A collection of other disorders that are not covered elsewhere and include separation anxiety, selective mutism, reactive attachment, and stereotypic movement disorders.

The disorders within each category have multiple inclusion and exclusion criteria related to the requisite symptoms, severity and duration, and patterns of onset (see DSM IV, APA, 1994). Details of the diagnoses are beyond the scope of this chapter.

categories are widely recognized and are useful because they do not depend on the vicissitudes and arbitrary cutoff criteria of diagnostic systems. In most treatment studies with children and adolescents, diagnostic assessment is not conducted. Of the categories listed in Table 12.2, externalizing and internalizing disorders constitute the most frequent bases of clinical referrals in children and adolescents. Clearly, externalizing disorders dominate both therapy research and clinical practice.

Several studies spanning different geographical locales (e.g., the United States, Puerto Rico, Canada, and New Zealand) have yielded rather consistent results on the prevalence of disorders

TABLE 12.2 Broad Categories of Problem Domains/Disorders

Externalizing Disorders: Problems that are directed toward the environment and others. Primary examples include oppositional, hyperactive, aggressive, and antisocial behaviors and are encompassed by the psychiatric diagnostic category, Attention-Deficit and Disruptive Behavior Disorders (in Table 12.1).

Internalizing Disorders: Problems that are directed toward inner experience. Primary examples include anxiety, withdrawal, and depression.

Substance-related Disorders: Impairment associated with any of a variety of substances including alcohol, illicit drugs, and tobacco. These disorders, though important in their own right, are also associated with other psychiatric disorders.

Learning and Mental Disabilities: A range of problems related to intellectual and academic functioning, including mental retardation and learning disorders. Such problems are probably underestimated in terms of both prevalence and impact on behavior among children and adolescents referred to treatment because of the more salient problems that serve as the basis for referral.

Severe and Pervasive Psychopathology: Disorders recognized to be the more severe forms of psychopathology that have pervasive influences in the areas of functioning they affect and in their long-term course. Examples include schizophrenia and autism.

among children and adolescents (e.g., ages 4 to 18). Between 17 and 22% suffer significant developmental, emotional, or behavioral problems (e.g., U.S. Congress, 1991; WHO, 2001). There are approximately 70 million children and adolescents in the United States (Snyder, Poole, & Wan, 2000; U.S. Bureau of Census, 1993). If a prevalence rate of 20% is assumed, then approximately 14 million of our nation's youth have significant impairment due to an emotional or behavioral problem.

The prevalence rate ought to be viewed as a general pattern rather than conclusions about the "real" rates of disorders among children. Diagnostic systems and definitions of disorders have changed considerably over the past two decades. In addition, different prevalence studies have drawn on different diagnostic systems or different editions of a particular system. Even when the diagnostic criteria are the same, different methods of assessing disorders can lead to quite different rates (Boyle et al., 1996; Kazdin, 1989; Offord et al., 1996). With these variations, the consistencies among the different studies are all the more remarkable.

Highlighting disorders and their prevalence rates does not fully represent the scope of impairment among children and adolescents. Many individuals meet criteria for two or more diagnoses, a phenomenon referred as *comorbidity* (see Angold, Costello, & Erkanli, 1999; Clark, Watson, & Reynolds, 1995). Among community samples, comorbidity rates are relatively high. For example, among youths who meet the criteria for one disorder, approximately one-half also meet the criteria for another disorder (Cohen et al., 1993; Greenbaum, Foster-Johnson, & Petrila, 1996). Among clinically referred samples, the rates of comorbidity are much higher. For example, among adolescents with a diagnosis of substance abuse, most (e.g., $\geq$ 70%) meet the criteria for other disorders (Milin, Halikas, Meller, & Morse, 1991; Weinberg, Rahdert, Colliver, & Glantz, 1998).

The high prevalence rates of psychiatric disorder (approximately one of five children) are likely to *underestimate* the range of mental disorders and impairment. Children who fail to meet the cutoff for a diagnosis because of the severity, number, or duration of symptoms can nonetheless suffer significant impairment. *Subsyndrome* is the term that refers to a set of symptoms that fall below or fail to meet the diagnostic criteria for a disorder. Individuals whose symptoms are subsyndromal (e.g., in relation to depression or conduct disorder) may still show significant impairment and untoward long-term prognoses (Boyle et al., 1996; Gotlib, Lewinsohn, & Seeley, 1995; Lewinsohn, Solomon, Seeley, & Zeiss, 2000; Offord et al., 1992). Clearly, prevalence rates, when based on meeting the criteria for diagnoses, may provide a conservative estimate of child impairment and the need for treatment.

Problem and At-Risk Behaviors

Problems other than psychiatric disorders also warrant intervention. During adolescence, there is an increase in a number of activities referred to as *problem* or *at-risk behaviors* (see DiClemente, Hansen, & Ponton, 1996; Ketterlinus & Lamb, 1994; U.S. Congress, 1991). Examples include use of illicit substances, truancy, school suspensions, stealing, vandalism, and precocious and unprotected sex. These are referred to as at-risk behaviors because they increase the likelihood of a variety of adverse psychological, social, and health outcomes. For example, alcohol abuse is associated with the three most frequent forms of mortality among adolescents: automobile accidents, homicides, and suicide (Windle, Shope, & Bukstein, 1996); approximately 90% of automobile accidents among adolescents involve the use of alcohol.

Many youths with problem behaviors might well meet the criteria for a disorder (e.g., substance abuse disorder). However, there is a larger group that would not; that is, they engage in problem behaviors, fit in with their peers, and manage daily functioning (e.g., at school). The prevalence rates of problem behaviors are relatively high. For example, in one survey 50.8% of twelfth grade students reported some alcohol use in the 30 days prior to the survey; 31.3% reported being drunk at least once; and 4.9% reported using marijuana daily or almost daily (Johnston, 1996). Other studies paint a similar picture, even though estimates of substance abuse vary as a function of the age of the sample, the types of substances (e.g., inhalants), the time frame (use in past week, month, year), the assessment method (e.g., self-report vs. medical emergency visits), and the impact of many other factors (e.g., social class, ethnicity, neighborhood). Even so, the rates of abuse and use are alarming. Moreover, current data suggest that rates of substance use are increasing, a trend that began in the early 1990s (Weinberg et al., 1998).

Substance abuse is merely one example of at-risk behavior. A number of other examples have been identified, including unprotected sexual activity and its risk for sexually transmitted diseases (including human immunodeficiency virus [HIV]) and teen pregnancy; delinquent, antisocial, and violent behavior; dropping out of school; and running away from home (DiClemente et al., 1996; Dryfoos, 1990). Multiple problem behaviors often go together (see Ketterlinus & Lamb, 1994). This does not mean that drug abuse, delinquent behavior, and academic dysfunction invariably co-occur. However, the behaviors often come in "packages." A sample of youth identified with one of the behaviors (e.g., early sexual activity) is likely to have higher rates of other problem behaviors (substance use and abuse, delinquent acts) than a comparison sample similar in age and sex.

Delinquency

Delinquency is a legal designation that includes behaviors that violate the law. Many acts are included such as robbery, drug use, and vandalism. Some of the acts are illegal for both adults and juveniles (referred to as *index* offenses) and encompass such serious offenses as homicide, robbery, aggravated assault, and rape. Other acts (referred to as *status* offenses) are illegal only because of the age at which they occur, namely, only for juveniles. Examples include underage drinking, running away from home, truancy from school, and driving a car.

Delinquent acts overlap with psychiatric disorders and problem behaviors mentioned previously. Indeed, the distinction between delinquency and mental disorder is not always sharp, and individuals can readily meet the criteria for both based on the same behaviors (e.g., conduct disorder symptoms). Moreover, individuals identified as delinquent often have high rates of diagnosable psychiatric disorders. Fifty to 80% of delinquent youths may show at least one diagnosable psychiatric disorder—with conduct, attention deficit, and substance abuse disorders being the most common (see Kazdin, 2000a).

The prevalence rates of delinquency in the population at large vary as a function of how delinquency is measured. Arrest records, surveys of victims, and reports of individuals about their own criminal activities are among the most common methods of measurement. Because much crime goes unreported and detected, self-report has often been used and detects much higher rates than official records. A large percentage of adolescents (e.g., 70%) engage in some delinquent behavior, usually status rather than index offenses (Elliott et al., 1985; Farrington, 1995). Most of these individuals do not continue criminal behavior. A much smaller group (e.g., 20 to 35%) engages in more serious offenses (robbery and assault) and may be identified through arrest or contact with the courts. There is a small group (e.g., 5%) of persistent or career criminals who engage in many different and more severe delinquent activities and are responsible for approximately half of the officially recorded offenses (Farrington, 1995; Tracy, Wolfgang, & Figlio, 1990).

General Comments

In highlighting the scope of the problems that children and adolescents experience, four conclusions are worth underscoring: (1) Children and adolescents experience many different types of problems; (2) they often experience multiple problems concurrently (e.g., comorbid disorders, multiple problem behaviors, academic and learning problems); (3) these problems can emerge at many different points over the course of development; and (4) several million children and adolescents could profit from and are in need of some intervention.

As mentioned previously, an estimated 20% of children and adolescents evince some form of psychiatric disorder. Even without adding problem behaviors and delinquent acts, the scope of problems in need of intervention is great. Psychotherapy is one of many interventions designed to address social, emotional, and behavioral problems. Other interventions (e.g., preventive interventions, school educational programs, and medication) are pertinent to the problems but are beyond the scope of this chapter.

SPECIAL CHALLENGES OF TREATING CHILDREN AND ADOLESCENTS

Salient among the special challenges in providing psychotherapy to children are identifying what problems warrant treatment, assessing child functioning, providing therapy when the child or adolescent may not see any need for treatment, deciding the focus of treatment, and retaining children and families in therapy.

Identifying Dysfunction

The initial task of identifying problems worthy of treatment raises special issues. Extreme and pervasive departures from normative functioning (e.g., autism and more severe forms of mental retardation), by definition, are readily identifiable as needing special intervention. Yet externalizing (e.g., oppositional, conduct, and hyperactivity) and internalizing (anxiety, depression, withdrawal) behaviors are the social, emotional, and behavioral problems most frequently seen in treatment. Most of the symptoms that comprise these problems are relatively common to some degree at different points in development. For example, fears, fighting, lying, difficulty in concentrating, and social withdrawal are symptoms of recognized disorders. Because many problems that warrant treatment are present in smaller or less intense doses in everyday life, identifying a pattern of behavior as a problem worthy of intervention is a problem that is difficult for parents, teachers, and mental health professionals. No easily administered measure can serve as a "psychological thermometer" to determine quickly whether a child has the equivalent of a social, emotional, or behavioral "fever."

Identifying a problem or dysfunction worthy of treatment is also difficult because it may not be the behavior or characteristic of the child that is deviant or significant at all. Rather, the significance of the behavior may stem from when the problem occurs over the course of development. For example, the implications and long-term outcome of a behavioral pattern (e.g., fighting and bedwetting) depend on the age of the child (e.g., 2 vs. 10 years old). Bedwetting in middle and later childhood but not in early childhood (before age 5) is a risk factor for later psychopathology (Rutter, Yule, & Graham, 1973). One ought to evaluate and intervene in middle to late childhood but probably not in early childhood. In general, one of the challenges of child and adolescent treatment is deciding whether the qualitative or quantitative characteristics of the behavior are maladaptive or are within the normative range for the child's period of development. These can be subtle judgments for trained and untrained individuals alike. The difficulty in making these judgments may be exacerbated by factors such as socioeconomic status, ethnicity, and culture, which can influence social, emotional, and behavioral development and expectations about what may warrant intervention.

Assessing Dysfunction

Measuring clinical problems in children and adolescents raises special challenges that affect treatment and treatment research. Children and adolescents are often asked to report on their own dysfunction. Children can report on their symptoms and their functioning in everyday life, but their ability to do so varies as a function of the nature of the problem and their individual characteristics (LaGreca, 1990). As a guideline, children are usually not considered to be reliable reporters in early childhood (e.g., < 5 years of age). Measures such as self-report questionnaires or interviews in which young children must report on their thoughts, feelings, and behaviors are unlikely to be reliable. The standard interpretation is that young children may not have sufficient levels of cognitive development to identify the behavior as a problem, to see that it is leading to or is associated with impairment, and to realize that something could be done about it. A blanket statement about the utility of self-report in young children is difficult to defend.

Few self-report measures are available and well tested for use in early childhood. This could be due in part to an accepted belief that children cannot report well on their behavior, but it also could be due to a recognition that others are better informants. For children ages 8 to 9 and older, considerable research is available indicating the concurrent and predictive validity of child report (e.g., LaGreca, 1990; Mash & Terdal, 1997). Self-report in young children cannot be discounted because of the child's age. Novelty in presenting the questions can make a great difference in the utility of self-report. For example, asking children to identify which of two puppets is more like them (as the puppets playfully self-disclose various characteristics, including social, emotional, and behavioral problems) yields information that is unlikely to emerge from simply asking questions directly (Measelle, Ablow, Cowan, & Cowan, 1998).

Parents are usually the primary source of information regarding child functioning because they are knowledgeable about the child's behavior over time and across situations and usually play a central role in the referral of children for treatment. Social, emotional, and behavioral problems often reflect a departure from behavior that is usual for the child (e.g., not interacting with friends, loss of interest in activities). Parents are in a unique position to comment on such changes. Parent evaluations usually are obtained on standardized rating scales (e.g., Behavior Problem Checklist, Child Behavior Checklist) that assess several domains of child functioning (e.g., aggression, hyperactivity, anxiety, depression). The information parents provide about their child's functioning raises its own interpretive problems. For example, parent (usually maternal) perceptions of child adjustment and functioning are related to parent psychopathology (especially anxiety and depression), marital discord, stressors, and social support outside of the home (see Kazdin, 1994). Parents with their own psychopathology or parents who are experiencing stress are more likely to rate their children as more deviant, even when independently obtained evidence suggests that the children are no more deviant than children of parents with fewer symptoms or stressors. In short, parent functioning may influence how deviant a child appears before and after treatment, at least on parent-report measures. Child improvement at the end of treatment may reflect actual changes in the child, reductions in parental stress, or some combination of the two.

The use of multiple informants and multiple methods of assessment (e.g., self-report, other report, direct observation) is routinely endorsed as a wise strategy for psychological research in general. In the context of treatment, this is no less important, but it raises a significant set of challenges. Key sources (e.g., parents, teachers, children) do not correspond very well in the information they provide about the child (Achenbach, McConaughy, & Howell, 1987; Kazdin, 1994). This means, of course, that children who appear deviant or who have problems on measures obtained from one source (e.g., parents) may not appear to have problems on measures obtained from another source (e.g., teachers) (see Kazdin 1989; Offord et al., 1996). In general, there is no gold standard, that is, laboratory test or rock-solid criterion, to judge clinical disorders for most problems that are brought to treatment. Realistically, many children referred for treatment are clearly having significant problems, which are readily detected on diagnostic interviews and parent-completed measures. At the same time, a child who appears to be deviant, or is deviant, in one context or on one measure may not be deviant in another context or on another measure.

Motivation for Seeking Treatment

Children rarely refer themselves for treatment or identify themselves as experiencing stress, symptoms, or problems. Young children may not have the perspective to identify their own psychological impairment and its impact on daily functioning, or to consider the possibility that therapy is a viable means to help. Also, problems most commonly referred for treatment involve externalizing or disruptive behavior (e.g., aggression, hyperactivity). Reports from adults (parents, teachers) serve as the impetus for treatment, so the focus may partially reflect someone else's stress other than that of the child. Children are less likely to report dysfunction or a problem in relation to their own experience. This is, of course, much less true of adolescents, although here, too, behavioral patterns that parents would see as problematic (e.g., behaviors related to substance use and abuse, unprotected sex, vandalism, talk of killing oneself, or excessive concern with body image and extreme dieting) are not usually considered by adolescents as being a reason for any intervention.

Parents, too, may not feel that their child needs help in many instances in which the data would suggest otherwise. For example, only 31% of the parents in a community sample of children with conduct disorders felt that assistance was needed (Boyle, 1991). Many parents believe that problems will resolve themselves with time, and therefore they are less likely to seek treatment (Pavuluri, Luk, & McGee, 1996). Consequently, not all the motivational obstacles for initiating child therapy reside in the children.

The absence of a perceived problem on the part of the child, adolescent, or parent affects motivation for seeking and remaining in treatment and for engaging in the tasks that the particular treatment approach requires. The challenge to the clinician and researcher is to engage the child in treatment. Getting the child to come to treatment is a significant obstacle. Although the parent is "in control" of the decision to come to treatment and to begin the treatment process, it is likely that the child may be much more interested in staying after school for soccer practice than using the time for therapy sessions.

Once at the treatment sessions, the therapist will implement various techniques that he or she considers to be the means of achieving the treatment goals. The techniques could involve talk, play, role-play, games, or a meeting with the entire family. Getting the child to participate in these activities is a challenge. Many therapists want the child to grasp the point of the activities. There is little motivation, interest, or incentive for the child to even be in treatment, particularly when contrasted with the other activities (hanging out, being with friends) that the child is sacrificing. Removing the child from school for the therapy sessions, when feasible, overcomes this objection for most children. Yet, the parent is likely to raise the same issue: namely, is treatment worth the loss of school time? Moreover, the logistics of transporting the child to and from school during the day for a treatment session raise their own and often insurmountable obstacles. In short, getting children to treatment and engaging them in the session pose special challenges.

Focus of Treatment

Many adverse contextual influences can be identified that affect child functioning and have direct implications for child adjustment and psychopathology. Familiar examples include physical and sexual abuse, and neglect of the child, parent substance abuse, and inept parenting. Some contextual influences are particularly important because they influence attendance to, participation in, and effects of the intervention. For example, among children and adolescents with externalizing problems, socioeconomic disadvantage, high levels of stress, and parent psychopathology can influence the likelihood that families will attend treatment and, among those who do attend, the extent to which the children will improve and maintain their improvements over time (see Kazdin, 2000d).

The child's dependence on parent and family influences and evidence that many of these influences are somehow involved in the child's problems raise questions about the appropriate focus of treatment. To whom should the treatment be directed? Major options include the child, parents, the family (as a unit), teachers, peers, and siblings. In clinical work, treatment of child or adolescent dysfunction usually incorporates the parent, family, and teacher in some way (Kazdin, Siegel, & Bass, 1990; Koocher & Pedulla, 1977). This may entail involving parents in the sessions with the child, seeing parents separately, meeting with the family, and using the teacher to assess or intervene at school (e.g., a behavior modification program in the classroom). The entire matter of where to intervene is especially complex in relation to child treatment in light of the range of options. If children are particularly dependent on the parent and family, perhaps the parent and family are the best place to intervene. Quite possibly, several of the forces or influences that promote or sustain the child's problems are within the family or interpersonal context. Also, no matter how the problem came about, changing aspects of the context might be an excellent way to effect change in the child.

Certain facets of the parents and family may warrant intervention as part of, or as a precondition for, effective treatment of the child. For example, marital conflict, spousal abuse, and substance abuse are often present among parents of children with externalizing problems. Some facets of these problems may directly influence concurrent child deviance (e.g., some of the child maltreatment and harsh discipline is in the context of marital conflict). Other facets of the context (e.g., substance abuse) may need to be incorporated into a treatment plan as well. Contextual influences are omnipresent and may be relevant to therapy for adults as well as children. In the case of children, treatment may be a bit more intricate because some of these influences may need to be incorporated directly into the treatment process (e.g., Dadds, Schwartz, & Sanders, 1987; Henggeler et al., 1998). There is very little in the way of empirical research to inform what influences ought to be incorporated into treatment and the extent to which, or indeed whether, including or neglecting a particular contextual influence on the child affects treatment outcome.

Remaining in Treatment

Retaining children and families in treatment is a significant challenge. Among children, adolescents, and adults who begin treatment, 40 to 60% drop out prematurely and against the advice of the clinician (Kazdin, 1996b; Wierzbicki & Pekarik, 1993). Perhaps the reasons can be deduced from points already highlighted. Thus, if the child is not motivated to come to treatment, this could easily create problems in attending and continuing in treatment. In addition, if there are many parent and family problems (e.g., marital conflict, stress in the home, parent clinical dysfunction) or difficult living circumstances (e.g., socioeconomic disadvantage), these, too, could add to the obstacles of remaining in treatment. Obstacles associated with coming to treatment, parental views that treatment is too demanding, and the parent's poor relationship with the therapist also contribute to dropping out early (e.g., Kazdin, Holland, & Crowley, 1997; Kazdin, Stolar, & Marciano, 1995).

Contextual influences play a role in remaining in treatment. Consequently, even if one is not focusing on the parents or family in ways that are intended to improve child functioning, parent and family factors may need to be addressed to ensure that families remain in treatment (Prinz & Miller, 1994; Szapocznik et al., 1988). This is somewhat different from the demands of providing therapy for adults.

In general, identifying effective treatments is not merely a matter of developing and testing an intervention that will reduce or eliminate the problems leading to clinical referral. There are challenges related to assessment of child dysfunction, the motivation of children to participate in treatment, and the decision of whom to include in treatment (child, parent, family). Parent and family functioning can play a large role in delivery of treatment. For example, parent dysfunction can influence assessment of clinical functioning of the child, adherence to and compliance with any treatment prescriptions, and attendance and completion of treatment (Kazdin, 2000d). The challenges of providing therapy to children are widely recognized; how to meet the challenges is not well studied.

Current Status of the Evidence

Reviews of Treatment Outcome Research

Historically, narrative or qualitative reviews of the evidence have served as the dominant way to examine the effects of child psychotherapy (e.g., Levitt, 1957, 1963). Meta-analysis has become the preferred way of reviewing the evidence because it integrates a large number of studies systematically and uses replicable procedures and explicit decision rules. Meta-analysis relies on effect size (ES), which provides a common metric across a variety of investigations. Effect size refers to the magnitude of the difference between two (or more) conditions or groups and is expressed in standard deviation units. For the case where there are two groups in the study, ES equals the differences between means (e.g., between treatment and control groups or two treatment groups) divided by the standard deviation (usually pooled for the groups). Because an ES can be computed for each outcome measure in a study, usually a mean ES across all measures is used to summarize the study. Effect size constitutes the *dependent measure* for the meta-analysis and is used as a summary statistic to examine the impact of type of treatment as well as other variables (e.g., type of clinical problem, age of the participants, experience of the therapist). Cohen (1988) has provided us with an admittedly arbitrary but quite useful guideline for interpreting ESs. Small, medium, and large ESs are .20, .50, and .80, respectively. (If the measure were r rather than ES, small, medium, and large effects would correspond to correlations of .10, .30, and .50.)

In the past 25 years, there have been scores of meta-analyses of psychotherapy. Although the bulk of these meta-analyses have focused on therapy with adults, many are available for treatment of children and adolescents and include reviews of therapy in general, specific treatment approaches such as cognitive behavior therapy, group therapy, and family therapy, therapies conducted in special settings such as schools, and therapies that target a specific focus such as preparing children for medical procedures (e.g., tests and surgery) (Kazdin, 2000d; Weisz, Huey, & Weersing, 1998; Weisz & Weiss, 1993). From the general analyses of child therapy, rather than those that focus on individual techniques, two main conclusions are clearly warranted: (1) Psychotherapy appears to be better than no treatment, and (2) the magnitude of the effects with children and adolescents closely parallels the magnitude obtained with adults. The ESs for treatment versus no treatment hover in the .70 range, and this is similar for child, adolescent, and adult therapy.

Other conclusions have emerged from the meta-analyses of child therapy. These conclusions might be regarded as somewhat secondary, in part because they are less consistently found than the main conclusions. These include findings that treatment differences, when evident, tend to favor behavioral rather than nonbehavioral techniques; that the effects of treatment are usually maintained from post-treatment (assessments at the end of treatment) to followup (approximately five to seven months later); that treatments tend to be more effective with adolescents than with children, although both are effective; that individual therapy is more effective than group therapy; and that treatment is equally effective for externalizing and internalizing problems (see Kazdin, 2000d). It is the main conclusions that have been most frequently replicated and provide the information needed here. Reiterated simply, we know from the meta-analyses that treatment with children is worth doing—that is, children get better, and some techniques tend to be more effective than others.

Meta-analyses have provided many benefits over the narrative reviews. The explicitness of the procedures of meta-analysis (e.g., how studies are selected, how dependent measures are converted to effect sizes, and whether coding of the studies is reliably accomplished) is specifiable. Meta-analyses have shown that therapy is more effective than no therapy. Also, meta-analysis has been enormously helpful in evaluating variables that are not easily addressed in any single investigation. For example, meta-analyses have suggested that treatments more likely to be preferred or favored by the investigator produce stronger effects than other treatments included in the study (Hoag & Burlingame, 1997; Luborsky et al., 1999). Allegiance of the investigator is very difficult to address in a single study. Consequently, the benefits of meta-analysis extend beyond establishing that treatment is effective.

Along with the benefits of meta-analysis are significant limitations (see Kazdin, 2000d). There are different ways of computing effect sizes and the different ways affect the conclusions that are reached (Matt, 1989, Matt & Navarro, 1997; Weisz, Weiss, et al., 1995). In addition, many decisions need to be made in a meta-analysis, and there is often no agreed upon standard for making these decisions. To date, most meta-analyses have included only a small fraction of the controlled outcome studies. As mentioned previously, 1,500 controlled trials of child and adolescent therapy are available. Individual meta-analyses of child therapy at best sample 100 to 300 studies, which might be as much as 10 to 20 % of the available literature.

Evidenced-Based Treatments

Currently Identified Treatments

Recent efforts to supplement the more general reviews have focused on identifying specific treatments that have evidence in their behalf for specific types of clinical problems. Separate and somewhat independent efforts have been made to identify such treatments by different professional organizations and committees spanning different countries (e.g., Chambless et al., 1996, 1998; *Evidence-Based Mental Health*, 1998; Nathan & Gorman, 2002; Roth & Fonagy, 1996; Task Force on Promotion and Dissemination of Psychological Procedures [TFPP], 1995). These efforts have used different terminology to delineate treatments that have evidence in their behalf (e.g., empirically validated treatments, empirically supported treatments, evidence-based treatments, evidence-based practice, and treatments that work). The criteria for making the delineation have also varied. Typically, the criteria include evidence in behalf of the treatment from studies that randomly assign subjects to conditions, carefully specify the client population, utilize treatment manuals, and evaluate treatment outcome with multiple measures completed by "blind" (experimentally naïve) raters (if raters were used). Also, replication of treatment effects beyond an initial study is often required, especially replication by an independent investigator or research team.

The search for evidence-based treatments has underscored a distinction between efficacy and effectiveness. In contemporary writings, *efficacy* refers to the extent to which treatment has been shown to produce change in well-controlled studies in which several conditions of treatment delivery depart from clinical practice; *effectiveness* refers to the extent to which change has been shown in the context of clinical settings in which several conditions are much less well controlled, and characteristics of the clients, therapists, and treatment usually depart from those in research settings (see Hoagwood, Hibbs, Brent, & Jensen, 1995). In the classification of evidence-based treatments, the focus is on findings from well-controlled research or efficacy studies.

Several reviews have identified evidence-based treatments for children and adolescents (see Kazdin & Weisz, 1998; Lonigan & Elbert, 1998). Committee work identifying such treatments and progress in research continue, so any statement at a fixed point in time is incomplete. Also, any list of evidence-based treatments identifies treatments that meet rather specific criteria. A different set of criteria or slight modifications in the criteria could change the list. However, there is value in enumerating and illustrating some of the evidence-based treatments because those that have been identified are not likely to lose their status, that is, be removed from the list. Table 12.3 provides a list of evidence-based psychotherapies for children and adolescents. The list has been culled from reviews based on problem domains (see Kazdin & Weisz, 1998; Lonigan & Elbert, 1998; Nathan & Gorman, 1998; TFPP, 1995). Because these different sources do not invoke the same criteria, any treatment identified as evidence-based by these reviews is included in the list.

A few points are conspicuous from the list. First, there are in fact evidence-based treatments. This initial point is rather important information for professionals, potential clients, and society at large. A child referred to treatment for severe anxiety (or other problem listed in Table 12.3) ought to receive one of the evidence-based treatments as the intervention of choice, barring unusual circumstances that would strongly argue otherwise. It is possible that other interventions, yet to be studied, would be very effective, but their use would be difficult to defend as a first line of attack based on current evidence.

Second, the list of evidence-based treatments is not that long, especially when viewed in the context of the 550+ available treatments and the 1,500+ controlled studies. The goal of psychotherapy research is not to generate long lists of effective treatment. Identifying a small set of effective treatments that are viable options for

TABLE 12.3 Treatments for Children and Adolescents That Are Evidence-Based for Key Problem Domains

Problem Domain	Treatment	For a Review, See
Anxiety, Fear, Phobias	Systematic desensitization Modeling Reinforced practice Cognitive behavior therapy	Ollendick & King (1998)
Depression	Cognitive behavior therapy Coping with depression course Interpersonal psychotherapy	Asarnow, Jaycox, & Tompson (2001) Cuijpers (1998) Kaslow & Thompson (1998)
Oppositional and Conduct Disorder	Parent management training Problem-solving skills training Multisystemic therapy	Brestan & Eyberg (1998) Kazdin (2002) Sheldrick et al. (2001)
Attention-Deficit/Hyperactivity	Psychostimulant medication Parent management training Classroom contingency management	Greenhill (1998) Pelham et al. (1998)

Note: The techniques noted here draw from different methods of defining and evaluating evidence-based treatments. The techniques are those that would meet criteria for well established or probably efficacious (Lonigan, Elbert, & Johnson, 1998) or those with randomized controlled trials in their behalf (Nathan & Gorman, 2002). Evaluation of treatments and identification of those that meet criteria for empirical support are ongoing; hence, the above is an illustrative rather than fixed or exhaustive list. Psychostimulant medication is mentioned because this is the standard treatment for attention-deficit/hyperactivity disorder.

children and adolescents referred with a particular type of problem would be quite fine. Even so, the discrepancy between treatments in use and treatments for which there are strong evidence is conspicuous.

Third, the list of evidence-based treatments is dominated by cognitive behavioral treatments. This is no coincidence; approximately 50% of child treatment studies investigate cognitive behavioral techniques (see Durlak, Wells, Cotten, & Johnson, 1995; Kazdin, Bass, Ayers, & Rodgers, 1990). In addition to be counted as evidence-based treatments, studies must include several methodological features (e.g., use of treatment manuals, random assignment). These characteristics are much more likely among contemporary studies than studies conducted 20 or 30 years ago, and cognitive behavioral techniques are more popular in contemporary work.

Issues in Identifying Treatments

The goal of identifying evidence-based treatments is clearly laudable and important. There might be value in making finer gradations and employing different ways of considering the evidence or lack thereof. For example, it might be useful to evaluate treatments by placing them on a continuum that reflects the extent to which they have been evaluated and shown to produce therapeutic change. To illustrate, based on evidence, a given treatment might be placed on the following continuum: (1) Not evaluated; (2) evaluated but unclear effects, no effects, or possibly negative effects at this time; (3) promising (e.g., some evidence in its behalf); (4) well established (e.g., criteria currently used for identifying evidence-based treatments); and (5) better/best treatments (e.g., studies shown to be more effective than one or more other well-established techniques).

Such a graded classification may help move treatments along, that is, encourage tests to see if an intervention can be advanced to a higher category of an established, effective treatment. Also, some treatments may not meet rigorous evidential standards for evidenced-based treatment but may still be the best available, and it would be important to delineate these explicitly. For example, the behavioral treatment for young autistic children has on its behalf controlled outcome research with long-term followup and clinical application with reports of success (Lovaas, 1987; McEachin, Smith, & Lovaas, 1993; Sheinkopf & Siegel, 1998). The evidence is not sufficient to make this an official "evidence-based" treatment, but it is probably the best treatment available and is the treatment of choice, if empirical evidence is used as the criterion (e.g., Rogers, 1998; Smith, 1999). There would be value in delineating the status of such treatments because of the implications for the next steps in research and for clinical practice.

Another issue associated with the search for evidenced-based treatment is the emphasis on treatment technique. The effectiveness of treatment can depend on many other variables, and failure to consider this would lead one to revert to the uniformity myths we have tried to eschew since therapy researchers were alerted to the problem (Kiesler, 1966, 1971). Uniformity myths reflect an assumption that treatment produces relatively homogeneous effects across all clients, therapists, and conditions of administration. For example, the characteristics of the therapist can influence outcome. Different therapists administering the same treatment, even if they are all following the manual, can produce different outcome effects (e.g., Luborsky et al., 1997; Shapiro, Firth-Cozens, & Stiles, 1989). Treatment outcome also depends on how well the therapist conducts the therapy. Well-executed treatment, as defined by adherence to a treatment manual or ratings of supervisors, influences treatment effectiveness (e.g., Frank, Kupfer, Wagner, McEachran, & Cornes., 1991; O'Malley et al., 1988; Rounsaville, O'Malley, Foley, & Weissman, 1988). Whether an evidence-based treatment is effective may depend on how it is implemented and not merely on what the treatment is.

Evidence-based treatments refer to interventions shown to produce therapeutic change in well-controlled laboratory settings and under conditions that depart from those of clinical practice. In research, investigators usually focus on less severely disturbed samples, utilize structured, manualized, and often inflexible treatments, train therapists well in the treatments they administer, monitor how treatment is administered to ensure the adherence of the therapist, and so on. This means that evidence-based treatments may or may not have similar impact when applied in clinical settings. This is not a new concern in psychotherapy research (e.g., Borkovec & Rachman, 1979; Heller, 1971; Kazdin, 1978), but it is no less salient now.

General Comments

Objections and concerns have been raised about the efforts to identify evidence-based treatments other than those mentioned here (see Garfield, 1998; Kazdin, 2000d; Persons & Silberschatz, 1998; Weisz & Hawley, 1998). These concerns ought not to detract from the important advance. As a method of reviewing the literature, the focus on evidence-based treatment provides a quite different yield from the general meta-analytic review. With the focus on evidence-based treatments, one can more readily consider the status of individual treatments as applied to specific problem areas. One can more easily consider what to do in clinical work. It is possible to quibble about some of the criteria that are used, but many efforts are made to identify evidence-based treatments, and singling out any particular effort ignores the larger movement within treatment research and the contribution it makes.

In terms of clinical application, if there are evidence-based treatments for a given problem (e.g., anxiety or conduct disorder), a very strong rationale will be needed for not using one of these treatments. As an example, the most frequently used treatment in clinical work for oppositional and aggressive behavior in children is relationship therapy based on psychodynamic or relationship-based, nondirective therapy (Kazdin, Siegel, & Bass, 1990). It is possible that these treatments are effective, although there is not strong support for such a conclusion in uncontrolled and controlled studies (e.g., Fonagy & Target, 1994; Kazdin, Bass, Siegel, & Thomas, 1989; Weiss, Catron, Harris, & Phung, 1999). Defenders of psychodynamic and relationship-based treatments could cogently note that the treatments have not been well or carefully studied and that it is premature to impugn their effectiveness. Nevertheless, the absence of solid data for these techniques is not a strong basis for continuing their use in clinical work. There *are* evidence-based treatments for conduct disorder (e.g., Bresten & Eyberg, 1998; Kazdin, 2002; Sheldrick, Kendall, & Heimberg, 2001). Although researchers argue about the interpretation of studies and criteria used to select the studies, in the day-to-day practice of therapy, treatments are being used that have no evidence in their behalf when there is evidence for the efficacy of other treatments.

Treatments That Work: Illustrations of Exemplary Research

Enumeration of evidence-based treatments does not convey concretely the advances and the high-quality research that has been completed to date. This section highlights four different treatments that are evidence-based and that have emerged from ongoing programs of research. The treatments focus on internalizing disorders (anxiety and depression) and externalizing disorders (oppositional and aggressive behavior, delinquency) and illustrate treatments with both children and adolescents.

Cognitive Behavioral Therapy for Child Anxiety

Characteristics of Treatment. Cognitive behavioral treatment (CBT) for anxiety in children focuses on dysfunctional cognitions and their implications for the child's subsequent thinking and behavior (see Kendall, Chu, Pimentel, & Choudbury, 2000; Kendall & Treadwell, 1996 for reviews). Key components of cognition are distinguished, including cognitive structures (memory and ways in which information is experienced); cognitive content (ongoing self-statements); cognitive processes (how experiences are processed and interpreted); and cognitive products (attributions that result from the above). In this treatment, cognitive distortions are considered to play a central role among children with anxiety (Kendall, Panichelli-Mindel, Sugarman, & Callahan, 1997). Cognitive distortions refer to information processes that are misguided and that lead to misperceptions of oneself or the environment. Treatment develops new skills, provides new experiences for the child to test dysfunctional as well as adaptive beliefs, and assists the child in processing new experiences. Strategies used in treatment focus directly on learning new behaviors through modeling and direct reinforcement. In addition, cognitive strategies such as the use of self-statements address processes (information processing style, attributions, and self-talk) considered to mediate anxiety.

The CBT program consists of 16 to 20 sessions administered individually to the child. Among the techniques that comprise treatment, modeling, role-playing, in vivo exposure, relaxation training, and reinforcement are used. In addition, practice efforts are provided to extend the treatment to anxiety-provoking situations at home and at school. Approximately the first half of treatment is devoted to learning steps for coping with anxiety and managing distress. These include recognizing the physiological symptoms of anxiety (e.g., internal signals for anxiety such as sensations of tension), challenging and altering anxiety-provoking cognitions and one's internal dialogue (e.g., expecting "bad" things to happen and generating alternatives of what else might happen); problem solving (e.g., devising a plan to cope with the anxiety, generating alternatives of what one can do, and selecting one of the courses of action); and evaluating the coping plan and administering consequences (e.g., self-evaluation and self-reinforcement).

The second half of treatment focuses on applying the newly learned skills by exposing children at first to imaginary and low-anxiety-provoking situations and then later to moderate and more highly anxiety-provoking situations. Exposure is also included as homework assignments in which the child rehearses application of the steps at home and at school. Rewards are earned for completion of these assignments. In the final session of treatment, the child makes a videotaped "commercial" describing the steps and their use in mastering anxiety-provoking situations.

Overview of the Evidence. Treatment has been evaluated with children 9 to 13 years of age in both group and single-case experimental studies (see Flannery-Schroeder & Kendall, 2000; Kendall, Panichelli-Mindell et al., 1997). In randomized controlled trials, treatment has been superior to waiting-list control conditions. Improvements are evident on multiple child-, parent-, and teacher-report measures of anxiety as well as other symptom domains, including aggression, social problems, hyperactivity, and depression, and on behavioral observations of child distress (Kendall, 1994; Flannery-Schroeder & Kendall, 2000; Kendall, Flannery-Schroeder et al., 1997). Treatment gains are reflected in returning many youths (64% in one of the studies) to within the normative range for anxiety. Followup data one year and over three years later have indicated that treatment effects are maintained (Kendall, Flannery-Schroeder et al., 1997; Kendall & Southam-Gerow, 1996). Another team of investigators (Barrett, 1998; Barrett, Dadds, & Rapee, 1996; Barrett, Duffy, Dadds, & Rapee, 2001; Dadds et al., 1999) has replicated the effects of treatment in randomized controlled trials and has shown the maintenance of treatment effects up to six years later.

The treatment research is exemplary in a number of ways. First, the studies have included children who meet criteria for a diagnosis of anxiety disorder, primarily generalized anxiety, separation anxiety, and social phobia. Second, the impact of treatment has been strong and consistent across studies, including replication of the main findings by a separate investigative team. Third, the clinical significance of treatment has been demonstrated repeatedly. Overall, CBT for anxiety disorders is one of the treatments considered to be evidence-based. The availability of a treatment manual (Kendall, Kane, Howard, & Siqueland, 1990) provides opportunities for extension in clinical work and, of course, for further research to develop the treatment.

Coping with Depression Course for Adolescents

Characteristics of Treatment. The coping with depression course for adolescents (CWD-A) draws on cognitive and behavioral conceptualizations of depression (see Lewinsohn & Clarke, 1999; Lewinsohn, Clarke, Rohde, Hops, & Seeley, 1996 for reviews). Depression is associated with multiple cognitions (e.g., hopelessness, helplessness) and restricted behavioral repertoires (e.g., limited participation in pleasant activities, few experiences of reinforcement from the environment). Disruptions of behavioral patterns in everyday life are accorded special importance in initiating depressive cognitions and the symptom patterns of the disorder (see Lewinsohn, Hops, Teri, & Hautzinger, 1985). The CWD-A is a cognitive behavioral treatment that combines these different views and treatment components. To address the cognitive features of depression, individuals are made aware of their often pessimistic, negative thoughts, beliefs, and self-blaming causal attributions. More constructive cognitions are substituted for these and are practiced outside of treatment. To address the behavioral features of depression, activities associated with positive reinforcement from the environment are increased. This is accomplished by teaching specific social skills.

CWD-A is a group treatment and is conceptualized as a course to emphasize the psychoeducational components in a way that eschews the stigma of treatment. The primary focus is on development of skills and the means to enhance the adolescent's ability to cope with problematic situations. Group activities and role-playing are central in the treatment sessions; between sessions there are homework assignments to extend the treatment beyond the classroom. Treatment includes 16 two-hour sessions over a period of eight weeks (see Lewinsohn et al., 1996). Up to 10 adolescents are included in the group. The course includes a workbook with brief readings, quizzes, structured learning tasks, and forms for the completion of practice (homework) assignments. The sessions are systematically planned and include skill training within the session and then extension to the home. The sessions focus on specific skills and themes, such as developing social skills, engaging in pleasant activities, and reducing negative cognitions. Throughout the sessions, skills are taught and practiced in the session and at home.

Other aspects of treatment have been included as well, but they are not necessarily central to the main treatment. A parent component has been added in which parents are trained to support and assist skills developed in the adolescent. During these sessions, separate from those provided to the adolescents, the parents are also taught communication and problem-solving skills. In addition, booster (additional) sessions for the adolescents have been provided at the end of the 16-week course. These sessions are offered at four-month intervals for a period of two years. These sessions address emergent issues individually tailored to each case. The focus is facilitated by a brief assessment that examines how the adolescent is doing in everyday life, current target complaints, and use of skills from the prior training course.

OVERVIEW OF THE EVIDENCE. Randomized controlled clinical trials of the CWD-A with adolescents have demonstrated that the course is significantly more effective in reducing depression than a wait list control treatment condition (Lewinsohn & Clarke, 1999; Lewinsohn, Clarke, Hops, & Andrews, 1990). Treatment effects have been maintained up to two years of followup. The studies have been consistent in demonstrating the effects of the basic treatment. Indeed, many (> 20) outcome studies, encompassing adolescents, adults, the elderly, minority groups, and caregivers of the elderly, and in the context of treatment and prevention, have demonstrated the effectiveness of this intervention (see Cuijpers, 1998). The parent component and booster sessions to the treatment of adolescents have not led to increases in effectiveness over the basic treatment without these features, although it may be premature to rule out these components (see Lewinsohn et al., 1996). Improvement in treatment has been associated with a number of characteristics of adolescents. Those who respond better tend to be male and younger, and to engage in more pleasant activities prior to treatment.

There are several notable features of this treatment. First, the focus has been on adolescents with diagnosable depression. Second, the impact of treatment has been impressive across a range of outcome domains (e.g., symptoms, functioning in everyday life, coping skills). Third, the clinical impact or significance of treatment has been demonstrated by evaluating the extent to which youths continue to meet diagnostic criteria for depression. At the end of treatment, the proportion of youths who still meet diagnostic criteria is significantly lower for treated than for wait list cases (e.g., 33 vs. 52%, respectively) (Lewinsohn et al., 1996). Fourth, the format of the treatment raises interesting prospects for dissemination. The intervention is presented as a course and an academic or educational experience rather than as psychotherapy or treatment. The course-like format may make this intervention disseminable to many depressed individuals who would not otherwise seek treatment because of any stigma, perceived or real, associated with seeking therapy or outpatient care. The availability of course materials including a treatment manual, videotapes, and workbooks (Clarke, Lewinsohn, & Hops, 1990; Lewinsohn et al., 1996) may also make the treatment disseminable among practitioners.

Parent Management Training for Oppositional and Aggressive Children

CHARACTERISTICS OF TREATMENT. Parent management training (PMT) refers to procedures in which parents are trained to alter their child's behavior in the home. Training is based on the general view that oppositional and aggressive behavior are inadvertently developed and sustained in the home by maladaptive parent-child interactions. Among the many interaction patterns, those involving coercion have received the greatest attention (Patterson, 1982; Patterson, Reid, & Dishion, 1992). Coercion refers to deviant behavior on the part of one person (e.g., the child) that is rewarded by another person (e.g., the parent). Aggressive children are inadvertently rewarded for their aggressive interactions and their escalation of coercive behaviors as part of the discipline practices that sustain aggressive behavior.

The primary goal of PMT is to alter the pattern of interchanges between parent and child so that prosocial, rather than coercive, behavior is directly reinforced and supported within the family. This requires developing several different parenting behaviors, such as establishing the rules for the child to follow, providing positive reinforcement for appropriate behavior, delivering mild forms of punishment to suppress behavior, negotiating compromises, and other procedures. These parenting behaviors are systematically and progressively developed within the sessions in which the therapist shapes (develops through successive approximations) parenting skills. The programs that parents eventually implement in the home also serve as the basis for the focus of the sessions in which the procedures are reviewed, modified, and refined.

Although many variations of PMT exist, several common characteristics can be identified. Treatment is conducted primarily with the parent(s) who implement several procedures at home. The parents meet with a therapist who teaches them to use specific procedures to alter interactions with their child, to promote prosocial behavior, and to decrease deviant behavior. Parents are trained to identify, define, and observe problem behaviors in new ways. Careful specification of the problem is essential for delivering reinforcing or punishing consequences and for evaluating whether or not the program is achieving the desired goals. The treatment sessions provide concrete opportunities for parents to see how the techniques are implemented, to practice and refine use of the techniques (e.g., through extensive role-playing), and to review the behavior-change programs implemented at home. Parent-managed reinforcement programs for child deportment and performance at school, completion of homework, and activities on the playground are routinely included with the assistance of teachers, as available.

Duration of treatment has varied depending on the severity of child dysfunction. Programs for young, mildly oppositional children usually last six to eight weeks. With clinically referred conduct-disordered children, the programs usually last 12 to 25 weeks. It is difficult to provide a firm statement of the required duration of treatment because of two competing trends, namely, efforts to develop more abbreviated and more cost-effective variations of treatment on the one hand (e.g., Thompson, Ruma, Schuchmann, & Burke, 1996) and to combine PMT with other treatment modalities (multimodal treatments) on the other hand (e.g., Webster-Stratton, 1996).

Overview of the Evidence. PMT is one of the most well-researched therapy techniques for children and adolescents. Treatment has been evaluated in scores of randomized controlled outcome trials with children and adolescents varying in age (e.g., 2 to 17 years old) and severity of oppositional and conduct problems (see Kazdin, 1997). Indeed, a review of treatments for conduct disorder has identified PMT as the only intervention that is well established, that is, has been shown to be effective in independently replicated controlled clinical trials (Brestan & Eyberg, 1998). The outcome studies show that PMT has led to marked improvements in child behavior, as reflected on parent and teacher reports of deviant behavior, direct observational measures of behavior at home and at school, and institutional records (e.g., school truancy, police contacts, arrest rates, institutionalization). The magnitude of change has placed conduct problem behaviors to within normative levels of functioning at home and at school, based on normative data from nonreferred peers (e.g., same age, sex). Treatment gains have been maintained in several studies one to three years after treatment, although one program reported maintenance of gains 10 to 14 years later (Long, Forehand, Wierson, & Morgan, 1994).

Family socioeconomic disadvantage, marital discord, high parental stress and low social support, single-parent families, harsh punishment practices, and parent history of antisocial behavior predict: (1) who remains in treatment; (2) the magnitude of change among those who complete treatment; and (3) the extent to which changes are maintained at followup (e.g., Dadds & McHugh, 1992; Dumas & Wahler, 1983; Kazdin, 1995; Kazdin & Wassell, 1999; Webster-Stratton, 1985; Webster-Stratton & Hammond, 1990). Those families at greatest risk often respond to treatment, but the magnitude of effects is attenuated as a function of the extent to which these factors are present. Among child characteristics, more severe and chronic antisocial behavior and comorbidity predict reduced responsiveness to treatment (e.g., Kazdin, 1995; Ruma, Burke, & Thompson, 1996).

Some evidence suggests that adolescents respond less well to PMT, when compared with preadolescents (Dishion & Patterson, 1992). This may be accounted for by the severity of symptoms at pre-treatment among adolescents (Ruma et al., 1996). Adolescents referred for treatment tend to be more severely and chronically impaired than preadolescents; once severity is controlled, the impact of age is less clear. Even so, developing contingencies in the home for children, compared to adolescents, is much easier because of the control parents can exert over reinforcing consequences.

In much of the outcome research, PMT has been administered to families individually in clinic settings. Group administration has been facilitated greatly by the development of videotaped materials that present themes, principles, and procedures to the parents. The use of these tapes has been rigorously evaluated and shown to be effective with parents of conduct problem children (see Webster-Stratton, 1996). PMT has been extended to community settings to bring treatment to those persons least likely to come to or remain in treatment. PMT is effective and highly cost effective when provided in small parent groups in neighborhoods where the families reside (e.g., Cunningham, Bremner, & Boyle, 1995; Thompson et al., 1996). Also, PMT has been effective in reducing conduct problems and increasing positive parenting behaviors when implemented on a large-scale as part of early school intervention (Head Start) programs (Webster-Stratton, 1998).

Perhaps the most important point to underscore is that no other technique for oppositional and conduct problem children has probably been studied as often or as well in controlled trials as has PMT (Brestan & Eyberg, 1998). Moreover, the procedures and practices that are used in PMT (e.g., various forms of reinforcement and punishment practices) have been widely and effectively applied outside the context of child conduct problems (e.g., autism, language delays, developmental disabilities, medical disorders) (see Kazdin, 2001a). Several resources are available to facilitate use of PMT clinically and in research. Treatment manuals are available for clinicians and convey the structure, content, and flow of treatment sessions (e.g., Forehand & McMahon, 1981; Forgatch & Patterson, 1989; Patterson & Forgatch, 1987; Sanders & Dadds, 1993). Books and pamphlets are also available for parents (e.g., Forehand & Long, 1996; Patterson, 1976) to convey basic concepts and to show how to apply various techniques. Already mentioned were videotapes that can also be used by professionals to guide group PMT. In short, several training materials are available for professionals as well as their clients.

Multisystemic Therapy for Antisocial and Delinquent Adolescents

Characteristics of Treatment. Multisystemic therapy (MST) focuses on systems in which behavior is embedded and on alteration of these systems in concrete ways that can influence behavior (Henggeler et al., 1998). The adolescent is influenced by a number of systems, including the family (immediate and extended family members), peers, schools, and neighborhoods. Multiple influences within these systems may be involved in development, maintenance, or amelioration of the problem. For example, within the context of the family, some tacit alliance between one parent and the adolescent may contribute to disagreement and conflict over discipline in relation to the adolescent. Treatment may be required to address the alliance and sources of conflict in an effort to alter adolescent behavior. Also, adolescent functioning at school may involve limited and poor peer relations; treatment may address these areas as well. The notion of a systems approach entails a focus on the individual's own behavior insofar as it affects others. Individual treatment of the adolescent or parents may be included in treatment.

The primary focus of treatment has been with delinquent adolescents, including seriously disturbed, repeat offenders. The focus of treatment is influenced in part by the factors that have been shown to influence and relate to development and maintenance of delinquent behavior. MST is not very concerned with past determinants of behavior but considers risk factors (e.g., family discipline, child problem-solving skills, parent conflict) that may reflect current areas worth redressing as part of treatment.

The goals of treatment are to help the parents develop the adolescent's behaviors, to overcome difficulties (e.g., marital) that impede the parents' ability to function as parents, to eliminate negative interactions between parent and adolescent, and to develop or build cohesion and emotional warmth among family members. Emphasis on systems and contexts requires mobilizing many influences and aspects of the interpersonal environment, as feasible and available. Consequently, treatment is multifaceted and draws on several different techniques, including PMT, contingency management, problem-solving skills therapy, marital therapy, and others. Domains may be addressed in treatment (e.g., parent unemployment) because they raise issues for one or more systems (e.g., parent stress, alcohol consumption) and affect how the adolescent is functioning (e.g., marital conflict, child-discipline practices). Much of the therapy is conducted outside of the treatment sessions in which parents and significant others engage in new strategies (e.g., reinforcement techniques) that alter behavior at home, at school, and in the community.

Treatment procedures are used on an as-needed basis directed toward addressing individual, family, and system issues that may contribute to problem behavior. The conceptual view focuses on multiple systems and their impact on the individual, which serves as a basis for selecting the different treatment procedures. The key focus of treatment is on present behavior and interventions that are directed toward concrete observable changes in the family and adolescent. Efforts are made to involve the family and to empower them as agents of change in relation to family interaction, the school, and peers. In some cases, treatment consists of helping the parents address a significant domain through practical advice and guidance (e.g., to involve the adolescent in prosocial peer activities at school, to restrict specific activities with a deviant peer group). Much of therapy is based on assessment and hypothesis testing. That is, an evaluation is made about how or what the adolescent is doing in a particular context, a hypothesis is generated by the therapist regarding what factors might be influencing these behaviors, and the hypothesis is tested by intervening to alter the factor to see if there are concrete changes in adolescent behavior.

Overview of the Evidence. There is strong evidence in behalf of MST. Treatment has been evaluated in multiple randomized controlled clinical trials with very seriously disturbed adjudicated delinquent youths and their families, including chronic juvenile offenders, juvenile sexual offenders, youths with substance use and abuse, and maltreating (abusing, neglectful) families (see Burns, Schoenwald, Burchard, Faw, & Santos, 2000; Henggeler et al., 1998, for reviews). The benefits of treatment, in comparison to other treatment and control conditions, have been evident on measures of adolescent and parent psychopathology, family relations and functioning, rearrest rates, severity of offenses, drug use, and reinstitutionalization (e.g., incarceration, hospitalization). Cost-effectiveness data have also shown that the treatment is a bargain in comparison to alternative diversion and institutional programs to which such youths are ordinarily assigned and other interventions with evidence on their behalf (e.g., functional family therapy, special foster care, parent problem solving) (see Burns et al., 2000).

Treatment influences key processes proposed to contribute to deviant behavior (Huey, Henggeler, Brondino, & Pickrel, 2000; Mann, Borduin, Henggeler, & Blaske, 1990). Specifically, decreases in adolescent symptoms are positively correlated with improved family functioning (e.g., improved communication, support, and affective expression and decreases in parental conflict). This work provides an important link between theoretical underpinnings of treatment and outcome effects. Also, evidence suggests that the fidelity with which MST is carried out influences treatment outcome (Henggeler, Melton, Brondino, Scherer, & Hanley, 1997; Huey et al., 2000).

The evidence in behalf of MST has several strengths, including the focus on very seriously disturbed adolescents, replication of treatment outcomes in several randomized controlled clinical trials, evaluation of clinically and socially important outcomes (e.g., arrest, criminal activity, reinstitutionalization), and assessment of long-term followup. In addition, conduct problems are conceptualized at multiple levels, namely, as dysfunction in relation to the individual, family, and extrafamilial systems and the transactions among these. Youths with conduct problems experience dysfunction at multiple levels, including individual repertoires, family interactions, and extrafamilial systems (e.g., peers, schools, employment among later adolescents). MST begins with the view that many different domains are likely to be relevant; they need to be evaluated and then addressed in treatment.

There remain important challenges for the approach. The administration of MST is demanding in light of the need to provide several different interventions in a high-quality fashion. Individual treatments alone are difficult to provide; multiple combinations of different treatments invite all sorts of challenges (e.g., therapist training, ensuring treatments of high quality, strength, and integrity). MST is an intensive treatment. In some projects, therapists are available 24 hours a day, 7 days a week; sometimes a team of therapists is involved rather than merely one therapist. Perhaps this model of treatment delivery is precisely what is needed for clinical problems that are multiply determined, protracted, and recalcitrant to more abbreviated interventions.

Overall Evaluation

The four treatments were highlighted rather than reviewed in detail; each of the treatments is part of an ongoing program of research that extends beyond questions of treatment outcome (e.g., child, parent, family factors associated with the disorder, longitudinal course). Many excellent features of these studies were identified, including recruitment of clinical samples, use of well-specified treatments, assessment of outcome in ways that reflect significant changes, and evaluation of followup. Studies of this quality are exceptions rather than the rule in child therapy research.

The treatments and their supportive research were highlighted to illustrate the accomplishments and benefits of child and adolescent therapy in more concrete ways than broad reviews of treatment research convey. The results convey that there are palpable effects of treatment on clinical problems and effects that are evident beyond post-treatment assessment. An objective of presenting these treatments was to see what the best research is accomplishing as a means of deciding what might be emulated in future studies and what is still in need of attention.

Characteristics and Limitations of Therapy Research

The limitations of contemporary research related to how therapy is studied greatly restrict the extent to which the results from therapy research are likely to be generalizable to clinical practice. In addition, key areas on which effective clinical application depends have been largely neglected.

Children and Families Seen in Treatment

In most investigations of therapy, children and families are actively recruited for participation in treatment (e.g., from advertisements, visits to local schools to announce the availability of special programs). The primary concern is that cases recruited for treatment research differ from cases seen in clinical work *and* that these differences influence the extent to which the results of treatment in research apply to clinically referred cases. Children recruited for therapy research tend to be less disturbed than children referred for treatment, as reflected in the severity and chronicity of the problem, the presence of comorbid disorders, and deficits in other areas of functioning likely to be correlated with impairment (peer relations, school functioning, participation in prosocial activities). One might expect less severely disturbed children with greater competence and prosocial attributes in other domains, as seen in research, to do much better in therapy than their more severely disturbed counterparts in clinical work. It is important not to oversimplify the distinction between recruited and clinically referred cases. Variation is likely to be a matter of degree and along multiple dimensions, and one can recruit cases whose clinical dysfunction and impairment are similar to or indeed are more extreme than a clinic sample. However, this is rarely the case in child therapy research.

Child dysfunction is likely to be correlated with parent dysfunction and characteristics of the situations in which children live. Consequently, recruiting less and mildly problematic cases for treatment research also is likely to yield families that are less seriously impaired, that live in environments that have fewer untoward influences on child dysfunction, and that are more responsive to treatment. For example, anxiety, mood, and conduct disorders tend to run in families (see Hammen, 1991; Klein & Last, 1989; Stoff, Breiling, & Maser, 1997). Parents of children referred for treatment with one of these disorders are themselves likely to have higher rates of the respective disorders and any features associated with those disorders than parents of nonreferred children. Referred children might be more difficult cases because of the strong set of influences (family history, whether biological, socioenvironmental, or some combination) in which their dysfunction is embedded. Also, in clinical work, parents are usually involved in the treatment of their children and adolescents, that is, participate in the sessions and carry out therapeutic strategies at home. Insofar as parents experience clinical dysfunction or impairment, implementation of and adherence to the treatment may be less evident among families of clinically referred than among families of recruited children. The benefits of treatment could be commensurately reduced.

Treatment and Treatment Administration

Types of Treatment. As mentioned previously, approximately one-half of outcome research for children and adolescents focuses on behavioral or cognitive behavioral techniques (Durlak et al., 1995; Kazdin, Bass, et al., 1990). Many approaches commonly practiced in clinical work (psychodynamic therapy, relationship-based treatment, generic counseling) have very sparse empirical literatures (e.g., Barrnett, Docherty, & Frommelt, 1991; Shadish et al., 1993). When reviews note that evidence supports the effects of psychotherapy, it is important to bear in mind that this applies to a small fraction of the treatments in use.

The type of treatment evaluated in research can be distinguished in another way. With few notable exceptions (e.g., MTA Cooperative Group, 1999a, 1999b), research focuses on relatively "pure" (single-type or modality) treatments. The investigator usually is interested in evaluating a particular type of treatment as applied to a relatively circumscribed problem. In clinical practice, on the other hand, therapists commonly mix and combine several different treatments; eclectic and combined treatments are the rule rather than the exception. In general, we have little idea about the effects of treatment that are administered in clinical practice and about whether the results obtained in research apply to clinical practice.

Characteristics of Administration. How treatment is administered in research departs from how it is administered in practice in ways that could readily influence outcome. In research, treatment is relatively brief (e.g., average of nine to ten sessions) and is administered in group format. The group format is one of convenience because many studies are conducted in school settings where children are recruited for participation. In clinical practice, treatment tends to be longer, to be administered individually, and, of course, in clinics. Conceivably, the "same" treatment (e.g., cognitive behavior therapy) might have quite different effects administered in a group format in schools rather than in clinical settings, assuming that all else (e.g., child severity of dysfunction) were equal.

Treatments as administered in research are often carefully described in treatment manuals. Manuals refer to written guidelines that convey the nature of treatment and how it is to be administered, and they can vary widely in degree of specificity. For example, a treatment manual may outline the general principles that guide the sessions, specify the themes, topics, skills, and tasks to be covered, and convey or specify mini-speeches or key aspects of what the therapist says during each session.

Along with treatment manuals, research usually includes supervision of the therapists during the study to ensure that the therapists actually follow or adhere to the manual. Supervision may take many forms, but typically one or more procedures are used, such as: (1) observing the treatment sessions (e.g., live through a one-way mirror or via audio- or videotaping); (2) reviewing sessions with the therapists; (3) discussing cases in treatment on a regular (e.g., weekly) basis to identify any problems in administering treatment; (4) repeatedly practicing or conducting retraining sessions with therapists during the study; and (5) having therapists complete checklists or forms regarding what they did during the session to prompt adherence to the procedures. Such rigorous specification of treatment and oversight of its execution are not at all like clinical work. One would expect that well-specified and closely monitored treatment would lead to greater adherence on the part of the therapist (i.e., administration of treatment more faithfully than would otherwise be the case). Indeed, therapist adherence to the prescribed treatment can increase effectiveness (e.g., Dobson & Shaw, 1988; Henggeler, Melton et al., 1997; Huey et al., 2000). Quite possibly, the findings from therapy research may pertain to therapy executed in a particular way and have little or unclear relation to the effects achieved in clinical practice.

Assessment of Treatment Outcome

Limited Outcome Focus. The usual impetus for seeking treatment is the presence of various symptoms, or maladaptive, disturbing, or disruptive behaviors. Naturally, the effects of treatment are measured by the extent to which the problems identified at the outset of treatment are reduced when treatment is completed. The reduction of symptoms identified at the outset of therapy is obviously central to the evaluation of outcome. However, the problems the individual brings to treatment are likely to involve many domains other than symptoms. For example, for a clinically depressed, anxious, or conduct-problem child, functioning in many domains (adult and peer relations, school performance, participation in activities, self-esteem) is likely to be problematic as well. In addition to symptom reduction, it is important to assess these other domains.

To illustrate the point, consider prosocial functioning as one domain likely to be of broad relevance for diverse clinical problems among children and adolescents. Prosocial functioning refers to the presence of positive adaptive behaviors and experiences such as participation in social activities, social interaction, and making friends. With children and adolescents, adjustment depends heavily on the positive adaptive behaviors or skills, given the significance of the peer group and prosocial experiences outside the home. Reducing symptoms no doubt can improve a person's functioning. Yet, the overlap of symptom reduction and positive prosocial functioning is not relatively small (e.g., $r = -.2$ to $-.3$; Kazdin, 1993a). Prosocial functioning as an important assessment domain is raised here merely to illustrate that a range of outcomes is relevant to evaluating therapy.

The effects of treatment are likely to be broad. Moreover, conclusions about a given treatment or the relative merits of different treatments may vary as a function of the outcome domain. Indeed, in some cases differential benefits of treatment are not evident or are less evident on symptoms than other outcome domains that are also clinically relevant (e.g., MTA Cooperative Group, 1999a; Szapocznik et al., 1989). Consequently, symptom reduction alone gives an incomplete picture of the benefits of treatment.

Clinical Significance and Impact of Treatment. *Clinical significance* refers to the practical value or importance of the effect of an intervention, that is, whether it makes any real difference in everyday life. Table 12.4 highlights the most commonly used ways of evaluating the clinical significance of treatment effects in child therapy research. These methods are applied in addition to the usual methods that test whether the changes from pre- to post-treatment and the differences between treatment and control groups are statistically significant.

The most frequently used method of assessing clinical significance is the extent to which treated patients are returned to normative levels of functioning. As noted in Table 12.4, to invoke this criterion, a comparison is made between treated patients and peers (e.g., same age, sex) who are functioning well or whose problems in everyday life are unremarkable. Prior to treatment, the patient sample presumably would depart considerably from their well functioning peers in the area identified for treatment (e.g., anxiety, social withdrawal, aggression). After treatment, presumably the treated individuals

Table 12.4 Primary Means of Evaluating Clinical Significance of Change in Intervention Studies

Type/Method	Defined	Criteria/Measures
Comparison Method	Client performance is evaluated in relation to the performance of others (e.g., normative sample, patient sample) (normative methods) or performance in comparison to one's own performance (ipsative methods)	1. Similarity to normative samples at the end of treatment 2. Statistical departure on a measure from scores of a dysfunctional sample 3. Amount of change from pre to post 4. No longer meeting criteria for a psychiatric diagnosis 5. Complete elimination of the problem or symptom
Subjective Evaluation	Impressions, judgments, opinions of the client or those who interact with the client	Ratings of: 1. Current functioning 2. Whether the original problem continues to be evident or affect functioning 3. Whether the change or changes produced in treatment make a difference
Social Impact	Change on a measure that is recognized or considered to be critically important in everyday life; usually not a psychological inventory or standardized measure	Change reflected on such measures as arrest, truancy, days missed from work, hospitalization, survival, and cost

Note: This list is not intended to exhaust all possibilities. Other methods and variants and their strengths and limitations have been addressed in other sources (see Foster & Mash, 1999; Gladis, Gosch, Dishuk, & Crits-Christoph, 1999; Jacobson, Roberts, Berns, & McGlinchy, 1999; Kazdin, 1977, 2003; Kendall, Marrs-Garcia, Nath, & Sheldrick, 1999; Lunnen & Ogles, 1998).

would be indistinguishable from, or within the range of, individuals functioning adequately to well in everyday life.

Efforts to assess clinical significance are important, although great ambiguity remains in interpreting what the measures mean (see Kazdin, 1999). For example, consider the use of normative data as a criterion for clinical significance. There is very little solid evidence (validity data) that individuals who return to normative levels of functioning on a symptom measure in fact are doing better in everyday life (e.g., are viewed differently by their peers, are less impaired) or are doing better than others who have not entered into the normative range at post-treatment assessment. Similarly, no longer meeting diagnostic criteria for a psychiatric disorder, another criterion for clinically significant change, may or may not reflect significant effects in patient functioning. One or two symptoms can determine whether diagnostic criteria are met so a slight change can lead investigators to conclude a clinically significant change was made. Moreover, as noted previously, individuals who fall right below diagnostic criteria can have significant social, emotional, and behavioral problems. Diagnostic criteria are rather arbitrary and meeting or not meeting them is interesting but not necessarily a measure of noticeable or palpable impact on the life of the child or adolescent.

More information is needed to develop the measures of clinical significance so that they can be incorporated into treatment research. The absence of well-validated measures is not a minor limitation. Even among those treatments regarded as empirically supported, it is not clear that the treatments make a difference that affects functioning in everyday life. Much more attention is needed to evaluate the impact treatment has on dimensions that make a difference in everyday life.

Timing of Outcome Assessment. Assessment immediately after treatment is referred to as *post-treatment* assessment; any point beyond that ranging from weeks to years typically is referred to as *followup* assessment. Conclusions about the efficacy of a treatment or relative efficacy of different treatments may vary greatly depending on when assessments are conducted. Thus, sometimes treatments that are significantly (statistically) different from each other or from controls at post-treatment are not different at followup or vice versa; sometimes changes over the course of treatment are small and nonsignificant but increase over time or vice versa (e.g., Heinicke & Ramsey-Klee, 1986; Kolvin et al., 1981; Meyers, Graves, Whelan, & Barclay, 1996; Newman, Kenardy et al., 1997). Clearly, the conclusions about the effects of a given treatment relative to a control condition or another treatment may vary at post-treatment and followup.

The majority of outcome studies do not report followup; among those that do the duration of followup is a matter of months (e.g., 5 to 7) (Durlak et al., 1995; Kazdin, Bass et al., 1990; Weisz & Weiss, 1993). When conclusions are reached about the effects of treatment, these pertain mostly to effects obtained immediately after treatment is completed. Reviews have suggested that the gains are maintained at followup for those studies in which data are available (see Weisz & Weiss, 1993). However, long-term followup data are rare and difficult to obtain.

Questions That Guide Therapy Research

Research on Treatment Moderators. Most child therapy studies are designed to evaluate one treatment versus a control condition or to compare two treatments. This type of research is obviously important, but by itself, unwittingly contributes to uniformity myths that need to be redressed. There is very little research on moderators of treatment, that is, the conditions on which the effects of treatment depend.

Many characteristics of the child are likely to influence treatment outcome. Severity, chronicity, and scope of dysfunction are obvious contenders. One might expect that treatment would be less effective as a function of how severe, chronic, and pervasive the problem is. Also, several influences related to onset or course of a particular disorder (e.g., various risk and protective factors) could influence treatment outcome. Ethnic, cultural, and racial identity may have an impact on treatment. Ethnicity and race have an impact on when and how children are identified for treatment, patterns of risk and protective factors, characteristic symptoms, age of onset, and course of symptoms (Gaw, 1993; Tharp, 1991). For example, consider substance use and abuse among children and adolescents. The substances used, family rules and monitoring of children in relation to substance use, and the number and type of risk factors that predict onset of substance use vary as a function of ethnic status (e.g., Catalano et al., 1993; Maddahian, Newcomb, & Bentler, 1988).

With differences in the factors that contribute to the emergence and maintenance of dysfunction, it may be reasonable to expect variation in responsiveness to treatment.

Clinical problems of the child are often associated with parent, family, and contextual influences such as parent psychopathology, family conflict, and socioeconomic disadvantage. Parent dysfunction and these other factors may play a central role in terms of maintaining child impairment or raise obstacles in the administration and delivery of treatment. Moreover, the influence of parent functioning on treatment outcome may vary for different types of treatment (e.g., family therapy versus individual child therapy). The range of possibilities regarding what moderators influence what treatments underscores the importance of theory as a guide of where to begin to unravel these possibilities.

Research processes and mechanisms. The question of how or why therapy works has received scant attention in child therapy research. In the long term, the greatest impact of treatment will derive from understanding how treatments work. What processes or characteristics within the child, parent, or family can be mobilized to foster therapeutic change? What events, processes, activities, and tasks in treatment can foster therapeutic change? If we knew the bases of therapeutic change, we might readily optimize the effectiveness of treatment.

Of the hundreds of available treatments, there are likely to be a few common bases or mechanisms of therapeutic change. Perhaps such key factors as rehearsal and practice (e.g., symbolic via language, imagery, or behavioral), catharsis (alleviation of the symptoms through expression and release), or mobilization of hope are some of the key or common factors that explain how all or most therapies work. Ideas for evaluating the basis of therapeutic change can come from all kinds of sources (e.g., various learning models, information processing, or social cognition views).

There is a need for much more research that attempts to explain how and why therapy achieves and induces change. Therapy research is largely restricted to identifying relations between various treatment and control conditions and outcome. This may be termed *descriptive research* and can be distinguished from *explanatory research*. Descriptive research tests relations, with little or no emphasis on explanation. Explanatory research includes an explicit component that focuses on mechanisms, understanding, processes, and why the effects are achieved. Consider descriptive and explanatory research as the end points of a continuum rather than as distinct categories. Indeed, when descriptions are fine-grained, elegant, and process related, they often *are* explanatory.

Implications

Many concerns about child therapy research focus on how the conditions of research depart from those of clinical practice. Do the results from therapy in more well-controlled laboratory-based research (efficacy studies) generalize to therapy in clinical settings (effectiveness studies)? The jury is still out—one meta-analysis suggests that treatment effects are stronger in controlled studies (Weisz, Weiss, & Donenberg, 1992); another analysis suggests that the effects are similar in both contexts (Shadish et al., 1997). Suffice it to say that the effectiveness of treatment in clinical practice is not at all clear. The reason is not just because treatments used in practice are not usually the ones investigated in research. The way in which treatment is studied is the key issue, and the cases to whom treatment is applied usually differ as well (see Weisz, Donenberg, Han, & Kauneckis, 1995; Weisz, Donenberg, Han, & Weiss, 1995).

The very special conditions of therapy research, as highlighted previously, may limit generality of the results to clinical practice. Yet, the main value of research is to test theory, propositions, and hypotheses in order to help understand the phenomenon of interest. Methodology and research design and all of the controlled conditions that compete with generalizing to clinical practice are assets in the context of efforts to isolate variables and test factors that could not be evaluated in other, more naturalistic situations. Testing causal hypotheses about treatment and tinkering with parameters of treatment or moderators (by matching clients to treatments) to test such hypotheses would be the natural focus of research.

Many leads for conceptually driven therapy research pose possible mechanisms of change. One can draw on theories and research on child and adolescent development and on specific clinical dysfunctions. Efforts to understand how therapy works may also draw on moderators. Predicting who will respond to treatment can test specific hypotheses about why treatment works. For example, if cognitive therapy really works because of changes in cognitions, one might test whether the initial level of specific cognitive processes or various distortions and deficiencies affect outcome.

Perhaps the greatest limitation of contemporary therapy research is the paucity of studies that attempt to understand why and how treatment works (Kazdin, 2001b; Kazdin & Nock, in press). In the long term, this will prove to be debilitating. More techniques will continue to be developed, pressures will increase to add to the list of evidence-based treatments, and more old techniques will be tested in new applications. If we knew how therapies worked, we might be able to select among treatments in a more informed fashion. Research could help us understand the processes and whether some treatments mobilized these processes better than others. Even the most effective treatments might be improved if we knew why they achieved their effects.

Developing Effective Treatments: Directions for Research

The limitations noted previously encompass major issues about child therapy research. Consider these stated somewhat bluntly. At this point in research, we have little idea about whether treatments are effective in clinical settings and with individuals referred for treatment, whether treatments with demonstrated efficacy make a genuine difference in the everyday lives of individuals who are treated, about the conditions that influence treatment outcome, and why or how treatment works. Current therapy research is not moving well or rapidly to redress these major gaps in knowledge.

Consider the task of child and adolescent therapy research more broadly. The key questions are: (1) What do we want to know about child and adolescent therapy? That is, what are the goals of the research? (2) What type of research is needed to obtain these goals? and (3) How can we evaluate that movement and determine whether we are making progress toward the goal(s)? The most significant limitation of child and adolescent psychotherapy research is not at the level of individual studies. Rather, the absence of a vision or plan prevents systematic progress toward the goals of therapy research. In order to fill this gap, a model or general framework is proposed here to develop the knowledge we need to understand and apply therapy effectively and to assess progress in research (see Kazdin, 2000d).

Table 12.5 Steps for Developing Treatment

1. *Theory and Research on the Nature of the Clinical Dysfunction*
   Proposals of key characteristics, processes, and mechanisms that relate to the development, onset, and course of dysfunction. Efforts to empirically test those processes.
2. *Theory and Research on the Change Processes or Mechanisms of Treatment*
   Proposals of processes and mechanisms through which treatment may achieve its effects and how the procedures relate to these processes. Studies to identify whether the intervention techniques, methods, and procedures within treatment actually affect those processes that are critical to the model.
3. *Specification of Treatment*
   Operationalization of the procedures, preferably in manual form, that identify how one changes the key processes. Material provided to codify the procedures so that treatment integrity can be evaluated and so that treatment can be replicated in research and practice.
4. *Tests of Treatment Outcome*
   Direct tests of the impact of treatment drawing on diverse designs (e.g., open studies, single-case designs, full-fledged clinical trials) and types of studies (e.g., dismantling, parametric studies, comparative outcome studies).
5. *Tests of the Boundary Conditions and Moderators*
   Examination of the child, parent, family, and contextual factors with which treatment interacts. The boundary conditions or limits of application are identified through interactions of treatment × diverse attributes.
6. *Tests of Generalization and Applicability*
   Examination of the extent to which treatment can be effectively applied to different problems, samples, and settings and variations of the treatment. The focus is explicitly on seeing if the results obtained in research can be obtained under other circumstances.

Steps to Develop Effective Treatments

There is a great deal we need to understand in order to make treatment effective and to ensure that it is applied optimally. Table 12.5 presents several steps to evaluate different facets of treatment, how treatment relates to what is known about clinical disorders, and how and to whom treatment can be applied to achieve optimal gains.

THEORY AND RESEARCH ON THE NATURE OF THE CLINICAL DYSFUNCTION. Treatment ought to be connected with what we know about the onset, maintenance, termination, and recurrence of the clinical problem that is the focus of treatment. Hypotheses about the likely factors leading to the clinical problem or pattern of functioning, the processes involved, and how these processes emerge or operate can contribute directly to treatment research. Many of the approaches to psychotherapy have originated from general models of treatment (e.g., psychoanalytic, family, and cognitive behavioral). Approaches often emphasize processes (e.g., thwarted impulses, maladaptive family processes, distorted cognitions) that have wide applicability across disorders rather than testable hypotheses about specific dysfunctions.

Tests of the processes hypothesized to be implicated in the clinical problem are needed. For example, if cognitions are proposed to play a pivotal role in the onset or maintenance of a disorder or pattern of functioning, direct tests are needed and ought to be part of the foundation leading toward the development of effective treatment. Research on the nature of the clinical problem is likely to identify subtypes, multiple paths leading to a similar onset, and various risk and protective factors. These characteristics are likely to influence treatment outcome and to serve as a basis for using different treatments with different types of children. An example of such research would be empirical efforts to distinguish among conduct disorder children based on the onset of disorder, patterns of comorbidity, and biological and neuropsychological correlates (Hill & Maughan, 2001). There are reasons to expect that these domains influence symptom patterns, clinical course, male and female prevalence rates, and, responsiveness to treatment. Connections of treatment research with psychopathology research could greatly enrich treatment by suggesting targets for intervention and moderators of therapeutic change.

THEORY AND RESEARCH ON THE CHANGE PROCESSES OR MECHANISMS OF TREATMENT. Conceptual views are needed about what treatment is designed to accomplish and through what processes or mechanisms. The guiding question is, how does this particular treatment achieve change? The answer may involve basic processes at different levels (e.g., neurotransmitters, stress hormones, memory, learning, information processing, motivation). In turn, these changes may be induced or activated by such therapeutic processes as gaining new insights, practicing new ways of behaving, or habituating to external events.

Theories of change must be followed by empirical tests. Do the intervention techniques, methods, and procedures within treatment sessions actually affect those processes considered to be critical to the treatment model? For example, it may be that parenting practices are critical to change for the oppositional child. If so, these parenting practices ought to change during treatment, and there ought to be a relation between change in parenting practices and child improvement. Tests of such processes are essential to ensure we understand why and how treatment works.

At least three steps are required to conduct the requisite research: (1) specifying the processes or factors responsible for change, (2) developing measures of these processes, and (3) showing that these processes change before therapeutic change. This latter requirement is needed to establish the time line; that is, processes are changing and are not merely concomitant effects of symptom improvement (see Kazdin, 2003). Thus, evidence that the putative process variable (e.g., parenting practices, cognitions, family interactions) and child symptoms have changed at the end of treatment will not do (i.e., demonstrate that one caused, led to, or mediated the other). The precise reasons that treatments work have been amply discussed but rarely studied. One way to bring order and parsimony to the 550+ treatments in use is to evaluate mechanisms of change. Some of the mechanisms are likely to have generality across multiple treatments.

SPECIFICATION OF TREATMENT. An important requirement for advances is specifying the focus of treatment and what actually is done with, to, or for the child, adolescent, parent, or family during the sessions. Treatments ought to be operationalized, preferably in manual form, so that the integrity of treatment can be evaluated, the material learned from treatment trials can be codified, and the treatment procedures can be replicated in research and clinical practice. Placing treatment into manuals does not rigidly fix treatment or provide a recipe book but rather codifies progress regarding what is essential to include. Much progress has been made on this front; that is, manuals have been developed for scores of child treatments (see Kazdin, 2000d).

The development of manuals, or at least of informed manuals, is closely related to research on the mechanisms of therapeutic change. Without knowing how therapy works and what the necessary, sufficient, and facilitative ingredients are and within what "dose" range, it is difficult to develop meaningful treatment manuals. That is, much of what is contained in treatment manuals may be low doses of effective practices, ancillary but important facets that make delivery more palatable, superstitious behavior on the part of those of us who develop manuals, and factors that slightly impede or fail to optimize therapeutic change. (Paradoxically, in the most rigorous clinical trials of psychotherapy, much of the content of the treatment manual[s], including core features of the treatment, is based on experience, anecdotal information, and broad conceptual views of critical components. When clinicians rely on these criteria for treatment decisions in their nonmanualized therapy, researchers are apt to criticize them.) The difficulty is that without understanding how treatment works, deciding which element in a manual falls in to which of these categories becomes a matter of conjecture. Manuals permit codification and accumulation of knowledge, so they represent an important step for research and clinical practice. Further work on manual development and the knowledge needed to develop informed manuals is needed.

TESTS OF TREATMENT OUTCOME. Obviously, in developing treatment, outcome studies are central. A wide range of treatment tests (e.g., open studies, single-case experiments, full-fledged randomized clinical trials, qualitative studies, and quasi-experiments) can provide evidence that change is produced and that treatment is responsible for the change (see Kazdin, 2003). Outcome studies are the most common forms of child therapy research, and hence this step does not represent a lacuna in research. At the same time, several different outcome questions can be addressed, as elaborated later. It is also important to mention outcome studies in the context of the present discussion to convey the idea that they represent one type of study needed to advance the knowledge base.

TESTS OF MODERATORS. Treatment effects may vary as a function of characteristics of the child, parent, family, context, therapist, and other influences. Moderators refer to characteristics on which outcome depends. The study of moderators reflects the "what works with whom" question (e.g., Fiske, 1977; Paul, 1967) that has often been considered to provide a cryptic statement of the agenda for therapy research. Although this question has guided *discussions* of research, it has not served as a basis for very many empirical studies in child therapy.

Theory and empirical findings can inform the search for moderators. For example, we know that many sexually abused children are likely to develop cognitions that the world is a dangerous place, that adults cannot be trusted, and that one's own efforts to influence the world are not likely to be effective (Wolfe, 1999). Based on this understanding of the problem, one might predict that sexually abused youths with these cognitions would respond less well to treatment, as measured by post-treatment prosocial functioning. If these cognitions are not altered in treatment, the children may be restricted in social activities compared to similar children without these cognitions. Perhaps another study using this information would evaluate whether the effectiveness of treatment could be enhanced by including a component that focuses on these cognitions.

Developmental processes and change constitute a broad set of moderators that may influence treatment outcome. For example, the level of cognitive development and the ability to plan, engage in abstract thinking, and take the perspective of others change markedly over the course of development and relate to clinical dysfunction. Although treatment that focus on these processes are effective for disruptive behavior disorders, improvements are greater for older (> 10 or 11 years old) than for younger children (Durlak, Fuhrman, & Lampman, 1991; Dush, Hirt, & Schroeder, 1989). The age effects might be due to the cognitive development of the children, although this has yet to be demonstrated. More generally, developmental processes need to be woven into the evaluation of treatment. Although age is a useful point of departure, specific processes with which age differences are associated must be identified and measured.

Clinical experience, too, is a good guide or source of potential moderators of treatment. For example, clinicians who provide services to children and adolescents believe that the degree of parent involvement in treatment, distress experienced by the child, and child motivation for treatment greatly influence treatment outcome (Kazdin, Siegel, & Bass, 1990). Although these proposed moderators are not theoretically based, their effects, if demonstrated in research, could serve to prompt theory to explain how and why they operate. The task is to end up with conceptual views of how, why, and for whom therapy is effective, along with supportive evidence, but we can begin with just good ideas, whatever their source. In general, moderators are infrequently evaluated in clinical research with children and adolescents. When they are, often they are moderators of convenience, that is, variables that are studied because they are available on intake or assessment forms (e.g., age, sex, socioeconomic status). When variables are shown to influence outcome, it is important to move to the next step to try to understand why or how these effects were obtained.

Tests of Generalization and Applicability. As the treatment is shown to produce change in a particular context or setting, it is valuable to assess the generality of the findings across other dimensions and domains. Can this treatment be applied clinically, and are the effects similar to those obtained in research? Tests of generality of a treatment are similar to tests of moderators, but they are less conceptually inspired and more application oriented; that is, can treatment be applied in different ways, to different people, and in different settings? The extension of findings across diverse samples is discussed further later in this chapter.

Mentioned in the prior discussion of limitations of child therapy research were the many ways in which treatment in research departs from treatment in clinical practice. This has led to an emphasis and seeming urgency to address whether effects can be obtained in clinical settings—an important priority to be sure. Yet, tests of generality will profit from knowing why and for whom treatment works, so one can ensure that the critical components of treatment are included and that a given client is a good candidate for the intervention.

General Comments. There are not many examples in child and adolescent therapy research in which one can illustrate progression through some subset of these steps. An example already mentioned that illustrates several key steps is research on parent management training as a means of treating oppositional and aggressive children (Patterson, 1982; Patterson et al., 1992). Conceptualization of conduct problems, research on family processes (inept and harsh discipline practices) that promote the problems, and outcome studies that establish the central role of these practices reflect many of the steps highlighted previously. A progression of studies has shown the association and influence of inept discipline practices on conduct problems (Dishion, Patterson, & Kavanagh, 1992; Forgatch, 1991). Also, many randomized controlled trials have shown that changes in parenting skills lead to reductions in child antisocial behavior (e.g., Dishion & Andrews, 1995; Dishion et al., 1992). This research not only establishes an effective treatment but provides a model of how the problem may develop for many children, how many domains of functioning are affected, what central foci of treatment are needed in cases where inept practices are evident, and what to monitor during treatment (e.g., parent progress) if the outcomes are to be achieved.

The steps outlined previously emphasize theoretical development of treatment, so that there is some connection to processes that can be investigated and established in their own right. The notion that there are steps and a progression of research provides opportunities for the literature to move systematically and permits evaluation of the field in a quite different way from the usual qualitative and quantitative reviews. Current reviews focus on what has been done in research. The accumulation of studies is haphazard, and what we can say is based on tracing the path through which the research has wandered. A more proactive stance for the field is one that begins with a model of what we need to know in moving from ignorance to knowledge about effective and disseminable interventions. Specifying some of the critical steps and movement from one step to another is likely to lead to much greater progress than has been achieved or is likely to be achieved with continuation of the status quo.

Progress depends not only on a plan but on some effort to evaluate the extent to which gains are being made. Existing methods of reviewing the literature (narrative, meta-analytic) attempt to chart progress. However, if we, as investigators, have ignored many critical questions about therapy, the conclusions from reviews will be quite limited. Reviews of the literature cannot be expected to bring to light new knowledge on such questions if the constituent studies continue to direct their attention to other issues.

A different type of review is recommended here: namely, a *progress review* that focuses on identifying precisely what progress has been made on the key questions. The purpose of review would be to consolidate gains in research, to identify whether some questions are not being addressed, and to determine whether more or indeed less research is needed in a particular area. A progress review provides a status report to underscore what has been accomplished. Of course, a review of progress itself could be proactive by modifying the research agenda and by providing, as it were, a midcourse correction.

Expanding the Range of Questions Addressed in Research

It is useful to consider in a more fine-grained fashion the range of questions that treatment research ought to address. Table 12.6 presents salient questions—that is, what we would like to know about treatment. Progress can be made by ensuring that for a given treatment and clinical problem these questions are addressed systematically. It is surprising how very little attention has been devoted to the questions related to the components of treatment that contribute to change, the treatment combinations that optimize change, the role of treatment processes, and the impact of child, parent, family, and contextual factors on therapy outcome (Durlak et al., 1995; Kazdin, Bass et al., 1990). The vast majority of research focuses on questions related to the treatment technique. This emphasis is likely to continue in light of the keen interest and pressures to identify evidence-based treatments. However, the emphasis is shortsighted if it is at the expense of other questions.

Each of the questions in Table 12.6 is important. However, we should not only expand the research focus to address these questions, but also track progress in a systematic way to ensure we are in fact developing the full set of answers. If, at this moment, we were asked to recommend which treatments might be useful for, say, separation anxiety or adjustment disorder in early childhood or substance abuse in adolescence, what studies would be cited to provide answers? Initial studies would be required to establish that treatments have an impact. To ensure we can advance the knowledge base in a more systematic fashion, we would want the field to move to some of the other questions. Indeed, some finite number of controlled studies might be all that is needed to address some of the questions, after which we could devote research to the more complex issues (e.g., therapy processes, boundary conditions). Deciding what treatments are evidence-based, would likely require knowing much more about treatment than a few studies designed to answer one or two questions.

Expanding Domains and Methods of Assessment

Identifying a range of questions inadvertently draws attention to the types of answers (i.e., outcome assessment). Three changes in assessment practices in research could greatly advance progress: (1) providing a comprehensive evaluation of the impact of treatment, (2) altering the way in which assessment is conducted so that it is more applicable to clinical work, and (3) evaluating characteristics of the treatment that can influence their adoption and use.

Range of treatment outcomes. Symptom reduction is usually the primary focus of treatment. Symptom measures are relevant, and no effort is made here to demean their importance. Yet, there is no need to restrict outcome to this

Table 12.6 Range of Questions to Guide Treatment Research

1. What is the impact of treatment relative to no treatment?
2. What components contribute to change?
3. What treatments can be added (combined treatments) to optimize change?
4. What parameters can be varied to influence (improve) outcome?
5. How effective is this treatment relative to other treatments for this problem?
6. What child, parent, family, and contextual features influence (moderate) outcome?
7. What processes or mechanisms mediate (cause, influence, are responsible for) therapeutic change?
8. To what extent are treatment effects generalizable across problem areas, settings, and other domains?

TABLE 12.7 Range of Outcome Criteria to Evaluate Treatment Effectiveness

1. *Child Functioning*
   a. Symptoms
   b. Impairment
   c. Prosocial competence
   d. Academic functioning
2. *Parent and Family Functioning*
   a. Dysfunction (e.g., symptoms)
   b. Contextual influences (e.g., stress, quality of life)
   c. Conditions that promote adaptation (e.g., family relations and organization)
3. *Social Impact Measures*
   a. Consequences on systems (e.g., school activities, attendance, truancy)
   b. Service use (e.g., reductions in special services, hospitalization)

focus. No compelling evidence has been found that symptom change (as opposed to improvements in prosocial functioning, family interaction, or adaptive cognitions) is the best predictor of long-term adjustment and functioning. Many other outcomes are critically important because of their significance to the child, family, and in many cases to society at large. Table 12.7 includes domains that are relevant for evaluating therapy outcomes. The relevance of any domain particular domain may vary by clinical problem (e.g., anxiety, hyperactivity) or indeed by subtype of the problem within a given disorder. However, multiple domains are likely relevant in any domain for a given clinical problem and the conclusions about what techniques are effective will vary somewhat by the outcome criteria.

Among the many criteria, perhaps special emphasis ought to be given to impairment, that is, the extent to which the individual's functioning in everyday life is impeded. Meeting role demands at home and at school, interacting prosocially and adaptively with others, and being restricted in the settings, situations, and experiences in which one can function can vary considerably among youths with a given disorder or problem. Impairment is related to, but distinguishable from, symptoms or meeting criteria for a disorder (Sanford et al., 1992) and contributes significantly to the likelihood that a child is referred for mental health services (Bird et al., 1990). Moving individuals toward reduced impairment may be a considerable accomplishment of treatment in addition to, but also independent of, symptom change.

Singling out impairment is not meant to imply that one criterion (impairment) ought to replace another (symptoms)—just the opposite, the full range of outcome criteria is relevant in developing and identifying effective treatments. One could make the case that other areas that tend to be neglected (e.g., social competence, academic functioning) are central as well because they predict long-term adjustment and clinical dysfunction. Indeed, the importance of understanding development and psychopathology in part derives from understanding what outcomes at one point in development predict (serve as a risk or protective factor for) outcomes at a later point.

The expanded range of outcome measures (in Table 12.7) focuses on domains of functioning of the child that are likely to be altered with treatment and that are likely to be pertinent to making conclusions about the effectiveness and relative effectiveness of treatment. One could expand the range of pertinent outcomes. For example, given the reciprocal and bidirectional nature of child and parent interactions, one might propose that changing the child will lead to therapeutic changes in the parents and family. Indeed, for children with externalizing disorders, we have found that treating the child leads to reductions in parental psychopathology and stress and to improved family relations (Kazdin & Wassell, 2000). The benefits of treatment are likely to extend beyond one domain of functioning of the child and perhaps as well to other domains among individuals in close contact with the child. The goal of expanded assessment is not to catalogue all of the possible measures affected by therapy. Some of the outcomes are centrally relevant to adjustment of the child (e.g., impairment, prosocial functioning), and others may be relevant to maintenance of changes in the child or are clinically important in their own right (e.g., reductions in parent depression, improved family relations).

PRE-POST VERSUS CONTINUOUS ASSESSMENT. A central feature of therapy research is assessment of the participants before and after treatment (pre-post treatment assessment). However, we do not want our evaluation of therapy to be restricted to when treatment is over. From the standpoint of research, understanding processes and mechanisms requires establishing a time line to see *how* change is occurring and through what processes. From the standpoint of clinical care, we want to see that change is occurring either on the outcomes of interest or on putative processes that will lead to the outcomes of interest.

There are clinically feasible guidelines and examples of monitoring client progress over the course of treatment (see Barlow, Hayes, & Nelson, 1984; Clement, 1999; Cone, 2000; Epstein, Kutash, & Duchnowski, 1998; Kazdin, 1993b). The guidelines utilize ongoing (repeated) assessment (i.e., multiple observations for individual cases), so that one can describe patterns in the data and see if there are changes associated with treatment in key processes in therapy or outcomes of treatment. Outcomes refer to interim changes (e.g., previews, trends, progress in a therapeutic direction) that portend the gains one would want to see at the end of treatment.

Pre-post assessments no doubt ought to continue in group designs that evaluate therapy. At the same time, it would be helpful to integrate periodic but regular interim assessments to monitor progress over the course of therapy. The purpose is to evaluate the change process and to provide measures that can be used clinically. In clinical work, the treatment cannot be evaluated at the end in the same way as in research in part because treatment regimens are less fixed and an effort is made to treat until progress is made. Also, in clinical work, one wants systematic information to make decisions as to when to end treatment or to provide different treatment. If the results of research are to be applicable to clinical practice, some interim assessments that can be used to assess progress will be very important to integrate into treatment research.

EVALUATING CHARACTERISTICS OF TREATMENT. A rather neglected area is evaluation of characteristics of treatment, particularly those features that may be related to adoption, use, or dissemination of treatment. Obviously, evaluating characteristics of treatment may be irrelevant if the treatment has not been shown to produce therapeutic change. However, can the treatments that have been shown to produce change be distinguished in important ways? Table 12.8 provides three criteria to evaluate treatment that are somewhat separate from the therapeutic changes produced in the clients.

The *disseminability of treatment* refers to the ease with which they may be extended beyond the confines of the research study, including extension to those who provide treatment (therapists) and to those who seek treatment (children, adolescents, and their families). The ease of dissemination encompasses many characteristics of treatment, including the complexity of the procedures, type and amount of training needed to implement the procedures, likelihood of adherence to the treatment among those who implement the procedures, and degree to which a departure from the prescribed procedures leads to a loss in effectiveness. Disseminability also encompasses the efficiency of treatment, as reflected in how many persons in need can be served and the medium through which treatment is delivered (e.g., Internet, videotapes, self-help books, individual versus group sessions).

TABLE 12.8 Criteria for Evaluating Treatment Procedures

1. *Disseminability*
   The extent or ease of extending the treatment widely to other clinicians and clients. This criterion may be related to complexity of the procedures, type and amount of training needed to implement the procedures, likelihood of adherence to those who implement the procedures, and degree to which departure from the prescribed procedures is associated with loss of effectiveness.
2. *Cost*
   The monetary costs of providing treatment and delivering services are pertinent measures of treatment. Cost is not usually a question of scientific interest in treatment evaluation but provides data that can influence dissemination, adoption, and policy. There are many ways to evaluate cost such as expenses in relation to obtained benefits or outcomes (e.g., cost-benefit analyses).
3. *Acceptability of Treatment*
   The extent to which those who participate in treatment (e.g., child, adolescents, families, but perhaps mental health professionals as well) view the treatment as reasonable, justified, and acceptable. Treatments that are more acceptable may be more frequently sought out, adhered to, and executed correctly than those that are less acceptable.

Some techniques may be widely disseminated because they can be implemented by clients themselves or because they might be able to be presented through the mass media (e.g., books, computer, television). For example, many self-help manuals are designed to treat diverse problems, including overeating, cigarette smoking, depression, stress, anger, sexual dysfunction, anxiety, social skills deficits, and conduct problems (Newman, 2000; Rosen, 1993; Santrock, Minnett, & Campbell, 1994). The use of media and communication technology, such as the television, computer, Internet, Palm computers, cell phones, and yet-to-be-invented devices will provide opportunities to disseminate treatment widely (e.g., Meyers et al., 1996; Ström, Pettersson, & Andersson, 2000; Zhu et al., 1996). The devices may provide information, help monitor behavior, and deliver therapeutic regimens (e.g., directives, practice assignments). Even though many people do not have such devices, many do and the reach of therapy can be extended widely. Access to such devices (e.g., and a clinic website) could reach a large number of individuals for a host of concerns (e.g., coping with stress, peer relations, body image), problems of living (e.g., divorce, bereavement), and clinical dysfunction (e.g., anxiety, depression). Computerized psychotherapy has been available in some form for decades and continues to develop in treatment outcome studies (Marks, Shaw, & Parkin, 1998; Newman, Consoli, & Taylor, 1997). Evidence suggests that self-administered and abbreviated treatments can be as effective as more costly therapist-administered treatments (Marrs, 1995). At present, few applications are available in clinical practice and for children or adolescents, but no doubt this will accelerate with advances in software and technology.

From the standpoint of research directions, disseminability is an important dimension to assess. There are no simple measures to assess the ease of disseminating a treatment. Elaboration of the construct and its constituent components and measures that can be integrated into assessment batteries are sorely needed. Disseminability is not an esoteric or incidental criterion and perhaps ought to be an initial consideration rather than an afterthought when developing treatment.

The *costs of providing treatment*, related to but distinguishable from disseminability, is important as well. Obviously, a less costly treatment is preferred to a more costly treatment, given evidence that both are effective. There are different ways of evaluating cost. *Cost-benefit analysis* is designed to evaluate the monetary costs of an intervention with the benefits that are obtained. The benefits must be measured in monetary terms also. This requirement makes cost-benefit analysis difficult to apply to many psychological interventions where the beneficial effects (e.g., increased harmony in the home) might extend well beyond monetary gains (Yates, 1995). In the treatment of adults, evidence that clients return to work, miss fewer days of work, have fewer car accidents, or stay out of hospitals or prison are examples that can be translated into monetary terms. Many of these are also pertinent to children and adolescents, with some changes (e.g., return to school, fewer days of missed school). Many measures may require little change; for example, child mental illness is likely to influence the number of days parents miss work.

Cost-effectiveness analysis does not require placing a monetary value on the benefits and can be more readily used for evaluating treatment. Cost-effectiveness analysis examines the costs of treatment relative to a particular outcome. The value for therapy evaluation is that it permits comparison of different treatment techniques if the treatment benefits are designed to be the same (e.g., reduction of drinking or delinquent offenses, increase in family harmony). Such information would be very useful and address important questions independently of debates about statistical differences that distinguish treatments. For example, one study compared two variations of parent training for parents of kindergarten children with behavior problems (Cunningham et al., 1995). One variation consisted of individual treatment provided at a clinical service site; the other consisted of group-based treatment conducted in the community (at community centers or schools). Both treatments were better than a wait list control condition. On several measures, the community-based treatment was more effective. Even if the treatments were equally effective, the monetary costs (e.g., start-up costs, travel time of families, costs of the therapist/trainer in providing treatment) of the individual treatment were approximately six times greater per family than the group treatment. Clearly, this is a significant criterion for evaluating the different ways of administering treatment.

Because any intervention costs something, the simple measure of cost—and this is an oxymoron—is not of interest or perhaps even important by itself. The interest in cost stems primarily from evaluating the cost of this treatment in relation to the alternatives. So, for example, among adults one could or could not treat alcoholism among workers at a major company. Both of these alternatives have costs. Treating alcoholism has the costs of the sort mentioned previously. Yet, not treating alcoholism has costs as well because alcoholism leads to many missed days at work, reduced worker productivity, and increased illness and injury (associated with alcoholism). Hence, the cost of treatment is not the issue but rather the cost of treatment versus no treatment, both of which may be expensive. A common statement that better reflects this is the notion that the cost of education in society is very high, but not that high when compared to the cost of ignorance. Similarly, the costs of not treating some problems (e.g., depression, substance use, conduct disorder) are enormous but must be weighed against the cost of not providing treatment. For example, the annual cost of anxiety disorders in the United States is estimated at $42.3 billion (or $1,542) per sufferer (Greenberg et al., 1999). These costs include lost productivity at work, psychiatric and nonpsychiatric treatment, and other costs. Clearly, mental health problems can have exorbitant costs. Studies have shown that the benefits of psychotherapy are reflected in reduced costs of subsequent treatment and reduced work impairment (see Gabbard, Lazar, Hornberger, & Spiegel, 1997), but cost outcomes are infrequently measured.

Within psychotherapy research, costs, cost-benefit, and cost-effectiveness measures are infrequently used, but the momentum has increased for considering cost as a critical part of treatment (Haaga, 2000; Newman, 2000; Simon et al., 2001). Estimating cost is not entirely straightforward because of the range of costs that can be included and the difficulty in translating benefits into monetary terms. Even so, efforts to describe the costs of different treatments represent a worthwhile addition to intervention research.

Treatment acceptability refers to judgments by laypersons, clients, and others of whether treatment procedures are appropriate, fair, and reasonable for the problem that is to be treated. Persons in a position to evaluate treatment, including review committees at institutions (e.g., hospital, university clinic), laypeople, and clients themselves, evaluate whether proposed treatment is reasonable. An assumption is made in this discussion that only treatments with demonstrated efficacy are considered. The reason is that there are many procedures (e.g., various diets, exercise regimens promoted in the media) that are readily acceptable to clients, even though they have little or no demonstrated efficacy. Different treatments that are effective for a given problem may not be equally acceptable to prospective clients, and this might be very important to know.

Those treatments that are acceptable are more likely to be sought and adhered to once clients have entered into treatment (e.g., Reimers, Wacker, Cooper, & DeRaad, 1992). Also, treatments that are highly acceptable are likely to be adopted more by professionals and hence influence disseminability of the treatment (Arndorfer, Allen, & Alijazireh, 1999). How well and carefully professionals carry out treatment is a function of the extent to which they view the intervention as acceptable (Allinder & Oats, 1997). It is likely that acceptability also influences the decision to remain in treatment. Seeing treatment as demanding or irrelevant contributes directly to dropping out of therapy (Kazdin, Holland, & Crowley, 1997). Clearly, professional and client views of the acceptability of treatment contribute to multiple aspects of treatment utilization and adherence.

Information on the acceptability of treatment can greatly supplement data on effectiveness. Moreover, acceptability may be an important dependent variable for developing effective treatments and for identifying factors that predict the extent to which treatment will be viewed as acceptable (e.g., Kazdin, 2000c). It will be useful to understand what can be done in the delivery of treatments to make them more acceptable (e.g., Foxx, Bremer, Schutz, Valdez, & Johndrow, 1996). The challenge for child therapy is that treatments probably need to be acceptable to both the child and the parent. Retaining cases in treatment may well depend on how acceptable the treatment is to both parties.

Needless to say, disseminability, cost, and acceptability are not the only characteristics of therapy that are critical to adoption and use. The utilization or utilizability of an intervention made available might be some mixture of the prior concepts but important in its own right. For example, in one study, school-based parent management training was made widely available to parents of 5- to 8-year-old children (Cunningham et al., 2000). Only 28% of the families utilized (enrolled in) the intervention, among those with children with extreme externalizing behavior (2 SDs above the mean). Understanding the utilization of treatment and the factors that influence participation is critical as well once an effective intervention is identified.

Expanding the Samples Included in Research

A critical priority for treatment research is greater attention to the treatment and mental health needs of the underserved. Reports already attest to the notion that children and adolescents constitute underserved populations (e.g., Institute of Medicine [IOM], 1989; U.S. Congress, 1991). Yet, in discussions of the underserved and underrepresented, minority group status is the delineation that first comes to mind. Minority groups within the United States are comprised primarily of African American, Hispanic American, Asian American, and Native American Indians. Minority groups tend to be underrepresented in psychotherapy services and research in general (Case & Smith, 2000) and perhaps especially so in relation to children and adolescents (Kazdin, Bass et al., 1990; Kazdin, Siegel, & Bass, 1990). In relation to the proportion of the population in the census (in the United States), some groups have been overrepresented (e.g., African Americans) and others have been quite underrepresented (e.g., Hispanic Americans) in psychological research (Case & Smith, 2000). However, a large proportion (approximately 40%) of investigations (sampling journals from clinical, counseling, and school psychology) does not even report the ethnicity of the participants. Consequently, the extent to which diverse groups are represented is difficult to discern. As a general point, greater attention to who is served and is included in treatment research and services is a high priority.

Separate issues dictate the priority of increased research with underserved and minority samples. First, it is important to ensure that findings obtained with one group generalize or extend to other groups. Second, often the direct benefits to participation in treatment or other intervention programs (e.g., prevention, educational interventions) are part of research. Inclusion in these programs gives access to the potential benefits they offer. Access ought not to be restricted to any particular group among those who can be identified as in need. Third, there is a broader scientific agenda. Researchers wish to know the extent to which findings extend to different groups and the principles or processes that can explain how various factors (e.g., ethnicity, culture) influence affect, cognition, behavior, development, and the family. It is important to understand the bases or processes that underlie and account for differences in findings that may emerge as a function of subject characteristics (and other potential moderators of treatment).

Beyond the scientific agenda, there are practical issues that also argue for the importance of understanding the bases for differences among various groups (and other moderators of treatment). It is not feasible to evaluate whether findings generalize across all subject or group characteristics. Consider the scope of the task. The most recent U.S. Census recognized over 60 different racial groups, including 6 single races (White, Black, Asian, American Indian or Alaska Native, Native Hawaiian or Other Pacific Islander, and Some Other), 15 possible combinations of 20 races, 20 combinations of 3 races, 15 combinations of 4 races, 6 combinations of 5 races, and one grand combination of all 6). Moreover, these racial categories were further combined with two ethnic categories (Hispanic or non-Hispanic), which led ultimately to 126 different combinations of race and ethnicity. Even remaining with the small number of the first delineation (i.e., six single races), distinctions that are important can be easily ignored. For example, the characteristics and responses of a given ethnic group to treatment can vary as a function of where they are currently living (e.g., country) and how recently they have immigrated, if they have moved (e.g., Lin, Poland, & Nagasaki, 1993). Beyond groupings within the United States, the richness of ethnic and cultural diversity increases. For example, some African countries can distinguish over 200 ethnic groups (see www.infoplease.com/ipa/A0855617.html.) Race, ethnicity, and culture leave out many other grouping variables (e.g., age, gender identity and preference, country of origin) that can make a difference in psychological and biological domains. Not all psychological (biological, health, and other) findings could be tested among these different groups.

Although not every group can be studied, this is not a rationale for limiting the study to one or two groups. Rather, efforts ought to be made to study different groups and to identify the bases of group differences. The bases are likely to point to broader issues that may help understand how treatment is moderated and what processes may facilitate broader extension and application, perhaps to many groups. A difficulty is that much research is based on just testing a novel group without even moving to suggest or explain why there might be differences. For example, a given effect may vary among different ethnic groups as a function of perception of the task, cultural meaning, context in which such influences ordinarily occur, accessibility to language use in the experiment, and other such influences (see Council of National Psychological Associations, 2000). Such influences would be important to hypothesize and evaluate.

Theory is very relevant as a way of suggesting what dimensions might influence the generality of the finding and of generating hypotheses about why the phenomenon would be evident in one set of circumstances or for some subjects but not for others. In the absence of a theory, it still can be quite useful to test whether the results obtained in the study (main effect) vary as a function of such other variables as sex, race, ethnicity, or social class. Although such comparisons may not initially be based on theory, differences that are found can be used to generate possible ideas for research as to why there might be such differences.

In the context of child and adolescent therapy, a few programs of research have developed and carefully evaluated treatment for underserved populations. For example, Malgady, Rogler, and Costantino (e.g., Costantino & Malgady, 1996) have developed treatments for Puerto Rican children and adolescents. The treatments are designed to integrate cultural values in the context of modeling (social learning) therapy. For young children, prosocial models are presented in the context of folktales *(cuentos)*; for adolescents, stories involving adult role models are based on biographies of heroic Puerto Ricans. The treatments are designed to develop prosocial behavior in ways that are culturally relevant, to foster ethnic pride, and to provide methods of coping with stresses common to the Puerto Rican community. As another example, Szapocznik and his colleagues (Kurtines & Szapocznik, 1996; Szapocznik & Williams, 2000) have examined family therapy with Hispanic youth. A family-based treatment approach was selected to focus on ethnically relevant family structure and values, to improve entry into treatment, to reduce attrition, and to augment therapeutic change. Both examples reflect programmatic studies that have tested the effects of treatment across age groups and clinical samples (referral problems).

A number of child and adolescent samples are underrepresented in treatment research. Among these samples are children of adults who have severe disorders (e.g., depression, alcohol abuse), children with physical handicap and chronic disease, children exposed to physical or sexual abuse and neglect, persons with mental retardation, and homeless youth, to mention a few examples (see Dryfoos, 1990; IOM, 1989; Kazdin, 2000d; U.S. Congress, 1991). Youth in these groups have higher rates of clinical dysfunction and represent a high priority for intervention for both treatment and preventive purposes.

A research priority is to extend treatment and treatment research to underserved populations. The task obviously involves more than recruiting a broader range of participants. Theoretical and empirical work are required to identify the extent to which special treatment and alternative service models are needed, what facets of existing treatments can be modified to extend the benefits to special groups, and what novel measures, modalities, and procedures are required. Research that follows from conceptualizing treatment and the factors that affect its cultural relevance, use, and adoption may be helpful to derive culturally relevant principles to guide treatment development and modification. The research agenda extends well beyond including diverse subject samples in a given outcome study. Providing and evaluating treatment for minorities are multifaceted because ethnic and racial status impact when and how youth are identified for treatment, manifestations of symptoms, help-seeking patterns, and treatment utilization (Tharp, 1991).

Expanding Models for Delivering Treatment

The implicit model for much of therapy research is that a limited number of sessions (usually eight to ten sessions) ought to achieve change and that treatment can end when these sessions are completed. For purposes of discussion, let us call brief and time-limited treatment a *conventional model of delivering therapy*. In the conventional model, the number of sessions is fixed, as required by the research project. Table 12.9 presents a number of other ways of delivering treatment than the conventional model. These other ways are likely to increase treatment effectiveness as well as our knowledge about treatment.

HIGH-STRENGTH TREATMENT. In the conventional model, treatment obviously is intended to have an impact, but rarely are the dose, strength, duration, and other parameters of treatment explicitly planned to maximize clinical impact.

TABLE 12.9 Models of Treatment Delivery

1. *Conventional Model*
   Current model of research in which a time-limited, usually brief treatment, is provided.
2. *High-strength Treatment*
   A test of a very strong intervention based on current knowledge. An effort to see what can be accomplished with the strongest available treatment.
3. *Amenability to Treatment*
   Identification of cases that are likely to vary in their responsiveness to treatment. The goal is to identify individuals for whom available treatments are likely to be very effective and, in the process, the factors that may moderate treatment response and hypotheses about what is needed for more recalcitrant cases.
4. *Broad-based Treatment*
   Use of multiple modalities, modules, components, or interventions to address the range of domains required to have significant impact on individual functioning.
5. *Continued Treatment*
   Treatment that is ongoing in some form, even after an initial period of a conventional treatment may have been provided. If dysfunction is likely to continue, an ongoing maintenance phase may be continued, perhaps on a more intermittent schedule or with a different format of delivering treatment, such as group rather than individual therapy, or treatment in different settings, such as at school rather than at a clinic.
6. *Periodic Monitoring and Treatment (Dental Model)*
   After a initial period of treatment, the intervention is suspended. The patient enters into a phase in which functioning is systematically assessed on a regular basis. Based on the assessment results, treatment is provided as needed.

The high-strength treatment model begins with an effort to maximize therapeutic change. For severe or recalcitrant clinical problems in particular, it may be valuable to test the strongest feasible version of treatment to determine whether the problem *can* be altered and, if so, to what extent. The high-strength model is an effort not only to maximize clinical change, but also to test the current limits of our knowledge.

For many problems (e.g., major depression, conduct disorder, attention-deficit/hyperactivity disorder), brief and time-limited interventions are likely to be weak in the outcomes they produce. Much longer treatments might seem more promising to maximize impact. Yet, few studies test variations of treatment strength or try to evaluate high-strength treatments. As an exception, Lovaas (1987) treated young autistic children for an average of 40 hours per week for two or more years and involved an intervention in the child's home, school, and community using parents and aides. The benefits at followup (mean of five years after treatment) were evident in classroom placement, adaptive behavior, and measures of IQ, compared to control cases with less intensive treatment (McEachin et al., 1993). This is an extreme illustration of the model but also a good example because many professionals would say that autism is resistant, given what we know at this point in time. Few treatments for the disorder have any evidence on their behalf (Rogers, 1998; Smith, 1999). Consequently, a question of interest is what can we accomplish with a strong treatment based on the best available knowledge?

It is exceedingly important to learn in controlled studies what we can accomplish based on a strong dose of our treatments. That dose may involve evaluating more intensive efforts to work with the child and family, involving others in the intervention, and encompassing more domains of the child's functioning (e.g., academic performance, social behavior). If the strongest version of the currently available treatment produces change, then it is reasonable to study whether less protracted, less costly, and less difficult-to-implement procedures can achieve similar outcomes and whether any loss in treatment gains is worth the savings in cost or ease of administration.

Although high-strength treatment studies are needed, the long-term goal is to develop a continuum of interventions that vary on such dimensions as efficiency, disseminability, cost, therapeutic effort or intensity, and restrictiveness on the client's life. A stepped-care model of therapy has been delineated to note the need to match patients to a continuum of services as needed (see Haaga, 2000; Newman, 2000). For many patients, low-cost interventions (e.g., self-help, brief) are effective; for others interventions of greater intensity are needed. In the current discussion, high-strength interventions are proposed to learn about the likely effects that can be obtained with the seemingly strongest version of treatment available. However long-term, this treatment may be reserved for those who do not respond to low-strength interventions.

Amenability to Treatment. Mentioned previously was the paucity of research on child, parent, family, contextual, therapist, and treatment factors that may moderate treatment outcome. The information on moderators is pertinent to identifying children and adolescents who vary in the extent to which they can be improved by treatment, that is, who vary in their amenability or responsiveness to treatment. It would be extremely valuable to identify the subgroup(s) of individuals whom we can treat effectively on a fairly reliable basis. Identifying subgroups in this fashion can contribute to knowledge by raising hypotheses about the reasons factors moderate outcome and contribute to practice and by permitting better triage of cases to treatments that are more likely to work.

Once subgroups of children who can be effectively treated are identified, a more concentrated focus can be provided to those less amenable and for whom effective treatments are unavailable. The approach of identifying children who are more or less amenable to treatment can be integrated into existing controlled outcome research. Within a given study, children can be identified as more or less amenable to the intervention based on characteristics of the sample and hypotheses about the interface of treatment and these characteristics. Analyses of outcome effects are then based on comparisons of subgroups within the investigation to assess responsiveness to treatment in planned or post-hoc comparisons.

Research on amenability to treatment can begin by identifying those children with a given problem who are likely to be the most responsive to treatment. Hypotheses might come from views about different subtypes of youths (e.g., those with early versus late onset), family loading for the problem (e.g., family history versus no family history of the disorder), and contextual influences (e.g., family adversity, untoward living conditions). Models of clinical dysfunction may also provide very useful guidelines regarding what factors (e.g., risk, protective; subtypes of the disorder) are likely to predict response to treatment.

Evaluation of amenability to treatment relies on empirically demonstrated or hypothesized moderators. However, the research may not merely be a study in which a moderator or two is evaluated in relation to outcome. The investigator may select several factors that have been studied in relation to a clinical problem and propose that individuals who are high (or low) on these several factors are more or less amenable to treatment. For example, in the treatment of children referred for aggressive and antisocial behavior, children who are less amenable to treatment are those who have more severe and chronic problems, comorbid disorders, and academic deficiencies; who come from socially disadvantaged backgrounds; and who live with parents who have current psychopathology and high levels of stress (Kazdin & Crowley, 1997; Kazdin & Wassell, 2000). These different variables can be combined to provide an amenability index. This is slightly different from research that evaluates a particular moderator insofar as multiple moderators are combined, but still addresses the same overall agenda.

Broad-Based-Treatment. Many dysfunctions encompass a broad range of symptoms, associated areas of dysfunction, and parent and family problems. Comorbidity among children and adolescents has received a great detail of discussion, but the range of problems that youths evince extends well beyond multiple symptoms and diagnoses. For example, attention-deficit/hyperactivity disorder may include many sources of impairment beyond attention problems, hyperactivity, and impulsiveness that are defining features. Academic dysfunction, poor peer relations, and aggressive and antisocial behavior are likely to be present as well. One reason for proposing systematic expansion of outcome criteria in treatment research is precisely because of evidence that symptoms are associated with dysfunction in other domains. In current approaches to treatment, a particular intervention is implemented to alter an important facet (e.g., psychic conflict, self-esteem, family processes) of the child and/or the system in which the child functions. The targeted domain is considered, on theoretical or clinical grounds, to be central to the child's problem. Yet, for many dysfunctions, associated (correlated) features of, or consequences resulting from, the disorder may require a broader range of interventions than any one treatment approach can reasonably provide.

Treatments can be conceived in a modular fashion where there are separate components (modules) woven into an overall treatment plan. Implementation initially requires evaluating child functioning in diverse domains (e.g., home, school, community; deviance, prosocial and academic functioning) and then providing multiple treatments or components of treatment to address these domains. An example is multisystemic therapy (MST), which was reviewed previously. This treatment consists of a package of interventions that are deployed with children and their families (Henggeler et al., 1998). The conceptual view is that multiple systems (e.g., family, school) impinge on the child as well as on each other. Domains are addressed in treatment (e.g., parent unemployment) because they raise issues for one or more systems (e.g., parent stress, increased alcohol consumption) and affect how the child is functioning (e.g., marital conflict, child disciplinary practices). Several different techniques (e.g., parent training, problem-solving skills training) and case management are combined to address these multiple domains. MST is an example of a broad-based treatment but does not of course exhaust the options.

An assumption in therapy research is that more treatments applied to a clinical problem or client are likely to be better (more effective). This is in part the rationale for eclectic combinations that often dominate clinical practice. Combinations of treatment are not invariably more effective. Indeed, one can conclude this on common-sense grounds. Squeezing multiple treatments within a fixed period (e.g., 10 weeks) of treatment can merely dilute the individual or constituent treatments because none of the components is presented at full dose. Common sense can be supplemented by research; there are cases in which combined treatments were actually less effective than treatments involving only one of the constituent interventions (see Kazdin, 1996a). On the other hand, in many instances combined treatments are likely to be more effective than their constituent treatments administered by themselves. Examples from medicine (e.g., for HIV, cancer, heart disease) can be readily cited. In the context of child and adolescent psychotherapy, broader-based treatments deserve more frequent tests, but selection of the modules or components of treatment ought to draw from theory and prior findings about why the combination is likely to be important, useful, or warranted.

An example of a broad-based and combined treatment was the multimodal treatment study of children with attention-deficit/hyperactivity disorder (MTA Cooperative Group, 1999a, 1999b). In this study, children (N = 579) were randomly assigned to careful medication management, intensive behavioral treatment, standard community care, or medication management and behavioral treatment combined. Although all four groups improved, the combined treatment was superior in a broader range of child outcomes (but not all outcomes) than the other treatments. Even with combined treatments, it may be important to identify for whom they are needed and when they ought to be deployed.

Continued Treatment. For several clinical dysfunctions or for a number of children with a particular disorder, the course of maladjustment may be life long. In such cases, continued treatment in some form may be required. Ongoing treatment or treatment in the same form may not be needed forever. Perhaps after the child is referred, treatment is provided to address the current crises and to have impact on functioning at home, at school, and in the community. After improvement is achieved, treatment is modified rather than simply terminated. At that point, the child could enter into maintenance therapy, that is, continued treatment perhaps in varying schedules ("doses"). Treatment would continue but perhaps on a more intermittent basis.

There are examples of the potential benefits of continued treatment. In the treatment of adult depression, the benefits of providing maintenance therapy following a treatment course have been carefully evaluated in controlled trials in which the maintenance therapy has included different treatments (e.g., half-dose of the original medication, interpersonal psychotherapy, cognitive therapy) (e.g., Frank et al., 1991, 1993). Patients who received maintenance therapy were much less likely to show a relapse. Findings suggest similar benefits of maintenance treatment (cognitive behavior therapy) in reducing relapse in depression among adolescents as well (Kroll et al., 1996). Maintenance therapies can provide intermittent treatment or treatment as needed and hence are not merely more sessions of the same treatment regimen. Needless to say, the use of ongoing treatment is not advocated in cases where there is evidence that brief and time-limited treatment is effective. Beginning with a model of brief and time-limited treatment may be quite reasonable, but heavy reliance on the conventional model will greatly limit what we can accomplish with treatment.

Periodic Monitoring and Treatment. An alternative to continued treatment is to provide treatment followed by systematic case monitoring. After initial treatment and demonstrated improvement in functioning in everyday life, treatment is suspended. At this point, the child's functioning begins to be monitored regularly (e.g., every three months) and systematically (with standardized measures). The assessment need not involve an extensive battery but may reflect screening items to assess the child's functioning at home and at school and along salient domains. Treatment could be provided as needed based on the assessment data or emergent issues raised by the family, teachers, or others. This is similar to the model for dental care in the United States in which "check-ups" are recommended every six months; an intervention is provided if, and as needed, based on these periodic checks.

The novel feature of this model is monitoring of child functioning and the use of additional treatment sessions on the basis of the resulting data. The model may capture the advantages of continued treatment but be deployed more specifically for individuals who are in need of some intervention. Many individuals who complete treatment may be functioning well; assessment can identify these individuals and not utilize resources for their continued treatment. For those doing less well, treatment can be offered as needed.

There is likely to be great value in this model. A difficulty in assessing the value is the paucity of data on a followup course for child and adolescent treatment. Indeed, the work on adult depression, as noted previously, came from evidence that there is a form of depression that is recurrent and that relapse is likely without treatment. With little evidence of how children are doing a year or two after treatment, the need for a maintenance therapy is unclear.

General Comments. The varied ways of evaluating and delivering treatment are designed to consider the different characteristics of clinical problems, the different types of treatment they may require, the differential responsiveness of some individuals, and the broad and enduring dysfunctions that clinically referred cases often bring to treatment. Typically, research on treatment of child and adolescent disorders is conducted in ways opposite from what might be needed to develop and to identify effective interventions. For example, the duration of treatment is relatively brief and thus probably not a test of a high-strength treatment. Child, parent, family, and other characteristics are rarely examined to identify who is more or less amenable or responsive to treatment. Individual techniques are usually contrasted with one another rather than combined to augment therapeutic change. Thus, broad-based treatments are not usually tested. Finally, treatment is usually terminated after the brief regimen is provided, so that continued care or treatment as needed is not evaluated. Overall, the very severe and enduring impairment of many childhood disorders may require reconsideration of the model that is used to investigate and evaluate treatment.

Some of the models presented here raise the prospect of treatments that are more extended than those currently included in research. The recommendations for longer treatments in research for more protracted problems seem to conflict directly with the move toward brief treatment prompted by managed care and cost containment considerations. It is essential to be sensitive to pressures and trends in clinical service delivery. Yet, the task for research is to identify what interventions can accomplish for the clinical problems of children and adolescents. If it turns out that more intensive and more extended treatments are required for some problems or some children, this will not necessarily mean more costly treatment. The costs to society, even purely monetary costs, are not merely those of treatment delivery. Cost savings and cost-benefit analyses are essential to consider as well. It may be premature to assume that using a broader range of models for treatment delivery would necessarily prove to be more costly. The models also include better matching of cases to treatments so that extended efforts, when needed, can be assigned to children for whom abbreviated treatments are not effective.

Conclusions

Progress in child and adolescent psychotherapy research has been remarkable, as reflected in the quantity and quality of outcome studies and the identification of evidence-based treatments. Currently, treatments are available for a wide range of clinical problems such as anxiety, depression, attention-deficit/hyperactivity disorder, oppositional and conduct disorder, eating disorders, and autism, to mention a few (e.g., Christophersen & Mortweet, 2001; Kazdin & Weisz, in press; Wasserman, Ko, & Jensen, 2001). Guidelines for clinical practice have begun to reflect the compelling evidence that some techniques are clearly the treatment of choice for the various problems that children and adolescents bring to treatment (American Academy of Child and Adolescent Psychiatry, 1997, 1998).

In this chapter, progress was illustrated by considering current reviews of therapy research, by enumerating evidence-based treatments identified for children and adolescents, and by illustrating exemplary programs of therapy research for internalizing and externalizing problems. Limitations were identified as well, and many of these focused on the characteristics of treatment research that depart from treatment as conducted in clinical practice. The departures encompass several critical dimensions (e.g., characteristics of the samples and treatments, methods for monitoring and implementing treatment) that raise questions about the generality of treatment effects obtained in research to clinical practice.

Perhaps of greater concern are the issues that have been neglected and are even less well discussed than the generalization problem. Fundamental questions about child therapy are rarely addressed in research. Prominent among these questions are those that pertain to the mechanisms of action or how and why therapy works and the moderators of treatment or for whom and under what conditions therapy works. Contemporary research is greatly concerned about how much treatment effects obtained in research generalize to practice. Concern for the mechanisms of action of therapy becomes even more important than concern for application in clinical practice. At this point, we do not understand why or how most treatments work, and hence we do not know those facets that are particularly important to extend to clinical practice. Not knowing the critical factors of therapy means we probably do not optimize those components that will effect change. This means that relatively weak or clearly less than optimal treatments are being tested in research and are being proposed for extension to clinical practice.

As mentioned previously, the three broad questions that might serve as a guide for child therapy research are: (1) What do we want to know about child and adolescent therapy? That is, what are the goals of the research? (2) What type of research is needed to obtain these goals? and (3) How can we evaluate the extent of movement and determine whether we are making progress toward the goal(s)? Although much of the chapter focused on the first two questions, the third is no less important and consists of monitoring and evaluating progress in a systematic way over the course of years. A given treatment or treatments for a given problem ought to progress through a series of studies, to establish not merely efficacy, but also the full range of questions about how the treatment works and why. Progress will be accelerated if a plan or model for the types of information we wish to know is put in place and then periodic evaluations are made of the extent to which gaps in knowledge have been addressed. There is no need to rigidly structure the research agenda, but currently the accumulation of studies is not tantamount to the accumulation of knowledge. Systematically neglecting key questions (e.g., mechanisms) and recycling the same old questions (Is technique *x* or *y* better than no treatment?) make genuine progress move at an unnecessarily geological pace. The present chapter has illustrated much of the progress that has been made, impediments to progress, and lines of work needed to provide the knowledge base for effective intervention.

Author Note

Completion of this article was facilitated by support from the Leon Lowenstein Foundation, the William T. Grant Foundation (98-1872-98), and the National Institute of Mental Health (MH59029).

FOOTNOTE

1. Throughout the chapter I use the term *children* to represent children and adolescents. The focus is on youth approximately 18 years of age and under. Where the distinction between children and adolescents is pertinent, this will be so noted.

REFERENCES

Achenbach, T. M., McConaughy, S. H., & Howell, C. T. (1987). Child/adolescent behavioral and emotional problems: Implications of cross-informant correlations for situational specificity. *Psychological Bulletin, 101*, 213–232.

Allinder, R. M., & Oats, R. G. (1997). Effects of acceptability on teacher's implementation of curriculum-based measurement and student achievement in mathematics computation. *Rase: Remedial and Special Education, 18,* 113–120.

American Academy of Child and Adolescent Psychiatry. (1997). Practice parameters. *Journal of the American Academy of Child and Adolescent Psychiatry, 36,* Whole issue 10 (Supplement).

American Academy of Child and Adolescent Psychiatry. (1998). Practice parameters. *Journal of the American Academy of Child and Adolescent Psychiatry, 37,* Whole issue 10 (Supplement).

American Psychiatric Association. (1994). *Diagnostic and statistical manual of mental disorders* (4th ed.). Washington, DC: APA.

Angold, A., Costello, E., & Erkanli, A. (1999). Comorbidity. *Journal of Child Psychology and Psychiatry, 40,* 55–87.

Arndorfer, R. E., Allen, K. D., & Aljazireh, L. (1999). Behavioral health needs in pediatric medicine and the acceptability of behavioral solutions: Implications for behavioral psychologists. *Behavior Therapy, 30,* 137–148.

Asarnow, J. R., Jaycox, L. H., & Tompson, M. C. (2001). Depression in youth: Psychosocial interventions. *Journal of Clinical Child Psychology, 30,* 33–47.

Barlow, D. H., Hayes, S. C., & Nelson, & R. O. (1984). *The scientist-professional: Research and accountability in clinical and research settings.* New York: Pergamon.

Barrett, P. M. (1998). Evaluation of cognitive-behavioral group treatments for childhood anxiety disorders. *Journal of Clinical Child Psychology, 27,* 459–468.

Barrett, P. M., Dadds, M. R., & Rapee, R. M. (1996). Family treatment of childhood anxiety: A controlled trial. *Journal of Consulting and Clinical Psychology, 64,* 333–342.

Barrett, P. M., Duffy, A. L., Dadds, M. R., & Rapee, R. M. (2001). Cognitive-behavioral treatment of anxiety disorders in children: Long-term (6-year) follow-up. *Journal of Consulting and Clinical Psychology, 69,* 135–141.

Barrnett, R. J., Docherty, J. P., & Frommelt, G. M. (1991). A review of psychotherapy research since 1963. *Journal of the American Academy of Child and Adolescent Psychiatry, 30,* 1–14.

Bird, H. R., Yager, T. J., Staghezza, B., Gould, M. S., Canino, G., & Rubio-Stipec, M. (1990). Impairment in the epidemiological measurement of psychopathology in the community. *Journal of the American Academy of Child and Adolescent Psychiatry, 29,* 796–803.

Borkovec, T., & Rachman, S. (1979). The utility of analogue research. *Behaviour Research and Therapy, 17,* 253–261.

Boyle, M. H. (1991). Children's mental health issues: Prevention and treatment. In L. C. Johnson & D. Barnhorst (Eds.), *Children, families, and public policy in the 90s* (pp. 73–104). Toronto: Thompson Educational.

Boyle, M. H., Offord, D., Racine, Y. A., Szatmari, P., Fleming, J. E., & Sanford, M. N. (1996). Identifying thresholds for classifying psychiatric disorder: Issues and prospects. *Journal of the American Academy of Child and Adolescent Psychiatry, 35,* 1440–1448.

Brestan, E. V., & Eyberg, S. M. (1998). Effective psychosocial treatment of conduct-disordered children and adolescents: 29 years, 82 studies, and 5275 kids. *Journal of Clinical Child Psychology, 27,* 180–189.

Burns, B. J., Schoenwald, S. K., Burchard, J. D., Faw, L., & Santos, A. B. (2000). Comprehensive community-based interventions with severe emotional disorders: Multisystemic therapy and the wraparound process. *Journal of Child and Family Studies, 9,* 283–314.

Case, L., & Smith, T. B. (2000). Ethnic representation in a sample of the literature of applied psychology. *Journal of Consulting and Clinical Psychology, 68,* 1107–1110.

Catalano, R. F., Hawkins, J. D., Krenz, C., Gillmore, M., Morrison, D., Wells, E., & Abbott, R. (1993). Using research to guide culturally appropriate drug abuse prevention. *Journal of Consulting and Clinical Psychology, 61,* 804–811.

Chambless, D. L., Baker, M. J., Baucom, D. H., Beutler, L. E., Calhoun, K. S., Crits-Cristoph, P., Daiuto, A., DeRubeis, R., Detweiler, J., Haaga, D.A.F., Johnson, S. B., McCurry, S., Mueser, K. T., Pope, K. S., Sanderson, W. C., Shoham, V., Stickle, T., Williams, D. A., & Woody, S. R. (1998). Update on empirically validated therapies, II. *The Clinical Psychologist, 51 (1),* 3–16.

Chambless, D. L., Sanderson, W. C., Shoham, V., Bennett-Johnson, S., Pope, K. S., Crits-Cristoph, P., Baker, M., Johnson, B., Woody, S. R., Sue, S., Beutler, L., Williams, D. A., & McCurry, S. (1996). An update on empirically validated treatments. *The Clinical Psychologist, 49(2),* 5–18.

Christophersen, E. R., & Mortweet, S. L. (2001). *Treatments that work with children: Empirically supported strategies for managing childhood problems.* Washington, DC: American Psychological Association.

Clark, L. A., Watson, D., & Reynolds, S. 1995. Diagnosis and classification of psychopathology: Challenges to the current system and future directions. *Annual Review of Psychology, 46,* 121–152.

Clarke, G. N., Lewinsohn, P. M., & Hops, H. (1990). *Adolescent coping with depression course: Leader's manual for adolescent groups.* Eugene, OR: Castalia.

Clement, P. W. (1999). *Outcomes and incomes: How to evaluate, improve, and market your practice by measuring outcomes in psychotherapy.* New York: Guilford Press.

Cohen, J. (1988). *Statistical power analysis for the behavioral sciences* (2nd ed.). Hillsdale, NJ: Erlbaum.

Cohen, P., Cohen, J., Kasen, S., Velez, C. N., Hartmark, C., Johnson, J., Rojas, M., Book, J., & Streuning, E. L. (1993). An epidemiological study of disorders in late childhood and adolescence—I. Age- and gender-specific prevalence. *Journal of Child Psychology and Psychiatry, 34,* 851–867.

Cone, J. D. (2000). *Evaluating outcomes: Empirical tools for effective practice.* Washington, DC: American Psychological Association.

Costantino, G., & Malgady, R. G. (1996). Culturally sensitive treatment: Cuento and hero/heroine modeling therapies for Hispanic children and adolescents. In E. Hibbs & P. Jensen (Eds.), *Psychosocial treatment research of child and adolescent disorders: Empirically based strategies for clinical practice* (pp. 639–669). Washington, DC: American Psychological Association.

Council of National Psychological Associations for the Advancement of Ethnic Minority Interests (2000). *Guidelines for research in ethnic minority communities.* Washington, DC: American Psychological Association.

Cuijpers, P. (1998). A psychoeducational approach to the treatment of depression: A meta-analysis of Lewinsohn's "Coping with Depression" course. *Behavior Therapy, 29,* 521–533.

Cunningham, C. E., Boyle, M., Offord, D., Racine, Y., Hundert, J., Secord, M., & McDonald, J. (2000). Tri-ministry Study: Correlates of school-based parenting course utilization. *Journal of Consulting and Clinical Psychology, 68,* 928–933.

Cunningham, C. E., Bremner, R., & Boyle, M. (1995). Large group community-based parenting programs for families of preschoolers at risk for disruptive behaviour disorders: Utilization, cost effectiveness, and outcome. *Journal of Child Psychology and Psychiatry, 36,* 1141–1159.

Dadds, M. R., Holland, D. E., Laurens, K. R., Mullins, M., Barrett, P. M., Spence, S. H. (1999). Early intervention and prevention of anxiety disorders in children: Results at 2-year follow-up. *Journal of Consulting and Clinical Psychology, 67,* 145–150.

Dadds, M. R., & McHugh, T. A. (1992). Social support and treatment outcome in behavioral family therapy for child conduct problems. *Journal of Consulting and Clinical Psychology, 60,* 252–259.

Dadds, M. R., Schwartz, S., & Sanders, M. R. (1987). Marital discord and treatment outcome in behavioral treatment of child conduct disorders. *Journal of Consulting and Clinical Psychology, 55,* 396–403.

DiClemente, R. J., Hansen, W. B., & Ponton, L. E. (Eds.) (1996). *Handbook of adolescent health risk behavior.* New York: Plenum Press.

Dishion, T. J., & Andrews, D. W. (1995). Preventing escalation in problem behaviors with high-risk young adolescents: Immediate and 1-year outcomes. *Journal of Consulting and Clinical Psychology, 63,* 538–548.

Dishion, T. J., & Patterson, G. R. (1992). Age effects in parent training outcomes. *Behavior Therapy, 23,* 719–729.

Dishion, T. J., Patterson, G. R., & Kavanagh, K. A. (1992). An experimental test of the coercion model: Linking theory, measurement, and intervention. In J. McCord & R. E. Tremblay (Eds.), *Preventing antisocial behavior* (pp. 253–282). New York: Guilford Press.

Dobson, K. S., & Shaw, B. F. (1988). The use of treatment manuals in cognitive therapy: Experience and issues. *Journal of Consulting and Clinical Psychology, 56,* 673–680.

Dryfoos, J. G. (1990). *Adolescents at risk: Prevalence and prevention.* New York: Oxford University Press.

Dumas, J. E., & Wahler, R. G. (1983). Predictors of treatment outcome in parent training: Mother insularity and socioeconomic disadvantage. *Behavioral Assessment, 5,* 301–313.

Durlak, J. A., Fuhrman, T., & Lampman, C. (1991). Effectiveness of cognitive-behavioral therapy for maladapting children. *Psychological Bulletin, 110,* 204–214.

Durlak, J. A., Wells, A. M., Cotten, J. K., & Johnson, S. (1995). Analysis of selected methodological issues in child psychotherapy research. *Journal of Clinical Child Psychology, 24,* 141–148.

Dush, D. M., Hirt, M. L., & Schroeder, H. E. (1989). Self-statement modification in the treatment of child behavior disorders: A meta-analysis. *Psychological Bulletin, 106,* 97–106.

Elliott, D. S., Huizinga, D., & Ageton, S. S. (1985). *Explaining delinquency and drug use.* Beverly Hills, CA: Sage.

Epstein, M. H., Kutash, K., & Duchnowski, A. J. (Eds.) (1998). *Outcomes for children and youth with emotional and behavioral disorders and their families: Programs and evaluation best practices.* Austin, TX: Pro-Ed.

Evidence-Based Mental Health (1998). (A journal devoted to evidence-based treatments and linking research to practice.) Volume 1, number 1.

Farrington, D. P. (1995). The development of offending and antisocial behaviour from childhood: Key findings from the Cambridge Study in delinquent development. *Journal of Child Psychology and Psychiatry, 36,* 929–964.

Fiske, D. W. (1977). Methodological issues in research on the psychotherapist. In S. Gurman & A. M. Razin (Eds.), *Effective psychotherapy: A handbook of research* (pp. 23–37). New York: Pergamon.

Flannery-Schroeder, E. C., & Kendall, P. C. (2000). Group and individual cognitive-behavioral treatments for youth with anxiety disorders: A randomized clinical trial. *Cognitive Therapy and Research, 24,* 251–278.

Fonagy, P., & Target, M. (1994). The efficacy of psychoanalysis for children with disruptive disorders. *Journal of the American Academy of Child Psychiatry, 33*, 45–55.

Fonagy, P., Target, M., Cottrell, D., Phillips, J., & Kurtz, Z. (2002). *What works for whom? A critical review of treatments for children and adolescents.* New York. Guilford Press.

Forehand, R., & Long, N. (1996). *Parenting the strong-willed child.* Chicago: Contemporary Books.

Forehand, R., & McMahon, R. J. (1981). *Helping the noncompliant child: A clinician's guide to parent training.* New York: Guilford Press.

Forgatch, M. S. (1991). The clinical science vortex: A developing theory of antisocial behavior. In D. J. Pepler & K. H. Rubin (Eds.). *The development and treatment of childhood aggression* (pp. 291–315). Hillsdale, NJ: Erlbaum.

Forgatch, M., & Patterson, G. (1989). *Parents and adolescents living together—Part 2: Family problem solving.* Eugene, OR: Castalia Publishing Co.

Foster, S., & Mash, E. J. (1999). Assessing social validity in clinical treatment research: Issues and procedures. *Journal of Consulting and Clinical Psychology, 67*, 308–319.

Foxx, R. M., Bremer, B. A., Schutz, C., Valdez, J., & Johndrow, C. (1996). Increasing treatment acceptability through video. *Behavioral Interventions, 11*, 171–180.

Frank, E., Kupfer, D. J., Perel, J. M., Cornes, C., Mallinger, A. G., Thase, M. E., McEachran, A. B., & Grochocinski, V. J. (1993). Comparison of full-dose versus half-dose pharmacotherapy in the maintenance treatment of recurrent depression. *Journal of Affective Disorders, 27*, 139–145.

Frank, E., Kupfer, D. J., Wagner, E. F., McEachran, A. B., & Cornes, C. (1991). Efficacy of interpersonal psychotherapy as a maintenance treatment for recurrent depression. *Archives of General Psychiatry, 48*, 1053–1059.

Gabbard, G. L., Lazar, S. G., Hornberger, J., & Spiegel, D. (1997). The economic impact of psychotherapy: A review. *American Journal of Psychiatry, 154*, 147–155.

Garfield, S. L. (1998). Some comments on empirically supported treatments. *Journal of Consulting and Clinical Psychology, 66*, 121–125.

Gaw, A. C. (Ed.) (1993). *Culture and ethnicity and mental illness.* Washington, DC: American Psychiatric Press.

Gladis, M. M., Gosch, E. A., Dishuk, N. M., & Crits-Cristoph, P. (1999). Quality of life: Expanding the scope of clinical significance. *Journal of Consulting and Clinical Psychology, 67*, 320–331.

Gotlib, I. H., Lewinsohn, P. M., & Seeley, J. R. (1995). Symptoms versus a diagnosis of depression: Differences in psychosocial functioning. *Journal of Consulting and Clinical Psychology, 63*, 90–100.

Greenbaum, P. E., Foster-Johnson, L., & Petrila, A. (1996). Co-occurring addictive and mental disorders among adolescents: Prevalence research and future directions. *American Journal of Orthopsychiatry, 66*, 52–60.

Greenberg, P. E., Sisitsky, T., Kessler, R. C., Finkelstein, S. N., Berndt, E. R., Davidson, J.R.T., Ballenger, J. C., & Fyer, A. J. (1999). The economic burden of anxiety disorders in the 1990s. *Journal of Clinical Psychiatry, 60*, 427–435.

Greenhill, L. L. (1998). Childhood attention deficit hyperactivity disorder: Pharmacological treatments. In P. E. Nathan & J. M. Gorman (Eds.), *A guide to treatments that work* (pp. 42–64). New York: Oxford University Press.

Haaga, D.A.F. (2000). Introduction to the special section on stepped-care models in psychotherapy. *Journal of Consulting and Clinical Psychology, 68*, 547–548.

Hammen, C. (1991). *Depression runs in families. The social context of risk and resilience in children of depressed mothers.* New York: Springer-Verlag.

Heller, K. (1971). Laboratory interview research as an analogue to treatment. In A. E. Bergin & S. L. Garfield (Eds.), *Handbook of psychotherapy and behavior change: An empirical analysis* (pp. 126–153). New York: John Wiley & Sons.

Heinicke, C. M., & Ramsey-Klee, D. M. (1986). Outcome of child psychotherapy as a function of frequency of session. *Journal of the American Academy of Child Psychiatry, 25*, 247–253.

Henggeler, S. W., Melton, G. B., Brondino, M. J., Scherer, D. G., & Hanley, J. H. (1997). Multisystemic therapy with violent and chronic juvenile offenders and their families: The role of treatment fidelity in successful dissemination. *Journal of Consulting and Clinical Psychology, 65*, 821–833.

Henggeler, S. W., Schoenwald, S. K., Borduin, C. M., Rowland, M. D., & Cunningham, P. B. (1998). *Multisystemic treatment of antisocial behavior in children and adolescents.* New York: Guilford Press.

Hill, J., & Maughan, B. (2001). *Conduct disorders in childhood and adolescence.* Cambridge: Cambridge University Press.

Hoag, M. J., & Burlingame, G. M (1997). Evaluating the effectiveness of child and adolescent group treatment: A meta-analytic review. *Journal of Clinical Child Psychology, 26*, 234–246.

Hoagwood, K., Hibbs, E., Brent, & Jensen, P. J. (1995). Efficacy and effectiveness in studies of child and adolescent psychotherapy. *Journal of Consulting and Clinical Psychology, 63*, 683–687.

Huey, S. J., Jr., Henggeler, S. W., Brondino, M. J., & Pickrel, S. G. (2000). Mechanisms of change in multisystemic therapy: Reducing delinquent behavior through therapist adherence and improved family and peer functioning. *Journal of Consulting and Clinical Psychology, 68*, 451–467.

Jacobson, N. S., Roberts, L. J., Berns, S. B., & McGlinchey, J. (1999). Methods for defining and determining the clinical significance of treatment effects in mental health research: Current status, new applications, and future directions. *Journal of Consulting and Clinical Psychology, 67,* 300–307.

Johnston, L. D. (1996, December). *The rise of drug use among American teens continues in 1996: Monitoring the Future Study,* Ann Arbor, MI: University of Michigan.

Kaslow, N. J., & Thompson, M. P. (1998). Applying the criteria for empirically supported treatments to studies of psychosocial interventions for child and adolescent depression. *Journal of Clinical Child Psychology, 27,* 146–155.

Kazdin, A. E. (1977). Assessing the clinical or applied importance of behavior change through social validation. *Behavior Modification, 1,* 427–452.

Kazdin, A. E. (1978). Evaluating the generality of findings in analogue therapy research. *Journal of Consulting and Clinical Psychology, 46,* 673–686.

Kazdin, A. E. (1989). Identifying depression in children: A comparison of alternative selection criteria. *Journal of Abnormal Child Psychology, 17,* 437–455.

Kazdin, A. E. (1993a). Changes in behavioral problems and prosocial functioning in child treatment. *Journal of Child and Family Studies, 2,* 5–22.

Kazdin, A. E. (1993b). Evaluation in clinical practice: Clinically sensitive and systematic methods of treatment delivery. *Behavior Therapy, 24,* 11–45.

Kazdin, A. E. (1994). Informant variability in the assessment of childhood depression. In W. M. Reynolds & H. Johnston (Eds.), *Handbook of depression in children and adolescents* (pp. 249–271). New York: Plenum.

Kazdin, A. E. (1995). Child, parent, and family dysfunction as predictors of outcome in cognitive-behavioral treatment of antisocial children. *Behaviour Research and Therapy, 33,* 271–281.

Kazdin, A. E. (1996a). Combined and multimodal treatments in child and adolescent psychotherapy: Issues, challenges, and research directions. *Clinical Psychology: Science and Practice, 3,* 69–100.

Kazdin, A. E. (1996b). Dropping out of child therapy: Issues for research and implications for practice. *Clinical Child Psychology and Psychiatry, 1,* 133–156.

Kazdin, A. E. (1997). Parent management training: Evidence, outcomes, and issues. *Journal of the American Academy of Child and Adolescent Psychiatry, 36,* 1349–1356.

Kazdin, A. E. (1998). Psychosocial treatments for conduct disorder in children. In P. E. Nathan & J. M. Gorman (Eds.), *A guide to treatments that work* (pp. 65–89). New York: Oxford University Press.

Kazdin, A. E. (1999). The meanings and measurement of clinical significance. *Journal of Consulting and Clinical Psychology, 67,* 332–339.

Kazdin, A. E. (2000a). Adolescent development, mental disorders, and decision making of delinquent youths. In T. Grisso & R. Schwartz (Eds.), *Youth on trial: A developmental perspective on juvenile justice* (pp. 33–84). Chicago: University of Chicago Press.

Kazdin, A. E. (2000b). Developing a research agenda for child and adolescent psychotherapy research. *Archives of General Psychiatry, 57,* 829–835.

Kazdin, A. E. (2000c). Perceived barriers to treatment participation and treatment acceptability among antisocial children and their families. *Journal of Child and Family Studies, 9,* 157–174.

Kazdin, A. E. (2000d). *Psychotherapy for children and adolescents: Directions for research and practice.* New York: Oxford University Press.

Kazdin, A. E. (2001a). *Behavior modification in applied settings* (6th ed.). Pacific Grove, CA: Wadsworth.

Kazdin, A. E. (2001b). Progression of therapy research and clinical application of treatment require better understanding of the change process. *Clinical Psychology: Science and Practice, 8,* 143–151.

Kazdin, A. E. (2002). Psychosocial treatments for conduct disorder in children. In P. W. Nathan & J. M. Gorman (Eds.) *A guide to treatments that work* (2nd ed., pp. 57–85). New York: Oxford University Press.

Kazdin, A. E. (2003). *Research design in clinical psychology* (4th ed.). Needham Heights, MA: Allyn & Bacon.

Kazdin, A. E., Bass, D., Ayers, W. A., & Rodgers, A. (1990). The empirical and clinical focus of child and adolescent psychotherapy research. *Journal of Consulting and Clinical Psychology, 58,* 729–740.

Kazdin, A. E., Bass, D., Siegel, T., & Thomas, C. (1989). Cognitive-behavioral treatment and relationship therapy in the treatment of children referred for antisocial behavior. *Journal of Consulting and Clinical Psychology, 57,* 522–535.

Kazdin, A. E., & Crowley, M. J. (1997). Moderators of treatment outcome in cognitively based treatment of antisocial children. *Cognitive Therapy and Research, 21,* 185–207.

Kazdin, A. E., Holland, L., & Crowley, M. (1997). Family experience of barriers to treatment and premature termination from child therapy. *Journal of Consulting and Clinical Psychology, 65,* 453–463.

Kazdin, A. E., & Nock, M. K. (in press). Delineating mechanisms of change in child and adolescent therapy: Methodological issues and research recommendations. *Journal of Child Psychiatry and Psychology.*

Kazdin, A. E., Siegel, T. C., & Bass, D. (1990). Drawing upon clinical practice to inform research on child and adolescent psychotherapy: A survey of practitioners. *Professional Psychology: Research and Practice, 21,* 189–198.

Kazdin, A. E., Stolar, M. J., & Marciano, P. L. (1995). Risk factors for dropping out of treatment among

White and Black families. *Journal of Family Psychology, 9*, 402–417.

Kazdin, A. E., & Wassell, G. (1999). Barriers to treatment participation and therapeutic change among children referred for conduct disorder. *Journal of Clinical Child Psychology, 28*, 160–172.

Kazdin, A. E., & Wassell, G. (2000). Therapeutic changes in children, parents, and families resulting from treatment of children with conduct problems. *Journal of the American Academy of Child and Adolescent Psychiatry, 39*, 414–420.

Kazdin, A. E., & Weisz, J. R. (1998). Identifying and developing empirically supported child and adolescent treatments. *Journal of Consulting and Clinical Psychology, 66*, 19–36.

Kazdin, A. E., & Weisz, J. R. (Eds.) (in press). *Evidence-based psychotherapies for children and adolescents.* New York: Guilford Press.

Kendall, P. C. (1994). Treating anxiety disorders in children: Results of a randomized clinical trial. *Journal of Consulting and Clinical Psychology, 62*, 100–110.

Kendall, P. C., Chu, B. C., Pimentel, S. S., & Choudbury, M. (2000). Treating anxiety disorders in youth. In P. C. Kendall (Ed.), *Child and adolescent therapy: Cognitive-behavioral procedures* (2nd ed.) (pp. 235–287). New York: Guilford Press.

Kendall, P. C., Flannery-Schroeder, E., Panichelli-Mindel, S. M., Southam-Gerow, M. A., Henin, A., & Warman, M. (1997). Therapy for anxiety-disordered youth: A second randomized clinical trial. *Journal of Consulting and Clinical Psychology, 65*, 366–380.

Kendall, P. C., Kane, M., Howard, B., & Siqueland, L. (1990). *Cognitive-behavioral therapy for anxious children: Treatment manual*, Department of Psychology, Temple University, Philadelphia, PA.

Kendall, P. C., Marrs-Garcia, A., Nath, S. R., & Sheldrick, R. C. (1999). Normative comparisons for the evaluation of clinical significance. *Journal of Consulting and Clinical Psychology, 67*, 285–299.

Kendall, P. C., Panichelli-Mindel, S. M., Sugarman, A., & Callahan, S. A. (1997). Exposure to child anxiety: Theory, research, and practice. *Clinical Psychology: Science and Practice, 4*, 29–39.

Kendall, P. C., & Southam-Gerow, M. A. (1996). Long-term follow-up of a cognitive-behavioral therapy for anxiety-disordered youth. *Journal of Consulting and Clinical Psychology, 64*, 724–730.

Kendall, P. C., & Treadwell, K.R.H. (1996). Cognitive-behavioral group treatment for socially anxious youth. In E. D. Hibbs & P. Jensen (Eds.), *Psychosocial treatment research of child and adolescent disorders: Empirically based strategies for clinical practice* (pp. 23–41). Washington, DC: American Psychological Association.

Ketterlinus, R. D., & Lamb, M. E. (Eds.), (1994). *Adolescent problem behaviors: Issues and research.* Hillsdale, NJ: Erlbaum.

Kiesler, D. J. (1966). Some myths of psychotherapy research and the search for a paradigm. *Psychological Bulletin, 65*, 110–136.

Kiesler, D. J. (1971). Experimental designs in psychotherapy research. In A. E. Bergin & S. L. Garfield (Eds.), *Handbook of psychotherapy and behavior change: An empirical analysis* (pp. 36–74). New York: John Wiley & Sons.

Klein, R. G., & Last, C. G. (1989). *Anxiety disorders in children.* Newbury Park, CA: Sage.

Kolvin, I., Garside, R. F., Nicol, A. E., MacMillan, A., Wolstenholme, F., & Leitch, I. M. (1981). *Help starts here: The maladjusted child in the ordinary school.* London: Tavistock.

Koocher, G. P., & Pedulla, B. M. (1977). Current practices in child psychotherapy. *Professional Psychology, 8*, 275–287.

Kroll, L., Harrington, R., Jayson, D., Frazer, J., & Gowers, S. (1996). Pilot study of continuation cognitive-behavior therapy for major depression in adolescents. *Journal of the American Academy of Child and Adolescent Psychiatry, 35*, 1156–1161.

Kurtines, W. M., & Szapocznik, J. (1996). Family interaction patterns: Structural family therapy in contexts of cultural diversity. In E. Hibbs & P. Jensen (Eds.). *Psychosocial treatment research of child and adolescent disorders: Empirically based strategies for clinical practice* (pp. 671–697). Washington, DC: American Psychological Association.

LaGreca, A. M. (Ed.) (1990). *Through the eyes of the child: Obtaining self-reports from children and adolescents.* Needham Heights, MA: Allyn & Bacon.

Levitt, E. E. (1957). The results of psychotherapy with children: An evaluation. *Journal of Consulting Psychology, 21*, 189–196.

Levitt, E. E. (1963). Psychotherapy with children: A further evaluation. *Behaviour Research and Therapy, 60*, 326–329.

Lewinsohn, P. M., & Clarke, G. N. (1999). Psychosocial treatments for adolescent depression. *Clinical Psychology Review, 19*, 329–342.

Lewinsohn, P. M., Clarke, G. N., Hops, H., & Andrews, J. (1990). Cognitive-behavioral treatment for depressed adolescents. *Behavior Therapy, 21*, 385–401.

Lewinsohn, P. M., Clarke, G. N., Rohde, P., Hops, H., & Seeley, J. R. (1996). A course in coping: A cognitive-behavioral approach to the treatment of adolescent depression. In E. D. Hibbs & P. Jensen (Eds.), *Psychosocial treatment research of child and adolescent disorders: Empirically based strategies for clinical practice* (pp. 109–135). Washington, DC: American Psychological Association.

Lewinsohn, P. M., Hops, H., Teri, L., & Hautzinger, M. (1985). An integrative theory of depression. In S. Reiss & R. Bootzin (Eds.), *Theoretical issues in behavior therapy* (pp. 331–359). San Diego, CA: Academic Press.

Lewinsohn, P. M., Solomon, A., Seeley, J. R., & Zeiss, A. (2000). Clinical implications of "subthreshold" depressive symptoms. *Journal of Abnormal Psychology, 109*, 345–351.

Lin, K., Poland, R. E., & Nagasaki, G. (Eds.) (1993). *Psychopharmacology and psychobiology of ethnicity.* Washington, DC: American Psychiatric Press.

Long, P., Forehand, R., Wierson, M., & Morgan, A. (1994). Does parent training with young noncompliant children have long-term effects? *Behaviour Research and Therapy, 32*, 101–107.

Lonigan, C. J., & Elbert, J. C. (Eds.) (1998). Special issue on empirically supported psychosocial interventions for children. *Journal of Clinical Child Psychology, 27(2).*

Lonigan, C. J., Elbert, J. C., & Johnson, S. B. (1998). Empirically supported psychosocial interventions for children: An overview. *Journal of Clinical Child Psychology, 27*, 138–145.

Lovaas, O. I. (1987). Behavioral treatment and normal educational/intellectual functioning in young autistic children. *Journal of Consulting and Clinical Psychology, 55*, 3–9.

Luborsky, L., Diguer, L., Seligman, D. A., Rosenthal, R., Krause, E. D., Johnson, S., Halperin, G., Bishop, M., Berman, J. S., & Schweizer, E. (1999). The researcher's own therapy allegiances: A "wild card" in comparisons of treatment efficacy. *Clinical Psychology: Science and Practice, 6*, 95–106.

Luborsky, L., McLellen, T., Diguer, L., Woody, G., & Seligman, D. A. (1997). The psychotherapist matters: Comparison of outcomes across twenty-two therapists and seven patient samples. *Clinical Psychology: Science and Practice, 4*, 53–65.

Lunnen, K. M., & Ogles, B. M. (1998). A multiperspective, multivariable evaluation of reliable change. *Journal of Consulting and Clinical Psychology, 66*, 400–410.

Maddahian, E., Newcomb, M. D., & Bentler, P. M. (1988). Risk factors for substance use: Ethnic differences among adolescents. *Journal of Substance Abuse, 1*, 11–23.

Mann, B. J., Borduin, C. M., Henggeler, S. W., & Blaske, D. M. (1990). An investigation of systemic conceptualizations of parent-child coalitions and symptom change. *Journal of Consulting and Clinical Psychology, 58*, 336–344.

Marks, I., Shaw, S., & Parkin, R. (1998). Computer-aided treatments of mental health problems. *Clinical Psychology: Science and Practice, 5*, 151–170.

Marrs, R. W. (1995). A meta-analysis of bibliotherapy studies. *American Journal of Community Psychology, 23*, 843–870.

Maser, J. D., Kaelber, C., and Weise, R. E. 1991. International use and attitudes toward DSM-III and DSM-III-R: Growing consensus in psychiatric classification. *Journal of Abnormal Psychology, 100*, 271–279.

Mash, E. J., & Terdal, L. G. (Eds.) (1997). *Assessment of childhood disorders* (3rd ed.). New York: Guilford Press.

Matt, G. E. (1989). Decision rules for selecting effect sizes in meta-analysis: A review and reanalysis of psychotherapy outcome studies. *Psychological Bulletin, 105*, 106–115.

Matt, G. E., & Navarro, A. M. (1997). What meta-analyses have and have not taught us about psychotherapy effects: A review and future directions. *Clinical Psychology Review, 17*, 1–32.

McEachin, J. J., Smith, T., & Lovaas, O. I. (1993). Outcome in adolescence of autistic children receiving early intensive behavioral treatment. *American Journal of Mental Retardation, 97*, 359–372.

Measelle, J. R., Ablow, J. C., Cowan, P. A., & Cowan, C. P. (1998). Assessing young children's views of their academic, social, and emotional lives: An evaluation of the self-perception scales of the Berkeley Puppet Interview. *Child Development, 69*, 1556–1576.

Meyers, A. W., Graves, T. J., Whelan, J. P., & Barclay, D. (1996). An evaluation of television-delivered behavioral weight loss program. Are the ratings acceptable? *Journal of Consulting and Clinical Psychology, 64*, 172–178.

Milin, R., Halikas, J. A., Meller, J. E., & Morse, C. (1991). Psychopathology among substance abusing juvenile offenders. *Journal of the American Academy of Child and Adolescent Psychiatry, 30*, 569–574.

MTA Cooperative Group. (1999a). A 14-month randomized clinical trial of treatment strategies for attention-deficit/hyperactivity disorder. *Archives of General Psychiatry, 56*, 1073–1086.

MTA Cooperative Group. (1999b). Moderators and mediators of treatment response for children with attention-deficit/hyperactivity disorder. *Archives of General Psychiatry, 56*, 1088–1096.

Nathan, P. E., & Gorman, J. M. (Eds.) (2002). *Treatments that work* (2nd ed.). New York: Oxford University Press.

Newman, M. G. (2000). Recommendations for a cost-offset model of psychotherapy allocation using generalized anxiety disorder as an example. *Journal of Consulting and Clinical Psychology, 68*, 549–555.

Newman, M. G., Consoli, A., & Taylor, C. B. (1997). Computers in assessment and cognitive behavioral treatment of clinical disorders: Anxiety as a case in point. *Behavior Therapy, 28*, 211–235.

Newman, M. G., Kenardy, J., Herman, S., & Taylor, C. B. (1997). Comparison of palmtop-computer-assisted brief cognitive-behavioral treatment to cognitive-behavioral treatment for panic disorder. *Journal of Consulting and Clinical Psychology, 65*, 178–183.

Offord, D., Boyle, M. H., Racine, Y. A., Fleming, J. E., Cadman, D. T., Blum, H. M., Byrne, C., Links, P. S., Lipman, E. L., MacMillan, H. L.,

Rae Grant, N. I., Sanford, M. N., Szatmari, P., Thomas, H., & Woodward, C. A. (1992). Outcome, prognosis, and risk in a longitudinal follow-up study. *Journal of the American Academy of Child and Adolescent Psychiatry, 31*, 916–923.

Offord, D., Boyle, M. H., Racine, Y. A., Szatmari, P., Fleming, J. E., Sanford, M. N., and Lipman, E. L. (1996). Integrating assessment data from multiple informants. *Journal of the American Academy of Child and Adolescent Psychiatry, 35*, 1078–1085.

Ollendick, T. H., & King, N. J. (1998). Empirically supported treatments for children with phobic and anxiety disorders. *Journal of Clinical Child Psychology, 27*, 156–167.

O'Malley, S. S., Foley, S. H., Rounsaville, B. J., Watkins, J. T., Sotsky, S. M., Imber, S. D., & Elkin, I. (1988). Therapist competence and patient outcome in interpersonal psychotherapy of depression. *Journal of Consulting and Clinical Psychology, 56*, 496–501.

Patterson, G. R. (1976). *Living with children: New methods for parents and teachers* (revised). Champaign, IL: Research Press.

Patterson, G. R. (1982). *Coercive family process.* Eugene, OR: Castalia.

Patterson, G. R., & Forgatch, M. (1987). *Parents and adolescents living together—Part 1: The basics.* Eugene, OR: Castalia Publishing Co.

Patterson, G. R., Reid, J. B., & Dishion, T. J. (1992). *Antisocial boys.* Eugene, OR: Castalia.

Paul, G. L. (1967). Outcome research in psychotherapy. *Journal of Consulting Psychology, 31*, 109–118.

Pavuluri, M. S., Luk, S. L., & McGee, R. (1996). Help seeking behavior problems by parents of preschool children: A community study. *Journal of the American Academy of Child and Adolescent Psychiatry, 35*, 215–222.

Pelham, W. E., Jr., Wheeler, T., & Chronis, A. (1998). Empirically supported psychosocial treatments for attention deficit hyperactivity disorder. *Journal of Clinical Child Psychology, 27*, 190–205.

Persons, J. B., & Silberschatz, G. (1998). Are results of randomized controlled clinical trials useful to psychotherapists? *Journal of Consulting and Clinical Psychology, 66*, 126–135.

Prinz, R. J., & Miller, G. E. (1994). Family-based treatment for childhood antisocial behavior: Experimental influences on dropout and engagement. *Journal of Consulting and Clinical Psychology, 62*, 645–650.

Reimers, T. M., Wacker, D. P., Cooper, L. J., & DeRaad, A. O. (1992). Clinical evaluation of the variables associated with treatment acceptability and their relation to compliance. *Behavioral Disorders, 18*, 67–76.

Rogers, S. J. (1998). Empirically supported treatment for young children with autism. *Journal of Clinical Child Psychology, 27*, 168–179.

Rosen, G. M. (1993). Self-help or hype? Comments on psychology's failure to advance self-care. *Professional Psychology: Research and Practice, 24*, 340–345.

Roth, A., & Fonagy, P. (1996). *What works for whom: A critical review of psychotherapy research.* New York: Guilford Press.

Rounsaville, B. J., O'Malley, S., Foley, S., & Weissman, M. (1988). Role of manual-guided training in the conduct and efficacy of interpersonal psychotherapy of depression. *Journal of Consulting and Clinical Psychology, 56*, 681–688.

Ruma, P. R., Burke, R. V., & Thompson, R. W. (1996). Group parent training: Is it effective for children of all ages? *Behavior Therapy, 27*, 159–169.

Rutter, M., Yule, W., & Graham, P. (1973). Enuresis and behavioural deviance: Some epidemiological considerations. In I. Kolvin, R. MacKeith, & S. R. Meadow (Eds.), *Bladder control and enuresis: Clinics in developmental medicine* (Vol. 48/49). London: Heinemann/SIMP.

Sanders, M. R., & Dadds, M. R. (1993). *Behavioral family intervention.* Needham Heights, MA: Allyn & Bacon.

Sanford, M. N., Offord, D. R., Boyle, M. H., Peace, A., & Racine, Y. A. (1992). Ontario Child Health Study: Social and school impairments in children aged 6–16 years. *Journal of the American Academy of Child and Adolescent Psychiatry, 31*, 60–67.

Santrock, J. W., Minnett, A. M., & Campbell, B. D. (1994). *The authoritative guide to self-help books.* New York: Guilford Press.

Shadish, W. R., Matt, G. E., Navarro, A. M., Siegle, G., Crits-Christoph, P., Hazelrigg, M. D., Jorm, A. F., Lyons, L. C., Nietzel, M. T., Prout, H. T., Robinson, L., Smith, M. L., Svartberg, M., & Weiss, B. (1997). Evidence that therapy works in clinically representative conditions. *Journal of Consulting and Clinical Psychology, 65*, 355–365.

Shadish, W. R., Montgomery, L. M., Wilson, P., Wilson, M. R., Bright, I., & Okwumabua, T. (1993). Effects of family and marital psychotherapies: A meta-analysis. *Journal of Consulting and Clinical Psychology, 61*, 992–1002.

Shapiro, D. A., Firth-Cozens, J., & Stiles, W. B. (1989). Therapists' differential effectiveness: A Sheffield Psychotherapy Project addendum. *British Journal of Psychiatry, 154*, 383–385.

Sheinkopf, S. J., & Siegel, B. (1998). Home based behavioral treatment of young children with autism. *Journal of Autism and Developmental Disabilities, 28*, 15–23.

Sheldrick, R. C., Kendall, P. C., & Heimberg, R. G. (2001). Assessing clinical significance: A comparison of three treatments for conduct disordered children. *Clinical Psychology: Science and Practice, 8*, 418–430.

Simon, G. E., Manning, W. G., Katzelnick, D. J., Pearson, S. D., Henk, H. J., & Helstad, C. P.

(2001). Cost-effectiveness of systematic depression treatment of high utilizers of general medical care. *Archives of General Psychiatry, 58,* 181–187.

Smith, T. (1999). Outcome of early intervention for children with autism. *Clinical Psychology: Science and Practice, 6,* 33–49.

Snyder, H., Poole, R., & Wan, Y. (2000). Easy access to juvenile populations—Online. Available: http://www.ojjdp.ncjrs.org/ojstatbb/ezapop.

Stoff, D. M., Breiling, J., & Maser, J. D. (Eds.) (1997). *Handbook of antisocial behavior.* New York: John Wiley & Sons.

Ström, L., Pettersson, R., & Andersson, G. (2000). A controlled trial of self-help treatment of recurrent headache conducted via the Internet. *Journal of Consulting and Clinical Psychology, 68,* 722–727.

Szapocznik, J., Perez-Vidal, A., Brickman, A., Foote, F. H., Santisteban, D. A., Hervis, O., & Kurtines, W. H. (1988). Engaging adolescent drug abusers and their families into treatment: A strategic structural systems approach. *Journal of Consulting and Clinical Psychology, 56,* 552–557.

Szapocznik, J., Rio, A., Murray, E., Cohen, R., Scopetta, M., Rivas-Vasquez, A., Hervis, O., Posada, V., & Kurtines, W. (1989). Structural family versus psychodynamic child therapy for problematic Hispanic boys. *Journal of Consulting and Clinical Psychology, 57,* 571–578.

Szapocznik, J., & Williams, R. A. (2000). Brief Strategic Family Therapy: Twenty-five years of interplay among theory, research and practice in adolescent behavior problems and drug abuse. *Child and Family Psychology Review, 3,* 117–134.

Task Force on Promotion and Dissemination of Psychological Procedures (1995). Training in and dissemination of empirically validated psychological treatments: Report and recommendations. *The Clinical Psychologist, 48(1),* 3–23.

Tharp, R. G. (1991). Cultural diversity and treatment of children. *Journal of Consulting and Clinical Psychology, 59,* 799–812.

Thompson, R. W., Ruma, P. R., Schuchmann, L. F., & Burke, R. V. (1996). A cost-effectiveness evaluation of parent training. *Journal of Child and Family Studies, 5,* 415–429.

Tracy, P. E., Wolfgang, M. E., & Figlio, R. M. (1990). *Delinquency careers in two birth cohorts.* New York: Plenum Press.

U.S. Bureau of Census, Current Population Reports. (1993). *U.S. population estimates by age, sex, race, and Hispanic origin: 1980–1991.* (P25-1095) Washington, DC: U.S. Government Printing Office.

U.S. Congress, Office of Technology Assessment. (1991). *Adolescent health.* (OTA-H-468). Washington, DC: U.S. Government Printing Office.

Wasserman, G. A., Ko, S. J., & Jensen, P. J. (2001). Columbia guidelines for child and adolescent mental health referral. *Emotional and Behavioral Disorders in Youth, 2,* 9–14, & 23.

Webster-Stratton, C. (1985). Predictors of treatment outcome in parent training for conduct disordered children. *Behavior Therapy, 16,* 223–243.

Webster-Stratton, C. (1996). Early intervention with videotape modeling: Programs for families of children with oppositional defiant disorder or conduct disorder. In E. D. Hibbs & P. Jensen (Eds.), *Psychosocial treatment research of child and adolescent disorders: Empirically based strategies for clinical practice* (pp. 435–474). Washington, DC: American Psychological Association.

Webster-Stratton, C. (1998). Preventing conduct problems in Head Start Children: Strengthening parenting competencies. *Journal of Consulting and Clinical Psychology, 66,* 715–730.

Webster-Stratton, C., & Hammond, M. (1990). Predictors of treatment outcome in parent training for families with conduct problem children. *Behavior Therapy, 21,* 319–337.

Weinberg, N. Z., Rahdert, E., Colliver, J. D., & Glanz, M. D. (1998). Adolescent substance abuse: A review of the past 10 years. *Journal of the American Academy of Child and Adolescent Psychiatry, 37,* 252–261.

Weiss, B., Catron, T., Harris, V., & Phung, T. M. (1999). The effectiveness of traditional child therapy. *Journal of Consulting and Clinical Psychology, 67,* 82–94.

Weisz, J. R., Donenberg, G. R., Han, S. S., & Kauneckis, D. (1995). Child and adolescent psychotherapy outcomes in experiments and in clinics: Why the disparity? *Journal of Abnormal Child Psychology, 23,* 83–106.

Weisz, J. R., Donenberg, G. R., Han, S. S., & Weiss, B. (1995). Bridging the gap between lab and clinic in child and adolescent psychotherapy. *Journal of Consulting and Clinical Psychology, 63,* 688–701.

Weisz, J. R., & Hawley, K. M. (1998). Finding, evaluating, refining, and applying empirically supported treatments for children and adolescents. *Journal of Clinical Child Psychology, 27,* 206–216.

Weisz, J. R., Huey, S. J., & Weersing, V. R. (1998). Psychotherapy outcome research with children and adolescents. In T. H. Ollendick & R. J. Prinz (Eds.), *Advances in clinical child psychology* (Vol. 20, pp. 49–91). New York: Plenum Press.

Weisz, J. R., & Weiss, B. (1993). *Effects of psychotherapy with children and adolescents.* Newbury Park, CA: Sage.

Weisz, J. R., Weiss, B., & Donenberg, G. R. (1992). The lab versus the clinic: Effects of child and adolescent psychotherapy. *American Psychologist, 47,* 1578–1585.

Weisz, J. R., Weiss, B., Han, S. S., Granger, D. A., & Morton, T. (1995). Effects of psychotherapy with children and adolescents revisited: A meta-analysis of treatment outcome studies. *Psychological Bulletin, 117,* 450–468.

Wierzbicki, M., & Pekarik, G. (1993). A meta-analysis of psychotherapy dropout. *Professional Psychology: Research and Practice, 24,* 190–195.

Windle, M., Shope, J. T., & Bukstein, O. (1996). Alcohol use. In R. J. DiClemente, W. B. Hansen, & L. E. Ponton (Eds.), *Handbook of adolescent health risk behavior* (pp. 115–159). New York: Plenum.

Wolfe, D. A. (1999). *Child abuse* (2nd ed.). Newbury Park, CA: Sage.

World Health Organization. (1992). *The ICD-10 classification of mental disorders.* Geneva: WHO.

World Health Organization. (2001). *The world health report: 2001: Mental health: New understanding, new hope.* Geneva: World Health Organization.

Yates, B. T. (1995). Cost-effectiveness analysis, cost-benefit analysis, and beyond: Evolving models for the scientist-manager-practitioner. *Clinical Psychology: Science and Practice, 2,* 385–398.

Zhu, S., Stretch, V., Balabanis, M., Rosbrook, B., Sadler, G., & Pierce, J. P. (1996). Telephone counseling for smoking cessation: Effects of single-session and multiple-session interventions. *Journal of Consulting and Clinical Psychology, 64,* 202–211.

CHAPTER 13

LEVELS OF EVIDENCE FOR THE MODELS AND MECHANISMS OF THERAPEUTIC CHANGE IN FAMILY AND COUPLE THERAPY

THOMAS L. SEXTON
Indiana University
JAMES F. ALEXANDER
University of Utah
ALYSON LEIGH MEASE
Indiana University

For over a quarter century, chapters in the volumes of this *Handbook* have chronicled the expanding knowledge and the evolving research practices of marital and family therapy (MFT). Previous chapters (Alexander, Holtzworth-Munroe, & Jameson, 1994; Gurman & Kniskern, 1977; Gurman, Kniskern, & Pinsof, 1986) have also served as historical documents that reflect the important theoretical developments, clinical issues, and research questions of the time. Despite the reliable and informative results of the cumulative research knowledge documented in these presentations, the persistent schism noted by Alexander et al. (1994) between the established findings of marital and family research and the practice and training of marital and family therapy continues. Indeed, now more than three decades after the publication of the first *Handbook* review, it is not uncommon to encounter concerns about the role of research in practice. As Gurman et al. (1986) noted, "despite numerous attempts at seduction and mutual courtship, it remains the case that clinicians and therapy researchers have failed to consummate a 'meaningful' and lasting relationship, as has been observed, commented on, and lamented repeatedly" (p. 490).

The practice–research schism has both conceptual and pragmatic roots. From the very beginning, the founding epistemological concepts of MFT challenged the traditional methods of science and questioned the place of that knowledge in clinical practice. The early conceptual shifts embodied in the founding theoretical models (Hoffman, 1981) brought with them a set of assumptions that questioned traditional linear "causal effect" and single variable research designs. These epistemological roots quite naturally led to criticism of traditional research methods. Clinicians and theorists openly questioned whether traditional methods could capture phenomena thought to be recursive, dynamic, multidirectional processes of openness and growth, interdeterminate dynamic system trajectories, and interpersonal transactions that absolutely could not be "dismantled" in a manner that represented the tradition of "good science."

Taking quite a different path, early marital and family researchers adopted traditional "gold standard" research approaches typified by randomized clinical trials (RCT) and well-controlled research designs. These methods were critical to establish the field as an empirically grounded, scientifically respected discipline (Pinsof & Wynne, 2000). Without the relentless early emphasis on an empirical foundation, MFT could easily have become a hot trend that then dissipated when the next hot trend emerged. However, this early research path has increasingly come in conflict with the systematic practice of MFT.

Rather than lamenting and verifying the schism, in this review we view the differences between the science and practice of MFT as a natural dialectic in which both are equally important and useful. The different epistemologies of research and practice are united by a common purpose that demands a more inclusive embodiment of methodologies, perspectives, and conceptual models. Such inclusivity and respect for different perspectives is nothing new and has been a central theme of MFT. Early theorists in the developing field of MFT certainly were not willing to accept that "more is less" when moving from an individual to a systems perspective. In fact, there was no sentiment for the position that family-based interventions represented a less powerful or less effective intervention than more traditional individual therapies, even though marriage and family therapy involved more people, was often shorter in duration, and often focused on changing relationship patterns more than individual insight. The progenitors of current MFT models thus asserted that "more is more," a more inclusive (systemic and multisystemic) perspective allows for just as much rigor as individual approaches and often even more efficacious and effective interventions (Alexander, Sexton, & Robbins, 2001). In order for this "have your cake and eat it too" situation to exist, however, the aura of oppositionality and "less than" must be replaced by a commitment to inclusion and integration (Alexander, Robbins, & Sexton, 2001; Lebow, 1999; Sexton & Alexander, 2002a). We must be able to "savor the dialectic" of the tensions that emerge when we integrate logical positivist and postmodern perspectives, manualized treatments, context-sensitive and responsible clinical transactions, quantitative databases, and the acceptance that the only true functional perspective is that experienced by the clients (Alexander, Robbins, & Sexton, 2001; see Slife, this volume, for a more extensive discussion of these issues).

To that end, our goal in this chapter is to present a systematic and comprehensive review of the clinical research literature of the fields of marital and family therapy published since the last *Handbook* chapter review. We hope that, like previous *Handbook* chapters, the chapter can represent a benchmark of the current knowledge in the field, a description of the current research questions and methods, a useful clinical reference, and the basis of continued theoretical and research development. This goal poses an interesting dilemma in light of the previous discussion. Although we insist on retaining the strong research criterion-based flavor of earlier reviews of MFT research as a model for this *Handbook* chapter, we do not wish to contribute to a process that could promote the "good science" aspects of MFT becoming anachronisms, if not the antithesis, of the majority of what is characteristic of the practice community. Thus, our goal is to review the research literature in a way that will build a bridge between the scientific basis and the clinical practice of MFT directed at the common purpose of enhancing the potency of clinical interventions.

In the sections that follow, we develop a context for our review, provide the details of our methodology, present the findings of our analysis, and provide a set of conclusions and recommendations. To establish a *context* for our discussions, we briefly discuss the history of the profession by reviewing the findings of the three previous *Handbook* chapters on marital and family therapy. Like others before us (Gurman, Kniskern, & Pinsof, 1986), we believe that it is important to provide a link between our findings and past concerns and thus gain a sense of the evolution of the knowledge base in the field. This new landscape brings into focus the issues of systematic practice models and ecologically valid research as a means to overcome the research practice gap. In our presentation of the *methodology* of the current review, we operationally define the domains that organize our effort and describe our method of analysis. We think our task requires a review of the findings and research trends of various levels of research, including both meta-analysis and individual studies in marital and family therapy published since the last *Handbook* chapter. Our goal is to focus on studies that are directly relevant for practice: efficacy, effectiveness, and process-outcome studies of recognizable marital and family therapy interventions that are directed toward the mitigation of specific clinical problems within clinical settings and with actual couples and families. We begin our discussion of *studies* in both marital and family therapy research, followed by an analysis of the notable *research-based practice trends* that emerge from these studies. We conclude with a discussion of future challenges for both research and practice in MFT.

The Current Context of Marital and Family Therapy

One of the hallmarks of marital and family therapy has always been its consideration of *context*. The context of clinical research is best understood through a consideration of the historical evolution of the ideas and questions of research in the field and the current "landscape" of research and practice in MFT.

Historical Evolution

The evolving knowledge base, research questions, and methods chronicled in the previous chapters of the *Handbook* form a historical context that documents the growth of knowledge as well as the fundamental research and clinical questions of the time. The combination of these chapters provides a way to identify the important developmental trends that are at the heart of the important questions, methods, and knowledge that set the stage for our work. Each chapter author adopted different review strategies to accomplish the task of delineating the state of the research because each of the chapter authors faced very different eras of MFT research and knowledge.

When the first MFT chapter appeared in the *Handbook* series (Gurman & Kniskern, 1981), several reviews of the MFT field had already appeared (Beck, 1976; Gurman, 1971, 1973). These reviews concluded, with cautious optimism, that marital and family therapies were efficacious therapeutic activities. This suggested a need for a comprehensive analysis of whether marital and family therapies had amassed reasonable evidence to argue that they were effective. Gurman and Kniskern (1981) set out to provide a detailed analysis of the population of outcome studies, identifying the trends and broad patterns of findings. They identified over 200 relevant studies in which marital or family treatment was explicitly focused on altering the interaction between family members. Their results clearly established that the broad approaches to MFT were efficacious and that family therapy was often as effective and possibly more effective than many individual treatments for problems attributed to family conflict. Furthermore, it appeared that both behavioral and nonbehavioral treatments produced beneficial outcomes that were superior to no-treatment controls in about two-thirds of the cases. They were even able to identify important therapist variables. For example, therapists who provide little structure in early sessions have more negative outcomes. Those therapists with a mastery of technical skills seemed better able to prevent the worsening of family interaction, whereas those therapists with high supportive and relational skills had more positive outcomes (Gurman & Kniskern, 1981).

When Gurman et al. (1986) began the second *Handbook* chapter, the field of MFT had changed considerably. The efficacy of marital and family therapy seemed well established, and the previous need to justify the existence of MFT was less important (Gurman et al., 1986). Instead, their emphasis was to "help delineate and forge closer linkages among theory, research, and clinical practice" (p. 570). Gurman et al. (1986) found the family therapy research field, to be "a good deal more mature developmentally, and (is), thus, more open to self-criticism and thoughtful self-reflection." Consequently, these authors did not review individual studies but instead concentrated on the results of 47 overlapping reviews of the marital and family literature from 1970 to 1984.

In their review, Gurman et al. (1986) focused much of their analysis on the efficacy of various "schools" of family and marital therapy. They identified "schools" of therapy that they believed to be common between therapist and educators as having "an enduring impact on the thinking and practices of significant number of clinicians, and which, in our judgment, are in regular use with genuine clinical help-seeking populations" (p. 593). In their analysis, they identified the evidence for each school in successfully intervening with various clinical problems. Interestingly, of 15 "schools" only 6 had at least moderately positive evidence of efficacy in treating at least one clinical problem, and the approaches with moderate or strong positive efficacy evidence were highly directive in nature. In addition, four different client problems (schizophrenia, substance abuse, juvenile delinquency, marital discord) had more than one method of high efficacy. Most interesting is that, of the possible method x problem combinations, only 23% had been empirically studied. From this review it seems clear that few "schools" of therapeutic intervention had been empirically tested, but when they were, the evidence of successful outcome was promising.

In the most recent version of the *Handbook*, Alexander et al. (1994) took a dramatically different approach than their predecessors by shifting the focus to the broad direction of marital and family therapy research programs. Their focus was on previously published reviews (both qualitative and meta-analytic) of family and marital therapy, with the primary emphasis on the identification of trends that set the stage for future advances in the field. In particular, they suggested that future research must pay careful attention to developmental issues, context and process, longitudinal patterns, and the clinical complexity and comorbidity of the problems presented by families and couples. In taking this approach, Alexander et al. (1994) were able to highlight the complex issues facing the future of marital and family therapy research in particular; the clinician's decision-making and intervention needs; the researcher's need for rigor and generalizability; and the clinician's and policymaker's need for accountability.

These results, like those from previous reviews, suggested that marital therapies seemed effective when compared to no-treatment control groups and that all treatments had about the same success rates. In regard to process studies, Alexander et al. (1994) found once again that "research into the process of marital therapy and its relationship with treatment outcome is still in its infancy" (p. 606). Relying on meta-analytic studies, they also found that family treatments were a viable and perhaps preferred vehicle for change when compared to no-treatment and alternative treatments. The "pragmatic" therapies—those relying on behavioral methods—had particularly strong support. However, Alexander et al. (1994) noted that global therapeutic orientations did not represent the important and distinguishing characteristics that differentiated effective and ineffective interventions. Instead, the differences were likely accounted for by specific techniques matched to specific clients. Alexander et al. (1994) suggested that the future focus of marital and family research be on specific, identifiable, and well-articulated systematic approaches to treatment in which (a) clinically meaningful problems are targeted; (b) there is a coherent conceptual framework underlying the clinical interventions; (c) there are specific interventions described in detail with an articulation of the therapist qualities necessary to follow them; (d) process research identifies how the change mechanisms work; and (e) outcome research demonstrates how well it works.

The Changing Landscape of Research and Practice

In addition to the history of ideas and research questions, our review is embedded in a context of a dramatically changing landscape of MFT research and practice. For example, managed care has pushed practitioners to consider the outcomes and costs of services, and, has ushered in an era of accountability that is now common in the world of practice (Sexton, Whiston, Bleuer, & Walz, 1997). In an effort to respond to the calls for accountability, professional organizations (e.g., the American Psychological Association, the American Psychiatric Association) have developed evidence-based practice guidelines identifying the scientific basis for psychological treatments. Empirically Supported Treatment (Chambless & Hollon, 1998) and Principles of Empirically Supported Interventions (Wampold, Lictenberg, & Waehler, in press) are both attempts to set a standard for what is "enough" research support for a psychological intervention to be reliable enough to be implemented by practitioners. In arenas outside the "professions" (e.g., juvenile justice, managed health care) the concept of "best practice" has become the criterion on which decisions are made regarding funding for treatment programs (Elliott, 1998). These efforts have brought empirical evidence and systematic treatment models into the forefront of consideration in MFT.

Over the last number of years we have also seen a growing push by model developers to link broad MFT theory to specific clinical actions. The "schools" of therapy approach has given way to more specific, systematic, and well-articulated clinical models intended to be therapeutic "maps" that directly guide practice with specific clinical foci (Alexander, Holtzworth-Munroe, & Jameson, 1994; Alexander, Robbins, & Sexton, 2001; Sexton & Alexander, 2002a). In some cases, these models are built on longstanding research programs that integrate theory (Lebow, 1999), and most are translated into practice by way of clinical manuals that create systematic guides that are also clinically responsive (Alexander et al., 2001). According to Liddle, Santisteban, Levant, and Bray (2001), these approaches represent the emergence of "family intervention science," which is predicated on the growing body of outcome and process research studies that meet the highest standards of research methodology.

The Need for "Matching to"

Despite the frequent conclusion that marital and family therapy produces some type of desirable outcomes, two significant issues remain elusive and contribute to the gap between research and practice. First, despite the considerable scientific knowledge gathered over the years, we have yet to come to a clear identification of what specific mechanisms are responsible for the successful changes found in outcome research (Alexander et al., 1994). In some cases, the mechanisms seem to refer to broad categories of action like marital and family therapy in general. In other cases, it seems to mean a specific clinical intervention program, or even individual interventions disconnected from a program's guiding conceptual and theoretical principles. The lack of clarity about the "it" becomes problematic when different consumers with different needs, goals, and objectives ask nonspecific questions of the research knowledge base. We suggest that the disconnect between research and practice comes about when consumers attempt to answer questions of varying levels of specificity with research findings that don't "match" the questions.

Second, there are continued questions surrounding the concept of what is appropriately considered an outcome and what constitutes "convincing empirical evidence" of clinically relevant and significant outcomes. This is a particularly understandable controversy given the diversity of context, clients, and interventionists that deliver MFT treatments. Does "works"—meaning "success"—refer to the nomothetic question regarding *most people* or does it refer to specific clients in specific situations? Furthermore, does "works" ask if an intervention program conducted under ideal clinical conditions with highly specialized interventions produces noticeable results, or does it refer to the actual practice of a real therapist in regular situations?

We suggest that the issue is one of "matching" the clinical question with the appropriate scientific knowledge best suited to answer the question. Different constituencies quite naturally ask different questions with differing levels of specificity (regarding both the "it" and the "works"), formulated in regard to the need to make different decisions. For example, political and policy questions require efficacy evidence regarding broad categories of action. Questions regarding the choice of treatments may require more specific and well-defined effectiveness evidence, including the clear identification of specific treatments, specific problems, and a clear delineation of the treatment context. Specific moment-to-moment clinical decisions that must be made by the MFT practitioner require an even more specific process-outcome type of study. We suggest that it is when the specific question is not matched with the appropriate research that research becomes difficult to use and the gap between research and practice grows.

THE CURRENT REVIEW

In this chapter we extend the "match-to" concept as a guiding principle to organize our review of the literature. To do so we first identify the domains we review, followed by the classification scheme that organizes the review process.

Domains of Review

To adequately understand the research literature, it is important to consider four *domains* of MFT practice: clinical treatments (the "it"), clinical outcomes (the "what"), types of research (the "how"), and the quality of the evidence. These domains are organized into a specific classification scheme described as follows.

1. SYSTEMATIC MFT TREATMENTS. Our primary interest is in the scientific basis of the identifiable intervention programs currently available in the fields of marital and family treatment. At the broadest category are general modalities that are unspecified but clearly represent a way of working. The general domain of 'marital and family therapy' fits this broad category of action. On the other end of the continuum are systematic intervention programs, or models of practice that meet the standard of a "treatment" (Alexander et al., 1994; Chambless & Hollon, 1998) or an intervention program (Wampold et al., in press).

In order to maintain continuity with previous work, we used the Alexander et al. (1994) criteria as our guiding definition of a "treatment." Accordingly, a treatment is defined as a clinical intervention that targets clinically meaningful syndromes or situations with a coherent conceptual framework underlying the clinical intervention, described in sufficient detail to explain the specific interventions and therapist qualities necessary to carry them out. This definition implies high treatment integrity brought about by clinical supervision, treatment manuals, and/or adherence verification throughout the course of therapy. In addition, we classify interventions according to Baucom et al. (1998) who differentiated couple therapies in three ways that we find useful in differentiating treatment types for both couple and family therapy. These ways consist of: (a) application of traditional marital and family therapies to address broad relationship issues thought to be part of maintaining the symptoms, (b) disorder-specific interventions in which the relational system of the couple or family are assumed to contribute to the maintenance of the symptom or impede the treatment, and (c) partner-assisted interventions in which the partner or family member serves as a surrogate therapist or coach with little attention to the relationship issues.

2. CLINICAL OUTCOMES. Defining the *outcomes* of MFT is also complex but broadly includes measures of client improvement. Different consumers of research are, however, interested in different outcomes. For example, policymakers are concerned with outcomes that address broad trends, based on social concerns and cost-benefit considerations. Those outcomes sought by clients and therapists in clinical practice settings are often related to Pinsof and Catherall's (1986) notion of "proximal" goals, or those immediate process steps that need to be taken for therapy to ultimately succeed.

In order to understand outcomes, three particularly salient issues must be considered: clinical significance, long-term sustainability of effects, and generalizability of outcomes to various contexts and settings. The debate regarding the meaning of "clinical significance" is well documented in the psychotherapy literature (Jacobson, Follette, & Ravensdorf, 1984; see Lambert & Ogles, this volume). Clinical significance is an absolute standard in which improved functioning based on more normative data is the primary standard. Based on this definition, change is clinically significant if it makes a difference in the functioning of the client whether that is in quality of life, reduction of experienced symptoms, elimination of environmental outcomes (e.g., arrest), or change in risky behaviors. For outcomes to be "important" they must be lasting. Issues of long-term sustainability have repeatedly been raised in the MFT research literature (Alexander et al., 1994). Finally, for results to be clinically useful, they must generalize to the context in which clients' lives. To meet this standard of generalizability, it is of increasing importance to identify the contexts in which treatments are effective for given problems. Context specifies the setting, the specific client, the specific community, and conditions of the treatment.

3. Types of research. Currently, three broad categories of research inform the MFT practitioners, trainers, and researchers. Meta-analytic research *reviews* give a broad perspective regarding important trends in the literature that carry the cumulative knowledge of studies previously conducted. *Clinical trial* studies provide more specific information about knowledge yet to be incorporated into the trends noted in reviews. Clinical trial research can be classified as varying along a continuum from high internal validity and control of variation (efficacy research) to high ecological validity and clinical relevance (process to outcome studies). Each type of research serves different purposes and has strengths and weaknesses. Efficacy studies answer questions about which treatments work under the most stringently controlled conditions. Efficacy studies have high methodological control but are limited because they are unrealistic of actual clinical conditions. Effectiveness studies answer questions regarding the power of therapeutic interventions in actual clinical settings with conditions that replicate those that clinicians actually face. Although there is decreased methodological control (in the traditional sense), these studies have high clinical relevance. But effectiveness is enormously difficult to establish (Wampold et al., in press). *Process-to-outcome* studies link the conditions of therapy (preexisting and specific within-session processes) with the outcome of family-based interventions. We classified process studies according to the process (mediator/predictor of change vs. moderator/mechanism of change) and the outcome to which it was linked (proximal-within therapy outcome and distal/ultimate post-therapy outcomes). Two types of processes are common in clinical research: mediational/or predictor variables and moderator/mechanisms of change. We believe that it is the combination of both that gives the best picture of a useful domain of knowledge to inform practice procedures and future research efforts.

4. Research quality. The quality of studies helps identify the degree of confidence that we might have in the findings. Research quality is a difficult dimension to classify when a diversity of research methods is considered. Most often, research quality is defined along the assumptions of logical positivist designs exemplified by randomized clinical trial studies. Unfortunately, the internal control required by these approaches may decrease the natural heterogeneity and diversity of the client, context, and problem. We suggest that each type of research requires *different criteria* for quality (Sexton & Alexander, 2002). In an efficacy study, the traditional criteria (control of client, random assignment, etc.) represent a useful and appropriate measure of quality. In effectiveness studies, with less control (in the traditional sense), the clear identification of the treatment (treatment integrity and fidelity) and significance of outcome is important. In process-outcome studies, the quality of studies also hinges on the ability to identify the change mechanism represented by the process variable. Despite differences, there is a common set of domains important in clinical research. It must be systematic in its design (clear questions that match appropriate methods) and be rigorous in its method. In addition, because MFT is a clinical process, there must be integrity of the treatment and the outcome. In the following review, we categorize the primary dimensions of research quality both as a mediator of our conclusions and as a statement about the status of MFT research.

Scope and Review Methodology

This review is a systematic analysis of all of the meta-reviews, clinical trial studies, and process investigations in MFT since the last *Handbook* chapter. To accomplish this task, we first identified all meta-analyses and clinical trial studies through a survey of the literature conducted through a systematic search of studies in all of the major professional publications (journal articles and book chapters). Meta-analyses were checked for additional studies. Studies included in the review articles *were not* included in order to avoid duplication of effects. We included the qualitative reviews, meta-analyses, and the individual clinical studies of MFT published since the last *Handbook* chapter (Alexander et al., 1994).

Figure 13.1 represents an organizational matrix for the review that is defined by the domains noted above. The first axis represents the *levels of scientific evidence* to which general or specific clinical questions can be matched, the second axis represents the different *types of research* that produce that knowledge, and the third represents the *research quality* necessary to have confidence in the results. It is important to note that we do not view these dimensions as independent. The dimensions delineated here certainly involve more than one domain (treatment and outcome). Increasingly specific levels of evidence require more specificity in research quality and research type. However, we think that the dimensions do create a classification scheme for organizing the research literature in a way that allows for a "matching" of clinical questions to the appropriate information available in the existing research.

In the text that follows, we organize our discussion in light of our "match-to" philosophy suggested previously. We present the different levels of research type and different treatment interven-

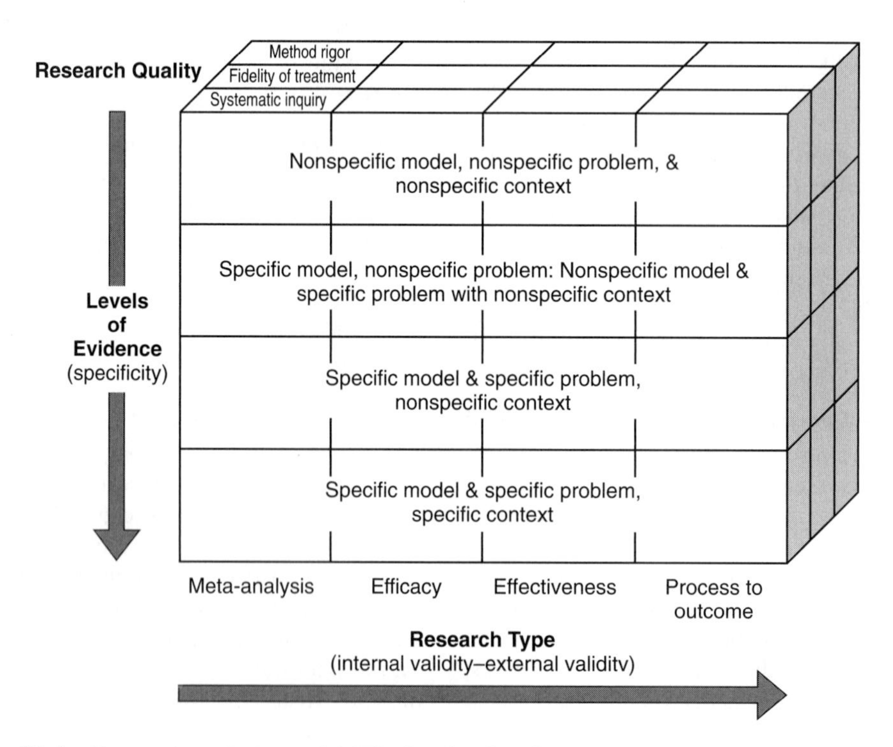

FIGURE 13.1 Research analysis model. The levels of evidence model for reviewing couple and family therapy research.

tions according to increasingly specific levels of clinical questions: "Does it work?", "What about it works?", "What does it work for?," "What works for which client with what concern in which setting?" The tables presented here contain the data driving our review. This matrix of studies not only organized the studies but also provided a new forum for bridging research and practice. The tables allow researchers and practitioners to access information about a range of clinical problems at a range of different levels (broad research to specific clinical models) determined through various types of research. They serve as parameters for carrying out our match-to philosophy by making such information accessible and responsive to a broad range of specific and broad clinical questions. This helps foster the match of researcher/ practitioner questions to the appropriate results and of stimulating further research conducted with the match-to philosophy in mind.

There are potential problems inherent in our organizational approach that require comment. First, organizing a major review of the marital and family therapy literature around the presenting problems of identified clients has, at least on the surface, potential epistemological conflicts given the systemic focus of the field. We believe that an organization focused on clinical issues does not mean that we abandon the systemic epistemological roots of the field. In fact, in the world of clinical practice, families and couples rarely come to us for help with systemically defined problems (e.g., the hierarchical relationship between my husband and son results in escalating patterns of interaction that often result in violence). Instead, it is the MFT practitioner who must translate presenting concerns that often focus on an individual in a relation system into the systemic meanings that are required in order to do marital and family therapy. Thus, this organization may actually match the realities of clinical work well. Second, like Alexander et al, (1994), we consider the research in marital and family therapy separately. There are a number of reasons for this decision. The origins of marital therapy are different from those of family therapy (Gurman et al., 1986). Despite the differences, martial therapy is often seen as a subtype of family therapy. In addition, unlike the eras that confronted early *Handbook* chapter authors, we find the overlap between marital therapy and family therapy research is small; research and model builders seem to restrict themselves to one or the other domain. This trend is apparent in reviews and meta-analyses (Hahlweg & Markman, 1988; Hazelrigg, Cooper, & Borduin, 1987; Shadish et al., 1993).

Couple Therapy

As a field of clinical research, couple therapy (CT) is unique in that it has had, in the form of the broad outcomes of "relationship satisfaction" and "distress," a common outcome target for research and treatment. The existence of a primary outcome target has allowed the couple therapy field to develop a finite number of well-defined treatment models that have come to "define" the domain of couple therapy. The benefit of this developmental trajectory is that it is possible to talk about couple therapy as a unified domain of practice. At the same time, the development of couple treatment models at more specific levels of evidence (specific approaches, for specific problems, in particular situations with specific clients) has been limited. Broad outcomes such as relationship distress or satisfaction might not capture the complexity of clinical problems couples present in therapy (where it works, who it works with, and what problems it helps). In the following section we review the evidence for the overall effectiveness of CT, the outcomes of the major models of CT, and the specific problems to which CT has been successfully applied, as well as the mechanisms that may contribute to successful CT. Our goal is to examine the "levels of evidence" for CT: the degree to which it is effective with specific clients, with specific problems, in particular contexts.

In our literature review, we identified three meta-analyses that evaluated the outcomes of CT. One of these was a meta-analysis of three major models of couple therapy (Dunn & Schwebel, 1995), another was a re-analysis of a former meta-analytic study addressing the general outcomes of CT and family therapy (Shadish, Ragsdale, Glaser, & Montgomery, 1995), and the other considered the outcomes of couple-involved and couple-assisted treatment of alcoholism (Edwards & Steinglass, 1995). Each of these meta-analyses relied primarily on efficacy studies, with a limited number of effectiveness studies. The conclusions of each are not independent because of the overlap in studies included for analysis. Our review of individual studies of CT found 10 effectiveness and 4 efficacy studies that considered three major approaches regarding problems *that were not included* in the meta-analyses. These studies are detailed below and summarized in Tables 13.1 and 13.2. An analysis of methodological issues found in these studies is included in the final section of this chapter.

The Outcomes of Couple Therapy: Does It Work?

Meta-analyses

In their reanalysis of marital and family studies from an earlier review, Shadish, Ragsdale, Glaser, and Montgomery (1995) identified 62 studies published through 1988 containing 71 treatments using couple therapy. Of those treatments comparing CT to no-treatment ($n = 27$) the effect size was $d = .60$, a moderate effect roughly equal to family therapy. Dunn and Schwebel (1995) reviewed 15 studies of marital therapy published between 1980 and 1993. Nine of these had been included in earlier meta-analytic studies of marital therapy outcome (Hahlweg & Markman, 1988); all of the studies between 1980 and 1988 were included in the Shadish et al. (1995) review. The combined effect of the 21 treatment conditions using three CT approaches suggested that, as a whole, CT was more effective than no treatment in fostering changes in various areas of couple relationships at post-treatment ($d = .79$) and followup ($d = .52$). These results were apparent for a variety of outcomes, including cognitions, affect, and measures of general attitudes toward relationship quality.

Despite what look to be large effect size differences, the clinical significance of couple therapy remains in question. The common conclusion from the qualitative and meta-analytic reviews is that, even among the most efficacious treatments, fewer than half of couples treated have clinically significant positive outcomes. This rate is surprisingly uniform across studies and modalities (Wesley & Waring, 1996). For example, in an analysis of their meta-analytic results Shadish et al. (1995) used a variation of the technique proposed by Jacobson, Follette, and Ravensdorf (1984) and looked at the percentage of couples who, following treatment, were no longer considered to be "distressed." The effects of CT were modest, with 41% of couples in treatment groups experiencing significant clinical improvement. Based on a systematic review of the CT literature, Christensen and Heavey (1999) concluded that "we can say with confidence that fewer than half of couples treated in therapy will move from distressed to nondistressed status" (p. 169).

Long-term sustainability has also been difficult to establish. Few studies included followup measures beyond immediate post-treatment. For example, Shadish et al. (1995) report only one study in their original meta-analysis of 163 marital and family studies that had a followup assessment conducted longer than nine months after treatment. Of the remaining, the median followup period was five months. Dunn and Schwebel (1995) found that while there were differences between treated and untreated groups at short-term followup, the followup periods ranged from .75 month to one year, with an average of only 9.2 months post-therapy. In their narrative review, Bray and Jouriles (1995) found only three studies with strong methodological characteristics that examined the long-term effectiveness of marital therapy for distressed couples. Their time frame for long-term followup was only 18 months post-therapy. In those studies where longer-term followup was present, the effects of CT deteriorated significantly at followup periods beyond six months (Christensen & Heavey, 1999).

Major Approaches to Couple Therapy: What Works?

A number of specific approaches to CT have been investigated. For the most part, this research considers broad outcome of marital distress and/or marital satisfaction as its clinical target from which to measure change. First, we present meta-analytic results that support CT as a broad category of intervention. Second, we review the specific meta-analytic and clinical trial research for the major approaches to CT.

Overall Meta-analytic Results

Dunn and Schwebel's (1995) meta-analysis focused on the impact of three categories of couple treatment: (1) behavioral marital therapy (BMT), (2) cognitive behavioral marital therapy (CBMT), and (3) insight-oriented marital therapy (IOMT, emotionally focused couple therapy, EFCT). They found that when compared to no-treatment conditions, these three approaches (BMT, EFCT, CBMT) produced significant positive changes in specific behaviors and relationship satisfaction measures at post-therapy and followup. Thus, it seems that BMT, CBMT, and IOMT approaches were more effective than no treatment in many areas of couple functioning. There were no differences between these models on measures of couple behavior change at either post-therapy or

TABLE 13.1 Couple Therapy Efficacy Studies

Study	Study Characteristics (*N*: Assignment; Setting; Population; Problem)	Treatment (IV)	Outcome Criteria (DV)	Primary Findings
Goldman & Greenberg (1992)	*N* = 42; random; CO; mostly Caucasian couples in Canada recruited or seeking help; conflictual relationship problems, 1 partner elevated DAS score	(1) Integrated Systemic Therapy (IST): 10 sessions, based on structural and strategic models based on Minuchin & Fishman (1981) and Fisch et al. (1982) (2) Emotionally Focused Therapy (EFT): 10 sessions, emphasis on affect, (Greenberg & Johnson, 1988) (CG) wait list control	(1) Alliance (2) Marital adjustment (3) Change/goal attainment (4) Conflict	*Clinical Significance:* (1) 67% of all couples finished with both partners in nondistressed range on the DAS[a] *Statistical Significance:* (1) Couples in both tx finished significantly better than controls on alliance, adjustment, conflict and amount of clinical change
Jacobson, Christensen, Prince, Cordova, & Eldridge (2000)	*N* = 21; random; CO; 21–60y couples requesting therapy; marital distress, score >58 on GDS of MSI	(1) Integrative Behavior Couple Therapy (IBCT): 10–26 sessions, acceptance-based and behavioral, Christensen et al. (1995) and Jacobson & Christensen (1996) (CG) Traditional Behavior Couple Therapy (TBCT): 10–26 sessions, solely behaviorally based, Jacobson & Margolin (1979)	(1) Marital satisfaction (2) Marital adjustment	*Clinical significance:* (1) 64% TBCT improved or recovered compared to 80% IBCT (2) IBCT couples reported greater marital satisfaction than TBCT at post-tx (3) TBCT and IBCT are distinct tx methods
Montag & Wilson (1992)	*N* = 30; random; CO or UO unspecified; Couples recruited through media; one spouse in distressed range (≤ 97 on DAS)	(1) Cognitive-Behavioral Marital Therapy Group (CBMT): 8 weekly 90 minute sessions, focus on cognitive and behavior change, based on Beck's (1976) cognitive therapy (2) Behavioral Group Treatment:8 wkly 90 min. group sessions, focus on behavior change (CG) Wait list control	(1) Satisfaction (2) Positive and negative behaviors (3) Cognitions (4) Relationship functioning (5) Individual functioning	*Clinical Significance:* 100% of Behav Group Tx couples were clinically improved at post-tx[b] *Statistical Significance:* Couples in both tx groups reported increased relationship satisfaction and functioning
Zimmerman Prest, & Wetzel (1997)	*N* = 36; nonrandom; CO; Volunteers, mostly Caucasian	(1) Solution-focused couples therapy: 6 weekly sessions, communication skills, problem-solving (CG) no-treatment control group	(1) Marital adjustment (2) Commitment to relationship	(1) Tx group significantly improved in overall affectional expression and satisfaction

Note: CO = Community Outpatient setting; UO = University Outpatient setting; DAS = Dyadic Adjustment Scale; GDS = Global Distress Scale; MSI = Marital Satisfaction Inventory; CG = Control Group.

[a] 100% of couples had one partner in distressed range pre-treatment.

[b] Clinical improvement = reliable change index ≥ + 1.96 (Jacobson, Follette, & Revensdorf, 1984; adapted by Christensen & Mendoza, 1986).

Table 13.2 Couple Effectiveness Studies

Author	Study Characteristics (*N*: Assignment; Setting; Population; Problem)	Treatment (IV)	Outcome Criteria (DV)	Principle Findings
Chernen & Friedman (1993)	*N* = 4; nonrandom; CO; Couples, 29–40y identified clients; Agoraphobic individuals w/comorbid personality disorder and their spouses	(1) Progressive Treatment for each identified client: (a) 3 sessions, intake, psychoeducation, relaxation training; (b) 10 session, individual treatment, in vivo exposure; (c) 10 sessions of BCT; (d) 3 sessions, followup consultation	(1) Symptomatology (2) Avoidance behavior (3) Marital adjustment (4) Family environment	(1) Those in discordant marriages experienced significant decrease in panic and agoraphobia symptoms after BCT phase, maintained at 3-month followup
Emanuels-Zuurveen & Emmelkamp (1996)	*N* = 27; random; CO; Recruited couples in Netherlands; Depressive clients and their spouses	(1) BCT: 16 one-hour sessions, relationship and communication focus based on Beach et al. (1990) and Emmelkamp et al. (1984) (2) Individual cognitive behavior therapy: 16 one-hour sessions, focus on mood and cognitions based on Lewinsohn (1975) and Beck et al. (1979)	(1) Depression (2) Pleasure (3) Marital and life satisfaction (4) Communication (5) Expressed emotion	(1) Relationships of those in BCT group were significantly more improved (2) BCT more effective in increasing marital satisfaction, increasing quality of communication, and decreasing level of expressed emotion in spouse (3) Both treatments were effective in improving mood, activity and pleasure
Fals-Stewart, Birchler & O'Farrell (1996)	*N* = 80; random; CO; 20–60y cohabitating or married males; Substance abuse	Both: 56 treatment sessions total over approx 25 weeks (1) BCT: 90 min/wk group therapy, 60 min/wk indiv therapy; 60 min/wk BCT w/partner (2) Individually Based Treatment (IBT): individual cognitive behavior therapy 2x/week plus 90 min/wk group therapy for substance abuser	(1) Relationship adjustment (2) Substance use	(1) BCT group improved significantly on all relationship measures and maintained these improvements at 3-month followup as compared to control group, which did not improve on any relationship measures. (2) Males in the BCT group had a significantly greater percentage of days abstinent at the 3- and 6-month followup assessment compared to controls (3) Husbands in BCT group slower to relapse in first 90 days post-treatment than those in control condition

Fals-Stewart, O'Farrell, & Birchler (1997)	N = 80; random; CO; 20–60y cohabitating or married males; Substance abuse	Both: 56 treatment sessions total over approx 25 weeks (1) BCT: 90 min/wk group therapy, 60 min/wk individual therapy; 60 min/wk BCT w/partner (2) Individually based treatment: Individual cognitive behavior therapy 2x/week plus 90 min per week group therapy for substance abuser	(1) Cost of each program (2) Social costs (3) Drug use	(1) Husbands in BCT group significantly lower costs than those in the individual therapy group at 1-year followup for inpatient hospitalizations and outpatient care (2) At 1-year followup, husbands in BCT group decreased in substance-abuse related care costs to 1/3 of baseline costs, whereas those in individual therapy group did not decrease significantly (3) Husbands in both groups generated significantly less criminal justice system costs at followup as compared to baseline, and BCT husbands significantly lower than individual therapy group on costs for arrest, incarceration, legal supervision and total system costs. (4) BCT group significant decrease in illegal income at followup (5) Only BCT husbands had a significant decrease in aggregate social costs from baseline to followup (6) Net benefit for BCT: $2,000 per patient, for individual therapy group: $550 per patient.
MacPhee, Johnson, & van der Veer (1995)	N = 64; random; UO; Couples in Canada; Female Inhibited Sex Desire, DAS > 70, Canada	(1) EFCT: 10 sessions, affect focus, conjoint, based on Greenberg & Johnson (1988) (CGI) Various other individual or couple therapies for NON-ISD issues: varied number of sessions (CG2) Wait list control	(1) Sexual functioning (2) Marital adjustment (3) Sexual desire	*Clinical Significance:* Greater percent of all females recovered or improved on all but one satisfaction variable in treatment group. *Statistical Significance:* Females report significantly more sexual desire and significantly less depressive symptoms than controls

(continues)

TABLE 13.2 Couple Effectiveness Studies *(Continued)*

Author	Study Characteristics (*N*: Assignment; Setting; Population; Problem)	Treatment (IV)	Outcome Criteria (DV)	Principle Findings
O'Farrell et al. (1993)	*N* = 59 couples; random; CO after CI; couples with male newly abstinent; substance abuse	Both, weekly BCT for 5–6 months (1) Relapse Prevention (RP): 15 sessions, conjoint over 12 months (CG) no relapse prevention	(1) Marital adjustment (2) Substance use (3) Consequence of using	(1) Couples receiving RP experienced significantly more days abstinent than the BCT only group at 6- and 12-month followups (2) Subjects in both groups improved on number of days abstinent through one-year followup (3) For husbands and wives with lower scores regarding marital adjustment at intake, BCT plus RP fostered significantly better scores on marital adjustment at the 3-month followup
O'Farrell et al. (1996)	*N* = 59 couples; random; CO; couples with male newly abstinent; substance abuse	Both, weekly BCT for 5–6 months (1) Relapse Prevention (RP): 15 sessions, conjoint over 12 months (CG) no relapse prevention	(1) Costs of RP vs. no RP service delivery (2) Costs re: health and legal due to substance use (3) Benefit to cost comparisons	(1) RP led to less drinking and better marital adjustment as compared to no RP, but did not decrease cost of legal and health expenses over non-RP group (2) BCT only (no RP) more cost-effective than BCT plus RP regarding abstinence from drinking (3) Greater cost of RP set off the benefits of this added intervention
O'Farrell et al. (1996a)	*N* = 36; random; CO; newly abstinent males; alcoholism	(1) Individual counseling plus BCT: supportive from paraprofessionals and 10 weekly sessions BCT couples group (2) Individual counseling plus Couples Interaction Group: supportive from paraprofessionals and 10 weekly sessions group therapy (CG) Individual counseling alone	(1) Marital satisfaction (2) Drinking activity (3) Costs of service delivery (4) Health and legal costs due to substance use (5) Benefit to cost comparisons	(1) Health and legal system costs decreased for control and BCT groups from baseline to 24-month followup. No significant difference between BCT and individual counseling alone (control). (2) Post-treatment health and legal costs savings were noted for both BCT ($5,800 per patient) and control groups ($7,600 per patient), but these costs increased for patients in the interaction group ($3100 extra per patient) (3) BCT significantly more favorable cost-benefit ratio than interaction group, but not better than individual counseling alone

Walker, Johnson, Manion, & Cloutier (1996)	*N* = 32; random; CO; Volunteer/recruited couples in Canada married average of 11.4y; chronically ill child diagnosed w/in last 12 mos., DAS score of 110 for one partner	(1) EFCT: 10 sessions-90 min each, focus on communication, conflict resolution, emotional expression, based on Walker & Manion (1991) (CG) wait list control	(1) Marital distress (2) Therapeutic alliance (3) Intimacy (4) Communication skills	*Clinical Significance:* Treatment group significantly more recovered and improved post and 5-month followup *Statistical Significance:* Treatment group significantly higher adjustment at post and 5 months (2) Treatment group significantly higher intimacy at 5 months (3) Treatment group significantly lower levels of negative communication at post
Wylie (1997)	*N* = 37; nonrandom; CO; couples w/ 21–64yo male, 22–59y female, referred by community mental health professionals and self-selected; Male Erectile Disorder	Both: sensate focus, homework, behaviorally oriented; Only introduce system interventions if needed by 3rd session (1) Combined treatment package maximum 6 sessions total: (a) Modified Modern Sex Therapy (MMST): sensate focus, homework, Matthews et al. (1983) (b) Behavioral Systems Couple Therapy (BSCT): systemic interventions, Crowe & Ridley (1990)	(1) Sex satisfaction (2) Change in symptoms (3) Marital satisfaction (4) Emotional well-being (5) Pleasant feelings	*Clinical Significance:* 10/23 had excellent outcome, 6/23 moderate outcome *Statistical Significance:* (1) Men reported significant reduction in infrequency of sex, avoidance of sex and noncommunication (2) Targeted symptoms (erections and sex enjoyment) significantly improved (3) Male history of psychological illness predicted poor outcome

Note. CO = Community Outpatient setting; UO = University Outpatient setting; CI = Community Inpatient setting; DAS = Dyadic Adjustment Scale; CG = Control Group; BCT = Behavioral Couple Therapy; EFCT = Emotionally Focused Couple Therapy: RP = Relapse Prevention.

followup. On measures of relationship quality, there were significant differences favoring insight-oriented therapies, but these differences disappeared at followup. Despite these positive results, Dunn and Schwebel note: "Whatever the form they take, a greater number of methodologically rigorous marital therapy outcome studies are needed to fully establish not only the short-term efficacy of marital therapy in increasing general satisfaction, but whether marital therapy approaches produce change across the many specific areas essential to spouses for the maintenance of healthy relationships." In addition, learning how to "match" therapy approaches to couples seems to be a valuable future direction.

Behavioral Marital/Couple Therapy

BMT (now behavioral couple therapy) is probably the most studied approach. The concepts of BMT (BCT), first articulated by Jacobson and Margolin (1979), are based on a social learning theory of human behavior. BCT views marital satisfaction and distress in terms of reinforcement: Couples are satisfied to the extent that there is more reinforcement than punishment in the relationship. BMT targets increasing caring behaviors and teaching communication and problem solving skills that enable couples to resolve conflicts in a constructive manner and cope with their differences in ways that increase reinforcement and decrease punishment within the couple interactions (Chernen & Friedman, 1993). BCT is typically a short-term treatment, ranging from 10 to 26 sessions, and is guided by a treatment manual.

META-ANALYSIS. Dunn and Schwebel (1995) examined 11 studies published between 1980 and 1993 that contained 13 BCT treatment groups. On measures of relationship quality, they found a weighted mean effect size for BCT of .78 at post-therapy and .54 at followup. On measures of marital behavior they found a weighted mean effect size of .79 at post-treatment and .52 at followup. The average follow-up was 8.75 months. This is similar, though somewhat lower than the earlier meta-analyses (ES = .95) conducted by Hahlweg and Markman (1988).

CLINICAL STUDIES. The current research regarding BCT contained a rather limited range of studies that focused on the efficacy of new elaborations of BMT, comparisons of BMT with other models, and the efficacy of the model with complex presenting problems such as depression (see Table 13.1).

Two studies investigated integrated behavior couple therapy (IBCT), a recent elaboration and variation of BMT (Christensen, Jacobson, & Babcock, 1995; Jacobson & Christensen, 1996). Jacobson, Christensen, Prince, Cordova, & Eldridge (2000) tested the efficacy of IBCT as compared to BMT in its traditional form, with a randomly assigned group of volunteer couples (n = 21) reporting marital distress. Results indicate that a majority of couples in both (IBCT or BMT) were clinically improved at post-treatment. Improvement rates were greater for the IBCT couples (80%) than the BMT couples (64%) in reductions of marital distress and increases in marital satisfaction. Emanuels-Zuurveen and Emmelkamp (1996) tested the effectiveness of BMT as compared to individual cognitive behavioral therapy (CBT) with a group of randomly assigned depressed individuals and their spouses. Participants in each group received 16 one-hour sessions (manual driven using supervision and monitoring for treatment fidelity). Post-treatment assessments indicated that both types of therapy led to improved activity, mood, and pleasure in the depressed patients. As compared to individual CBT, BMT was significantly more effective in improving marital satisfaction, decreasing the level of expressed negative emotion in the depressed client's spouse and improving the quality of communication in the marital dyad. This research points to the utility of BMT in alleviating depressive symptoms. However, small sample size (n = 27) limits the generalizability of these results and points to the need for replication studies of marital therapies in the treatment of depression.

Emotionally Focused Couple Therapy

EFCT was first described by Walker (Walker & Manion, 1991) and further developed by Greenberg and Johnson (1998) and Johnson and Greenberg (1998). Although variations of this type of therapy differ somewhat, the basic component characterizing EFCT throughout its various implementations is the focus on uncovering unresolved emotions that affect and maintain negative interaction patterns between couples (Walker, Johnson, Manion, & Cloutier, 1996). EFCT is based on attachment theory (Bowlby, 1969) and considers relationship distress to be a failure of the attachment relationship to provide a secure base for one or both partners. This disruption of attachment bonds leads to relationship distress, which stimulates strong emotions (e.g., fear of abandonment) and their negative behaviors. The two main tasks of EFCT are (1) to access and reprocess the emotional experience of partners and (2) to restructure the interactional patterns (Johnson & Greenberg, 1998). As partners experience and voice emotions, they encounter new aspects of themselves and the other and are thus able to develop more functional interaction patters to satisfy their attachment needs.

META-ANALYSIS. Dunn and Schwebel (1995) found five studies they defined as insight-oriented marital therapy, four of which specifically examined EFCT. The last study examined Snyder and Wills's insight-oriented marital therapy, which is similar to EFCT. The weighted effect size for marital behavior was .87 at post-treatment and .69 at followup. Effect sizes for relationship quality outcomes were 1.37 at post-treatment and 1.04 at followup. The average followup time was 12.4 months. Studies in this analysis included both control group and prepost test designs.

CLINICAL STUDIES. The current research into EFCT includes both efficacy (EFCT as compared to another approach) and effectiveness of EFCT studies with specific presenting problems (see Tables 13.1 and 13.2). In all empirical studies reviewed here, therapists implementing EFCT were trained, supervised, and checked for adherence to the treatment manual. In general, therapy was carried out over 10 to 15 sessions and was conducted by therapists with a range of professional degrees and experience. This high degree of treatment fidelity makes EFCT an exemplary model of marital therapy as it may be replicated and subjected to empirical scrutiny.

Goldman and Greenberg (1992) examined the efficacy of both EFCT and IST (integrated systematic therapy) with maritally distressed couples. IST integrates structural and strategic/interactional components. In this random-assignment, wait list control design with ten sessions of each therapy, couples in both treatment conditions improved over control couples on all measured dimensions. Furthermore, in regards to clinical significance, 67% of couples in treatment groups (EFCT and IST) finished treatment in the "nondistressed" range of marital adjustment on the Global Adjustment Scale. It is unclear how many couples began treatment in the depressed range. No difference between treatments was reported. Walker et al. (1996) focused on couples with a chronically ill child who were experiencing marital distress. After ten 90-minute sessions of EFT, couples demonstrated significantly lower levels of negative communication. At both post-treatment and the five-month followup assessment, significantly more couples in the EFT condition were clinically "improved" or "recovered" than those in the control group. Finally, EFT couples reported significantly higher levels of intimacy at the five-month followup assessment than those on the wait list.

Cognitive Behavioral Couple Therapy (CBCT)

Cognitive techniques have been used as a set of primary CT interventions and as a supplement to BCT. CBCT uses cognitive restructuring techniques to alter the cognitive patterns of partners using logical analysis, disputing, and challenging. Baucom and Epstein (1990) suggested that cognitive restructuring, similar to that used with individuals, might be helpful to aid partners in identifying and changing dysfunctional cognitions.

META-ANALYSES. Dunn and Schwebel (1995) found three outcome studies involving a total of 74 different couples that examined the effectiveness of cognitive interventions alone or in combination with behavioral procedures. On measures of marital behavior the weighted effect size was .54 at post-treatment and .75 at followup. In regard to relationship quality, the weighted effects size was .71 at post-treatment and .54 at followup. Only two of these studies included followup assessment, with an average followup time of six months.

CLINICAL STUDIES. We found one study that investigated the outcome of CBCT. Montag and Wilson (1992) integrated components of Baucom's (Baucom, Shoham, Mueser, Daiuto, & Stickle, 1998) cognitive restructuring for couples and Beck's (1976) individual cognitive therapy, in addition to communication/behavioral strategies characteristic of BMT, into a CBMT treatment protocol. CBMT was conducted in a group format (n = 30) and compared to pure behavioral group therapy as well as a wait list control group. (All CBMT couples were in one group; all behavioral treatment couples were in the other.) Treatment was administered according to a treatment manual and included treatment adherence checks. The authors reported that 100% of the behavioral therapy group were clinically "improved" at post-test and that couples in both treatment groups demonstrated significant increases in relationship satisfaction and level of functioning after treatment. Thus, positive results were observed, but these results were not specifically related to CBMT. Both treatments, which incorporate behavioral techniques and interventions, seemed to foster improvements in some of the couples in treatment. The results of this study would suggest that cognitive interventions add little above and beyond what is gained from BMT. Replication is needed in order to draw stronger conclusions about CBMT as an effective form of marital therapy.

Couple Therapy for Specific Clinical Problems

Couple therapy (CT) has been used to treat a variety of relationship and individual adult and child problems as both a direct intervention and as an adjunct to individually oriented interventions. The clinical problems studied range from general categories of concern like relationship distress (see the previous discussion) to specific clinical problems such as depression. When applied to specific clinical problems, CT is most frequently used as part of a multicomponent treatment intervention package for specific disorders. When used in this way, CT is often an adjunct to the primary individual treatments that do not assume that relationship difficulties are part of or require attention in the treatment of the individual problem. What is surprising is that the *least* commonly used format for the treatment of specific clinical problems (outside of relational adjustment and distress) was CT as a primary treatment. Baucom et al. (1998) found that CT was the primary treatment for only one specific problem, depression. Our analysis of meta-analyses and current clinical trials confirms this observation. In the following discussion, we review the broad meta-analytic findings, followed by a review of meta-analytic and clinical trial evidence for the effectiveness of CT with specific clinical problems.

Meta-analysis. The meta-analysis considered in this review shed little light on the effect of CT on specific client problems. Most consider broad problem areas such as marital distress and dissatisfaction. Shadish et al. (1995) considered global marital dissatisfaction (n = 16, d = .71) and communication and specific problem-solving complaints (n = 7, d = .52). In an analysis of CT for specific clinical problems, Shadish et al. were unable to find effects of CT that clearly exceeded the control conditions for major affective disorders, divorce problems, sexual dysfunction, and coping with medical illness.

Depression

Studies into the impact of CT as a treatment for depression have a long history. Early studies established CT (generally defined) as a potentially helpful treatment for depression. A second generation of research that focused on well-specified marital therapy and compared CT to control groups suggested that CT is better than no treatment and more effective than alternative approaches within a distressed couple with a depressed member (Beach, Finchan, & Katz, 1998). In fact, according to Baucom et al. (1998), marital therapy might be preferable to individual psychotherapy among maritally distressed couples with a wife that is depressed because it leads to an improvement in both depression and marital adjustment.

Clinical studies. Only one study regarding the effectiveness of marital therapy in treating depression has appeared since the last review. Emanuels-Zuurveen and Emmelkamp (1996) examined the effectiveness of BMT versus individual cognitive behavior therapy and a wait list control. Participants in the BMT group made significantly greater improvements than the cognitive therapy and control groups on measures of marital satisfaction, spousal-expressed emotion, and quality of communication between spouses but not in levels of depression. Thus, marital therapy—specifically BMT—had somewhat positive effects on these clients in the Netherlands suffering from depression. In order to further support the utility of this and other couple-oriented approaches in the treatment of depression, a greater volume of effectiveness studies are needed, including replications in the United States and across cultures, with outcomes specifically tailored to clinical problems.

Sexual Disorders

The research into the treatment of sexual disorders illustrates the complex intervention x problem interaction in many complex clinical issues. For example, partner-assisted treatment of female primary orgasmic disorder may both alter the sexual disorder and increase relationship satisfaction, while the effects of the most specific treatment programs (e.g., Masters and Johnson treatment program) seem specific to couples who were compliant, who got along well, and who did not have other psychological problems. The treatment of sexual disorders through general CT (specifically EFCT) does not seem to produce results any greater than those reported by waiting list controls. However, the combination of BMT with disorder-specific treatment of female secondary sexual dysfunction with maritally distressed couples does seem to be effective both statistically and clinically.

CLINICAL STUDIES. We found two studies investigating the effectiveness of couple interventions in treating Male Erectile Disorder (MED) as well as Inhibited Sexual Desire (ISD) in females. Wylie (1997) examined the effectiveness of behavioral systems couple therapy in combination with modified modern sex therapy in treating MED. Results suggest that the men in the treatment group experienced significant improvements in frequency of and ability to have erections, increases in sexual enjoyment, and a significant reduction in infrequency of sex, avoidance of sex, and noncommunication with partner about sex (Wylie, 1997). Unfortunately, the self-selective nature of the subject pool, small sample size (n = 37), and lack of experimental control inhibit the generalizability of these results. MacPhee, Johnson, and van der Veer (1995) investigated the females with ISD treated with emotionally focused couples therapy (EFCT) compared to a wait list control group. Subjects in the EFCT group made clinically and statistically significant gains in symptomatology and sexual desire in comparison to the control group. Thus, ISD, which has been deemed quite difficult to treat (MacPhee et al., 1995), appears to be decreased with EFCT marital therapy. Despite these positive results regarding the treatments of ISD and MED, the literature on the use of marital therapies for treating sexual disorders is minimal and lacking in generalizability. This is a surprising predicament given the widespread nature of sexual dysfunction and the likely positive effects of couple therapy in general.

Alcohol and Drug Problems

Alcohol and drug abuse and dependence are not only difficult individual problems but can have a major impact on the couple relationship (Edwards & Steinglass, 1995). In addition to the devastating and costly effects of alcohol and drugs on individuals, these problems seem associated with higher rates of physical and psychological problems among nondrinking spouses, marital dissatisfaction, and violence within couple relationships (Baucom et al., 1998).

META-ANALYSIS. Edwards and Steinglass (1995) conducted a meta-analysis of 21 studies of what they call family-involved therapy for alcoholism. In almost all cases, these studies investigated the outcome of partner-assisted and partner-involved CT interventions. The results of their investigation suggest that it is useful to involve family, mostly spouses, in all phases of alcohol treatment. Four couple-involved CT studies that attempted to engage and involve alcoholics in treatment demonstrated powerful effects (ES = 1.83; pre-post comparison), with rates for entering treatment ranging from 57% to 86% (as compared to 0% to 31% for control groups). Thus, partner-assisted CT is very effective in helping alcoholics enter treatment and sometimes reduce drinking before other formal treatment has begun. Studies of CT as a primary treatment modality showed less clear-cut results. Of the 15 studies that considered CT as the primary treatment, the overall mean effect size was .86. When compared to individual treatment, two approaches to CT demonstrated results superior to individual treatment, with 8 of 13 comparisons demonstrating the superiority of CT. Unfortunately, when followup periods extended beyond one year, the CT treatment was no longer superior to individual treatment.

Despite the reported efficacy and effectiveness of CT, a number of important questions remain regarding the role of the spouse or partner in treatment. Edwards and Steinglass (1995) note that these results are moderated by a number of factors, including gender of the alcohol-involved spouse, investment by spouses in the relationship, and family commitment to abstinence. These factors need further study. In addition, the degree to which partner involvement is helpful is yet to be determined. Baucom et al. (1998) reported that studies of both approaches did not find significant improvement in outcomes when partners were involved. In fact, Baucom et al. (1998) concluded that minimal spouse involvement might be just as effective as conjoint BMT.

PROCESS STUDIES IN COUPLE THERAPY

In its present state, the trends and specific findings of couple therapy process research provide no more than provocative possibilities and avenues for further exploration rather than definite conclusions (Lebow & Gurman, 1986). It became evident in our review of the marital process literature that studies in this category had a wide range of research questions. As already noted, process studies could be classified as either examining *moderators* (predictor variables) or *mediators* (mechanisms) of clinical change. Each of these processes may be linked to either proximal (short term within therapy outcomes) or distal outcomes (post-treatment and followup outcomes). Our review identified 12 studies of the process of couple therapy as defined in the above categories (see Table 13.3). Half of these provided findings derived within the context of a systematic treatment approach (manualized and/or supervised, structured treatment program requiring training prior to implementation). Results from these studies provide the most useful information because they are replicable according to the specific treatment approach. Although information from other studies adds to our literature base, a lack of attachment to specific treatment protocols leaves the results unclear and difficult to replicate. Findings discussed in the next section provide a range of implications for future research and practice in the field of couple therapy. Unfortunately, studies of the moderators and mechanisms of CT are sparse and currently provide little specific information regarding ways in which to improve CT.

Moderators of Change in CT

Moderators point us in the direction of being able to better match treatments with clients. Results from meta-analysis shed little light on the treatment factors that might moderate CT. The few clinical process studies can be organized into two areas of study: preexisting client and therapist factors that impact the outcome of CT (see Table 13.3).

1. Preexisting Client Characteristics. Four preexisting client characteristics were investigated in the studies we reviewed: Marital Satisfaction, Depression, Problem-Solving, and Career Status. Snyder et al. (1993) found that lower Dyadic Adjustment Scale (DAS) satisfaction scores at intake were predictive of poorer outcome immediately following treatment as well as at four years after termination. In addition, couples with higher rates of depressive symptoms in at least one spouse prior to treatment were more likely to be distressed at both the termination and four-year followup assessments. Johnson and Talitman (1997) found that the Dyadic Adjustment Scale was a predictor of post-treatment satisfaction for distressed couples receiving 12 sessions of EFCT, while the wife's initial level of faith in her partner's caring (measured on a subscale of the Relationship Trust Scale) was a predictor of marital satisfaction for husbands at the three-month followup assessment. The work on CT for depression is a good example of how the identification of moderators is moving us closer to a "matching" of treatment approach within specific presenting problems. For example, CT appears to reduce depression if the couple is experiencing and reporting marital problems. This finding does not seem important in individual therapy of depression. Beach et al. (1998) suggested that, based on their review of methodologically sound articles of couple therapy for depression, there were a number of prescriptive indicators for marital therapy. These factors would suggest that marital therapy might be the treatment of choice if: (1) the depressed partner is relatively more concerned about marital problems than about depression, (2) marital problems are viewed by the depressed partner as having preceded and perhaps having caused the depression, or (3) individual cognitive symptoms are less salient to the depressed partner than her marital problems.

2. Preexisting Therapist Factors. Raytek, McCrady, Epstein, and Hirsch (1999) investigated the relationship between therapist experience (as measured in hours of clinical work and divided into three levels of high, moderate, and low experience) on a random sample of 66 couples seeking treatment for one spouse's alcohol abuse or dependency. Sessions with more experienced therapists were rated as significantly higher on alliance and significantly lower on number of errors in technique. In addition, therapists with the highest level of experience had a significantly greater percentage of clients who completed treatment than both groups of less experienced therapists. These results indicate that in this population, the therapist's greater clinical experience may be influential in developing a stronger therapeutic alliance and in maintaining couples in treatment. Interestingly, levels of alliance were not found to be associated with the number of days the alcoholic spouse was abstinent from alcohol following treatment. Thus, the importance of alliance in reaching the long-term goal of decreased alcohol use is unclear despite the indicators that alliance and maintenance in treatment are related to initial levels of therapist experience.

TABLE 13.3 Process to Outcome Studies in Couple and Family Therapy

Couple Therapy

Moderators/Predictors

Therapist Factors—Proximal Outcomes

- Raytek, McCrady, Epstein, & Hirsch (1999): Therapist Experience—Alliance

Client Characteristics—Distal

- Snyder et al. (1993): Marital Satisfaction, Depression, Problem-solving, Career Status—Marital Distress; *BCT*
- Waldron et al. (1997): Marital Adjustment/Satisfaction—Marital Adjustment/Satisfaction; *no specific model*
- Johnson & Talitman (1997): Trust in Partner—Marital Satisfaction; *EFT*
- Gray-Little et al. (1996): Power Structure—Marital Satisfaction; *BMT*

Mediators/Mechanisms:

Behavior/Interactional Changes—Distal

- Halford, Sanders & Behrens (1993): Negative Communication and Blaming—Marital Satisfaction; *BMT*
- Christensen et al. (1998): Affect, Cognitions, and Communication—Therapeutic Change; *no specific model*
- Kelly and Halford (1995): Behavioral Negativity—Marital Satisfaction; *CBMT*
- Cordova, Jacobson, and Christensen (1998): Change in Problem Description—Marital Satisfaction; *BMT*

Therapist Variables—Distal

- Raytek et al. (1999): Number of Errors in Therapist Technique—Number of Sessions Attended; *ABMT*
- Raytek et al. (1999): Alliance—Number of Sessions Attended; *ABMT*
- Waldron et al. (1993): Therapist Defensiveness—Marital Satisfaction; *no specific model*
- Christensen et al. (1998): Various therapist behaviors—Therapeutic Change; *no specific model*
- Johnson & Talitman (1997): Alliance—Marital Satisfaction; *EFT*
- Estrada & Holmes (1999): Effective and Ineffective Therapist Interventions—Therapeutic Change/Success; *IPCT (no manual mentioned)*
- Bischoff & McBride (1996): Therapist techniques—Perceived helpfulness of therapy; *no specific model*
- Quinn et al. (1997): Alliance—Goal attainment and perception of duration of therapeutic effects; *no specific model*

Therapist Variables—Proximal

- Butler & Wampler (1999): Therapist Control and Structure—Struggle vs. Cooperation in Therapeutic Relationship; *no specific model*
- Coupland & Serovich (1999): Session control by therapist vs. couple—Therapeutic Alliance; *no specific model*

Other

Client Characteristics (Descriptive)

- Aniol & Snyder (1997): Characteristics of clients in financial, marital, and no counseling; *no specific model*

Family Therapy

Moderators/Predictors:

Client Characteristics and Therapy Conditions—Proximal

- Diamond & Liddle (1996): Family pessimism, conflict, depressive symptomatology—Resolution of in-session impasse; *MDFT*
- Tompson et al. (2000): Family-expressed emotion, client symptomatology—Family resistance in session; *psychoeducation based on Falloon et al. (1984)*

(continues)

TABLE 13.3 (*Continued*)

Client Characteristics and Therapy Conditions—Distal
- Montero (1999): Age and symptom history—Therapy dropout; *BFT (modeled on Falloon, et al., 1986)*
- Hampson & Beavers (1996a): Family competency—Dropout and therapy goal attainment; *Beavers Systems Model*
- Hampson & Beavers (1996b): Family competency—Goal attainment; *Beavers Systems Model*
- Hampson & Beavers (1996b): Number of sessions attended—Goal attainment; *Beavers Systems Model*
- Allgood et al. (1995): Pre-treatment change—Planned termination; *no specific model*
- Linszen et al. (1996): Family expressed emotion—Relapse; *psychoeducation based on Falloon, et al. (1984)*
- Linszen et al. (1996): Patient diagnosis—Relapse; psychoeducation *based on Falloon et al. (1984)*

Therapist Characteristics—Proximal
- Lawson & Sivo (1998): Therapist shares conjoint family experience—Alliance; *no specific model*
- Weisman et al. (1998): Therapist adherence/competence—family expressed emotion, resistance in therapy; *psychoeducation based on Falloon, et al. (1984)*

Mediators/Mechanisms:

Therapist Variables—Proximal
- Newell et al. (1996): Therapist techniques—Reduction of family negativity; *FFT*
- Robbins et al. (1996): Therapist techniques—Reduction of family negativity; *FFT*
- Robbins et al. (2000): Therapist reframing—Family defensive response; *FFT*
- Huey et al. (2000): Adherence—Family functioning, delinquent peer affiliation; *MST*
- Coulehan et al. (1998): Therapist techniques—Redefinition of presenting problem; *Constructivist Narrative Therapy*
- Diamond & Liddle (1999): Therapist techniques—Redefinition of presenting problem; *MDFT*
- Diamond et al. (1999): Therapist techniques—Improved alliance; *MDFT*
- Barbera & Waldron (1994): Therapist techniques—Family cooperation; *no specific model*
- Friedlander et al. (1994): Therapist techniques—Sustained engagement; *no specific model*

Therapist Variables—Distal
- Hampson & Beavers (1999): Therapist techniques—Goal attainment; *Beavers Systems Model*
- Huey et al. (2000): Adherence—Delinquent Behavior; *MST*
- deKemp & Van Acker (1997): Therapist collaboration w/family—Decrease in presenting problems; *Family Project Approach*
- Schoenwald et al. (2000): Adherence, structuring, collaboration—Parental monitoring, peer relations, family functioning; *MST*

Reduction of Negativity—Distal
- Simoneau et al. (1999): Increase in positive communication—Symptom Improvement; *Family Focused Psychoeducational Therapy*
- Coulehan et al. (1998): Reduction in blaming—Redefinition of presenting problem; *Constructivist Narrative Therapy*

Improved Competencies/Symptoms—Proximal
- Diamond & Liddle (1996): Increase in understanding—Resolution of in-session impasse; *MDFT*

Improved Competencies/Symptoms—Distal
- Harrington et al. (2000): Family functioning, symptomatology—Success in therapy; *manualized treatment for suicide attempters*
- Schmidt et al. (1996): Parenting—Adolescent drug use; *MDFT*
- Robbins et al. (1996): Family interactions—Adolescent conduct disorder; *SSFT*

Other

Process Methods
- Hogue et al. (1998): Description of steps in adherence process research; *MDFT*

Mechanisms (Mediators) of Change in CT

There have been two approaches to the study of mechanisms of change in CT. The first looks at general nonspecific therapeutic processes. For example, the early work by Greenberg and colleagues focused on the analysis of key therapeutic events. They found that successful outcomes were associated with higher levels of client experiencing, showing more affective actions, and "softening" of feelings toward their partner (Johnson & Greenberg, 1988). The second approach considered looked at theoretically linked mechanisms of change. Most of the work in the area of mechanisms of change has been done with behavioral interventions (Whisman & Snyder, 1997). Behavior therapy consistently results in changes in observational measures of interaction patters (e.g., toward more positive and constructive interaction). Unfortunately, researchers have been unable to find an association between interaction change and marital satisfaction or between relationship skill acquisition (e.g., communication skills) and satisfaction, or between changes in cognitions and marital satisfaction. To identify mechanisms, researchers will need to better articulate more specific meditation pathways and more specific targets of change that are hypothesized to result in improvement.

We identified three categories of mechanisms of change supported by studies in our review: reduction of negative communication, therapist control, and the therapeutic alliance (see Table 13.3).

1. Reduction of negative communication/blaming. Halford, Sanders, and Behrens (1993) examined the effectiveness of BMT in reducing negativity in communication and cognitions in a group of 26 Australian couples randomly assigned to either BMT or Enhanced BMT (BMT plus cognitive restructuring; Baucom & Epstein, 1990; Baucom & Lester, 1986) treatment groups. After 12 to 15 weekly sessions of either treatment, both forms of BMT were successful in decreasing negativity in the domains mentioned above. However, success in these proximal outcomes was not linked to overall marital satisfaction (measured by the Dyadic Adjustment Scale) at the termination of treatment in this study. These results suggest that BCT may be effective through mechanisms other than reducing negativity in communication and cognitions.

Studies of more distal outcomes generally examined the relationship between the reduction of negativity and blaming, therapists' control, and the therapeutic alliance, in regard to changes in overall treatment outcomes. For example, three studies considered negativity or blaming reduction as related to outcome. Using Alexander's (1973) communication coding technique, Waldron et al. (1993) found that therapist defensiveness in one early session was associated with lower levels of marital satisfaction post-treatment for both husbands and wives. Cordova, Jacobson, and Christensen (1998) focused on whether or not increases in nonblaming problem definitions on the part of spouses were significantly associated with higher post-treatment marital satisfaction. Although not causal in nature, this finding highlights the need for further study of the relationship between this proximal outcome variable and marital satisfaction in trials of behavioral therapy with couples. Kelly and Halford's (1995) finding that decreasing negative couple interaction resulted in increases in marital satisfaction provides useful preliminary information about the factors comprising therapy in this approach.

2. Therapist control and structure. Butler and Wampler (1999) found a positive association between couple-responsible (CR) therapeutic processes (those in which clients were allowed to guide the therapeutic session) and cooperation between therapist and clients. In the therapist-responsible (TR) condition in which the therapist guided session activities, the struggle between the therapist and the couple occurred in clients who perceived the therapist as usually taking a CR approach to therapy. Across both conditions of therapeutic processes, a negative correlation existed between perceived responsibility and the proximal outcome of struggle in the therapeutic relationship. Couples reported more struggles with the therapist when they perceived themselves as having less responsibility in the process.

3. Therapeutic alliance. The relationship between therapeutic alliance and therapy outcome was investigated in three studies. Johnson and Talitman (1997) explored therapeutic processes in EFT with distressed couples. After 12 sessions of treatment, 79% of the sample had made clinically significant improvements in marital satisfaction as measured by the Dyadic Adjustment Scale. The couple's perception of the therapist and interventions as helpful and personally relevant was significantly related to higher post-treatment and followup levels of marital satisfaction. Taking a different approach, Christiansen, Russell, Miller, and Peterson (1998) found that a number of therapist behaviors commonly associated with the therapeutic alliance were deemed facilitative of therapeutic change: fostering hope, avoiding alignment with only one spouse, pacing progress appropriately, and normalizing the marital problems. These couples also saw safety and trust in the therapeutic alliance as important in fostering therapeutic change.

Family Therapy

Family therapy (FT) research has evolved in different ways than couple therapy. Because there is no common outcome target, specific treatment intervention programs have developed for specific clinical problems rather than for broad approaches directed at general outcomes (such as relationship distress or satisfaction). The different evolutionary track of FT has resulted in practice that is more *diverse*, involves more integration among models, and is tied more directly to specific clinical problems than is CT (Alexander & Barton, 1995). Liddle (1999) notes that, while the traditional approaches to FT still have an impact on the field, the new family therapy models extend beyond traditional theoretical boundaries, are more comprehensive, and have included the role of ecological factors outside the family in understanding the etiology of problems. The positive result of this situation is that the evidence to support family therapy exists at *specific* "levels of evidence." As such, family therapy is widely applicable to many types of clients, clinical problems, and settings, and is increasingly seen as the most viable treatment for many mental health problems, conduct and behavior disorders, and other psychological and interpersonal difficulties that strike children, adolescents, and adults through their lives (Pinsof & Wynne, 1995, 2000; Sexton & Alexander, 2002).

Like couple therapy, family therapy has evolved to the point that systematic family-based treatment programs have undergone numerous evaluations within the traditional research literature, resulting in a growing knowledge base regarding family interventions. Unlike most any other area of psychological practice, entities outside the traditional research arena (e.g., consumers, communities, government agencies) are taking an increasingly active role in an effort to identify "best practices." For example, with the growing social concern for children and adolescents (e.g., conduct disorder, juvenile delinquency, adolescent drug abuse), recent efforts have been devoted to identifying effective approaches to youth violence (Elliott, 1998; Surgeon General's Report, 2001) and adolescent drug abuse (Model Programs for Substance Abuse and Delinquency Prevention; Center for Substance Abuse Prevention; Alvarado, Kendall, Beesley, Lee-Cavaness, 2000). These efforts are notable in that they combine rigorous methodological standards traditionally associated with efficacy studies with the needs for replicability across diverse clients and in diverse treatment settings that are more traditionally characteristic of effectiveness studies. Because of these efforts there are now a number of effectiveness-based reviews of the outcomes and cost-effectiveness reviews not typically found in the psychotherapy literature that are available to inform the family therapy knowledge base. As a result of these efforts, family therapy research knowledge can inform clinical practice at high levels of ecological validity perhaps unmatched by any other psychological intervention.

In the following sections, we review family therapy (FT) research using our "levels of evidence" model. We consider the results of meta-analyses as well as specific clinical trial studies identified in our review. The evidence for FT is complete enough that specific models can be reviewed for specific problems. Sometimes, evidence for specific models with specific clients in settings can also be identified. We found four meta-analyses that evaluated the outcomes of either FT in general or specific problems treated by FT approaches. We also draw on three reviews of FT literature conducted outside typical refereed journal articles (Aos & Barnoski, 1998; Elliott, 1998; Surgeon General's Report, 2001). These reviews present a unique view of FT in that each combines high methodological quality while addressing the effectiveness and cost benefits of FT approaches in community settings in evaluating the impact of family therapy with conduct-disordered and delinquent adolescents. Our review of clinical trials studies found 22 effectiveness and 8 efficacy studies that considered four major approaches regarding eight major clinical problems. These studies are detailed below and summarized in Tables 13.4 and 13.5. An analysis of the methodological issues of these studies is included in the final section of this chapter.

TABLE 13.4 Family Therapy Efficacy Studies

Author	Study Characteristics (N; Assignment; Setting; Population; Problem)	Treatment (IV)	Outcome Criteria (DV)	Principle Findings
Beardslee et al. (1992)	N = 14 parents (7 families); random; CO; Families with ≥ 1 child 8–14yo; ≥ 1 parent with affective disorder in recent past	(1) Clinician-based psychoeducation: 6–10 sessions total, cognitively based (CG) Lecture group: 2 sessions, lectures on psychoeducation regarding affective disorder	(1) Adult psychopathology (2) Marital adjustment (3) Therapeutic alliance (4) Intervention success	Parents reported being significantly less upset about presenting concerns at post-treatment (2) 86% parents report ≥ 1 behavior change due to intervention (3) No harm from treatment reported = treatment is safe
Beardslee et al. (1993)	N = 12; random; CO; Families with ≥ 1 child 8–14 yo; ≥ 1 parent diagnosed with affective disorder in past year	(1) Clinician-based psychoeducation: 6–10 sessions, cognitive orientation, increase awareness of illness (2) Lecture: 2 sessions, one-hour lectures for parents' psychoeducation regarding depression	(1) Parental concern/ upset (2) Treatment satisfaction (3) Behavior/attitude change	(1) Clinician-based reported significantly more attitude and behavior changes in family, with especially high changes in family attitudes about illness as compared to 0% reporting changes in this area in lecture group (2) Both groups reported significantly less "upset" about concerns at post-treatment (3) Both groups reported satisfaction with intervention, with clinician-based reporting significantly higher satisfaction than lecture group
Beardslee et al. (1996)	N = 54 parents (28 families; random; CO; Families ≥ 1 child 8–14 yo; ≥ 1 parent diagnosed w/affective disorder in past yr	Both assessed at 3–6 wks, 9–12 months, 2yr post-previous assessment (1) Clinician-based psychoeducation: 6–10 sessions, cognitive orientation, increase awareness of illness (2) Lecture: 2 sessions, one-hour lectures for parents' psychoeducation regarding depression	(1) Adult pathology (2) Parental concern/ upset (3) Treatment satisfaction (4) Behavior/attitude change	(1) More behavior and attitude change reported by families in clinician-facilitated group at post and followups

(continues)

TABLE 13.4 Family Therapy Efficacy Studies *(Continued)*

Author	Study Characteristics (*N*; Assignment; Setting; Population; Problem)	Treatment (IV)	Outcome Criteria (DV)	Principle Findings
Brent et al. (1997)	*N* = 107; random; CO; 13–18yo referred by clinicians or media; Major Depressive Disorder	(1) Cog Behavior Therapy (CBT): 12–16 sessions (2) Systemic Behavioral Family Therapy (SBFT): 12–16 sessions, family therapy w/techniques from FFT (Alexander & Parsons, 1982) & problem-solving approaches (Robin & Foster, 1989) (3) Nondirective Supportive Therapy (NST): 12–16 sessions, individual therapy w/focus on rapport, therapeutic relationship	(1) Depression (adolescent) (2) Suicidality (3) Functional impairment	(1) CBT reduced symptoms faster than other treatments per K-SADS interviews and had significantly higher clinical remission rates of MDD than other groups. (2) Significant decreases in suicidality across all groups (3) Significant improvement in functioning across all groups
Griff (1999)	*N* = 18; random; CO, Midwestern community; 2–6yo children and their parents; behavior problems	BOTH treatments: structured, brief play therapies (1) Intergenerational Play Therapy: 9 weekly sessions, play therapy with parent and one grandparent (2) Family Play Therapy: 9 sessions, no grandparents (CG) Wait list control	(1) Parental stress (2) Dysfunctional parenting (3) Child competency and behavior problems	(1) Fewer external behavior problems per parent report (2) Reduction in child behaviors that interfere with good parenting

Hahlweg & Wiedemann (1999)	N = 48; random; CO post d/c; 17–50yo identified clients in Germany; previously admitted 1 + times for treatment of schizophrenia or schizo-affective disorder	Both based on Behavioral Family Management of Falloon et al. (1984): psychoeducation weekly (3months), bimonthly (3 months), monthly (1 y) post-discharge (1) Behavioral Family Mgmt plus Standard Dose medication (BFMSD): maintenance on consistent dosage throughout (2) BFM plus targeted medication (BFMTM) TM: gradual decrease in dosage throughout	(1) Relapse of symptoms (2) Medication dosage (3) Psychopathology (4) Social adjustment	(1) BFMSD group had significantly fewer relapses at 18-month followup (2) Both groups consistently improved on pathology and social functioning up through 18-month followup (3) Relatives in both groups consistently decreased in self-rated pathology through 18 months (4) BFM efficacious cross-culturally
Harrington et al. (1998)	N = 162; random; CI and CO (admitted just after attempt); ≤ 16yo, England; suicide attempters	(1) Family Therapy: Assessment session plus 4 home visits, problem-solving focus (CG) Routine care: avg. 3.6 sessions, clinical family visits at hospital	(1) Family functioning (2) Problem-solving (3) Symptomatology	Reduced suicidal ideation as compared to control for NON-depressed patients only
Xiong et al. (1994)	N = 63; random; CI and CO; Schizophrenic patients in China	(1) Individual and Group Family Treatment: varied # of sessions up to 2 years of treatment, inpatient and outpatient psychoeducation: problem-solving (CG) Standard Care: sessions upon request only plus 2 months of medication	(1) Symptomatology (2) Clinical functioning (identified client) (3) Social functioning (identified client and family)	(1) Significantly lower frequency and duration of rehospitalization at 12 and 18 months in treatment group (2) Significantly more months of employment at 18 months in treatment group

Note: CO = Community Outpatient setting; CI = Community Inpatient setting; CG = Control Group; MDD = Major Depressive Disorder

TABLE 13.5 Family Therapy Effectiveness Studies

Author	Study Characteristics (*N*; Assignment; Setting; Population; Problem)	Treatment (IV)	Outcome Criteria (DV)	Principle Findings
Beardslee et al. (1997)	*N* = 37; random; CO; Families; parental affective disorder diagnosed by clinician in past yr	(1) Clinician-based psychoeducation: 6–10 sessions, cognitive orientation, increase awareness of illness (2) Lecture: 2 one-hour lectures for parents, psychoeducation regarding depression	(1) Attitude and behavior change (2) Treatment satisfaction (3) Family functioning (4) Psychopathology symptoms (child and parents)	(1) Participants in both groups reported illness-related attitude and behavior change and some level of change due to and satisfaction with the intervention As compared to the lecture only group, participants in the clinician facilitated group: (1) Parents reported significantly more marital supportiveness, more understanding of parental affective disorder, and improved communication with children about the disorder (2) Experienced significantly greater change in attitudes and beliefs about the parental affective disorder—especially regarding communication between spouses and with children about the disorder (3) Children reported a greater understanding of the parental affective disorder due to program participation
Birmaher et al. (2000)	*N* = 107; random; CO; 13–18yo referred to Pitt, PA anx center by media or clinicians; MDD	(1) Cognitive behavior therapy (CBT): 12–16 weekly sessions (2) Systemic behavior family therapy (SBFT): 12–16 weekly sessions; based on FFT (Alexander & Parsons, 1982) & problem-solving approaches (Robin & Foster, 1989) (3) Nondirective Supportive Therapy (NST): 12–16 weekly sessions; individual, focus on rapport and therapeutic relationship	(1) Depression (adolescent and parent) (2) Functional impairment (3) Cognitive distortion (4) Family environment *assessed at 2yr post-treatment for long-term comparison across treatments	*Clinical Significance:* Most (84%) of all participants recovered *Statistical Significance:* No differences in long-term advantages/improvements on dependent variables across treatments

Borduin et al. (1995)	N = 176; random; CO; 12–17yo, 67.5% male, 70% Cauc; juvenile offenders	(1) MST: averaged 23.9 hours of treatment, usually at family's home (CG) Individual treatment: averaged 28.6 hours of treatment, psychodynamic, client-centered, and/or behavioral, individual focus	(1) Individual adjustment (2) Family relations (3) Peer relations (4) Criminal activity	As compared to individual treatment, MST completers AND dropouts at post- through 4-yr followup: (1) Had lower recidivism rates (2) Committed less serious crimes (3) Committed less violent crimes *Several process-oriented moderators possible
Geist et al. (2000)	N = 25; random; CI; 12–17 yo anorexic women and families	(1) Generic family therapy: 8 sessions, 4 months, focus on adolescent's problems (2) Family group psychoeducation: 8 sessions, 4 months, education regarding eating disorder	(1) Depression (2) Eating disorder behaviors (3) Symptomatology (4) Family functioning	(1) Both groups experienced significant weight restoration—no difference between groups (2) Adolescents in both groups reported an increase in family pathology post-treatment
Gordon et al. (1995)	N = 45; random then nonrandom quasi-experimental design; CO; adolescents, white; court-referred juvenile delinquents	(1) FFT (2) Probation SEE Gordon et al. (1988) for length of treatments	(1) Offenses committed between 28- and 60-month followup	(1) FFT rate of recidivism = 9% vs. probation = 41% as adults
Henggeler et al. (1993)	N = 84; random; CO; 77% male, 44% Caucasian, 56% African American; Juvenile delinquents w/prior placement risk for placement	(1) MST: average 33 hours of direct contact over 13 weeks (CG) Treatment as usual: various hours, through local community youth services department	2.4 yrs post-referral: (1) Re-arrest rates (2) Incarceration rates	(1) MST superior to control in prolonging time to rearrest
Henggeler et al. (1996) *F99*	N = 118; random; CO (home or clinic); average 15.9yo, lower SES, 50% African American, 47% Caucasian, 1% Asian, 1% Hispanic, 1% Native American; subst abusing or dependent adolescents w/comorbid Axis I disorder	BOTH: monthly phone interview re: use & services (1) MST: average 40 contact hours, home-based (CG) Treatment as usual: various number of contact hours, referred by probation officer to 12-step programs, adolescent support groups, other services	(1) Dropout rates (dropout = never seen or incomplete treatment) (2) Contact hours (therapy)	(1) 98% of MST completed full treatment (2) 78% in treatment as usual group were never seen in 5mos post-referral (3) Significantly more treatment contact hours in MST group

(continues)

TABLE 13.5 Family Therapy Effectiveness Studies *(Continued)*

Author	Study Characteristics (*N*; Assignment; Setting; Population; Problem)	Treatment (IV)	Outcome Criteria (DV)	Principle Findings
Henggeler, et al. (1997)	*N* = 155; random; CO; 11–17yo, 81.9% male, 80.6% African American, 19.4% Caucasian, urban and rural dwellers; violent offenders	(1) MST: various locations (CG) Treatment as usual: referrals from probation officer, meetings w/probation officer monthly	(1) Emotional adjustment (2) Adolescent behavior problems (3) Family relations (4) Parental monitoring (5) Peer relations	(1) Behavior problems significantly decreased in both groups (2) MST group incarcerated significantly fewer days from pre-1.7y post-followup (3) MST group significantly lowered symptomatology, control group increased symptoms (4) Higher MST adherence associated w/greater treatment benefits: adherence is a moderator for effectiveness
Henggeler et al. (1999)	*N* = 116; random; CI vs. CO; California, 10–17 yo; psychiatric emergency status: homicidal, suicidal, psychotic	(1) MST: average 97 contact hours, 123 days of services over 4 months post-recruitment, home-based (2) Inpatient hospitalization: various numbers of days hospitalized, various types and hours of services provided: psych evaluation, acute stabilization, behavior management, aftercare planning	(1) Symptomatology (2) Antisocial behavior (3) Self-esteem (4) Family relations (5) Peer relations (6) School attendance (7) Consumer satisfaction	(1) MST more effective in decreasing externalizing symptoms at post-treatment (2) Hospitalization more effective in increasing self-esteem at post-treatment (3) Family cohesion and structure increased more in the MST group (4) MST participants missed significantly fewer days of school (5) Youths and caregivers in MST reported significantly greater treatment satisfaction
Henggeler et al. (1999)	*N* = 118; random; CO; 12–17yo, 79% male; juvenile offenders w/substance abuse or dependence	(1) MST: average 40 direct contact hours over 130 days, in home and community settings (CG) Usual Community Services: varied number of contact hours, referrals to 12-step groups, inpatient, residential programs, outpatient, school-based	(1) Drug use (2) Criminal activity (3) Out-of-home placement	(1) MST reduced alcohol, marijuana, and other drug use at post-treatment, not sustained at 6-mo followup (2) MST reduced total days in out-of-home placement by 50% at 6-mo followup

McFarlane et al. (1995)	*N* = 172; random; CO and CI; 18–45yo, NY; acute psychotics and families	Both psychoeducation based on Anderson et al. (1986) & Falloon et al. (1984): Meetings w/ and w/o identified clients, problem-solving focus, coping skills (1) Multiple Family Group (MFG): 4 initial sessions plus biweekly multifamily group sessions (2) Single Family Group (SFG): 4 initial sessions plus biweekly single family group sessions	(1) Relapse/ rehospitalization (2) Positive and negative symptoms (3) Medication dosage and compliance (4) Client employment status	(1) Rehospitalization and psychotic symptoms significantly decreased, and medication compliance was equally high in both treatments (2) MFG groups had significantly lower total relapse rates across two years of study (3) MFG cost benefit ratio compared to SFG is up to 1:34
Nutger et al. (1997)	*N* = 52; random; CI then CO; Netherlands, male, 15–26yo; recent onset schizophrenia or related disorder	(1) BFM: 18 sessions post d/c, modeled on Falloon et al. (1984) (CG) Individual contact w/nurse for 12 months post-discharge: psychoeducation	(1) Levels of expressed emotion (2) Relapse rates	(1) Higher relapse rates in individual treatment group were significantly related to EE instability over time (2) No effect of individual treatment on EE
Randolph et al. (1994)	*N* = 41; random; CO; male, 18–55yo; Schizophrenic clients w/previous admissions to a veterans hospital	BOTH: Medication management (1) BFM plus customary care: average of 21 sessions over 12 months (Falloon et al., 1984), plus customary care described below (CG) Customary Care: Monthly clinical services, evaluation and medication management, referrals, crisis services, recreation and occupational therapy groups, skills training	(1) Psychopathology (2) Expressed emotion (all family members)	(1) BFM treatment equally effective for pts from Hi and Lo EE families (2) BFM group experienced significantly fewer symptom exacerbations (psychoses)

(continues)

Table 13.5 Family Therapy Effectiveness Studies *(Continued)*

Author	Study Characteristics (*N*; Assignment; Setting; Population; Problem)	Treatment (IV)	Outcome Criteria (DV)	Principle Findings
Robin et al. (1994)	*N* = 22; random; CO; 12–19yo females referred by physician, teachers, mental health professionals; anorexia nervosa	(1) BFST: weekly 72-minute family sessions for 12–18 months, parents taught to control adolescent's eating, then focus on cognitive restructuring and family functioning, then return eating control to adolescent (2) Ego-Oriented Individual Therapy (EOIT): 12–18 months of weekly 45-min individual sessions w/adolescent focusing on ego strength, coping skills and developmental issues, and bimonthly, approximately 54-min family sessions for psychoeducation of parents and help in coping	(1) Weight (2) Eating attitudes/ Body dissatisfaction (3) Family conflict (4) Ego functioning (5) Depression/ internalizing behavior disorders	[Clinical Significance: (no significant differences between percentages below)] (1) 73% of BFST and 45% of EOIT reached 50th percentile BMI and/or resumed menstruation (2) 89% BFST and 60% EOIT resumed menstruation (3) 67% BFST and 30% EOIT reached 50th percentile BMI and resumed menstruation Statistical Significance: (1) Perceived family conflict significantly decreased in both groups (2) Both groups significantly improved in weight gain; BFST group improved significantly more
Robin et al. (1999)	*N* = 37; Random; CO; Adolescents; anorexia nervosa	(1) BFST: weekly 72-minute family sessions for 12–18 months, parents taught to control adolescent's eating, then focus on cognitive restructuring and family functioning, then return eating control to adolescent (2) EOIT: 12–18 months of weekly 45-min individual sessions w/adolescent focusing on ego strength, coping skills and developmental issues, and bimonthly, approximately 54-min family sessions for pyschoeducation of parents and help in coping	(1)Body mass (2) Eating attitudes (3) Ego functioning (4) Depressive affect (5) Family conflict	(1) Adolescents in BFST demonstrated significantly more weight gain at post and 1-yr followup (2) BFST group reestablished menstruation at higher rates than EOIT group at post-treatment (3) Both treatment groups experienced improvements in depressive affect, eating attitudes, and family conflict related to eating

Santisteban et al. (1996)	*N* = 193; random; CO; 12–17y adolescents at risk of drug abuse, 70% male, 54% Cuban, 46% non-Cuban Hispanic	ALL: unlimited amount of contacts across four weeks (1) Engagement Family Therapy: brief structural family therapy (Szapocznik & Kurtines, 1989), plus SSSE (Szapocznik et al., 1988) (2) Family Therapy as usual: no attempt to restructure resistance (3) Group therapy w/o SSSE: adolescent only, process-oriented group	(1) Engagement of family (2) Maintenance in therapy (don't dropout)	SSSE group had significantly more successful engagements than both other groups, but less success was observed for Cubans than non-Cubans, which may be attributable to parental resistance in Cuban families.
Santisteban et al. (1997)	*N* = 122; nonrandom; CO; 12–14 yo, African American or Hispanic; conduct or antisocial personality disorders or both, risk of drug use initiation, referred by school counselor	(1) Brief Structural/Strategic Family Therapy: 12–16, 90-minute sessions for 4–6 months	(1) Adolescent behavior problems (2) Family functioning (3) Adolescent alcohol & drug use	*Clinical Significance:* for those starting at clinical levels (1) 47% improved and 36% nonclinical on conduct disorder scales at post-treatment (2) 24% improved and 12% nonclinical on socialized aggression at post-treatment (3) 29% reliable change on clinical levels of anxiety by post-treatment *Statistical Significance:* (1) Conduct disorder, social aggression, family functioning all predictors of AOD use initiation (2) Significant decrease in use of adolescent users post-treatment (3) Significant decrease in conduct disorder and social anxiety behavior at post-treatment *all results may be mediated by ethnicity

(continues)

TABLE 13.5 Family Therapy Effectiveness Studies *(Continued)*

Author	Study Characteristics (*N*; Assignment; Setting; Population; Problem)	Treatment (IV)	Outcome Criteria (DV)	Principle Findings
Sayger et al (1993)	*N* = 43; random; CO; 2–6th grade boys; aggressive w/ oppositional-defiant or conduct disorder, parents with high or low marital satisfaction at outset	(1) Social Learning Family Therapy: 10 sessions over 9 months (Fleischman et al; 1983; Horne & Sayger, 1990) (CG) wait list control (not used in comparisons for this repeated measures analysis)	(1) Problem behaviors (2) Marital satisfaction (3) Family interactions (4) Depression (parents)	*Clinical Significance:* (1) In pre-treatment to marital satisfaction group, 68% made clinically significant change, 12.5% became clinically functional *Statistical Significance:* (1) Both hi and lo marital satisfaction groups demonstrated significant improvements on depressive symptoms (2) Significant decrease in parent and teacher reported disruptive behavior sustained at 9mos (3) Child's aggressive behavior not necessarily a symptom of a dysfunctional marriage
Schoenwald et al. (2000)	*N* = 113; random; CO vs. CI; 10–17yo, 65% male, 64% African American, 34% White, 1% Asian, 1% Hispanic; suicidal or homicidal ideation or psychosis, approved for psychiatric hospitalization	(1) MST: Average of 97 contact hours (SD = 57 hours), approximately 4 months of intensive home-based treatment (CG) Hospitalization: Various lengths of stay in a milieu program including crisis stabilization, psychiatric evaluation, aftercare planning	(1) Treatment service utilization (2) Restrictive quality of placement environment	(1) MST group significantly fewer days in hospital between referral and crisis stabilization (initial 2-week period) (2) Compared to hospitalization, MST reduced group total days hospitalized by 72% from initial referral time to MST treatment completion 3–4 months post-referral (3) MST group experienced significantly fewer changes of out-of-home placement and significantly fewer changes to more restrictive placements than youth in control group.

Schooler et al. (1997)	*N* = 528; random; CI and CO; 18–55yo, recruited during hospitalization or acute outpatient symptom exacerbation; schizophrenia or related disorders	(1) Supportive Family Management (SFM): (initial psychoeducational workshop, 2 yrs monthly support meetings w/clients and families (Anderson et al., 1986) (2) Applied Family Management (AFM): maximum of 32 sessions, individual assessment and family psychoeducation, problem-solving, communication skills training (Falloon et al., 1988) * varied medication management across treatments	(1) Clinical and social functioning (2) Symptomatology (3) Med side effects 6, 12, 18, & 24 months (and 20 wks post-rescue meds if needed)	(1) Attendance at psychoeducational workshop predicted continuation of therapy to maintenance stage (2) No difference in effectiveness of treatments, variations of med dosage significantly moderated effects of both treatments on relapse
Spoth et al. (1998)	*N* = 523 families; random; CO; Families of 6th graders in 33 rural schools in a Midwest state	(1) Preparing for Drug Free Years (PDFY): 5-sessions, 2hr group w/other families (kids included 1x), skills/competence training (Catalano et al., 1996) (2) Iowa Strengthening Families Program (ISFP): 7 sessions; biopsychosocial approach to enhance family resilience (DeMarsh & Kumpfuer, 1986) (CG) minimal contact control	(1) Parent-child affective quality (2) General child mgmt (3) Targeted parenting behaviors	(1) Targeted parenting skills were directly improved by both interventions, which indirectly influenced parent-child affective quality and general child management
Sundelin & Hansson (1999)	*N* = 109; nonrandom; CO Swedish, low SES, families w/children averaging 10.8 yo; 60% kids have conduct problems	(1) Intensive Family Therapy: Day treatment for one month plus 6 months maximum followup, modeled on Henggeler et al. (1995) (CG) none	(1) Family climate (2) Family functioning	(1) IFT improved family functioning, especially for mothers

Note: CO = Community Outpatient setting; CI = Community Inpatient setting; FFT = Functional Family Therapy; MST = Multisystemic Family Therapy; SES = Socioeconomic Status; BFST = Behavioral Family Systems Therapy; Behavioral Family Management; Ego Oriented Individual Therapy; SSSE = Strategic Structural Systems Engagement; IFT = Intensive Family Therapy; EE = Expressed Emotion; SFG = Single Family Group treatment; MFG = Multiple Family Group treatment.

The Outcomes of Family Therapy: Does It Work?

Meta-analysis

The results of meta-analyses suggest that FT, broadly considered, is an effective intervention for a variety of specific clinical problems. In the reanalysis of their previous meta-analysis, Shadish et al. (1995) reported on 101 controlled studies of family therapy conducted through 1988. Of the FT studies, the weighted mean effect size was .47, somewhat lower but not significantly different than the ES for CT (.60). They do, however, report a number of important differences between the two treatments. First, FT studied more kinds of presenting problems that were considered to be more difficult than those treated by CT. Unfortunately, no measures of clinical significance were available for FT, making it difficult to compare it with CT and other treatment modalities. As noted above, most of the studies included were efficacy studies conducted in highly controlled laboratory settings. Three meta-analyses investigated FT interventions in the treatment of specific problems (Cuijpers, 1994; DeJesus, Mari & Streiner, 1994; Stanton & Shadish, 1997). Each of these studies is reviewed in more detail in the appropriate section below. Taken together, they also provide evidence for the overall efficacy of FT.

Major Approaches to Family Therapy; What Works?

The majority of recent family therapy research has been directed toward systematic family-based treatment intervention programs developed to treat specific clinical problems rather than toward broad, general, and theoretically based "schools" of family therapy. The movement toward systematic clinical models for specific clinical problems is an important one because it provides research information at the most specific levels of evidence.

Meta-analysis

In their meta-analysis, Shadish et al. (1995) found significant positive effects for all orientations (behavioral-psychoeducational, systemic, psychodynamic, eclectic, and a broad group of other approaches). Only those orientations classified as "humanistic" produced no differences when compared to control groups. They did not find any particular orientation demonstrably superior to any other, with the exception of some small advantage for behavioral approaches, when compared to eclectic and unclassified orientations. These findings led Shadish et al. to conclude "that if all treatments were equally designed, implemented and reported, significant differences among orientations might not be found" (p. 350).

These findings are, however, not supported by the results of two systematic reviews of the literature that suggest all approaches may not be equal when specific intervention programs for specific clinical problems are considered. In a review of conduct-disorder treatment, Kazdin (1997) identified three family-based programs that could be considered promising in regard to these essential criteria of an "intervention" program: Parent management training, functional family therapy (Alexander & Sexton, in press; Sexton & Alexander, 2002), multisystemic therapy (Henggeler, Borduin, et al., 1991), and cognitive problem solving skills training (PSST; Feindler & Ecton, 1986). In a similar effort, Sexton and Alexander (2002) and Alexander, Robbins, and Sexton (2001) identified a group of well-defined family-based interventions that met criteria similar to those used by Kazdin. Labeled family-based empirically supported treatments (FBest), each approach includes specific treatment protocols (manuals) developed with realistic client populations, in actual clinical settings, within ongoing, systematic programs of research and evaluation. Currently, four clinical interventions meet these FBest criteria: functional family therapy (Alexander & Sexton, in press; Sexton & Alexander, 2002), multidimensional family therapy (Liddle, 1995), multisystemic therapy (Borduin, Henggeler, Blaske, & Stein, 1990; Henggeler et al., 1991), and structural family therapy (as developed by Szapocznik & Kurtines, 1989). To date, both the promising programs identified by Kazdin (1997) and the FBest intervention programs noted by Alexander et al. (2001) are concentrated in the area of adolescent disruptive disorders and the specific accompanying problems of delinquency, drug abuse, and family conflict.

Family Therapy Intervention Programs for Specific Clinical Problems

In the following sections, we consider the four major areas of clinical problems with the most accumulated evidence. In each section we describe the problem and the intervention programs with demonstrated successful outcomes. In each case, we follow our "levels of evidence" scheme and note the conclusions of meta-analyses and specific efficacy and effectiveness studies identified in our review. It is important to note that our review identified more studies than are described in detail here. Tables 13.4 and 13.5 include a complete listing of family therapy efficacy and effectiveness studies identified in the review.

Conduct Disorder/Oppositional Defiant Problems

The acting out, externalizing behavior problems of children and adolescents, most often termed "conduct disorders," is one of the most frequent clinical referrals for children and adolescents to psychological treatments (Kazdin, 1997). Because of the comorbid nature of the problems (e.g., behavior, drug, delinquency), many systems and therefore many seemingly distinct populations of clients are often involved. Kazdin (1997) suggested that conduct disorder problems usually represent a very broad domain of systems including the child, parent, family, and context.

Two systematic qualitative reviews from outside traditional research settings are important to consider because they provide a unique picture of the extent of the evidence for FT with conduct disorders. Elliott (1998) conducted a systematic search of existing intervention programs for youth violence for the Center for the Study and Prevention of Violence (CSPV). The review was the basis for the "Blueprint" program, a collaborative venture between CSPV, the Centers for Disease Control, and the Office of Juvenile Justice and Delinquency Prevention (OJJDP) to identify best practices in the treatment of adolescent behavior problems. The review used four criteria to select effective programs: (1) strong research designs, (2) significant positive effects, (3) replication of the effects at multiple sites, and (4) evidence that the treatment effect was sustained for at least one year post-treatment. Of the 500 programs reviewed, only 10 interventions met these strict standards. Three approaches would be considered FT: functional family therapy, multisystemic therapy, and therapeutic treatment foster care (Chamberlain & Rosicky, 1995). The Surgeon General's report (2001) used a methodology similar to that adopted by CSPV. In this analysis, they identified four "level I" programs that were effective in the treatment of juvenile violence. These approaches included functional family therapy and multisystemic therapy.

The Public Policy Institute of the state of Washington recently completed an economic analysis of the outcome and cost-effectiveness of various approaches to reduce delinquency (Aos & Barnoski, 1998). The goal of the project was to find cost-effective programs (based on costs to taxpayers and crime victims) that worked (highest effect sizes of studies using sound research designs that were published in peer reviewed journals). First, they systematically reviewed published research to determine potentially effective intervention programs. From those studies, they calculated average effect size for each program, which they combined with the costs to implement the program, justice system costs averted, crime victim costs avoided if implemented, and years it would take to recover the cost of program implementation to determine the economic effectiveness of intervention programs. Two family-based intervention programs, functional family therapy and multisystemic therapy, had among the strongest effectiveness ratings and high cost savings when compared to other juvenile offender programs. The *cost savings* (taxpayer and crime victim cost) for MST and FFT ranged from $13,908 to $21,863 (per adolescent treated), respectively.

Meta-Analyses. No meta-analytic review specifically addresses the impact of family-based interventions on child and adolescent behavior disorders. In their broad review of FT, Shadish et al. (1995) suggested that family-based interventions were not as successful as individually based treatments for conduct disordered children. Unlike the reviews noted above, Shadish et al. did not note the number of studies or the specification of treatments used in this analysis. The Stanton and Shadish (1997) review evaluated adolescent drug abuse, a common problem with conduct-disordered and delinquent adolescents, and found FBT to be more successful than individual treatments (see drug abuse section below).

Clinical Studies. Family therapy for the treatment of conduct disorder, oppositional defiant disorder, and related problems of violence and juvenile delinquency in children and adolescents was tested in several empirical studies (see Tables 13.3 and 13.4). We found seven studies considering five different intervention approaches. The majority of participants in these studies were male and from a variety of racial and cultural backgrounds (e.g., Caucasian, African American, and Hispanic). Target behaviors were defined in a variety of ways ranging from American Psychiatric Association criteria for oppositional-defiant and conduct disorders to family-reported presenting problems of behavior. Many of the studies of conduct disorder (CD) and opposition defiant disorder (ODD) targeted juvenile delinquency as the primary outcome measure. Few studies investigated changes in family dynamics and functioning that might be related to these outcomes. Overall, the family treatment of oppositional-defiant and conduct disorders appears successful across a variety of intervention types.

Specific Approaches for the Treatment of Conduct Disorders

Two treatment approaches are represented in our review of the research into the treatment of childhood and adolescent acting out conduct disorders. Both of these approaches (functional family therapy and multisystemic therapy) are also effective interventions for other problems (adolescent drug abuse) but will be reviewed here because it is the primary area of application (see Tables 13.4 and 13.5 for more specific details). It is important to note that some intervention programs (e.g., Parent Management Training), have been previously identified as effective interventions but are not represented by current published research and are therefore not reviewed here.

***Functional family therapy* (FFT).** FFT is a multisystemic family therapy intervention that has as its primary focus and therapeutic entry point the family relational system. FFT focuses on diverse domains of client functioning (emotional, cognitive, and behavioral) and views clinical "problems" as representative of individual, family, and community risk factors that manifest themselves within ineffective but functional family relational processes. FFT assumes that the symptom is both mediated by and embedded in complex relational sequences involving all other family members and that it has come to serve some legitimate relational outcome (closeness, distance, hierarchy). Change is a phasic process in which each of the three phases of intervention (engagement/motivation, behavior change, and generalization) has a set of therapeutic goals, related change mechanisms that help accomplish those goals, and therapist interventions most likely to activate these change mechanisms. The goal is for change to be systematically guided while clinically responsive. As a *treatment* program, FFT has been applied successfully to a wide range of problem youth and their families in various contexts (Alexander et al., 2001; Elliott, 1998; Sexton & Alexander, 2002). As a *prevention* program, FFT has demonstrated its efficiency in diverting the trajectory of at-risk adolescents away from entering the mental health and justice systems (Alexander, Robbins, & Sexton, 2000). In both contexts, the target populations are generally youth aged 11–18, although younger siblings of referred adolescents may also be seen. Thus, the youth range from preadolescents who are at-risk to older youth with very serious problems such as conduct disorder, drug involvement, risky sexual behaviors, and truancy. The families represent multiethnic, multicultural populations living in diverse communities. FFT is a short-term intervention averaging roughly 8 to 12 sessions for mild to moderate cases and 26 to 30 hours of clinical service for more difficult cases.

The results of published studies suggest that FFT is effective in reducing recidivism (between 26% and 73% with status offending, moderate, and seriously delinquent youth) as compared to both no-treatment and juvenile court probation services (Alexander et al., 2000). Of most interest is the range of community settings and client ethnicities that have composed these studies (a more complete list can be found in Alexander et al., 2000). These positive outcomes of FFT remain relatively stable even at followup times as long as five years (Gordon, Arbuthnot, Gustafson, & McGreen, 1988) and the positive impact also affects siblings of the identified adolescent (Klein, Alexander, & Parsons, 1977).

In two studies by Gordon et al. (1988, 1995), the long-term effectiveness of FFT was investigated. Gordon et al. (1988) investigated whether FFT was effective in reducing recidivism compared to regular probation services up to 60 months after termination of the treatment. These authors used the adult criminal records of the lower socioeconomic status, white, Midwestern juveniles who received family treatment as adolescents for status offense. Adult records demonstrated a 9% recidivism rate for individuals previously treated with FFT. In contrast, the 41% of a comparison group who received probation as usual services had been rearrested as adults. These results further the support for FFT as an effective intervention and add to the strength of this intervention in affecting long-term change in a population of juvenile delinquents. It is important to note that recidivism was the primary outcome variable studied. Additional measures of family functioning should also be studied since family functioning change is also an important outcome.

MULTISYSTEMIC THERAPY (MST). MST is a systematic, manual-driven family-based intervention for youth and families facing problems of juvenile delinquency, adolescent conduct disorder, and substance abuse (Henggeler, Pickrel, & Brondino, 1999). MST is an approach derived from social-ecological models of behavior, family systems, and social learning theories (Henggeler et al., 1999). It highlights the strengths of individuals, families, and social systems affecting the family in order to raise the level of family functioning and curtail adolescent involvement in delinquent or problem behaviors. Targets of change in MST include individual and family-level behaviors as well as outside system dynamics and resources, including the adolescent's social network. Treatment interventions are on an "as-needed" basis and focus on whatever it takes to alter individual, family, and systems issues that contribute to the problem behavior. The typical treatment course for MST implementation ranges from two to four months.

An impressive series of outcome studies have evaluated MST in various contexts among adolescents with varying problems (drug abuse, delinquency, conduct problems, etc.). The randomized clinical trials of MST demonstrate improved family relations and family functioning, improved school attendance, decreased drug use, and reductions of 25% to 70% in long-term rearrest rates (Henggeler, 1999). These trials focused on a wide variety of adolescent problems including violent and chronic juvenile delinquency (Borduin et al., 1995; Henggeler et al., 1997; Henggeler, Melton, & Smith, 1992), substance abuse with high rates of psychiatric comorbidity (Henggeler, Melton, Brondino, Scherer, & Hanley, 1997), psychiatric emergencies (Henggeler, 1999), maltreatment, neglect (Brunk, Henggeler, & Whelan, 1987), and sexual offenses (Borduin, Henggeler, Blaske, & Stein, 1990). Followup studies suggest that the initial recidivism rate decreases continue up to five years post-treatment.

Two studies by Henggeler et al. (1996, 1999) provided separate findings regarding the effectiveness of MST with one randomized sample (*n* = 118) of juvenile delinquents and their families. The first of these studies investigated the effectiveness of this treatment in preventing dropout with this historically difficult population (substance-abusing/dependent juvenile delinquents). Results suggest that 98% of families in the MST group completed treatment, whereas 78% of adolescents referred for usual community services had never been seen for services within five months after the referral. Results of the second study suggested that MST reduced alcohol, marijuana, and other drug use at post-test. However, these reductions were not sustained at the six-month followup. In regards to preventing out-of-home placement, at the assessment taken six months post-treatment, adolescents in the MST group had spent 50% fewer days in out-of-home placements (incarceration facilities, residential centers, or inpatient units) than the treatment as usual group.

Drug Abuse

Adolescent and adult drug abuse is a serious public health problem, with consequences that extend beyond the drug user to their families and communities. Family therapy approaches have long been considered one of the viable treatment interventions for this category of problems. Family therapy is increasingly considered successful because of its ability to engage and retain youth and their families in drug treatment (from 16% to 28% dropouts) when compared to peer-group and individual therapy. It also has been shown to be successful in reducing drug use, with abstinence rates ranging from 73% (white middle-class youth using marijuana) to 44% (for hard drug users) when compared to treatment as usual and other treatments (e.g., peer-group therapy, individual therapy, other family-based treatments, parent training, and multifamily therapy groups. These reductions appear to be maintained at followup periods up to one year. Three categories of family-based intervention models seem most effective among family systems models (structural-strategic models, functional family therapy), behavioral family models, and ecological family-based intervention models (multisystemic therapy) (Waldron, 1997). Waldron notes: "Taken together, the results of randomized clinical trials provide ample evidence that family therapy is an effective treatment for adolescent substance abusers," and "The consistency of support for family therapy interventions is remarkable, given the problems, limitations, and widely varying theoretical models, design, approaches to measurement, and other methodological issues"

(p. 224). The outcomes of family therapy treatment for adult alcohol and drug use were less encouraging.

META-ANALYSIS. Stanton and Shadish (1997) conducted a comprehensive analysis of family-based interventions in the treatment of adolescent and adult drug abuse from 15 studies published through 1997 which involved 1,571 cases and 3,500 clients and family members. Those adult clients receiving family and couple therapy had significantly lower drug use after treatment than did those in nonfamily alternative treatments ($d = .48, p < .01$). Results for adolescents treated with family interventions were also significantly different from nonfamily alternatives ($d = .39, p < .01$). Though not clear cut, there also appeared to be evidence that family-based interventions were more cost effective than other approaches to drug abuse treatment. One of the most pertinent findings was that substantially more family therapy clients stayed in treatment as compared to those in nonfamily treatments. In a qualitative analysis attempting to understand the common mechanisms of treatment, they note that the nonblaming and nonjudgmental approach of many of these treatments (e.g., functional family therapy) was an important factor in the success and differences in treatment engagement.

Specific Approaches for the Treatment of Drug Abuse

The two approaches described here illustrate the current intervention models available. Two of the approaches described earlier (FFT and MST) also have evidence to suggest their efficacy with adolescent drug abuse. Like the approaches to conduct disorder problems noted above, these are systematic treatment intervention programs that are manual driven, with comprehensive models of the etiology and treatment mechanisms of drug use. As already mentioned, systematic FT approaches for adult alcohol and drug abuse have yet to emerge (Liddle & Dakof, 1995). We were unable to find any efficacy and effectiveness studies of other well-known treatment models (e.g., multidimensional family therapy, MDFT) in our review (see Tables 13.3 and 13.4). Process studies into MDFT have significantly contributed to our understanding of the mechanism of FT, but outcome studies were missing.

BRIEF STRUCTURAL STRATEGIC FAMILY THERAPY. Szapocznik and his colleagues at the University of Miami were the first to publish a systematic study of a family therapy intervention for adolescent drug use (Szapocznik et al., 1983; Szapocznik & Coatsworth, 1997). The approach was an elaboration of the early structural family therapy approaches. They reported changes in abstinence rates from 7% at admission to 80% at termination. These results were maintained up to the 12-month followup.

Santisteban et al. (1997) tested the effectiveness of his brief structural strategic family therapy (BSSFT) delivered in 12 to 16 sessions in a nonrandom sample ($n = 122$) of African American and Hispanic families, with 12- to 14-year-old adolescents experiencing both problem behaviors (such as conduct disorder and socialized aggression) and substance use (including alcohol, marijuana, cocaine, opiates, and nine other drugs not mentioned). Of the adolescents beginning treatment in a clinical range, 83% finished treatment clinically improved or recovered on levels of conduct disorder symptoms, 36% of subjects improved or recovered clinically on assessments of socialized aggression, and 29% made reliable clinical change in levels of anxiety at post-treatment assessments. Although these results appear positive, the lack of control groups and possibly low treatment integrity (no supervision, manual or therapist training, or adherence checks mentioned) pose a problem for deriving supportive conclusions for the effectiveness of BSSFT in the prevention and treatment of adolescent substance use for this population.

Schizophrenia

The role of family relational interactions in the development and maintenance of schizophrenia has been of long interest to family systems researchers and theorists. This interest went virtually unstudied until the late 1970s when a renewed interest in the role of family-oriented interventions reemerged. This interest was linked to the recognition by clinicians and now researchers that families play a potentially important role in the stabilization phase of treatment for schizophrenia. These family intervention programs are psychoeducational in nature and are intended to be an adjunct to pharmacotherapy.

META-ANALYSIS. Two meta-analyses studied the impact of various family-assisted and family therapy interventions with families in which one member suffered from a major mental illness (most often schizophrenia). de Jesus Mari and

Streiner (1994) investigated the impact of family interventions on the relapse of schizophrenic patients in six random assignment clinical trials of 350 clients in published results that appeared in the literature between 1966 and 1992. Since the dependent measure was relapse, the authors calculated the relative and absolute risk reduction, as well as the odds ratio of relapse at 6 months, 9 months, and 24 months post-treatment. This calculation results in a probability rather than an effect size. The family interventions included in these studies ranged from family therapy (crisis-oriented family therapy, home-based family therapy, and general family counseling) to various family-assisted educational treatments. The treatments were generally delivered in conjoint settings (one treatment was the family group). In addition, all studies included an educational component. The results suggest that the clients in the family-assisted interventions were less likely to relapse when compared to control groups. Risks of relapse among those treated in FT were between 6% and 41% at nine months and between 14% and 33% at two years. Two additional findings are also important. The overall state of expressed emotionality was lower, the compliance with mediation regimes was higher, and the hospitalization rate was lower for those in the FBT as compared to controls.

Cuijpers (1999) found that a broad category of family-based interventions was successful in decreasing the degree of relative perceived sense of burden and stress, while improving the relationship between relatives and the schizophrenic client in 15 studies of family-assisted treatment published between 1966 and 1993. The effect size of all studies was .46 at post-test and .23 at followup. However, when studies were clustered into groups of studies with significantly different effect sizes (for improvement in psychological distress), the five studies with the largest overall effect sizes (d = 1.0 at post-test; d = .73 at followup) had more sessions (average 13 vs. 9) compared to the eight studies with small effect sizes (d = .09 at post-test; d = .05 at followup). Improvements in psychological distress (d = .08–1.15 post-test; d = .22–.86 followup), for relationship improvement (d = .32; followup, d = .02 to d = .51), and for measures of family distress (d = .02 – 1.07; followup d = .22 to .48) were substantial. Although a reasonable number of studies were included, there were a limited number of comparisons with widely varying family treatments and outcomes.

Specific Approaches for the Treatment of Schizophrenia

The most common category of interventions for schizophrenia are family-assisted psychoeducational interventions programs. Since these approaches share a common set of procedures, they will be reviewed together in the following section.

FAMILY EDUCATION/INTERVENTION. A set of family-intervention programs with common intervention procedures have demonstrated efficacy in reducing relapse in schizophrenic clients. These approaches include specific models developed by Goldstein, Rodnick, Evans, May, and Steinberg (1978), Falloon, Boyd, and McGill (1982), and Tarrier, Barrowclough, Porceddu, and Watts (1988). Despite a number of unique variations, each of these models shares a number of common ingredients including early family engagement, education about schizophrenia, strategies for coping, communication and problem-solving training, and crisis intervention strategies (Goldstein & Miklowitz, 1995). Most approaches ranged from approximately 15 sessions to a maximum of 32 sessions over the course of one to two years (Linszen et al., 1996; Nutger, Dingemans, Van der Does, Linszen, & Gersons, 1997; Randolph et al., 1994; Schooler et al., 1997). Most outcome studies included the reduction of relapse as the central outcome measure. As a whole, these approaches demonstrated a significant reduction in relapse rates beyond that attributable to antipsychotic maintenance medication alone. Relapse rates ranged from 0% to 17%, compared to approximately 50% for those conditions without a family intervention.

Clinical studies support these conclusions. Hahlweg and Weidemann (1999) investigated behavioral family therapy (BFM) along with both standard dosage (BFMSD: consistent levels of medication throughout treatment) and targeted medication (BFMTM: gradual decrease in) dosage across time in treatment as maintenance interventions. Both treatment groups demonstrated improvements on measures of psychopathology of the identified patient and social functioning through the 18-month followup assessment. The BFMSD group had significantly fewer relapses by the 18-month followup assessment compared to patients receiving BFM with targeted medication reduction. In their effectiveness studies, Nutger et al. (1997) and Randolph et al. (1994) found similar positive results for BFM compared to individual therapy and customary care, respectively, for outpatient clients with schizophrenic disorders. In these studies, clients in BFM treatment reported significantly fewer relapses and psychotic symptom exacerbations than those in comparison groups. Xiong et al. (1994) investigated the efficacy of general family psychoeducation and problem-solving sessions up to two years after inpatient discharge of clients with schizophrenia compared to treatment as usual that included post-discharge family or individual meetings only upon request. This randomized sample of 63 clients and families in China revealed that those in the psychoeducational group reported a significantly lower frequency and duration of rehospitalization at 12 and 18 months post-discharge. In addition, subjects in the treatment group reported significantly more hours of employment at the 18-month followup assessment.

Additional studies examined the effectiveness of more specific, manualized psychoeducational treatments. Interventions in these studies were modeled on Falloon (1984), which incorporated workshop materials from Anderson's (1986) model developed for educating family members of clients with schizophrenia. In their comparison of applied family management and the less intensive supportive family management, Schooler et al. (1997) reported no differences in effectiveness between groups. Instead, it was observed that differentiations in medication dosages (standard dose, low dose, targeted reduction) significantly moderated the effects of both treatments on symptom relapse. McFarlane et al. (1995) tested the effectiveness of multiple (MFG) versus single family group (SFG) treatments for schizophrenia and relapse prevention. Both interventions were aimed at educating family members and fostering positive coping skills. Clients in both groups reported significantly fewer rehospitalizations and psychotic symptoms post-treatment. In addition, medication compliance was equally high in both treatment groups. The MFG group demonstrated significantly lower relapse rates across the two years included in this study. Because the cost/benefit ratio for MFG/SFG was 1:34, this highly structured, high-integrity treatment regimen (MFG) holds promise for curbing relapse and maintaining medication and treatment compliance in a cost-effective way for clients with schizophrenia.

Specific Disorders of Childhood

Much of the work on childhood mental health problems has focused on the externalizing conduct and oppositional defiant behavior problems already reviewed. To date, none of the meta-analyses of family therapy has specifically considered effect sizes for other specific disorders of childhood. Estrada and Pinsof (1995) comment that "there is a stunning lack of research on what has classically been defined as family therapy in regard to childhood disorders" (p. 433). They note that their review initially sought to cover family interventions for a wide range of childhood problems (schizophrenia, depression, suicide, and learning disabilities), but they could not locate appropriate studies. We found FT studies investigating adolescent depression and eating disorder treatment. It is clear that more research on a wider range of family therapy interventions is needed in these important areas of family life.

Two studies focused on the efficacy and effectiveness of family therapy in the treatment of depression (Brent et al., 1997; Birmaher et al., 2000) with adolescents (13–18) who were primarily outpatient females. The goal of these studies was to compare the efficacy (Brent et al., 1997) and then effectiveness (Birmaher et al. 2000) of the systemic behavioral family therapy (SBFT) model to individual cognitive behavioral therapy and nondirective supportive therapies in the treatment of adolescent depression. In their comparison of the efficacy of SBFT, individual CBT, and nondirective supportive therapies, Brent et al. (1997) found significant decreases in adolescent suicidality and improvements in functioning across all groups. Birmaher et al. (2000) reported followup data on the effectiveness of the same three treatment interventions on the Brent et al. (1997) sample of 107 13- to 18-year-old adolescents. The authors reported no differences in long-term improvements between groups on any dependent variables (depression in adolescent and parents, functional impairment, cognitive distortion, and family climate). Clinically, 84% of all participants across treatments were "recovered" post-treatment. Although these results do not provide direct support for SBFT or the other treatments tested, this intervention was reported to have positive effects on this population of families and merits further investigation.

Eating disorders, primarily among adolescent females, is a serious problem with both long-term physical and psychological consequences. Anorexia nervosa is associated with high morbidity, with recent long-term studies indicating that up to 30% of clients remain chronically ill and 15% die from the complications of the disorder. Behavioral family systems therapy (BFST), a treatment model for anorexia nervosa in adolescent females has been studied a number of times. Developed by Robin et al. (1994, 1999), BFST incorporates behavioral methods such as skill building for parents to establish a weight management program for their adolescent and cognitive techniques such as restructuring the adolescent's distortions around eating. Robin et al. (1994, 1999) also compared BFST with ego-oriented individual therapy (EOIT). BFST clients gained significantly more weight by posttest (1994) and one-year followup assessments (1999) than did those subjects in EOIT. However, no significant differences appeared between groups for percentage of clients reaching a targeted body mass, resuming menstruation, or reaching both of these outcome criteria.

Mediators and Moderators of Family Therapy

FT intervention programs have a particularly impressive record of process research that investigates both the factors that mediate change (usually considered predictors of change) and those within session mechanism that moderate the change process. Meta-analyses have yet to provide any insight into these critical mechanisms. Thus, specific process research studies provide the best evidence to make causal attributions about the mechanisms of therapeutic change within family-based intervention programs. Factors such as preexisting client characteristics and factors related to the structure of therapy (e.g., number of sessions) are common mediators. Mechanisms of change include a consideration of the role of the redefinition of initial presenting problems, resolution of therapeutic impasses, the therapeutic alliance, within-family negativity, family interaction, and family competency and interaction change, and the relationship between program adherence and treatment fidelity on therapeutic outcome. In each of these areas, the studies identified differ according to type of process variable (mediator/moderator) and type of outcome (proximal vs. distal).

We identified 20 family-based process studies found in our review. These studies are summarized in Table 13.3. In several studies, more than one level of research question was posed. Therefore, summaries of findings from these studies appear under both headings to report the respective results.

Mediators of FT

Three studies describe client pre-treatment characteristics (client demographic characteristics, preexisting behavioral competency, and the amount of post-referral change) and one therapy characteristic (number of sessions) as predictors of dropout/early termination (proximal outcomes) and degree of therapeutic success (distal outcomes). No specific trends emerge from this literature. Taken as a whole, however, these studies suggest that certain client factors do provide significant therapeutic challenges, which, unattended, will result in either early termination (dropout) or decreased outcomes. What is important is that these client characteristics need not be seen as factors that predetermine the outcome of treatment. Instead, we suggest that these studies are important in that they point out important characteristics of the family that should become therapeutic targets. It is the responsibility of program developers to identify methods to reduce potential negative effects and inform therapists of the importance of such methods.

Mechanisms (Mediators) of Family Therapy Change

Five therapeutic change mechanisms were investigated in the studies in this review (see Table 13.3). Most of these studies identified in this review were conducted within a manualized and systematic treatment program (MDFT, FFT, MST). When considered within systematic change models, change mechanisms are specifically identified as agents likely to produce change. Thus, the successful identification of a relationship between the change mechanism and some outcome provides support for the change model. These mechanisms represent a common set of factors that contribute to successful therapeutic change in family therapy.

1. Redefinition of the presenting problem. Coulehan, Friedlander, and Heatherington (1998) investigated the relationship between various family characteristics and success in changing the problem definition in the first session of constructivist narrative family therapy. Successful redefinition of the problem within the first session of therapy occurred after family members were able to provide multiple perspectives regarding the problem. In addition, families in which members were able to shift blame from any one individual were more likely to experience a successful redefinition of the problem in the first session of therapy. In cases where a successful shift occurred, it was preceded by the therapist encouraging the involvement of all family members and placing responsibility on all family members for changing the problem.

2. IMPASSE RESOLUTION. The resolution of the therapeutic impasse is hypothesized to be a point at which therapy may turn toward a positive or negative outcome. Liddle and colleagues conducted a series of studies of multidimensional family therapy (MDFT) in which they studied the importance of successful impasse resolution as well as the factors that contribute to positive resolution. For example, Diamond and Liddle (1996) found that successful and unsuccessful cases could be differentiated in session change events in which the family moved from a problem state (parents and adolescents argued over behavior management issues) to a resolution (session focus shifted to the interpersonal/relational nature of the problem).

3. THERAPEUTIC ALLIANCE. The therapeutic alliance is one of the few therapeutic processes consistently linked to outcome in both individual and family counseling (Horvath & Symonds, 1991; Sexton & Whiston, 1994). Diamond and colleagues (1999) looked at factors associated with an improved therapeutic alliance as measured from the first to third sessions of MDFT with substance-abusing adolescents and their families. The population in this sample (n = 10) was mostly African American, male, and representative of a low socioeconomic status group. Alliance was defined here as collaborative efforts between therapists and clients rather than simply as the result of a therapist technique. Previous research suggests that this definition represents the type of alliance most influential in distal treatment outcomes and needed to examine the specific techniques used to create a strong alliance (Frieswyk et al. 1986). In this small sample, therapists who acted as the adolescent's ally in session had higher levels of alliance.

4. REDUCTION OF WITHIN-SESSION NEGATIVITY. Negative or conflicted family interactions in therapy have been associated with poor therapy outcome and premature dropout. The work of Alexander and colleagues provides the most longstanding series of investigations into within-session negativity and its impact on proximal and distal outcomes of family therapy. In two studies of functional family therapy, Newell, Alexander, and Turner (1996) and Robbins, Alexander, Newell, and Turner (1996) looked at the impact of therapist interventions (e.g., reframing, directiveness, supportiveness) on the negativity of verbalizations by family members and found that greater frequency of therapist reframes and balanced style of structure and support were linked to more verbal and less defensive involvement of the family in therapy, as well as to successful therapy outcomes. Results indicate that reframing was significantly more effective than other therapist interventions in lowering defensiveness in all family members' response to therapist speech acts.

5. IMPROVED INTERACTIONAL AND BEHAVIORAL COMPETENCY. It has long been posited that positive modifications in parent–adolescent communications and other within-family interactions were associated with the reduction of behavior problems in adolescents. We identified a number of studies that support this claim. For example, in a recent study of multidimensional family therapy (MDFT), Schmidt, Liddle, and Dakof (1996) linked improvements in parenting to reductions in drug abuse and behavior problems. Robbins, Mitrani, Zarate, Coatsworth, and Szapocznik (1996) demonstrated a relationship between improvements in family interaction over the course of family therapy and outcome with conduct-disorder diagnosed adolescents and their families during the course of strategic structural family therapy (SSFT) intervention.

6. TREATMENT ADHERENCE. With the increased development of systematic intervention programs, treatment adherence is becoming a particularly important, albeit unstudied, process issue. To what degree does a therapist need to adhere to an efficacious program to duplicate the successful outcomes previously demonstrated? Henggeler et al. (1997) was the first to empirically link treatment adherence and clinical outcomes in the family literature. Therapist adherence was measured based on parent, adolescent, and therapist reports on a standardized MST adherence questionnaire. The level of therapist adherence was significantly related to absolute outcomes like rearrest and incarceration rates. High adherence predicted favorable outcomes, while low adherence predicted poor outcomes. This study highlights the potentially important role of treatment adherence in the outcomes of family-based counseling interventions, although the data are also consistent with the idea that more difficult cases who are not improving make it difficult for the therapist to adhere to techniques that are not working. Huey, Henggeler, Brondino, and Peckrel (2000) measured therapist adherence as it related to both proximal and distal outcomes of MST. Using the MST Adherence Measure and indices of delinquent peer affiliation and family functioning, these authors found that therapist adherence was positively associated with improved family cohesion and family functioning. In addition, higher levels of MST adherence on the part of the therapist were related to decreased delinquent peer affiliation.

STATUS OF THE COUPLE AND FAMILY THERAPY RESEARCH

The findings from these studies provide a substantial base for understanding the outcomes and mechanism of change in MFT. The research that produced these findings has grown in comprehensiveness, type, and quality when compared to the previous *Handbook* chapter. The following section contains a summary of the salient findings of the research that can inform practice, followed by an analysis of the research.

Practice Findings from the MFT Research

A number of conclusions can be drawn from the findings of both the CT and FT literature. With regard to CT:

1. Evidence could not be found on the majority of couple therapy treatments.
2. Those with enough evidence suggest that CT improves general marital distress/satisfaction in about 40% of treated couples. Improvements decline at followups that extend beyond six months. Despite these modest outcomes, treated couples, as a group, are better off than their nontreated peers. The degree of improvement seems to be similar to or somewhat smaller than that found in other treatment modalities (see Lambert and Ogles, this volume).
3. CT has not been studied as a primary treatment for most DSM disorders. However, there is some evidence suggesting it is effective for women who have depressive illness, although it is not more effective than individual therapy in most cases. Its effectiveness in treatment of sexual dysfunction is mixed.
4. Using CT as an adjunctive treatment in adults with alcohol and drug problems seems to enhance outcomes, especially at post-treatment. CT appears to be superior to individual therapy in about half the studies that were reviewed, but its superiority is not maintained at followup periods of one year.
5. The effectiveness of CT treatments seems to confirm the importance of premorbid adjustment as a predictor of outcome. In addition, better outcome is associated with reduction of blaming partner for problems, better alliance, and early agreement in process-outcome goals.
6. There is evidence to suggest that a limited number of CT treatments can be considered empirically supported treatments (EST). Baucom et al. (1998) applied the empirically supported treatment criteria developed by Chambless and Hollon (1998) to CT treatments and concluded that only three intervention programs met EVT/EST criteria. Of these, they classified behavioral marital therapy (BMT) and emotionally focused couple therapy (EFCT) as efficacious interventions for treating relationship distress.

With regard to FT:

1. Family therapy has been applied across a wide range of client disorders.
2. Despite numerous types of FT, only a few have undergone substantial study of outcome. Even fewer of those with outcome support have undergone process study.
3. Of those that have been studied, three models have substantial support in the treatment of specific disorders. FT models have had a substantial impact on conduct disorders and related problems of acting out (e.g., substance abuse). Adolescents with these problems show reductions in target behavior and improved family relations. The effect is impressive when one considers the difficulties encountered with samples commonly treated (delinquent youths, schizophrenic disorders) and the poor outcomes seen in control clients.
4. The positive effects found with conduct-disordered youth are most commonly found in systematic treatment programs with both outcome and process research.
5. The results of these treatments appear to be maintained in relation to treatment-as-usual control groups but have not been found to be superior to other alternative treatments.
6. The process literature in family therapy may also point to a common set of change mechanisms that might be operative in successful

family therapy. Treatment effects appear to be mediated by the therapist's ability to help the family redefine the presenting problem (shifting blame from the identified client) and solve impasses in family dynamics by shifting problem solving, reducing negativity within therapy sessions, and fostering improved communication. The therapeutic alliance was found to be an important mediator of outcome as is early structuring of treatment sessions.

7. There is evidence to suggest that some systematic family therapy models (e.g., MST, FFT) meet the criteria of empirically supported treatments. A "horse race" comparison of these models, where models are compared in a single study, has not been done.

Marital and Family Therapy Research

The current status of the MFT research is best summarized by considering three questions: (1) Is the research comprehensive enough to answer important and complex questions of clinical practice (clinical decisions, questions of policy, and resource allocation) and guide and direct future research? This question is answered by an analysis of the levels of evidence in MFT. (2) Is there a range of study types such that they are methodologically sound yet clinically relevant? (3) Is the research of high enough quality that we can have confidence in its results?

Comprehensiveness of the Research in MFT. The dimension of levels of evidence considers the specificity of the treatments, the problems/target outcomes of treatment, and the specificity of context in which those treatments and problems apply. The analysis shows that there is a range of evidence in MFT. Compared with the breadth of research in previous *Handbook* chapters, as already noted, this is a change for the MFT literature, reflecting a move toward more specific levels of evidence. The levels of specificity do, however, differ significantly between couple therapy and family therapy. Family therapy provides more specific, more contextual, and broader evidence to guide clinical practice. It is also important to note the missing cells. On the one hand, some cells received attention in the past and are no longer relevant for the field (e.g., nonspecific models with nonspecific problems). On the other hand, some empty cells represent areas in which research has not and is not being done. For example, from this analysis it seems that CT, and to a lesser extent FT, research has yet to move its research to the level of specificity of model, problem, and context. Thus, although the current research does have the potential to provide valuable guidance, it is currently limited in its ability to provide specific answers to "local" or ideographic questions of the clinician.

Types of Studies. Our review of the literature identified 7 meta-analyses and 82 couple and family therapy efficacy, effectiveness, and process to outcome studies published since the last *Handbook* chapter. Of those 43% focused on process-outcome connections, 38% were effectiveness studies and 15% were efficacy studies. These totals reflect a significant departure from past research literature and an increased emphasis on studying treatments in actual clinical settings. Significant attention was also given to process studies. There were also significant differences between CT and FT in regard to the range of study types. CT remains more focused on nonspecific models, nonspecific problems, or nonspecific context and is less likely than FT to study mechanism of change.

Quality of the Research. The studies reviewed have a wide range of research quality (see Table 13.6). We counted the studies according to whether they used random assignment, had adequate sample size, utilized measures of treatment fidelity, and included measures of clinical significance in regard to change. Although this is not a complete list of quality indices, it does represent the most basic, identifiable dimensions for good clinical research. It is encouraging to see the extent to which important elements of clinical research have been included in the study of MFT. Numerous studies included measures of clinical significance in their interpretation of the findings (n = 17, 22.0% of total clinical studies). Most studies used random assignment (n = 39; 51.3% of total clinical studies). In regard to the integrity of the treatment, a wide range of methods were used. The encouraging news is that of the 76 clinical studies, over 90% (n = 69) included some measure of treatment integrity. Fifteen of these studies relied on an extensive array of treatment integrity measures, including a manual, supervision, adherence checks, and therapist training. Most studies still considered very small sample sizes and consequently had low power to detect differences within and between groups.

TABLE 13.6 Frequency of Efficacy and Effectiveness Studies Incorporating Various Research Quality Dimensions

	Couple Therapy		Family Therapy	
Research Quality Dimensions	**Efficacy Studies**	**Effectiveness Studies**	**Efficacy Studies**	**Effectiveness Studies**
Random assignment	3	8	8	20
Clinical significance outcomes	3	3	5	6
Treatment integrity measure				
Manual	1	6	3	10
Training	0	1	4	9
Adherence	1	0	1	5
Supervision	1	3	1	6
All methods	2	2	1	6
No methods	0	1	2	4
Sample size				
<10	0	1	0	0
<20	0	0	3	0
<30	2	1	0	2
<50	2	3	1	5
<75	0	3	2	1
<100	0	2	0	1
>100	0	0	2	12

CONCEPTUAL AND METHODOLOGICAL ISSUES

Despite the impressive accumulation of MFT research, there continues to be a need for conceptual and methodological specification of the treatments, outcomes, and quality of MFT research. These limitations are not new or unexpected but instead represent challenges by a field of research attempting to capture the complex process of relational change in clinical settings. Next we discuss these limitations and make recommendations for MFT research based on the findings of the review and the clinical studies identified.

1. *Expand the range of treatments studied.* There was a relatively narrow range of treatments studied, particularly in couple therapy. Including more treatments in the MFT research literature would be of value to clinicians, researchers, and the profession. As noted by Alexander and Barton (1995), without a more inclusive research agenda, the evidence-based literature would remain irrelevant to many clinicians. A more inclusive research agenda would also benefit researchers by expanding our understanding of different treatments, the potential differences in treatments, and the mechanisms by which those treatments work.

2. *Expand the clinical problems to which couple and family treatments are applied.* Our review identified what seem to be two very different approaches to the treatment of specific clinical problems. Couple therapy developed models of treatment for broad clinical problems (e.g., marital distress) that are just now being applied to the specific clinical problems presented by clients (e.g., depression, alcohol and drug abuse). To date, the range of problems to which the major models of CT intervention have been applied is quite limited. Our guess is that by specifying the treatment first, it can be conceptually difficult to expand that treatment to address relational processes not initially anticipated or identified as treatment objectives. Family therapy began with specific problem areas and developed integrative treatments thought to be effective in treating specific problems. Those treatments are now being extended to other similar clinical problems that are part of the comorbid nature of certain disorders (e.g., conduct disorder and drug abuse). This approach has yielded a broader range of problems to which family treatments apply. It may be that

developing models of treatment around a cluster of clinical problems from the outset enhances the applicability of approaches. We suggest that future treatment model development follow the lead of family therapy and set the treatment x clinical problem level of specificity as the most basic level of evidence accepted.

3. *Expand the heterogeneity of clinical problems studied.* By definition, efficacy studies limit the heterogeneity of the client problem in order to decrease error variance. Unfortunately, this also reduces the clinical relevance of the findings. MFT, particularly couple therapy, needs to expand the heterogeneity of the problems of clients under study. Clients with co-occurring and comorbid disorders should be included rather than excluded from studies in order to approximate actual community samples. Family therapy studies of delinquent and conduct-disordered youth are a good example of the way in which heterogeneity can be used to enhance clinical relevance and to understand moderators and mechanisms of successful treatment.

4. *Increase the study of relationship outcomes.* Too few CT or FT investigations have studied relationship system outcomes. The study of relationship change is difficult and many times does not fit within the parameters of traditional research design. However, without a relational focus, changes in certain symptoms and the determination of clinical significance may become more difficult to understand and operationalize. For example, CT remains focused on relationship distress, satisfaction, and adjustment as its most common outcome measure. Unfortunately, it is difficult to know what changes in marital satisfaction and adjustment may mean. In some cases, marital distress that leads to divorce may not be negative outcomes, while in other cases they are. In family therapy the reduction of symptoms in an adolescent may actually be accompanied by increases in individual symptoms in a parent. Friedlander and Tuason (2000) suggest moving to a "problem" rather than a symptom focus that would consider relationship patterns and ideographic concerns. To move in this direction, instruments would need to be developed to look at communication patterns, in a systematic way that many researchers could share. Understanding the different domains, the different perspectives, and the relational connection between couples and families is critical if clinical change in MFT patients is to be clearly measured.

5. *Study the relationship between the proximal outcomes of some measure of relationship functioning (e.g., communication improvements) and more distal outcomes (e.g., relationship satisfaction, effective parenting).* This problem is compounded by the use of nomothetic, *a priori*, and external operationalization of outcome rather than idiosyncratic ones. These difficulties have led to difficulty in determining the operational definition of successful treatment. The problems of adequate operational definitions of therapeutic success and outcome are not unique to MFT. The solution may lie in clearer articulation of proximal and distal outcome goals of particular treatment programs based on notions of relationship functioning rather than particular states of existence. This would allow for client-specific and model congruent outcomes.

6. *Study systematic interventions programs.* The existence of specific, systematic, and integrated intervention models that incorporate the common factors of successful therapy while providing clinical direction and strong research support is a strength of MFT. Despite the fact that meta-analyses find no difference between "schools" of therapy, clinical trial studies and research reviews suggest that when specific client problems are considered, all models are not equal. In fact, the qualitative reviews conducted of empirical research and evaluation projects in real-world settings suggest that only a select and specific set of FT treatments models have been demonstrated to be successful in the treatment of some clinical problems, including adolescent externalizing behavior problems (conduct disorder) and adolescent drug abuse. These findings are not a surprise given that most meta-analytic studies mix levels of evidence that are likely to obscure differences that do occur. Identifying a range of successful programs for specific problems is a more important and more inclusive outcome rather than the traditional "who is best" approach called for in many research circles. Studying specific therapeutic models allows practitioners and researchers to understand change at specific levels of evidence and thus integrate a clear set of therapeutic principles into process and outcome research. These models provide a framework for future research and practices that allow us to systematically move the knowledge of MFT forward.

7. *Expand the range, diversity, and type of client studied.* This is both a research and a treatment issue. Our review found that most participants in

CT research were white, middle class, heterosexual, and came from mainstream cultures and ethnic groups. Few, if any, CT studies have included large samples of ethnic minority couples. From a research perspective, this is clearly not a random sample of the population. As a result, it is currently unclear whether successful CT interventions can be expected to offer the same benefits to clients with other cultural backgrounds. (See Chapter 17, this volume, for a more complete discussion of this issue.) There is an apparent gender bias in the study and treatment of certain clinical problems. For example, most studies of CT and the treatment of alcohol or schizophrenia are based on male clients; studies of the treatment of depression tend to be on women. At the present time, it is difficult to generalize results anywhere except to the limited gender representation in the studies. Family therapy research has done a better job of studying diverse populations.

8. *Increase the statistical power of MFT studies.* The current MFT research is based on small sample sizes. With small sample sizes statistical power is low, and it becomes very difficult to identify treatment differences of any kind. As a result, we may be making numerous type II errors and not finding differences between treatment approaches that do exist. According to Kazdin and Bass (1989), power can be increased by "selecting homogeneous sets of patients, ensuring the integrity of treatment, standardizing the assessment conditions, carefully choosing outcome measures and similar practices" (p. 145). Unfortunately, some of these practices result in reduced clinical utility. Power is also improved by increasing sample size. Wesley and Waring (1996) suggest a power level of 0.80 to protect against acceptance of the null hypothesis. That power level would require the study to have 63 families or couples per group in order to detect a medium effect size of 0.50. Sample sizes this large are likely only in community-based effectiveness research.

9. *Expand the scope of process studies to include additional moderators and mediators of change.* Expanding the range of moderator variables helps match treatments to clients and to inform treatments about necessary proximal treatment goals. Whisman and Snyder (1997) suggest that a better understanding of moderators and mediators would allow a "capitalization" approach in which the skills and relational style of the couple are matched to a specific change mechanism or treatment model. Once again, the family literature has been somewhat more successful than the couple research in identifying the factors that may moderate therapeutic interventions. However, both literatures have yet to adequately identify the risk factors that might impede even the most powerful therapeutic interventions. When this work is done, it is usually in the area of preexisting client variables. Though interesting, these moderating factors are not changeable and thus might provide us with limited information regarding how to improve therapeutic outcomes. If we can identify changeable moderators, it will be important because they could become early treatment goals. A particularly important moderator variable that has yet to be studied is the way in which treatments are delivered. Without attention to this area we may be unable to improve the way therapy is delivered. Understanding moderators of successful interventions can also help match treatments to clients.

10. *Study treatment implementation.* As MFT treatments move into community settings, a new type of translational research has become important. Community-based studies by the Surgeon General (2001) and the Center for the Study and Prevention of Violence (Elliott, 1997) suggest that effective treatment intervention programs are not useful unless they can be successfully replicated in community settings. Replication requires treatment manuals, systematic intervention programs, systematic and comprehensive training, and treatment adherence and monitoring to be successful (Sexton & Alexander, 2002). Research into the principles that may guide implementation is in its infancy, and we suggest it is the most important future challenge of MFT research and practice.

The Challenge of the Future: Adopting and Investigating Evidence-based Practice

The era of MFT research reviewed here is different from that seen by previous *Handbook* chapter authors. The field has moved well beyond questions of "Does MFT work?" and even beyond questions of which "school" of therapy is best. Instead, the field, as represented in its research, has now matured to the point where there are a number of long-term systematic research programs investigating well-articulated models of practice that have accumulated efficacy, effectiveness, and process research. The research reviewed here is both useful and credible. As a useful guide, the research can help answer many of the clinical questions of practitioners, the policy questions of administrators, and the resource allocation questions of communities and agencies. As a credible knowledge base, it is comprehensive in its scope, specific in its levels of evidence, and of high methodological quality. As a comprehensive research-based profession, MFT can, in some cases, provide specific levels of evidence that inform the treatment x problem x content decisions called for by many (Alexander et al., 1994).

Despite the advances in MFT research, certain methodological and conceptual challenges, as well as knowledge limitations, need to be addressed. These challenges are to be expected given that MFT is a dynamic field in which the fundamental questions of clinical change evolve and new research questions and methodological dilemmas arise. However, the persistence of the research-practice schism suggests that even a comprehensive and evolving knowledge base may be only one of the steps necessary to unify research and practice. Unification also requires an appreciation that research and practice are different routes to the same end—dialectic—"different sides of the same coin."

We suggest that the systematic and evidence-based practices evolving in MFT offer a bridge, with the potential to unite research and practice on a foundation of theoretically sound clinical models and valid and reliable scientific knowledge. Models like behavioral couple therapy, emotionally focused couple therapy, functional family therapy, and multisystemic therapy (among others) have demonstrated effectiveness for a wide range of clients with various clinical problems and can be replicated in local communities. Each has articulated change mechanisms and at least some degree of supporting process research. In addition, because of their systematic nature, they lend themselves to research and have become and probably will remain the primary focus of clinical research studies. Many of these models of practice are systematic enough that they may meet the test of any of the current criteria of "best practices" or empirically supported treatment. These models also have the opportunity for widespread adoption as many communities, funding agencies, and service providers are moving toward mandating and requiring "best practices" with demonstrated outcomes.

Embracing the research and practice opportunities available, current and future models will, however, require researchers and practitioners to change. For MFT researchers, this step may require rethinking traditional models of developing and researching these and other models of practice. Research will need to move toward more specific levels of evidence that is most likely gained through effectiveness research rather than efficacy research. To make this shift, effectiveness research will need to be viewed as an alternative and legitimate pathway for establishing treatment programs rather than a second step or a "less than perfect" choice that either follows or substitutes for a randomized clinical trial. Such a step may require that other types of research (e.g., community effectiveness research) join the randomized clinical trial as the new "gold standard" of intervention research in MFT. Clinical research may even need to take further steps toward individualized study of change by adopting models like the "progress research" approach suggested by Pinsof and Wynne (2000). It requires programs of systematic research that follow model-specific lines of questions over time. Despite an impressive start, researchers have yet to provide a substantive body of research that impacts MFT treatments (in specific contexts) such that individual clinicians can use the evidence-based knowledge for the programmatic and clinical decisions they must make. For the practice community, the biggest challenge will come in the acceptance and adoption of the systematic change models as the primary lens of clinical decision making (Sexton & Alexander, 2000). Moving from therapist-based to model-based clinical decision making is an enormous shift, which in many ways is in opposition to the decades of training and practice in the field of MFT.

References

Alexander, J. F. (1973). Defensive and supportive communications in normal and deviant families *Journal of Consulting and Clinical Psychology, 40,* 223–231.

Alexander, J. F., & Barton, C. (1995). Family therapy research. In R. Mikesell, D., Lusterman, S., McDaniel (Eds.), *Integrating family therapy: Handbook of family psychology and systems Theory.* Washington DC: American Psychological Association.

Alexander, J. F., Holtzworth-Monroe, A., & Jameson, P. (1994). The process and outcome of marital and family therapy: Research review and evaluation. In A. E. Bergin & S. L. Garfield (Eds.), *Handbook of Psychotherapy and Behavior Change* (pp. 594–630). New York: John Wiley & Sons.

Alexander, J. J., Robbins, M. S., & Sexton, T. L. (2000). Family-based interventions with older, at-risk youth: From promise to proof to practice. *Journal of Primary Prevention (42)*, 185–205.

Alexander, J. F., Robbins, M., & Sexton, T. (2001). The developmental evolution of Family Therapy. In H. A. Liddle, D. Santisteban, R. Levant, & J. Bray (Eds.), *Family Psychology Intervention Science.* Washington, DC: American Psychological Association.

Alexander, J. F., & Sexton, T. L. (in press). Functional Family Therapy as an integrative, mature clinical model for treating high risk, acting out youth. Wiley Series in Couple and Family Dynamics and Treatment, *Comprehensive Handbook of Psychotherapy, Volume IV: Integrative Therapies* (J. Lebow, Ed.).

Allgood, S. M., Parham, K. B., Salts, C. J., & Smith, T. A. (1995). The association between pretreatment change and unplanned termination in family therapy. *American Journal of Family Therapy, 23(3)*, 195–202.

Alvarado, R., Kendall, K., Beesley, S., & Lee-Cavaness, (2000). *Strengthening America's families: Model family program for substance abuse and delinquency prevention.* Washington, DC: Office of Juvenile Justice and Delinquency Prevention.

Anderson, C., Hogarty, G., & Reiss, D. (1986). *Schizophrenia and the family.* New York: Guilford Press.

Aniol, J. C., & Snyder, D. K. (1997). Differencial assessment of financial and relationship distress: Implications for couples therapy. *Journal of Marital and Family Therapy, 23(3)*, 347–352.

Aos, S., & Barnoski, R. (1998). *Watching the bottom line: Cost-effective interventions for reducing crime in Washington.* Washington State Institute for Public Policy: RCW 13.40.500.

Azrin, N. H. (1976). Improvements in the community-reinforcement approach to alcoholism. *Behavior Research and Therapy, 14*, 339–348.

Bakely, J. (1996). Couples therapy outcome research: A review. In B. J. Brothers et al. (Eds.), *Couples and change* (pp. 83–94). New York: Haworth Press.

Barbera, T. J., & Waldron, H. B. (1994). Sequential analysis as a method of feedback for family therapy process. *The American Journal of Family Therapy, 22(2)*, 156–163.

Barton, C., & Alexander, J. F. (1981). Functional family therapy. In A. Gurman and D. Kniskern (Eds.), *Handbook of family therapy* (pp. 403–443). New York: Brunner/Mazel.

Baucom, D. H., & Epstein, N. (1990). *Cognitive behavioral marital therapy.* New York: Brunner/Mazel.

Baucom, D. H., & Lester, G. W. (1986). The usefulness of cognitive restructuring as an adjunct to behavioral marital therapy. *Behavior Therapy, 17*, 385–403.

Baucom, D. H., Shoham, V., Mueser, K. T., Daiuto, A. D., & Stickle, T. R. (1998). Empirically supported couple and family interventions for marital distress and adult mental health problems. *Journal of Consulting and Clinical Psychology, 66*, 53–88.

Beach, S. R., Fincham, F. D., & Katz, J. (1998). Marital therapy in the treatment of depression: Toward a third generation of therapy and research. *Psychology Review, 18(6)*, 635–661.

Beach, S.R.H., Sandeen, E. E., & O'Leary, K. D. (1990). *Depression in marriage: A model for etiology and treatment.* New York: Guilford Press.

Beardslee, W. R., Hoke, L., Wheelock, I., Rothberg, P. C., van de Velde, P., & Swatling, S. (1992). Initial findings on preventive intervention for families with parental affective disorders. *American Journal of Psychiatry, 149(10)*, 1335–1340.

Beardslee, W. R., Salt, P., Porterfield, K., Rothberg, P. C., Van de Velde, P., Swatling, S., Hoke, E., Moilanen, D. L., & Wheelock, I. (1993). Comparison of preventive interventions for families with parental affective disorder. *Journal of the American Academy of Child and Adolescent Psychiatry, 32*, 254–263.

Beardslee, W. R., Versage, E. M., Wright, E. J., & Salt, P. (1997). Examination of preventive interventions for families with depression: Evidence of change. *Development and Psychopathology, 9(1)*, 109–130.

Beardslee, W. R., Wright, E., Rothberg, P. C., Salt, P., & Versage, E. (1996). Response of families to two preventive intervention strategies: Long-term differences in behavior and attitude change. *Journal of the American Academy of Child and Adolescent Psychiatry, 35*, 774–782.

Beck, A. T. (1976). *Cognitive therapy and the emotional disorders.* New York: International Universities.

Beck, A. T., Rush, A. J., Shaw, B. F., et al. (1979). *Cognitive therapy of depression.* New York: Guilford Press.

Birmaher, B., Brent, D. A., Kolko, D. Baugher, M., Bridge, J., Holder, D., Iyengar, S., & Ulloa, R. E. (2000). Clinical outcome after short-term psychotherapy for adolescents with major depressive disorder. *Archives of General Psychiatry, 57(1)*, 29–36.

Bischoff, R. J., & McBride, A. (1996). Client perceptions of couples and family therapy. *The American Journal of Family Therapy, 24(2)*, 117–128.

Borduin, C. M., Henggeler, S. W., Blaske, D. M., & Stein, R. (1990). Multisystemic treatment of adolescent sexual offenders. *International Journal of Offender Therapy and Comparative Criminology, 34*, 105–113.

Borduin, C. M., Mann, B. J., Cone, L. T., Henggeler, S. W., Fucci, B. R., Blaske, D. M., & Williams, R. A. (1995). Multisystemic treatment of serious juvenile offenders: Long-term prevention of criminality and violence. *Journal of Consulting and Clinical Psychology, 63(4)*, 569–578.

Bowlby, J. (1969). *Attachment and loss, Vol. 1, Attachment.* New York: Basic Books.

Bray, J. H., & Jouriles, E. N. (1995). Treatment of marital conflict and prevention of divorce. *Journal of Marital and Family Therapy, 21(4)*, 461–473.

Brent, D. A., Holder, D., Kolko, D., Birmaher, B., Baugher, M., Rothe, C., Iyengar, S., & Johnson, B. A. (1997). A clinical psychotherapy trial for adolescent depression comparing cognitive, family, and supportive treatments. *Archives of General Psychiatry, 54*, 877–885.

Brunk, M., Henggeler, S. W., & Whelan, J. P. (1987). A comparison of multisystemic therapy and parent training in the brief treatment of child abuse and neglect. *Journal of Consulting and Clinical Psychology, 55*, 311–318.

Butler, M. H., & Wampler, K. S. (1999). A meta-analytical update of research on the couple communication program. *American Journal of Family Therapy, 27(3)*, 223–237.

Carr, A. (2000). Evidence-based practice in family therapy and systemic consultation: I: Child-focused problems. *Journal of Family Therapy, 22(1)*, 29–60.

Catalano, R. F., Kosterman, R., Hawkins, J. D., Newcomb, M. D., & Abbott, R. D. (1996). Modeling the eitology of adolescent substance use: A test of the social development model. *Journal of Drug Issues, 26*, 429–455.

Chamberlain, P., & Rosicky, J. G. (1995). The effectiveness of family therapy in the treatment of adolescents with conduct disorders and delinquency. *Journal of Marital and Family Therapy, 21(4)*, 441–459.

Chambless, D. L., & Hollon, S. D. (1998). Defining empirically supported therapies. *Journal of Consulting and Clinical Psychology, 66*, 7–18.

Chernen, L., & Friedman, S. (1993). Treating the personality disordered agoraphobic patient with individual and marital therapy: A multiple replication study. *Journal of Anxiety Disorders, 7(2)*, 163–177.

Christensen, A., & Heavey, C. L. (1999). Interventions for couples. *Annual Review of Psychology, 50*, 165–190.

Christensen, A., Jacobson, N. S., & Babcock, J. C. (1995). Integrative behavioral couple therapy. In N. S. Jacobson & A. S. Gurman (Eds.), *Clinical handbook of couples therapy* (pp. 31–64). New York: Guilford Press.

Christensen, L., & Mendoza, J. L. (1986). A method of assessing change in a single subject: An alteration of the RC index. *Behavior Therapy, 17*, 305–308.

Christensen, L. L., Russell, C. S., Miller, R. B., & Peterson, C. M. (1998). The process of change in couples therapy: A qualitative investigation. *Journal of Marital and Family Therapy, 24(2)*, 177–188.

Cordova, J. V., Jacobson, N. S., & Christensen, A. (1998). Acceptance versus change interventions in behavioral couple therapy: Impact on couples' in-session communication. *Journal of Marriage and Family Counseling, 24(4)*, 437–455.

Coulehan, R., Friedlander, M. L., & Heatherington, L. (1998). Transforming narratives: A change event in constructivist family therapy. *Family Process, 37(1)*, 17–33.

Coupland, S. K., & Serovich, J. M. (1999). Effects of couples' perceptions of genogram construction of therapeutic alliance and session impact: A growth curve analysis. *Contemporary Family Therapy, 21(4)*, 551–572.

Craske, M. G., & Zoellner, L. A. (1995). Anxiety disorders: The role of marital therapy. In N. S. Jacobson, A. S. Gurman (Eds.), *Clinical handbook of couple therapy* (pp. 394–410). New York: Guilford Press.

Crowe, M. J., & Ridley, J. (1990). *Therapy with couples.* London: Blackwell.

Cuijpers, P. (1999). The effects of family interventions on relatives' burden: A meta-analysis. *Journal of Mental Health—UK, 8(3)*, 275–285.

de Jesus Mari, J., & Streiner, D. L. (1994). An overview of family interventions and relapse on schizophrenia: Meta-analysis of research findings. *Psychological Medicine, 24(1)*, 565–578.

de Kemp, R.A.T., & Van Acker, C. A. (1997). Therapist-parent interaction patterns in home-based treatments: Exploring family process. *Family Process, 36(1)*, 281–295.

DeMarsh, J., & Kumpfuer, K. L. (1986). Family-oriented interventions for the prevention of chemical dependency in children and adolescents. *Prevention, 18*, 117–151.

Diamond, G. M., Hogue, A., Liddle, H. A., Dakof, G. A. (1999). Alliance-building interventions with adolescents in family therapy: A process study. *Psychotherapy, 36(4)*, 355–367.

Diamond, G. S., & Liddle, H. A. (1996). Resolving a therapeutic impasse between parents and adolescents in multidimensional family therapy. *Journal of Consulting and Clinical Psychology, 64(3)*, 481–488.

Diamond, G. S., & Liddle, H. A. (1999). Transforming negative parent-adolescent interactions: From impasse to dialogue. *Family Process, 38(1)*, 5–26.

Diamond, G. S., Liddle, H. A., Hogue, A., & Dakof, G. A. (1999). Alliance-building interventions with adolescents in family therapy: A process study. *Psychotherapy, 36(4)*, 355–368.

Diamond, G. S., Serrano, A. C., Dickey, M., & Sonis, W. A. (1996). Current status of family-based outcome and process research. *Journal of the American Academy of Child and Adolescent Psychiatry, 35(1)*, 6–16.

Dixon, L. B., & Lehman, A. F. (1995). Family interventions for schizophrenia. *Schizophrenia Bulletin, 21*, 631–643.

Dunn, R. L., & Schwebel, A. I. (1995). Meta-analytic review of marital therapy outcome research. *Journal of Family Psychology, 9(1),* 58–68.

Edwards, M. E., & Steinglass, P. (1995). Family therapy treatment outcomes for alcoholism. *Journal of Marital and Family Therapy, 21(4),* 475–509.

Elliott, D. S. (1998). Editor's introduction: In D. Elliott (Series Ed.), *Book Three: Blueprints for violence prevention.* Golden, CO: Venture Publishing and Denver, CO: C & M Press.

Elliot, R. (1997). Therapy with remarried couples: A multitheoretical perspective. *Australian and New Zealand Journal of Family Therapy, 18(4),* 181–193.

Emanuels-Zuurveen, L., & Emmelkamp, P. M. (1996). Individual behavioural-cognitive therapy v. marital therapy for depression in maritally distressed couples. *British Journal of Psychiatry, 169(2),* 181–188.

Emmelkamp, P.M.G., ban der Helm, M., & MacGillavry, D. (1984). Marital therapy with clinically distressed couples: A comparative evaluation of system theoretic, contingency contracting and communication skills approaches. In K. Hahlweg & N. Jacobson (Eds.), *Marital interaction analysis and modification* (pp. 36–70). New York: Guilford Press.

Estrada, A. U., & Holmes, J. M. (1999). Couples' perceptions of effective and ineffective ingredients of marital therapy. *Journal of Sex and Marital Therapy, 25(2),* 151–162.

Estrada, A. U., & Pinsof, W. M. (1995). The effectiveness of family therapies for selected behavioral disorders of childhood. *Journal of Marital and Family Therapy, 21,* 403–440.

Falloon, I. Mueser, K., Gingerich, S. Rappaport, S., McGill, C., & Hole, V. (1988). *Behavioural family therapy: A workbook.* Buckingham, England: Buckingham Mental Health Services.

Falloon, I.R.H., Boyd, J. L., & McGill, C. W. (1982). Family management in the prevention of exacerbations of schizophrenia: A controlled study. *New England Journal of Medicine, 306,* 1437–1440.

Falloon, I.R.H., Boyd, J. L., & McGill, C. W. (1984). *Familycare of schizophrenia.* New York: Guilford Press.

Fals-Stewart, W., Birchler, G. R., & O'Farrell, T. J. (1996). Behavioral couples therapy for male substance-abusing patients: Effects on relationship adjustment and drug-using behavior. *Journal of Consulting and Clinical Psychology, 64(5),* 959–972.

Fals-Stewart, W., O'Farrell, T. J., & Birchler, G. R. (1997). Behavioral couples therapy for male substance-abusing patients: A cost outcomes analysis. *Journal of Consulting and Clinical Psychology, 65(5),* 789–802.

Feindler, E. L., & Ecton, R. B. (1986). *Adolescent anger control: Cognitive-behavioral techniques.* Elmsford, NY: Pergamon.

Fisch, R., Weakland, L., & Segal, L. (1982). *Tactics of change: Doing therapy briefly:* San Francisco: Jossey-Bass.

Fleischman, M. J., Horne, A. M., & Arthur, J. (1983). *Troubled families: A treatment program.* Champaign, IL: Research Press.

Freidlander, M., Heatherington, L., Johnson, B., & Skowron, E. A. (1994). Sustaining engagement: A change event in family therapy. *Journal of Counseling Psychology, 41,* 438–448.

Friedlander, M., & Tuason, M. T. (2000). Process and outcomes in couples and family therapy. In S. D. Brown & R. Lent (Eds.), *Handbook of counseling psychology* (pp. 797–824). New York: John Wiley & Sons.

Frieswyk, S. H. (1986). Therapeutic alliance: Its place as a process and outcome variable in dynamic psychotherapy research. *Journal of Consulting and Clinical Psychology, 54(1),* 32–38.

Frieswyk, S. H., Allen, J. G., Colson, D. B., Coyne, L., Gabbard, G. O., Horwitz, L., & Newsom, G. (1986). Therapeutic alliance: Its place as a process and outcome variable in dynamic psychotherapy research. *Journal of Consulting and Clinical Psychology, 54(1),* Special Issue: Psychotherapy Research, 32–38.

Geist, R., Heinmaa, M., Stephens, D., Davis, R., & Katzman, D. K. (2000). Comparison of family therapy and group psychoeducation in adolescents with anorexia. *Canadian Journal of Psychiatry, 45(2),* 173–178.

Goldman, A., & Greenberg, L. (1992). Comparison of integrated systemic and emotionally focused approaches to couples therapy. *Journal of Consulting and Clinical Psychology, 60(6),* 962–969.

Goldstein, M. J., & Miklowitz, D. J. (1995). The effectiveness of psychoeducational family therapy in the treatment of schizophrenic disorders. *Journal of Marital and Family Therapy, 21,* 361–376.

Goldstein, M. J., Rodnick, E. H., Evans, J. R., May, P. R. A., & Steinberg, M. R. (1978). Drug and family therapy in the aftercare of acute schizophrenics. *Archives of General Psychiatry, 43,* 633–642.

Gordon, D. A., Arbuthnot, J., Gustafson, K., & McGreen, P. (1988). Home-based behavioral systems family therapy with disadvantaged juvenile delinquents. *American Journal of Family Therapy, 16,* 243–255.

Gordon, D. A., Graves, K., & Arbuthnot, J. (1995). The effect of functional family therapy for delinquents on adult criminal behavior. *Criminal Justice and Behavior, 22(1),* 60–73.

Gray-Little, B., Baucom, D. H., & Hamby, S. L. (1996). Marital power, marital adjustment, and therapy outcome. *Journal of Family Psychology, 10(3),* 292–303.

Greenberg, L., & Johnson, S. (1988). *Emotionally focused therapy for couples.* New York: Guilford Press.

Griff, M. D. (1999). Intergenerational play therapy: The influence of grandparents in family systems. *Child and Youth Services, 20(1–2)*, 63–76.

Guerney, B. G. (1977). *Relationship Enhancement.* San Francisco: Jossey-Bass.

Gurman, A. S. (1971). Group marital therapy: Clinical and empirical implications for outcome research. *International Journal of Group Psychotherapy, 21(2)*, 174–189.

Gurman, A. S. (1973). Instability of therapeutic conditions in psychotherapy. *Journal of Counseling Psychology, 20(1)*, 16–24.

Gurman, A. S., & Kniskern, D. P. (1977). Enriching research on marital enrichment programs. *Journal of Marital and Family Therapy, 3(2)*, 3–11.

Gurman, A. S., & Kniskern, D. P. (1981). Family therapy outcome research: knowns and unknowns. *Handbook of family therapy* (pp. 742–746). New York: Bruner-Mazel.

Gurman, A. S., Kniskern, P. D., & Pinsof, W. M. (1986). Research on the process and outcome of marital and family therapy. In S. L. Garfield & A. E. Bergin (Eds.), *Handbook of psychotherapy and behavior change.* New York: John Wiley & Sons.

Hahlweg, K., & Markman, H. J. (1988). Effectiveness of behavioral marital therapy: empirical status of behavioral techniques in preventing and alleviating marital distress. *Journal of Consulting and Clinical Psychology, 56*, 440–477.

Hahlweg, K., & Weidemann, G. (1999). Principles and results of family therapy in schizophrenia. *European Archives of Psychiatry and Clinical Neuroscience, 249*(Suppl. 4), 108–115.

Halford, W. K., Sanders, M. R., & Behrens, B. C. (1993). A comparison of the generalization of behavioral marital therapy and enhanced behavioral marital therapy. *Journal of Consulting and Clinical Psychology, 61(1)*, 51–60.

Hampson, R. B., & Beavers, W. R. (1996). Measuring family therapy outcome in a clinical setting: Families that do better or do worse in therapy. *Family Process, 35(3)*, 347–361.

Hampson, R. B., & Beavers, W. R. (1996a). Family therapy and outcome: Relationships between therapist and family styles. *Contemporary Family Therapy, 18(3)*, 345–370.

Harrington, R. C., Kerfoot, M., Dyer, E., McNiven, F., Gill, J., Harrington, V., Woodham, A., & Byford, S. (1998). Randomized trial of a home based family intervention for children who have deliberately poisoned themselves. *Journal of the American Academy of Child and Adolescent Psychiatry, 37*, 512–518.

Hazelrigg, M. D., Cooper, H. M., & Borduin, C. M. (1987). Evaluating the effectiveness of family therapies: An integrative review and analysis. *Psychological Bulletin, 101*, 428–442.

Henggeler, S. W., Borduin, C. M., Melton, G. B., Mann, B. J., Smith, L. A., Hall, J. A., Cone, L., & Fucci, B. R. (1991). Effects of multisystemic therapy on drug use and abuse in serious juvenile offenders: A progress report from two outcome studies. *Family Dynamics of Addiction Quarterly, 1*, 40–51.

Henggeler, S. W., Melton, G. B., Brondino, M. J., Scherer, D. G., & Hanley, J. H. (1997). Multisystemic therapy with violent and chronic juvenile offenders and their families: The role of treatment fidelity in successful dissemination. *Journal of Consulting and Clinical Psychology, 65*, 821–833.

Henggeler, S. W., Melton, G. B., & Smith, L. A. (1992). Family preservation using multisystemic therapy: An effective alternative to incarcerating serious juvenile offenders. *Journal of Consulting and Clinical Psychology, 60(6)*, 953–961.

Henggeler, S. W., Melton, G. B., Smith, L. A., Schoenwald, S. K., & Hanley, J. H. (1993). Family preservation using multisystemic treatment: Long-term follow-up to a clinical trial with serious juvenile offenders. *Journal of Child and Family Studies, 2*, 283–293.

Henggeler, S. W., Pickrel, S. G., & Brondino, M. J. (1999). Multisystemic treatment of substance abusing and dependent delinquents: Outcomes, treatment fidelity, and transportability. *Mental Health Services Research, 1*, 171–184.

Henggeler, S. W., Pickrel, S. G., Brondino, M. J., & Crouch, J. L. (1996). Eliminating (almost) treatment dropout of substance abusing or dependent delinquents through home-based multisystemic therapy. *American Journal of Psychiatry, 153(3)*, 427–428.

Henggeler, S. W., Rodick, J. D., Borduin, C. M., Hanson, C. L., Watson, S. W., & Urey, J. R. (1986). Multisystemic treatment of juvenile offenders: Effects on adolescent behavior and family interactions. *Developmental Psychology, 22*, 132–141.

Henggeler, S. W., Rowland, M. D., Randall, J., Ward, D. M., Pickrel, S. G., Conningham, P. B., Miller, S. L., Zealberg, J. J., Hand, L. D., & Stanos, A. B. (1999). Home-based multisystemic therapy as an alternative to hospitalization of youths in psychiatiric crisis: Clinical outcomes. *Journal of the American Academy of Child and Adolescent Psychiatry, 38*, 1331–1339.

Henggeler, S. W., Schoenwald, S., & Pickrel, S. (1995). Multisystemic therapy: Bridging the gap between university and community-based treatment. *Journal of Consulting and Clinical Psychology, 5*, 709–717.

Hinshaw, S. (1994). *Attention deficits and hyperactivity in children.* Thousand Oaks, CA: Sage.

Hinshaw, S., Klein, R., & Abikoff, H. (1998). Childhood attention deficit hyperactivity disorder: nonpharmacological and combination approaches. In P. Nathan & J. Gorman (Eds.), *A Guide to treatments that work* (pp. 26–41). New York: Oxford University Press.

Hoffman, L. (1981). *Foundations of family therapy.* New York: Basic Books.

Horne, A. M., & Sayger, T. M. (1990). *Treating conduct and oppositional defiant disorders in children.* Elmsford, NY: Pergamon.

Horvath, A. O., & Symonds, B. D. (1991). Relation between working alliance and outcome in psychotherapy: A meta-analysis. *Journal of Counseling Psychology, 38(2),* 139–149.

Huey, S. J., Henggeler, S. W., Brondino, M. J., & Peckrel, S. G. (2000). Mechanisms of change in multisystemic therapy: Reducing delinquent behavior through therapist adherence and improved family and peer functioning. *Journal of Consulting and Clinical Psychology, 68(3),* 451–467.

Jacobson, N. S., & Addis, M. E. (1993). Research on couples and couple therapy: What do we know? Where are we going? *Journal of Consulting and Clinical Psychology, 61,* 85–93.

Jacobson, N. S., & Christensen, A. (1996). *Integrative couple therapy.* New York: W.W. Norton.

Jacobson, N. S., Christensen, A., Prince, S. E., Cordova, J., & Eldridge, K. (2000). Integrative behavioral couple therapy: An acceptance-based, promising new treatment for couple discord. *Journal of Consulting and Clinical Psychology, 68(2),* 351–355.

Jacobson, N. S., Follette, W. C., & Ravensdorf, D. (1984). Psychotherapy outcome research: Methods for reporting variability and evaluating clinical significance. *Behavior Therapy, 15,* 336–352.

Jacobson, N. S., & Gurman, A. S. (1995). *Clinical handbook of couple therapy.* New York: Guilford Press.

Jacobson, N. S., & Margolin, G. (1979). *Marital therapy: Strategies based on social learning and behavior exchange principles.* New York: Brunner/Mazel.

Johnson, S. M., & Greenberg, L. S. (1988). Relating process to outcome in marital therapy. *Journal of Marital and Family Therapy, 14,* 175–183.

Johnson, S. M., & Lebow, J. (2000). The "coming of age" of couple therapy: A decade review. *Journal of Marital and Family Therapy, 14,* 175–183.

Johnson, S. M., & Talitman, E. (1997). Predictors of success in emotionally focused marital therapy. *Journal of Marital and Family Therapy, 23(2),* 135–152.

Kazdin, A. E. (1997). Practitioner review: Psychosocial treatments for conduct disorder in children. *Journal of Child Psychology and Psychiatry, 38(2),* 161–178.

Kelley, A. B., & Halford, W. K. (1995). The generalisation of cognitive behavioural marital therapy in behavioural, cognitive and physiological domains. *Behavioural and Cognitive Psychotherapy, 23(4),* 381–398.

Klein, N., Alexander, J., & Parsons, B. (1997). Impact of family systems interventions on recidivism and sibling delinquency: A model of primary prevention and program evaluation. *Journal of Consulting and Clinical Psychology, 45,* 469–474.

Lawson, D. M., & Sivo, S. (1998). Trainees' conjugal family experience, current intergenerational family relationships, and the therapeutic alliance. *Journal of Marital and Family Therapy, 24(2),* 225–231.

Lebow, J. (1999). Building a science of couple relationships. *Family Process, 38(2),* 27–57.

Lebow, J., & Gurman, A. S. (1995). Research assessing couple and family therapy. *Annual Review of Psychology, 46,* 27–57.

Lewinsohn, P. M. (1975). The behavioral study and treatment of depression. In M. Hersen, R. M. Eisler, & P. M. Miller (Eds.), *Progress in behavior modification, Vol. I* (pp. 19–64). New York: Academic Press.

Liddle, H. A. (1995). Conceptual and clinical dimensions of a multidimensional, multisystems engagement strategy in family-based adolescent treatment (Special issue: Adolescent Psychotherapy). *Psychotherapy: Theory, Research, and Practice, 32,* 39–58.

Liddle, H. A. (1999). Theory development in a family-based therapy for adolescent drug abuse. *Journal of Clinical Child Psychology, 28(4),* 521–532.

Liddle, H. A., & Dakof, G. A. (1995). Efficacy of family therapy for drug abuse: Promising but not definitive. *Journal of Marital and Family Therapy, 21(4),* 511–543.

Liddle, H. A., Dakof, G. A., & Diamond, M. A. (1992). Adolescent substance abuse: Multidimensional family therapy in action. In E. Kauf & P. Kaufman (Eds.), *Family therapy of drug and alcohol abuse* (2nd ed.). Boston, MA: Allyn and Bacon.

Liddle, H. A., Santisteban, D., Levant, R., & Bray, J. (2001). *Family psychology intervention science.* Washington, DC: American Psychological Association.

Linszen, D., Dingemans, J., Van Der Does, J. W., Nutger, A., Scholte, P., Lenior, R., & Goldstein, M. J. (1996). Treatment, expressed emotion and relapse in recent onset schizophrenic disorders. *Psychological Medicine, 26,* 333–342.

MacPhee, D. C., Johnson, S. M., & van der Veer, M. M. (1995). Low sexual desire in women: The effects of marital therapy. *Journal of Sex and Marital Thearpy, 21(3),* 159–182).

Matthews, A., Whitehead, A., & Kellett, J. (1983). Psychology and hormonal factors in the treatment of female sexual dysfunction. *Psychological Medicine, 13,* 83–93.

McFarlane, W. R., Lange, A., & Pettigrew, T. F. (1990). Effectiveness of family therapy: A meta-analysis. *Journal of Family Therapy, 12(3),* 205–221.

McFarlane, W. R., Lukens, E., Link, B., Dushay, R., Deakins, S. A., Newmark, M., Dunne, E. J., Horen, B., Toran, J. (1995). Multiple-family groups and psychoeducation in the treatment of schizophrenia. *Arch General Psychiatry, 52(1),* 679–687.

Minuchin, S., & Fishman, H. (1981). *Family therapy techniques*. Cambridge, MA: Harvard University Press.

Montag, K. R., & Wilson, G. L. (1992). An empirical evaluation of behavioral and cognitive-behavioral group marital treatments with discordant couples. *Journal of Sex and Martial Therapy, 18(4)*, 255–272.

Montero, I., Asencio, A. P., Ruiz, I., & Hernandez, I. (1999). Family interventions in schizophrenia: An analysis of non-adherence. *Acta Psychiatrica Scandinavica, 100(2)*, 136–141.

Newell, R. M., Alexander, J. F., & Turner, C. W. (1996). The effects of therapist divert and interrupt on family members' reciprocity of negativity in delinquent families. Poster session presented at the Annual Convention of the American Family Therapy Academy, San Francisco, June.

Nutger, A., Dingemans, P., Van der Does, J. W., Linszen, D., & Gersons, B. (1997). Family treatment, expressed emotion and relapse in recent onset schizophrenia. *Psychiatry Research, 72(1)*. 23–31.

O'Farrell, T. J., Choquette, K. A., Cutter, H.S.G., Brown, E. D., & McCourt, W. F. (1993). Behavioral marital therapy with and without additional couples relapse prevention sessions for alcoholics and their wives. *Journal of Studies and Alcohol, 54*, 652–666.

O'Farrell, T. J., Choquette, K. A., Cutter, H.S.G., Brown, E. D., McCourt, W. F., Lowe, J., Chan, A., & Deneault, P. (1996a). Cost-benefit and cost-effectiveness analyses of behavioral marital therapy with and without relapse prevention sessions for alcoholics and their spouses. *Behavior Therapy*, 27, 7–24.

O'Farrell, T. J., Choquette, K. A., Cutter, H. S. G., Brown, E. D., McCourt, W. F., Lowe, J., Chan, A., & Deneault, P. (1996b). Cost-benefit and cost-effectiveness analyses of behavioral marital therapy as an addition to outpatient alcoholism treatment. *Journal of Substance Abuse, 8(2)*, 145–166.

Pinsof, W. M., & Catherall, D. R. (1986). The integrative psychotherapy alliance: Family, couple and individual therapy scales. *Journal of Marital and Family Therapy, 12(12)*, 137–151.

Pinsof, W. M., & Wynne, L. C. (1995). The efficacy of marital and family therapy: An empirical overview, conclusions, and recommendations. *Journal of Marital and Family Therapy, 21(4)*, 585–613.

Pinsof, W. M., & Wynne, L. C. (2000). Toward progress research: Closing the gap between family therapy practice and research. *Journal of Martial and Family Thearpy, 26(1)*, 1–8.

Quinn, W. H., Dotson, D., & Jordan, K. (1997). Dimensions of therapeutic alliance and their associations with outcome in family therapy. *Psychotherapy Research*, 7(4), 429–438.

Randolph, E. T., Eth, S., Glynn, S. M., Paz, G. G., Leong, G. B., Shaner, A. L., Strachan, A., Van Vort, W., Escobar, J. I., & Liberman, R. P. (1994). Behavioral family management in schizophrenia: Outcome of a clinic-based intervention. *British Journal of Psychiatry, 164*, 501–506.

Raytek, H. S., McCrady, B. S., Epstein, E. E., & Hirsch, L. S. (1999). Therapeutic alliance and the retention of couples in conjoint alcoholism treatment. *Addictive Behaviors, 24(3)*, 317–330.

Robbins, M. S., Alexander, J. F., Newell, R. M., & Turner, C. W. (1996). The immediate effect of reframing on client attitude in family therapy. *Journal of Family Psychology, 10(1)*, 28–34.

Robbins, M. S., Alexander, J. F., Turner, C. W. (2000). Disrupting defensive family interactions in family therapy with delinquent adolescents. *Journal of Family Psychology, 14(4)*, 688–701.

Robbins, M. S., Mitrani, V., Zarate, M., Coatsworth, D., & Szapocznik, J. (1996, June). Linking process to outcome in structural family therapy with drug using youth: An examination of the process of family therapy in successful and unsuccessful outcome cases. Paper presented at the 27th Annual meeting of the Society for Psychotherapy Research (SPR), Amelia Island, FL.

Robin, A. L., & Foster, S. L. (1989). *Negotiating parent-adolescent conflict: A behavioral family systems approach*. New York: Guilford Press.

Robin, A. L., Siegel, P. T., Koepke, T., Moye, A. W., & Tice, S. (1994). Family therapy versus individual therapy for adolescent females with anorexia nervosa. *Journal of Developmental and Behavioral Pediatrics, 15(2)*, 111–116.

Robin, A. L., Siegel, P. T., Moye, A. W., Gilroy, M., Dennis, A. B., & Sikand, A. (1999). A controlled comparison of family versus individual therapy for adolescents with anorexia nervosa. *Journal of the American Academy of Child and Adolescent Psychiatry, 38(12)*, 1482–1489.

Santisteban, D. A., Coatsworth, J. D., Perez, V. A., Mitrani, V., Jean-Gilles, M., & Szapocznik, J. (1997). Brief structural/strategic family therapy with African American and Hispanic high-risk youth. *Journal of Community Psychology, 25(5)*, 453–471.

Schmidt, S. E., Liddle, H. A., & Dakof, G. A. (1996). Changes in parenting practices and adolescent drug abuse during multidimensional family therapy. *Journal of Family Psychology, 10(1)*, 12–27.

Schoenwald, S. K., Henggeler, S. W., Brondino, & M. J., Rowland, M. D. (2000). Multisystematic therapy: Monitoring treatment fidelity. *Family Press, 39(1)*, 83–103.

Schooler, M. R., Keith, S. J., Severe, J. B., Matthews, S. M., Bellack, A. S., Click, I. D., Hargreaves, W. A., Kane, J. M., Ninan, P. T., Frances, A. Jacobs, M., Lieberman, J. A., Mance, R., Simpson, G. M., & Woerner, M. G. (1997). Relapse and rehospitalization during maintenance treatment of schizophrenia: The effects of dose reduction and family treatment. *Archives of General Psychiatry, 54,* 453–463.

Sexton, T. L., & Alexander, J. F. (2000). *Functional Family Therapy.* Juvenile Justice Bulletin. Washington DC: U.S. Department of Justice.

Sexton, T. L., & Alexander, J. F. (2002). Family-based Empirically Supported Interventions. *The Counseling Psychologist.*

Sexton, T. L., & Alexander, J. F. (2002). Functional family therapy: An empirically supported, family-based intervention model for of risk adolescents and their families. Wiley Series in Couples and Family dynamics and Treatment, *Comprehensive handbook of psychotherapy. Volume II: Cognitive/behavioral/functional* (T. Patterson, Ed.). New York: John Wiley & Sons.

Sexton, T. L., & Whiston, S. C. (1994). The status of the counseling relationship: An empirical review, theoretical implications, and research directions. *Counseling Psychologist, 22(1),* 6–78.

Sexton, T. L., Whiston, S. C., Bleuer, J. C., & Walz, G. R. (1997). *Integrating outcome research into counseling practice and training.* Alexandria, VA: American Counseling Association.

Shadish, W., Montgomery, L., Wilson, P., Wilson, M., Bright, I., & Okwumabua, T. (1993). Effects of family and marital psychotherapies: A meta-analysis. *Journal of Consulting and Clinical Psychology, 61,* 992–1002.

Shadish, W. R., Ragsdale, K., Glaser, R. R., & Montgomery, L. M. (1995). The efficacy and effectiveness of marital and family therapy: A perspective from meta-analysis. *Journal of Marital and Family Therapy, 21(4),* 345–360.

Simoneau, T. L., Miklowitz, D. J., Richards, J. A., Saleem, R., & George, E. L. (1999). Bipolar disorder and family communication: Effects of a psychoeducational treatment program. *Journal of Abnormal Psychology, 108(4),* 588–597.

Snyder, D. K., Mangrum, L. F., Wills, R. M. (1993). Predicting couples' response to marital therapy: A comparison of short- and long-term predictiors. *Journal of Consulting and Clinical Psychology, 61(1),* 61–69.

Stanton, M. D., & Shadish, W. R. (1997). Outcome, attrition, and family-couples treatment for drug abuse: A meta-analysis and review of the controlled, comparative studies. *Psychological Bulletin, 122(2),* 170–191.

Surgeon General. (2001). *Youth violence: A report of the Surgeon General.* Department of Health and Human Services. Washington, DC: US Government Printing Office.

Szapocznik, J., & Coatsworth, D. (1999). *An ecodevelopmental framework for organizing the influences on drug abuse: A developmental model of risk and protection.* In M. D. Glantz & C. R. Hartel (Eds.), Drug abuse: Origins & Interventions (pp. 331–366). Washington, DC: American Psychological Association.

Szapocznik, J., & Kurtines, W. (1989). *Breakthroughs in family therapy with drug abusing problem youth.* New York: Springer.

Szapocznik, J., Kurtines, W., Foote, F., Perez-Vidal, A., & Hervis, O. (1983). Conjoint versus one-person family therapy: Some evidence for the effectiveness of conducting family therapy through one person. *Journal of Consulting and Clinical Psychology, 51(6),* 889–899.

Szapocznik, J., Kurtines, W. M., Foote, F., Perez-Vidal, A., & Hervis, O. E. (1986). Conjoint versus one-person family therapy: Further evidence for the effectiveness of conducting family therapy through one person with drug-abusing adolescents. *Journal of Consulting and Clinical Psychology, 54(3),* 395–397.

Szapocznik, J., Perez-Vidal, A., Brickman, A. L., Foote, F. H., Santisteban, D. A., Hervis, O. E., & Kurtines, W. M. (1988). Engaging adolescent drug abusers and their families into treatment: A strategic structural systems approach. *Journal of Consulting and Clinical Psychology, 56,* 552–557.

Tarrier, N., Barrowclough, C., Porceddu, K., & Watts, S. (1988). The assessment of psychophysiological reactivity to the expressed emotion of the relatives of schizophrenic patients. *British Journal of Psychiatry, 152,* 618–624.

Waldron, H. (1997). Adolescent substance abuse and family therapy outcome: A review of randomized trials. In T. H. Ollendick & R. J. Prinz (Eds.), *Advances in Clinical Child Psychology,* Vol., 19 (pp. 199–234). New York: Plenum Press.

Waldron, H. B., Turner, C. W., Alexander, J. F., & Barton, C. (1993). Coding defensive and supportive communications: Discriminant validity and subcategory convergence. *Journal of Family Psychology, 7(2),* 197–203.

Waldron, H. B., Turner, C. W., Barton, C., Alexander, J. F., & Cline, V. B. (1997). Therapist defensiveness and marital therapy process and outcome. *American Journal of Family Therapy, 25(3),* 233–243.

Walker, J. G., & Johnson, S., Manion, I., & Cloutier, P. (1996). Emotionally focused marital intervention for couples with chronically ill children. *Journal of Consulting and Clinical Psychology, 64(5),* 1029–1036.

Walker, J. G., & Manion, I. G. (1991). Marital interactions and family coping in pediatric chronic illness: Assessment of needs. Paper presented at the Third Florida Conference on Child Health Psychology, Gainesville, FL.

Wampold, B. E., Lictenburg, J. W., & Waehler, C. A. (in press). Principles of empirically-supported interventions in counseling psychology. *The Counseling Psychologist.*

Wampold, B. E., Mondin, G. W., Moody, M., Stich, F., Benson, K., & Ahn, H. (1997). A meta-analysis of outcome studies comparing bona fide psychotherapies: Empirically "all must have prizes." *Psychological Bulletin, 122(3)*, 203–215.

Weisman, A. G., Okazaki, S., Gregory, J., Goldstien, M. J., & Miklowitz, D. J. (1998). Evaluating therapist competency and adherence to behavioral family management with bipolar patients. *Family Process, 37(1)*, 107–121.

Wesley, S., & Waring, E. M. (1996). A critical review of marital therapy outcome research. *Canadian Journal of Psychiatry, 41(7)*, 421–428.

Whisman, M. A., & Snyder, D. K. (1997). Evaluating and improving the efficacy of conjoint couple therapy. In W. K. Halford & H. J. Markman (Eds.), *Clinical handbook of marriage and couples interventions.* New York: John Wiley & Sons.

Wylie, K. R. (1997). Treatment outcome of brief couple therapy in psychogenic male erectile disorder. *Archives of Sexual Behavior, 26(5)*, 527–545.

Xiong, W., Phillips, M. R., Hu, X., et al. (1994). Family based intervention for schizophrenia patients in China: A randomized controlled trial. *British Journal of Psychiatry, 165*, 239–247.

Zimmerman, T. S., Prest, L. A., & Wetzel, B. E. (1997). Solution-focused couples therapy groups: An empirical study. *Journal of Family Therapy, 19(2)*, 125–144.

CHAPTER 14

SMALL-GROUP TREATMENT: EVIDENCE FOR EFFECTIVENESS AND MECHANISMS OF CHANGE

GARY M. BURLINGAME
Brigham Young University
K. ROY MACKENZIE
University of British Columbia
BERNHARD STRAUSS
Frederick Schiller University

Beginning group therapists face several challenges as they attempt to master the group psychotherapy literature. The first is a definitional conundrum. Extremely divergent models of treatment find their home under the rubric of group psychotherapy. For instance, the traditional North American psychotherapy group—reflected by Irvin Yalom's (1995) classic text—has been an important force in the literature for several decades. This genre of treatment gives emphasis to therapeutic properties that are unique to the group format. High value is placed on the interpersonal and interactional climate of the group, undergirded by the belief that the group is the vehicle of change and that member-to-member interaction is a primary mechanism of change (Fuhriman & Burlingame, 1990). This type of psychotherapy group is often referred to as a "process group" designated in part by the dynamic focus of the group on here-and-now (i.e., immediate group interaction) exchanges among group members.

Another type of group psychotherapy relies on a far more structured approach to guide in-session group activity. In contrast to the dynamic focus of process groups, preplanned session activities associated with specific change strategies characterize these group treatments. Cognitive and cognitive behavioral therapy (CBT) groups provide one example of these more structured group treatments. Here, session plans that focus on a specific change strategy (e.g., cognitive restructuring) guide in-session activities. Structured groups have typically evolved as an extension of a treatment initially developed for the individual format (e.g., CBT for major depression). This genealogy may explain why the unique properties of group are seldom incorporated into protocols of structured group treatments (Fuhriman & Burlingame, 1994).

A related challenge facing the beginning group therapist is a literature that "suffers with and is blessed by multiple origins" (Fuhriman & Burlingame, 1994, p. 6). Theoretical principles relating to the group format emanate not only from the clinical realm but also from personality theory, field theory, social psychology, and general systems theory. Existing models of patient change reflect nearly every psychotherapeutic approach. Moreover, multidisciplinary contributions, including psychiatry, psychology, social work, nursing, education, and organizational behavior, create a daunting number of publication venues for group research.

Thus, the imprint of the group psychotherapy literature is blurred by variegated definitions that have emerged from diverse theoretical sources. Expositions regarding the therapeutic forces operative in the group format come from traditional individual psychotherapeutic models and academic research that are outside the clinical arena. Collectively, these challenges can overwhelm beginning group therapists as they identify the major therapeutic influences of the group format and try to understand how they interrelate. This diversity is supported by the authors' collective experience of training group clinicians on two continents. To address these challenges, we propose a model of the multiple therapeutic influences operative in the group format (Figure 14.1). This model emerges from principles articulated in previous reviews of the group literature (Burlingame, Fuhriman, & Johnson, 2002; Fuhriman & Burlingame, 1994) and attempts to bridge the artificial gap that is often found between outcome and process studies. More often, reviews of group psychotherapy separately present and discuss studies within two groupings: those that test the efficacy or effectiveness of group treatment (outcome studies) and those that describe or predict theoretical mechanisms of change operative within the group (process studies). This separation often leaves the neophyte group therapist with no understanding of how to wed interventions drawn from formal change theories with those suggested by the process literature. The model proposed herein provides one way to organize and bring meaning to a literature that often feels conceptually and empirically disjointed.

Conceptualizing Group Treatments

A firm empirical foundation exists to support the general therapeutic effectiveness of group psychotherapy (Bednar & Kaul, 1994; Fuhriman & Burlingame, 1994; Burlingame, Ellsworth, Richardson, and Cox, 2000; Burlingame, Fuhriman & Mosier, in press). Accordingly, Figure 14.1 starts with these beneficial therapeutic effects at the top of the diagram and asks the question: What components of group treatment might explain observed patient benefits?

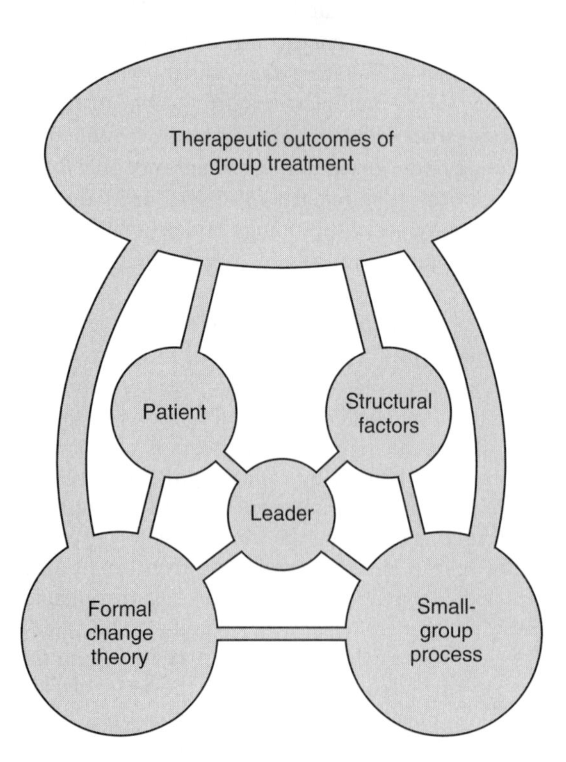

FIGURE 14.1 Forces that govern the therapeutic outcomes of group psychology.

The first major arena—*formal change theory*—encapsulates the majority of group therapy outcome studies that test either the general efficacy or differential efficacy of specific "brands" of group treatment. All of the major models of psychotherapy are present in the group treatment literature (e.g., psychodynamic, interpersonal, cognitive, behavioral, cognitive behavioral, humanistic, etc.). Equally important, the particular theoretical model is often applied in the same manner across treatment formats (i.e., individual and group). Tests of formal change theories are the most plentiful and straightforward aspect of the empirical literature and are summarized later in this chapter. Finally, with rare exception (e.g., process and psychodrama groups), formal change theories typically originate from the individual rather than group psychotherapy literature. The unidirectional transfer of formal change theories from the individual to group format explains why some have felt that group treatments have a "borrowed identity" when it comes to the principles underlying patient change (cf. Fuhriman & Burlingame, 1990; Kaul & Bednar, 1986).

The second arena—*principles of the small-group process*—reflects the unique features of the group format that have been theoretically or empirically related to patient outcome. These group-based principles offer a counterpoint to the concern regarding the "borrowed identity" of group therapy. However, the conceptual and empirical foundation of the small-group process principles has evolved in neither a linear nor a unified fashion and reflects the confluence of research from both clinical and nonclinical sectors (e.g., social psychology). Thus, mastery of this literature is no small undertaking since it is scattered across a host of publication venues.

Therapists who focus on small-group processes begin with an appreciation of the *group* as a noun and how its collective properties can have strong effects on members that extend well beyond those associated with the formal change theory. Examples of accepted small-group processes include group development, therapeutic factors, degree and timing of group structure, and interpersonal feedback. Leaders guided by small-group process principles understand that the therapeutic environment of the group is a potent and independent source of patient change. For instance, members who experience a greater sense of acceptance, belonging, and support from their group, regardless of formal change theory, typically report more post-treatment improvement (Burlingame et al., 2002). Moreover, since the group is an evolving entity, group process principles (e.g., timing of feedback) must be understood and differentially applied to potentiate this therapeutic environment over the life of the group. Group therapy is not merely individual therapy offered in the context of a group!

The nexus of the formal change and small-group process theories lies in the third force that governs the effectiveness of group treatment—*the group leader.* The independent effects of specific leader characteristics have been studied as they relate to small-group processes and outcomes. For instance, attributes such as warmth, openness, and empathy have been associated with more cohesive groups and better patient outcomes, essentially replicating the impact of nonspecific factors found in the individual literature (Burlingame, Fuhriman, & Johnson, 2002). More unique to the group format are studies of differences in leadership style. Unfortunately, definitive conclusions are often elusive since most studies hopelessly confound leader style with the specific interventions that formal theories of change dictate (Dies, 1994).

Nonetheless, the leader is the pivotal force in determining the degree to which the theoretical components of the formal change theory are thoughtfully integrated with small group process principles. This decision (reflected by the smaller lines in Figure 14.1) is fundamental to whether the group is used as a vehicle of change to enhance the active ingredients of the formal change theory or if the therapist will conduct individual therapy in a group setting without regard for the unique features of the group format (Fuhriman & Burlingame, 1994). Wilfley and colleagues (1998) provide an excellent example of how to systematically modify a formal change theory (interpersonal psychotherapy) from the individual to group format. They raise issues such as preserving effective change processes, patient and therapist roles, modification of techniques, and how change theory interventions relate to important group processes. Moreover, a byproduct of engaging in this process is a more careful articulation of the leader style that may be determined by the formal change theory (e.g., level of activity and directiveness) as well as parameters that might be independent (e.g., personal versus technical dimensions of leadership). This greater clarity can eliminate the confound between leadership style and interventions dictated by the change theory, but such thoughtful efforts are rare in research studies.

A fourth component associated with the effectiveness of group treatment is the *patient.* The identification of specific patient characteristics has held a primary position in formulations regarding those who improve or deteriorate in group treatment (Yalom, 1995). For instance, the basic skills of listening and the ability to understand, empathize, and help others have been shown to be important patient factors (Braaten, 1990; Trad, 1993). However, the sheer number of permutations when different groups of patients, treatment approaches, and therapists are combined has significantly limited our ability to arrive at empirically supported guidelines for ideal combinations. On the other hand, Piper (1994) persuasively argues that promising developments in group treatment are emerging from studies that test for interactions between patient characteristics and treatment model. As will become evident, the past decade has seen a slow accumulation of these studies.

The final parameter in understanding the impact of group treatment is *group structural factors.* Considerations such as treatment dosage (number and length of sessions), sequencing of sessions (weekly, monthly, bimonthly), size of the group, setting, and need for a co-leader are illustrative of this dimension. Structural features of a group can affect the durability of treatment effects. For instance, adding a booster session to a treatment protocol can significantly increase the long-term effects of group treatment.

The complexity of group treatment is the result of the interaction of forces depicted in Figure 14.1. For instance, structure will interact with group process (e.g., increased size will decrease member interaction), change strategies may compete with group process principles (e.g., in-depth individual exploration vs. shared floor time), and patient characteristics will interact with change strategies and therapist characteristics (e.g., highly resistant clients may do better with particular models and therapists). In short, the group format is comprised of multiple interactive parts and these multifaceted relationships change over the course of time.

Nevertheless, the complexity of the group format has not deterred its impact on clinical service delivery systems. There is growing evidence that the demand for group treatment in clinical practice may be increasing in North America (Cox, Ilfeld, Ilfeld, & Brennan, 1999; MacKenzie, 2001a; Taylor et al., 2001). This increase is undoubtedly due to its general efficacy and favorable cost-benefit ratio when compared to individual treatment (Heinzel, Breyer, & Klein, 1998). Within the context of these positive developments, coupled with the humility created by the complexity of the phenomena of group treatment, we enter into this review.

CHAPTER ORGANIZATION AND REVIEW APPROACH

This review includes studies published in both European and North American journals because significant differences exist between the modal groups on the two continents. The typical North American group is time-limited (10 to 12 sessions) and of homogeneous composition, whereas groups conducted abroad are long-term (sometimes six months to a year or more) and are composed of diagnostically heterogeneous patients. Long-term groups are a core part of the clinical practice in North America but are underrepresented in the empirical literature. Thus, findings from the European literature may be of particular import. This review also highlights theory-based programmatic research. Although isolated reports make up a significant portion of the empirical literature, a number of research teams have systematically explored outcome and process using well-articulated theoretical models. These teams receive special attention because their work exemplifies how significant advances can be made in the group literature. Finally, given space limitations, this review emphasizes high-quality studies or topics where an adequate number of papers (five or more) were available.

The efficacy and effectiveness literature is presented first, organized by treatments that address explicit psychiatric disorders (e.g., mood and schizophrenia) or medical disorders (e.g., cancer and HIV). Treatments for client populations that have received considerable empirical effort are also included (e.g., elderly and domestic violence). We then provide a model to assist the reader in understanding the process studies that explore mechanisms of change as well as predictors of in-session behavior or outcome. Since the frequent absence of important information significantly limits many of our conclusions, we provide a list of the minimal data needed to derive meaningful conclusions and to assist future replications. Finally, we provide recommendations regarding future effectiveness/efficacy research, mechanisms of change, and process research.

We conducted a computer search of PsychLit and Medline to identify outcome research using the search terms of group psychotherapy, group counseling, and group therapy. We then filtered citations with a health or mental health emphasis yielding 1,823 citations. Outcome studies that met the following criteria were included in the analysis: (a) empirical studies published between January 1990 and January 2001; (b) studies of treatment offered to clinically relevant populations; and (c) designs that used randomized assignment of patients to an active treatment or control condition, nonrandomized matched or wait list controls, or pre-post only (no control group). We excluded case studies as well as studies that (a) relied exclusively on unstandardized measures because findings from such are impossible to evaluate (cf. Burlingame, Lambert, Reisinger, Neff, & Mosier, 1995); (b) had small sample sizes ($n < 12$); (c) either did not use statistical procedures or used them inappropriately; (d) focused on self-help, mutual support, or 12-step programs—except when used as controls; and (e) had attrition rates that seriously compromised the meaning of findings.

After establishing the primary areas of outcome research, we returned to the literature to identify recent meta-analyses of treatment effectiveness that would extend findings beyond the coverage period and also provide a quantitative index on overall effectiveness. The final sample included 107 studies and 14 meta-analyses across six disorders (mood, anxiety, eating, substance abuse, personality, and psychotic) and four patient populations (elders, domestic violence, sexual abuse, and medical illness). A team composed of three advanced graduate students and the senior author rated the articles using a set of predetermined categories that have proved useful in previous reviews and meta-analyses (Burlingame, Fuhriman & Mosier, in press; Burlingame, Kircher, & Taylor, 1994; Hoag & Burlingame, 1997; McRoberts, Burlingame, & Hoag, 1998). Finally, we applied a modified version of the Periodic Health Examination classification system for rating the quality of evidence (Kusumakar et al., 1997), with the highest weight given to studies using random assignment, followed by matched control and pre-post only designs.

The manner in which groups were employed in the treatment of patients varied considerably, leading to the following organizational scheme for the outcome research. Papers classified under *group as the primary* include diagnostic groupings where a patient typically received no treatment beyond the group, or in some cases, group plus concurrent medication. Group treatment continues to be used as an augment for structured inpatient and outpatient treatment programs. If the patient participated in a multicomponent treatment regimen (individual, family, group, milieu therapy, and medication), the treatment was cataloged under *group as an augment.* There are a significant number of studies assessing the effectiveness of *group treatment for severe mental illness.* Although identical in form to the *group as an augment,* the chronicity of the disorders often dictates a very different group approach with this patient population. Finally, there continues to be a steady flow of studies published that test the differential effectiveness of the *individual versus group* format. Thus, we provide and discuss a compilation of recent meta-analyses that have explicitly tested this effect.

Evidence for Effectiveness of Group Treatment

Group versus Individual

The comparative effectiveness of the group versus individual format has been a continuing interest in the psychotherapy literature. Fuhriman and Burlingame (1994) reviewed seven meta-analyses that focused on this question and concluded that the majority report no differential effectiveness between the two modalities. They note that the two meta-analyses (Dush, Hirt, & Schroeder, 1983; Nietzel, Russell, Hemmings, & Gretter, 1987) that supported the superiority of individual therapy were primarily composed of studies that did not incorporate group process principles into treatment, but rather used group as a "convenient, cost effective, vehicle for the delivery of a treatment package originally designed for individual therapy" (Fuhriman & Burlingame, 1994, p. 16). Fuhriman and Burlingame argue that if the unique interactive properties of groups were left untapped, one would expect poorer outcomes in the group condition. Bretz, Heekerens, and Schmitz (1994) conducted the only meta-analyses addressing format differences based on the European literature and arrived at a different conclusion. Investigations were limited to effectiveness studies of Gestalt therapy. Reliable differences between formats were found with individual yielding the smallest pre-to-post-treatment gains (ES = .22) while group psychotherapy and personal growth groups produced the largest treatment gains (ES = .52 and .68, respectively).

The mixed findings from these two reviews are partially clarified by two recent reviews. McRoberts, Burlingame, and Hoag (1998) point out that all but one (Tillitski, 1990) of the seven meta-analyses included in the Fuhriman and Burlingame review failed to directly compare group and individual therapy within the same experiment. To address this concern, they conducted a meta-analysis of 23 outcome studies that directly compared the effectiveness of the individual and group therapy formats within the *same* study. Results were consistent with the majority of previous reports: the two modalities produced indistinguishable patient outcomes (ES = .01). It is important to note that both formats produced large pre-to-post treatment gains supporting the beneficial effects of each (ES group = .90; ES individual = .76).

In the most recent review of this question, Tschuschke (1999) summarized 22 controlled studies published between 1973 and 1999 that compared the effectiveness of group versus individual therapy. Half report no reliable differences between the two formats, five found individual therapy to be more effective, and six showed the opposite pattern. Interestingly, the few studies where group was more effective, used outcome measures that might be related to the specific benefits of the group modality (e.g., increase in social support for substance abuse patients). However, it is important to note that McRoberts et al. (1998) tested for these same effects and found no reliable aggregate difference.

At face value, the findings from multiple meta-analytic studies portray a very persuasive argument regarding the general equivalence of the two formats. In short, the aggregate message is that the literature does not support differential effectiveness between the two formats. On the other hand, the meta-analyses cited above often do not separately test for differential effectiveness of format by patient diagnosis. Even when these tests are conducted (e.g., McRoberts, Burlingame, & Hoag, 1998) the findings are limited since the number of studies in the most frequent categories seldom rises above three or four (e.g., chemical dependency and depression). Small sample sizes limit the power of a statistic to detect real differences, leading us to conclude that it is premature to accept the equivalence finding at the individual diagnosis level. Moreover, even if there were a sufficient number of studies, the reliability and uniformity of assigning patient diagnoses across studies would be essential to establish. Thus, we are left with a predicament. The collective evidence strongly supports the "no difference" conclusion in the aggregate but is weak with respect to format by diagnosis interactions. Since investigators continue to test for format differences across a variety of psychiatric disorders and treatment models, future research will undoubtedly shed further light on this point.

Group as Primary

The conclusion that group psychotherapy is potent enough to be the sole or primary treatment for patients suffering from a psychiatric disorder has emerged from three decades of research (Fuhriman & Burlingame, 1994). Reviews prior to the 1970s suggested that groups provided a strong complementary role to more robust therapists (typically individual or milieu). However, research in the 1970s and 1980s applied standardized treatment protocols, randomization, and control groups and led to far more optimistic estimates of the independent efficacy of the group format. In this section, group treatments that are used as primary treatment for six patient populations accrued enough empirical evidence throughout the 1990s to tender empirically based conclusions.

Mood disorders. Over a decade ago, the Robinson, Berman, and Neimeyer (1990) meta-analysis concluded that (1) depressed clients who were treated with a wide variety of treatment models (cognitive, cognitive behavioral, and general verbal) showed substantial improvement over untreated controls, (2) different treatment models were equivalent after controlling for experimenter allegiance, and (3) no differences in patient improvement were evident when the individual and group formats were compared. In many respects, these conclusions are replicated and extended by recent research (Table 14.1). Specifically, significant pre-post treatment improvement was evident when the active treatment conditions were compared with wait list controls (Burlingame & Barlow, 1996; Kuhns, 1997; Murphy, 1997; Scott & Stradling, 1990). No differential effectiveness was found for cognitive behavioral, process/interactional, and mutual support groups (Bright, Baker, & Neimeyer, 1999; Kuhns, 1997). The group and individual formats appear equivalent (Scott & Stradling, 1990). If the findings from the past decade of group research ended here, the main conclusion would be that the Robinson, Berman, and Neimeyer findings were supported and extended to different patient populations (e.g., depressed primary care patients). However, further meaning is evident when this research is viewed through the putative forces operative in group treatment (Figure 14.1).

Nearly half (5) of the mood studies (Table 14.1) tested formal change theories that do not appear to incorporate group process principles. For patients suffering from major depression, cognitive behavioral therapy (CBT) was found to produce reliable pre-to-post treatment gains (Peterson & Halstead, 1998) and proved to be more effective than manualized Gestalt group treatment (Beutler et al., 1991, 1993). No differential effectiveness was found for cognitive therapy by treatment format (group or individual), although patients in both active treatments demonstrated significantly more improvement than wait list controls (Scott & Stradling, 1990). Tests of the combined and independent effects of medication and CBT are mixed. Stravynski and colleagues (1994) found that imipramine did not enhance the therapeutic effects of group CBT, while Ravindran et al. (1999) reported that group CBT alone was not significantly more effective than the placebo in reducing symptoms of dysthymia, nor did it enhance the effectiveness of sertraline.

Together, these studies support the efficacy of group CBT models that do not formally include group process principles for patients suffering from mood disorders (i.e., major depression and dysthymia). Further confidence in this conclusion comes from the quality of the designs (i.e., three used random assignment to comparison condition) and adequate sample size (average n is nearly 90 patients/study). Less clarity is evident for the efficacy of CBT when compared to medication. The Ravindran et al. (1999) study is methodologically stronger (i.e., sample size and double-blind procedure), and its findings are in agreement with past reviews (Dush, Hirt, & Schroeder, 1983; McRoberts, Burlingame, & Hoag, 1998; Nietzel, Russell, Hemmings, & Gretter, 1987). On the

TABLE 14.1 Summary of Group as Primary Studies by Patient Population

	Study	Patient Characteristics[a]	Treatment Description[b]	Study Characteristics[c]	Results[d]
Mood Disorders	Bright et al. (1999) Ravindran et al. (1999) Peterson & Halstead (1998) Kuhns (1997) Murphy (1997) Burlingame & Barlow (1996) McNamee et al. (1995) Stravynski et al. (1994) Konen et al. (1992) Beutler et al. (1991, 1993) Robinson et al. (1990) Scott & Stradling (1990)	n = 1051, 63% solicited; Major depression (66%). Grief (25%), and dysthynia (9%); female (65%) avg. 40 years of age (18–54); outpatient (82.4%) primary care (10%) and inpatient (7.6%)	Closed membership, 10 sessions (6–15) avg. 90-minutes (30–120); CT & CBT (7), PS & PE (4), P-IG (3), MSG (3), I (1); GPP (5)	69 studies: MA (58), RAAT (3), RAWC (4), PPWC (1), & PPNC (3); Avg. attrition for therapy (n = 6) 20% (0–38), and f/u (n = 3) 15.5% (0–35), Avg. length of f/u (n = 8) 9 months (3–18)	Mixed 0 (4), +(3), ++(4)
Panic Disorders	Martinsen et al. (1998) Oei et al. (1997) Telch et al. (1995) Lidren et al. (1994) Telch et al. (1993) Scheibe et al. (1993)	n = 475, 55% solicited, 23% referred, 22% archival; Panic disorder with (93%) or without agorophobia (7%); female (72%) avg. 35 years of age (17–65); some samples (2) had patients on medication (39–50+%); COD ranged from 3 to 8 years.	Primarily closed membership, 11 sessions (8 sessions to 1 year) avg. 90 minutes (75 min.-4 hours); CBT (4), ST (1), BBT (1), P-IG (1); GPP (1)	6 studies: RAWC (3), PPNC (3); Avg. attrition for therapy (n = 5) 5.8% (0–15) and f/u (n = 2) 12.5% (6–19); Avg. length of f/u (n = 4) 15 months (6–38)	Good + (3), ++ (3)
OCD	Van Noppen et al. (1998) Van Noppen et al. (1997) Fals-Stewart et al. (1993) Enright (1991) Krone et al. (1991)	n = 286 all referred; female (64%) avg. 33.5 years of age (31–38); COD 11 years (6.6–19)	Closed membership; 12 sessions (7–24) avg. 120 minutes (90–120); BT (4), MFG (1), I (1) CBT (1); GPP (1)	5 studies: RAWC (1), PPWC (1), PPNC (3); Avg. attrition for therapy (n = 5) 10% (3–19) and f/u (n = 1) 41%; Avg. length of f/u (n = 5) 10 months (3–24)	Promising 0 (1), + (4)

(continues)

TABLE 14.1 (Continued)

	Study	Patient Characteristics[a]	Treatment Description[b]	Study Characteristics[c]	Results[d]
Social Phobia	Hayward et al. (2000) Fanget (1999) Heimberg et al. (1998) Hope et al. (1995) Scholing & Emmelkamp (1993) Heimberg et al. (1990)	*n* = 403; 55% solicited; excluded comorbid depression, panic, substance, psychoses, organic, and Axis II disorder; female (55%) avg. 30 years of age (16–35); some samples (2) had patients on medication (27–30%); COD 15 years (6–19)	Closed membership, 15 sessions (12–23) avg. 135 minutes (90–150); CBT (5), ST (2), CT (1), IE (2), I(1); GPP (3)	6 studies: RAAT (2), RAWC (3), PPNC (1); Avg. attrition for therapy (*n* = 6) 13.3% (2–19), and f/u (*n* = 3) 17.6% (12–26); Avg. length of f/u (*n* = 6) 17 months (2–60)	Very good ++ (5), + (1)
Eating Disorders	Peterson et al. (1998) Davis et al. (1997) Mitchell et al. (1993) Wilfley et al. (1993) Fettes & Peters (1992) Hartmann et al. (1992) Olmsted et al. (1991) Davis et al. (1990) Mitchell et al. (1990)	*n* = 646; 66% solicited; 91% bulimia nervosa, 9% binge eating disorder; female (100%) avg. 30 years of age (24–44); COD 11 years (6–24)	Closed membership, 15 (5–22) sessions avg. 90 minutes (1–5 hours); CBT (5), CBT & PE (2), MSG (1), IPT (1), I (1); GPP (3)	56 studies; MA (49); RAAT (1); RAWC (3); PPWC (3); Avg. attrition for therapy (*n* = 7) 19% (11–33); and f/u (*n* = 1) 18%; Avg. length of f/u (*n* = 2) 7.5 months (3–12)	Excellent 0 (1), + (4), ++ (2), +++ (2)
Elders	Rokke et al. (2000) Pinquart (1998) Engels & Vermey (1997) Toseland et al. (1997) Arean & Miranda (1996) Scogin & McElreath (1994) Leung & Orrell (1993) Abraham et al. (1992) Gorey & Cryns (1991)	*n* = 409; 30% solicited; 25% referred; 45% archival; major depression (77%), physical/verbal aggression (23%); female (70%) avg. 74 years of age	Therapy length is highly variable (5–160 hours) and covaries with setting; CBT (25%), CT (22%), RT (22%), PT (20%), BT (12%), ET (7%)	151 studies; MA (146); RAWC (3); PPWC (1); PPNC (1); Attrition range (16–23%)	Mixed 0 (2), + (3)

[a] Total *n* across studies: patient description and *n* does not include patients in meta-analysis; solicited patients using medic, referred patients were walk-ins; COD = Chronicity of disorder.

[b] Excluding meta-analysis: CT = cognitive therapy; CBT = Cognitive behavior therapy; BT = Behavior therapy; P—IG = Process-interactional group; MSG = Mutual support group; PS = Problem solving; PE = Psychoeducational; GPP = Incorporate group process principles, I = Individual therapy; BBT = Bibliotherapy; ST = Supportive therapy; MFG = Multi-family groups; IE = In vivo exposure; RT = Reminiscent; PT = Psychodynamic; ET = Eclictic.

[c] MA = Meta-Analysis; RAAT = Random Assignment to Active Treatment; RAWC = Random Assignment with Control; PPWC = Pre-Post with comparison group; PPNC = Pre-Post with No Control; f/u = follow-up; attrition n reflects the number of studies with tx % based on those who started treatment & f/u % based on those who completed treatment and then were subsequently assessed, value in parentheses is range.

[d] O = both active and control show equivalent gains, + pre-post gains for tx, ++ tx gains from randomized clinical trials, +++ strong meta-analytic support.

other hand, the two studies (Ravindran et al., 1999; Stravynsky et al., 1994) investigated different patient populations, medications, and treatments, making direct comparisons problematic. Although there appears to be some evidence to suggest caution regarding the effectiveness of CBT when compared to sertraline, definitive conclusions await future replication.

A minority of studies (three) tested group models that deliberately incorporate group process principles into treatment. Konen, Simoneau, Hughes, Ruoss, and Gabris (1992) examined the effectiveness of a CBT group protocol that emphasized group member interaction and process, reporting pre-to-post treatment improvement for over half of the patients. Improvement was maintained at six-month followup. Murphy (1997) studied a two-hour structured bereavement group treatment for mothers and fathers who had lost a child, where the first hour of each session was problem-focused and the second hour was emotion/process focused. When compared to a delayed treatment condition, no significant benefits accrued for fathers, although mothers significantly decreased in grief and post-traumatic stress symptoms and reported several therapeutic factors (cohesion, universality, hope, and catharsis) as important aspects of the group. Finally, McNamee, Lipman, and Hicks, (1995) found that process groups modeled after Yalom (1995) resulted in reliable improvement on measures of depression, self-esteem, and family functioning for depressed single mothers.

The evidence from these three studies is not as persuasive as that from CBT investigations. The designs are weaker (two pre-post only studies), and the overall improvement is simply less convincing. In addition, the patients being treated (grieving parents and inpatients) are markedly different from the depressed outpatients treated in the CBT studies. Although a conclusion favoring CBT over treatments emphasizing group process principles seems enticing, an inferentially sound conclusion requires a direct comparison with the same population. This requirement was partially met in one study (Bright et al., 1999) that compared leader experience and training.

Four investigative teams (Beutler et al., 1991, 1993; Bright, Baker, & Neimeyer, 1999; Burlingame & Barlow, 1996; Kuhns, 1997) compared groups led by professionals and nonprofessionals with depressed outpatients randomly assigned to treatment condition. Several theoretical orientations (cognitive behavioral, existential, process, Gestalt, & Yalom) were tested, and in two studies (Burlingame & Barlow; Kuhns), a wait list control group was included. Consistent with past reviews (e.g., Stein & Lambert, 1995), patient improvement in professionally led groups was equivalent to both self-help groups (Beutler et al., 1991, 1993; Bright et al., 1999; Kuhns, 1997) and paraprofessional group conditions (Burlingame & Barlow, 1996). Moreover, patients in all treatment conditions demonstrated more improvement than the wait list control condition (Burlingame & Barlow; Kuhns). Bright et al. speculated that leader experience might explain the equivalent results. (In their study, experienced group leaders led self-help groups, whereas half of the CBT leaders had no formal group experience.) However, this explanation is challenged by the Beutler et al. (1991, 1993) studies in which graduate students offered self-help treatment and the Burlingame and Barlow (1996) report where patient outcomes in the "expert" therapist groups were virtually indistinguishable from patient outcomes in groups led by untrained age-matched college professors. Nonetheless, those studies were constrained by ethical concerns to treat only patients with lower levels of depression. Such patients respond more readily to both medication and psychotherapy, making the clinical meaning of these comparisons uncertain.

Is the group literature merely replicating the weak support for therapist experience found in the general outcome literature (Lambert & Bergin, 1994)? Perhaps. However, an alternative explanation lies in the proposed patient change model (Figure 14.1). Group process theory would predict that when a group is operating as a therapeutic unit, members take greater responsibility, group member interaction becomes an important agent of change, and leader effects are diminished (Fuhriman & Burlingame, 1994; Yalom, 1995). The Bright et al. (1999) study, describes self-help leaders as shifting "their responsibilities to allow the group to develop independence and autonomy [creating an atmosphere made up of] interpersonal insight ... sharing of feedback and advice ... expression of emotion, and informal brainstorming about shared problems" (pp. 493–494). More specifically, this study appears to be directly contrasting a formal change theory (CBT) with factors ascribed to group process theory (self-help), finding equivalent patient improvement. We are suggesting that the equivalence of self-help and nonprofessional groups might be attributed to the therapeutic effectiveness of small-group processes rather than the formal change theories being less effective. This explanation finds support in the Burlingame and Barlow (1996) study where the professionally and nonprofessionally led groups had similar therapeutic factors operating (e.g., cohesion, insight, and catharsis). Collectively, these four studies suggest that when small-group processes are manifest, the necessary and sufficient conditions for patient change resulting from the therapeutic group climate are present but may be independent of a formal theory of change.

Overall, we have labeled the empirical evidence for group treatment of mood-disordered patients as mixed. Although nearly two-thirds of the investigations of various change models produced beneficial effects (Table 14.1), results from four studies (Bright et al., 1999; Burlingame & Barlow, 1996; Kuhns, 1997; & Ravindran et al., 1999) did not establish that group treatment provided any additional benefit beyond that realized by patients in control (placebo) or comparison groups (nonprofessional treatment). However, the action of small-group process principles was proffered as one explanation for the results of these four studies.

Agoraphobia/Panic Disorders. The dominant change theory tested with patients suffering from panic disorder was CBT. There was no evidence for the incorporation of group process principles in treatment protocols. Thus, these studies are considered tests of a formal change theory that consisted of: (a) education and corrective information concerning etiology and maintenance of the disease (b) cognitive techniques, for example, identifying faulty appraisals of threat; (c) diaphragmatic breathing; and (d) interoceptive exposure to feared body cues. In three controlled studies (Lidren et al., 1994; Telch et al., 1993, 1995) patients treated in CBT groups showed significantly higher levels of improvement than wait list controls at post-treatment assessment on measures of anxiety, fear, depression, frequency and severity of panic attacks, agoraphobic avoidance, and catastrophic cognitions. Within-subject analysis revealed that CBT patients demonstrated reliable post-treatment gains, with as many as 81% being classified as recovered. The uncontrolled studies reported similar gains (Martinsen, Olsen, Tonset, Nyland, & Aarre, 1998; Oei, Llamas, & Evans, 1997). The concordance of findings between randomized comparative trials and field experiments provided good evidence for the efficacy of CBT when compared to wait list controls. This conclusion is buttressed by the strength of the research designs (e.g., randomization, low attrition, sample size).

Nevertheless, two studies sound a cautionary note concerning ascribing treatment gains to solely group CBT. In the only active treatment comparison, Lidren et al. (1994) reported equivalent rates of improvement for patients receiving either self-help bibliotherapy or group CBT, with both treatment conditions posting more improvement than a wait list control. Another team (Oei, Llamas, & Evans, 1997) reported significant pre-to-post improvement for patients who attended a three-day CBT workshop. Should patient improvement be ascribed to the formal change theory (CBT) regardless of treatment format (bibliotherapy, massed practice, traditional group therapy), or could some of this improvement result from group process principles? Although Scheibe, Albus, Walther, and Schmauss (1993) found reliable improvement using a model that emphasized group process principles, we found no investigation that directly compared a formal change model with one emphasizing group process principles.

Finally, investigations of the differential efficacy of group CBT and pharmacological treatments (Oei et al., 1997; Telch et al., 1993) have concluded that medication does not significantly enhance or detract from patient outcomes. Unfortunately, these studies suffer from weak designs (e.g., post-hoc and retrospective analyses), and future experimental comparisons of medication and group CBT are necessary to support any conclusions. In addition, the existence of a comorbid diagnosis may be related to the differential effectiveness of group treatment. Two studies (Martinsen et al., 1998; Scheibe et al., 1993) reported less improvement for patients with comorbid depressive disorders. Higher levels of post-treatment depression predicted poorer outcome at one-year followup, and severe personality disorder and substance abuse/dependence may be related to poor outcomes and dropout (Martinsen, Olsen, Tonset, Nyland, & Aarre, 1998). Although suggestive, these findings must be tested by prospective designs to rule out potential confounds.

Obsessive-Compulsive Disorders (OCD). The typical OCD patient was a female (55 to 67%) in her mid- to late 30s with chronic symptoms (Table 14.1). The principal change theory was a behavioral group approach (BG) that emphasized response prevention, in vivo or imaginal exposure, and modeling. Most included an educational component to help patients understand OC symptoms and the cognitive and behavioral mechanisms of change underlying the treatment protocol. One investigator explicitly acknowledged the importance of group process principles (Van Noppen, Pato, Marsland, & Rasmussen, 1998). Overall, the rigor of the designs was low (Table 14.1), although a notable strength was the use of a common measure (Yale-Brown Obsessive Compulsive Scale, YBOCS) across four studies, thus making direct comparisons feasible.

In the only controlled study (Fals-Stewart, Marks, & Schafer, 1993), group and individual formats were found to be equivalent in significantly reducing pre-to-post-treatment symptoms on the YBOCS. Similarly positive findings were reported in three of the four uncontrolled pre-post investigations. In the remaining study, Enright (1991) found that BG treatment did not reduce specific OC symptoms and concluded that it should be only used for clients awaiting individual therapy. However, this investigation did not use the YBOCS, providing one explanation for the discrepant findings.

The limitations of the current research warrant considerable restraint in endorsing behavioral groups for OCD. A single controlled trial does not yield sufficient evidence for an endorsement, even when supplemented by three uncontrolled pre-post designs. Because uncontrolled trials of behavior therapy with this population extend back two decades (e.g., Epsie, 1986), continuation of this design in future investigations seems counterproductive. Future controlled trials are needed to test the efficacy and differential efficacy of BG treatment against treatments that have incorporated group process principles and found significant patient improvement (e.g., Van Noppen, Pato, Marsland, & Rasmussen, 1998).

Social phobia. Richard Heimberg and colleagues have been a dominant force in the group treatment of social phobia (Table 14.1) developing and refining a group-based CBT protocol over the past 15 years. Accordingly, all but one investigation reviewed relies on a group CBT protocol with the outlier (Scholing & Emmelkamp, 1993) testing the differential efficacy of CBT components: in vivo exposure versus cognitive interventions.

The typical group begins with a session devoted to presenting a CBT model of social anxiety emphasizing the learned nature and reciprocal influence of cognitive, behavioral, and physiological components. This is followed by a didactic presentation of CBT concepts, with the remaining sessions devoted to exposure (simulated or in vivo), cognitive restructuring, homework assignments, and skill acquisition in identifying, categorizing, and disputing problematic cognitions. Again, there is no acknowledged incorporation of group process principles in the group CBT protocols except for the placebo-attention group. More specifically, Heimberg and colleagues (1990) developed an educational support (ES) group to serve as a credible placebo control. Matched for treatment dosage, ES members experience one hour of lectures on social phobia (e.g., definitions, theories, and physiology) followed by an unstructured hour where members share with one another (e.g., concerns about the past week or upcoming situations and how the group might assist them in managing their anxiety).

Both CBT and ES groups produced statistically and clinically significant reductions in social phobic anxiety, depression, and cognitions (Heimberg, Salzman, Holt, & Blendell, 1993). CBT was superior to ES on several measures at post-treatment and maintained these gains at followup (six-month and five-year; Heimberg, Salzman, Holt, & Blendell, 1993). However, ES patients showed more within-subject change on two measures (heart rate and performance anxiety). Perceived confidence in and credibility of treatment did not vary between conditions. To test the purported mechanisms of change, the Heimberg team (Hope, Heimberg, & Bruch, 1995) employed a dismantling strategy (Kazdin, 1998). One condition received the entire CBT package, whereas another received exposure alone (EA). As expected, both CBT and EA patients improved more than the wait list patients on measures of anxiety, social phobia, and behavioral performance, and the two groups demonstrated equivalent levels of cohesion. Surprisingly, the EA patients achieved more broad-based change on measures of social phobia and cognition. Although they proffered alternative explanations, the authors suggested that "the experiential learning that accompanies exposure may provide ample evidence [for patients] to counter dysfunctional beliefs without direct intervention" (p. 648). This conclusion is further supported by the Scholing and Emmelkamp (1993) study where separate exposure and cognitive therapy conditions produced equivalent reductions in irrational cognitions.

The efficacy of group CBT has been compared with pharmacotherapy (phenelzine: PZ; Heimberg et al., 1998). As expected, both CBT and PZ led to superior outcomes on most measures when compared to two control conditions (ES and pill placebo), while in-session assessments of ES indicated comparable levels of cohesion and treatment credibility. Patients receiving PZ responded faster than those in the CBT. Based on this finding, the value of extending CBT treatment was tested in a followup paper (Liebowitz et al., 1999) using a six-month maintenance phase that consisted of continued medication (PZ dose unchanged) or participation in a monthly CBT booster session. Most patients maintained the clinical gains attained during the acute phase of treatment; however subsequent to the maintenance phase, PZ patients continued to relapse, whereas CBT group patients did not. The authors point out that while CBT patients may have less chance of relapse, the PZ nonrelapsers post greater gains.

Overall, the evidence for group CBT being an efficacious treatment for social phobia is compelling. Findings from five rigorous studies (Heimberg et al., 1993, 1998; Hope et al., 1995; Scholing and Emmelkamp, 1993; Liebowitz et al., 1999) carried out at four sites using three different research teams all conclude that CBT treatment produced reliable improvement in salient symptoms of social phobia when compared to wait list controls. However, challenges exist for this line of inquiry. Significant improvement has been repeatedly found for patients randomly assigned to unstructured discussion groups (ES). Although labeled attention-placebo conditions, features of these groups resemble the group process principles previously described. Because the effectiveness of these groups has, at times, rivaled the effect of CBT (cf. Heimberg et al., 1990), careful exploration of alternative forces of therapeutic effectiveness appears to be the next logical step for this line of research.

Bulimia Nervosa. Group treatment has played an integral role in the treatment of patients with eating disorders (Harper-Guiffre & MacKenzie, 1992). Our analysis uncovered two meta-analytic studies that focus on group research conducted in the 1980s and seven empirical studies representing 56 nonoverlapping investigations (Table 14.1).

Investigations conducted in the 1980s support the general post-treatment effectiveness of group treatment, with effect sizes ranging from ES = .75 to .93 (Fettes & Peters, 1992; Hartmann, Herzog, & Drinkmann, 1992, respectively). No aggregate advantage was found for specific theoretical models, with cognitive behavioral models representing the bulk. More improvement for group (e.g., ES = 1.25; cf. Fettes & Peters) resulted when group was combined with other treatments (e.g., individual, pharmacotherapy, etc.), and larger effects were associated with more hours of therapy. Typically, between 9 and 15 sessions were needed for reliable effects.

The dominant change theory tested in the 1990s was cognitive behavioral. Three investigations incorporated and tested group process principles (Davis, Olmsted, Rockert, Marques, & Dolhanty, 1997; Peterson et al., 1998; Wilfley et al., 1993). Four studies tested a formal change theory (Davis, Olmsted, & Rockert, 1990; Peterson et al., 1998; Wilfley et al., 1993, in press), concluding that patients participating in group CBT report lower rates of bingeing and vomiting when compared to controls (no- or delayed-treatment). Although gains emerged from two closed-group formats (a 15-session traditional group and a 5-session psychoeducational group using lectures on the sequelae of bulimia and self-care strategies), the two approaches cannot be considered equivalent because they were not directly compared. The importance of direct comparison for treatments with differing dosages is demonstrated by a study that tested whether patient improvement was due to the intensity of group treatment and the early interruption of disordered eating behaviors (Mitchell et al., 1993). This study defined intensity by dose (22.5 vs. 45 hours) and examined early interruption by clustering more visits focused on controlling eating behavior toward the beginning of therapy versus an even distribution over the entire course of treatment. Greater improvement was associated with high-intensity and early interruption conditions, an approach that is not typical of the weekly protocols found in many outpatient settings.

Although there is a growing body of evidence to support the efficacy of group CBT, there is no support for it being more effective than other treatments. For instance, Wilfley et al. (1993) contrasted CBT (Telch, Agras, Rossiter, Wilfley, & Kenard, 1990) and interpersonal (IPT: Fairburn et al., 1991) treatments and found that both conditions posted more improvement than the wait list control but were not different from each other on measures of bingeing and disinhibition (emotional eating). A recent replication of this study (Wilfley et al., in press) confirmed the equivalence of the two approaches. Olmsted et al. (1991) compared a 5-session CBT psychoeducational group with 19 sessions of individual CBT and found equivalent improvement in bingeing and purging for most patients, although individual therapy was more effective for patients with severe symptoms. Unfortunately, patients in individual therapy received $2^1/_2$ times more treatment, and since greater improvement has been shown to be associated with treatments of longer duration (Fettes & Peters, 1992; Hansen, Lambert, & Forman, 2002; Hartmann et al., 1992), one must entertain dosage as an alternative explanation for differential improvement. Finally, Mitchell et al. (1990) compared the efficacy of an intensive cognitive behavioral group treatment against imipramine hydrochloride and a pill placebo. All active treatment conditions (medication, group + placebo, and group + medication) resulted in significant reduction in pathological eating behaviors and mood (anxiety and depression) when compared to a placebo condition. The group plus placebo condition posted superior outcomes in terms of pathological eating behavior when compared to medication alone, but the group plus medication condition resulted in superior outcomes on mood.

Two studies compared CBT with treatments that incorporated group process principles and arrived at different results. Using a sequential cohort design, Davis, Olmsted, Rockert, Marques, & Dolhanty (1997) contrasted the five-session CBT psychoeducational group with and without a followup seven-session process group. No incremental gain was found on objective measures for patients who participated in the process group, and the authors concluded that the "process sessions are almost completely devoid of any potency" (p. 32). Nonetheless, members who participated in these process sessions described them as "extremely helpful" when compared to psychoeducational treatment factors. On the other hand, Peterson et al. (1998) explored the relative efficacy of combining a 14-session CBT group program with a process/discussion component using three delivery formats. Equivalent benefit was found for therapist-led, partial self-help, and self-help formats, and all three conditions produced more improvement than the control group.

The Davis et al. (1997) study was the only direct test of the differential effectiveness between group process principles and a formal change theory (CBT) and thus merits closer attention. The process sessions were guided by sequentially shared member agendas, with the task defined as helping "members deal with their agendas by engaging in cognitive-restructuring and problem-solving strategies at the group level" (p. 28). Moreover, members left each session with homework for the upcoming week based on these agendas. In short, the process sessions tested in this study maintained a high and constant level of structure throughout the life of the group. This is in direct contrast to group process principle literature (Burlingame, Fuhriman & Johnson, 2002; Fuhriman & Burlingame, 1994; Yalom, 1995) that recommends incorporating high structure at the beginning of a group followed by less structure, more emphasis on interpersonal feedback, and greater member control in mid-to-late group sessions. In short, the more fluid here-and-now focus of process groups may have been absent from this study, making it an incomplete test of these two forces in group treatment.

Collectively, the evidence for the efficacy of group CBT with eating disorders (especially BN) is excellent, with strong support from both meta-analytic and rigorous studies. The effect of treatment may be associated with dosage as well as the intensity and timing of interventions. Though sparse, the evidence does not support the superiority of CBT over other formal change theories (e.g., IPT) and greater improvement in patient mood may be achieved by combining CBT with medication. Little can be concluded regarding the differential efficacy of the group and individual format due to unequal dose.

Groups for Elders. Elders are a rapidly increasing proportion of the North American and European populations. Although diagnosable mood disorders occur less frequently in elders than in younger adults, depressive symptoms and adjustment disorders are more prevalent (Scogin & McElreath, 1994). To address these disorders, cognitive and cognitive behavioral techniques are most frequently employed, followed by reminiscent, psychodynamic, behavioral, and eclectic treatments (Table 14.1). Virtually all focus on resolving problems, sharing memories and feelings, and increasing self-esteem and life satisfaction.

A "promising," in contrast to good, efficacy rating was given to this literature, due in part to the dissimilar conclusions drawn from the four meta-analyses. The most significant discrepancy was between the Engels and Vermey (1997) and

Scogin and McElreath (1994) reviews. When compared to no-treatment control conditions, individual treatment (ES = .76) was shown to be superior to group (ES = .16) by Engels and Vermey. However, Scogin and McElreath reported virtually identical values for the two modalities (ES = .77 and .74, respectively). These divergent results appear to be due to differences in the studies sampled as well as to effect size calculation. For instance, the Engels and Vermey study contains more than twice as many studies (57%) where group produced equivalent or less favorable improvement, with two studies posting very large negative effects for group treatment (Sallis, Lichstein, Clardson, Stalgaitis, & Campbell, 1983; Johnson & Wilborn, 1991; ES = –.90 and –.89, respectively). The most recent meta-analysis (Pinquart, 1998) contained the most studies and reported effect sizes that fell between the above estimates, suggesting that group therapy (ES for depression = .33 and well-being = .41) may be marginally less effective than individual therapy (ES for depression = .56 and well-being = .64). Finally, similar but slightly higher estimates for group (ES = .68) were reported by an earlier meta-analysis (Gorey & Cryns, 1991).

More agreement can be found regarding the positive pre-to-post treatment gains resulting from group treatment. Pre-to-post-treatment gains are slightly larger, ranging from .74 to .92 (Gorey & Cryns, 1991; Scogin & McElreath, 1994). Although a few studies report group treatment as ineffectual (Abraham, Neundorfer, & Currie, 1992; Toseland et al., 1997), studies continue to replicate positive effects (Arean & Miranda, 1996; Leung & Orrell, 1993; Rokke, Tomhave, & Jocic, 2000).

The aforementioned heterogeneity in patient improvement led to a search for predictors of differential outcome. Scogin and McElreath (1994) report no effect for treatment orientation. Engels and Vermey (1997) conclude that cognitive and behavioral treatments are more effective than cognitive behavioral, reminiscent, and anger control. Unfortunately, both conclusions rest on a small number of studies, making acceptance of either conclusion premature. Treatment effectiveness appears to be independent of client age, gender, length, and setting of treatment (Gorey & Cryns, 1991; Scogin & McElreath, 1994). There is mixed support for the association of greater treatment gains and more severe levels of depression (Engels & Vermey; Gorey & Cryns) and in some studies, elders diagnosed with major depression appeared to benefit more from CBT than those with dysthymic or cyclothymic disorders (Leung & Orrell, 1993). Finally, comparative studies using placebo-attention groups have found improvement that is comparable to active treatment (Rokke, Tomhave, & Jocic, 2000).

The methodological context of the literature on elders sets a cautious interpretive frame. Many studies have small *n*'s, poorly defined samples, unstandardized treatments, and patients who received concurrent medical interventions. Nonetheless, the collective findings from over 100 independent studies on group treatment for depressed elders are mixed with respect to differential efficacy (individual vs. group), yet supportive of positive pre-to-post treatment improvement. Less clear are what specific factors might account for this improvement, with at least one recent investigation finding placebo-attention groups posting equivalent improvement when compared to active treatments. The next challenge for research on elders is rigorous comparative designs that can provide more definitive answers regarding differential effectiveness rather than simply reaffirming pre-post-treatment gains. Greater clarity is needed regarding treatment, group process, and patients and leader characteristics (Figure 14.1).

General Conclusions for Group as Primary Research. Several evidence-based conclusions emerge from the group as primary literature. Treatment gains that exceed wait list control groups have been reported for the majority of patient populations (mood, panic, social phobia, bulimia nervosa, elders). These findings are important because they not only rule out plausible alternative explanations for patient gains (e.g., regression to the mean, maturation, history, etc.; cf. Cook & Campbell, 1979) but also provide disorder-specific support for the efficacy of group treatment. This type of design needs to be extended to OCD treatment models to further test its efficacy.

The majority of studies reviewed support the efficacy of formal change theories (e.g., CBT, BT, and CT) that do not formally incorporate group process principles. This finding appears to be robust across patient disorders and supports the efficacy of change theories that are initially developed for individual treatment and then transferred to a group format.

Very few studies were found that tested the effectiveness of group models that are primarily based on the group process principles. Even fewer studies contrast such models with group treatments guided by a formal change theory. However, a large number of studies contrasted formal change theories with control groups that deliberately or inadvertently incorporated group process principles. In virtually every case, patient improvement in the control group rivaled active treatment. The replication of this intriguing finding across three patient populations (mood, social phobia, and elders) and different research teams argues for its robustness. Moreover, this finding casts the aforementioned efficacy of formal change theories in a new light, partially explained by the putative forces described in Figure 14.1. If patient change is indeed equivalent when models that employ formal change and group process theories are independently compared, a critical next step is to experimentally test the combined and independent effects of these forces (formal change and group process principles) in the same study. One study conducted such a comparison (Davis et al., 1997) and did not find support for the incremental value of group process. However, we question the degree to which the process sessions in this study emulate group process principles articulated in the literature.

The differential efficacy studies are dominated by comparisons of the individual and group format, which, for the most part, replicate the equivalence findings from recent meta-analyses. The findings from studies of elders and eating disorders are less definitive on this point and require future analysis and research. There is a paucity of investigations that examine the differential efficacy of different models of group treatment, making it impossible to arrive at a definitive conclusion. Similarly, the mixed findings from comparative studies of pharmacotherapy, coupled with weak research designs (e.g., archival), make conclusions premature. However, stellar examples of such research exist (Heimberg et al., 1998; Liebowitz et al., 1999; Ravindran et al., 1999) and should be replicated. Finally, promising work on differential predictors of patient outcome has begun as investigators study patient (Beutler et al., 1991, 1993) and disease characteristics (Scheibe et al., 1993; Martinsen et al., 1998).

Group as Augment

Substance-Related Disorders. The typical substance abuse program is multimodal, relying on individual, family, group, 12-step, pharmacotherapy, and psychoeducational treatment components (Stinchfield, Owen, & Winters, 1994). Group is often a central component of these programs because it can break through an addict's denial, especially when it is composed of fellow addicts (Galanter, Castaneda, & Franco, 1991). It is also a successful component of aftercare programs (Fisher & Bentley, 1996; Kaminer, Burleson, Blitz, Sussman, & Rounsaville, 1998; McKay et al., 1997, 1999; Shaffer, LaSalvia, & Stein, 1997). In general, patients who participate in group treatment exhibit more improvement on typical measures of outcome (e.g., abstinence and use rates, objective measures, urinalysis) when compared to standard care without group (Burtscheidt, Schwarz, Rdner, & Gaebel, 1999; Fisher & Bentley, 1996) and those who refuse or drop out of treatment (Sandahl, Herlitz, Ahlin, & Roennberg, 1998).

The majority of reports test the differential effectiveness of formal change theories for patients using alcohol or illicit drugs. Although family therapy outperformed unstructured peer discussion groups (Joanning, Quinn, Thomas, & Mullen, 1992; Stanton & Shadish, 1997), equivalent outcomes were found when psychodynamic groups were contrasted with Hatha yoga (Shaffer et al., 1997) or cognitive behavioral groups (Sandahl et al., 1998) and when behavioral and cognitive groups were compared (Burtscheidt et al., 1999). Studies of the dually diagnosed have found that CBT is effective for those suffering from post-traumatic stress, equivalent to disease recovery models for personality disorders (Fisher & Bentley, 1996), and superior to interaction groups (Yalom, 1995) for externalizing and internalizing adolescents (Kaminer, Burleson, Blitz, Sussman, & Rounsaville, 1998). Crits-Christoph et al. (1999) found that a combination of individual and group drug counseling that was based on a less formal change theory (i.e., 12-step model) produced superior outcomes when compared to group and group plus individual treatment conditions that were guided by two empirically supported change theories (cognitive and supportive-expressive). Finally, the research on differential effectiveness of the group versus individual format is mixed, with group producing better outcome in some studies (Bowers & Al-Redha, 1990; McKay et al., 1997, 1999) and equivalence in others (Weinstein, Gottheil, & Sterling, 1997).

Reliable patient improvement occurred in every study, although differences in formal change theories do not seem to explain variations in patient outcome. Whereas equivalence of change theory is one plausible explanation, another may lie in the strong relationship found between dosage and outcome (Shaffer et al., 1997; Weinstein et al., 1997). For instance, this relationship might explain the superiority of a couples group (Bowers & Al-Redha, 1990) that received 170% more treatment than the individual condition. Unfortunately, the average rate of attrition across studies is very high (43%, range 18–82), creating a challenge for patients receiving an adequate dosage. Finally, we must take notice of the unexpected finding from a rigorous multisite study where empirically supported models were found to be inferior to individual and group counseling approaches based on a 12-step model. One explanation may lie in the strong emphasis placed on creating a "supportive group atmosphere" (Crits-Christoph et al., 1999, p. 495) in the latter condition, suggesting the potential operation of group process principles.

Trauma-Related Disorders. A plethora of group models have emerged to treat the effects of sexual abuse. The typical study treats adult females abused as children using a time-limited approach that combines psychoeducation and process interventions. When compared to random and nonequivalent control groups at posttreatment, group members posted lower levels of depression (Bagley & Young, 1998; Morgan & Cummings, 1999; Richter, Snider, & Gorey, 1997), lower levels of dissociative and PTSD symptoms (Morgan & Cummings, 1999; Zlotnick et al., 1997), as well as higher levels of self-esteem (Bagley & Young, 1998; Richter et al., 1997) and social adjustment (Morgan & Cummings, 1999). Similar gains were reported in uncontrolled studies (Lubin, Loris, Burt, & Johnson, 1998; Stalker & Fry, 1999), with one investigation demonstrating the equivalence of group and individual treatments (Stalker & Fry). These positive findings find further support in a meta-analysis of earlier research (De Jong & Gorey, 1996), with a posttreatment effect size estimate of .79 that was maintained at followup. Given that half of the clients in these studies received concurrent individual or psychotropic treatment, some have attempted to tease apart the independent effect of group treatment (Morgan & Cummings, 1999; Zlotnick et al., 1997). This research supports the additive value of group, but this conclusion needs additional replications.

A number of group models appearing in the 1990s focused on victims and perpetrators of domestic violence. Post-treatment improvements were reported with cognitive behavioral (Brannen & Rubin, 1996; Saunders, 1996), mixed educational and process (Brannen & Rubin; Johannson & Tutty, 1998; Petrik, Gildersleeve-High, McEllistrem, & Subotnik, 1994), and psychodynamic groups (Saunders, 1996). CBT produced lower physical abuse ratings than educational-process oriented groups with patients who had a history of alcohol abuse (Brannen & Rubin).

Two dominant models exist in the domestic violence literature. One begins with gender-specific groups to ensure the safety of the spouse and increase the likelihood that the perpetrator will assume responsibility for the abusive behavior (Philpot, 1991; Rosenbaum & O'Leary, 1986). In this approach, gender-specific treatment for men focuses on violence prevention, with concurrent supportive group treatment for women (Tutty, Bidgood, & Dothery, 1993; Weidman, 1986). Two studies (Johannson & Tutty, 1998; Weidman, 1986) illustrate the potential effectiveness of this model. The second approach begins with conjoint group treatment and has also been shown to be effective (Brannen & Rubin, 1996; Schlee, Heyman, & O'Leary, 1998). Unfortunately, a direct test of the differential effectiveness of these two models could not be found.

Regrettably, testimonials and case studies eclipse the number of controlled evaluations for group treatment with trauma-related disorders in the 1990s. Although the effectiveness of group treatment seems promising, it is premature to heartily endorse these treatments at this time. A common set of outcome measures will significantly strengthen future research, as will studies testing the differential effectiveness and potential interactions between treatment and client characteristics. One reason for the paucity of controlled studies may be the ill-defined treatment models in existence. The absence of well-articulated change models impedes the advancement of knowledge, clinical application, and replication.

Patients with Medical Illness. Joseph Pratt, an oft-cited pioneer of group treatment (Barlow, Burlingame, & Fuhriman, 2000), was the first physician to use group treatments in a medical setting, believing that if the mind improved the body would follow. The remarkable increase in the application of group treatment within primary care medicine confirms Dr. Pratt's initial impression. Although there is enormous diversity in the groups applied in medical settings, two areas of practice and research, cancer and HIV, dominate the published literature.

Group interventions for cancer patients appear in three primary formats: psychoeducation, time-limited therapy, and support groups. Frequent goals include emotional adjustment, information regarding the disease and treatment, coping skills, existential issues, and functional adjustment. Patients reflect a mix of diagnoses, although breast cancer is the most frequent (Cwikel & Behar, 1999; Meyer & Mark, 1995). Support groups are most common, followed by educational, cognitive behavioral, general psychotherapy, and behavioral techniques. Most emphasize multiple goals.

Changes in emotional distress and coping skills (e.g., nausea and pain) are the largest and most consistent improvements associated with group treatment (Baider, Uziely, & DeNour, 1994; Forester, Kornfeld, Fleiss, & Thompson, 1993; Meyer & Mark, 1995; Roberts, Piper, Denny, & Cuddeback, 1997; Sheard & Maguire, 1999; Spiegel et al., 1999). For instance, a recent meta-analysis (Sheard & Maguire) reported improvement in anxiety and depression (ES = .42 and .36, respectively) that was substantiated by two concurrent reviews composed of 46 nonoverlapping studies (Cwikel & Behar, 1999; Fawzy & Fawzy, 1998; Goodwin et al., 2000). However, some individual studies have failed to replicate these outcomes (Beem et al., 1999; Evans & Connis, 1995). Significant, yet smaller, improvements result in quality of life and patient knowledge (Cwikel & Behar, 1999; Dolgin, Somer, Zaidel, & Zaizov, 1997; Fawzy, Fawzy, Arndt, & Pasnau, 1995; Sheard & Maguire, 1999), and mixed support exists for effects on immune system functioning, disease recurrence, and survival rates (Fawzy et al., 1995; Meyer & Mark, 1995). Although Spiegel's early work (1981, 1989) on increased survival time for women participating in groups has been replicated (Fawzy et al., 1993), others' attempts have failed (Beem et al., 1999; DeVries et al., 1997; Linn, Linn, & Harris, 1982; Morgenstern, Gellert, Walter, Ostfeld, & Siegel, 1984). Finally, there are mixed findings for the association between stage of treatment and patient improvement. Cwikel and Behar (1999) suggest that the *middle* stage of the disease is the optimal time for psychosocial intervention, although Sheard and Maguire found the greatest effect for depression during the *last* stage.

Overall, there is good evidence for the general effectiveness of group for cancer patients on measures of emotional distress and coping as well as promising evidence for quality of life and knowledge gains. The "jury is out" regarding the direct effect of group treatment on disease recurrence, survival and immune system functioning, and the association between stage of disease and patient improvement. Adequate tests of these latter effects are hampered by the complexity created when different treatments, goals, and stages of cancer are combined. A partial answer may lie in emerging conceptual models that link clinical theory with empirical findings and then suggest specific matches between treatment format, goals, and stage of cancer (Cunningham, 1995; Simonton & Sherman, 2000; Spira, 1997).

Group models for human immunodeficiency virus (HIV) and acquired immunodeficiency syndrome (AIDS) have two foci: prevention and treatment. Prevention protocols typically emphasize reduction of high-risk behaviors (e.g., multiple partners, unprotected sex), increased knowledge of the disease, and modification of attitudes, while treatment protocols focus on psychosocial factors (stress, psychological distress, coping, and social support). Most last three to four hours and rely on a single session (Choi et al., 1996; Cohen, MacKinnon, Dent, Mason, & Sullivan, 1992). Others (Roffman et al., 1998) employ more traditional group formats (e.g., 17 sessions).

Group-based prevention interventions have been associated with a decrease in unprotected sex (Branson, Peterman, Cannon, Ransom, & Zaidi, 1998; Choi et al., 1996; Roffman et al., 1998), number of sexual partners (Branson et al., 1998; Choi et al., 1996), and new infections (Branson et al.; Choi et al.), with dosage related to treatment effects (Branson et al.). Some (e.g., Roffman et al.) have found that self-efficacy, coping skills, positive treatment expectancies, and knowledge of safe alternatives predict outcome, while others (e.g., Choi et al.) have not.

Kelly et al. (1993) describe their study as the first randomized trial of group treatment with HIV patients, providing an indication of the nascent nature of the treatment literature. Nonetheless, the collective findings from the 1990s support the benefit of using some form of structured or supportive group treatment to alleviate psychological distress found in HIV/AIDS patients. CBT and support groups outperformed wait list patients on measures of depression, anxiety, hostility, and somatization (Kelly et al.; Mulder et al., 1994, 1995). However, no effect was found on immunological parameters (CD4 and

NK cell counts; Mulder et al., 1995; Targ et al., 1994) or for medication (fluoxetine), adding to the gains that result from structured group treatment (Targ et al.). We are cautiously optimistic about the effectiveness of these treatments and await future comparative research with larger sample sizes and more diverse patients before offering a more confident judgment.

Groups for Severe Mental Illness

SCHIZOPHRENIA. Confidence in the use of group treatment for schizophrenia has waxed and waned as psychological models of etiology have ignored or emphasized brain disease models (Bellak & Mueser, 1993). However, the widespread acceptance of interactive etiological models (e.g., diathesis-stress) linking psychosocial stress to relapse (Huxley, Rendall, & Sederer, 2000), coupled with the marginal effect of medication on negative symptoms and social skills (Liberman et al., 1998), have all contributed to the revitalization of group approaches. Four dominant group models appear in the literature: social skills, psychoeducation, cognitive-information processing, and cognitive behavioral.

The most researched form of group treatment with schizophrenic patients is social skills training (Mueser, Wallace, & Liberman, 1995). The underlying premise of this approach is that deficits in social functioning lead to social isolation, which, in turn, can exacerbate symptom and disease management. The modal social skills approach breaks complex interpersonal skills into discrete modules and trains patients in each with behavioral techniques. The UCLA *Social and Independent Living Skills* program (UCLA-SILS; Liberman et al., 1998) continues to dominate North American and European social skills protocols (e.g., Chambon & Marie-Cardine, 1998; Spaulding, Reed, Sullivan, Richardson, & Weiler, 1999).

An early meta-analysis of the effectiveness of social skills treatment (Benton & Schroeder, 1990) indicated strong pre-to-post-treatment improvement (ES = .76) on behavioral measures of social skill, assertiveness, and hospital discharge rates. Similar, though smaller overall gains (ES = .41), were reported in a recent meta-analysis (Mojtabai, Nicholson, & Carpenter, 1998). More specifically, social skills groups outperformed comparison groups (e.g., support and discussion groups) on measures of general and specific social skills (Chambon & Marie-Cardine, 1998; Smith, Hull, Romanelli, Fertuck, & Weiss, 1999), grooming (Wallace, Liberman, MacKain, Blackwell, & Eckman, 1992), and social adjustment and leisure activities (Chambon & Marie-Cardine; Marder et al., 1996; Wallace et al.). Others report few differences using similar comparative group conditions (Dobson, McDougall, Busheikin, & Aldous, 1995; Hayes, Halford, & Varghese, 1995); some (e.g., Huxley et al., 2000) have proposed that the most consistent effects result from the UCLA-SILS model (Liberman et al., 1993).

The distinguishing feature between social skills and psychoeducational groups is the emphasis on acquisition of disease-related information and an opportunity to discuss and engage in general problem solving. Beneficial effects have been associated with psychoeducational groups composed primarily of patients (e.g., Atkinson, Coia, Gilmour, & Harper, 1996; Buccheri, Trygstad, Kanas, Waldron, & Dowling, 1996). This approach is frequently used with the family of individuals with schizophrenia (Hogarty et al., 1991; Mills & Hansen, 1991). An example of this approach is McFarlane's multiple family group (MFG) treatment, which has been shown to produce equivalent improvement in symptoms, social and vocational functioning, and treatment compliance when compared to single-family therapy, yet result in lower relapse rates (McFarlane, Dushay, Stastny, Deakins, & Link, 1996; McFarlane, Link et al., 1995; McFarlane, Lukens et al., 1995).

Since cognitive dysfunction plays a central role in describing the pathognomonic characteristics of schizophrenia, cognitive-information processing rehabilitation models have emerged addressing specific information-processing deficits and remediation strategies. For instance, Brenner et al. (Brenner et al., 1992a, 1992b; Roder, Jenull, & Brenner, 1998) developed a five-module group-based *integrated psychological therapy* (IPT) program to ameliorate cognitive and social-behavioral deficits—not to be confused with interpersonal psychotherapy (IPT). Findings from European (Brenner et al., 1992a) and North American studies (Spaulding et al., 1999) suggest that IPT produces improvement in both cognitive and psychopathology measures. For instance, Spaulding and colleagues reported on the initial findings of a five-year study showing that IPT had greater incremental improvement on measures of social competence and attentional processing when compared to patients receiving supportive group treatment and standard psychiatric rehabilitation treatment. However, significant and equivalent improvement resulted in both conditions on measures of attention, memory, and executive functioning.

Cognitive and cognitive behavioral models challenge the discontinuity between psychosis and normality by suggesting that "normal" psychological processes maintain specific psychotic symptoms (Dickerson, 2000). Interventions include belief modification and coping strategies for positive symptoms (hallucinations, delusions, thought disorder, etc.), as well as modeling, rehearsal, exposure, and homework. When compared to other active treatments (supportive or social skills groups), group CBT was associated with more improvement on positive symptoms and mixed findings for negative symptoms (Drury, Birchwood, Cochrane, & Macmillan, 1996; Pinto, La Pia, Mennella, Giorgio, & DeSimone, 1999; Wykes, Parr, & Landau, 1999). One study (Lewandowski, Buchkremer, & Stark, 1994) reported lower rehospitalization and relapse rates for cognitive versus social skills groups.

Although the four group approaches (social skills, psychoeducation, cognitive-information processing, and CBT) are presented separately, in practice most treatment programs combine two or more other treatment components (medication, individual, family). Overall, there is very good evidence that the effectiveness of social skills groups has a reliable effect on the acquisition and maintenance of targeted skill sets (Mueser et al., 1995) and promising evidence that these skills may generalize to later community functioning (Liberman et al., 1998). Thus, standard practice should include social skills group treatment. In contrast, the cumulative evidence for psychoeducational groups is rather small (Huxley et al., 2000), yet the cost-effectiveness of this approach makes it a particularly attractive option. The partial replication of European findings for cognitive-information processing groups in North America is also encouraging, although the specific and nonspecific improvements in cognitive functioning associated with *both* standard care and targeted cognitive treatment suggests the need for future research on these methods. The cognitive and CBT treatments have a handful of studies that rely on weaker designs, making these findings only suggestive. Finally, the traditional verbal therapies characterized by psychodynamic, Gestalt, and process groups (Kanas, 1986; Klein, Brabender, & Fallon, 1994) were most frequently used as the "traditional treatment" comparison or combined with a formal change theory (e.g., CBT plus process; Daniels, 1998, or CBT plus social skills; McQuaid et al., 2000) rather than tested as independently efficacious treatments. In the present evidence-based zeitgeist, the dramatic reduction of studies on traditional verbal therapies with schizophrenia is disquieting since they continue to be frequently applied in clinical practice even as they are losing ground on the empirical front.

Personality disorders. Several group models have been developed to treat personality disorders (MacKenzie, 2001b). Some are based on detailed manuals such as interpersonal group psychotherapy (IGP: Marziali & Munroe-Blum, 1994), dialectical behavior therapy (Linehan, Heard, & Armstrong, 1993), cognitive analytic therapy (CAT; Ryle et al., 1997), or experiential group psychotherapy (EGP; Budman & Gurman, 1988). Others are modifications of psychodynamic (Wilberg, Friis, Karterud et al., 1998), interpretive (Joyce, McCallum, & Piper 1999), or client-centered group models (Eckert & Biermann-Ratjen, 1998). Current research focuses on two groupings: outpatient and day or inpatient group milieu protocols.

Among the studies with homogeneous groups, the majority deal with borderline personality disorder (BPD). Results from controlled and uncontrolled studies indicated that extant group models result in a reduction of depression and suicidal tendencies (Linehan et al., 1991, 1993, 1999; Munroe-Blum & Marziali, 1995), disorder specific symptoms (Eckert & Wuchner, 1996; McCallum, Piper, & O'Kelly, 1997; Wilberg et al., 1998), increased interpersonal functioning (Joyce et al., 1999; Munroe-Blum & Marziali), and life satisfaction and adjustment (Joyce et al.; Munroe-Blum & Marziali). Although groups were typically time-limited and closed, some extended treatment over a two-year period, with gains maintained for up to two years (e.g., Eckert & Wuchner; Munroe-Blum & Marziali). A recent study focusing on antisocial personality disorders (MacKenzie et al., 1999) reports similar results.

Studies of groups comprised of mixed personality-disordered patients are more commonly found in inpatient day- or evening-treatment programs, although exceptions do occur (e.g., Budman, Demby, Soldz, & Merry, 1996). The duration of these treatment programs ranges from six weeks to eight months and includes a variety of change theories. Patients participating in such programs show improvement on a variety of outcome measures, including interpersonal functioning, psychiatric symptoms, and life satisfaction (Dazord, Gerin, Seulin, Duclos, & Amar, 1997; Karterud, 1992; Piper, Rosie, Joyce, & Azim, 1996). In several European countries (e.g., Germany, Switzerland), patients suffering from severe Axis I pathology and/or personality disorders (mainly BPD) are commonly treated within inpatient programs that incorporate group treatment components. Most studies rely on pre-post designs, with outcome related to the entire treatment program. Nonetheless, reliable patient improvement has been evident (Davies-Osterkamp, Strauss, & Schmitz, 1996; Janssen, 1987; Strauss, 1992, 2001; Strauss & Burgmeier-Lohse, 1994a), with at least one study suggesting that group independently contributes to patient improvement (Schmidt, Nübling, Lamprecht, & Wittmann, 1994).

Compared to other clinical syndromes, the efficacy research on group treatment of personality disorders is restricted. Comparative summaries (e.g., meta-analyses) are difficult owing to the diversity of the models, lack of controlled studies, and limited number of studies. Since group is often one of several components comprising institutional programs, the construction of control conditions is constrained by ethical principles. Nevertheless, the available evidence indicates that group can be a beneficial and economic approach to the treatment of PD.

Group Psychotherapy Process

Process studies reflect an attempt to describe or predict theoretical mechanisms of change operative within the group. In past editions of this chapter (Bednar & Kaul, 1994; Kaul & Bednar, 1986), process was largely defined by studies that focused on pregroup training, early group structure, and feedback. The number of studies focusing on these topics has significantly decreased, and summative reviews have emerged reflecting the stability of evidence regarding their properties (e.g., Burlingame et al., 2002; Morran, Stockton, & Teed, 1998). Accordingly, we find little merit in endorsing further work on these topics and instead concentrate on emerging trends in process research.

A recent definition of group psychotherapy process, adopted in this review, describes it as

> the study of the group-as-a-whole system and changes in its development, the interactions within the patient and therapist subsystems, the patient and patient (dyadic or subgroup) subsystems, the therapist and therapist subsystem if there are co-leaders, and the way each of the subsystems interacts with and is influenced by the group as a whole (Beck & Lewis, 2000, p.8).

The use of this definition presents one with an array of interesting studies from the 1990s that are not easy to summarize given the broad spectrum of populations (patient & nonpatient) and therapy models. Further heterogeneity emerges because studies are split between North American and European psychotherapy research centers that typically emphasize time-limited or inpatient group programs, respectively. Finally, the predominant change theories are psychodynamic and interpersonal, in contrast to the outcome studies where structured models (CBT) prevail.

We employ three organizational techniques to bring meaning to this diverse and seemingly disordered process literature. We offer a conceptual model to further define the small-group process principles introduced in Figure 14.1. Boundary dimensions are briefly described to establish a common language for group process. We then describe three complex programs of group process research to provide an integrated view of how a range of significant process findings relate to boundary conditions. These programs are models for the type of process research that is likely to be particularly productive. Next, we present a large number of individual process studies organized by common small-group process themes (e.g., group development, therapeutic factors) and type of research design employed (e.g., predicting outcome using process). Unfortunately, the study of group processes continues to lack cohesion. Accordingly, we end with special focus on an organizational scheme that may bring heuristic and clinical value to the literature. We are hopeful that this approach will make the process literature both exciting and useful.

Group as a System

The organization of this chapter is based partly on the premise that group process theories might explain an independent portion of improvement in group treatment. Ingredient to this premise is the realization of the group as an entity, evident in part by identifiable patterns of connections among the members that can, in turn, be described by systemic boundaries. Durkin, an influential figure

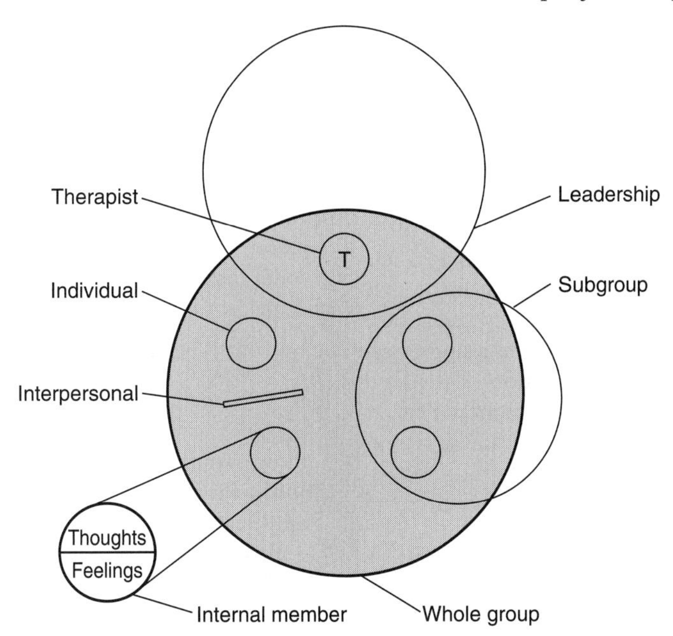

FIGURE 14.2 Forces that govern the boundaries of treatment groups. Group boundary structure (The *whole group boundary* defines the properties that must bc dcalt with as a collective, including criteria for inclusion/exclusion as well as the number of members. The *subgroup boundary* recognizes that clusters of members may form that can have helpful or hindering effects on a group. The *leadership boundary* recognizes the formal theoretical approach and technical style used to deliver that model. *Therapist boundary* recognizes that the therapist is also an individual with personal characteristics that may have an important impact on the group or some of its members. The *interpersonal boundary* reflects the complex interplay of relationships among the individual members. *Internal member boundaries* reflect covert processes (thoughts and feelings) for individual members.

in the early group literature, observed that "Organized complexities, or 'systems' as they came to be called, are the product of the dynamic interaction among their parts rather than the sum of their absolute characteristics. Neither the resultant whole nor its new characteristics can be explained by the nature of the parts themselves" (Durkin, 1972, p. 161). The "dynamic interaction" that Durkin identifies can be understood as the flow of factual and emotional information across boundaries, with general systems theory providing a framework for identifying boundaries for the psychotherapy group.

Figure 14.2 identifies and defines six boundary structures, adding greater specificity to small-group process principles (Figure 14.1). The term *boundary* is used in a double sense. Boundaries can be conceptualized in physical terms: closing the door of the group for the first session is a powerful message that a group has been created. But of greater interest to an understanding of group process is the idea of a boundary being created by an awareness of transactions across the boundary and particularly of differences on either side of the boundary. For example, an early phenomenon in therapy groups is the awareness of universality; that is, the members understand that they share many common symptoms, experiences, or emotions. Technically, this could be seen as the development of an external boundary to the group: "we in this room are a special category of people who can understand each other," as opposed, perhaps, to the perceived lack of understanding of spouses or friends outside of the group. The nature of boundary regulation is expected to vary over time as the group proceeds. The format of a time-limited closed group provides an ideal model for applying group systems concepts. The boundary structures form a hierarchy of levels: a minimum list includes the whole group as a unit in its external context, interactional phenomena between members including the leader(s), and the internal processes within each member. These levels are used to organize and integrate findings from diverse process studies.

Complex Research Programs

Research programs that hypothesize and test relationships between pre-therapy characteristics of the patients, specific process patterns believed to moderate change, formal change theories, and comprehensive outcomes are labeled "complex." Given that these research teams pay heed to many of the components identified in Figures 14.1 and 14.2, their work holds great promise for understanding the complexity of group treatment effects. Reviewing multiple studies as a single program allows us a better appreciation of the linkages between studies and the interactional nature of programmatic research. Interestingly, most programs focus on psychodynamic group models using detailed process and outcome measures.

Vancouver/Edmonton Research Project. Piper and colleagues have pursued three distinct, yet linked, programs of research involving systematic process and outcome analysis. The first (Piper et al., 1992) involved the study of pathological grief using an interpretive group approach. Findings from this study led to the development of a second (Piper et al., in press) program thrust: the inclusion of a supportive model along with an interpretive treatment approach. Finally, a parallel set of studies (Piper et al., 1996) was conducted with a personality-disordered sample, using a milieu approach. Table 14.2 describes the process measures used, arranged according to the boundary each addresses, while Table 14.3 outlines the major findings related to the three sets of studies.

Piper, McCallum, and Azim (1992) used a 12-session closed-interpretive group therapy model for pathological grief. Pathological grief is associated with substantial levels of symptomatic distress, especially depression, and is a very common psychiatric presentation (according to Piper et al., in press, 33.3% in a sample of 729 psychiatric patients). The research design addressed methodological weaknesses in previous studies and included: (1) a large sample, (2) patients with clinical levels of disturbance, (3) matching and random assignment to condition, (4) experienced therapists, (5) manualized therapy, (6) process analysis to ensure integrity of technique, (7) personality assessment (e.g., psychological mindedness) to investigate patient X treatment interactions, and (8) comprehensive outcome with followup.

Patients with low psychological mindedness (PM) had a high likelihood of terminating prematurely, but there was a relatively weak correlation between PM and outcome for those who stayed (Table 14.3). Following the successful demonstration of the general efficacy of the interpretive model, a series of studies addressed more subtle effects. This work examined the comparative effects between: (1) an interpretive group model that focused on unconscious processes and early relationships that increase anxiety and regression and (2) a supportive group model that emphasized basic group common factors such as universality, altruism, and cohesion, and that focused on adaptation to the patient's current life (Piper, McCallum, Joyce, & Rosie, in press). The question of supportive or interpretive therapy is an important theme in the clinical literature concerning the choice of a therapeutic model. Finally, a measure of relational functioning, Quality of Object Relations (QOR; Table 14.2), was added to the assessment battery.

A parallel set of studies applied the same measures to a more severely dysfunctional patient population consisting of treatment-resistant mood and personality disorders. These patients received treatment in intensive small groups in day or evening intensive milieu programs that occupied several days per week for six to eight months. Parallel studies provide an opportunity to compare the therapeutic course of two different populations on the same instruments, thus permitting a broader view of the efficacy of the model.

The cumulative findings from the studies on pathological grief shed light on the boundary conditions of process research (Table 14.3). For instance, in the pathological grief group at the *group boundary*, the positive outcome in both the supportive and interpretive treatments provided further support for the equivalence hypothesis. This highlighted the importance of identifying patient variables to enhance treatment outcome. All group patients received the same pre-therapy preparation, but patients with lower QOR dropped out at a higher rate in the interpretive condition. The interpretive groups were designed to confront the expectation of deepening psychological understanding. This may have set up a "competitive framework" in which the high QOR members were superior to the low QOR members as they addressed the goals of the interpretive group. On the other hand, high QOR shares conceptual similarities with other predictors of outcome in psychodynamic psychotherapy (such as self-reflective or interpersonal functioning) and may have been a better match with the interpretative model.

TABLE 14.2 Description of Vancouver and Edmonton Milieu and Process Measures

Group	Leadership	Interpersonal	Individual
Community Oriented Programs Environment Scale (COPES) (Moos, 1974)	Therapist Intervention Rating Scale (TIRS) (Piper, Debbanme, de Carufel, & Bienvu, 1987)	Psychodynamic Work and Object Rating System (PWORS) (Piper, McCallum, & Azim, 1992)	Quality of Object Relations (QOR) (Azim, Piper, Segal, Nixon, & Duncan, 1991)
Designed to assess the environment of milieu programs. Factor analysis of 10 subscales yields two factors: (1) Positive therapeutic climate: characterized by exploration of personal issues within a clear program structure. Resembles a "good enough" containing environment. (2) Anger and staff control: reflects permission to express anger in safety, an important issue for a personality disorder population.	A content analysis system that assigns each therapist intervention to 1 of 10 categories. A dynamic component is defined as one part of a patient's conflict that exerts an internal force on some other part of the patient (e.g., a wish, anxiety, or defense).	Used to rate each statement by a patient or therapist for the presence of work and reference to persons (objects). Work is defined as an attempt to understand the problems of one or more members of the group, or the group as a whole. It is described in terms of conflict among dynamic components dealing with wishes, anxiety, and defenses. Any affect, behavior, or cognition may serve as a dynamic component if it is presented as an internal force that is part of conflict.	Defined as a person's internal enduring tendency to establish certain life-long types of relationships that range from primitive to mature; one semistructured interview provides information to rate patient on a nine-point scale, using four criteria: behavioral manifestations, affect regulation, self-esteem regulation, and antecedent (etiological) factors. Psychological Mindedness Assessment Procedure (PMAP) (McCallum & Piper, 1990) Defined as "the ability to identify dynamic (intrapsychic) components and relate them to a patient's difficulties," based on the patient's opinions of a brief videotape of a simulated patient-therapist interaction. Scored on dynamic components as such conflictual wishes and fears, defensive maneuvers, and parallels between internal and external events using a nine-point scale.

TABLE 14.3 Summary of Process Findings from Three Complex Research Programs Related to Group, Interpersonal, and Individual Boundaries*

Studies	Group Boundary	Interpersonal Boundary	Individual Boundary
Vancouver/Edmonton Grief Study (Piper et al., 1992) (McCallum et al., 1992)	Overall outcome statistically and clinically significant for patients serving as a wait list control, greater improvement was found during the treatment phase	PM predicts Work, and Work predicts Outcome. Catharsis of negative affect, that is, "the pain of grief," most effective when associated with evidence of Work.	Low PM and greater symptomatic severity strongly predicts a high dropout rate. PM does not predict outcome.
Vancouver/Edmonton Supportive/Interpretive Study (Piper et al., in press)	No overall statistical difference in outcome for patients in supportive or interpretative groups. Higher dropout rate in interpretive groups		PM predicts outcome in all conditions, Patients high on QOR improve more in interpretive groups, patients low on QOR improve more in supportive groups. Positive affect predicts outcome.
Vancouver/Edmonton Milieu Study (Piper et al., 1996)	Overall outcome statistically and clinically significant. Staff and patients agree on 8 of 10 COPES subscales. Anger expression and staff control reflecting permission to express anger in safety independently predicts outcome. Positive therapeutic climate characterized by exploration of personal issues independently predict outcome.	Work independently predicts outcome. Patients rated low on PM who rate other patients as high on Work have a better outcome. With Borderline PD, PM was not related to Work or Outcome, and Work was not associated with Outcome. Self-rated level of personal Work by patients with Paranoid PD increases the predictive ability of PM. Dependent PD is associated with higher levels of Work as seen by both other members and therapists, but not by self.	QOR independently predicts outcome and lower dropout rate. Level of PM independent of level of psychological disturbance and personality disorders.

Stuttgart project (Tschuschke & Dies, 1994, 1997) (Mackenzie & Tschuschke, 1993) (Tschuschke & MacKenzie, 1989) (Tschuschke et al., 1992) (Tschuschke et al., 1996) (Catina & Tschuschke, 1993)	Group Cohesiveness and the individual member's sense of Relatedness to the group predicts outcome. Working Alliance does not predict outcome. Moving through standard theorized stages of group development is correlated with better treatment outcome for the group members.	Self-Disclosure and Feedback (highly correlated) predict outcome. Interpersonal Work scores in first half of the group (not in later sessions) predict outcome. Members showing no early positive response in the first 10–15 sessions have poor outcome even if their Interpersonal Work improves. Patients with positive outcome received more (critical) feedback in the first half of the group. Less involved patients begin to receive more supportive and positive feedback in second half of the group, but have poorer outcome.	Only successful patients make significant changes in their perceptions of important relationship. On the Repertory Grid better treatment outcome is associated with changes in three aspects of the Repertory Grid (closer distances between "Mother" and "Me", "Me, as I want to be" (Ideal Self), "Me, as I am" (Real Self).
Kiel project (Strauss & Burgmeier-Lohse, 1994a, b) (Strauss et al., 1996) (Strauss & Burgmeier-Lohse, 1994a) (Davies-Osterkamp, 1996) (Strauss & Burgmeier-Lohse, 1995) (Strauss, 2000) (Strauss & Burgmeier-Lohse, 1994b)	Evidence of systematic group development (KGPS) not found. Relatedness to the group, autonomy, assertiveness, activity, and self-disclosure (GEQ, Stuttgarter Bogen) predict outcome.	Alpha (influential) and beta (realistic) sociometric position predict better: omega (negative) position poorer outcome. Dismissing attachment pattern predicts lower process ratings of altruism and cohesion.	Ambivalent attachment pattern predicts better, dismissing attachment pattern poorer outcome. IIP, CCRT, and SASB do *not* predict outcome.

[a] *Note:* no measure of leadership was used.

Leadership boundary implications were tested by using the same therapist to deliver both the supportive and interpretive models. Process rating measures (Piper, Debbanme, de Carufel, & Bienvu, 1987) indicate that therapists were successful in adhering to each model. *Interpersonal boundary* findings were evident for both clinical populations. Specifically, psychological mindedness predicted psychodynamic work, and work predicted outcome, providing additional support for the stability of the measures. The effectiveness of emotional catharsis was more predictive when it was combined with work. This finding suggested that neither a unitary focus on affect expression nor an emphasis solely on cognitive understanding would be likely to optimize outcome.

Several findings related to the *individual boundary* show that patients with low psychological mindedness and greater symptom severity are at high risk of dropping out in early sessions. The differentiated outcome between high and low QOR scores is a new and important finding and is bidirectional: high QOR predicted better outcome in the interpretive model and poorer outcome in the supportive model. Low QOR scores predicted better outcome in supportive treatment and poorer outcome in interpretive treatment. This finding agrees with the general psychotherapy literature (Horowitz et al., 1984) where those having greater psychological resources use psychotherapy more effectively.

These findings have immediate implications for group therapists. For instance, the *group-level* findings regarding effectiveness are sharpened by two *individual-level* considerations (i.e., PM and dropout, QOR and improvement; Table 14.3). Although some attrition is inevitable, the ability to predict dropout suggests the need for targeting at-risk patients with programmatic intervention. Premature termination not only signals the end of possibly helpful therapy, but the loss of members can also demoralize a group and result in further dropouts or inhibit future work. The treatment by patient interaction lends more precision concerning choice of a therapeutic model than previous findings allowed (Piper, 1994), honing clinicians' ability to prescribe helpful treatment approaches.

Milieu groups. Findings from the studies of milieu groups (Piper et al., 1996) are related to three boundary categories (Table 14.3). At the *group level*, the general agreement by patients and staff on the group environment subscales (COPES, Table 14.2) suggests that a reliable group-level process measure was achieved. The discrepancy between patient and staff rating on the milieu scales (patients reported higher levels of anger and aggression and lower levels of program clarity than staff) are understandable given the high proportion of personality disorders, especially borderline patients, where issues surrounding affect management and boundary structure are dominant. Moreover, group environment (COPES) independently contributed to outcome after considering the effects of *individual-level* processes (QOR and PM) that predicted outcome (Table 14.3). These group-level results not only support the efficacy of a psychodynamic model for a severely dysfunctional patient population, but also support the power of *group-level* processes on treatment outcome.

Several unique findings linked *interpersonal boundary* concerns to various personality disorders (Table 14.3). For all three of the personality disorders, a positive relationship was found between work and outcome, which is an encouraging finding given the challenging nature of this patient population. Psychological mindedness was not related to work or outcome for borderline patients. This finding distinguishes the borderline diagnosis from the other personality disorders in terms of response patterns. Other members see dependent personality disorder patients as hard at work, and, as one might expect, higher work predicted better outcome with this patient group. However, the patient's own self-reports of work were significantly lower, presumably reflecting the low self-esteem typical of dependent personality-disordered patients. Paranoid personality-disordered patients rated themselves more highly on work than did therapists or other patients; however, for these patients, work does not predict outcome regardless of the point of view. Patients' self-rating on work interacts with psychological mindedness levels such that patients rated low on psychological mindedness who rate other patients as high on work had a better outcome. This interesting finding suggests that perceiving other members as working may, to some extent, compensate for low psychological mindedness. This has possible relevance to the value of having a mix of psychological mindedness levels in each group.

Stuttgart Psychodynamic Inpatient Project. Tschuschke and colleagues have published a number of studies of patients treated in a European intensive milieu inpatient program with a patient population comparable to Piper's milieu patients (Table 14.3). Daily intensive small groups that extended over five to six months were considered the core of this program. Two *group boundary* process measures were used. The Stuttgarter Bogen (SB: Lerner & Ermann, 1976) has a seven-item measure of "cohesion" using the whole group as the unit of observation and an eight-item measure of "relatedness to the group." The Engaged subscale of the Group Climate Questionnaire (GCQ; MacKenzie, 1983) used a similar observational frame tapping the working alliance. In addition, two *interpersonal boundary* measures were employed. The Kelly Repertory Grid (cf. Tschushke et al., 1992) requests group participants to rate other group members and themselves on a series of descriptive dimensions. In this study, the grid was used as a process measure by correlating personal object grids with the initial grid of each group member. An act-by-act analysis of video/transcripts of each session using the Systematic and Multiple Level Observation of Groups Method SYMLOG (Bales, Cohen, & Williams, 1979) tapped self-disclosure, feedback, interpersonal work, and interpersonal learning-output.

This study was designed to test whether a closed-group environment from a "here-and-now" perspective would predict a "corrective emotional experience." Outcome measures included standard symptomatic measures as well as a measure of family reenactment as assessed by the *Kelly Repertory Grid* method. Changes in the Kelly Grid suggest significant shifts in relationship attitudes toward family members (past and present) and to self. Findings suggested that successful patients do experience a predictable sequence of process events (Table 14.3). Both *relatedness* to the group and group *cohesiveness* predicted better outcome. However, the *working alliance* in the whole group did not predict outcome. This discrepancy was related to a subgroup of patients who saw the group as working productively, yet did not feel part of it, highlighting the value of using both individual and group level measures of process.

Kiel Group Psychotherapy Study. The Kiel Group Psychotherapy project (Strauss & Burgmeier-Lohse, 1994a,b) was designed to study an inpatient psychodynamic slow open group (i.e., open group with members infrequently added) setting that was similar to the Stuttgart study. The patients suffered from severe Axis-I pathology (eating disorders and major depression) and/or personality disorders (borderline and schizotypical personal disorder) and attended group for six to seven months. Outcome was assessed on 10 scales, while process measures tapped four boundary conditions. The *group-level* process measures included cohesion (SB), GCQ, Group Experience Questionnaire (GEQ; Strauss & Eckert, 1994) and the Kiel Group Process Scales (KGPS; Strauss, Rohweder, Wienands, & Burgmeier-Lohse, 1996). The *therapist* boundary was assessed by the Helping Alliance Questionnaire (HAQ; Alexander & Luborsky, 1986), with *interpersonal* relations measured by both sociometric analysis (Hess, 1996) and the Duesseldorf Questionnaire of Therapeutic Factors (DQTF; Davies-Osterkamp, 1996). Finally, *individual* boundaries were assessed with the Inventory of Interpersonal Problems (IIP; Horowitz, Rosenberg, Baer et al., 1988), Core Conflictual Relationship Theme (CCRT; Luborsky et al., 1996), and Structural Assessment of Social Behavior (SASB; Benjamin, 1974).

Findings at the *group boundary* level were mixed. The KGPS failed to detect evidence of systematic group development. This finding may be related to the slow open format where membership changes push group development back to an engagement level, inhibiting group climate evolution. Nonetheless, *group-level* measures of cohesion (SB), group climate (GCQ), and member experience (GEQ) significantly predicted outcome. Interestingly, patients with a better outcome increasingly perceived the group as high on conflict and avoidance, suggesting an evolving perception of interpersonal work.

A test of the *leadership boundary* emerged from the fit between the treatment concepts of the therapist and the patient's experience of therapeutic factors. Congruence between therapists' and patients' views predicted better outcome at the end of treatment and at followup (Strauss & Burgmeier-Lohse, 1995). These results support Eckert and Biermann-Ratjen's (1990) notion that the "theory of the therapist" is an important factor in group treatments. Thus, what the therapist is thinking may permeate the therapeutic climate in unobtrusive ways that go beyond technical interventions (cf. Kivlighan & Tarrant, 2001).

A sociogram generated by members rating each other on a session-by-session basis, capturing the *interpersonal* boundary, predicted eventual outcome (Table 14.3). Sociometric measurement may be a powerful way of understanding group process but is seldom used despite its ease of implementation. Moreover, members who are not viewed in a positive manner on the sociogram may be at risk for poor outcome (Hess, 1992) and could be identified to ward off this event. Finally, three *individual boundary* measures were not associated with outcome (Kaspar, Sievers, Burgmeier-Lohse, & Strauss, 2000). However, attachment patterns were linked to outcome (Strauss, 2000), creating an opportunity for future treatment selection research. For instance, while strongly autonomous patients might do better in individual therapy (Robins et al., 1994), we know less about how many negatively valenced members a group can manage without undue damage to its effectiveness.

Individual Process Investigations

The past decade has seen a steady flow of singular group process studies with a variety of themes. Some appear to address a particular issue in the literature, using a design recommended by past reviewers (process outcome). Others are serial, yet unrelated, studies that follow a common, small-group process topic (group development). Although each study provides valuable information, the collective findings are difficult to integrate because different methodologies, measures, and content domains are employed. To the extent possible, individual process investigations with a sufficient number of studies to render tentative conclusions have been clustered by topic and design. We begin with two dominant themes in the small-group process literature (group development and therapeutic factors) that illustrate unique properties of the group format followed by two designs used to predict outcome (patient characteristic and process).

Group Development. Ingredient to theories of group development is the acceptance of the group as a *noun*, an entity having properties (i.e., group process principles) that are independent of the formal change theory (Figure 14.1). A host of different group development theories have been proffered and recently summarized (MacKenzie, 1994). However, each theory reflects the assumption that there will be a systematic deepening of the group's work requiring the use of stage-specific therapeutic strategies, regardless of the formal change theory that guides treatment. Successful groups are expected to show predictable features over time, and unsuccessful groups are thought to experience interruptions or developmental blocks that result in a return to earlier stage patterns or even disintegration.

The idea of group development brings with it two theoretical concepts. The first is epigenetic progress, which assumes that mastery of early stages is requisite to mastery of succeeding ones. There is considerable variability in the number and content of developmental stages proposed (cf. MacKenzie, 1994); however, most follow the basic outline proposed by Tuckman (1965), which includes forming (orientation and dependence), storming (intragroup conflict and differentiation), norming (interpersonal intimacy and cohesion), performing (work and functional role-relatedness), and adjourning (loss and autonomy). The second concept states that the group system will simultaneously increase in complexity across the different levels of the group system, including the total group, interpersonal interactions, and internal phenomena of individual members (cf. Figure 14.2). The isomorphy across levels of group describes, in part, why small-group process writers view the group as greater than the sum of its parts (i.e., group-as-a-whole perspective).

Although it is impossible to prove the existence of group development, substantial process literature has demonstrated phenomena that are compatible with the basic stages listed above, especially when closed time-limited groups are studied. The reports can be divided into two categories: those showing linear changes over the course of a group and those finding evidence of stage alterations, particularly a conflict/differentiation stage characterized by negativity and resistance that follows an early positive engagement phase. These two stages are then followed by a deepening of interpersonal work.

In addition to the developmental patterns noted in the preceding "complex programs of research" section, linear patterns showing progression have been identified: from casual familiarity to interpersonal intimacy (Barker, 1991); from low cohesion to high cohesion (Castonguay, Pincus, Agras, & Hines, 1998); from low to high engagement and high to low avoiding scores (Kivlighan & Goldfine, 1991); from cohesiveness associated with outside-group statements to cohesiveness negatively associated with such statements (Budman, Soldz, Demby, Davis, & Merry, 1993); from low to high use of positive and empathic statements (Wheeler & Kivlighan, 1995); from high to low use of outside and advice topics (Wheeler & Kivlighan 1995); from cognitive learning to interpersonal learning to behavioral application (Kivlighan & Mullison, 1988); and from leader tasks to relationship orientation (Kivlighan, 1997).

Patterns of group stage development are also evident in the group literature. Most rely on the subscales (engaged, avoiding, and conflict) of the Group Climate Questionnaire and test the stage model proposed and refined by MacKenzie (1983). A phasic pattern (low-high-low) of conflict has been shown to predict patient improvement (Brossart, Patton, & Wood, 1998; Castonguay, Pincus, Agras, & Hines, 1998; Kivlighan & Goldfine 1991; Kivlighan & Lilly, 1997), and high conflict and avoiding scores have been associated with patient termination (Brossart et al., 1998). Tschuschke and Dies (1994) report that patient improvement results from the following sequence of processes: an early positive emotional relationship to the group leads to self-disclosure, disclosure promotes feedback from other members, feedback results in changes to the interpersonal behavior within the group, and changes in group behavior are followed by an internal shift in pathological attitudes. Similarly, Kivlighan and Lilly (1997) found that *patterns* of process change were more predictive of improvement than *absolute* levels. Better outcome was found when cohesion and interpersonal work showed a continuous increase, and measures of conflict showed an early but brief increase. Brossart et al.'s study (1998) was the only report that did not find a positive link between process patterns and outcome. However, inexperienced therapists in the study may have had trouble managing early conflict and the stress of termination.

Finally, three papers used complex nonlinear dynamical analysis (chaos theory) to identify subtle underlying process patterns that were unencumbered by the usual assumptions of linearity. Fuhriman and Burlingame (1994) and Burlingame et al. (1995) rated every verbal utterance in eight time-limited psychotherapy groups using the Hill Interaction Matrix (Hill, 1965) and found increasing order and complexity in the therapeutic work of the group that is compatible with linear group development. However, Lichtenberg and Knox (1991) measured chaos trends in four therapy groups using only the response patterns to each speaker without consideration of verbal content and found no significant patterns. This complex analytic tool is in its infancy but offers a novel approach to studying the complexity of group process.

The collective evidence of these papers is very persuasive. Process patterns congruent with group development theory have been found using different measures, patient populations, and formal change theories. These results not only argue for the importance of group development theory but, on a larger scale, argue for the significance of considering *group-level* properties regardless of formal change theory. However, not all papers support the existence of developmental stages. Structural factors (Figure 14.1) such as open versus closed, time-limited versus time-unlimited group formats (Strauss & Burgmeier-Lohse, 1994a,b), and therapist factors (Brossart et al., 1998) may inhibit or annal developmental processes. Given the robust evidence for group development, it seems important to clarify the conditions that interfere with it.

Therapeutic Mechanisms. Over the last decade, the most commonly used process measurement has been some form of Yalom's Therapeutic Factors instrument (Yalom, 1995). This broad acceptance should have signaled a major step toward establishing an empirical base for understanding helpful process patterns. Unfortunately, several problems have inhibited progress. First, the literature consists of a large number of "modified" versions of the original instrument, making it impossible to reliably collate findings. Second, the typical study simply lists the therapeutic factors in order of aggregate member endorsement without connection to outcome. For instance, variation in rank orders have been assembled by nationality (Netherlands; Colijin, Hoencamp, Snijders, Van der Spek, & Duivenvoorden, 1991), ethnicity (Native American; Wilson, 1998), patient population (incest survivors; Wheeler, O'Mallcy, Waldo, Murphy, & Blank, 1992), treatment setting (acute; Hoge & McLoughlin, 1991), type of group (AA; Ciepialkowska, 1994), and group leader (occupational therapy; Webster & Schwartzberg, 1992). Finally, the typical modus operandi—a single rating without regard to group development—is unlikely to be representative of the group experience, especially considering the abundant evidence that members' views vary over time.

The dubious value of this collective literature leads us to endorse more advanced designs incorporating sequential measurement of therapeutic factors and possible covariates. For instance, Kivlighan, Multon, and Brossart, in their 1996 factor analytic study, uncovered four underlying therapeutic factor dimensions (relationship-climate, other versus self-focus, emotional awareness-insight, and problem solving-behavior change) that were differentially related to group leadership. Hurley (1997) used sequential measurement of self- and other-acceptance, demonstrating that a positively accelerating linear trend was related to leader and group climate measures, while Slavin (1993) reported here-and-now disclosure to be correlated with cohesion but not there-and-then disclosure. Promising psychometric developments have also been made. For instance, MacNair-Semands and Lese (2000) developed the Therapeutic Group Interaction Factors Scale, which is sensitive to group development and differentially correlates with interpersonal problems of individual members.

Overall, the therapeutic factors literature is mixed. The accrual of additional studies that rank order therapeutic factors will not measurably add to our clinical or theoretical knowledge and should be forsaken. On the other hand, the advent of instruments and advanced methodologies are a harbinger for a better understanding of the mechanisms of change.

Predicting Process and Outcome from Patient Characteristics. Patient characteristics were identified as a critical component to explain the effects of group treatment (Figure 14.1). Although diagnosis continues to be a frequently studied characteristic, Piper's (1994) review of 83 studies revealed interpersonal style to be the most promising predictor of treatment process and outcome. Several recent studies support this conclusion. For instance, patients with higher levels of interpersonal functioning have better outcome as measured by higher scores on the QOR (McCallum, Piper, & O'Kelly, 1997), Inventory of Interpersonal Problems (Davies-Osterkamp, 1996; Davies-Osterkamp et al., 1996; Liedtke 2001; Strauss, Eckert, & Ott 1993; Strauss et al., 1993), ego strength (Sexton, 1993), and secure attachment (Mosheim, Zachhuber, Scharf et al., 2000; Strauss, Eckert, & Ott, 1993; Strauss, Lobo-Drost, & Pilkonis, 1999).

Five studies investigated related personality styles, with three reporting better outcome when therapy was aligned to style. More specifically, Beutler et al. (1991) reported that "externalizing" patients improved more with group CBT (CBT-G) and those with inhibiting "resistance potential" did better with self-directed therapy. MacKenzie (2001b) found better outcomes for patients who rated themselves high on relationship seeking (Personal Style Inventory; Robins et al., 1994), and Saunders (1996) found that men with antisocial traits did better in CBT groups, while dependent men benefited more in process groups. However, two studies report findings that were not directly supportive of this pattern. Tasca, Russell, and Busby (1994) asked patients to choose between a structured activity-oriented program and process-oriented group psychotherapy and found that those with externalizing defenses chose the process group, while those with inhibiting defenses chose the more structured group. Using the Interpersonal Checklist, Kivlighan and Goldfine (1991) found that members rating themselves as more affiliative endorsed significantly more cognitive items on the Critical Incident Questionnaire. However, those rating themselves as nonaffiliative members endorsed more behavioral items, putting themselves in the aligning category.

Kordy and Senf (1992) studied 445 patients who dropped out of 58 inpatient groups to identify potential predictors; two clusters resulted. The first was a *group-related* cluster, suggesting that patients who were in an isolated position in the group with respect to their diagnosis, assigned to a larger group size (10 to 11 members compared to a mean of 7.7 members), admitted into an existing closed group, or waited for more than one year for treatment were more likely to drop out. The second cluster was *patient-related* and consisted of low motivation, physical symptoms, chronic course of illness, and geographical distance from hospital.

The patient is of paramount importance in understanding the effects of treatment. Unfortunately, it is not possible to draw firm conclusions due to variability in measures, patients, and treatments. There is a hint of support for aligning treatment approaches with patient characteristics, and this remains an important area for further research. More consistency is found in research on interpersonal characteristics. However, the lack of a common definition or measure is inhibiting progress on this construct. The study with the most discrepant results (Tasca et al., 1994) measured treatment preference rather than outcome, and it is unclear whether this variable is related to improvement. Finally, the issue of dropouts is an important one that results in underutilization of treatment resources and the possibility of demoralization of remaining members (and therapists). Regrettably, little interest in dropouts was evident during the last decade and this neglect needs to be rectified.

Process-Outcome Studies. The importance of linking specific mechanisms of action to patient improvement has been advocated by a host of past reviewers (Bednar & Kaul, 1994; Burlingame et al., 1994; Strauss & Burgmeier-Lohse, 1994b). The majority of these studies were reviewed in the preceding "complex programs of research" section; however, a small number that can further our understanding remain.

Several small-group processes have been related to outcome. For instance, patient improvement has been associated with early group cohesion (Strauss, 1992), early confrontation (Strauss, 1992), later positive alliance (Marziali, Munroe-Blum, & McCleary, 1997), later affective confrontation (Marziali et al., 1997; Soldz, Budman, & Demby, 1992; Strauss, 1992), and a greater abstinence of leader interventions in later sessions (Strauss, 1992). Moreover, Kivlighan and Tarrant (2001) found that group climate modulated the effect of therapist intentions. For instance, in the absence of active engagement (a measure of group work), therapeutic work and a safe environment did not have the expected positive effect on outcome.

Five studies investigating cognitive behavioral groups (CBT) are of particular interest, given that this model often does not emphasize group process strategies. Castonguay et al. (1998) reported that early positive affect (individual level), working atmosphere, and early cohesion (group level) predicted better outcome in binge eating disorder groups. Interestingly, elevations in midsession conflict scores were also predictive of better outcome, a phenomenon predicted by group development theory. Two studies (Free, Oei, & Appleton, 1998; Oei & Sullivan, 1999) of CBT for depression found that lower rates of participation predicted premature dropouts. Hamblin, Beutler, Scogin, and Cobishley (1993) reported that patient responsivity to therapist values was significantly related to improvement. Finally, Glass and Arnkoff (2000) found that common factors such as listening to others, talking in a group, and having homework assignments were as important to group members as the formal change theory. Although patients ranked formal change theory interventions highest with respect to value, group processes such as support, catharsis, and universality were ranked second with patients attributing improvement to participation in a cohesive group.

The cumulative value of findings from this small series of CBT-G process studies is provocative, yet by no means definitive. Small-group processes (cohesion, member participation, and therapeutic factors) were predictive of patient improvement at both the individual and group level. Moreover, at least one study (Castonguay et al., 1998) suggests that CBT groups follow patterns predicted by group development theory. Collectively, the authors argue for the need to be alert to the impact that process has on outcome in CBT groups, the most commonly used time-limited group approach. There is a clear need for further research studying the interplay between formal change theory strategies (e.g, cognition change) and group process principles. Finally, unstudied processes (affective confrontation, diminished leader interventions) provide fertile ground for future investigations.

Conceptual and Measurement Issues

Past reviews have made calls for greater conceptual clarity and measurement precision in the process literature (Bednar & Kaul, 1994; Burlingame et al., 1994; Fuhriman & Burlingame, 1994; MacNair-Semands, 1998). These advances must take place before individual process studies can accumulate into a body of knowledge that can guide our practice of group treatment. Accordingly, conceptual and measurement issues rise to the forefront in guiding future research.

Most of the process studies published over the past decade measure cohesion, alliance, or group climate. Unfortunately, ambiguity exists regarding these concepts (Budman et al., 1987; Dion, 2000; Kivlighan & Lilly, 1997; MacNair-Semands, 2000). For instance, Burlingame et al. (in press) uncovered 23 different measures of cohesion and group climate, each varied in definition, source (e.g., member & leader), and method of measurement (e.g., self-report, observation, sociometry, statement-by-statement analysis). Nonetheless, most consider cohesion to be a measure of belonging and acceptance at the group level. Accordingly, we contend that the proper procedure is to measure cohesion at the whole group level, regardless of whether the rater is a member, leader, or observer. When rated as such, results can be presented in terms of the group mean, and within-group agreement can be inspected to judge the reliability of the mean. There may be value in having cohesion assessed by multiple sources since ratings from independent observers and group members can vary (Piper et al., in press). On the other hand, alliance is a measure of interpersonal work factors, and it too can be measured at group, therapist, or member level, although it is usually restricted to the leader(s) (Piper et al., 1983).

Table 14.4. Belongingness, Attraction, and Work: Definitions and Theoretical Implications

	Common Belonging and Acceptance Factors			Common Interpersonal Work Factors		
	Group Cohesion	**"Pseudo" Cohesion**	**Alliance to Leader**	**Group Working Alliance**	**Individual Working Alliance**	**Group Climate**
Definition	Members rate the WHOLE GROUP on belongingness or attraction. Data is aggregated and reported as group mean with standard deviation.	Members rate the WHOLE GROUP on belongingness and attraction. Data is reported at individual level.	Members rate attraction to leader.	Members rate level or importance of psychological Work in the WHOLE GROUP.	Members rate personal level of work.	Members rate dimensions of the WHOLE GROUP (e.g., conflict, avoidance).
Illustrative Measures	CCI and CIQ		SQ and CALPAS-G	CCI	CALPAS-G	GCQ
Theoretical Implication	Cohesive groups have more members with better outcome.	Members who rate cohesion highly have better outcome.	Members with higher alliance to leader have better outcome.	Groups with higher mean ratings of work have more members with better outcome.	Members with higher personal ratings of work have better outcome.	Groups with a low-high-low pattern of conflict have more members with better outcome.

Note: CCI = Curative Climate Instrument; CIQ = Critical Incident Questionnaire; SQ = Stultgart Questionnaire; CALPAS-G = California Psychotherapy Alliance Scale; GCQ = Group Climate Questionnaire.

Table 14.4 attempts to clarify the closely related concepts of cohesion, alliance, and group climate found in the research and clinical literature. The three columns on the left side of the table assess the sense of acceptance and belonging to the *whole group* and/or to the *leader*. They might be measured by instruments such as the cohesion scale on the Curative Climate Instrument (CCI: Fuhriman, Drescher, Hanson, Henrie, & Rybicki, 1986), the understanding and involvement scale on the California Psychotherapy Alliance Scale (CALPS-G; Gaston, 1991; Gaston & Marmar, 1991); the alliance to the leader scale on the Stuttgart Questionnaire (SQ: Tschuschke, 1996), or the therapeutic factor of acceptance on the Critical Incident Questionnaire (CIQ: Hurd, 1996). These properties reflect "common factors" associated with an accepting and safe group environment that has been related to low dropout rates and patient improvement in nearly every group process-outcome report.

The three columns on the right side of Table 14.4 deal with the interpersonal work dimension of group treatment. They address cognitive efforts to learn about self and might be measured by instruments such as the insight scale on the CCI (Fuhriman et al., 1986); patient working capacity and commitment scales on the CALPAS-G (Gaston, 1991); and engaged, conflict, and avoiding scales on the Group Climate Questionnaire (GCQ: MacKenzie, 1983). These scales address psychological work that could be termed "common working factors" and are closely related to the concept of interpersonal learning. The technical skills of the therapist in promoting a working environment may play a particularly important role in groups for more severely dysfunctional patients, while common supportive factors may be adequate for change in groups with lower levels of dysfunction.

Although much can be learned from process measures designed to score act-by-act interactions from videotapes and/or transcripts (e.g., the Hill Interaction Matrix: Fuhriman & Burlingame, 2000; SYMLOG: Bales et al., 1979), the extensive training and labor-intensive rating required may explain why they are seldom used in the group process literature. Flowers, Boorgem, and Schwartz (1993) suggested that process measures that are simple, short, and easily scored result in more frequent use, higher member satisfaction, and greater clinical impact. The measures identified in Table 14.4 meet these requirements and could be thought of as a "beginning" process assessment battery. Moreover, they reflect therapeutic factors that have been frequently endorsed across multiple process studies (Hoge & McLoughlin, 1991).

General Observations and Recommendations

Eight years ago Bednar and Kaul (1994) concluded that the orderly evolution of knowledge in the group disciplines had produced evidence that group treatment was more effective than no-treatment, placebo-attention, and nonspecific treatment comparison conditions. Given this foundation, has the past decade of research taken us any further along the evolutional trail? We believe that the answer to this question is a qualified yes.

Our organization of outcome investigations by disorder and patient population exposed variability in evidence regarding the efficacy of different treatment models. In some cases, specific treatment models designed for particular patient populations have been tested with rigorous designs, resulting in high efficacy marks (panic, social phobia, and schizophrenia). In other instances, multiple models appear to be equally effective (mood, bulimia nervosa, and cancer). In still other cases, the evidence was promising, yet not compelling (OCD and substance abuse), or the treatment models were underdeveloped or tested with unsophisticated research designs (elders, domestic violence, sexual abuse, and HIV/AIDS). A recent meta-analysis of 111 studies provides support for the differential effectiveness of group protocols for different psychiatric disorders (Burlingame, Fuhriman & Mosier, in press). We believe that it is no longer acceptable to describe group treatment as effective in a generic sense. The cumulative evidence can now *begin* to support specific statements regarding differential effectiveness of treatment models for specific disorders.

The emergence of research teams devoted to the systematic study of mechanisms of action in group treatment is a harbinger of a new and exciting age in the process literature. There is incalculable benefit in systematically studying a treatment model with the same population using theoretically relevant process and outcome measures. What is different and exciting about these research programs is that they have gone beyond the study of general group process principles (structure, feedback, etc.). More specifically, the process measures of key mechanisms have been carefully developed and applied to understand *how* change takes place, with whom, and when, using a specific model of group treatment. These efforts are in stark contrast to the single-shot process studies that are not carefully connected to the theoretical and empirical literature, which, in turn, add very little to our knowledge. Unfortunately, the latter describes the bulk of the process literature.

A cumulative effect of these promising evolutionary developments is that substantive conclusions are now focused on the treatment model and its application to specific patient populations as reflected in the preceding pages. However, having some specific treatment and patient evidence does not exclude the value of general recommendations. We believe that if future researchers heed the following recommendations, a stronger and more substantive knowledge base will result.

Recommendation 1. Report a basic minimal amount of information regarding the salient aspects of the study.

The increasing specificity in the literature provides an opportunity for establishing outcome conclusions related to group treatments for specific populations. However, the large number of studies that fail to provide the basic details of the study and its components significantly attenuates the possibility of offering substantive conclusions. Accordingly, we have developed a list of recommended data needed to evaluate group studies (Table 14.5) to raise the quality of research reports and to help future reviewers capture a more complete picture of the group. The requirements relate to the basic "who, what, when, where, and how questions" in research and can be divided into information related to the sample of patients, the group leader(s), the treatment approach, group characteristics, and methodological aspects (cf. Strauss, Burlingame, & MacKenzie, in press).

The following questions should be answered in research reports: What is the *sample* size, how was it created (referred or solicited), and were there any obvious selection effects? The *patients* should be characterized with respect to gender, age, education, socioeconomic status, and ethnicity. Diagnostic information should not be restricted to primary diagnoses, and a better understanding of the source of the diagnoses (clinical, based on diagnostic interviews such as the SCID), comorbidities, and duration of the problem is needed. The number of *leaders*, gender, experience (e.g., number of groups run, total number of group experience hours), and training should be provided as well as whether a coleader was present.

Studies should explicitly specify the *theoretical model* of the treatment, including information about the use of treatment manuals, session characteristics, or session outlines and their structure. The *group setting* should be described, including the number, length, and frequency of the group sessions as well as group format (closed, slow open, or open). Finally, detailed descriptions of the criteria of membership and the composition of the group(s) are required, including the sex ratio, the distribution of diagnosis in heterogeneous groups, and the distribution of further relevant features.

Methodologically, the type of the study design should be noted, and reports should contain detailed information on followup assessments; the presence, magnitude, and attrition effect on the group (during treatment and at followup); process and outcome measures; the source of the measures (self, other); and psychometric data. The *presentation of the results* should clearly differentiate the unit of analysis and, optimally, include both total group and individual group results (e.g., how many individual groups had poor outcomes). Similarly, outcome should be reported by the individual patient indicating whether clinically significant change has occurred. Procedures for estimating group dependency should be reported (e.g., intraclass correlation), and since the results will probably be included in future meta-analyses, effect size estimates or at least the information necessary to compute effect sizes (means *and* variances) should be included. Evidence of this basic information should be included in every group report.

Recommendation 2. Select a research design that aligns with the state of knowledge and is likely to add substantively to the literature.

Scientific knowledge follows a somewhat orderly progression (Burlingame et al., 1994) and investigators should have an adequate understanding of the maturity of their field and match their research design accordingly. We have noted several examples where further use of a specific design (e.g., pre-post, outcome, or ranking of therapeutic factors) was unlikely, in our opinion, to contribute to the literature. In other cases, investigators have employed research designs that were far more rigorous than their treatment model warranted. Tests of ill-defined treatment models with an experimental design are far too frequent in the group literature.

TABLE 14.5 Recommended Data for the Publication of Group Psychotherapy Studies

Sample/patients	Sample size Demographic (gender, age, ethnicity, and socioeconomic status) Dx. info. (Diagnosis and source, e.g. comorbidity and duration, clinical interview or standardized measure) Experiences with mental health treatment — before entering group — subsequent to group therapy (in case of followup) Recruited patients vs. walk-ins
Therapists/Leaders	Number of therapists Gender Training and experience Adherence Coleadership
Treatment model/groups	Theoretical model (manualized, session outline) Duration, number, frequency of sessions, and groups Group composition (gender, age, diagnoses, criteria for membership) Group size Group format (closed, slow open, open)
Methodology	Research design Sample selection throughout the study (i.e., attrition) Measures Followup Information necessary to compute effect sizes (M, SD) Both total group & individual group results Intraclass correlation coefficients to ascertain dependency

An overly simplistic set of steps would be to first develop and *pilot* a group treatment, carefully, examining pilot data to determine *potential* benefits as well as necessary modifications in the model. If the pilot data suggested patient benefit, the model could then be submitted to *repeated* testing with pre-post designs to determine its effectiveness. During this phase, the investigator could collect pertinent patient and process information that might interact with the success of the treatment and develop clear and testable hypotheses. Only those models that have been shown to be *empirically effective* should be submitted to rigorous experimental designs to test their efficacy in contrast to comparison groups (no-treatment, placebo, or active treatment). A similar progression of design sophistication is operative for process research (cf. Burlingame et al., 1994). In the group literature, too many studies skip one or more of these steps, invariably resulting in experimental noise (e.g., variability in treatment implementation, patient response, etc.) that rivals the effects of treatment. Another frequent occurrence is the failure to move beyond the pilot or case study phase of development, resulting in a disproportionately high number of small *n* studies.

Recommendation 3. Study efficacious models for potential interaction effects.

Several examples were provided (e.g., mood, pathological grief, substance) that demonstrated the value of testing for interactions between patient characteristics and treatment models. For instance, the work of the Vancouver/Edmonton team demonstrates the clinical value of theoretically matching relevant patient characteristics to specific treatments to achieve optimal improvement. We contend that after a group treatment has empirical support for effectiveness or efficacy at the *aggregate* level, an important next step is to determine its effect at the *individual* patient level. Although there are a plethora of models meeting the effectiveness or efficacy criteria, there is a paucity that test for such interactions. Tests of interactions should include not only patient characteristics, but also other relevant treatment considerations (e.g., the well-established effect of psychotropic medication is often ignored).

Recommendation 4. Report durability of change and patient retention systematically since they have methodological and clinical import.

Although significant progress has been achieved in incorporating followup assessments over the past decade, there is room for improvement. Given recent evidence, it is untenable to assume that treatment gains will be maintained after the termination of active treatment. We suggest 6- and 12-month followup periods as a minimum, recognizing that this time frame may need to be extended based on the chronicity of the disorder. An excellent example of the clinical implications of adequate followup emerges from the work of Heimberg and colleagues (1998; Liebowitz et al., 1999). Followup data, in part, led this team to add four booster sessions of group, resulting in more durable treatment effects that eventually rivaled the effects of medication. A similar pattern resulted in the use of aftercare group treatment for more severe disorders (e.g., schizophrenia, borderline PD).

In the studies we reviewed, retention of group members ranged from 18 to 100%. Although differential attrition has obvious implications for the generalizability of findings (Cook & Campbell, 1979), high attrition can also be a disruptive influence for those who remain in treatment (Yalom, 1995). Groups that systematically suffer from problems of high attrition should leverage against known group properties and techniques that might be of assistance. For instance, higher levels of retention have been associated with cohesion, which, in turn, can be facilitated by group and interpersonal-level interventions (cf. Burlingame et al., in press). In short, salient aspects of group theory may offer some solutions to the problem of differential attrition noted in the literature.

Recommendation 5. Increase attention on the theoretically predicted mechanisms of change (process-outcome links) to explain treatment results.

Previous editions of this chapter (e.g., Bednar & Kaul, 1994) have decried the lack of empirical support for purported mechanisms of change. This concern is echoed in the counterintuitive findings of a few studies in which placebo-attention and mutual support groups posted equivalent or superior findings when compared to active treatment. What is responsible for these effects? Although the administration of one or two self-report process measures (e.g., cohesion) is laudable, it falls far short of the scrutiny needed to establish even the most cursory causal links for mechanisms of change. Moreover, global process measures that are not carefully linked to the goals of group treatment can yield theoretically barren results. There is good evidence that process patterns evolve over time; therefore, process should be repeatedly assessed over the life of the group.

A few exemplary research programs were noted that have begun to fill this gap using two divergent approaches. The Heimberg team (Hope et al., 1995) tackled the mechanisms of change question by testing the underlying change strategy of the treatment model. More specifically, they first identified the theoretically potent components of the *treatment model* (e.g., exposure, cognitive restructuring) and then tested the differential efficacy of each on patient outcome. The Stuttgart program took a different tact by focusing on the group-as-a-whole as the mechanism of change. Accordingly, they measured the impact of theoretically potent aspects of *group properties* (interpersonal feedback, cohesion, self-disclosure) on patient outcome. Finally, the Vancouver/Edmonton team reflects a combination of both approaches, with measures testing components of the *treatment model* and *group* as possible mechanisms of change.

Since placebo-attention or paraprofessional groups are likely to contain active ingredients found in the formal change theories (e.g., unplanned in vivo exposure to distressing stimuli or cohesion), investigators would be wise to investigate both types of mechanisms focusing on the systemic (leader and group) and treatment components (Figures 14.1 and 14.2). In many studies, fidelity checks are routinely conducted with inferential statistics, demonstrating that the therapist is engaging in *more* of the desired interventions. This test does not entirely address the point we are raising. In *group* treatment, the therapist is only one change agent, and even if he or she has a lower mean on a particular intervention type, it does not rule out the operation of other mechanisms of change. In the measurement literature, there is a scaling model labeled "partial credit" which is intended to capture variance due to the fractional presence of a phenomena. What we are suggesting is that fractional mechanisms of change may be operative in two sources—leader and group—and that assessment of both is essential for a comprehensive understanding of process-outcome links.

Recommendation 6. Give greater attention to the process of transferring formal theories of change from individual to group formats.

A common concern that has been repeatedly raised in the group literature is the inattentive transfer of individual treatment models into the group format (Fuhriman & Burlingame, 1990). Groups have unique systemic properties (Burlingame et al., in press), and in many cases interventions designed for dyadic treatment simply don't "play well" in the group setting. For instance, the Castonguay et al. (1998) study provides some evidence that important supportive group properties emerge in highly structured models that were initially developed for individual treatment (e.g., CBT). In fact, these properties may emerge even if the treatment model does not formally facilitate them.

We see the Wilfley et al. (1998; in press) work in modifying CBT and IPT models as they migrate to the group format as a very promising contribution. As noted earlier, there has been a significant shift of treatment models in the empirical group literature over the past 10 years, with more traditional group approaches (e.g., process, nondirective, psychodynamic) giving way to cognitive and behavioral models. We believe that patient improvement may be compromised if careful attention is not given to the unique and inherently therapeutic properties of the group when empirically supported individual models are offered in a group format.

Recommendation 7. Focus considerable conceptual and empirical attention on the technical and personal aspects of group leadership.

The paucity of papers devoted to exploring the characteristics of effective leadership of *clinical groups* is disquieting. In some cases, the conceptual and empirical knowledge base on this topic is dated, extending back nearly 30 years. This is particularly problematic given that many of the treatment models in use today did not exist when the leadership knowledge base was created. Although general principles may transfer from this literature, the current dominance of highly structured group treatments demands that we give immediate empirical attention to understanding the role of the leader. Does the leader manage multiple relationships differently in a high- versus low-structure group treatment? If so, what effect does this have on treatment outcome? Given that cohesion has been defined as the therapeutic relationship in group psychotherapy (Burlingame et al., in press; Fuhriman & Barlow, 1983) and that it has been linked to patient outcome in most studies, careful attention needs to be given to the role of the leader in fostering this important group process principle. Group leadership has remained a dynamic topic in social psychology and organizational behavior and this literature may be a valuable source in guiding future clinical inquiries on this topic.

Recommendation 8. Direct efforts toward building consensus on core process and outcome measures are needed.

Confidence in evidence-based inferences regarding efficacy and mechanisms of action is directly tied to the rigor and common variance in measurement protocols. Too much variability was evident in the measures being used to evaluate the efficacy and effectiveness of group treatments within diagnostic categories, and near independence exists between the same clinical populations. Over 160 standardized measures were used to assess patient improvement in the 106 outcome studies reviewed. Instrument variability motivated the proposal of a "core" set of brief process measures. Consensus of measures will increase knowledge overlap between investigations. This recommendation, of course, does not address the need for continued development of observational measures (e.g., HIM, SYMLOG) that track similar or related group processes.

The American Psychological Association recently sponsored a large collaborative conference aimed at generating a core set of measures for quantifying patient outcome (Strupp, Horowitz, & Lambert, 1997). Would a similar conference aimed at identifying a core battery of outcome and process measures be useful for the group psychotherapy literature? Perhaps. The core battery proposed by the American Group Psychotherapy Association nearly three decades ago had modest success in the empirical literature. However, this historical success must be balanced by the complexity and diversity of the current group literature that presents an entirely different challenge.

Recommendation 9. Direct more empirical attention on group treatments for severely and persistently mentally ill (SPMI) patients.

Without a doubt, SPMI patients consume a disproportionate percentage of the mental health resources and the cost-effectiveness of the group format argues for further refinement and study of models for these patients. The good news is that we have a few well-developed and tested models for individuals with schizophrenia (e.g., Brenner et al., 1990, 1992a, 1992b; Liberman et al., 1993, 1998; Spaulding et al., 1999) and personality disorders (Dazord et al., 1997; Linehan et al., 1999; Piper et al., 1996). The bad news is that simply too little empirical work is being conducted in this vital area.

Summary

After reviewing hundreds of group psychotherapy outcome and process studies, we are guardedly optimistic. The literature has become stronger and deeper and is capable of supporting evidence-based treatment recommendations for some patient populations. On the other hand, we face considerable challenges in bolstering our treatment models for some patient populations and refining our understanding of mechanisms of action to explain the change associated with group treatment. The unique features of group treatment articulated in Figures 14.1 and 14.2 outline the minimum dimensions for consideration. We hope that the recommendations herein provide useful guidance for current and future investigators as we enter a new millennium of group research.

References

Abraham, I. L., Neundorfer, M. M., & Currie, L. J. (1992). Effects of group interventions on cognition and depression in nursing home residents. *Nursing Research, 41(4)*, 196–202.

Alexander, L. B., & Luborsky, L. (1986). The Penn helping alliance scales. In L. S. Greenberg & W. S. Pinsof (Eds.), *The psychotherapeutic process* (pp. 325–364). New York: Guilford Press.

Arean, P., & Miranda, J. (1996). The treatment of depression in elderly primary care patients: A naturalistic study. *Journal of Clinical Geropsychology, 2(3)*, 153–160.

Atkinson, J., Coia, D. A., Gilmour, W. H., & Harper, J. P. (1996). The impact of education groups for people with schizophrenia on social functioning and quality of life. *British Journal of Psychiatry, 168*, 199–204.

Azim, H.F.A., Piper, W. E., Segal, P. M., Nixon, G.W.H., & Duncan, S. C. (1991). The quality of object relations scale. *Bulletin of the Menninger Clinic, 55*, 323–343.

Bagley, C., & Young, L. (1998). Long-term evaluation of group counselling for women with a history of child sexual abuse: Focus on depression, self-esteem, suicidal behaviors and social support. *Social Work with Groups, 21(3)*, 63–73.

Baider, L., Uziely, B., & DeNour, A. K. (1994). Progressive muscle relaxation and guided imagery in cancer patients. *General Hospital Psychiatry, 16(5)*, 340–347.

Bales, R. F., Cohen, S. P., & Williams, S. A. (1979). *SYMLOG: A system for the multiple level observation of groups*. New York: Free Press.

Barker, D. B. (1991). The behavioral analysis of interpersonal intimacy in group development. *Small Group Research, 22*, 76–91.

Barlow, S., Burlingame, G., & Fuhriman, A. (2000). The therapeutic application of groups: From Pratt's thought control classes to modern group psychotherapy. *Group Dynamics: Theory, Research, and Practice, 4(1)*, 115–134.

Beck, A. P., & Lewis, C. M. (Eds.). (2000). The process of group psychotherapy: Systems for analyzing change. Washington, DC: American Psychological Association.

Bednar, R. L., & Kaul, T. J. (1994). Experiential group research: Can the cannon fire? In A. E. Bergin & S. L. Garfield (Eds.), *Handbook of psychotherapy and behavior change* (4th ed.) (pp. 631–663). New York: John Wiley & Sons.

Beem, E. E., Hooijkaas, H., Cleiren, M. H., Schut, H. A., Garssen, B., Croon, M. A., Jabaaij, L., Goodkin, K., Wind, H., & de Vries, M. J. (1999). The immunological and psychological effects of bereavement: Does grief counseling really make a diffrence? A pilot study. *Psychiatry Research, 85(1)*, 81–93.

Bellak, A. S., & Mueser, K. T. (1993). Psychosocial treatment for schizophrenia. *Schizophrenia Bulletin, 19(2)*, 317–336.

Benjamin, L. S. (1974). Structural analysis of social behavior. *Psychological Review, 81*, 392–425.

Benton, M. K., & Schroeder, H. E. (1990). Social skills training with schizophrenics: A meta-analytic evaluation. *Journal of Consulting and Clinical Psychology, 58(6)*, 741–747.

Beutler, L. E., Engle, D., Mohr, D., Daldrup, R. J., Bergan, J., Meredith, K., & Merry, W. (1991). Predictors of differential response to cognitive, experiential, and self-directed psychotherapeutic procedures. *Journal of Consulting and Clinical Psychology, 59(2)*, 333–340.

Beutler, L. E., Machado, P. P., Engle, D., & Mohr, D. (1993). Differential patient treatment maintenance among cognitive, experiential, and self-directed psychotherapies. *Journal of Psychotherapy Integration, 3(1)*, 15–31.

Bowers, T. G., & Al-Redha, M. R. (1990). A comparison of outcome with group/marital and standard/individual therapies with alcoholics. *Journal of Studies on Alcohol, 51(4)*, 301–309.

Braaten, L. J. (1990). The different patterns of group climate and critical incidents in high and low cohesion sessions of group psychotherapy. *International Journal of Group Psychotherapy, 40(4),* 477–493.

Brannen, S. J., & Rubin, A. (1996). Comparing the effectiveness of gender-specific and couples groups in a court-mandated spouse abuse treatment program. *Research on Social Work Practice, 6(4),* 405–424.

Branson, B. M., Peterman, T. A., Cannon, R. O., Ransom, R., & Zaidi, A. A. (1998). Group counseling to prevent sexually transmitted disease and HIV: A randomized controlled trial. *Sexually Transmitted Disease, 25(10),* 553–560.

Brenner, H. D., Hodel, B., Genner, R., Roder, V., & Corrigan, P. W. (1992a). Biological and cognitive vulnerability factors in schizophrenia: Implications for treatment. *British Journal of Psychiatry, 161(18),* 154–163.

Brenner, H. D., Hodel, B., Roder, V., & Corrigan, P. (1992 b). Treatment of cognitive dysfunctions and behavioral deficits in schizophrenia. *Schizophrenia Bulletin, 18(1),* 21–26.

Brenner, H. D., Kraemer, S., Hermanutz, M., & Hodel, B. (1990). Cognitive treatment in schizophrenia. In E. R. Straube & K. Hahlweg (Eds.), *Schizophrenia: Concepts, vulnerability and interventions* (pp. 161–192). New York: Springer-Verlag.

Bretz, H. J., Heekerens, H. -P., & Schmitz, B. (1994). Eine Metanalyse zur Wirksamkeit von Gestalttherapie [Metanalytical assessment of the effectiveness of Gestalt therapy]. *Zeitschrift für Klinische Psychologie, Psychiatrie und Psychotherapie, 42,* 241–260.

Bright, J. I., Baker, K. D., & Neimeyer, R. A. (1999). Professional and paraprofessional group treatments for depression: A comparison of cognitive-behavioral and mutual support interventions. *Journal of Consulting and Clinical Psychology, 67(4),* 491–501.

Brossart, D., Patton, M., & Wood, P. (1998). Assessing group process: An illustration using Tuckerized growth curves. *Group Dynamics: Theory, Research, and Practice, 2(1),* 3–17.

Buccheri, R., Trygstad, L., Kanas, N., Waldron, B., & Dowling, G. (1996). Auditory hallucinations in schizophrenia: Group experience in examining symptom management and behavioral strategies. *Journal of Psychosocial Nursing, 34(2),* 12–25.

Budman, S. H., Demby, A., Feldstein, M., Redondo, J. Scherz, B., Bennett, M. J., Koppenaal, G., Daley, B. S., Hunter, M., & Ellis, J. (1987). Preliminary findings on a new instrument to measure cohesion in group psychotherapy. *International Journal of Group Psychotherapy, 37,* 75–94.

Budman, S. H., Demby, A., Soldz, S., & Merry, J. (1996). Time-limited group psychotherapy for patients with personality disorders: Outcomes and dropouts. *International Journal of Group Psychotherapy, 46,* 357–377.

Budman, S., & Gurman, A. (1988). *Theory and practice of brief therapy.* New York: Guilford Press.

Budman, S. H., Soldz, S., Demby, A., Davis, M., & Merry, J. (1993). What is cohesiveness? An empirical examination. *Small Group Research, 24,* 199–216.

Burlingame, G. M., & Barlow, S. H. (1996). Outcome and process differences between professional and nonprofessional therapists in time-limited group psychotherapy. *International Journal of Group Psychotherapy, 46(4),* 455–478.

Burlingame, G. M., Ellsworth, J. R., Richardson, E. J., & Cox, J. C. (2000). How effective is group psychotherapy: A review and synthesis of treatment outcomes. *Ricerche Sui Gruppi, 10,* 7–35.

Burlingame, G. M., Fuhriman, A., & Barnum, K. R. (1995). Group therapy as a nonlinear dynamical system: Analysis of therapeutic communication for chaotic patterns. In F. D. Abraham & A. R. Gilgen (Eds.), *Chaos theory in psychology.* Westport, CT: Praeger Publisher/Greenwood Publishing Group.

Burlingame, G. M., Fuhriman, A., & Johnson, J. (2002). Cohesion in group psychotherapy. In J. Norcross (Ed.), *A guide to psychotherapy relationships that work* (pp. 71–88). Oxford: Oxford University Press.

Burlingame, G. M., Fuhriman, A., & Mosier, J. (in press). The differential effectiveness of group psychotherapy: A meta-analytic perspective. *Group dynamics: Theory, research & practice.*

Burlingame, G. M., Kircher, J. C., & Taylor, S. (1994). Methodological considerations in group psychotherapy research: Past, present, and future practices. In A. Fuhriman & G. M. Burlingame (Eds.), *Handbook of group psychotherapy: An empirical and clinical synthesis* (pp. 41–80). New York: John Wiley & Sons.

Burlingame, G. M., Lambert, M., Reisinger, C., Neff, W., & Mosier, J. (1995). Pragmatics of tracking mental health outcome in managed care settings. *Journal of Mental Health Administration, 22(3),* 226–235.

Burtscheidt, W., Schwarz, R., Rdner, C., & Gaebel, W. (1999). Verhaltenstherapeutische Verfahren in der ambulanten Behandlung von Alkoholabhängigen [Behavioral approaches to the outpatient treatment of alcoholism]. *Forschritte der Neurologie und Psychiatrie, 67,* 274–280.

Castonguay, L. G., Pincus, A. L., Agras, W. S., & Hines, C. E. (1998). The role of emotion in group cognitive-behavioral therapy for binge eating disorder: When things have to feel worse before they get better. *Psychotherapy Research, 8(2),* 225–238.

Catina, A., & Tschuschke, V. (1993). A summary of empirical data from the investigation of two psychoanalytic groups by means of repertory grid technique. *Group Analysis, 26(4)*, 433–447.

Chambon, O., & Marie-Cardine, M. (1998). An evaluation of social skills training modules with schizophrenia inpatients in France. *International Review of Psychiatry, 10(1)*, 26–29.

Choi, K. H., Lew, S., Vittinghoff, E., Catania, J. A., Barrett, D. C., & Coates, T. J. (1996). The efficacy of brief group counseling in HIV risk reducation among homosexual Asian and Pacific Islander men. *AIDS, 10(1)*, 81–87.

Ciepialkowska, L. (1994). Therapeutic factors in AA and Al-Anon groups. *Polish Psychological Bulletin 25(1)*, 59–73.

Cohen, D. A., MacKinnon, D. P., Dent, C., Mason, H. R., & Sullivan, E. (1992). Group counseling at STD clinics to promote use of condoms. *Public Health Report, 107(6)*, 727–731.

Colijn, S., Hoencamp, E., Snijders, H.J.A., Van der Spek, M.W.A., & Duivenvoorden, H. J. (1991). A comparison of curative factors in different types of group psychotherapy. *International Journal of Group Psychotherapy, 41(3)*, 365–377.

Cook, T. D., & Campbell, D. T. (1979). *Quasi-experimentation: Design and analysis issues for field settings.* Chicago: Rand McNally.

Cox, P., Ilfeld, F., Ilfeld, B. S., & Brennan, C. (1999). Group therapy program development: Clinician-administrator collaboration in new practice settings. *International Journal of Group Psychotherapy, 50(1)*, 3–24.

Crits-Christoph, P., Siqueland, L., Blaine, J., Frank, A., Luborsky, L., Onken, L. S., Muenz, L. R., Thase, M. E., Weiss, R. D., Gastfriend, D. R., Woody, G. E., Barber, J. P., Butler, S. F., Daley, D., Salloum, I., Bishop, S., Najavits, L. M., Lis, J., Mercer, D., Griffin, M. L., Moras, K., & Beck, A. T. (1999). Psychosocial treatments for cocaine dependence: National Institute on Drug Abuse Collaborative Cocaine Treatment Study. *Archives of General Psychiatry, 56(6)*, 493–502.

Cunningham, A. J. (1995). Group psychological therapy for cancer patients: A brief discussion of indicators for its use and the range of interventions available. *Journal of Supportive Care in Cancer, 3*, 244–247.

Cwikel, J. G., & Behar, L. C. (1999). Social work with adult cancer patients: A vote-count review of intervention research. *Social Work in Health Care, 29(2)*, 39–67.

Daniels, L. (1998). A group cognitive-behavioral and process-oriented approach to treating the social impairment and negative symptoms associated with chronic mental illness. *Journal of Psychotherapy Practice and Research, 7(2)*, 167–176.

Davies-Osterkamp, S. (1996). Der Duesseldorfer Wirkfaktorenfragebogen. In B. Struss, J. Eckert, & V. Tschuschke (Eds.), *Methoden der empirischen Gruppentherapieforschung—Ein Handbuch.* Wiesbaden: Westdeutscher Verlag.

Davies-Osterkamp, S., Strauss, B., & Schmitz, N. (1996). Interpersonal problems as predictors of symptom-related treatment outcome in longterm psychotherapies. *Psychotherapy Research, 6*, 164–176.

Davis, R., Olmsted, M. P., & Rockert, W. (1990). Brief group psychoeducation for bulimia nervosa: Assessing the clinical significance of change. *Journal of Consulting and Clinical Psychology, 58(6)*, 882–885.

Davis, R., Olmsted, M., Rockert, W., Marques, T., & Dolhanty, J. (1997). Group psychoeducation for bulimia nervosa with and without additional psychotherapy process sessions. *International Journal of Eating Disorders, 22(1)*, 25–34.

Dazord, H., Gerin, P., Seulin, G., Duclos, A., & Amar, A. (1997). Day-treatment evaluation: Therapeutic outcome after a treatment in a psychiatric day-treatment center. *Psychotherapy Research, 7(1)*, 57–69.

De Jong, T. L., & Gorey, K. M. (1996). Short-term versus long-term group work with female survivors of childhood sexual abuse: A brief meta-analytic review. *Social Work with Groups, 19(1)*, 19–27.

De Vries, M. J., Schilder, J.M.N., Mulder, C. L., Vrancken, A. M., Remie, M., & Garssen, B. (1997). Phase II study of psychotherapeutic intervention in advanced cancer. *Psycho-oncology, 6(2)*, 129–137.

Dickerson, F. B. (2000). Cognitive behavioral psychotherapy for schizophrenia: A review of recent empirical studies. *Schizophrenia Research, 43*, 71–90.

Dies, R. (1994). Therapist variables in group psychotherapy research. In A. Fuhriman & G. M. Burlingame (Eds.), *Handbook of group psychotherapy: An empirical and clinical synthesis* (pp. 114–154). New York: John Wiley & Sons.

Dion, K. L. (2000). Group cohesion: From "field of forces" to multidimensional construct. *Group Dynamics: Theory, Research, and Practice, 4(1)*, 7–26.

Dobson, D.J.G., McDougall, G., Busheikin, J., & Aldous, J. (1995). Effects of social skills training and social milieu treatment on symptoms of schizophrenia. *Psychiatric Services, 46(4)*, 376–380.

Dolgin, M. J., Somer, E., Zaidel, N., & Zaizov, R. (1997). A structured group intervention for siblings of children with cancer. *Journal of Child and Adolescent Group Therapy, 7(1)*, 3–18.

Drury, V., Birchwood, M., Cochrane, R., & Macmillan, F. (1996). Cognitive therapy and recovery from acute psychosis: A controlled trial, impact on psychotic symptoms. *British Journal of Psychiatry, 169*, 593–601.

Durkin, H. E. (1972). General systems theory and group therapy: An introduction. *International Journal of Group Psychotherapy, 22*, 159–166.

Dush, D. M., Hirt, M. L., & Schroeder, H. E. (1983). Self-statement modification with adults: A meta-analysis. *Psychological Bulletin, 94(3)*, 408–422.

Eckert, J., & Biermann-Ratjen, E. M. (1990). Die Theorie des Therapeuten als Wirkfaktor in der Gruppentherapie. In V. Tschuschke & D. Czogalik (Eds.), *Psychotherapie—Welche Effekte veraendern?* Heidelberg: Springer.

Eckert, J., & Biermann-Ratjen, E. M. (1998). The treatment of borderline personality disorder. In L. S. Greenberg, J. C. Watson, & G. Lietaer (Eds.), *Handbook of experiential psychotherapy*. New York: Guilford Press.

Eckert, J., & Wuchner, M. (1996). Long-term development of borderline personality disorder. In R. Hutterer, G. Pawlosky, P. Schmid, & R. Stipsits (Eds.), *Client-centered and experiential psychotherapy*. Frankfurt am Main: Lang.

Engels, G. I., & Vermey, M. (1997). Efficacy of nonmedical treatments of depression in elders: A quantitative analysis. *Journal of Clinical Geropsychology, 3(1)*, 17–35.

Enright, S. J. (1991). Group treatment for obsessive compulsive disorder: An evaluation. *Behavioral Psychotherapy, 19*, 183–192.

Epsie, C. A. (1986). The group treatment of obsessive-compulsive ritualizers: Behavioral management of identified patterns of relapse. *Behavioral Psychotherapy, 14*, 21–33.

Evans, R. L., & Connis, R. T. (1995). Comparison of brief group therapies for depressed cancer patients receiving radiation treatment. *Public Health Report, 110(3)*, 306–311.

Fairburn, C. G., Jones, R., Peveler, R. C., Carr, S. J., Solomon, R. A., O'Connor, M. E., Burton, J., & Hope, R. A. (1991). Three psychological treatments for bulimia nervosa: A comparative trial. *Archives of general Psychiatry, 48*, 463–469.

Fals-Stewart, W., Marks, A. P., & Schafer, J. (1993). A comparison of behavioral group therapy and individual behavior therapy in treating obsessive-compulsive disorder. *Journal of Nervous and Mental Disease, 181*, 189–193.

Fanget, F. (1999). Treatment of social phobias: Efficacy of cognitive and behavioral group therapy. *Encephale, 25*, 158–168.

Fawzy, F. I., & Fawzy, N. W. (1998). Group therapy in the cancer setting. *Journal of Psychosomatic Research, 45(3)*, 191–200.

Fawzy, F. I., Fawzy, N. W., Arndt, L. A., & Pasnau, R. O. (1995). Critical review of psychosocial intervention in cancer care. *Archives of General Psychiatry, 52*, 100–113.

Fawzy, F. I., Fawzy, N. W., Hyun, C. S., Elashoff, R., Guthrie, D., Fahey, J. L., & Morton, D. L. (1993). Malignant melanoma: Effects of an early structured psychiatric intervention, coping, and affective state of recurrence and survival 6 years later. *Archives of General Psychiatry, 50*, 681–689.

Fettes, P. A., & Peters, J. M. (1992). A meta-analysis of group treatments for bulimia nervosa. *International Journal of Eating Disorders, 11(2)*, 97–110.

Fisher, M. S., Sr., & Bentley, K. J. (1996). Two group therapy models for clients with a dual diagnosis of substance abuse and personality disorder. *Psychiatric Services, 47(11)*, 1244–1250.

Flowers, J. V., Boorgem, C. D., Schwartz, B. (1993). Impact of computerized rapid assessment instruments on counselors and client outcome. *Computers in Human Services, 10(2)*, 9–18.

Forester, B., Kornfeld, D. S., Fleiss, J. L., & Thompson, S. (1993). Group psychotherapy during radiotherapy: Effects on emotional and physical distress. *American Journal of Psychiatry, 150(11)*, 1700–1706.

Free, M. L., Oei, T. P., & Appleton, C. (1998). Biological and psychological processes in recovery from depression during cognitive therapy. *Journal of Behavior Therapy & Experimental Psychiatry, 29(3)*, 213–26.

Fuhriman, A., & Barlow, S. H. (1983). Cohesion: Relationship in group therapy. In M. J. Lambert (Ed.), *Psychotherapy and patient relationships* (pp. 263–289). Homewood, IL: Dorsey Press.

Fuhriman, A., & Burlingame, G. M. (1990). Consistency of matter: A comparative analysis of individual and group process variables. *The Counseling Psychologist, 18(1)*, 6–63.

Fuhriman, A., & Burlingame, G. M. (1994). Group psychotherapy: Research and practice. In A. Fuhriman & G. M. Burlingame (Eds.), *Handbook of group psychotherapy: An empirical and clinical synthesis* (pp. 3–40). New York: John Wiley & Sons.

Fuhriman, A., & Burlingame, G. (2000). The Hill Interaction Matrix: Therapy through dialogue. In A. P. Beck & C. Lewis (Eds.), *The process of group psychotherapy: Systems for analyzing change* (pp. 135–174). Washington, DC: American Psychological Association.

Fuhriman, A., Drescher, S., Hanson, E., Henrie, R., & Rybicki, W. (1986). Refining the measurement of curativeness: An empirical approach. *Small Group Behavior, 17*, 186–201.

Galanter, M., Castaneda, R., & Franco, H. (1991). Group therapy and self-help groups. In R. J. Frances & S. I. Miller (Eds.), *Clinical textbook of addictive disorders* (pp. 431–451). New York: Guilford Press.

Gaston, L. (1991). Reliability and criterion-related validity of the California Alliance Scales—patient version. *Psychological Assessment: A Journal of Consulting and Clinical Psychology, 3*, 68–74.

Gaston, L., & Marmar, C. (1991). *Manual of California Psychotherapy Alliance Scales (Form G)*. San Francisco: University of California, San Francisco.

Glass, C. R., & Arnkoff, D. B. (2000). Consumers' perspectives on helpful and hindering factors in mental health treatment. *Journal of Clinical Psychology, 56(11)*, 1467–1480.

Goodwin, P. J., Leszcz, M., Quirt, G., Koopmans, J., Arnold, A., Dohan, E. Hundeley, M., Chochinov, H. M., & Navarro, M. (2000). Lessons learned from enrollment in the BEST study: A multicenter, randomized trial of group psychosocial support in metastatic breast cancer. *Journal of Clinical Epidemiology, 53(6)*, 605–614.

Gorey, K. M., & Cryns, A. G. (1991). Group work as interventive modality with the older depressed client: A meta-analytic review. *Journal of Gerontological Social Work, 16(1–2)*, 137–157.

Hamblin, D. L., Beutler, L. E., Scogin, F., & Cobishley, A. (1993). Patient responsiveness to therapist values and outcome in group cognitive therapy. *Psychotherapy Research, 3(1)*, 36–46.

Hansen, N. B., Lambert, M. J., & Forman, E. M. (2002). Comparisons of clinically significant change in clinical trials and naturalistic practice settings: The dose-effect relationship and its implication for practice. *Clinical Psychology: Science and Practice, 9*, 329–343.

Harper-Guiffre, H., & MacKenzie, K. R. (Eds.). (1992). *Group psychotherapy for eating disorders.* Washington, DC: American Psychiatric Press.

Hartmann, A., Herzog, T., & Drinkmann, A. (1992). Psychotherapy of bulimia nervosa: What is effective? A meta-analysis. *Journal of Psychosomatic Research, 36(2)*, 159–167.

Hayes, R. L., Halford, W. K., & Varghese, F. T. (1995). Social skills training with chronic schizophrenic patients: Effects on negative symptoms and community functioning. *Behavior Therapy, 26(3)*, 433–449.

Hayward, C., Varady, S., Albano, A. M., Thienemann, M., Henderson, L., & Schatzberg, A. F. (2000). Cognitive-behavioral group therapy for social phobia in female adolescents: Results of a pilot study. *Journal of the American Academy of Child and Adolescent Psychiatry, 39(6)*, 721–726.

Heimberg, R. G., Dodge, C. S., Hope, D. A., Kennedy, C. R., Zollo, L. J., & Becker, R. J. (1990). Cognitive behavioral group treatment for social phobia: Comparison with a credible placebo control. *Cognitive Therapy and Research, 14*, 1–23.

Heimberg, R. G., Liebowitz, M. R., Hope, D. A. Schneier, F. R., Holt, C. S., Welkowitz, L. A., Juster, H. R., Campeas, R., Bruch, M. A., Cloitre, M., Fallon, B., & Klein, D. F. (1998). Cognitive behavioral group therapy versus phenelzine therapy for social phobia: 12-week outcome. *Archives of General Psychiatry, 55(12)*, 1133–1141.

Heimberg, R. G., Salzman, D., Holt, C. S., & Blendell, K. (1993). Cognitive behavioral group treatment for social phobia: Effectiveness at five-year follow-up. *Cognitive Therapy & Research, 17*, 325–339.

Heinzel, R., Breyer, F., & Klein, T. (1998). Ambulante analytische Einzel- und Gruppenpsychotherapie [Outpatient psychoanalytic therapy in Germany]. *Gruppenpsychotherapie und Gruppendynamik, 34*, 135–152.

Hess, H. (1992). Affektives Erleben im Gruppenprozess und Therapieerfolg. *Psychotherapie Psychosomatik, Medizinische Psychologie, 42*, 120–126.

Hess, H. (1996). Das Soziogramm von Hess and Hoeck. In B. Strauss, J. Eckert, & V. Tschuschke (Eds.), *Methoden der empirischen Gruppentherapieforschung—Ein Handbuch.* Wiesbaden: Westdeutscher Verlag.

Hill, W. F. (1965). *Hill Interaction Matrix* (rev. ed.). Los Angeles, CA: Youth Studies Center, University of Southern California.

Hoag, M. J., & Burlingame, G. M. (1997). Evaluating the effectiveness of child and adolescent group treatment: A meta-analytic review. *Journal of Clinical Child Psychology, 26(3)*, 234–246.

Hogarty, G. E., Anderson, C. M., Reiss, D. J., Kornblith, S. J., Greenwald, D. P., Ulrich, R. F., & Carter, M. (1991). Family psychoeducation, social skills training, and maintenance chemotherapy in the aftercare treatment of schizophrenia: Two-year effects of a controlled study on relapse and adjustment. *Archives of General Psychiatry, 48*, 340–347.

Hoge, M. A., & McLoughlin, K. A. (1991). Group psychotherapy in acute treatment settings: Therapy and technique. *Hospital and Community Psychiatry, 42(2)*, 153–158.

Hope, D. A., Heimberg, R. G., & Bruch, M. A. (1995). Dismantling cognitive-behavioral group therapy for social phobia. *Behavior Research and Therapy, 33*, 637–650.

Horowitz, M., Marmar, C., Krupnick, J., Wilner, N., Kaltreider, N., & Wallerstain, R. (1984). *Personality styles and brief psychotherapy.* New York: Basic Books.

Horowitz, L. M., Rosenberg, S. E., Baer, B. A., et al. (1988). Inventory of Interpersonal Problems: Psychometric properties and clinical applications. *Journal of Consulting and Clinical Psychology, 56*, 885–892.

Hurd, L. J. (1996). A task analysis of change episodes in group psychotherapy. *Dissertation Abstracts International: Section B. The Sciences and Engineering, 57*(3-B), 2153.

Hurley, J. (1997). Interpersonal theory and measures of outcome and emotional climate in 111 personal development groups. *Group Dynamics: Theory, Research, and Practice, 1(1)*, 86–97.

Huxley, N. A., Rendall, M., & Sederer, L. (2000). Psychosocial treatments in schizophrenia: A review of the past 20 years. *Journal of Nervous and Mental Disease, 188(4)*, 187–201.

Janssen, P. L. (1987). *Psychotherapie in der Klinik* [Psychotherapy in the hospital]. Stuttgart: Klett-Cotta.

Joanning, H., Quinn, W., Thomas, F., & Mullen, R. (1992). Treating adolescent drug abuse: A comparison of family systems therapy, group therapy, and family drug education. *Journal of Marital and Family Therapy, 18(4)*, 345–356.

Johannson, M. A., & Tutty, L. M. (1998). An evaluation of after-treatment couple's groups for wife abuse. *Family Relations, 47(1)*, 27–35.

Johnson, W. Y., & Wilborn, B. (1991). Group counseling as an intervention in anger expression and depression in older adults. *Journal for Specialist in Group Work 16*, 133–142.

Joyce, A. S., McCallum, M., & Piper, W. B. (1999). Borderline functioning, work and outcome in intensive evening group treatment. *International Journal of Group Psychotherapy, 49(3)*, 343–368.

Kaminer, Y., Burleson, J. A., Blitz, C., Sussman, J., & Rounsaville, B. J. (1998). Psychotherapies for adolescent substance abusers: A pilot study. *Journal of Nervous and Mental Disease, 186(11)*, 684–690.

Kanas, N. (1986). Group psychotherapy with schizophrenics: A review of controlled studies. *International Journal of Group Psychotherapy, 36*, 339–351.

Karterud, S. (1992). Day hospital therapeutic community treatment for patients with personality disorders: An empirical evaluation of the containment function. *Journal of Nervous and Mental Disease, 180*, 238–243.

Kaspar, J., Sievers, K., Burgmeier-Lohse, M., & Strauss, B. (2000). Indentifikation und Veranderung von Interaktionsmustern bei Patienten einer stationaren Gruppenpsychotherapie—Eine Erkundungsstudie mit der Structural Analysis of Social Behavior (SASB). *Gruppenpsychotherapie und Gruppendynamik, 36*, 333–354.

Kaul, T. J., & Bednar, R. L. (1986). Experiential group research: Results, questions, and suggestions. In S. L. Garfield & A. E. Bergin (Eds.), *Handbook of psychotherapy and behavior change: An empirical analysis* (pp. 671–714). New York: John Wiley & Sons.

Kazdin, A. E. (1998). *Research design in clinical psychology* (3rd ed.). Boston: Allyn & Bacon.

Kelly, J. A., Murphy, D. A., Bahr, G. R., Kalichman, S. C., Morgan, M. G., Stevenson, L. Y., Koob, J. J., Brasfield, T. L., & Bernstein, B. M. (1993). Outcome of cognitive-behavioral and support group brief therapies for depressed, HIV-infected persons. *American Journal of Psychiatry, 150(11)*, 1679–1686.

Kivlighan, D. M. (1997). Leader behavior and therapeutic gain: An application of situational leadership theory. *Group Dynamics: Theory, Research, and Practice, 1(1)*, 32–38.

Kivlighan, D. M., & Goldfine, D. C. (1991). Endorsement of therapeutic factors as a function of stage of group development and participant interpersonal attitudes. *Journal of Counseling Psychology, 38*, 150–158.

Kivlighan, D. M., & Lilly, R. L. (1997). Developmental changes in group climate as they relate to therapeutic gain. *Group Dynamics: Theory, Research, and Practice, 1(3)*, 208–221.

Kivlighan, D. M., & Mullison, D. (1988). Participants' perception of therapeutic factors in group counseling: The role of interpersonal style and stage of group development. *Small Group Behavior, 19(4)*, 452–468.

Kivlighan, D. M., Multon, K. D., & Brossart, D. F. (1996). Helpful impacts in group counseling: Development of a multidimensional rating system. *Journal of Counseling Psychology, 43(3)*, 347–355.

Kivlighan, D. M., & Tarrant, J. M. (2001). Does group climate mediate the group leadership-group member outcome relationship? A test of Yalom's hypotheses about leadership priorities. *Group Dynamics: Theory, Research, and Practice, 5(3)*, 220–234.

Klein, R. H., Brabender, V., & Fallon, A. (1994). Inpatient group therapy. In A. Fuhriman & G. M. Burlingame (Eds.), *Handbook of group psychotherapy: An empirical and clinical synthesis* (pp. 370–415). New York: John Wiley & Sons.

Konen, A., Simoneau, J. F., Hughes, J., Ruoss, B., & Gabris, G. (1992). Combined cognitive group treatment for depressed in-patients. *Schweizerische Rundschau Medizin, 81*, 1192–1195.

Kordy, H., & Senf, W. (1992). Therapieabbrecher in geschlossenen Gruppen. *Psychotherapie, Psychosomatik, Medizinische Psychologie, 42*, 127–135.

Krone, K. P., Himle, J. A., & Nesse, R. M. (1991). A standardized behavioral group treatment program for obsessive compulsive disorder: Preliminary outcomes. *Behavioral Research and Therapy, 29*, 627–631.

Kuhns, M. L. (1997). Treatment outcomes with adult children of alcoholics: depression. *Advanced Practical Nursing Quarterly, 3(2)*, 64–69.

Kusumakar, V., Yatham, L. N., Haslam, D. R., Parikh, S. V., Matte, R., Silverstone, P. H., & Sharma, V. (1997). Treatment of mania, mixed state, and rapid cycling *Canadian Journal of Psychiatry, 42* (Suppl. 2), pp. 79s–86s.

Lambert, M. J., & Bergin, A. E. (1994). The effectiveness of psychotherapy. In A. E. Bergin & S. L. Garfield (Eds.), *The handbook of psychotherapy and behavior change* (4th ed.). New York: John Wiley & Sons.

Lerner, S. P., & Ermann, G. (1976). Der Stuttgart Bogen (SB) zur Erfassung des Erlebens in der Gruppe (The Stuttgarter Bogen: A questionnaire for describing group experience). *Gruppendynamik, 2*, 133–140.

Lese, K. P., & MacNair-Semands, R. R. (2000). The Therapeutic Factors Inventory: Development of a scale. *Group, 24(4)*, 303–317.

Leung, S. N., & Orrell, M. W. (1993). A brief cognitive behavioural therapy group for the elderly: Who benefits? *International Journal of Geriatric Psychiatry, 8(7)*, 593–598.

Lewandowski, L., Buchkremer, G., & Stark, M. (1994). Das Gruppenklima un die Therapeut-Patient-Beziehung bei zwei Gruppentherapiestrategien für schizophrene Patienten – Ein Beitrag zur Klärung differentieller Therapieeffekte [Group atmosphere and the therapist-patient relationship in two therapeutic group settings for schizophrenic patients—A contribution to the clarification of differential therapeutic effects]. *Psychotherapie, Psychosomatik, Medizinische Psychologie, 44*, 115–121.

Liberman, R. P., Wallace, C. J., Blackwell, G., Eckman, T. A., Vaccaro, J. V., & Kuehnel, T. G. (1998). Innovations in skills training for the seriously mentally ill: The UCLA social and independent living skills (SILS) modules. *Innovations and Research, 2(2)*, 43–59.

Liberman, R. P., Wallace, C. J., Blackwell, G., Kopelowicz, A., Vaccaro, J. V., & Mintz, J. (1993). Skills training versus psychosocial occupational therapy for persons with persistent schizophrenia. *American Journal of Psychiatry, 155(8)*, 1087–1091.

Lichtenberg, J. W., & Knox, P. L. (1991). Order out of chaos: A structural analysis of group therapy. *Journal of Counseling Psychology, 38(3)*, 279–288.

Lidren, D. M., Watkins, P. L., Gould, R. A., Clum, G. A., Asterino, M., & Tullock, H. L. (1994). A comparison of bibliotherapy and group therapy in the treatment of pani disorder. *Journal of Consulting and Clinical Psychology, 62*, 865–869.

Liebowitz, M. R., Heimberg, R. G., Schneier, F. R., Hope, D. A., Davies, S., Holt, C. S., Goetz, D., Juster, H. R., Lin, S. H., Bruch, M. A., Marshall, R. D., & Klein, D. F. (1999). Cognitive-behavioral group therapy versus phenelzine in social phobia: Long-term outcome. *Depression and Anxiety, 10(3)*, 89–98.

Liedtke, R., & Geiser, F. (2001). Veränderungen interpersonaler probleme während und zwei Jahre nach stationärer Psychotherapie. *Gruppenpsychotherapie und Gruppendynamik, 37*, 214–228.

Linehan, M. M. (1993). *Skills training manual for treating borderline personality disorder.* New York: Guilford Press.

Linehan, M. M., Armstrong, H. E., Suarez, A., Allmon, D., & Heard, H. L. (1991). Cognitive-behavioral treatment of chronically parasuicidal borderline patients. *Archives of General Psychiatry, 48*, 1060–1064.

Linehan, M. M., Heard, H. L., & Armstrong, H. E. (1993). Naturalistic follow-up of a behavioral treatment of chronically parasuicidal borderline patients. *Archives of General Psychiatry, 50*, 971–974.

Linehan, M. M., Schmidt, H., Dimeff, L. A., Craft, J. C., Kanter, J., & Comtois, K. A. (1999). Dialectical behavior therapy for patients with borderline personality disorder and drug dependence. *American Journal on Addictions, 8*, 279–292.

Linn, M. W., Linn, B. S., & Harris, R. (1982). Effects of counseling for late-stage cancer patients. *Cancer, 49*, 1048–1055.

Lubin, H., Loris, M., Burt, J., & Johnson, D. R. (1998). Efficacy of psychoeducational group therapy in reducing symptoms of posttraumatic stress disorder among multiply traumatized women. *American Journal of Psychiatry, 155(9)*, 1172–1177.

Luborsky, L., Barber, J. P., Siqueland, L., Johnson, S., Najavitz, L. M., Frank, A., & Daley, D. (1996). The revised Helping Alliance Questionnaire: Psychometric Properties. *Journal of Psychotherapy Practice and Research, 5(3)*, 260–271.

MacKenzie, K. R. (1983). The clinical application of group measure. In R. R. Dies & K. R. MacKenzie (Eds.), *Advances in group psychotherapy: Integrating research and practice* (pp. 159–170). New York: International Universities Press.

MacKenzie, K. R. (1994). Group development. In A. Fuhriman & G. M. Burlingame (Eds.), *Handbook of group psychotherapy: An empirical and clinical synthesis* (pp. 223–268). New York: John Wiley & Sons.

MacKenzie, K. R. (2001a). Group psychotherapy. In W. J. Livesley (Ed.), *Handbook of Personality Disorders* (pp. 497–526). New York: Guilford Press.

MacKenzie, K. R. (2001b). An expectation of radical change in the future of group psychotherapy. *International Journal of Group Psychotherapy, 51(2)*, 175–180.

MacKenzie, K. R., Brink, J., Hills, A. L., Jang, K., Livesley, J., Smiley, W. C., & McHattie, L. (1999). Group treatment outcome for psychopathic inmates. Paper presented at the American Psychiatric Association Annual Conference, Chicago, IL.

MacKenzie, K. R., & Tschuschke, V. (1993). Relatedness, group work, and outcome in long-term inpatient psychotherapy groups. *Journal of Psychotherapy: Practice and Research, 2*, 147–156.

MacNair-Semands, R. R. (1998). Encompassing the complexity of group work. *Journal for specialists in group work, 23(2)*, 208–214.

MacNair-Semands, R. R. (2000). Examining the beneficial components of groups: Commentary on Estabrooks and Carron (2000) and Terry et al. (2000). *Group Dynamics: Theory, Research, and Practice, 4(3)*, 254–258.

MacNair-Semands, R. R., & Lese, K. P. (2000). Interpersonal problems and the perception of therapeutic factors in group therapy. *Small Group Research, 31(2)*, 158–174.

Marder, S. R., Wirshing, W. C., Mintz, J., McKenzie, J., Johnston, K., Eckman, T. A., Lebell, M., Zimmerman, K., & Liberman, R. P. (1996). Two-year outcome of social skills training and group psychotherapy for outpatients with schizophrenia. *American Journal of Psychiatry, 153(12),* 1585–1592.

Martinsen, E. W., Olsen, T., Tonset, E., Nyland, K. E., & Aarre, T. F. (1998). Cognitive-behavioral group therapy for panic disorder in the general clinical setting: A naturalistic study with 1-year follow-up. *Journal of Clinical Psychiatry, 59(8),* 437–442.

Marziali, E., & Munroe-Blum, H. (1994). *Interpersonal group psychotherapy for borderline personality disorder.* New York: Basic Books.

Marziali, E., Munroe-Blum, H., & McCleary, L. (1997). The contribution of group cohesion and group alliance to the outcome of group psychotherapy. *International Journal of Group Psychotherapy, 47(4),* 475–497.

McCallum, M., & Piper, W. E. (1990). The psychological mindedness assessment procedure. *Psychological Assessment: Journal of Consulting and Clinical Psychology, 2,* 412–418.

McCallum, M., Piper, W. E., & Joyce, A. S. (1992). Dropping out from short-term group therapy. *Psychotherapy, 29,* 206–215.

McCallum, M., Piper, W. E., & O'Kelly, J. G. (1997). Predicting patient benefit from a group oriented evening treatment program. *International Journal of Group Psychotherapy, 47,* 291–314.

McFarlane, W. R., Dushay, R. A., Stastny, P., Deakins, S. M., & Link, B. (1996). A comparison of two levels of family-aided assertive community treatment. *Psychiatric Services, 47(7),* 744–750.

McFarlane, W. R., Link, B., Dushay, R., Marchal, J., & Crilly, J. (1995). Psychoeducational multiple family groups: Four-year relapse outcome in schizophrenia. *Family Process, 34*(June), 127–144.

McFarlane, W. R., Lukens, E., Link, B., Dushay, R., Deakins, S. A., Newmark, M., Dunne, E. J., Horen, B., & Toran, J. (1995). Multiple-family groups and psychoeducation in the treatment of schizophrenia. *Archives of General Psychiatry, 52,* 679–687.

McKay, J. R., Alterman, A. I., Cacciola, J. S., O'Brien, C. P., Koppenhaver, J. M., & Shepard, D. S. (1999). Continuing care for cocaine dependence: Comprehensive 2-year outcomes. *Journal of Consulting and Clinical Psychology, 67(3),* 420–427.

McKay, J. R., Alterman, A. I., Cacciola, J. S., Rutherford, M. J., O'Brien, C. P., & Koppenhaver, J. (1997). Group counseling vs individualized relapse prevention aftercare following an intensive outpatient treatment for cocaine dependence. *Journal of Consulting and Clinical Psychology, 65(5),* 778–788.

McNamee, J. E., Lipman, E. L., & Hicks, F. (1995). A single mothers' group for mothers of children attending an outpatient psychiatric clinic: preliminary results. *Canadian Journal of Psychiatry, 40(7),* 383–388.

McQuaid, J. R., Granholm, E., McClure, F. S., Roepke, S., Pedrelli, P., Patterson, T. L., & Jeste, D. V. (2000). Development of an integrated cognitive-behavioral and social skills training intervention for older patients with schizophrenia. *Journal of Psychotherapy Practice and Research, 9(3),* 149–156.

McRoberts, C., Burlingame, G. M., & Hoag, M. J. (1998). Comparative efficacy of individual and group psychotherapy: A meta-analytic perspective. *Group Dynamics, 2(2),* 101–117.

Meyer, T. J., & Mark, M. M. (1995). Effects of psychosocial intervention with adult cancer patients: A meta-analysis of randomized experiments. *Health Psychology, 14,* 101–108.

Mills, P. D., & Hansen, J. C. (1991). Short-term group interventions for mentally ill young adults living in a community residence and their families. *Hospital and Community Psychiatry, 42(11),* 1144–1150.

Mitchell, J. E., Pyle, R. L., Eckert, E. D., Hatsukami, D., Pomeroy, C., & Zimmerman, R. (1990, February). A comparison study of antidepressants and structured intensive group psychotherapy in the treatment of bulimia nervosa. *Archives of General Psychiatry, 47,* 149–157.

Mitchell, J. E., Pyle, R. L., Pomeroy, C., Zollman, M., Crosby, R., Seim, H., Eckert, E. D., & Zimmerman, R. (1993). Cognitive-behavioral group psychotherapy of bulimia nervosa: Importance of logistical variables. *International Journal of Eating Disorders, 14(3),* 277–287.

Mojtabai, R., Nicholson, R. A., & Carpenter, B. N. (1998). Role of psychosocial treatments in management of schizophrenia: A meta-analytic review of controlled outcome studies. *Schizophrenia Bulletin, 24(4),* 569–587.

Moos, R. H. (1974). *Community Oriented Programs Environment Scale.* Manual. Palo Alto, CA: Consulting Psychologists Press.

Morgan, T., & Cummings, A. L. (1999). Change experienced during group therapy by female survivors of childhood sexual abuse. *Journal of Consulting and Clinical Psychology, 67(1),* 28–36.

Morgenstern, H., Gellert, G. A., Walter, S. D., Ostfeld, A. M., & Siegel, B. S. (1984). The impact of a psychosocial support program on survival with breast cancer: The importance of selection bias in program evaluation. *Journal of Chronic Disease, 37(4),* 273–282.

Morran, D. K., Stockton, R., & Teed, C. (1998). Facilitating feedback exchange in groups: Leader interventions. *Journal for Specialists in Group Work, 23,* 257–268.

Mosheim, R., Zachhuber, U., Scharf, L., Hofmann, A., Kemmler, G., Danzl, G., Kinzl, J., Biebl., W., & Richter, R. (2000). Bindung und Psychotherapie. *Psychotherapeut, 45*, 223–229.

Mueser, K. T., Wallace, C. J., & Liberman, R. P. (1995). New developments in social skills training. *Behavior Change, 12(1)*, 31–40.

Mulder, C. L., Antoni, M. H., Emmelkamp, P.M.G., Veugelers, P. J., Sandfort, T.G.M., van de Vijver, F.A.J.R., & de Vries, M. J. (1995). Psychosocial group intervention and the rate of decline of immunological parameters in asymptomatic HIV-infected homosexual men. *Psychotherapy and Psychosomatics, 63(3–4)*, 185–192.

Mulder, C. L., Emmelkamp, P. M., Antoni, M. H., Mulder, J. W., Sandfort, T. G., & DeVries, M. J. (1994). Cognitive-behavioral and experiential group psychotherapy for HIV-infected homosexual men: A comparative study. *Psychosomatic Medicine, 56*, 423–431.

Munroe-Blum, H., & Marziali, E. (1995). A controlled trial of short-term group treatment for borderline personality disorder. *Journal of Personality Disorder, 9*, 190–198.

Murphy, S. A. (1997). A bereavement intervention for parents following the sudden, violent deaths of their 12–28-year-old children: Description and applications to clinical practice. *Candian Journal of Nursing Research, 29(4)*, 51–72.

Nietzel, M. T., Russell, R. L., Hemmings, K. A., & Gretter, M. L. (1987). Clinical significance of psychotherapy for unipolar depression: A meta-analytic approach to social comparison. *Journal of Consulting and Clinical Psychology, 55(2)*, 156–161.

Oei, T.P.S., Llamas, M., & Evans, L. (1997). Does concurrent drug intake affect the long-term outcome of group cognitive behaviour therapy in panic disorder with or without agoraphobia. *Behaviour Research and Therapy, 35(9)*, 851–857.

Oei, T. P., & Sullivan, L. M. (1999). Cognitive changes following recovery from depression in a group cognitive-behaviour therapy program. *Australian and New Zealand Journal of Psychiatry, 33(3)*, 407–415.

Olmsted, M. P., Davis, R., Rocker, W., Irvine, M. J., Eagle, M., & Garner, D. M. (1991). Efficacy of a brief group psychoeducational intervention for bulimia nervosa. *Behaviour Therapy and Research, 29(1)*, 71–83.

Peterson, A. L., & Halstead, T. S. (1998). Group cognitive behavior therapy for depression in a community setting: A clinical replication series. *Behavior Therapy, 29(1)*, 3–18.

Peterson, C., Mitchell, J. E., Engbloom, S., Nugent, S., Mussell, M. P., & Miller, J. P. (1998). Group cognitive-behavioral treatment of binge eating disorder: A comparison of therapist-led versus self-help formats. *International Journal of Eating Disorders, 24*, 125–136.

Petrik, N. D., Gildersleeve-High, L., McEllistrem, J. E., & Subotnik, L. S. (1994). The reduction of male abusiveness as a result of treatment: Reality or myth? *Journal of Family Violence, 9(4)*, 307–316.

Philpot, C. L. (1991). Gender sensitive couples' therapy: A systemic definition. *Journal of Family Psychotherapy, 2(3)*, 19–40.

Pinquart, M. (1998). Wirkungen psychosozialer und psychotherapeutischer Interventionen auf das Befinden und das Selbstkonzept im höheren Erwachsenenalter – Ergebnisse von Metaanalysen [Effects of psychosocial and psychotherapeutic interventions on well-being and self concept in late adulthood—Meta-analytical results]. *Zeitschrift für Gerontologie und Geriatrie, 31*, 120–126.

Pinto, A., La Pia, S., Mennella, R., Giorgio, D., & DeSimone, L. (1999). Cognitive-behavioral therapy and clozapine for clients with treatment-refractory schizophrenia. *Psychiatric Services, 50(7)*, 901–904.

Piper, W. E. (1994). Client variables. In A. Fuhriman & G. M. Burlingame (Eds.), *Handbook of group psychotherapy: An empirical and clinical synthesis* (pp. 83–113). New York: John Wiley & Sons.

Piper, W. E., Debbanme, E. G., de Carufel, F. L., & Bienvu, J. P. (1987). A system for differentiating therapist interpretations and other interventions. *Bulletin of the Menninger Clinic, 51*, 532–550.

Piper, W. E., Marrache, M., Lacroix, R., Richardsen, A. M., & Jones, B. D. (1983). Cohesion as a basic bond in groups. *Human Relations, 36*, 93–108.

Piper, W. E., McCallum, M., & Azim, H.F.A. (1992). *Adaptation to loss through short-term group psychotherapy.* New York: Guilford Press.

Piper, W. E., McCallum, M., Joyce, A. S., & Rosie, J. S. (In press). Patient personality and time-limited group psychotherapy for complicated grief. *International Journal of Group Psychotherapy.*

Piper, W. E., Rosie, J. S., Joyce, A. S., & Azim, H.F.A. (1996). *Time-limited day treatment for personality disorders: Integration of research design and practice in a group program.* Washington, DC: American Psychological Association.

Ravindran, A. V., Anisman, H., Merali, Z., Charbonneau, Y., Telner, J., Bialick, R. J., Wiens, A., Ellis, J., & Griffiths, J. (1999). Treatment of primary dysthymia with group cognitive therapy and pharmacotherapy: Clinical symptoms and functional impairments. *American Journal Psychiatry, 156(10)*, 1608–1617.

Richter, N. L., Snider, E., & Gorey, K. M. (1997). Group work intervention with female survivors of childhood sexual abuse. *Research on Social Work Practice, 7(1)*, 53–69.

Rile, A., Leighton, T., & Pollock, P. (1997). *Cognitive analytic therapy and borderline personality disorder.* New York: John Wiley & Sons.

Roberts, C. S., Piper, L., Denny, J., & Cuddeback, G. (1997). A support group intervention to facilitate young adult's adjustment to cancer: *Health & Social Work, 22(2)*, 133–141.

Robins, C. J., Ladd, J., Welkowitz, J., Blaney, P. H., Diaz, R., & Kutcher, G. (1994). The Personal Style Inventory: Preliminary validation studies of new measures of sociotropy and autonomy. *Journal of Psychopathology and Behavioral Assessment, 16*, 277–300.

Robinson, L. A., Berman, J. S., & Neimeyer, R. A. (1990). Psychotherapy for the treatment of depression: A comprehensive review of controlled outcome research. *Psychological Bulletin, 108(1)*, 30–49.

Roder, V., Jenull, B., & Brenner, H. D. (1998). Teaching schizophrenic patients recreational, residential and vocational skills. *International Review of Psychiatry, 10*, 35–41.

Roffman, R. A., Stephen, R. S., Curtin, L., Gordon, J. R., Craver, J. N., Stern, M., Beadnell, B., & Downey, L. (1998). Relapse prevention as an interventive model for HIV risk reduction in gay and bisexual men. *AIDS Education and Prevention, 10(1)*, 1–18.

Rokke, P. D., Tomhave, J. A., & Jocic, Z. (2000). Self-management therapy and educational group therapy for depressed elders. *Cognitive Therapy and Research, 24(1)*, 99–119.

Rosenbaum, A., & O'Leary, F. D. (1986). The treatment of marital violence. In N. Jacobson & A. Gurman (Eds.), *Clinical handbook of mental therapy* (pp. 385–405). New York: Guilford Press.

Sallis, J. F., Lichstein, K. L., Clardson, A. D., Stalgaitis, S., & Campbell, M. (1983). Anxiety and depression for the elderly. *International Journal of Behavioral Geriatrics, 1*, 3–12.

Sandahl, C., Herlitz, K., Ahlin, G., & Roennberg, S. (1998). Time-limited group psychotherapy for moderately alcohol dependent patients: A randomized controlled clinical trial. *Psychotherapy Research, 8*, 361–378.

Saunders, D. G. (1996). Feminist cognitive-behavioral and process-psychodynamic treatments for men who batter: Interaction of abuser traits and treatment models. *Violence and Victims, 11(4)*, 393–413.

Scheibe, G., Albus, M., Walther, A. U., & Schmauss, M. (1993). Gruppenpsychotherapie bei Patienten mit Panikstoerung and Agoraphobie [Group psychotherapy in patients with panic disorders and agoraphobia]. *Psychotherapie, Psychosomatik, Medizinische Psychologie, 43*, 238–244.

Schlee, K. A., Heyman, R. E., & O'Leary, K. D. (1998). Group treatment for spouse abuse: Are women with PTSD appropriate participants? *Journal of Family Violence, 13(1)*, 1–20.

Schmidt, J., Nübling, R., Lamprecht, F., & Wittmann, W. W. (1994). Patientenzufriedenheit am Ende psychosomatischer Reha-Behandlungen. [Patient satisfaction at the end of psychosomatic rehabilitation]. In: F. Lamprecht & R. Johnen (Eds.), *Salutogenese* (pp. 271–283). Frankfurt am Main: Verlag für akademische Schriften.

Scholing, A., & Emmelkamp, E. (1993). Exposure with and without cognitive therapy for generalized social phobia: Effects of individual and group treatments. *Behavior Research Therapy, 31*, 667–681.

Scogin, F., & McElreath, L. (1994). Efficacy of psychosocial treatments for geriatric depression: A quantitative review. *Journal of Consulting and Clinical Psychology, 62(1)*, 69–74.

Scott, M. J., & Stradling, S. G. (1990). Group cognitive therapy for depression produces clinically significant reliable change in community-based settings. *Behavioral Psychotherapy, 18*, 1–19.

Sexton, H. (1993). Exploring a psychotherapeutic change sequence: Relating process to intersessional and posttreatment outcome. *Journal of Consulting and Clinical Psychology, 61(10)*, 128–136.

Shaffer, H. J., LaSalvia, T. A., & Stein, J. P. (1997). Comparing Hatha yoga with dynamic group psychotherapy for enhancing methadone maintenance treatment: A randomized clinical trial. *Alternative Therapies in Heath and Medicine, 3(4)*, 57–66.

Sheard, T., & Maguire, P. (1999). The effect of psychological interventions on anxiety and depression in cancer patients: Results of two meta-analyses. *British Journal on Cancer, 80(11)*, 1770–1780.

Simonton, S., & Sherman, A. (2000). An integrated model of group treatment for cancer patients. *International journal of Group Psychotherapy, 50(4)*, 487–506.

Slavin, R. L. (1993). The significance of here-and-now disclosure in promoting cohesion in group psychotherapy. *Group, 17(3)*, 143–150.

Smith, T. E., Hull, J. W., Romanelli, S., Fertuck, E., & Weiss, K. A. (1999). Symptoms and neurocognition as rate limiters in skills training for psychotic patients. *American Journal of Psychiatry, 156(11)*, 1817–1818.

Soldz, S., Budman, S., & Demby, A. (1992). The relationship between main actor behaviors and treatment outcome in group psychotherapy. *Psychotherapy Research, 2(1)*, 52–62.

Spaulding, W. D., Reed, D., Sullivan, M., Richardson, C., & Weiler, M. (1999). Effects of cognitive treatment in psychiatric rehabilitation. *Schizophrenia Bulletin, 25(4)*, 657–676.

Spiegel, D., Bloom, J., & Yalom, I. (1981). Group support for patients with meta-static cancer. *Archives of General Psychiatry, 38*, 527–533.

Spiegel, D., Bloom, J. R., Kraemer, H. C., & Gottheil, E. (1989). Effect of psychosocial treatment on survival of patients with meta-static breast cancer. *Lancet, 2*, 888–891.

Spiegel, D., Morrow, G. J., Classen, C., Raubertas, R., Stott, P. B., Mudaliar, N., Pierce, H. I., Flynn, P. J., Heard, L., & Riggs, G. (1999). Group psychotherapy for recently diagnosed breast cancer patients: a multicenter feasibility study. *Psycho-oncology, 8(6)*, 482–493.

Spira, J. (1997). *Group therapy for medically ill patients.* New York: Guilford Press.

Stalker, C. A., & Fry, R. (1999). A comparison of short-term group and individual therapy for sexually abused women. *Canadian Journal of Psychiatry, 44(2)*, 168–174.

Stanton, M. D., & Shadish, W. R. (1997). Outcome, attrition, and family-couples treatment for drug abuse: A meta-analysis and review of the controlled, comparative studies. *Psychological Bulletin, 122(2)*, 170–191.

Stein, D. M., & Lambert, M. J. (1995). Graduate training in psychotherapy: Are therapy outcomes enhanced? *Journal of Consulting and Clinical Psychology, 63*, 182–196.

Stinchfield, R., Owen, P. L., & Winters, K. C. (1994). Group therapy for substance abuse: A review of the empirical research. In A. Fuhriman & G. M. Burlingame (Eds.), *Handbook of group psychotherapy: An empirical and clinical synthesis* (pp. 458–488). New York: John Wiley & Sons.

Strauss, B. (1992). Empirische Untersuchungen zur stationären Gruppentherapie. *Gruppenpsychotherapie und Gruppendynamik, 28*, 125–149.

Strauss, B. (2000). Attachment and group psychotherapy. *Ricerche sui gruppi, 5(10)*, 41–53.

Strauss, B. (2001). Behandlung seffekte in therapeutischen Gruppen. In: V Tschuschki (Ed), *Pravis der Gruppenpsychotherapie* (pp. 180–187) Stuttgart, Thieme.

Strauss, B., & Burgmeier-Lohse, M. (1994a). Prozess-Ergebnis-Zusammenhänge in der analytisch orientierten Gruppenpsychotherapie: Eine Erkundungsstudie im stationären Rahmen. *Psychotherapeut, 39*, 239–250.

Strauss, B., & Burgmeier-Lohse, M. (1994b). *Stationäre Langzeitgruppenpsychotherapie.* Heidelberg: Asanger.

Strauss, B., & Burgmeier-Lohse, M. (1995). Merkmale der "Passung" zwischen Patienten und Therapeut als Determinante des Behandlungsergebnisses in der stationärer Gruppenthearpie. *Zeitschrift für Psychosomatische Medizin und Psychoanalyse, 41*, 127–140.

Strauss, B., Burlingame, G., & MacKenzie, K. R. (in press). Wer, was, wann, wo, wie? Minimalanforderungen für die Veröffentlichung gruppentherapiebezogener Forschungsergebnisse [Who, what, when ,where and how? Minimal requirements for the publication of group related research results]. *Gruppenpsychotherapie und Gruppendynamik, 37*, 207–213.

Strauss, B., & Eckert, J. (1994). Dimensionen des Gruppenerlebens: Zur Skalenbildung im Bruppenerfahrungsbogen. *Zeitschrift für klinische Psychologie, 23(3)*, 188–201.

Strauss, B., Eckert, J., & Ott, J. (1993). Interperaonle probleme in der stationären gruppenpsychotherapie. *Gruppenpsychotherapie und Gruppendynamik, 29*, 223–298.

Strauss, B., Lobo-Drost, A., & Pilkonis, P. A. (1999). Einschätzung von Bindungsstilen bei Erwachsenen—erste Erfahrungen mit der deutschen Version einer Prototypenbeurteilung. *Zeitschrift für Klinische Psychologie, Psychiatrie und Psychotherapie, 7*, 347–364.

Strauss, B., Rohweder, R., Wienands, H., & Burgmeier-Lohse, M. (1996). Die Kieler Gruppenpsychotherapieprozess-Skala (KGPPS). In B. Strauss, J. Eckert, & V. Tschuschke (Eds.), *Methoden der emprischen Gruppentherapieforschung—Ein Handbuch.* Wiesbaden: Westdeutscher Verlag.

Stravynski, A., Verreault, R., Gaudette, G., Landglois, R., Gagnier, S., & Larose, M. (1999). The treatment of depression with group behavioral-cognitive therapy and imipramine. *Canadian Journal of Psychiatry, 39*, 387–390.

Strupp, H. H., Horowitz, L. M., & Lambert, M. J. (Eds.). (1997). *Measuring patient changes in mood anxiety and personality disorders: Toward a core battery.* Washington, DC: American Psychological Association Press.

Targ, E. F., Karasic, D. H., Diefenbach, P. N., Anderson, D. A., Bystritsky, A., & Fawzy, F. I. (1994). Structured group therapy and fluoxetine to treat depression in HIV-positive persons. *Psychosomatics, 35(2)*, 132–137.

Tasca, G. A., Russell, V., & Busby, K. (1994). Characteristics of patients who choose between two types of group psychotherapy. *International Journal of Group Psychotherapy, 44(4)*, 499–508.

Taylor, N. T., Burlingame, G. M., Fuhriman, A., Kristensen, K. B., Johansen, J., & Dahl, D. (2001). A survey of mental health care provider and managed care organization attitudes toward, familiarity with, and use of group interventions. *International Journal of Group Psychotherapy, 51(2)*, 243–263.

Telch, C. F., Agras, W. S., Rossiter, E. M., Wilfley, D., & Kenard, J. (1990). Group cognitive-behavioral treatment for the nonpurging bulimic: An initial evaluation. *Journal of Consulting and Clinical Psychology, 58*, 629–635.

Telch, M. J., Lucasm, J. A., Schmidt, N. B., Hanna, H. H., Jaimez, T. L., & Lucas, R. A. (1993). Group cognitive behavioral treatment of panic disorder. *Behavioral Research and Therapy, 31*, 279–288.

Telch, M. J., Schmidt, N. B., Jamimez, T. L., Jacquin, K. M., & Harrington, P. J. (1995). Impact of cognitive behavioral treatment on quality of life in panic disorder patients. *Journal of Consulting and Clinical Psychology, 63(5)*, 823–830.

Tillitski, L. (1990). A meta-analysis of estimated effect sizes for group versus individual versus control treatments. *International Journal of Group Psychotherapy, 40(2)*, 215–224.

Toseland, R. W., Diehl, M., Freeman, K., Manzanares, T., Naleppa, M., & McCallion, P. (1997). The impact of validation group therapy on nursing home residents with dementia. *Journal of Applied Gerontology, 16(1)*, 31–50.

Trad, P. V. (1993). Using the prospective approach as an adjunct to established models of group psychotherapy. *Group, 17*, 43–60.

Tschuschke, V. (1996). Der Stuttgarter Bogen. In B. Strauss, J. Eckert, & V. Tschuschke (Eds.), *Methoden der empirischen gruppentherapieforschung: ein handbuch* (pp. 218–228). Opladen, Germany: Westdeutcher Verlag.

Tschuschke, V. (1999). Gruppentherapie versus Einzeltherapie—gleich wirksam? [Group versus individual psychotherapy—equally effective?]. *Gruppenpsychotherapie und Gruppendynamik, 35*, 257–274.

Tschuschke, V., Catina, A., Beckh, T., & Salvini, D. (1992). Therapeutic factors of inpatient analytic group psychotherapy. *Psychotherapie, Psychosomatik, Medizinische Psychologie, 42*, 91–101.

Tschuschke, V., & Dies, R. R. (1994). Intensive analysis of therapeutic factors and outcome in long-term inpatient groups. *International Journal of Group Psychotherapy, 44(2)*, 187–211.

Tschuschke, V., & Dies, R. R. (1997). The contribution of feedback to outcome in long-term group psychotherapy. *Group, 21*, 3–15.

Tschuschke, V., & MacKenzie, K. R. (1989). Empirical analysis of group development: A methodological report. *Small Group Behavior, 20*, 419–442.

Tschuschke, V., MacKenzie, K. R., Haaser, B., & Janke, G. (1996). Self-disclosure, feedback, and outcome in long-term inpatient psychotherapy groups. *Journal of Psychotherapy: Practice and Research, 5*, 35–44.

Tuckman, B. W. (1965). Developmental sequence in small groups. *Psychological Bulletin, 63*, 384–399.

Tutty, L., Bidgood, B., & Dothery, M. (1993). Support groups for battered women: Research on their efficacy. *Journal of Family Violence 8(4)*, 325–343.

Van Noppen, B. L., Pato, M. L., Marsland, R., & Rasmussen, S. A. (1998). A time-limited behavioral group for treatment of obsessive-compulsive disorder. *Journal of Psychotherapy Practice and Research, 7(4)*, 272–280.

Van Noppen, B., Steketee, G., McCorkle, B. H., & Pato, M. (1997). Group and multifamily behavioral treatment for obsessive compulsive disorder: A pilot study. *Journal of Anxiety Disorders, 11(4)*, 431–446.

Wallace, C. J., Liberman, R. P., MacKain, S. J., Blackwell, G., & Eckman, T. A. (1992). Effectiveness and replicability of modules for teaching social and instrumental skills to the severely mentally ill. *American Journal of Psychiatry, 149(5)*, 654–658.

Webster, G. D., & Schwartzberg, P. E. (1992). Patients' perception of curative factors in occupational therapy groups. *Occupational Therapy in Mental Health, 12(1)*, 3–7.

Weidman, A. (1986). Family therapy with violent couples. *Social Casework: The Journal of Contemporary Social Work, 67*, 211–218.

Weinstein, S. P., Gottheil, E., & Sterling, R. C. (1997). Randomized comparison of intensive outpatient vs. individual therapy for cocaine abusers. In E. Gottheil & B. Stimmel (Eds.), *Intensive outpatient treatment for the addictions* (pp. 41–56). New York: Haworth Press.

Wheeler, J. L., & Kivlighan, D. M. (1995). Things unsaid in group counseling: An empirical taxonomy. *Journal of Counseling and Development, 73(6)*, 586–591.

Wheeler, I., O'Malley, K., Waldo, M., Murphy, J., & Blank, C. (1992). Participant's perception of therapeutic factors in groups for incest survivors. *The Journal for Specialists in Group Work, 17(2)*, 89–95.

Wilberg, T., Friis, S., Karterud, S., Mehlum, L., Urnes, O., & Vaglum, P. (1998). Outpatient group psychotherapy: A valuable continuation treatment for patients with borderline personality disorder treated in a day hospital. *Nordisk Journal of Psychiatry, 52(3)*, 213–221.

Wilfley, D. E., Agras, W. S., Telch, C. F., Rossiter, E. M., Schneider, J. A., Cole, A. G., Sifford, L., & Raeburn, S. D. (1993). Group cognitive-behavioral therapy and group interpersonal psychotherapy for the nonpurging bulimic individual: A controlled comparison. *Journal of Consulting and Clinical Psychology, 61(2)*, 296–305.

Wilfley, D. E., Frank, M. A., Welch, R., Spurrell, E. B., & Rounsaville, B. J. (1998). Adapting interpersonal psychotherapy to a group format (IPT-G) for binge eating disorder: Toward a model for adapting empirically supported treatments. *Psychotherapy Research, 8(4)*, 379–391.

Wilfley, D. E., Welch, R. R., Stein, R. I., Spurrell, E. M., Cohen, L. R., Saelens, B. E., Dounchis, J. Z., Frank, M. A., Wiseman, C. V., & Matt, G. E. (in press). A randomized comparison of group cognitive-behavioral and group interpersonal psychotherapy for the treatment of binge eating disorder. *Archives of General Psychiatry.*

Wykes, T., Parr, A. M., & Landau, S. (1999). Group treatment of auditory hallucinations: Exploratory study of effectiveness. *British Journal of Psychiatry, 175*, 180–185.

Yalom, I. D. (1995). *The theory & practice of group psychotherapy* (4th ed.). New York: Basic Books.

Zlotnick, C., Shea, T. M., Rosen, K., Simpson, E., Mulrenin, K., Begin, A., & Pearlstein, T. (1997). An affect-management group for women with posttraumatic stress disorder and histories of childhood sexual abuse. *Journal of Traumatic Stress, 10(3)*, 425–436.

CHAPTER 15

HEALTH PSYCHOLOGY

THOMAS L. CREER
Ohio University
KENNETH A. HOLROYD
Ohio University
RUSSELL E. GLASGOW
AMC Cancer Research Center, Denver, Colorado
TIMOTHY W. SMITH
University of Utah

A chapter in the third edition of this *Handbook* featured a broad focus on health psychology and behavioral medicine (Pomerleau & Rodin, 1986). The topics were highlighted by providing in-depth coverage of a few selected areas. A more limited aspect of behavioral medicine—intervention or treatment research—was described by Blanchard (1994) in the fourth edition of the book. He discussed a band of empirical investigations in behavioral medicine that were conducted in the previous decade. Both chapters achieved their aim; in addition, both chapters (Blanchard, 1994; Pomerleau & Rodin, 1986) serve as benchmarks in the evolution and progression of health psychology and behavioral medicine.

We are taking a different approach to health psychology and behavioral medicine for three reasons. First, the number of topics encompassed by behavioral medicine and health psychology has exploded in the past three decades. We could not cover all of these areas or the research they generated even if we wished; what we would end up with would be little more than a list of topics with limited value to anyone. In addition, there are more current or forthcoming reviews of many areas of behavioral medicine or health psychology (e.g., Smith, Kendall, & Keefe, 2002). Therefore, to review any disease or condition in depth would not only be redundant but, in most cases, outdated. We will, however, describe pertinent research in health psychology and behavioral medicine where it is appropriate to do so. We do not distinguish between the terms *health psychology* and *behavioral medicine* but treat them as synonyms.

Second, we opted to take a global perspective in writing the chapter. Diseases as common as the cold and as rare as Ebola now circle around our globe with near telephonic speed (Angier, 2001). We don't need to touch someone because by living in the homeothermic biomass, we can be reached and touched by microbes that cause disease. Whereas it took a few weeks or months for sailors to deliver a ship of rats carrying the bubonic plague from the Orient to Europe, today microbes "travel by land, sea, air, nose, blows, glove, love, sewage, steerage, rat backs, hat racks, uncooked burritos, overlooked mosquitoes. ... Nowadays, a mosquito infested with the malaria parasite can be buzzing in Ghana at dawn and dining on an airport employee in Boston by cocktail hour" (Angier, 2001, p. 68). Outbreaks of HIV/AIDS, West Nile fever, and, to an increasing extent, tuberculosis reflect the increasing globalization of disease and illness.

Finally, we wish to describe the role health psychologists play or could play within the context of health care. Given the short history of our discipline, we have made impressive strides in developing and applying techniques for the treatment of an array of physical disorders, in contributing to the success of interdisciplinary treatment teams, in assessing change, and in helping patients cope with illness. Our skills and expertise have been applied in the worldwide battle against HIV/AIDS but have been ignored with respect to another global infectious disease, tuberculosis (TB). By bringing our competencies to the treatment of TB, we could make a significant contribution to the control of the disease. In discussing our role, we will emphasize topics of research that are likely to be prominent in health psychology and behavioral medicine in the future.

HEALTH CARE

The annual report of the World Health Organization (2000a) noted that in today's complex world, it is difficult to say exactly what a *health system* is, what it consists of, and where it begins and ends. The report defines a health system to include "*All the activities whose primary purpose is to promote, restore, or maintain health*" (p. 5). The definition is amplified:

> Formal health care services, including the professional delivery of personal medical attention, are clearly within these boundaries. So are the actions by all traditional healers, and all use of medication, whether prescribed by a provider or not. So is home care of the sick, which is now somewhere between 70% and 90% of all sickness is managed. Such traditional public health activities as health promotion and disease prevention, and other health-enhancing interventions like road and environmental safety improvements, are also part of the system. Beyond the boundaries of this definition are those activities whose primary purpose is something other than health—education, for example—even if these activities have a secondary, health-enhancing benefit. Hence, the general education system is outside the boundaries, but specifically health-related education is included. (p. 5)

The definition includes activities performed by physicians and allied health personnel; equally important, it includes activities performed by behavioral scientists whether they practice health psychology, behavioral medicine, or health education. As the type of system establishes the context, including both the freedom and constraints under which we apply our skills and expertise, a brief discussion of systems of health care is warranted.

SYSTEMS OF HEALTH CARE

In describing systems, Ackoff (1994) provided the following definition: "A system is a whole consisting of two or more parts (1) each of which can affect the performance or properties of the whole, (2) none of which can have an independent effect on the whole, and (3) no subgroup of which can have an independent effect on the whole. In brief, then, a system is a whole that cannot be divided into independent parts or subgroups of parts" (p. 175). Systems are further defined as mechanical, organismic, or social systems. Ackoff (1994) noted that "Social systems—of which organizations, institutions, and societies are examples—are open system systems that (1) have purposes of their own, (2) at least some of whose essential parts have purposes of their own, and (3) are parts of larger (containing) systems that have purposes of their own" (p. 176). No one working in health care would argue with the definition: it fits the framework within which we treat patients or conduct research in health psychology. At the same time, however, it is important to emphasize the importance of the word *open*. In most instances, whatever changes occur are a result of our actions. If we take an aspirin when we have a headache, for example, the headache may disappear. However, there are other instances where the openness of the system permits other variables to produce change. An illustration of what is meant by open is provided by an asthma attack which, according to the current definition, is an airway obstruction that is "reversible (but not completely in some patients) either spontaneously or with treatment" (National Institutes of Health, 1991, p. 1). The fact that asthma attacks can spontaneously remit reinforces the point that we are never absolutely certain that our actions produced any changes we see. Uncertainty is particularly relevant with chronic health conditions where both the course of a disorder and its treatment are unpredictable in individual patients (e.g., Cassell, 1997).

Because a system as a whole cannot be divided into independent parts, its performance is never equal to the sum of its individual parts; rather, what is significant is the interaction of the parts (Ackoff, 1994). Even when each part of a healthcare system independently performs as well as possible, however, the system does likely not achieve optimal performance. Optimal performance in health care demands that each member of a treatment team not apply his or her specific talents separately, but do so in concert with others on the team. When these interactions take place, synergy may occur. As Ackoff explained, "Synergy is an increase in the value of the parts of a system that derive from their membership in the system, that is, from their interactions with other parts of the system. Such an increase in value can obviously only occur if the parts can do something of value together that they cannot do alone" (p. 181).

Along with most health psychologists, we perceive synergy as a goal rather than as a *fait accompli.* There are two reasons for our skepticism. First, although synergy may occur with a multidisciplinary team approach—when each member of a healthcare team independently applies his or her particular expertise and skills—synergy is more apt to occur when members perform their skills in an interdisciplinary manner. An interdisciplinary approach, however, is more often the ideal than the reality of health care provided by treatment teams. Second, each health team member must acquire a basic understanding of the knowledge and skills of all members of the interdisciplinary team. It requires us as health psychologists, for example, to have a working and current knowledge regarding a condition and how it is treated by our medical colleagues. This knowledge, in turn, permits us as part of an interdisciplinary team to provide optimal treatment to patients. Equally important, we are able to avoid causing harm, such as improving adherence to an inappropriate or potentially dangerous treatment regimen.

Participating in an interdisciplinary team represents a paradigmatic shift in providing health care (Creer, 2000). Each group of professionals is used to perceiving what they do through their own pair of spectacles that narrowly focuses on what that group does. However, the success of any given group, whether psychologists or physicians, is a function of the performance of all groups involved in the team. Creating an effective interdisciplinary team cannot be a one-sided exercise on our part; others, particularly physicians and allied health personnel, must have a working knowledge of our skills and how they can be applied to ameliorate problems faced by patients. A metaphor would be that instead of a group of musicians separately playing their instruments in a chaotic and cacophonous manner, the musicians concentrate on playing together whatever piece they select to play. We emphasize the distinction between multidisciplinary and interdisciplinary because the value of our actions requires that we work with others on a healthcare team in a coordinated fashion to provide maximally effective treatment to patients. At one time or another, each of us is a patient; therefore, it behooves us to strive for a healthcare system that provides maximum benefit to whoever is being treated, including ourselves (Sontag, 1978).

The World Health Organization's (2000a) report of the definition of health will be expanded by organizing the chapter to focus on the topics of (1) promotion and prevention; (2) restoration or control, and (3) maintenance of change.

HEALTH PROMOTION AND PREVENTION

Health Promotion

Wurtele (1995) defined health promotion as the "process of enabling individuals to increase control over and improve their health" (p. 200). It involves encouraging health-enhancing behaviors, such as engaging in regular exercise, and avoiding health-compromising behaviors, such as smoking. Health promotion is aimed not only at changing behaviors in healthcare settings, but at improving healthy behaviors in schools, homes, the workplace, and the community. The overall goal in the past decade has been to attain objectives outlined in *Healthy People 2000* (U.S. Department of Health and Human Services, 1991). Objectives centered on: (a) increasing physical fitness and activity, (b) improving nutrition, (c) reducing tobacco use, (d) decreasing alcohol and other drug abuse, and (e) enhancing educational and community-based health programs. In most instances, the objectives set for the year 2000 were not achieved. The conclusion is reflected by following health indicators as assessed over the past decade (U.S. Department of Health and Human Services, 2000):

PHYSICAL ACTIVITY. There was a slight rise in exercise and physical activity by adolescents, but a sharp decrease in physical activity by adults.

OVERWEIGHT AND OBESITY. At the end of the last decade, over half the adults in the United States were estimated to be overweight or obese; 11% of children and adolescents were considered overweight or obese.

TOBACCO USE. After years of steady decline, rates of smoking among adults leveled off in the 1990s. However, the percentage of adolescents in grades 9 through 12 who smoked increased in the 1990s. Every day, an estimated 3,000 young persons started smoking.

ALCOHOL AND SUBSTANCE ABUSE. For adolescents, the trend from 1994 to 1998 showed fluctuations, with about 77% of adolescents aged 12 to 17 years reporting they were both alcohol-free or drug-free during the past month. Binge drinking remained at the same approximate level (17%) for all adults since 1988, with the highest current rate of 32% among adults aged 18 to 25 years.

RESPONSIBLE SEX BEHAVIOR. In the past six years, both an increase in abstinence among all youth and an increase in condom use occurred among sexually active youth. Nevertheless, approximately one million teenage girls in the United States have unintended pregnancies each year. Nearly half of these unintended pregnancies ended in abortion.

INJURY AND VIOLENCE. Motor vehicle crashes, particularly among the age group 15 to 24 years, remained high. Although the latter group comprised only 10% of the U.S. population in 1996, they accounted for 15% of deaths from motor vehicle crashes. Although homicide rates fell to their lowest level in three decades, 32,436 individuals died from firearm injuries in 1997, of this number, 42% were homicide victims.

Healthy People 2010 (U.S. Department of Health & Human Services, 2000) proposed two overarching goals: (1) increasing quality and years of healthy life, as measured by health-related quality of life, global assessment, healthy days, and years of healthy life; and (2) eliminating health disparities among segments of the population, including differences that occur because of gender, race or ethnicity, education or income, disability, geographic location, or sexual orientation. The nation's progress in achieving the two goals of *Healthy People 2010* will be monitored through 467 objectives in 28 focus areas. Significant behavioral change in the majority of focus areas, similar to those adopted in *Healthy People 2000*, can only be achieved through a national commitment that, heretofore, has been absent. Any treatment approach taken will require multilevel prevention interventions that extend beyond the individual to systems, organizations, and community factors.

Prevention

Prevention is defined as the act of preventing or impeding a particular result. In a thoughtful discussion, Kaplan (2000) explained that there are two pathways to prevention: primary and secondary. In many instances, health promotion and primary prevention overlap (e.g., the development and dissemination of community programs targeted for the prevention of smoking). These programs have the goal of promoting healthy lifestyles and preventing smoking, particularly in adolescents and young adults who may experience peer pressure to start smoking.

Primary Prevention

Kaplan (2000) pointed out that "primary prevention almost always involves behavioral change, therefore, successful primary prevention must use behavioral theories and behavioral intervention" (p. 382). A number of behavioral approaches may be taken in primary prevention; in addition, a number of other factors, including public policy, educational, economic, and contextual variables, are prominent. Application of these factors will be illustrated by describing cigarette smoking, a behavior that is influenced, one way or another, by all these variables.

SUCCESS OF PRIMARY PREVENTION. Tobacco consumption fell between 1981 and 1991 in most high-income countries, including the United States (World Health Organization, 1999). The goal of smoking reduction was achieved by the adoption of a wide range of policy, educational, economic, and behavioral measures. The result is illustrated in data gathered from both developed and developing countries.

UNITED STATES. In the United States, the prevalence of smoking increased steadily from the 1930s. It reached a peak in 1964 when more than 40% of all Americans, including 60% of men, smoked. Since that time, smoking among adults in the United States has leveled off (Centers for Disease Control, 2000a,b,c). In 1988, one-fourth of U.S. adults smoked cigarettes; in 1999, one in 10 U.S. middle school students and nearly one in three high school students smoked (Centers for Disease Control, 2000b). Reductions in smoking were due not only to changes in public policy and education approaches to prevent smoking, but to behavioral programs that resulted in smoking cessation (e.g., Kaplan, 2000).

The World Health Organization (1999) estimated that in the United States, health education campaigns combined with smoke-free polices enacted between 1965 and 1985 resulted in 40 million people either not starting to smoke or abandoning the habit. The World Health Organization projected that although there were 50 million smokers in the United States in 1985, the number would have been 90 million had primary care measures not been taken.

The role of primary prevention in preventing and reducing tobacco use is illustrated by smoking cessation programs spurred by the recent tobacco settlement. Bauer, Johnson, Hopkins, and Brooks (2000), for example, described the progress made following implementation of the Florida Pilot Program on Tobacco Control. The main outcome variables were changes in use status, intentions, and behavior among large groups of students over a two-year period. The results of the study led Bauer and her colleagues to conclude that a comprehensive statewide program could be effective in preventing and reducing youth tobacco use. Similar types of programs designed to prevent smoking may be adopted by other states as a result of the Master Tobacco Agreement between the tobacco industry and state attorney generals. Any success that occurs, however, is dependent on whether funds are spent by individual states in the development and implementation of smoking prevention programs and not diverted by state legislatures to other projects.

Contextual variables are significant in the control of smoking in the United States. For example, the Centers of Disease Control (2000c) reported that the lowest smoking prevalence rates were found in Puerto Rico (13.7%), followed by Utah (13.9%). Puerto Rico and Utah were, in fact, the only two parts of the United States that achieved the national health objective for 2000 of reducing the prevalence of cigarette smoking in adults to $\leq$ 15% (U.S. Department of Health and Human Services, 1991). However, the report by the Centers of Disease Control (2000c) noted that Puerto Rico's overall median prevalence of 13.7% was far lower than the 26.9% prevalence among persons of Puerto Rican descent living in the United States. Since tobacco-producing states not only have higher rates of smoking, but lower excise taxes and less restrictive clean-air requirements (Emont, Choi, Novotny, & Giovino, 1993), the states are less apt to generate and implement tobacco prevention or smoking cessation programs.

United Kingdom. The United Kingdom (UK) has reduced smoking substantially through economic and other measures (World Health Organization, 1999). From 1965 to 1995, annual UK sales fell from 150 billion to 80 billion cigarettes; annual tobacco-related deaths in the 35- to 69-year age group decreased from 80,000 to 40,000. A national smoking prevention campaign, initiated in December of 1998, is targeted at helping an additional 1.5 million people quit smoking by the year 2010.

Norway. Norway enforced a total ban on all advertising for tobacco products in 1975, provided health warnings about smoking, and prohibited the sales of cigarettes to minors (World Health Organization, 1999). The approach has had a strong impact on tobacco sales, particularly among young teenagers. If cigarette consumption had continued to rise in Norway, it is estimated that the rate of smoking would be 80% higher than current estimates.

Less progress in reducing smoking has been made in developing countries (World Health Organization, 1999):

Thailand. Beginning in the 1970s, Thailand adopted a comprehensive control program; it consisted of curbing smoking in some public areas, banning national cigarette advertising, requiring tobacco companies to reveal the ingredients of their cigarettes, and enacting other antismoking measures. The result has been a decline in smoking prevalence by 4% among males and by almost 3% among 15- to 19-year-olds.

Latin America. Among Latin American countries, advertising controls on tobacco products only apply in Chile, Colombia, Costa Rico, Mexico, and Panama. However, no estimates of smoking reductions have been reported (World Health Organization, 1999).

Barriers to Primary Prevention

By the end of the third decade of this century, smoking is expected to kill 10 million people worldwide each year. The rate of mortality is more than the total of deaths from malaria, maternal and major childhood conditions, and tuberculosis combined (World Development Report, 1993). Murray and Lopez (1996) pointed out that 70% of these deaths will be in developing countries. The World Health Report (World Health Organization, 1999) described three barriers to tobacco control: (1) lack of information on risks of smoking, (2) addiction to nicotine in cigarettes, and (3) profits to tobacco companies.

Lack of Information on Risks. Whereas smoking prevalence has decreased in developed countries, it has steadily increased by 3.4% per annum in developing countries. Overall, the World Health Organization (1999) estimated that the prevalence of smoking among men in developing countries is 48%. Education alone, as a tool to change the risks of tobacco use, is unlikely to be effective. Reduction in smoking in the United States relied on a combination of components, including increased taxes, restrictions on tobacco promotion, warning labels on tobacco products, restrictions on smoking in public, and the increased availability of behavioral smoking cessation programs (Houston & Kaufman, 2000). A similar approach—blending together multiple components into a treatment package—will be required to reduce smoking everywhere in the world, including those nations labeled developing countries.

Nicotine Addiction. The World Heath Report (World Health Organization, 1999) fails to recognize the function of behavioral techniques in halting smoking. A type of stage approach described by Murray and Lopez (1996) is mentioned, but it is the only time that any behavioral component is discussed with respect to smoking cessation. Rather, the World Health Report (World Health Organization, 1999) declared that cigarettes are refined vehicles designed to give peak nicotine levels. The report further noted that while social and psychological influences were important in the initiation of smoking, the "addictive nature of nicotine is the main reason why many smokers maintain their tobacco use, leading to tobacco-related ill-health, disability and premature death" (p. 70). There is little discussion of the central role played by health psychologists or other behavioral scientists in designing, tailoring, and implementing smoking cessation programs. Rather, the authors of the report concluded their discussion of smoking cessation by suggesting, "Although nicotine is the addictive substance in tobacco, it causes relatively little harm itself. For many current smokers, continued use of nicotine—through patches, tablets, inhalers or other means—offers the best practical approach to cessation" (p. 74). Although the conclusion is true for some smokers, others quit smoking only with a combination of pharmacological and behavioral counseling. A recent report by the Centers of Disease Control (2000d), for example, noted that pharmacological treatment, combined with behavioral support, will enable 20% to 25% percent of smokers to remain abstinent at least one-year post-treatment; physician advice alone can produce cessation rates of 5% to 10% each year. A comprehensive review of the various techniques applied in smoking cessation programs is described by Niaura and Abrams (2002).

Profits to Tobacco Companies. Tobacco is big business throughout the world. According to the World Health Report (World Health Organization, 1999), twice as many cigarettes were smoked in 1999 than were smoked 30 years ago. The tobacco industry is expanding, with the world retail market in cigarettes worth $300 billion. Tobacco firms will continue to make profits currently estimated at more than $20 billion a year. The largest tobacco company was the China National Tobacco Corporation with sales of 1,700 billion cigarettes; the Corporation accounted for 24.6% of the cigarette production in 1997. Huge increases in cigarette advertising, accompanied by a 10% increase in total sales, occurred in four Asian countries when U.S. companies entered these markets. Two companies were Philip Morris, with sales of 947 billion cigarettes accounting for 13.7% of the market, and R.J. Reynolds, with sales of 316 billion cigarettes accounting for 4.6% of the market (Jha & Chaloupka, 1999).

Principles of control of tobacco sales proposed by the World Health Organization (1999) include: (a) creating a "fair information" environment regarding the health consequences of smoking, (b) using taxes and regulations to reduce consumption, (c) encouraging cessation of tobacco use, and (d) building tobacco control coalitions to diffuse opposition to control measures. Application of these principles faces numerous obstacles generated by tobacco companies, including the use of public relations campaigns, buying scientific and other expertise to generate controversy over established facts, hiring lobbyists to influence policy, and preempting strong legislation for the adoption of voluntary codes or weaker laws (e.g., Saloojee & Dagli, 2000). In addition, the loss of potential revenue creates ambivalence among state and federal officials. DiFranza and Librett (1999), for example, pointed out that an estimated 3.76 million daily smokers, aged 12 through 17 years, consume an estimated 924 million packs of cigarettes per year in the United States. This generates $222 million in federal tax revenues and $293 in state tax revenues; it also produces $480 million in tobacco company profits. Finally, recognition that global tobacco control is the only way to stem the epidemic of tobacco-associated diseases has, to this point, been a failure. A recent editorial in the *Lancet* (2001) noted that global efforts to change smoking patterns have met with lukewarm acceptance; there simply was a lack of support for a strong draft treaty to regulate tobacco consumption. Furthermore, continued the editorial, an agreement reached between British and American Tobacco (BAT) with China permits BAT to build a large plant in the western Szhewan Province. The coup for BAT further challenges efforts to control the spread of tobacco use.

Secondary Prevention

Kaplan (2000) noted that secondary prevention is often referred to as medical prevention. The medical approach is built on linear thinking in that it involves diagnosing a disease at an early stage and, in a stepwise manner, eliminating or restricting it before it gets out of control. At the outset, it should be noted that the distinction between primary and secondary prevention is not always clear. For example, smoking cessation techniques used in primary prevention are apt to be a treatment component for smokers diagnosed with chronic obstructive pulmonary disease. Once diagnosed, control over a condition may or may not be established; in the latter case, the final result is often death. The World Health Report (World Health Organization, 1999) noted that, although studies in the 1960s suggested that one in four long-term smokers died from their habit, surveys of smoking mortality in the 1990s showed that the ratio is now about one in two. Smokers dying between ages 35 and 69 lose about 10 to 25 years of life versus nonsmoker life expectancy, and smokers dying over age 70 lose about 8 years of life. It is estimated that in developed countries, smoking caused about 62 million deaths between 1950 and 2000. It is expected that tobacco will cause about 150 million deaths in the first quarter of the twenty-first century and 300 million deaths in the second quarter of the century.

Three conditions closely linked to tobacco use are lung cancer, irreversible respiratory disease, and coronary heart disease.

LUNG CANCER. Parkin, Pisani, Lopez, and Masuyer (1994) estimate that 85% of the 676,000 cases of lung cancer among men in developed countries are attributable to smoking. More cases of lung cancer in men occurred in areas where cigarette smoking had been established the longest: North America, Europe, and Australia/New Zealand. Pisani, Parkin, Bray, and Ferlay (1999) estimated that, overall, there were 5.2 million deaths from cancer in 1990. Lung cancer remained the most common cause of death from cancer, with over 900,000 deaths per year. Pisani and his colleagues echo Kaplan (2000) in emphasizing the potential impact of primary prevention. Pisani and colleagues (1999) concluded that 20% of all cancer deaths (approximately 1 million per year) could be prevented by adoption of preventive measures.

Lung cancer remains the leading cause of cancer deaths in both men and women in the United States and Canada (Landis, Murray, Bolden, & Wingo, 1998). Approximately one out of every five deaths in the United States results from smoking. In Australia, France, Germany, Scandinavia, Spain, and the United Kingdom, lung cancer is the leading cause of cancer death in men and the second or third cause in women (Midthun & Jett, 1999).

Evidence shows that a combination of primary and secondary prevention can reduce deaths from lung cancer. During the period between 1988 to 1997, for example, per capita cigarette smoking in California declined more than twice as rapidly as occurred in the rest of the country (Pierce et al., 1998). Pierce and colleagues suggested that these results were related to the California Tobacco Control Program created by Proposition 99 and approved in 1988 by California voters. The Centers for Disease Control (2000e) noted that several states, including Arizona, Florida, Maine, Massachusetts, and Oregon, implemented smoking cessation programs based on the California model. Many of these states have shown substantial declines in per capita cigarette consumption and/or changes in the prevalence of adult or youth smoking rates. A summary of psychological interventions for cancer patients, including those with lung cancer, was presented by Anderson (2002).

CHRONIC RESPIRATORY PULMONARY DISORDERS. In China, which has the highest number of tobacco-related deaths in the world, more deaths occur from respiratory diseases than from cardiovascular disease. Forty-five percent of deaths are due to respiratory disease, specifically *chronic obstructive pulmonary disease* (COPD), compared to 15% for lung cancer (Liu et al., 1998). If current smoking rates persist in China, where about two-thirds of men but few women smoke, Liu and colleagues estimated that tobacco will kill about 100 million of the 0.3 billion males now aged zero to 29 years, with half the deaths occurring in middle age and half occurring in old age. A prospective study by Niu and colleagues (1998) indicated that smoking caused 12% of mortality in middle-aged men in China. Smokers have a large selection of cigarette brands to chose from in that more than 1,000 brands of cigarettes are available in China. They are not cheap: the average smoker is estimated to spend 24% of his or her income on cigarettes (Yang et al., 1999). Yang and colleagues also strongly advocate primary prevention and, for those who smoke, smoking cessation programs. They suggest that steps be taken to maintain or decrease the currently low smoking prevalence in women. Taxation of cigarettes is a major source of income in China (World Health Organization, 1999); thus, a shift in priorities toward primary or secondary prevention is unlikely in the foreseeable future.

COPD is defined as slowly progressive airflow obstruction that, when possible, is only partially reversible (Senior & Anthonisen, 1998). It is estimated that 80 to 90% of those at risk for COPD smoke cigarettes (American Thoracic Society, 1995). The risk of COPD, in turn, increases as a function of the number of cigarettes a person smokes daily. Smoking is associated with three types of lesions: emphysema, small-airways inflammation and fibrosis, and mucus gland hyperphasia (Senior & Anthonisen, 1998). Bronchitis is defined as the amount of coughing that occurs so many months each year. Bronchitis can also be produced by smoking; it, along with emphysema, is a major form of COPD.

It is estimated that the overall prevalence of COPD in adult white populations in the United States is 4 to 6% in men and 1 to 3% in women; in people older than 55 years, COPD is recognized in approximately 10 to 15% of individuals. In 1990, COPD emerged as the fourth leading cause of death in the United States; in the age group 55 to 74 years, COPD was ranked third in men and fourth in women as a cause of death (Joint ACCP/AACVPR Evidence-Based Guidelines, 1997).

Pulmonary rehabilitation as an effective treatment for COPD is still debated. Recently, for example, Albert (1997) argued that it was ineffective, but Celli (1997) argued that it was effective. Gradually, however, the idea of attempting to rehabilitate patients with COPD is gaining credence. Initial attempts to rehabilitate patients with COPD focused on providing exercise training to improve physical function and, in turn, the quality of life of patients. These studies have often been regarded as inconclusive and controversial because of methodological weaknesses (Barry & Walschlager, 1998), although a meta-analysis of pulmonary rehabilitation and COPD found that positive benefits occurred in programs where exercise was the main rehabilitative component (Lacasse et al., 1996). At the same time that exercise for the rehabilitation of COPD patients was investigated, success at helping COPD patients to quit smoking was reported. Exercise and smoking cessation have emerged as two components, albeit major ingredients, in an overall program developed for the pulmonary rehabilitation of COPD patients. It is likely that the concurrent performance of exercise and smoking cessation produces, as occurs with weight loss (Jeffrey et al., 2000), a positive outcome that would not occur with performance of only exercise or smoking cessation. Programs that offer a variety of options that can be selected and tailored for individual patients have been most successful (e.g., Cambach, Wagenaar, Koelman, van Keimpema, & Kemper, 1999; Scherer, Schmieder, & Shimmel, 1998; Young, Dewse, Ferguson, & Kolbe, 1999).

Today, pulmonary rehabilitation is regarded as a set of tools and skills that can be packaged to address the multiple needs of COPD patients (Ries, Kaplan, Limberg, & Prewitt, 1995; Tiep, 1997). It expands treatment beyond traditional medical care by attempting to alter, through the application of behavioral techniques, disabling features of chronic and progressive lung disease. The skills described by Tiep (1997) are familiar to behavioral scientists no matter what conditions they treat; they include self-management, exercise promotion, functional training, building and enhancement of social skills, and methods to optimize the medical management of COPD. Other components of successful rehabilitation programs for COPD include patient and family education (Ferguson, 1998), training in coping with the condition (Young et al., 1999), and development of self-efficacy (Scherer et al., 1998). All these techniques have a role in a programmatic approach to the rehabilitation of COPD patients (Kaptein, 1997).

There remain several challenges to the implementation of rehabilitation programs for COPD patients. First, smoking cessation must continue to be at the forefront of any rehabilitative effort, even though the goal is often hard to attain (Celli, 1998). Even smokers with airflow obstruction can benefit from quitting despite previous heavy smoking, advanced age, poor baseline lung function, or airway hyper-responsiveness (Scanlon et al., 2000). Second, rehabilitation of COPD is often regarded as a one-time intervention rather than as an ongoing effort that occurs over time. If continual efforts do not occur, Tiep (1997) lamented, any benefits from brief rehabilitation programs are likely to fade quickly. Participation of healthcare providers in an ongoing partnership with their patients is required to strengthen rehabilitation outcomes in COPD. Such alliances also increase the chance of maintenance and generalization of change, a point Mahler (1998) cited as important for future rehabilitation programs. Third, Mahler described the need to establish levels of training intensity, particularly with respect to exercise, during formal training and in the maintenance of behavioral skills. Considering the number of rehabilitation programs being developed and implemented for COPD, these levels may soon be established. Finally, rehabilitation is currently available to only a small percentage of patients with COPD. Tiep (1997) argued that optimal management of COPD will require redesigning standard care for the heterogeneous disorder by integrating components of rehabilitation into a system centered around patient self-management and regular exercise for all patients.

Coronary heart disease. *Coronary heart disease* (CHD), often referred to as *coronary artery disease* (CAD), is a condition wherein fatty deposits accumulate in the cells lining the walls of coronary arteries and obstruct bloodflow. CHD is the leading cause of death in the United States and most industrialized nations. Each year about 450,000 people in the United States die from CHD, about 1 million experience an initial or recurrent coronary event, and about 12 million live with documented CHD often with a diminished quality of life (Smith & Ruiz, 2002).

The relationship between smoking and cardiovascular disease has long been established (Department of Health and Human Services, 1983). Stein et al. (1998) pointed out that angina is precipitated by inhalation of tobacco smoke, which can also increase heart rate, blood pressure, and myocardial oxygen demand. Consequently, smoking is often a primary cause of mortality from heart disease. The inhalation of tobacco smoke can also increase coronary vascular resistance and impair myocardial perfusion, and interfere with the efficacy of antianginal drugs. For these reasons, Stein and colleagues recommended that all patients with coronary heart disease be strongly urged and counseled to quit smoking. In another study, Gabbay et al. (1996) examined triggers (physical and mental exercise, anger, and smoking) of myocardial ischemia during the daily life in patients with coronary artery disease. It was found that the percentage of diary entries associated with ischemia was more than five times as high when patients reported smoking than when they did not.

If smoking can be prevented, the risk of heart disease in many individuals will also be reduced. Fichtenberg and Glanz (2000) described how the California Tobacco Control Program, a large, aggressive antitobacco program implemented and funded by a voter-enacted surtax, accelerated the decline in cigarette consumption and the prevalence of smoking in California. Specifically, Fichtenberg and Glanz hypothesized that because the risk of heart disease falls rapidly with smoking cessation, the program would be associated with lower risks of death from coronary heart disease. Results indicated that between 1989 and 1992, the rates of decline in per capita cigarette consumption and mortality from heart disease in California, relative to the rest of the United States, were significantly greater than the pre-1989 rates. The rates of decline in packs smoked and deaths, however, significantly rebounded when the program was cut back in 1992. Despite the cutback, Fichtenberg and Glanz (2000) concluded that the program was associated with 33,300 fewer deaths from heart disease between 1989 and 1997 than would have been expected in California relative to the rest of the United States. Even so, the diminished effectiveness of the program after 1992 resulted in 8,300 more deaths than would have been expected had the initial program continued.

A programmatic approach to the secondary prevention of heart disease was described by Smith and Ruiz (2002). Components of the program include exercise, smoking cessation, stress management, and modification of coronary prone behavior. Coordinated comprehensive care with prioritized intervention efforts can assist patients to avoid becoming overwhelmed and confused by multiple demands and conflicting advice. A prioritized list suggested by Smith and Ruiz included, in decreasing importance, (a) adherence to medication regimens, (b) smoking cessation (where relevant), (c) regular exercise, (d) a sensible diet, (e) stress management, and (f) additional interventions for depression and anger augmented by psychopharmacological consultation if needed.

Dramatic demonstrations of comprehensive behavioral approaches to coronary heart disease have been reported. In a controlled trial of a program involving regular exercise, low-fat diet, stress management, and group support, Ornish and colleagues (1998) found that more regression of atherosclerosis occurred after five years than after one year in the experimental group. In contrast, coronary atheroschlerosis continued to progress in the control group. The control group also had twice as many cardiac events. A similar study by Gould et al. (1995) showed that a program incorporating lifestyle and risk factor change was associated with decreased (improved) size and reduced severity of perfusion abnormalities on dipyridamole positive emission topography images.

Restoration or Control

In assessing health systems, the World Health Organization (2000a) emphasized that, above all, a health system contributes to good health. Good health, in turn, is the defining objective for the health system. Achieving the objective requires that the health status of the entire population be as good as possible over the person's entire life cycle, taking account of both premature mortality and disability. Whether a person's health can be fully restored is a function of the condition experienced by the patient and healthcare resources available to him or her; with appropriate treatment, many infectious diseases can be cured and the patient's health restored. With chronic conditions, all we can do is intervene to help individuals to control a condition; establishing control, in turn, may assist patients to live healthier and happier lives. The World Health Organization (2000a) described health in terms of infectious diseases and noninfectious or chronic disorders.

Infectious Diseases

Infectious Diseases in Developing Countries

Overcoming Antimicrobial Resistance, a report on infectious diseases, was recently issued by the World Health Organization (2000b). The report proclaimed that we are the first generation ever to have the means of protecting ourselves from the most deadly and common infectious diseases. We possess the knowledge to prevent or cure diseases such as malaria, tuberculosis, HIV, diarrheal diseases, pneumonia, and measles. These diseases can be prevented with tools and techniques that cost a few dollars or, in many cases, a few cents. The costs of effective interventions for different infectious diseases are depicted in Table 15.1. It is difficult to imagine that so little money could achieve so much for so many people throughout the world.

Despite these lifesaving drugs, interventions, and control strategies, they have not been put to wide use in combating disease. In disease-endemic countries, global efforts have remained embarrassingly low. Only 3% of Africa's children

TABLE 15.1 Effective Interventions for Infectious Diseases and Their Approximate Costs (Adapted from the World Health Organization, 2000b)

Intervention	Prevention or Treatment Cost in U.S. Dollars	Effectiveness When Used Consistently and Correctly
Six months of chemotherapy to treat tuberculosis	$20	95%
Year's supply of condoms to prevent HIV	$14[a]	99%
Antimalarials	$0.05	95%
Rehydration salts to treat diarrheal diseases	$0.33	Highly effective
Five days of antibiotics to treat pneumonia	$0.27	90%
One dose of vaccine to prevent measles	$0.26	98%

[a] The cost of 100 condoms in prevention programs ranges anywhere from $1.30 to $1.50 in Cambodia or Rwanda to $17 in Central America, Brazil, or Bolivia. The $14 cost per person is high in most developing countries.

have bednets or effective anti-TB medicines, and treatment strategies only reach 25% of the world's TB cases, and only half of developing countries have adopted the Integral Management of Childhood Illnesses (IMCI) package proven to be effective in preventing deaths among children.

The underuse and misuse of health breakthroughs has been catastrophic for people who live in developing countries. Almost two out of three deaths among people in the poorest countries of Africa and Asia continue to result from just seven illnesses. The illnesses and the percentage of deaths they cause worldwide include AIDS (13%); maternal and perinatal conditions (11%); diarrheal diseases (9%); acute respiratory conditions (9%); malaria (6%); measles (5%); and tuberculosis (4%). Worldwide, more than 11 million people, mainly young parents and children, die each year from preventable or curable afflictions. Infectious diseases account for one-half of the deaths in the world each year. Angier (2001) noted that half of these deaths are due to three "pedestrian" diseases: malaria, HIV/AIDS, and tuberculosis (TB).

***HIV/AIDS* IN DEVELOPING COUNTRIES.** Throughout the world, 22 million have died from AIDS, and another 36 million, mainly in developing countries, have become infected with HIV (Schwartlander et al., 2001). In the 20-year history of the HIV/AIDS epidemic, few resources were available to provide assistance to the millions with HIV/AIDS in developing countries. At recent meetings of the United Nations, however, commitments were made to intensify the fight against AIDS and, specifically, to reduce HIV in young people. The approach that will be taken is based on 34 studies in 18 countries that met rigorous inclusion criteria (Merson, Dayton, & O'Reilly, 2000) and focuses on primary prevention of HIV. The activities and aims of the campaign are ambitious. The program centers around 12 essential prevention steps ranging from teacher education to supplying condoms to men and women, and from conducting harm reduction programs to providing peer counseling. In addition, the costs of achieving these steps, mainly behavioral in nature, have been calculated for each country. For the first time, countries, private foundations, and pharmaceutical companies have pledged financial assistance for the program. This led Schwartlander et al. (2001) to proclaim that "Acting individually and collectively, the world's highest income countries have also signaled that they recognize the need for an extraordinary boost in the fight against AIDS" (p. 2436).

Three questions should be asked with respect to the potential control of HIV/AIDS throughout the world. First, are developed countries concerned enough to expend the $7 billion required for a global program (Das, 2001)? We already spend $11 billion annually for HIV/AIDS treatment in the United States (Pear, 2001); whether we are willing to add more to the pool of resources for global HIV/AIDS treatment may be a different matter. Second, will financial support alone erase HIV/AIDS from developing countries? Such an outcome is unlikely. Das (2001) emphasized that money alone is not enough to keep infectious diseases under control. He warned that unless there is a paradigmatic shift in the way we shape global health policies, particularly through spending more money to train providers in Third World communities, our efforts may backfire with the emergence of more drug-resistant diseases. Das pointed out that "if there is one thing that AIDS has taught us, it is to be wary of interactions between medical technology and sociocultural factors" (2001, p. 23). Finally, are people willing to make whatever behavioral changes are required, a hallmark of primary prevention (Kaplan, 2000)? A leitmotif that is repeated throughout this chapter is that it is difficult both to change and to maintain behavioral change.

***TB* IN DEVELOPING COUNTRIES.** TB is a disease caused by a potentially deadly form of bacteria. Until the 1940s when environmental and behavioral changes controlled the disease, it was a leading cause of death in both developed and developing countries. It was thought that TB was a thing of the past but, in recent years, it returned with a vengeance. A strain—*multidrug-resistant tuberculosis* (MDRTB)—is rapidly increasing on five continents. Four drugs used to treat MDRTB produce high cure rates in areas of low drug resistance; MDRTB is more difficult to treat, however, in areas that have high levels of drug resistance. These areas, unfortunately, are usually found in poorer regions of the world; in developing countries, it causes 25% of preventive mortality among young people and is a leading killer of young women worldwide (World Health Organization, 1999). Dye, Scheele, Dolin, Pathania, and Raviglione (1999) presented data collected from 212 countries by the WHO Global

Surveillance and Monitoring Project in 1997. The data indicated that the global prevalence of TB and *mycobacterium tuberculoses* (MTB) continues unabated. The MTB infection was found in 32% or 1.86 billion people in the world. Although dormant in most patients, approximately 10% of those infected with MTB can be expected to develop active tuberculosis (Broughton & Bass, 1999).

Globally, the burden of TB is enormous, mainly because of poor control in Southeast Asia, sub-Saharan Africa, and Eastern Europe, and because of high rates of MTB/HIV co-infection in south African countries. The World Health Organization (1999) has relied on generalities such as a global initiative, *Stop TB*, rather than introducing proven behavioral procedures to help stem the sweeping tide of tuberculosis. However, as TB is closely linked to HIV/AIDS (e.g., Schwartlander et al., 2001), greater attention will likely be paid in the future to both the primary and secondary prevention of TB.

Infectious Diseases in Developed Countries

Populations of developed countries have been perched on a knife's edge with respect to infectious diseases. We were fortunate in the United States, for example, to have dodged the full impact of HIV and AIDS, now ranked among history's worst epidemics (773,474 persons had been reported with AIDS in the United States as of December 31, 2000; 448,060 of these persons have died) (Centers for Disease Control, 2001a). The rapid spread of HIV/AIDS throughout the world in the past 20 years, however, signals that developed countries will not be so lucky in the future. As pointed out by Angier (2001), "the world is moving beyond the old polarities of ancient and modern, global and vernacular, high-tech and no tech" (p. 69).

An example of the globalization of our world can be found in looking at recent trends with infections in developed countries. The World Health Organization (2000b) highlighted what it referred to as the Big Guns of Resistance. The Big Guns respect no borders and include penicillin-resistant pneumococci (identified in Spain), salmonella resistance (identified in Germany), staphylococcus resistance to methicillan (identified in the United Kingdom), multidrug-resistant Streptococcus pneumonia (identified in the United States), and declining resistance to antimalarial drugs found throughout the world. Consequences of antimicrobial resistance include: (a) increased mortality (resistant infections are more often fatal), (b) increased morbidity (with prolonged illness, there is a greater chance for resistant organisms to spread to other people), (c) increased costs of care and more expensive drugs, and (d) limited solutions (there are no new drugs on the horizon). Two examples of the worldwide spread of infectious diseases in developed countries are HIV/AIDS and TB.

HIV/AIDS in Developed Countries. The twentieth anniversary of the HIV/AIDS epidemic was recently commemorated by the Centers for Disease Control in an issue of *Morbidity and Mortality Weekly Report* (available on-line at www.cdc.gov). One article reviewed medical and behavioral approaches taken to control HIV/AIDS in the United States (Centers for Disease Control, 2001b); a second article described the global HIV/AIDS epidemic and steps taken to curtail the disease (Centers for Disease Control, 2001a). More than 448,000 Americans are known to have died from AIDS, but with the development of new drugs, the number of yearly deaths declined from 50,610 in 1995 to 16,273 in 1999 (Pear, 2001).

Kelly and Kalichman (2002) described significant advances made in behavioral research over the past decade to help patients or potential patients both to prevent HIV infections (primary prevention) and to reduce or alleviate adverse consequences among those living with HIV disease (secondary prevention). In primary prevention, Kelly and Kalichman cite research that has shown the effectiveness of multilevel risk reduction interventions with individuals, couples, small groups, and communities; changes in social policy and, at the structural level, other prevention measures have been taken to prevent HIV/AIDS. Advances in medical care have resulted in establishing some control over HIV/AIDS, while presenting challenges to behavioral scientists with respect to secondary prevention of HIV. Kelly and Kalichman describe such challenges as helping patients (a) to adhere to complex medication regimens, (b) to cope with the successes and setbacks in their health, and (c) to live with the uncertainty that surrounds what is, in many cases, fast becoming both an infectious and a chronic disease. In marking the twentieth anniversary of the HIV/AIDS crisis in the United States, Pear (2001) enumerated four changes in federal policy and operations prompted by AIDS: (a) huge increases in federal spending in biomedical research, including the development of new vaccines; (b) swifter approval of prescription drugs for all sorts of illness; (c) a deeper appreciation of the importance of social and behavioral science in preventing diseases; and (d) the growing recognition that infectious diseases threaten the economic and political stability of many countries.

Specific counseling and behavioral techniques used in developed countries with HIV/AIDS patients were enumerated by Chippendale and French (2001). They list a number of strategies that involve: (a) establishing specific aims of counseling of HIV/AIDS patients, (b) selecting a tactic from among an array of HIV counseling programs and services, (c) dealing with uncertainty in HIV/AIDS patients, (d) teaching coping strategies; and (e) becoming aware of psychological issues in HIV/AIDS counseling. These techniques will likely be used in helping to resolve key issues that Kelly and Kalichman (2002) describe as emergent directions in behavioral research with HIV/AIDS patients. The issues include: (a) tailoring prevention approaches to reach all populations with a high incidence of HIV/AIDS, (b) improving prevention intervention exchange between investigators and service providers, (c) better integrating HIV prevention and care services, and (d) maintaining a sense of urgency in fighting the HIV/AIDS epidemic.

There is increasing evidence that the battle against HIV/AIDS in developed countries presents different challenges than those found in the battle against the disease in developing countries. Imrie et al. (2001) conducted a randomized control trial, with a 12-month followup, to determine the effectiveness of a brief cognitive behavioral intervention in reducing the incidence of sexually transmitted infections among gay men. The study involved 343 men who reported they had an acute sexually transmitted infection, had engaged in unprotected anal intercourse in the past year, or expressed concern about their sexual activities. All participants received a brief one-to-one counseling session about sexual risk behavior. In addition, those assigned to the intervention group were invited to a one-day workshop that drew on the transtheoretical model of behavior change, the model of relapse prevention, and elements of social learning theory and motivational interviewing.

Imrie and colleagues (2001) pointed out that this was the first trial in a population of gay men to measure both clinical and behavioral outcomes. The main outcome measures were the number of new sexually transmitted infections diagnosed during the 12-month followup and self-reported incidence of unprotected anal intercourse. At baseline, 37% of the intervention group and 30% of the control group reported having unprotected anal intercourse in the past month. At 12 months, the proportions for the two groups were 27% and 32%, respectively. However, 31% of the intervention group and 21% of the control group had presented with at least one new infection that was diagnosed at the clinic. In considering only men who requested a checkup for sexually transmitted infections, the proportion diagnosed with a new infection was 58% for men in the intervention group and 43% for men in the control group.

The findings led Imrie et al. (2001) to declare that the behavioral intervention they used was acceptable and feasible to deliver. However, they pointed out, the higher risk of acquiring a sexually transmitted infection among participants in the intervention group was unexpected and clearly a cause of concern. Although the findings supported a previous study (Stephenson, Imrie, & Sutton, 2000), Imrie et al. (2001) indicated that the results support the conclusion that, "Despite its promise and acceptability, the brief cognitive intervention aimed at gay men at high risk of sexually transmitted infections did not reduce their risk of acquiring new infections" (p. 1455). The statement suggests that even carefully designed behavioral interventions cannot be assumed to benefit patients over time. With improved medical treatments, patients with HIV/AIDS are likely to perceive that they can be less vigilant in performing behaviors required to manage their condition; the consequence of these perceptions is apt to make future studies of behavioral interventions for HIV/AIDS more complex and more difficult to treat because of the development of drug-resistant strains of the disease.

TB in Developed Countries. In the United States, TB is untreated in many adults and children because of the failure to find and treat adult cases, and failure to completely evaluate and properly treat children exposed to TB (Lobato, Mohle-Boetani, & Royce, 2000). The disease has been prevalent among foreign-born persons living in the United States. In 1999, 43% of the TB cases reported in the United States were among foreign-born persons, compared with 24% of the cases reported in 1990 (Centers for Disease

Control, 2001c). The finding should not be construed, however, to suggest that only foreign-born persons are at risk for TB. Clusters of TB have been found in jails, where it is readily transmitted to inmates and jail personnel (e.g., Jones, Craig, Valway, Woodley, & Schaffner, 1999), and in a group of women who worked as exotic dancers (Centers for Disease Control, 2001d). In the latter case, TB was transmitted both among the dancers and to their customers. The Centers for Disease Control (2001d) warned that the findings underscore the need for all states, including those with low TB incidence, to maintain control capability, including plans for outbreaks of TB. All cases of TB are acquired through person-to-person contact via droplets nuclei; prevention occurs by use of ultraviolet radiation in a patient's room, or by covering the mouth and nose of patients' by having them wear a mask or cough into a handkerchief (Broughton & Bass, 1999). As a patient with tuberculosis may infect 10 to 15 other people, there is the potential for anyone in the United States to become a TB patient. It is only our good fortune that clusters of TB have not yet been found in overcrowded classrooms, the workplace, and among passengers flying on packed airplanes with inadequate air circulation.

Once detected, TB can only be controlled through aggressive medical treatment. A type of supervised strategy—*direct observed therapy* (DOT)—is accepted by over 100 countries in the world. Thus far, one million patients have been treated with the approach (World Health Organization, 1999). DOT calls for TB patients to report to a medical facility and receive treatment directly from healthcare personnel, an approach that Garner (1998) refers to as "supervised swallowing." It does not ask TB patients to accept the program, a factor that undermines patient compliance (Heyman, Sell, & Brewer, 1998), and to accept any responsibility for self-care (Garner, 1998). The acceptance of DOT as a gold standard for the treatment of TB is senseless for the following reasons:

First, the World Health Organization (1999) admitted that optimal treatment of TB is not occurring throughout the world. The World Health Organization observed that progress has been too slow—the only possible conclusion when considering the one million patients treated versus almost half a billion patients who could end up with TB—and credit this state to a lack of political commitment within countries with a high rate of the disease.

Second, a series of studies on the cost-effectiveness of DOT are unconvincing. The results, in part because they are not based on randomized clinical trials (e.g., Palmer, Miller, Halpern & Geiter, 1998), are mixed. On one hand, a decision analysis by Burman, Dalton, Cohn, Butler, and Reves (1997a) suggested that DOT is more effective than *self-administered therapy* (SAT). Other investigators (e.g., Gourevitch, Alcabes, Wasserman, and Arno, 1998; Snyder et al., 1999) have reported similar findings. No actual data on self-administered therapy data were presented in these studies, however. The truth, argued Garrett (1994), is that no nation does a worse job than the United States in identifying TB cases, successfully treating these cases, and keeping track of the outcome.

Third, noncompliance to DOT is common, particularly among alcoholics and the homeless (Burman et al., 1997b); in only half of the cases do TB patients complete their treatment (Volmink & Garner, 2001). Approaches taken to improve compliance have ranged from sending the noncompliant to jail (e.g., Gasner, Maw, Feldman, Fujiwara, & Frieden, 1999), where TB is further spread, to using established behavioral techniques to enhance compliance. Evidence presented by Tulsky and her colleagues (2000), for example, found that a $5 biweekly cash incentive improved adherence to TB treatment. The application of behavioral technology is a more palliative approach to changing behavior than the catch-22 approach of sending noncompliant TB patients to jail where they infect others.

Fourth, two investigations have compared DOT with SAT in randomized control trials. Zwarenstein, Schoeman, Vundule, Lombard, and Tatley (1998) found that treatment of TB was more successful among patients who performed SAT (60%) than among those treated with DOT (54%). Retreatment patients had significantly more successful treatment with SAT (74%) than with DOT (42%). Zwarenstein and his colleagues suggested that SAT achieved equivalent outcomes to clinic-based DOT at a lower cost. In a second study, Walley, Khan, Newell, and Khan (2001) randomly assigned 497 adults with TB to one of three groups: (1) 170 were assigned to DOTs by health workers; (2) 165 were assigned to DOTs by family workers; and (3) 162 were assigned to SAT. Health-worker DOTs, family-member DOTs, and SAT had similar outcomes, with cure rates of 64%, 55%, and 62%, respectively, and cure or treatment-completion rates of 67%, 62%, and

65%, respectively. The findings led Walley and colleagues (2001) to declare that none of the three strategies was superior to the others and that DOT did not give any additional improvement in cure rates. An introduction to the article asked the question, "Is DOT not so hot?"

Finally, the Cochrane Collaboration is composed of experts who regularly review the literature and prepare articles about specific diseases and disorders. (Periodic reviews of diseases and treatments, as well as abstracts of the reviews, are available on-line at www.software-update.com.) In a recent review of interventions for promoting adherence to TB management, Volmink and Garner (2001) analyzed 14 trials and reported that reminder cards sent to defaulters, a combination package of a monetary incentive and health education, and more supervision of clinic staff increased the number of people completing TB treatment. Return to the clinic for reading of a tuberculin skin test was enhanced by monetary incentives, assistance by lay health workers, contracts, and telephone prompts. No single strategy, especially DOTs, was responsible for turning the tide against TB in New York. Rather, Farmer, Becerra, and Kim (1999) concluded that several interventions were made, "including more rapid diagnosis, active case finding in epicenters of transmission, more rapid detection and treatment of MDR-TB, and, for a minority of patients, directly observed therapy" (p. 176). These conclusions reinforce findings by McKeown (1976; 1997), who analyzed the decrease in deaths from TB in the United States and Britain in the nineteenth and twentieth centuries. He found that the decline in tuberculosis occurred from 1838 onward, although the first effective therapy for TB, the antibiotic streptomycin, was not available until 1948. These findings led McKeown to conclude the decrease in TB in the United States and Britain was entirely due to environmental and behavioral changes, a verdict echoed by Magner (1992).

Control of Chronic Disorders

The World Health Organization (1997) reported that chronic diseases are responsible for more than 24 million deaths a year, or almost half of the global total. The leading causes are circulatory diseases, including heart disease and stroke; cancer; and COPD. As life expectancy in developing countries continues to increase—the life expectancy at birth reached 65 years in 1996—there is the likelihood that an aging population will begin to experience chronic diseases and conditions. This situation is referred to as *epidemiology transition*—the changing pattern of health in which poor countries inherit the problems of the rich, including not merely illness but also the harmful effects of tobacco; alcohol and drug use; and accidents, suicide, and violence. The phenomenon is also referred to as *the double burden* because of the continuing weight of endemic infectious diseases.

Types of conditions, particularly chronic illnesses and their consequences, are shown in Table 15.2. As will be described, many behavioral actions can be taken to reduce the impact of chronic illness in most of the categories.

The number of people aged 65 and older increased to 380 million, a 14% increase in that age group, between 1990 and 1995 (World Health Organization, 1997). Between 1996 and 2020, it is projected that the over-65 aged population will increase over 82% globally, or by about 110% in the least developed countries and developing countries, and by about 40% in developed countries. Longer life can be both a penalty and a prize, an irony emphasized by describing characteristics of chronic diseases.

Most health psychologists are involved with chronic conditions; the duties they perform range from applying behavioral techniques in smoking cessation programs to developing treatment plans for diabetes control. In one way or another, what we do as behavioral scientists is dictated by characteristics of the chronic conditions. The importance of each of these characteristics varies from disorder to disorder and from patient to patient. Nevertheless, all behavioral scientists who work with chronic illness are familiar with the characteristics of chronic disease.

Restoration versus Control

A crucial difference between infectious and chronic diseases is that infectious diseases can be cured by destroying the infectious agent, thus restoring the health of the individual. There are few, if any, cures for chronic conditions. The best we can hope for is to control the disorder. As succinctly summarized in the report by the World Health Organization (1997): "Chronic diseases ... do not spread from person to person. Every case of chronic disease represents a burden borne by one individual who, depending on circumstances, may or may not have access to treatment or support" (p. 2). This stark explanation demands

TABLE 15.2 Major Chronic Conditions and, in Most Cases, Causes of Death Throughout the World in 1996 (World Health Organization, 1997)

Cancer	More than 10 million people developed cancer in 1996; 6 million people with cancer died that year. Eight leading cancer killers are the eight most common in terms of incidence: cancers of the lung, stomach, breast, colon-rectum, mouth, liver, cervix, and esophagus.
Circulatory diseases	Account for over 15 million deaths, or about 30% of the global total. Include diseases of the heart and circulation—cardiovascular and cerebrovascula—such as heart attacks and stroke.
Rheumatic fever/rheumatic heart disease	Most common cardiovascular disease in children and young adults. Affects at least 12 million people, causing 400,000 deaths a year.
Chronic nonspecific lung diseases	COPD and asthma kill about 3 million people annually.
Diabetes mellitus	Approximately 135 million people have diabetes in the world; this number is expected to increase to almost 300 million by the year 2025.
Nutrition-related disorders	Malnutrition underlies more than half of the deaths among children in developing countries.
Human genetics, hereditary diseases and birth defects	Congenital and genetic disorders are second only to perinatal factors as the most common cause of infant and childhood death. Category includes thalassaemia, sickle cell anemia, cystic fibrosis, and hemophilia.
Muscular diseases	The category includes approximately 200 conditions affecting joints, bones, soft tissues, and muscles.
Mental and neurological disorders	The category includes epilepsy; dementia, of which Alzheimer's disease is the most common form (there are 29 million people with the disease); and mood disorders.
Violence	During 1993, at least 4 million deaths resulted from unintentional or intentional injury, including 300,000 murders.
Occupational and risk factors	There may be up to 160 million cases a year of occupational diseases stemming from exposure to chemical, biological and physical agents, and other environmental factors. Category includes household and road accidents.
Other issues	The category includes blindness, hearing loss, and oral health.

a realistic response in that if the majority of chronic diseases cannot be cured, the emphasis must be on (a) preventing their premature onset, (b) delaying their development in later life, (c) reducing the suffering they cause, and (d) providing the social environment to care for those disabled by them.

Costs

The economic burden of chronic conditions is enormous. Hoffman, Rice, and Sung (1996) reported that in the United States alone, over 45% of the population have one or more chronic condition; the direct costs of these conditions account for three-fourths of U.S. healthcare expenditures. A recent report from the National Academy of Sciences (2001) noted that 70% of healthcare expenditures, estimated to be $1.1 trillion in 1998 (Levit et al., 2001), are for the management of chronic illness. The report from the National Academy of Sciences (2001) listed 25 chronic conditions, such as heart disease, diabetes, asthma, and arthritis, and pointed out that focusing attention on these conditions could result in sizable improvements in the quality of care provided all patients.

Duration

Verbrugge and Patrick (1995) argue that duration is the defining characteristic of chronic illness. Once patients are diagnosed with a chronic illness, they can expect to experience the condition for the rest of their lives. The best hope is that control be established over the condition. For this reason, it is imperative that steps be taken to promote good health and to prevent, wherever possible, chronic diseases from developing (e.g., Kaplan, 2000).

Uncertainty

Perhaps the most insidious factor that intrudes upon care of chronic conditions is the uncertainty that affects both patients and their healthcare teams. Specific factors that contribute to uncertainty include:

Rhythm of the Disorder. Although patients with chronic conditions must constantly deal with the disorder, the rhythm of the disorder itself may wax and wane. Fluctuating symptoms occur with many chronic conditions, including arthritis, asthma, cystic fibrosis, diabetes, migraine headache, and multiple sclerosis. Periods of quiescence are interspersed between exacerbations of the condition; alleviation of the episodic flareups requires extra medications, additional treatment, and, in some cases, hospitalization. The temporal fluctuations of a condition only contribute to increased uncertainty both to patients and healthcare personnel.

Beliefs of Patients. The diagnosis of a chronic condition is often difficult to accept by patients, members of their family, or others in their environment. The thought is that if it could only be located, there is a silver bullet that would cure the disorder. For this reason, patients often shop around in seeking the nonexistent silver bullet. They grasp at any breaking news regarding their condition; a cover story in the newspaper, *USA Today* or on the Web will lead patients to run to their physicians to see if the new breakthrough would help them. It rarely does. When they finally realize there is no cure for their condition, patients may find it difficult to accept the reality that their condition can only be controlled. Patients may feel a sense of hopelessness and be ill-prepared to eschew denial and move to an effective strategy (e.g., the performance of effective self-care skills) required to control their condition.

A number of investigators (e.g., Brownlee, Leventhal, & Leventhal, 2000; Horne, 1997) have studied the beliefs of patients. The emphasis on the dynamics of illness cognition, temporal aspects of illness, and the interaction of affective and cognitive processes led Brownlee et al. (2000), for example, to reemphasize what may be their most basic proposition: peoples' judgments as to whether they are sick or well are based on their appraisals of experiences of somatic change and physical, affective, and cognitive function. People's perceptions, in turn, reflect the action of decision heuristics or rules that are tied to schemata of illness, life events, and the self.

Beliefs of Healthcare Providers. Cassell (1997) contended that a barrier to the management of a chronic illness occurs because our healthcare system is not set up to deal with such conditions. In his words, "Medicine in the United States, in terms of its institutions, payment mechanisms, goals, practices, technology, training, myths, and symbols is a profession concerned primarily with acute disease" (p. 22). The shortcomings of training healthcare professionals to work mainly with acute conditions were reinforced in the report by the National Academy of Sciences (2001). Although acute diseases remove people from normal life, the demise of the illness usually restores the patient's health. Chronic conditions, noted Cassell (1997), "have an insidious onset, a variable expression throughout their existence, and usually last the lifetime of the patient" (p. 23). The foremost difference between acute and chronic diseases is that the treatment of a chronic condition is not against death but against disability.

Beliefs of Others. It is often difficult to attend school or to work because of a chronic condition. A teacher may look askance at a student who misses school with an asthma attack, thinking "She was fine yesterday. It's all in her head." Similarly, a worker may find it is necessary to remain in bed because of an exacerbation of his arthritis. "He just wants to miss work," may be what the man's supervisor thinks. These beliefs, usually erroneous, further complicate the lives of those with chronic conditions, as well as generate unnecessary guilt about their plight.

Uncertainty of Treatment. In arriving at a treatment regimen for chronic illness, members of the treatment team must share their knowledge and expertise in an attempt to arrive at a plan that will provide optimal control over a condition.

However, even if each member possessed all the knowledge in his or her respective field—an impossible scenario—there would still be uncertainty surrounding treatment (e.g., Cassell, 1997). The hope is that the plan will work, but there is always the probability that it will not. Such uncertainty is rarely conveyed to patients; they are certain that if they adhere to the regimen, their condition will be controlled. When it fails to do so, the level of frustration and helplessness of patients and their families increases. Perceptions of care, including the uncertainty of treatment, can influence patient performance. The personal models that patients have toward illness, for example, have been shown to be independent predictors of self-care behaviors, including compliance to treatment regimens (Hampson, Glasgow, & Toobert, 1990).

Patients as caregivers. Perhaps the most vexing problem in treating chronic conditions is the realization that patients are the ones who must adhere to the treatment regimen and treat themselves. Anderson (1995), for example, estimated that patients with diabetes provide 95% of the treatment they receive for their condition. The same comment could be made about most chronic illnesses. Who provides the treatment is a topic that presents overlapping problems: Physicians and other healthcare professionals are, as noted, trained to manage acute diseases. They may believe that all they need to do is write a prescription and that will take care of the patient's problem. These same healthcare providers are often unwilling to recognize that, in order to be effective, they need both to provide daily treatment and to enter into a partnership with the patient to control his or her condition. Patients, on the other hand, may want "to leave it to the doc," and be unwilling to accept responsibility for providing day-to-day care for their condition. They may not accept the fact that their diabetes, arthritis, or asthma will be present even if they take steps to remedy exacerbations and perform the daily skills required to establish and maintain control over a condition.

Under the best case scenario, patients with a chronic disease become allies with their physician in the management of the condition. *Collaborative management* is defined by Von Korff, Gruman, Schaefer, Curry, and Wagner (1997) as "care that strengthens and supports self-care in chronic illness while assuring that effective medical, preventive, and health maintenance interventions take place" (p. 1097). Elements of corroborative management include: (1) collaborative definitions of problems by patients and healthcare providers, (2) targeting, goal setting, and planning between patients and healthcare providers, (3) creation of a continuum of self-management training and support for patients, and (4) active and sustained followup. The premise and elements of collaborative care are being integrated into change programs designed and implemented by health psychologists.

Controlling Chronic Conditions

It has been 35 years since Ullmann and Krasner (1965) published their book describing case studies in behavior modification. The book included cases on anorexia nervosa and hysterical blindness, two topics that today would be of interest to health psychology and behavioral medicine. Since 1965, other approaches to behavioral change have evolved. We will describe four: behavioral, cognitive behavioral, transtheoretical, and self-management. Before doing so, we would like to emphasize several points: First, the distinction among the four approaches is more theoretical than real. The distinction among terms in discussing intervention procedures, for example, is often blurred. For example, Ullmann and Krasner included studies on systematic desensitization by reciprocal inhibition (Wolpe, 1958); this technique was considered a behavioral method in 1965 whereas because of self-induced relaxation and imagery, it could today be considered a cognitive behavioral method. Another illustration is provided by the process referred to as self-reinforcement. Although often considered in purely behavioral terms, what reinforces patients to change and maintain their behavior has a cognitive component.

Second, there is commonality across approaches in the selection of assessment and outcome measures. Those who categorize themselves as cognitive behaviorists, for example, are as apt to use the rate of behavior as an outcome measure as are the behaviorists who popularized the method. By the same token, many investigators who refer to themselves as behaviorists often include a measure of self-efficacy, a construct developed by Bandura (1977; 1997).

Third, being comprehensive in selecting techniques to produce behavioral change is appropriate for three reasons: First, the response reflects the complex context within which we operate by participating in the treatment of ill patients, particularly those with a chronic condition. We may be asked to desensitize a patient to taking daily shots of insulin for diabetes, for example, or to develop a contingency contract for home treatment of cystic fibrosis. We have to consider what we think will work, not whether the technique is a pure example of any one treatment model. Second, only by picking and choosing can we tailor a treatment plan for a given patient and his or her illness. *Tailoring treatment plans* for individual patients is an aim explicitly described in the treatment guidelines for most chronic conditions. Finally, use of any available technique to change behavior should be considered not only in designing and implementing treatment techniques, but in developing a research or clinical program for behavioral change.

Finally, we will use research to illustrate each behavioral or cognitive behavioral technique. Although we recognize that most readers are well versed in the techniques that will be described, they are discussed in order to describe current uses of the techniques in health psychology or behavioral medicine.

BEHAVIORAL TECHNIQUES

Behavioral and cognitive behavioral scientists use a wide array of behavioral techniques. We will first focus on techniques that emerged from operant and classical conditioning. The techniques have either been used singularly (e.g., the use of extinction to decrease an inappropriate behavior) or, as is more likely today, in combination with other behavioral methods (e.g., in conjunction with contingency contracting). It is common, for example, for behavioral techniques to be used across all the models of behavioral change we will describe.

Operant Conditioning

Operant conditioning is a type of learning in which behavior is controlled by its consequences. Behaviors affected by their consequences are, in turn, modified by these consequences (e.g., Skinner, 1953). Specific techniques emerging from research in operant conditioning include the following:

POSITIVE REINFORCEMENT. *Positive reinforcement* is defined as the strengthening or maintenance of the future probability of a behavior as a function of the contingent occurrence of a stimulus that follows the behavior. The stimulus that increases or maintains the behavior because of its presence is empirically defined as a positive reinforcer. For example, Sloan and Mizes (1996) reported on the successful behavioral treatment of an older person with psychogenic vomiting. The approach taken was to reward independent behavior by praise and attention.

We are in a period that could be characterized as reinforcement redux: positive reinforcement has recaptured the interest it had several decades ago in generating and maintaining behavioral change. As noted, Tulsky and her colleagues (2000) found that a $5 biweekly cash incentive improved adherence to TB treatment; moreover in their periodic review for the Cochrane Collaboration, Volmink and Garner (2001) analyzed 14 trials and reported that a combination package that included a monetary incentive increased the number of people completing TB treatment. Volmink and Garner also found that returning to a clinic for a tuberculin skin test was enhanced by monetary incentives. Finally, Koffman, Lee, Hopp, and Emont (1998) reported that in a workplace smoking cessation program, an incentive competition component was significantly better at 6 months than a multicomponent or a traditional program. At 12 months, however, there was little difference between a multicomponent program with telephone counseling and the program that offered incentives.

Other techniques requiring the manipulation of positive reinforcers include the following:

1. EXTINCTION. *Extinction* is a decrease in the probability of a behavior that occurs with the withdrawal or discontinuance of positive reinforcement. Two studies illustrate the use of extinction. Benoit, Wang, and Zlotkin (2000) sought to obviate the need for enteral feeding in infants with resistance to feeding. Sixty-four children receiving enterostomy tube feeding were randomly assigned to either a behavioral or nutritional intervention group. Intervention consisted of the use of extinction. Results indicated that elimination of the need for tube feeding was achieved in 15 (47%) of 32 children in the behavioral group versus none in the nutritional group. Yody et al. (2000) provided a general discussion of the effective use of applied behavioral management, including reducing unwanted behaviors through extinction, in patients with acquired brain injury.

2. SHAPING. *Shaping* is a procedure whereby new behaviors are acquired by systematically reinforcing successive approximations toward a behavioral goal. Shaping was illustrated by Gutentag and

Hammer (2000) who successfully used shaping of oral feeding with a gastronomy tube-dependent child in natural settings. Shaping consisted of providing social praise and access to a favorite toy with food acceptance. In a review of the literature on environmental tobacco smoking (ETS), Hovell, Zakarian, Wahlgren, and Matt (2000) found three studies where repeated counseling/shaping procedures reduced quantitative estimates of ETS exposure in children with asthma.

3. STIMULUS CONTROL. Stimulus control is the influence that a stimulus or set of stimuli has on the probability that a behavior will occur. Stimuli are referred to as discriminative when, after being reliably present when a response was reinforced, their presence or absence systematically alters the probability of a response. Stimulus control is a major component of behavioral treatments of insomnia. Morin, Culbert, and Schwartz (1994) conducted a meta-analysis of 59 treatment studies involving 2,102 patients who experienced insomnia. Stimulus control, coupled with sleep restriction during the day, was the most effective single-therapy procedure. A review by Morin et al. (1999) revealed that on the basis of a review of 48 clinical trials and two meta-analyses, nonpharmacological therapies produced reliable and durable changes in several parameters of chronic insomnia. The data indicated that between 70% and 80% of patients treated with nonpharmacological interventions benefited from treatment. Stimulus control was found to be a major technique to reduce insomnia. For these reasons, stimulus control was the technique proposed to be standard in any nonpharmacological treatment of chronic insomnia (Chesson et al., 1999).

4. CHAINING. Chaining is a procedure whereby responses are reinforced sequentially to form more complex behaviors. When the step-by-step linkage of responses is complete, the chain appears as a single cohesive behavior. Chaining was demonstrated to be an integral part of the following studies: Hagopian, Farrell, and Amari (1996) described a 12-year-old boy with a history of gastrointestinal problems who displayed total liquid and food refusal. Backward shaping was used to shape drinking from a cup; a fading procedure was used to increase the quantity of water the boy drank. Second, Domel, Thompson, Baranowski, and Smith (1994) found that 82 children reportedly used behavioral chaining, as well as visual imagery, usual practice behavior, and preferences, to remember the foods they consumed at meals. The technique has promise in the treatment of childhood diabetes. Finally, Giles and Morgan (1989) employed chaining in the development of personal hygiene skills in a patient with five years of post-herpes simplex encephalitis. The program consisted of chaining a series of nine discrete activities by using linking phrases. The approach allowed the patient to structure his behavior and wash in a well-organized, nonrepetitive manner.

5. PREMACK PRINCIPLE. The *Premack Principle* states that for any pair of behaviors, the more probable one will reinforce the least probable one. The principle, proposed by David Premack (1959), has been used in a number of studies in health psychology. Amari, Grace, and Fisher (1995) used the principle to reduce noncompliance to a ketogenic diet in a 15-year-old girl with uncontrolled epilepsy. A ketogenic diet is difficult to introduce because it is often perceived to be unpalatable. Amari and colleagues, however, used stimulus-choice to assess relative preferences in 33 foods from the diet; they then developed two treatments based on the Premack principle. This resulted in increased compliance that generalized across settings and was associated with a 40% reduction in seizures. The Premack principle also proved of value in developing eating programs in children who exhibit failure to thrive or who had developmental disabilities (O'Brien, Repp, Williams, & Christophersen, 1991).

Another example of the Premack Principle was reported by Goldfield, Kalakanis, Ernst, and Epstein (2000). Thirty-four obese children, aged 8–12 years, were randomly assigned to one of three groups: two experimental groups had to accumulate 750 or 1,500 pedometer counts, respectively, to earn 10 minutes of access to video games or movies; access to sedentary behaviors was provided on a noncontingent basis to a control group. Results indicated that children in the 750 and 1,500 count contingency groups engaged in significantly more physical activity and spent more time in moderate or higher intensity activity compared to the control group. Furthermore children in the 1,500 count group engaged in more activity and spent more time in moderate or greater intensity activity compared to children in the 750 count group.

NEGATIVE REINFORCEMENT. Negative reinforcement is a consequence that strengthens or maintains a behavior by being subtracted or removed from the environment. Kitfield and Masalsky

(2000) used negative reinforcement to increase weight gain in a 22-year-old woman with developmental disabilities. The negative reinforcement intervention involved escape from eating and the dining area contingent on the consumption of food. Increased weight was maintained at one and three months. Other examples of the use of negative reinforcement are avoidance and escape learning.

1. ***Avoidance learning.*** *Avoidance learning* refers to the performance of behaviors to avoid the possibility of an unpleasant consequence. Harper, Brown, Triplett, Villasenor, and Gatchel (2000) conducted a study on 44 children with juvenile rheumatoid arthritis (JRA) who did or did not experience temporomandibular joint pain (TMJ). Thirty-four children without JRA served as the control group. Results indicated that children with JRA who experience TMJ may compromise their masticatory function as a pain avoidance mechanism. These findings may have profound implications with respect to the nutritional status of the children. Al-Obaidi, Nelson, Al-Awadhi, and Al-Shuwaie (2000) described pain variables as experienced by 63 patients with chronic low back pain. Al-Obaidi and colleagues found chronicity of pain is not explained solely by the sensory perception of pain. Rather, the anticipation and fear-avoidance about physical activities were the strongest predictors of the variation in physical performance.

2. ***Escape learning.*** *Escape learning* refers to the performance of behaviors that terminate an unpleasant consequence. Escaping from the consequences strengthens or maintains the behaviors. Escape learning was used by Hagopian and Thompson (1999) with an 8-year-old boy with cystic fibrosis (CF), mental retardation, and autism who exhibited noncompliance with respiratory treatments for CF. Treatment involved shaping cooperation while still allowing escape for other behaviors; the procedure improved compliance to the CF regimen. Ghaderi and Scott (2000) analyzed coping in dieting and eating disorders in five groups, including subjects with no past history of dieting or an eating disorder (ED). It was found that subjects with past or current ED reported significantly higher levels of escape avoidance.

Punishment. *Punishment* is a procedure whereby an aversive stimulus (or punisher) is presented immediately after the occurrence of a behavior. Punishment is rarely used in health psychology, although it was noted that patients with TB who failed to report for treatment have been incarcerated. As found by Gasner et al. (1999), jail time proved to be an ineffective strategy to use with these patients. Punishment (e.g., aversive smoking procedures such as rapid smoking, rapid puffing, and other smoke exposure) has been found to be significantly related to smoking cessation (Niaura & Abrams, 2002). Two other forms of punishment are time-out and response cost.

*1. **Time-out.*** *Time-out* (T.O.) refers to a procedure whereby access to varied sources of reinforcement are removed or reduced for a given period of time contingent upon a specified behavior. In a study using time-out with asthmatic children, Hochstadt, Shepard, and Lulla (1980) showed that by reducing potential reinforcers in a hospital setting, they significantly reduced frequency of hospitalizations in a group of asthmatic children considered to unnecessarily prolong their hospital stay. The findings replicated an earlier study by Creer (1970) and demonstrated that, besides reducing unnecessary hospitalizations, T.O. altered a major outcome measure of asthma: the frequency and duration of hospitalizations.

*2. **Response cost.*** *Response cost* (RC) is a procedure whereby a specified amount of available reinforcers are withdrawn contingent on the occurrence of a specified behavior. A common use of response cost was the approach taken in some weight reduction programs. At the outset, a client would pay a certain amount to the program; he or she could then have part of the money returned if they achieved specified goals. Jeffrey et al. (2000), however, reported that response cost is ineffective in motivating individuals to lose weight. Response cost was used as part of a comprehensive program employed to improve adherence to medication regimens in children with asthma (da Costa, Rapoff, Lemanek, & Goldstein, 1997).

Classical Conditioning

Classical conditioning occurs via the pairing of a neutral stimulus and an unconditioned stimulus. Following the systematic pairing of these stimuli, the neutral stimulus acquires properties similar to the unconditioned stimulus. Classical conditioning has been offered as the framework for a number of conditions that are of interest in health psychology, including conditioning of avoidance in burn patients (Thurber, Martin-Herz, & Patterson, 2000), acquisition of idiopathic environmental intolerance (Giardino & Lehrer, 2000), and age-related declines in associative learning and memory in the aged (Powell, 1999).

SYSTEMATIC DESENSITIZATION. There are three separate components to the procedure (Wolpe, 1958). First, hierarchies—consisting of descriptions of stimulus events that cause fear, anxiety, or other emotional responses—are developed. Second, patients learn a response pattern that is incompatible with the what they described in the hierarchies (e.g., self-generated relaxation skills). Finally, there is a juxtaposition of the two events, with patients attempting to relax while imagining items selected from the hierarchies. Systematic desensitization has long been a staple of behavior therapy (e.g., Paul, 1966). The technique has been used, as part of a multimodal treatment package, to treat children with cancer (DuHamel, Redd, & Vickberg, 1999), to reduce chemotherapy-induced nausea and vomiting in cancer patients (Morrow & Hickok, 1993), to reduce oral hypersensitivity in a 36-year-old man with a closed head injury (Brown, Nordloh, & Donowitz, 1992), and to reduce vaginismus in women (Biswas & Ratnam, 1995).

COGNITIVE BEHAVIORAL TECHNIQUES

The behavioral techniques described are also used in *cognitive behavioral therapy* (CBT). In addition to verifiable and public behaviors that can be objectively assessed, however, CBT approaches consider private and nonverifiable thoughts and beliefs. Identifying and changing distortions in thinking, for example, has long been a part of CBT (e.g., Beck, Rush, Shaw, & Emery, 1979; Ellis, 1973). Allen (1995) pointed out that various CBT models "all share the same three fundamental tenets: (a) cognitive activity affects behavior, (b) cognitive behavior may be monitored and altered, and (c) desired behavior may be effected through behavioral change" (p. 508). CBT incorporates diverse psychotherapeutic procedures, is sensitive to a biopsychological perspective of medical and psychiatric disorders, and is wed to empirically proven interventions (Meichenbaum, 1997). The biopsychosocial perspective emphasizes the reciprocal interaction that takes place among cognitive, behavioral, physical, and environmental variables as described in social cognitive theory by Bandura (1986). The reciprocal determination of variables is adaptable as the basis for self-management.

CBT is invaluable in health psychology and behavioral medicine because having taught patients the skills needed to manage a physical disorder, cognitive processes help patients mediate the translation of the skills into performance. Cognitive variables (e.g., self-monitoring and decision making) are particularly prominent processes. Personal feedback regarding behavioral change, in turn, permits patients to assess the effects of their performance and to acquire the confidence that they can perform whatever skills they may need in the future.

Specific Cognitive Behavioral Techniques

CBT techniques often used by health psychologists include the following:

SELF-MONITORING. Self-monitoring consists of self-observation of an activity and the recording of the observed findings. Self-monitoring is the single most important component of many cognitive behavioral interventions, including self-management. Whether it is monitoring cognitive processes, such as thoughts, or observing what one eats, such as occurs with diabetes, self-monitoring is key to any success attained by individuals in using cognitive behavioral skills. Laffel (2000) accentuated the need to use self-monitoring of blood glucose levels during diabetic exacerbations. Skeie, Thue, and Sandberg (2001) found that such data, when gathered with appropriate tools, met the expectations of patients. Finally, Quaglietti, Atwood, Ackerman, and Froelicher (2000) found that self-monitoring was a key tool in the successful management of congestive heart failure. Even though they may cease to record data, many individuals who fail to perform other self-management skills report they continue to observe some aspects of their behavior. Their response is useful when there are frequent and longer periods of quiescence between exacerbations of a chronic disorder (e.g., Caplin & Creer, 2001). Self-monitoring of behavior is one of the most consistent predictors of long-term success in controlling a chronic illness, leading Fenwick (1994) to declare that self-monitoring is the engine that drives the creation of countermeasures and their application to halting epileptic seizures.

SELF-STATEMENTS. Self-statements are statements or thoughts people make to themselves to guide their behavior. Several types are important: (a) statements that they make to themselves to take action when exposed to various stimuli, particularly to those stimuli that precipitate or control their behavior, (b) negative statements that come when thinking distressing thoughts when faced with a particular situation, and (c) positive statements people make to themselves in perceiving their performance or in reinforcing themselves (e.g., Beck et al., 1979; Ellis, 1973). Patients have used self-statements in coping with a variety of chronic conditions, including low back pain (Lin & Ward, 1996), the long-term followup of an outpatient interdisciplinary pain management program (Lynch, Agre, Powers, & Sherman, 1996), as a coping strategy by patients with rheumatoid arthritis (Gustafsson, Gaston-Johansson, Aschenbrenner, & Merboth, 1999), and as a way to control body dysmorphic disorder (Looper & Kirmayer, 2002).

Self-statements can be combined with other procedures in an attempt to control a situation or our own behavior.

1. Self-statements plus distraction. Self-statements can be combined with three other techniques to change behavior. *External distraction* means that people attempt to divert their attention away from a situation by focusing on a stimulus in their immediate environment. Dentists, for example, often mount a TV screen in the ceiling of a room that can be viewed by patients during a dental visit. *Internal distraction* means that people attempt to divert their attention away from a situation by focusing on some thought or physical sensation. If they are around friends who smoke when they are attempting to quit smoking, for example, they may focus on the healing that is occurring in their lungs because they stopped smoking. Finally, *imagery* can be used as a method of distraction. In the presence of tempting desserts while on a diet, people might imagine how they will look when wearing a size smaller dress or trousers. Self-statements plus distraction have been used with chronic illnesses. Distraction techniques have included focusing on positive expectations by patients with chronic pain in performing coping skills (Lynch et al., 1996; VanDalfsen & Syrjala, 1990).

2. Reperception of situation. When suddenly faced with a situation, such as someone offering a person a cocktail when they are trying to quit drinking alcoholic beverages, they may need to quickly *reperceive the situation* and decline the drink. Failure to avoid or escape from stimuli that formerly controlled their behavior may lead to a relapse of whatever change the people have made. Reperceiving a stimulus or stimuli is important in managing acute pain (VanDalfsen & Syrjala, 1990) and in coping with rheumatic arthritis (Gustafsson et al., 1999; Keefe et al., 2002).

3. Thought stopping. Thought stopping is an established behavioral change technique. When thoughts of a discriminative stimuli for a behavior people are trying to change begin to creep into their consciousness (e.g., thinking of a cigarette to go with their coffee), they use a variety of techniques ranging from snapping a rubber band they have around their wrist to exclaiming, either overtly or covertly, "Halt!". Thought stopping has been linked with *thought substitution* (e.g., substituting another thought for an undesired thought) in studies on acute pain (VanDalfsen & Syrjala, 1990), rheumatic arthritis (Gustafsson et al., 1999), and chronic low back pain (Lin & Ward, 1996).

4. Relaxation. Relaxation is a coping technique used in both behavioral and cognitive behavioral programs. People learn to relax on self-cue, often using the exercises promulgated by Jacobson (1938), in order to relax in the face of a stimulus or situation they find aversive. Relaxation is widely used by patients with chronic conditions, including the control of acute pain (VanDalfsen & Syrjala, 1990), chronic pain (Pan, Morrison, Ness, Fugh-Berman, & Leipzig, 2000; Peters, Simon, Folen, Umphress, & Lagana, 2000), and as a management tool in the preoperative treatment of proctological patients (Renzi, Peticca, & Pescatori, 2000).

5. Meditation. Meditation can achieve the same effect as relaxation in that it produces relaxation and, in many cases, a renewed sense of vigor. Meditation differs from relaxation in that instead of focusing on the body and concentrating on the release of physical tension, meditation accentuates detachment from physical states and from feelings and thoughts (Rudestam, 1980). A number of techniques may be used in meditation, including the use of a *mantra*, the name of a deity, a melodic word, a phrase, or a prayer (e.g., Benson, 1975). Meditation was a key technique used by Speca, Carlson, Goodey, and Angen (2000) with cancer patients. In a randomized controlled trial, Speca and colleagues reported that a meditation program was effective in decreasing mood disturbance and stress in cancer patients; the patients represented a wide array of cancer diagnoses, stages of illness, ages, stress, and mood. In recent years, patients have reported successful meditation through personal prayers to cope with fibromyalgia (e.g., Bernard, Prince, & Edsall, 2000).

6. IMAGERY. *Imagery* may be used with other behavioral techniques, particularly systematic desensitization by reciprocal inhibition. If imagery is to be used successfully, it is suggested that people: (a) escape from distracting stimuli, (b) relax, (c) listen to soothing music (if helpful), and (d) decide what type of imagery they wish to use. Three types of imagery can be used, including *receptive imagery*, a technique that consists of relaxing, creating an ambiguous scene, asking a question, and waiting for a response; *programmed imagery* consisting of generating an image complete with everything that might be present in visualizing the scene; and *guided visualization* or imaging a scene or procedure in detail. In their review, Pan and associates (2000) found that relaxation and imagery were effective in reducing oral mucositis pain.

Behavioral and CBT procedures are the foundation of health psychology and behavioral medicine. Illustrations of the use of the techniques in programmatic research follow.

Empirical Applications

Behavioral scientists have applied CBT procedures to a wide array of physical and psychological problems. Topics of interest range from insomnia to geriatric problems and from chronic diseases to depression that often accompanies a chronic condition. We will focus on two topics—pain and headache—because CBT research has been successful with the two chronic conditions. Moreover, the research has yielded information on the number and type of concurrent variables that occur in using CBT procedures, as well as methods of assessing change in both behavior and outcome measures of a chronic illness.

PAIN. Kole-Snijders and colleagues (1999) combined cognitive techniques with operant-behavioral treatment for individuals with low back pain. The latter patients formed what was labeled the complete package (OPCO) group. The patients were compared with those in two other groups: an operant-behavioral program plus group discussion (OPDI) group and a waiting list control (WLC) group. In comparison to the WLC group, both the OPCO and OPDI groups showed less negative affect, higher activity tolerance, less pain behavior, and higher pain coping and pain control. At post-treatment, the OPCO group showed better coping with pain. A number of studies have examined cognitive CBT procedures in relation to pain and depression. Burns, Johnson, Mahoney, Devine, and Pawl (1998) utilized a number of measures, including pain helplessness, walking endurance, depression, pain severity, and activity in 94 patients with chronic pain. Data were gathered at pre- and post-treatment and at three- to six-month followup evaluations. Results showed that decreases in pain helplessness were linked to pain severity reduction, whereas walking endurance increases were related to improvements in activity levels even after controlling for the effects of decreased depression. Sullivan, Reesor, Mikail, and Fisher (1992) urged that in designing programs for patients with clinical depression and pain, both problems be targeted for change by the use of CBT techniques. Other studies have examined the importance of sleep and pain (e.g., Lewin & Dahl, 1999; Currie, Wilson, Pontefract, & de Laplante, 2000). In the study by Currie and colleagues (2000), 60 patients with insomnia secondary to chronic pain were randomly assigned to either a CBT group or a self-monitoring/waiting list control group. The results provided evidence that CBT is an effective treatment for insomnia that occurs secondary to chronic pain.

A number of studies have expanded our knowledge of the treatment of pain, assessment of the condition, and characteristics of patients with pain. Williams and Keefe (1991) found that pain patients who believed that pain was enduring and mysterious were less likely to use cognitive behavioral coping strategies than patients who believed pain was understandable and of a short duration. In another study, Keefe, Dunsmore, and Burnett (1992) described the importance of the social context of pain, the relationship of chronic pain to depression, cognitive variables affecting pain, and methods for assessing these topics. Other studies have found that behavioral and CBT interventions for increasing pain coping efficacy are useful adjuncts in treating pain in children with chronic arthritis (Schanberg, Lefebvre, Keefe, Kredich, & Gil, 1997), and examined differences in gender and emotion-focused strategies in men and women (Affleck et al., 1999). In the study by Affleck and colleagues (1999) of 71 patients with osteoarthritis (OA) and 76 patients with rheumatoid arthritis (RA), it was found that women, regardless of their disease, and RA patients, regardless of their gender, reported more daily pain. Women used more emotion-focused strategies each day than did men, regardless of their disease, and even after controlling for their greater pain. Men were more likely than women to report an increase in negative mood the day after an especially painful day. RA patients' pain improved following a day when they were able to cope by using emotion-focused coping strategies.

Keefe and co-workers (1997) analyzed pain-coping strategies that predict patients' and spouses' ratings of the patients' coping. In addition, Keefe (2000) examined different observation strategies—behavior sampling methods, naturalistic observation methods, and self-observation—with chronic pain. Keefe advocated the need (a) to develop clinical methods to better observe pain behavior, (b) to study the social context of pain, (c) to examine the predictive validity of pain behavior, and (d) to identify pain behavior within heterogeneous chronic pain populations.

As noted, behavioral scientists working with pain have felt free to select and apply whatever behavioral or CBT techniques fit the purpose of the investigators. The band of potential interventions for pain is further accentuated by the meta-analyses of pain research conducted in recent years. The analyses range from evaluating smooth muscle relaxants in the treatment of irritable bowel syndrome (e.g., Poynard, Regimbeau, & Benhamou, 2001) to assessing patient education in arthritis (e.g., Superio-Cabuslay, Ward, & Lorig, 1996). A number of topics related to pain are regularly updated on the Cochrane Library. The reviews provide invaluable information to behavioral scientists, particularly to those who wish to design and implement programmatic research to compare medical to behavioral or CBT procedures.

Headache. Johnson and Thorn (1989) randomly assigned 22 patients with chronic headache into three conditions: (1) group-administered CBT, (2) individually administered CBT group, or (3) a waiting list control group. Results showed that were no differences between the patients administered CBT in the group or individual format. Other investigators have described intervention procedures used with headache, as well as the variables that influence the application of these techniques. In one study, Holroyd, Nash, Pingel, Cordingley, and Jerome (1991) found no difference in 41 patients randomly assigned to either a CBT group or to a group receiving amitriptyline, a mild antidepressent. In instances where differences in treatment effectiveness were observed, CTB yielded somewhat more positive outcomes. In another study, it was found that, in comparison to relaxation-biofeedback training alone or to limited-contact control groups, relaxation-thermal biofeedback training plus propranolol hydrochloride was more effective. In addition, the latter group showed larger reductions in analgesic medication use and greater improvements in quality of life (Holroyd et al., 1995). Finally, Holroyd and co-workers (Holroyd, Malinoski, Davis, & Lipchik, 1999; Holroyd et al., 2000) concluded that affective distress was a major dimension, comparable to pain and disability, with respect to its impact on chronic headache.

Programmatic research on headache highlights the armamentarium of behavioral and CBT techniques available in designing and implementing interventions for patients with the disorder. In addition, a number of current reviews of different aspects of headache are available at the Cochrane Library. These are particularly useful in comparing various treatment modalities singly or in combination with one another. An example of the latter study was described by Holroyd et al., 2001. They randomly assigned 203 adults to one of four groups: (1) tricyclic antidepressant, (2) stress management with placebo, (3) placebo, or (4) stress management therapy plus antidepressant medication. Results indicated that antidepressant medications and stress management therapy are each modestly effective in treating chronic tension-type headache. Combined therapy of stress management and antidepressants, however, may improve outcomes relative to monotherapy.

Transtheoretical Model

Criteria for Model

The *transtheoretical* (TTM) or *stages of change model* is based on four central criteria (Prochaska, 1979; 1995): First and foremost, the model has to be empirical, thus permitting each fundamental variable to be validated and measured. An example might be the assessment of weight loss by someone on a diet. Second, the model has to account for how people change with and without therapy. The criteria of the model were established to detect not only changes that occur as a result of an intervention, but self-changes generated by people themselves. Third, the model has to generalize to a broad range of human problems. It had to explain not only psychopathology, but also such behaviors as smoking. Finally, the model was created to enable eclectic and integrative therapists to become innovators and not just followers. The resulting model was "developed within the spirit of a search for synthesis, of trying to identify and integrate the best of what different therapy systems had to offer" (Prochaska, 1995, p. 405).

Stages of Change

The TTM model is based on six stages of change and related processes of change that characterize each stage. Consequently, the model implies ordering or sequence (Sutton, 1997). Prochaska (1995) emphasized that stages are fundamental to understanding change for several reasons: (a) stages provide a temporal dimension of change that unfolds over time, (b) stages are at a middle level of abstraction in that they may be both stable and dynamic, and (c) stages offer a dimension for synthesizing core constructs from across diverse systems of psychotherapy and behavioral change.

An understanding of the TTM requires a more thorough description of each stage. Although the stage model has been closely identified with Prochaska (1995) predominantly in work with individuals, organizational and diffusion theorists (e.g., Rogers, 1995; Vaughan & Rogers, 2000) have used similar constructs with somewhat different names and stages of organizational change. The latter models may be useful to many health psychologists, although we will focus only on the TTM outlined by Prochaska (1995).

Precontemplation. At the *precontemplation stage*, people have no intention of changing their behavior in the foreseeable future. They may have heard others, such as employers, tell them they should change or they themselves may wish to change, but they lack the intention to do so. Resistance to recognize or modify a problem is a hallmark of precontemplation (Prochaska, 1995).

Contemplation. The *contemplation stage* is where people are aware that a problem exists and seriously begin to think of how it might be changed. Still, they lack the commitment to take action to modify the problem.

Preparation. The *preparation stage* combines intention with some attempt, however weak, by individuals to change behavior. People at this stage intend to take immediate action, and, in some cases, they may do so. However, their efforts fall short of any criterion for change, such as abstaining from smoking or going on a diet to lose weight.

Action. At the *action stage*, individuals attempt to alter their behavior, experiences, and/or environment in order to overcome their problems. Behavioral actions tend to be the most visible and to receive the greatest recognition. Prochaska (1995) classified a person as being in the action stage if he or she successfully altered a problem behavior from one day to six months.

Maintenance. At the *maintenance stage*, people work to consolidate the gains they made in the action stage and prevent relapse of their gains. Maintenance is described as a continuation, not an absence, of change.

Termination. At the *termination stage*, people have 100% confidence in themselves or the self-efficacy that they will not engage in any previous problem behaviors across all situations. Sutton (1997) pointed out that termination has been omitted from recent descriptions of the transtheoretical model. Given the description of maintenance, it would seem extraneous in the stage approach.

In the TTM, change moves in a linear manner. However, cautioned Prochaska (1995), linear progress in the stage model is a relatively rare phenomenon. Anyone who has tried to diet might agree with this sentiment. Sutton (1997) went further with the caveat that forward progressive movement through the stages is far from being the modal pattern of change that occurs in self-generated change.

Processes of Change

Processes are, in Prochaska's (1995) words, "the covert or overt activities that people engage in to alter affect, thinking, behavior, or relationships related to particular problems or patterns of living" (p. 408). The processes of change are assumed to be common to behavior change that occurs within a formal treatment program (Sutton, 1997). Examples include consciousness raising (increasing information about one's self and the problem behavior), self-reevaluation (assessing how one feels and thinks about a problem), counterconditioning (substituting alternatives for problem behaviors), and reinforcement management (rewarding one's self or being rewarded by others for making change). Sutton further accentuates the point that processes of change are integrated with the steps of change in that it assumes different processes will be emphasized in different stages. Specifically, the application of TTM makes recommendations or prescriptions of different "stage-appropriate processes" for patients at different steps of change.

Empirical Research

Sutton (1997) commented that TTM has been applied mainly to smoking cessation, although it has been used with other problem behaviors such as cocaine use, condom use, and weight control (Prochaska, 1994). Recent applications of the model have been to identify subtype groups within each stage of change (Norman, Velicer, Fava, & Prochaska, 2000), to determine the effectiveness of physician smoking cessation practices (Goldstein et al., 1998), and to assess readiness to apply self-management techniques by patients with chronic pain (Kerns & Rosenberg, 2000). Others have advocated use of TTM by patients with chronic illness (Cassidy, 1999) and by women to improve their health (Peipert & Ruggiero, 1998).

Perhaps the most comprehensive study of TMM was conducted by Steptoe, Kerry, Rink, and Hilton (2001) in assessing stages of change in fat intake, physical activity, and cigarette smoking during a randomized controlled trial of behavioral counseling. Twenty general practices were randomly assigned either to lifestyle counseling by behavioral methods or to usual health promotion. A total of 833 patients were selected for the presence of one or more of the risk factors (e.g., cigarette smoking, high cholesterol, or a combination of a high body mass index and low physical activity). Stage of change (precontemplation, contemplation, preparation, and action/maintenance) was assessed at baseline and after 4 and 12 months. Steptoe and colleagues (2001) found that the odds of moving to action/maintenance for behavioral intervention versus control at four months were 2.15 for fat reduction, 1.89 for increased physical activity, and 1.77 for smoking cessation. The likelihood of achieving action/maintenance was related to baseline stage for all three behaviors. The findings led Steptoe et al. (2001) to conclude that behavioral counseling, based on advice matched to stage of readiness for change, may be valuable in encouraging healthy lifestyles among patients in primary care who are at risk of cardiovascular disease.

Although the TTM has been praised in helping to generate a focus on population-based interventions, criticism has been voiced regarding the model (Bandura, 1997; Davidson, 1992; Sutton, 1996). One major criticism is the lack of empirical evidence, outside of smoking cessation, to support the model. This criticism, however, is blunted somewhat by the Steptoe et al. (2001) investigation. Sutton (1997) suggested that evidence, particularly from longitudinal studies, does not strongly support the model. He noted that use of particular processes in particular stages fails to consistently predict movement to subsequent stages. Many of the findings interpreted as supporting the TTM, Sutton continued, are consistent with other models (e.g., Social-Cognitive Theory, the Theory of Reasoned Action, etc.). Finally, Sutton noted that a major problem with the TTM is that it is not specified clearly enough.

Self-Management Model

In the past three decades, patients, particularly those with chronic illness, have been taught to perform most of the care needed to control their condition. Their performance, in turn, has been labeled as self-care, self-regulation, self-supervision, self-directed action, or the term we will use, self-management (e.g., Holroyd & Creer, 1986). *Self-management* is a distinctive human attribute in that we not only react to external events, but are self-reactors with the capacity for self-evaluation and self-managed action. Self-managed capabilities permit us to exercise a degree of control over our cognitive abilities, motivation, and action.

The self-management of any physical disorder requires two necessary conditions. First, any control over a condition occurs only as a function of the reciprocal interaction of physical, cognitive, behavioral, and environmental variables. This ongoing interaction of variables, referred to as "reciprocal determinism" by Bandura (1997), is necessary but not sufficient for individuals to experience success in controlling a physical condition across time and contexts. Second, individuals must become allies with health-care personnel and behavioral scientists if they are to attain any control over their condition. The relationship between patients and health-care providers, referred to as collaborative management (Von Korff et al., 1997; Wagner et al., 2001), is also necessary but not sufficient for successful self-management. Although collaborative management has been emphasized in treatment guidelines for chronic conditions, true collaboration between medical personnel and their patients remains an elusive goal in most instances (e.g., Glasgow & Anderson, 1999).

Specific Self-Management Skills

Self-management is based on empirically established behavioral and CBT techniques. Behavioral techniques, particularly those selected from operant learning, are an integral part of many self-management programs. At times, behavioral techniques may serve, almost alone, as components for a self-management intervention. Kotses, Stout, McConnaughy, Winder, and Creer (1996), for example, compared an individualized self-management program for asthma based on stimulus control—peak-flow readings that served as an antecedent condition regarding the probability of asthma attacks occurring in a specified period of time—to both a self-management group and a control group. Patients in the individualized self-management and group self-management groups showed equivalent improvement in pulmonary function; those in the former group, however, showed a significant decrease in number of asthma attacks when compared to the group self-management condition. A component of CBT—self-monitoring—was used across conditions.

CBT techniques are also integral to self-management programs. Self-monitoring, for example, is an essential part of all self-management programs; equally important, however, is the use of self-instruction, relaxation, and imagery in many of these programs. Self-efficacy is often used as an outcome measure in many self-management programs, whether the basis is more behavioral than cognitive behavioral, or vice versa. For example, the assessment of self-efficacy was used in another asthma self-management program that featured the integration of behavioral and CBT techniques (Kotses et al., 1995). It is likely that no matter what type of self-management program is designed and applied, those conducting the study should review both behavioral and CBT techniques with respect to their appropriateness for a specific program.

Processes of Self-Management

The processes of self-management have been described by others (e.g., Karoly, 1993). Despite different terminology, however, there is considerable commonality about the events being described; differences emerge from the way various events are defined, not from basic differences in conceptualization (Creer & Holroyd, 1997). Processes salient in the self-management of health problems include the following:

Goal selection. Goal selection can occur only after careful preparation. In particular, two preparatory actions must occur: First, patients need to acquire information about their condition and how it can be managed. They must understand and accept the major role they will be expected to play with respect to themselves and their condition. Second, patients must then meet with their healthcare providers to establish realistic goals that can only be achieved by collaboratively working together. There are four positive consequences of goal selection: (1) it establishes preferences about desirable outcomes for both patients and their healthcare providers, (2) it enhances the commitment to perform goal-oriented skills, (3) it establishes expectancies on the part of patients that can trigger their effort and performance, and (4) it enhances consistency across different healthcare professions in treating the patient.

Goal selection is the only activity where there is true collaboration between patients and their physicians or other healthcare providers (Creer & Holroyd, 1997; Von Korff et al., 1997; Wagner et al., 2001). The process of selecting goals is often misunderstood by both physicians and patients. Many physicians—likely the majority—believe that they are guiding patients in performing whatever skills are required to control a condition. In reality, however, the term *guided self-management* is an oxymoron; patients perform "self-generated self-management." (Creer, 2001). They alone perform the skills needed to manage a chronic disorder, including exacerbations of the condition; all physicians and allied health personnel can do is track the outcomes of self-management. On the other hand, patients are often reluctant to accept the reality of chronic illness (e.g., they must perform most actions needed to control a chronic condition). As was noted, patients may cling to the belief that their condition is similar to an acute disease or condition and that treatment should be left in the hands of their healthcare provider. Only through collaborative goal setting, however, can the responsibilities of patients and healthcare providers be explicitly spelled out. In doing so, the probability of achieving mutually set goals is increased.

Information collection. *Self-monitoring*, or the self-observation and self-recording of data, is the foundation of information collection. Accurate self-monitoring by patients is a necessary condition for self-management; it also provides information that can be assessed and interpreted by both patients and healthcare professionals. There are two ways to obtain accurate data in information collection (Creer & Holroyd, 1997). First, patients should attend only to phenomena that have been precisely defined and spelled out when establishing goals with their healthcare providers. If possible, an objective measure, such as a device to monitor blood glucose in diabetic patients, should be added to enhance the reliability and validity of collected information. Second, in gathering data on themselves, it is imperative that patients gather data on a regular and established schedule; whenever possible, it is desirable that data be gathered for specified periods of time. Information collection can be arduous and tedious for many patients. For this reason, only data necessary for the control of a patient's condition, particularly a chronic illness, should be gathered. There is no need either to overwhelm patients with too many tasks in gathering information or to have data collection shift to the center of their lives. Whatever data are gathered must be the result of careful consideration and agreement by healthcare providers and patients.

Information processing and evaluation. Individuals must learn to process and evaluate the information they collect about themselves and their condition. There are five factors to consider with this component of self-management. First, patients must be able to quickly detect any changes in their condition. This may be easy for diabetic patients who see change in their blood glucose or in asthma patients who see changes in their peak-flow readings. The process of information processing and evaluation becomes more difficult when patients observe changes in some subjective measure, such as is used with pain or migraine headache. Second, patients must be able to compare the changes they observe against a set standard. This is easy with hypertensive patients, for example, who can compare their data against standardized criteria for hypertension provided by a meter. Again, however, the problem becomes more difficult when comparing any collected data against what, in most cases of pain, are idiosyncratic standards established by patients themselves. Third, processing and evaluating data on themselves requires that patients make judgments about any changes they see. Again, this may be easy with an objective standard, such as a blood glucose monitor or a peak-flow meter. However, matching-to-standard is often difficult when comparing one set of subjective data to another set of such data in making accurate judgments. Fourth, individuals should make any judgments within the context of the stimuli that could have produced change, the action they should take, and the potential consequences of their action. By doing so, they should increase the accuracy of their judgments. Finally, the reciprocal interaction that occurs among contextual factors and self-management skills should be considered. The interaction among these variables, including setting events and establishing stimuli, is significant in information processing and evaluation.

Decision making. A critical function in self-management involves decision making. After patients collect, process, and evaluate the information they have gathered about themselves and their condition, they need to make appropriate decisions based on the data. Making appropriate decisions or action plans underlies much of the success achieved in the acquisition and maintenance of asthma self-management skills (Caplin & Creer, 2001; Creer, 2001). Patients who perform and continue to perform self-management skills use advanced cognitive strategies, coupled with remarkable flexibility, in processing and evaluating the information they gather on themselves. Any decisions regarding self-management actions are based on this information.

Action. *Action* entails the performance of self-management skills by patients to promote health or to control a physical disorder or condition. Self-instruction, including the prompting, directing, and maintaining of behavioral skills, is crucial to the success of action. Self-instruction is used in two ways: First, self-instruction permits patients to institute the strategies they have worked out and agreed upon with their healthcare provider to control a condition. The action they take often requires performing a series, often in sequence, of different behaviors (Creer & Holroyd, 1997). Second, self-instruction can prompt the patient to perform other strategies or steps needed to control the disorder. For example, in the study by Caplin and Creer (2001), individual patients indicated they had developed strategies that were effective for them in controlling asthma; at the same time, the number of behaviors performed by the patients in establishing control became more established over time.

Self-reaction. *Self-reaction* refers to the attention individuals direct toward evaluating their performance (Bandura, 1986). On the basis of their evaluation, patients can establish realistic expectations about their performance, as well as evaluate what they need to do to achieve these expectations. *Self-efficacy* is the belief of individuals that they can adequately perform specific skills in a given situation (Bandura, 1977); it influences the performance of self-management skills by patients.

Problem solving often serves as an element of behavioral or CBT interventions (e.g., Perri, Sears, & Clark, 1993). The aim of problem solving is to teach patients to solve problems that arise and interfere with their attempt to manage a physical condition. Specific problem-solving skills include (a) defining the problem, (b) gathering and interpreting information on the problem, (c) making decisions based on the data, (d) taking action, and (e) evaluating the outcome of action. The skills are often taught in self-management programs. An example of the use of problem solving in a self-management program was described in *Living with Asthma* (1986; 1987), a program for childhood asthmatics and their families. Participating families were asked what they would do if on a camping trip, they forgot to take along a quick relief medication and a member of the family began to experience an asthma attack. After proclaiming that could never happen inasmuch as they kept a spare inhaler with quick relief medication in their car specifically for such a situation, participants were nevertheless asked how they would solve this hypothetical problem. The families invariably came up with a solution: they would brew up a pot of strong coffee to give to the patient. Because coffee and theophylline-based asthma drugs are both xanthine compounds, coffee can be taken to manage mild asthma episodes. Participants added that, concurrent with the use of coffee, they would try to keep calm and, if necessary, seek help.

The use of self-management skills has often been considered, much like the practice of medicine (Kaplan, 2000), as a linear process. The reality of self-management, however, is that in successful programs, a reciprocal interaction is continually taking place among the different processes of self-management. What occurs is depicted in Figure 15.1. The relationship among the processes of self-management permits patients to take whatever action they deem necessary to manage a chronic or acute condition. As patients are experiencing the condition, they are the ones who often know the best way to manage it. The model accounts for both linear and nonlinear variables that may be involved in the execution of self-management processes needed to manage a condition successfully. The multidirectional interaction taking place among the variables can become highly complex, particularly at the level of assessment and causal explanation. However, as noted by Thoresen and Kirmil-Gray (1983), "the tradeoff may be worthwhile insofar as the model more closely fits the experience of people" (p. 599).

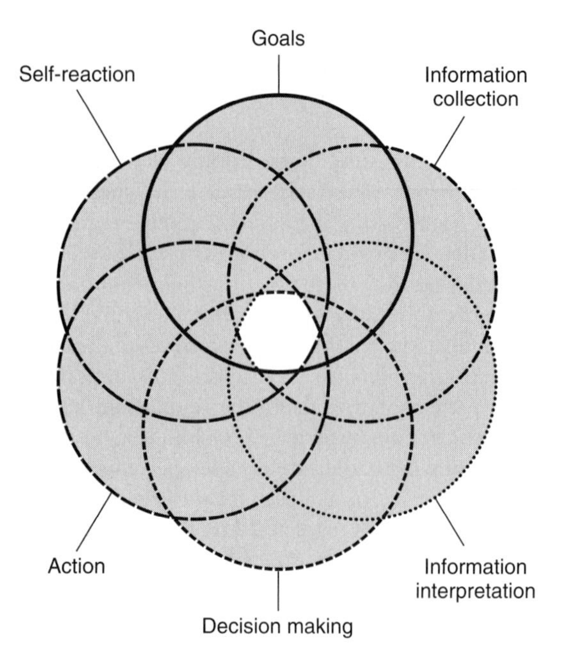

FIGURE 15.1 Reciprocal interactions between and among components of self-management.

Empirical Research

There has been a burst of research on self-management, particularly in the treatment of chronic conditions. These studies report a wide array of characteristics; four characteristics include the variety of conditions investigated, mode of instruction, assessment of needs and changes in self-management, and the cost-benefits of self-management programs.

VARIETY OF CONDITIONS. Well-designed studies with appropriate controls have shown the effectiveness of self-management techniques to treat people living with AIDS (PLWAs) who experience chronic diarrhea (Henry, Holzemer, Weaver, & Stotts, 1999), to enhance the effectiveness of abortive therapy in patients with recurrent headache (Holroyd et al., 1989), and to reduce psychological distress and increase psychological adjustment one year after coronary artery bypass graft surgery (Ai, Dunkle, Peterson, Saunders, & Bolling, 1998). Self-management skills have also been used to reduce decline in function, number of hospitalizations, total number of inpatient hospital days, use of psychoactive medications, and to increase significantly higher levels of physical activity and senior center participation in frail, older adults with chronic illness (Leveille et al., 1998).

Other randomized control trials have shown that self-management substantially reduced distress and increased self-efficacy in elderly adults who experienced vision loss due to macular degeneration (Brody et al., 1999), decreased use of emergency rooms and greater reduction in mean number of hospitalizations in children with asthma (Clark et al., 1986), and lowered interdialytic weight gain in patients with end-stage renal disease (Christensen & Ehlers, 2002). Self-management skills are also linked to lower asthma attack frequency, reduced medication use, increased use of self-management skills, and increased self-efficacy in adults with asthma (Kotses et al., 1995). Moreover, self-management was shown to produce improvements in frequency of exercise, cognitive symptoms management, communication with physicians, self-reported health, health distress, fatigue, disability, and social/role activities across patients with heart disease, lung disease, stroke, and arthritis (Lorig et al., 1999).

Mode of instruction. Teaching self-management skills has usually taken the form of group or individual instruction. These two approaches often served as independent variables in intervention studies (e.g., Kotses et al., 1996). Recently, however, there have been a number of studies using computer-based or Internet-based teaching technology. Gustafson et al. (1999), for example, described the use of a computerized system to provide HIV-positive patients with information, decision support, and connection to HIV/AIDS experts and other patients. In a randomized control trial, it was found that the computer-based system improved patients' quality of life and promoted more efficient use of health care. A study by Glasgow et al. (1997) found that a brief intervention using touchscreen computer-assisted assessment and immediate feedback on key barriers to dietary self-management, goal setting, and problem-solving produced significantly greater improvement in diabetic patients than did usual care. Shegog et al. (2001) described how a theory-based CD-ROM educational technology improved clinical outcomes in 76 children with asthma between the ages of 9 and 13 years. Finally, Tate, Wing, and Winett (2001) described a comprehensive study whereby the Internet and e-mail were shown to be viable methods for delivery of structured behavioral weight loss programs.

Assessment of change. Webster and Brennan (1998) examined self-management of interstitial cystitis, a chronic illness that primarily affects women. They found that the effectiveness of behavioral and cognitive self-care strategies correlated differentially with dimensions of health. Kerns and Rosenberg (2000) utilized an instrument, based on the TTM, to predict responses to self-management treatments for chronic pain. They reported that precontemplation and contemplation scores discriminated among those who did or did not complete self-management training. Sandstrom and Keefe (1998) examined the use of formal coping skills training and exercise training in the self-management of fibromyalgia; the investigators found that they were able to identify key individual and contextual variables related to treatment outcome in patients with the condition. By analyzing diabetes self-management in seven studies, Toobert, Hampson, and Glasgow (2000) revised and refined a standardized measure, the Summary of Diabetes Self-Care Activities (SDSCA), which can be used across studies of diabetes. Finally, Glasgow and Strycker (2000) assessed the level of physician performance on the American Diabetes Association Recognition Program. Considerable variability was found in levels of performance regarding activities recommended by the Program, leading Glasgow and Strycker to emphasize that greater attention be focused on self-management and patient-focused care to control diabetes. An in-depth discussion of self-management in the treatment of diabetes was provided by Gonder-Frederick, Cox, and Ritterband (2002).

Economic analyses. Self-management studies of chronic disorders have sometimes provided cost data (e.g., Clark et al., 1986). In doing so, investigators have often reported cost economic analyses by comparing costs of the program to the obtained results. Cost-analysis data gathered in managed care settings were described in two recent investigations. Groessl and Cronan (2000) studied 363 participants with osteoarthritis, 60 years or older, who were enrolled in a health maintenance organization. The patients were assigned to one of three self-management groups—social support, education, or a combination of social support and education—or to a control group. All intervention groups showed increased self-efficacy and overall health status. In addition, however, healthcare costs increased less in the intervention groups than in the control groups. Cost analysis was used to demonstrate that the monetary savings of intervention greatly outweighed the costs of the procedure. In a second study on high-risk patients, Lynch, Forman, Graff, and Gunby (2000) conducted a time sequence study of program intervention across an entire managed care population and compared costs with prior baseline years. Intervention consisted of focus on the high-risk group, an integrated clinical and psychological approach to assessment, a self-care management program, secured Internet applications, and population-based outcome metrics from widely used measures of resource utilization and functional status. Lynch and colleagues (2000) found that this subgroup's costs dropped 35.7% from pre-program levels, while cross-sectional functional status rose 12.5%.

MAINTENANCE

The report on health systems, compiled and issued by the World Health Organization (2000a), contained the following:

> Assessing how well a health system does its job requires dealing with two large questions. The first is how to measure the outcomes of interest—that is, to determine what is achieved with respect to the three objectives of good health, responsiveness and fair financial contribution *(attainment)*. The second is how to compare these attainments with what the system should be able to accomplish—that is the best that could be achieved with the same resources *(performance)*. Although progress is feasible against many of society's health problems, some of the causes lie completely outside even a broad notion of what health systems are. Health systems cannot be held responsible for influences such as the distribution of income and wealth, any more than for the impact of climate. But avoidable deaths and illness from childhood measles, malaria or tobacco consumption can properly be laid at their door. A fair judgment of how much health damage it should be possible to avoid requires an estimate of the best that can be expected, and of the least that can be demanded, of a system. (p. 23)

A theme repeatedly sounded by the World Health Organization (2000a) is that performance is the *raison d'etre* of the report; performance, in turn, is often used as a synonym for better health. A second theme is the importance of patient expectations regarding a health system. More formally, it is stated that "Similarly, as in any system, people have expectations which society regards as legitimate, as to how they should be treated, both physically and psychologically. Responsiveness is therefore always a social goal" (p. 23).

With respect to health psychology, we have described impressive strides in developing and applying techniques that help alleviate human suffering. It can be convincingly argued that we make a significant difference in applying these techniques to many of the health issues we face. Whether we can always satisfy the expectations of individual patients is, however, another matter. If the expectations are that we can intervene and help someone stop smoking, we may attain success; whether the individual remains a nonsmoker, however, is equivocal. The conundrum we face in health psychology and behavioral medicine is that, while we can change many behaviors in many cases, there is no guarantee that the change will be maintained. We control only a few variables that contribute to relapse. Nevertheless, our goal should be to strengthen the behavior we change in order to increase the probability that it will be maintained. In addition, we need to collaborate with individual patients to make reasonable changes in themselves and their environment to enhance maintenance (e.g., Wagner et al., 2001).

Marlatt (1985a) used the term *maintenance* with respect to addictive behaviors. He suggested there were two ways to conceptualize the term. First, maintenance was considered as the stage following initial treatment where changes resulting from intervention gradually wore off. Relapse rates could be expected to increase over time, unless some type of booster sessions was provided to slow the rate of relapse. Second, the maintenance stage was viewed as an opportunity for new learning to occur. In place of retaining maladaptive behaviors, they would be extinguished as new, more adaptive behaviors are learned and performed. Orleans (2000) pointed out that, although Marlatt (1985b) effectively used the metaphor of a "journey" to describe the process of change from initial behavior change, he stopped short at the maintenance stage, which he described as "the final destination" (Marlatt, 1985b, p. 212). In addition, continued Orleans (2000), although most of CBT approaches to behavior change and maintenance could be readily expanded to encompass powerful social-environmental variables, they "have not been systematically incorporated in past health behavior change or maintenance research" (p. 79).

Other investigators have attempted to study maintenance of behavioral change. The purpose of a workshop, sponsored by the National Heart, Lung, and Blood Institute, was to summarize "the current state of science related to achieving long-term behavior change across risk behaviors (smoking, diet, obesity, and physical activity) and to develop recommendations for future research in these areas" (Wing, 2000, p. 3). In the remainder of the section, we will discuss reports concerning two areas—weight loss and smoking—as well as describe a retrospective followup of the use of asthma self-management skills by adults.

Maintenance of Weight Loss

Obesity in the United States is up by 57% since 1991; currently, over half of the adult population in the United States is considered as overweight or obese. Jeffrey et al. (2000) defined obesity as "an unhealthy amount of body fat" (p. 5). They pointed out that the natural history of weight loss and regain among patients who participate in behavioral intervention is remarkably consistent. "The rate of initial weight loss is rapid and then slowly declines. The point of maximum weight loss is usually reached approximately 6 months after the initial treatment" (p. 7). For this reason, six months is suggested as a time point for assessing initial weight loss, although trends in weight gain are usually visible at 18 to 30 months. For maintenance assessment, a five-year followup is desirable. Long-term maintenance of weight loss described by Jeffrey and colleagues includes a discussion of four processes.

1. *Increasing the intensity of initial treatment*
   "Intensifying initial treatments for obesity by encouraging more severe restriction of energy intake can produce larger weight losses" (Jeffrey et al., 2000, p. 9). Increasing weight losses in this manner, however, has little effect on long-term maintenance of weight loss and may be associated with reduced participation rates.
2. *Extending the length of treatment*
   Treating people for longer periods of time is associated with more weight loss. After active treatment, however, weight regain was observed; the rate of weight regain was comparable to that found in short and long treatment conditions. Jeffrey and colleagues suggested that programs that emphasized weight loss over long periods of time deserve more study. They warned, however, that patients are often unwilling to participate in programs conducted over longer periods of time (e.g., one year).
3. *Modifying behavioral approaches to energy balance*
   One approach has been to modify nutritional habits by curbing the intake of foods that contribute to body fat. The experimental evidence with this approach has been disappointing with respect to improving long-term weight loss. A second approach has been to combine a weight loss program with exercise. Emphasizing exercise as a component of obesity treatment appears to enhance weight loss at all time points and may slow weight regain after treatment.
4. *Enhancing motivation*
   Two approaches have been taken to enhance motivation: direct payment from external funds for weight loss and repayment of deposits made by patients at the beginning of treatment contingent upon weight loss. Overall, efforts to increase motivation for weight maintenance have not been successful in enhancing long-term outcomes. Direct incentives and repayment of deposits have also been shown to be ineffective. These outcomes suggest the need to investigate nonmonetary approaches (e.g., social support) to enhance motivation.

Summary and Recommendations

The number of weight reduction studies that included maintenance-specific skills, such as relapse prevention skills, is limited; the findings to date have not been impressive. Weight control medications have shown maximum efficiency when combined with traditional weight modification programs. Moreover, Jeffrey and colleagues reported that recommendations to decrease dietary fat and increase exercise seem to be synergistic with respect to weight control.

Jeffrey et al. (2000) offered several suggestions for future study that are based on available data. Recommendations include investigating: (a) methods for keeping overweight patients in long-term treatments, (b) observational studies of the natural history of intentional weight loss, (c) physical activity and social support in regard to long-term weight loss, and (d) the development of safer and more effective drugs that can be included in effective weight control programs.

Maintenance of Smoking Cessation

Data on smoking throughout the world were summarized earlier. As a counter to the bad news, Ockene et al. (2000) noted that almost 70% of smokers want to stop smoking. Ockene and her colleagues reviewed research on maintenance of cessation and relapse in adults. The key topics they addressed are three stages of cessation: maintenance, relapse, and recycling.

Maintenance

Ockene and colleagues (2000) indicated that the maintenance of change starts at six months. *Short-term maintenance* covers the period between 6 and 12 months after cessation; *long-term maintenance* starts after one year of abstinence. The definition of maintenance allows for the possibility that ex-smokers may have isolated lapses and still be considered abstinent provided the initial criterion of seven consecutive days of abstinence is achieved.

Relapse and Recycling

The rapidity of relapse is well documented. Ockene and colleagues pointed out that in one study of smokers who had relapsed within six months of quitting, half of the smokers had resumed smoking within the first 30 days. Relapse rates among smokers participating in formal treatment are lower than those of self-quitters, but the same pattern of relapse is seen. Even after one year, relapse continues to occur, although at a lower rate.

Traveling along the road to cessation is slippery for most smokers. Data indicate that 88% of smokers who lapse eventually relapse. Clearly, slips increase the probability of relapse. Ockene et al. (2000) categorized precipitants of lapses and relapses into the following domains: (a) personal-demographic, affective (e.g., depression, stress); (b) cognitive (e.g., self-efficacy, knowledge); (c) physiological (e.g., level of dependence, withdrawal symptoms); and (d) social context (e.g., social support). Cognitive factors, such as higher confidence and self-efficacy, are related to both short- and long-term maintenance for self-quitters. It was also pointed out that although relapse is common, it is important for smokers to know that all is not lost: many smokers recycle and try again. Ockene and colleagues emphasized that it is imperative to maintain contact with those going through a smoking cessation program. Close contacts with those in a program permits relapses to be caught early and facilitates recycling in those smokers with high motivation to quit after relapse. In addition, close contacts provide an opportunity to rebuild self-efficacy and motivation before further attempts to quit smoking are initiated.

Summary and Recommendations

Ockene and her colleagues (2000) concluded their discussion by recommending that approaches taken in smoking cessation should include (a) the development and testing of more intensive treatment programs; (b) incorporating such techniques as self-help, telephone counseling, pharmocotherapy, and physician-delivered interventions into comprehensive smoking cessation programs; and (c) treating slips seriously by detecting them early, alerting clients to the problem, and using slips as an opportunity for increased intervention. The greatest challenge in smoking cessation, cautioned Ockene et al. (2000), may be the ability to apply what we already know, and to rapidly translate research findings into effective practices and policies to assist smokers who wish to quit.

Many suggestions for research were similar with respect to the maintenance of weight loss and smoking cessation. Orleans (2000) pointed out that in contrast to interventions that produce short-term behavior change, maintenance interventions, as well as the theories and models that drive maintenance, have not improved significantly over the past 20 years. She suggested that to move the field forward, "we need (a) more comprehensive and social-ecological models of population-based health behavior change and maintenance, (b) a broader view of maintenance as a dynamic process rather than a static state or result, and (c) more theory-based research combined with efforts to reinvigorate the theories and paradigms guiding maintenance research and practice" (p. 82). Since social-environmental variables have been consistently shown to be associated with maintenance, greater attention needs to be directed toward creating ways to intervene to determine how these variables can maintain behavior (e.g., Stokols, 1996).

Maintenance of Asthma Self-Management

The development and application of a self-management program for adult asthma was reported by Kotses et al. (1995). In the study, 76 patients with confirmed asthma, including 49 women and 27 men, served as subjects. Two salient aspects of the program included, first, avoiding the concurrent manipulation of two major treatments (e.g., both medical and self-management interventions). This distinction was achieved by determining that the asthma of all the subjects was under medical control before introducing them to asthma self-management. Second, the program was conducted over an eight-week period; the period of time permitted patients more time to acquire self-management skills and allowed investigators to determine whether the patients were performing the skills.

Subjects and Assessment of Maintenance

An average of six years after the last followup of subjects (seven years after their participation in the self-management program), an attempt was made to contact subjects in the original program (Caplin & Creer, 2001). Fifty-three subjects—70% of the group involved in the study by Kotses et al. (1995)—agreed to participate and answer questions posed on an open-ended questionnaire. The questionnaire could be either completed by subjects or administered over the telephone. The questions assessed a number of specific domains that addressed cognitive, behavioral, and affective experiences of patients maintaining or relapsing in the performance of asthma self-management skills (Caplin & Creer, 2001). The four criteria selected for relapse were: (1) estimated percentage of time patients reported they engaged in self-management since the completion of their participation in the program; (2) a monitoring index, calculated for the 12 weeks prior to the survey, on the performance of subjects; (3) a dichotomous rating by patients who identified themselves as "relapsers" or "continuers;" and (4) relapse in that subjects went for more than 30 days with no performance of self-management skills.

Maintenance of Skills

According to the criteria used, 33 of the subjects were classified as continuers and 20 were classified as relapsers. Compared to those who relapsed, those who continued described a number of characteristics about themselves, including their motivation to change, their higher degree of self-efficacy, their ability to manage interfering factors to self-management, their greater flexibility in treating themselves, and their experienced improvement in their asthma. All of the subjects monitored their behavior to some degree; the finding might have been expected because asthma patients detect significant changes in their breathing. An unexpected finding was that half of those who fell into the relapse group claimed they no longer experienced asthma. Therefore, they added, they no longer needed to perform self-management skills on a regular basis. The result led to the conclusion that all patients should have been queried regarding the current state of their asthma, particularly as it is likely that both a larger number of continuers and relapsers may have experienced a remission of their asthma (Caplin & Creer, 2001). The unexpectedly high degree of remission of asthma at followup suggests that optimal medical treatment, combined with optimal self-management by the patients, generated a remission of a disorder heretofore considered to have no known cure.

Summary and Conclusion

The findings by Caplin and Creer (2001) may be unique: developmental changes that could have contributed to remission of asthma cannot be ruled out as factors in the study (e.g., Bernstein, 2000). In the meantime, the problem of maintaining behavioral change in chronic illness requires greater research attention. Rather than teaching patients behavioral and self-management skills and sending them out into world, we need to determine the effective cognitive strategies and environment-ecological variables that can assist patients to maintain their change. We also need to determine how these factors interact with any given chronic illness to interfere with or maintain behavioral change.

Conclusions

This chapter described several themes in health psychology and behavioral medicine. The first is found in the general description of progress in the field. This theme is reflected by an increasing breadth of subject matter, the imaginative use of behavioral and CBT techniques, and the development and implementation of sophisticated techniques to assess change. In describing progress, the chapter traced the continuing evolution of health psychology and behavioral medicine reflected in past chapters of the handbook (e.g., Blanchard, 1994; Pomerleau & Rodin, 1986).

Another theme emphasized the need to work in an interdisciplinary manner with others, particularly medical colleagues, in caring for patients. Collaborative management is important for three reasons: First, as noted by Jeffrey et al. (2000), in describing the synergy that may result from combining exercise with weight loss techniques, interdisciplinary programs can be more than the sum of their individual parts. Synergy was illustrated by the significant improvement in weight loss found by combining lifestyle modification with pharmacological management (Wadden, Berkowitz, Sarwer, Prus-Wisniewski, & Steinberg, 2001). We argued that synergy is less the rule than the exception in combining elements from different fields to generate change. Nevertheless, synergy of components will only occur with interdisciplinary research and teamwork. Second, different models of assessment are required in interdisciplinary research. An example would be the increased use of multilevel models to assess change. Such models include the role of multilevel growth modeling in epidemology-based prevention research (Kellam, Koretz, & Moscicki, 1999) and multilevel pyramid models to evaluate outcomes in diabetes (Glasgow, 1999). Finally, what amounts to a paradigmatic shift is taking place in health care (Creer, 2000). The shift requires that those in health psychology and behavioral medicine learn about the effects and potential side-effects of actions taken by other members of an interdisciplinary team. Although we do not advocate that the skills of health psychologists attempt to mirror the skills of physicians and healthcare personnel, we suggest that health psychologists acquire a basic knowledge of the skills and expertise of all members of an interdisciplinary team. Such a background would enhance the research and clinical skills we bring to health care. In addition, the background would make us less open to doing harm to patients (e.g., improving adherence to a dangerous medication regimen, such as the so-called Fen-Phen diet). Fortunately, treatment guidelines for many diseases and conditions have been issued in the past two decades. These guidelines can serve as the blueprint for interdisciplinary teams in the management of most conditions. Moreover, the guidelines are readily available to anyone. (Over 150 sets of guidelines can be found on-line at www.healthfinder.gov.)

A third theme emerged in the discussion of primary and secondary prevention (Kaplan, 2000). With respect to primary prevention of smoking, the data show that smoking can be curbed through the adoption of a wide range of policy, educational, economic, and behavioral measures. As noted, however, these strategies are not being adopted in developing countries. If anything, contingencies in these areas of the world reinforce smoking in men and, to an increasing degree, women. Progress made in applying behavioral techniques to the secondary prevention of three health consequences of smoking—lung cancer, COPD, and coronary heart disease—was described. The actions we take may be limited with respect to lung cancer, COPD, and coronary heart disease because the course of the conditions is often irreversible. However, research evidence concerning COPD and coronary heart disease suggests we can play a more significant role in improving the health of those with the conditions than has heretofore been known or acknowledged.

A fourth theme concerned the growing threat of infectious diseases, as well as the overuse of antibiotics in treating many conditions. In particular, we focused on the HIV/AIDS epidemic and the potential crisis posed by TB. In doing so, we accentuated the point that the globalization of disease and health is here; we in developed countries can no longer pretend otherwise. In addition, we cannot escape the fact that further globalization will provide even more challenges in health psychology and behavioral medicine.

The final theme was integrated into a brief discussion of behavioral maintenance. As stimuli in our society tend to promote failure of behavioral change with such health problems as smoking and obesity, we must intervene not only to change behavior but to structure social environments in order to promote the maintenance of healthy behaviors. Two events are pushing us in this direction. First, the growing acceptance of evidence-based medicine (e.g., Sackett, Straus, Richardson, Rosenberg, & Haynes, 2000) will force us to more accurately assess and document the changes we do attain. In an environment that is increasingly being dominated by managed care, we have no option other than to be more precise in delineating our actions and the consequences and outcomes of our actions. Second, a related theme suggests the need to become more programmatic in practicing health psychology or behavioral medicine. Achieving this goal would make the data we help produce more prominent in health care. A myriad of possibilities exist for health psychologists, including making full use of available epidemiological data (e.g., on HIV/AIDS) and gathering data on specific diseases (e.g., diabetes), groups of diseases (e.g., respiratory disorders), or methods used across diseases (e.g., medication compliance procedures). What we do is a function of the context within which we work, but we will increasingly be asked to justify our actions and the results that occur as a consequence of our actions.

In a book she wrote on writing and life, Anne Lamott (1994) described how her brother failed to write an essay on birds until the night before it was due. Panicking, the boy ran to his father to ask what he should do. After thinking awhile, his father responded by putting his arm around his son's shoulders and saying, "Bird by bird, buddy. Just take it bird by bird" (p. 19). In many ways, what we have done in health psychology is treat physical disorder by physical disorder, one by one, and, as health psychologists, one by one. Despite progress, the approach has stymied the full integration of our discipline into the mainstream of health care (e.g., Coyne, Thompson Klinkman, & Nease, 2002). Furthermore, once admitted into the sacrosanct mainstream of health care, we repeatedly have to explain why we are there, even with a disorder such as diabetes where we have made significant behavioral contributions (e.g., Glasgow & Anderson, 1999). Perhaps the most disheartening event is to have a healthcare colleague reinvent the wheel by proclaiming that he or she can solve a behavioral problem when health psychologists have developed, applied, collected empirical evidence, and described in the literature a behavioral technique or way of assessing the very problem being reinvented.

In a book on global inequality and the health of the poor, Millen, Irwin, and Kim (2000) noted:

> In its 1998 annual report, the United Nations Development Program (UNDP) calculated that it would take less than four percent of the combined wealth of the 225 richest individuals in the world to achieve and maintain access to basic education, basic health care, reproductive health care, adequate food, safe water, and adequate sanitation for all people living on the planet. (pp. 7–8)

Although it depicts a seemingly simple scenario, it is unlikely to happen. Yet, the description illustrates that improved health can only occur through the cooperation of medical scientists, public health specialists, and behavioral scientists, working together with all people on the globe, to make necessary medical, environmental, and behavioral changes. With increasing globalization, the goal of better health for all people on earth must become a priority. The rich empirical history, including both skills and database, we have built in health psychology and behavioral medicine must be applied if there is to be any success in achieving this goal.

REFERENCES

Ackoff, R. L. (1994). Systems thinking and thinking systems. *Systems Dynamics Review, 10,* 175–188.

Affleck, G., Tennen, H., Keefe, F. J., Lefebvre, J. C., Kashikar-Zuck, S., Wright, K., Starr, K., & Caldwell, D. S. (1999). Everyday life with osteoarthritis or rheumatoid arthritis: Independent effects of disease and gender on daily pain, mood, and coping. *Pain, 83,* 601–609.

Ai, A. L., Dunkle, R. E., Peterson, C., Saunders, D. G., & Bolling, S. F. (1998). Self-care and psychosocial adjustment of patients following cardiac surgery. *Social Work and Health Care, 27,* 75–95.

Albert, R. K. (1997). Is pulmonary rehabilitation an effective treatment for chronic obstructive pulmonary disease? No. *American Journal of Respiratory and Critical Care Medicine, 155,* 784–785.

Allen, F. (1995). Feminist theory and cognitive behaviorism. In W. O'Donohue & L. Krasner (Eds.), *Theories of behavioral therapy: Exploring behavior change* (pp. 495–528). Washington, DC: American Psychological Association.

Al-Obaidi, S. M., Nelson, R. M., Al-Awadhi, S., & Al-Shuwaie, N. (2000). The role of anticipation and fear of pain in the persistence of avoidance behavior in patients with chronic low back pain. *Spine, 25,* 1126–1131.

Amari, A., Grace, N. C., & Fisher, W. W. (1995). Achieving and maintaining compliance with the ketogenic diet. *Journal of Applied Behavior Analysis, 28,* 341–342.

American Thoracic Society. (1995). Standards for the diagnosis and care of patients with chronic obstructive pulmonary disease. *American Journal of Respiratory and Critical Care Medicine, 152,* S77–S122.

Anderson, B. L., (2002). Biobehavioral outcomes following psychological intervention for cancer patients. In T. W. Smith, P. C. Kendall, & F. J. Keefe (Eds.), Health psychology. *Journal of Consulting and Clinical Psychology 70,* 590–610.

Anderson, R. M. (1995). Patient empowerment and the traditional medical model. *Diabetes Care, 18,* 412–415.

Angier, N. (2001, May 6). Together, in sickness and health. *New York Times Magazine,* pp. 67–69.

Bandura, A. (1977). Self-efficacy: Toward a unifying theory of behavioral change. *Psychological Review, 84,* 191–215.

Bandura, A. (1986). *Social foundations of thought and action. A social cognitive perspective.* Englewood Cliffs, NJ: Prentice-Hall.

Bandura, A. (1997). *Self-efficacy. The exercise of control.* New York: W. H. Freeman.

Barry, M. J., & Walschlager, S. A. (1998). Exercise training and chronic obstructive pulmonary disease: past and future research directions. *Journal of Cardiopulmonary Rehabilitation, 18,* 181–191.

Bauer, U. E., Johnson, T. M., Hopkins, R. S., & Brooks, R. G. (2000). Changes in youth cigarette use and intentions of a tobacco control program. Findings from the Florida Youth Tobacco Survey, 1998–2000. *Journal of the American Medical Association, 284,* 723–728.

Beck, A., Rush, J., Shaw, B., & Emery, G. (1979). *Cognitive therapy of depression.* New York: Guilford Press.

Benoit, D., Wang, E. E., & Zlotkin, S. H. (2000). Discontinuance of enterostomy tube feeding by behavioral treatment in early childhood: A randomized control trial. *Journal of Pediatrics, 137,* 498–503.

Benson, H. (1975). *The relaxation response.* New York: William Morrow.

Bernard, A. L., Prince, A., & Edsall, P. (2000). Quality of life issues for fibromyalgia patients. *Arthritis Care, 13,* 42–50.

Bernstein, D. I. (2000). The natural history of adult asthma: what do we know? *Annals of Allergy, Asthma, and Immunology, 84,* 469–470.

Biswas, A., & Ratnam, S. S. (1995). Vaginismus and outcome of treatment. *Annals of Academic Medicine of Singapore, 24,* 755–758.

Blanchard, E. B. (1994). Behavioral medicine and health psychology. In A. E. Bergin & S. L. Garfield (Eds.), *Handbook of psychotherapy and behavior change* (4th ed.) (pp. 701–733). New York: John Wiley & Sons.

Brody, B. L., Williams, R. A., Thomas, R. G., Kaplan, R. M., Chu, R. M., & Brown, S. I. (1999). Age-related macular degeneration: a randomized clinical trial of a self-management intervention. *Annals of Behavioral Medicine, 21,* 322–329.

Broughton, W. A., & Bass, J. B., Jr. (1999). Tuberculosis and diseases caused by atypical mycobacteria. In: R. K. Albert, S. G. Shapiro, & J. R. Jett (Eds.), *Comprehensive respiratory medicine* (pp. 29.1–29.16). St Louis: C. V. Mosby.

Brown, G. E., Nordloh, S., & Donowitz, A. J. (1992). Systematic desensitization of oral hypersensitivity in a patient with a closed head injury. *Dysphagia, 7,* 138–141.

Brownlee, S., Leventhal, H., & Leventhal, E. A. (2000). Regulation, self-regulation, and construction of the self in the maintenance of physical health. In M. Boekaerts, P. R. Pintrich, & M. Zeidner (Eds.), *Handbook of self-regulation* (pp. 369–416). San Diego: Academic Press.

Burman, W. J., Cohn, D. L., Rietmeijer, C. A., Judson, F. N., Sbarbaro, J. A., & Reves, R. R. (1997b). Noncompliance with directly observed therapy for tuberculosis. Epidemiology and effect in the outcome of treatment. *Chest, 111,* 1168–1173.

Burman, W. J., Dalton, C. B., Cohn, D. L., Butler, J. R., & Reves, R. R. (1997a). A cost-effectiveness analysis of directly observed therapy vs self-administered therapy for treatment of tuberculosis. *Chest, 112,* 63–70.

Burns, J. W., Johnson, B. J., Mahoney, N., Devine, J., & Pawl, R. (1998). Cognitive and physical capacity process variables predict long-term outcome after treatment of chronic pain. *Journal of Consulting and Clinical Psychology, 66,* 434–439.

Cambach, W., Wagenaar, R. C., Koelman, T. W., van Keimpema, A. R., & Kemper, H. C. (1999). The long-term effects of pulmonary rehabilitation in patients with asthma and chronic obstructive pulmonary diseases: A research synthesis. *Archives of Physical and Medical Rehabilitation, 80,* 103–111.

Caplin, D. L., & Creer, T. L. (2001). A self-management program for adult asthma. Part III. Maintenance and relapse of skills. *Journal of Asthma, 38,* 343–356.

Cassell, E. J. (1997). *Doctoring: The nature of primary care medicine.* New York: Oxford University Press.

Cassidy, C. A. (1999). Using the transtheoretical model to facilitate behavior change in patients with chronic illness. *Journal of the American Academy of Nurses, 11,* 281–287.

Celli, B. R. (1997). Is pulmonary rehabilitation an effective treatment for chronic obstructive pulmonary disease? Yes. *American Journal of Respiratory and Critical Care Medicine, 155,* 784–785.

Celli, B. R. (1998). Standards for optimal management of COPD: A summary. *Chest, 113,* 283S–287S.

Centers for Disease Control. (2000a). Cigarette smoking among adults—United States, 1998. *Morbidity and Mortality Weekly Report, 49,* 881–884.

Centers for Disease Control. (2000b). Youth tobacco surveillance—United States, 1998–1999. *Morbidity and Mortality Weekly Report, 49,* No. SS-10.

Centers for Disease Control. (2000c). State-specific prevalence of current cigarette smoking among adults and the proportion of adults who work in a smoke-free environment—United States, 1999. *Morbidity and Mortality Weekly Report, 49,* 978–982.

Centers for Disease Control. (2000d). Reducing tobacco use: A report of the surgeon general. Executive report. *Morbidity and Mortality Weekly Report, 49,* No. RR-16.

Centers for Disease Control. (2000e). Declines in lung cancer rates – California, 1988–1997. *Morbidity and Mortality Weekly Report, 49,* 1066–1069.

Centers for Disease Control. (2001a). The Global HIV and AIDS Epidemic, 2001. *Morbidity and Mortality Weekly Report, 50,* No. 21, 434–439. Centers for Disease Control (2001a).

Centers for Disease Control. (2001b). HIV and AIDS—United States, 1981–2000. *Morbidity and Mortality Weekly Report, 50,* No. 21, 430–434.

Centers for Disease Control. (2001c). Preventing and controlling tuberculosis along the U.S.-Mexico border. *Morbidity and Mortality Weekly Report, 50,* No. RR-1.

Chesson, A. L., Jr., Anderson, W. M., Littner, M., Davila, D., Hartse, K., Johnson, S., Wise, M., & Rafecas, J. (1999). Practice parameters of the nonpharmacologic treatment of chronic insomnia. An American Academy of Sleep Medicine report. Standards of Practice Committee of the American Academy of Sleep Medicine. *Sleep, 22,* 1128–1133.

Chippendale, S., & French, L. (2001). HIV counseling and the psychological management of patients with HIV or AIDS. *British Medical Journal, 322,* 1533–1535.

Christensen, A. J., & Ehlers, S. L. (2002). Psychological factors in end-stage renal disease: an emerging context for behavioral medicine research. In T. W. Smith, P. C. Kendall, & F. J. Keefe (Eds.), Health psychology. *Journal of Consulting and Clinical Psychology, 70,* 712–724.

Clark, N. M., Feldman, C. H., Evans, D., Levison, M. J., Wasilewski, Y., & Mellins, R. B. (1986). The impact of health education on frequency and cost of health care use by low income children with asthma. *Journal of Allergy and Clinical Immunology, 78,* 108–115.

Coyne, J. C., Thompson, R., Klinkman, M. S., & Nease, D. E., Jr. (2002). Emotional disorders in primary care. In T. W. Smith, P. C. Kendall, & F. J. Keefe (Eds.), Health psychology. *Journal of Consulting and Clinical Psychology, 70,* 798–809.

Creer, T. L. (1970). The use of a time-out from positive reinforcement procedure with asthmatic children. *Journal of Psychosomatic Research, 14,* 117–120.

Creer, T. L. (2000). Self-management and the control of chronic pediatric illness. In D. Drotar (Ed.), *Promoting adherence to medical treatment in chronic childhood disease* (95–129). Hillsdale, NJ: Lawrence Erlbaum Associates.

Creer, T. L. (2001, May). Assessment of decision-making in asthma maintenance and relapse. Paper presented at 97th International Conference of the American Thoracic Society, San Francisco.

Creer, T. L., & Holroyd, K. A. (1997). Self-management. In A. Baum, S. Newman, J. Weinman, R. West, & C. McManus (Eds.), *Cambridge handbook of psychology, health and medicine* (pp. 255–258). Cambridge: Cambridge University Press.

Currie, S. R., Wilson, K. G., Pontefract, A. J., & de Laplante, L. (2000). Cognitive-behavioral treatment of insomnia secondary to chronic pain. *Journal of Consulting and Clinical Psychology, 68,* 407–416.

da Costa, I. G., Rapoff, M. A., Lemanek, K., & Goldstein, G. L. (1997). Improving adherence to medication regimens for children and its effect on children outcome. *Journal of Applied Behavior Analysis, 30,* 687–691.

Das, S. (2001). Epidemic proportions. Money isn't enough to keep infectious diseases under control. *American Prospect, 12,* 23–26.

Davidson, R. (1992). Prochaska and DiClemente's model of change: A case study? *British Journal of Addiction, 87,* 821–822.

Department of Health and Human Services (1983). *The health consequences of smoking: cardiovascular disease. A report of the Surgeon General* (DHHS publication no. 84-50204). Washington, DC: U.S. Government Printing Office.

DiFranza, J. R., & Librett, J. J. (1999). State and federal revenues from tobacco consumed by minors. *American Journal of Public Health, 89,* 1106–1108.

Domel, S. B., Thompson, W. O., Baranowski, T., & Smith, A. F. (1994). How children remember what they have eaten. *Journal of American Diet Association, 94,* 1267–1274.

DuHamel, K. N., Redd, W. H., & Vickberg, S. M. (1999). Behavioral interventions in the diagnosis, treatment and rehabilitation of children with cancer. *Acta Oncology, 38,* 719–734.

Dye, C., Scheele, S., Dolin, P., Pathania, V., & Raviglione, M. C. (1999). Global burden of tuberculosis. *Journal of the American Medical Association, 282,* 677–686.

Editorial: Tobacco control needs help. (2001). *Lancet, 357,* 1459.

Elk, R., Mangus, L., Rhoades, H., Andres, R., & Grabowski, J. (1998). Cessation of cocaine use pregnancy: effects of contingency management interventions on maintaining abstinence and complying with prenatal care. *Addictive Behavior, 23,* 57–64.

Ellis, A. (1973). *Humanistic psychotherapy.* New York: McGraw-Hill.

Emont, S. L., Choi, W. S., Novotny, T. E., & Giovino, G. A. (1993). Clean indoor air legislation, taxation, and smoking behavior in the United States: an ecological analysis. *Tobacco Control, 2,* 13–17.

Farmer, P. E., Becerra, M. C., & Kim, J. Y. (1999). Conclusions and recommendations. *The global impact of drug-resistant tuberculosis.* Boston: Program in Infectious Disease and Social Change, Harvard University.

Fenwick, P. (1994). The behavioral treatment of epilepsy generation and inhibition of seizures. *Neurological Clinics, 12,* 175–202.

Ferguson, G. T. (1998). Management of COPD. Early identification and active intervention are crucial. *Postgraduate Medicine, 103,* 136–141.

Fichtenberg, C. M., & Glanz, S. A. (2000). Association of the California Tobacco Control Program with decline in cigarette consumption and mortality from heart disease. *New England Journal of Medicine, 343,* 1772–1777.

Gabbay, F. H., Krantz, D. S., Kop, W. J., Hedges, S. M., Klein, J., Gottdiener, J. S., & Rozanski, A. (1996). Triggers of myocardial ischemia during daily life in patients with coronary artery disease: Physical and mental activities, anger and smoking. *Journal of the American College of Cardiology, 27,* 585–592.

Garner, P. (1998). What makes DOT work? *Lancet, 352,* 1326–1327.

Garrett, L. (1994). *The coming plague. Newly emerging diseases in a world out of bounce.* New York: Farrar, Straus & Giroux.

Gasner, M. R., Maw, K. L., Feldman, G. E., Fujiwara, P. I., & Frieden, T. R. (1999). The use of legal action in New York City to ensure treatment of tuberculosis. *New England Journal of Medicine, 340,* 359–366.

Ghaderi, A., & Scott, B. (2000). Coping in dieting and eating disorders: A population-based study. *Journal of Nervous and Mental Disorders, 188,* 273–279.

Giardino, N. D., & Lehrer, P. M. (2000). Behavioral conditioning and idiopathic environmental intolerance. *Occupational Medicine, 15,* 519–528.

Giles, G. M., & Morgan, J. H. (1989). Training functional skills following herpes simplex encephalitis: a single case study. *Journal of Clinical and Experimental Neuropsychology, 11,* 311–318.

Glasgow, R. E. (1999). Outcomes of and for diabetes education research. *Diabetes Education, 25 (Suppl.),* 74–88.

Glasgow, R. E., & Anderson, R. M. (1999). In diabetes care, moving from compliance to adherence is not enough. Something entirely different is needed. *Diabetes Care, 22,* 2090–2092.

Glasgow, R. E., La Chance, P. A., Toobert, D. J., Brown, J., Hampson, S. E., & Riddle, M. C. (1997). Long-term effects and costs of brief behavioral dietary intervention for patients with diabetes delivered from the medical office. *Patient Education and Counseling, 32,* 175–184.

Glasgow, R. E., & Strycker, L. A. (2000). Preventive care practices for diabetes management in two primary care samples. *American Journal of Preventive Medicine, 19,* 9–14.

Goldfield, G. S., Kalakanis, L. E., Ernst, M. M., & Epstein, L. H. (2000). Open-loop feedback to increase physical activity in obese children. *International Journal of Obese Related Metabolism Disorders, 24,* 888–892.

Goldstein, M. G., DePue, J. D., Monroe, A. D., Lessne, C. W., Rakowski, W., Prokhorov, A., Niaura, R., & Dube, C. E. (1998). A population-based survey of physician smoking cessation counseling practices. *Preventive Medicine, 27,* 720–729.

Gonder-Frederick, L. A., Cox, D. J., & Ritterband, L. M. (2002). Diabetes and behavioral medicine: The second decade. In T. W. Smith, P. C. Kendall, & F. J. Keefe (Eds.), Health psychology. *Journal of Consulting and Clinical Psychology, 70,* 611–625.

Gould, K. L., Ornish, D., Scherwitz, L., Brown, S., Edens, R. P., Hess, M. J., Multani, N., Bolomey, L., Dobbs, F., & Armstrong, W. T. (1995). Changes in myocardial perfusion abnormalities by position emission tomography after long-term, intense risk factor modification. *Journal of the American Medical Association, 274,* 894–901.

Gourevitch, M. N., Alcabes, P., Wasserman, W. C., & Arno, P. S. (1998). Cost-effectiveness of directly observed chemoprophylaxis of tuberculosis among drug users at high risk for tuberculosis. *International Journal of Tuberculosis and Lung Disease, 2,* 531–540.

Groessl, E. J., & Cronan, T. A. (2000). A cost analysis of self-management programs for people with chronic illness. *American Journal of Community Psychology, 28,* 455–480.

Gustafson, D. H., Hawkins, R., Bobert, E., Pingree, S., Serlin, R. E., Graziano, F., & Chan, C. L. (1999). Impact of a patient-centered, computer-based health information/support system. *American Journal of Preventive Medicine, 16,* 43–45.

Gustafsson, M., Gaston-Johansson, F., Aschenbrenner, D., & Merboth, M. (1999). Pain, coping and analgesic medication usage in rheumatoid arthritis patients. *Patient Education and Counseling, 37,* 33–41.

Gutentag, S., & Hammer, D. (2000). Shaping oral feeding in a gastronomy tube-dependent child in natural settings. *Behavior Modification, 24,* 395–410.

Hagopian, L. P., Farrell, D. A., & Amari, A. (1996). Treating total liquid refusal with backward chaining and fading. *Journal of Applied Behavioral Analysis, 29,* 573–575.

Hagopian, L. P., & Thompson, R. H. (1999). Reinforcement of compliance with respiratory treatment in a child with cystic fibrosis. *Journal of Applied Behavior Analysis, 32,* 233–236.

Hampson, S. E., Glasgow, R. E., & Toobert, D. J. (1990). Personal models of diabetes and their relations to self-care activities. *Health Psychology, 9*, 632–646.

Harper, R. P., Brown, C. M., Triplett, M. M., Villasenor, A., & Gatchel, R. J. (2000). Masticatory function in patients with juvenile rheumatoid arthritis. *Pediatric Dentistry, 22*, 200–206.

Henry, S. B., Holzemer, W. L., Weaver, K., & Stotts, N. (1999). Quality of life and self-care management strategies of PLWAs with chronic diarrhea. *Journal of the Association of Nurses AIDS Care, 10*, 46–54.

Heyman, S. J., Sell, R., & Brewer, T. F. (1998). The influence of program acceptability on the effectiveness of public health policy: A study of directly observed therapy for tuberculosis. *American Journal of Public Health, 88*, 442–445.

Hochstadt, N. J., Shepard, J., & Lulla, S. H. (1980). Reducing hospitalizations of children with asthma. *Journal of Pediatrics, 97*, 1012–1015.

Hoffman, C., Rice, D., & Sung, H. Y. (1996). Persons with chronic conditions. Their prevalence and cost. *Journal of the American Medical Association, 276*, 1473–1479.

Holroyd, K. A., Cordingley, G. E., Pingel, J. D., Jerome, A., Theofanous, A. G., Jackson, D. K., & Leard, L. (1989). Enhancing the effectiveness of abortive therapy: A controlled evaluation of self-management training. *Headache, 29*, 148–153.

Holroyd, K. A., & Creer, T. L. (Eds.). (1986). *Self-management of chronic disease: Handbook of clinical interventions and research.* Orlando, FL: Academic Press.

Holroyd, K. A., France, J. L., Cordingley, G. E., Rokicki, L. A., Kvaal, S. A., Lipchik, G. L., & McCool, H. R. (1995). Enhancing the effectiveness of relaxation-thermal biofeedback training with propranolol hydrochloride. *Journal of Consulting and Clinical Psychology, 63*, 327–330.

Holroyd, K. A., Malinoski, P., Davis, M. K., & Lipchik, G. L. (1999). The three dimensions of headache impact: Pain, disability and affective distress. *Pain, 83*, 571–578.

Holroyd, K. A., Nash, J. M., Pingel, J. D., Cordingley, G. E., & Jerome, A. (1991). A comparison of pharmacological (amitriptyline HCL) and nonpharmacological (cognitive-behavioral) therapies for chronic tension headache. *Journal of Consulting and Clinical Psychology, 59*, 387–393.

Holroyd, K. A., O'Donnell, F. J., Stensland, M., Lipchik, G. L., Cordingley, G. E., & Carlson, B. W. (2001). Management of chronic tension-type headache with tricyclic antidepressant medication, stress management therapy, and their combination. *Journal of the American Medical Association, 285*, 2208–2215.

Holroyd, K. A., Stensland, M., Lipchik, G. L., Hill, K. R., O'Donnell, F. S., & Cordingley, G. (2000). Psychosocial correlates and impact of chronic tension-type headaches. *Headache, 40*, 3–16.

Horne, R. (1997). Representation of medication and treatment: advances in theory and measurement. In K. J. Petrie & J. A. Weinman (Eds.), *Perceptions of health and illness: Current research and applications* (pp. 155–188). London: Harwood Academics Press.

Houston, T., & Kaufman, N. J. (2000). Tobacco control in the 21st century. Searching for answers in a sea of change. *Journal of the American Medical Association, 284*, 752–753.

Hovell, M. F., Zakarian, J. M., Wahlgren, D. R., & Matt, G. E. (2000). Reducing children's exposure to environmental tobacco smoke: The empirical evidence and directions for future research. *Tobacco Control, 9*, 40–47.

Imrie, J., Stephenson, J. M., Cowen, F. M., Wanigararate, S., Billington, A. J., Copas, A. J., French, L., French, P. D., & Johnson, A. M. for the Behavioral Intervention in Gay Men Project Study Group. (2001). A cognitive behavioral intervention to reduce sexually transmitted infections among gay men: randomized trial. *British Medical Journal, 322*, 1451–1456.

Jacobson, E. (1938). *Progressive relaxation.* Chicago: University of Chicago Press.

Jeffrey, R. W., Drewnowski, A., Epstein, L. H., Stunkard, A. J., Wilson, G. T., Wing, R. R., & Hill, R. H. (2000). Long-term maintenance of weight loss: current status. *Health Psychology, 19*, 5–16.

Jha, P., & Chaloupka, F. J. (Eds.) (1999). *Tobacco control policies in developing countries.* New York: New York, University Press.

Johnson, P. R., & Thorn, B. E. (1989). Cognitive behavioral treatment of headache: Group versus individual treatment format. *Headache, 29*, 358–365.

Joint ACCP/AACVPR Evidence-Based Guidelines. (1997). Pulmonary rehabilitation. *Chest, 112*, 1363–1396.

Jones, T. F., Craig, A. S., Valway, S. E., Woodley, C. L., & Schaffner, W. (1999). Transmission of tuberculosis in a jail. *Annals of Internal Medicine, 131*, 557–563.

Kaplan, R. M. (2000). Two pathways to prevention. *American Psychologist, 55*, 382–396.

Kaptein, A. A. (1997). Behavioral interventions in COPD: A pause for breath. *European Respiratory Journal, 7*, 88–91.

Karoly, P. (1993). Mechanisms of self-regulation: a systems view. *Annual Review of Psychology, 44*, 23–52.

Keefe, F. J. (2000). Pain behavior observation: current status and future directions. *Current Review of Pain, 4*, 12–17.

Keefe, F. J., Dunsmore, J., & Burnett, R. (1992). Behavioral and cognitive-behavioral approaches to chronic pain: Recent advances and future directions. *Journal of Consulting and Clinical Psychology, 60*, 528–536.

Keefe, F. J., Kashikar-Zuck, S., Robinson, E., Salley, A., Beaupre, P., Caldwell, D., Baucom, D., & Haythornthwaite, J. (1997). Pain coping strategies that predict patients' and spouses' ratings of patients' self-efficacy. *Pain, 73*, 191–199.

Keefe, F. J., Smith, S. J., Buffington, A.L.H., Gibson, J., Studts, J. L., & Caldwell, D. S. (2002). Recent advances and future directions in the biopsychosocial assessment and treatment of arthritis. In T. W. Smith, P. C. Kendall, & F. J. Keefe (Eds.), Health psychology. *Journal of Consulting and Clinical Psychology, 70*, 640–655.

Kellam, S. G., Koretz, D., & Moscicki, E. K. (1999). Core elements of developmental epidemiologically based prevention research. *American Journal of Community Psychology, 27*, 463–482.

Kelly, J. A., & Kalichman, S. C. (2002). Behavioral research in HIV/AIDS primary and secondary prevention: Recent advances and future directions. In T. W. Smith, P. C. Kendall, & F. J. Keefe (Eds.), Health psychology. *Journal of Consulting and Clinical Psychology, 70*, 626–639.

Kerns, R. D., & Rosenberg, R. (2000). Predicting response to self-management treatments for chronic pain: Application of the pain stages of change model. *Pain, 84*, 49–55.

Kitfield, E. B., & Masalsky, C. J. (2000). Negative reinforcement-based treatment to increase food intake. *Behavior Modification, 24*, 600–608.

Koffman, D. M., Lee, J. W., Hopp, J. W., & Emont, S. L. (1998). The impact of including incentives and competition in a workplace smoking cessation program on quit rates. *American Journal of Health Promotion, 13*, 105–111.

Kole-Snijders, A. M., Vlaeyen, J. W., Goossens, M. E., Rutten-van Molken, M. P., Heuts, P. H., van Breukelen, G., & van Eek, H. (1999). Chronic low-back pain: What does cognitive coping skills training add to operant behavioral treatment? Results of a randomized clinical trial. *Journal of Consulting and Clinical Psychology, 67*, 931–944.

Kotses, H., Bernstein, I. L., Bernstein, D. I., Reynolds, R. V., Korbee, L., Wigal, J. K., Ganson, E., Stout, C., & Creer, T. L. (1995). A self-management program for adult asthma. Part I: development and evaluation. *Journal of Allergy and Clinical Immunology, 95*, 529–540.

Kotses, H., Stout, C., McConnaughy, K., Winder, J. A., & Creer, T. L. (1996). Evaluation of individualized asthma self-management programs. *Journal of Asthma, 33*, 113–118.

Lacasse, Y., Wong, E., Guyatt, G. H., King, D., Cook, D. J., & Goldstein, R. S. (1996). Meta-analysis of respiratory rehabilitation in chronic obstructive pulmonary disease. *Lancet, 348*, 1115–1119.

Laffel, L. (2000). Sick-day management in Type 1 diabetes. *Endocrinology Metabolism, 29*, 707–723.

Lamott, A. (1994). *Bird by bird. Some instructions on writing and life.* New York: Pantheon Books.

Landis, S. H., Murray, T., Bolden, S., & Wingo, P. A. (1998). Cancer statistics 1998. *CA: A Cancer Journal for Clinicians, 48*, 6–29.

Leveille, S. G., Wagner, E. H., Davis, C., Grothaus, L., Wallace, J., LoGerfo, M., & Kent, D. (1998). Preventing disability and managing chronic illness in frail older adults: A randomized trial of a community-based partnership with primary care. *Journal of the American Geriatric Society, 46*, 1191–1198.

Levit, K., Cowan, C., Lazenby, H., Sensenig, A., McDonnell, P., Stiller, J., Martin, A., & the Health Accounts Team (2001). Health spending in 1998: Signals of change. *Health Affairs, 19*, 124–132.

Lewin, D. S., & Dahl, R. E. (1999). Importance of sleep in the management of pediatric pain. *Journal of Developmental Behavioral Pediatrics, 20*, 244–252.

Lin, C. C., & Ward, S. E. (1996). Perceived self-efficacy and outcome expectancies in coping with chronic low back pain. *Research in Nursing Health, 19*, 299–310.

Liu, B. Q., Peto, R., Chen, Z. M., Boreham, J., Wu, Y. P., Li, J. Y., Campbell, T. C., & Chen, J. S. (1998). Emerging tobacco hazards in China: 1. Retrospective proportional mortality study of one million deaths. *British Medical Journal, 317*, 1411–1422.

Living with Asthma. Part 1. Manual for teaching parents the self-management of childhood asthma. (1986). U.S. Department of Health and Human Services (NIH publication No. 87-2364). Washington, DC: U.S. Department of Health and Human Services

Living with Asthma. Part 2. Manual for teaching children the self-management of childhood asthma. (1987). U.S. Department of Health and Human Services (NIH publication No. 86-2364). Washington, DC: U.S. Department of Health and Human Services.

Lobato, M. N., Mohle-Boetani, J. C., & Royce, S. E. (2000). Missed opportunities for preventing tuberculosis among children younger than five years of age. *Pediatrics, 106*, E75.

Looper, K. J., & Kirmayer, L. J. (2002). Cognitive behavioral therapy for somatoform disorders. In T. W. Smith, P. C. Kendall, & F. J., Keefe (Eds.), Health psychology. *Journal of Consulting and Clinical Psychology, 70*, 810–827.

Lorig, K. R., Sobel, D. S., Stewart, A. L., Brown, B. W., Jr., Bandura, A., Ritter, P., Gonzalez, V. M., Laurent, D. D., & Holman, H. R. (1999). Evidence suggesting that a chronic disease self-management program can improve health status while reducing hospitalization: A randomized trial. *Medical Care, 37*, 5–14.

Lynch, J. P., Forman, S. A., Graff, S., & Gunby, M. C. (2000). High-risk population health management—achieving improved patient outcomes and near-term financial results. *American Journal of Managed Care, 6,* 781–791.

Lynch, R. T., Agre, J., Powers, J. M., & Sherman, J. (1996). Long-term follow-up of outpatient interdisciplinary pain management with a no-treatment comparison group. *American Journal of Physical Medicine and Rehabilitation, 75,* 213–322.

Magner, L. N. (1992). *A history of medicine.* New York: Marcel Dekker, Inc.

Mahler, D. A. (1998). Pulmonary rehabilitation. *Chest, 113,* 263S–268S.

Marlatt, A. G. (1985a). Relapse prevention: Theoretical, rationale, and overview of the model. In A. G. Marlatt & J. R. Gordon (Eds.), *Relapse prevention: Maintenance strategies in the treatment of addictive behaviors* (pp. 3–70). New York: Guilford Press.

Marlatt, A. G. (1985b). Cognitive assessment and intervention procedures for relapse prevention. In A. G. Marlatt & J. R. Gordon (Eds.), *Relapse prevention: Maintenance strategies in the treatment of addictive behaviors* (pp. 201–279). New York: Guilford Press.

McKeown, T. (1976). *The role of medicine: Dreams, mirage, or nemesis.* London: The Nuffield Provincial Hospitals Trust.

McKeown, T. (1997). Determinants of health. In P. R. Lee & C. Estes (Eds.), *The nations's health* (5th ed.) (pp. 136–156). Boston: Jones and Bartlett.

Meichenbaum, D. (1997). Cognitive behavior therapy. In A. Baum, S. Newman, J. Weinman, R. West, & C. McManus (Eds.), *Cambridge handbook of psychology, health and medicine* (pp. 200–203). Cambridge: Cambridge University Press.

Merson, M. H., Dayton, J. M., & O'Reilly, K. (2000). Effectiveness of HIV prevention interventions in developing countries. *AIDS, 14 (Suppl.),* S68–S84.

Midthun, D. J., & Jett, J. R. (1999). Lung tumors. In R. Albert, S. Spiro, & J. Jett (Eds.), *Comprehensive respiratory medicine* (pp. 43.1–43.23). London: Harcourt Brace.

Millen, J. V., Irwin, A., & Kim, J. Y. Introduction: What is growing? Who is dying. (2002). In J. Y. Kim, J. V., Millen, A. Irwin, & J. Gershman (Eds), *Dying for growth: Global inequity and the health of the poor* (pp. 3–10). Monroe, MA: Common Courage Press.

Morin, C. M., Culbert, J. P., & Schwartz, S. M. (1994). Nonpharmacological interventions for insomnia: A meta-analysis of treatment efficiency. *American Journal of Psychiatry, 151,* 1172–1180.

Morin, C. M., Hauri, P. J., Espie, C. A., Spielman, A. J., Buysse, D. J., & Bootzin, R. R. (1999). Nonpharmacologic treatment of chronic insomnia. An American Academy of Sleep Medicine review. *Sleep, 22,* 1134–1156.

Morrow, G. R., & Hickok, J. T. (1993). Behavioral treatment of chemotherapy-induced nausea and vomiting. *Oncology, 7,* 83–89.

Murray, C.J.E., & Lopez, A. D. (1996). *The global burden of disease.* Cambridge, MA: Harvard University Press.

National Academy of Sciences. (2001). *Crossing the quality chasm: a new health system for the 21st century.* Washington, DC: National Academy Press.

National Institutes of Health. (1991). *Executive summary: Guidelines for the diagnosis and management of asthma* (NIH Publication No. 91-3042A). Washington, DC: U.S. Department of Health and Human Services.

Niaura, R., & Abrams, D. B. (2002). Smoking cessation: Progress, priorities, and prospectus. In T. W. Smith, P. C. Kendall, & F. J. Keefe (Eds.), Health psychology. *Journal of Consulting and Clinical Psychology, 70,* 494–509.

Niu, S. R., Yang, G. H., Chen, Z. M., Wang, G. H., H, X. Z., Schoerpff, H., Boreham, J., Pan, H. C., & Peto, R. (1998). Emerging tobacco hazards in China: 2. Early mortality results from a prospective study. *British Medical Journal, 317,* 1425–1424.

Norman, G. J., Velicer, W. F., Fava, J. L., & Prochaska, J. O. (2000). Cluster subtypes within stage of change in a representative sample of smokers. *Addictive Behaviors, 25,* 183–204.

O'Brien, S., Repp, A. C., Williams, G. E., & Christophersen, E. R. (1991). Pediatric feeding disorders. *Behavior Modification, 15,* 394–418.

Ockene, J. K., Emmons, K. M., Mermelstein, R. J., Perkins, K. A., Bonollo, D. S., Voorhees, C. C., & Hollis, J. F. (2000). Relapse and maintenance issues for smoking cessation. *Health Psychology, 19 (Suppl.),* 17–31.

Orleans, C. T. (2000). Promoting the maintenance of health behavior change: Recommendations for the generation of research and practice. *Health Psychology, 19 (Suppl.),* 76–83.

Ornish, D., Scherwitz, L. W., Billings, J. H., Brown, S. E., Gould, K. L., Merritt, T. A., Sparler, S., Armstrong, W. T., Ports, T. A., Kirkeeide, R. L., Hogeboom, C., & Brand, R. J. (1998). Intensive lifestyle changes for reversal of coronary heart disease. *Journal of the American Medical Association, 280,* 2001–2007.

Palmer, C. S., Miller, B., Halpern, M. T., & Geiter, L. J. (1998). A model of the cost-effectiveness of directly observed therapy for treatment of tuberculosis. *Journal of Public Health Management Practice, 4,* 1–13.

Pan, C. X., Morrison, R. S., Ness, J., Fugh-Berman, A., & Leipzig, R. M. (2000). Complementary and alternative medicine in the management of pain, dyspnea, and nausea and vomiting near the end of life. A systematic review. *Journal of Pain Symptom Management, 20,* 374–387.

Parkin, D. M., Pisani, P., Lopez, A. D., & Masuyer, E. (1994). At least one in seven cases of cancer is caused by smoking. Global estimates for 1985. *International Journal of Cancer, 59*, 494–504.

Paul, G. L. (1966). *Insight in therapy.* Stanford, CA: Stanford University Press.

Pear, R. (2001, June 5). Advocates for patients barged in, and the federal government changed. *New York Times* (On-line). Available at www.nytimes.com.

Peipert, J. F., & Ruggiero, L. (1998). Use of the transtheoretical model for behavioral change in women's health. *Women's Health, 8*, 304–309.

Perkins, K. A., Sanders, M., D'Amico, D., & Wilson, A. (1997). Nicotine discrimination and self-administration in humans as a function of smoking status. *Psychopharmacology, 131*, 361–370.

Perri, M. G., Sears, S. F., Jr., & Clark, J. E. (1993). Strategies for improving maintenance of weight loss. Toward a continuous care model of obesity management. *Diabetes Care, 16*, 200–209.

Peters, L., Simon, E. P., Folen, R. A., Umphress, V., & Lagana, L. (2000). The COPE program: Treatment efficacy and medical utilization outcome of a chronic pain management program at a major military hospital. *Military Medicine, 165*, 954–960.

Pierce, J. P., Gilpin, E. A., Emery, S. L., White, M. M., Rosbrook, B., Berry, C. C. (1998). Has the California tobacco control program reduced smoking? *Journal of the American Medical Association, 280*, 893–899.

Pisani, P., Parkin, D. M., Bray, F., & Ferlay, J. (1999). Estimates of the worldwide mortality from 25 cancers in 1990. *International Journal of Cancer, 83*, 18–29.

Pomerleau, O. F., & Rodin, J. (1986). Behavioral medicine and health psychology. In A. E., Bergin & S. L., Garfield (Eds.), *Handbook of psychotherapy and behavior change.* (3rd ed.) (pp. 483–522). New York: John Wiley & Sons.

Powell, D. A. (1999). A behavioral stages model of classical (Pavlovian) conditioning: Application to cognitive aging. *Neuroscience and Biobehavior Review, 23*, 797–816.

Poynard, T., Regimbeau, C., & Benhamou, Y. (2001). Meta-analysis of smooth muscle relaxants in the treatment of irritable pain syndrome. *Pharmacological Therapy, 15*, 355–361.

Premack, D. (1959). Toward empirical behavioral laws: Positive reinforcement. *Psychological Review, 66*, 219–233.

Prochaska, J. O. (1979). *Systems of psychotherapy: A transtheoretical analysis.* Chicago: Dorsey.

Prochaska, J. O. (1994). Strong and weak principles for progressing from precontemplation to action on the basis of twelve problem areas. *Health Psychology, 13*, 47–51.

Prochaska, J. O. (1995). An eclectic and integrative approach: Transtheoretical therapy. In: A. S. Gurman & S. B. Messer (Eds.), *Essential psychotherapies. Theory and practice* (pp. 403–440). New York: Guilford Press.

Quaglietti, S. E., Atwood, J. E., Ackerman, L., & Froelicher, V. (2000). Management of the patient with congestive heart failure using outpatient, home, and palliative care. *Progress in Cardiovascular Disease, 43*, 259–274.

Renzi, C., Peticca, L., & Pescatori, M. (2000). The use of relaxation techniques in the perioperative management of proctological patients: Preliminary results. *International Journal of Colorectalogy, 15*, 313–316.

Ries, A. L., Kaplan, R. M., Limberg, T. M., & Prewitt, L. A. (1995). Effects of pulmonary rehabilitation on physiologic and psychosocial outcomes in patients with chronic obstructive pulmonary disease. *Annals of Internal Medicine, 122*, 823–832.

Rogers, E. M. (1995). *Diffusion of innovations.* New York: Free Press.

Rudestam, K. E. (1980). *Methods of self-change; an ABC primer.* Monterrey, CA: Brooks/Cole.

Sackett, D. L., Straus, S. E., Richardson, W. S., Rosenberg, W., & Haynes, R. B. (2000). *Evidence-based medicine: how to practice and teach EBM* (2nd ed.). London: Churchill Livingstone.

Saloojee, Y., & Dagli, E. (2000). Tobacco industry tactics for resisting public policy on health. *Bulletin of the World Health Organization, 78*, 902–910.

Sandstrom, M. J., & Keefe, F. J. (1998). Self-management of fibromyalgia: The role of formal coping skills and physical exercise training programs. *Arthritis Care and Research, 11*, 432–447.

Scanlon, P. D., Connett, J. E., Waller, L. A., Altose, M. D., Bailey, W. C., & Buist, A. S. (2000). Smoking cessation and lung function in mild-to-moderate chronic obstructive pulmonary disease. The Lung Health Study. *American Journal of Respiratory and Critical Care Medicine, 161*, 281–390.

Schanberg, L. E., Lefebvre, J. C., Keefe, F. J., Kredich, D. W., & Gil, K. M. (1997). Pain coping and the pain experience in children with juvenile chronic arthritis. *Pain, 73*, 181–189.

Scherer, Y. K., Schmieder, L. E., & Shimmel, S. (1998). The effects of education alone and in combination with pulmonary rehabilitation on self-efficacy in patients with COPD. *Rehabilitation Nursing, 23*, 71–77.

Schwartlander, R., Stover, J., Walker, N., Bollinger, L., Gutierre, J. P., McGreevey, W., Opuni, M., Forsythe, S., Kumaranayake, L., Watts, C., & Bertozzi, S. (2001). Resource needs for HIV/AIDS. *Science, 292*, 2434–2436.

Senior, R. M., & Anthonisen, N. R. (1998). Chronic obstructive pulmonary disease (COPD). *American Journal of Respiratory and Critical Care Medicine, 157*, S139–S147.

Skeie, S., Thue, G., & Sandberg, S. (2001). Patient-derived quality specifications for instruments used in self-monitoring of blood glucose. *Clinical Chemistry, 47*, 67–73.

Skinner, B. F. (1953). *Science and human behavior.* New York: Macmillan.

Sloan, D. M., & Mizes, J. S. (1996). The use of contingency management in the treatment of a geriatric nurse home patient with psychogenic vomiting. *Journal of Behavioral Therapy and Experimental Psychiatry, 27*, 57–65.

Smith, T. W., Kendall, P. C., & Keefe, F. J. (Eds.) (2002). Health psychology. *Journal of Consulting and Clinical Psychology, 70*, 459–856.

Smith, T. W., Nealey, J. B., & Hamann, H. A. (2000). Health psychology. In C. R. Snyder & R. E. Ingram (Eds.), *Handbook of psychological change: Psychotherapy processes and practice for the 21st Century* (pp. 562–590). New York: John Wiley & Sons.

Smith, T. W., & Ruiz, J. M. (2002). Coronary heart disease. In A. J. Christensen & M. Antoni (Eds.), *Chronic Medical Disorders: Behavioral Medicine's Perspective* (pp. 83–111). Oxford, UK: Blackwell Publishers Limited.

Snyder, D. C., & Chin, D. P. (1999). Cost-effectiveness analysis of directly observed therapy for patients with tuberculosis at low risk for treatment default. *American Journal of Respiratory and Critical Care Medicine, 160*, 582–586.

Snyder, D. C., Paz, E. A., Mohle-Boetaini, J. C., Fallstad, R., Black, R. L., & Chin, D. (1999). Tuberculosis prevention in methadone maintenance clinics. Effectiveness and cost-effectiveness. *American Journal of Respiratory and Critical Care Medicine, 160*, 178–185.

Sontag, S. (1978). *Illness as metaphor.* New York: Farrar, Straus & Giroux.

Speca, M., Carlson, L. E., Goodey, E., & Angen, M. (2000). A randomized, wait-list controlled clinical trial: The effect of mindfulness mediation-based stress reduction program on mood and symptoms of stress in cancer outpatients. *Psychosomatic Medicine, 62*, 613–622.

Stein, J. H., Eisenberg, J. M., Hutton, J. J., Klippel, J. H., Kohler, P. O., LaRosso, N. F., O'Rourke, R. A., Reynolds, H. Y., Samuels, M. A., Sande, M. A., & Zvaifler, N. J. (1998). *Internal medicine.* St. Louis: C. V. Mosby.

Stephenson, J. M., Imrie, J., & Sutton, S. R. (2000). Rigorous trials of sexual behavioral interventions in STD/HIV preventions: What have we learned from them? *AIDS, 2000, 14 (suppl)*, S115–S124.

Steptoe, A., Kerry, S., Rink, E., & Hilton, S. (2001). The impact of behavioral counseling on stage of change in fat intake, physical activity, and cigarette smoking in adults at increased risk of coronary heart disease. *American Journal of Public Health, 91*, 265–269.

Stokols, D. (1996). Translating social ecological theory into guidelines for community health promotion. *American Journal of Health Promotion, 10*, 282–298.

Sullivan, M. J., Reesor, K., Mikail, S., & Fisher, R. (1992). The treatment of depression in chronic low back pain: Review and recommendations. *Pain, 50*, 5–13.

Superio-Cabuslay, E., Ward, M. M., & Lorig, K. R. (1996). Patient education interventions in osteoarthritis and rheumatoid arthritis: A meta-analytic comparison with nonsteroidal anti-inflammatory drug treatment. *Arthritis Care, 9*, 292–301.

Sutton, S. R. (1996). Can "stages of change" provide guidance in the treatment of addictions? A critical examination of Prochaska and DiClemente's model. In G. Edwards & C. Dare (Eds.), *Psychotherapy, psychological treatments, and the addictions* (pp. 189–205). Cambridge: Cambridge University Press.

Sutton, S. (1997). Transtheoretical model of behavior change. In A. Baum, S. Newman, J. Weinman, R. West, & C. McManus (Eds.), *Cambridge handbook of psychology, health and medicine* (pp. 180–183). Cambridge: Cambridge University Press.

Tate, D. F., Wing, R. R., & Winett, R. A. (2001). Using internet technology to deliver a behavioral weight loss program. *Journal of the American Medical Association, 285*, 1172–1177.

Thoresen, C. E., & Kirmil-Gray, K. (1983). Self-management psychology and the treatment of childhood asthma. *Journal of Allergy and Clinical Immunology, 72*, 596–606.

Thurber, C. A., Martin-Herz, S. P., & Patterson, D. R. (2000). Psychological principles of burn wound pain in children. I: Theoretical framework. *Journal of Burn Care Rehabilitation, 21*, 376–387.

Tiep, B. L. (1997). Disease management of COPD with pulmonary rehabilitation. *Chest, 112*, 1630–1656.

Toobert, D. J., Hampson, S. E., & Glasgow, R. E. (2000). The summary of diabetes self-care activities measure: Results from 7 studies and a revised scale. *Diabetes Care, 23*, 943–950.

Tulsky, J. P., Pilote, L., Hahn, J. A., Zolopa, A. J., Burke, M., Chesney, M., & Moss, A. R. (2000). Adherence to isoniazid prophylaxis in the homeless. A randomized controlled trial. *Archives of Internal Medicine, 160*, 697–702.

Ullmann, L. P., & Krasner, L. (1965). *Case studies in behavior modification.* New York: Holt, Rinehart & Winston.

U.S. Department of Health and Human Services (DHHS). (1991). *Healthy people 2000: National health promotion and disease prevention objectives* (DHHS Publication No. PHS 91-50213). Washington DC: U.S. Government Printing Office.

U.S. Department of Health and Human Services (DHHS). (2000). *Healthy People 2010: Understanding and improving health* (2nd ed.). Washington, DC: U.S. Government Printing Office.

VanDalfsen, P. J., & Syrjala, K. L. (1990). Psychological strategies in acute pain management. *Critical Care Clinics, 6,* 421–431.

Vaughan, P. W., & Rogers, E. M. (2000). A staged model of communication effects: Evidence from an entertainment-education radio soap opera in Tanzania. *Journal of Health Communication, 5,* 203–227.

Verbrugge, L. M., & Patrick, D. L. (1995). Seven chronic conditions: Their impact on U.S. adults' activity levels and use of medical services. *American Journal of Public Health, 85,* 173–182.

Volmink, J., & Garner, P. (2001). Interventions for promotion adherence to tuberculosis management (Cochrane Review). In *The Cochrane Library, 2.* Oxford: Update Software.

Von Korff, M., Gruman, J., Schaefer, J., Curry, S. J., & Wagner, E. H. (1997). Collaborative management of chronic illness. *Annals of Internal Medicine, 127,* 1097–1102.

Wadden, A., Berkowitz, R. J., Sarwer, D. B., Prus-Wisniewski, R., & Steinberg, C. (2001). Benefits of lifestyle modification in the pharmacologic treatment of obesity. *Archives of Internal Medicine, 161,* 218–227.

Wagner, E. H., Glasgow, R. E., Davis, C., Bonomi, A. E., Provost, L., McCulloch, D., Carver, P., & Sixta, C. (2001). Quality improvement in chronic illness care: A collaborative approach. *The Joint Commission Journal on Quality Improvement, 27,* 63–80.

Walley, J. D., Khan, M. A., Newell, J. N., & Khan, M. H. (2001). Effectiveness of the direct observation component of DOTS for tuberculosis: A randomized controlled trial in Pakistan. *Lancet, 356,* 664–669.

Webster, D. C., & Brennan, T. (1998). Self-care effectiveness and health outcomes in women with interstitial cystitis: Implications for mental health clinicians. *Issues in Mental Health, 19,* 495–519.

Williams, D. A., & Keefe, F. J. (1991). Pain beliefs and the use of cognitive-behavioral coping strategies. *Pain, 46,* 185–190.

Wing, R. R. (2000). Maintenance of behavior change in cardiorespiratory risk reduction: Introduction to proceedings from the National Heart, Lung, and Blood Institute Conference. *Health Psychology, 19 (Suppl.),* 3–4.

Wolpe, J. (1958). *Psychotherapy by reciprocal inhibition.* Stanford, CA: Stanford University Press.

World Development Report. (1993). *Investing in health.* New York: Oxford University Press.

World Health Organization. (1997). *The World Health Report, 1999: Conquering suffering, enriching humanity.* Geneva: World Health Organization.

World Health Organization. (1999). *The World Health Report, 1999: Making a difference.* Geneva: World Health Organization.

World Health Organization. (2000a). *Health systems: Improving performance.* Geneva: World Health Organization.

World Health Organization. (2000b). Overcoming antimicrobial resistance. *Report on Infectious Diseases.* Geneva: World Health Organization.

Wurtele, S. K. (1995). Health promotion. In M. C. Roberts (Ed.), *Handbook of pediatric psychology* (2nd ed.) (pp. 200–216). New York: Guilford Press.

Yang, G., Fan, L., Tan, J., Qi, G., Zhang, Y., Samet, J. M., Taylor, C. E., Becker, K., & Jing, X. (1999). Smoking in China. Findings of the 1996 national prevalence survey. *Journal of the American Medical Association, 282,* 1247–1253.

Yody, B. B., Schaub, C., Conway, J., Peters, S., Straus, D., & Helsinger, S. (2000). Applied behavioral management and acquired brain injury: Approaches and assessment. *Journal of Head Trauma Rehabilitation, 15,* 1041–1060.

Young, P., Dewse, M., Ferguson, W., & Kolbe, J. (1999). Improvements in outcomes for chronic obstructive pulmonary disease (COPD) attributable to a hospital-based respiratory rehabilitation program. *Australian and New Zealand Journal of Medicine, 29,* 59–65.

Zwarenstein, M., Schoeman, J. H., Vundule, C., Lombard, C. J., & Tatley, M. (1998). Randomized controlled trial of self-supervised and directly observed treatment of tuberculosis. *Lancet, 352,* 1340–1343.

CHAPTER 16

Combining Psychotherapy and Psychopharmacology for Treatment of Mental Disorders

MICHAEL E. THASE
RIPU D. JINDAL
University of Pittsburgh Medical Center, Western Psychiatric Institute and Clinic

In this chapter we discuss the conceptual and empirical basis for treatment plans that combine medication and psychotherapy. Psychotherapy–pharmacotherapy combinations, hereafter referred to as the combined treatments, generally receive high marks from consumers (Seligman, 1995) and are frequently recommended by the expert consensus panels that review therapeutics for specific DSM-IV mental disorders (e.g. American Psychiatric Association, 1993, 1997, 1998; Ballenger et al., 1998; Depression Guidelines Panel, 1993). Therefore, all mental health professionals should know the indications for and evidence pertaining to the efficacy of combined treatment.

At the beginning of the twenty-first century, concerns about the costs of mental health interventions are paramount. The direct costs of combined treatment are generally greater during the first 6 to 12 weeks than those of either of the monotherapies. Moreover, routine provision of combined treatment to everyone seeking mental health care would overwhelm the capacities of existing health services. Now, more than ever before, there is the need for convincing evidence that combined treatment is superior to component monotherapies, before that approach can be recommended. Such evidence must be obtained for each major mental disorder.

In some areas, however, the weight of research evidence from comparative studies that have already been completed does not clearly establish the superiority of combination treatments over monotherapies. Before assuming that these studies have yielded negative data (as opposed to false negative results), there is a need to evaluate the research methodologies to ensure the validity of findings. Specifically, we will argue that recent advances in understanding clinical trial design and statistical methods permit a reexamination of these data, which reveals a systematic underestimation of the benefits of combined treatment for subgroups of patients with serious mental disorders. A new generation of properly controlled and adequately powered investigations is therefore needed before the even thornier questions of cost-effectiveness can be addressed.

The Rationale for Psychotherapy–Pharmacotherapy Combinations

Although combined treatment approaches have come to be accepted by a large proportion of mental health professionals, there has been an enduring concern that alleviation of symptoms with medication would reduce the motivation for gaining the understanding or making lifestyle changes needed to bring about a sustainable "cure" (see, e.g., discussions by Gregory & Jindal, 2001; Klerman et al., 1994; Nesse, 2000).

Historically, the psychodynamically oriented mental health professionals have also debated the impact of the act of prescribing medication on the therapeutic relationship. Some suggested that the prescribing therapist could be seen as authoritarian or dictatorial. Others perceived a therapist who was unwilling to write a prescription as potentially "withholding" or even sadistic. In an earlier era in which the transference between patient and therapist was considered to be the prime vehicle for successful psychotherapy, the intrusion of medical monitoring into the therapeutic relationship was viewed as, at best, distracting and, at worst, deleterious.

With the emergence of evidence regarding the efficacy of pharmacotherapies for treatment of severe mental disorders such as schizophrenia, bipolar disorder, obsessive-compulsive disorder, and depression with psychotic features, pharmacotherapy began to be viewed more favorably as a way to hasten recovery and to help patients make better use of psychotherapy (Klerman et al., 1994). Some of the earliest clinical trials of combined treatments showed no evidence of negative interaction in combining treatment modalities (see, for example, the review by Rounsaville, Klerman, & Weissman, 1981). Moreover, in the earlier studies of schizophrenia, psychotherapy was ineffective unless combined with antipsychotic pharmacotherapy (Hogarty, Ulrich, Mussare, & Aristigueta, 1976; May, 1968). Subsequently, it was assumed that psychotherapy, alone, would be ineffective for any form of psychosis, including mania and depression with psychotic features. However, pharmacotherapy alone did not seem to address psychotic patients' underlying vulnerabilities and, even when treated effectively with medication, many patients continued to be impaired by interpersonal difficulties, lower than expected vocational attainment, and poor problem-solving skills. The addition of psychotherapy to pharmacotherapy could be aimed at lessening psychosocial dysfunction or improving quality of life without having a direct effect on the core psychotic symptoms of the mental disorder. Additional symptomatic benefits also might be expected over time, however, as a consequence of less demoralization, improved coping with adverse life events, or better adherence with medication. Combining treatments thus became viewed as the best way to broaden the spectrum of efficacy as compared to single treatments.

As evidence that at least some forms of focused psychotherapies had significant, symptom-reducing effects for various anxiety and nonpsychotic depressive disorders, attention turned to the possibility of truly additive effects. Theoretically, one might even expect a synergistic interaction between treatments used in the combination (i.e., .5 + .5 = 1.2). Such synergy, though highly desirable, has not been evident in studies of combined treatment (Thase, 2000). Rather, the largest effect size ever observed favoring combined treatment is rather modest (i.e., .5 + .5 = .8) (Keller et al., 2000). There are both statistical and practical reasons for the failure to demonstrate synergistic or fully additive effects.

One of the best-known reasons for "incomplete summation" of additive effects is a methodologic artifact known as the ceiling effect. This refers to a progressive loss of measurement sensitivity as symptomatic improvements evolve over time. A ceiling effect may occur because outcome is measured in terms of symptom severity rather than the presence of indicators of wellness (e.g., mirth, equanimity, flexibility, reciprocity, or patience). Without capturing these indicators of "better than average" functioning, it is often difficult to distinguish between the higher grades of response.

A different kind of ceiling effect is also imposed in studies of patient groups that include a fair proportion of treatment-resistant cases. In this case, the ceiling has been lowered. In depression studies, for example, about 10% to 20% of a typical patient group will develop chronic syndromes that persist for two years or longer despite attempts at treatment (Keller & Boland, 1998). In studies of mania or schizophrenia, fully 50% of a typical study group will not respond to a medication with known efficacy. These patients will thus continue to manifest high symptom scores, which inflate the standard deviations of the outcome measures. The standard deviations of measures such as the Hamilton (HAM-D; Hamilton, 1960) or Beck (BDI; Beck, Ward, Mendelson, Mack, & Erbaugh, 1961) depression rating scales, the Young Mania Rating Scale (YMRS; Young, Biggs, Siegler, & Meyer, 1978), or the Brief Psychiatric Rating Scale (BPRS; Overall & Gorham, 1961) typically double across a four- to eight-week randomized control trial (RCT), greatly reducing the sensitivity to detect small to moderate differences in symptom ratings. This problem is amplified when the last observation carried forward (LOCF) method is used to impute the outcomes of study dropouts (Lavori, 1992). Although an "intent-to-treat" (ITT) approach to data analysis

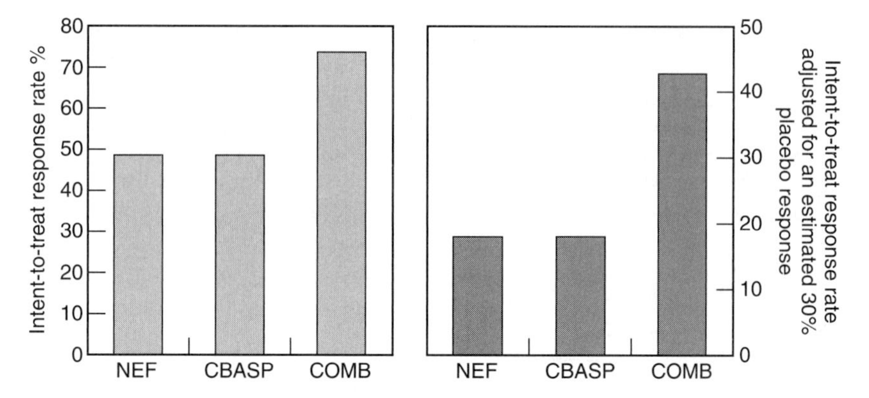

FIGURE 16.1 *Left Panel:* The apparent additive effects of CBASP and nefazodone were large (52% relative advantage) in one study of chronic depression but did not approach a full summation of the benefits of the monotherapies. *Right Panel:* Removal of the common response rate to placebo-expectancy factors (estimated here as a 30% response rate) reveals a fully additive and possibly synergistic effect for combined treatment (139% relative advantage). (Adapted from Keller et al., 2000)

is preferred, the assumption that dropouts would have the same high scores across multiple time points can grossly distort the variance structure of a longitudinal data set.

A second and more widely recognized factor is the failure to take into account the magnitude of the effects of common or nonspecific elements of helping relationships, which are sometimes minimized by the term *placebo (PBO) effects.* In randomized RCTs of antidepressant medications, for example, PBO effects consistently account for 50% to 75% of the response to pharmacotherapy (Khan, Warner, & Brown, 2000; Thase, 1999). There is every reason to believe that such nonspecific effects similarly dwarf the specific elements of the depression-focused therapies (Elkin et al., 1989; Jacobson et al., 1996).

The PBO effect actually has very little to do with the specific sham intervention utilized (Hróbjartssonh & Gøtzsche, 2001). Rather, the PBO effect encompasses spontaneous remission (in this case, the probability of improvement within a fixed time period without *any* intervention. The spontaneous remission rate may thus be viewed as a reflection of the prognostic status of a given research sample), reactivity to repeated measurement, and the beneficial effects of hope, expectation, and support derived from a helping, professional relationship (Thase, 1999). In one RCT, a measure of the strength of the helping alliance was as predictive of success in pharmacotherapy, either with imipramine *or* placebo, as it was with cognitive and interpersonal psychotherapies (Krupnick et al., 1996).

Appreciation of the limitations of ceiling effects and the magnitude of nonspecific effects opens new horizons for interpretation of existing studies of combined treatment. Drawing on the largest and most recent study of combined treatment of depression as an example, the left panel of Figure 16.1 illustrates the apparent "incomplete summation" observed by Keller et al. (2000). After taking into account the design considerations discussed above (see right panel), it appears that a fully additive effect or even, possibly, the first example of synergy was documented favoring combined treatment. This difference in interpretation shows that allowances have been made for approximately 30% of this study group who would have responded to a credible PBO-expectancy intervention (cf. Ravindran et al., 2000; Thase, Fava, Halbreich, Kocsis, & Koran, 1996), as well as a 10% risk of treatment resistance. Thus, the "active" components of pharmacotherapy and psychotherapy each delivered about a 20% response rate, so that a full addition of therapeutic effects should have resulted in a 70% intent-to-treat (ITT) response rate (i.e., 30% + 20% + 20%); a 72% ITT response rate actually was observed.

With respect to planning new studies, it will be vital to design studies that have the statistical power necessary to reliably detect the small-to-modest differences likely to be associated with specific therapies. If a 15% difference in response or remission rates is anticipated, then at least 250 patients will need to be enrolled into *each* arm of the study (Kraemer & Thiemann, 1987). If an even more modest 10% difference is anticipated

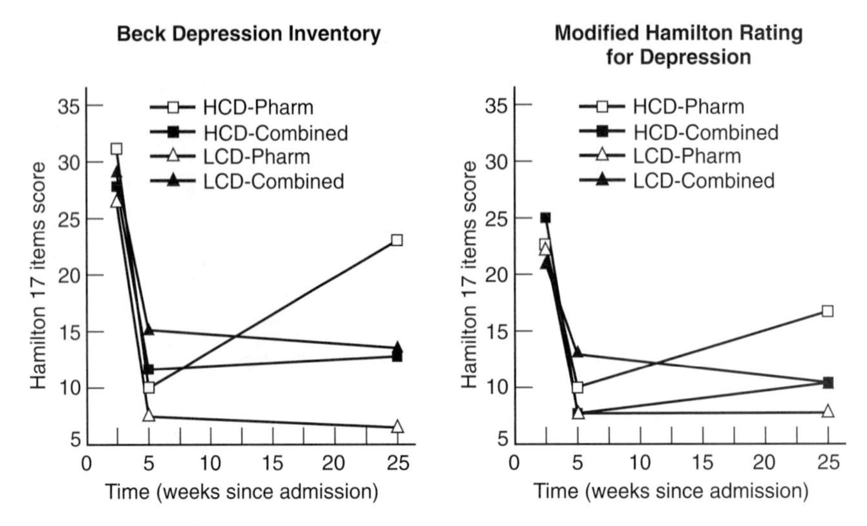

FIGURE 16.2 Miller, Norman, and Keitner (1990) found that the combination of CBT and antidepressant medication was particularly effective among patients with high levels of dysfunctional attitudes. (Reprinted from Miller et al., 1990, with permission.)

(i.e., partial summation), then at least 500 patients per group will be needed (see, for example, Thase, Entsuah, & Rudolph, 2001).

The assumption that psychotherapy and pharmacotherapy have dissimilar specific mechanisms of action provides another rationale for the combining treatments. This "hitting-two-targets-simultaneously" approach is particularly attractive in terms of a two-stage strategy: rapid alleviation of patients' suffering, followed by slower improvements in social functioning and vulnerability. There is evidence, for example, than an estimation of neuropsychological disturbance associated with depression is associated with the probability of response to cognitive (Thase, Simons, & Reynolds, 1996) and interpersonal (Thase, Buysse et al., 1997) psychotherapy, but not response to pharmacotherapy (Thase, Greenhouse et al., 1997). This pattern of disturbance was observed on polysomnographic recordings and included reduced eye movement (REM) sleep latency, poor sleep efficiency, and increased phasic REM activity (Thase, Kupfer et al., 1997). These disturbances are thought to reflect hyperarousal of limbic and brain stem circuits and show some degree of state dependence during acute episodes of depression (Thase, Fasiczka, Berman, Simons, & Reynolds, 1998). Direct suppression of REM sleep with the use of antidepressant medications is thought to represent the dampening of these overly active circuits. Elevated indices of the stress-sensitive hormone cortisol, another set of indicators of exaggerated or prolonged dysphoric arousal in the central nervous system, similarly have been shown to be associated with poorer response to psychotherapy (McKnight, Nelson-Gray, & Barnhill, 1992; Thase & Friedman, 1999; Thase et al., 1996), but not pharmacotherapy (Ribeiro, Tandon, Grunhaus, & Greden, 1993). Again, antidepressant medications appear to suppress such abnormal stress responses more directly (Barden, Reul, & Holsboer, 1995; Carroll, 1991; DeBellis, Gold, Geracioti, Listwak, & Kling, 1993).

An opposite pattern of additive effects has been observed when the outcome moderator is drawn from the psychosocial domain. Miller, Norman, and Keitner (1990) reported that a moderate additive effect for the combination of pharmacotherapy and cognitive and behavioral therapies was actually a sum of two distinctly different response profiles. In this study of relatively severe depression, four weeks of inpatient treatment was followed by six months of ambulatory therapy. Among the subgroup of patients with elevated scores on a measure of dysfunctional attitudes, a large effect favored the group receiving cognitive behavior therapy in addition to pharmacotherapy as compared with the group receiving only medication management. No such additive effect was observed among the subgroup with lower (more normal) dysfunctional attitude scores—both groups did equally well (see Figure 16.2; Miller, Norman, & Keitner, 1990).

Another potential benefit of combination treatments lies in the targeting of specific deficits that are associated with chronic mental disorders. In this case, the addition of a psychosocial intervention may not result in greater improvements in core psychotic symptoms but may aid in rehabilitation.

The addition of psychotherapy to pharmacotherapy may also be aimed at improving medication adherence and, possibly, may permit use of lower dosages of medication (e.g., Hersen, Bellack, Himmelhoch, & Thase, 1984). If true, the latter effect would translate into cost-savings and a better side-effects profile. Poor adherence with medication is known to be a major risk factor for nonresponse, inadequate response, and subsequent relapse. Nonadherence is attributable to a number of factors, including side effects, inadequate psychoeducation, avoidant coping with issues of stigma or shame associated with the illness, and strains in the physician-patient alliance. When the prescriber is also the psychotherapist, more time is available within sessions to address these matters. More commonly, a nonmedical psychotherapist is collaborating with a physician, who as often as not works in primary care rather than psychiatry. Given the brevity and infrequency of medication management in most community settings, as well as the low ratings for consumer satisfaction associated with this model of care (Seligman, 1995), the collaborating psychotherapist may contribute importantly by helping to address issues raised by pharmacotherapy. The key here is communication with the physician and effective management of the triadic relationship to ensure clear communications. The beneficial effect of a strong therapeutic alliance on adherence does not seem to be limited only to psychotropic medication. For example, provider-patient relationship has been shown to be a predictor of glycemic-control in diabetes (Sherbourne, Hays, Ordway, DiMatteo, & Kravitz, 1992).

Despite these potential additive benefits of combined treatment, quality of care, whether pharmacotherapy or psychotherapy, is a key determinant of efficacy. Indeed, there is evidence that poorly executed pharmacotherapy adds little additional benefit to skillfully applied psychotherapy (Blackburn, Bishop, Glen, Whalley, & Christie, 1981; Teasdale, Fennell, Hibbert, & Amies 1984). Similarly, poorly executed psychotherapy may add little, if any, to the benefits from competent supportive care (Elkin et al., 1989; Frank, Kupfer, Wagner, McEchran, & Cornes, 1991; Spanier, Frank, McEachran, Grochocinski, & Kupfer, 1996). Regrettably, it is not at all clear that psychotherapists and pharmacotherapists know when they are providing poor care. It would therefore seem reasonable to obtain a second opinion when treatment is not progressing (i.e., strategies that usually work have failed).

Practical Issues

There are two ways to provide combination treatments: (1) an integrated model, in which a psychiatrist provides both therapies, and (2) a split treatment model, in which a psychotherapist collaborates with the primary care physician or psychiatrist. As noted in the introduction, both economic concerns and the relative scarcity of psychiatrists necessitate that most healthcare systems offer the split-care model. There is paucity of evidence regarding the superiority of one approach over the other. Psychiatrists (and, in all likelihood, the prescribing psychologists in New Mexico) often believe that the integrated model is optimal. The argument can be made that a single provider would be more likely to impart clear, nonconflicting psychoeducation about the treatment plan than a pair of providers. Moreover, a single provider functionally precludes the possibility of splitting communication (Thase, 1996). The evidence that such splitting commonly disrupts care provided by a psychiatrist and psychotherapist is strictly anecdotal, however. Also, psychiatrists need to recognize that substantial proprietary or guild-based advantages are associated with the belief that integrated care is the best approach.

Ethical nonmedical therapists would not knowingly treat a person with schizophrenia or bipolar disorder without concomitant medical collaboration, and most already "share" the care of a number of patients treated with antidepressants, anxiolytics, mood stabilizers, or antipsychotics. The occasional problems that arise because of miscommunication are usually remedied by e-mail, a telephone call, or (very rarely) a conjoint session.

The split treatment model is also favored by most managed care organizations as a means to save costs because the hourly fee of a psychiatrist is generally higher than that of other providers. However, when compared to nonmedical therapists, psychiatrists tend to treat more severely ill patients for longer periods of time (Wells, Burnam, Rogers, Hays, & Camp, 1992) and, after controlling for case complexity, the presumed extra cost of care provided by psychiatrists actually disappears (Goldman et al., 1998). In one study of an insurance database, Dewan (1999) found that integrated care by a psychiatrist was somewhat less costly than split treatment. Certainly, psychiatrists who are skilled at psychotherapy should not be barred from providing this intervention. Studies using random assignment to integrated or split treatment are needed to resolve the issue of the cost-effectiveness of the two models.

Regardless of the ultimate outcome of such research, there simply will never be enough psychiatrists to treat all of the patients who might benefit from combined therapy. Service utilization data reveals that psychiatrists provide no more than 10% of psychotherapy and only about 35% of the pharmacotherapy provided to patients with mental disorders in the United States (Regier et al., 1988; Wells et al., 1992). A psychopharmacologically oriented physician working with a group of four nonmedical psychotherapists can effectively manage a caseload comparable to five or six psychiatrists. Even larger efficiencies could be achieved by greater use of group therapies when there are data to document efficacy that approaches the effectiveness of individual therapies (Depression Guidelines Panel, 1993).

To our knowledge, there has never been a RCT that compared the pharmacotherapy outcomes of psychiatrists with those of primary care physicians. There is some evidence regarding the superiority of pharmacotherapy as provided by a psychiatrist (Blackburn, Bishop, Glen, Whalley, & Christie, 1981), but this study did not employ random assignment to the two treatment settings. Specifically, Blackburn and colleagues found that antidepressant pharmacotherapy was virtually ineffective in the subset of patients treated by primary care physicians, whereas it was quite effective in the subset of patients treated by psychiatrists. The outcome of the treatment as usual (as provided by primary care physicians) was also poor in the studies by Teasdale et al. (1984) and Schulberg et al. (1996). However, in the latter study a second medication management condition that included advanced training and a carefully outlined pharmacotherapy protocol yielded outcomes comparable to those obtained in studies employing psychiatrists. On the basis of very limited data, it has been suggested that patients with complex, comorbid disorders, such as an episode of major depression superimposed on longstanding posttraumatic stress disorder or substance abuse, would be the most suitable candidates for combined treatment provided by a psychiatrist (Thase, 1997).

Pharmacotherapy: Issues of Approval and Regulation

The United States Food and Drug Administration (FDA) requires three phases of research before approving psychotropic medications for the treatment of specific mental disorders. Documentation of safety and estimation of daily dosage are the main aims during the first phase, which principally involves normal volunteers. The second and third phases are larger in scope and employ progressively more sophisticated research designs. All of these studies are conducted double-blind; the first goal is to establish the efficacy of the study medication in comparison with an inert placebo. A number of the later third-phase studies also include a standard antidepressant as an active comparator. Although some consider the use of placebo control as unethical once an active medication has shown efficacy (e.g., Michaels, 2000), the FDA continues to require that at least two positive placebo-controlled studies be completed before granting approval for general use of a psychotropic medication. To ensure that this goal is accomplished, the manufacturer of a promising new medication typically conducts 6 to 10 such studies prior to submission to the FDA.

The FDA does not require evidence that the new medication is more effective than already available medications. As a result, most psychotropic medications are approved before there is a substantial amount of data concerning relative efficacy. No FDA-approved medication approaches universal efficacy, and the effect sizes of antidepressant and antianxiety medications are usually only modestly (i.e., .2 to .4) superior to placebo. In fact, FDA-approved medications fail to show a statistically significant drug-placebo difference in approximately 50% of controlled clinical trials of antidepressants and anxiolytics (Thase, 1999). The proportion of failed trials of antimanic and antipsychotic medications has been smaller (on the order of 25% to 35%) because patients with these more severe and disabling disorders typically have a lower likelihood of responding to placebo-expectancy interventions.

The approval criteria are relatively stringent with respect to safety and are typically based on data from 1,000 to 2,000 patients treated with the novel compound. By excluding patients with severe medical conditions or those taking other medications, however, Phase 2 and Phase 3 clinical trials tend to overestimate the safety of novel medications. After FDA approval for general use, post-marketing or Phase 4 trials are ongoing surveillance efforts to gain further information on side-effects, toxicities, and tolerability. Definitive post-marketing studies of relative efficacy, with the statistical power to detect modest but clinically significant differences (i.e., 10% to 15%), are rarely, if ever, conducted (Thase, 2002).

Although FDA approval for new medications is sought and granted initially for a specific disorder, the therapeutic benefits of many psychotropics extend across diagnostic boundaries, prompting off-label use by physicians eager to have additional options for their harder-to-treat patients. For example, although most antipsychotic medications are FDA-approved only for treatment of schizophrenia, they are widely and successfully used (in combination with other medications) in the treatment of mania and psychotic depression. Other current examples of off-label use are prescription of anticonvulsant carbamazepine in mania, the antidepressant trazodone as a hypnotic, and the anticonvulsant lamotrigine for the treatment of bipolar depression. In addition to their well-known antidepressant effects, several members of the widely used class of medications known as selective serotonin reuptake inhibitors (SSRIs) have received approval for treatment of panic, obsessive compulsive, and generalized anxiety disorders, as well as premenstrual dysphoric disorder and bulimia. Off-label use sometimes precedes eventual FDA approval, as was the case with anticonvulsant divalproex and antipsychotic olanzapine as treatments of mania. Conversely, off-label use may continue for years or even decades without formal approval (e.g., tricyclic antidepressants for treatment of panic disorder). This is because a manufacturer's decision to seek FDA approval for a specific indication involves commitment of up to $40 million in research and development costs. The manufacturer must weigh such costs against the prospects for a return on the investment, a calculation that involves the prevalence of the disorder, the amount of competition, and the number of remaining years of patent life.

THE GENERAL APPROACH TO PHARMACOTHERAPY

The decision to prescribe a psychotropic medication to treat a specific condition is made after determining that the benefits of taking the medication outweigh any potential risks. Psychiatrists are more likely than other physicians to base the decision to prescribe psychotropic medication on the presence of one or more well-characterized mental disorders described in the DSM-IV (American Psychiatric Association, 1994). By contrast primary care physicians more commonly prescribe treatment based on a less precise diagnosis (i.e., depression, anxiety, or mixed anxiety-depressive disorder) or a readily recognizable constellation of symptoms (e.g., insomnia and crying spells or anxiety "attacks" and increasing avoidance). It is the physician's responsibility to ensure that a patient's newly diagnosed mental disorder is not a consequence of an occult or unrecognized general medical disorder or adverse response to a medication. Although such "organic" mental disorders are not common, a thorough medical evaluation typically yields relevant new information in 5% to 10% of cases (Depression Guidelines Panel, 1993). An even higher yield would be expected in assessments of the elderly or the medically ill.

Physicians vary widely in their approach to medical differential diagnosis. The minimum evaluation should include a medical history, ascertainment of current medications, and a review of physical systems (i.e., neurologic, digestive, respiratory, musculoskeletal, and urologic functioning). Pertinent positives on the review of systems and/or discrepant aspects of the history should then lead to a more detailed examination and, when appropriate, to judicious selection of laboratory tests. Most psychiatrists do not perform physical examinations but instead refer their patients to a primary care provider.

The pharmacotherapy of chronic diseases is generally palliative. No psychotropic medication is truly curative; similar dilemmas must be faced in treatment of hypertension, diabetes, and arthritis. The aim of pharmacotherapy is to suppress symptoms, achieve return to premorbid ("normal self") functioning, and prevent relapses or chronicity. Response to pharmacotherapy is assessed by monitoring the frequency and severity of signs and symptoms of the specific disorder. Most physicians do not use formal rating scales to gauge outcomes, relying instead on global impressions and patient reports of benefits.

For most mental disorders pharmacotherapy can be viewed as involving three distinct phases: acute, continuation, and maintenance phases. The acute phase of pharmacotherapy may last only a few weeks, or it may extend for months if a patient is not responsive to multiple interventions. Frequency of visits usually ranges from weekly to monthly, with the former preferred for patients with suicidal ideation or marked impairment. Inpatient care is now generally reserved for crises (e.g., suicidal ideations with intent), detoxification from illicit drugs or alcohol, or florid and incapacitating psychosis (e.g., catatonia or wandering, nude and incoherent, down a thoroughfare). Cost-containment efforts have reduced typical inpatient lengths of stay from weeks or even months to seven days or less. Yet each medication trial should take four to six weeks to evaluate, and, if there is partial response, an even longer course of therapy may be considered before switching to an alternative strategy. Therefore, the practice of pharmacotherapy, even during the acute phase of management, is predominantly an outpatient endeavor.

The acute phase ends with full remission or a marked global response to treatment. During the subsequent continuation phase, the goals are prevention of relapse and consolidation and generalization of improvements. The visit frequency decreases, and the focus of medical management shifts to issues such as adherence and longer-term side-effect concerns, such as weight gain or sexual dysfunction. For disorders at relatively low risk of relapse (e.g., a first lifetime episode of depression or panic disorder at age 35 in the context of a difficult divorce), pharmacotherapy may be tapered and discontinued after 6 to 12 months of sustained remission. For more chronic and/or highly recurrent disorders, the continuation phase is followed by an indefinite course of maintenance phase therapy. Maintenance phase visits are usually even less frequent: quarterly, twice yearly, or even annually. Although some pharmacotherapists view maintenance phase therapy as a lifelong proposition, there are some grounds for optimism that advances in neuroscience could lead to development of more curative treatments.

Although pharmacotherapy for most mental disorders generally follows a medical or disease-management model, there are a number of differences in the treatment of medical and psychiatric conditions. Foremost, well-trained psychiatrists generally view psychopathology from a broad biopsychosocial perspective. The relevance of social support, adversity, and coping styles is explicitly recognized, and the treatment plan should be individualized on the basis of a multiaxial case formulation. The various disorders are viewed as syndromes of multifactorial origins; it is assumed that conditions such as schizophrenia, bipolar disorder, or obsessive-compulsive disorder ultimately will be subdivisable into more discrete subtypes on the basis of a better understanding of genetic vulnerabilities and alterations in brain physiology related to protracted activation of stress responses or the effects of illness duration.

Psychiatric conditions also differ because they are associated with greater societal stigma than general medical disorders. Some people still associate mental illness with moral or character weakness, and, from this vantage point, psychotropic medication may be viewed as a "crutch" or a cop-out. Imagine a situation in which a presumably caring family member taunts the person with early onset diabetes about being "hooked" on twice daily insulin injections or a person with chronic renal failure being confronted with the view that dialysis would not be necessary if only more willpower could be exercised. Moreover, the cognitive deficits and impairment in judgment associated with the more severe psychiatric disorders affect treatment adherence and compromise informed consent. Together, these problems underscore the importance of making the family a vital part of the treatment team whenever possible. Finally, mental health treatment is still hampered by relatively limited access. There is still incomplete parity in insurance benefits between mental health treatment and general medical care, and despite the intended provisions of the community mental health act, high-quality and low-cost mental health care for the indigent and working poor remains more of an illusion than a reality.

Disorders That May Respond Better to Combined Treatment Than to Psychotherapy Alone

As reviewed elsewhere in this volume, a number of DSM-IV mental disorders can be effectively treated by psychotherapy alone. Controlled clinical studies show that 40% to 70% of patients with major depressive disorder (nonpsychotic nonmelancholic subtype), dysthymia, panic disorder, obsessive compulsive disorder, social phobia, generalized anxiety disorder, bulimia, and primary insomnia will achieve a satisfactory response with a procedurally specified form of psychotherapy alone. Such outcomes clearly outstrip the spontaneous remission rates observed in waiting list control groups and usually surpass the gains observed in pseudotherapy or attentional control conditions. Demonstration of similar effects outside of RCTs may be soon forthcoming. Regrettably, it is not clear that the evidence derived from these RCTs of well-specified therapies pertains to the most commonly provided eclectic psychotherapies. Concerns about the generalizability of the findings of studies of evidence-based psychotherapies are just as relevant to the practice of combined therapy.

The existence of effective pharmacotherapies for these conditions increases options for consumers and providers, and issues such as patient preference, availability, and cost must be considered in making treatment decisions.

Major Depressive Disorder

Two forms of psychotherapy, cognitive behavioral (CBT) and interpersonal (IPT) are the most widely studied in RCTs of combined strategies. We are not aware of any published, controlled study of a combination of psychodynamic psychotherapy, with pharmacotherapy employing a rigorous clinical trial design.

Meta-analyses of RCTs of depressed outpatients have shown relatively small additive effect sizes (Conte, Plutchik, Wild, & Karasu, 1986; Depression Guidelines Panel, 1993). As noted earlier, the modest nature of such additive effects should not be misinterpreted because each monotherapy also has a small advantage relative to a shared placebo expectancy intervention. Our group in Pittsburgh completed a large pooled analysis of nearly 600 depressed patients (Thase, Greenhouse et al. 1997). Among the patients with milder depressive episodes, the addition of pharmacotherapy to IPT improved remission rates by about 15% (when compared to IPT and CBT alone). For those in an acute, initial lifetime depressive episode, the additive value of pharmacotherapy may be even smaller (Thase, 1997). Combined treatment yielded a much more impressive additive effect among the patients with more severe, recurrent, depressive episodes (see Figure 16.3).

DiMascio et al. (1979) conducted the single, most influential study of combined treatment of major depressive disorder. They studied IPT and amitriptyline, singly and in combination, and they used a low-contact treatment on demand condition as the comparison group. They concluded that the two component monotherapies were superior to the control group and that the combination was superior to monotherapies on symptom measures. A further analysis of the data from the same study (Prusoff, Weissman, Klerman, & Rounsaville, 1980) suggested that the three active treatment groups were comparably effective for the subset of patients who met Research Diagnostic Criteria (Spitzer, Endicott, & Robins, 1978) for situational, nonendogenous major depressive disorder, whereas combined treatment was superior to monotherapies among the patients with nonsituational, endogenous depression (see Thase, 2000, for a graphical presentation of the possible interaction). Although the number of subjects involved in these post-hoc analyses was too small to exclude chance variation, the findings parallel exactly those of Thase, Greenhouse et al. (1997). It is therefore suggested that a severity/recurrence (i.e., endogenous) grouping can be used to select patients for whom combined treatment is likely to be more cost-effective than either pharmacotherapy or psychotherapy alone.

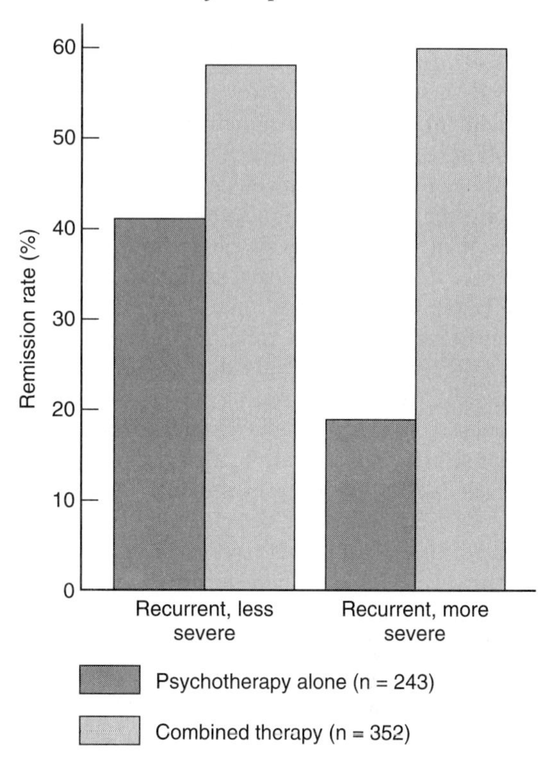

Figure 16.3 Recovery rates in patients in midlife (younger than 60 years) with recurrent major depression as a function of severity and treatment type. (Reprinted from Thase, Greenhouse et al., 1997, with permission)

Most of the first wave of individual studies employing cognitive or behavioral therapies have failed to show a statistically significant additive benefit of combined treatment approach (Beck, Hollon, Young, Bedrosian, & Budenz, 1985; Hersen, Bellack, Himmelhoch, & Thase, 1984; Hollon et al., 1992; Murphy, Simons, Wetzel, & Lustman, 1984). As reviewed previously, Blackburn et al.'s (1981) early trial appeared to be confounded by the poor performance of the pharmacotherapy alone condition in the primary care site. Inspection of published means certainly suggests a treatment *x* setting interaction, with a modest advantage for the combined condition treated in a specialty psychiatric clinic (also see Thase, 2000, for a fuller discussion).

These studies were designed and completed before the concepts of statistical power and design were widely appreciated. None of the these trials enrolled enough subjects to give adequate statistical power to detect even moderate additive effects (i.e., a 15% to 20% difference in remission rates). Moreover, that generation of research was plagued by the necessity of using tricyclic antidepressants (TCA), which have been shown to be less effective in the treatment of younger women with mild-to-moderate depression (Thase, Frank, Kornstein, & Yonkers, 2000). This is particularly true for depressed patients with reverse neurovegetative features (i.e., overeating or oversleeping), for whom TCAs may be ineffective (Stewart et al., 1998) or, at best, minimally effective (Quitkin et al., 1993).

Two relatively small studies of hospitalized depressed patients found evidence favoring combined strategy over medication management (Bowers, 1990; Miller, Norman, & Keitner, 1989). As discussed previously, Miller et al. (1990) observed a particularly large additive effect among the patients with high levels of dysfunctional attitudes. Patients with pessimistic and distorted patterns of thinking have been shown to be at high risk of chronicity and relapse and are often overrepresented among treatment resistant populations (Thase, 1996). Furthermore, patients with this pattern of thinking also tend to respond less favorably to CBT alone (Whisman, 1993). Although the data from controlled trials are sparse, it appears that the combination of CBT and pharmacotherapy may be especially useful for depressed patients following an acute psychiatric hospitalization.

There have been only two published RCTs of combined treatment in chronically depressed outpatients. Ravindran et al. (1999) found little evidence of an additive effect for group CBT and sertraline in a study of 97 outpatients with dysthymia. The group CBT intervention was no more effective than placebo, however, which calls into question the adequacy of this intervention. In a multicenter trial of over 650 patients with chronic forms of depression, Keller et al. (2000) compared the Cognitive Behavior Analysis System of Psychotherapy (CBASP, an individual therapy specifically developed for treatment of chronic depression; McCullough, 2000) and pharmacotherapy with nefazodone, both singly and in combination. The aims of the study did not justify inclusion of a placebo control group in the acute phase of the study, which limits the interpretability of the monotherapy group's outcomes. Nevertheless, Keller et al. found that the group receiving combined treatment had substantially better response and remission rates than both of the monotherapies, which had virtually identical outcomes (see Figure 16.1).

An earlier study of continuation therapy by Klerman, DiMascio, Weissman, Prusoff, and Paykel (1974) concluded that combined treatment was no more effective than pharmacotherapy alone in preventing relapses. There was a later-emerging trend suggesting that the patients who had received individual psychotherapy (a forerunner of IPT) and who had not relapsed obtained a significantly higher level of social adjustment. Moreover, this study does not fully represent the therapeutic potential of IPT because all of the patients had responded to amitriptyline before they began psychotherapy. (The specific criticism is that the study group was preselected for responsiveness to pharmacotherapy, not psychotherapy.)

Two more recent studies have evaluated the efficacy of combined treatment in the maintenance phase of recurrent depression. In both of these studies, all patients received combined treatment during the acute and continuation phase. In the first study (Frank et al., 1990), which involved 125 patients aged 19 to 65, continued monthly IPT sessions in combination with high-dose imipramine had no greater benefit than imipramine alone during a 36-month blinded maintenance phase. Monthly IPT sessions alone did provide some prophylaxis against recurrent depressive episodes when compared to a placebo condition (i.e., patients who were withdrawn from both pharmacotherapy and psychotherapy). The benefit of IPT alone was also significantly stronger when therapist-patient dyads were able to sustain focus on key interpersonal problems (Frank et al., 1990; Spanier, Frank, McEachran, Grochocinski, & Kupfer, 1996). Said another way, if IPT "devolved" into support and unfocused conversation it had no demonstrable prophylactic benefit.

In the second study, 107 elders (age 60 and above) who had stabilized during acute and continuation phases of treatment with notriptyline and IPT participated in the double-blind, placebo-controlled maintenance phase study (Reynolds et al., 1999). The findings of this study differed from the first (Frank et al., 1990) in several important ways. First, the group that remained on combination treatment was less likely to suffer a recurrence than either of the monotherapy conditions. Second, the efficacy of pharmacotherapy alone was less pronounced, especially among those aged 70 and older.

Another important line of research is to combine treatments in sequence, such as adding psychotherapy to treat the residual symptoms after incomplete remission or pharmacotherapy. Fava et al. (1994) demonstrated a significant additive effect when a three-month course of CBT was added to the treatment of patients who remitted incompletely in response to pharmacotherapy. In a followup report on this study, the group that received CBT had a significantly better chance of discontinuing medication without relapse (Fava, Grandi, Zielezny, Rafanelli, & Canestrari, 1996), as well as a sustained decrease in recurrence risk (Fava et al., 1998a). Paykel et al. (1999) partially replicated these findings in a larger multicenter study of incompletely remitted patients receiving continuation pharmacotherapy. The group that received CBT in addition to ongoing pharmacotherapy had about a 50% reduction in relapse risk. The protective effect of sequential CBT treatment in recurrent depression was also shown in another study by the Bologna group (Fava et al., 1998b). In this small but informative trial, 20 fully remitted patients with a history of highly recurrent depression received either a 14-session course of CBT or supportive medication management during the initial months of a planned withdrawal of antidepressant pharmacotherapy. Again, the sequenced addition of CBT significantly reduced the risk of recurrence over the following two years.

Thase, Buysse et al. (1997) reported on the opposite strategy—adding an antidepressant (either imipramine or fluoxetine) after nonresponse or incomplete remission with 8 to 16 weeks of individual IPT. A 76% remission rate was observed among 38 patients in this case series. Although interpretation of this study was constrained by the lack of a placebo control, it seems highly unlikely that such a high remission rate on pharmacotherapy could be attributed to nonspecific factors after two to four months of unsuccessful psychotherapy (see, e.g., Stewart, Mercier, Agosti, Guardino, & Quitkin, 1993). Frank et al. (1999) subsequently observed similar results in a second group of IPT nonresponders. Thus, it seems reasonable to add antidepressant pharmacotherapy if patients have not experienced substantial symptomatic progress after two months of psychotherapy.

PANIC DISORDER

A number of treatments including several forms of CBT, most antidepressants, and potent benzodiazepines have been found to be effective in treating panic disorder. Comparisons between different treatment modalities typically show parity, and consequently, treatment preference for CBT is driven by the side-effects of medications and an apparently greater durability of gains after treatment termination (American Psychiatric Association, 1998).

Benzodiazepines are a particularly rapid and effective acute treatment of panic disorder. However, liability for abuse and the potential for development of tolerance of therapeutic effects are drawbacks to longer-term benzodiazepine therapy. Sequenced therapy with CBT facilitates discontinuation of benzodiazepines without relapse (Otto et al., 1993; Spiegel, Bruce, Gregg, & Nuzzarello, 1994).

Studies of combination treatments using benzodiazepines as the pharmacotherapy have failed to show any meaningful additive effect (Spiegel & Bruce, 1997). For example, studies using moderate doses of lower potency benzodiazepines such as diazepam did not show additive effects (Hafner & Marks, 1976; Wardle, 1990), and concerns were raised that medication effects might compromise memory and learning during exposure therapy (Curran, 1986). A two-center (London and Toronto) randomized trial comparing alprazolam (versus placebo) and exposure therapy (versus relaxation) in 154 patients with panic disorder and agoraphobia suggested that addition of active alprazolam (up to 5 mg per day) did little to the beneficial effects of exposure therapy beyond the first four weeks of treatment

(Marks et al., 1993). Furthermore, combination treatment was superior to alprazolam alone, leading the authors to conclude that the behavior therapy had the stronger relative effect.

Even if there is an early advantage for combined treatment with benzodiazepines and CB, such gains have to be weighed against longer-term outcomes. For example, the relapse rate following discontinuation of alprazolam was approximately 50%, as compared with only 12% for patients who received therapy and placebo (Basoglu et al., 1994b). Further evaluation of these data revealed a link between relapse risk and a patient's attribution of improvement to the benzodiazepine (Basoglu, Marks, Kilic, Brewin, & Swinson, 1994a).

It is possible that addition of a benzodiazepine to CBT does not actually disrupt learning per se, but it may decrease confidence in the in vivo exposure strategies that are crucial in the success of treatment. If one chooses to add a benzodiazepine to CBT in an attempt to hasten symptomatic improvement, it seems important to help the patient recognize the relatively greater value of the psychotherapy and to discourage overvaluation of pharmacotherapy. Subsequently, the benzodiazepine should be tapered gradually while continuing with in vivo exposure or CBT strategies.

Most experts now favor antidepressants for combined treatment for panic disorder (American Psychiatric Association, 1998). In the largest study of combined treatment including antidepressant therapy comparisons, Barlow, Gorman, Shear, and Woods (2000) evaluated the outcomes of 312 outpatients with panic disorder. The study followed a 2 × 2 factorial design (placebo versus imipramine; CBT versus clinical management), and included a fifth cell, CBT alone, to ensure that placebo did not adversely affect therapy durability. Results were presented for the acute (three-month) and continuation (six-month) phases, as well as a six-month post-continuation followup. Both monotherapies were significantly effective in the intent-to-treat analyses, and placebo did not diminish the utility of CBT. The addition of CBT to imipramine therapy was significantly more effective than imipramine alone but no more effective than CBT plus placebo. The advantages of combined treatment dissipated after withdrawal of imipramine. Though most of these studies used tricyclic antidepressants, it appears virtually certain that results will generalize to the selective serotonin-reuptake inhibitors (SSRIs). Unlike benzodiazepines, antidepressants do not rapidly suppress somatic cues of arousal, and therefore do not undercut the value of exposure. Therefore, antidepressants can be used for longer periods of time (than benzodiazepines) in the treatment of panic disorder. Nevertheless, discontinuation of effective antidepressants is still associated with a risk of relapse, which may justify the use of sequential treatment strategies. In our view, CBT alone should be offered as a first-line treatment for most patients, reserving combination treatments for more severe, chronic, or disabling cases, as well as those with significant comorbid panic symptoms.

Obsessive Compulsive Disorder

Behavior therapy and selected antidepressants with strong serotonergic activity are the best established treatments for obsessive compulsive disorder (OCD). Controlled studies of behavior therapy and pharmacotherapy with either selective serotonin reuptake inhibitors or the TCA clomipramine have consistently failed to show better than 60% response rates in OCD. Moreover, some patients decline participation in exposure plus response prevention, the most reliable form of behavior therapy (Mavissakalian, 1995). There are parallel drawbacks to pharmacotherapy. For example, at the doses at which serotonergic antidepressants are effective in OCD, 10% to 15% of patients experience intolerable side effects (Griest, Jefferson, Kobak, Katzelnick, & Serlin, 1995). An even larger proportion of patients experience problematic longer term side-effects such as weight gain or sexual dysfunction. And, as was the case in studies of both depression and panic disorder, the benefits of maintenance phase pharmacotherapy dissipate rapidly when the medication is discontinued.

Several studies (Marks, Stern, Mawson, Cobb, & McDonald, 1980; Mawson, Marks, & Ramm, 1982; O'Connor, Todorov, Robillard, Borgeat, & Brault, 1999) of combined therapy of OCD have shown significant additive effects. However, van Balkom and colleagues (1998) did not observe an advantage in a smaller study comparing cognitive and behavioral therapies with and without concomitant fluvoxamine. Emerging data from several still ongoing, larger investigations will allow a better assessment of the magnitude of such additive effects. Drawing upon the research conducted with depressed patients, it seems likely that the best evidence of additive effects will come from studies of patients with more chronic, severe, or relapsing forms of OCD.

Other Anxiety Disorders

Other anxiety disorders such as social phobia, generalized anxiety disorder (GAD), and posttraumatic disorder can be effectively treated with focused forms of psychotherapy or pharmacotherapy. The best-studied forms of psychotherapies are, yet again, behavior therapy and CBT. Pharmacotherapies supported by literature include most types of antidepressants, buspirone (GAD only), benzodiazepine (GAD only), and β-blockers (social phobia only).

Few pivotal studies support the additive effects of combined treatment in these prevalent but less well-studied anxiety disorders (Beaudry, 1991; Mavissakalian, 1995). In the largest study published to date ($n = 387$) social phobia was more responsive to sertraline than placebo and, although a brief exposure intervention was not effective alone, it did enhance outcomes on a number of dependent measures (Blomhoff et al., 2001). The poorer longitudinal outcomes of patients suffering from more chronic and severe forms of these disorders make it logical to consider combined treatments.

Bulimia Nervosa and Other Eating Disorders

Although there is evidence that bulimia nervosa is responsive to a number of different treatments, including IPT (Fairburn et al., 1991), supportive-dynamic therapy (Freeman, Barry, Dunkeld-Turnbull, & Henderson, 1988), and antidepressant medication (Walsh & Devlin, 1995), many consider CBT to be the treatment of first choice. Notwithstanding some individual differences in treatment responsiveness, the results of several head-to-head comparisons have favored CBT over pharmacotherapy (Agras et al., 1992; Mitchell et al., 1990).

There have been three published RCTs of combined treatment of bulimia. Mitchell et al. (1990) found a more pronounced improvement on measures of depression and anxiety with a combination of imipramine and CBT than with CBT plus a placebo pill in a relatively large ($n = 171$) factorial (2 × 2) study. The combined group did not produce greater improvements in frequency of binge eating or vomiting, however, which could be the result of a ceiling effect imposed by the marked improvement observed in the CBT plus placebo group. Combined treatment also did better than pharmacotherapy alone on a number of outcome measures, even though patients in the monotherapy group received a higher average dose of medication (mean 267 mg per day versus 217 mg per day).

Walsh et al. (1997) enrolled 120 bulimic patients in a 16-week trial comparing five treatment cells. Four treatment cells received two types of psychotherapy, CBT and psychodynamic supportive therapy, in combination with either active pharmacotherapy or a placebo pill (in a 2 × 2 design). The fifth treatment cell received unblinded pharmacotherapy alone. The pharmacotherapy consisted of a two-stage intervention: up to 300 mg per day of desipramine (a noradrenergically active TCA), followed when necessary by up to 60 mg per day of the SSRI fluoxetine. At the end of the acute phase trial, CBT was more effective than supportive-dynamic psychotherapy, and active pharmacotherapy was superior to placebo. There was also evidence of an additive effect for the combination of CBT and active pharmacotherapy over medication alone. The combination of supportive-dynamic therapy and medication did not result in additive effects.

In the third trial of combined treatment, Agras et al. (1992) compared CBT plus desipramine with both monotherapies in a sample of 71 bulimic outpatients. The combined approach was initially more effective than CBT alone, but there were few significant differences by week 16. By contrast, combined treatment performed better than medication alone on most measures. Continued CBT sessions also had a protective role for prevention of relapse after discontinuation of medication. The study was probably weakened by the relatively low serum level of desipramine (a mean dose of 156.7 mg per day produced a mean serum level of only 131 mg/ml). Again, the study was not large enough to have adequate statistical power to detect anything other than a huge additive effect.

On the basis of these studies, it is concluded that CBT, either alone or in combination with pharmacotherapy, is superior to pharmacotherapy alone. Although the results of the several extant studies were far from conclusive, it does appear that a subset of patients gain extra benefit from the combined strategy. Further studies are needed to determine whether patients who gain more benefit from combined treatment can be identified at the time of initial treatment. Further research using multistage sequential treatment strategies is needed.

Substance Abuse Disorders

Methadone maintenance and naltrexone are approved for use in the treatment of opiate dependence. For treatment of alcoholism, naltrexone, disulfiram, and acamprosate are approved for suppression of cravings and relapse prevention, respectively. There are no pharmacotherapies approved for the treatment of either cocaine or marijuana dependence.

Several psychotherapies also have received support from clinical trials of substance-dependent patients. The addition of CBT or supportive-dynamic psychotherapy to methadone improved outcomes in one study of opiate-dependent patients (Woody et al., 1983). This additive effect was largely observed among the subgroup of patients with higher levels of anxiety or depressive symptoms (Woody, McLellan, & Luborsky, 1984). The combination of CBT and tricyclic desipramine similarly was found to have additive effects in the treatment of cocaine-dependent patients, with concomitant depressive symptoms (Carroll et al., 1994). Similarly, addition of disulfiram to a contingency-based behavioral intervention improved treatment outcome for alcohol abusers (Higgins et al., 1991). These types of studies provide promising leads for further development of cost-effective psychosocial treatments but do not necessarily imply that more is always better. For example, in a recent well-controlled study of more than 400 cocaine-dependent patients, the addition of CBT or supportive-dynamic therapy to a standard regimen of group drug counseling did not improve outcome (Crits-Christoph et al., 1999). Moreover, adding professional psychotherapy to group drug counseling was actually significantly less effective than adding sessions of individual drug counseling (Crits-Christoph et al., 1999).

Combining Treatments: Conditions That Should Not be Treated with Psychotherapy Alone

Patients with the most severe mental disorders, such as schizophrenia or mania, should not be treated with psychotherapy alone (Thase, 2000). This rigid position is taken because pharmacotherapy has established efficacy in these disorders, whereas there is virtually no evidence that psychotherapy alone is effective. To knowingly withhold pharmacotherapy from patients with these disorders thus could amount to malpractice. Exceptions may be made if a psychotic patient makes an informed decision to refuse pharmacotherapy, though most states provide for involuntary treatment of patients with severe mental disorders when it is clear that the patient's competence to make an informed choice is impaired by the illness. Guardianship procedures also may be a necessary option when lifesaving treatment is indicated. Some states also allow mental health advance directives, thus balancing principles of autonomy and beneficence.

Psychotherapy as an Adjunctive Therapy: Schizophrenia and Related Disorders

The principal adjunctive psychosocial interventions now used with people with schizophrenia include milieu therapy, CBT, behavior therapy aimed at improving social skill, and various types of family intervention. The scope of these interventions has been evaluated at different stages of treatment, including during acute hospitalization, immediately following discharge, and during long-term maintenance care.

The effectiveness of adjunctive inpatient psychosocial interventions for schizophrenia has been extensively evaluated (Lauriello, Bustillo, & Keith, 1999). Several early, large inpatient studies did show modest additive effects for insight-oriented psychotherapy in combination with antipsychotic medications (Grinspoon, Ewalt, & Shader, 1972; May, 1968). The extended length of hospitalizations in these studies (months), however, make the findings of these studies virtually irrelevant to current practice. Other studies conducted during the same era suggested that longer hospital stays did not add to the benefit of briefer hospitalizations (e.g., Caffey, Galbrecht, & Klett, 1971; Herz, Endicott, & Spitzer, 1977). A subsequent meta-analysis of 26 controlled studies revealed a lack of benefit of psychosocial interventions during shorter, acute care hospitalization (Lauriello, Bustillo, & Keith, 1999).

The trend of deinstitutionalization of schizophrenia throughout the 1960s and 1970s led to greater focus on the impact of outpatient psychosocial interventions. The goals of intervention in this generation of studies were improved medication adherence, reduction in relapse and rehospitalization rates, improved social function, and better tolerance of psychosocial stressors. It is important to note that until recently, psychosocial interventions did *not* aim to directly reduce the positive symptoms of schizophrenia (i.e., delusions and hallucinations). Perhaps the most noteworthy modifiable risk factor was recognition that residing with significant others who manifested a high level of expressed emotion greatly increased the risk of psychotic relapse and rehospitalization (Brown, Birley, & Wing, 1972; Butzlaff & Hooley, 1998; Vaughn & Leff, 1976).

A number of outpatient studies of specific psychosocial interventions have been completed. In such studies, supportive individual interventions such as major role training (Schooler et al., 1980), occupational therapy (Liberman et al., 1998), and personal therapy (Hogarty et al., 1997) have yielded modest additive effects of questionable generalizability. Interestingly, Hogarty et al. (1997) found that personal therapy had a modest beneficial effect for patients living with families but actually increased the risk of relapse for those living alone. The reasons for this unexpected finding remain unclear. One possibility is that schizophrenic patients who choose to live alone have done so because they are less tolerant of interpersonal interaction. The well-meaning attempts of the therapist thus may be perceived as aversive or threatening. In contrast, those who continue to live with families are better able to maintain significant social relations and, hence, may be better able to engage in therapy.

Of the various psychosocial interventions, family-focused treatments have shown a more consistent and substantial additive effect in reducing risk of relapse and improving social function (Falloon et al., 1985; Penn & Mueser, 1996; Randolph et al., 1994). In the study by Randolph and colleagues, for example, addition of a 25-session behavior family management program reduced the risk of relapse from 55% to 14%. Curiously, the added benefits of the family intervention were not limited to the subset with high expressed emotion, and were extended to patients across other living arrangements. One recent study suggests that benefit of family involvement can be achieved by a relatively low-intensity, once a month group intervention (Schooler et al., 1997).

Another line of research effort has focused on social skills training. In controlled studies, social skills training scored over supportive therapy control conditions on measures of residual symptoms, social adjustment, and in vivo behavioral tests (Hogarty et al., 1986; Liberman et al., 1998; Marder et al., 1996). Moreover, in the study by Hogarty and colleagues, an additive effect was evident between individual skills training and psychoeducational family therapy. In a recent report, the beneficial effects of social skills training were sustained across a two-year followup (Liberman et al., 1998). Overall, the addition of social skills training to medication management seems to reduce the risk of re-hospitalization (Benton & Schroeder, 1990), although results were not consistent across various studies.

A modified version of Beck's CBT (1976) has also attracted the attention of researchers as an adjunctive treatment for schizophrenic patients who are already stabilized on medication. Specifically, this version of CBT is geared toward helping patients learn to use the techniques of rational discourse to challenge and modify psychotic experiences (Perris, 1989). This approach showed considerable promise in two British studies (Drury, Birchwood, Cochrane, & MacMillan, 1996; Kuipers et al., 1997). In both trials, the addition of weekly individual sessions of CBT to antipsychotic treatment regimen improved symptomatic outcomes. Moreover, further analysis of the data obtained from one trial revealed that improvement following CBT was associated positively with the strength of delusions prior to treatment. This was striking because the severity of psychotic symptoms typically implies poorer response to a wide range of interventions for schizophrenia. Replication studies are underway in both the United Kingdom and the United States.

Most psychosocial interventions have not shown impressive results in the treatment of chronically ill, institutionalized patients (Lauriello, Bustillo, & Keith, 1999). In perhaps the most intensive study of such patients, a systematic program based on contingency management principles resulted in improvement on a number of symptomatic and functional measures (Paul & Lentz, 1977; Paul, Tobias, & Holly, 1972). Furthermore, many patients in the program were able to decrease doses and even discontinue antipsychotic medication. Although it is possible that many, if not most, of these patients were not responsive to the antipsychotic medication that was withdrawn (and hence lost no benefit when the medication was stopped) (Schooler, 1978), their participation in an intensive psychosocial program certainly facilitated the withdrawal of medication. Intensive, contingency-based interventions thus could prevent unnecessary prolonged exposure to antipsychotic medication, and hence lower the risk of tardive dyskinesia, a potentially irreversible and disabling neurological condition. Unfortunately, less costly alternatives to the extensive (and expensive) program developed by Paul and Lentz (1977) have not been evaluated in the modern era.

Recently, Rosenheck et al. (1998) conducted a study of treatment utilization in chronically ill schizophrenics. Their study of treatment-resistant, institutionalized veterans compared 122 patients treated with novel antipsychotic clozapine with 169 patients treated with conventional antipsychotics. Patients receiving clozapine were more likely to participate in supplemental psychosocial therapies. Furthermore, patients participating in those therapies had better outcomes on symptomatic and measures of quality of life. Thus, clozapine treatment facilitated greater involvement in available psychosocial intervention, which in turn, further improved outcome. Although clozapine has a proven therapeutic superiority over conventional antipsychotics, higher cost and greater side-effects (including a potentially fatal bone marrow dysfunction, agranulocytosis) limit its use to patients who have failed other antipsychotic medications. It would be interesting to see if the results of this study could be replicated using other novel antipsychotics (e.g. risperidone, olanzapine, etc.) in lieu of clozapine.

There is enough evidence to conclude that a range of individual and family-focused psychotherapeutic interventions have definite beneficial effects when provided in combination with antipsychotic medications. Recent evidence in support of CBT makes it a promising option for improving the course of schizophrenia.

BIPOLAR DEPRESSION

When compared to schizophrenia, bipolar disorder has received much less attention with respect to studies of combined therapy. This is perhaps because the therapeutic benefits of lithium salts were overvalued until the late 1980s and early 1990s (Sachs & Thase, 2000). Today it is recognized that, though not as disabling as schizophrenia, bipolar disorder is more often than not a recurrent and life-disrupting, severe mental illness with profound associated morbidity and increased mortality (Angst, Sellaro, & Merikangas, 2000). Moreover, evidence about the pathogenic effects of stressful life events (Johnson & Roberts, 1995), high levels of expressed emotion (Butzlaff & Hooley, 1998), marital discord (Miklowitz, 1998), and social support (Johnson, Winett, Meyer, Greenhouse, & Miller, 1999) provide a compelling case for study of the impact of various modalities of psychosocial interventions that can also be adapted to improve knowledge about, and enhance adherence to, pharmacotherapy (Cochran, 1984).

At present, the results of three large studies of psychotherapy added to pharmacotherapy have been published, and additional studies are underway. In the first such report, Perry, Tarrier, Morriss, McCarthy, and Limb (1999) evaluated a brief individual psychoeducation intervention (average duration: seven sessions). The intervention provided information about the disorder and its treatment and helped patients to identify early warning signs of impending relapse and to develop relapse prevention plans. When compared to a treatment as usual condition, patients who received the additional psychoeducational sessions had a significant reduction in manic relapses.

The second study (Miklowitz et al., 2000) evaluated a longer-term model for family-focused therapy (FFT). Participants were recently hospitalized for treatment of an acute episode of mania (n = 51), depression (n = 15), or a mixed state (n = 35) and were assigned randomly to receive pharmacotherapy and either clinical management (n = 70) or 21 sessions of FFT across a nine-month duration. A preliminary study of this method involving nine patients had yielded promising results in relation to a historical control group (i.e., 1 relapse [11%] versus 14 relapses [61%] among 23 controls). Results of the prospective study confirmed the benefit of FFT (n = 31) over the comparison group (n = 70) across the first year, both in terms of fewer depressive relapses and lower levels of depressive symptoms. Of note, these effects were not mediated by improved medication adherence or reduced levels of expressed emotion (both of which contributed to outcome but are independent of treatment assignment). The advantage of FFT was, however, most pronounced among patients living in high expressed emotion households, particularly if they had not fully recovered from the index episode. Perhaps in the context of the sample's good overall medication adherence, FFT did not reduce the risk of manic relapse.

The third study examined a modified form of IPT, adapted to include lifestyle management strategies intended to help patients develop more stable social rhythms (Interpersonal Social Rhythms Therapy or IPSRT; Frank, Swartz, & Kupfer, 2000). This study used a 2×2 sequential design, with one-half of the acute ill patients initially receiving IPSRT for acute phase management (the remainder received clinical management). All patients received appropriate pharmacotherapy for their index episodes following Expert Consensus Guidelines (American Psychiatric Association, 1993). During the maintenance phase of the study, one-half of the remitted patients in each group continued to receive the same treatment strategy, whereas one-half were switched (i.e., from IPSRT to clinical management or vice versa).

The principal findings of the trial include: (1) IPSRT did indeed significantly enhance patient's lifestyle regularity (Frank et al., 1997), (2) IPSRT did not improve acute phase treatment outcomes or speed time to remission (Cole et al., 2002; Hlastala et al., 1997); (3) discontinuation of acute phase IPSRT led to an increase in relapse risk, whereas the addition of maintenance IPSRT did not lower relapse risk (Frank et al., 1999); and (4) patients receiving maintenance IPSRT experienced a significant, later-emerging reduction in depressive symptoms and an increase in "well" or euthymic days (Frank et al., in press).

Individual and group cognitive therapy is also receiving increasing attention as an adjunctive treatment for bipolar disorder (e.g., Basco & Rush, 1995; Scott, 1996). Although the results of definitive studies have not yet been published, illustrative case series and pilot studies have suggested antidepressant effects (Zaretsky, Segal, & Gemar, 1999) and lower relapse risk (Fava, Bartolucci, Rafanelli, & Mangelli, 2001; Lam et al., 2000; Palmer, Williams, & Adams, 1995).

In aggregate, the results of these initial larger trials provide consistent support for the addition of focused psychosocial treatment for patients receiving pharmacotherapy for bipolar disorder. Family- and interpersonal-oriented interventions appear to help protect against depression, both in terms of syndromal and subsyndromal difficulties. By contrast, psychoeducation and relapse prevention training may help reduce risk of manic relapse (as compared to a low-intensity, usual care program). It may be that the "control" conditions of Miklowitz et al. (2000) and Frank et al. (in press) provided sufficient therapeutic support and psychoeducation to match the outcomes of the experimental group of Perry et al. (1999).

Summary and Conclusions

There is now ample evidence that focused psychosocial interventions have significant benefit when added to pharmacotherapy of patients with a number of persistent and severe mental disorders. The conditions for which a combined effect is best established include schizophrenia; severe, recurrent, and chronic major depressive disorder; obsessive-compulsive disorder; and (most recently) bipolar affective disorder. Additive effects also have been observed in some studies of bulimia and panic disorder, although the results are less conclusive. The added benefits of psychotherapy are partly disorder-specific (e.g., social skills training for schizophrenia) and partly domain-focused (e.g., reduction of expressed emotion in a household or improved medication adherence). It remains to be seen if there are also therapy-specific outcomes.

As previously noted (Thase, 2000), there is no evidence that psychotherapy–pharmacotherapy combinations should be considered a routine standard of care for less pervasive or milder depressive and anxiety disorders, that is, the most prevalent conditions for which people currently seek treatment. We believe that the lack of a definite additive effect justifies selection of the monotherapies first, based on availability and patient preference, with the alternative strategy considered in sequence or in combination for those who are less responsive to treatment.

Several areas remain fertile ground for future research. At one extreme, determining whether there are *any* relative indications for combined treatment provided by a single provider is an important topic that (despite much opinion and speculation) has never been properly studied. We would predict that patients with severe Axis II pathology may gain the most benefit from a single provider, largely because we believe that people who had longstanding problems in interpersonal relations may have the hardest time negotiating and shifting alliances with two mental healthcare givers.

At the other end of the pharmacotherapy spectrum, the effectiveness of primary care physicians as prescribers is worrisome, mainly from the standpoint of low ratings of patient satisfaction (Seligman, 1995) and poorer outcomes in clinical trials (e.g., Blackburn, Bishop, Glen, Whalley, & Christie, 1981; Schulberg et al., 1996; Teasdale, Fennell, Hibbert, & Amies, 1984). Because there are too few psychiatrists to provide all the pharmacotherapy for mental disorders, improving the collaborative care provided by psychotherapist-generalist teams will continue to be a public health priority.

Finally, evidence of additive efficacy conveys the need for a new generation of research that evaluates the translation and dissemination of findings from specialty research clinics to everyday practice settings. Treatments that convey benefit only when provided by hand-picked, highly skilled expert therapists offer little value to patients treated in busy urban clinics or community mental health centers. Much work remains to be done.

References

Agras, W. S., Rossiter, E. M., Arnow, B., Schneider, J. A., Telch, C. F., Raeburn, S. D., Bruce, B., Perl, M., & Koran, L. M. (1992). Pharmacologic and cognitive-behavioral treatment for bulimia nervosa: A controlled comparison. *American Journal of Psychiatry, 149*, 82–87.

American Psychiatric Association. (1993). Practice guidelines for major depressive disorder in adults. *American Journal of Psychiatry, 150* (Suppl. 4), 1–26.

American Psychiatric Association. (1994). *Diagnostic and statistical manual of mental disorders*, Washington, DC: American Psychiatric Press.

American Psychiatric Association. (1997). Practice guidelines for the treatment of patients with schizophrenia. *American Journal of Psychiatry, 154* (Suppl. 4), 1–63.

American Psychiatric Association. (1998). Practice guidelines for the treatment of patients with panic disorder. *American Journal of Psychiatry, 155* (Suppl. 5), 1–34.

Angst, J., Sellaro, R., & Merikangas, K. R. (2000). Depressive spectrum diagnoses. *Comprehensive Psychiatry, 41*, 39–47.

Ballenger, J. C., Davidson, J.R.T., Lecrubier, Y., Nutt, D. J., Baldwin, D. S., Den Boer, J. A., Kasper, S., & Shear, M. K. (1998). Consensus statement on panic disorder from the International Consensus Group on Depression and Anxiety. *Journal of Clinical Psychiatry, 59* (Suppl. 8), 47–54.

Barden, N., Reul, J.M.H.M., & Holsboer, F. (1995). Do antidepressants stabilize mood through actions on the hypothalamic-pituitary-adrenocortical system? *Trends in Neuroscience, 18*, 6–11.

Barlow, D. H., Gorman, J. M., Shear, M. K., & Woods, S. W. (2000). Cognitive-behavioral therapy, imipramine, or their combination for panic disorder. A randomized controlled trial. *JAMA, 283*, 2529–2536.

Basco, M. R., & Rush, A. J. (1995). Compliance of pharmacotherapy in mood disorders. *Psychiatric Annals, 25*, 269–270/276–279.

Basoglu, M., Marks, I. M., Kilic, C., Brewin, C. R., & Swinson, R. P. (1994a). Alprazolam and exposure for panic disorder with agoraphobia attribution of improvement of medication predicts subsequent relapse. *British Journal of Psychiatry, 164*, 652–659.

Basoglu, M., Marks, I. M., Swinson, R. P., Noshirvani, H., O'Sullivan, G., & Kuch, K. (1994b). Pretreatment predictors of treatment outcome in panic disorder and agoraphobia treated with alprazolam and exposure. *Journal of Affective Disorders, 30*, 123–132.

Beaudry, P. (1991). Generalized anxiety disorder. In B. D. Beitman, B. D., & Klerman, G. L. (Eds.), *Integrating pharmacotherapy and psychotherapy* (pp. 211–230). Washington, DC: American Psychiatric Press.

Beck, A. T. (1976). *Cognitive therapy and the emotional disorders.* New York: International Universities Press.

Beck, A. T., Hollon, S. D., Young, J. F., Bedrosian, R. C., & Budenz, D. (1985). Treatment of depression with cognitive therapy and amitriptyline. *Archives of General Psychiatry, 42*, 142–148.

Beck, A. T., Ward, C. H., Mendelson, M., Mack, J., & Erbaugh, J. (1961). An inventory for measuring depression. *Archives of General Psychiatry, 4*, 561–571.

Benton, M. K., & Schroeder, H. E. (1990). Social skills training with schizophrenics: A meta-analytic evaluation. *Journal of Consulting and Clinical Psychology, 58*, 741–747.

Blackburn, I. M., Bishop, S., Glen, A.I.M., Whalley, L. J., & Christie, J. E. (1981). The efficacy of cognitive therapy in depression: A treatment trial using cognitive therapy and pharmacotherapy, each alone and in combination. *British Journal of Psychiatry, 139*, 181–189.

Blomhoff, S., Haug, Hellström, K., Holme, I., Humble, M., Madsbu, H. P., & Wold, J. E. (2001). Randomised controlled general practice trial of sertraline, exposure therapy and combined treatment in generalized social phobia. *British Journal of Psychiatry, 179*, 23–30.

Bowers, W. A. (1990). Treatment of depressed inpatients cognitive therapy plus medication, relaxation plus medication, and medication alone. *British Journal of Psychiatry, 156*, 73–78.

Brown, G. W., Birley, J.L.T., & Wing, J. K. (1972). Influence of family life on the course of schizophrenic disorders: A replication. *British Journal of Psychiatry, 121*, 241–258.

Butzlaff, R. L., & Hooley, J. M. (1998). Expressed emotion and psychiatric relapse: A meta-analysis. *Archives of General Psychiatry, 55*, 547–552.

Caffey, E. M. Jr., Galbrecht, C. R., & Klett, C. J. (1971). Brief hospitalization and aftercare in the treatment of schizophrenia. *Archives of General Psychiatry, 24*, 81–86.

Carroll, B. J. (1991). Psychopathology and neurobiology of manic-depressive disorders. In B. J. Carroll & J. E. Barrett (Eds.), *Psychopathology and the brain* (pp. 265–285). New York: Raven Press.

Carroll, K. M., Rounsaville, B. J., Gordon, L. T., Nich, C., Jatlow, P., Bisighini, R. M., & Gawin, R. H. (1994). Psychotherapy and pharmacotherapy for ambulatory cocaine abusers. *Archives of General Psychiatry, 51,* 177–187.

Cochran, S. D. (1984). Preventing medical noncompliance in the outpatient treatment of bipolar affective disorders. *Journal of Consulting and Clinical Psychology, 52,* 873–878.

Cole, D. P., Thase, M. E., Mallinger, A. G., Soares, J. C., Luther, J. F., Kupfer, D. J., & Frank, E. (2002). Slower treatment response in bipolar depression predicted by lower pretreatment thyroid function. *American Journal of Psychiatry, 159,* 116–121.

Conte, H. R., Plutchik, R., Wild, K. V., & Karasu, T. B. (1986). Combined psychotherapy and pharmacotherapy for depression: A systematic analysis of the evidence. *Archives of General Psychiatry, 43,* 471–479.

Crits-Christoph, P., Siqueland, L., Blaine, J., Frank, A., Luborsky, L., Onken, L., Muenz, L., Thase, M. E., Weiss, R. D., Gastfriend, D. R., Woody, G., Barber, J. P., Butler, S. F., Daley, D., Salloum, I., Bishop, S., Najavits, L. M., Lis, J., Mercer, D., Griffin, M. L., Moras, K., & Beck, A. T. (1999). Psychosocial treatments for cocaine dependence: Results of the National Institute on Drug Abuse collaborative cocaine treatment study. *Archives of General Psychiatry, 56,* 493–502.

Curran, H. V. (1986). Tranquillizing memories: A review of the effects of benzodiazepines on human memory. *Biological Psychology, 23,* 179–213.

DeBellis, M. D., Gold, P. W., Geracioti, T. D., Listwak, S. J., & Kling, M. A. (1993). Association of fluoxetine treatment with reductions in CSF concentrations of corticotropin-releasing hormone and arginine vasopressin in patients with major depression. *American Journal of Psychiatry, 150,* 656–657.

Depression Guidelines Panel. (1993). Clinical practice guideline number 5. *Depression in primary care, vol 2. Treatment of major depression* (AHCPR Publication No. 93-0551). Rockville, MD: U.S. Department of Health and Human Services Agency for Health Care Policy and Research.

Dewan, M. (1999). Are psychiatrists cost-effective? An analysis of integrated versus split treatment. *American Journal of Psychiatry, 156,* 324–326.

DiMascio, A., Weissman, M. M., Prusoff, B. A., Neu, C., Zwiling, M., & Klerman, G. L. (1979). Differential symptom reduction by drugs and psychotherapy in acute depression. *Archives of General Psychiatry, 36,* 1450–1456.

Drury, V., Birchwood, M., Cochrane, R., & MacMillan, F. (1996). Cognitive therapy and recovery from acute psychosis: A controlled trial. I. Impact on psychotic symptoms. *British Journal of Psychiatry, 169,* 593–601.

Elkin, I., Shea, M. T., Watkins, J. T., Imber, S. D., Sotsky, S. M., Collins, J. F., Glass, D. R., Pilkonis, P. A., Leber, W. R., Docherty, J. P., Fiester, S. J., & Parloff, M. B. (1989). National Institute of Mental Health Treatment of Depression Collaborative Research Program: General effectiveness and treatments. *Archives of General Psychiatry, 46,* 971–982.

Fairburn, C. G., Jones, R., Peveler, R. C., Carr, S. J., Solomon, R. A., O'Connor, M. E., Burton, J., & Hope, R. A. (1991). Three psychological treatments for bulimia nervosa. A comparative trial. *Archives of General Psychiatry, 48,* 463–469.

Falloon, I. R., Boy, J. L., McGill, C. W., Williamson, M., Razani, J., Moss, H. B., Gilderman, A. M., & Simpson, G. M. (1985). Family management in the prevention of morbidity of schizophrenia: clinical outcome of a two-year longitudinal study. *Archives of General Psychiatry, 42,* 887–896.

Fava, G. A., Bartolucci, G., Rafanelli, C., & Mangelli, L. (2001). Cognitive-behavioral management of patients with bipolar disorder who relapsed while on lithium prophylaxis. *Journal of Clinical Psychiatry, 62,* 556–559.

Fava, G. A., Grandi, S., Zielezny, M., Canestrari, R., & Morphy, M. A. (1994). Cognitive behavioral treatment of residual symptoms in primary major depressive disorder. *American Journal of Psychiatry, 151,* 1295–1299.

Fava, G. A., Grandi, S., Zielezny, M., Rafanelli, C., & Canestrari, R. (1996). Four-year outcome for cognitive behavioral treatment of residual symptoms in major depression. *American Journal of Psychiatry, 153,* 945–947.

Fava, G. A., Rafanelli, C., Grandi, S., Canestrari, R., and Morphy, M. A. (1998a). Six-year outcome for cognitive behavioral treatment of residual symptoms in major depression. *American Journal of Psychiatry, 155,* 1443–1445.

Fava, G. A., Rafanelli, C., Grandi, S., Conti, S., & Belluardo, P. (1998b). Prevention of recurrent depression with cognitive behavioral therapy. Preliminary findings. *Archives of General Psychiatry, 55,* 816–820.

Frank, E., Hlastala, S., Ritenour, A., Houck, P., Tu, X. M., Monk, T. H., Mallinger, A. G., & Kupfer, D. J. (1997). Inducing lifestyle regularity in recovering bipolar patients: results from the maintenance therapies in bipolar disorder protocol. *Biological Psychiatry, 41,* 1165–1173.

Frank, E., Kupfer, D. J., Gibbons, R., Houck, P., Kostelnik, B., Mallinger, A. G., Swartz, H. A., & Thase, M. E. (in press). Interpersonal and social rhythm therapy prevents depressive symptomatology in patients with bipolar I disorder. *Archives of General Psychiatry.*

Frank, E., Kupfer, D. J., Perel, J. M., Cornes, C., Jarrett, D. B., Mallinger, A. G., Thase, M. E., McEachran, A. B., & Grochocinski, V. J. (1990).

Three-year outcomes for maintenance therapies in recurrent depression. *Archives of General Psychiatry, 47,* 1093–1099.

Frank, E., Kupfer, D. J., Wagner, E. F., McEachran, A. B., & Cornes, C. (1991). Efficacy of interpersonal psychotherapy as a maintenance treatment of recurrent depression. Contributing factors. *Archives of General Psychiatry, 48,* 1053–1059.

Frank, E., Swartz, H. A., & Kupfer, D. J. (2000). Interpersonal and social rhythm therapy: Managing the chaos of bipolar disorder. *Biological Psychiatry, 48,* 593–604.

Frank, E., Swartz, H. A., Mallinger, A. G., Thase, M. E., Weaver, E. V., & Kupfer, D. J. (1999). Adjunctive psychotherapy for bipolar disorder: Effects of changing treatment modality. *Journal of Abnormal Psychology, 108,* 579–587.

Freeman, C.P.L., Barry, F., Dunkeld-Turnbull, J., & Henderson, A. (1988). Controlled trial of psychotherapy for bulimia nervosa. *British Medical Journal, 296,* 521–525.

Goldman, W., McCulloch, J., Cuffel, B., Zarin, D. A., Suarez, & Burns, B. J. (1998). Outpatient utilization patterns of integrated and split psychotherapy and pharmacotherapy for depression. *Psychiatric Services, 49,* 477–482.

Gregory, R. J., & Jindal, R. D. (2001). Ethical dilemmas in prescribing antidepressants. *Archives of General Psychiatry, 58,* 1085–1086.

Griest, J. H., Jefferson, J. W., Kobak, K. A., Katzelnick, D. J., & Serlin, R. C. (1995). Efficacy and tolerability of serotonin transport inhibitors in obsessive-compulsive disorder. *Archives of General Psychiatry, 52,* 53–60.

Grinspoon, L., Ewalt, J. R., & Shader, R. I. (1972). *Schizophrenia: Pharmacotherapy and psychotherapy.* Baltimore, MD: Williams & Wilkins.

Hafner, J., & Marks, I. (1976). Exposure in vivo of agoraphobics: contributions of diazepam, group exposure, and anxiety evocation. *Psychological Medicine, 6,* 71–88.

Hamilton, M. (1960). A rating scale for depression. *Journal of Neurology, Neurosurgery, and Psychiatry, 23,* 56–62.

Hersen, M., Bellack, A. S., Himmelhoch, J. M., & Thase, M. E. (1984). Effects of social skill training, amitriptyline, and psychotherapy in unipolar depressed women. *The Behavior Therapist, 15,* 21–40.

Herz, M. I., Endicott, J., & Spitzer, R. L. (1977). Brief hospitalizations: A two-year follow-up. *American Journal of Psychiatry, 134,* 502–507.

Higgins, S. T., Delaney, D. D., Budney, A. J., Bickel, W. J., Hughes, J. R., Foerg, F., & Fenwick, J. W. (1991). A behavior approach to achieving initial cocaine abstinence. *American Journal of Psychiatry, 148,* 1218–1224.

Hlastala, S. A., Frank, E., Mallinger, A. G., Thase, M. E., Ritenour, A. M., & Kupfer, D. J. (1997). Bipolar depression: an underestimated treatment challenge. *Depression and Anxiety, 5,* 73–83.

Hogarty, G. E., Anderson, C. M., Reiss, D. J., Kornblith, S. J., Greenwald, D. P., Javna, C. D., Madonia, M. J., & Environmental/Personal Indicators in the Course of Schizophrenia Research Group. (1986). Family psychoeducation, social skills training, and maintenance chemotherapy in the aftercare treatment of schizophrenia. *Archives of General Psychiatry, 43,* 633–642.

Hogarty, G. E., Greenwald, D., Ulrich, R. F., Kornblith, S. J., DiBarry, A. L., Cooley, S., Carter, M., & Flesher, S. (1997). Three-year trials of personal therapy among schizophrenic patients living with or independent of family, II: Effects on adjustment of patients. *American Journal of Psychiatry, 154,* 1514–1524.

Hogarty, G. E., Ulrich, R. F., Mussare, F., & Aristigueta, N. (1976). Drug discontinuation among long term, successfully maintained schizophrenic outpatients. *Diseases of the Nervous System, 37,* 494–500.

Hollon, S. D., DeRubeis, R. J., Evans, M. D., Wiemer, M. J., Garvey, M. J., Grove, W. M., & Tuason, V. B. (1992). Cognitive therapy and pharmacotherapy for depression singly and in combination. *Archives of General Psychiatry, 49,* 774–781.

Jacobson, N. S., Dobson, K. S., Truax, P. A., Addis, M. E., Koerner, K., Gollan, J. K., Gortner, E., & Prince, S. E. (1996). A component analysis of cognitive-behavioral treatment for depression. *Journal of Consulting and Clinical Psychology, 64,* 295–304.

Johnson, S. L., & Roberts, J. E. (1995). Life events and bipolar disorder: implications from biological theories. *Psychological Bulletin, 117,* 434–449.

Johnson, S. L., Winett, C. A., Meyer, B., Greenhouse, W. J., & Miller, I. (1999). Social support and the course of bipolar disorder. *Journal of Abnormal Psychology, 108,* 558–566.

Keller, M. B., & Boland, R. J. (1998). Implications of failing to achieve successful long-term maintenance treatment of recurrent unipolar major depression. *Biological Psychiatry, 44,* 348–360.

Keller, M. B., McCullough, J. P., Klein, D. N., Arnow, B., Dunner, D. L., Gelenberg, A. J., Markowitz, J. C., Nemeroff, C. B., Russell, J. M., Thase, M. E., Trivedi, M. H., & Zajecka, J. (2000). A comparison of nefazodone, the cognitive behavioral-analysis system of psychotherapy, and their combination for the treatment of chronic depression. *The New England Journal of Medicine, 342,* 1462–1470.

Khan, A., Warner, H. A., & Brown, W. A. (2000). Symptom reduction and suicide risk in patients treated with placebo in antidepressant clinical trials. An analysis of the Food and Drug Administration database. *Archives of General Psychiatry, 57,* 311–317.

Klerman, G. L., DiMascio, A., Weissman, M., Prusoff, B., & Paykel, E. (1974). Treatment of depression by drugs and psychotherapy. *American Journal of Psychiatry, 131,* 186–191.

Klerman, G. L., Weissman, M. M., Markowitz, J., Glick, I., Wilner, P. J., Mason, B., & Shear, M. K. (1994). Medication and psychotherapy. In A. E. Bergin & S. L. Garfield (Eds.), *Handbook of psychotherapy and behavior change* (pp. 734–782). New York: Raven Press.

Kraemer, H. C., & Thiemann, S. (1987). *How many subjects? Statistical power analysis in research.* Newbury Park: Sage Publications.

Krupnick, J. L., Sotsky, S. M., Simmens, S., Moyer, J., Elkin, I., Watkins, J., & Pilkonis, P. A. (1996). The role of therapeutic alliance in psychotherapy and pharmacotherapy outcome: findings in the National Insitute of Mental Health treatment of depression collaborative research program. *Journal of Consulting and Clinical Psychology, 64,* 532–539.

Kuipers, E., Garety, P., Fowler, D., Dunn, G., Bebbington, P., Freeman, D., & Hadley, C. (1997). London-East Anglia randomised controlled trial of cognitive-behavioural therapy psychosis. *British Journal of Psychiatry, 171,* 319–327.

Lam, D. H., Bright, J., Jones, S., Hayward, P., Schuck, N., Chisholm, D., & Sham, P. (2000). Cognitive therapy for bipolar illness—a pilot study of relapse prevention. *Cognitive Therapy and Research, 24,* 503–520.

Lauriello, J., Bustillo, J., & Keith, S. J. (1999). A critical review of research on psychosocial treatment of schizophrenia. *Biological Psychiatry, 46,* 1409–1417.

Lavori, P. W. (1992). Clinical trials in psychiatry: Should protocol deviation censor patient data? *Neuropsychopharmacology, 6,* 39–48.

Liberman, R. P., Blackwell, G., Wallace, C. J., & Mintz, J. (1994). Reducing relapse and rehospitalization in schizophrenic patients treated in a day hospital: A controlled study of skills training vs psychosocial occupational therapy. Presented at the 147th Annual Meeting of the American Psychiatric Association, May 22–26, Philadelphia, Pennsylvania.

Liberman, R. P., Wallace, C. J., Blackwell, G., Kopelowicz, A., Vaccaro, J. V., & Mintz, J. (1998). Skills training versus psychosocial occupational therapy for persons with persistent schizophrenia. *American Journal of Psychiatry, 155,* 1087–1091.

Marder, S. R. Wirshing, W. C., Mintz, J., McKenzie, J., Johnston, K., Eckman, T. A., Lebell, M., Zimmerman, K., & Liberman, R. P. (1996). Two-year outcome of social skills training and group psychotherapy for outpatients with schizophrenia. *American Journal of Psychiatry, 153,* 1585–1595.

Marks, I. M., Stern, R. S., Mawson, D., Cobb, J., & McDonald, R. (1980). Clomipramine and exposure for obsessive-compulsive rituals: I. *British Journal of Psychiatry, 136,* 1–25.

Marks, I. M., Swinson, R. P., Basoglu, M., Kuch, K., Noshirvani, H., O'Sullivan, G., Lelliott, P. T., Kirby, M., McNamee, G., Sengun, S., & Wickwire, K. (1993). Alprazolam and exposure alone and combined in panic disorder with agoraphobia: A controlled study in London and Toronto. *British Journal of Psychiatry, 162,* 776–787.

Mavissakalian, M. R. (1995). Combined behavioral and pharmacological treatment of anxiety disorders. In L. J. Dickstein, M. B. Riba, & J. M. Oldham (Eds.), *Review of psychiatry,* vol. 15 (pp. 565–584). Washington, DC: American Psychiatric Press.

Mawson, D., Marks, I. M., & Ramm, L. (1982). Clomipramine and exposure for chronic obsessive-compulsive rituals: III. Two year follow-up and further findings. *British Journal of Psychiatry, 140,* 11–18.

May, P.R.A. (1968). *Treatment of schizophrenia.* New York: Science House.

McCullough, J. P., Jr. (2000). *Treatment for chronic depression. Cognitive behavioral analysis system of psychotherapy.* New York: Guilford Press.

McKnight, D. L., Nelson-Gray, R. O., & Barnhill, J. (1992). Dexamethasone suppression test and response to cognitive therapy and antidepressant medication. *Behavior Therapist, 23,* 99–111.

Michaels, K. B. (2000). The placebo problem remains. *Archives of General Psychiatry, 57,* 321–322.

Miklowitz, D. J. (1998). Psychosocial approaches to the course and treatment of bipolar disorder. *CNS Spectrums, 3,* 48–52.

Miklowitz, D. J., Simoneau, T. L., George, E. L., Richards, J. A., Kalbag, A., Sachs-Ericsson, N., & Suddath, R. (2000). Family-focused treatment of bipolar disorder: 1-year effects of a psychoeducational program in conjunction with pharmacotherapy. *Biological Psychiatry, 48,* 582–592.

Miller, I. W., Norman, W. H., & Keitner, G. I. (1989). Cognitive-behavioral treatment of depressed inpatients: Six- and twelve-month follow-up. *American Journal of Psychiatry, 146,* 1274–1279.

Miller, I. W., Norman, W. H., & Keitner, G. I. (1990). Treatment response of high cognitive dysfunction depressed inpatients. *Comprehensive Psychiatry, 30,* 62–71.

Mitchell, J. E., Pyle, R. L., Eckert, E. D., Hatasukami, D., Pomeroy, C., & Zimmerman, R. (1990). A comparison study of antidepressants and structured intensive group psychotherapy in the treatment of bulimia nervosa. *Archives of General Psychiatry, 47,* 149–157.

Murphy, G. E., Simons, A. D., Wetzel, R. D., & Lustman, P. J. (1984). Cognitive therapy and pharmacotherapy. Singly and together in the treatment of depression. *Archives of General Psychiatry, 41,* 33–41.

Nesse, R. M. (2000). Is depression an adaptation? *Archives of General Psychiatry, 57,* 14–20.

O'Connor, K., Todorov, C., Robillard, S., Borgeat, F., & Brault, M. (1999). Cognitive-behaviour therapy and medication in the treatment of obsessive-compulsive disorder: A controlled study. *Canadian Journal of Psychiatry, 44,* 64–71.

Otto, M. W., Pollack, M. H., Sachs, G. S., Reiter, S. R., Meltzer-Brody, S., & Rosenbaum, J. F. (1993). Discontinuation of benzodiazepine treatment: Efficacy of cognitive-behavioral therapy for patients with panic disorder. *American Journal of Psychiatry, 150,* 1485–1490.

Overall, J. E., & Gorham, D. E. (1961). The brief psychiatric rating scale. *Psychology Reports, 10,* 799–812.

Palmer, A. G., Williams, H., & Adams, M. (1995). CBT in a group format for bi-polar affective disorder. *Behavioural and Cognitive Psychotherapy, 23,* 153–168.

Paul, G. L., & Lentz, R. J. (1977). *Psychosocial treatment of chronic mental patients.* Cambridge, MA: Harvard University Press.

Paul, G. L., Tobias, L. L., & Holly, B. L. (1972). Maintenance psychotropic drugs in the presence of active treatment programs. *Archives of General Psychiatry, 27,* 106–115.

Paykel, E. S., Scott, J., Teasdale, J. D., Johnson, A. L., Garland, A., Moore, R., Jenaway, A., Cornwall, P. L., Hayhurst, H., Abbott, R., & Pope, M. (1999). Prevention of relapse in residual depression by cognitive therapy. *Archives of General Psychiatry, 56,* 829–835.

Penn, D., & Mueser, K. (1996). Research update on the psychosocial treatment of schizophrenia. *American Journal of Psychiatry, 153,* 607–617.

Perris, C. (1989). *Cognitive therapy of schizophrenia.* New York: Guilford Press.

Perry, A., Tarrier, N., Morriss, R., McCarthy, E., & Limb, K. (1999). Randomised controlled trial of efficacy of teaching patients with bipolar disorder to identify early symptoms of relapse and obtain treatment. *British Medical Journal, 318,* 149–153.

Prusoff, B. A., Weissman, M. M., Klerman, G. L., & Rounsaville, B. J. (1980). Research diagnostic criteria subtypes of depression. Their role as predictors of differential response to psychotherapy and drug treatment. *Archives of General Psychiatry, 37,* 796–801.

Quitkin, F. M., Stewart, J. W., McGrath, P. J., Tricamo, E., Rabkin, J. G., Ocepek-Welikson, K., Nunes, E., Harrison, W., & Klein, D. F. (1993). Columbia atypical depression. A subgroup of depressives with better response to MAOI than to tricyclic antidepressants or placebo. *British Journal of Psychiatry, 163* (Suppl. 21), 30–34.

Randolph, E. T., Eth, S., Glynn, S. M., Paz, G. G., Leong, G. B., Shaner, A. L., Strachan, A., Van Vort, W., Escobar, J. L., & Liberman, R. P. (1994). Behavioural family management in schizophrenia. Outcome of a clinic-based intervention. *British Journal of Psychiatry, 164,* 501–506.

Ravindran, A. V., Anisman, H., Merali, Z., Charbonneau, Y., Telner, J., Bialik, R. J., Weins, A., Ellis, J., & Griffiths, J. (1999). Treatment of primary dysthymia with group cognitive therapy and pharmacotherapy: clinical symptoms and functional impairments. *American Journal of Psychiatry, 156,* 1608–1617.

Regier, D. A., Boyd, J. H., Burke, J. D., Jr., Rae, D. S., Myers, J. K., Kramer, M., Robins, L. N., George, L. K., Karno, M., & Locke, B. Z. (1988). One-month prevalence of mental disorders in the United States: based on five epidemiological catchment area sites. *Archives of General Psychiatry, 45,* 977–986.

Reynolds, C. F., III, Frank, E., Perel, J. M., Imber, S. D., Cornes, C., Miller, M. D., Mazumdar, S., Houck, P. R., Dew, M. A., Stack, J. A., Pollock, B. G., & Kupfer, D. J. (1999). Nortriptyline and interpersonal psychotherapy as maintenance therapies for recurrent major depression: A randomized controlled trial in patients older than 59 years. *Journal of the American Medical Association, 281,* 39–45.

Ribeiro, S.C.M., Tandon, R., Grunhaus, L., & Greden, J. F. (1993). The DST as a predictor of outcome in depression: a meta-analysis. *American Journal of Psychiatry, 150,* 1618–1629.

Rosenheck, R., Tekell, J., Peters, J., Cramer, J., Fontana, A., Xu, W., Thomas, J., Henderson, W., Charney, D., for the Department of Veterans Affairs Cooperative Study Group on Clozapine in Refractory Schizophrenia. (1998). Does participation in psychosocial treatment augment the benefit of clozapine? *Archives of General Psychiatry, 55,* 618–625.

Rounsaville, B. J., Klerman, G. L., & Weissman, M. M. (1981). Do psychotherapy and pharmacotherapy for depression conflict? Empirical evidence from a clinical trial. *Archives of General Psychiatry, 38,* 24–29.

Sachs, G. S., & Thase, M. E. (2000). Bipolar disorder therapeutics: Maintenance treatment. *Biological Psychiatry, 48(6),* 573–581.

Schooler, N. R. (1978). Antipsychotic drugs and psychological treatment in schizophrenia. In M. A. Lipton, A. DiMascio, & K. F. Killam (Eds.), *Psychopharmacology: A generation of progress* (pp. 1155–1168). New York: Raven Press.

Schooler, N. R., Keith, S. J., Severe, J. B., Matthews, S. M., Bellack, A. S., Glick, I. D., Hargeaves, W. A., Kane, J. M., Ninan, P. T., Frances, A., Jacobs, M., Lieberman, J. A., Mance, R., Simpson, G. M., & Woerner, M. G. (1997).

Relapse and rehospitalization during maintenance treatment of schizophrenia. The effects of dose reduction and family treatment. *Archives of General Psychiatry, 54*, 453–463.

Schooler, N. R., Levine, J., Severe, J. B., Brauzer, B., DiMascio, A., Klerman, G. L., & Tuason, V. B. (1980). Prevention of relapse in schizophrenia: An evaluation of fluphenazine decanoate. *Archives of General Psychiatry, 37*, 16–24.

Schulberg, H. C., Block, M. R., Madonia, M. J., Scott, C. P., Rodriguez, E., Imber, S. D., Perel, J., Lave, J., Houck, P. R., & Coulehan, J. L. (1996). Treating major depression in primary care practice. Eight-month clinical outcomes. *Archives of General Psychiatry, 53*, 913–919.

Scott, J. (1996). Cognitive therapy of affective disorders: A review. *Journal of Affective Disorders, 37*, 1–11.

Seligman, M.E.P. (1995). The effectiveness of psychotherapy. The Consumer Reports study. *American Psychologist, 50*, 965–974.

Sherbourne, C. D., Hays, R. D., Ordway, L., DiMatteo, M. R., & Kravitz, R. L. (1992). Antecedents of adherence to medical recommendations: Results from medical outcomes study. *Journal of Behavioral Medicine, 15*, 447–468.

Spanier, C., Frank, E., McEachran, A. B., Grochocinski, V. J., & Kupfer, D. J. (1996). The prophylaxis of depressive episodes in recurrent depression following discontinuation of drug therapy: Integrating psychological and biological factors. *Psychological Medicine, 26*, 461–475.

Spiegel, D. A., & Bruce, T. J. (1997). Benzodiazepines and exposure-based cognitive behavior therapists for panic disorder: Conclusion from combined treatment trials. *American Journal of Psychiatry, 154*, 773–781.

Spiegel, D. A., Bruce, T. J., Gregg, S. F., & Nuzzarello, A. (1994). Does cognitive behavior therapy assist in slow-taper alprazolam discontinuation in panic disorder? *American Journal of Psychiatry, 151*, 876–881.

Spitzer, R. L., Endicott, J., & Robins, E. (1978). Research diagnostic criteria. Rationale and reliability. *Archives of General Psychiatry, 35*, 773–782.

Stewart, J. W., Garfinkel, R., Nunes, E. V., Donovan, S., & Klein, D. F. (1998). Atypical features and treatment response in the National Institute of Mental Health Treatment of Depression Collaborative Research Program. *Journal of Clinical: Psychopharmacology, 18*, 429–434.

Stewart, J. W., Mercier, M. A., Agosti, V., Guardino, M., & Quitkin, F. M. (1993). Imipramine is effective after unsuccessful cognitive therapy: Sequential use of cognitive therapy and imipramine in depressed outpatients. *Journal of Clinical Psychopharmacology, 13*, 114–119.

Teasdale, J. D., Fennell, M.J.V., Hibbert, G. A., & Amies, P. L. (1984). Cognitive therapy for major depressive disorder in primary care. *British Journal of Psychiatry, 144*, 400–406.

Thase, M. E. (1996). The role of axis II comorbidity in the management of patients with treatment resistant depression. *Psychiatric Clinics of North America, 19*, 287–309.

Thase, M. E. (1997). Integrating psychotherapy and pharmacotherapy for treatment of major depressive disorder. Current status and future considerations. *The Journal of Psychotherapy Practice and Research, 6*, 300–306.

Thase, M. E. (1999). How should efficacy be evaluated in randomized clinical trials of treatments for depression. *Journal of Clinical Psychiatry, 60* (Suppl. 4), 23–31.

Thase, M. E. (2000). Recent developments in the pharmacotherapy of depression. *Psychiatric Clinics of North America: Annual of Drug Therapy, 7*, 151–171.

Thase, M. E. (2002). Studying new antidepressants: If there was a light at the end of the tunnel could we see it? *Journal of Clinical Psychiatry, 63* (Suppl. 2), 24–28.

Thase, M. E., Buysse, D. J., Frank, E., Cherry, C. R., Cornes, C. L., Mallinger, A. G., & Kupfer, D. J. (1997). Which depressed patients will respond to interpersonal psychotherapy? The role of abnormal electroencephalographic sleep profiles. *American Journal of Psychiatry, 154*, 502–509.

Thase, M. E., Dubé, S., Bowler, K., Howland, R. H., Myers, J. E., Friedman, E., & Jarrett, D. B. (1996). Hypothalamic-pituitary-adrenocortical activity and response to cognitive behavior therapy in unmedicated, hospitalized depressed patients. *American Journal of Psychiatry, 153*, 886–891.

Thase, M. E., Entsuah, A. R., & Rudolph, R. L. (2001). Remission rates during treatment with venlafaxine or selective serotonin reuptake inhibitors. *British Journal of Psychiatry, 178*, 234–241.

Thase, M. E., Fasiczka, A. L., Berman, S. R., Simons, A. D., & Reynolds, C. F., III. (1998). Electroencephalographic sleep profiles before and after cognitive behavior therapy of depression. *Archives of General Psychiatry, 55*, 138–144.

Thase, M. E., Fava, M., Halbreich, U., Kocsis, J. H., & Koran, L. (1996). A placebo-controlled randomized clinical trial comparing sertraline and imipramine for the treatment of dysthymia. *Archives of General Psychiatry, 53*, 777–784.

Thase, M. E., Frank, E., Kornstein, S., & Yonkers, K. A. (2000). Gender differences in response to treatments of depression. In E. Frank (Ed.), *Gender and its effects on psychopathology* (pp. 103–129). Washington, DC: American Psychiatric Press.

Thase, M. E., & Friedman, E. S. (1999). Is psychotherapy, alone, an effective treatment for melancholia and other severe depressive states? *Journal of Affective Disorders, 54*, 1–19.

Thase, M. E., Greenhouse, J. B., Frank, E., Reynolds, C. F., III, Pilkonis, P. A., Hurley, K., Grochocinski, V., & Kupfer, D. J. (1997). Treatment of major depression with psychotherapy or psychotherapy–pharmacotherapy combinations. *Archives of General Psychiatry, 54,* 1009–1015.

Thase, M. E., Kupfer, D. J., Fasiczka, A. L., Buysse, D. J., Simons, A. D., & Frank, E. (1997). Identifying an abnormal electroencephalographic sleep profile to characterize major depressive disorder. *Biological Psychiatry, 41,* 964–973.

Thase, M. E., Simons, A. D., & Reynolds, C. F., III. (1996). Abnormal electroencephalographic sleep profiles in major depression. *Archives of General Psychiatry, 53,* 99–108.

van Balkom, A.J.L.M., De Haan, E., Van Oppen, P., Spinhoven, Ph., Hoogduin, K.A.L., & Van Dyck, R. (1998). Cognitive and behavioral therapies alone versus in combination with fluvoxamine in the treatment of obsessive-compulsive disorder. *Journal of Nervous and Mental Disease, 186,* 492–499.

Vaughn, C. E., & Left, J. P. (1976). The influence of family and social factors on the course of psychiatric illness. A comparison of schizophrenic and depressed neurotic patients. *British Journal of Psychiatry, 129,* 125–137.

Walsh, B. T., & Devlin, M. J. (1995). Psychopharmacology of anorexia nervosa, bulimia nervosa, and binge eating. In F. E. Bloom & D. J. Kupfer (Eds.), *Psychopharmacology: The fourth generation of progress* (pp. 1581–1589). New York: Raven Press.

Walsh, B. T., Wilson, G. T., Loeb, K. L., Devlin, M. J., Pike, K. M., Roose, S. P., Fliess, J., & Waternaux, C. (1997). Medication and psychotherapy in the treatment of bulimia nervosa. *American Journal of Psychiatry, 154,* 523–531.

Wardle, J. (1990). Behavior therapy and benzodiazepines: Allies or antagonists? *British Journal of Psychiatry, 156,* 163–168.

Wells, K. B., Burnam, M. A., Rogers, W., Hays, R., & Camp, R. (1992). The course of depression in adult outpatients. Results from the Medical Outcomes Study. *Archives of General Psychiatry, 49,* 788–794.

Whisman, M. A. (1993). Mediators and moderators of change in cognitive therapy of depression. *Psychological Bulletin, 114,* 248–265.

Woody, G. E., McLellan, A. T., & Luborsky, L. (1984). Psychiatric severity as a predictor of benefits from psychotherapy. *American Journal of Psychiatry, 141,* 1171–1177.

Woody, G. E., McLellan, A. T., Luborsky, L., O'Brien, C. P., Beck, A. T., Blaine, J., Herman, I., & Hole, A. (1983). Psychotherapy for opiate addicts: Does it help? *Archives of General Psychiatry, 40,* 639–645.

Young, R. C., Biggs, J. T., Siegler, V. E., & Meyer, D. A. (1978). A rating scale for mania: Reliability, validity and sensitivity. *British Journal of Psychiatry, 133,* 429–435.

Zaretsky, A. E., Segal, Z. V., & Gemar, M. (1999). Cognitive therapy for bipolar depression: A pilot study. *Canadian Journal of Psychiatry, 44,* 491–494.

CHAPTER 17

RESEARCH ON PSYCHOTHERAPY WITH CULTURALLY DIVERSE POPULATIONS

NOLAN ZANE
University of California, Davis
GORDON C. NAGAYAMA HALL
University of Oregon
STANLEY SUE
University of California, Davis
KATHLEEN YOUNG
Palomar College, San Diego
JOEL NUNEZ
Pennsylvania State University

The analysis of research on psychotherapy with ethnic minority clients (i.e., African Americans, American Indians, Asian Americans, and Latino/a Americans) is important. If we can identify those psychotherapeutic conditions that have universal applicability, then these conditions should prove to be effective with different populations. If, however, current treatment practices work well only with certain populations, we need to know about these limitations and devise strategies to address the mental health needs of culturally diverse groups. Such tasks are not only theoretically meaningful (i.e., knowing the generality and limitations of theories and practices) but also consistent with psychology's goal to promote human welfare.

There are other reasons why it is important to consider psychotherapy research on ethnic minorities. First, about 30% of the population of the United States in 2000 was composed of ethnic minorities, and in California, ethnic minorities constitute the majority of the state's population (U.S. Census Bureau, 2001). Given the rapidly growing ethnic population, we are increasingly likely to encounter individuals from a variety of ethnic groups as clients. Intercultural skills in our roles as researchers and psychotherapists are important to develop in an increasingly diverse society, yet few systematic investigations into these skills have been conducted, and training programs in clinical psychology have not fully utilized what is known about intercultural skills (Bernal & Castro, 1994). Second, there is evidence that ethnic minority groups are experiencing significant mental health problems. It is beyond the scope of our review to analyze the prevalence of psychopathology. However, available data suggest that overall prevalence rates for these groups are comparable to, or higher than, those in the general population (Hall, Bansal, & Lopez, 1999; Kessler et al., 1994; Vega & Rumbaut, 1991). Immigrant/refugee background, encounters with prejudice and discrimination, cultural differences, and other experiences associated with minority group status may act as stressors that influence mental health. In addition, some of the groups are disproportionately represented in vulnerable populations such as the homeless and poor (U.S. Surgeon General's Supplement to the Report on Mental Health, in press). Considerable controversy has existed for the past three decades over the effectiveness of traditional psychotherapeutic approaches for members of ethnic minority clients. Specifically, what evidence is there for the efficacy of psychotherapy? What are the conditions that promote effectiveness? This chapter addresses these two questions. Psychotherapy research with ethnic minority groups helps determine the generalizability of psychological principles that have been developed primarily by and for European Americans.

We engage in a critical analysis of psychotherapy research on ethnic minorities, identifying the major empirical trends as well as discussing the major methodological and conceptual challenges. The present analysis is an update of our earlier review of research in this area (Sue, Zane, & Young, 1994). We continue to be impressed by the pioneering work of scholars in this area who strive to define and debate issues.

ETHNIC MINORITY GROUPS

Our discussion has relevance especially for groups that traditionally have been considered ethnic minorities. Such groups are commonly defined by cultural characteristics, ethnic identity, and minority group status. Other groups may indeed be included as ethnics or minorities. However, we shall focus on four groups along with Whites (which we define as non-Latino/a Whites). Although we recognize cultural differences between other groups such as White ethnics vs. non-White ethnics, people who live in urban and rural areas, Christians and Jews, men and women, and so on, it is beyond the scope of this chapter to include these groups.

It should be noted that the very terms used to refer to groups vary—for example, "Blacks" versus "African American"; "Native American" versus "American Indian"; "Asian" versus "Oriental"; "Hispanic" versus "Latino/a"; "Caucasian" versus "White." Although variations exist, we have decided to use the terms *African American*, *American Indian*, *Asian American*, *Latino/a American*, and *White* to refer to the groups. Furthermore, the term *ethnic minority* refers collectively to the four non-White groups because the phrase conveys culture and identity (ethnicity) as well as race and social status (minority status). *Ethnicity* involves shared social and cultural characteristics that have a bearing on psychological functioning (Sue, 1991). *Race* is a biologically based concept that may have some bearing on one's sociocultural identity but is dependent on the context in which one's sociocultural identity is developed. For example, the amount of social and cultural similarity between one person from a particular racial group and other racial groups often depends on the amount of contact the person has had with persons from the particular group. For our purposes, ethnicity is more germane than is race. Thus, the terms *ethnicity* and *ethnic minority* will be used in this chapter.

Knowing the cultural values of each ethnic group is only one critical facet of understanding the group. What must also be acquired is knowledge of the history of racial/ethnic relations in this country. Problems in mental health service delivery may occur not only because ethnic minority groups have different cultural values, but also because certain relationships have developed between majority and minority group individuals. In addition, all four groups and Whites exhibit heterogeneity in terms of identification with their group, socioeconomic status, education, acculturation, psychopathology, and the like. (Jones, 1991; Phinney, 1996). Given this heterogeneity, discussions concerning groups such as American Indians, Asian Americans, and Whites often have a stereotypic quality. The different levels of discourse—whether the intent is to discuss between-group cultural differences or within-group variability—are important to distinguish (Phinney, 1996; Sue, 1991). At one level, when between-group comparisons are made, generalizations about group characteristics may be needed. In this case, for ethnicity and culture to have meaning, between-group differences in values and traits have to be highlighted in an abstract manner.

Inkeles and Levinson (1969) introduced the notion of "modal personality" to describe average characteristics of different ethnic groups. Members of a particular group may exhibit heterogeneity. However, the modal (i.e., average) characteristics of groups may show meaningful differences when between-group comparisons are made (Kwon, 1995). For example, Asians and Whites may exhibit differences on certain measures of individualism and collectivism. These differences provide the context for understanding ethnic groups. However, the context or modal patterns must not be confounded with the characteristics of individual members of a group who may or may not possess the modal group patterns. Otherwise, individuals are stereotyped according to their culture.

At another level of communication, we may wish to emphasize within-group heterogeneity. Not all White Americans are individualistic, even though they may as a group place a higher value on individualism than members of other groups.

By understanding the purpose of communication and by recognizing these levels of discourse, we can discuss both between- and within-ethnic group differences with more clarity and precision.

As mentioned previously, ethnic minority groups are quite heterogeneous. For example, Latino/a's are composed of individuals whose origin or family of origin is Mexico, the Caribbean, or Central or South America. American Indians are composed of hundreds of different tribes, and discussions of American Indians often include Alaskan Natives. Asian Americans include Chinese, Japanese, Koreans, Filipinos, Southeast Asians, and Pacific Islanders. Given this diversity, there are restrictions in terms of our ability to generalize findings even from a study of one subgroup to other subgroups within the same ethnic minority. In addition, research on a group (e.g., Latino/a Americans) may be largely based on one particular subgroup (e.g., Mexican Americans). For some subgroups within a designated ethnic group, little research may be available (e.g., among the Asian and Pacific Islander American group, not much research has been conducted on Samoans).

Finally, the designation of "ethnic minority" has also been challenged in that some feel the term conveys a sense of inferiority. We acknowledge that the designation of "ethnic minority" is arbitrary. Their "minority" status is relative (i.e., Whites are not in the majority relative to the world population) and should not be interpreted to imply the sense of inferiority, separateness, or "minor" status sometimes associated with the term. Thus we clarify our intentions because we use a term that, by custom, is subject to misinterpretation.

Issues Discussed

There are few studies comparing the outcomes of treated and untreated groups of ethnic minority clients. Moreover, most researchers and practitioners have reformulated the therapeutic effectiveness question into specifics: What type of treatment by which therapist is effective for which client with what specific problem under what conditions? Because we simply do not have much research into the specifics of psychotherapy with ethnic minorities, we can only provide glimpses into the answers to these questions. For heuristic purposes, we address five questions: (1) Do ethnic minority clients improve after undergoing psychotherapy (show positive pre-post treatment changes), (2) do clients from a particular ethnic group fare as well as other clients after treatment (e.g., compared to Whites or compared to other ethnic groups), (3) are certain types of treatments more or less effective with ethnic minority clientele, (4) what client, therapist, situational, and treatment variables are associated with treatment outcomes and with progress in psychotherapy, and (5) what conceptual and methodological issues must be addressed in psychotherapy research on culturally diverse populations? The first three questions deal directly with the treatment outcome issue. We include a discussion not only of direct measures of outcome and treatment improvement but also indirect indices such as utilization of services and treatment dropout rates. The fourth question largely involves process research. Research findings pertinent to client characteristics such as acculturation and preferences, to therapist characteristics such as ethnicity and therapeutic style, to features of the treatment process such as pretherapy orientations and the incorporation of purportedly culturally relevant elements, or to situational variables such as the service delivery setting are included. Finally, a critique of research methodology and conceptual schemes is presented.

Much has been written about the problems faced by ethnic minorities in finding adequate psychotherapeutic services. Skepticism regarding the value of psychotherapy for ethnic minority clients is based largely on conceptual models and anecdotal/experiential reports. Conceptual models derived from research on cross-cultural or ethnic/racial issues suggest that culture plays a critical role in the assessment, etiology, symptom expression, and treatment of mental disorders (e.g., Betz & Fitzgerald, 1993; Ramirez, 1999; Sue & Sue, 1999). Because the majority of ethnic minority clients are likely to see White therapists, and because many of these therapists are unfamiliar with the cultural values and lifestyles of various ethnic clients, performing valid clinical assessments and conducting effective psychotherapy for these clients presumably is problematic. Furthermore, it is likely that ethnic and race relations in the United States, often occurring in a context of prejudice and discrimination, may be reflected in the mental health profession. Therapist biases, stereotypes, discomfort, and so on, may exist with clients who are dissimilar in ethnicity, race, or culture (Clark, 1972; Garb, 1997; Whaley, 1998).

Much of the research on utilization indices related to treatment outcomes offers comparisons of the four different groups (often including

Whites as a comparison), so the groups are examined together rather than separately. However, in presenting the research on actual treatment outcome and treatment process, each group is discussed separately. The reason for this is that outcome and process research on each group has proceeded more or less separately, with certain issues esteemed as more salient for some groups than for others. Indeed, it is difficult to compare ethnic groups on most variables because the extent of research varies from group to group and not all of the same variables have been studied for each group. Although this methodology limits an accurate assessment of between-group comparisons, it affords the opportunity to discuss the outcome and process research separately for each group in order to see the level of work conducted on each group. Nevertheless, the quality of treatment process affects treatment outcome.

Client and therapist variables are categorized separately in this chapter based on the foci of the studies presented. However, it should be noted that most client variables are related implicitly to one or more therapist variables and vice versa. For example, preference for ethnicity of therapist is classified as a client variable, when ethnic match obviously depends on a given therapist characteristic—in this case, ethnicity. Similarly, therapeutic alliance depends on a relationship between therapist *and* client, implying that client variables are involved.

INDIRECT MEASURES OF OUTCOME FOR ETHNIC MINORITY GROUPS

Utilization rates, premature treatment termination, and length of treatment are commonly used as "indirect" indices of outcome. Utilization is defined as a help-seeking behavior in which the services of the mental health system are used. Premature termination occurs when the client drops out of treatment, presumably before receiving substantial psychotherapeutic benefits. Length of treatment is defined as the number of treatment sessions attended. Most studies have defined utilization as a comparison of the proportion of a population using services with the proportion of that population comprising the area being served. Thus references to under- or overutilization of services are based on population comparisons and not on the actual psychiatric need for services. Also, the view that premature termination (whether defined by the therapist or by failure to attend a certain minimum number of sessions) results in unfavorable outcomes is only an assumption. In addition, in most ethnic comparisons, the White population has been used as the comparison group because it is the majority group. The wisdom of these assumptions and comparative procedures is debatable. However, ethnic differences on these indirect indices of outcome per se are important to investigate because they may reveal different patterns of effectiveness of services by ethnic group.

Utilization of Services

The results of utilization studies vary depending on the ethnic minority group examined. Some studies reveal that African Americans and American Indians overutilize services, whereas Asian Americans and Latino/a Americans underutilize services. One study involving 17 community mental health facilities in Seattle (Sue, 1977) found a pattern in which African Americans and American Indians overutilized services and Asian Americans and Latino/a's underutilized services. A second study of outpatient services in the entire Los Angeles County Mental Health System (Sue, Fujino, Hu, Takeuchi, & Zane, 1991) found a similar pattern in which African Americans overutilized services and Asian Americans and Latino/a's underutilized services. In a followup to the Sue (1977) study, O'Sullivan, Peterson, Cox, and Kirkeby (1989) also found overutilization by African Americans and American Indians but no underutilization by Asian Americans and Latino/a Americans. Other community studies have suggested that African Americans are less likely than are Whites to use mental health services (Kessler et al., 1994). Thus, there is evidence of ethnic differences in the utilization of mental health services, but consistent patterns of overutilization and underutilization have been found for only certain groups such as underutilization for Asian Americans. There is also evidence of ethnic differences in the referral process into mental health care. In a study of community mental health clinics that served predominantly poor populations in Los Angeles, African Americans (particularly men) were more likely than other ethnic groups to be involuntarily placed in psychiatric facilities (Takeuchi, Bui, & Kim, 1993; Takeuchi & Cheung, 1998).

Why do utilization differences exist? In Snowden and Cheung's (1990) analysis of hospitalization, several possible explanations were discussed, but none was considered sufficient to explain the results. These differences included racial differences in socioeconomic background and rates of insurance for medical/mental health services, rates of psychopathology, help-seeking tendencies, diagnostic bias, and involuntary hospitalization. In addition, mental health providers are located primarily in urban areas, whereas many members of certain ethnic minority groups are located in rural areas of the country. Thus, access to facilities may hinder utilization rates by ethnic minorities. Utilization of inpatient and outpatient services may involve these factors and many others such as knowledge about and accessibility of facilities, attitudes, and values (e.g., feelings of shame or stigma), familiarity with Western forms of treatment, and presence of bilingual-bicultural staff. Indeed, Asian Americans and Latino/a Americans who show underutilization are predominantly foreign born and speak English as a second language or don't speak English at all. Furthermore, there is evidence that among minority groups utilization is directly related to the number of minority group staff available at mental health facilities. The most appropriate conclusion at this time is that ethnic differences exist in utilization patterns and that a number of factors may account for these differences.

Length of Treatment

Length of treatment can be considered an indirect indicator of treatment outcome because it has been consistently associated with treatment effects (Luborsky, Chandler, Auerbach, Cohen, & Bachrach, 1971; see Lambert & Ogles, Chapter 5, this volume). A dose-response relationship has been identified in that clients' self-reported improvement is positively associated with their number of therapy sessions (Lambert et al., 2001). O'Sullivan and his colleagues (1989) did not find any consistent differences in dropout rates between ethnics and Whites at community mental health centers in Seattle. In the previously mentioned Los Angles County study, Sue et al. (1991) found that 19.4% of African Americans, 15.3% of Whites, 14.6% of Mexican Americans, and 10.7% of Asian Americans dropped out of treatment after one session. The group averages for number of treatment sessions attended were 6.3 for Asian Americans, 5.1 for Mexican Americans, 5.1 for Whites, and 4.0 for African Americans. These ethnic differences were statistically significant and suggest that relative to other groups, African Americans prematurely terminate services. In a similar study, length of treatment at various inpatient facilities did not show consistent differences between ethnic groups and Whites (Snowden & Cheung, 1990). However, in examining the treatment of depression with cognitive-behavioral therapy, Organista, Munoz, and Gonzalez (1994) found that even among low-income patients, ethnic minority status was associated with a higher dropout rate, although specific ethnic group data on dropouts were not reported.

The results of research to date suggest that, although some differences have emerged in number of sessions, they have not been consistent. The results could reflect the influence of specific and local factors (e.g., regional, community, and service system differences), or time period differences (e.g., between 1977 and 1991 when many culturally oriented community programs were developed), or individual differences in generation level, a possible shift in values and attitudes toward mental health services, or changes in degree of identity with the dominant culture.

Psychotherapy Outcome Research with Ethnic Minority Groups

A major movement in clinical psychology has been the identification and development of empirically supported therapies (ESTs). ESTs are treatments that have been demonstrated to be superior in efficacy to a placebo or another treatment (Chambless & Hollon, 1998). The criteria for *well-established* effective treatments are at least two good between-group design experiments or 10 or more single-case design experiments by at least two different investigators demonstrating superiority to pill or psychological placebo or to another treatment, or equivalence to an already established treatment. Treatment manuals are required in the experiments, and client characteristics must be clearly specified. The criteria for *probably efficacious* treatments are two experiments showing that the treatment is more effective than a waiting list control group, or one or more experiments meeting the well-established treatment criteria, or four or more single-case design experiments. Well-established and probably efficacious treatments have been identified for anxiety and stress, depression, health problems, childhood psychological disorders, marital discord, and sexual dysfunction (Chambless et al., 1996; DeRubeis & Crits-Christoph, 1998). However, there is limited empirical support for the efficacy of ESTs with ethnic minority groups (Sue, 1998).

Hall (2001) has contrasted EST with culturally sensitive therapy (CST). CST involves the modification of psychotherapy to specific cultural contexts. Persons from one cultural group may require a form of psychotherapy that differs from psychotherapy found to be effective for another cultural group. Several models of culturally sensitive therapy have been developed (e.g., Betz & Fitzgerald, 1993; Ivey, Ivey, & Simek-Morgan, 1993; Ramirez, 1999; Sue, Ivey, & Pedersen, 1996). Although there are ethical and conceptual rationales for CST, a review of the literature suggested that there is no more empirical support for the efficacy of CST than for EST with ethnic minorities (Hall, 2001). We will review the available evidence for the efficacy of ESTs and CSTs with ethnic minority groups. In addition, we will review outcome and process research on the four ethnic minority groups: African Americans, American Indians, Asian Americans, and Latino/a Americans.

Research on African Americans

African Americans are currently the largest ethnic minority group in the United States, with a population of 35 million in 2000 (U.S. Census Bureau, 2001). The general public has been exposed to statistics regarding African Americans in terms of income, unemployment, crime, health, and education, but unfortunately, the statistics often are misinterpreted to reinforce popular stereotypes. Actually, in contrast to the stereotypes, about half of all African Americans are members of the middle or upper classes. In addition, a great deal of within-group heterogeneity exists in terms of family structure, socioeconomic status, educational background, cultural identity, and reactions to racism (Jones & Gray, 1983). Although African Americans as a group hold certain values such as the importance of the collective, sensitivity to interpersonal matters, and cooperation among peers (Nobles, 1980), these values have been influenced by culture, social class, and exposure to racism. Given these influences, it is not surprising that African Americans are quite diverse. This diversity has implications for our analysis of treatment outcomes and client, therapist, and situational/treatment variables that affect psychotherapeutic processes.

Treatment Outcome

Reviews of the literature on the effectiveness of psychotherapy with African Americans have been evaluated in different ways, with various conclusions reflecting the methodology and focus of each study. Two studies have demonstrated poorer outcomes among African Americans. Brown, Joe, and Thompson (1985) examined the outcomes of African American, Mexican American, and White American clients seen in different drug abuse treatment programs—residential programs, methadone programs, and drug-free outpatient programs. Particularly in outpatient programs, ethnic clients were retained in treatment longer than Whites and had less favorable outcomes at discharge. In a study of thousands of ethnic minority clients (African Americans, Asian Americans, and Mexican Americans) treated in the Los Angeles County Mental Health System, Sue et al. (1991) analyzed the pre- and post-treatment Global Assessment Scale (GAS) scores of clients. The GAS was a rating given by therapists to clients in order to indicate clients' overall functioning, with higher scores indicating better functioning. It is very similar to the Global Assessment of Functioning scale used on Axis V of the *Diagnostic and Statistical Manual of Mental Disorders-III-R* (American Psychiatric Association, 1987). GAS scores at the termination of treatment, adjusted for initial GAS scores, were: 47.9 for Mexican Americans, 46.8 for Whites, 46.7 for Asian Americans, and 45.8 for African Americans. These scores suggest moderate levels of adaptive functioning. Although these ethnic group differences were statistically significant, such differences in large samples would not necessarily be clinically significant (Maramba & Hall, in press).

Specific types of therapy have been investigated for depressed African American clients. Both interpersonal therapy and nortriptyline have been found to be effective in reducing depression among African American adults in studies at the outpatient clinic of the University of Pittsburgh School of Medicine (Brown, Schulberg, Sacco, Perel, & Houck, 1999; Stack et al., 1995). Interpersonal therapy focuses on problems in interpersonal relationships as the basis of depression. Nortriptyline is an antidepressant drug. In both trials, these treatments were equally effective for African Americans and European Americans. Cognitive behavioral treatment, which primarily involves interventions to change a person's thoughts and perceptions that are assumed to be the basis of depression, has also been demonstrated to reduce depression in African American adults, although the reductions were not as great as had been reported in previous research with

European Americans (Organista et al., 1994). Among the African Americans in the study, Beck Depression Inventory (BDI) scores were reduced from 27.1 pretreatment to 19.6 at treatment completion, which represents a change from severe to moderate depression. In most other studies with European Americans, BDI scores were in the mild depression range at termination. It is possible that the relatively small amount of change in the Organista et al. (1994) study was a function of sample characteristics. All were low-income and may have had few coping resources. Moreover, none of these three studies on African Americans included a control group and thus would not meet the criteria for EST validation studies (Chambless & Hollon, 1998).

Cognitive behavioral therapy has also been demonstrated to be equally effective in reducing anxiety among African American and European American children and adults (Friedman, Paradis, & Hatch, 1994; Treadwell, Flannery-Schroeder, & Kendall, 1995). Behavior therapy formulated to restructure clients' problem behaviors has fared less well in the treatment of anxiety disorders among African Americans. Exposure therapy designed to desensitize clients to their anxiety-inducing situations and physiological responses was shown to be ineffective in reducing panic attacks in a sample of African American adults (Williams & Chambless, 1994). Similar to the above studies on depression, none of these studies on anxiety included a control group, and conclusions are tentative.

It is difficult to compare previous studies because of the differences in outcome measures used as well as possible differences in the demographic characteristics of African Americans, types of clients seen, treatments received, and so on. Furthermore, relatively few investigators have examined the effects of treatment for African Americans. As a general conclusion, in no studies have African Americans been found to exceed White Americans in terms of favorable treatment outcome. Some investigations have revealed no ethnic differences, whereas other studies have supported the notion that treatment outcomes are less beneficial for African Americans.

Treatment Process

Client variables, therapist variables, and situational or treatment variables may affect the treatment process. Client variables include expectancies, preferences, attitudes, and characteristics that are pertinent to the progress of psychotherapy. Research on client characteristics points to important differences within the African American population and the influence of these characteristics on treatment. Therapist variables also affect the psychotherapeutic process. These include ethnic match between client and therapist, training, therapist style (e.g., directiveness), and background. Indeed, one of the major controversies in the ethnic mental health field is the issue of whether African American therapists are more effective than White therapists in working with African American clients. Finally, situational or treatment variables are also important to consider. Are certain forms of treatment more effective than others in promoting favorable therapeutic outcomes among African Americans? And are there pretreatment variables such as cultural sensitivity training that may impact therapeutic process and outcome? These questions have been widely discussed, although little research has actually been devoted to the matter.

Client Variables

As mentioned previously, scholars have recognized that African Americans exhibit considerable variation in cultural background and in ethnic identity and that recommendations for "culturally appropriate" or "culturally specific" forms of treatment may be applicable for some but not all African Americans (Sue, 1988).

Preferences for Ethnicity of Therapist

The most commonly addressed question in research on culturally specific counseling or therapy has been whether African Americans prefer same-race or same-ethnicity therapists, whether within-group characteristics are associated with these preferences, and whether ethnic preferences are a part of a more encompassing desire to find therapists who share similar background characteristics (Helms & Carter, 1991). Some investigators have concluded that many clients prefer ethnically similar therapists (Atkinson, 1983; Fuertes & Gelso, 1998; Kenney, 1994; Okonji, Ososkie, & Pulos, 1996), particularly in the case of African American clients. Based on Cross's (1971) model of racial identity, Helms has been in the forefront of developing identity measures and of stimulating research on stages of racial identity (e.g., Helms, 1984). Parham and Helms (1981) and Morten and Atkinson (1983) found some evidence of a stage effect on preferences, with African Americans who accept an African American identity and who are skeptical of White values most likely to want a therapist of the same race. Obviously, preference for a therapist of the same race may be a salient variable. However, given the array of possible variables that may influence preferences for a particular therapist (e.g., attitude similarity, attractiveness of therapist, social class, etc.), perhaps therapist race is only one of several variables that should be considered.

Other Research on Client Variables

Although the issue of preference for the race of the therapist has dominated the literature, other client variables among African Americans have also been discussed. Cultural differences between African Americans and Whites on values such as individualism versus the importance of the collective have been found (Nobles, 1980)—values that may affect the attitudes, expectations, and behavior of clients and therapists. For example, most psychotherapies focus on solutions to problems at the individual level. However, solutions at the individual level may not address the social context of a problem. Furthermore, the relationship between client and therapist may also be influenced by the minority group status of African Americans and the accompanying prejudice and discrimination often experienced in society. Gibbs and Huang (1989) have noted the difficulties in establishing a therapeutic alliance with many ethnic minority clients. In their view, African American clients may encounter therapists, especially non-African American therapists, who operate with different orientations. For example, African Americans often work from an interpersonal orientation, and psychotherapists are evaluated by the client based on their interpersonal perspective. Consequently, the therapist's ability to evoke positive attitudes and to obtain favorable reactions is deemed important to the African American client. The client sizes up the therapist and behaves in a "cool" manner in order to observe the therapist and to minimize expressions of distrust that may be present. If the therapist has evoked favorable responses from the client, the client becomes personally and not just professionally involved in the relationship as evidenced by increasing commitment and engagement. African American therapists tend to approach therapy in an interpersonal manner. On the other hand, it has been suggested that White therapists, particularly those who are not familiar with culturally diverse clients, frequently have an instrumental orientation in which value is placed on the goal or task-related aspects in the relationship between therapist and client (Ramirez, 1999). The incompatibility of these two different orientations may cause misunderstandings and problems in communication during psychotherapy because the therapist and client may be seeking different goals, evaluating the relationship in discrepant ways, and failing to understand each other. These issues have been addressed at a theoretical level and have yet to be empirically evaluated.

Research on client variables clearly indicates the importance of such variables as attitudes and preferences and of the heterogeneous nature of the African American population. However, because of the relatively small number of studies conducted, the empirical knowledge base lags markedly behind the ideas, conceptual analyses, and theoretical/applied contributions of scholars in the field. In addition, most of the empirical investigations have been based on students rather than on the general population of clients and on analogue rather than on actual studies of psychotherapy. For instance, evidence for a therapist race effect has been found more frequently in clinical analogue studies than in actual treatment studies (Atkinson, 1986). Despite the problems and limitations of research on the interface between African Americans and psychotherapy, the increase in the number and sophistication of studies conducted on African Americans is encouraging, but there is a need to move toward hypothesis testing and away from conceptual schemes that currently remain untested.

Therapist Variables

Research on therapist variables includes characteristics, attitudes, values, knowledge, experience, and therapist behaviors that influence the treatment outcomes or processes of African American clients. One of the most salient controversies in this area has been the importance of therapist ethnicity: Is it better for African American clients to see an ethnically similar therapist?

Ethnic Match Between Client and Therapist

Studies on variables such as therapeutic alliance and race effect presumably take into account both client and therapist variables. Yet at the same time, such research assumes that one variable (e.g., therapist style) is more salient. An investigative approach that does not attempt to differentiate client and therapist variables, but rather attempts to determine possible effects and interactions of ethnicity is the study of ethnic match between the client and the therapist. The effects of ethnic match based on a large-scale study of the length of treatment and on outcomes of African American outpatients seen in the Los Angeles County Mental Health System were reported (Sue et al., 1991). Outcomes for African American clients who were matched with therapists on ethnicity were compared with outcomes for clients not matched on ethnicity (i.e., African American clients seen by a non-African American therapist). Results revealed that African Americans who saw an African American rather than a non-African American therapist attended a greater number of therapy sessions. However, on the Global Assessment Scale (GAS), no differences in treatment outcome were found as a function of match. Therefore, ethnic match appeared to affect the number of treatment sessions but not outcome as reported on the measure used. The investigators speculated that perhaps the GAS is not a very sensitive measure or that ethnic match may influence interpersonal attraction, which results in a greater number of sessions but fails to affect outcomes. There is no consistent evidence from studies of actual clients that ethnic match enhances outcomes among African Americans. Another neglected issue is that the preferences for therapist ethnicity by clients were not assessed. It is unknown if the African American clients preferred to have African American therapists.

The previous study failed to find consistent evidence in support of a therapist-client ethnic match. However, other more recent studies have found supportive evidence. Recent data from the same Los Angeles County Mental Health System (Yeh, Eastman, & Cheung, 1994) suggest that therapist-client ethnic matching in general may have beneficial effects on treatment utilization and outcome. African American adolescents who were ethnically matched with therapists were less likely to drop out of treatment after a single session, attended more treatment sessions, and were judged to have better psychological functioning at discharge than those who were ethnically mismatched with therapists. Moreover, African American adults who were ethnically matched with therapists were judged to have better psychological functioning following treatment than those African American adults who were ethnically mismatched (Russell, Fujino, Sue, Cheung, & Snowden, 1996). In a national study of Veterans Administration outpatient settings, African American veterans had higher rates of early termination and received fewer treatment sessions when treated by White therapists, but not when treated by African American therapists (Rosenheck, Fontana, & Cottrol, 1995). When African Americans had White therapists, they failed to return for a second session 29% of the time. However, the premature termination rate was only 14% when African Americans had African American therapists. African American clients averaged 17 sessions with White therapists versus 25 sessions with African American therapists. African American therapists also appeared to positively impact White clients, as premature termination rates were lower and number of sessions higher when White clients were treated by African American therapists versus White therapists. In none of these studies, however, were actual client preferences for therapist ethnicity assessed.

Contrary to the findings in the mental health and Veterans Administration settings, ethnic matching of therapists and African American clients in outpatient substance abuse programs has not been associated with better outcomes (Fiorentine & Hillhouse, 1999; Sterling, Gottheil, Weinstein, & Serota, 1998). Although ethnic match was associated with perceived counselor credibility (Fiorentine & Hillhouse, 1999), ethnic matching was not associated with longer treatment utilization or better outcomes. Effective substance abuse treatment may be particularly critical for African Americans, for there is evidence that more African Americans may seek substance abuse treatment than Whites do (Nebeker, Lambert, & Huefner, 1995). It is possible that other variables, such as therapist competence in drug abuse treatment or high rates of recidivism, were more influential than ethnic match. For instance, evidence suggests that a method to enhance counselor communication with African American substance abusers involving individually tailored diagrams results in fewer drug-positive urine tests and clients missing fewer scheduled counseling sessions relative to clients who underwent a standard drug treatment program (Dansereau, Joe, Dees, & Simpson, 1996). These diagrams represent interrelationships among personal issues and related plans, accompanied by alternatives or solutions. For example, a diagram of a choice to do drugs leads to a need for money, which leads to stealing and a dependence on one's mother. Stealing leads to jail, and a dependence on one's mother may interfere with future opportunities for independent functioning. Conversely, a diagram of a choice not to do drugs leads to positive consequences, including feeling good about oneself and getting a job. Such individualized efforts to enhance communication through illustrative interpretation of the problem and its related consequences and alternatives were more effective for African Americans and Mexican Americans than for European Americans.

A recent meta-analysis of the previously cited and other therapist-client ethnic match studies suggested that the statistically significant effects of ethnic match are small and in some of these studies may be a function of the large sample sizes (Maramba & Hall, in press). These small effect sizes may reflect weak outcome measures or the possibility that an ethnic match is not necessarily a cultural match (Sue & Zane, 1987). Components of cultural match include a shared language, understanding the client's cultural background, and openness to modifying treatment. Cultural match and ethnic match are not necessarily synonymous. Some therapist-client ethnic matches are also cultural matches, but others are not, which may account for the statistically significant but small effect sizes for outcome differences in the ethnic match studies. In the Sue et al. (1991) study, although large effect sizes were found for ethnic match and dropout, the base rates for dropping out were low for ethnically matched and ethnically mismatched therapist-client pairings. However, the study did provide evidence that ethnic match may be beneficial for certain kinds of ethnic clients, such as those who are less acculturated to the mainstream culture or who have limited English proficiency.

Other Therapist Variables

Although ethnic match has dominated the pertinent literature (and in some respects, could be considered a therapist variable), other therapist variables have also been studied. These therapist variables include cultural sensitivity training, attitudes and behaviors, and physical characteristics.

In the past, cross-cultural mental health scholars and practitioners have devised strategies and programs to help train therapists to work with culturally different clients. For example, the Cross-Cultural Training Institute for Mental Health Professionals, developed by Lefley (1985), was designed to enhance the diagnostic, therapeutic, and administrative skills of mental health professionals in providing culturally responsive services to African American and Latino/a communities. The intensive eight-day training program evaluated changes in trainees' abilities and changes in the agency's functioning. The program was favorably evaluated—without a control group—and found to be effective in enhancing therapeutic skills and in effecting positive changes in mental health agencies, but its effects on individual clients were not assessed.

In a similar study, Wade and Bernstein (1991) investigated the effects of therapist cultural sensitivity training on African American clients. These researchers assigned experienced African American or White therapists to either a cultural sensitivity training program or a control group (with no additional training given). Therapists then saw female African American clients from the community who presented for counseling. A main effect for training (but not therapist race) was found in that clients who saw culturally trained therapists rated the therapists as having greater expertise, trustworthiness, attractiveness, empathy, and unconditional positive regard than the clients whose therapists were not exposed to this training. In terms of the number of treatment sessions, main effects for training and therapist race were found. Clients of trained therapists and of therapists who were African American attended more sessions than those with nontrained or White therapists. The effects of training appear to be dramatic, particularly because the training program only lasted *four* hours. If the results are replicated, the implications for programs and policies may be immense. It is surprising that there has not been a published replication over the ensuing 10 years since this study was published.

In another study, D'Andrea, Daniels, and Heck (1991) assessed the efficacy of three approaches to multicultural training with graduate students, based on the same content but varied by time format. In the first condition, the effects of a multicultural training course were examined, in which the three-hour class met once a week during a 15-week semester. In the second condition, a multicultural training course that took place twice weekly for three hours per session over a six-week period was examined. Finally, a third condition focused on a weekend workshop format involving intensive weekends of training for three consecutive weekends. The results of the three conditions indicate that each multicultural training format led to significant improvement in therapists' self-reported cross-cultural knowledge, awareness, and skill acquisition between pre- and post-test administration (D'Andrea et al., 1991). These findings suggest that the specific length of multicultural training programs is not influential in determining the effectiveness of these programs.

In contrast to the previous study, Pope-Davis, Prieto, Whitaker, and Pope-Davis (1993) and Pope-Davis and Dings (1995) both found limited gains from workshops, and the gains that were made were in multicultural awareness but not in knowledge or skills. Thus, these researchers asserted a need for longer training programs. However, the studies by Pope-Davis and colleagues were retrospective and asked about any workshop training the respondents had, whereas D'Andrea et al. (1991) evaluated programs with similar content, structure, and length. The findings of D'Andrea et al. suggest that perhaps as long as the training is sufficiently intense, the specific length and number of sessions will have little or no effect on outcome. They also demonstrated that the acquisition of the multicultural skills component, though significantly improved across all conditions, was generally less affected than the knowledge and awareness components. This finding suggests that the skills component may be more difficult or time-consuming to promote. None of these studies tested to see if training had any effect on therapeutic outcome.

At a minimum, cultural sensitivity may involve therapists' willingness to address issues of race and ethnicity. For example, two African American female and two White female counselors were trained to increase their levels of awareness of African American clients and of the experiences of African Americans (Thompson, Worthington, & Atkinson, 1994). These counselors addressed issues of being an African American woman with some clients and did not with others. Ratings of videotapes suggested that African American college women were more willing to reveal intimate information to female counselors who addressed issues of being an African American woman than to those who avoided these issues. Moreover, the women were more willing to return to see counselors who addressed these issues.

Rather than simply examine preferences for African American or White therapists, Helms and Carter (1991) assessed how racial identity and demographic variables of African Americans and Whites predicted preferences for therapists who differed according to race and gender. Using African American male and female and White male and female therapists, a large number of variables and analyses were conducted. Only a brief presentation of the results pertinent to our discussion is given. For White participants, racial identity and gender (but not social class) were important in predicting preferences for a White therapist. However, predicting preferences for an African American therapist was not possible from the variables examined. Among African American participants, predictors of preference for African American therapists failed to reach significance, although racial identity attitudes did predict their preferences for White male therapists.

The overall findings suggest that predictors of preferences may be quite complex and interact according to the ethnicity and gender of participants and therapists. Research on ethnic preferences has become increasingly systematized and specific. Several conclusions seem appropriate: (1) Research has evolved from simply ascertaining the ethnic preferences to identifying the individual differences that are associated with ethnic as well as other preferences among African Americans; (2) ethnicity of the therapist is but one of many characteristics preferred by African Americans; (3) in general, African Americans prefer therapists who are similar in a wide range of characteristics; and (4) research has not yielded consistent findings regarding the role of identity and values in influencing preferences for the ethnicity of the therapist. Perhaps the most obvious and yet the most unappreciated fact is that African Americans represent a very heterogeneous group. Most psychotherapy studies have not examined this within-group heterogeneity along dimensions such as ethnic identity.

In summary, the research literature on therapist variables has yielded mixed findings. Ethnic matching of clients with therapists in the case of African Americans results in more favorable outcomes in general mental health and Veterans Administration settings, but not in substance abuse settings. However, the positive effect sizes of ethnic match are small, and it is possible that cultural match is more predictive of positive outcomes than ethnic match per se. Finally, a few studies demonstrate success in training therapists to be culturally sensitive, open, and willing to self-disclose, and to deal with cultural issues in working with African American clients.

Situational or Treatment Variables

Have certain situations or types of programs or therapies been found to be especially effective with African Americans? Many scholars have discussed the kinds of mental health services that may be culturally appropriate for African Americans. For example, Lefley and Bestman (1984) established a comprehensive mental health program with staff that included personnel indigenous to the community and who were headed by a cultural broker. A cultural broker is someone familiar with two cultures who can serve as a liaison between the two cultures. The investigators reported that dropout rates in this program were low and that consumer satisfaction and treatment outcomes were high when a cultural broker was involved as an interpreter during therapy. However, further research on this program has not been forthcoming since the original report. Still others have recommended that ethnic-specific services (i.e., those that are specifically designed for African Americans) or services provided by indigenous healers be more fully incorporated into the mental health system (Sue, 1977; White, 1984). Although most scholars have offered suggestions regarding psychotherapy with African Americans, few have empirically tested the effects of such suggestions.

One important modification, which appears to be very helpful in the provision of services, is pre-therapy intervention. Ethnic minority clients may not know what psychotherapy is, how psychotherapy can help, what to do in therapy, or what to expect from therapy. Some pre-therapy interventions may be beneficial. Acosta, Yamamoto, and Evans (1982) have devised client orientation programs aimed at familiarizing clients with psychotherapy. By using slides, audiotapes, or videotapes, the investigators showed clients the process of seeing a therapist, means by which to express problems and self-disclose, and possible ways of communicating needs. Acosta, Yamamoto, Evans, and Skilbeck (1983) conducted an evaluation of the effectiveness of the orientation program. They presented, prior to the first treatment session, low-income African American, Latino/a American, and White outpatients with either the orientation program or a program that was neutral with regard to psychotherapy. Knowledge of and attitudes toward psychotherapy were assessed prior to and immediately after the programs. Results indicated that exposure to the orientation program increased knowledge and favorable attitudes toward psychotherapy. Therapist orientation programs have also been devised to familiarize therapists with ethnic minority clients. Reviews of client and therapist preparation programs have been favorable (see Jones & Matsumoto, 1982). However, pre-therapy training, though effective, has not been studied since the mid-1980s, and it is not widely employed despite its apparent value.

In general, many scholars have made suggestions concerning treatment or situational variables that are important in working with African Americans. However, few empirical studies are available that point to effective treatment strategies. The impact of ethnic specific services has not yet been tested.

RESEARCH ON AMERICAN INDIANS

American Indians and Alaska Natives are a culturally heterogeneous population consisting of over 510 federally recognized tribes, including more than 200 Alaska Native villages (Bureau of Indian Affairs, 1991). The American Indian population in 2000 was 2.4 million. Between 1990 and 2000, the population grew by 7%. The nation's American Indian, Eskimo, and Aleut resident population is relatively young, with an estimated median age of 27.6 years, which is nearly eight years younger than the median of the U.S. population as a whole (U.S. Census Bureau, 2001).

As a group, when compared to the U.S. population at large, American Indians and Alaska Natives are economically impoverished and educationally disadvantaged. American Indians tend to be unaffected by national economic cycles, as their unemployment tends to be chronically high (LaFromboise, 1988). From 1997 to 1999, 26% of the nation's American Indian, Eskimo, and Aleut households had incomes that placed them below the poverty line (U.S. Census Bureau, 1999b). Unemployment ranged from 20% to 70%, depending on the community; their 9.6 mean years of formal education was the lowest of any ethnic group in the United States. Social and psychological problems within the American Indian and Alaska Native population include the highest arrest rates in the United States (10 times the arrest rate of Whites), high rates of alcohol abuse and alcohol-related deaths, and high rates of serious psychiatric problems including post-traumatic stress (Manson, Walker, & Kivlahan, 1987). However, tribes vary in terms of familial and social organizations, religious practices, economic resources, and rates of social and psychological problems. There are 200 American Indian and Alaska Native languages still in use by tribal members (LaFromboise, 1988). Besides linguistic and cultural differences between tribes, individuals affiliated with particular tribes differ in their acculturation to tribal or Anglo-American values. Furthermore, significant within-tribe differences include whether individuals live on or off a reservation. Thus, generalizations about the population need to be qualified.

Although generalizations about American Indians and Alaska Natives are difficult to make because of the diversity of these groups, it appears that American Indian and Alaska Natives differ from Whites in world views and value orientations. Such value differences have included American Indians' and Alaska Natives' preferences for sharing and redistribution rather than acquisition, cooperation instead of competition, noninterference instead of intervention, harmony with nature instead of controlling nature, present time orientation rather than future planning, and promotion of an extended family network instead of promotion of a nuclear family network (Sue & Sue, 1999; Trimble & LaFromboise, 1985). Other differences, which have been suggested as relevant in psychotherapy with American Indians and Alaska Natives, include culturally based faith in tribal rituals, ceremonial practices, Indian medicine and traditional healing practices, causes of mental health problems, and ways such problems should be solved. In addition, culturally specific mental disorders and culturally specific manifestations of mental disorders are salient issues (Manson, Shore, & Bloom, 1985; Neligh, 1988; Trimble & LaFromboise, 1985).

Treatment Outcome

Very few empirical studies have been conducted on the effectiveness of psychotherapy in the treatment of American Indians and Alaska Natives, and no research has investigated the relative effectiveness of different therapeutic modalities (Manson et al., 1987; Neligh, 1988). The need for outcome research is apparent given the proliferation and funding of a wide variety of treatment and prevention programs that have arisen to target the serious mental health needs of many American Indians and Alaskan Natives. Given these efforts, the lack of research on outcomes must be considered a serious problem.

The most researched American Indian mental health problem has been drug and alcohol use and abuse, although even here few treatment evaluation studies of this problem have been conducted. A comparative study (Query, 1985) between White and American Indian youth in an inpatient chemical dependency treatment program at a North Dakota State Hospital found that American Indian youth were disproportionately represented in the unit as would be expected by their percentage in the population. The youths received an unspecified form of "reality therapy" for four to six weeks. Before treatment, 64% of the White youth and 55% of the American Indian youth had contemplated suicide. Thirty-two percent of the White youth and 30% of the American Indian youth had actually attempted suicide. Upon followup six months after release from treatment, Whites were found to be functioning much better than American Indian youth on various outcome measures. Since their discharge from treatment, 42% of the American Indian youth had contemplated suicide and 25% had attempted suicide, compared to 21%, and 16%, respectively, of the White youth. Findings from this study suggest that the treatment program had resulted in more positive change in White than in American Indian youth.

Other alcohol and drug abuse programs have been studied. For instance, a substance abuse program for American Indians has been developed that combines family systems approaches, individual and group counseling, and Alcoholics Anonymous and Narcotics Anonymous meetings with Indian cultural and spiritual methods of healing. Two common methods include the sweat lodge and talking circle (Gutierres & Todd, 1997). The sweat lodge—a ritual in which participants sit near hot rocks sprinkled with water and subsequently experience sweat while engaging in fasting and prayer—promotes a feeling of kinship with all living things and the universe as the participants are exposed to the steam. The talking circle is a form of group therapy focused on the circle as a symbol of physical and psychological connectedness among individuals, a connectedness that requires that members are heard and not criticized. When evaluated relative to a no treatment control group, this culturally enhanced program increased the likelihood of treatment completion and significantly decreased depression (Gutierres, Russo, & Urbanski, 1994; Gutierres & Todd, 1997). The effects of the program on additional substance abuse, however, were not reported.

Substance abuse and suicide prevention programs for American Indians also have been advocated (see Manson, 1982; and Moncher, Holden, & Trimble, 1997, for reviews of the prevention programs). Although prevention programs are not normally discussed in terms of treatment outcome, because of the dearth of treatment outcome research with American Indians and Alaska

Natives, and because prevention approaches appear to be the trend in American Indian research, they are discussed here. Bobo, Gilchrist, Cvetkovich, Trimble, and Schinke (1988) developed a culturally tailored drug prevention program targeting American Indian youth, which included extensive collaboration within the American Indian community and in which researchers delivered the program to six groups of American Indian youth. Even highly traditional parents consented to their children's participation. In addition, the youth themselves evaluated the program favorably. However, of the six outcome variables (drug use opinions, drug knowledge, alcohol use identity, tobacco use identity, inhalant use identity, marijuana use identity), only one, "alcohol use identity," which was a measure of self-identification as a current or future alcohol user, was found to have changed significantly following the prevention program. Bobo et al. (1988) attributed this lack of statistically significant change on all but one variable to a small sample size (N = 35) and resulting insufficient power to detect change. Also, these researchers speculated that American Indian culture in general has a resistance to outside influences. Thus the study's design may have confounded the results.

Social skills training for client bicultural competence is another prevention approach. LaFromboise and Rowe (1983) outlined the process of culturally adapting an assertiveness training program for American Indians. The training combined general assertiveness skills (e.g., refusing an unreasonable request, presenting an idea to a superior) with assertiveness skills in dealing with racism (e.g., challenging employers who stereotype Indians, maintaining composure when called derogatory names). Behavioral skills (e.g., eye contact, timing, loudness of voice) were emphasized for interactions with Whites, whereas cultural appropriateness (e.g., the impact of assertiveness on the group) was emphasized in interactions with Indians. The authors contended that skills training is less culturally biased than other approaches in that it is less prescriptive in its conceptualization of appropriate behaviors. The approach can be tailored to the context and thus is less culturally imposing on American Indian culture. In addition, skills training is flexible, allowing for the selection of target behaviors to be changed. This presumably facilitates culturally appropriate modifications of the program.

Schinke and colleagues (1988) compared a bicultural competence skills training approach, which taught competence in American Indian and mainstream U.S. cultures, with a no-treatment control condition for preventing substance abuse in American Indian adolescents. They found that there were greater post-test and followup improvements with the bicultural skills program than with the no-treatment group on measures of knowledge about the health and social effects of substance use, self-control, assertiveness, and substance use rates.

In addition to substance abuse prevention, suicide prevention programs have been developed for American Indians. The Zuni Life Skills Development Curriculum was designed to prevent suicide among American Indian high school students (LaFromboise & Howard-Pitney, 1995). The program involved: (a) building self-esteem; (b) identifying emotions and stress; (c) increasing communication and problem-solving skills; (d) recognizing and eliminating self-destructive behaviors such as pessimistic thoughts or anger reactivity; (e) receiving suicide information; (f) receiving suicide intervention training; and (g) setting personal and community goals. Zuni students who were exposed to this curriculum had better suicide intervention skills as measured by a role-play assessment, and significantly lower suicide probability and hopelessness ratings, as measured by self-report, than did students who did not receive the intervention. Unfortunately, no followup data have been published showing that it affected suicide rates.

It is apparent that research on interventions with American Indians for problems such as substance abuse and suicide has proceeded very slowly, and it would be premature to try to address the question of the efficacy of mental health interventions.

Treatment Process

Client Variables

In terms of expectancy and preferences, it has often been stated that American Indians distrust non-Indian therapists (LaFromboise, 1988). However, the empirical investigation of such a claim, especially as it relates to American Indian expectancy and preferences for ethnically similar therapists, has yielded mixed results (see Atkinson, 1983, for a review). For example, LaFromboise, Dauphinais, and Rowe (1980), in a study of American Indian high school students who were attending boarding, urban, and rural schools in Oklahoma, had the students rate their preferences of qualities of a helpful person. The ethnicity of a person, in terms of being an American Indian, was found to be relatively less important than other qualities such as trustworthiness. No differences in ratings were found between students from boarding, urban, or rural schools.

In another study, LaFromboise and Dixon (1981) had American Indian reservation high school students in Nebraska observe and rate previously videotaped segments of one of four counseling conditions, within which the interviewer's ethnicity was crossed with the interviewer's performance. The interviewer's ethnicity was either American Indian or non-Indian, and the interviewer acted according to a trustworthy or nontrustworthy model of counseling. Ratings of trustworthiness, expertness, or attractiveness were found to be unrelated to the interviewer's ethnicity.

By contrast, Dauphinais, Dauphinais, and Rowe (1981) studied American Indian high school students from two federal boarding schools in Oklahoma and one tribally controlled boarding school in South Dakota (40 tribal affiliations were represented in the sample). Students were randomly assigned to listen to one of three tape-recorded conditions, which differed only in that counselor responses reflected either a directive, nondirective, or American Indian culturally oriented counseling style. For each condition, half of the students were told that the counselor was American Indian, and half were told that the counselor was non-Indian. Dauphinais et al. (1981) found that students gave more positive ratings on the Counselor Effectiveness Scale to counselors who were introduced as American Indian. Furthermore, the culturally oriented counseling style was rated as more credible than the nondirective approach, but not the directive approach.

Havilland, Horswill, O'Connell, and Dynneson (1983) studied American Indian college students in Montana, who represented 11 American Indian tribes, with a range of 3% to 100% American Indian blood quantum, with nearly 70% of the sample having lived on a reservation some time during their lives. The researchers found that American Indian students showed a strong preference for an ethnically similar counselor, and that students' willingness to use a counseling center where an American Indian was on staff related directly to students' preferences for an ethnically similar counselor. Furthermore, Havilland et al. (1983) found that American Indian students tended to report a preference for an American Indian counselor for personal, educational, and vocational problems. Blood quantum and percentage of life spent on a reservation were not found to influence students' preferences.

Bennett and BigFoot-Sipes (1991) found that, although therapist-client ethnic match was more important to American Indian college students than to White students, especially to those American Indian students who were more involved in American Indian culture, having a counselor who shared similar attitudes and values was even more important for both American Indians and Whites. These findings were supported in a subsequent study (BigFoot-Sipes, Dauphinais, LaFromboise, Bennett & Rowe, 1992).

Cultural commitment may also influence American Indians' attitudes toward mental health services. In a study of American Indian college students, those strongly committed to their native Indian culture displayed more negative attitudes toward counseling and mental health professionals than those strongly committed to White culture or to both cultures (Price & McNeill, 1992). American Indian women in all groups showed more positive attitudes toward counseling than did men.

The studies to date on American Indian expectancies and preferences have been analogue studies and have yielded mixed results. However, inconsistent results may have been caused by the method employed. Thus, it would be useful for future expectancy and preference research to take into account the type of problem with which a client presents and counselor characteristics other than ethnicity alone. These could include client and therapist attitudes, personality, education, and especially American Indian ethnic identity or cultural commitment (Bennett & BigFoot-Sipes, 1991; BigFoot-Sipes et al., 1992). Finally, a pragmatic factor to consider is that ethnic preference studies may not reflect what services are actually available to the American Indian and Alaska Native population. For example, many American Indians and Alaska Natives simply have few therapist choices available to them, despite the preferences they may have. In 1993, only 22 American Indians received a doctoral degree in psychology (Commission on Ethnic Minority Recruitment, Retention, and Training in Psychology, 1997). Findings that American Indians prefer American Indian therapists may provide additional justification for funding the education of American Indian and Alaska Native researchers and therapists, for there currently are so few American Indian and Alaska Native mental health professionals. However, further research is needed to clarify American Indian expectancies and preferences within the therapeutic setting.

Therapist Variables

The paucity of empirical research also is evident with respect to the impact of therapist variables, and what has been evaluated to date has yielded mixed results. Dauphinais, LaFromboise, and Rowe (1980) surveyed American Indian eleventh and twelfth grade students (from a variety of tribal affiliations such as Choctaw, Creek, Kiowa, Chickasaw, Comanche, Cherokee, Sioux, Cheyenne/Arapahoe) attending Bureau of Indian Affairs boarding schools and urban and rural public schools in Oklahoma. These researchers found that the students' satisfaction with previous counseling was not related to whether the counselor's race was American Indian or non-Indian. However, as mentioned previously, in the Dauphinais et al. (1981) study with American Indian high school students, counselors were rated as more credible on the Counselor Effectiveness Rating Scale when the counselor used a culturally relevant counseling style. In addition, independent of counseling style, the counselor who was introduced as American Indian received more positive ratings. This suggests that the ethnicity of the counselor may be an important factor in the counseling of American Indians. Treatment outcome was not assessed in these studies. Thus, the effects of therapist variables may be obscured by client preferences.

Another line of research suggests that American Indians may initially turn to community support systems for help. Similar to White students, Zuni high school students were more likely to seek help from a friend, parent, or relative than professional sources for personal problems (Bee-Gates, Howard-Pitney, LaFromboise, & Rowe, 1996). When Zuni students did seek professional help, it was primarily for academic and career issues. Thus, academic and career counselors should be alert to potential psychological problems among American Indian youth, as these problems are not likely to come to the attention of mental health clinicians.

Situational or Treatment Variables

There is little empirical evidence that validates the effectiveness of specific modes of psychotherapy with American Indian or Alaska Native populations, and no information was found comparing the efficacy of different psychotherapeutic approaches. However, this has not impeded the proliferation of program development, most particularly, prevention interventions (see Manson, 1982) and group treatment. The majority of these programs target the most salient mental and social problem in many American Indian communities: alcohol and drug abuse and dependence.

In addition, family-network therapy, traditional healing practices, and bicultural skills training programs have been described in the literature as possible culturally appropriate modalities to be considered in working with American Indians. For instance, Manson et al. (1987), in their review of psychiatric assessment and treatment of American Indians and Alaska Natives, propose that family-network therapy may be culturally appropriate for some American Indians and Alaska Natives, given a cultural context of an extended family social organization. LaFromboise (1988) notes that American Indian communities have traditionally used extended families as sources of care and psychological support, and has described work utilizing the extended family in a therapeutic setting.

Basic knowledge of psychotherapy processes and outcomes for American Indians and Alaska Natives is being established very slowly. The population is a particularly difficult one to study, given not only its cultural and linguistic heterogeneity, but its geographical range across the United States, including varied locations such as cities, rural areas, and reservations. Another problem (which is not, by any means, unique to American Indian research) is the tendency for researchers to use nonclinical populations, a methodology that limits the generalizability of findings. In addition, there have been so few empirical psychotherapy studies on American Indians, and none on Alaska Natives, that those that have been conducted do not allow for broad generalizations. The literature on psychotherapy with American Indians and Alaska Natives predominantly consists of descriptive reports and theoretical program suggestions. However, the recent trend in American Indian research, which utilizes and extends the methodologies developed to study other ethnic groups, appears to have potential to further the field. Because the methodologies are similar, comparisons now can be made across ethnic groups, and methodological and theoretical advances can be shared.

Research on Asian Americans

Asian American groups are the fastest growing ethnic minority populations in the United States.

As a whole, the Asian American population grew by 45% between 1990 and 1999 to 11.2 million (U.S. Census Bureau, 2001). This increase can be attributed largely to immigration to the United States from China, the Philippines, India, Korea, Southeast Asia, and secondarily to natural increases (births minus deaths and departures from the United States). The largest groups are Chinese Americans (22%), Filipino Americans (19%), Japanese Americans (12%), South Asians or Asian Indians (11%), Korean Americans (11%), Vietnamese Americans (8%), and Hawaiian Americans (3%) (U.S. Bureau of the Census, 1993). Most Asian Americans (70%) live in just five states—namely, California, Hawaii, New York, Illinois, and Texas.

Asian Americans have a higher median household income ($45,248) than Whites ($40,576). However, this is probably because 14% of European American households have no income earners versus only 9% in Asian American households (U.S. Census Bureau, 1999). In addition, 20% of Asian American households have three or more income earners versus 12% of European American households. Per capita median income for Asian Americans ($22,398) is somewhat lower than it is for European Americans ($23,191). Moreover, Asian Americans have more persons living in their households than do other groups. Whereas 47% of European Americans have two-member households, only 28% of Asian Americans do (U.S. Census Bureau, 1999). Forty-eight percent of Asian American households have four or more members versus 31% for European Americans. In addition, over 90% of Asian Americans live in metropolitan areas, where the cost of living is highest (Lee, 1998). Thus, living expenses are higher for Asian Americans than for other groups who are less densely populated in metropolitan areas.

An important characteristic of the Asian American population is the diversity among groups (U.S. Census Bureau, 1993). For example, the vast majority of Vietnamese, Koreans, Asian Indians, Filipinos, and Chinese in the United States were born overseas. However, Samoans, Japanese, Guamanians, and Hawaiians were largely born in the United States. Japanese and Asian Indians had median ages that exceeded the national average, but other Asian groups had median ages lower than the national average. The median family income of Japanese Americans ($27,400) was strikingly higher than that of Vietnamese Americans ($12,800). Great variation also exists among Asian groups in educational attainment and achievement. The high school dropout rates for Filipinos are substantially higher than those for other Asian groups and White Americans. There is also a great deal of within-group variability. For example, a majority of the Chinese are foreign born but over one-third of them are American born (37%). Moreover, foreign-born Chinese come from different parts of the world (e.g., mainland China, Taiwan, Hong Kong) and speak different dialects of Chinese, adding to the within-group diversity.

Both the diversity between and within Asian American groups must be considered in the interpretation and generalizability of treatment process and outcome findings. Most of these studies have focused on the larger and more acculturated Asian American groups such as Chinese and Japanese and have primarily used student samples that tend to be more acculturated and homogeneous than those drawn from Asian communities. Some investigations have included different groups within the rubric of "Asian Americans," so that differences among the groups are masked (i.e., it is unclear which Asian American groups are being studied).

Treatment Outcome

Few studies have directly examined psychotherapy outcomes for Asian American clients. Zane, Enomoto, and Chun (1994) assessed White and Asian outpatients at a community mental health center at the first and fourth sessions using both client self-report (Symptom Checklist) and therapist-rated (Brief Psychiatric Rating Scale) outcome measures. The results indicated poorer short-term treatment outcomes for Asian American outpatients relative to their White American counterparts after controlling for pre-treatment level of severity. Asian clients reported greater depression ($\beta = .20$), hostility ($\beta = .44$), and anxiety ($\beta = .15$) after four sessions of treatment and were less satisfied than White clients on five satisfaction indices (βs = –.29 to –.40). There was also a tendency for therapists to evaluate Asian clients as having lower levels of psychosocial functioning ($\beta = -.14$) than White clients after short-term treatment. Most outcome studies have aggregated across different Asian groups with the exception of research on Southeast Asians. Mollica et al. (1990) reported improvement in depression among Cambodian clients following six months of psychotherapy, whereas no significant improvements in depression or anxiety were found for Vietnamese or Hmong/Laotian clients.

In terms of differential outcome, two studies have examined clinical outcome among Asian outpatients using the Global Assessment Scale (GAS), a measure of general psychosocial functioning as rated by the client's therapist. Zane, Hatanaka, Park, and Akutsu (1994) found no differences between Asians and Whites on post-treatment GAS scores, adjusted for pre-treatment GAS. Sue et al. (1991) obtained similar results as Asian outpatients showed similar improvement compared with White clients. Other studies have found some evidence of differential outcome. Lee and Mixson (1995) asked clients at a university counseling center to rate the effectiveness of counseling and of their therapists and to indicate the reasons they sought treatment. Despite presenting with a similar number of concerns prior to treatment, Asians rated both the counseling experience and therapists as less effective than did Whites. Statistically significant differences were found between Asian Americans and Whites on ratings of helpfulness for personal problems (Asian American mean = 4.03, White mean = 4.63 on a 7-point scale), therapist competence (Asian American mean = 4.01, White mean = 4.57 on a 5-point Scale), and likelihood of returning to the therapist (Asian American mean = 4.28, White mean = 4.87 on a 7-point scale).

An intervention to enhance parent-child relationships and to reduce parental overcontrol was examined among Chinese American parents who were not necessarily experiencing psychological distress (Chau & Landreth, 1997). Parents in two metropolitan churches were assigned either to a filial therapy intervention or a no-treatment control group. Parents in the intervention group significantly increased in their empathic interactions and acceptance of their children and experienced a significant decrease in stress. However, it is unknown if group assignments were random, and children's outcomes were not assessed.

Any conclusions about the effectiveness of treatment for Asians would be premature given the limited data, but several empirical trends should be noted. First, some evidence suggests that certain Asian groups improve with psychotherapy. Second, with respect to differential outcomes, divergent trends are found, and these are associated with the type of outcome measure used. Studies reporting no differential outcome between Asians and Whites relied on a measure of general psychological functioning (e.g., GAS), whereas differential outcomes were found in studies that used client satisfaction measures and/or specific symptom scales. It is possible that the null results may reflect the unreliability and insensitivity of the global outcome measure used. The GAS essentially constitutes a one-item measure. It is highly reliable if raters are extensively trained in its use (Endicott, Spitzer, Fleiss, & Cohen, 1976), but there appeared to be no such training conducted with the therapists in either study. In sum, Asian clients appear to derive less positive experiences from therapy than Whites, but it is unclear if this difference in client satisfaction actually reflects ethnic differences in actual treatment outcomes (e.g., symptom reduction).

Treatment Process

The empirical work that has addressed psychotherapy issues has focused primarily on variables such as client preferences and mental health beliefs, treatment and therapist credibility, and ethnic match.

Client Variables

In view of the great heterogeneity that exits between and within Asian American groups, client variables presumably would be an important area of focus for process research on Asian Americans. To date, the major empirical efforts have addressed acculturation influences and client preferences and expectancies. At times, these variables have been examined concurrently.

Asian American Ethnic Group Differences

Combining Asian Americans as a single group may obscure important between-group differences in psychopathology. Ying and Hu (1994) examined public outpatient mental health services for Chinese, Japanese, Filipino, Korean, and Southeast-Asian American adults in the San Francisco area. Filipinos were underrepresented in the system, whereas Southeast Asians were overrepresented and had higher utilization rates, but showed less improvement than did the other groups. It is possible that Southeast Asians had more acculturation stressors as a function of refugee status and had less community coping resources than the other groups, though this hypothesis was not studied.

In a study of inpatient and outpatient mental health facilities in Hawaii, Leong (1994) found that Chinese and Japanese Americans underutilized both types of facilities. It was suggested that this general underutilization was partially a function of the stigma associated with mental health problems for both ethnic groups. However, Filipino clients tended to underutilize outpatient facilities somewhat less than they did inpatient facilities. It was suggested that Filipinos may feel less stigma regarding mental health services than other Asian American groups.

In a study of outpatients in the public mental health system in Seattle, the percentages of all Asian Americans and European Americans diagnosed with schizophrenia and with major affective disorders (e.g., major depression, bipolar disorder) were approximately the same (Uehara, Takeuchi, & Smukler, 1994). However, an analysis of individual Asian American ethnic groups revealed striking differences. Japanese and Chinese American clients were diagnosed with significantly greater rates of schizophrenia than major affective disorders. The opposite was true for Laotian Americans and Filipino Americans. Rates of diagnoses for schizophrenia and major affective disorders for Vietnamese Americans were approximately the same. These findings may reflect a reluctance of Japanese and Chinese Americans to seek public mental health services for major affective disorders. The findings also suggest that those Japanese and Chinese Americans who do seek public mental health services may be more psychologically disturbed than other groups of Asian American or European American clients. Japanese and Chinese Americans who are less psychologically disturbed may seek support from family or community sources other than the public mental health system. The Japanese and Chinese American communities in Seattle and in other areas of the West Coast and Hawaii have existed longer and are better established than many of the other Asian American ethnic communities. These well-established communities may be better able to provide alternative sources of support for mental health problems than other less established Asian American communities.

Thus, it appears that Asian Americans generally tend to underutilize mental health services, although utilization rates vary across specific Asian American ethnic groups. However, the reasons for different rates of utilization are unknown. Investigation of potential cultural mechanisms or environmental stressors such as acculturation is needed.

Client Preferences and Expectancies

A number of studies have examined the preferences of Asian Americans for ethnicity of the therapist and type of counseling approach. This research has primarily relied on nonclinical samples of Asian American or foreign Asian students. There is recent evidence that Asian Americans may not prefer traditional psychotherapy methods. Atkinson, Kim, and Caldwell (1998) have identified eight counselor helping roles for work with ethnic minority clients: adviser, consultant, counselor, psychotherapist, advocate, change agent, facilitator of indigenous support systems, and facilitator of indigenous healing methods. For problems of external etiology (e.g., a Korean immigrant being taken advantage of by an employer), Asian American students preferred a counselor in a consultant role. For problems of internal etiology (e.g., depressed thoughts), the students preferred a counselor who facilitated indigenous support systems. The psychotherapist role was perceived by the students as the least helpful of the eight roles for internal and external problems. Thus, effective interventions with Asian Americans may involve therapists who engage in methods other than traditional psychotherapy. However, this conclusion is based on analogue research with nonpatient samples.

Similar to the pretherapy interventions discussed above in the section on African Americans, a pretherapy intervention was developed for immigrant clients at a community mental health center in Hawaii (Lambert & Lambert, 1984). Clients in the intervention condition listened to a recorded message that explained role expectations for therapy, therapy processes, expectations for verbal disclosure, problems encountered by clients in psychotherapy, misconceptions about psychotherapy, and the need for regular attendance. Clients in the control condition listened to a recorded message about why people have trouble coping with problems and demands in their lives. Relative to the clients in the control condition, clients in the experimental condition had lower dropout rates, were more satisfied with therapy, rated themselves as more changed, and became less dependent on the therapist for support, advice, and direction.

Acculturation Influences

Important variations in the way Asians seek, respond to, or experience psychotherapy may depend on the individual's level of acculturation. Acculturation refers to the extent to which members of an ethnic minority group have learned or adopted the cultural patterns of the majority group (Sue & Morishima, 1982). In one of the few studies of Asian clients, Tracey, Leong, and Glidden (1986) examined the presenting problems of Whites and of seven Asian groups (Chinese, Filipino, Hawaiian, Korean, Japanese, Asian-White, and Asian-Asian Americans) at a university counseling center. The most acculturated groups, Asian-Whites and Filipinos, were more likely to perceive their major presenting problem as involving emotional/interpersonal issues (e.g., "feel lonely and alienated from others, have difficulty with close personal relationships") and less likely to perceive their major presenting problem as involving academic/vocational concerns (e.g., "don't know how to study, don't know what my interests are").

Other Variables

There is some evidence that Asians define and think about mental health and emotional problems somewhat differently than those from other cultures. Clinicians have noted that Asians tend not to make a strong distinction between emotional and physical problems and attribute both to bodily imbalances (Flaskerud & Soldevilla, 1986). This holistic tendency was reflected in findings in which Asians believed that emotional problems were more influenced by organic and somatic factors than did Whites (Sue, Wagner, Ja, Margullis, & Lew, 1976). On the other hand, Asians were more likely to believe that mental health is enhanced by the avoidance of negative thinking and/or using self-discipline (Lum, 1982; Sue et al., 1976). Given that the practice of psychotherapy often requires clients to focus on painful or negative thoughts, relies on emotional catharsis, and tends to deemphasize somatic interventions, it has been hypothesized that many Asian American clients may find the initial stage of psychotherapy which relies most heavily on these processes (cf. Meichenbaum, 1976), inconsistent with their conceptualization of positive mental health benefits (Zane & Sue, 1991).

In addition to causal attributions and conceptualizations of illness, symptom patterns of Asian clients in treatment have been examined. Asians (particularly those with depressive disorders) tend to present with more somatic complaints than non-Asian clients, and this has been interpreted as evidence of somatization in which physical symptoms are expressed in place of psychological symptoms (Kleinman, 1977; Marsella, Kinzie, & Gordon, 1973). Tanaka-Matsumi and Marsella (1976) suggested that the experience of depression may, indeed, be somewhat different for Asians. In a word association study, Japanese nationals associated more external referent and somatic terms to the word "depression," whereas White Americans associated terms that referred to internal mood states. The associations of a seemingly highly acculturated Japanese American sample were very similar to the White responses. Some research suggests that these somatic tendencies have resulted from help-seeking practices in which Asians have tended to use medical services for psychological disorders (Cheung, 1982; Cheung & Lau, 1982). One study suggests that Asian Americans are no more likely to experience somatic discomfort than are Whites (Zhang, Snowden, & Sue, 1998). However, when considering somatic symptoms, including the culture-bound syndrome such as neurasthenia (a disorder similar to Chronic Fatigue Syndrome and characterized by persistent and distressing mental fatigue or bodily weakness with symptoms of muscular pain, dizziness, tension headaches, sleep disturbance, extreme tenseness, irritability, or dyspepsia), it appears that Asian Americans are more likely to show somatic symptoms (*U.S. Surgeon General's Supplement to the Report on Mental Health*, 2001). Regardless of the causal pathway, the process by which basic psychological problems are presented and/or experienced appears to be somewhat different for Asians.

Culture-specific symptom presentation suggests that culture-specific psychotherapy methods may be most useful for many Asian Americans. Western psychotherapy relies on verbal expressiveness and open self-disclosure as the primary means for resolving psychological problems. These aspects can conflict with the tendency of Asians to be less verbal and to refrain from the public expression of feelings (Kim, 1973). Indeed, Asian Americans have been found to be more reticent than White Americans to discuss psychological problems with professionals, family, or friends (Zhang et al., 1998). In many East Asian cultures, the "language of emotion" for Asians is somewhat different in that affection is conveyed by the use of gestures, often involving the exchange of material goods and services that enhance the person's well-being (Chang, 1985). Also, metaphors are frequently used to communicate feelings. Thus, it is possible that differences in the communication styles of Asian Americans may influence the therapeutic relationship and the development of rapport in psychotherapy. However, more research is needed to clarify the roles such differences may have and their possible relationship to outcomes.

Therapist Variables

Match Between the Client and Therapist

The match between client and therapist has been considered to be an important factor in psychotherapy. For those Asian American clients who are non-English speaking, language match would also be crucial.

Sue et al. (1991), in the previously described study of Los Angeles County Mental Health System, found that ethnic match between client and therapist was associated with increased use of mental health services and a lower likelihood of dropout for Asian American clients. In addition, for those Asian Americans for whom English was not a primary language, ethnic match, language match, and gender match were associated with a decrease in the likelihood of premature termination and an increase in the number of sessions. Thus, at least in terms of indirect indices of treatment efficacy, ethnic match exerted a significant influence with Asian American clients. Moreover, in terms of outcome, non-English-speaking Asian Americans were found to have better outcomes, as measured by GAS change, when matched with a therapist of similar ethnicity and language.

Language match may be a lowest common denominator for effective communication in psychotherapy (Rogler, Malgady, Costantino, & Blumenthal, 1987). However, a language match does not necessarily ensure that the therapist is culturally competent. As with other aspects of ethnic matching, language match has shown statistically significant but small effects on mental health services utilization and outcome among Asian Americans. Thus, language match is a starting point rather than an endpoint for culturally competent mental health services. Considering that the growth of the Asian American population in the United States is due, in large part, to immigration and that those immigrants tend to be non-English speaking, the availability of therapists who are of the same ethnicity and/or who speak the same language as Asian American clients is important for service utilization and, to some extent, treatment outcome. However, further research is needed to replicate Sue et al.'s (1991) findings and to investigate potential differences in the significance of match among Asian American groups.

Situational or Treatment Variables

It has often been hypothesized that modifications in the approach to psychotherapy are needed to adequately treat Asian American clients (Chin, 1998; Lee, 1997). For example, Lee (1997) and others have noted important differences in family structure, value orientation, and beliefs about mental health and illness between Asian and White American cultures. Compared with Western culture, which typically focuses on the nuclear family unit, involves somewhat egalitarian relationships, and emphasizes values of individualism, competition, self-worth, and direct expression of emotions, many Asians have strong ties to nonegalitarian societies that center on extended family arrangements based on structured, hierarchical role relationships and that stress values of collectivism, group achievement, "face," and emotional restraint. Murase (1977) has recommended that treatment approaches for Asians should recognize the family as an integral part of treatment, establish an active, highly personalized therapeutic relationship, focus on survival-related tasks to facilitate the engagement process, address the possible conflict between the cultural dynamic of "loss of face" and the confessional character of psychotherapy, differentiate between cultural behavioral propensities and pathology, reevaluate the self-determination construct, permit flexibility in session scheduling and duration, and recognize the ameliorative effect of a familiar and predictable cultural milieu.

Despite the extensive amount of published recommendations for the modification of Western psychotherapeutic approaches, there have been no empirical comparisons of efficacy between mainstream Western modalities and culturally modified modalities in the treatment of Asian Americans, nor have there been empirical studies of the effectiveness of culturally specific treatments or culturally modified treatments themselves. Most research has focused on aspects of "culturally sensitive services" for Asian Americans, such as ethnic and language match discussed in the previous section.

Nevertheless, ethnic and language match are only part of "culturally sensitive services." Sue (1977) suggested parallel services, which entail not only ethnic and language match, but a systemic change of integration into the community, altering the situations in which services are rendered. That is, parallel services should be based in the community, staffed by a bilingual and bicultural staff, and designed in a way that would be more culturally responsive to Asian American clientele.

Such parallel services appear to have increased utilization by Asian American clients. In a study of community mental health care centers in Southern California, Flaskerud (1986) found that culturally compatible factors such as ethnic and language match and location within the community contributed to increased utilization of mental health services by Asian Americans. Lau and Zane (2000) compared patterns of the cost-utilization and outcomes of 3,178 Asian American outpatients using ethnic-specific services (ESS) to those Asians using mainstream services. Consistent with earlier studies, cost-utilization for ESS Asian clients was higher than that for mainstream Asian clients. However, better treatment outcome was found for ESS clients compared to their mainstream counterparts after controlling for certain demographics, pre-treatment symptom severity, diagnosis, and type of reimbursement. Moreover, there was a significant relationship between cost-utilization and outcome for ESS clients, whereas for mainstream clients, this relationship was not significant. Nevertheless, statistically significant effects in a large database are not necessarily substantive. Overall, these studies suggest that parallel services have increased the utilization and, in some cases, the effectiveness of mental health services with some Asian American groups.

Although these studies are limited in that treatment outcome was not often measured, the impact of parallel services on indirect indices for Asian Americans is apparent. Preliminary studies strongly suggest that parallel services have increased the utilization and efficacy of mental health services with most Asian American groups, but there are no outcome studies on interventions for psychological disorders and very little research conducted in the 1990s.

RESEARCH ON LATINO/A AMERICANS

Latino/a Americans number 32.4 million and make up approximately 12% of the United States population (U.S. Census Bureau, 2001). They are the second largest ethnic minority group in the United States, preceded only by African Americans. However, the Latino/a American population is projected to become the nation's largest ethnic minority group by 2005 and to comprise 24% of the population by 2050 (U.S. Census Bureau, 2000a). The nation's Latino/a population increased by 10.1 million people between 1990 and 2000 (U.S. Census Bureau, 2001). The tremendous growth in the Latino/a population has been due to the high levels of Latino/a immigration into the United States. Nearly two-thirds (63%) of Latino/a Americans in 1997 were of Mexican origin, whereas 14 percent were of Central or South American origin, 11 percent of Puerto Rican origin and 4 percent of Cuban origin (U.S. Census Bureau, 1998). California (10.5 million) and Texas (6 million) are home to over half of the Latino/a's in the United States (U.S. Census Bureau, 2000b). Latino/a Americans are relatively young, with the median age of the population being 27 years.

Compared to the non-Latino/a White population of the United States, Latino/a's have lower levels of income, education, and occupational status, although their disadvantage varies greatly by Latino/a group. In 1998, approximately 26% of Latino/a Americans were poor, as defined by individual annual earnings of less than $8,500 (U.S. Census Bureau, 1999). The reasons for these differences are partly attributable to the educational and economic status of immigrants prior to their arrival in the United States. Cubans, for example, tend to be from the middle or upper class, whereas some Latino/a groups come from impoverished economic backgrounds (Gurak & Rogler, 1983).

Although the general question of the degree of psychotherapy effectiveness with Latino/a's remains, research in this area has attempted to clarify this question. Specifically, what kinds of psychotherapy are most effective with Latino/a's? What are the client, therapist, and situational factors that influence psychotherapy with Latino/a's? How do within-group differences affect client preferences leading to differential outcomes? And finally, given what is known, how can treatment programs be modified or developed to encourage service utilization and increase treatment effectiveness?

Treatment Outcome

It is generally assumed that mainstream mental health therapies are less effective with Latino/a's. This assumption, though not always tested directly, has been supported by indirect measures of treatment outcome such as treatment utilization, premature termination, and treatment duration of Latino/a's in the mental health care system. Accordingly, there has been a movement toward "culturally sensitive" mental health services that consist of various strategies such as increasing the accessibility of treatment, selecting available treatments deemed most appropriate for Latino/a values or cultural orientation, modifying current therapies for Latino/a's, and developing therapies that utilize elements of Latino/a culture (Rogler et al., 1987).

Much emphasis has been given to investigating the efficacy of therapies, which have been modified to fit Latino/a culture. These studies will be discussed. However, research focusing on the treatment outcomes of Latino/a's, given current Western modes of treatment, has received less attention. One large-scale study in Los Angeles County (described earlier) measured treatment outcome using pre- and post-treatment scores on the GAS; Mexican Americans were found most likely to improve after treatment when compared to Whites, African Americans, and Asian Americans (Sue et al., 1991). Thus, at least in this study, based on data from a large metropolitan area, Mexican Americans do appear to improve in their GAS scores. However, Mexican Americans tend to underutilize services, so at this time it is unclear what the effect of underutilization may have been on the sample. Thus, conclusions drawn from this study must be interpreted with caution.

Treatment Process

Client Preferences

Client preference studies among Latino/a Americans have explored (1) the relationship between client ethnicity and acculturation, (2) ratings of therapists of similar and different ethnicities, and (3) client ratings of therapeutic style. In a review of the research on the role of ethnic similarity in psychotherapy, Atkinson (1983) concluded that for Latino/a's, there did not appear to be a preference for therapist ethnicity. Likewise, no therapist ethnicity effect on therapy process variables was found. These variables included perceived therapist credibility, perceived therapist effectiveness, and client verbal behavior.

Ruelas, Atkinson, and Ramos-Sanchez (1998), in an analogue study, found that perception of therapist credibility among Mexican American community college students was positively associated with therapist adherence to Mexican cultural attitudes and behavior. Conversely, acculturation to North American culture was not associated with ratings of counselor credibility. These findings contradict the "cultural barrier" hypothesis that Latino/a cultural values prevent Latino/a Americans from help-seeking. The aspects of Latino/a cultures that may facilitate help-seeking require additional investigation.

Therapist Variables

Match Between Client and Therapist

In a previously discussed study of clients in Los Angeles County, Sue et al. (1991) found that ethnic match predicted a greater number of sessions for Mexican American clients. The Mexican American clients were divided into two groups based on whether English was their primary language. For those whose primary language was not English, ethnic match was found to significantly predict a decrease in premature termination, an increase in the number of sessions, and more positive treatment outcomes in terms of therapist ratings. Thus, it appears that ethnic and language matches are important factors in the psychotherapeutic process, especially for Mexican Americans whose primary language is not English. These findings have been replicated in subsequent analyses of the clients at the same Los Angeles clinics (Russell et al., 1996; Yeh et al., 1994). In a previously described study of culturally compatible mental health services in Los Angeles, Flaskerud (1986) found that language match, ethnic-racial match, and community location made the largest contribution in discriminating between dropout and non-dropout status. As discussed previously, the effect sizes of the ethnic match studies have been small. This suggests that ethnic matching is not a guarantee that mental health services will be effective for Latino/a's (Maramba & Hall, in press).

In addition to ethnic match, language match is a particularly important factor in the treatment of monolingual Spanish-speaking Latino/a clients. The Bilingual Interpreter Program in Los Angeles trained bilingual-bicultural community aides to become interpreters for English-speaking therapists (Acosta & Cristo, 1981). Spanish-speaking clients who used an interpreter were found to feel more helped and understood than bilingual Mexican American clients who spoke to the therapist in English (Kline, Acosta, Austin, & Johnson, 1980). More research needs to be conducted in this area. However, available evidence suggests that language match is important in understanding psychotherapy and its outcomes among Latino/a's.

In other studies, variables in addition to ethnic match have been examined. Similar to the results with African Americans, Latino/a Americans who were matched with substance abuse counselors on gender and ethnicity did not utilize services more frequently or have better outcomes than those who were not matched on these variables (Fiorentine & Hillhouse, 1999). Nevertheless, individually tailored methods to enhance counselor communication with Mexican American substance-abusing clients have been found to be more effective in reducing positive drug urine tests and enhancing treatment attendance (Dansereau et al., 1996). These methods were described previously in the section on African Americans. Individual tailoring of treatment methods may be a means of increasing the therapist-client cultural match (Sue & Zane, 1987).

Therapist Style

The effect of therapist style is a more recently investigated area in Latino/a psychotherapy research. Preliminary evidence supports the claim that Latino/a's prefer a directive counseling style over a nondirective style. Ponce and Atkinson (1989) found that Mexican American students gave more positive ratings to a directive counseling style than a nondirective style. Pomales and Williams (1989) found Puerto Rican and Mexican American students to have an overall preference for a directive counseling style. This preference for a directive style was found to exert a stronger influence than acculturation on the ratings of the counselor's knowledge of psychology, on counselor willingness to help, and on the students' own willingness to see a counselor.

Cultural Sensitivity Training

As mentioned earlier, development of cultural sensitivity training for therapists has been an important trend in providing effective services to minority populations (Acosta, 1984; Acosta et al., 1982; Lefley, 1985). In reviewing clinical and empirical findings on psychotherapy with Mexican Americans, Acosta (1984) described a research project that investigated the orientation of therapists to low-income and minority patients at the Los Angeles County-University of Southern California Medical Center's Adult Psychiatric Outpatient Clinic. The orientation program consisted of a series of seminars with topics drawn from the book *Effective Psychotherapy for Low-Income and Minority Patients* (Acosta et al., 1982). Post-program evaluations showed that therapists significantly increased their knowledge and sensitivity in dealing with low-income and minority patients, and patient followup data suggested that therapists may have been more effective, according to self- and patient reports, as a result of the orientation program (Yamamoto, Acosta, Evans, & Skilbeck, 1984). Another brief, intensive training program mentioned earlier in the section on African Americans—Cross Cultural Training for Mental Health Professionals, also has been evaluated positively in increasing the effectiveness of therapists in servicing Latino/a's (Lefley, 1985). Thus preliminary research supports the efficacy of cultural sensitivity training. However, further empirical research needs to be conducted to replicate the findings of these studies. Moreover, the effects of cultural sensitivity training on psychotherapy outcome also need to be evaluated.

Situational or Treatment Variables

The need for culturally sensitive treatments for minority populations has been argued. However, research on the effectiveness of services for Latino/a's has been limited to indirect indices. No direct comparisons between the effectiveness of mainstream services and culturally sensitive services were found. Previous research has focused either on mainstream treatments or on culturally sensitive treatments. However, recent studies on cultural modification of treatments have begun to bridge the gap between mainstream and culturally sensitive treatments.

Cognitive Behavioral Therapy

Cognitive behavioral therapy (CBT) has been found to be an effective, well-established treatment for depression in European American adults (DeRubeis & Crits-Christoph, 1998). Three studies in medical centers and outpatient university settings that have focused specifically on Latino Americans have reported similar results, suggesting that cognitive behavioral therapy reduces depression in Latino/a American adults and adolescents. One study did not include a control group (Organista et al., 1994), but two others demonstrated superior effects for CBT versus no-treatment control groups (Muñoz et al., 1995; Rossello & Bernal, 1999). A class for groups of clients based on CBT principles reduced Beck Depression Inventory (BDI) scores by 2 points but did not impact Center for Epidemiological Studies depression scores (Muñoz et al., 1995). This small effect on BDI scores may be a function of the class format without individualized attention. In the Rossello and Bernal (1999) study involving Puerto Rican adolescents, the effect size for cognitive behavioral therapy was .43. The evidence from the latter two studies qualifies CBT as a probably efficacious treatment for depression among Latino/a American groups by EST standards. CBT has also been found to reduce panic symptoms among Latino/a American adults in a community medical center setting

(Sanderson, Raue, & Wetzler, 1998). All 30 clients experienced two or more panic attacks before treatment. However, 15 clients were panic free at the end of treatment, and 24 experienced one or no panic attacks per week following treatment. However, this study did not include a control group. Cognitive behavioral therapy clearly shows promise in treating depression among Latino/a Americans and could become an effective, well-established treatment with one more well-designed outcome study.

Interpersonal Therapy

Another effective, well-established treatment for depression in European American adults is interpersonal therapy (DeRubeis & Crist-Cristoph, 1998). Rossello and Bernal (1999) compared the effects of CBT, interpersonal therapy, and a waiting list control group on depressed Puerto Rican adolescents. Cognitive behavioral therapy and interpersonal therapy were equally effective in reducing depression, and both treatments were more effective than no treatment. It is possible that the two treatments were equally effective because components of Puerto Rican culture, including *respeto* (respect for elders) and *familismo* (emphasis on family), were incorporated into both treatments. Rossello and Bernal (1999) suggested that the interpersonal approach is more consistent with Puerto Rican values and hence is the more culturally sensitive of the two treatment approaches. Because interpersonal therapy was not demonstrated to be superior to CBT, it awaits additional validation as a probably efficacious treatment by EST standards.

Family Therapy

A number of scholars believe that the family plays an essential role for Latino/a's as a source of help and support (Acosta, 1984; Padilla & Salgado de Snyder, 1987; Rogler et al., 1983; Rogler, Malgady, & Rodriguez, 1989). Nonetheless, in a study comparing structural family therapy, individual psychodynamic child therapy, and a recreational control condition for Latino/a boys with behavioral and emotional problems, Szapocznik et al. (1989) found that both structural family therapy and individual psychodynamic child therapy were more effective than the control condition in terms of limiting therapy dropout. During the study's duration, no significant differences were found in the reduction of emotional and behavioral problems between the treatment conditions. However, upon followup, families whose child had been in the individual psychodynamic child therapy condition were found to have deteriorated with regard to family functioning. In direct contrast, those families in the structured family therapy condition displayed improvement in family functioning. Those families in the control condition remained the same in terms of family functioning.

Group Therapy

The group therapy format has been advocated as useful with Latino/a's in certain contexts (Acosta & Yamamoto, 1984). An empirical study by Comas-Diaz (1981) compared the effects of cognitive and behavioral group therapy for depressed Puerto Rican women. Both treatment groups were found to have improved significantly more than a control condition. More recent studies with Puerto Rican children and adolescents, which did compare different types of group interventions, have demonstrated the efficacy of a group format (Costantino, Malgady, & Rogler, 1986; Malgady, Rogler, & Costantino, 1990b). Kay, de Zapien, Wilson, and Yoder (1993) randomly assigned elderly Mexican American widows to a no intervention control group or to a support group conducted primarily in Spanish. The support group also incorporated Mexican American cultural elements. Women in the support group showed significant decreases in anxiety, somatization, and affective symptoms, whereas the control group did not. Because there was no comparison treatment, it is unclear if the treatment effects were a function of the group format or of the cultural elements. Thus group therapy appears to be beneficial for Latino/a's, but it is unclear if group therapy is more effective than individual therapy.

Patient Orientation Programs

Clients of low socioeconomic backgrounds have been found to be more likely to drop out of treatment, and Rogler et al. (1983) propose that this factor may be of relevance for many Latino/a's. Acosta, Evans, Yamamoto, and Wilcox (1980) developed a brief audiovisual orientation program for low-income clients to enable clients to understand the process of psychotherapy and act upon that understanding in therapy (e.g. an open expression of problems and needs). As noted earlier, low-income, Latino/a, African American, and White patients who participated in the orientation program were found to be more knowledgeable and positive in their attitudes toward psychotherapy than those who participated in a control condition (Acosta et al., 1983). Little research on this topic has been published in the last 20 years, despite the positive effects reported earlier.

Culturally Specific Treatments

One of the most innovative areas of psychotherapy research with Latino/a's has been the development of culturally sensitive treatment modalities. Although the effectiveness of many of these culturally-specific treatments remains to be determined, some of them have been subject to empirical study and have been shown to be useful.

Cuento therapy utilizes cuentos, or folktales, to convey morals and models of adaptive behavior to children. The effectiveness of two types of cuento therapy was compared with art/play therapy and with no intervention for high-risk kindergarten through third grade Puerto Rican children (Costantino et al., 1986). There was a significant effect due to cuento therapy treatment, and a significant interaction between treatment and grade level, with differences between treatments only at the first grade level. First grade children who received cuento therapy showed significantly less trait anxiety than those in the other groups after 20 weeks of treatment. Cuento therapy was more effective in reducing trait anxiety than no intervention but did not significantly differ from art/play therapy. In addition, cuento therapy significantly increased scores on the Wechsler Intelligence Scale for Children-Revised (WISC-R) comprehension subtest compared to art/play therapy and the no intervention controls.

In a study supporting the effectiveness of cuento therapy for Puerto Rican children, Malgady, Rogler, and Costantino (1990a; 1990b) found that cuento therapy significantly decreased anxiety and aggression, and significantly increased social judgment. Relative to an attention control group, cuento therapy has also been found to reduce anxiety and phobic symptoms, and results in better school conduct among Puerto Rican, Dominican, and Central American children, and adolescents (Costantino, Malgady, & Rogler, 1994).

Because cuento therapy seemed most effective with younger children and was perhaps age-inappropriate for older children, Malgady et al. (1990a) developed hero/heroine modeling for Puerto Rican adolescents who were at high risk for mental health problems. This social learning-based intervention used biographies of famous Puerto Rican historical individuals to convey appropriate adult role models. Although there was no significant treatment effect on distress symptoms, treatment did significantly affect ethnic identity. Interestingly, the effect of treatment on adolescents' self-concept (which is different than ethnic identity) varied as a function of gender and with the presence or absence of the adolescent's father in the household. In household where the father was absent, self-concept was increased by treatment. However, for adolescents whose father was present, treatment did not affect the self-concept for boys but adversely affected the self-concept for girls. Malgady et al. (1990a; 1990b) speculate that the presentation of heroic figures may have resulted in negative outcomes because those who did have parental role models in the home may have compared their parents to the heroic figures, which resulted in subsequent feelings of inadequacy.

The effect sizes in the above studies of cuento therapy versus a control condition were generally in the medium range. These studies qualify cuento therapy as a probably efficacious therapy for Puerto Rican children according to EST criteria. One more controlled outcome study with children demonstrating the superior effects of cuento therapy versus another treatment, similar to the Costantino et al. (1986) study, but conducted by investigators other than Costantino and his colleagues, would qualify cuento therapy as a well-established treatment.

Social skills training has been adapted for Latino/a's by translating patient and therapist manuals and videos into Spanish and by having participants' families integrated into the treatment process in order to increase sensitivity to Latino/a cultural values of *respeto* and *familismo* (Kopelowicz, 1998). Adult Latino/a schizophrenics who received this culturally sensitive treatment exhibited better acquisition of social skills and a reduction of schizophrenic symptoms relative to a group who had monthly visits to psychiatrists. However, it is unknown if the cultural adaptation of the social skills training approach would have been superior to social skills training that was not culturally adapted. Moreover, the specific Latino/a groups in the study were not specified.

Summary of Findings for African Americans, American Indians, Asian Americans, and Latino/a Americans

Across the four ethnic groups discussed above, there are some common findings. Many ethnic minority persons tend to prefer therapists of their own ethnicity. In mental health service settings, ethnic matching of clients and therapists has been associated with longer service utilization and better outcomes, as measured by clinician ratings. These results have been found in large studies and are not necessarily substantive. It is possible that ethnic matching is an imperfect measure of cultural match (e.g., same language, similar values, similar world views) between clients and therapists, and that cultural matching is more substantively associated with positive treatment outcomes. There is some evidence that cultural sensitivity training for therapists and pre-therapy orientation for clients may help improve client-therapist cultural match.

Cognitive behavioral and interpersonal therapy appear to have promise in treating depression among African Americans and Latino/a Americans. The interpersonal approach may be more consistent with the interdependent cultural characteristics of ethnic minority cultures (Rosello & Bernal, 1999). Additional comparative studies are needed to determine the effects of cognitive behavioral versus interpersonal therapy with ethnic minority groups. The results of research on specific psychotherapy approaches with American Indians and Asian Americans are equivocal.

An overall conclusion is that much more psychotherapy research is needed with ethnic minority populations. Much of the published literature on psychotherapy with ethnic minorities is conceptual without actual hypothesis testing (Hall, 2001). A notable exception is the empirical work on cuento therapy, which utilizes cultural folktales to convey morals and models of adaptive behavior to children. Cuento therapy appears to be effective in reducing children's anxiety. In general, the potential benefits of integrating conceptually based, culturally relevant treatment into treatments established for Whites remain to be investigated (Hall, 2001).

Evaluation of Research Methods and Theories for Culturally Diverse Populations

Numerous methodological difficulties complicate any empirical inquiry into the process and efficacy of psychotherapy, and these have been well documented elsewhere (e.g., Kazdin, 1994). These problems include inadequate sample selection, inappropriate outcome criteria, ambiguity over the types of therapists and treatments used, nonconvergence among outcome criteria, observational biases, incorrect statistical analyses of change, inappropriate designs for the outcome question being addressed, inadequate control groups, uncertainty over the clinical and social value of the treatment-produced magnitude of change, and inadequate power in terms of design sensitivity. We now focus on the specific methodological and conceptual problems that have limited or complicated efforts to examine the influence of ethnicity and culture on psychotherapy processes and outcomes. These issues include types of research questions asked, reliance on analogue studies, types of samples used, selection of appropriate measures, interethnic versus intraethnic comparison designs, and controlling for potential confounds with ethnicity/culture.

Research Strategies and Issues

Research Questions

Selection of a certain research strategy is partially guided by the initial conceptualization of culturally related variables in the study. Studies have varied greatly in the manner by which they have operationalized cultural variables. It has often been assumed that ethnic affiliation is an adequate representation of cultural variation. However, ethnic differences and cultural differences are not equivalent, and a distinction must be made between the two. Ethnic differences involve differences in group membership (i.e., a type of social identity) that *imply* differences in culture. Cultural differences refer to variations in actual attitudes, values, and perceptual constructs that result from different cultural experiences. As Zane and Sue (1991) have noted,

> Whereas the former simply involves group membership, the latter constitutes a host of cognitive variables that are linked to different cultural lifestyles and perspectives. These cognitive variables, and not ethnic membership, have been the ones implicated in culture-related problems for psychotherapists. . . . Ethnic match research, although important, has not directly tested the cultural difference hypothesis of treatment (p. 52).

Ethnic differences are only indirect indices of the more important cultural differences, which tend to be more proximal to psychotherapy processes and outcomes. The question usually asked is, "Does a certain ethnic group (compared to other ethnic groups) benefit more or less from treatment?" It would be far more informative to address the question: "Do differences between ethnic groups on culturally relevant variables (e.g., values, role relationships) affect a certain process or outcome in treatment?" Essentially, the study of cultural influences is the study of individual difference variables that are associated with ethnic group experiences.

Use of Analogue Studies

There has been a great reliance on analogue studies involving: (a) the use of simulated rather than actual treatment sessions, (b) the sampling of students instead of clients, (c) the assessment of change over one treatment session rather than over the course of many sessions, and (d) the examination of client preferences for certain personal characteristics of the therapist (e.g., ethnicity, professional status, attitude similarity) and for certain types of therapist approach (directiveness, trustworthiness, pro-assimilation versus pro-pluralism, culture-salience vs. culture-blind). Excellent discussions of the advantages and disadvantages of using analogue strategies have been presented elsewhere (Kazdin, 1986).

Related to these issues are specific problems that result from the examination of cultural influences. First, it is questionable whether the brevity and simulated nature of the treatment sessions in most analogue designs allow for the sensitive testing of cultural or ethnic effects. For example, studies of Latino/a's have found few ethnic effects in therapist credibility (e.g., Furlong, Atkinson, & Casas, 1979; Hess & Street, 1991). However, Acosta et al.(1980) have noted how many ethnic minority and low-income clients have little familiarity with the process of psychotherapy. With little understanding of this process, the rating of one's therapist in credibility may have little functional meaning for many ethnic minority clients at the initial stages of treatment. Second, the reliance of analogues on student samples may restrict variation in acculturation and ethnic identity. Both of these variables have been identified as important predictors of the treatment process. Most student samples tend to be more acculturated but also more ethnically conscious. The restriction of range on acculturation and ethnic identity limits generalizability but, more importantly, limits the design's sensitivity to cultural effects as operationalized by these two variables.

Finally, analogues may curtail the range of clinical problems that are typically presented by ethnic clients suffering from real problems. Issues such as racism, cultural adjustment, ethnic identity conflicts, and intergenerational difficulties are more frequently presented by ethnic clients. These areas may also be the most problematic for nonethnic therapists who likely would be less familiar with these experiences. These are complex issues that may not be discussed by ethnic clients until trust and rapport have been established (Ridley, 1984). Again, the brevity and focus on initial sessions of analogues tend to exclude many clinical situations in which cultural differences may have their most impact. The reliance on analogue studies stems partially from the earlier tendency in psychotherapy research to concentrate on efficacy issues. In efficacy studies, the focus is primarily on the intervention and on the rigorous evaluation of intervention effects under highly controlled conditions (Barlow, 1996). To optimize internal validity and replicability, the effects of factors that may obscure treatment effects are minimized. For example, factors such as differential treatment expectations, variations in therapist behaviors and skills, and client heterogeneity are controlled as much as possible through the use of nonspecific control groups, treatment manuals, and very restrictive inclusion and exclusion criteria for client selection (Nathan, Stuart, & Dolan, 2000).

Within this approach, analogue studies can be useful in that they can examine, under very controlled conditions, the specific aspects of the treatment that may account for some of its effects. Although much has been learned from efficacy studies about which particular treatments actually improve client symptoms and functioning, there is growing appreciation for the need for effectiveness research to complement efficacy investigations. Effectiveness studies determine whether treatments have favorable and useful effects with clients who typically use mental health services in real-life community settings and circumstances. A major interest in the study of effectiveness centers on how certain contextual and individual difference variables moderate the effects of treatment. Factors often considered sources of error in efficacy studies are allowed to vary or are systematically varied to assess their impact. It should be noted that sociocultural factors essentially constitute a subset of these variables. Much of the research reviewed here points to the importance of determining how variables that map onto important ethnic and cultural differences on the part of clients and/or therapists can moderate the effects of treatment and services.

Samples Selected

The heterogeneity within each ethnic minority group has often been noted by researchers (e.g., Clark, 1972; Leong, 1986). For each group there are important variations in sociodemographic and psychosocial characteristics that include country of origin, immigration history (length of stay in refugee camps, immigrant versus refugee status), place of residence (urban versus rural, urban versus reservation), education level (both in the United States and the country of origin), motivation for leaving country of origin, acculturation level, socioeconomic level, English proficiency, ethnic identification, and preferred language. Despite this documented diversity, few studies have articulated the specific samples used in the research. When efforts are made to examine this within-group diversity, important relationships are frequently found. For example, Pomales and Williams (1989) assessed the acculturation level of Puerto Rican and Mexican college students in both Latino/a and Anglo American culture. In responding to a directive or nondirective style, Latino/a-acculturated students rated the nondirective therapist as more credible than did bicultural students. On the other hand, Anglo-acculturated students found the therapist more trustworthy than did bicultural or Latino/a-acculturated students regardless of therapist style. By not identifying subgroup characteristics (e.g., level of acculturation, tribal affiliation, different Asian groups, and different Latino/a groups), it is difficult to determine to what extent the findings can truly be generalized to the various subpopulations within a particular ethnic group. Moreover, the systematic investigation of critical treatment processes is difficult because it is unclear if studies of a particular ethnic group are comparable.

One of the most significant reasons for sampling difficulties is the relatively small population of ethnic minority groups. Small population size creates problems in trying to find not only representative samples for study but also adequate numbers of participants. For example, finding a sufficient sample of American Indians who are using mental health services is extremely difficult.

Selection of Appropriate Measures

Ethnic and cultural differences can be obscured by the use of unreliable, invalid, or insensitive measures. Many investigators have pointed to methodological and conceptual problems in the assessment of ethnic minority group individuals. These problems include: clinical assessments that overpathologize or underpathologize the symptoms of ethnic clients; evaluations based on norms developed on White populations; conceptual and scale nonequivalence of measures across different cultural groups; difficulties in administering instruments to limited-English speaking clients or in making adequate translations; and cultural differences in approaching assessment tasks (Okazaki & Sue, 1995). Despite widespread concern over the cross-cultural validity of assessment measures, the nature of cultural bias has not been empirically examined to any great extent, and solutions for cultural bias have been difficult to find. In the past, clinical and personality assessments of ethnic minorities have proceeded without the benefit of validation studies, and diagnosticians and clinicians have simply been admonished to take into account cultural differences and to avoid making strong conclusions on the basis of the assessment results. Often, when a popularly used instrument is finally tested on ethnic minority populations, the instrument is not widely used among these ethnic groups because another, more recent, and sophisticated measure is developed for the rest of the country and may also be used with ethnic minority groups without validation. This results in the situation in which the assessment of ethnic minority populations frequently lags behind, and ethnic minorities are given new assessment instruments of unknown validity for their particular ethnic group.

Inter- and Intraethnic Comparison Designs

Two general strategies have dominated the examination of cultural influences in psychotherapy. Studies have used either interethnic designs involving comparisons between ethnic groups (usually ethnic minorities with Whites) or intraethnic designs in which comparisons are made within a group with respect to different levels of acculturation or ethnic identity. Some studies have used a combination of these two approaches. Interpretations of the research have implicitly assumed that interethnic comparisons are an extension of the intraethnic approach in that the White comparison group represents the most acculturated level of the culture variable. Usually, it is assumed that Whites are a homogeneous, highly acculturated group. As indicated earlier, ethnic affiliation appears to be a more distal variable than acculturation with respect to treatment process and outcome.

Therefore, it is unclear if the two approaches are functionally related.

Potential Confounds

Many studies have failed to control for variables that may be confounded with ethnicity or culture. Research has consistently found that variables such as socioeconomic status, education level, type of living environment, and English proficiency covary with ethnicity or culture. By not assessing these variables, questions of internal validity can be raised about much of the previous research. Moreover, these studies have missed opportunities for increasing design sensitivity (by covarying out their effects) because some of these variables have been identified as correlates of treatment outcome (Luborsky et al., 1971).

Role of Culture

Probably the most challenging issue for ethnic mental health researchers has been the development of viable strategies for specifically examining the role of culture in psychotherapy process and outcome. In other words, it often has been difficult to incorporate variables directly related to cultural experiences into psychotherapy research designs. Three conceptual issues have complicated this task: the distal nature of ethnicity, limitations of traditional outcome designs, and the lack of conceptual or theoretical approaches to guide the research.

Distal Nature of Ethnic Variables

Earlier it was noted that ethnicity implies certain cultural differences, and it is these cultural differences that should serve as the focus of process and outcome studies. Ethnicity and race often are used as proxies or as distal variables for a set of other, not explicitly measured, variables (Walsh, Smith, Morales, & Sechrest, 2000). The focus on the broad concept of ethnicity has frequently obscured important variations that could be related to treatment outcome within both the ethnic minority *and* White groups. Moreover, intervening cultural variables tend to exist between the ethnicity of the client and clinical outcomes. The cultural difference approach facilitates the integration of cultural findings with other psychotherapy research because many of these variables (e.g., coping styles) also have been the focus of previous studies on process and outcome. Ultimately, the meaningfulness of race or ethnicity and of more proximal cultural variables is an empirical/theoretical issue.

Concluding Comments

We now know that ethnic and cultural group variations are related to certain processes and outcomes in psychotherapy. However, the exact nature of these effects seems less clear. There is limited research on ethnic minority groups, and the research is not highly programmatic. Because of the paucity of knowledge and baseline information, many studies have been descriptive and problem oriented rather than theoretical in nature. Questions have been posed by researchers, such as: (1) Is psychotherapy effective for ethnic minority clients; (2) what are utilization and dropout rates; (3) which kind of individual differences affect treatment; and (4) how can therapy be modified and improved? Addressing these basic questions is important because they lay the foundation for other, more specific research issues that have not been adequately researched even now, and have implications for programs and policies. Nevertheless, there is a need for programmatic research that focuses on more theoretical issues. For instance, why do we see underutilization of services by some ethnic groups, and why are culturally responsive or culturally congruent forms of treatment effective? A more theoretical focus is occurring in some areas. For example, we do see some research issues in which descriptive and theoretical advances are being made by groups of researchers (e.g., preferences for the ethnicity of the therapist and client's stage of ethnic identity). The field is in need of this kind of programmatic research that helps to improve ideas, theories, and methodologies and to stimulate other research.

Second, many researchers and practitioners believe that psychotherapy is relatively ineffective with members of ethnic minority groups. Subsequently, they believe that providing a definitive answer based on research findings is not possible. The reason for this is that only a few empirical studies are available and the question of psychotherapy effectiveness is complex, requiring more than an affirmative or negative response. If we put aside the subtleties and complexities involved in the question of overall effectiveness, we have some reason to believe that certain conditions are related to aspects of effectiveness: ethnic similarity for clients and therapists of some ethnic minority groups; the use of some culturally responsive forms of treatment; pre-therapy intervention with ethnic clients; and the training of therapists to specifically work with members of culturally diverse groups. It is yet unclear if the therapies that have been proven efficacious are actually effective with ethnic minority individuals. Although they may well be beneficial for all groups, the paucity of rigorous research findings leaves open the question of whether the empirically supported therapies (ESTs) for major depression such as cognitive behavioral therapy or interpersonal psychotherapy actually are effective with most ethnic minority individuals. Clearly, more effectiveness studies are needed to address these basic questions of generalizability before these ESTs can be considered as "best practice" interventions for minority clientele. It should be noted that we are not suggesting that ethnic minority clients avoid the use of psychotherapy, even in the absence of rigorous empirical research on outcomes. Our position includes the following: that therapy can be very helpful, but the factors underlying culturally competent services should be identified, and more research should be conducted on treatment outcomes.

Third, research on ethnic minority groups is difficult to conduct. Throughout this chapter, we have noted the problems in conducting research—for example, difficulties in finding adequate samples, achieving representativeness in sampling, devising cross-culturally valid measures, applying existing theories. Ethnic researchers must often confront additional methodological and conceptual problems that other researchers do not encounter to the same extent. These problems mean that for ethnic research to be more programmatic, rigorous, and sophisticated, greater resources are needed (e.g., personnel, training, and research funding).

Fourth (and related to the second point), the heterogeneity of ethnic minority groups is an increasingly salient characteristic to consider. The current research is going beyond the evaluation of treatment issues for African Americans, American Indians, Asian Americans, and Latino Americans as ethnic groups. Rather, the focus is now on individual differences within a particular group.

These four points, as well as our analysis of conceptual and methodological problems, have been well recognized by researchers who study ethnic issues. As mentioned in the introductory comments, this critical review should be placed in proper perspective. Major advances in ethnic minority research have been made, knowledge has improved substantially because of the pioneering work of many scholars, and the viewpoints of "insiders" to the groups (i.e., those who conduct ethnic minority research) have increasingly been expressed. In closing, we offer some personal comments and observations about ethnic minority research.

Ethnic minority research in general, and ethnic psychotherapy research in particular, were largely initiated on African Americans because of the long oppressive history of African Americans by Whites in this country and the need to address these relations. This early research established the major parameters for investigation: differences in cultural values and lifestyles between African Americans and White Americans, and the effects of racism. Indeed, these parameters are pertinent to the study of American Indians, Asian Americans, and Latino/a Americans, and much work on these groups has been patterned after the research and theories developed on African Americans.

More recent literature on the different ethnic groups demonstrates a greater ethnic-specific focus. That is, each group is beginning to more clearly define its own concerns and needs and to focus research efforts on these needs. For example, the responsiveness of government agencies that control mental health services is of concern for African Americans. The nature of services is also of concern to the other groups, but other additional issues such as the underutilization of services among Asian Americans and Latino/a Americans are especially salient for these ethnic groups. Unlike African Americans and American Indians, Asian Americans and Latino/a Americans are largely voluntary immigrants to this country. Language differences, separation from other kin who reside in the "old country," and adjustment to a new culture are important factors to consider. American Indians who live on reservations are more isolated from mainstream American culture than are, say, Latino/a Americans living in urban ethnic communities. Many have experienced cultural genocide—the destruction of traditional folkways. Using culturally based psychotherapy approaches may serve not only to increase treatment effectiveness, but also to reaffirm the cultural folkways. As indicated previously, much research on the role of ethnic identity in psychotherapy among African Americans has been conducted by Helms and her colleagues (e.g., Helms & Carter, 1991; Parham & Helms, 1981). For Latino/a Americans, ethnic identity is also important but it is part of a larger issue—acculturation and assimilation (Padilla, 1980). With the continuing immigration of

Latino/a's to this country, there is a constant source of cultural values coming from Latino/a "homelands." Also, many first-generation individuals, born and raised in another country, do not seem to have the identity issues faced by American-born ethnics who grow up as members of a minority group. Issues of undocumented aliens are also pertinent to Asian Americans and Latino/a Americans. The point is, that in trying to understand ethnic populations, ethnicity, culture, and minority group status are important variables that are being redefined for each group.

Finally, there has been a move away from population-focused studies in which research has examined ethnic or cultural between-group differences on psychotherapy process and outcome. Although this parameter-based research has provided important information about the treatment experiences of ethnic minorities, the focus on between-group differences has obscured important variations among members of a particular minority group. More significantly, the descriptive nature of this research has precluded determining exactly how culture affects the treatment experience and eventual outcomes. Recently, greater emphasis has been placed on variable-focused studies in which the research examines how specific psychological elements associated with ethnic or cultural group differences (namely, the specific aspects of culture) affect treatment or moderate treatment effectiveness. This shift to studying culturally based variables such as cultural value orientation, cultural identity, control orientation and shame and stigma, allows us to better explain and understand the specific effects of cultural influences.

REFERENCES

Acosta, F. X. (1984). Psychotherapy with Mexican Americans: Clinical and empirical gains. In J. L. Martinez, Jr., & Richard H. Mendoza (Eds.), *Chicano Psychology* (pp. 163–189). Orlando, FL: Academic Press.

Acosta, F. X., & Cristo, M. H. (1981). Development of a bilingual interpreter program: An alternative model for Spanish-speaking services. *Professional Psychology, 12,* 474–482.

Acosta, F. X., Evans, L. A., Yamamoto, J., & Wilcox, S. A. (1980). Helping minority and low-income psychotherapy patients "Tell it like it is." *The Journal of Biocommunication,* 7, 13–19.

Acosta, F. X., & Yamamoto, J. (1984). The utility of group work practice for Hispanic Americans. *Social Work with Groups,* 7, 63–73.

Acosta, F. X., Yamamoto, J., & Evans, L. A. (1982). *Effective psychotherapy for low-income and minority patients.* New York: Plenum.

Acosta, F. X., Yamamoto, J., Evans, L. A., & Skilbeck, W. M. (1983). Preparing low-income Hispanic, Black, and White patients for psychotherapy: Evaluation of a new orientation program. *Journal of Clinical Psychology, 39,* 872–877.

American Psychiatric Association. (1987). *Diagnostic and statistical manual of mental disorders* (3rd Ed.—Revised). Washington, DC: American Psychiatric Association.

Atkinson, D. R. (1983). Ethnic similarity in counseling psychology: A review of research. *The Counseling Psychologist, 11,* 79–92.

Atkinson, D. R. (1986). Similarity in counseling. *The Counseling Psychologist, 14,* 319–354.

Atkinson, D. R., Kim, B.S.K., & Caldwell, R. (1998). Ratings of helper roles by multicultural psychologists and Asian American students: Initial support for the three-dimensional model of multicultural counseling. *Journal of Counseling Psychology, 45,* 414–423.

Atkinson, D. R., Wampold, B. E., Lowe, S. M., Matthews, L., & Ahn, H. (1998). Asian American preferences for counselor characteristics: Application of the Bradley-Terry-Luce model to paired comparison data. *Counseling Psychologist, 26,* 101–123.

Barlow, D. H. (1996). Health care policy, psychotherapy research, and the future of psychotherapy. *American Psychologist, 51,* 1050–1058.

Bee-Gates, D., Howard-Pitney, B., LaFromboise, T., & Rowe, W. (1996). Help-seeking behavior of Native American Indian high school students. *Professional Psychology: Research & Practice, 27,* 495–499.

Bennett, S. K., & BigFoot-Sipes, D. S. (1991). American Indian and white college student preferences for counselor characteristics. *Journal of Counseling Psychology, 38,* 440–445.

Bernal, M. E., & Castro, F. G. (1994). Are clinical psychologists prepared for service and research with ethnic minorities? Report of a decade of progress. *American Psychologist, 49,* 797–805.

Betz, N. E., & Fitzgerald, L. F. (1993). Individuality and diversity: Theory and research in counseling psychology. *Annual Review of Psychology, 44,* 343–381.

BigFoot-Sipes, D. S., Dauphinais, P., LaFromboise, T. D., Bennett, S. K., & Rowe, W. (1992). American Indian secondary school students' preferences for counselors. *Journal of Multicultural Counseling and Development, 20,* 113–122.

Bobo, J. K., Gilchrist, L. D., Cvetkovich, G. T., Trimble, J. E., & Schinke, S. P. (1988). Cross-cultural service delivery to minority communities. *Journal of Community Psychology, 16,* 263–272.

Brown, B. S., Joe, G. W., & Thompson, P. (1985). Minority group status and treatment retention. *International Journal of the Addictions, 20,* 319–335.

Brown, C., Schulberg, H. C., Sacco, D., Perel, J. M., & Houck, P. R. (1999). Effectiveness of treatments for major depression in primary medical care practice: A post hoc analysis of outcomes for African American and white patients. *Journal of Affective Disorders, 53*, 185–192.

Bureau of Indian Affairs. (1991). *American Indians Today* (3rd ed.). U.S. Department of the Interior.

Chambless, D. L., & Hollon, S. D. (1998). Defining empirically supported therapies. *Journal of Consulting and Clinical Psychology, 66*, 7–18.

Chambless, D. L., Sanderson, W. C., Shoham, V., Johnson, S. B., Pope, K. S., Crits-Christoph, P., Baker, M., Johnson, B., Woody, S., Sue, S., Beutler, L., Williams, D. A., & McCurry, S. (1996). An update on empirically validated therapies. *Clinical Psychologist, 49*, 5–18.

Chang, W. (1985). A cross-cultural study of depressive symptomatology. *Culture, Medicine, & Psychiatry, 9*, 295–317.

Chau, I. Y., & Landreth, G. L. (1997). Filial therapy with Chinese parents: Effects on parental empathic interactions, parental acceptance of child and parental stress. *International Journal of Play Therapy, 6*, 75–92.

Cheung, F. M. (1982). Psychological symptoms among Chinese in urban Hong Kong. *Social Science & Medicine, 16*, 1339–1344.

Cheung, F. M., & Lau, B.W.K. (1982). Situational variations of help-seeking behavior among Chinese patients. *Comprehensive Psychiatry, 23*, 252–262.

Chin, J. L. (1998). Mental health services and treatment. In L. C. Lee & N.W.S. Zane (Eds.), *Handbook of Asian American psychology* (pp. 485–504). Thousand Oaks, CA: Sage.

Clark, K. B. (1972). Foreword. In A. Thomas & S. Sillen (Eds.), *Racism and psychiatry*. New York: Brunner/Mazel.

Comas-Diaz, L. (1981). Effects of cognitive and behavioral group treatment on the depressive symptomatology of Puerto Rican women. *Journal of Consulting and Clinical Psychology, 49*, 627–632.

Commission on Ethnic Minority Recruitment, Retention, and Training in Psychology. (1997). *Visions and transformations: The final report*. Washington, DC: American Psychological Association.

Costantino, G., Malgady, R. G., & Rogler, L. H. (1986). Cuento therapy: A culturally sensitive modality for Puerto Rican children. *Journal of Consulting and Clinical Psychology, 54*, 639–645.

Costantino, G., Malgady, R. G., & Rogler, L. H. (1994). Storytelling through pictures: Culturally sensitive psychotherapy for Hispanic children and adolescents. *Journal of Clinical Child Psychology, 23*, 13–20.

Cross, W. E., Jr. (1971). The Negro-to-black conversion experience: Toward a psychology of black liberation. *Black World, 20*, 13–27.

D'Andrea, M., Daniels, J., & Heck, R. (1991). Evaluating the impact of multicultural counseling training. *Journal of Counseling and Development, 70*, 143–148.

Dansereau, D. F., Joe, G. W., Dees, S. M., & Simpson, D. D. (1996). Ethnicity and the effects of mapping-enhanced drug abuse counseling. *Addictive Behaviors, 21*, 363–376.

Dauphinais, P., Dauphinais, L., & Rowe, W. (1981). Effect of race and communication style on Indian perceptions of counselor effectiveness. *Counselor Education and Supervision, 21*, 72–80.

Dauphinais, P., LaFromboise, T., & Rowe, W. (1980). Perceived problems and sources of help for American Indian students. *Counselor Education and Supervision, 20*, 37–46.

DeRubeis, R. J., & Crits-Christoph, P. (1998). Empirically supported individual and group psychological treatments for adult mental disorders. *Journal of Consulting and Clinical Psychology, 66*, 37–52.

Endicott, J., Spitzer, R. L., Fleiss, J. L., & Cohen, J. (1976). The global assessment scale: A procedure for measuring overall severity of psychiatric disturbance. *Archives of General Psychiatry, 33*, 766–771.

Fiorentine, R., & Hillhouse, M. P. (1999). Drug treatment effectiveness and client-counselor empathy. *Journal of Drug Issues, 29*, 59–74.

Flaskerud, J. H. (1986). The effects of culture-compatible intervention on the utilization of mental health services by minority clients. *Community Mental Health Journal, 22*, 127–141.

Flaskerud, J. H., & Soldevilla, E. Q. (1986). Filipino and Vietnamese clients: Utilizing an Asian mental health center. *Journal of Psychosocial Nursing, 24*, 32–36.

Friedman, S., Paradis, C. M., & Hatch, M. (1994). Characteristics of African-American and White patients with panic disorder and agoraphobia. *Hospital and Community Psychiatry, 45*, 798–803.

Fuertes, J. N., & Gelso, C. J. (1998). Asian-American, Euro-American, and African-American students' universal-diverse orientation and preferences for characteristics of psychologists. *Psychological Reports, 83*, 280–282.

Furlong, M. J., Atkinson, D. R., & Casas, J. M. (1979). Effects of counselor ethnicity and attitudinal similarity on Chicano students' perceptions of counselor credibility and attractiveness. *Hispanic Journal of Behavioral Science, 1*, 41–53.

Garb, H. N. (1997). Race bias, social class bias, and gender bias in clinical judgment. *Clinical Psychology: Science and Practice, 4*, 99–120.

Gibbs, J. T., & Huang, L. N. (1989). *Children of color: Psychological interventions with minority youths*. San Francisco: Jossey-Bass.

Gurak, D. T., & Rogler, L. H. (1983). Hispanic diversity in New York City. In L. H. Rogler, R. C. Santana, G. Costantino, B. F. Earley, B. Grossman,

D. T. Gurak, R. Malgady, & O. Rodriguez (Eds.), *A conceptual framework for mental health research on Hispanic populations* (pp. 59–65). Bronx, NY: Hispanic Research Center, Fordham University.

Gutierres, S. E., Russo, N. F., & Urbanski, L. (1994). Sociocultural and psychological factors in American Indian drug use: Implications for treatment. *International Journal of the Addictions, 29*, 1761–1786.

Gutierres, S. E., & Todd, M. (1997). The impact of childhood abuse on treatment outcomes of substance users. *Professional Psychology: Research and Practice, 28*, 348–354.

Hall, G.C.N. (2001). Psychotherapy research with ethnic minorities: Empirical, ethical, and conceptual issues. *Journal of Consulting and Clinical Psychology, 69*, 502–510.

Hall, G.C.N., Bansal, A., & Lopez, I. R. (1999). Ethnicity and psychopathology: A meta-analytic review of 31 years of comparative MMPI/MMPI-2 research. *Psychological Assessment, 11*, 186–197.

Havilland, M. G., Horswill, R. K., O'Connell, J. J., & Dynneson, V. V. (1983). Native American college students' preference for counselor race and sex and the likelihood of their use of a counseling center. *Journal of Counseling Psychology, 30*, 267–270.

Helms, J. E. (1984). Toward a theoretical explanation of the effects of race on counseling: A Black and White model. *Counseling Psychologist, 12*, 153–164.

Helms, J. E., & Carter, R. T. (1991). Relationships of White and Black racial identity attitudes and demographic similarity to counselor preferences. *Journal of Counseling Psychology, 38*, 446–457.

Hess, R. S., & Street, E. M. (1991). The effect of acculturation on the relationship of counselor ethnicity and client ratings. *Journal of Counseling Psychology, 38*, 71–75.

Inkeles, A., & Levinson, S. J. (1969). National character: The study of modal personality and sociocultural systems. In G. Lindzey and E. Aronson (Eds.), *The handbook of social psychology*. Reading, MA: Addison-Wesley.

Ivey, A. E., Ivey, M. B., & Simek-Morgan, L. (1993). *Counseling and psychotherapy: A multicultural perspective*. Boston: Allyn & Bacon.

Jones, B. E., & Gray, B. A. (1983). Black males and psychotherapy: Theoretical issues. *American Journal of Psychotherapy, 37*, 77–85.

Jones, E. E., & Matsumoto, D. R. (1982). Psychotherapy with the underserved. In L. Snowden (Ed.), *Services to the underserved* (pp. 207–228). Los Angeles, CA: Sage Publications.

Jones, J. M. (1991). Psychological models of race: What have they been and what should they be? In J. D. Goodchilds (Ed.), *Psychological perspectives on human diversity in America* (pp. 3–46). Washington, DC: American Psychological Association.

Kay, M. J., de Zapien, J. G., Wilson, C. A., & Yoder, M. (1993). Evaluating treatment efficacy by triangulation. *Social Science and Medicine, 36*, 1545–1554.

Kazdin, A. E. (1986). Comparative outcome studies of psychotherapy: Methodological issues and strategies. *Journal of Consulting and Clinical Psychology, 54*, 95–105.

Kazdin, A. E. (1994). Psychotherapy for children and adolescents. In A. E. Bergin & S. L. Garfield (Eds.), *Handbook of psychotherapy and behavior change* (4th ed.) (pp. 543–594). New York: John Wiley & Sons.

Kenney, G. E. (1994). Multicultural investigation of counseling expectations and preferences. *Journal of College Student Psychotherapy, 9*, 21–39.

Kessler, R. C., McGonagle, K. A., Zhao, S., Nelson, C. B., Hughes, M., Eshleman, S., Wittchen, H., & Kendler, K. S. (1994). Lifetime and 12-month prevalence of DSM-III-R psychiatric disorders in the United States. *Archives of General Psychiatry, 51*, 8–19.

Kim, B.L.C. (1973). Asian-Americans: No model minority. *Social Work, 18*, 44–54.

Kleinman, A. M. (1977). Depression, somatization and the new cross-cultural psychiatry. *Social Science and Medicine, 11*, 3–10.

Kline, F., Acosta, F. X., Austin, W., & Johnson, R. G. (1980). The misunderstood Spanish-speaking patient. *American Journal of Psychiatry, 137*, 1530–1533.

Kopelowicz, A. (1998). Adapting social skills training for Latino/a's with schizophrenia. *International Review of Psychiatry, 10*, 47–50.

Kwon, P. (1995). Application of social cognition principles to treatment recommendations for ethnic minority clients: The case of Asian Americans. *Clinical Psychology Review, 15*, 613–629.

LaFromboise, T. D. (1988). American Indian Mental Health Policy. *American Psychologist, 43*, 388–397.

LaFromboise, T. D., Dauphinais, P., & Rowe, W. (1980). Indian students' perceptions of positive helper attributes. *Journal of American Indian Education, 19*, 11–16.

LaFromboise, T. D., & Dixon, D. N. (1981). American Indian perception of trustworthiness in a counseling interview. *Journal of Counseling Psychology, 28*, 135–139.

LaFromboise, T. D., & Howard-Pitney, B. (1995). The Zuni life skills development curriculum: Description and evaluation of a suicide prevention program. *Journal of Counseling Psychology, 42*, 479–486.

LaFromboise, T. D., & Rowe, W. (1983). Skills training for bicultural competence: Rationale and application. *Journal of Counseling Psychology, 30*, 589–595.

Lambert, R. G., & Lambert, M. J. (1984). The effects of role preparation for psychotherapy on immigrant clients seeking mental health services in

Hawaii. *Journal of Community Psychology, 12,* 263–275.

Lambert, M. J., Whipple, J. L., Smart, D. W., Vermeersch, D. A., Nielsen, S. L., & Hawkins, E. J. (2001). The effects of providing therapists with feedback on patient progress during psychotherapy: Are outcomes enhanced? *Psychotherapy Research, 11,* 49–68.

Lau, A., & Zane, N. (2000). Examining the effects of ethnic-specific services: An analysis of cost-utilization and treatment outcome for Asian American clients. *Journal of Community Psychology, 28,* 63–77.

Lee, E. (1997). *Working with Asian Americans: A guide for clinicians.* New York: Guilford Press.

Lee, L. C. (1998). An overview. In L. C. Lee & N.W.S. Zane (Eds.), *Handbook of Asian American psychology* (pp. 1–20). Thousand Oaks, CA: Sage.

Lee, W.M.L., & Mixson, R. J. (1995). Asian and Caucasian client perceptions of the effectiveness of counseling. *Journal of Multicultural Counseling and Development, 23,* 48–56.

Lefley, H. P. (1985). Mental health training across cultures. In P. Pedersen (Ed.), *Handbook of cross-cultural counseling and therapy* (pp. 259–266). Westport, CT: Greenwood Press.

Lefley, H. P., & Bestman, E. W. (1984). Community mental health and minority: A multi-ethnic approach. In Sue & T. Moore (Eds.), *The pluralistic society: A community mental health perspective* (pp. 116–148). New York: Human Sciences Press.

Leong, F.T.L. (1986). Counseling and psychotherapy with Asian-Americans: Review of the literature. *Journal of Counseling Psychology, 33,* 196–206.

Leong, F.T.L. (1994). Asian Americans' differential patterns of utilization of inpatient and outpatient public mental health services in Hawaii. *Journal of Community Psychology, 22,* 82–96.

Luborsky, L., Chandler, M., Auerbach, A. H., Cohen, J., & Bachrach, H. M. (1971). Factors influencing the outcome of psychotherapy: A review of quantitative research. *Psychological Bulletin, 75,* 145–408.

Lum, R. G. (1982). Mental health attitudes and opinions of Chinese. In E. E. Jones & S. J. Korchin (Eds.), *Minority mental health* (pp. 165–189). New York: Praeger.

Malgady, R. G., Rogler, L. H., & Costantino, G. (1990a). Hero/heroine modeling for Puerto Rican adolescents: A preventive mental health intervention. *Journal of Consulting and Clinical Psychology, 58,* 469–474.

Malgady, R. G., Rogler, L. H., & Costantino, G. (1990b). Culturally sensitive psychotherapy for Puerto Rican children and adolescents: A program of treatment outcome research. *Journal of Counsulting and Clinical Psychology, 58,* 704–712.

Manson, S. M. (1982). *New directions in prevention among American Indian and Alaska Native communities.* Portland, OR: Oregon Health Sciences University.

Manson, S. M., Shore, J. H., & Bloom, J. D. (1985). The depressive experience in American Indian communities: A challenge for psychiatric theory and diagnoses. In A. Kleinman & B. Good (Eds.), *Culture and depression* (pp. 331–368). Berkeley: University of California Press.

Manson, S. M., Walker, R. D., & Kivlahan, D. R. (1987). Psychiatric assessment and treatment of American Indians and Alaska natives. *Hospital and Community Psychiatry, 38,* 165–173.

Maramba, G. G., & Hall, G.C.N. (in press). Meta-analysis of ethnic match as a predictor of drop-out, utilization, and outcome. *Cultural Diversity and Ethnic Minority Psychology.*

Marsella, A. J., Kinzie, D., & Gordon, P. (1973). Ethnic variations in the expression of depression. *Journal of Cross-Cultural Psychology, 4,* 435–458.

Meichenbaum, D. (1976). Toward a cognitive theory of self-control. *Consciousness and Self-Regulation, 1,* 1–66.

Mollica, R. F., Wyshak, G., Lavelle, J., Truong, T., Tor, S., & Yang, T. (1990). Assessment symptom change in Southeast refugee survivors of mass violence and torture. *American Journal of Psychiatry, 147,* 83–88.

Moncher, M. S., Holden, G. W., & Trimble, J. E. (1997). Substance abuse among Native-American youth. In G. A. Marlatt & G. R. VandenBos (Eds.), *Addictive behaviors: Readings on etiology, prevention, and treatment* (pp. 841–856). Washington, DC: American Psychological Association.

Morten, G., & Atkinson, D. R. (1983). Minority identity development and preference for counselor race. *Journal of Negro Education, 52,* 156–161.

Muñoz, R. F., Ying, Y., Bernal, G., Perez-Stable, E. J., Sorensen, J. L., Hargreaves, W. A., Miranda, J., & Miller, L. S. (1995). Prevention of depression with primary care patients: A randomized controlled trial. *American Journal of Community Psychology, 23,* 199–222.

Murase, K. (1977). Minorities: Asian-Americans. *Encyclopedia of Social Work, 2,* 953–960.

Nathan, P. E., Stuart, S. P., & Dolan, S. L. (2000). Research on psychotherapy efficacy and effectiveness: Between Scylla and Charybdis? *Psychological Bulletin, 126,* 964–981.

Nebeker, R. S., Lambert, M. J., & Huefner, J. C. (1995). Ethnic differences on the Outcome Questionnaire. *Psychological Reports, 77,* 875–879.

Neligh, G. (1988). Major mental disorders and behavior among American Indians and Alaska Natives. In *Behavioral health issues among American Indians and Alaska Natives: Explorations on the frontiers of the biobehavioral sciences.* American Indian and Alaska Native Mental Health Research. Monograph *1,* 116–159.

Nobles, W. W. (1980). African philosophy: Foundations for Black psychology. In R. Jones (Ed.), *Black Psychology* (pp. 99–105). New York: Harper & Row.

Okazaki, S., & Sue, S. (1995). Methodological issues in assessment research with ethnic minorities. *Psychological Assessment*, 7, 367–375.

Okonji, J.M.A., Ososkie, J. N., & Pulos, S. (1996). Preferred style and ethnicity of counselors by African American males. *Journal of Black Psychology*, *22*, 329–339.

Organista, K. C., Munoz, R. F., & Gonzalez, G. (1994). Cognitive-behavioral therapy for depression in low-income and minority medical outpatients: Description of a program and exploratory analyses. *Cognitive Therapy and Research*, *18*, 241–259.

O'Sullivan, M. J., Peterson, P. D., Cox, G. B., & Kirkeby, J. (1989). Ethnic populations: Community mental health services ten years later. *American Journal of Community Psychology*, *17*, 17–30.

Padilla, A. M. (1980). *Acculturation: Theory, models, and some new findings*. Boulder, CO: Westview Press.

Padilla, A. M., & Salgado de Snyder, N. (1987). Counseling Hispanics: Strategies for effective intervention. In P. Pedersen (Ed.), *Handbook of cross-cultural counseling and therapy* (pp. 157–164). Westport, CT: Greenwood.

Parham, T. A., & Helms, J. E. (1981). The influence of Black students' racial identity attitudes on preferences for counselor's race. *Journal of Counseling Psychology*, *28*, 250–257.

Phinney, J. S. (1996). When we talk about American ethnic groups, what do we mean? *American Psychologist*, *51*, 918–927.

Pomales, J., & Williams, V. (1989). Effects of level of acculturation and counseling style on Hispanic students' perceptions of counselor. *Journal of Counseling Psychology*, *36*, 79–83.

Ponce, F. Q., & Atkinson, D. R. (1989). Mexican-American acculturation, counselor ethnicity, counseling style, and perceived counselor credibility. *Journal of Counseling Psychology*, *36*, 203–208.

Pope-Davis, D. B., & Dings, J. G. (1995). The assessment of multicultural counseling competencies. In J. G. Ponterotto, J. M. Casas, L. A. Suzuki, & C. M. Alexander (Eds.), *Handbook of multicultural counseling*. Thousand Oaks, CA: Sage.

Pope-Davis, D. B., Prieto, L. R., Whitaker, C. M., & Pope-Davis, S. A. (1993). Exploring multicultural counseling competencies of occupational therapists: Implications for education and training. *American Journal of Occupational Therapy*, *47*, 838–844.

Price, B. K., & McNeill, B. W. (1992). Cultural commitment and attitudes toward seeking counseling services in American Indian college students. *Professional Psychology: Research and Practice*, *23*, 376–381.

Query, J.M.N. (1985). Comparative admission and follow-up study of American Indians and Whites in a youth chemical dependency unit on the North Central Plains. *The International Journal of the Addictions*, *20*, 489–502.

Ramirez, M. (1999). *Multicultural psychotherapy: An approach to individual and cultural differences* (2nd ed.). Boston: Allyn & Bacon.

Ridley, C. R. (1984). Clinical treatment of the nondisclosing Black client: A therapeutic paradox. *American Psychologist*, *39*, 1234–1244.

Rogler, L. H., Cooney, R. S., Costantino, G., Earley, B. F., Grossman, B., Gurak, D. T., Malgady, R., & Rodriguez, O. (1983). *A conceptual framework for mental health research on Hispanic populations*. Bronx, NY: Fordham University, Hispanic Research Center.

Rogler, L. H., Malgady, R. G., Costantino, G., & Blumenthal, R. (1987). What do culturally sensitive mental health services mean?: The case of Hispanics. *American Psychologist*, *42*, 565–570.

Rogler, L. H., Malgady, R. G., & Rodriguez, O. (1989). *Hispanics and mental health: A framework for research*. Malabar, FL: Krieger Publishing Company.

Rosenheck, R., Fontana, A., & Cottrol, C. (1995). Effect of clinician-veteran racial pairing in the treatment of posttraumatic stress disorder. *American Journal of Psychiatry*, *152*, 555–563.

Rossello, J., & Bernal, G. (1999). The efficacy of cognitive-behavioral and interpersonal treatments for depression in Puerto Rican adolescents. *Journal of Consulting and Clinical Psychology*, *67*, 734–745.

Ruelas, S. R., Atkinson, D. R., & Ramos-Sanchez, L. (1998). Counselor helping model, participant ethnicity and acculturation level, and perceived counselor credibility. *Journal of Counseling Psychology*, *45*, 98–103.

Russell, G. L., Fujino, D. C., Sue, S., Cheung, M., & Snowden, L. R. (1996). The effects of therapist-client ethnic match in the assessment of mental health functioning. *Journal of Cross-Cultural Psychology*, *27*, 598–615.

Sanderson, W. C., Raue, P. J., & Wetzler, S. (1998). The generalizability of cognitive behavior therapy for panic disorder. *Journal of Cognitive Psychotherapy*, *12*, 323–330.

Schinke, S. P., Orlandi, M. A., Botvin, G. J., Gilchrist, L. D., Trimble, J. E., & Locklear, V. B. (1988). Preventing substance abuse among American-Indian adolescents: A bicultural competence skills approach. *Journal of Counseling Psychology*, *35*, 87–90.

Snowden, L. R., & Cheung, F. K. (1990). Use of inpatient mental health services by members of ethnic minority groups. *American Psychologist*, *45*, 347–355.

Snowden, L. R., & Hu, T. W. (1997). Ethnic differences in mental health service use among the severely mentally ill. *Journal of Community Psychology*, *25*, 235–247.

Stack, J. A., Paradis, C. F., Reynolds, C. F., Houck, P. R., Frank, E., Anderson, B., Mayo, A. L., Miller, A. D., Rifai, A. H., Perel, J. M., &

Kupfer, D. J. (1995). Does recruitment method make a difference? Effects on protocol retention and treatment outcome in elderly depressed patients. *Psychiatry Research, 56*, 17–24.

Sterling, R. C., Gottheil, E., Weinstein, S. P., & Serota, R. (1998). Therapist/patient race and sex matching: Treatment retention and 9-month follow-up outcome. *Addiction, 93*, 1043–1050.

Sue, D. W., Ivey, A. E., & Pedersen, P. B. (1996). *A theory of multicultural counseling and therapy.* Pacific Grove, CA: Brooks/Cole.

Sue, D. W., & Sue, D. (1999). *Counseling the culturally different: Theory and practice* (3rd ed.). New York: John Wiley & Sons.

Sue, S. (1977). Community mental health services to minority groups: Some optimism, some pessimism. *American Psychologist, 32*, 616–624.

Sue, S. (1988). Psychotherapeutic services for ethnic minorities: Two decades of research findings. *American Psychologist, 43*, 301–308.

Sue, S. (1991). Ethnicity and culture in psychological research and practice. In J. D. Goodchilds (Ed.), *Psychological perspectives on human diversity in America* (pp. 47–85). Washington, DC: American Psychological Association.

Sue, S. (1998). In search of cultural competence in psychotherapy and counseling. *American Psychologist, 53*, 440–448.

Sue, S., Fujino, D. C., Hu, L. T., Takeuchi, D. T., & Zane, N.W.S. (1991). Community mental health services for ethnic minority groups: A test of the cultural responsiveness hypothesis. *Journal of Counseling Psychology, 59*, 533–540.

Sue, S., & Morishima, J. K. (1982). *The mental health of Asian-Americans.* San Francisco: Jossey-Bass.

Sue, S., Wagner, N., Ja, D., Margullis, C., & Lew, L. (1976). Conceptions of mental illness among Asian and Caucasian- American students. *Psychological Reports, 38*, 703–708.

Sue, S., & Zane, N. (1987). The role of culture and cultural techniques in psychotherapy: A critique and reformulation. *American Psychologist, 42*, 37–45.

Sue, S., Zane, N., & Young, K. (1994). Research on psychotherapy with culturally diverse populations. In A. E. Bergin & S. L. Garfield (Eds.), *Handbook of psychotherapy and behavior change* (4th ed.) (pp. 783–817). New York: John Wiley & Sons.

Szapocznik, J., Rio, A., Murray, E., Cohen, R., Scopetta, M., Rivas-Vazquez, A., Hervis, O., Posada, V., & Kurtines, W. (1989). Structural family versus psychodynamic child therapy for problematic Hispanic boys. *Journal of Consulting and Clinical Psychology, 57*, 571–578.

Takeuchi, D. T., Bui, K. T., & Kim, L. (1993). The referral of minority adolescents to community mental health centers. *Journal of Health and Social Behavior, 34*, 153–164.

Takeuchi, D. T., & Cheung, M. (1998). Coercive and voluntary referrals: How ethnic minority adults get into mental health treatment. *Ethnicity and Health, 3*, 149–158.

Tanaka-Matsumi, J., & Marsella, A. J. (1976). Cross-cultural variations in the phenomenological experience of depression: I. Word association studies. *Journal of Cross-Cultural Psychology, 7*, 379–396.

Thompson, C. E., Worthington, R., & Atkinson, D. R. (1994). Counselor content orientation, counselor race, and Black women's cultural mistrust and self-disclosures. *Journal of Counseling Psychology, 41*, 155–161.

Tracey, T. J., Leong, F.T.L., & Glidden, C. (1986). Help seeking and problem perception among Asian Americans. *Journal of Counseling Psychology, 33*, 331–336.

Treadwell, K.R.H., Flannery-Schroeder, E. C., & Kendall, P. C. (1995). Ethnicity and gender in relation to adaptive functioning, diagnostic status, and treatment outcome in children from an anxiety clinic. *Journal of Anxiety Disorders, 9*, 373–384.

Trimble, J. E., & LaFromboise, T. (1985). American Indian and the counseling process: Culture, adaptation, and style. In P. Pedersen (Ed.), *Handbook of cross-cultural counseling and therapy* (pp. 127–134). Westport, CT: Greenwood Press.

Uehara, E. S., Takeuchi, D. T., & Smukler, M. (1994). Effects of combining disparate groups in the analysis of ethnic differences: Variations among Asian American mental health service consumers in level of community functioning. *American Journal of Community Psychology, 22*, 83–99.

U.S. Census Bureau. (1993). *1990 Census of the Population, Asians and Pacific Islanders in the United States.* Washington, DC: U.S. Government Printing Office.

U.S. Census Bureau. (1998). *Current population survey, March 1997*, Ethnic and Hispanic Statistics Branch, Population Division. Retrieved July 25, 2001, from http://www.census.gov./sociodemo/hispanic/cps97/.

U.S. Census Bureau. (1999). *Household Income at Record High; Poverty Declines in 1998, Census Bureau Reports* [on-line]. Available Internet: http://www.census.gov/Press-Release www/1999/cb99-188.html.

U.S. Census Bureau (1999b). *Statistical Abstract of the United States:* The National Data Book. Washington, DC. Author.

U.S. Census Bureau. (2000a). *Census Bureau Projects Doubling of Nation's Population by 2100* [on-line]. Available Internet: http://www.census.gov/Press-Release/www/2000/cb00-05.html.

U.S. Census Bureau. (2000b). *Census Bureau Releases 1999 State and County Population Estimates by Age, Sex, Race and Hispanic Orgin* [on-line]. Available Internet: http://www.census.gov/Press-Release/www/2000/cb00-126.html.

U.S. Census Bureau. (2001). *Resident Population Estimates of the United States by Sex, Race, and Hispanic*

Origin: April 1, 1990 to July 1, 1999, with Short-Term Projection to November 1, 2000 [on-line]. Available Internet: http://www.census.gov. population-project-natsum-T3.html

U.S. Surgeon General. (2001). Mental health: Culture, race, and ethnicity. A supplement to *Mental Health: A Report of the Surgeon General.* Rockville, MD: U.S. Department of Health and Human Services.

U.S. Surgeon General's Supplement to the Report on Mental Health. (2001). Washington, DC: U.S. Government Printing Office.

Vega, W. A., & Rumbaut, R. G. (1991). Ethnic minorities and mental health. *Annual Review of Sociology, 17,* 351–383.

Wade, P., & Bernstein, B. (1991). Culture sensitivity training and counselor's race: Effects on Black female clients' perceptions and attrition. *Journal of Counseling Psychology, 38,* 9–15.

Walsh, M., Smith, R., Morales, A., & Sechrest, L. (2000). *Ethnocultural research: A mental health researcher's guide to the study of race, ethnicity, and culture.* Cambridge, MA: Health Services Research Institute.

Whaley, A. L. (1998). Racism in the provision of mental health services: A social-cognitive analysis. *American Journal of Orthopsychiatry, 68,* 47–57.

White, J. L. (1984). *The psychology of blacks: An Afro-American perspective.* Englewood Cliffs, NJ: Prentice Hall.

Williams, K. E., & Chambless, D. L. (1994). The results of exposure-based treatment in agoraphobia. In S. Friedman (Ed.), *Anxiety disorders in African Americans* (pp. 149–165). New York: Springer.

Yamamoto, J., Acosta, F. X., Evans, L. A., & Skilbeck, W. M. (1984). Orienting therapists about patients' needs to increase patient satisfaction. *American Journal of Psychiatry, 141,* 274–277.

Yeh, M., Eastman, K., & Cheung, M. K. (1994). Children and adolescents in community health centers: Does the ethnicity or the language of the therapist matter? *Journal of Community Psychology, 22,* 153–163.

Ying, Y., & Hu, L. (1994). Public outpatient mental health services: Use and outcome among Asian Americans. *American Journal of Orthopsychiatry, 64,* 448–455.

Zane, N., Enomoto, K., & Chun, C. (1994). Treatment outcomes of Asian and White American clients in outpatient therapy. *Journal of Community Psychology, 22,* 177–191.

Zane, N., Hatanaka, H., Park, S., & Akutsu, P. (1994). Ethnic-specific mental health services: Evaluation of the parallel approach for Asian American clients. *Journal of Community Psychology, 22,* 68–81.

Zane, N., & Sue, S. (1991). Culturally-respective mental health services for Asian Americans: Treatment and training issues. In H. Myers, P. Wohlford, P. Guzman, & R. Echemendia (Eds.), *Ethnic minority perspectives on clinical training and services in psychology* (pp. 49–58). Washington, DC: American Psychological Association.

Zhang, A. Y., Snowden, L. R., & Sue, S. (1998). Differences between Asian and White Americans' help seeking and utilization patterns in the Los Angeles area. *Journal of Community Psychology, 26,* 317–326.

CHAPTER 18

OVERVIEW, TRENDS, AND FUTURE ISSUES

MICHAEL J. LAMBERT
Brigham Young University
SOL L. GARFIELD
Washington University
ALLEN E. BERGIN
Brigham Young University

Similar to its predecessors, this fifth edition of the *Handbook* provides the reader with a comprehensive and evaluative review of developments and research that have taken place since the previous edition was published in 1994. Many important issues discussed in past *Handbook* editions continue to be discussed in the current decade. Important changes and new trends are evident, however, and in this final chapter we shall offer our appraisal of these as well as past developments.

Although we use the term *psychotherapy* as though it reflected a uniform field, the reality is quite different. The extraordinary diversity of viewpoints, theories, techniques, emphases, and values evident in the field of psychotherapy does not appear to have lessened since the previous edition was published. The diversity of practitioners, the types and length of training programs, and views concerning the importance of research appraisal of psychotherapy also vary widely (Garfield, 1998). The major approaches considered in this book provide analyses of some of the best-known variants of psychotherapy, but there are literally hundreds of other lesser-known approaches. The followers of most approaches have their own journals and books, but most have reported little or no research. Thus, it is difficult to generalize about the field as a whole or even such aspects as the training of psychotherapists, the length of therapy, or even the effectiveness of treatment methods. So herein we have assessed the few approaches that have been empirically evaluated. Presumably they are among the most promising ones, having been selected on the basis of professional judgments.

This *Handbook* gained its reputation and influence as a standard reference because it took a position of openness to diverse perspectives and insisted on an empirical appraisal of them. Today, this viewpoint appears to dominate the field. The demand of Health Maintenance Organizations (HMOs), insurance companies, and government agencies for empirical evidence of treatment safety and efficacy now drive the psychotherapy marketplace. Consequently, economic factors have become a strong force in driving an expansion of research evaluations of psychotherapy. Economic, academic, and professional interests now combine to exclude treatments that have no empirical support. So a new hegemony rules, which has the potential to significantly benefit consumers if implemented wisely. Although we have always supported an empirical ethic, it is not clear that it is being applied judiciously, a problem to which we shall return shortly (see also, Slife, Chapter 3, in this volume).

ECLECTICISM AND INTEGRATION

Surveys suggest that most professionals in North America prefer some form of eclecticism (Garfield, 1994; Jensen, Bergin, & Greaves, 1990; Norcross, Karg, & Prochaska, 1997). The empirical analysis and merging of behavioral and cognitive perspectives are the most notable examples. But leaders of this movement have also come from a diversity of other schools of thought. They prefer the term *integration* over *eclecticism* because integration implies a more systematic use of concepts and techniques from different approaches. Similar trends can be seen in many countries, with much of the development being prompted and documented by the Society for Exploration of Psychotherapy Integration. One of the world's largest and most successful centers for integration is in Rome, Italy, under the direction of Edoardo Giusti (Giusti, Montanari, & Iannazzo, 2001). Another important schema is Cognitive Analytic Therapy from Britain's Tony Rile; this method uses themes from all major orientations but goes beyond synthesis to an original conceptual and clinical strategy (Rile, 1995; 1997).

Even in managed care settings practitioners have indicated a clear need to become more eclectic in their therapy (Austad, Sherman, Morgan, & Holstein, 1992). The chapters in this volume reflect this trend. For instance, Elliot, Greenberg, and Lietear (Chapter 11) show how the "nondirective approach" of Carl Rogers and others can be enhanced by its integration with more directive and expressive techniques, while Beutler and colleagues (Chapter 7) suggest that nondirectiveness itself has special value with some cases and is counterproductive with others. There is even a trend, as noted by Hollon and Beck (Chapter 10), that suggests integrated approaches such as CBT are further expanding and incorporating important aspects of psychodynamic and experiential approaches in the form of concepts such as self-schemas (McCullough, 2000). Clearly, CBT is not a single crystallized approach but one that continues to change by incorporating concepts and interventions similar to, if not borrowed from, a variety of other approaches.

As Thase and Jindal (Chapter 16) point out, combinations of medication and psychotherapy may have additive effects and should be used in combination with each other for the treatment of severe depression and a variety of other disorders. It is clear that much research is needed before we fully understand the best way to manage integration of medication and psychotherapy, how they should be sequenced, and when the combination is ill advised. Though not strictly integrative, many treatments (such as group and family therapies) when used in combination with others, best serve a multitude of clients. This is clearly illustrated by the uses of group treatments in combination with theoretically diverse individual psychotherapies (see Burlingame, MacKenzie, & Strauss, Chapter 14), and family and couple interventions with individuals who have clinical disorders exacerbated by or concurrent with marital distress (Sexton, Alexander, & Mease, Chapter 13).

Theoretically derived treatment interventions that are open to empirical analysis are fluid rather than stagnant. Such flexible approaches, undergirded by careful empirical evaluation, mark the maturation of the field. Nevertheless, there are still some who adhere, at least formally, to a single orientation or perspective, such as the relatively few remaining classical analysts, strict behaviorists, or biomedical reductionists (see Slife, Chapter 3).

Micro Theories Replace Macro Theories

Commensurate with the foregoing trends has been a steady decline in strict adherence to traditionally dominant theories of personality and therapeutic change, such as behavioral, psychoanalytic, humanistic, and other major approaches. Questions today are being asked at the micro level (What works with this type of case?) rather than at the macro level (What is the nature of human personality?). This trend has been dictated partly by consumer, government, and insurance company pressures for evidence of prompt efficacy and partly by the failure of macro theories to yield definable practices that are clinically and empirically tenable. Empirical research has speeded up this process because many assumptions of the macro theories simply have not held up to scrutiny or have not been translatable into operations that will bear scrutiny.

Efforts today are more pragmatic and are guided by minitheories, such as "the therapeutic alliance should have certain characteristics in order to facilitate outcome," or "cognitive retraining adds to the effect of relaxation in reducing panic responses" (Emmelkamp, Chapter 9). One cannot help but be impressed with the systematic evaluation of hypotheses and rejection of theoretically cherished beliefs that are clear from reading the chapters of research on experiential, cognitive, and behavior therapies. These chapters document the vitality and utility of the scientific approach adopted by researchers and by the authors of these chapters.

The Gap Between Research and Practice

The trend toward eclectic practice found in clinical services and fostered by research findings stands in stark contrast to research that is aimed at identifying particular treatments that are effective with specific disorders. The 1980s and 1990s were replete with clinical trails that attempted to isolate "pure-form" treatments that were efficacious for specific "disorders." This research trend has resulted in considerable friction between practitioners and researchers (e.g., Andrews, 2000; Bohart, O'Hara, & Leitner, 1998; Golfried & Wolfe, 1995; Ingram, Hayes, & Scott, 2000). This friction is well documented in scientific and professional publication outlets (also see Chapters, 5, 6, 7, and 8, this volume).

Task Forces on Psychological Interventions and Criteria for Evaluating Treatments: The Generation of Empirically Supported Psychotherapies and Treatment Guidelines

The mental health professions and funding agencies have responded to pressures for accountability by advocating the development and employment of empirically supported psychotherapies. These are presumably effective treatments for specific disorders that have at least minimal evidence, based on controlled research: A worthy goal, indeed. Since the early 1990s, Division 12 of the American Psychological Association (Society of Clinical Psychology) has focused considerable attention on identifying "treatments that work" and on promoting so-called evidence-based practice in the form of empirically supported psychotherapies (ESTs). The members of the current Division 12 task force (Committee on Science and Practice) are well aware of the many issues they face (e.g., evolving treatments, evolving diagnostic classification system, variations in treatment fidelity across studies; Weisz, Hawley, Pilkonis, Woody, & Follette, 2000) and the growing criticism from researchers and practitioners about the committee's former attempts to provide criteria of effectiveness and lists of effective treatments (e.g., Garfield, 1996).

Bohart, O'Hara, and Leitner (1998) went so far as too suggest that the attempt could be relabeled as empirically "violating" psychotherapies rather than empirically validating them. They suggest that the proposed criteria are not only inappropriate for judging psychotherapy, but will also stifle research by forcing it into a medical-like model. Henry (1998) argued along similar lines—that the long-term consequences of generating ESTs would be negative for practice, training, and research. He sees the Task Force work as unnecessarily narrowing training and treatment options, giving greater power to third-party payers as de facto untrained supervisors, and disseminating findings that don't advance knowledge because the recommendations ignore the limits of research and entrench an outmoded set of designs that have outlived their usefulness. Silverman (1996) observed that the recommendations were akin to "painting by numbers," stripping psychotherapy of its richness and flexibility.

Addis, Wade, and Hatgis (1999) note that the assumption that treatment quality would improve by decreasing variability in treatment approaches and increasing accountability in mental health care has led to the rapid proliferation of treatment guidelines over the past decade. They have suggested that it is time to reduce the gap between researchers and practitioners by listening more carefully to practitioner concerns: That manuals reduce the quality of the therapeutic relationship, limit focus on some important client needs, assume broad levels of competence and confidence in various treatments that are not present (nor possible to achieve), reduce job satisfaction, and restrict clinical innovation. In general, bridging the gap between practitioners and researchers will be accomplished only when practitioners' concerns are heard and addressed. Considerable effort at communication and cooperation is needed in this area. Practitioners are not mere technicians who offer treatments for disorders. Task force lists of empirically supported treatments, treatment manuals, and practice guidelines are essential to the research setting but not necessarily to the practice setting because they suggest a degree of precision and knowledge that has not been (nor perhaps ever will be) attained. The generation of treatment lists is premature.

Despite the objections of some researchers and clinicians, ESTs continue to be advocated. Calhoun, Moras, Pilkonis, and Rehm (1998), for example, have even suggested that the longer term and exploratory therapies of the past are not essential and even outdated. Clinical trials researchers have advocated criteria for judging the degree to which a treatment is found to be supported by research evidence, limiting practice to the use of such treatments, and insisting that training programs teach such treatments (see also Abrahamson, 1999, on "leading horses to water").

Practitioners (and many psychotherapy researchers) have recoiled at such agendas and have noted the many weaknesses and limitations of using a medical model of clinical trials research to drive practice. In the history of psychotherapy research, no issue has generated more heated debate or caused more clear lines to be drawn between practitioners and researchers. This debate has been well documented by Lambert and Ogles (Chapter 5). At the root of differences between practitioners and researchers is the adequacy of research methods to provide the primary foundation for effective clinical practice, a topic that is also dealt with from a philosophical point of view by Slife (Chapter 3). Among the more problematic methodological findings in this area is the presence of an allegiance effect in comparative outcome studies.

Luborsky et al. (1999) reevaluated the tendency of comparative outcome studies to show results that favor the psychotherapy preferred by researchers who conduct a study. Their review was consistent with earlier reviews (e.g., Robinson, Berman, & Neimeyer, 1990) in finding a researcher "allegiance effect" that, when factored in to the analysis of treatment differences, appreciably reduces any differences found between treatments. Such an effect was interpreted as distorting research results.

The Luborsky et al. (1999) review was accompanied by seven commentaries by leading researchers in the field who all accepted the reality of the effect but differed in their interpretation of its meaning and importance. Most agreed that it represented phenomena that undermined the degree to which clinical trials reflect true differences between treatments and that it diminishes confidence in comparative studies. Hollon (1999), for example, stated: "my own opinion is that allegiance effects are most likely to occur (and be most problematic) when investigators compare some preferred modality in which they have both interest and expertise with some other alternative intervention in which they have neither" (p. 107). This view was shared by other commentators (e.g., Thase, 1999) and leads to an important methodological implication: That comparative research studies involve investigators with expertise and commitment to the treatments under investigation. In addition, Jacobson (1999) pointed out that even in the best controlled studies (which often take years to complete and involve multiple sites) the independent variable is not as clear as research reports imply: "There are gaping holes in the process of testing manual-based treatments that allow for drift and the potential of bias to creep in" (p. 118). Slife in Chapter 3 also notes this pattern of ignoring the limitations of research.

Westen and Morrison (2001) have offered an essay and meta-analysis on the limitations of empirically supported therapies. They observe that clinical trials exclude around two-thirds of eligible clients from study because of rigorous selection criteria and seldom provide followup results that report on the outcomes of individual patients. In commentaries on their article, four reviews responded with various reactions. All agreed that much more research is needed before confidence can be placed in what is currently known about effective treatments. In this dialogue, Lambert (2001b) suggested that outcomes in clinical trials are equivalent to those found in clinical practice even though they are not "pure-form" or manual driven, but only when patients receive similar amounts of treatment and regardless of whether empirically supported therapies are offered.

We applaud the growing movement toward basing practice on empirical evidence. However, the generation of lists of empirically supported therapies appears to be misguided and overvalued. In response to the impact of EST research on practice, a committee sponsored by Division 29 of the American Psychological Association was created: The Task Force on Empirically Supported Therapy Relationships. The Task Force, under the leadership of John Norcross, published its first report (Norcross 2001) and a book (*Psychotherapy Relationships That Work*, Norcross, 2002). The efforts of this committee are aimed at documenting the importance of relationship variables in therapy and the necessity of emphasizing relationship factors in clinical training and practice. Generally speaking, the research on psychotherapy relationships is not experimental but limited to correlational studies. The best research designs for enhancing psychotherapy effectiveness is a topic that we will return to later, but first we deal with an issue of related importance: the apparent equivalence of outcomes across treatments.

The sufficiency of clinical trials research, the treatment guidelines they have spawned, and the manual-based interventions advocated will continue to be a controversial area in the early part of this century. Although many schools of therapy rush to show that their systems of treatment meet criteria for being empirically supported, practitioners and many researchers will continue to argue that empirical methods have serious limitations that need to be acknowledged and that lessen the importance of using "empirically supported therapies" in practice and in training programs (also see Chapter 8, this volume).

Equal Outcomes and Common Factors of Diverse Techniques

One of the most difficult findings to conceptualize theoretically or to use practically is the continuing and frequent lack of difference in the outcomes of various techniques. Certainly behavior therapy is very different from psychoanalytically oriented psychotherapy. Thus, Freudian psychoanalysts generally do not focus on behaviors and reinforcement, and behavior therapists spend little or no time analyzing a patient's dreams or countertransference problems. With some important exceptions which are discussed later, there is conclusive evidence that psychotherapeutic techniques do not have specific effects that are *uniquely* effective. Yet, there is tremendous resistance to accepting this finding as a legitimate one. Numerous interpretations of the data have been given in order to preserve the idea that technical factors have substantial, unique, and specific effects. Those therapists who are strongly committed to or identified with one specific form of psychotherapy cannot accept such evaluative results. As Bergin and Garfield (1994) have pointed out: "The reasons for this are not difficult to surmise. Such pronouncements essentially appear to be rationalizations that attempt to preserve the role of special theories, the status of leaders of such approaches, the technical training programs for therapists, the professional legitimacy of psychotherapy, and the rewards that come to those having supposedly curative powers" (p. 822). One might have expected that the impressive number of studies and meta-analytic reviews suggesting equivalence to have had some impact on the therapist's views of the effectiveness of other forms of therapy. Such has not been the case. Rather, school loyalties and identifications remain strong for a significant number of psychotherapists. What is the answer?

First, we have to recognize that in a majority of studies, different approaches to the same symptoms (e.g., depression) show little difference in efficacy (see Chapter 5). Group and family treatment methods show few differences in results between and within themselves, or as compared with individual methods (see Chapters 13 and 14). The cognitive approaches show little advantage over behavioral approaches or over combinations of both in many instances (see Chapter 9). Within the same system, different subtechniques often manifest few differences. This is true despite the fact that the research procedures that have been employed maximize finding any differences that might exist. If one observes therapy sessions or listens to tapes, one can note that regardless of the type of therapy conducted, the therapy will include cognitive elements, emotional elements, behavior elements, relationship elements, and the like. Klein, Dittman, Parloff, and Gill (1969) for example, after observing two behavior therapists at work, were struck by the degree to which the therapists used suggestion and managed patients' expectations and attitudes.

It is important to emphasize that none of this means that therapy is ineffective. We know that it generally is, but we do not always know precisely why. There are probably many ways to health. The issue is whether we can isolate and identify the ingredients of practice and then enhance their influence. Some theoretical guidelines would help in deciding what to look for. The main theoretical interpretations assume that common factors exist in all or most therapies, that these account for a considerable amount of the change that occurs, and that is why no differences occur.

Three main traditional views have been advocated as explanations of this phenomenon. One derives from learning theories. It argues that mental disorders are generally acquired via learning processes and that positive change consists of "un-learning" old response patterns and acquiring new ones. Two of the main mechanisms used in this view are desensitization or extinction of anxiety-associated responses and learning of mastery behaviors via rehearsal, positive reinforcement, or self-enactment of adaptive actions. It is said that all of these occur whether wittingly or unwittingly in all therapies.

The second view, the humanistic, phenomenological perspective, suggests that the common factor is a caring relationship characterized by warmth, support, attention, understanding, and acceptance. These ingredients are said to have direct healing properties somewhat like the effects of good nutrition or solar radiation, which strengthen the organism and stimulate growth. The therapeutic relationship is thus seen as a "condition" that leads to the dropping of defenses and the reintegration of conflicted aspects of thought, feeling, and action that makes growth or the healthful blossoming of self possible. The position is central to a recent influential book, *The Heart and Soul of Change* (Hubble, Duncan, & Miller, 1999).

A third major perspective has argued that all therapies provide a cathartic release of turbulent affect; a rationale or belief system for understanding and explaining one's troubles; a set of rituals or procedures for enacting an alternative, healthier lifestyle; and faith in the wisdom of the sanctioned healer. This view embraces the social psychology of persuasion and culturally defined social role behavior. Psychotherapies are all thus viewed as merely special cases of more general cultural phenomena having to do with religious beliefs and practices and cultural roles and norms.

All three of these views have merit and all three may apply to some degree, but none has held up as a complete explanation of the findings of psychotherapy research. Therapeutic change has been found to be far more cognitively guided than simple "reconditioning" via learning implies. There is evidence that cognitive changes are brought about through changes in behavior as well as medication without the benefit of focus on cognitions themselves (Chapters 9 and 16, this volume). Therapeutic healing conditions have not been sufficient in causing or explaining change. The dramatic effects of "faith," alternate beliefs, and newfound role conformity appear limited to certain kinds of people and may not be lasting.

Contemporary views amalgamate and refine these viewpoints in attempts to more precisely identify the common ingredients that, together, may add up to an optimal change process. Much of this work is discussed in Chapters 5, 7, and 8 of this volume; Table 5.8 (p. 173) summarizes a general perspective. There, the common ingredients are seen to be a combination of affective experiencing, cognitive mastery, and behavioral regulation. Techniques deriving from the different schools are subsumed under these categories. This table, and the thinking it represents, provides a template for pursuing the ingredients that may be the key factors in change. But there are, as yet, no precise description of all these factors and no empirical tests of the effectiveness of combinations or integrations of the ingredients.

A second perspective is provided in Chapter 8 where a "generic model" of therapy is proposed as an overarching conceptual system. All therapies thus construed involve a formal aspect (therapeutic contract), a technical aspect (therapeutic operations), an interpersonal aspect (therapeutic bond), an intrapersonal aspect (self-relatedness), a clinical aspect (in-session impacts and therapeutic realizations), and a temporal aspect (sequential processes). A massive amount of data is summarized in Chapter 8 using this system and showing the statistical relations among its different aspects under the overall heading of "Process and Outcomes."

The Value of Specific Interventions

Although there are many instances in which no differences occur between therapeutic approaches or in comparisons of specific techniques with attention-placebo conditions, there are also a number of results showing such differences. How do we account for these? What are the mechanisms or processes involved? It appears that certain kinds of cases respond well to the factors that are common to all conditions. When symptoms are not too severe, they seem to respond to the influence of common factors that facilitate change. Greater severity, however, tests the limits of the common factors. When more severe cases of depression, anxiety, and so on are considered, technique differences sometimes emerge. There appear to be specific and superior effects of some behavioral and cognitive methods with some otherwise difficult problems such as severe phobia (e.g., agoraphobia and panic), compulsions, bulimia nervosa, tension headaches, insomnia, and other health-related dysfunctions. It is particularly important to note the long history and current success that exposure treatments of various kinds have with anxiety disorders (see Emmelkamp, Chapter 9, this volume). Patients with severe and chronic disorders, such as schizophrenia and bipolar disorder, seem to respond well to specific medications, while their response to psychotherapy is less dramatic (see Chapter 16). Family-based interventions have been shown to be especially effective in slowing relapse in schizophrenia and in treating conduct disorder in adolescents (see Chapters 12 and 13, this volume). Behavior therapy has been shown to be more effective than nonbehavioral treatments with disturbed children (see Chapter 12, this volume). Active and specifically targeted interventions have clearly added something unique to the therapeutic repertoire that should not be lost in arguments over "no differences" in some studies or in global meta-analyses (Garfield, 1997). In addition, psychoeducational interventions that do not depend on theoretical positions or on relationship factors often result in substantial improvement (see Chapters 14 and 15 on Group Therapy and Health Psychology).

Given the large number and variety of techniques and client problems, as well as the changing nature of interventions themselves, one can only applaud efforts aimed at discovering the unique effects of treatments. Thase and Jindal (Chapter 16, this volume) provide an interesting summary of such efforts with specific medications and specific disorders that show clear effects of specific treatments across disorders but limited evidence for the unique effects of specific medications within disorders. In addition, the failure of such different treatments as antidepressant medications and psychotherapy to have specific effects is sometimes reversed when subsamples are examined. As Thase and Jindal point out, there is some evidence that combined treatments are superior to either treatment alone with severe, nonsituational, endogenous depression and possibly with recurrent depression. This finding, if it holds up, has important implications for routine practice and increases the importance of diagnostic evaluations in the clinical setting. It also implies that many variables beyond diagnosis might be useful for differentiating patient subgroups that have unique responses to specific types of interventions.

As Beutler and colleagues point out in Chapter 7 (see also Chapter 6), certain client personality traits may interact with therapy techniques or therapist characteristics to produce specific interaction effects in relation to outcome (so-called aptitude by treatment interactions, or ATI). For instance, depressed clients who are resistance prone appear to do better with a less directive technique than a directive one. If replicated and extended, such findings could prove to be of great importance because they suggest that techniques may not show an effect by themselves but their effect is overlooked by researchers. At this time, there is little evidence that effective matching can be routinely achieved, but without the search for interaction effects many aspects of effective interventions may remain hidden.

In addition, the search for unique effects of specific interventions goes on in a context in which an alternative treatment is being compared with a treatment that has already been shown to be effective. Thus, the treatment of interest is considered to be uniquely effective only if it surpasses the comparison treatment. Studies of this nature often require large numbers of patients in each group and measures of outcome that have room for detecting differences at the scale's extreme (healthy end). The use of larger treatment samples and the more sensitive measures may be necessary for the most effective treatments to be identified.

Changes in the Nature of the Major Orientations

It appears that psychotherapy research has had a noticeable effect on how the major traditional orientations to therapy are being construed. Research evidence of the efficacy of cognitive interventions has had a dramatic influence on the way the behavioral movement is conceptualized, and the redefinition of the behavioral approach as "cognitive behavioral" represents a major shift in thought and practice. Most of the people who used to consider themselves behavioral therapists now identify themselves as cognitive behavioral. Also, most people who once considered themselves strictly cognitive practitioners now are willing to take on the cognitive behavioral label as well. Although many influences have produced such changes, it is pleasing to note that the effect of research has been substantial. There continues to be friction between advocates of the behavioral and cognitive behavioral positions, and many attempts have been made to clarify which aspects of these treatments are central to their positive impact.

The person-centered orientation has also been greatly influenced by research. Even though Beutler and colleagues have suggested that a nondirective technique may be a good match for certain resistant clients, overall the trend has been away from the nondirective orientation. This has been due, in part, to evidence indicating that therapy oriented entirely toward the traditional client-centered, nondirective notion of treatment has not produced large effect sizes. Despite making significant contributions in demonstrating the importance of empathy, respect, and other therapist characteristics, this orientation has significantly declined in the United States so far as its technical comparative efficacy is concerned. How does this trend fit with the surprisingly large effect sizes summarized in Chapter 11 on experiential therapies where research on various approaches is summarized?

The review by Elliot, Greenberg, and Lietaer shows rather dramatic new evidence supporting the efficacy of the humanistic experiential therapies; this is important because it may become an influential force in resurrecting the credibility of this orientation. However, the evidence presented in Chapter 11 shows that it is not the traditional nondirective, client-centered aspect of experiential therapy that is producing the largest effect sizes. The effect sizes are being produced by more "directive" interventions. These include the process-experiential, the Gestalt, and so forth. So, it may be the action-oriented and specific targeting aspects of this orientation that are coming to the front and providing evidence of effects that rival those from behavioral and cognitive orientations.

At the same time, we need to view some of the large effect sizes noted in Chapter 11 with a note of caution because many of them were produced by innovative therapists, like Greenberg, whose allegiance to the viewpoint is strong. We know from previous research that strong allegiances produce larger effect sizes in research studies (Luborsky et al. 1999). There is essentially nothing wrong with this. This phenomenon has been noted with respect to each of the major orientations, but we do find that over time the size of these large effects tends to decline somewhat and become more like those of other approaches. Indeed, the overall result of the Elliot, Greenberg, and Lietaer meta-analysis showed no differences in the outcomes of experiential and other major approaches. In any case, a major shift seems to have occurred in the way that experiential therapy is construed and implemented, and research studies of process and outcome have been central in such changes.

There has also been a dramatic change in the way psychodynamic psychotherapy is practiced today, at least in the United States. It has become much more eclectic, abbreviated, and specifically targeted. Therapy manuals for use with specific problem behaviors (such as cocaine and heroine addiction) have been developed, tested, and applied to patients with these difficult and destructive problems. Research evidence has also significantly undermined the notion that interpretation in general, and transference interpretation in particular, is the key to efficacy in this approach. It is difficult to underestimate the significance of this shift in thought, which has been brought about largely by careful therapy research.

At the same time, innovative work on the therapeutic alliance has shown considerable promise and significant correlations with psychotherapy outcome and is now being widely applied inside and outside of psychodynamic research. The concept of the alliance denotes an active collaboration between therapist and client where the client is not seen so much as the object of the therapist's empathy but as a partner in the work of therapy. So, the old directivism that used to be attributed to the psychodynamic approach, with interpretation as the key, has shifted to a new kind of directivism that is closer to a cognitive behavioral orientation but retains an important focus on the depth of the therapeutic relationship and resolution of defenses as clinical tools. It should also be mentioned that psychodynamic therapy is a broad designation that can be used to cover a variety of different emphases. Not only do the new changes described here apply mainly to recent developments featuring certain types of manual-guided brief therapies, but within this group there is also a fair amount of diversity (Garfield, 1990). These developments, however, are quite distinct from classical long-term psychoanalysis and psychoanalytically oriented psychotherapy. In these latter categories, very little systematic empirical research has been conducted. Evaluations of long-term psychodynamically oriented psychotherapies are still being conducted in Europe (e.g., Blomberg, Lazar, & Sandell, 2001) where these treatments continue to be routinely and widely practiced.

Overall, however, the changes described in this section show a growth in the precision, discipline, and focusing of the major orientations, and all of these have been substantially influenced by research. They also have laid the basis for the new eclectic and integrative movements because similarities are emerging from each of the main viewpoints, and it is becoming empirically visible that these changes are important in helping clients to improve. Even within distinct orientations there are modifications over time that have led particular theories to appropriate important aspects of other theories. Consider the emphasis on changing schemas that is evident within some cognitive behavior therapy, making these approaches more similar to dynamic and humanistic treatments. The fluidity evident in the evolution of treatments is a positive phenomenon but presents a serious challenge to identifying empirically supported therapies. Lists of efficacious interventions may therefore fall years behind contemporary practice and research.

The Therapist and Client

There is some evidence that, in addition to common factors and specific techniques, the therapist as an individual is responsible for differences in outcome. Variations in therapists' skills are frequently correlated with variations in outcome. The use of therapy manuals has greatly assisted the refinement of interventions, improving outcomes in some instances. On the other hand, when the therapist variable is allowed to vary uncontrollably, the influence of therapist factors becomes more dramatic.

Identification of the therapist as an important variable mediating change, semi-independent of technique and orientation, has been an important research endeavor. Until recently, the research focus has tended to be on the form of psychotherapy, thus minimizing the importance of therapist variability. At the same time, the use of therapy manuals to ensure that a specific type of therapy is actually being conducted does raise the issue of external validity—that is, are the results obtained in the research study applicable to everyday practice in the clinical setting? This issue has come to the forefront and requires further study and thought. However, there is little question that research on the efficacy of psychotherapy should use competent therapists, but this does not solve the problem of the therapist's contribution to outcome, which is still understudied (Elkin, 1999).

Although a great deal of variability exists within the medical profession, as a whole it embraces a standard of performance and quality control that has emphasized study of actual practice. In psychotherapy, older research studies examined the efficacy of therapy "as practiced" in a variety of clinical agencies where quality control was minimal. But even in these older studies the individual therapist was seldom the focus of research. The psychotherapy professions would be wise to achieve and maintain standards that include evaluation of each individual therapist's personal practice. Evaluations in this context are much more threatening than studies that focus on comparisons between theory-based interventions. As threatening as such evaluations can be, if the therapist is important to positive and negative outcomes, then routine self-evaluations of practice are an important component of offering the highest quality services. The value of therapeutic techniques is best judged on the basis of carefully controlled studies and not on evaluations of ordinary practices that may include mediocre work. But the evaluation of services as offered to clients in routine practice and its immediate improvement will require assessment of the individual therapist's work. One can only hope that practicing clinicians will have the confidence and security to allow evaluations of their patients' outcomes and contrasts with other therapists. Perhaps though, the most important determining force in outcome is the client her- or himself.

As Chapter 6 clearly shows, client characteristics make a sizable difference with respect to outcomes, and diagnosis per se may not be the key variable in understanding treatment response. Chapters 6 and 7 point out that interaction among therapists, techniques, and clients results in different types of outcomes. When these possible interactions are not taken into account, the overall outcome data may gloss over rather divergent results. In addition, outcomes may be divergent across clients from diverse cultural groupings. The extent of the actual effects of this diversity has not been well documented in the research literature.

There is an abundance of speculation about the importance of racial and ethnic group differences, but the empirical investigation of these speculations lags well behind the rhetoric. One problem in this area is the difficulty of gathering large samples of patients within minority groups. Paradoxically, those who work in the area insist on a high level of sophistication in properly describing minority clients' ethnicity (e.g., measuring degree of acculturation) and thereby make demands of researchers that cannot be met in most routine outcome studies. This results in limiting information on the effects of therapy on ethnic minorities when the information comes from researchers who do not have a primary interest in ethnic issues but who have data on the outcome of treatment where demographics are limited to ethnic group. There also seems to be a bias in this area of inquiry towards assuming (insisting) that ethnically diverse clients have poorer outcomes than their majority counterparts, in the absence of evidence that supports this conclusion. As pointed out by Zane and colleagues (Chapter 17, this volume) progress has been slow and unsystematic, despite the clear importance of advancements in understanding client variables. It is surprising to see the amount of money spent on treatment programs for the underserved (e.g., Native Americans) in the absence of well-designed outcome research. It would be a welcome change to see as much attention and energy devoted to research investigations of ethnic group "outcomes" as has been devoted to speculations about the special needs of these patients. Actual research results, rather than mere speculation, would help us better serve these important members of our community.

Another important observation regarding clients is that it is the client more than the therapist who implements the change process. If the client does not absorb, utilize, and follow through on the facilitative efforts of the therapist's change process, then nothing happens. In this regard, we need to reform our thinking about the efficacy of psychotherapy. Clients are not inert objects or diagnostic categories on whom techniques are administered. They are not dependent variables on which independent variables operate (see Chapter 3). As Bandura (1986) has so clearly shown, people are agentive beings who are effective forces in the complex of casual events.

Studies of early response to therapy (e.g., response in the first three sessions) show that early response to treatment occurs in many clients *before* they have received a major portion of the treatment being offered. Despite our belief in the causal influence of our theories of change, our treatment plan, and the interventions we have designed to help clients, many clients show a substantial positive response before the treatment has been implemented. This positive response may be achieved before the client has received a substantial portion of therapist-offered therapeutic conditions. These early responders are not only overrepresented among those who attain clinically significant change at termination but also tend to maintain their gains at followup (Haas, Hill, Lambert, & Morrell, 2002). Given the rapidity and size of this response, it would appear to be due to client variables rather than therapy per se. These rapidly responding clients appear to be especially resourceful. Identification of the rapidly responding client would allow clinicians to terminate treatment rapidly, with these cases freeing up resources and allowing for greater focus on those clients that are not so fortunate.

Methods for helping clients maintain their gains have shown some positive effects, but relapse prevention is dependent on the client playing a significant role in implementing the change procedures. Relapse prevention would be more feasible and widespread if there were a way of specifying, beforehand, who is most in need of this kind of help. An important task of future research is to identify specific persons who need followup interventions.

Brief Therapies the Norm

Trends in psychotherapy research indicate that almost all the psychotherapies studied in the United States are brief. This has been dictated in part by economic factors, but it is also influenced by the fact that a good deal of change can be stimulated in a much shorter time than previously thought. The dose-response work (see Chapter 5) indicated that about half of the patients who undergo psychotherapy show reliable improvement by the eighth session; that about half the cases obtain clinically significant improvement within about 18 sessions or 5 months at once a week; and that about 75% of cases show a return to normal functioning within a year (Hansen & Lambert, 2003). Thus, much of the change for many cases occurs in a relatively brief time. This needs to be clearly recognized, and it supports the trend initiated by the behavior therapy movement several decades ago. Even so, the number of sessions attended by the majority of clients falls well below these "doses" and well below the 12 to 14 sessions typically studied in clinical trials research. Efforts need to be made to make therapy available to clients in doses large enough to give them a chance to work. Managed care organizations that purportedly engage in quality assurance activities should look closely at patient utilization figures and make efforts to keep many clients in treatment for longer rather than shorter time periods (Hansen, Lambert, & Forman, 2002). The allocation of treatment sessions should not be based on arbitrary limits or even theoretical predilections. Those patients who respond to treatment quickly can be terminated after just a few sessions, but more slowly responding patients are in need of more sessions. However, these slow-responding patients cannot be recognized unless their progress is monitored. Response to treatment, rather than insurance coverage or theoretical considerations, should be emphasized by third-party payers, government agencies, and clinicians, if the outcome of treatment is to be optimized and cost effective.

We also need to acknowledge that there are intractable cases, such as those that have comorbid disorders and certain kinds of personality disorders, which may require more than a year of treatment or who may not respond to therapy at all. Despite such complications, it is important to recognize that empirical evidence shows major improvements being achieved by means of psychotherapy in far less than the two years that were once hypothesized as the norm. This, of course, does not mean that all change occurs in a few months, but rather, that a process of change has been effected that can be maintained and even improved upon by continued independent actions of the client and, in some cases, by occasional booster sessions with the therapist. It is important to emphasize this latter point, for psychotherapy is no longer viewed as a long-term process that, once completed, implies a lifetime period of mental health and adjustment.

The Meta-analysis Epidemic

Until the 1980s, reviews of the effects of psychotherapy were based on a careful reading of research studies followed by commentaries and conclusions. A methodological advance was the application of statistical methods initiated by Smith, Glass, and Miller (1980). Their book on the effects of psychotherapy, based on calculating and summing effect size statistics across studies, marked a change in reviewing procedures that significantly impacted the review process. Other reviewers followed their procedures and made advances in calculation methods (e.g., Cooper & Hedges, 1994) and software developments to ease the task (e.g., SPSS/PC+, SYSTAT). Today the meta-analytic review is considered the gold standard for integrating research reports. The effect size statistic has become a standard way of expressing the size of therapeutic effects and is now routinely reported within individual studies.

Hundreds of research reviews based on meta-analytic procedures are now available. These reviews have the advantage of being replicable, provided that the same calculation procedures are used. Unfortunately, meta-analytic reviewers still must make an extremely large number of decisions (e.g., inclusion and exclusion of studies for review, which effect sizes to calculate, how effect sizes will be summed). The promise of a "totally objective review" that appeared to come with meta-analytic procedures is clearly an unrealistic expectation.

Meta-analytic reviews have increased precision but are open to many of the same biases as narrative reviews. Many of the same controversies that were apparent before meta-analytic procedures continue today, despite the fact that meta-analytic procedures are employed. Examples of the failure of meta-analytic reviews to be more "objective" than narrative reviews and thereby resolve disagreements about the size of treatment effects (Lipsey & Wilson, 1993), the effectiveness of the placebo controls (Prioleau, Murdock, & Brody, 1983), and differences between treatments (Anderson & Lambert, 1995; Crits-Christoph, 1992; Svartberg & Stiles, 1991), to name just a few, are plentiful.

Unfortunately, meta-analytic reviews do not give definitive answers to the most important questions that are of interest to the field, yet they proliferate unabated. Among the more problematic issues that have come with this methodology is the failure of the scholars who conduct them to attend to the limitations inherent in this methodology. The elaborate and even elegant statistical procedures of meta-analysis have become a substitute for careful thought about the studies under consideration and their implications for practice. Although meta-analysis adds significantly to our methods of inquiry, we urge caution in relying too heavily on the assumed objectivity of such reviews (e.g., Westen & Morrison, 2001) and suggest that journal editors insist on full discussion of the limitations of each review that is published.

CLINICAL SIGNIFICANCE

One of the most important innovations in the field has been the renewed emphasis on clinical significance as opposed to statistical significance of results (see Chapters 2, 4, and 5). Clinical significance can be determined by establishing a normative reference criterion based on the absence of symptoms or the status of a "normal" group to which the patient's improvement can be compared. It is an index of outcome that is useful to researchers who study treatments, especially with regard to quality management and dose-effect relationships. Clinical significance is also important to practitioners and to agencies that may be paying the fees for treatment and judging its success. Of course, it is ultimately most significant to the client, who must live with whatever results occur as a consequence of therapy. As criteria for clinical significance become more stringent, the proportion of patients who are judged "improved" decreases significantly. Whereas 70 to 80 percent of patients may be judged improved by traditional statistical methods and effect size estimates, far lower percentages are improved by the more stringent standards of clinical significance.

The use of clinical significance standards to judge treatment outcomes has grown in popularity since their introduction in the 1980s. Some kind of clinical significance is now an expected analysis in outcome research. In contrast to earlier editions of this *Handbook*, clinically significant change is now widely discussed and presented, enabling the reader to grasp more clearly the practical consequences of treatments for individual patients and the degree to which current treatment practices are fulfilling expectations.

Generally, the modern efforts at evaluating clinical significance constitute another rather important advance in psychotherapy research and one that can effect practical decisions. In this sense, the practitioner can benefit more fully from the results of research, narrowing the gap between practice and research. This research innovation is still in its infancy, and more research on the validity of statistical definitions is needed.

Negative Effects

Readers will note that the topic of negative effects arises in various chapters in this book, and researchers seem to have no doubt that deterioration or negative outcomes can and do occur. The seriousness of the problem has diminished somewhat in research studies as a result of new and stricter controls, manual-guided therapies, and training and selection of therapists for studies. Negative effects are much less evident in such carefully designed and executed projects. On the other hand, when such controls do not exist, negative effects persist as a significant problem (see Chapter 5). There is probably no system of intervention in any profession that cannot be misused or does not, by inept application, produce useless or negative outcomes. The problem is not unique to the psychotherapies or to the mental health profession in general. It is important to note that there have been improvements in this area over time. Training programs are more assiduously taking into account the potential for damage that can occur as a result of poor therapy. In many training programs, inexperienced therapists are more carefully initiated into client contacts, and this is often preceded by a period of skills training. In addition, the videotaping and supervision processes are more rigorous, and accrediting agencies are more demanding of quality control on the part of supervising faculties. Where there is less rigorous management of quality in agencies and training programs, there is the likelihood of more negative outcomes.

Although the problem of negative effects persists, it is encouraging to observe that, to some degree, this liability has been recognized and actions have been taken in formal training settings to contain negative outcomes. Yet, it is surprising, and even disheartening, to see that few training programs have introduced independent systems to measure and monitor treatment response in the clients of trainees. Such monitoring systems can be implemented with minimal effort (Lambert & Hawkins, 2001) and would strengthen the effects of supervision and quality control efforts.

It is also a matter of continuing concern that so many new therapies that have no empirical support (or advocates who have active programs for validating such treatments) are invented and introduced by licensed practitioners, but even more so by entrepreneurial unlicensed persons. Numerous treatments are also applied by people who have merely attended a workshop or two in a procedure and then consider themselves to be experts. It is also unfortunate that fads continue to dot the landscape of the mental health professions and that a fair amount of magical thinking regarding the power to change people is associated with such movements. Fortunately, when these "innovations" are empirically evaluated, claims of extraordinary results are eventually tempered (see, for example, Emmelkamp's comments on Eye Movement Desensitization Therapy in Chapter 9). This leveling of claims has to be viewed as one of the more significant contributions of psychotherapy research as well as an impetus to continue such research.

Measurement

Apparently, scientific advancements are frequently dependent on the invention of measuring devices that consolidate certain insights regarding nature, in our case, human nature. In the physical sciences, Nobel prizes have been won by people who have developed ingenious ways of measuring or monitoring phenomena. However, precise measurement of clinical phenomena continues to be a problem in evaluating psychotherapy processes and outcomes. Chapter 4 is devoted to this issue and represents the importance of this topic for advancing our understanding of outcomes and the process mechanisms that cause them.

In addition, several recent books are devoted to the topic of measuring outcome. These books are a response to worldwide demand for outcome assessment that characterizes current concerns over accountability. Most provide listings and summaries of specific measures and recommended procedures. Chapter 4 by Hill and Lambert (this volume) note several volumes, including Maruish's *The Use of Psychological Testing for Treatment Planning and Outcome Assessment* (1999), Cone's *Evaluating Outcomes: Empirical Tools for Effective Practice* (2001), and Ogles, Lambert, and Masters' *Assessing Outcome in Clinical Practice* (1996). These volumes, as well as the many others that have been recently published, provide much needed information for those who want to measure outcome.

Measurement innovations continue. However, as pointed out in Chapters 4 and 5, many of the new measures are essentially homemade devices that are used only once or only a few times. The number of devices has also exploded into the hundreds. Some of these devices, such as some of the new alliance scales and some of the careful work on depression measurement, reflect significant progress, while many of the efforts lack the rigor and precision that would ordinarily be expected of people who understand the psychological and methodological requirements of good measurement. It is conceivable that better innovation in the measurement area awaits better theoretical insights concerning the phenomena under consideration. Such insights might be followed by ingenious new constructions for estimating the effects of techniques or for describing phenomenological processes. In any case, we wish to clearly identify the measurement area as a problem area that presents special challenges. For the vigorous and rigorous researcher who can produce creative innovations in this area, great rewards are likely to follow.

Process Research

Along with the growing interest in clinical significance and measurement of outcomes, there has been a burst of energy devoted to process studies. A new level of sophistication has become evident that is way beyond the earlier focus on rudimentary aspects of therapy processes. The new developments, which are documented in many chapters in this book (e.g., Chapters 4, 8, and 11), indicate a good deal of original thought. With a number of the outstanding issues regarding outcome settled to some degree, much more focus has shifted to the "mechanisms" of change. Elliot, Greenberg, and Lietaer's section in Chapter 11, "Specific Therapeutic Task Interventions," illustrates the point, as does the work of Burns and Spangler (2000) using path analysis.

As processes are more clearly defined in relation to outcome in the therapies that currently exist, we may be able to refine techniques based on such research in order to center them on those aspects that are most clearly correlated with positive change. This is the quest, and, as indicated in many places in the book, significant progress is being made. This progress will eventually trickle down to training and practice settings.

Spiritually Based Change

Spiritual and religious change variables have been alluded to briefly in the present and previous editions of this handbook. Spiritual change has become a major mental health growth industry (Miller, 1999; Richards & Bergin, 1997, 2000; Shafranske, 1996). A substantial research literature has emerged documenting the relationship of such phenomena to physical and mental health (Larson, Sawyers, & McCollough, 1998), but the field of psychotherapy research has hardly touched this potential source of therapeutic effects.

The limited therapy research available has been summarized by Worthington and colleagues (Worthington, Kurusu, McCullough, & Sandage, 1996; Worthington & Sandage, 2002). Data indicate that religious/spiritual clients prefer therapists who address change within a spiritual framework. If such therapists are not available, many avoid treatment altogether. Findings also show that religious cognitive therapy for depression works as well or better than secular therapy for a religious clientele (McCullough, 1999); and, equally challenging, that pastoral counselors achieve outcomes equal to or better than those professionally trained in cognitive methods (Propst, Ostrom, Watkins, Dean, & Mashburn, 1992). Of course, much more research needs to be completed before sound conclusions can be drawn about how the spiritual life of the client can be addressed so as to facilitate recovery. Given the large number of clients who subscribe to a religious belief system and the importance of such a system to their functioning, it is surprising to see the degree to which discussions and research are missing from the literature on psychotherapy process and outcome.

Sophisticated inquiries (Miller & C'deBaca, 2001) continue on a small scale, but a new $2.5 million research grant program, funded by the John Templeton Foundation, provides the promise of larger data-gathering efforts (see:www.spiritualtransformationresearch.org). Perhaps the therapy research establishment will become part of this developing area of inquiry.

Methodological Pluralism

In Chapters 2 and 3, the term *methodological pluralism* is used in a positive way to indicate the desirability of using multiple distinct methodologies. We endorse this view, and it seems to be supported by more and more people who are studying clinical phenomena. Sexton et al. (Chapter 13) as well as Kazdin (Chapter 12), echo these sentiments and call for qualitative research as well as more creative use of traditional strategies. It seems that traditional experimental and multivariate methodologies have not consistently or adequately addressed the phenomenon of therapeutic change. Numerous writings have been intensely critical of the standard methodologies, but granting agencies, journal editors, and promotions committees still seem to focus primarily on them. As noted in Chapter 1, however, there has been a significant change in the thinking of researchers and theorists on this subject (Bergin, 1997).

The growing endorsement of narrative, descriptive, and qualitative approaches represents a rather significant shift in attitude that is likely to become increasingly manifest in the conduct and reporting of inquiries. We find ourselves endorsing a kind of pluralism that does not throw out the virtues of the traditional approaches of research but complements those with a variety of flexible techniques for getting at the complexity of the phenomena we deal with. We anticipate seeing much more along this line in the future. At the same time, we are not advocating a reversion to nineteenth-century phenomenology and hermeneutics, but, rather, an objective approach to subjective phenomena that can be addressed qualitatively and descriptively using rigor and, in many cases, quantification. The tremendous surge of single-case studies that occurred within the behavioral movement in the 1960s and 1970s is one form of intensive design that goes in the right direction, but the contemporary movements address much more complex phenomena than single specified target responses. Although this movement (and it has become a movement) does hold promise, its promise has to be demonstrated by showing fruitful additions to research findings from traditional methodologies.

Future Directions

Psychotherapy research has been a distant cousin of clinical practice. It has often taken years for research findings to impact training and clinical practice. With the current emphasis on accountability brought on by economic concerns about the costs of healthcare worldwide, outcome research is beginning to play a larger role in clinical practice. This is especially noticeable with the advent of so-called empirically supported psychotherapies, with research providing the justification for selecting intervention methods for patients with particular disorders. Reliance on offering empirically supported treatments, as a method of assuring positive outcomes, does not appear to be a particularly hopeful direction for future research. Although it does provide possibilities for rooting out poorly conceived treatment plans and practices, in the long run offering empirically supported therapies is only a first step in improving treatment and patient outcome.

A necessary and productive direction for psychotherapy researchers involves methods of monitoring patient treatment response in real time and modifying ongoing treatment when its intended positive impact fails to materialize. Such research is beginning to be seen in various settings across the world and has been highlighted in a recent special issue of the *Journal of Clinical and Consulting Psychology* (Lambert, 2001a). We call for more such research and encourage those in the field to give special consideration to engaging in this "patient-focused" or "outcome-focused" research. Research directed toward identifying potential treatment failure and methods to change the course of failure during ongoing treatment should become a high priority in the next decade.

Conclusion

Psychotherapy research has resulted in a large body of findings which indicate that the treatments offered to clients are helpful and surpass the effects of informal social support networks and placebo controls. The effects of psychotherapy are often enduring, but research has also made it clear that psychotherapy is not a panacea; the limits of services are painfully obvious to those who engage in research. Many patients show little benefit from routine practice. Methods have been developed for identifying negative treatment response and, to some degree, for reversing this decline before termination of services occurs. Research has helped to identify causal factors in outcome and to maximize the likelihood that effective treatments will be offered while damping the claims of those who would oversell the consequences of seeking professional help. This latter contribution of the research enterprise should not be undervalued because it bolsters the credibility of the professional practitioner and of psychological services generally.

The search for effective treatments and their limitations goes on worldwide and promises to enhance practice. We believe that the current emphasis on anchoring professional therapeutic work in empirical research is a healthy trend for the field that will pay big dividends to the patient. At the same time, we do not foresee any major new theoretical developments along the line of global, comprehensive theories that attempt to explain all aspects of personality, psychopathology, and psychotherapy, as we have in the past. It is more likely that the trend toward minitheories centered on specific problem domains and empirical evaluations will continue. Research on psychotherapy will continue to focus on casual factors that can be modified to enhance client functioning. In addition, the complexity of the phenomenon will likely be addressed in new and interesting ways that will include sophisticated statistical methods made possible by advances in computer technology. The use of computer-based applications is also likely to increase, including Internet-based efforts to connect with people in their homes by providing information and direct services as well as assessment and research.

Efforts to attain greater precision and to have clear and valid measurement of therapy effects, both within sessions and as estimates of outcome, will likely continue. External pressures from government and insurance agencies as well as the natural trend of scientific advancement are likely to continue to improve both precision and comprehension with regard to the phenomenon of therapeutic change.

We would also expect the trend toward manual-guided therapy to continue, with the refinements that are needed to accommodate applications in routine practice. This will include greater care in the design of manuals, inclusion of a rigorously defined flexibility to accommodate differences in therapist style, more attempts to address the complexity of therapeutic transactions, and greater emphasis on the client-therapist relationship.

We hope that in the future both federal and state agencies as well as professional organizations and private granting agencies will become more concerned with psychotherapy research as they determine funding for treatments, accredit training programs, and license practitioners. Although mental disorders are enormously costly to our society and are pervasive throughout it, the funding allotted for research is quite minor compared with the enormous sums devoted to the natural and biological sciences. Keeping therapy research in the role of a "cottage industry" is a scandalous state of affairs. Although there have been a few collaborative programs on the treatment of depression, anxiety, and substance abuse disorders, more could be done. Currently, the number of researchers is far too few, it takes too long to complete projects, and the accumulation of information is dreadfully slow with respect to the factors that assist in altering mental disorders.

A significant increase in funding for research in psychotherapy is a critical need, and a positive response to it could dramatically accelerate our ability to assist persons in mental distress. The general disregard of this issue by public and private agencies and by state and federal legislatures is a tragic state of affairs made painfully obvious by the pervasive problems that affect children, adolescents, and the family in our culture. It is our hope that in the coming years, a new edition of this or a similar volume will include reference to scores of new major inquiries involving large numbers of new researchers that will show significant progress due to concerted effort and adequate financial support.

Despite the great need for improvement with respect to future research support, we are pleased to acknowledge that over the past quarter-century substantial progress has been made. The burden of that progress has been carried by a relatively small number of dedicated researchers who have been idealistic, hard working, open to change, and unusually free from vain ambition. We commend them, and we hope for many more like them in a future characterized by greater recognition of the significant contribution that psychotherapy research can make to human welfare.

References

Abrahamson, D. (1999). Outcomes, guidelines, and manuals: On leading horses to water. *Clinical Psychology: Science and Research, 6*, 467–471.

Addis, M. E., Wade, W. A., & Hatgis, C. (1999). Barriers to dissemination of evidence-based practices: Addressing practitioners' concerns about manual-based psychotherapies. *Clinical Psychology: Science and Practice, 6*, 430–441.

Anderson, E. M., & Lambert, M. J. (1995). Short-term dynamically oriented psychotherapy: A review and meta-analysis. *Clinical Psychology Review, 15,* 503–514.

Andrews, G. A.(2000). A focus on empirically supported outcomes: A commentary on search for empirically supported treatments. *Clinical Psychology: Science and Practice,* 7, 264–268.

Austad, C. S., Sherman, W. O., Morgan, T., & Holstein, L. (1992). The psychotherapist and the managed care setting. *Professional Psychology: Research & Practice, 23,* 329–332.

Bandura, A. (1986). *Social foundations of thought and action: A social cognitive theory.* Englewood Cliffs, NJ: Prentice Hall.

Bergin, A. E. (1997). Neglect of the therapist and the human dimensions of change: A commentary. *Clinical Psychology: Science and Practice, 4,* 83–89.

Bergin, A. E., & Garfield, S. L. (Eds.) (1994). *Handbook of psychotherapy & behavior change* (4th ed.). New York: John Wiley & Sons.

Blomberg, J., Lazar, A., & Sandell, R. (2001). Long-term outcome of long-term psychoanalytically oriented therapies: First findings of the Stockholm outcome of psychotherapy and psychoanalysis study. *Psychotherapy Research, 11,* 361–382.

Bohart, A. C., O'Hara, M., & Leitner, L. M. (1998). Empirically violated treatments: Disenfranchisement of humanistic and other psychotherapies. *Psychotherapy Research, 8,* 141–147.

Burns, D. D., & Spangler, D. L. (2000). Does psychotherapy homework lead to improvements in depression in cognitive-behavioral therapy or does improvement lead to increased homework compliance? *Journal of Consulting and Clinical Psychology, 68,* 45–56.

Calhoun, K. S., Moras, K., Pilkonis, P. A., & Rehm, L. P. (1998). Empirically supported treatments: Implications for training. *Journal of Consulting and Clinical Psychology, 66,* 151–162.

Cone, D. (2001). *Evaluating outcomes: Empirical tools for effective practice.* Washington, DC: APA.

Cooper, H., & Hedges, L. V. (Eds.). (1994). *The handbook of research synthesis.* New York: Russell Sage Foundation.

Crits-Christoph, P. (1992). The efficacy of psychodynamic psychotherapy: A meta-analysis. *American Journal of Psychiatry, 149,* 151–158.

Elkin, I. (1999). A major dilemma in psychotherapy outcome research: Disentangling therapists from therapies. *Clinical Psychology: Science and Practice, 6,* 10–32.

Garfield, S. L. (1990). Issues and methods in psychotherapy research. *Journal of Consulting and Clinical Psychology, 58,* 273–280.

Garfield, S. L. (1994). Eclecticism and integration in psychotherapy: Developments and issues. *Clinical Psychology: Science and Practice, 1,* 123–137.

Garfield, S. L. (1996). Some problems associated with "validated" forms of psychotherapy. *Clinical Psychology: Science and Practice, 3,* 218–229.

Garfield, S. L. (1997). Brief psychotherapy: The role of common and specific factors. *Clinical Psychology and Psychotherapy, 4,* 217–225.

Garfield, S. L. (1998). *The practice of brief psychotherapy* (2nd ed.). New York: John Wiley & Sons.

Giusti, E., Montanari, C., & Iannazzo, A. (2001). *Piscoterapie integrate.* Milan, Italy: Masson.

Goldfried, M., & Wolfe, B. (1995). Psychotherapy practice and research: Repairing a strained alliance. *American Psychologist, 51,* 1007–1016.

Haas, E., Hill, R., Lambert, M. J., & Morrell, B. (2002). Do early responders to psychotherapy maintain treatment gains? *Journal of Clinical Psychology, 58,* 1157–1172.

Hansen, N. B., & Lambert, M. J. (2003). The dose-effect relationship: A survival analysis across treatment centers. Mental Health Services Research, 5, (1).

Hansen, N. B., Lambert, M. J., & Forman, E. M. (2002). Comparisons of clinically significant change in clinical trials and naturalistic practice settings: The dose-effect relationship and its implications for practice. *Clinical Psychology: Science and Practice, 9,* 329–343.

Henry, W. P. (1998). Science, politics, and the politics of science: The use and misuse of empirically validated treatment research. *Psychotherapy Research, 8,* 126–140.

Hollon, S. D. (1999). Allegiance effects in treatment research: A commentary. *Clinical Psychology: Science and Practice, 6,* 107–112.

Hubble, M. A., Duncan, B. L., & Miller, S. D. (Eds.) (1999). *The heart and soul of change.* Washington, DC: American Psychological Association Press.

Ingram, R. E., Hayes, A., & Scott, W. (2000). Empirically supported treatments: A critical analysis. In R. Ingram and C. R. Synder (Eds.), *Handbook of psychological change* (pp. 40–60). New York: John Wiley & Sons.

Jacobson, N. S. (1999). The role of the allegiance effect in psychotherapy research: Controlling and accounting for it. *Clinical Psychology: Science and Practice, 6,* 116–119.

Jensen, J. P., Bergin, A. E., & Greaves, D. W. (1990). The meaning of eclecticism: New survey and analysis of components. *Professional Psychology: Research and Practice, 12,* 124–130.

Klein, M. H., Dittman, A. T., Parloff, M. B., & Gill, M. M. (1969). Behavior therapy: Observations and reflections. *Journal of Consulting and Clinical Psychology, 33,* 259–266.

Lambert, M. J. (2001a). Psychotherapy outcome and quality improvement: An introduction to the special section on patient-focused research. *Journal of Consulting and Clinical Psychology, 69,* 147–149.

Lambert, M. J. (2001b). The status of empirically supported psychotherapies: Comment on Westen and Morrison's (2001) multidimensional meta-analysis. *Journal of Consulting and Clinical Psychology, 69*, 910–913.

Lambert, M. J., & Hawkins, E. J. (2001). Using information about patient progress in supervision: Are outcomes enhanced? *Australian Psychologist, 36*, 131–138.

Larson, D. B., Sawyers, J. P., & McCullough, M. E. (1998). *Scientific research on spirituality and health: A consensus report.* Rockville, MD: National Institute for Healthcare Research.

Lipsey, M. W., & Wilson, D. B. (1993). The efficacy of psychological, educational, and behavioral treatment: Confirmation from meta-analysis. *American Psychologist, 48*, 1181–1209.

Luborsky, L., Diguer, L., Seligman, D. A., Rosenthal, R., Krause, E. D., Johnson, S., Halperin, G., Bishop, M., Berman, J., & Schweizer, E. (1999). The researcher's own therapy allegiances: A "wild card" in comparisons of treatment efficacy. *Clinical Psychology: Science and Practice, 6*, 95–106.

Maruish, M. A. (Ed.) (1999). *The use of psychological testing for treatment planning and outcome assessment* (2nd ed). Mahwah, NJ: Lawrence Erlbaum.

McCullough, J. P. (2000). *Treatment for chronic depression: Cognitive behavioral analysis system of psychotherapy.* New York: Guilford Press.

McCullough, M. E. (1999). Research on religion-accommodative counseling: Review and meta-analysis. *Journal of Counseling Psychology, 46*, 92–98.

Miller, W. R. (1999). *Integrating spirituality into treatment: Resources for practitioners.* Washington, DC: APA.

Miller, W. R., & C'deBaca, J. (2001). *Quantum Change.* New York: Guilford Press.

Norcross, J. D. (2001). Empirically supported therapy relationships: Summary report of the Division 29 Task Force. *Psychotherapy, 38(4)*, 495–497.

Norcross, J. D. (Ed.). (2002). *Psychotherapy relationships that work.* New York: Oxford University Press.

Norcross, J. D., Karg, R. S., & Prochaska, J. O. (1997). Clinical psychologists in the 1990s: Part I. *The Clinical Psychologist, 50(2)*, 4–9.

Ogles, B. M., Lambert, M. J., & Masters, K. S. (1996). *Assessing outcome in clinical practice.* Boston: Allyn & Bacon.

Prioleau, L., Murdock, M., & Brody, N. (1983). An analysis of psychotherapy versus placebo studies. *The Behavioral and Brain Sciences, 6*, 275–310.

Propst, L., Ostrom, R., Watkins, P., Dean, T., & Mashburn, W. (1992). Comparative efficacy of religious and non-religious cognitive-behavioral therapy for the treatment of clinical depression in religious individuals. *Journal of Consulting and Clinical Psychology, 60*, 94–103.

Richards, P. S., & Bergin, A. E. (1997). *A spiritual strategy for counseling and psychotherapy.* Washington, DC: American Psychological Association.

Richards, P. S., & Bergin, A. E. (Eds.) (2000). *Handbook of psychotherapy and religious diversity.* Washington, DC: American Psychological Association.

Rile, A. (1995). *Cognitive analytic therapy: Developments in theory and practice.* New York: John Wiley & Sons.

Rile, A. (1997). *Cognitive analytic therapy and borderline personality disorder.* New York: John Wiley & Sons.

Robinson, L., Berman, J., & Neimeyer, R. (1990). Psychotherapy for the treatment of depression: A comprehensive review of controlled outcome research. *Psychological Bulletin, 108*, 30–49.

Shafranske, E. P. (Ed.) (1996). *Religion and the clinical practice of psychology.* Washington, DC: American Psychological Association.

Silverman, W. H. (1996). Cookbooks, manuals, and paint-by-numbers: Psychotherapies in the 1990's. *Psychotherapy, 33*, 207–215.

Smith, M. L., Glass, G. V., & Miller, T. I. (1980). *The benefits of psychotherapy.* Baltimore, MD: Johns Hopkins University Press.

Svartberg, M., & Stiles, T. C. (1991). Comparative effects of short-term psychodynamic psychotherapy: A meta-analysis. *Journal of Consulting and Clinical Psychology, 59*, 704–714.

Thase, M. E. (1999). What is the investigator allegiance effect and what should we do about it? *Clinical Psychology: Science and Practice, 6*, 113–115.

Weisz, J. R., Hawley, K. M., Pilkonis, P. A., Woody, S. R., & Follette, W. C. (2000). Stressing the (other) three Rs in the search for empirically supported treatments: Review procedures, research quality, relevance to practice and public interest. *Clinical Psychology: Science and Practice, 7*, 243–258.

Westen, D., & Morrison, K. (2001). A multidimensional meta-analysis of treatments of depression, panic, and generalized anxiety disorder: An empirical examination of the status of empirically supported psychotherapies. *Journal of Consulting and Clinical Psychology, 69*, 875–889.

Worthington, E. L., Jr., Kurusu, T. A., McCullough, M. E., & Sandage, S. J. (1996). Empirical research on religion and psychotherapeutic processes and outcomes: A ten-year review and research prospectus. *Psychological Bulletin, 119*, 448–487.

Worthington, E. L. Jr., & Sandage, S. J. (2002). Religion and spirituality. In J. C. Norcross (Ed.), *Psychotherapy relationships that work.* New York: Oxford University Press.

Name Index

Subject Index